THE NIGERIAN DIRECTORY

"The LIST"

A Complete Directory of Notable Companies
and Federal Establishments in Nigeria

1st WORLD
PUBLISHING

THE NIGERIAN DIRECTORY

5, Adelabu Close, off Ola Ayinde St,
Ikeja, Lagos, Nigeria
234-1-722-1830
234-802-323-5100

Published by 1stWorld Publishing
1100 North 4th St. Suite 131, Fairfield, Iowa 52556
tel: 641-209-5000 • fax: 641-209-3001
web: www.1stworldpublishing.com

LCCN: 2005908465

ISBN: 1-59540-964-5

FROM THE EDITOR

We, Hannahsgate Ltd, Lagos, Nigeria in partnership with 1st World Publishing Inc., Fairfield, Iowa, USA, congratulate you for getting a copy of this edition of our great Directory - **THE LIST**. Nigeria's social and economic life has remained vibrant. With a population of 154 million people (United Nations' estimate), and 'the happiest and most religious people on earth' (British Broadcasting Corporation survey) that is to be expected. Democratic Governance has thrown up a lot of challenges and opportunities. Government as a matter of policy is putting emphasis on attaining a private-sector-driven economy. Privatisation and/or commercialisation of Government-owned Commercial ventures and deregulation of the economy are on course. Although these exercises have experienced some hiccups here and there, the deregulation of the Telecommunication sector and the subsequent introduction of Global System for Mobile Telecommunication is simply a revolution in the country.

Small- and Medium-scale Investment Equity Scheme (SMIES), a policy that require Commercial Banks to put aside ten percent to their profit-before-tax for joint equity investment has erected a favourable situation of cash chasing after investors.

Moreover with the recent directive from the Central Bank of Nigeria requiring operating banks to have a minimum paid-up Share Capital of 25 billion naira by December 2005, the country will have stronger investment-friendly banking services

We advise that you use this directory deligently to reach our Corporate community - manufacturers, providers of equipment, machineries, services, and even the banks and other financial institutions that have the funds.

Investment opportunities are bound in Nigeria especially in the Real Sector - Agrculture, Manufacturing, Solid Mineral and Tourism. All you need is **THE LIST** to meet your marketing, communications, strategic planning and overall business interaction.

We sincerely thank our numerous advertisers for their faith in this medium.

Do make the very best use of "**THE LIST**". A Nigerian Directory compiled in Nigeria, printed, published, distributed and marketed world-wide from the United States of America.

Daniel I. Omoruyi
HANNAHSGATE LIMITED

TABLE OF CONTENTS

The Pillars
As pillars would support a building,
so we grant you succor by paying your claims promptly.
nfi
RC 96658
Nfi Insurance Company Limited
(Formerly Nigerian-French Insurance Company Ltd.)
...The ultimate in underwriting excellence
203/205 Apapa Oshodi Expressway, Isolo, Lagos.
Tel: 4526870, 4524970, 4520649, 4811410, 4523462 Fax: 4526773
website: www.nfinigeria.com e-mail: nfinigeria@linkserve.com

What is it they know
that you don't ?
Motorists who know, understand that Dunlop Elite Tubeless is the result of computer optimised product design plus a highly technological approach to manufacturing process.
This special performance tubeless tyre has the following unique attributes:
• Long tread life that guarantees durability and reliability.
• Zigzag edges and deep tread grooves that give good grip on all road surfaces, wet or dry.
• Wide tread shoulder grooves for rapid water dispersal
• Large tread blocks that deliver stable handling.
• Reinforced casing for the ultimate safety advantage.
• High load capacity that ensures tyres do not burst when subjected to heavy loads.
• No matter the type of road, Dunlop Elite Tubeless can weather its condition.
Now that you know what majority of motorists know, why don't you join them!
DUNLOP
DUNLOP ELITE TUBELESS
The Ultimate Safety Advantage
Full Complimentary After-Sales Service Available
ISO 9002
For farther enquiries contact: Service Department, Dunlop Nigeria Plc HEAD OFFICE: Oba Akran Avenue, P.M.B. 21079, Ikeja, Lagos, Nigeria.
Tel: 4978910-19, 4962666-7.
Victoria Island - 2622063.

gopn/0045

MAERSK
SEALAND
MAERSK
SEALAND
.COM

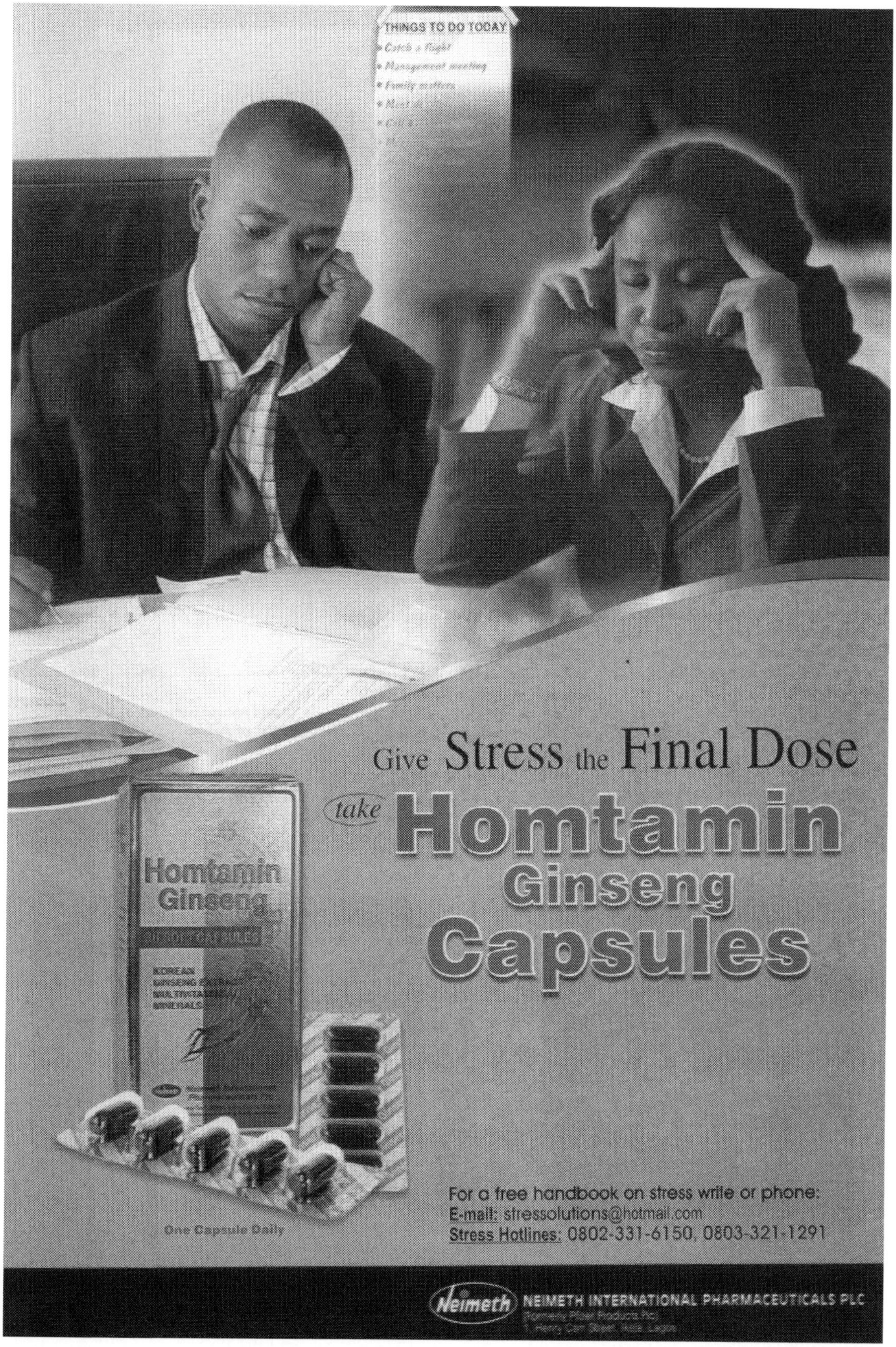

THINGS TO DO TODAY
Give Stress the Final Dose
take Homtamin Ginseng Capsules
Homtamin Ginseng
One Capsule Daily
For a free handbook on stress write or phone:
E-mail: stressolutions@hotmail.com
Stress Hotlines: 0802-331-6150, 0803-321-1291
Neimeth
NEIMETH INTERNATIONAL PHARMACEUTICALS PLC

Our
future
is not a
gift.
Whatever we are today was planned and shaped yesterday. Nothing fortuitous.
We came into printing from the top end, single-minded on delivering unsurpassed quality prints. So we pioneered cutting edge technology DI (Direct Imaging) press. Since then printing has not been the same in Nigeria.
We download and print straight from the Internet, Zip, CD, etc **without colour separation on films;** yet in offset ink. What you get are impeccable prints that wow you to ask "were these printed in Nigeria?"
Planet Press Ltd.
443 Badagry Express Road, Alakija, Lagos
Tel: 01-2885323, 01-4701279, 7731699, 08023157658
Email: press@planetpressltd.com Website: www.planetearthltd.com
...we Print by Direct Imaging

DREDGING AND CIVIL ENGINEERING

SECURITY

For further enquiry visit our office at

INDEX OF COMPANIES (A - Z)

ACCOUNTING SERVICES
AKINTOLA WILLIAMS DELOITTE & TOUCHE.
BABINGTON ASHAYE & COMPANY.
KPMG PROFESSIONAL SERVICES
LEGEND CONSULTING
MICHAEL STEVENS & ASSOCIATES LTD
PANNELL KERR FOSTER
PRICEWATERHOUSECOOPERS.
SAGE BUSINESS GROUP (Robert Ade-Odiachi & Co.)

ADVERTISING AGENCIES (OUTDOOR)
ABIOK PUBLICITY LTD
ADPEAK EXPOSURES LTD
ADSPACE COMMUNICATIONS LTD
BEN-AD LTD
BENJAMIN BLACK & CO. LTD
CHARELLA NIGERIA LTD
COLOUR IMAGE PUBLICITY LTD
DELUXE COLOUR PRODUCTIONS LTD
FOLHAM NIGERIA LTD
FRANCIS STILLWATERS NIGERIA LTD
FRANK MARKETRING COMMUNICATIONS LTD
FRISTOTUNE NIGERIA LTD
GAP PUBLICITY LTD
GRAPHIC PROJECTS LTD
GREENLAND PUBLICITY LTD
INVENTMEDIA LTD
JACSIL & SONS ENTERPRISES LTD.
KINSCO LTD
KONTACTPOINT LTD
KTFB LTD
LOOKOUT COMMUNICATIONS LTD
MAINE VENTURES LTD
MARKETING + MEDIA LTD
MEDIA LINK LTD
MEDIA SPACE LTD
NIGERIA ADVERTISING SERVICE LTD
OPTIMUM EXPOSURES LTD
OUTDOOR COMMUNICATIONS LTD
OUTREACH COMMUNICATION LTD
PANAFY LTD
PRACAM PRODUCTIONS LTD
PRESTO DISPLAY SERVICE LTD
RAILAD LTD
ROCANA NIGERIA LTD
ROYAL COMMUNICATIONS LTD
SADEL INTERNATIONAL LTD
VISUAL ADVERTISING CO. LTD

ADVERTISING, MARKETING & PUBLIC RELATIONS AGENCIES/MEDIA CONSULTING SERVICES
ADMIX COMMUNICATIONS LTD
ADPURE LTD
ADVENT COMMUNICATIONS LTD
ADVERTISING TECHNIQUES LTD
ALDER CONSULTING LTD
ALL SEASONS MEDIACOM LTD
ANGELS COMMUNICATIONS LTD
BARBWILLOMS LTD
BENDEL NEWSPAPER CO. LTD
BENJAMIN BLACK & CO. LTD
BLUEBIRD COMMUNICATIONS LTD
BTAS COMMUNICATIONS LTD
BURTOMLINE LTD
CAMPAIGN + CONCEPTS LTD
CAMPAIGN PALACE LTD
CANDID COMMUNICATIONS LTD
CARDINAL CONCEPTS ADVERTISING LTD
CENTRESPREAD FCB LTD
CENTURY 21 SYSTEMS LTD
CMC CONNECT LAGOS
COMEX LTD
CONCEPT UNIT LTD
CONIC GROUP OF COMPANIES
CORPORATE PRESS SERVICES INC
CREATIVE PLUS LTD
CT & ASSOCIATES LTD.
DAWN FUNCTIONS NIGERIA LTD
DDB CASERS LTD
DIRECT MARKETING COMMUNIATIONS (NIG) LTD
DKK & ASSOCIATES LTD
ELO-PEE WORLDWIDE TELEVISION LTD
EMINENT COMMUNICATIONS LTD
EXPLICIT COMMUNICATIONS LTD
FORUM ADVERTISING LTD
FRANCHISE COMMUNICATIONS LTD1
FRISTOTUNE NIGERIA LTD
FSG COMMUNICATIONS NIGERIA LTD
GENPROGETTI NIGERIA LTD
GOLDMARK LTD
GRANT ADVERTISING NIGERIA LTD.
GREENGATE & CO. LTD
GROUP AFRICA LTD
GUY SARIES LTD
HEARTLINK VENTURES LTD
HUNTERS PUBLICITY LTD
IMAGELINK COMMUNICATIONS LTD
IMPACTPLUS COMMUNICATIONS LTD
INSIGHT COMMUNICATIONS LTD.
INTERMARK ASSOCIATES LTD
INTERPUBLIC NIGERIA LTD
JOEMEDIA & CO. LTD
JSP CORPORATE COMMUNICATIONS LTD
LINTAS LTD
LTC ADVERTISING LTD
MACSELL ASSOCIATES LTD
MAHASSA ADVERTISING LTD
MARKETING + MEDIA LTD
MART LINK ADVERTISING LTD
MASTERPIECE LTD
MC & A LTD
MEDIA PLANNING SERVICES
MEDIA TRUST NIGERIA LTD.
MEDIA WOLRD LTD
MEDIAPLUS INTERNATIONAL LTD
M-GOLD COMMUNICATIONS LTD
NIGERIA ADVERTISING SERVICE LTD
NOVITAS LTD
OGA WILLIAMS LTD
OGINS ADVERTISING LTD
OLU ADEKOYA PRESS AGENCY LTD
OMNI COMMUNICATIONS LTD
OPTIMUM EXPOSURES LTD
PALCOMMS LTD
PATIKE COMMUNICATIONS LTD
PMI DIRECT LTD

PRESTIGE COMMUNICATIONS LTD.
PRIMA GARNET COMMUNICATIONS LTD.
PULSAR LTD.
RICHLAND COMMUNICATIONS LTD
RIZROSE COMMUNICATIONS LTD.
ROSABEL ADVERTISING LTD
SA & C LTD
SAAL ADVERTISING LTD
SATELLITE COMMUNICATIONS LTD
SO & U LTD.
STB-McCANN LAGOS
SUNBEAM ADVERTISING & PUBLICITY LTD
SUNRISE D'ARCY
TAIJO WONUKABE LTD
TANUS COMMUNICATIONS LTD
THE SHOPS LTD.
TIE COMMUNICATIONS LTD
TOTAL MARKETING COMMUNICATIONS LTD
TRANS-MEDIA GROUP
TWENTY-FIRST CENTURY COMMUNICATIONS LTD
TWT COMMUNICATIONS LTD
UNIMARK LTD.
UNIWORLD LTD
USP COMMUNICATIONS LTD
XLR8 LIMITED
ZEPOL ADVERTISING LTD
ZUS BUREAU LTD

AGRICULTURAL COMMODITY MERCHANTS/EXPORTERS

AFCOTT NIGERIA PLC
AFPRINT NIGERIA PLC
AGRO ALLIED DEV. ENTERPRISES LTD
ALL GRAINS (WEST AFRICA) LTD
BAO MOTORS (NIGERIA) LTD
BEST STORE LTD
BIZGATE LTD
C C & M LTD
CASH FLOW LTD
COMAGRI NIGERIA LTD
COMMODITIES SUPPORT SERVICE LTD
DAVOF TRADING COMPANY (NIGERIA) LTD.
ED & F MAN NIGERIA LTD
ELEPHANT GROUP LTD
FAIR BOND GROUP OF COMPANIES
FATBOL OJIKUTU NIGERIA LTD
FIDELITY INTRA AFRICA LTD.
GABIMO HOLDINGS LTD
GOLDCHAINS INTERNATIONAL LTD
I.B.N. NIGERIA LTD
JAGAL GROUP OF COMPANIES
JOF IDEAL FAMILY FARMS LTD
KODA TRADING COMPANY LTD
KOPEK LTD8
LADGROUP LTD
MOTAYO FOODS & HEALTH PRODUCTS LTD
NIGERIA ENGINEERING WORKS LTD
OLAM NIGERIA LTD
P. S. MANDRIDES PLC
PACIFIC FARMS LTD
RAFAKAN NIGERIA LTD
TATEC INTERBIZ LTD
THE ASSOC. OF NIG. CO-OPERATIVE EXPORTERS LTD
THE OKOMU OIL PALM COMPANY PLC
TOMBIZ GROUP OF COMPANIES
TRIMCO LTD
UNIGLOBAL COMMODITIES PLC
U-NUEL & CO. LTD
VENUS PROCESSING & PACKAGING LTD
VIKREN CORPORATION NIGERIA LTD

AGRICULTURAL FARMS

ADLAD GROUP
ADOKA HOLDINGS LTD
AFRICAN FARMS LTD
ALLIED RANCH NIGERIA LTD
CHELLARAMS PLC
COMPLETE PROJECTS ENGINEERING CONSULTIUM
DALA AGRICULTURAL & ALLIED PRODUCTS LTD.
DANGOTE GROUP.
EKWENIBE & SONS TRADING CO. LTD
EZERA INTERNATIONAL GROUP OF CO
FOLAWIYO FARMS LTD
GARBS ORGANISATION LTD
GOLDEN GUINEA BREWERIES PLC
HAMZA HOLDINGS LTD
HARDEL & ENIC GROUP OF COMPANIES
IBIKUNLE LAWAL ORGANISATION LTD
IBRU SEA FOODS LTD
J. UDEAGBALA HOLDINGS (NIGERIA) LTD
J. J. SCOT GROUP OF COMPANIES
JOF IDEAL FAMILY FARMS LTD
JONES GROUP OF COMPANIES
LADIPO DANIEL FARMS LTD
LOTTO INTERNATIONAL LTD
LUBONA NIGERIA LTD
MATBENY HOLDINGS LTD
MIC-MERAH INTERNATIONAL AGENCY LTD
NORDY GROUP LTD
OBA PAPER PRODUCTS INDUSTRIES LTD
OBASANJO FARMS (NIGERIA) LTD
OJEMAI FARMS LTD.
OKAM INTERNATIONAL GROUP OF CO
OKITIPUPA OIL PALM PLC
OZDE GROUP OF COMPANIES.
PACIFIC FARMS LTD
PINEWOOD INVESTMENTS LTD
PRESCO OIL-MILLS PLC
PROJECT STRUCTURES LTD
RISONPALM LTD.
SAMROSE AGRO-INDUSTRIAL COMPANY LTD
SHOREMAN GROUP OF COMPANIES
SYKOBIN INVESTMENT LTD4
TALON NIGERIA LTD
THE OKOMU OIL PALM COMPANY PLC
TUNS HOLDINGS LTD

AIRCRAFT CHARTER

AFRI-AIR INTERNATIONAL LTD
ASSOCIATED AVIATION LTD
BRISTOW HELICOPTERS (NIGERIA) LTD
CHROME AIR SERVICES LTD
EXECUTIVE AIRLINES SERVICES LTD (EAS Airlines)
FRESH AIR LTD
PAN AFRICAN AIRLINES (NIGERIA) LTD
SOSOLISO AIRLINES LTD
UNITED AIR EXPRESS LTD

AIRLINES (FOREIGN/INTERNATIONAL)
AIR AFRIQUE
AIR FRANCE
AIR GABON
AIR INDIA
ALITALIA
BRITISH AIRWAYS
CAMEROON AIRLINES
CATHAY PACIFIC AIRWAYS
EGYPT AIR.
ETHIOPIAN AIRLINES
GHANA AIRWAYS
KLM ROYAL DUTCH AIRLINES
LUFTHANSA GERMAN AIRLINES
MIDDLE EAST AIRLINES
OKADA AIRLINES LTD
SOUTH AFRICAN AIRWAYS
SWISSAIR/SABENA
VIRGIN ATLANTIC AIRLINE

AIRLINES (LOCAL)
AERO CONTRACTORS CO. OF NIGERIA LTD
AFRIJET AIRLINES LTD
ALBARKA AIR PLC
ASSOCIATED AVIATION LTD
BELLVIEW AIR SERVICES LTD
BRISTOW HELICOPTERS (NIGERIA) LTD.
CAPITAL AIRLINES LTD
CHANCHANGI AIRLINES NIGERIA LTD
EXECUTIVE AIRLINES SERVICES LTD (EAS Airlines)
KABO AIR LTD
ORIENTAL AIRLINES LTD
PREMIUM AIR SHUTTLE LTD
SOSOLISO AIRLINES LTD

ALUMINIUM EXTRUSION MILLS
ALUMINIUM EXTRUSION IND. PLC
ALUMINIUM ROLLING MILLS
ALUMINIUM SMELTER CO. NIGERIA LTD
FIRST ALUMINIUM NIGERIA PLC
NIGERIAN ALUMINIUM EXTRUSIONS LTD
ROBICON NIGERIA LTD
TOWER EXTRUSIONS NIGERIA PLC

ALUMINIUM PRODUCTS FABRICATION
ALL SEASONS INDUSTRIES LTD
ALTIMAX METAL INDUSTRIES LTD
ALUCON BUILDING PRODUCTS LTD
ALUMINIUM FABRICATION CO. LTD (ALFACO)
ALUMINIUM METAL TECHNOLOGIES LTD
ALUMINIUM PRODUCTS LTD
ALUMINIUM TECHNOLOGY PRODUCTS PLC
APEX ALUMINIUM LTD
ARCHITECTURAL PRODUCTS LTD
ASABA ALUMINIUM CO. LTD
BEST ALUMINIUM (MANUFACTURING) CO. LTD
BORNO ALUMINIUM CO. LTD
BROSSETTE (NIG.) LTD
CARAT ALUMINIUM LTD
CHAMPION ALUMINIUM & METAL PRODUCTS LTD
CHARTERED ALUMINIUM SYSTEMS LTD
COGEMAT NIGERIA LTD
COMMEDOR NIGERIA LTD
CRITTALL-HOPE NIGERIA LTD
E.B.M SYSTEMS NIGERIA LTD
EURO-TECH ALUMINIUM LTD
FAWAZ STEELWOOD & CHEMICAL CO. LTD
FINE ALUMINIUM LTD
FRAB & COMPANY (NIG.) LTD
GAMJI-TEC GROUP OF COMPANIES
GENERAL METAL PRODUCTS LTD
GINPAT ALUMINIUM PRODUCTS LTD
GREATGATE INVESTMENT LTD
HASSAN STEEL PRODUCTS (NIG.) LTD
IMPERIAL ALUMINIUM PRODUCTS LTD
JIMEX INDUSTRIES (NIG.) LTD
JOICO INDUSTRIES LTD
JONES GROUP OF COMPANIES
KAL GROUP OF COMPANIES
LENTO NIGERIA PLC
MEGA ALUMINIUM & BUILDING SERVICES LTD
MICHAEL OLUSEGUN ENTERPRISES LTD
MID-EAST (NIG.) LTD
NALMAC ALUMINIUM PRODUCTS LTD
NORTHERN INDUSTRIES LTD
OMNIA NIGERIA LTD
ONITSHA ALUMINIUM MANUFACTURING CO. LTD
OWIPS INTERNATIONAL CO. LTD
PAULLY JAJA ALUMINIUM INDUSTRIES LTD
STANDARD SYSTEMS INTEGRATED
ARCHITECHTURAL PRODUCTS LTD
SYNDICATED METAL INDUSTRIES LTD
TAFAK INDUSTRIES NIGERIA LTD
TOWER BUILDING PRODUCTS.
TOWER HOLLOWARE (Div. of Tower Aluminium Plc)
UGEN & ASSOCIATES CO. LTD
UTC NIGERIA PLC
ZENBOOK INTERIOR CONSTRUCTION LTD

AQUARIUM & WATER FOUNTAIN
DEXDEE FOUNTAINS LTD
EDDY MOORE MARBLE AND FURNISHING LTD
OLATECH BOREHOLES LTD
OX4 SYSTEMS LTD

ARCHITECTURAL CONSULTANTS
ARCHCON NIGERIA LTD
ARCHI-HIVES (Architect + Planners)
BUILDING & TECHNICAL INFO. CONSULTANTS
DEZACHI CONSTRUCTION LTD
ECAD DESIGN GROUP LTD
FEMI MAJEKODUNMI ASSOCIATES LTD
GODWIN HOPWOOD KUYE LTD
HAVILAH CONSULT LTD
INCHSCAPE ACHITECT VO
JAMES CUBITT ARCHITECTS
QUARRY DESIGN GROUP
TOWRY-COKER ASSOCIATES
VOEN ASSOCIATES

AUDIO-VISUAL EQUIPMENT & TRAINING AIDS SALES
BIOTECH AUDIO VISUAL (NIG.) LTD
BONAMA NIGERIA LTD
CHAMS NIGERIA LTD
FINLAB NIGERIA LTD.
INFORMATION DISPLAY EXHIBIT & SYSTEM LTD

INFORTRONICS NIGERIA LTD
MAC-TAY TACK CONSULTING
MINNESOTA NIGERIA LTD
NEWBRAND INDUSTRIES LTD
OPEN LEARNING ASSOCIATES LTD
RAPIDO VENTURES LTD
TESNIC NIGERIA LTD
WESTCOTT NIGERIA LTD

AVIATION CONSULTANCY SERVICES
AEROCONTROL LTD
AEROSPACE SYSTEMS (NIG.) LTD
AVIATION LOGISTIC & MANAGEMENT LTD
EXPERT AVIATION AGENCY NIGERIA LTD
GOGINS TRAVELS LTD
LANDROVER CO. LTD
SKYLINE LTD
YASAVA LTD

BAKERS/CONFECTIONERS
ADOKA HOLDINGS LTD
ALLIANCE INTERNATIONAL (NIG.) LTD
BAKERS WORLD LTD
BIG TREAT CONFECTIONERIES LTD
DALLAS BAKERY & CONFECTIONERIES IND. LTD
FAMILY FOODS LTD
FRENCHIES LTD
LEVENTIS FOODS LTD
NASCO GROUP.
NIDOCO LTD
NIGER BISCUIT CO. LTD
TANU GROUP

BANKS
ACCESS BANK NIGERIA PLC
AFRIBANK NIGERIA PLC
AFRIBANK INTERNATIONAL LTD (Merchant Bankers)
AFRICAN EXPRESS BANK PLC
AFRICAN INTERNATIONAL BANK LTD
ALLSTATES TRUST BANK PLC
ASSURANCE BANK NIGERIA LTD
BANK OF INDUSTRY LTD
BANK OF THE NORTH LTD
BROAD BANK OF NIGERIA LTD
CAPITAL BANK INTERNATIONAL LTD
CENTREPOINT BANK PLC
CHARTERED BANK PLC
CITIBANK NIGERIA
CITIZENS INTERNATIONAL BANK LTD
CITY EXPRESS BANK PLC
CO-OPERATIVE BANK PLC
CO-OPERATIVE DEVELOPMENT BANK PLC
CONTINENTAL TRUST BANK LTD
DEVCOM BANK LTD
DIAMOND BANK LTD
EAGLE BANK LTD
ECOBANK NIGERIA PLC
EIB INTERNATIONAL BANK PLC
EQUITORIAL TRUST BANK LTD
EQUITY BANK OF NIGERIA LTD
FBN (MERCHANT BANKERS) LTD
FEDERAL MORTGAGE BANK OF NIGERIA
FIDELITY BANK PLC
FIRST ATLANTIC BANK PLC
FIRST BANK OF NIGERIA PLC
FIRST CITY MONUMENT BANK LTD
FORTUNE INTERNATIONAL BANK PLC
FOUNTAIN TRUST BANK LTD
FSB INTERNATIONAL BANK PLC
GATEWAYBANK PLC
GLOBAL BANK PLC
GUARANTY TRUST BANK PLC
GUARDIAN EXPRESS BANK PLC
GULF BANK OF NIGERIA PLC
HABIB NIGERIA BANK LTD
HALLMARK BANK PLC
IMB INTERNATIONAL BANK PLC
INLAND BANK (NIGERIA) PLC
INTERCITY BANK PLC
INTERCONTINENTAL BANK PLC
INTERNATIONAL TRUST BANK PLC
INVESTMENT BANKING & TRUST COMPANY LTD
LEAD BANK PLC
LIBERTY BANK LTD
LION BANK OF NIGERIA PLC
MAGNUM TRUST BANK LTD
MANNYBANK PLC
MARINA INTERNATIONAL BANK LTD
MBC INTERNATIONAL BANK LTD
METROPOLITAN BANK LTD
MIDAS BANK PLC
NAL BANK PLC
NATIONAL BANK OF NIGERIA LTD
NBM BANK LTD
NIGERIAN AGRIC. CO-OP. & RURAL DEV. BANK
NIGERIAN EXPORT-IMPORT BANK (NEXIM)
NIGERIAN-AMERICAN BANK LTD
NNB INTERNATIONAL BANK PLC
NUB INTERNATIONAL BANK LTD
OCEANIC BANK INTERNATIONAL (NIGERIA) LTD
OMEGABANK PLC
PLATINUM BANK LTD
PRUDENT BANK PLC
REGENT BANK LTD
RELIANCE BANK LTD
SOCIETE GENERALE BANK NIGERIA LTD
STANBIC BANK NIGERIA LTD
STANDARD CHARTERED BANK NIGERIA LTD
STANDARD TRUST BANK LTD
TRADE BANK PLC
TRANS INTERNATIONAL BANK PLC
TRIUMPH MERCHANT BANK PLC
TROPICAL COMMERCIAL BANK PLC
TRUST BANK OF AFRICA LTD (Merchant Bankers)
UNION BANK OF NIGERIA PLC
UNION MERCHANT BANK LTD
UNITED BANK FOR AFRICA PLC
UNIVERSAL TRUST BANK PLC
WEMA BANK PLC
ZENITH INTERNATIONAL BANK PLC

BATHROOM EQUIPMENT & PRODUCTS SALES
ALLIED BOND STANDARD CO. LTD
CAPPA HOLDINGS LTD
GENERAL b.m. LTD
HAGENE ASSOCIATES LTD

MEGER NIGERIA LTD
NEW COMEX TRADING CO. NIGERIA LTD
PORTLAND PAINTS & PRODUCTS NIGERIA LTD
POSH INTERNATIONAL CO. LTD
ROYAL SUITES LTD
UNITED PREFAB CO. (NIG.) LTD
ZABADNE & CO. LTD

BITUMEN PRODUCTION/SALES
WEST AFRICAN BITUMEN EMULSION CO. LTD

BOAT, BARGE & SHIP BUILDING, REPAIRS & CONSULTANCY
GIBRALTAR CONSTRUCTION (NIG.) LTD
MARINETEC LTD
MODANT MARINE LTD
MOUDACO LTD
PYTHON ENGINEERING CO. LTD
RAYCON & COMPANY (NIG.) LTD
STEELWAYS NIGERIA LTD

BOOKSHOPS & BOOKS DISTRIBUTION/SALES
ABIOLA BOOKSHOPS LTD
CSS LTD
FLORIDA BOOKSHOP LTD
GLENDORA INTERNATIONAL (NIG.) LTD
INTERLINGUA LTD
NIGERIAN BAPTIST BOOKSTORE LTD
ODUSOTE BOOKSTORES LTD
READERSWORLD.COM LTD

BOREHOLE (Water) DRILLING, EQUIPMENT SALES
HOLMAN BROTHERS (NIG.) LTD
IFOY NIGERIA LTD
KINGSMAT CO. LTD
SHEBAG HOLDINGS LTD
STRUCTEC (Div. of CFAO Nigeria Plc)

BOTTLERS (Carbonated Drinks And Spring Water)
AZUMA BOTTLING CO. LTD
COASTAL BOTTLERS LTD
INTERLAND INDUSTRIES LTD
J. NWANKWU GROUP OF COMPANIES
LIFE BREWERIES CO. LTD
LIMCA BOTTLERS PLC
NIGERIAN BOTTLING CO. PLC
NIGERIAN MINERAL WATER INDUSTRIES LTD
PHARMA-DEKO PLC
RAGOLIS WATERS LTD
SAVANNAH BEVERAGES LTD
SEVEN-UP BOTTLING CO. PLC
SONA BREWERIES PLC
SPRING WATERS (NIGERIA) LTD
UNITED BEVERAGES CO. LTD
WARRI BOTTLING CO. LTD

BREWERIES
BENDEL BREWERY LTD
BENUE BREWERY LTD
CHURCHGATE GROUP
CONSOLIDATED BREWERIES PLC
DIL/MAL TEX (NIGERIA) PLC
GOLDEN GUINEA BREWERIES PLC
GUINNESS NIGERIA PLC
INTERNATIIONAL BEER & BEVERAGES IND. LTD
INTERNATIONAL BREWERIES PLC
JOS INTERNATIONAL BREWERIES PLC
LIFE BREWERIES CO. LTD
NIGERIAN BREWERIES PLC.
SONA BREWERIES PLC
VITAMALT PLC

BUILDING & CIVIL ENGINEERING SERVICES
A.G. FERRERO CO. LTD
AB PETERS (NIGERIA) LTD
ABDULAI & AWOMOLO CONSTRUCTION CO. LTD
ACME BUILDERS LTD
AGRIC INT'L TECHNOLOGY & TRADE (NIG) LTD
AKAROLO GROUP OF COMPANIES
ALH. YAHAYA UMARU & CO. LTD
ALINACO NIGERIA LTD
AMAFO ENGINEERING LTD
AMALGAMATED GROUP OF COMPANIES
AMBER RESOURCES NIGERIA LTD
ARAB CONTRACTORS O.A.O. NIGERIA LTD
ARBICO PLC
ARC (NIG.) LTD
ARCHARRIS ENGINEERING CONSTRUCTION LTD
ARFO CONSTRUCTION COMPANY NIGERIA LTD
ARIZONA CONSTRUCTION LTD
ASI BUILDING SYSTEMS LTD
BEC FRERES NIGERIA LTD
BECHTEL (NIG.) LTD
BELTECO ENGINEERING LTD
BENCOV CONSTRUCTION CO. LTD
BENJACK TRANSWORLD AGENCIES LTD
BETCY GROUP OF COMPANIES
BIMKOL NIGERIA LTD
BIOINVEST ENGINEERING CO. LTD
BKI BUILDING & CIVIL ENGINEERING CO. LTD
BMA NIGERIA LTD
BORINI PRONO & CO. (NIGERIA) LTD
BRUNELLI CONSTRUCTION COMPANY (NIG.) LTD
BUILDING DEVELOPMENT & CONSTRUCTION LTD
BUILDWELL PLANTS & EQUIPMENT INDUSTRIES LTD
BULET INTERNATIONAL (NIGERIA) LTD
BUOSHISHI HOLDINGS LTD
BUSINESS CONTRACTING LTD
BUSSDOR & CO. LTD
C & C CONSTRUCTION CO. LTD
C. G. C. NIGERIA LTD
CACHEZ GROUP
CAPPA & D'ALBERTO PLC
CENTRE-LINE CONSTRUCTION NIGERIA LTD
CHARVET NIGERIA LTD
CHASTE PROJECT GROUPE
CHINA HARBOUR ENGINEERING CO. LTD
CHROME OIL SERVICES LTD
CIKA GROUP OF COMPANIES
COMPLETE PROJECTS ENGINEERING CONSORTIUM
CONIC GROUP OF COMPANIES
CONSTRUCTION PRODUCTS NIGERIA LTD
CONTRANSIMEX NIGERIA LTD
CORNESTONE CONSTRUCTION (NIG.) LTD
CREMOTRADE CO. LTD
CROWN TRUST LTD
D. S. D. (NIGERIA) LTD

DAGMAR NIGERIA LTD
DALEX CO.LTD
DANFODIO CONSTRUCTION & COMMERCIAL CO
DANTATA & SAWOE CONSTRUCTION CO. (NIG) LTD
DATUN CONSTRUCTION (NIG.) LTD
DELATTRE BEZONS (NIG.) LTD
DEZACHI CONSTRUCTION LTD
DRAGETANOS CONSTRUCTION (NIG.) LTD
DUMEZ (NIGERIA) PLC
DYS TROCCA VALSESIA & CO. LTD. (DTV & CO. LTD
EAGLE CONSTRUCTION LTD
EBIMO NIGERIA LTD
ECO-BUILDING SYSTEMS NIGERIA LTD
ENOSCO NIGERIA LTD
F. K. CONSTRUCTION LTD
FALACOL GROUP OF COMPANIES
FERROSTAL NIGERIA LTD
FHOMO NIGERIA LTD
FOLBEN NIGERIA LTD
FOLIO CONSTRUCTION LTD
FOUGEROLLE NIGERIA LTD
FRANCHISE PARTICIPATION LTD
FUGRO-IGN LTD
FUND-TAI ENGINEERING CO. LTD
G. CAPPA PLC
G.E.C. OBIAMALU & SONS LTD
GENPROGETTI NIGERIA LTD
GLOBE ENGINEERING & CONSTRUCTION CO. LTD
GRAMEN PETROSERVE NIGERIA LTD
GREATGATE INVESTMENT LTD
GUFFANTI (NIG.) PLC
H.F.P. ENGINEERING (NIGERIA) LTD
HABIBU ENGINEERING NIGERIA LTD
HALCON ENGINEERING LTD
HAMZAS HOLDINGS LTD
HAPEL (NIG.) LTD
HARDEL & ENIC GROUP OF COMPANIES
HARIESCOCAN & ASSOCIATES LTD
HAVILAH CONSULT LTD
HENSMOR GROUP OF COMPANIES
HONEYWELL GROUP OF COMPANIES
HYDROWORKS LTD
ICON MARINE SERVICES LTD
INNOCHRIS NIGERIA LTD
INTEK GROUP LTD
INTER ROOF (NIG.) LTD
INTER-BAU CONSTRUCTION (NIG.)LTD
INTERKEL NIGERIA LTD
IPCO (NIG.) LTD
J. NWAKWU GROUP OF COMPANIES
J.D.P. CONSTRUCTION (NIG.) LTD
JAFCO CONSTRUCTION LTD
JAGAL NIGERIA LTD
JAJO NIGERIA LTD
JANGO INTERNATIONAL LTD
JISACO (NIG.) LTD
JONES GROUP OF COMPANIES
JULIUS BERGER NIGERIA PLC
KENCHENZ NIGERIA LTD
KNORR CONSTRUCTION COMPANY (NIG.) LTD
LAUTAI ENTERPRISES LTD
LEE ENGINEERING & CONSTRUCTION CO. LTD
LEE NOBEC NIGERIA LTD
LINK WOOD & METAL LTD
LODIGIANI (NIG.) LTD
MADONA ORGANISATION LTD
MAIJAMA'A INTERNATIONAL LTD
MANDARA GROUP OF COMPANIES
MAYSSA INTERNATIONAL NIGERIA LTD
MEGAPROJEKT CONSORTIUM
MERCURY ENGINEERING & CONSTRUCTION CO. LTD
METAL CONSTRUCTION (WEST AFRICA) LTD
MONIER CONSTRUCTION CO. (NIGERIA) LTD
MOSAF NIGERIA LTD
MOTHERRCAT LTD
MOULDS (NIG.) LTD.
MULTILINE INVESTMENT LTD
NAHMAN CONSTRUCTION CO. LTD
NIGER DIESEL ENGINEERING SERVICES LTD
NIGER HOPE ENTERPRISES NIGERIA LTD
NIGERIAN ROAD CONSTRUCTION LTD
NIGERNORTH LTD.
NOVACOKE BUILDERS LTD
OILFIELD & WATERWAYS SERVICES CO. LTD
OZIGBU ENGINEERING CO. LTD
P.G.H. LTD
P.W. NIGERIA LTD
PECCOLO BRUNELLI ENGINEERING LTD
PEDROCCHI & CO. LTD
PET JIBSON & CO. LTD
PHOENIX ENGINEERING & CONTRACTOR LTD
PORTLAND RENOVATIONS & CONSTRUCTION LTD
POWERLINES LTD
PREST GROUP LTD
PRIMUS NIGERIA LTD
PROCON GROUP AFRICA
PURIFICATION TECHNIQUES (NIG.) LTD
RAHUSA VENTURES NIGERIA LTD
RAYCON & COMPANY (NIG.) LTD
REYNOLDS CONSTRUCTION CO. (NIGERIA) LTD
ROADS NIGERIA PLC
ROTIMI OBEISUN INVESTMENT LTD
S.OJOLOWO TECHNICAL CO. LTD
SABIU BAKO GROUP OF COMPANIES
SAFE NIGERIA LTD
SALINI NIGERIA LTD
SANDERTON VENTURES LTD
SANS FRONTIERS INVESTMENT LTD
SETRACO ENGINEERING CONSTRUCTION CO. LTD
SHELTER WORKS LTD
SIECON NIGERIA LTD
SINGAFRIQUE ENGINEERING LTD
SOLEL BONEH (NIGERIA) LTD
SPARKLIGHT ENGINEERING CO. LTD
STABILINI VISINONI LTD
STANDARD CONSOLIDATED DREDGING&CONSTR. CO
STANDARD CONSTRUCTION LTD
STIRLING CIVIL ENGINEERING (NIG.) LTD
STRABAG CONSTRUCTION (NIGERIA) LTD
SYKOBIN INVESTMENT LTD
TILLEY GYADO & COMPANY (NIG.) LTD
TITAN ENGINEERS & CONSTRUCTION LTD
TRAB INVESTMENTS NIGERIA LTD
TRANSPROJECT NIGERIA LTD
TRANSRAPID NIGERIA LTD
TRANTER INTERNATIONAL LTD

TRIACIA CONSTRUCTION LTD
TYME RESOURCES AND CO. LTD
UNITY CONTINENTAL NIGERIA LTD
U-NUEL & CO. LTD
UREN CONSTRUCTION ENGINEERING CO. LTD
VITA CONSTRUCTION LTD
WEMTRACO (NIG.) LTD
WESCO ENGINEERING LTD
ZAKHEM CONSTRUCTION NIGERIA LTD

CAR HIRE/RENTAL SERVICES
A.V.I. SERVICES LTD
ATS TRAVEL NIGERIA LTD
EXPERT AVIATION AGENCY NIGERIA LTD
GLOBAL VIEW TRAVELS & TOURS LTD
LAMBIC TECHNIC & GENERAL SERVICES LTD
RUTAM TRAVELS LTD
SANTA SEDE NIGERIA LTD

CARGO SUPERINTENDENTS & SURVEYORS
AIR SEA FREGHTERS LTD
ALFA LABORATORIES LTD
AUDIT CONTROL & EXPERTISE (NIG.) LTD (ACE)
BUREAU VERITAS NIGERIA LTD
CARGO INSPECTION & FREIGHT (LTD)
FLA RISK SURVEYS LTD
JAROS INSPECTION SERVICES LTD
K-MARINE & BUSINESS NETWORK LTD
MARINE TECHNICAL SERVICES INTER'L (NIG.) LTD
MERYT ADVERTISING LTD
MESO INDUSTRIES LTD
PROVIDENCE CONSULT & SERVICEES LTD
SGS INSPECTION SERVICES NIGERIA LTD
SUPERMARITIME (NIG.) LTD
SWEDE CONTROL INTERTEK LTD

CATERING SERVICES
BEMIL NIGERIA LTD
COURDEAU NIGERIA LTD
DE-FRIENDSHIP CATERING SERVICES LTD
DOUBLE ZERO CHINESE RESTAURANT LTD
FAVOURITES LTD
FLAMINGO (NIG.) LTD
FOREMOST CATERERS LTD
GOLDEN GATE PARADISE NIGERIA LTD
HOTEL & CATERING SERVICES LTD
HOTEL SUPPORT SERVICES LTD
JUICE & GRILLADE LTD
LAGOS TRAVEL INN
MAMA CASS RESTAURANTS LTD
NANET HOTELS LTD
NIGERIAN CATERERS & SUPERMARKET LTD
PELLEGRINI NIGERIA CATERING LTD
PETRONELLA NIGERIA LTD
RAYCON & COMPANY (NIG.) LTD
SAIDI STARGATE HOTELS LTD
SODEXHO NIGERIA LTD
STAR MOTELS (NIG.) LTD
TASTEE POT LTD
TOURIST COMPANY OF NIGERIA PLC
WEST END LTD
WHASSAN-EUREST (NIG.) LTD
ZENITH HOTELS LTD

CLEANING SERVICES (Industrial)
AMAFO ENGINEERING LTD
CONTACT LINK LTD
DURACLEAN SERVICES (NIG.) LTD
DURACLEAN SPECIALISTS (NIG.) LTD
DUSTMEN CLEANING SERVICES LTD
FIRST EKIMOGUN NIGERIA LTD
FLOOROSIL CLEANING SERVICES LTD
KLEENOL NIGERIA LTD
MICHANI ENTERPRISES LTD
O'LA-KLEEN NIGERIA LTD
PATOVILKI INDUSTRIAL PLANNERS LTD
RENENT LTD
WESTOWN NIGERIA LTD
YARESH INTERNATIONAL LTD

CLEARING & FORWARDING AGENCIES
ABSAF GROUP OF COMPANIES
ADE KOMOLAFE (NIG.) LTD
AEI (NIG.) LTD
AFRICA PORT SERVICES LTD
AFRICA SHIPPING LTD
AIR SEA FREIGHTERS LTD
AJE & BAWORA (NIG.) LTD
AJELENJE NIGERIA LTD
AKWIWU MOTORS LTD
ALL-ROUTES SERVICES LTD
ALPHA & BETA MERCHANTS CO. LTD
ANGLO NORMAN SHIPPING NIGERIA LTD
AROLAK (NIG.) LTD
BAFLINE NIGERIA LTD
BAKFAJ INTERNATIONAL LTD
BEMS LTD
BENIGAN FORWARDERS LTD
BENJACK TRANSWORLD AGENCIES LTD
BHN TRANSPORT & LOGISTIC LTD
BRAWAL SHIPPING (NIG.) LTD
BROADLINE SERVICES LTD
CARLDOM INTERCONTINENTAL AGENCIES LTD
CASMAN LTD
CHRISMATEL SHIPPING COMPANY (NIG.) LTD
CHUKABEN AGENCIES NIGERIA LTD
CITECO TECHNICAL CO. LTD
CLOVERLEAF SHIPPING LTD
COASTAL SERVICES LTD
CONAIR CARGO SERVICES LTD
CONTACT INTERNATIONAL NIGERIA LTD
CRESEADA INTERNATIONAL LTD
CRISP INTERNATIONAL LTD
DADDO MARITIME SERVICES LTD
DE NATUMAS INTERCONT. FREIGHT AGENCY LTD
DEBUK (NIG.) LTD
DELTA BROTHERS LTD
DENCA SERVICES LTD
DER KURIER (AIR ACTION COURIERS)
DEROS MARITIME LTD
DOKU AND SONS ENTERPRISES NIGERIA LTD
DONMARINE AND TRADING LTD
DUNCAN MARITIME NIGERIA LTD
EASY EMPEROR AGENCIES LTD
EBUNY SHIPPING AGENCIES LTD
EJIX MARITIME LTD
EXCELLENCE ALL FREIGHT LTD

FANO SHIPPING AGENCIES LTD
FIRST MARINE AND ENGINEERING SERVICES LTD
FLEMING INTERNATIONAL AGENCIES LTD
GEETEE NIGERIA LTD
GEONNASONS INTERNATIONAL GROUP NIGERIA LTD
GLOBE SHIPPING LINES NIGERIA LTD
GULF AGENCY & SHIPPING (NIG.) LTD
HAMADAH SHIPPING SERVICES LTD
HAMSTANG NIGERIA LTD
HARLINK INVESTMENT LTD
HENSMOR GROUP OF COMPANIES.
HIMMA FREIGHT LTD
HUGE INVESTMENT LTD
IAL NIGERIA LTD
INTER-SERVICE NIGERIA LTD
IYAYI MARITIME NIGERIA LTD
JOE-EBOJE INTERNATIONAL AGENCIES LTD
JOHN HOLT SHIPPING SERVICES (Div. of John Holt Plc)
JOKI (NIG.) LTD
JONATEX & COMPANY NIGERIA LTD
KERILDBERT HOLDINGS LTD
K-MARINE & BUSINESS NETWORK LTD
LAAS LTD
LABANA GLOBAL VENTURES LTD
LAGOS & NIGER SHIPPING AGENCIES LTD. (LANSAL).
LIAS FREIGHT AGENCIES LTD
MAC-TONNEL (NIG.) LTD
MADSON (NIG.) LTD
MADUAKO TRANSPORT CO. LTD
MAIDEN SHIPPING LINES LTD
MALIP SERVICES LTD
MARI TRANS NIGERIA LTD
MASMA NIGERIA LTD
MASPHALA COMPANY NIGERIA LTD
MERIT SHIPPING COMPANY (NIG.) LTD
MICHELLE BONDED TERMINAL NIGERIA LTD
MIPPERS INTERNATIONAL LTD
MONZINA COASTAL AGENCIES LTD
MORLAP SHIPPING CO. LTD
MURHI INTERNATIONAL COMPANY (NIG.) LTD
MURPHY SHIPPING & COMMERCIAL SERVICES LTD
NAPAK SERVICES (NIG.) LTD
NATIONAL CLEARING & FORWARDING AGENCY.
NIGERIAN MARITIME SERVICES LTD
NSU INTERNATIONAL CO. LTD
OCEAN TRANSPORT & SHIPPING LTD
OGO OLUWA KITAN TRADING CO. LTD
OGUBETH INDUSTRIES NIGERIA LTD
OJOKORO CEMENT INDUSTRY LTD
ONIBUDO HOLDINGS LTD
PANAT NIGERIA LTD
RAINBOW MARITIME (NIG.) LTD
red\line NIGERIA LTD
ROTIMI OBEISUN INVESTMENT LTD
S.G. INTERNATIONAL AGENCIES LTD
SABRU NIGERIA LTD
SAFRA VENTURES LTD
SAIL SEA SHIPPING LINES LTD
SALLYMAN (NIG.) LTD
SALTAJ NIGERIA LTD
SAMCHAM HOLDINGS LTD
SAPID AGENCIES LTD
SHIPPING MAGNATE LTD
SIFAX NIGERIA LTD
SKYROUTE AGENCY LTD
SON INTENATIONAL AGENCIES (NIG.) LTD
SOTAEN NIGERIA LTD
SPEEDY WORLD LTD
SUPERMARITIME (NIG.) LTD
SYKOBIN INVESTMENT LTD
TANO AGENCY & SHIPPING CO. LTD
THE ASSOC. OF NIG. CO-OP. EXPORTERS LTD
THE COOPERS GROUP LTD
TOKKE MARITIME SERVICES LTD
TRANE AGENCIES
TRANS ATLANTIC SHIPPING AGENCY LTD
TRANSALTIC NIGERIA LTD
TRANS-CLASS WORLD SERVICES NIGERIA LTD
TRANSMARINE NIGERIA LTD
UNICENT ENTERPRISES LTD
UNITED FREIGHT SERVICES LTD
VAN INVESTMENTS LTD
VERITAS & COMPANY (NIG.) LTD
WARRY-GEE MAYO & COMPANY (NIG.) LTD
WORLD MARITIME LTD
YODESONS GROUP OF COMPANIES
YOUNESCO LTD
ZEALETT CARGOES LTD
ZENITH SHIPPING CO. LTD

COCOA PROCESSORS & EXPORTERS
AGRO ALLIED DEVELOPMENT ENTERPRISES LTD
ALL GRAINS (WEST AFRICA) LTD
BEEB HOLDINGS LTD
CARGILL VENTURES LTD
COCOA INDUSTRIES LTD
EBUN INDUSTRIES LTD
ED & F MAN NIGERIA LTD
OLAM NIGERIA LTD
SARO AGROCHEMICALS LTD
STANMARK COCOA PROCESSING CO. LTD
UNICONTROL COMMODITY NIGERIA LTD
WATYEM-DKS ENTERPRISE LTD

COLOUR SEPARATION, IMAGING & PRE-PRESS SERVICES
CLEAR IMPRESSIONS LTD
HEPTAGON VENTURES LTD
HYWILLS GRAPHIC LTD
INTEC PRINTERS LTD
JIMMY VIRGO PRESS LTD
LITHOTEC LTD
PHILIP TRIMNELL PRODUCTIONS LTD
PLANET GRAFFIX (NIG.) LTD
PROGRAFIK LTD
ROYAL PRESS LTD
STAR MODERN PAPER MILL LTD
TDT LTD
THEMES & SCHEMES LTD
TRANSCAN GRAPHICS LTD
TRYFAM NIGERIA LTD
VICODA LTD

COMPANY REGISTRARS/SECRETARIAL STUDIES
COSEC SERVICES LTD
DANLON ASSOCIATES
DTT SERVICES LTD

EKO NOMINEES LTD
EXCEL SECURITIES LTD
GENASEC NOMINEES NIGERIA LTD
MARINA NOMINEES LTD
NIDB TRUSTEES LTD

COMPUTER/INFORMATION TECHNOLOGY CONSULTANCY SERVICES

AB TECHNOLOGIES (NIG.) LTD
ACCOUNTING SOLUTIONS
ADVANCED DIGITAL TECHNOLOGY NIGERIA LTD
AFRO SYSTEMS & TECHNOLOGY LTD
ALASCO COMPUTERS (NIG.) LTD
ALLIED TECHNOLOGIES & DIVERSIFIED SERVICES LTD
ANSA SYSTEMS LTD
APPLEBY NIGERIA LTD
ASONNET TECHNOLOGIES LTD
ASSOCIATED DATA SYSTEMS LTD
AVANCE SYSTEMS LTD
B & M COMPUTER SERVICES NIGERIA LTD
BELLAN ASSOCIATES LTD
BI-TRAX COMPANY INCORPORATED
BUILDING & TECHNICAL INFORMATN CONSULTANTS
CAPITAL TECHNOLOGICAL SOLUTION LTD
CASAC NIGERIA LTD
CITI COMMUNICATIONS LTD
CITILINK GROUP
CITY BUSINESS COMPUTER LTD
CLONE CONCEPT LTD
COMMERCIAL & SCIENTIFIC COMPUTING NIG. LTD
COMMUNICATION WAYS & MEANS LTD
COMPLETE NETWORKS NIGERIA LTD
COMPUSCOPE INTERNATIONAL LTD
COMPUTER SYTEMS ASSOCIATES LTD
COMPUTER WAREHOUSE GROUP
COMPUTER-RITE SYSTEMS LTD
COMTEL SYSTEMS LTD
CONNECTIVITY RESOURCES LTD
DADA SADARE CONSULTANTS
DEBIS (NIG.) LTD
DEVICES & TECHNIQUES LTD
DIGITRUST (NIG.) LTD
EDP AUDIT & SECURITY ASSOCIATES
ENTERPRISES INFORMATION TECHNOLOGIES LTD
EPIDATA CONSULTING LTD
FALCON COMPUTERS LTD
GAFUNK NIGERIA LTD
GENESYS INTERNATIONAL LTD
GIGABYTES SYSTEMS (NIG.) LTD
GLOBAL INTERNET LTD
HCN TECHNOLOGIES LTD
ICON eTECHNOLOGIES LTD
IDEA KONSULT LTD
IMAGE TECHNOLOGIES LTD
IMPEXX RESOURCES LTD
INFORMATION MANAGEMENT RESOURCES NIG. LTD
INTEGRATED DATA SERVICES LTD
INTER SYSTEMS NIGERIA LTD
INTERNATIONAL COMPUTERS (NIG.) LTD (ICL)
INTERNATIONAL CONSULTING GROUP LTD
INTERNATIONAL DATA MANAGEMT SERVICES LTD
ITEC SOLUTIONS LTD
ITECO (NIG.) LTD
JETLINK LTD
KES COMPUTER ENGINEERS LTD
KPMG CONSULTING LTD
LABYET POLARIS NIGERIA LTD
LEADING EDGE LTD
MANKRIS VENTURES LTD
MICRO PRODUCTS INTERNATIONAL (NIG.) LTD
MICROBYTE INTERNATIONAL (NIG.) LTD
MICROTECH SYSTEMS LTD
MICROWORKS NIGERIA LTD
MULTIMESH COMMUNICATION LTD
MYLOID TELECOMMUNICATIONS LTD
NCR (NIG.) PLC
NSL CONSULTING LTD
OMICRON IMAGING TECHNOLOGIES LTD
OSIQUIP BUSINESS AIDS LTD
OXFORD TECHNOLOGIES LTD
PHAREZ LTD
POTOMAC COMPUTERS LTD
PROGENICS CORP.LTD
RDM LTD
RESOURCERY LTD
ROSS CLAYTON LTD
S & D GROUP
SAAP-TECH NIGERIA LTD
SCIENTIFIC INFORMATION LTD
SIMBA TECHNOLOGY (NIG.) LTD
SIMOCH INTERNATIONAL LTD
SOLUTION TECH LTD
SPRADIT COMPUTERS LTD
SPRINGFOUNTAIN LTD
SUPERIOR EQUIPMENT LTD
SYBASE NIGERIA LTD
SYNERCOM LTD
SYNERGY SYSTEMS LTD
TECHNOLOGY EXCHANGE LTD
THEOBECK SYSTEMS LTD
TINEX NIGERIA LTD
TOPCLASS COMPUTERS (NIG.) LTD
TRANTER INTERNATIONAL LTD
TRIPPLE "E" SYSTEMS ASSOCIATES LTD
USG TECHNOLOGY LTD
WADOF SOFTWARE CONSULTING LTD
WEARNESS NIGERIA LTD
WECO COMPUTER SERVICES LTD

COMPUTER SOFTWARE DEVELOPMENT & MARKETING

A-Z COMPUTER WOLRD LTD
ACCOUNTING SOLUTIONS.
ALASCO COMPUTERS (NIG.) LTD
ALLIED TECHNOLOGIES & DIVERSIFIED SERVICES LTD
APPLIED-TECH MANAGEMENT CONSULTANTS LTD
ASSOCIATED DATA SYSTEMS LTD
AVANCE SYSTEMS LTD
AXIS INFORMATION SYSTEMS LTD
BELLAN ASSOCIATES LTD
BENCHMARCK COMPUTER SOLUTIONS LTD
BITCOM SYSTEMS (NIG.) LTD
BI-TRAX COMPANY INCORPORATED
BUSINESS NETWORKS LTD
CASAC NIGERIA LTD
CEETADEL COMPUTER LTD
CHAMS NIGERIA LTD

CHIPS, BITS & BYTES LTD
CITY BUSINESS COMPUTERS LTD
COMMERCIAL & SCIENTIFIC COMPUTING NIG. LTD
COMMUNICATION WAYS & MEANS LTD
COMPUSCOPE VENTURES LTD
COMPUSOLVE INTERNATIONAL LTD
COMPUTER & INFO. MANAGEMENT CENTRE LTD
COMPUTER SYSTEMS ASSCIATES (NIG.) LTD
COMPUTER WAREHOUSE GROUP
COMPUTE-RITE SYSTEMS LTD
CONSOLIDATE ACE LTD
COSCHARIS TECHNOLOGIES LTD
DATA & TELECOMMUNICATIONS (NIG.) LTD
DATANET SYSTEMS LTD
DE HAASTRUP COMMUNICATION NIGERIA LTD
EDP AUDIT & SECURITY ASSOCIATES
EPIDATA CONSULTING LTD.
FINANCE APPLICATION SYSTEMS LTD
FUTURE TECHNOLOGY SYSTEMS LTD
GAFUNK NIGERIA LTD.
GHOTEK TECHNOLOGIES LTD
GIGABYTE SYSTEMS (NIG.) LTD
ICON eTECHNOLOGIES LTD
INFO SOFT NIGERIA LTD.
INFORMATION MANAGEMENT RESOURCES NIG. LTD
INNOVATIVE SYSTEMS LTD
INTELI-TECH LTD
INTER SYSTEMS NIGERIA LTD
INTERNATIONAL DATA MANAGEMT SERVICES LTD
KES COMPUTER ENGINEERS LTD
LABYET POLARIS NIGERIA LTD
MAGIC SOFTWARE ENTERPRISES NIGERIA LTD
MEGA SOURCE NETWORK INCORPORATED
MEGATECH SOFTWARE LTD
MICRONET TECHNOLOGIES (NIG.) LTD
MICROTECH SYSTEMS LTD
MICROWARE NIGERIA LTD
MULTISOLF LTD
NIGERIANET TECHNOLOGY SERVICES LTD
OMICRON IMAGING TECHNOLOGY LTD
ORBITAL COMPUTER SERVICES LTD
PHAREZ LTD
PI NIGERIA LTD
POTOMAC COMPUTERS LTD
PROGENICS CORP LTD
RESOURCERY LTD
RIPPCON NIGERIA LTD
SAFOLE NIGERIA LTD
SAGE BUSINESS GROUP (Robert Ade-Odiaci & Co.).
SAP (SYSTEMS APPLICATION PRODUCTS) NIG LTD.
SIDMACH TECHNOLOGIES NIGERIA LTD
SOFT SOLUTIONS LTD
SOUTHGATE TECHNOLOGIES LTD
SUNCOAST (NIG.) LTD
SYNERCOM LTD
SYNERGY SYSTEMS LTD
SYSTEMCARE & SOFTWARE LTD
SYSTEMTECH SERVICES LTD
TECHNO-LOGIC NIGERIA LTD
TEEOMY SYSTEMS LTD
THEOBECH SYSTEMS LTD
TOEM TECHNOLOGIES LTD
TOPCLASS COMPUTERS (NIG.) LTD
TRITECH COMPUTERS LTD
WADOF SOFTWARE CONSULTING LTD
WECO COMPUTER SYSTEMS LTD
X-CEL COMPUTER CO. LTD

CONFERENCE CENTRES & FACILITIES

D'ROVANS HOTEL LTD
EKO HOTEL & SUITES
FESTAC '77 HOTEL PLC
GOLDEN GATE PARADISE NIGERIA LTD
GRAND HOTEL, ASABA
HILL STATION HOTEL LTD
IMO CONCORDE HOTEL LTD
LAGOS AIRPORT HOTEL LTD
LAGOS HILTON HOTEL LTD
LAGOS TRAVEL INN
PORT HARCOURT INT'L AIRPORT HOTEL LTD
PREMIER HOTEL, IBADAN
ROCKVIEW HOTEL, ABUJA
SHAGALINKU HOTEL AND CONFERENCE CENTRE
SHERATON LAGOS HOTEL & TOWERS
SHONNY INVESTMENT & PROPERTY CO. LTD
STOP OVER MOTELS LTD
THE LAGOON RESTAURANT
TRAINING & CONFERENCE CENTRE, LAGOS.

CORPORATE GIFTS SUPPLIERS

ADSPACE COMMUNICATIONS LTD
AL-BRETT INTERNATIONAL LTD
ALIBAN GROUP LTD
A-ONE (SOFISTICAT) LTD
BIOTECH AUDIO VISUAL (NIG.) LTD
BURTOMLINE LTD
CARDINAL CONCEPTS ADVERTISING LTD
CHARELLA NIGERIA LTD
COLOURS IN AFRICA
DELTA COLOUR PRODUCTION NIGERIA LTD
EDNEL NIGERIA LTD
EL & KAY NIGERIA LTD
FEMEB NIGERIA LTD
FINIDEL NIGERIA LTD
FRANCIS STILL WATERS NIGERIA LTD
GINO RESOURCES LTD
GONAC GROUP
HAMBLESIDE NIGERIA LTD
HEROES FURNITURE LTD
HOLE 19 INVESTEMENT LTD
JIMMY VIRGO PRESS LTD
KINDELL LTD
KOGGI INDUSTRIES LTD
LEATHER CREATIONS LTD
LEMANSHE MANUF. & CONSULTANCY (NIG) LTD
LITERAMED PUBLICATIONS (NIG.) LTD
MUNDIAL ENTERPRISES LTD
OAKWOOD NIGERIA LTD
OUTDOOR COMMUNICATIONS LTD
POLO LTD
REECHMONDZ CO. LTD
RENART PRINTS LTD
ROGA GROUP OF COMPANIES
ROSAAB INDUSTRIAL DESIGN LTD
ROYAL COMMUNICATIONS LTD
SAINT FLAIRS AWARDS LTD

SEA SANDY INVESTMENTS LTD
SEVELLE NIGERIA LTD
THE PEN SHOP LTD
UMM VENTURES LTD
VIGEO LTD
WEST AFRICAN BOOK PUBLISHERS LTD
ZACCHI & KROME LTD

COURIER AND FREIGHT SERVICES
ABEX EXPRESS PARCEL SERVICES
BEMS LTD
BLUE CHIP EXPRESS LTD
BROADLINE SERVICES LTD
CITY MESSENGERS NIGERIA LTD
CLIENTS INTERNATIONAL LTD
CROWN COURIER SERVICES LTD
DHL INTERNATIONAL (NIGERIA) LTD
EMS/SPEEDPOST.
EXCELLENCE ALL FREIGHT LTD
FedEx REDSTAR EXPRESS.
FENWAY COURIER EXPRESS SERVICES (NIG.) LTD
GLOBAL EXPRESS LTD.
GRAYLINK FLEXFREIGHT SERVICES NIGERIA LTD
MIC-MERAH INTERNATIONAL AGENCY LTD
OGIDI AVIATION SERVICES LTD
PRECISION COURIER SERVICES LTD
red\line NIGERIA LTD
SUMMIT PARCEL SERVICE LTD
TNT/IAS CARGO AIRLINES (NIGERIA) LTD
TRANS AFRICA AIR EXPRESS LTD
TRANS-NATIONAL EXPRESS PLC
TRANSCONTINENTAL EXPRESS SERVICES LTD
TROPICAL EXPRESS NIGERIA LTD
UNITED COURIER LTD
UNITED PARCEL SERVICE
XPRESS PARTNERS LIMITED
WADOYE NIGERIA LTD

CREDIT CARDS & DISCOUNT SERVICES
ETN DISCOUNT NETWORK NIGERIA LTD
GEMCARD NIGERIA LTD
SMARTCARD NIGERIA PLC

CRUDE OIL REFINING
ELEME PETROCHEMICALS CO. LTD
KADUNA REFINING & PETROCHEMICALS CO. LTD
PORT HARCOURT REFINING CO. LTD
WARRI REFINING & PETROCHEMICALS CO. LTD

CUSTOMS-BONDED TERMINAL OPERATORS
BRAWAL LINES LTD
C.J. TERMINAL & STEVEDORES LTD
CARGO VISION NIGERIA LTD
CRESEADA INTERNATIONAL LTD
DUNCAN MARITIME NIGERIA LTD
INLAND CONTAINERS (NIG.) LTD
JOINCROWN EXPRESS LTD
MICHELLE BONDED TERMINAL NIGERIA LTD
MID MARITIME SERVICES LTD
SAIL SEA SHIPPING LINES LTD
SAPID AGENCIES LTD
SIFAX NIGERIA LTD

DAIRY PRODUCTS MANUFACTURERS/DISTRIBUTIONS
AJOKE STORES LTD
AKRON (NIG.) LTD
BRIGHTWAY INTERNATIONAL (NIG.) LTD
CARNCO FOODS (NIG.) LTD
CONSOLIDATED FOOD & BEVERAGES LTD
CONTINENTAL FEEDERS (NIG.) LTD
ESCO SUPERSTORES LTD
FAN MILK PLC
JAWA GROUP OF COMPANIES
KNEIPE NIGERIA LTD
MALDESA NIGERIA LTD
PROMASIDOR NIGERIA LTD
SABEANAT NIGERIA LTD
SANTANA FOODS LTD
UAC OF NIGERIA PLC
WEST AFRICA MILK CO. (NIG) PLC

DEPARTMENTAL STORES/SUPERMARKETS
A DIFFERENT WORLD LTD
CASH 'N' CARRY (NIG.) LTD
COMMERCIAL GIVE 'N' TAKE (NIG.) LTD
MEGA INVESTMTS LTD (Mega-Plaza Century 21 Mall)
PARK 'n' SHOP (Div. of Artee Ind. Ltd)
STOP CENTRE (Div. of Eta Noel Ltd.)
TRY 'N' CARRY (NIG.) LTD

DISTILLERIES & VINTNERS
DEEBEE CO. LTD
EASTERN DISTILLERIES & FOOD INDUSTRIES LTD
ELCHEM LTD
FLUREX INDUSTRIES (NIG.) LTD
INTERCONTINENTAL DISTILLERIES LTD
KERLIN PRODUCTS NIGERIA LTD
KP BEVERAGES CO. LTD
NIGERIA DISTILLERIES LTD
OZDE GROUP OF COMPANIES
UNITED DISTILLERS & VINTNERS NIGERIA LTD

DREDGING & LAND RECLAMATION ENGINEERING
AGRO-INDUSTRIES & DEVELOPMENT SCHEME LTD
BALLAST HAM NIGERIA
BENEK ENGINEERING CO. LTD
CONTRANSAR INTERNATIONAL NIGERIA LTD
DREDGING INTERNATIONAL SERVICES NIGERIA LTD
ENOSCO NIGERIA LTD
ESSENTIAL MARINE OIL SERVICES LTD
FOUNDATION CONSTRUCTION LTD
FUNG-TAI ENGINEERING CO. LTD
GIORGIO DREDGING LTD
ICON MARINE SERVICES LTD
JM DREDGING & MARITIME LTD
NIGERIAN WESTMINISTER DREDGING & MARINE LTD
OZIGBU ENGINEERING CO. LTD
RAPHA SERVICES CO. LTD
SHORELINE CHEMICALS & OIL SERVICES LTD
SMIEC CHEMICAL ENGINEERING & CONST. CO. LTD
YESIN INTERNATIONAL NIGERIA LTD

DRYCLEANING & LAUNDRY SERVICES
EMBASSY DRYCLEANING & LAUNDRY SERVICES LTD
FIRST EKIMOGUN NIGERIA LTD.
GARMENT CARE LTD

INSTANT CLEANERS LTD
MICHANI ENTERPRISES LTD
NATHAN'S DRYCLEANERS
WASHAMAN DRYCLEANERS NIGERIA LTD

DYESTUFF & PIGMENTS MANUFACTURERS & MARKETERS
ADEJUMO FAM (NIG.) LTD
BASF (NIG.) LTD
CENTURY DYES & CHEMICALS LTD
DYECHEM NIGERIA LTD
FINE CHEMICALS NIGERIA LTD
JAWA GROUP OF COMPANIES
MULTICHEM INDUSTRIES LTD
PRINT INKS NIGERIA LTD
SWISS COLOUR NIGERIA LTD
UNICHEM NIGERIA LTD

ELECTRIC CABLE & WIRE MANUFACTURERS
ALIND (NIG.) LTD
BENMAX CABLES LTD
COLEMAN TECHNICAL INDUSTRIES LTD
CUTIX PLC
GEOELIS CABLES LTD
MicCom CABLES & WIRES LTD
MMAB CABLE MANUFACTURING INDUSTRIES LTD
NEXANS KABELMETAL NIGERIA PLC
NIGERCHIN ELECTRICAL DEV. CO. LTD
NIGERIAN WIRE AND CABLE PLC
NORTHERN CABLE PROCESSING & MANUF. CO. LTD

ELECTRICAL ENGINEERING/CONSULTANCY SERVICES
AIRFLOW ENGINEERING WORKS LTD
AKOWHO SERVICES LTD
AMAFO ENGINEERING LTD
AMCO TECHNICAL ENGINEERING CO. LTD
ARIZONA CONSTRUCTION LTD
ASCENT LTD
BAFANI ENGINEERING CO. LTD
BECTHEL (NIG.) LTD
BETCY GROUP OF COMPANIES
BMA NIGERIA LTD
BOLAMAK ENGINEERING LTD
BUOSHISHI HOLDINGS LTD
CHROME OIL SERVICES LTD
CLEMESSY NIGERIA LTD
CONSTRUCTION PRODUCTS NIGERIA LTD
D.S.D (NIG.) LTD
DANBRITE COMPANY NIGERIA LTD
DANELEC LTD
DASAT NETWORK SYSTEMS LTD
DRAKE & SCULL (NIG.) LTD
DREK CO. LTD
ELECTRA TECHNICAL CO. LTD
ELEKTRIM (NIG.) LTD
ELEKTRINT (NIG.) LTD
ELGAR (NIG.) LTD
ENERGY & COMMUNICATIONS INT'L (NIG.) LTD
ENGINEERING & TECHNICAL COMPANY (NIG.) LTD
ESE-TECH (NIG.) LTD
FENIKOH NIGERIA LTD
FRANCHISE PARTICIPATION LTD
FRANK'S COMET GROUP
FRIGOTERMICA NIGERIA LTD
GAMA ENGINEERING LTD
GILCO NIGERIA LTD
GLENYORK NIGERIA LTD
GRAHAM BELL (NIG.) LTD
H.F. SCHROEDER (WEST AFRICA) LTD
HADEMEC LTD
ICON eTECHNOLOGIES LTD
INDUSTRIAL PORTS ENGINEERING SERVICES LTD
INTERLINKED TECHNOLOGIES PLC
JAGAL NIGERIA LTD
JIYODA ENGINEERING NIGERIA LTD
JOHN-RAY LTD
JOMANNAG NIGERIA LTD
JONAC ENGINEERING PLANTS (NIG.) LTD
KASTEL NIGERIA LTD
LATRASAK NIGERIA LTD
MADONA ORGANISATION LTD
MECHANICAL & ELECTRICAL CONTRACTORS LTD
MEKIOS LTD
MINESFIELD ENGINEERING LTD
MOTHERCAT LTD
NAIRDA LTD
ORRI TECH NIGERIA LTD
PHOENIX ENGINEERING & CONTRACTOR LTD
PIVOT ENGINEERING CO. LTD
PORTLAND RENOVATIONS & CONSTRUCTION LTD
POWER SYSTEMS TECHNOLOGY LTD
POWERLINES LTD
POWERTRON (NIG.) LTD
RAHUSA VENTURES NIGERIA LTD
REAL TIME TECHNOLOGY (NIG.) LTD
SARM NIGERIA LTD
SEFAM CO. LTD
SENIL POWER PROTECTION SYSTEMS LTD
SOKO-TECH (NIG.) LTD
STAG ENGINEERING (NIG.) LTD
SUDELETTRA NIGERIA LTD
TAG (NIG.) LTD
TRANTER INTERNATIONAL LTD
TYME RESOURCES AND CO. LTD
UNITED SWITCHGEARS & CONTROLS LTD
UREN CONSTRUCTION ENGINEERING CO. LTD
WECO ENGINEERING & CONSTRUCTION CO. LTD
WEMTRACO (NIG.) LTD
WESTRON GROUP OF COMPANIES
YINKA FOLAWIYO ELECT. & MECHANICAL CO. LTD
YODESONS GROUP OF COMPANIES

ELECTRICAL MATERIALS & EQUIPMENT MARKETERS
AMASAYE INVESTMENT LTD
BANIT INVESTMENT LTD
BOLAMARK ENGINEERING LTD
C.N. OKOLI INVESTMENT COMPANY NIGERIA LTD
CABLE & SATELLITE COMMUNICATIONS LTD
CAPERNAUM VENTURES LTD
DOFAS TECHNICAL NIGERIA LTD
DOMAX INTERNATIONAL LTD
EMO-TIMEX LTD
FABROS ENTERPRISES LTD
GEE WILLIAMS NIGERIA LTD
IBRON LTD
INCOMTEL NIGERIA LTD
INTERNATIONAL CONTROL SYSTEMS LTD

INTERNATIONAL TOOLS LTD
J. O. ASUZU BROS & COMPANY (W.A) LTD
JANGO INTERNATIONAL (NIG.) LTD
JAZOM INTERNATIONAL (NIG.) LTD
JOMANNAG NIGERIA LTD
KASTEL NIGERIA LTD
LANCO NIGERIA LTD
MIC-MIBE & BROTHERS NIGERIA LTD
MINNESOTA NIGERIA LTD
NAJICO IRON & STEEL CO. LTD
NNEJI & SONS ELECTRIC LTD
NUDAL NIGERIA CO. LTD
ON-LINE PRODUCTS EQUIPMENTS & SERVICES LTD
OSCARTE NIGERIA LTD
P & J ELECTRICAL & INDUSTRIAL CO. (NIG.) LTD
POWER CONTROL & APPLIANCES LTD
SIMS NIGERIA LTD
SKEIN NIGERIA LTD
SOCATEC ELECTRICAL INDUSTRIES NIGERIA LTD
THE WEST AFRICAN ENGINEERING CO. (NIG.) LTD
WHITEHALL MULTINATIONAL LTD
YODESONS GROUP OF COMPANIES

ELECTRICITY ENGINEERING/PRODUCTS SALES (Generation/Transmission/Distribution)
ABULICO NIGERIA LTD
AES NIGERIA BARGE LTD
AGCOMEX LTD
AMASAYE INVESTMENT LTD
BEST & CROMPTON ENGINEERING (NIG.) LTD
COUTINHO CARO & COMPANY (NIG.) LTD
DAYAKAS NIGERIA LTD
ELEKTRIM (NIG.) LTD
ENERGY COMPANY NIGERIA LTD
GILCO NIGERIA LTD
GRAHAM BELL (NIG.) LTD
H.F. SCHROEDER (WEST AFRICA) LTD
JIYODA ENGINEERING NIGERIA LTD
MAYOK ENGINEERING WORKS LTD
MUNAK GROUP LTD
NATEC NIGERIA LTD
NIGERIAN ELECTRICITY SUPPLY CORP. (NIG.) LTD
OZIGBU ENGINEERING CO. LTD
PLANTGERIA CO. LTD
POWER SYSTEMS TECHNOLOGY LTD
SAFE NIGERIA LTD
SAGAOLA MINING & ENGINEERING (NIG.) LTD
SALINI NIGERIA LTD
SILICON ENGINEERING LTD
VOEST-ALPINE (NIG.) LTD
YF POWER NIGERIA LTD
ZIATECH NIGERIA LTD

ELECTRICITY GENERATORS SALES & SERVICE
AADE INDUSTRIA L & INVESTMENTS CO. LTD
AFROCOMMERCE (W.A.) LTD
AMABROS TECHNICAL CO. LTD
BARNAX ENGINEERING COMPANY (NIG.) LTD
BENLOCK NIGERIA LTD
BHN PLC
BRISCOEatlascopco (Div. of R.T. Briscoe Nig. Plc)
C. JOE KANNON INTERNATIONAL LTD
C. WOERMANN (NIG.) LTD
CAMPLANT ENGINEERING SALES AND SERVICE LTD
CASTLAT GROUP OF COMPANIES
CHRIS EJIK GROUP OF COMPANIES LTD
CHRISTON INVESTMENT LTD
CICA NIGERIA LTD
CNEICO (NIG.) LTD
CONVEYYANCER (NIG.) LTD
DAVOF TRADING COMPANY (NIG.) LTD
DONNATEC ENGINEERING CO. LTD
ENERGIE NIGERIA LTD
ESCRAVOS PROJECTS LTD
ESTENDO POWER PRODUCTS CO. LTD
EUNIBROWN (WEST AFRICA) LTD
FAR EAST TECHNICAL NIGERIA LTD
FOREST CITY LTD
FOTOKLINIC NIGERIA LTD
FRANK'S COMET GROUP
GABIMO HOLDINGS LTD
GENTECH POWER SUPPLY NIGERIA LTD
GEOBI (NIG.) LTD
GOCUS GROUP LTD
GOKAS NIGERIA LTD
H.B.M. GENERAL SUPPLIES LTD
INCAR (NIG.) PLC
JOHN BEDOLA ENTERPRISES LTD
JOHN HOLT ENGINEERING (Div. of John Holt Plc)
JUBAILI BROS. ENGINEERING LTD
JUBAILI MOUKARIM GROUP LTD. (JMG LTD)
KRESTA LAUREL LTD
L.N. TECHNOLOGIES LTD
L.W. LAMBOURN NIGERIA LTD
LANRE SHITTU GROUP OF COMPANIES
LEVENTIS POWER SYSTEMS LTD
MASONS GROUP1
MIKANO INTERNATIONAL LTD
MUNAK GROUP LTD
NIODA LTD
NIZAK TECHNICAL (SUPPLY) CO. LTD
OMENI GROUP LTD.
OOSY INDUSTRIES LTD
PHILPET VENTURES LTD
POWERGAS (NIG.) LTD
POWERLINE ENGINEERING SERVICES LTD
PRIME ENERGY & ENGINEERING LTD
RADIO COMMUNICATIONS (NIG.) LTD
RAYBROS ENTERPRISES (NIG.) LTD
REAL TIME TECHNOLOGY (NIG.) LTD
SCOA TRAC (Div. of SCOA Nigeria Plc)
SEG. MAHSEN & COMPANY (NIG.) LTD
SKEIN NIGERIA LTD
SPARK POWER GENERATORS LTD
STAG ENGINEERING (NIG.) LTD
TOP NOTCH ENGINEERING LTD
UNIVERSAL POWER SYSTEMS NIGERIA LTD
WITT & BUSCH LTD
YIFA NIGERIA LTD
ZIATECH NIGERIA LTD

ELECTRONIC & INSTRUMENTATION ENGINEERING SERVICES
ABB ELECTRICAL SYSTEMS LTD
ABG COMMUNICATIONS LTD
ASEA BROWN BOVERI LTD

BAFANI ENGINEERING CO. LTD
DANELEC LTD
ELGAR (NIG.) LTD
FRANCHISE PARTICIPATION LTD
GAMA ENGINEERING LTD
GENERAL TELEPHONES & ELECTRONICS LTD
GENUSS INVESTMENTS LTD
GRAHAM BELL (NIGERIA) LTD
INDUSTRIAL PORTS ENGINEERING SERVICES LTD
MOTU-TEC LTD
NUMERIQUE LTD
OVERSEAS TECHNICAL SERVICE NIGERIA LTD
SIEMENS LTD
WECO ENGINEERING & CONSTRUCTION CO. LTD

ENGINEERING CONSULTANCY SERVICES
AIM GROUP
ALLOTT NIGERIA LTD
AMANA CONSULTING ENGINEERS
AOP-CONSULT LTD
BEST & CROMPTON ENGINEERING (NIG.) LTD
BMA NIGERIA LTD
CIV-STRUCT ASSOCIATES
COMPLETE PROJECTS ENGINEERING CONSORTIUM
COMPREHENSIVE PROJECT MGT SERVICES LTD
DE-CROWN (WEST AFRICA) LTD
DEO MAKRO LTD
EL-BEZALEEL CONSULTS LTD
ENPLAN GROUP
ETTEH ARO & PARTNERS
FINCO ENGINEERS.
HANCOCK OGUNDIYA & PARTNERS
HASKONING ENGINEERING CONSULTANTS (NIG.) LTD
HAY, BARRY, ODUNSI & ASSOCIATES
JIYODA ENGINEERING NIGERIA LTD
KEMENG SERVICES LTD
KRISCO ENGINEERING SERVICES LTD
KUNLE OGUNBAYO & ASSOCIATES
LINKSO NIGERIA LTD
LUBESERVICES ASSOCIATES
McADOG & ASSOCIATES
MEC CONSULT
MORGAN, OMONITAN & ABE LTD.
NATIONAL ENGINEERING & TECHNICAL CO. LTD
OBI OBEMBE & ASSOCIATES
OVE ARUP & PARTNERS NIGERIA
PINCONSULT ASSOCIATES
PROGRESS ENGINEEERS
REID CROWTHER NIGERIA LTD
SAMPAL ENGINEERING SERVICES INTERNATIONAL
SHELTER WORKS LTD
SHONUBI MEK-IND ASSOCIATES
SOLID BASE NIGERIA LTD
TATEC INTERBIZ LTD
TEMPAS CONSULTANTS
TORNADO INTERNATIONAL ASSOCIATES LTD
TRIPLE "E" SYSTEMS ASSOCIATES LTD
UNECON ASSOCIATES LTD
VISION RESERVOIR MGT TECH. (VRMT) INT'L

ENGRAVING, CASTING & MONOGRAMMING SERVICES
ABBEY SPECIAL JEWELLERS LTD
ABEKOGOLD LTD
AL-BRETT INTERNATIONAL LTD
EMCAST WORKS LTD
FERDINAND TECHNICAL & TRADING CO. LTD
FIMCO LTD
GRAPHITEK VENTURES LTD
HYDRALINK LTD
INTERNATIONAL UNIFORMS NIGERIA LTD
MONOGRAMM & LOGO CREATIONS LTD
NIGERIAN PRECISION ENGRAVERS LTD
PROMOMART NIGERIA LTD
QUARTERMASTERS LTD
RENART PRINTS LTD
ROGA GROUP OF COMPANIES
ROSAAB INDUSTRIAL DESIGN LTD8
XLEVEL LTD
ZACCHI PLANNERS LTD

ENVIRONMENTAL CONSULTANCY SERVICES
ALBA NIGERIA LTD
ALFA LABORATORIES LTD
ALKO LTD
ASH-BERT (NIG.) LTD
ATLANTIC WASTE MANAGEMENT LTD
AUGIAS ENVIRON. & CONSULTING SERVICES LTD
BALLAST HAM NIGERIA
CINO NIGERIA LTD
DAVCO INTERNATIONAL (NIG.) LTD
DEO MAKRO LTD
DUBI (NIG.) CO. LTD
el-RUFAI & PARTNERS LTD
ENVIRONMENTAL RESOURCES MANAGERS LTD
FALCON PETROLEUM LTD
GEOMATICS NIGERIA LTD
GLITZ PETROLEUM LTD
GLOBAL ENVIRONMENTAL CONSULTANTS LTD
GLOBAL ENVIRONMENTAL TECHNOLOGY LTD
HARMONY PROJECTS LTD
HYDRO CONSTRUCTION & ENGINEERING CO. LTD
JAROS INSPECTION SERVICES LTD
MAIL-IN OILFIELDS SERVICES LTD
MASSOIL FIELD SERVICES LTD
NESTOIL LTD
PAMAQUE NIGERIA LTD
PRAKLA GEOMECHANIK INTERNATIONAL LTD
PRIME ENERGY RESOURCES LTD
PRODEC-FUGRO LTD
PROVIDENCE CONSULT & SERVICES LTD
SAFETY ENGINEERING & FIRE CONSULTANTS LTD
SCHWARTZ GROUP OF COMPANIES
SPECIALTY DRILLING FLUIDS LTD
STILLWATER GROUP OF COMPANIES
TEMEC NIGERIA LTD
THERMOSTEEL NIGERIA LTD
TOMBULCO (NIG.) LTD
TRIPLE 'E' SYSTEMS ASSOCIATES LTD
TRITHEL INTERNATIONAL CO. LTD
VIGEO LTD
WORLD ENVIRONMENTAL SYSTEMS (NIG.) LTD
ZENITH NIGERGROUP CO. LTD
ZITADEL LTD

FASHION HOUSES & DESIGNERS
ALREN TRADING COMPANY (L'Uomo Lifestyle Plus)

A-ONE (SOFISTICAT) LTD
BEVISTA & CO. LTD
CASTARIO LTD
CHALLENGER NIGERIA LTD (Wrangler Shop)
COLLECTIBLES
CORPORATE CLOTHIERS LTD
DENLYN NIGERIA LTD
FAGBOHUN & CO LTD
LABENELLA INDUSTRIES LTD
LAMBADA VENTURES LTD
LARRUTTI CREATIONS NIGERIA LTD
MAHANAIM & HAVTACHA LTD
MEN'S AFFAIR LTD
NIKKY AFRICANA FASHIONS NIGERIA LTD
OKEMADU INTERNATIONAL LTD
PEACOCK CREATIONS NIGERIA LTD
RUFF 'n' TUMBLE
SILKY TOUCH EMPORIUM
TEXEN LTD
THE ROSE OF SHARON
TOPKLASS BOUTIQUE.
VIVID IMAGINATION

FAST-FOOD PRODUCERS/VENDORS
DOMINO STORES LTD
FAVOURITES LTD
FOREMOST CATERERS LTD
FRENCHIES LTD
NISTECH GROUP
SHAFOL INVESTMENT LTD
SWEET SENSATION CONFECTIONERY LTD
TANTALIZERS NIGERIA LTD
TASTEE POT LTD
UAC FOODS (Div. of UAC of Nigeria Plc)

FIRE CONTROL, DETECTION & PREVENTION EQUIPMENTS MARKETERS
ALPH DESIGNERS (NIG.) LTD
ANALYSED DATA LTD
ANOFENCO (NIG.) LTD
APTICS LTD
BORODO & COMPANY (NIG.) LTD
BUFAMBRA INDUSTRIES LTD
COMATEL INDUSTRIES LTD.
COSPAM (NIG.) LTD
DE-LOUIS TECHNOLOGIES LTD
DREK CO. LTD
ENGINEERING & TECHNICAL COMPANY (NIG.) LTD
FIRESTOP INTERNATIONAL LTD
FIREWORKS INVESTMENTS LTD
GAMA EGINEERING LTD
HENSEN TRUST LTD
HOLMAN BROTHERS (NIG.) LTD
IBA c.m. SYSTEMS (WEST AFRICA) LTD
IPBC NIGERIA LTD
ISIWAS NIGERIA LTD
JAMATAL INDUSTRIES (NIG.) LTD
JKPEEZ IMPEX CO. LTD
LAI SECURITY & INVESTIGATION SERVICES LTD
LOGIC SCIENCES LTD
MICHAEL HAMMOND ENGINEERING CO. LTD
OMOT FIRE PROTECTION ENGINEERING LTD
PINECREST SERVICES (NIG.) LTD
PIVOT ENGINEERING CO. LTD.
RESOURCES TRADES & TECHNOLOGIES LTD
S. OJOLOWO TECHNICAL CO. LTD
SAFEQUIP (NIG.) LTD
SAFETECH LTD
SAFETY ENGINEERING & FIRE CONSULTANTS LTD
SANACO MOTORS NIGERIA LTD
SARM NIGERIA LTD
SOFITAM NIGERIA LTD
STONEHILL NIGERIA LTD
THE WEST AFRICAN ENGINEERING CO. (NIG.) LTD
TROPICAL FIRE PREVENTION SERVICES LTD
URBAN FIRE LTD

FISH FARMING
AKIA AGRO ALLIED PRODUCTS LTD
FRONTLINE FARMS LTD
SAMROSE AGRO-INDUSTRIAL CO. LTD
TALON NIGERIA LTD

FISH TRAWLING & SHRIMPING
BANARLY (NIG.) LTD
BANUSO FISHERIES LTD
COSMOS FISHING CO. LTD
DAVRO (NIG.) LTD
DOLPHINE FISHERIES LTD
EVEN-EZRA NIGERIA LTD
FOLAWIYO FISHERIES LTD
GLOBE FISHING INDUSTRIES LTD
GUSTO INTEGRATED LTD
HENSMOR GROUP OF COMPANIES
HONEYWELL FISHERIES LTD
IBRU SEA FOODS LTD
INTERCONTINENTAL FISHING (NIG.) LTD
MANUCOM FISHING CO. LTD
NOKOY INVESTMENT NIGERIA LTD
OCEAN FISHERIES (NIG.) LTD
ORC FISHING & FOOD PROCESSING LTD
PETRO MED. OILS NIGERIA LTD
SOTONIA FISHERIES LTD
STALLION SEAFOODS LTD
TARABAROZ FISHERIES LTD
TRAWL ATLANTIC LTD
UNITED FISHERIES LTD

FLOUR MILLS
ADOKA HOLDINGS LTD
AKIA AGRO ALLIED PRODUCTS LTD
BENDEL FEED & FLOUR MILS LTD
CROWN FLOUR MILLS LTD
DANGOTE INDUSTRIES LTD
EZERA INTERNATIONAL GROUP OF CO. LTD
FLOUR MILLS OF NIGERIA PLC
GRAIN PROCESSING COMPANY NIGERIA LTD
HONEYWELL FLOUR MILLS LTD
IDEAL FLOUR MILLS LTD
JOS FLOUR MILLS LTD
LIFE FLOUR MILLS LTD
LISTER FLOUR MILLS (NIG.) LTD
MIX & BAKE FLOUR MILLS LTD
MODANDOLA GROUP OF COMPANIES
NIYYA FARMS LTD
NORTHERN NIGERIA FLOUR MILLS PLC

PIONEER MILLING CO. LTD
POKOBROS FOOD & CHEMICAL INDUSTRIES LTD
PORT HARCOURT FLOUR MILLS LTD
SHOREMAN GROUP OF COMPANIES
STANDARD FLOUR MILLS LTD

FOOD PROCESSORS
AJELENJE NIGERIA LTD
AMALGAMATED GROUP OF COMPANIES
AMSEL LTD
ASSOCIATED PHARMA., FOODS & CHEMICALS LTD
BAUCHI MEAT PRODUCT CO. LTD
BEST FOODS GLOBAL (NIG.) LTD
CADBURY NIGERIA PLC
CARNCO FOODS (NIG.) LTD
CHOCOLATE ROYAL LTD
CONSOLIDATED FOOD & BEVERAGES LTD
DANGOTE GROUP.
DANICO (WEST AFRICA) LTD
DANSA FOODS LTD
DE-UNITED FOOD INDUSTRIES LTD
EGHIEMAI INDUSTRIES LTD
EVANS MEDICAL PLC
FAN MILK PLC
FREEDOM (DEVELOPMENT) GROUP LTD
FRENCHIES LTD
GRAND CEREALS & OIL MILLS LTD
INT'L FRACTIONATN & MARGARINE PRODUCTS LTD
J.NWANKWU GROUP OF COMPANIES
JUNO FOODS LTD
KAURA BISCUIT & MACARONI FACTORY LTD
LISABI MILLS (NIG.) LTD
M.A. JOBITEX NIGERIA LTD
MARSTON BARROW FOODS LTD
METALOBA INDUSTRIES LTD
MICHANI ENTERPRISES LTD
NASCO FOODS (NIG.) LTD
NESTLE NIGERIA PLC
NIGERIA ASSOCIATED BEST FOODS LTD
OMATHA HOLDINGS NIGERIA LTD
PRIMLAKS NIGERIA LTD
SANTANA FOODS LTD
UAC FOODS (Div. of UAC of Ngeira Plc)
UNILEVER NIGERIA PLC
UREN UNITED FOOD PROCESSING CO. LTD
UTC NIGERIA PLC
WEST AFRICA MILK CO. (NIGERIA) PLC.
WILLMERR LA CUISSON LTD
ZARTECH LTD

FOOD-BEVERAGES DRINK MANUFACTURERS/MARKETERS
AMSEL LTD
BETTER FOODS LTD
CADBURY NIGERIA PLC
COCOA INDUSTRIES LTD
CONSOLIDATED FOOD & BEVERAGES LTD
DALA FOODS NIGERIA LTD
DANICO (WEST AFRICA) LTD
HARBURY NIGERIA LTD
MARSTON BARROW FOODS LTD
NESTLE NIGERIA PLC
NIGERIA ASSOCIATED BEST FOODS LTD
NIGERIAN BEVERAGES PRODUCTION CO. LTD
NUTRIFOOD & BEVERAGES LTD
SCIRROCCO INTERNATIONAL LTD

FOOD-FLAVOURS, SEASONING & PROCESSING RAW MATERIAL MARKETERS
AMESI COMMERCIAL ENT. LYD
ASSOCIATED BIOTECHNOLOGY LTD
BIO-ORGANICS (NIGERIA) LTD
CADBURY NIGERIA PLC
CONSOLIDATED FOOD & BEVERAGES LTD
DANGOTE INDUSTRIES
DANTATA ORGANISATION LTD
EUROBRIDGE INDUSTRIES LTD
INDUSTRIAL FLAVOURS & COLOURS LTD
KNIGHT CLASS NIGERIA LTD
MARC & MEI (NIGERIA) LTD
NESTLE NIGERIA PLC
SWISS PHARMA NIGERIA LTD
UNION DICON SALT PLC

FORKLIFTS/PALLET TRUCK SALES & SERVICES
CICA NIGERIA LTD
CONVEYANCER (NIG.) LTD
HENRY STEPHENS ENGINEERING CO. LTD

FOUNDATION ENGINEERING SERVICES
BRUNELLI CONSTRUCTION COMPANY (NIG.) LTD
FOUNDATION ENGINEERING SERVICES LTD
TREVI FOUNDATION NIGERIA LTD

FOUNDERIES & CASTING MANUFACTURERS/MARKETERS
BAMFORDS INTERNATIONAL NIGERIA LTD
CANPLAS LTD
EASITECH PROJECTS (NIG.) LTD
GALBA LTD
J. NWANKWU GROUP OF COMPANIES
JOHN-RAY LTD
KADUNA MACHINE WORKS LTD
KENQUIP GROUP OF COMPANIES
MART CHEM INDUSTRY NIGERIA LTD
METALOCK NGIERIA LTD
MINESFIELD ENGINEERING LTD
NIGERIA MACHINE TOOLS LTD
ROCH TOOLS AND PRODUCTS LTD
SAULAWA MACHINERY & FABRICATION IND. LTD
TECO LTD

FRUIT-JUICE DRINK PRODUCERS/MARKETERS
CROWN DRINKS LTD
DEEBEE CO. LTD
FUMMAN AGRICULTURAL PRODUCTS IND. LTD
JOKKY CO. LTD
OCM NIGERIA LTD
SANTANA FOODS LTD
TENEX GROUP NIGERIA LTD

FURNITURE MANUFACTURERS & MARKETERS
AGATHA'S INTERIOR DESIGNS LTD
AMAHAJ LTD
AMERICAN FURNITURE GALLERIES LTD
ANSBREED INVESTMENT LTD. (Numerouno)
ANTHOG DECORATIONS NIGERIA LTD
AUSKEN INTERNATIONAL (NIG.) LTD

CACHE HOMES LTD
CARONC INVESTMENTS LTD
CASTILLA LTD
CHESTERFIELD RESOURCES LTD
CHOICE FINISHING & FURNISHING PRODUCTS LTD
DATEC INTERNATIONAL (NIG.) LTD
EDDY MOORE MARBLE & FURNISHING LTD
EQUINOX INTERNATIONAL RESOURCES LTD
EZE MUSTAFA INDUSTRIES LTD
FILMORE FURNITURE & FITTINGS LTD
FINISHING MARBLE PRODUCTS CO. NIGERIA LTD
FITTING FINISHES LTD
GUSTO INTEGRATED LTD
HEROES FURNITURE LTD
ILLUMINAIRE LTD
ITEX (NIG.) LTD
JEKKY NIGERIA LTD
LEATHERWORLD LTD
MEGER NIGERIA LTD
MSM MICRODEVICES LTD
NIGER HOLDINGS LTD
NOVAFOAM CHEMICAL & WIRE MANUF. NIG. LTD
NOVENA MAJESTY FURNITURE INDUSTRIES LTD
PATED (NIG.) LTD
PELLETTERIA LTD
PORCHESTER INVESTMENTS NIGERIA LTD
PURIFICATION TECHNIQUES (NIG.) LTD
ROYAL SUITES LTD
ROYAS EXCLUSIVE FURNISHINGS LTD
SAFIRE FURNISHINGS NIGERIA LTD
SANS FRONTIERS INVESTMENT LTD
SCOA EQUIP (Div. of SCOA Nigeria Plc)
TECNOBAT FITTINGS & FIXTURES LTD
TEKNO NIGERIA LTD
THE CHAIR CENTRE LTD
THE PEACH CO. LTD
TOTAL OFFICE CONCEPT LTD
VICTORIA LIGHTS & FURNITRE (NIG.) LTD

GAS PRODUCERS, BOTTLERS & MARKETERS
AIR LIQUIDE NIGERIA PLC
ASCON OIL CO. LTD
BOC GASES PLC
DELMAN GROUP OF COMPANIES
DOZZY OIL & GAS LTD
FIRST VENTURES LTD
FLAME PETROLEUM & GAS CO. LTD
GRENIGAS LTD
ILODI GROUP OF COMPANIES
JACOBOD NIGERIA LTD
LOPA ENERGY CO. LTD
MAJOR GAS & INDUSTRIAL LTD
NIDOGAS CO. LTD
NIGERIAN & OVERSEAS GAS CO. LTD (Utilgas)
REAMS NIGERIA LTD
SUNGAS COMPANY NIGERIA LTD
TOM-TAN LTD
TUDAKA PETROLEUM & GAS CO. LTD

GEOLOGICAL/REMOTE SENSING CONSULTANCY SERVICES
AFREX VENTURES LTD
ALOLIS GEO-SCIENCES NIGERIA LTD
FOUNDATION ENGINEERING SERVICES LTD
GEOMATICS NIGERIA LTD
GEOQUEST
GEOSERVICES NIGERIA LTD
GLOBAL ENERGY CO. LTD
HYDRO CONSTRUCTION & ENGINEERING CO. LTD
INTEGRATED ALLIED APPLICATNS ENGINEERING LTD
INTEGRATED DATA SERVICES LTD
LAND & SEA DRILLING CO LTD
MABON LTD
MASSOIL FIELD SERVICES LTD
NIGERIAN LOGGING & SUPPORT SERVICES LTD
PRAKLA GEOMECHANIK INTERNATIONAL LTD
SCANA LTD
UNITED GEOPHYSICAL (NIG.) LTD
VISION RESERVOIR MANAGEMT TECH. (VRMT) INT'L.410
ZENITH NIGERGROUP CO. LTD

HATS MANUFACTURERS & MARKETERS
BIMBY LADS LTD
GRACES HATS LTD
HEADWORKS LTD
JOHN 3V3 HATS LTD

HEALTH & FITNESS CLUBS & CENTRES
CLAIR RESOURCES LTD
HEALTHY LIVING SERVICES LTD
HOME GYMS EQUIPMENT LTD
PRO-FLEX.
VENI VICI

HUMAN RESOURCES CONSULTANTS
ACCENTURE
ACCOUNTING SOLUTIONS
AFRICAN DEVELOPMENT CONSULTING GROUP LTD
AGROVOG LTD
AGUSTO & CO. LTD
BBc CONSULTING LTD
BOYLE-STREET CONSULTING LTD
CHANGE MANAGEMENT ASSOCIATES LTD
CONSOLIDATED MANAGEMENT CONSULTANTS LTD
DELOITTE & TOUCHE MANAGEMENT SOLUTIONS
HUMAN EDGE LTD
INTERGRATED CORPORATE SERVICES LTD
INTERNATIONAL CONSULTING GROUP LTD
INTERNATIONAL DATA MANAGEMT SERVICES LTD
KPMG CONSULTING LTD
LEADING EDGE CONSULTING SERVICES LTD
MAC-DIGITON RESOURCES LTD
McFORD CONSULTING LTD
MICHAEL STEVENS & ASSOCIATES LTD
NEWMAN INVESTMENT CO. LTD
NIDB CONSULTANCY AND FINANCE LTD
OVERSEAS TECHNICAL SERVICES NIGERIA LTD
PHILLIPS CONSULTING LTD
PRICEWATERHOUSECOOPERS CONSULTANTS LTD
RESTRAL CONSULTING LTD
SCG CONSULTING
TELEDOM INTERNATIONAL LTD
VIC LAWRENCE & ASSOCIATES LTD

INDUSTRIAL & PHARMACEUTICAL CHEMICALS MANUFACTURERS/MARKETERS
AADE INDUSTRIAL & INVESTMENTS CO. LTD

ABEOKUTA COMMERCIAL & INDUSTRIAL CO. LTD
ADEJUMO FAM (NIG.) LTD
ADLAD GROUP
AGILITY & BROTHERS ENTERPRISES NIGERIA LTD
AGUATECNICA CO. LTD
AMARILO INDUSTRIES LTD
ASCON OIL CO. LTD
ASSOCIATED BIOTECHNOLOGY LTD
BASF (NIG.) LTD
BHOJSONS & COMPANY (NIGERIA) PLC
BUSSDOR & CO. LTD
CAPITAL OIL PLC
CHEMCOM INDUSTRIES LTD
CHEMICAL AND ALLIED PRODUCTS PLC
CHEMLAP NIGERIA LTD
CHRIS IMPEX LTD
CHURCHGATE GROUP
CIKA GROUP OF COMPANIES
CLARIANT (NIG.) LTD
COMBINED BUSINESS LTD. (PAKTEL)
COMBINE CHEMICAL CO. LTD
COSMIC FOAM & CHEMICAL INDUSTRIES (NIG.) LTD
CUSAL INDUSTRIES LTD
DAT MERCHANT INVESTMENTS LTD
DEROTECH INTERNATIONAL LTD
DOBLINK KREDIT & COMMERCE LTD
DRUG AND HEALTHCARE LTD
DRURY INDUSTRIES LTD
DUNLOP NIGERIA PLC
DYECHEM NIGERIA LTD
ELESON INDUSTRIES NIGERIA LTD
EMMYSON NIGERIA LTD
ENCEE ENTERPRISES NIGERIA LTD
EUROBRIDGE INDUSTRIES LTD
FENGURU NIGERIA LTD
FINE CHEMICALS NIGERIA LTD
FRAMAN ENTERPRISES (NIG.) LTD
FUMMAN (NIG.) LTD
GARNET INDUSTRIES (NIG.) LTD
GENERAL OIL LTD
GOODWILL IMPEX INTERNATIONAL LTD
GORA NIGERIA LTD
GREAT AFRICA TRUST LTD
IBACHEM (Ibafon Chemicals) LTD
IBIMO INDUSTRIES LTD
INDUSTRIAL FLAVOURS & COLOURS LTD
INTERNATIONAL CONSULTING GROUP LTD
INTERNATIONAL STARCHEM INDUSTRIES LTD
JAWA GROUP OF COMPANIES
JUMBO NOMINEES LTD
KEMENG SERVICES LTD
KILOSKA VENTURES LTD
KRAINE INVESTMENTS LTD
KUNLE-OLA ENTERPRISES (NIG.) LTD
LANRE SHITTU GROUP OF COMPANIES LTD
LUKE & JUDE (NIG.) LTD
M.B.K. NIGERIA LTD
MACDAVINSON INTERNATIONAL LTD
MARKSON CHEMICAL IND. (WEST AFRICA) LTD
MARTINS BROTHERS (NIG.) LTD
MEADGROVE (NIG.) LTD
METOXIDE NIGERIA LTD
MEZ INDUSTRIES LTD
MOSENG NIGERIA LTD
NIGERIAN-GERMAN CHEMICALS PLC
NNIL COMMERCIAL CO. LTD
NOSAK AGENCIES LTD
NOVAFOAM-CHEMICAL & WIRE MANUF. NIG. LTD
NYCIL LTD
OBIKE INDUSTRIES NIGERIA LTD
ORIENTAL RESOURCES LTD
OSCARTE NIGERIA LTD
PARAMOUNT TRADING & INDUSTRIES (NIG.) LTD
PARCO ENTERPRISES (NIG.) LTD
PAU-LOAD LTD
REAMS NIGERIA LTD
RHODIA NIGERIA LTD
RODCO NIGERIA LTD
ROGA GROUP OF COMPANIES
ROTIMI OBEISUN INVESTMENT LTD
SAVANNAH CHEMICAL INDUSTRIES LTD
SIFUL NIGERIA LTD
SIPERCO NIGERIA LTD
TANO AGENCY & SHIPPING CO. LTD
THERAPEUTIC LABORATORIES (NIG.) LTD
THERMOSTEEL NIGERIA LTD
TRANSCHEM NIGERIA LTD
TRANSRAPID NIGERIA LTD
TRIDOK NIGERIA LTD
UGOCHUKWU GROUP OF COMPANIES.
UNICHEM NIGERIA LTD

INDUSTRIAL ENGINEERING CONSULTANCY & SERVICES

AFROCAT (NIG.) CO. LTD
AFROCOMMERCE (W.A.) LTD
AFRO-EQUIP NIGERIA LTD.
ANALYSED DATA LTD
ASCENT LTD
BEARING SERVICES LTD
BREWTECH NIGERIA LTD
BROSSETTE (NIG.) LTD
CHINA CIVIL ENGINEERING CONSTR. CORP. NIG. LTD
CHIYODA NIGERIA LTD
CITECO TECHNICL CO. LTD
COMERINT (NIG.) LTD
COUTINHO CARO & COMPANY (NIG.) LTD
DEO MAKRO LTD
DRESSER-RAND NIGERIA LTD
DTD SERVICES NIGERIA LTD
FALCON PETROLEUM LTD
GLOEDE & HOFF NIGERIA LTD
HANBAT NIGERIA LTD
HAVILAH CONSULT LTD
INDEV LTD
INDUSTRIAL PORTS ENGINEERING SERVICES LTD
INTEK GROUP LTD
INTERNATIONAL TECHNICAL & ENGINEERING CO
IPTC (WEST AFRICA) LTD
JONAC ENGINEERING PLANTS (NIG.) LTD
KOTCO LTD
LUBESERVICES ASSOCIATES
MET NIGERIA LTD
OFEIMU ENGINEERING (NIG.) LTD
RURU ENGINEERING SERVICES LTD
VOEST-ALPINE (NIG.) LTD

INDUSTRIAL MACHINES, PLANTS & EQUIPMENT SALES & SERVICE

A.M.H. ENTERPRISES LTD
ABEOKUTA COMMERCIAL & INDUSTRIAL CO. LTD
ADIMEX VENTURES LTD
AFROCAT (NIG.) CO. LTD
AFROCOMMERCE (W.A.) LTD
AFRO-EQUIP NIGERIA LTD
AGRO-TYRES & INDUSTRIAL EQUIPMENT NIG LTD.
AGUBAS NIGERIA LTD
AIR SEPARATION (NIG.) LTD
ALZICO LTD
AMAFO ENGINEERING LTD
AMINEX INDUSTRIAL MACHINES LTD
AUSTIN SHERIF LTD
AUSTON REED INTERNATIONAL LTD
B.N. NATSON CO. LTD
BEARING SERVICES LTD
BENLOCK NIGERIA LTD
BINDALO AGRICULTURAL & INDUSTRIAL CO. LTD
BOSKEL NIGERIA LTD
BRISCOEatlascopco (Div. of R.T. Briscoe Nig Plc)
BROSSETTE (NIG.) LTD
C. WOERMANN (NIG.) LTD
C. ZARD & CO. LTD.
CHASTE PROJECT GROUPE
COUTINHO CARO & COMPANY (NIG.) LTD
DAID NIGERIA LTD
DAT MERCHANT INVESTMENT LTD
EBUNSO NIGERIA LTD
EVO (NIG.) LTD
GANI INTERNATIONAL SERVICES LTD
HANBAT NIGERIA LTD
HIUNA ELECTRONICS NIGERIA LTD
HOLMAN BROTHERS (NIG.) LTD
INDEV LTD
INVANSIL INVESTMENTS LTD
JIMBEST AUTO SUPPLY CO. LTD
JOHN WHITE INDUSTRIES LTD
KADUNA MACHINE WORKS LTD
KAELER TECHNICAL SERVICES LTD
KAN-DOKI LTD
KEMEK NIGERIA LTD
KENCHEZ NIGERIA LTD
KILOSKA VENTURES LTD
KINGSMAT CO. LTD
LUKE & JIDE (NIG.) LTD
M.B.K. NIGERIA LTD
MAJOR GAS & INDUSTRIAL LTD
MARCON TECHNICAL CO. LTD
NIGERIAN MOTORS INDUSTRIES LTD
OBEV SYSTEMS LTD
ODKA NIGERIA LTD
OZED VENTURES LTD
PHARMAPLASTIC (NIG.) LTD
POULTRY EQUIPMENT FACCO (WEST AFRICA) LTD
POWERLINE ENGINEERING SERVICES LTD
R.T. BRISCOE (NIGERIA) PLC
ROBEY BOILER & SITE SERVICES LTD
ROCKPETERS NIGERIA LTD
RURU ENGINEERING SERVICES LTD
SEBAYA GROUP LTD
SIFUL NIGERIA LTD
SOFITAM NIGERIA LTD
STAG ENGINEERING (NIG.) LTD
STONEHILL NIGERIA LTD
SULTEC INTERNATIONAL CO. LTD
SUNGAS COMPANY NIGERIA LTD
TAHIR OIL MILLS LTD
TECHO-QUIP LTD
TECK TRUCKS & EQUIPMENT CO. (W.A.) LTD
TECO LTD
THERAPEUTIC LABORATORIES (NIG.) LTD
THERMOSTEEL NIGERIA LTD
TRACMASTER LTD
TRACTOR & EQUIPMENT NIGERIA LTD
UNITED TECH SUPPLY CO.LTD
VIDAC EQUIPMENT NIGERIA LTD
WATA TIMBER CO. LTD

INSPECTION SERVICES/CARGO SURVEYORS

AUDIT CONTROL & EXPERTISE (NIG.) LTD. (ACE)
BUREAU VERITAS NIGERIA LTD
CARGO INSPECTION & FREIGHT LTD
COMMODITIES SUPPORT SERVICES LTD
COTECNA INSPECTION LTD
JAROS INSPECTION LTD
JOINCROWN EXPRESS LTD
LINKSO NIGERIA LTD
MOODY INTERNATIONAL NIGERIA LTD
PETRONELLA NIGERIA LTD
SGS INSPECTION SERVICES NIGERIA LTD
SWEDE CONTROL INTERTEK LTD

INSURANCE & RE-INSURANCE SERVICES

ACEN INSURANCE CO. LTD
AFRICAN ALLIANCE INSURANCE CO. LTD
AFRICAN DEVELOPMENT INSURANCE CO. LTD
AFRICAN PRUDENTIAL INSURANCE CO. LTD
AFRICAN SAFETY INSURANCE CO. LTD
AIICO INSURANCE PLC9
ALLIANCE & GENERAL INSURANCE CO. LTD
ANCHOR INSURANCE CO.LTD
ASSET & LIABILITY INSURANCE CO.LTD
ATLANTIC INSURANCE CO. LTD
BAICO INSURANCE PLC
BENDEL INSURANCE PLC
CAPITAL EXPRESS INSURANCE CO. LTD
CONFIDENCE INSURANCE PLC
CONTINENTAL REINSURANCE CO. LTD
CORAL INTERNATIONAL INSURANCE CO. LTD
CORPORATE IDEALS INSURANCE LTD
CORNERSTONE INSURANCE PLC
CRUSADER INSURANCE CO. LTD
DESTINY INSURANCE (NIGERIA) PLC
ELMAC ASSURANCE (NIGERIA) LTD
EQUITY INDEMNITY INSURANCE CO. LTD
EQUITY LIFE INSURANCE CO. LTD
FIRE EQUITY & GENERAL INSURANCE CO. LTD
FIRST CHARTERED INSURANCE CO. LTD
FORTUNE ASSURANCE CO. LTD
GLOBAL COMMERCE & GENERAL ASSURANCE LTD
GLOBE REINSURANCE PLC
GOLD STANDARD INSURERS LTD
GOLDEN INSURANCE CO. LTD
GOLDLINK INSURANCE CO. LTD

GREAT NIGERIA INSURANCE CO. LTD
GUARDIAN TRUST INSURANCE CO. LTD
GUINEA INSURANCE PLC
HALLMARK ASSURANCE PLC.
HERITAGE ASSURANCE CO. LTD
HONESTY INSURANCE CO. LTD
INDUSTRIAL AND GENERAL INSURANCE CO. LTD
INTER-CONTINENTAL ASSURANCE CO. LTD
INTERNATIONAL ENERGY INSURANCE CO. LTD
INVESTMENTS & ALLIED ASSURANCE CO. LTD
KAPITAL INSURANCE CO. LTD
LAMDA INSURANCE CO. LTD
LASACO ASSURANCE PLC
LAW UNION AND ROCK INSURANCE CO. OF NIG. PLC
LEADWAY ASSURANCE PLC
LEXINGTON INTERNATIONAL INSURANCE CO. LTD
LINKAGE ASSURANCE CO. LTD
LISTER INSURANCE COMPANY (NIG.) LTD
LOMBARD INSURANCE CO. LTD
METROPOLITAN TRUST INSURANCE CO. LTD
MUTUAL ASSURANCES LTD
MUTUAL BENEFITS ASSURANCE PLC
NASAL INSURANCE CO. LTD
NEW LINE INSURANCE CO. LTD
NICON INSURANCE CORPORATION
NIGER INSURANCE PLC
NIGERIA REINSURANCE CORPORATION
NIGERIAN AGRICULTURAL INSURANCE CORP.
NIGERIAN ALLIANCE ASSURANCE CORP. LTD
NIGERIAN-FRENCH INSURANCE CO. LTD
OASIS INSURANCE CO. LTD
OLYMPIA INSURANCE CO. LTD
PERPETUAL ASSURANCE CO. LTD
PHOENIX OF NIGERIA ASSURANCE PLC
PICCADILLY INSURANCE CO. LTD
POSTAL LIFE & GENERAL INSURANCE CO. LTD
PRESIDENTIAL INSURANCE CO. LTD
PRESTIGE ASSURANCE PLC
REFUGE INSURANCE CO. LTD
REGENCY INSURANCE CO. LTD
RIVBANK INSURNACE CO. LTD
ROYAL EXCHANGE ASSURANCE (NIGERIA) PLC
ROYAL PROPERTY & CASAULTY ASSURANCE LTD
SHELTER INSURANCE CO. LTD
SOVEREIGN TRUST INSURANCE CO. LTD
STANDARD LIFE ASSURANCE PLC
STERLING ASSURANCE NIGERIA LTD
SUMMIT INSURANCE CO. LTD
SUN INSURNACE NIGERIA PLC
THE LION OF AFRICA INSURANCE CO. LTD
THE NIGERIAN GENERAL INSURANCE CO. LTD.
TRANS-NIGERIA ASSURANCE CO. LTD
TRUST-WORLD INSURANCE CO. LTD
UNIC INSURANCE PLC
UNITRUST INSURANCE CO. LTD
VIGILANT INSURANCE CO.LTD.
WAPIC INSURANCE PLC
WORLDWIDE INSURANCE CO. LTD
YANKARI INSURANCE CO. LTD

INSURANCE BROKING & CONSULTANCY

A.B. ALHASSAN & CO. INSURANCE BROKERS LTD
A.O. RICHARDS INSURANCE BROKERS LTD
ACCURATE INSURANCE BROKERS LTD
AFN BROKERS LTD
AFRIBANK INSURANCE BROKERS LTD
AFRICAN GENERAL INSURANCE BROKERS LTD
AFRICAN INSURANCE BROKERS LTD
AFRI-OVIS INSURANCE BROKERS LTD
ALFAM INSURANCE BROKERS LTD
ALLIED TRUST INSURANCE BROKERS LTD
ALPHA BROKERS LTD
ALRISK INSURANCE BROKERS LTD
AMANA INSURANCE BROKERS & CONSULTANTS
ARK INSURANCE GROUP
ASHMOUNT INSURANCE BROKERS LTD
ATLANTIC INSURANCE BROKERS LTD
AUSTIN & ASSOCIATES LTD
AXIS INSURANCE BROKERS LTD
B.C. MADIEBO & CO. LTD
BOFF & COMPANY INSURANCE BROKERS LTD
BOOF AFRICA INSURANCE BROKERS LTD
BRIGHTWAYS INSURANCE BROKERS LTD
CARRIER INSURANCE BROKERS LTD
CAUTIOUS INSURANCE RBOKERS LTD
CHASE INSURANCE BROKERS LTD
CITILADS INSURANCE BROKERS LTD
CLARKSON, EDU & CO. LTD
CLASSIC INSURANCE BROKERS LTD
CLIMAX INSURANCE BROKERS LTD
COBAL INSURANCE BROKERS LTD
COLXIMATE INSURANCE BROKES LTD
COMMERCIAL MARINE INSURANCE BROKES LTD
COMPETENT INSURANCE BROKES LTD
CONFLUENCE INSURANCE BROKES LTD
CORPORATE CITIZENS INSURANCE BROKES LTD
COSMIC INSURANCE BROKES LTD
COUNTRY & CITY INSURANCE BROKES LTD
CROWN INSURANCE BROKES LTD
CYRSTAL TRUST INSURANCE BROKES LTD
CTI INSURANCE BROKERS LTD
DINTA RISK & INSURANCE BROKERS LTD
DIPOD INSURANCE BROKERS LTD
DUTEE INSURANCE BROKES LTD
DYKES INSURANCE BROKES LTD
ECLONA INSURANCE BROKERS LTD
EFT INSURANCE BROKERS LTD
EMAT INSURANCE BROKES LTD
EMERALD INSURANCE BROKES LTD
EMINENT INSURANCE BROKES CO. LTD
EQUITY PROVIDERS INSURANCE BROKES LTD
ESENARD INSURANCE BROKES LTD
EXPRESS SECURITY INSURANCE BROKES LTD
FAIR DEAL INSURANCE BROKES LTD
FBN INSURANCE BROKERS LTD
FCN INSURANCE BROKERS LTD
FEMI JOHNSON & COMPANY LTD
FENGATE INSURANCE BROKERS LTD
FIDEI INSURANCE BROKERS LTD
FIDELITY BOND OF NIGERIA LTD
FIRST ATLANTIC SECURITIES LTD
FIRST DOMINION INSURANCE BROKERS LTD
FIRST-LINK INSURANCE BROKERS LTD
FORESIGHT INSURANCE BROKERS LTD
FOUNTAIN INSURANCE BROKERS LTD
FRANCO NIG. INS. BROKERS & CONSULTANTS LTD

G & V INSURANCE BROKES LTD
G.N. BISHOP INSURANCE BROKERS (NIG.) LTD
GLANVILL ENTHOVEN LIFE & PENSIONS CONSULTS
GLANVILL ENTHOVEN REINSURANCE BROKERS LTD
GLOBAL RISK ASSOCIATES LTD
GOLD STANDARD INSURANCE BROKERS LTD
GRACECHURCH INSURANCE BROKERS LTD
GREENLINK INSURANCE BROKERS LTD
GUARDIAN INTERNATIONAL BROKERS LTD
HAKASH & CO. LTD
HAN'S INSURANCE BROKERS LTD
HARRIS & JONES INSURANCE BROKERS LTD
HARVARD INTERNATIONAL INSURANCE BROKERS
HELMSMAN INSURANCE BROKERS LTD
HIGHGATE INSURANCE BROKERS LTD
HOGG ROBINSON NIGERIA LTD
IDEAL INSURANCE BROKERS LTD
IFEBOGUN & CO. LTD
IMPERIAL TRUST INSURANCE BROKERS LTD
INFINITY INSURANCE BROKERS LTD
INLAND INSURANCE BROKERS LTD
INSURANCE BROKERS OF NIGERIA LTD
INTERLINK ASSOCIATES & CO. LTD
INTERNATIONAL INSURANCE BROKERS LTD
INTRA-NIGER INSURANCE BROKERS LTD
J. AKIN-GEORGE & CO. LTD
JAASNA CITY INSURANCE BROKERS LTD
JONADS INSURANCE BROKERS LTD
JONES SIMPLIX & CO. LTD
KAL & KAY INSRUANCE BROKES CO LTD
KAPEX INSURANCE BROKES LTD
KAYOK INSURANCE BROKERS LTD
KOGUNA BABURA INSURANCE BROKERS LTD
KOLKUF INSURANCE BROKERS LTD
KUK INSURANCE BROKERS LTD
LAMBERT WILLIS & ASSOCIATES LTD
LANDGOLD INSURANCE BROKERS LTD
LANTOS INSURANCE BROKERS LTD
LEKTOL INSURANCE BROKERS LTD
LEVERAGE INSURANCE BROKERS LTD
LIBRA INSURANCE BROKERS LTD
LINKALL INSURANCE BROKERS LTD
M & M INSURANCE BROKERS LTD
MADISON INSURANCE BROKERS LTD
MAGNUM TRUST INSURANCE BROKERS LTD
MAN-MOUNTAIN & CO. LTD
MARHABAN INSURANCE BROKERS LTD
MAYFAIR BROKERS LTD
MENTOR & HOPKINS INSURANCE BROKERS LTD
MERCYFAITH INSURANCE BROKERS LTD
METRIC INSURANCE BROKERS LTD
METRO PERIL INSURANCE BROKERS LTD
MIDRON INSURANCE BROKERS LTD
MILESTONE INSURANCE BROKERS LTD
MINET NIGERIA LTD
MONITOR INSURANCE BROKERS LTD
MULTILATERAL INSURANCE BROKERS LTD
MUSTARD INSURANCE BROKERS LTD
NALEX ASSOCIATES INSURANCE BROKERS LTD
NAMKAN INTEGRATED INSURANCE BROKERS LTD
NATIONWIDE & GLOBE INSURANCE BROKERS LTD
NELSON UTI INSURANCE BROKERS LTD
NETWORK INSURANCE BROKERS LTD
NEW PLANET INSURANCE BROKERS LTD
NICHEK INSURANCE BROKERS LTD
NIGERIAN LIFE & PENSIONS CONSULTANTS LTD
NOBEL & LESLEY INSURANCE BROKERS LTD
OLA ESAN INSURANCE BROKERS LTD
OPEX INSURANCE BROKERS LTD
ORIWU INSURANCE BROKERS LTD
PEAK INSURANCE BROKERS LTD
PECUNIARY & TRUST INSURANCE BROKERS LTD
PERFECT INSURANCE BROKERS LTD
PETRA INSURANCE BROKERS LTD
PHILEX INSURANCE BROKERS LTD
PINNACLE INSURANCE BROKERS LTD
PLUM INSURANCE BROKERS LTD
PERMIER BROKERS LTD
PREMIUM INSURANCE BROKERS LTD
RAHIMBOD INSURANCE BROKERS LTD.
RISK CONSULTANTS LTD
RISK WATCH INSURANCE BROKERS LTD
RISKTECH INSURANCE BROKERS LTD
ROOMANS ENELI FLYNN INSURANCE BROKERS LTD
ROSEAT INSURANCE BROKERS LTD
ROYAL TRUST INSURANCE BROKERS LTD
SANFORD INSURANCE BROKERS LTD
SANRISK INSURANCE BROKERS LTD
SCIB NIGERIA & CO. LTD
SENFORCE INSURANCE BROKERS LTD
SHEPHERDS INSURANCE BROKERS LTD
SHIELD INSURANCE BROKERS LTD
SILVERTRUST INSURANCE BROKERS LTD
SMOOTHWAY INSURANCE BROKERS LTD
SOLID TRUST INSURANCE BROKERS LTD
SOUND INSURANCE BROKERS LTD
SOURCHE INSURANCE BROKERS LTD
STANDARD INSURANCE CONSULTANTS LTD
STANLEY MORGAN INSURANCE BROKERS LTD
STAR INSURANCE BROKERS LTD
SUPREME INSURANCE BROKERS LTD
T.A. BRAITHWAITE (INSURANCE BROKERS) & CO
THE UNITED AFRICAN INSURANCE BROKERS LTD
THOMAS INSURANCE BROKERS CO. LTD
TIDY INSURANCE BROKERS LTD
TIME INSURANCE BROKERS LTD
TRANSGLOBAL INSURANCE BROKERS LTD
UNI-CHARTERED INSURANCE BROKERS LTD
UNIMAG INSURANCE BROKERS LTD
UNION COMMERCIAL INSURANCE BROKERS LTD
UNITED MODERN INSURANCE BROKERS LTD
UNITED VANGUARD INSURANCE BROKERS LTD
VIBRANT INSURANCE BROKERS LTD
VIVA INSURANCE BROKERS LTD
VTL INSURANCE BROKERS LTD
WHITESANDS INSURANCE BROKERS LTD
WISEWAY INSURANCE BROKERS LTD
WORLDMARK INSURANCE BROKERS LTD

INTERIOR & EXTERIOR DECORATORS/DESIGNERS

ACME BUILDERS LTD
AGATHA'S INTERIOR DESIGSN LTD
ANON FURNITURE CO. LTD
ANTHOG DECORATIONS NIGERIA LTD
BOUSSALLE GROUP LTD
C.S.A. NIGERIA LTD

CACHE HOMES LTD
CONTACT LINK LTD
CURTAIN WORLD INC
DATEC INTERNATIONNAL (NIG.) LTD
EXCLUSIVE INTERIORS (NIG.) LTD
FITTING FINISHES LTD
FRAB & COMPANY (NIG.) LTD
G.E.C. OBIAMALU & SONS LTD
HARIESCOCAN & ASSOCIATES LTD
IDEAL HOME FINISHES & FIXTURES LTD
INDIGROID FUNRISHINGS LTD
INTERBASIC PRODUCTS CO. LTD
INTERIOR OPTIONS LTD
JAMES CUBITT ARCHITECTS
KES KARPET LTD
KOLMAB FURNITURE LTD
LABANELLA INDUSTRIES LTD
LEATHERWORLD LTD
LINK WOOD & METAL LTD
MANGROVE FURNISHING CO. LTD
MICHAEL OLUSEGUN ENTERPRISES LTD
MID-EAST (NIG.) LTD
MILLENNIA INTERIORS
NICKS NIGERIA LTD
NORTHERN FURNITURE INDUSTRIES LTD
NTCN LTD
OAKWOOD NIGERIA LTD
OHKAN & DEAN LTD
OTI CARPETS & FURNTURE INDUSTRIES LTD
OX4 SYSTEMS LTD
PELLETTERIA LTD
PETRONELLA NIGERIA LTD
ROYAS EXCLUSIVE FURNISHINGS LTD
SUNFLEX NIGERIA LTD
SVENGALI DESIGNS LTD
TOTAL OFFICE CONCEPT LTD
WOODPECKERS NIGERIA LTD
ZENBROOK INTERIOR CONSTRUCTIONS LTD
ZIKLAG LTD

IRRIGATION ENGINEERING SERVICES & EQUIPMENT SALES

BALLAST HAM (NIG.) LTD
BROSSETTE (NIG.) LTD
CFAO (NIGERIA) PLC
CROWN TRUST LTD
IBRU SEA FOODS LTD
OBASANJO FARMS (NIG.) LTD
S.C.C. (NIGERIA) LTD

JEWELLERS AND GOLDSMITHS

ABEKOGOLD LTD
LABANELLA INDUSTRIES LTD
STANLEY BRIDAL SHOP

KITCHEN EQUIPMENT, CABINETS & FURNITURE SALES

AINONISE (NIG.) LTD
AMARILO INDUSTRIES LTD
ARBON LTD
BENGAS INDUSTRIES (NIG.) LTD
C.H.F. HERON NIGERIA LTD
COMPENSATIONS (NIG.) LTD
ELPINA ASSOCIATES LTD
FAMILY FOODS LTD
FENLAB & COMPANY (NIG.) LTD
FINIDEL NIGERIA LTD
FOLD NIGERIA LTD
GRENIGAS LTD
GROUP FOUR COMPANY OF NIGERIA LTD
HARRYMAG VENTURES LTD
IEC NIGERIA LTD
KOLINTON TECHNICAL INDUSTRIES LTD
LUKE & JUDE (NIG.) LTD
MANDILAS ELECTROGAS APPLIANCES LTD
NEATIDY ENTERPRISES LTD
NIDOGAS CO. LTD
NIGERIAN & OVERSEAS GAS CO. LTD (Utilgas)
TRY 'N' CARRY (NIG.) LTD
UNION PRODUCTS LTD
WESTON PORKKA NIGERIA LTD

LABORATORY ANALYTICAL SERVICES

ALFA LABORATORIES LTD
ATLANTIC WASTE MANAGEMENT LTD
AUGIAS ENVIRONMENTAL & CONSULTING SERVICES
CARGO INSPECTION & FREIGHT LTD
GLOBAL ENVIRONMENTAL CONSULTANTS LTD
GLOBAL ENVIRONMENTAL TECHNOLOGY LTD
INTERNATIONAL ENERGY SERVICES LTD
LIGHTHOUSE PETROLEUM ENGINEERING CO. LTD
MAIL-IN OILFIELDS SERVICES LTD
MARINE TECHNICAL SERVICES INT'L (NIG.) LTD
QUALITY CONTROL & TESTING LABORATORIES LTD
WINELIGHT ANALYTICAL SYSTEMS (NIG.) LTD

LABORATORY EQUIPMENT, CHEMICALS & FURNITURE/FITTING SALES

ABJ CONSOLIDATED NIGERIA LTD
ANDY MEDICAL SUPPLIES LTD
AROLAB NIGERIA LTD
ASTRA INSTRUMENTS LTD
AUGIAS ENVIRONMENTAL & CONSULTING SERVICES
BRUME SANKEY MEDICAL LTD
CES NIGERIA LTD
CHRISTELA CHEMICAL WORKS LTD
CUSAL INDUSTRIES LTD
DANSPITAL NIGERIA LTD
DARLEZ NIGERIA LTD
DEUX PROJECT LTD
DRUG AND HEALTHCARE LTD
DUTSI LABORATORY ENGINEERING LTD
FARADAY NIGERIA LTD
FINLAB NIGERIA LTD
FOBAC EQUIPMENT MANUFACTURING CO. LTD
GRACE FOUNTAINS INTERNATIONAL LTD
I.F. JOHNSON LTD
JAGEE NIGERIA LTD
JOFFIN SCIENTIFIC INSTRUMENTS NIGERIA LTD
KATCHEY CO. LTD
KROLLENE LABORATORIES LTD
NAAFCO (SCIENTIFIC SUPPLIES) LTD
NEW SUMTECH LTD
NZEMAT NIGERIA LTD
QUALITY CONTROL & TESTING LABORATORIES LTD
RAPHSON LABORATORIES LTD
SALENAB NIGERIA LTD
TRANSRAPID NIGERIA LTD

UNIQUE INSTRUMENTS & SCIENCE CO. LTD
UNITED SURGICALS LTD
VOSAN & BAACON LTD
WESTON PORKKA NIGERIA LTD
WINELIGHT ANALYTICAL SYSTEMS (NIG.) LTD

LAND, MARINE & AERIAL SURVEYORS
AERIAL & SATELLITE RESOURCES LTD
FUGRO SURVEY NIGERIA LTD
GOEMATICS NIGERIA LTD
LANSAR GROUP SURVEYORS & ENGINEERS
ZENITH NIGERGROUP CO. LTD

LANGUAGE SERVICES & TRAINING
LIAISON FRANCAIS NIGERIA LTD

LEASING, HIRE & RENTAL SERVICES
AGRO-INDUSTRIES & DEVELOPMENT SCHEME LTD
AIKON ENGINEERING LTD
ALL MANAGEMENT SERVICES CO. LTD (AMSCO LTD)
APOL PETROLEUM NIGERIA LTD
BENEK ENGINEERING CO. LTD
BENLOCK NIGERIA LTD
BFCL ASSETS & SECURITIES LTD
BUILDWELL PLANTS & EQUIPMENT INDUSTRIES LTD
C & I LEASING PLC
CAPITAL BANCORP LTD
CARIBBEAN FINANCE LTD
CASHLINK FINANCE & INVESTMENT PLC
COMPACK FINANCE & SECURITIES LTD
CORNERSTONE TRUSTEES LTD
EME TECHNICAL CO. LTD
FUNDTECH FINANCE & INVESTMENT LTD
FUNTEB NIGERIA LTD
GEORGE COHEN (NIG.) LTD
GERIZIM GROUP
GERMAINE AUTO CENTRE LTD
GREAT AFRICA TRUST LTD
INTERNATIONAL TECHNICAL & ENGINEERING CO
JUBAILI BROS. ENGINEERING LTD
JUBAILI MOUKARIM GROUP LTD. (JMG LTD)
KENCHEZ NIGERIA LTD
LAMBIC TECHNICAL & GENERAL SERVICES LTD
LEASING SERVICES DIVISION (Div. of John Holt Plc)
MADUAKO TRANSPORT CO. LTD
MINGI SERVICES LTD
NIGER DIESEL ENGINEERING SERVICES LTD
NIHOL CRANE & EQUIPMENT HIRE CO. LTD
OCO INDUSTRIAL SERVICES LTD
ON-LINE PRODUCTS EQUIPMENTS & SERVICES LTD
OPTICOM LEASING CO. LTD
OZIGBU ENGINEERING CO .LTD
PAN SECURITIES LTD
PEBETO VENTURES LTD
PETRONELLA NIGERIA LTD
SANTA SEDE NIGERIA LTD
SCOA MOTORS (Div. of SCOA Nigeria Plc)
SEA PETROLEUM and GAS CO. LTD
SHORELINE CHEMICAL & OIL SERVICES LTD
UBINI INDUSTRIAL (NIG.) LTD
VIKING CONTAINER & MARINE SERVICES LTD
VT LEASING LTD
W.W. WHYTE INTERNATIONAL LTD
WALL STREET TRUST CO. LTD

LIBRARY SERVICE
BOOK SERVICES (WEST AFRICA) LTD
CHELIS BOOKAZINE LTD
FLORIDA BOOKSHOP LTD
LAKE VAL LTD
READERSWORLD.COM LTD

LIFTS, ESCALATORS & CONVEYORS INSTALLATION
BAFANI ENGINEERING CO. LTD
BARRI ELEVATORS NIGERIA LTD
ELEVATOR TECHNOLOGIES CO. LTD
FEEZY ENGINEERING NIGERIA LTD
KRESTA LAUREL LTD
MIDLANDS LTD
WINCOTECH LIFTS LTD

LIVESTOCK FEEDMILING & PREMIXES
AFRICAN FARMS LTD
AMO SANDERS (NIG.) LTD
ANIMAL CARE SERVICES KONSULT (NIG.) LTD
BALUFON ANIMAL FEEDS LTD
BENDEL FEED & FLOUR MILLS LTD
CAPS FEED LTD
ECWA RURAL DEVELOPMENT LTD
EZERA INTERNATIONAL GROUP OF CO. LTD
FEEDEX (NIG.) LTD
GRAND CEREALS & OIL MILLS LTD
KANO AGRICULTURAL SUPPLY CO.LTD
LIFE FLOUR GROUP
LIVESTOCK FEEDS PLC
NEIMETH INT'L PHARMACEUTICALS PLC
NIYYA FARMS LTD
NOMA OIL & CAKE MILLS LTD
P.S. MANDRIDES PLC
POKOBROS FOOD & CHEMICAL INDUSTRIES LTD
PORT HARCOURT FLOUR MILLS LTD
RESOURCES IMPROVEMENT & MANUF. CO. LTD
SAMROSE AGRO-INDUSTRIAL CO. LTD
SEEPC NIGERIA LTD
TOP FEEDS LTD

LUBRICANT BLENDING & MARKETING
A-Z PETROLEUM PRODUCTS LTD
AFRICAN PETROLEUM PLC.
AFROCOMMERCE (W.A.) LTD
AGIPNIGERIA PLC
CHICASON GROUP OF COMPANIES
CONOIL PLC
DEZERN NIGERIA LTD
DOZZY OIL & GAS LTD
ETERNA OIL & GAS PLC
EWEKE NIGERIA LTD
FAIRWINDS LTD
HONEYWELL OIL & GAS LTD
IBETO GROUP LTD
LUBCON LTD
MOBIL OIL NIGERIA PLC
OANDO NIGERIA PLC
OCEAN & OIL SERVICES LTD
OENIC INDUSTRIAL LTD
OKAI INTEGRATED CO. LTD

PETRALPHA LTD
TECHNO OIL LTD
TEXACO NIGERIA PLC
TONIMAS NIGERIA LTD
TOTALFINAELF NIGERIA PLC
WEST AFRICAN BITUMEN EMULSION CO. LTD
YINKA OMILANI ASSOCIATES

MACHINE TOOLS SALES & SERVICE
AFROCOMMERCE (W.A.) LTD
AMIN BROTHERS ENGINEERING CO. LTD
BERTOLA MACHINE-TOOL LTD
C. WOERMANN (NIG.) LTD
CNEICO (NIG.) LTD
DROCHESSY LTD
GOCUZ GROUP LTD
INTERNATIONAL TOOLS LTD.
JASPER COMMERCIAL ENTERPRISES (W.A.) LTD
MARCON TECHNICAL CO. LTD
ROCKPETERS NIGERIA LTD
STEEL & WIRE MANUFACTURING CO. LTD
TOOLS & ALLIED PRODUCTS NIGERIA LTD
WATA TIMBER CO. LTD

MARINE ENGINEERING SERVICES
ALBANS INTERNATIONAL (NIG.) LTD
AMAZON ENERGY LTD
BASILMAN & COMPANY (NIG.) LTD
BOUSSALLE GROUP LTD
CONTINENTAL SHIPYARD LTD
FOMENE MARITIME INTERNATIONAL LTD
HYDRODIVE NIGERIA LTD
ICON MARINE SERVICES LTD
INTERNATIONAL OILFIELD SERVICES LTD
INTEROIL SERVICES LTD
JM DREDGING & MARITME LTD
KENT RESOURCES LTD
M.GHALAYINI NIGERIA LTD
METALOCK NIGERIA LTD
NIGER DIVE LTD
NIGER-BENUE TRANSPORT CO. LTD
NIGERIA SUBMARINE DIVERS LTD
OCEANSIDE ENGINEEERING SERVICES LTD
OFEIMU ENGINEEERING (NIG.) LTD
RADAM MARITIME SERVICES LTD
RAPHA SERVICES CO. LTD
SHIP & SHORE SERVICES LTD
TETHYS PLANTGERIA CO. LTD
UNDERWATER ENGINEERING (CO.) NIGERIA LTD
YESIN INTERNATIONAL NIGERIA LTD

MARINE ENGINES, EQUIPMENT & PRODUCTS SALES
GANI INTERNATIONAL SERVICES LTD
GOCUZ GROUP LTD
MERIT SHIPPING COMPANY (NIG.) LTD
MOUDACO LTD
SCOA TRAC (Div. of SCOA Nigeria Plc)
SEA PETROLEU & GAS CO. LTD
YAMACO (Div. of John Holt Plc)

MARKETING CONSULTANCY & RESEARCH SERVICES
AFRICAN DEVELOPMENT CONSULTING GROUP LTD
CONTACT MARKETING SERVICES LTD
CORPORATE DIAMOND SECURITIES & INV. LTD
CORPORATE PRESS SERVICES INC.
DECISION SUPPORT CONSULTANCY LTD
EQUINOX ASSETS MANAGEMENT LTD
FIRST RESEARCH NIGERIA LTD
INTERNATIONAL DATA MANAGEMT SERVICES LTD
MARKET TRENDS RESEARCH INTERNATIONAL
MICHAKINSON (WEST AFRICA) CO. LTD
NEO-TROPICAL INV. & EXPORT MARKETING CO. LTD
RESEARCH & MARKETING SERVICES LTD
THE MARKET RESEARCH CONSULTANCY LTD

MECHANICAL ENGINEERING SERVICES
AKOWHO SERVICES LTD
AMCO TECHNICAL ENGINEERING CO. LTD
ARIZONA CONSTRUCTION LTD
ASCENT LTD
BAFANI ENGINEERING CO. LTD
BEARING SERVICES LTD
BECHTEL (NIG.) LTD
BETCY GROUP OF COMPANIES
BHN PLC
BMA NIGERIA LTD
CHROME OIL SERVICES LTD
CONSTRUCTION PRODUCTS NIGERIA LTD
CONVEYANCE (NIG.) LTD
D.S.D (NIG.) LTD
DELATTRE BEZONS (NIG.) LTD
DRAKE & SCULL (NIG.) LTD
DREK CO. LTD
ELEKTRIM (NIG.) LTD
ELEKTRINT (NIG.) LTD
ENOSCO NIGERIA LTD
ESE-TECH (NIG.) LTD
FENIKOH NIGERIA LTD
FRANCHISE PARTICIPATION LTD
FRANK'S COMET GROUP
FRIGOTERMICA NIGERIA LTD
FUGRO-IGN LTD
GENERAL MERCHANDISE & TECHNICAL CO. LTD
GILCO NIGERIA LTD
GLENYORK NIGERIA LTD
ICON MARINE SERVICES LTD
INDUSTRIAL PORTS ENGINEERING SERVICES LTD
INTERLINKED TECHNOLOGIES PLC
INTERNATIONAL TECHNICAL & ENGINEERING CO.
JAGAL NIGERIA LTD
JOHN-RAY LTD
KENCHEZ NIGERIA LTD
LATRASAK NIGERIA LTD
MADONA ORGANISATION LTD
MARK IV NIGERIA LTD
MEKIOS LTD
METALOCK NIGERIA LTD.
MINESFIELD ENGINEERING LTD
MOTHERCAT LTD
NAIRDA LTD
NIGER DIESEL ENGINEERING SERVICES LTD
PHOENIX ENGINEERING & CONTRACTOR LTD
POWERLINES LTD9
POWERTRON (NIG.) LTD
RAYCON & COMPANY (NIG.) LTD
SARM NIGERIA LTD

SOKO-TECH (NIG.) LTD
STAG ENGINEERING (NIG.) LTD
SUDELETTRA NIGERIA LTD
TAG (NIGERIA) LTD
TRANTER INTERNATIONAL LTD
TYME RESOURCES AND CO. LTD
UNIVERSAL MOTORS & ENGINEERING CO. LTD
UREN CONSTRUCTION ENGINEERING CO. LTD
W.W. WHYTE INTERNATIONAL LTD
WECO ENGINEERING & CONSTRUCTION CO. LTD
WEMTRACO (NIG.) LTD
WESCO GROUP OF COMPANIES
YINKA FOLAWIYO ELECT. & MECHANICAL CO. LTD
ZAKHEM CONSTRUCTION NIGERIA LTD

MEDICAL & HEALTH-CARE SERVICES
AJANAKU GROUP OF COMPANIES
AJAYI MEMORIAL HOSPITAL LTD
ALBA CLINICS & MEDICAL CENTRE LTD
BARNES DIAGNOSTIC & HEART CENTRE
COUNTY HOSPITAL LTD
DR. ABIMBOLA AWOLIYI MEMORIAL HOSPITAL CONSULTANTS LTD
DURO SOLEYE HOSPITALS
EKOCHIN LTD
EKOCORP PLC
FALACO GROUP OF COMPANIES
FIRST DOMINICAN HOSPITAL LTD
GOLD CROSS HOSPITAL LTD
HYGEIA NIGERIA LTD..
KING'S CARE HOSPITAL LTD
LIFE SUPPORT SYSTEMS LTD
MOTAYO HOSPITAL LTD
MOUNT SINAI HOSPITAL LTD
PROVIDENCE HOSPITALS LTD
SAINT NCHOLAS HOSPITAL
SHOREMAN GROUP OF COMPANIES
TEJU GROUP OF COMPANIES
THE CARDIAC CENTRE
THE HUMANA HOSPITAL.
TOTAL HEALTH TRUST LTD
VICTORIA IS. CONSULTANCY HOSPITAL SERVICES.

MEDICAL AIR AMBULANCE SERVICES
FUNTAI LTD
TOCARO EMERGENCY MEDICAL SERVICES LTD

MEDICAL LABORATORY DIAGNOSTIC SERVICES
BARNES DIAGNOSTIC & HEART CENTRE
CLINA-LABS NIGERIA LTD
HEPTAGON VENTURES LTD
IMMUNOASSAY LABORATORIES (NIGERIA) LTD
JMW INTERSCAVON UNITED LABORATORIES LTD
LIFE SUPPORT SYSTEMS LTD
NIVCO INTERNATIONAL LTD
PHONICS HEARING CENTRE
RADMED DIAGNOSTIC CENTRE LTD
RAPHSON LABORATORIES LTD

MERCHANDISE DISTRIBUTION & MARKETING SERVICES
GENERAL IMPORT (Div. of CFAO Nig. Plc)
JOHN HOLT DISTRIBUTION
MARKETORCH NIGERIA LTD
MICHAKINSON (WEST AFRICA) CO. LTD
PANAFY LTD

METAL FABRICATION & CONSTRUCTION WORKS
ACME BUILDERS LTD
AMINEX INDUSTRIAL MACHINES LTD
AREWA METAL CONTAINERS LTD
BOTNIC METALCRAFT (NIGERIA) LTD
CISCON LTD
DADDO INDUSTRIES LTD
DDS MINES LTD
DOLMECH ENGINEERING NIGERIA LTD
EASITECH PROJECTS (NIGERIA) LTD
EASTERN WROUGHT IRON LTD
FUMMAN (NIGERIA) LTD
GENERAL METALWARE CO. LTD
GIBRALTAR CONSTRUCTION (NIGERIA) LTD
HAC INTERNATIONAL NIGERIA LTD
HASSAN STEEL PRODUCTS (NIGERIA) LTD
ILLUMINAIRE LTD
INDEV LTD
INDUSTRIAL & FARM EQUIPMENT CO. LTD
INDUSTRIAL METAL PROCESSING CO. LTD
INDUSTRIAL METALLIZING & PACKAGING CO. LTD
INVANSIL INVESTMENTS LTD
JONAC ENGINEERING PLANTS (NIG.) LTD
KADUNA MACHINE WORKS LTD
KANO ELECTRODES & ALLIED PRODUCTS LTD
M. GHALAYINI NIGERIA LTD
METAL CONSTRUCTION (WEST AFRICA) LTD
MOSAF NIGERIA LTD
OBIEFUNA MODERN BUS INDUSTRIES (NIG) LTD
OX4 SYSTEMS LTD
PAMAQUE NIGERIA LTD
PHOENIX ENGINEERING & CONTRACTOR LTD
POWERTRIM NIGERIA LTD
PROFAB ENGINEERING LTD
ROCH TOOLS & PRODUCTS LTD
SAULAWA MACHINERY & FABRICATION IND. LTD
SDEM ERECTORS NIGERIA LTD
SHONGAI PACKAGING INDUSTRY LTD
SKYBRIGHT INDUSTRIES LTD
STEEL WORKS LTD
STI STEPHENSON LTD
SUPASTEEL LTD
SVENGALI DESIGNS LTD
TECHO-QUIP LTD
TOWER GALVANISED PRODUCTS (NIGERIA) LTD
TYME RESOURCES & CO. LTD
VIKING CONTAINER & MARINE SERVICES LTD

MINERAL MINING, PROCESSING, MARKETING/ CONSULTANCY SERVICES
AFO-TIN MINES LTD
AGRO-ALLIED DEVELOPMENT ENTERPRISES LTD
AMINEX INDUSTRIAL MACHINES LTD
ANNIG & NOWAS GROUP LTD
CASTLAT GROUP OF COMPANIES
CONSOLIDATED TIN MINES LTD
DDS MINES LTD
DELTA PROSPECTORS LTD
EDEWOR INTERNATIONAL LTD
FREEDOM (DEVELOPMENT) GROUP LTD

HARIESCOCAN & ASSOCIATES LTD
JAKURA MARBLE INDUSTRY LTD
KAVITEX MILLS LTD
KEMMAPP NIGERIA LTD
KNIGHTS HOLDINGS LTD
MINING & GRANITE CO. LTD
MINOR METALS & MINERALS LTD
MOOREGATE LTD
NASARAWA MINERALS DEVELOPMENT CO. LTD
NIGERIAN COAL CORPORATION
NORDIC INDUSTRIES LTD
OILCHEM LTD
PIONEER SPECTRUM MINERALS NIGERIA LTD
PLATEAU MINERALS DEVELOPMENT CO. LTD
REGAL MINERAL INDUSTRIES LTD
SAGAOLA MINING & ENGINEERING (NIG) LTD
SOLID BASE NIGERIA LTD
TATEC INTERBIZ LTD
TOMBULCO (NIGERIA) LTD
WEST AFRICAN FERTILIZER CO. LTD
YCN MINERAL PROCESSING CO. LTD

MINING EQUIPMENT SALES
ALZICO LTD
MOOREGATE LTD
NITRO ATLASCO NIGERIA LTD
SCOA TRAC (Div of SCOA Nig Plc)

MOTOR VEHICLE ASSEMBLY/BODY BUILDING
ADDIS ENGINEERING LTD
FRIGOGLASS NIGERIA LTD
INCAR (NIGERIA) PLC
LAMBERT INTERNATIONAL LTD
LAMCL INTERNATIONAL LTD
MANUFACTURING & TECHNICAL CO. NIGERIA LTD
OBIEFUNA MODERN BUS INDUTRIES (NIGERIA) LTD
ROAD TRUCKERS (NIGERIA) LTD
SCOA INDUSTRIES
UGEN & ASSOCIATES CO. LTD
VAN VLIET TRUCK (NIGERIA) LTD

MOTOR VEHICLE DISTRIBUTION, SALES & SERVICE
A.C. OKOCHA MOTORS LTD
A.S.D. GROUP OF COMPANIES
ACCREDITED TRUST & AUTOMOBILE LTD
AFFORDABLE CARS LTD
ALL MANAGEMENT SERVICES CO. LTD (AMSCO LTD
AURA WEST AFRICA LTD
AUTOMOBILE MANUFACTURERS CO. LTD
BANILUX GROUP OF COMPANIES
BAO MOTORS (NIGERIA) LTD
BAP SERVICES LTD
BENLOCK NIGERIA LTD
BHN PLC
BHOJWANI BROS. (NIGERIA) LTD
BORG & HESS MOTORS LTD
BRAS MOTORS LTD
BRIGHT MOTORS LTD
BRISCOEmotors (Div of R.T. Briscoe Nig. Plc)
C.N. OKOLI INVESTMENT CO. NIGERIA LTD
CAR LINK LTD
CFAO MOTORS
CONCEITO MOTORS (NIGERIA) LTD
CONIC GROUP OF COMPANIES
COSCHARIS MOTORS LTD
DAAYAD CAR & ACCESSORIES LTD
DAZZ MOTORS LTD
DE-KOMPASS VENTURES LTD
DONE MOTORS & AUTO SERVICES NIGERIA LTD
EMALESSON ENTERPRISES LTD
EXOTIC CARS LTD
FIRST MOTORS LTD
GARAGES LTD
GERMAINE AUTO CENTRE LTD
HOLGATE HAULAGE LTD
HYUNDAI MOTORS NIGERIA LTD
IMMAC GROUP
INEH-MIC HOLDINGS LTD
JUDEK NIGERIA LTD
KUNLE-OLA ENTERPRISES (NIGERIA) LTD
L.E. EJINKEONYE NIGERIA LTD
LABANA GLOBAL VENTURES LTD
LAMBIC TECHNICAL & GENERAL SERVICES LTD
LANRE SHITTU GROUP OF COMPANIES.
LEASING SERVICES DIVISION (Div of John Holt Plc)
LEVENTIS MOTORS
M-B AUTOMOBILE SERVICES LTD
MACK AMERICAN TRUCK CO. LTD
MADUNKA INTERNATIONAL LTD
MANDILAS MOTORS
MILLENNIUM AUTOMOBILES LTD
MINGI SERVICES LTD
MITOB MOTORS LTD
MONS MOTORS LTD
MOTOR PARTS INDUSTRY LTD
NIGERIAN TECHNICAL CO. LTD
NISSAN NIGERIA LTD
NORDY GROUP LTD
NUEL OJEI HOLDINGS LTD
OGO OLUWA KITAN TRADING CO. LTD
OLUWALOGBON MOTORS LTD
OWODUNNI & SONS MOTORS LTD
QUALITY MOTORS LTD
RAHUSA VENTURES NIGERIA LTD
RYDER FENDT NIGERIA LTD
SACKS & MOTORS NIGERIA LTD
SCOA MOTORS (Div of SCOA Nig. Plc)
SHANNA NIGERIA LTD
SIO MOTORS LTD
SKYMIT MOTORS LTD
SOTAEN NIGERIA LTD
STALLION MOTORS LTD
SUNNY MOTORS AND CO. LTD
SUPERIOR MOTORS (NIGERIA) LTD
TECK TRUCKS & EQUIPMENT CO. (W.A.) LTD
TEEM MOTORS LTD
TODAY'S CARS LTD
UNION AUTOMOBILES LTD
VAN VLIET TRUCKS (NIGERIA) LTD
VOLKSWAGEN OF NIGERIA LTD
WINBAZ TRACTOR EQUIPMENT LTD

MUSICAL INSTRUMENT & EQUIPMENT SALES
AFRIKANA INVESTMENTS LTD
ANAMIKE NIGERIA LTD
BEN HOLDINGS LTD

DENSINE INDUSTRIES (W.A.) LTD
HOMELAND HOLDINGS LTD
MIKE DAD NIGERIA LTD
ORPHEUS CO. LTD

OFFICE EQUIPMENT & MACHINES SALES & SERVICE

AFRILINKS NIGERIA LTD
AIRCOM (NIGERIA) LTD
ALH. J. SULEIMAN & SONS (NIGERIA) LTD
AMAHAJ LTD
APPLIED SERVICES LTD (APPSERV
ASSAY NIGERIA LTD
BIOTECH AUDIO VISUAL (NIGERIA) LTD
C. J. MARTINS (WEST AFRICA) LTD
CFAO TECHNOLOGIES LTD
COMPLETE BUSINESS MACHINES (NIGERIA) LTD
COMPUTER SOLUTIONS LTD
CONYBIRD NIGERIA LTD
COPYCAT LTD
CSS LTD
DALEX CO. LTD
DATAMATICS COMPANY (NIGERIA) LTD
DATLEX CO. LTD
DEGOAL INVESTMENT LTD
DEN-HARRIS AND CO. LTD
DEPENDABLE SYSTEMS NIGERIA LTD
DEVELOP OFFICE PRODUCTS LTD
DOLLY BUSINESS MACHINES LTD
DOLPHIN OTIS INVESTMENT LTD
EQUIFAX COMPUTER & OFFICE EQUIPMENT LTD
F & F GROUP
FAIR BOND GROUP OF COMPANIES
FERDINAND TECHNICAL & TRADING CO. LTD
FERDISON HOLDINGS LTD
FOTO CHRIS INTERBIZ LTD
FOTO PIE GROUP LTD
GAMMA-RAD NIGERIA LTD
GEOMESAF & CO LTD
GLOBECOM INTEGRATED SYSTEMS LTD
GRACE FOUNTAINS INTERNATIONAL LTD
GRUNZ LINK LTD
GUBABI & CO. LTD
HANACO NIGERIA LTD
HENVACO LTD
IDEAL INFOSYSTEMS (Div. of Leventis Group)
INTERCOMM LTD
JAYBEST INTERNATIONAL LTD
JOE-HAN NETWORK MARKETING LTD
JOHN BEDOLA ENTERPRISES LTD
JOKAS INTERNATIONAL LTD
JOLAJ OFFICE PRODUCTS NIGERIA LTD
KENDO NIGERIA LTD
McQUINTUS LTD
MEGA-PLAZA CENURY 21 MALL
MOS OFFICE PRODUCTS LTD
NEET (NIGERIA) LTD
NETWORK TECHNOLOGIES LTD
OEP INTERNATIONAL LTD
OFFICE DEVICES LTD
OFFICETRON CO. LTD
OKECHINA NIGERIA LTD
OLACO NIGERIA LTD
OSADEMEY TRADING CO. NIGERIA LTD
OSIQUIP BUSINESS AIDS LTD
PANA/SHARP LTD
PANABIZ INTERNATIONAL LTD
PRAGMATIC TECHNOLOGIES LTD
RADIO COMMUNICATIONS (NIGERIA) LTD
ROBERT-JOHNSON NIGERIA LTD
SFICO LTD
SUPREME TRADING CO. LTD
TAAK LTD
TESNIC NIGERIA LTD
TICON INVESTMENT LTD
TOTAL OFFICE CONCEPT LTD
TRINICLE NIGERIA LTD
VIMBA INTERNATIONAL NIGERIA LTD
WESTCOTT NIGERIA LTD
WORLDMARK (NIGERIA) LTD
YAOLAT TECHNOLOGIES NIGERIA LTD

OIL & GAS EXPLORERS & PRODUCERS

ADDAX PETROLEUM DEVELOPMENT (NIGERIA) LTD
ALFRED JAMES PETROLEUM LTD
AMNI INTERNATIONAL PETROLEUM DEV. CO. LTD
ATLAS PETROLEUM INTERNATIONAL LTD
CAVENDISH PETROLEUM NIGERIA LTD
CHEVRONTEXACO NIGERIA LTD
CONOCO ENERGY NIGERIA LTD
CONSOLIDATED OIL LTD
DUBRI OIL CO. LTD
ESSO EXPLORATION & PRODUCTION (NIGERIA) LTD
EXPRESS PETROLEUM & GAS CO. LTD
FAMFA OIL LTD
ICON MARINE SERVICES LTD
MOBIL PRODUCING NIGERIA UNLTD
NEXEN PETROLEUM EXPLORATN & PRODUCTN LTD
NIGER DELTA EXPLORATION & PRODUCTION PLC
NIGERIA LNG LTD
NIGERIAN AGIP EXPLORATION LTD
NIGERIAN AGIP OIL CO. LTD
ONIBUDO HOLDINGS LTD
OPTIMUM PETROLEUM DEV. CO. LTD
PAN OCEAN OIL CORPORATION NIGERIA LTD
PHILLIPS OIL CO. (NIGERIA) LTD
PHOENIX OIL COMPANY (NIGERIA) LTD
QUEEN'S PETROLEUM LTD
SCHWARTZ GROUP OF COMPANIES
SHELL NIGERIA EXPLORATN & PRODUCTN CO. LTD
SOLGAS PETROLEUM LTD
STATOIL NIGERIA LTD
SUMMIT OIL INTERNATIONAL LTD
TEXACO NIGERIA OUTER SHELF LTD
THE SHELL PETROLEUM DEV. CO. OF NIGERIA LTD
TOTAL UPSTREAM NIGERIA LTD
YINKA FOLAWIYO PETROLEUM CO. LTD

OILFIELD ENGINEERING SERVICES

A.C.M OF NIGERIA LTD
AB JOSEF INTERNATIONAL & CO. LTD
ABB LUMMUS GLOBAL NIGERIA LTD
ADAMACGROUP
ADLAD GROUP
AFRICA OILFIELD SERVIVES LTD
AIKON ENGINEERING LTD
AKER NIGERIA LTD

AKOWHO SERVICES LTD
ALAN UNIVERSAL ENGINEERING CO. LTD
ALBAN'S INTERNATIONAL (NIGERIA) LTD
ALBERDIN ENERGY SERVICES LTD
ALCON NIGERIA LTD
AMAZON ENERGY LTD
ANADRILL (NIGERIA) LTD
APOL PETROLEUM NIGERIA LTD
ARCO PETROLEUM ENGINEERING CO. LTD
ASA CEILINGS LTD
ASCOT OIL & GAS NIGERIA LTD
ATLANTIC MARINE & PETROLEUM MGT LTD
ATLANTIC MARINE & OILFIELD SERVICES LTD
ATLANTIC MEDITERRANEAN OIL SERVICES LTD
ATLANTIC MERIDEAN LTD
BAKER HUGHES NIGERIA LTD
BAKER NIGERIA LTD
BAROID OF NIGERIA LTD
BASILMAN & COMPANY (NIGERIA) LTD
BATEX NIGERIA LTD
BAYWOOD CONTINENTAL LTD
BENEK ENGINEERING CO. LTD
BEST LAND & SEA SERVICES LTD
BHI LTD
BOUSSALLE GROUP LTD
CAKASA (NIGERIA) CO. LTD
CALTA CONSTRUCTION (NIGERIA) LTD
CAMCO NIGERIA LTD
CASCHE NIGERIA LTD
CASTLAT GROUP OF COMPANIES
CENTURY OIL SERVICES LTD
CENTURY TECHNOLOGY LTD
CEOTI LTD
CHASTE PROJECT GROUPE
CHIFY (NIGERIA) LTD
CHROME OIL SERVICES LTD
CINO NIGERIA LTD
CISCON LTD
COMERINT (NIGERIA) LTD
COMPLETE PROJECTS ENGINEERING CONSORTIUM
COOPER CAMERON CORPORATION NIGERIA LTD
CORELAB NIGERIA LTD
DANBA OIL LTD
DELATTRE BEZONS (NIGERIA) LTD
DENVER PETROLEUM SERVICES LTD
DEUTAG (NIGERIA) LTD
DOWELL (NIGERIA) LTD
DREDGING INTERNATIONAL SERVICES NIGERIA LTD
DRESSER-RAND NIGERIA LTD
DRILLOG PETRO-DYNAMICS LTD
DSV TECHNOLOGIES LTD
DUBI (NIGERIA) CO. LTD
DUPRE INTERNATIONAL NIGERIA LTD
EBIMO NIGERIA LTD
ELEPHANT GROUP LTD
ENERGY TECHNIQUES NIGERIA LTD
ESCRAVOS PROJECTS LTD
EUROBASE CONSULTS LTD
EXCEL ENERGY SERVICES LTD
FAIR BOND GROUP OF COMPANIES
FALCON PETROLEUM LTD
FIELD OFF-SHORE DESIGN ENGINEERING (NIG) LTD
FLOW PRECISION LTD
FOLBEN NIGERIA LTD
FORSTER WHEELER NIGERIA LTD
FRANK'S INTERNATIONAL OILFIELD SERVICES LTD
FUGRO-IGN LTD
FUTURE CONCERNS NIGERIA LTD
G.C.O. GROUP OF COMPANIES
G.E.N.P. NIGERIA LTD
GALBA LTD
GEOQUEST
GEOSERVICES NIGERIA LTD
GLITZ PETROLEUM LTD
GLOBAL OFFSHORE DRILLING LTD
GLOBESTAR ENGINEERING CO. (NIGERIA) LTD
GRAMEN PETROSERVE NIGERIA LTD
GROUP PRECISION INDUSTRY LTD
HALLIBURTON ENERGY SERVICES LTD
HOMAN ENGINEERING CO. LTD
HYDRIL TECHNICAL DRILLING & PRODUCTION SERVICES NIGERIA LTD
HYDRODIVE NIGERIA LTD
HYSON (NIGERIA) LTD
ICON MARINE SERVICES LTD
INDEV LTD
INDUSTRIAL TRUST ENGINEERING LTD
INTEGRATED ALLIED APPLICATNS ENGINEERING LTD
INTEGRATED DATA SERVICES LTD
INTELS NIGERIA LTD
INTER ROOF (NIGERIA) LTD
INTERDRILL NIGERIA LTD
INTERNATIONAL CONSULTING GROUP LTD
INTERNATIONAL ENERGY SERVICES LTD
INTERNATIONAL OILFIELD SERVICES LTD
INTEROIL SERVICES LTD
INTERTEC ENGINEERING (NIGERIA) LTD
IPCO (NIGERIA) LTD
J.J. SCOT GROUP OF COMPANIES
JAKKOS ENGINEERING LTD
JGC NIGERIA LTD
JKPEEZ IMPEX CO. LTD
JUCHI NIGERIA LTD
KEEDAK NIGERIA LTD
KENQUIP GROUP OF COMPANIES
KING & PEARLS INTERNATIONAL LTD
KNIGHTSBRIDGE LTD
LADUNNI INTERNATIONAL LTD
LANDOVER CO. LTD
M.F. KENT ENGINEERING LTD
M.G.S. GROUP LTD
MABON LTD
MALLARD BAY DRILLING NIGERIA LTD
MARS ENERGY SERVICES LTD.
MASSOIL FIELD SERVICES LTD
MATRIX PETRO-CHEM LTD
MEDITTERRANEAN ENGINEERING SERVICE LTD
MEGASTER TECHNICAL & CONSTRUCTION CO. LTD
MIDEN SYSTEMS LTD
MONCRIEF OIL INTERNATIONAL LTD
MORPOL INDUSTRIAL CORPORATION LTD
MOSAF NIGERIA LTD
NAUTILUS (NIG) ENGINEERING & CONSTRUCTN LTD
NEGRIS LTD
NESTOIL LTD
NEW OILFIELD & ALLIED SERVICES LTD

NIGER-GLOBAL ENGINEERING & TECHNICAL CO. LTD
NIGERIAN LOGGING & SUPPORT SERVICES LTD
NIGERIAN WESTMINISTER DREDGING & MARINE LTD
NIGERIAN SERVICES & SUPPLY CO. LTD
NIODA LTD
NISSHO IWAI (NIGERIA) LTD
NUCLEUS GROUP NIGERIA LTD
O.I.A. SERVICES LTD
OCEANSIDE ENGINERRING SERVICES LTD
OIL & INDUSTRIAL SERVICES LTD
OIL TECH (NIGERIA) LTD
OILDATA WIRELINE SERVICES LTD
OILFIELD & WATERWAYS SERVICES CO. LTD
OILSCAN LTD
OILTEST SERVICES NIGERIA LTD
ONAHSONS HOLDINGS LTD
OVERSEAS TECHNICAL SERVICE NIGERIA LTD
OZARCO (NIGERIA) LTD
P. PAIVE ASSOCIATES LTD
P.G.H. LTD
PEAK PETROLEUM LTD
PENEL INVESTMENTS LTD
PETROLEIGH O.G.O. INTERNATIONAL LTD
PETROLOG LTD
PETRONELLA NIGERIA LTD
PINL OIL & MARINE SERVICES LTD
PRIME ENERGY RESOURCES LTD
PYTHON ENGINEERING CO. LTD
REMM OIL SERVICES LTD
RITZOIL LTD
ROBEY BOILER & SITE SERVICES LTD
ROMSON OILFIELD SERVICES LTD
SAFA STEEL & CHEMICAL MANUFACTURING LTD
SAIPEM CONTRACTING NIGERIA LTD
SANTA FE DRILLING CO. LTD
SCHLUMBERGER NIGERIA LTD
SCHONWELD TRIAD TECHNICAL SERVICES LTD
SCOA PETROLEUM
SDEM ERECTORS NIGERIA LTD
SEA TRUCKS GROUP
SEALAND OILFIELD SERVICES LTD
SEDCO FOREX OF NIGERIA LTD
SEG. MAHSEN & COMPANY (NIGERIA) LTD
SHIP & SHORE SERVICES LTD
SHORELINE CHEMICALS & OIL SERVICES LTD
SINO GROUP OF COMPANIES LTD
SIRPI ALUSTEEL CONSTRUCTION LTD
SLOK GROUP
SMIEC CHEMICAL ENGINEERING & CONSTR. CO LTD
SMIT NIGERIA LTD
SNC LAVALIN NIGERIA LTD
SNIG NIGERIA LTD
SOLUS SCHALL NIGERIA LTD
SOVERAN NIGERIA LTD
SOWSCO WELL SERVICES (NIGERIA) LTD
STAN TECH LTD
STEELWAYS NIGERIA LTD
SUDELETTRA NIGERIA LTD
TECO LTD
TECON OIL SERVICES LTD
TETHYS PLANTGERIA CO. LTD
THE OIL RESOURCES DEVELOPMENT CO. (NIG) LTD
TITAN ENGINEERS & CONSTRUCTORS LTD
TOE INDUSTRIES LTD
TORNADO INTERNATIONAL ASSOCIATES LTD
TRAB INVESTMENTS NIGERIA LTD
TRANSCOASTAL NIGERIA LTD
TRANSCON GROUP OF COMPANIES
TRICONTINENTAL OIL SERVICES LTD
TRIDENT STEEL WORKS (NIGERIA) LTD
TYPHA CENIA NIGERIA LTD
UNITED GEOPHYSICAL (NIGERIA) LTD
VALKAN PETROLEUM SERVICES LTD
W.W. WHYTE INTERNATIONAL LTD
WASCO OIL SERVICES CO. NIGERIA LTD
WEATHERFORD NIGERIA LTD
WECO ENGINEERING & CONSTRUCTION CO. LTD
WELTEK LTD
WESCO ENGINEERING LTD
WEST AFRICA OFFSHORE LTD
WEST AFRICAN OILFIELD SERVICES LTD
WEST ATLANTIC SYSTEMS NIGERIA LTD
WESTERN AFRICA WELL SERVICES NIGERIA LTD
WESTERN ATLAS INTERNATIONAL NIGERIA LTD
WILLBROS (NIGERIA) LTD
WORLDWIDE PETROLEUM SERVICES (W.A.) LTD
YESIN INTERNATIONAL NIGERIA LTD
ZUKUS INDUSTRIES LTD

OPTICAL CARE PRODUCTS MARKETERS & SERVICES

ALIBAN GROUP LTD
CHARIS OPTICIANS LTD
CLEAR VIEW OPTICS LTD
DURO SOLEYE HOSPITALS
EYEWARE LTD
INSIGHT EYE CLINIC & OPTICAL SERVICES LTD
ISIJOLA OPTICAL SERVICES (NIGERIA) LTD
METRO EYES NIGERIA LTD
NIGER OPTICAL SERVICES CO. (NIGERIA) LTD
OCULUS PHARMACARE LTD
OMNIVISION LTD
TRUVISION LTD

PAINT & VARNISHES MANUFACTURERS & MARKETERS

ACELAND INDUSTRIES LTD
AFRICAN PAINTS (NIGERIA) PLC
ALINCO STEEL & METAL CONSTRUCTION CO. LTD
APEX PAINTS LTD
ASKAR PAINTS (NIGERIA) LTD
BANEX GROUP LTD
BERGER PAINTS NIGERIA PLC
BIASOWL NIGERIA LTD
BILLAND CHEMICALS & PAINTS INDUSTRIES LTD
CHEMICAL AND ALLIED PRODUCTS PLC
CHEMSTAR PAINTS INDUSTRY (NIGERIA) LTD
DELMAN GROUP OF COMPANIES
DN MEYER PLC
DURACLEAN CHEMICALS & ALLIED PRODUCTS LTD
EAGLE PAINTS NIGERIA LTD
EBONY PAINTS LTD
FENICOM CHEMICAL INDUSTRIES NIGERIA LTD
IPWA PLC
LYDOLINE PAINTS LTD
McDON INTERNATIONAL LTD
MEMMS WEST AFRICA LTD
MICHAEL OLUSEGUN ENTERPRISES LTD

NIGER CEDAR INDUSTRIES (NIGERIA) LTD
NIGER STANDARD INDUSTRIES LTD
OLUMO RECORDS LTD
PCI LTD
PODA PAINTS NIGERIA LTD
PORTLAND PAINTS & PRODUCTS NIGERIA LTD
PREMIER PAINTS PLC
PRESIDENT PAINTS NIGERIA LTD
REGENCY (OVERSEAS) CO. LTD
STAR PAINTS INDUSTRIES LTD
TOKY CHEMICAL MANUFACTURERS LTD
TRINTAS INTERNATIONAL LTD
UNION COLOURS & CHEMICALS LTD
WEATHERHEAD INDUSTRIES LTD
WEST AFRICAN PORTLAND CEMENT PLC
ZENINA LTD

PALM PRODUCE PROCESSORS
ADEOLA ODUTOLA INDUSTRIES PLC
CAMELA PURE VEGETABLE OIL CO. LTD
CROWN TRUST LTD
ENVOY OIL INDUSTRIES LTD
FIMCON LTD
GENERAL AGRO OIL INDUSTRIES LTD
MAC-TONNEL (NIGERIA) LTD
OKITIPUPA OIL PALM PLC
POKO OIL MILLS (WEST AFRICA) LTD
PRESCO INDUSTRIES PLC
RESOURCES IMPROVEMENT & MANUF. CO. LTD
RISONPALM LTD
RIVERS VEGETABLE OIL CO. LTD
STELLAN INDUSTRIES NIGERIA LTD
TRIMCO LTD

PAPER & BOARD PACKAGING MANUFACTURERS
BPP-KALAMAZOO
FUNLAYO ADEBO ENTERPRISES LTD
GATEWAY PLASTIC & PAPER PACKAGING LTD
INDUSTRIAL PRINTING & PACKAGING CO. LTD
INTERCAP LTD
INTERNATIONAL CONVERTERS OF NIGERIA LTD.
INTERNATIONAL PACKAGING IND. OF NIGERIA PLC
ITUA PACK LTD
NASCO PACK LTD
NIGERIA KRAFT BAGS LTD
POLYTHENE ENTERPRISES (NIGERIA) LTD
RIGIDPAK CONTAINERS LTD
SMURFIT CASES NIGERIA LTD
TETRA PAK (WEST AFRICA) LTD
TRIUMPH NIGERIA LTD
WAHUM PACKAGING LTD

PAPER CONVERTERS & PRODUCTS MANUFACTURERS
A & H INDUSTRIES LTD
A. N. EJEAGWU & SONS LTD
ADEXSON NIGERIA CO. LTD
B. C. IFEGBO & ASSOCIATES LTD
BEL-PAPYRUS LTD
BENCOD PRESS LTD
BENGAS INDUSTRIES (NIGERIA) LTD
DAZEINE PRESS LTD
DENSON PAPER MILL LTD
EPESOK PAPER MILL LTD
FUNLAYO ADEBO ENTERPRISES LTD
HALLMARK PAPER PRODUCTS PLC
INDUSTRIAL PRINTING & PACKAGING CO. LTD
INTERNATIONAL ENVELOPES LTD
INTERNATIONAL PACKAGING IND. OF NIGERIA PLC
INTERNATIONAL STARCHEM INDUSTRIES LTD
ISAACSTAN LTD
KAZOGA NIGERIA LTD
LEE NOBEC NIGERIA LTD
MAI-NASARA & SONS LTD
MEMMS WEST AFRICA LTD
NADINA INDUSTRIES LTD
NICETOP PAPER INDUSTRIES LTD
NIGER PAPER INDUSTRIES LTD
NIGER SANITARY INDUSTRY LTD
NOKOSING PAPER MILL LTD
ONWARD STATIONERY STORES LTD
OYO STATE PAPER MILL LTD
PAPERCRAFT NIGERIA LTD
PEFAC PAPER INDUSTRIES LTD
RELIANCE HOLDINGS NIGERIA LTD
STAR MODERN PAPER MILL LTD
THOMAS WYATT & SONS (NORTHERN NIGERIA) LTD
TOFA GENERAL ENTERPRISES LTD

PEST CONTROL SERVICES & EQUIPMENT/ PRODUCTS SALES
AUGIAS ENVIRONMENT & CONSULTING SERV. LTD
AUREOL SERVICES LTD
BRICKFIELD CONCERNS LTD
BUG BUSTERS LTD
DURACLEAN SERVICES (NIGERIA) LTD
DURACLEAN SPECIALISTS (NIGERIA) LTD
DUSTMEN CLEANING SERVICES LTD
FIRST EKIMOGUN NIGERIA LTD
FLOOROSIL CLEANING SERVICES LTD
HARMONY PROJECTS LTD
KLEENOL NIGERIA LTD
MICHANI ENTERPRISES LTD
NIGERIA CLEANING SERVICE LTD
NIGERMERI EXTERMINATING & PEST CONTROL CO
NOVAT ANIMAL HOSPITAL LTD
O'LA-KLEEN NIGERIA LTD
PESTKIL (NIGERIA) LTD
SCHUKAS RAPIDKIL LTD
SELINA VENTURES LTD
TEKNOKLEEN LTD
ZEE HOLDINGS LTD

PETROCHEMICAL PRODUCTS MANUFACTURERS /MARKETERS
CHRISTOVAL INDUSTRIAL CO. LTD
ELEME PETROCHEMICALS CO. LTD
KADUNA REFINING & PETROCHEMICALS CO. LTD
MULTI-VENTURES LTD
WARRI REFINING & PETROCHEMICALS CO. LTD

PIPES (Metal) MANUFACTURERS & MARKETERS
AREWA METAL CONTAINERS LTD
ELDORADO (NIG.) LTD
HOMAN INDUSTRIES LTD
SEG. MAHSEN & COMPANY (NIG.) LTD
TOWER GALVANISED PRODUCTS (NIG.) LTD

ULTIMATE SUNNY INTERNATIONAL LTD
WEST AFRICAN BUILDING MATERIALS LTD

PIPES & FITTINGS (PVC) MANUFACTURERS & MARKETERS
BENGAS INDUSTRIES (NIG.) LTD
CICO HOLDINGS LTD
DANMAN PLASTICS & PACKAGING INDUSTRIES LTD
DURAPLAST NIGERIA INDUSTRIES LTD
E.A. ABIMBOLA & CO. LTD
ESLON (NIG.) LTD
FITTINGS & ACCESSORIES LTD
HOMUS INDUSTRIES LTD
J. UDEAGBALA HOLDINGS (NIG.) LTD
LOMBARDY PLASTICS (NIG.) LTD
MAJOR ELECTRODES INDUSTRIES LTD
NIGERIA PIPES LTD
Om LTD
POLO SACKS LTD
SAFETY PRODUCTS MANUFACTURING CO. LTD
TUNS HOLDINGS LTD

PLASTIC PACKAGING PRODUCTS MANUFACTURERS
A.A. MUDALLABI ABDULLAHI & SONS LTD
ADIG PLASTICS LTD
BEN HOLDINGS LTD
BETA ADAMA PLASTICS LTD
CAPHI NIGERIA LTD
CELPLAS INDUSTRIES NIGERIA LTD
CHRISLIEB PLC
CONTECH NIGERIA LTD
CONTROLLED PLASTICS LTD
COSMOT NIGERIA LTD
CPL INDUSTRIES LTD
DANMAN PLASTICS & PACKAGING INDUSTRIES LTD
DANSY INDUSTRIES (NIG.) LTD
DELTA MANUFACTURING CO. LTD
FERTECHO INDUSTRIES LTD
GATEWAY PLASTIC & PAPER PACKAGING LTD
GEEPEE INDUSTRIES LTD
GEES DENVER CO. LTD
GIMNS INDUSTRIAL CO. LTD
GOLDEN GATE PLASTICS INDUSTRIES LTD
HARDEEP (NIG.) LTD
HOMUS INDUSTRIES LTD
IBACHEM (Ibafon Chemicals) LTD
INTERNATIONAL ENAMELWARE INDUSTRIES LTD
IVORY PRODUCTS NIGERIA LTD
J. NWANKWU GROUP OF COMPANIES
JOHNNY INDUSTRIES NIGERIA LTD
KARAMU PLASTIC INDUSTRIES LTD
KGM INDUSTRIES (NIG.) LTD
KHUSHBU WATERS LTD
KRS INVESTMENT LTD
LOGIC INVESTMENTS LTD
LOVLEEN TOYS INDUSTRIES LTD
MONAPLEX INDUSTRIES (NIG.) LTD
NAMOH INDUSTRIES NIGERIA LTD
NIGER HYGIENE LTD
OBASANJO FARMS LTD
OZALLA PLASTICS ENTERPRISES LTD
PARAMOUNT TRADING & INDUSTRIES (NIG.) LTD
PETER'S & DANIELS ENTERPRISES LTD
PHARMACEUTICAL SERVICES LTD
PHARMAPLASTIC (NIG.) LTD
PLASTIC CONTAINERS & CHEMICAL SPECIALTIES
PLASTIC PACKAGING INDUSTRIES LTD
POLYBAGS INDUSTRIES (NIG.) LTD
QUALITY RADIATORS LTD
ROBATEK NIGERIA LTD
ROCHALCHET NIGERIA LTD
SA'ADATU PLASTICS MANUFACTURING CO. LTD
SAFETY PRODUCTS MANUFACTURING CO. LTD
SCOTTS INDUSTRIES LTD
SHONGAI PACKAGING INDUSTRY LTD
ST. MARY'S INDUSTRIAL COMPLEX LTD
STANDARD PACKAGING NIGERIA LTD
SUPERFINE INDUSTRIES (NIG.) LTD
UNION ADHESIVE & CHEMICAL CO. LTD
UNITAB NIGERIA LTD
VIK INDUSTRIES LTD

PLASTICWARE PRODUCTS MANUFACTURERS
AFROMEDIA PLASTICS AND ENGINEERING LTD
ALLIANCE INTERNATIONAL (NIG.) LTD
ALTAK INDUSTRIES LTD
AMAFCO ENTERPRISES LTD
AMALGAMATED PLASTIC INDUSTRIES LTD
AMBED INTERNATIONAL (NIG.) LTD
ANGELA PLASTICS INDUSTRIES LTD
APRICOT PLASTIC INDUSTRIES LTD
AWUTOLO INDUSTRIES LTD
BENGAS INDUSTRIES (NIG.) LTD
BETA ADAM PLASTICS LTD
BLACK HORSE PLASTIC INDUSTRIES LTD
BRIGHT PRODUCTS LTD
CELPAS INDUSTRIES NIGERIA LTD
CLEMCO PLASTICS LTD
CONTINENTAL PLASTIC (WEST AFRICA) LTD
CORONA PLASTIC INDUSTRIES LTD
COSMOT NIGERIA LTD
DANCO MANNYON INDUSTRIES LTD
DANSY INDUSTRIES (NIG.) LTD
DYNAMIC INDUSTRIES LTD
ENKAY PLASTICS LTD
EVA RUBBER & PLASTIC PRODUCTS NIGERIA LTD
FACILITY PRODUCTS (NIG.) LTD
FATAHI PLASTIC INDUSTRIES LTD
FEDERATION PRODUCTS (NIG.) LTD
FERTECHO INDUSTRIES LTD
GARBS ORGANISATION LTD
GATEWAY PLASTIC & PAPER PACKAGING LTD
GENERAL METALWARE CO. LTD
GLOBAL CONCEPTS (WEST AFRICA) LTD
GLOBAL PLASTIC INDUSTRIES (NIG.) LTD
HARDEEP (NIG.) LTD
HASSAN PLASTIC INDUSTRIES LTD
HENSMOR GROUP OF COMPANIES
HOMUS INDUSTRIES LTD
IKOLABA INDUSTRIES LTD
IVORY PRODUCTS NIGERIA LTD
JACOBOD NIGERIA LTD
JID-BOD INDUSTRIES LTD
JOBIKAN NIGERIA LTD
JOHNNY INDUSTRIES NIGERIA LTD
KRISEL INVESTMENT LTD
LAYAL INDUSTRIES LTD

LIBERTY INDUSTRIES LTD
LOUIS CARTER GROUP OF COMPANIES
LOVLEEN TOYS INDUSTRIES LTD
MAPLE PLASTICS INDUSTRIES LTD
METROPLAST LTD
MONUMENT PLASTICS INDUSTRIES LTD
N.O. JOHN GREAT (NIG.) LTD
NAMOH INDUSTRIES NIGERIA LTD
NIGER PAPER INDUSTRIES LTD
NIPOL LTD
OK PLAST LTD
OZALLA PLASTICS ENTERPRISES LTD
PANAR LTD
PAPILON INDUSTRY LTD
PHARCO (PRODUCTIONS) PLC
REEVE PLASTICS LTD
ROBATEK NIGERIA LTD
ROCHALCHET NIGERIA LTD
SA'ADATU PLASTICS MANUFACTURING CO.LTD
SABIU BAKO GROUP OF COMPANIES
SAFETY PRODUCTS MANUFACTURING CO. LTD
SAWYERR GROUP NIGERIA LTD
SCOTTS INDUSTRIES LTD
SHAGOYA NIGERIA LTD
SILVER PLASTICS LTD
STALLION PLASTICS LTD
SUPERFINE INDUSTRIES (NIG.) LTD
T.A.C. (TIGER) PLASTICS INDUSTRIES NIGERIA LTD
UDEZE INVESTMENTS & INDUSTRIAL COMPLEX LTD
YALO DALA PLASTICS LTD
YOUNESCO LTD

PNEUMATIC EQUIPMENT SALES & SERVICE

HOLMAN BROTHERS (NIG.) LTD
INDUSTRIAL PORTS ENGINEERING SERVICES LTD
KOJACO INDUSTRIAL SUPPLIES LTD
KRESTA LAUREL LTD
MET NIGERIA LTD
NITRO ATLASCO NIGERIA LTD
OCO INDUSTRIAL SERVICES LTD
P. PAIVE ASSOCIATES LTD
SULTEC INTERNATIONAL CO. LTD
WAYNE (WEST AFRICA) LTD

POLYMER PRODUCTS (Polyltene/Propylene/Ureathane) MANUFACTURERS

ABBSTAL LTD
ADAOBI NIGERIA LTD
ALIDOT NIGERIA LTD
ANGELA PLASTICS INDUSTRIES LTD
BAJABURE INDUSTRIAL COMPLEX LTD
BEST BAGS LTD
BOGO SACKS NIGERIA LTD
CAMEL STAR LTD
CENTRAL BAGS MANUFACTURING CO. NIGERIA LTD
CICO HOLDINGS LTD
CONTROLLED PLASTICS LTD
DABENO ENTERPRISES LTD
DANGOTE AGRO SACKS LTD
DECENT BAG INDUSTRY LTD
FAS AGRO INDUSTRIAL LTD
GOLDEN GATE PLASTICS INDUSTRIES LTD
HOMUS INDUSTRIES LTD
JID-BOD INDUSTRIES LTD
JOHNNY INDUSTRIES LTD
KANO SACKS INDUSTRIES LTD
KOREA MACHINERY LTD
KRISEL INVESTMENT LTD
MADRATEX LTD
METROPLAST LTD
MONUMENT PLASTICS INDUSTRIES LTD
NIGER PAPER INDUSTRIES LTD
NIGERIAN POLYVINYL CHLORIDE PRODUCTS LTD
PHARMADEX NIGERIA LTD
PLASCO SHEETS (NIG.) LTD
POLO SACKS LTD
POLYBAGS INDUSTRIES (NIG.) LTD
PORT HARCOURT SACKS LTD
PYRAMID BAG MANUFACTURING CO. LTD
SACKS & MOTORS NIGERIA LTD
SILAS POLYPLASTIC INTERNATIONAL LTD
SIO INDUSTRIES LTD
SIVACO LTD
ST. MARY'S INDUSTRIAL COMPLEX LTD
STANDARD PACKAGING COMPLEX LTD
TAJU INDUSTRIES NIGERIA LTD
VK PLASTIKS LTD
WESTMART NIGERIA LTD
YCN MINERAL PROCESSING CO. LTD
ZENITH CONTAINERS CO. LTD

PREFABRICATED ACCOMMODATION (Portakabin) MANUFACTURERS/MARKETERS

CHARVET NIGERIA LTD
ECO-BUILDING SYSTEMS NIGERIA LTD
GENPACO LTD
MANUFACTURING & MARKETING CO. (NIG.) LTD
PYTHON ENGINEERING CO. LTD
STEELWAYS NIGERIA LTD
STEEL WORKS LTD
VINA INTERNATIONAL LTD

PRINTING & LITHOGRAPHIC SERVICES

ADAMAWA PRESS LTD
ADSPACE COMMUNICATIONS LTD
AMANA PRINTING & ADVERTISING LTD
AWK-PRINT LTD
BANILUX GROUP OF COMPANIES
BARAKA PRESS & PUBLISHERS LTD
BAUCHI PUBLISHING & PRINTING CO. LTD
BENCOD PRESS LTD
BENDEL NEWSPAPER CO. LTD
BENUE PRINTING & PUBLISHING CORPORATION
BERTIE-JOHN (NIG.) PRINTERS LTD
BRILA LTD
BUOSHISHI HOLDINGS LTD
C & A PRINTS NIGERIA LTD
CLEAR IMPRESSIONS LTD
CORPORATE PRESS SERVICES INCORPATED
CSS LTD
DANCO MANNYON INDUSTRIES LTD
DAZEINE PRESS LTD
DDB CASERS LTD
DELTA COLOUR PRODUCTION NIGERIA LTD
ECWA PRODUCTIONS LTD
EL & KAY NIGERIA LTD

FRED GAY INTERNATIONAL LTD
FUNLAYO ADEBO ENTERPRISES LTD
GABUMO PUBLISHING CO. LTD
GOLDSTAR PUBLISHERS (NIG.) LTD
HEARTLINK VENTURES LTD
IBUKUNOLA PRINTERS (NIG.) LTD
ICIC (DIRECTORY PUBLISHERS) LTD
INTEC PRINTERS LTD
INTEGRATED PRESS LTD
INVENTMEDIA LTD
JACSIL & SONS ENTERPRISES LTD
JIMMY VIRGO PRESS LTD
JO-GENE INTERNATIONAL LTD
JOHN WEST PACKAGING LTD
KENDO NIGERIA LTD
KING & GEORGE (NIG.) LTD
LITERAMED PUBLICATIONS (NIG.) LTD
LITHO PACKAGES (NIG.) LTD
LITHO-CHROME LTD
LOTTO INTERNATIONAL LTD
LUKAB NIGERIA LTD
MAFE PRINTING WORKS LTD
MAI-NASARA & SONS LTD
MASTERSTROKE PACKAGES LTD
MESHICO ENTERPRISES LTD
MINAJ PRINTERS LTD
MODERN DESIGNS LTD
NASARAWA PUBLISHING CO. LTD
NATIONHOUSE PRESS LTD
NAYEE COMMUNICATIONS LTD
NEW NIGERIAN NEWSPAPERS LTD
NIGERIA ADVERTISING SERVICE LTD
NIGERIAN OFFICE STATIONERY SUPPLY STORES LTD
OAKWOOD NIGERIA LTD
ODU'A PRINTING CO. LTD
OGEKPO INDUSTRIES LTD
OUTDOOR COMMUNICATIONS LTD
OXFORD TECHNOLOGIES LTD
OYO STATE PAPER MILL LTD
PHILIP TRIMNELL PRODUCTIONS LTD
PLANET PRESS LTD
PRESY & ADENSON LITHOGRAPHIC PACKAGING LTD.321
PRINCE OF PRINTS LTD
PRINTEX (NIG.) LTD
PRINTS SPECIALITY LTD
PRISMA NIGERIA LTD
PROMPT ENTERPRISES LTD
RAMADAN PRESS LTD
RENART PRINTS LTD
RO-MARONG (NIG.) LTD
ROCANA NIGERIA LTD
ROSAN VENTURES LTD
ROYAL PRESS LTD
SAMAKOL PRINTERS NIGERIA LTD
SKETCH PRESS LTD
SMAGH & COMPANY NIGERIA LTD
STUDIO PRESS (NIG.) PLC
SUPERFLUX INTERNATIONAL LTD
TANUS COMMUNICATIONS LTD
THE CAXTON PRESS (WEST AFRICA) LTD
THEMES & SCHEMES LTD
TIMES PRESS LTD
TRANSCAN GRAPHICS LTD
TRIUMPH PUBLISHING CO. LTD
TRYFAM NIGERIA LTD
TULIP PRESS LTD
U. I. VENTURES LTD
VICODA LTD
WYTAK PRESS LTD
YUSFAITH LITHOGRAPHIC INDUSTRIES LTD
ZACCHI & KROME LTD
ZIKLAG LTD

PRINTING EQUIPMENT & MACHINERY SALES & SERVICES

CIVILETIS NIGERIA LTD
CPI-MOORE (NIG.) LTD
DALEWARES LTD
HAMBLESIDE NIGERIA LTD
HEIDELBERG NIGERIA LTD
HEPTAGON VENTURES LTD
MONOTYPE NIGERIA LTD
RAISERS INTERNATIONAL LTD
RO-MARONG (NIG.) LTD

PRINTING INKS & CHEMICALS MANUFACTURERS/ MARKETERS

AULT & WIBORG (NIG.) LTD
COATES BROTHERS (WEST AFRICA) LTD
FINE CHEMICALS NIGERIA LTD
INTERNATIONAL STARCHEM INDUSTRIES LTD
MULTICHEM INDUSTRIES LTD
OLYMPIC INKS LTD
PRINT INKS NIGERIA LTD
TOKY CHEMICAL MANUFACTURERS LTD
ZENINA LTD

PUBLISHERS (General Educational/Literary)

AFRICAN UNIVERSITIES PRESS LTD
AFRICANA-FEP PUBLISHERS LTD
BISSO NIGERIA LTD
FOURTH DIMENSION PUBLISHING CO. LTD
GABUMO PUBLISHING CO. LTD
IBIKUNLE LAWAL ORGANISATIONS (NIG.) LTD
LITERAMED PUBLICATIONS (NIGERIA) LTD
NELSON PUBLISHERS LTD
NPS EDUCATIONAL PUBLISHERS LTD
WEST AFRICAN BOOK PUBLISHERS LTD

PUBLISHERS (Newspaper/Magazines)

ADAMAWA PRESS LTD
AFRICAN NEWSPAPERS OF NIGERIA LTD
BAUCHI PUBLISHING & PRINTING CO. LTD
BENDEL NEWSPAPER CO. LTD
BENUE PRINTING & PUBLISHING CORPORATION
CHAMPION NEWSPAPERS LTD
COMPLETE COMMUNICATIONS LTD
ENCOMIUM VENTURES LTD
FAME PUBLICATIONS LTD
HEALTHCARE COMMUNICATIONS LTD
INDEPENDENT COMMUNCATIONS NETWORK LTD
INDEPENDENT NEWSPAPERS LTD
LACOM COMMUNICATIONS LTD
LAGOS HORIZON PUBLISHING CO. LTD
MADIBA (NIGERIA) LTD
MEDIA TECHNIQUES NIGERIA LTD
MEDIA TRUST NIGERIA LTD

MILLENNIUM HARVEST LTD
NASARAWA PUBLISHING CO. LTD
NEW NIGERIAN NEWSPAPERS LTD
NEWSWATCH COMMUNICATIONS LTD
SATELLITE COMMUNICATIONS LTD
SKETCH PRESS LTD
SOUL PUBLICATIONS LTD
SUB-SAHARAN PRESS LTD
SUMMIT PUBLICATIONS LTD
TELL COMMUNICATIONS LTD
THE MONITOR NEWSPAPERS LTD
THE POST PUBLISHING CO. LTD
TNT NEWSPAPERS LTD
TRIUMPH PUBLISHING CO. LTD
TRUE TALES PUBLICATIONS LTD
TURNING-POINT NEWSPAPERS LTD
WORLD INFORMATION AGENTS LTD
ZUS BUREAU LTD

PUBLISHERS (Professional Books/Journals/Directories)
BRAINPOWER LTD
BRANDS INTERNATIONAL CO. LTD
CENTURY 21 SYSTEMS LTD
CIKA GROUP OF COMPANIES
DSC PUBLICATIONS LTD
FSG COMMUNICATIONS NIGERIA LTD
GLENDORA INTERNATIONAL (NIG.) LTD
GOLDSTAR PUBLISHERS (NIGERIA) LTD
HANNAHSGATE LTD
ICIC (DIRECTORY PUBLISHERS) LTD
LAW & BUSINESS PUBLICATIONS LTD
LAWBREED LTD
LEGAL TEXT PUBLISHING CO. LTD
LEX LTD
METALOBA INDUSTRIES LTD
MFI & ASSOCIATES LTD
NIGERIAN INTERNATIONAL BIOGRAPHICAL CENTRE
NIGERIAN LAW PUBLICATIONS LTD
PATIKE COMMUNICATIONS LTD
RESEARCH & DATA SERVICES LTD
TRYFAM NIGERIA LTD

RECREATIONAL & RESORT FACILITIES
ASH-BERT (NIG.) LTD
D'ROVANS HOTEL LTD
FANTANSYLAND
JOEDONE INTERNATIONAL LTD
NIKE LAKE RESORT
NITESHIFT COLISEUM
PARKWAY RIDES & SERVICES LTD
PENINSULA WATERFRONT LTD
ROJENNY GAMES & TOURIST VILLAGE
WATERPARKS LTD
WHISPERING PALMS HOLIDAY RESORT, IWORO

RESTAURANTS
CEASER'S PALACE HOTELS
DE-FRIENDSHIP CATERTING SERVICES LTD
DOUBLE ZERO CHINESE RESTAURANT LTD
FLAMINGO (NIG.) LTD
FOREMOST CATERERS LTD
FRENCHES LTD
GOLDEN CROWN CHINESE RESTAURANTS LTD
GOLDEN GATE PARADISE NIGERIA LTD
IMPERIAL CHINESE CUISINE LTD
JAGAL FOODS LTD
MAMA CASS RESTAURANTS LTD
OCEAN VIEW RESTAURANTS
SAVANNAH SUITES & RESTUARANT LTD
STAR MOTEL (NIG.) LTD
THE LAGOON RESTAURANT
WHASSAN-EUREST (NIG.) LTD
ZENITH HOTELS LTD

ROOFING & WATERPROOFING SERVICES
MARBLETON GROUP OF COMPANIES
SIGNFRIQUE ENGINEERING LTD
STRUTEC (A Div. of CFAO Nigeria Plc

ROOFING MATERIALS MANUFACTUERERS & MARKETERS
ALL SEASONS INDUSTRIES LTD
ALLIANCE INTERNATIONAL (NIG.) LTD
ALO ALUMINIUM MANUFACTURING CO. LTD
ARCON ALUMINIUM NIGERIA LTD
ASABA ALUMINIUM CO. LTD
BEST ALUMINUM CO. LTD
BORNO ALUMINIUM CO. LTD
CARAT ALUMINIUM LTD
CHARTERED ALUMINIUM SYSTEMS LTD
CICO HOLDINGS LTD
EMENITE LTD
EURO-TECH ALUMINIUM LTD
GALVANIZING INDUSTRIES LTD
GINPAT ALUMINIUM PRODUCTS LTD
GIWARITE LTD
GREATGATE INVESTMENT LTD
HST SYSTEMS LTD
IMPERIAL ALUMINIUM PRODUCTS LTD
INDUSTRIAL MINERAL PRODUCTS
MEGA ALUMINIUM PRODUCTS LTD
NALMAC ALUMINIUM PRODUCTS LTD
ONITSHA ALUMINIUM MANUFACTURING CO. LTD
PIONEER METAL PRODUCTS COMPANY PLC
PRIMLAKS GALVANIZING LTD
QUALITEC INDUSTRIES LTD
QUEENWAY ALUMINUM CO. LTD
ROOFCO NIGERIA LTD
SANUSI BROTHERS (NIG.) LTD
STANDARD SYSTEMS INTEGRATED
ARCHITECTURAL PRODUCTS LTD
SUPERCOR INDUSTRIES LTD
TOTAL ALUMINIUM SYSTEMS LTD
TOWER BUILDING PRODUCTS
UNITED STEEL CONVERTERS LTD
WEST AFRICAN BUILDING MATERIALS LTD

ROPES & TWINES MANUFACTURERS
BOGO SACKS NIGERIA LTD
COATS WEST AFRICAN THREAD CO. LTD
INTERNATIONAL POLYWORKS CO. LTD
NIGERIAN ROPES PLC
POLYBAGS INDUSTRIES (NIG.) LTD
ROPE & RIGGING NIGERIA LTD
SIO INDUSTRIES LTD

SAFE DEPOSIT SERVICES
MONTGORMERY SECURITY VAULTS (NIGERIA) LTD

SAFETY EQUIPMENT & SYSTEMS SALES/SERVICES
AMAHAJ LTD
C.F. CANUTE LTD
COMATEL INDUSTRIES LTD
DE-LOUIS TECHNOLOGIES LTD
ELECTRICARE LTD
EME TECHNICAL CO. LTD
FIREWORKS INVESTMENTS LTD
FOLBEN NIGERIA LTD
FUTURE CONCERNS NIGERIA LTD
HIUNA ELECTRONICS NIGERIA LTD
INTERTEC ENGINEERING (NIG.) LTD
JKPEEZ IMPEX CO. LTD
MASTERPLAN INVESTMENTS LTD
MINNESOTA NIGERIA LTD
OBF-HI-TEKNOLOGIES LTD
OSCARTE NIGERIA LTD
SAFETECH LTD
SAFETY ENGINEERING & FIRE CONSULTANTS LTD
SCOA EQUIP (Div. of SCOA Nigeria Plc)
SOFITAM NIGERIA LTD
STONEHILL NIGERIA LTD
TROPICAL FIRE PREVENTION SERVICES LTD
UNITED TECH SUPPLY CO. LTD
URBAN FIRE LTD
VIGEO LTD

SATELLITE COMMUNICATION ENGINEERING SERVICES
AVSATEL COMMUNICATIONS LTD
COMMUNICATION TRENDS NIGERIA LTD
SAHARA BELLS COMMUNICATIONS LTD
SCHLUMBERGER NETWORK SOLUTIONS
UNITED TELESYS LTD
WARSUN NETWORK SOLUTIONS LTD

SCIENTIFIC ANALYTICAL EQUIPMENT SALES
ANDOMEZ LTD
ASTRA INSTRUMENTS LTD
BUSSDOR & CO. LTD
CHIBEK OIL TOOLS LTD
DARLEZ NIGERIA LTD
EVO (NIGERIA) LTD
GAMLA NIGERIA LTD
JAGEE NIGERIA LTD
NAAFCO (SCIENTIFIC SUPPLIES) LTD
QUALITY CONTROL & TESTING LABORATORIES LTD
WINTECK (NIG.) LTD

SECURITY SERVICES & CONSULTANCY
ABG COMMUNICATIONS LTD
AKAROLO GROUP OF COMPANIES
ALARM CENTRE LTD
ARKSEGO NIGERIA LTD
ARMOUR GUARDS NIGERIA LTD
ASHAKA SECURITY CO. LTD (ASCO)
BEMIL NIGERIA LTD
BEVERLY COPS & SECURITY SERVICES LTD
CAPITAL SECURITY & SURVELLANCE LTD
CASCHE NIGERIA LTD
CORPORATE GUARDS LTD
DAMOG NIGERIA LTD
DE-LOUIS TECHNOLOGIES LTD
EXECUTIVE GUARDS LTD
FENCE TECHNOLOGY NIGERIA LTD
GUARDSMARK NIGERIA LTD
HALOGEN SECURITY CO. LTD
INTER-FALCON SECURITY SERVICES LTD
KEK NIGERIA LTD
KEMEK NIGERIA LTD
KINGS GUARDS NIGERIA LTD
KWAJAFA SECURITY & INVESTIGATION SERVICES
LADUNNI INTERNATIONAL LTD
LAI SECURITY & INVESTIGATION SERVICES LTD
McDRILLE RESOURCES LTD
MONTGOMERY SECURITY VAULTS (NIG.) LTD
MUNAK GROUP LTD
PORTCULLIS SECURITY (NIGERIA) LTD
RAPID VIGIL LTD
ROYALSEC SERVICES CO. LTD
TECHNOCRIME SECURITY SYSTEMS LTD
TEPSI (INVESTMENT) LTD
TRANS-WORLD SECURITY & INVESTIGATN SERVICES
VIGILANT INTERNATIONAL AGENCIES (NIG.) LTD
WAFO NIGERIA LTD
ZEE HOLDINGS LTD
ZITADEL LTD

SHIP CHARTERS, BROKERS & MANAGERS
ATLANTIC MARINE & PETROLEUM MGT LTD
BLUE FUNNEL NIGERIA LTD
CARGO INSPECTION & FREIGHT LTD
CITITRUST INVESTMENT LTD
CLOVERLEAF SHIPPING LTD
DADDO MARITIME SERVICES LTD
DONMARINE & TRADING LTD
EAST WEST COAST MARINE SERVICES LTD
EXPO SHIPPING LINE (NIG.) LTD
FAGET NIGERIA LTD
GILOLA INTERNATIONAL AGENCIES LTD
GLOBE SHIPPING LINES NIGERIA LTD
HAMSTANG NIGERIA LTD
JAROS SHIPPING LINE LTD
KARLANDER NIGERIA LTD
KNIGHTSBRIDGE LTD
KODA INTERNATIONAL LTD
MARI TRANS NIGERIA LTD
MORLAP SHIPPING CO. LTD
NIGERBRAS SHIPPING LINE LTD
NIGERIA UNITY LINE PLC
RO/RO OCEANIC SHIPPING SERVICES (NIG.) LTD
SABRU NIGERIA LTD
SAMCHAM HOLDINGS LTD
STOIRIN MARITIME SERVICES LTD
SUPERMARITIME (NIG.) LTD
TRANSMARINE NIGERIA LTD

SHIPPING AGENCIES & SERVICES
ABSAF GROUP OF COMPANIES
ADE KOMOLAFE (NIGERIA) LTD
AEI (NIGERIA) LTD
AEROMARITIME GROUP OF COMPANIES
AFRICA PORT SERVICES LTD
AIR SEA FREIGHTERS LTD
AKWIWU MOTORS LTD
ALL-ROUTES SERVICES LTD
AMBED INTERNATIONAL (NIGERIA) LTD

AROLAK (NIGERIA) LTD
ATLANTIC INTERNATIONAL VENTURES LTD
BAKFAJ INTERNATIONAL (NIGERIA) LTD
BEMS LTD
BLUE FUNNEL NIGERIA LTD
BRAWAL SHIPPING (NIGERIA) LTD
C.M.A. LTD
CARLDOM INTERCONTINENTAL AGENCIES LTD
CHRISMATEL SHIPPING COMPANY (NIG.) LTD
CITI TURST INVESTMENT LTD
CLOVERLEAF SHIPPING LTD
COMET SHIPPING AGENCIES NIGERIA LTD
CONAIR CARGO SERVICES LTD
CRISP INTERNATIONAL LTD
DANAA SHIPPING CO. LTD
DAT MERCHANT INVESTMENTS LTD
DE NATUMAS INTERCONTINENTAL FREIGHT AGENCY
DELE GROUP INTERNATIONAL LTD
DELTA BROTHERS LTD
DELTA MARINE SHIPPING CO. LTD
DEROS MARITIME LTD
DUNCAN MARITIME NIGERIA LTD
EAST WEST COAST MARINE SERVICES LTD
EJIX MARITIME LTD
EXPO SHIPPING AGENCIES LTD
F. G. N. OKOYE & SONS GROUP LTD
FIDDIL NIGERIA LTD
FIDEPAT INTERNATIONAL CO. LTD
FIRST MARINE & ENGINEEERING SERVICES LTD
FREIGHT FORWARDERS (NIG.) LTD
GEETEE NIGERIA LTD
GENESIS WORLDWIDE SHIPPING CO. LTD
GEONNASONS INTERNATIONAL GROUP NIGERIA LTD
GILOLA INTERNATIONAL AGENCIES LTD
GLOBE SHIPPING LINES NIGERIA LTD
GMT SHIPPING NIGERIA LTD
GOLDEN SHIPPING COMPANY NIGERIA LTD
GULF AGENCY & SHIPPING (NIG.) LTD
HAASTRUP LINE (WEST AFRICA) LTD
HAMADAH SHIPPING SERVICES LTD
HARLINK INVESTMENT LTD
HENSMOR GROUP OF COMPANIES
HIMMA FRIEHGT LTD
IAL NIGEIRA LTD
IBRU TRANSPORT CO. LTD
IDEKE SHIPPING LTD
INLAND CONTAINERS (NIG.) LTD
INTERFREIGHT NIGERIA LTD
INTER-SERVICE NIGERIA LTD
IYAYI MARITIME NIGERIA LTD
IZZI INDUSTRIES NIGERIA LTD
JAROS SHIPPING LINE LTD
JOE-EBOJE INTERNATIONAL AGENCIES LTD
JOHN HOLT SHIPPING SERVICES (Div. of John Holt Plc)
JOKI (NIG.) LTD
KABAYAN INTERNATIONA LTD
KERILDBERT HOLDINGS LTD
K-MARINE & BUSINESS NETWORK LTD
KODA INTERNATIONAL LTD
LAAS LTD
LAGOS & NIGER SHIPPING AGENCIES LTD. (LANSAL)
LIAS FREIGHT AGENCIES LTD
LINKTEL SHIPPING LTD
M.G.S. GROUP LTD
MAC-TONNEL (NIG.) LTD
MAIDEN SHIPPING LINES LTD
MAMBILLA SHIPPING COMPANY (NIG) LTD
MERIT SHIPPING COMPANY (NIG.) LTD
MIGFO NIGERIA LTD
MIPPERS INTERNATIONAL LTD
MOFAS SHIPPING LINE (NIG.) LTD
MONZINA COASTAL AGENCIES LTD
MORLAP SHIPPING CO. LTD
MURPHY SHIPPING & COMMERCIAL SERVICES LTD
NIGERIA AMERICA LINE LTD
NIGERIA UNITY LINE PLC
NIGERIAN FORWARDERS LTD
NIGERIAN GREEN LINES LTD
NSU INTERNATIONAL CO. LTD
OAN OVERSEAS AGENCY NIGERIA LTD
OCEAN STEAMSHIP (NIG.) LTD
OCEAN TRANSPORT & SHIPPING LTD
OGUBETH INDUSTRIES NIGERIA LTD
OJOKORO CEMENT INDUSTRY LTD
ONIBUDO HOLDINGS LTD
PALM LINE AGENCIES (NIG.) LTD
PRIME MARKETING ASSOCIATES LTD
REAL SHIPPING CO. LTD
red\line NIGERIA LTD1
RO/RO OCEANIC SHIPPING SERVICES (NIG.) LTD
ROTIMI OBEISUN INVESTMENT LTD
S.G. INTERNATIONAL AGENCIES LTD
SABRU NIGERIA LTD
SAFMARINE NIGERIA LTD
SAIL SEA SHIPPING LINES LTD
SALLYAMN (NIG.) LTD
SALTAJ NIGERIA LTD
SAMCHAM HOLDINGS LTD
SAPID AGENCIES LTD
SEAWAVE GROUP OF COMPANIES
SHIPPING MAGNATE LTD
SIFAX NIGERIA LTD
SON INTERNATIONAL AGENCIES (NIG.) LTD
SOUTHERN STAR SHIPPING COMPANY (NIG.) LTD
STOIRIN MARITIME SERVICES LTD
SUNGLAD NIGERIA LTD
SUPERMARITIME (NIG.) LTD
SYKOBIN INVESTMENT LTD
TANO AGENCY & SHIPPING CO. LTD
TOKKE MARITIME SERVICES LTD
TOMBIZ GROUP OF COMPANIES
TRANE AGENCIES
TRANS ATLANTIC SHIPPING AGENCY LTD
TRANS-NATIONAL EXPRESS PLC
TRANSMARINE NIGERIA LTD
TRIANA LTD
VERITAS & COMPANY NIGERIA LTD
WORLD MARITIME LTD
YESIN INTERNATIONAL NIGERIA LTD
ZENITH SHIPPING CO. LTD

SHIPPING LINES

ALRAINE SHIPPING AGENCIES (NIGERIA) LTD
BRAWAL LINES LTD
FAGET NIGERIA LTD
HULL BLYTH NIGERIA

MAERSK NIGERIA LTD
MODANT MARINE LTD
NIGERBRAS SHIPPING LINE LTD
NIGERIA UNITY LINE PLC
NIGERIAN GREEN LINES LTD
PANALPINA WORLD TRANSPORT (NIGERIA) LTD
SAFMARINE NIGERIA LTD
SDV NIGERIA LTD
TRANSCAP NIGERIA LTD
UMARCO NIGERIA PLC
WASA-DELMAS NIGERIA LTD

SOLAR ENERGY EQUIPMENT SALES & INSTALLATION
HILLRICH LTD
MICKMONIS MULTI-SYSTEMS & INVESTMT CO. LTD
NEW COMEX TRADING CO.NIGERIA LTD
PENEL INVESTMENTS LTD
PRIME ENERGY VENTURES LTD
ROLAY ENGINEERING CO. LTD
SOLAR ELECTRIC SYSTEMS LTD
SOLAR ENERGY ADVANCED POWER SYSTEMS LTD
SOLAR ENERGY SYSTEMS & PRODUCTS CO. LTD
SOLARMATE ENGINEERING LTD
SOLLATEK (NIG.) LTD
STRUCTEC (Div. of CFAO Nigeria Plc)
TLG ENGINEERING NIGERIA LTD

SPORTS SHOPS
BIDAT SPORTWEAR CO. LTD
GRAND OLYMPUS (NIG.) LTD
HOLE 19 INVESTMENTS LTD
HOME GYMS EQUIPMENT LTD
JAGAL SPORTS LTD
PLANET SPORTS LTD
PROSPORTS LTD
SIO INDUSTRIES LTD
VAST INTERNATIONAL CO. LTD

STEEL FABRICATION & CONSTRUCTION SERVICES
ALCON NIGERIA LTD
ALINCO STEEL AND METAL CONSTRUCTION CO. LTD
AREWA METAL CONTAINERS LTD
AREWA STEEL WORKS CO. LTD
BEMAR DMP LTD
CONTINENTAL SHIPYARD LTD
D.S.D. (NIGERIA) LTD
DORMAN LONG & AMALGAMATED ENGINEERING
ELDORADO (NIG.) LTD
FAWAZ STEEL WOOD & CHEMICAL CO. LTD
FRAB & COMPANY (NIG.) LTD
GIBRALTAR CONSTRUCTION (NIG.) LTD
HASSAN STEEL PRODUCTS (NIG.) LTD
HOMAN ENGINEERING CO. LTD
INDUSTRIAL METAL PROCESSING CO. LTD
KENQUIP GROUP OF COMPANIES
LOPA ENERGY CO. LTD
MAZIN ENGINEERING LTD
MEKIOS LTD
METAL CONSTRUCTION (WEST AFRICA) LTD
OBA GROUP INTERNATIONAL CO. LTD
OBIEFUNA MODERN BUS INDUSTRIES (NIG.) LTD
OIL & INDUSTRIAL SERVICES LTD
OMARS ROYAL CO. LTD
PEBETO VENTURES LTD
POWERTRIM NIGERIA LTD
PRISMA NIGERIA LTD
PROJECT STRUCTURES LTD
SAFA STEEL & CHEMICAL MANUFACTURING LTD
SIRPI ALUSTEEL CONSTRUCTION LTD
SNIG NIGERIA LTD
SODIK ELECTRICAL AND ENGINEERING LTD
STEEL & ENGINEERING SERVICES (W. A.) LTD
STEEL WORKS LTD
STEELWAYS NIGERIA LTD
SUPASTEEL LTD
TOWER GALVANISED PRODUCTS (NIG.) LTD
TRANSCOASTAL NIGERIA LTD
TRIDENT STEEL WORKS (NIG.) LTD
UNION PRODUCTS LTD
VAN VLIET TRUCKS (NIG.) LTD
VIKING CONTAINER AND MARINE SERVICES LTD
WECO ENGINEERING & CONSTRUCTION CO. LTD

STEEL MILLS
AJAOKUTA STEEL CO. LTD
DELTA STEEL CO. LTD
JOS STEEL ROLLING CO. LTD
KATSINA STEEL ROLLING CO. LTD
OSHOGBO STEEL ROLLING CO. LTD

TANNERIES
AKKAD TANNING CO. LTD
FINE LEATHER PROCESSING CO. LTD
GASHASH TANNERIES LTD
GOD'S LITTLE TANNER LTD
GREAT NORTHERN TANNING CO. LTD
HARMATTAN TANNERY LTD
INTERNATIONAL TANNERY LTD
K.T.L. TANNERIES LTD
M.A. KRISHT INDUSTRIES NIGERIA LTD
MAHAZA CO. LTD
MARIO-JOSE ENTERPRISES LTD
MULTI-TAN LTD
NAKUDU TANNERY LTD
PROCO LTD
SULE GALADIAM & SONS LTD
TANORTH TANNER LTD
TRENDS VENERATE LTD
USAMA INDUSTRIES LTD
WHITE COLT TANNERY LTD

TELECOMMUNICATION ENGINEERING SERVICES
ABG COMMUNICATIONS LTD
ALKO LTD
ASONNET TECHNOLOGIES LTD
BOD-GEE VENTURES NIGERIA LTD
BTN (NIGERIA) LTD
CABLE & SATELLITE COMMUNICATIONS LTD
CEE BEN NIGERIA LTD
CHEZPAQ LTD
CITI COMMUNICATIONS LTD
CLEMESSY NIGERIA LTD
COMPUSOLVE INTERNATIONAL LTD
DASAT NETWORK SYSTEMS LTD
DEO MAKRO LTD
DEVICES & TECHNOLOGIES LTD

DIGITEK ENGINEERING COMPANY (NIG). LTD
DIZECO (Div. of Dizengoff West Africa Ltd)
DUCAT LTD
ECAS TELECOMMUNICATIONS & SYSTEMS LTD
EIL TELECOM LTD
EMMANUEL ELECTRONICS LTD
EXPOMA NIGERIA LTD
FRESHFONES NIGERIA LTD
GENERAL TELEPHONES & ELECTRONICS LTD
GENUSS INVESTMENTS LTD
GRAHAM BELL (NIGERIA) LTD
HADACON INTERNATIONAL LTD
HAVILAH COMMUNICATIONS LTD
HIPOTEL COMMUNICATIONS LTD
ICON eTECHNOLOGIES LTD
INTEGRATED WIRELESS TECHNOLOGIES (NIG.) LTD
ITALTEL (NIGERIA) LTD
ITT NIGERIA LTD
LEVEL '2' NIGERIA LTD
MF COMMUNICATIONS LTD
MURHI INTERNATIONAL COMPANY (NIG.) LTD
NSL CONSULTING LTD
ONAHSONS HOLDINGS LTD
PREST GROUP LTD
RDM LTD
REECHMONDZ CO. LTD
SCHLUMBERGER NETWORK SOLUTIONS
SEFAM CO. LTD
SIMBA TECHNOLOGY (NIGERIA) LTD
SKYLINK TELECOMMUNICATIONS LTD
SOKO-TECH (NIGERIA) LTD
SYSTEMS FOR TELECOMMUNICATIONS INT'L LTD
TAYLOR COMMUNICATION SOLUTIONS LTD
TELECOM TECHNOLOGIES INTERNATIONAL LTD
TELEDOM INTERNATIONAL LTD
TELEMOBILE (NIG.) LTD
TELNET NETWORK SERVICES LTD
THEOBECH SYSTEMS LTD
TLG ENGINEERING NIGERIA LTD
UNITEX TELECOMMUNICATIONS LTD
VIRGIN TECHNOLOGIES LTD
VISTAR SERVICES LTD

TELECOMMUNICATION EQUIPMENT & SYSTEMS SALES

ACCAT (NIGERIA) LTD
AFRICAN TELECOMMUNICATIONS NETWORK LTD
AFRILINKS NIGERIA LTD
AIRCOM (NIG.) LTD
ALMAS LTD
BACOM COMMUNICATIONS LTD
BANILUX GROUP OF COMPANIES
BASSCOM NIGERIA LTD
BENWILS CELLULAR CONSULTANTS LTD
BI-TRAX COMPANY INCORPORATED
BOI-TEAC (NIG.) LTD
BTN (NIG.) LTD
BUSINESS COMPUTERS & INFORMATION SYSTEMS
BUSINESS NETWORK LTD
CABLE & SATELLITE COMMUNICATIONS LTD
CALLNET TELECOMMUNICATIONS LTD
CAPITAL TECHNOLOGY SOLUTIONS LTD
CEE BEEN NIGERIA LTD
CENTRAL DYNAMICS LTD
CHEZPAQ LTD
CHOIZCOM LTD
CHYZOB ENTERPRISES LTD
CITI COMMUNICATIONS LTD
CITILINK GROUP
COMBINED BUSINESS LTD. (PAKTEL
COMMUNICATIONS ASSOCIATES OF NIGERIA LTD
COMPUTER SOLUTIONS LTD
CONIC GROUP OF COMPANIES
DEGOAL INVESTMENT LTD
DELTATEL COMMUNICATIONS LTD
DERIN (NIG.) LTD
DEVICES & TECHNOLOGIES LTD
DIGICOM TRENDS LTD
DIGITEK ENGINEERING COMPANY (NIG.) LTD
DISC COMMUNICATIONS LTD
DIZECO (Div. of Dizengoff West Africa Ltd.)
EIL TELECOM LTD
EKLIPPS TELEPHONE SYSTEMS LTD
ELECTRICARE LTD
el-RUFAI & PARTNERS LTD
EMMANUEL ELECTRONICS LTD
ENERGY & COMMUNICASTIONS INT'L (NIG.) LTD
ENGINEERING & TECHNICAL CO. (NIG.) LTD
FIRST LINK NIGERIA LTD
FRESHFONES NIGERIA LTD
GERIZM GROUP
GLOBECOM INTEGRATED SYSTEMS LTD
GOCUZ GROUP LTD
GS TELECOM NIGERIA LTD
HADACON INTERNATIONAL LTD
HITECH (NIGERIA) LTD
HYPERTRONIX NIGERIA LTD
IBA c.m. SYTEMS (WEST AFRICA) LTD
ICON eTECHNOLOGIES LTD
IMPERIAL TELECOMMUNICATIONS LTD
IMPEXX RESOURCES LTD
INCOMTEL NIGERIA LTD
INFINITE HOLDINGS LTD
INTEGRATED WIRELESS TECHNOLOGIES NIG. LTD
INTERFINISH GROUP
INTERGLOBAL LTD
INTERNATIONAL CONTROL SYSTEMS LTD
ITALTEL (NIGERIA) LTD
ITT NIGERIA LTD
JETLINK LTD
MEDCOM NIGERIA LTD
MICKMONIS MULTI-SYSTEMS & INVESTMT CO. LTD
MIKE DAD NIGERIA LTD
MINNESOTA NIGERIA LTD
MOBILE SYSTEMS LTD
M-SYSTEMS LTD
MULTIMESH COMMUNICATION LTD
NATELCO NIGERIA LTD
NEET (NIGERIA) LTD
NEOTERIC ELECTRONICS & TECHNOLOGY (NEAT) LTD
PAGING SERVICES (NIGERIA) LTD
PANA/SHARP LTD
PANABIZ INTERNATIONAL LTD
PAYBACK LTD
PAYPHONE COMPANY NIGERIA LTD
PHILIPS PROJECTS CENTRE LTD
PINEWOOD INVESTMENTS LTD

POWERLINE ENGINEERING SERVICES LTD
RADIAL CIRCLE TELECOMMUNICATIONS LTD
RADIO COMMUNICATIONS (NIG.) LTD
RAMLAX COMMUNICATION LTD
RANC LTD
REYOMS NIGERIA LTD
RIPPCON NIGERIA LTD
RTB TELECOM LTD
SAHARA BELLS COMMUNICATIONS LTD
SATELLITE TELECOMMUNICATIONS LTD
SCIENTIFIC INFORMATION LTD
SIGNAL & CONTROL SYSTEMS LTD
SIMBA TECHNOLOGY (NIG.) LTD
SKYLINK TELECOMMUNICATIONS LTD
SOUTHGATE TECHNOLOGIES LTD
SPAR AEROSPACE (NIG.) LTD
SPEAKEEZEE (Cellular & Paging Systems)
SPECTRUM COMMUNICATIONS SERVICES LTD
STARCOM INTERNATIONAL LTD
SUPERFLUX INTERNATIONAL LTD
SYSTEMPLUS LTD
SYSTEMS for TELECOMMUNICATIONS INT'L LTD (STI)
TALAFON TELECOMMUNICATIONS LTD (Talatel)
TALINET LTD
TALKLAND TRADE ALLIANCE LTD
T-COMMS NIGERIA LTD
TELEMOBILE (NIG.) LTD
TIMICOM TELECOMMUNICATIONS LTD
TORNADO INTERNATIONAL ASSOCIATES LTD
TRANS-CLASS WORLD SERVICES NIGERIA LTD
WEST ATLANTIC SYSTEMS NIGERIA LTD
WINDSBROW CONSULT LTD
YABAK TELECOMMUNICATIONS LTD
YEMTOS NIGERIA LTD

TELEPHONY SERVICE PROVIDERS
BOURDEX TELECOMMUNICATION LTD
CELL COMMUNICATIONS LTD
MTS FIRST WIRELESS LTD
RELIANCE TELECOMMUNICATIONS NIGERIA LTD
STARCOMMS LTD
VICTORIA GARDEN CITY COMMUNICATIONS CO. LTD

TELEVISION BROADCASTING SERVICES
ABG COMMUNICATIONS LTD
AIM GROUP
CHANNELS INCORPORATED LTD
COMMUNICATION TRENDS NIGERIA LTD
DAAR COMMUNICATIONS LTD
DBN LTD
MINAJ GROUP
MULTICHOICE NIGERIA
MURHI INTERNATIONAL COMPANY (NIG.) LTD
NIGERIAN TELEVISION AUTHORITY
PREST GROUP LTD
SCHWARTZ GROUP OF COMPANIES

TOBACCO PROCESSORS & MARKETERS
BRITISH AMERICAN TOBACCO (NIG.) LTD
DIAMOND TOBACCO PROCESSING CO. LTD
INTERNATIONAL TOBACCO COMPANY PLC
LAGOS TOBACCO DISTRIBUTION CO. LTD
OLIVE FOUNDATION (NIG.) LTD

TRADE AGENCIES, CENTRES & REPRESENTATIVES
ELO-PEE WORLDWIDE TELEVISION LTD
MISR (NIG.) LTD
MITSUBISHI SHOJI KAISHA (NIG.) LTD
WORLD TRADE CENTRE OF NIGERIA Ltd/Gte

TRANSPORTERS (Goods)
A.B. MANU LTD
A.G.S. BARMA LTD
A.J.K. NIGERIA LTD
AEI (NIG.) LTD
AFROCAT (NIG.) CO. LTD
AIR SEA FREIGHTERS LTD
AJE & BAWORA (NIG.) LTD
AKROSAMIK INVESTMENTS LTD
AKWIWU MOTORS LTD
ALPHA & BETA MERCHANTS CO. LTD
ASH-BERT (NIG.) LTD
ASSOCIATED BUS CO. LTD (ABC Transport)
BABS ANIMASHAUN HOLDINGS LTD
BAKFAJ INTERNATIONAL (NIG.) LTD
BONIMAS NIGERIA LTD
BOUSSALLE GROUP LTD
C.M.A. LTD
CHRISMATEL SHIPPING COMPANY (NIG.) LTD
COASTAL SERVICES (NIG.) LTD
CONAIR CARGO SERVICES LTD
CRESEADA INTERNATIONAL LTD
CRISP INTERNATIONAL LTD
DADDO MARITIME SERVICES LTD
DANGOTE NIGERIA LTD (Transport Division)
DAT MERCHANT INVESTMENTS LTD
DELMAN GROUP OF COMPANIES
DENCA SERVICES LTD
DEROS MARITIME LTD
DIMARS INDUSTRIES LTD
DOHAGRO GROUP OF COMPANIES
DOKU & SONS ENTERPRISES NIGERIA LTD
EJIX MARITIME LTD
EKENE DILI CHUKWU NIGERIA LTD
EKWENIBE & SONS TRADING CO. LTD
EXCELLENCE ALL FREIGHT LTD
F.A. ONWUACHU ENTERPRISES LTD
GEETEE NIGERIA LTD
GERMAINE HAULAGE LTD
GREMA MOHAMMED GROUP OF COMPANIES
GULFLINK LTD
GUSTO INTEGRATED LTD
HARLINK INVESTMENT LTD
HIMMA FREIGHT LTD
HOLGATE HAULAGE LTD
IBRU TRANSPORT CO. LTD
IKE GOD GROUP OF COMPANIES (NIG.) LTD
IMPERIAL SERVICES LTD
INTERPLAND TRANSPORT LTD
IWUOHA BESTWAY ELECTRONICS LTD
IZU CHUKWU TRANSPORT NIGERIA LTD
IZZI INDUSTRIES NIGERIA LTD
J.I. IBEKWE (WEST AFRICA) LTD
JAESON INTERBIZ AGENCIES LTD
JOKI (NIG.) LTD
KERILDBERT HOLDINGS LTD
KHALI & DIBBO TRANSPORT LTD

K-MARINE & BUSINESS NETWORK LTD
L.E.EJINKEONYE NIGERIA LTD
LABANA GLOBA VENTURES LTD
LUBONA NIGERIA LTD
MADUAKO TRANSPORT CO. LTD
MAIDEN SHIPPING LINES LTD
MAIJAMA'A INTERNATIONAL LTD
MALIP SERVICES LTD
MERIT SHIPPING COMPANY (NIG.) LTD
MESO INDUSTRIES LTD
MIPPERS INTERNATIONAL LTD
MONZINA COASTAL AGENCIES LTD
MOSCOL TRANSPORT CO. LTD
MOSENG NIGERIA LTD
MU'AZU INLAND TRANSPORT LTD
MULTIMART LTD
MURPHY SHIPPING & COMMERCIAL SERVICES LTD
NAJICO IRON & STEEL CO. LTD
NAPAK SERVICES (NIG.) LTD
NIGERIAN MARITIME SERVICES LTD
NUCLUES VENTURES LTD
O.I.A. SERVICES LTD
OCEAN TRANSPORT & SHIPPING LTD
OGUBETH INDUSTRIES NIGERIA LTD
OIL BATH NIGERIA LTD
ORPET NIGERIA LTD
PACIFIC FREIGHTLINERS LTD
PETRANOL NIGERIA LTD
PHILPET VENTURES LTD
PREMIER PLANT LEASE NIGERIA LTD. (PPL)
RAINBOW MARITIME (NIG.) LTD
RAYFIELD TRAVELS & TOURS LTD
RIMI HOLDINGS LTD
ROADMARKS NIGERIA LTD
SALLYMAN (NIG.) LTD
SAMCHAM HOLDINGS LTD
SANTA SEDE NIGERIA LTD
SAPID AGENCIES LTD
SON INTERNATIONAL AGENCIES (NIG.) LTD
SOTAEN NIGERIA LTD
SPIDER INTERNATIONAL LTD
STOIRIN MARITIME SERVICES LTD
SUPERMARITIME (NIG.) LTD
SYKOBIN INVESTMENT LTD
TECK TRUCKS & EQUIPMENT COMPANY (W.A.) LTD
TOKKE MARITIME SERVICES LTD
UNICENT ENTERPRISES LTD
USAMA INDUSTRIES LTD
WADOYE NIGERIA LTD
WARRY-GEE MAYO & COMPANY (NIG.) LTD
ZENITH SHIPPING CO. LTD

TRANSPORTERS (Passengers)
ASSOCIATED BUS CO. LTD (ABC Transport)
C.N. OKOLI INVESTMENT COMPANY NIGERIA LTD
CHISCO GROUP OF COMPANIES
CHUKWU DI TRANSPORT SERVICES (NIG.) LTD
DAN DOLLARS GROUP LTD
E. EKESONS BROTHERS NIGERIA LTD
EDEGBE MOTORS CO. LTD
EDO LINE TRANSPORT SERVICES LTD
F.G. ONYENWE MOTORS NIGERIA LTD
G.U. OKEKE & SONS LTD
IFESINACHI INDUSTRIES LTD
INNOCHRIS NIGERIA LTD
IZU CHUKWU TRANSPORT NIGERIA LTD
J.J. SCOT GROUP OF COMPANIES
MIC-MERAH INTERNATIONAL AGENCY LTD
NEW TARZAN MOTORS LTD
P.N. EMERAH & SONS (NIG.) LTD
RIVERS TRANSPORT CO. LTD
ROADMARKS NIGERIA LTD

TRAVEL & TOURS AGENCIES
ABBEY TRAVELS & TOURS (NIG.) LTD
ATS TRAVEL NIGERIA LTD
BELLVIEW TRAVELS LTD
BHN TRANSPORT & LOGISTICS LTD
BISCORDINT TRAVEL AGENCY LTD
BITTS TRAVEL & TOURS LTD
BUOSHISHI HOLDINGS LTD
CAZOGIE TRAVELS & TOURS LTD
COASTAL SERVICES (NIG.) LTD
CONNECTIONS TRAVEL & TOURS LTD
CRESTWOOD HOLDINGS LTD
CRISP INTERNATIONAL LTD
DANIEL TRAVELS AGENCY LTD
EXPERT AVIATION AGENCY NIGERIA LTD
FAFINC NIGERIA LTD
FIRST STANDARD TRAVELS & TOURS LTD
FIVE STAR TRAVEL LTD./BTI-Nigeria
GALLIEO NIGERIA
GLOBAL VIEW TRAVELS & TOURS LTD
GOGINS TRAVELS LTD
HRN TRAVEL LTD
JETA TRAVEL AGENCY LTD
JOEDONE INTERNATIONAL LTD
KALIFE TRAVEL BUREAU LTD
KRAINE INVESTMENTS LTD
L'ARISTOCRATE TRAVEL & TOURS LTD
LANDOVER CO. LTD
LIAISON FRANCAIS NIGERIA LTD
MAGNIFICENT TRAVELS & TOURS LTD
MANDILAS TRAVELS LTD8
MASSARRAH AIR SERVICES
MONARCH TRAVELS LTD
NATIONAL CLEARING & FORWARDING AGENCY
NUSRA TRAVELS & TOURS LTD
OMICRON INTERNATIONAL LTD
PARADISE TRAVELS & TOURS LTD
PARAMOUNT AIRLINES & TRAVEL SERVICES LTD
PLATEAU STATE TOURISM CORPORATION
PLATINUM TRAVEL LTD
POINTVIEW TRAVELS & TOURS LTD
PRIME UNION TRAVELS & TOURS LTD
RAYFIELD TRAVELS & TOURS LTD
REWARD TRAVELS & TOURS LTD
RUTAM TRAVELS LTD
SAFEPOINT INVESTMENTS CO. LTD
SELINA VENTURES LTD
SILMA TRAVELS LTD
SOLTAN TRAVELS & TOURS LTD
TARGET TRAVELS LTD
TRANS-NATIONAL EXPRESS PLC
TRANSCAP TRAVEL BUREAUX (Div of CFAO Nig. Plc)
TUNG TRAVEL & TOURS LTD

VOYAGER TRAVELS LTD
ZENITH TRAVELS & TOURS LTD

VEGETABLES OIL MILLS/PROCESSORS
A.A. MUDALLABI ABDULLAHI & SONS LTD
ASSAN OIL MILLS LTD
BEBEJI OIL & ALLIED PRODUCTS LTD
CAMELA PURE VEGETABLE OIL CO. LTD
ENVOY OIL INDUSTRIES LTD
GENERAL AGRO OIL INDUSTRIES LTD
GOMBE OIL SEED PROCESSORS LTD
GRAND CREALS OIL MILLS LTD
INTERNATIONAL FRACTIONATION & MARGARINE PRODUCTS LTD
JOF IDEA FAMILY FARMS LTD
KATSINA OIL MILL LTD
NAMALCO OIL MILLS LTD
NOMA OIL & CAKE MILLS LTD
Om OIL INDUSTRY LTD
POKO OIL MILLS (WEST AFRICA) LTD
PRESCO INDUSTRIES LTD
REAL OIL MILLS (NIG.) LTD
RESOURCES IMPROVEMENT & MANUF. CO. LTD
RIVERS VEGETABLE OIL CO. LTD
SAVANNAH CHEMICAL INDUSTRIES LTD
SUNSEED NIGERIA PLC
TAHIR OIL MILLS PLC
TRIMCO LTD
TUNS HOLDINGS LTD

VETERINARY SERVICES
HARMONY PROJECTS LTD
NOVAT ANIMAL HOPSITAL LTD
PVC GROUP
ZEE HOLDINGS LTD

WASTE MANAGEMENT SERVICES
ATLANTIC WASTE MANAGEMENT LTD
DAVCO INTERNATIONAL (NIG.) LTD
DURACLEAN SERVICES (NIG.) LTD
ENVIRONMENTAL RESOURCES MANAGERS LTD
GEOMATICS NIGERIA LTD
GLOBAL ENVIRONMENTAL TECHNOLOGY LTD
HIGHWAY MANAGERS LTD
NIGERIA CLEANING SERVICES LTD
SATEC WATER TREATMENT (NIG.) LTD
SCHWARTZ GROUP OF COMPANIES
SEAVIEW PROPERTIES LTD
TOMBIZ GROUP OF COMPANIES
WASCO NIGERIA LTD
WASTE MATTERS NIGERIA LTD
ZITADEL LTD

WATER ENGINEERING SERVICES
AMCO TECHNICAL ENGINEERING CO. LTD
ARCHBODE ENGINEERING LTD
AREWA METAL CONTAINERS LTD
BAZEE NIGERIA LTD
BEE DRILLING SERVICES LTD
BETCY GROUP OF COMPANIES
BRAITHWAITE WATER RESOURCES (NIG.) LTD
CHARVET NIGERIA LTD
CLEANAQUA AFRICA LTD
CLOVIC NIGERIA LTD
CONSTRUCTION PRODUCTS NIGERIA LTD
CROSSAIDS LTD
DANBRITE COMPANY NIGERIA LTD
DEGREMONT NIGERIA LTD
EAUXWELL NIGERIA LTD
GEODEZ NIGERIA LTD
HCP WATER SERVICES LTD
HOLD-TRADE DRILLING CO. (NIGERIA) LTD
HYDRO CONSTRUCTION & ENGINEERING CO. LTD
HYDROWORKS LTD
JAGAL NIGERIA LTD
JOS. HANSEN & SOEHNE (NIG.) LTD
KAYFEM KONSULT LTD
KEMENG SERVICES LTD
LATRASAK NIGERIA LTD
NIGERNORTH LTD
NOKU KONSULT LTD
O.B.BAKER LTD
OLATECH BOREHOLES LTD
ONAHSONS HOLDINGS LTD
PANITEX NIGERIA LTD
PARI NIGERIA LTD
PIVOT ENGINEERING CO. LTD
PRAKLA GOEMECHANIK INTERNATIONAL LTD
SAFE NIGERIA LTD
SAGAOLA MINING & ENGINEERING (NIG.) LTD
SAKEY ENGINEERING SERVICES LTD
SATEC WATER TREATMENT (NIG.) LTD
SCANA LTD
SCANWATER (NIGERIA) LTD
SDEM ERECTORS NIGERIA LTD
SEG. MAHSEN & COMPANY (NIG.) LTD
STRUCTEC (Div. of CFAO Nigeria Plc)
TOMBULCO (NIG.) LTD
UNILINKS NIGERIA LTD
VELTROP LTD
WATER SEARCH NIGERIA LTD
WATER SERVICES ENGINEERING LTD
ZAKHEM CONSTRUCTION NIGERIA LTD
ZIATECH NIGERIA LTD

WATER PURIFICATION & DISPENSING SYSTEMS SALES
ASTRAL WATERS LTD
BILL + BROTHERS LTD
CEPCO COMMUNICATION SYSTEMS LTD
CLEANAQUA AFRICA LTD
C-WAY DRINKING WATER SCIENCE & TECHNOLOGY CO. NIGERIA LTD
DOFAS TECHNICAL NIGERIA LTD
EMIC VENTURES LTD
FROSS INVESTMENT LTD
H20 INTERNATIONAL NIGERIA LTD
KINGSMAT CO. LTD
NIMBUS WATER SYSTEMS INC
OZED VENTURES LTD
SAKEY ENGINEERING SERVICES LTD
UNIPUMPS NIGERIA LTD
WATERTECH (NIG.) LTD

WATER/SEWAGE TREATMENT PLANTS & ENGINEERING
ADIMEX VENTURES LTD
ARCHBODE ENGINEERING LTD

BEMAR DMP LTD
BRAITHWAITE WATER RESOURCES (NIG.) LTD
CINO NIGERIA LTD
CONSTRUCTION PRODUCTS NIGERIA LTD
CROSSAIDS LTD
DEGREMONT NIGERIA LTD
DUMSON NIGERIA LTD
EAUXWELL NIGERIA LTD
KAYFEM KONSULT LTD
MEKIOS LTD
NOKU KONSULT LTD
OLATECH BOREHOLES LTD
SAKEY ENGINERING SERVICES LTD
SATEC WATER TREATMENT (NIG.) LTD
SCANA LTD
SCANWATER (NIG.) LTD
SEG. MAHSEN & COMPANY (NIG.) LTD
TITAN ENGINEERS & CONSTRUCTORS LTD
UNILINKS NIGERIA LTD
VELTROPS LTD
VOEST-ALPHINE (NIG.) LTD
WATER SEARCH NIGERIA LTD
WATER SERVICES ENGINEERING LTD

WEIGHING EQUIPMENT & SCALES SALES
AVERY NIGERIA LTD
GOLDEN CROSS TECHNICAL LTD
INDUSTRIAL AUTOMATION (NIG.) LTD

WELDING EQUIPMENT & MATERIALS SALES
A.M.H. ENTERPRISES LTD
ANBUS WELDSERV (NIG.) LTD
BESTLINE NIGERIA LTD
DANDICKINS ENYEOBI & CO. LTD
HOLMAN BROTHERS (NIG.) LTD
KRESTA LAUREL LTD
MAJOR ELECTRODES INDUSTRIES LTD
OCO INDUSTRIAL SERVICES LTD
SCOA TRAC (Div. of SCOA Nigeria Plc)
UNITED WIRE PRODUCTS LTD

WIRE PRODUCTS MANUFACTURERS/SALES
EUREKA METALS LTD
HIGHLAND STEEL & ALLIED INDUSTRIES LTD
ILODI GROUP OF COMPANIES
J. IRORUN ENTERPRISES NIGERIA LTD
TRIDENT STEEL WORKS (NIG.) LTD
UDEZE INVESTMENTS & INDUSTRIAL COMPLEX LTD
UNITED WIRE PRODUCTS LTD
VIDEPAT ENTERPRISES NIGERIA LTD

THE PRESIDENCY

Executive Offices

MINISTRIES AND EXTRA-MINISTERIAL DEPARTMENTS IN THE PRESIDENCY

NATIONAL ASSEMBLY

Executive Offices

Administrative Offices

FEDERAL JUDICIARY

Federal Courts

Judicial Bodies

FEDERAL MINISTRIES AND EXTRA-MINISTERIAL DEPARTMENTS

FEDERAL PARASTATALS AND AGENCIES

FEDERAL RESEARCH AND DEVELOPMENT INSTITUTES AND CENTRES

FEDERAL GOVERNMENT-OWNED COMMERCIAL ENTERPRISES

MILITARY/PARA-MILITARY ORGANISATIONS

Armed Forces

Para-Military Services

FEDERAL HOSPITALS

FEDERAL UNIVERSITIES/POSTGRADUATE INSTITUTIONS

FEDERAL VOCATIONAL COLLEGES AND SCHOOLS

THE PRESIDENCY (Executive Offices)

OFFICE OF THE PRESIDENT OF THE FEDERAL REPUBLIC
Address: Aso Rock Villa, Asokoro District, Abuja.
Tel: (09) 5232127-8 (2L), 5232136, 5234080, 2343662
Fax: (09) 2347546
E-mail: admin@nopa.net
public@nopa.net
ssa@nopa.net
Website: www.nopa.net
Contact: Snr Special Assistant (Media)

OFFICE OF THE VICE-PRESIDENT OF THE FEDERAL REPUBLIC
Address: Aso Rock Villa, Asokoro District, Abuja.
Tel: (09) 2340011, 5231167, 5231777, 5231867
Fax: (09) 5235277
Contact: Special Assistant (Media)

OFFICE OF THE SECRETARY TO THE GOVERNMENT OF THE FEDERATION
Address: Federal Secretariat Towers (11th Floor), Shehu Shagari Way, Maitama District, Abuja
Tel: (09) 5233540
Contact: Deputy Director (Press & Public Relations)

OFFICE OF THE HEAD OF CIVIL SERVICE OF THE FEDERATION
Address: Federal Secretariat Complex, Phase II, Bulet House (4th Floor), Shehu Shagari Way, Maitama District, Abuja
Tel: (09) 2348250 - 5(5L), 2348279, 2348284, 2348354
Contact: Chief Press Secretary

MINISTRIES AND EXTRA-MINISTERIAL DEPARTMENTS IN THE PRESIDENCY

MINISTRY FOR CO-OPERATION AND INTEGRATION IN AFRICA (The Presidency)
Address: Federal Secretariat Annex (1st Floor), Shehu Shagari Way, Maitama District, Abuja
Tel: (09) 5234150, 5232968
Fax: (09) 5235638
Contact: Senator Lawan Gana Guba - Honourable Minister

MINISTRY OF ECONOMIC MATTERS & SPECIAL PROJECTS (The Presidency)
Address: Federal Secretariat Complex, Phase II, Bulet Buiding (Right Wing, 3rd Floor), Shehu Shagari Way, Maitama District, Abuja
Tel: (09) 2344422, 2345624
Contact: The Permanent Secretary

MINISTRY OF INTER-GOVERNMENTAL AFFAIRS & NDDC MONITORING (The Presidency)
Address: Federal Secretariat Complex, Phase II, Bulet Buiding (Right Wing, 2nd Floor), Shehu Shagari Way, Maitama District, Abuja
Tel: (09) 2349907 - 8(2L)
Contact: Col. Musa Mohammed (rtd) - Honourable Minister

MINISTRY OF SPECIAL DUTIES (The Presidency)
Address: Federal Secretariat Complex, Phase II, Bulet Buiding (Left Wing, 3rd Floor), Shehu Shagari Way, Maitama District, Abuja
Tel: (09) 2349911, 2349912
Fax: (09) 2349939

NATIONAL PLANNING COMMISSION (The Presidency)
Address: Federal Secretariat Complex, Annex III (4th Floor), Shehu Shagari Way, Maitama District, Abuja
Tel: (09) 5232924, 5236628
* Federal Secretariat Complex, Phase I (5th & 6th Floors), Lagos. **Tel:** (01) 686273
Contact: Assistant Director (Public Affairs)

NATIONAL ASSEMBLY
Executive Offices:

OFFICE OF THE PRESIDENT OF THE SENATE
Address: National Assembly Complex, Three Arms Zone, Abuja
Tel: (09) 2340000, 2340009, 2340505, 2340622, 2341217, 5234900 - 5(6L)
Fax: (09) 2341214
Contact: Personal Assistant to the Senate President

OFFICE OF THE DEPUTY PRESIDENT OF THE SENATE
Address: National Assembly Complex, Three Arms Zone, Abuja
Tel: (09) 2340020, 2340373
Fax: (09) 2340217
Contact: Special Assistant (Media)

OFFICE OF THE SPEAKER OF THE HOUSE OF REPRESENTATIVES
Address: National Assembly Complex, Three Arms Zone, Abuja
Tel: (09) 2340009, 2340087, 2340393
Fax: (09) 2340303
E-mail: speaker@ngspeaker.org
Website: www.ngspeaker.org
Contact: Public Liaison Officer

OFFICE OF THE DEPUTY SPEAKER OF THE HOUSE OF REPRESENTATIVES
Address: National Assembly Complex, Three Arms Zone, Abuja
Tel: (09) 2340018, 2340278
Fax: (09) 2341446
E-mail: deputyspeaker@deputyspeaker-nass-nig.org
Website: www.deputyspeaker-nass-nig.org
Contact: Special Assistant (Media Relations)

Administrative Offices:

OFFICE OF THE CLERK OF THE NATIONAL ASSEMBLY
Address: National Assembly Complex, Three Arms Zone, Abuja
Tel: (09) 2340082, 2342269
Fax: (09) 2342157
Contact: Clerk of the National Assembly

OFFICE OF THE CLERK OF THE SENATE
Address: National Assembly Complex, Three Arms Zone, Abuja
Tel: (09) 2340013, 2340038, 2340274
Fax: (09) 2340274
Contact: Clerk of the Senate

OFFICE OF THE CLERK OF THE HOUSE OF REPRESENTATIVES
Address: National Assembly Complex, Three Arms Zone, Abuja
Tel: (09) 2340273
Contact: The Clerk of the House

FEDERAL JUDICIARY
Federal Courts:

SUPEME COURT OF NIGERIA
Address: Supreme Court Complex, Three Arms Zone, Abuja
Tel: (09) 2344762, 5236841
Fax: (09) 2346717, 6700649
E-mail: supremecourt@cyberspace.net.ng
* Old Supreme Court Building, Igbosere Road, Lagos
Tel: (01) 2636452
* 2, Waff Road, Kaduna.
Tel: (062) 240453
Contact: The Chief Registrar, Supreme Court of Nigeria.

COURT OF APPEAL OF NIGERIA
Address: Behind former Open University Complex, off Orlu Street, off Tafawa Balewa Way, Area 3, Garki, Abuja
Tel: (09) 2346643, 2346645
Fax: (09) 2345290
* Old Supreme Court Building, Igbosere Road, Lagos
Tel: (01) 2600491, 2600493
* 13, Moscow Road, Port Harcourt.
Tel: (084) 232131
* Kawo Road, Ali Akilu Road, by Nigerian Defence Academy Junction, Kaduna.
Tel: (062) 312716
* Independence Layout, Enugu
Tel: (042) 453898, 458883, 459999
* Quarter 749, Iyanganku G.R.A., Ibadan
Tel: (02) 2310386, 2310444, 2312573, 2312713, 2315668, 2318411-2(2L)
* 1, Kano Road, near Challenge Bookshop, Jos
Tel: (073) 453734 **Fax:** (073) 452356
* Sapele Road, Benin City.
Tel: (052) 201041, 253716
* Gari Alimi Road, Ilorin.
Tel: (031) 223160, 226802
* Government House Road, Calabar
Tel: (087) 232297, 232607, 232649
Contact: The Chief Registrar, Federal Court of Appeal.

FEDERAL HIGH COURT OF NIGERIA
Address: 24, Oyekan Abayomi Drive, Ikoyi, Lagos
Tel: (01) 2691006, 2691439, 2671260
Fax: (01) 2691006
* 1B, Bourdillon Road, Falomo, Ikoyi, Lagos
Tel: (01) 685047
* O.A.U. Quarters (Restaurant Building), off Kashim Ibrahim Way, Maitama, Abuja.
Tel: (09) 4138995
* Usuma Street, off Gana Street, Maitama, Abuja
Tel: (09) 4136833
* Station Okrika Road, Port Harcourt
Tel: (084) 232189, 335777
* New Court Road, Gyadi-Gyadi, Kano
Tel: (064) 665140, 667823
* New Adeoyo Hospital Road, off Ring Road, Ibadan
Tel: (02) 2319891, 314162
* Independence Layout, Enugu.
Tel: (042) 250596, 459662
* Old Court of Appeal Premises, Ali Akilu Road, opp. NDA, Kaduna.
Tel: (062) 210194, 312041
* 3, Toro Road, offShehu Laminu Way, Old G.R.A., Maiduguri.
Tel: (076) 235046, 236321
* IBB Boulevard, Kobape Road, adj. Federal Secretariat, Oke-Mosan, Abeokuta.
Tel: (039) 242894, 243542
* Ahmadu Bello Way, Old G.R.A, Makurdi
Tel: (044) 534124, 534125
* Quarter 33, Alfred Rewane Road, Alagbaka, G.R.A., Akure.
Tel: (034) 241645
* Gwandu Road, Sokoto.
Tel: (060) 232803
* Abia State High Court Premises, Ikot Ekpene Road, Umuahia.
Tel: (088) 220049
* 9A, Kashim Ibrahim Road, Jimeta-Yola.
Tel: (075) 624344, 627644
* 1, Iwogban Road, off Benin-Auchi Road, Ikpoba Hill, Benin City.
Tel: (052) 259672
* Fate Road, Ilorin.
Tel: (031) 221797, 220937 **Fax:** (031) 220937
* Murtala Mohammed Highway, Calabar
Tel: (087) 230220, 232335
* 21, Club Road, near Court of Appeal/CBN, Jos
Tel: (073) 453845
Contact: The Chief Registrar, Federal High Court.

NATIONAL INDUSTRIAL COURT
Address: Plot 670, Port Harcourt Crescent, Gimbiya Street, off Ahamdu Bello Way, Area II, Garki, Abuja.
Tel: (09) 3140363
* 22, Oju-Olobun Close, Victoria Island, Lagos
Tel: (01) 2625829, 2625831, 611131
Fax: (01) 610946
Contact: The Chief Registrar, National Industrial Court

Judicial Bodies:

INDUSTRIAL ARBITRATION PANEL
Address: Tofa House (4th & 5th Floors), Central Business Distrct, Garki, Abuja
Tel: (09) 5231525
* 15A, Awolowo Road, S.W., Ikoyi, Lagos
Tel: (01) 2673516, 2694106
Fax: (01) 2694106
Contact: The Chief Registrar, Industrial Arbitration Panel

NATIONAL JUDICIAL INSTITUTE
Address: Supreme Court Complex, Three Arms Zone, Abuja
Tel: (09) 2346864-5 (2L), 2347786
Fax: (09) 2347554
* Court of Appeal Premises, Igbosere Road, Lagos.
Tel: (01) 2636376, 2647552
Contact: The Administrator

FEDERAL MINISTRIES AND EXTRA-MINISTERIAL DEPARTMENTS

FEDERAL MINISTRY OF AGRICULTURE AND RURAL DEVELOPMENT

Address: Block A, FCDA Secretariat Complex, Area II, Garki, Abuja
Tel: (09) 3141458, 3141931, 3142405, 3142622, 3142728 3142914, 3143987, 3146509
Fax: (09) 3140347, 3140945, 3141185, 3142207, 3144392
* Glass House (2rd Floor), Former National Assembly Complex, Tafawa Balewa Square, Lagos
Tel: (01) 2632880, 2636473
Fax: (01) 2632880
Contact: Alh. Adamu Bello - Honourable Minister

FEDERAL MINISTRY OF AVIATION

Address: Federal Secretariat Complex, Annex 2, Shehu Shagari Way, Maitama District, Abuja.
Tel: (09) 5232052, 5232053, 5232112, 5232118, 5232132
Fax: (09) 5237603
* 14, Broad Street, Lagos. **Tel:** (01) 2600942-7 (6L)
Contact: Dr Babalola Borishade - Honourable Minister

FEDERAL MINISTRY OF COMMERCE

Address: Block H & G, Old Federal Secretariat, Area 1, Garki, Abuja
Tel: (09) 2341490, 2341661, 2341687, 2348454
Fax: (09) 2341351
Contact: Amb. Idris Waziri - Honourable Minister

FEDERAL MINISTRY OF COMMUNICATIONS

Address: Block 5B (2nd & 3rd Floor), Federal Secretariat Complex, Shehu Shagari Way, Maitama District, Abuja.
Tel: (09) 5232836, 5237135, 5237183, 5237250, 5237260, 5238245 **Fax:** (09) 5232834
* P & T Building, Lafiaji, Lagos.
Tel: (01) 2633476, 2646761
Contact: Chief Cornelius Adebayo - Honourable Minister

FEDERAL MINISTRY OF CULTURE AND TOURISM

Address: Federal Secretariat Complex, Phase II, Bulet Buiding (Block A, 1st Floor & Block B, 5th Floor), Shehu Shagari Way, Maitama District, Abuja
Tel: (09) 2348297, 2348311 **Fax:** (09) 2348257
E-mail: culturetourism@yahoo.com
Contact: Chief Franklin Ogbuewu - Honourable Minister

FEDERAL MINISTRY OF DEFENCE

Address: Ship House, Olusegun Obasanjo Way, Central Business Area, Garki, Abuja
Tel: (09) 2340534, 2348955, 2348970, 2348975, 2349143
Fax: (09) 2340714
* Defence Headquarters, 1/3, Moloney Street, Onikan, Lagos. **Tel:** (01) 2647139
Contact: Dr Rabiu Musa Kwankwaso - Honourable Minister

FEDERAL MINISTRY OF EDUCATION

Address: Federal Secretariat Complex, (Block 5A, 3rd Floor), Shehu Shagari Way, Maitama District, Abuja
Tel: (09) 5230720, 5232800, 5237487-9 (3L)
* Federal Min. of Education Building, Ahmadu Bello Way (Legico Bus-Stop), Victoria Island, Lagos
Contact: Mrs Chinwe Obaji - Honourable Minister

FEDERAL MINISTRY OF EMPLOYMENT, LABOUR AND PRODUCTIVITY

Address: Federal Secretariat Complex, (Block 4A, 2nd Floor), Shehu Shagari Way, Maitama District, Abuja
Tel: (09) 5235980, 5235988, 5235994
Fax: (09) 5235973
* Federal Secretariat Complex, Phase I (7th Floor), Ikoyi, Lagos.
Contact: Permanent Secretary

FEDERAL MINISTRY OF ENVIRONMENT

Address: Federal Secretariat Complex, (9th Floor), Shehu Shagari Way, Maitama District, Abuja
Tel: (09) 5234014, 5234119, 5234931-2 (2L)
Fax: (09) 5234014, 5234119
E-mail: fmenv@hyperia.com
* Federal Ministry of Environment, Games Complex, Bode Thomas Street, Surulere, Lagos
Tel: (01) 5850120, 5850122, 5850124, 5851570-1 (2L)
* Brown Office Building, Independence Way South, Central Area, Garki, Abuja
Tel: (09) 2342808 **Fax:** (09) 2342807
* Green Office Building, Aguiyi Ironsi Street, opp. Raw Material Research & Dev. Council, Wuse II, Abuja. **Tel:** (09) 4135972-3 (2L)
Contact: Dr Iyorchia Ayu - Honourable Minister

FEDERAL MINISTRY OF FEDERAL CAPITAL TERRITORY

Address: Area 11, Garki, Abuja
Tel: (09) 3141019, 3141295, 3141525, 3148135
Fax: (09) 3143859
* 15B, Awolowo Road, S.W., Ikoyi, Lagos
Tel: (01) 2673618, 2673619, 2673620
Contact: Mallam Nasir'el-Rufai - Honourable Minister

FEDERAL MINISTRY OF FINANCE

Address: Federal Ministry of Finance Complex, Ahmadu Bello Way, Central Business District, Garki, Abuja
Tel: (09) 2340946, 2343787, 2346291-4 (4L), 2346928, 2346930-1 (2L)
* Federal Secretariat Complex, Phase I, (10th Floor), Ikoyi, Lagos.
Tel: (01) 683608, 688659 **Fax:** (01) 685222
Contact: Mrs. Ngozi Okonjo-Iweala - Honourable Minister

FEDERAL MINISTRY OF FOREIGN AFFAIRS

Address: Maputo St, off Abdjan Street, Wuse Zone 3, Abuja
Tel: (09) 5230208-10 (3L), 5230185-9 (5L), 5234467
Fax: (09) 5230361, 5234467
* 23, Marina (4th Floor), Lagos
Tel: (01) 2620315, 2630023
Contact: Amb. Olu Adeniyi - Honourable Minister

FEDERAL MINISTRY OF HEALTH

Address: Federal Secretariat Complex, (Block 4A, 3rd Floor), Shehu Shagari Way, Maitama District, Abuja
Tel: (09) 5231511, 5234590, 5238362
Fax: (09) 5234590
E-mail: minhealth@fmoh.gov.ng
* Federal Secretariat Complex, Phase II (9th Floor), Ikoyi, Lagos.
Tel: (01) 684488 **Fax:** (01) 684409
Contact: Prof. Eyitayo Lambo - Honourable Minister

FEDERAL MINISTRY OF HOUSING & URBAN DEVELOPMENT
Address: Mabushi, Abuja
Tel: (09) 5211637-8 (2L)
* Tafawa Balewa Square, Lagos
Tel: (01) 2631915
Contact: Dr Rahman Mimiko - Honourable Minister

FEDERAL MINISTRY OF INDUSTRY
Address: Block C & D, Old Federal Secretariat, Area 1, Garki, Abuja
Tel: (09) 2341367, 2341570, 2341690, 2341721, 2343998
Fax: (09) 2341690, 2341919
* Federal Secretariat Complex, Phase II, Ikoyi, Lagos.
Tel: (01) 2672945
Contact: Amb. Fidelis Tapgun - Honourable Minister

FEDERAL MINISTRY OF INFORMATION & NATIONAL ORIENTATION
Address: Radio House, Herbert Macaulay Way (South), Area 10, Garki, Abuja
Tel: (09) 2340717, 2340787, 2344107, 2345793, 2346351, 2346353-6 (4L), 2346358
Fax: (09) 2344106
E-mail: webmaster@nig.com.ng
Website: www.nig.gov.ng
* 15C, Awolowo Road, Ikoyi, Lagos
Tel: (01) 681857, 2694978
Fax: (01) 2694978
Contact: Mr Frank Nweke Jr - Honourable Minister

FEDERAL MINISTRY OF INTERNAL AFFAIRS
Address: Block F, Old Federal Secretariat, Area 1, Garki, Abuja
Tel: (09) 2341934-6 (3L), 2341298, 2341953, 2343369, 2349128
Fax: (09) 2342029
* Prison Department Complex, Alagbon Close, off Ikoyi, Lagos.
Tel: (01) 2692944-5 (2L)
Contact: Amb. Magaji Muhammed - Honourable Minister

FEDERAL MINISTRY OF JUSTICE
Address: Federal Secretariat Towers, (5th & 10th Floors), Shehu Shagari Way, Maitama District, Abuja
Tel: (09) 5235039, 5235194
Fax: (09) 5235208
* Old Federal Secretariat, Joseph Street/Marina, Lagos
Tel: (01) 2630026
Fax: (01) 2634552
Contact: Chief Bayo Ojo (SAN) - Honourable Minister

FEDERAL MINISTRY OF PETROLEUM RESOURCES
Address: Federal Secretariat Complex, (1st Floor), Shehu Shagari Way, Maitama District, Abuja
Tel: (09) 5230926, 5237571, 5237581
Fax: (09) 5230763, 5237332
* 41, Glover Road, Ikoyi,Lagos.
Tel: (01) 2691039
Contact: The Chief Press Secretary

FEDERAL MINISTRY OF POLICE AFFAIRS.
Address: Federal Secretariat Complex, (8th Floor), Shehu Shagari Way, Maitama District, Abuja
Tel: (09) 5230549, 5234783 **Fax:** (09) 5232450
* 2, Kofo Abayomi Street, Victoria Island, Lagos.
Tel: (01) 615194
Contact: Mr. Broderick Bozimo - Honourable Minister

FEDERAL MINISTRY OF POWER AND STEEL
Address: Federal Secretariat Complex, Annex 3 (3rd & 4th Floors), Shehu Shagari Way, Maitama District, Abuja
Tel: (09) 5237064, 5237065, 5237066, 5239462, 5239465
* Federal Secretariat Complex, Phase I (1st Floor), Ikoyi, Lagos.
Tel/Fax: (01) 687233
Contact: Senator Liyel Imoke - Honourable Minister

FEDERAL MINISTRY OF SCIENCE & TECHNOLOGY
Address: Federal Secretariat Towers "B" (4th, 5th & 9th Floors), Shehu Shagari Way, Maitama District, Abuja
Tel: (09) 5233397, 5233903, 5235204, 5235768-9 (2L)
Fax: (09) 5235204
Contact: Prof. Turner Isoun - Honourable Minister

FEDERAL MINISTRY OF SOLID MINERALS DEVELOPMENT
Address: Federal Secretariat Complex, Annex 3 (5th Floor), Shehu Shagari Way, Maitama District, Abuja
Tel: (09) 5235830, 5235831, 5236454, 5236517
Fax: (09) 5236519
* Federal Secretariat Complex, Phase I (2nd & 12th Floors), Ikoyi, Lagos.
Tel: (01) 26900048
Contact: Mrs Obiageli Ezekwesili - Honourable Minister

FEDERAL MINISTRY OF SPORTS & SOCIAL DEVELOPMENT
Address: Federal Secretariat Complex, (Block 3, 1st Floor), Shehu Shagari Way, Maitama District, Abuja
Tel: (09) 5232272, 5235903, 5235905, 5235907
* National Stadium Premises, Surulere, Lagos.
Tel: (01) 2885099, 5454472
Fax: (01) 4931972
Contact: Alhaji Saidu Sama'ila - Honourable Minister

FEDERAL MINISTRY OF TRANSPORT
Address: Bukar Dipcharima House, off Third Avenue, off Tofa House, Central Business District, Garki, Lagos
Tel: (09) 2340319, 2340850, 2347470-6 (7L), 2347478, 2347452 **Fax:** (09) 2347452, 2347470
* 1, Joseph Street/Marina, Lagos.
Tel: (01) 2645411
Contact: Dr. Precious Sekibo - Honourable Minister

FEDERAL MINISTRY OF WATER RESOURCES
Address: Block A, Old Federal Secretariat, Area 1, Garki, Abuja
Tel: (09) 2342376, 2342415, 2342684, 2344436;
* (01) 2631841 **Fax:** (09) 2342370
Contact: Alh. Muktar Shagari - Honourable Minister

FEDERAL MINISTRY OF WOMEN AFFAIRS & YOUTH DEVELOPMENT
Address: New Federal Secretariat, Annex 2, Shehu Shagari Way, Maitama District, Abuja
Tel: (09) 5233642, 5233644, 5237112, 5237115, 5237278, 5238341, 5238864
Fax: (09) 5233644
Contact: Hadjia Mariam Ciroma - Honourable Minister

FEDERAL MINISTRY OF WORKS
Address: Mabushi, Abuja.
Tel: (09) 5211637-8 (2L), 5239622-6 (5L)
* Tafawa Balewa Square, Lagos.
Tel: (01) 2631915
Contact: Senator Adeseye Ogunlewe - Honourable Minister

FEDERAL CIVIL SERVICE COMMISSION
Address: Abidjan Street, Wuse Zone 3, Abuja
Tel: (09) 5231021, 5233504, 5237234-5 (2L)
* Federal Secretariat Complex, Phase II (11th Floor), Ikoyi, Lagos.
Tel: (01) 686475
Contact: Chief Press Secretary/Head (Press & Public Rel.)

INDEPENDENT NATIONAL ELECTORAL COMMISSION (INEC)
Address: Plot 436, Zambezi Crescent, off Aguiyi Ironsi Street, Cadastral Zone A5, Maitama District, Abuja
Tel: (09) 4133339, 4133843, 4134368, 4134416, 4134565, 4135230
Tel/Fax: (09) 4133339, 4133843
Contact: The Executive Secretary

OFFICE OF THE ACCOUNTANT-GENERAL OF THE FEDERATION
Address: Zaria St, opp.Central Bank of Nigeria, Garki II, Abuja
Tel: (09) 2340494, 2340632, 2340672
* Old Federal Secretariat, Area 1, Garki, Abuja
Tel: (01) 2341040, 2341933
Contact: Head (Public Relations)

OFFICE OF THE AUDITOR-GENERAL OF THE FEDERATION
Address: Plot 849, Koforidua Street, off Michael Okpara Street, Wuse Zone 2, Abuja
Tel: (09) 5235752, 5237792, 5237797
Fax: (09) 5235322
* 5, Mobolaji Bank-Anthony Street, Lagos Island, Lagos.
Tel: (01) 2632335 **Fax:** (01) 2635857
Contact: The Auditor-General

STATES & LOCAL GOVERNMENT AFFAIRS
Office of the Vice President (The Presidency)
Address: Radio House (10-12th Floors), Herbert Macaulay Way (South), Area 10, Garki, Lagos
Tel: (09) 2343402, 2343403-5 (3L), 2343449
Fax: (09) 2343447, 2343453
Contact: The Permanent Secretary/Overseeing Director

FEDERAL PARASTATALS AND AGENCIES

ABUJA INTERNATIONAL CONFERENCE CENTRE & EAGLE SQUARE
Address: Herbert Macaulay Way (South), Central Business District, Abuja
Tel: (09) 2345090-9 (10L), 2345523
Contact: The Sole Administrator

ANAMBRA-IMO RIVER BASIN DEVELOPMENT AUTHORITY
Address: Km. 10, Owerri-Aba Road, Agbala Town, Owerri.
Tel: (083) 233147, 233886, 233987
Contact: Public Relations Officer

BENIN-OWENA RIVER BASIN DEVELOPMENT AUTHORITY
Address: Km. 24, Sapele Road, Obayantor, Benin City
Tel: (052) 230017, 254415, 258868-9 (2L)
Fax: (052) 254415
* Plot 3796, Cadastral Zone A6, off Danube Street, Maitama, Abuja.
Tel: (09) 4139504-5 (2L).
* Alagbaka G.R.A., Akure.
Tel: (034) 241076, 242734
* 55, Ezenei Avenue, Asaba.
Tel: (056) 280780
* Benin-Owena Housing Estate, Ise Road, Ikere-Ekiti
Tel: (030) 61005
Contact: Public Relations Officer

BUREAU OF PUBLIC ENTERPRISES (BPE)
(National Council on Privatisation)
Address: 1, Osun Crescent, off IBB Way, Maitama, Abuja
Tel: (09) 4134636-46 (11L)
Fax: (09) 4134655-7 (3L), 4134671
E-mail: bpe@bpeng.org
Website: www.bpeng.org
Contact: Deputy Director (Public Affair)

CALABAR FREE TRADE ZONE (CFTZ)
Address: Ikot Utan, Calabar
Tel: (087) 210000-1 (2L)
Fax: (087) 210010
E-mail: cftz@infoweb.abs.net
Contact: The Administrative Officer

CENTRAL BANK OF NIGERIA (CBN)
Address: Zaria Street, off Ladoke Akintola Boulevard, Garki II, Abuja.
Tel: (09) 2343132-7 (6L), 2343191, 2342516
E-mail: info@cenbank.org
Website: www.cenbank.org
* Tinubu Square, Lagos.
Tel: (01) 2660624, 2660647, 2660934
Contact: Assistant Director (Corporate Affairs)

CHAD BASIN DEVELOPMENT AUTHORITY
Address: Dikwa Road, Maiduguri
Tel: (076) 231036, 231630
Fax: (076) 231036

CITIZENSHIP AND LEADERSHIP TRAINING CENTRE (Man O' War)
Address: Plot 150, Oke Agbe Close, off S. L. Akintola Boulevard, Garki II, Abuja
Tel: (09) 2347760, 2347831
Fax: (09) 2347761
* Federal Secretariat Complex, Phase I (3rd Floor), Ikoyi, Lagos.
Tel: (01) 2618221
Contact: The Director General/CEO

CODE OF CONDUCT BUREAU (The Presidency)
Address: Federal Secretariat Complex, (Block 5, 5th Floor), Shehu Shagari Way, Maitama District, Abuja
Tel: (09) 5230168, 5231320
Fax: (09) 5231320
Contact: The Secretary to the Bureau

CONSUMER PROTECTION COUNCIL
Address: A2, Herbert Macaulay Way, Plot 2215, Wuse Zone 6, Abuja
Tel: (09) 5230343, 5233915
Fax: (09) 5230343
E-mail: cpc_p@hotmail.com
Contact: The Public Relations Officer

CORPORATE AFFAIRS COMMISSION (CAC)
Address: Plot 565, Ndola Square, Cadastral Zone AZ, Wuse Zone 5, Abuja
Tel: (09) 5241016-7 (2L), 5241020, 5241022, 5241026, 5241028-9 (2L), 5241046-50 (5L)
E-mail: info@cac.giv.ng
Website: www.company-reg.com
* UBA House, Marina, Lagos
* Elephant Cement House (4th & 5th Floors), ASSBIFI Road, Alausa, Ikeja, Lagos.
Tel: (01) 4968256, 7744799
Fax: (01) 4922944
Contact: Head (Public Relations)

CROSS RIVER BASIN & RURAL DEVELOPMENT AUTHORITY
Address: P.M.B. 1249, Calabar
Tel: (087) 233163, 237942 **Fax:** (087) 233163
Contact: The Chief Admin. Officer (Information)

DEBT MANAGEMENT OFFICE (The Presidency)
Address: NDIC Building (1st Floor), Plot 447/448, Constitution Avenue, Central Business District, Abuja
Tel: (09) 5237405 **Fax:** (09) 5237396
Contact: The Team Leader (Public Relations)

DEPARTMENT OF NATIONAL CIVIC REGISTRATION
Address: 3, Sokode Crescent, off Dalaba St, Wuse Zone 5, Abuja
Tel: (09) 5230637-8 (2L), 5230667-9 (3L)
Fax: (09) 5230638
* Prison Department Complex, Alagbon Close, off Ikoyi, Lagos.
Tel: (01) 2694865
Contact: The Director

DEPARTMENT OF PETROLEUM RESOURCES (DPR)
Address: 7, Kofo Abayomi Street, Victoria Island, Lagos
Tel: (01) 2612320, 2616869, 2618228, 2622205, 3200440-9
Fax: (01) 2622408
Website: www.nigeria-licenseround.com
* 49, Haile Sellasie Street, Asokoro District, Abuja
Tel: (09) 3148358-60 (3L) **Fax:** (09) 3148359
Contact: Assistant Director (Public Affairs)

DIRECTORATE OF PILGRIMS AFFAIRS
Address: 6 (Plot 2117), Suez Crescent, Ibrahim Abacha Housing Estate, off Ladi Kwali Way, Wuse Zone 4, Abuja
Tel: (09) 5233116, 5235079, 5235156, 5235804
Fax: (09) 5235157
Contact: The Principal Public Relations Officer

DIRECTORATE OF TECHNICAL AID CORPS
Address: Block 28, Gaborone Street, Wuse Zone 2, Abuja
Tel: (09) 5230755, 5231502, 5232770
Fax: (09) 5232770
Contact: The Director/CEO

DIRECTORATE OF TECHNICAL CO-OPERATION IN NIGERIA
Address: Ministry of Co-operation & Integration in Africa, Federal Secretariat Complex, Annex 3, Shehu Shagari Way, Maitama District, Abuja.
Tel: (09) 5235372
E-mail: tcf@mciang.net
Website: www.mciang.net
Contact: The Director-General

ECONOMIC & FINANCIAL CRIMES COMMISSION
Address: Ibrahim Taiwo Road, Aso Rock Villa, Abuja.
Tel: (09) 3141791, 6717419
* 70, Awolowo Road, S.W., Ikoyi, Lagos
Tel: (01) 2624189, 2621293
E-mail: info@efccnigeria.com

EDUCATION TAX FUND
Address: 13/16, Azores Street, off Aminu Kano Crescent, Wuse II, Abuja
Tel: (09) 4132105, 4139111-2 (2L)
Fax: (09) 4139101
E-mail: etf@beta.linkserve.com
Website: www.eductiontaxfund.org
Contact: The Executive Secretary/CEO

ENERGY COMMISSION OF NIGERIA (The Presidency)
Address: Plot 701C, Central Business Area, opp. the Central Mosque, Abuja
Tel: (09) 5234920
Fax: (09) 5234925
E-mail: ecn@hyperia.com
Contact: The Director-General/CEO

FEDERAL AIRPORTS AUTHORITY OF NIGERIA (FAAN)
Address: Murtala Mohammed Airport, Ikeja, Lagos
Tel: (01) 4970336-8 (3L), 4971129, 4971132
Fax: (01) 4970342
E-mail: md@faan.com.ng
Contact: The Managing Director/CEO

FEDERAL CHARACTER COMMISSION
Address: First Avenue, off Shehu Shagari Way, Maitama, Abuja
Tel: (09) 5238515-7 (3L), 5238524, 5238528, 5238530-1 (2L)
Contact: The Executive Chairman

FEDERAL FIRE SERVICE
Address: Command Headquarters, Muhammadu Buhari Way, Area 10, Garki, Abuja
Tel: (09) 2341299, 2341399
Fax: (09) 2346897
E-mail: ffireservices@yahoo.com
* 6, Campos Street, Lagos Island, Lagos
Tel: (01) 2630040, 2633251, 2633355
Contact: The Comptroller-General/CEO

FEDERAL HOUSING AUTHORITY (FHA)
Address: Julius Nyerere Crescent, off Yakubu Gowon Crescent, opp. ECOWAS Secretariat, Asokoro District, Abuja
Tel: (09) 3144962, 3144964
Fax: (09) 3144963
* 202 Road, B Close, Festac Town, Lagos
Tel: (01) 5892489
Contact: The Managing Director/CEO

FEDERAL INLAND REVENUE SERVICE (FIRS)
Address: Revenue House, Plot 522, Sokode Crescent, off Dalaba St, off Michael Okpara St, Wuse Zone 5, Abuja
Tel: (09) 5236593-4 (2L), 5236598, 5236605, 5236611
Fax: (09) 5236612
Website: www.firs-nigeria.org
* Federal Secretariat Complex, Phase I (12th Floor), Ikoyi, Lagos.
Tel: (01) 2673331, 2673332 **Fax:** (01) 2673336
Contact: The Executive Chairman

FEDERAL MORTGAGE BANK OF NIGERIA (FMBN)
Address: Plot 124, Moshood Abiola Road, Area 2, Garki, Abuja
Tel/Fax: (09) 2344212-3 (2L), 2349537
Contact: The Managing Director/CEO

FEDERAL OFFICE OF STATISTICS (FOS)
Address: Plot205, Bacita Close, off J. S. Tarka Road, Area 2, Section 2, Garki, Abuja
Tel: (09) 2344816, 2346760-2 (3L)
Fax: (09) 2346761
E-mail: fos@infoweb.abs.net
* 36/38, Broad Street, Lagos
Tel: (01) 2601710-4 (5L), 2647258
Fax: (01) 2635077
* Federal Secretariat Complex, Phase II (3rd Floor), Ikoyi, Lagos.
Tel: (01) 680709, 683326
Contact: The Managing Director/CEO

FEDERAL RADIO CORPORATION OF NIGERIA (FRCN)
Address: Radio House, Herbert Macaulay Way (South), Area 10, Garki, Abuja
Tel: (09) 2341023, 2346484, 2346487 **Fax:** (09) 2346485
E-mail: frcnhq@alpha.linkserve.com
* FRCN Abuja, Broadcasting House, Kutunku, Gwagwalada, FCT
Tel: (09) 8821065, 8822192 **Fax:** (09) 8821040
* FRCN Lagos, Broadcasting House, Ikoyi, Lagos
Tel: (01) 2690301-5 (5L) **Fax:** (01) 2673438
* FRCN Kaduna, Broadcasting House, 7, Yakubu Gowon Way, Kaduna.
Tel: (062) 245390 **Fax:** (062) 245392
* FRCN Ibadan, Broadcasting House, Oba Adebimpe Road, Dugbe, Ibadan.
Tel: (02) 2414093, 2414106 **Fax:** (02) 2413930
E-mail: frcnibadan@yahoo.com
* FRCN Enugu, Broadcasting House, Onitsha Road, Enugu.
Tel: (042) 254400 **Fax:** (042) 254137
Contact: The Director-General/CEO

FEDERAL ROAD SAFETY CORPS (FRSC)
Address: Plot 2032, Olusegun Obasanjo Way, Wuse Zone 7, Abuja
Tel: (09) 5230150, 5231857, 5236662 **Fax:** (09) 5231867
Contact: The Corp Marshal/CEO

FEDERAL SCHOLARSHIP BOARD
Address: Block 46, Yaounde Street, Wuse Zone 6, Abuja
Tel: (09) 5230493 **Fax:** (09) 5237995
E-mail: fedscholarshipabj@yahoo.com
* NITEL Building, 1/3, Moloney St, Onikan, Lagos
Contact: The Secretary to the Board/CEO

HADEJIA-JAMA'ARE RIVER BASIN DEVELOPMENT AUTHORITY
Address: Maiduguri Road, Horoto, Kano
Tel: (064) 668183-4 (2L), 668237
Fax: (064) 666631
E-mail: hjrbda@infoweb.abs.net
Contact: The Managing Director/CEO

INDUSTRIAL TRAINING FUND (ITF)
Address: ITF Office Complex, Miango Road, Jos
Tel: (073) 461731, 463827, 465297 **Fax:** (073) 465297
E-mail: info@itf-nigeria.com
* 28, Olorunfunmi Street, beh. Philips Factory, off Oregun Road, Ojota, Lagos
Tel: (01) 4964428, 4964733
Contact: The Director-General/CEO

JOINT ADMISSIONS & MATRICULATION BOARD (JAMB)
Address: Suleja Road, Bwari, Abuja
Tel: (09) 8501756-7 (2L)
Fax: (09) 5238803, 8501284
E-mail: jamb@hyperia.com
Website: www.jambng.com
* 11, Ojora Road, Ikoyi, Lagos
Tel: (01) 2694751-2 (2L) **Fax:** (01) 2694098
E-mail: jambconsult@hyperia.com
* 79, Tafawa Balewa Way, near Rimi College, Kaduna
Tel: (062) 240405, 241497, 241655 **Fax:** (062) 240405
Contact: The Registrar/CEO

JOINT TAX BOARD
Address: Revenue House, Plot 522, Sokode Crescent, off Dalaba St, off Michael Okpara St, Wuse Zone 5, Abuja
Tel/Fax: (09) 5238827
Contact: The Chairman

LAGOS INTERNATIONAL TRADE FAIR COMPLEX MANAGEMENT BOARD
Address: Lagos-Badagry Expressway, Abule-Osun, Lagos
Tel: (01) 5890797-8 (2L) **Fax:** (01) 5890796
Website: www.litfc.org
Contact: The Executive Director/CEO

LEGAL AID COUNCIL OF NIGERIA
Address: 11, Adetokunbo Ademola Crescent, Wuse II, Abuja
Tel: (09) 5238477-9 (2L), 5238481-3 (3L)
Fax: (09) 5238477
* 10, Okotie-Eboh Street, S.W., Ikoyi, Lagos.
Tel: (01) 2692560
Contact: The Director-General/CEO

LOWER BENUE RIVER DEVELOPMENT AUTHORITY
Address: Km 10, Makurdi-Otukpo Road, Makurdi
Tel: (044) 531567 **Fax:** (044) 533247
Contact: The Managing Director/CEO

LOWER NIGER RIVER BASIN DEVELOPMENT AUTHORITY
Address: Lower Niger River Basin Estate, Basin Road, off Fate Roundabout, Ilorin
Tel: (031) 220430, 224561, 224565
Fax: (031) 224561
E-mail: lnrbda@yahoo.com
Contact: The Managing Director/CEO

NATIONAL AGENCY FOR FOOD & DRUG ADMINISTRATION AND CONTROL (NAFDAC)

Address: Plot 1057, Ikeja Crescent, off Oyo Street, Area 2, Section 1, Garki, Abuja
Tel: (09) 2346380-3 (4L), 2346405, 5241102
Fax: (09) 2346380, 2346383
E-mail: nafdac@linkserve.com
nafdac@yahoo.com
Website: www.nafdac.org
* Federal Secretariat Complex, Phase II (2nd Floor, Rooms 219, 220 & 224), Ikoyi, Lagos.
E-mail: nafdac.lagos@alpha.linkserve.com
Tel: (01) 2671635, 2693105
* Nafdac Laboratory/Office Complex, Oshodi Bus-Stop, 3/4, Oshodi-Apapa Expressway, Oshodi, Lagos
Tel: (01) 4521212, 4521218, 4524259
Contact: The Director-General/CEO

NATIONAL AGENCY FOR SCIENCE AND ENGINEERING INFRASTRUCTURE (NASENI)

Address: Idu Industrial Area, Idu, Abuja
Tel: (09) 5212474-5 (2L), 5239649
Fax: (09) 5232698
E-mail: naseni@beta.linkserve.com
* NASENI Ventures Ltd, Idu Industrial Area, Idu, Abuja.
Tel: (09) 5235161, 5232698
* 9, Kofo Abayomi Street, Victoria Island, Lagos.
Tel: (01) 2622049
Contact: The Director-General/CEO

NATIONAL ARCHIVES OF NIGERIA

Address: Ikoyi Road, near Federal Secretariat, Ikoyi, Lagos
Tel: (01) 2670807
Contact: The Director-General/CEO

NATIONAL AUTOMOTIVE COUNCIL (NAC)

Address: Plot 1322, Parakou Crescent, off Aminu Kano Crescent, Wuse II, Abuja
Tel/Fax: (09) 5233771, 5233963, 5239312
E-mail: nac@infoweb.abs.net
Contact: The Executive Secretary/CEO

NATIONAL BIOTECHNOLOGY DEVELOPMENT AGENCY

Address: Plot 2284, Accra Street, Wuse Zone 5, Abuja
Tel: (09) 5237954-5 (2L)
E-mail: natbiotech@hotmail.com
Contact: The Director/CEO

NATIONAL BOARD FOR COMMUNITY BANKS

Address: 48 (Plot 564), Usuma Street, off Gana Street, Cadastral Zone A5, Maitama District, Abuja
Tel: (09) 4132244, 4132377, 4132660-2 (3L)
Fax: (09) 4132500
* 54, Saka Tinubu Street, Victoria Island, Lagos
Tel: (01) 611491, 614603, 615832
Fax: (01) 615203
Contact: The Executive Secretary/CEO

NATIONAL BOARD FOR TECHNICAL EDUCATION (NBTE)

Address: Plot B, Bida Road, Kaduna
Tel: (062) 246554, 247609, 247877
Fax: (062) 240974, 247507
E-mail: es@nbte.edu.ng
Website: www.nbte.edu.ng
* Plot 644, Aguiyi Ironsi Street, Maitama, Abuja
Contact: The Executive Secretary/CEO

NATIONAL BOUNDARY COMMISSION (The Presidency)

Address: Federal Secretariat Complex, (Ground Floor), Shehu Shagari Way, Maitama District, Abuja
Tel: (09) 5235170, 5236509
Fax: (09) 5235169
* Federal Secretariat Complex, Phase II (Ground Floor), Ikoyi, Lagos.
Tel: (01) 680286
Contact: The Director-General/CEO

NATIONAL BROADCASTING COMMISSION (NBC)

Address: Plot 807, Ibrahim Taiwo Road, Asokoro, Abuja
Tel: (09) 3140484-5 (2L) 3142458, 3147521, 3147523-8 (6L)
Fax: (09) 3147522
E-mail: info@nbc.ng.org
* Red Brick Building, former National Assembly Complex, Tafawa Balewa Square, Lagos
Tel: (01) 2647861, 2647864, 2647867
Fax: (01) 2647868
Contact: The Director-General/CEO

NATIONAL BUSINESS AND TECHNICAL EXAMINATION BOARD (NABTEB)

Address: Ikpoba Hill, near Ramat Park, Benin City
Tel: (052) 255972, 258182, 258197
Fax: (052) 255972
E-mail: enquire@nabtebhq.org
registrar@nabtebhq.org
staff@nabtebhq.org
Website: www.nabtebhq.org
* Plot 650, Aminu Kano Crescent, Wuse II, Abuja.
Tel: (09) 5239676
Contact: The Registrar/CEO.

NATIONAL CENTRE FOR WOMEN DEVELOPMENT

Address: Better Life Street, Central Area, Garki, Abuja
Tel: (09) 2340960-4 (5L), 2340629, 2342481
Fax: (09) 2340628
E-mail: dgncwd@yahoo.com
prsncwd@yahoo.com
Contact: The Director-General/CEO

NATIONAL COMMISSION FOR COLLEGES OF EDUCATION (NCCE)

Address: Plot 829, Ralph Shodeinde Street, off Ahmadu Bello Way, by Federal Min. of Finance Complex, Central Area, Garki, Abuja
Tel: (09) 2345484, 2346531, 5239283
E-mail: info@ncce.edu.ng
Website: www.ncce.edu.ng
Contact: The Executive Secretary/CEO

NATIONAL COMMISSION FOR MASS EDUCATION

Address: Former Open University Building, Block A (3rd Floor), Area 3, Garki, Abuja
Tel: (09) 2342635, 2344030
E-mail: nmec@wwlkad.com
Contact: The Executive Secretary/CEO

NATIONAL COMMISSION FOR MUSEUMS AND MONUMENTS
Address: Plot 2018, Cotonou Crescent, Wuse Zone 6, Abuja
Tel: (09) 5230823 **Fax:** (09) 5238254
* National Museum, Onikan, Lagos.
Tel: (01) 2663005, 631934, 632844, 636075
Contact: The Director-General/CEO

NATIONAL COMMISSION FOR NOMADIC EDUCATION
Address: 9, Kashim Ibrahim Road, Kaduna
Tel: (062) 242672, 249175 **Fax:** (062) 240613
E-mail: info@nomadic-edu.org
Website: www.nomadic-edu.org
Contact: The Executive Secretary/CEO

NATIONAL COUNCIL FOR REFUGEES (NCRF) (The Presidency)
Address: Federal Secretariat Complex, Shehu Shagari Way, Maitama District, Abuja.
Tel: (09) 5235254-6 (3L) **Fax:** (09) 5235256
* 13, Awolowo Road, Ikoyi, Lagos
Tel: (01) 2693298 **Fax:** (01) 2692745
Contact: Hon. Federal Commissioner/CEO

NATIONAL COUNCIL FOR ARTS AND CULTURE (NCAC)
Address: Arts Centre Complex, Moshood Abiola Way, Area 10, Garki, Abuja
Tel: (09) 2342360, 2344181, 2346164, 2347908
Fax: (09) 2342360
Contact: The DIrector/CEO

NATIONAL DIRECTORATE OF EMPLOYMENT (NDE)
Address: Evarist House, 1 (Plot 1529), Nouakchott Street, off Olusegun Obasanjo Way, Wuse Zone 1, Abuja
Tel: (09) 5232226, 5238308-10 (3L) **Fax:** (09) 5234312
* Federal Secretariat Complex, Phase II (2nd Floor), Ikoyi, Lagos. **Tel:** (01) 2672539
Contact: The Director-General/CEO

NATIONAL DRUG LAW ENFORCEMENT AGENCY (NDLEA)
Address: 4, Shaw Road, Ikoyi, Lagos
Tel: (01) 2692091, 686193 **Fax:** (01) 2693850, 686193
* Federal Secretariat Complex, (Wing B, 5th Floor), Shehu Shagari Way, Maitama District, Abuja
Tel: (09) 5233995-6 (2L)
Contact: The Hon. Chairman/CEO

NATIONAL ECONOMIC INTELLIGENCE COMMITTEE
Address: Federal Secretariat Complex, (Phase 3), Shehu Shagari Way, Maitama District, Abuja
Tel: (09) 5234047, 5234085, 5234102 **Fax:** (09) 5234102

NATIONAL EMERGENCY MANAGEMENT AGENCY (NEMA) (The Presidency)
Address: Plot 439, Adetokunbo Ademola Crescent, opp. NICON Hilton Hotel, Maitama, Abuja
Tel/Fax: (09) 4134340, 4137290, 4137640
E-mail: nema@rosecom.net
Website: www.ngnema.org
* The Presidency, Glass House, former National Assembly Complex, Tafawa Balewa Square, Lagos
Tel: (01) 2636482
Contact: The Director-General/CEO

NATIONAL EXAMINATIONS COUNCIL (NECO)
Address: Former SDP Secretariat, Dr Nnamdi Azikiwe Road, Western Bye-Pass, Minna, Niger State.
Tel: (066) 224732 **Fax:** (066) 224182
E-mail: nbem@alpha.linkserve.com
Website: www.neconigeria.org
* 20, Coker Road, Ilupeju, Lagos
Contact: The Registrar/CEO

NATIONAL FILM AND VIDEO CENSORS BOARD
Address: Plot 730, Alexandria Crescent, Cadastral Zone A7, Wuse II, Abuja
Tel/Fax: (09) 4138940
E-mail: edfilmvideo@premiernet.com
Contact: The Executive Director/CEO

NATIONAL GALLERY OF ART
Address: Plot 6A/796, Ahmadu Bello Way, Garki II, Abuja
Tel: (09) 2340003, 2345511
* National Theatre Complex, Iganmu, Lagos
Tel: (01) 836730, 802060-5 (6L) (Ext. 223)
Contact: The Executive Director/CEO

NATIONAL HEALTH INSURANCE SCHEME (NHIS)
Address: Plot 782, Adetokunbo Ademola Crescent, Wuse II, Abuja
Tel: (09) 4130027-8 (2L) **Fax:** (09) 4130026
* Plot 314A, Akin Ogunlewe Street, off Ligali Ayorinde Street, Victoria Island, Lagos
Contact: The Executive Secretary/CEO

NATIONAL HUMAN RIGHTS COMMISSION (NHRC)
Address: Gidan Aisha, Plot 800, Blantyre Street, off Adetokunbo Ademola Crescent, Wuse II, Abuja
Tel: (09) 5231774, 5238656, 5239393-6 (4L)
Fax: (09) 5238657
E-mail: nhrc@linkserve.com
Website: www.nhrc-ng.org
Contact: The Executive Secretary/CEO

NATIONAL INFORMATION TECHNOLOGY DEVELOPMENT AGENCY (NITDA)
Address: Plot 695, Port Harcourt Crescent, off Gimbiya Street, off Ahmadu Bello Way, Area II, Garki, Abuja
Tel: (09) 3142924-5 (2L) **Fax:** (09) 3142924
E-mail: info@nitda.gov.ng
Website: www.nitda.gov.ng
Contact: The Director-General/CEO

NATIONAL INLAND WATERWAYS AUTHORITY (NIWA)
Address: Mohammed Ibrahim Road, Adankolo New Layout, Lokoja, Kogi State.
Tel: (058) 221011, 221606 **Fax:** (058) 250888
E-mail: niwa@alpha.linkserve.com
* C.M.S., Ferry Terminal, Marina, Lagos
Tel: (01) 2631587
Contact: The Managing Director/CEO

NATIONAL INSTITUTE FOR CULTURAL ORIENTATION (NICO)
Address: Plot 338, Sirasso Crescent, off Kigoma Street, Wuse Zone 7, Abuja
Tel: (09) 5233728-9 (2L) **Fax:** (09) 5233728
* National Theatre Complex, Iganmu, Lagos.
Tel: (01) 5835095

NATIONAL INSURANCE COMMISSION (NAICOM)
Address: Shipper's Plaza, Michael Okpara Street, Wuse Zone 5, Abuja
Tel: (09) 5238268-9 (2L) **Fax:** (09) 5238260
E-mail: naicom@abuja.rcl.nig.com
* Federal Secretariat Annex, Ikoyi Road, Alagbon, Ikoyi, Lagos
Contact: The Commissioner for Insurance/CEO

NATIONAL LIBRARY OF NIGERIA
Address: Sanusi Dantata House, beh. NICON Plaza, Central Business District, Garki, Abuja
Tel: (09) 2341062, 2346772-4 (3L), 2347714
Fax: (09) 2346772
E-mail: nlo@rcl.nig.com
nln.rusd@rcl.nig.com
Website: www.nlbn.org
* 4, Wesley Street,off Joseph Street, Lagos Island, Lagos. **Tel:** (01) 2656004
Contact: The National Librarian/CEO

NATIONAL MANPOWER BOARD
Address: Plot 192, R. B. Dikko Road, off Shehu Shagari Way, Asokoro, Abuja
Tel: (09) 2341106
* Federal Secretariat Complex, Phase I (3rd & 4th Floors), Ikoyi, Lagos.
Tel: (01) 2690632, 2691138, 2692661 **Fax:** (01) 2692661
Contact: The Executive Secretary/CEO

NATIONAL MARITIME AUTHORITY (NMA)
Address: Maritme House, 4, Burma Road, Apapa, Lagos
Tel: (01) 5804800-4 (5L)
Fax: (01) 5450722, 5451430
E-mail: natmaritime@infoweb.abs.net
Website: www.nma-ng.com
* Plot 2891, Taraba Close, off Limpopo Street, Maitama, Abuja.
Tel: (09) 4139662 **Fax:** (09) 4125239
Contact: The Director-General/CEO

NATIONAL OFFICE FOR TECHNOLOGY ACQUISITION & PROMOTION (NOTAP)
Address: Plot 168, Cotonou Crescent, Wuse Zone 6, Abuja
Tel: (09) 5236954, 5239776
Fax: (09) 5239823
E-mail: e_notap@email.com
notap2@yahoo.com
* Federal Secretariat Complex, Phase II (1st Floor), Ikoyi, Lagos
Tel: (01) 2695452, 2696123 **Fax:** (01) 2696123
Contact: The Director-General/CEO

NATIONAL ORIENTATION AGENCY (NOA)
Address: Block B, Old Federal Secretariat, Area 1, Garki, Abuja
Tel: (09) 2341010, 2341711, 2341722, 2341744, 2341766
Fax: (09) 2341722
Contact: The Director-General/CEO

NATIONAL PARK SERVICE
Address: Nnamdi Azikiwe Airport Expressway, Abuja
Tel: (09) 2345507-8 (2L)
Contact: The Conservator-General/CEO

NATIONAL POPULATION COMMISSION (NPC)
Address: Former FEAP Building, Plot 2031, Olusegun Obasanjo Way, Wuse Zone 7, Abuja
Tel: (09) 5239449, 5239450, 5239453
Contact: The Director-General/CEO

NATIONAL PRIMARY HEALTH CARE DEVELOPMENT AGENCY
Address: Plot 681/682, Port Harcourt Crescent, off Gimbiya Street, off Ahamdu Bello Way, Area 11, Garki, Abuja
Tel: (09) 3143626, 3143632, 6701740-1 (2L), 6701743-4 (2L)
Fax: (09) 3143632
E-mail: nphcdaabuja@yahoo.com
* Central Medical Library Compound, Yaba Bus-Stop, Yaba, Lagos
Contact: The Executive Director/CEO

NATIONAL PRODUCTIVITY CENTRE
Address: Plot 1498, Abidjan Street, Wuse Zone 3, Abuja
Tel: (09) 5237752-3 (2L), 5238680-1 (2L)
Fax: (09) 5238682
Contact: The Director-General/CEO

NATIONAL SALARIES, INCOMES & WAGES COMMISSION
Address: Federal Secretariat Towers, (3rd Floor), Shehu Shagari Way, Maitama District, Abuja
Tel: (09) 5239524-5 (2L) **Fax:** (09) 5233291
*Plot 209, Shehu Shagari Way, Asokoro District, Abuja. **Tel:** (09) 2341110, 2349704, 2349706-8 (3L)
Contact: The Secretary to the Commission

NATIONAL SPACE RESEARCH & DEVELOPMENT AGENCY
Address: Plot 555, Misau Street, off Ahmadu Bello Way, Garki II, Abuja
Tel: (09) 2342069, 2342203, 2342220 **Fax:** (09) 2342220
E-mail: nasrda_nig@yahoo.co.uk
Website: www.nasrda.gov.ng
Contact: The Director-General/CEO

NATIONAL STEEL RAW MATERIALS EXPLORATION AGENCY
Address: 18, Rabah Road, Malali Village, opp. Federal Government College, Kaduna
Tel: (062) 246634, 247792, 247798
Fax: (062) 236450
E-mail: nsrmea@wwlkad.com
Website: www.nsrmea.org
* Plot 481, Ipele Close, thro' Jere Close, off Funmilayo Ransome-Kuti Road, Area 3, Garki, Abuja
Tel: (09) 2349875
Contact: The Director/CEO

NATIONAL SUGAR DEVELOPMENT COUNCIL
Address: Plot 1112, Emeka Anyaoku Street, opp. Radio House, Area 11, Garki, Abuja
Tel: (09) 2345617 **Fax:** (09) 2345622
Contact: The Executive Secretary/CEO

NATIONAL THEATRE
Address: Iganmu, Lagos
Tel: (01) 5850968, 802060-8 (9L)
Fax: (01) 5850968
* c/o Federal Ministry of Culture and Tourism, Federal Secretariat Complex, Phase II, Abuja
Contact: The General Manager/CEO

NATIONAL TROUPE OF NIGERIA
Address: National Theatre Complex, Iganmu, Lagos
Tel: (01) 4707552
E-mail: nationaltroupe@yahoo.com
Contact: The Artistic Director/CEO

NATIONAL UNIVERSITIES COMMISSION (NUC)
Address: Aja Nwachukwu House, Plot 430, Aguiyi Ironsi Street, Maitama District, Abuja
Tel: (09) 4133176-81 (6L) **Fax:** (09) 4133520
E-mail: es@nuc.edu.ng
Website: www.nuc-nigeria.org
* 10, James George Street, off Alagbon Close, Ikoyi Road, Ikoyi Lagos
Tel: (01) 2691536 **Fax:** (01) 2694879
Contact: The Executive Secretary/CEO

NATIONAL WAR MUSEUM
Address: Uzuakoli Road, Umuahia
Tel: (088) 222458
Contact: The Curator/CEO

NATIONAL WATER REHABILITATION PROJECT
Address: Co-operative Building, Plot 2789, Aguiyi Ironsi Street, Maitama District, Abuja
Tel: (09) 4138504
E-mail: nwater@infoweb.abs.net
Contact: The Project Manager/CEO

NATIONAL YOUTH SERVICE CORPS (NYSC)
Address: J. S. Tarka Street, off Moshood Abiola Road, Area 3, Garki, Abuja
Tel: (09) 2340952-3 (2L), 2341438, 2341465
Fax: (09) 2340240
E-mail: nysc.dhq@milestonesnigeria.com
nysc.dhq@hotmail.com
Contact: The Director-General/CEO

NEWS AGENCY OF NIGERIA (NAN)
Address: Block 29, Benue Crescent, Area 1, Section 1, Garki, Abuja
Tel: (09) 2341189, 2343196, 2344901, 2349730-1 (2L), 5239054 **Fax:** (09) 2349734, 2349735
E-mail: abuja@nan.com.ng
Contact: The Managing Director/CEO

NIGER DELTA BASIN & RURAL DEVELOPMENT AUTHORITY
Address: 21, Nnamdi Azikiwe Road, Port Harcourt
Tel: (084) 230024, 233971 **Fax:** (084) 235610
Contact: The General Manager/CEO

NIGER DELTA DEVELOPMENT COMMISSION (NDDC)
Address: 6, Olumini Street, off Forces Avenue, by UTC Junction, G.R.A. Phase I, Port Harcourt
Contact: The Managing Director/CEO

NIGERIA DEPOSIT INSURANCE CORPORATION (NDIC)
Address: NDIC Building, Plot 447/448, Constitution Avenue, Central Business District, Garki, Abuja
Tel: (09) 5236740, 5237710-21 (12L) **Fax:** (09) 5237718
E-mail: info@ndic-ng.com
Website: www.ndic-ng.com
* Mamman Kontagora House, 23A, Marina, Lagos.
Tel: (01) 2647840-7 (8L) **Fax:** (01) 2647848
Contact: The Managing Director/CEO

NIGERIA NATIONAL MERIT AWARD
Address: Merit House, Aguiyi Ironsi Street, Maitama, Abuja
Tel: (09) 4134528, 4134530, 4134537

NIGERIA NATURAL MEDICINE DEVELOPMENT AGENCY
Address: 9, Kofo Abayomi Street, Victoria Island, Lagos
Tel: (01) 616187, 619827, 7737817 **Fax:** (01) 619827

NIGERIA SECURITY AND CIVIL DEFENCE CORPS
Address: Gombi Close, Area 1, Section 2, Garki, Abuja
Tel/Fax: (09) 2341402
E-mail: nscdc59@yahoo.com
* 19, Alfred Rewane Road, Ikoyi Lagos.
Tel: (01) 2671716
Contact: Commandant-General/CEO

NIGERIA SOCIAL INSURANCE TRUST FUND (NSITF)
Address: Plot 794, Muhammadu Buhari Way, Central Business District, Garki, Abuja
Tel: (09) 2340121-3 (3L) **Fax:** (09) 2340112
E-mail: nsitf@infoweb.abs.net
Website: www.nsitf.com
* 9, Ijora Causeway, Ijora, Lagos
Tel: (01) 4707107, * 08033497698
Contact: The Managing Director/CEO

NIGERIAN ACCOUNTING STANDARDS BOARD (NASB)
Address: Elephant Cement House (3rd Floor), ASSBIFI Road, Alausa, Ikeja, Lagos
Tel: (01) 4922944-5 (2L), 4812099, 7747828
Fax: (01) 4922945
E-mail: technicalenquires@nasb.org
Website: www.nasb.org
Contact: The Executive Secretary/CEO

NIGERIAN AIRSPACE MANAGEMENT AGENCY (NAMA)
Address: NAMA Headquarters, Murtala Mohammed Airport, Ikeja, Lagos
Tel: (01) 4931140-9 (10L), 4931310 **Fax:** (01) 4937443
E-mail: namahdq@nama-nig.com
Website: www.nama-nig.com
Contact: The Managing Director/CEO

NIGERIAN CIVIL AVIATION AUTHORITY (NCAA)
Address: Aviation House, M. Mohammed Airport, Ikeja, Lagos
Tel: (01) 4930026-7 (2L), 4930030 **Fax:** (01) 4930030
E-mail: nigeriancaa@hyperia,com
Website: www.nigeriancaa.com
Contact: The Director-General/CEO

NIGERIAN COMMUNICATIONS COMMISSION (NCC)
Address: Plot 72, Ahmadu Bello Way, Central Business Disrict, Garki, Abuja
Tel: (09) 2340330, 2344591-2 (2L) **Fax:** (09) 2344589
E-mail: ncc@ncc.gov.ng
Website: www.ncc.gov.ng
* 48, Saka Tinubu Street, Victoria Island, Lagos.
Tel: (01) 26622620-9 (10L) **Fax:** (01) 2622631, 2622635
Contact: The Executive Vice Chairman

NIGERIAN COPYRIGHT COMMISSION
Address: Federal Secretariat Complex, Annex II, (Ground Floor), Shehu Shagari Way, Maitama District, Abuja
Tel: (09) 5235771, 5235773 **Fax:** (09) 5235772
* 16, Aloba Street, Ebute-Metta (West), Lagos
Tel: (01) 5836748
Contact: The Director-General/CEO

NIGERIAN EDUCATIONAL RESEARCH & DEVELOPMENT COUNCIL (NERDC)
Address: Lokoja-Kaduna Road, Sheda, FCT
Tel: (09) 8821114, 8822204 **Fax:** (09) 8821047
* Plot 3 & 4, Block B, NERDC Road, Central Business District, Agidingbi, Ikeja, Lagos. **Tel:** (01) 4710909
Contact: The Executive Secretary/CEO

NIGERIAN EXPORT PROCESSING ZONES AUTHORITY (NEPZA)
Address: Plot 211, Shehu Shagari Way, beh. Bulet Garden, Asokoro District, Abuja
Tel: (09) 3142945-8 (4L)
Fax: (09) 3142943, 3142957
E-mail: cepz@infoweb.abs.net
Website: www.nepza.com
* 5, Billingsway, opp. Neimeth Factory, Oregun Ind. Estate, Oregun, Ikeja, Lagos. **Tel/Fax:** (01) 4705430
* Calabar Free Trade Zone, off Murtala Mohammed Highway, Ikot Utan, Calabar.
Tel: (087) 210001-5 (5L), 210012-4 (3L)
Fax: (087) 210010
Contact: The Managing Director/CEO

NIGERIAN EXPORT PROMOTION COUNCIL (NEPC)
Address: Export House, Block 312, Kunmba Street, Wuse Zone 2, Abuja
Tel: (09) 5230933, 5233380, 5233386, 5233388
Fax: (09) 5230931, 5230938, 5230983
* 13/15, Ladipo Oluwole Road, Apapa, Lagos.
Tel/Fax: (01) 5872335
Contact: The Executive Director/CEO

NIGERIAN INVESTMENT PROMOTION COMMISSION (NIPC)
Address: Plot 1181, Aguiyi Ironsi Street, Maitama, Abuja
Tel: (09) 4130582, 4131403, 4132344, 4134317, 4134373, 4134380 **Fax:** (09) 4134306
E-mail: nipc@nipc-nigeria.org
Website: www.nipc-nigeria.org
Contact: The Chief Operating Officer

NIGERIAN LAW REFORM COMMISSION
Address: Plot 1977, Orlu Street, Area 3, Garki, Abuja
Tel: (09) 2342799, 2349461
E-mail: nlrc@linkserve.com
* Federal Secretariat Complex, Phase I (4th Floor), Ikoyi, Lagos. **Tel:** (01) 683275
Contact: The Chairman/CEO

NIGERIAN NUCLEAR REGULATORY AUTHORITY (The Presidency)
Address: Plot 701C, near Central Mosque, Central Area, Garki, Abuja
Tel/Fax: (09) 5234920, 5234924
E-mail: nnra@linkserve.com
Contact: The Director-General/CEO

NIGERIAN PORTS AUTHORITY (NPA)
Address: NPA House, 26/28, Marina, Lagos
Tel: (01) 2600620-31 (12L) **Fax:** (01) 2630306, 2636719
E-mail: telnpa@infoweb.abs.net
Website: www.nigeriaports.com
* Plot 665, Jere Street, Area A3, Garki, Abuja.
Tel/Fax: (09) 2348030
Contact: The Managing Director/CEO

NIGERIAN POSTAL SERVICE (NIPOST)
Address: Sanusi Dantata House, behind NICON Plaza, Central Business District, Garki, Abuja
Tel: (09) 2342162, 2346432, 2347621, 2341704
Fax: (09) 2342313
* P & T Building, Lafiaji, Lagos. **Tel:** (01) 2634091
Contact: The Postmaster-General/CEO

NIGERIAN PRESS COUNCIL
Address: Plot 772, Ikot Ekepene Close, off Emeka Anyaoku Street, Area 11, Garki, Abuja
Tel: (09) 2346527, 2340185 **Fax:** (09) 2340185
E-mail: presscouncil@nigerianet.com
Contact: The Managing Director/CEO

NIGERIAN SHIPPERS' COUNCIL
Address: Shipper's Tower, 4, Park Lane, Apapa, Lagos
Tel: (01) 5451799, 5452307-9 (3L), 5451797, 5452981, 5451351, 5451352-4 (3 L) **Fax:** (01) 5452906
E-mail: info@shipperscouncil.com
E-mail: nsc@shipperscouncil.com
Website: www.shipperscouncil.ccom
Website: www.shipperscouncil.org
Contact: The Managing Director/CEO

NIGERIAN TOURISM DEVELOPMENT CORPORATION (NTDC)
Address: Block H, Old Federal Secretariat, Area I, Garki, Abuja
Tel: (09) 2342779, 2342764, 2342775 **Fax:** (09) 2342775
E-mail: ntdc@metrong.com
Website: www.nigeriatourism.net
Contact: The Executive Director/CEO

OGUN-OSHUN RIVER BASIN DEVELOPMENT AUTHORITY
Address: Alabata Road, Abeokuta
Tel: (039) 240568, 240570, 241629
Fax: (039) 241628
Contact: Managing Director/CEO

PETROLEUM EQUALISATION FUND (MANAGEMENT) BOARD
Address: AP Plaza, Adetokunbo Ademola Crescent, Wuse II, Garki, Abuja
Tel: (09) 5239085-6 (2 L), 5232409 **Fax:** (09) 5232872
Website: www.pef(m)b.org
* Plot 887, Balarabe Musa Crescent, Victoria Is.Lagos
Contact: The Executive Secretary/CEO

PETROLEUM TECHNOLOGY DEVELOPMENT FUND
Address: Plot 762, Ahmadu Bello Way, Area 11, Garki, Abuja
Tel: (09) 3142167

POPULATION INFORMATION & COMMUNICATION BUREAU
Address: 15A, Awolowo Road, (Annex), S.W. Ikoyi, Lagos
Tel/Fax: (01) 2694779
* Federal Min. of Information & National Orientation,

Radio House (3rd Floor), Area 10, Garki, Abuja
Tel: (09) 2340807
Contact: The Project Director/CEO

PUBLIC COMPLAINTS COMMISSION
Address: Plot 426, Aguiyi Ironsi Street, Maitama, Abuja
Tel: (09) 4137270, 4137271, 4136374
Fax: (09) 4136093, 4133465
Contact: The National Sercetary/CEO

RAW MATERIALS RESEARCH AND DEVELOPMENT COUNCIL (RMRDC)
Address: Plot 427, Aguiyi Ironsi Street, Maitama, Abuja
Tel: (09) 4137416-7 (2 L), 4137420
Fax: (09) 4136034
E-mail: ceo@rmrdc.nig.com
Contact: The Director-General/CEO

REVENUE MOBILISATION, ALLOCATION AND FISCAL COMMISSION (The Presidency)
Address: Plot 210, Francis Adekunle Fajuyi Street, Central Business District, Garki, Abuja
Tel: (09) 2348922, 2348914, 2346189, 2348923
Fax: (09) 2346189
* Federal Secretariat Complex, Phase II (1st Floor, Rooms 154 - 160), Ikoyi, Lagos.
Tel: (01) 2672510
* 6, Aggrey Road, Port Harcourt.
Tel: (084) 331656
Contact: The Chairman/CEO

SECURITIES AND EXCHANGE COMMISSION (SEC)
Address: Labour House, behind Federal Ministry of Finance Complex, Central Business District, Abuja
Tel: (09) 2346272-5 (4 L) **Fax:** (09) 2346276
E-mail: sec-ng@compuserve.com
Website: www.secngr.org
Contact: The Director General/CEO

SHEDA SCIENCE AND TECHNOLOGY COMPLEX
Address: Tower B (1st Floor), Federal Secretariat Complex, Shehu Shagari Way, Maitama District, Garki, Abuja
Tel: (09) 5233916, 5233917, 5233918 **Fax:** (09) 5233919
E-mail: shedascience@hyperia.com
Contact: The Director-General /CEO

SOKOTO-RIMA RIVER BASIN DEVELOPMENT AUTHORITY
Address: Km. 10, Gusau Road, Sokoto
Tel: (060) 236878, 231742, 235774, 231744, 231790
Fax: (060) 231765
Contact: The Managing Director/CEO

STANDARDS ORGANISATION OF NIGERIA (SON)
Address: Plot 1687, Lome Street, off Olusegun Obasanjo Way, Zone 7, Wuse, Abuja
Tel: (09) 5239353, 5239187 **Fax:** (09) 5239353
E-mail: sonnis_ng@yahoo.com
* Federal Secretariat Complex, Phase I (9th Floor), Ikoyi, Lagos.
Tel: (01) 2696177-8 (2L) **Fax:** (01) 2696178
* 11, Kofo Abayomi Street, Victoria Island, Lagos
Tel: (01) 615867
Contact: The Director-General /CEO

STRATEGIC GRAIN RESERVE
Address: NAIC Building, Plot 590, off Independence Avenue, Zone AO, Central Business District
Tel: (09) 2344827, 2344958 **Fax:** (09) 2344382
E-mail: nsgrfma@hotmail.com
Contact: The Director

UNIVERSAL BASIC EDUCATION (UBE)
Address: Plot 532, IBB Close, off IBB Way, Zone 4, Wuse, Abuja
Tel: (09) 5230089, 5237899 **Fax:** (09) 5230089
Contact: The National Co-ordinator/CEO

UPPER BENUE RIVER BASIN DEVELOPMENT AUTHORITY
Address: Fufore Road, Yola
Tel: (075) 624469, 625460, 625541
Contact: The Managing Director

UPPER NIGER RIVER & RURAL DEVELOPMENT AUTHORITY
Address: Tudun Fulani, Km. 5, Zungeru Road, Minna
Tel: (066) 223148, 222953, 222942, 223445
Fax: (066) 223019
Contact: The Managing Director

UTILITIES CHARGES COMMISSION
Address: Block 17, Meknes Street, off Loma Mansa Street, Zone 4, Wuse, Abuja
Tel: (09) 5237538 **Fax:** (09) 5237502
E-mail: uccng@yahoo.com
Contact: The Executive Secretary/CEO

VOICE OF NIGERIA CORPORATION (VON)
Address: Radio House (6th & 7th Floors), Herbert Macaulay Way (South), Area 10, Garki, Abuja
Tel: (09) 2346973, 2344016, 2344017, 2346971, 2346972, 2346974, 2347802, 2347802, 2347803, 2347804
Fax: (09) 2346970
* Broadcasting House, Ikoyi Road, Ikoyi, Lagos.
Tel: (01) 2692074, 2692628-30 (3L), 2693074-5 (2L), 2693078, 2694647, 2694846, 2694848.
Fax: (01) 2691944, 2692630, 2693076, 2693078
Contact: The Director-General/CEO

FEDERAL RESEARCH AND DEVELOPMENT INSTITUTES AND CENTRES

ADMINISTRATIVE STAFF COLLEGE OF NIGERIA (ASCON)
Address: ASCON Complex, Topo, Badagry, Lagos State
Tel: (01) 732300, 732304, 732307, 7736836-7 (2 L)
Fax: (01) 2882907
* Annex 2 (3rd Floor), Federal Secretariat Complex, Shehu Shagari Way, Maitama District, Garki, Abuja
Tel: (09) 5236883, 2348324
Fax: (09) 5236883
Contact: The Director-General/CEO

AGRICULTURAL AND RURAL MANAGEMENT TRAINING INSTITUTE (ARMTI)
Address: Km. 18, Ilorin/Ajase-Ipo Highway, Ilorin
Tel: (031) 221183 **Fax:** (031) 222322
E-mail: armti@ilorin.skannet.com
Contact: The Director/CEO

CENTRAL MEDICAL LIBRARY
Address: Murtala Mohammed Way (opp. Yaba Bus-Stop),
Tel: (01) 7735511
Contact: The Chief Medical Labrarian

CENTRE FOR ADAPTATION OF TECHNOLOGY (CAT)
Address: 16, Igweze Street, Akwa
Tel: (048) 553402, 552630 **Fax:** (048) 552630
E-mail: cat_awka@yahoo.com
Website: www.naseni.org
Contact: The Director/CEO

CENTRE FOR BLACK AND AFRICAN ARTS AND CIVILISATION (CBAAC)
Address: National Arts Theatre Complex, Iganmu, Lagos
Tel: (01) 4705667, 5852173 **Fax:** (01) 5852173
E-mail: cbaac@infoweb.abs.net
Website: www.cbaac.org
Contact: The Director/CEO

CENTRE FOR ENERGY RESEARH AND DEVELOPMENT ILE-IFE (CERD)
Address: Obafemi Awolowo University, Ile-Ife, Osun State
Tel: (036) 233638 **Fax:** (036) 232975
E-mail: cerd@cerdoauife.edu.ng
Contact: The Director/CEO

CENTRE FOR ENERGY RESEARH & TRAINING (CERT)
Address: Ahmadu Bello University, Samaru, Zaria
Tel: (069) 550397, 551397, 551424, 553135
E-mail: cert@cyberspace.net.ng
Contact: The Director/CEO

CENTRE FOR MANAGEMENT DEVELOPMENT (CMD)
Address: Management Village, Shangisha, off Old Lagos/ Ibadan Expressway Toll-Gate, Ikeja, Lagos
Tel: (01) 7748165, 4978391 **Fax:** (01) 4978390
E-mail: cmd@nipost.com.ng
Contact: The Director-General/CEO

CENTRE FOR SPACE SCIENCE & TECHNOLOGY EDUCATION
Address: Obafemi Awolowo Unversity, Ile-Ife, Osun State
Tel: (036) 230454 **Fax:** (036) 233973
E-mail: cessted@oauife.edu.ng

COCOA RESEARCH INSTITUTE OF NIGERIA (CRIN)
Address: Idi-Ayunre, Ibadan
Tel: (02) 2414820, 2410040
Fax: (02) 2413121
E-mail: flourish@skannet.com
Contact: The DirectorCEO

ENGINEERING MATERIALS DEVELOPMENT INSTITUTE
Address: Km. 4, Ondo Road, Akure
Tel: (034) 243800, 244929, 244884, 242450
Fax: (034) 243800
Contact: The Director/CEO

FEDERAL INSTITUE OF INDUSTRIAL RESEARCH, OSHODI (FIIRO)
Address: Blind Centre Street, via Cappa Bus Stop, off Agege Motor Road, Oshodi
Tel: (01) 522760, 523880, 523260, 4522905, 523205
Fax: (01) 4525880
E-mail: fiiro@rcl.nig.com
Website: www.fiiro.gov.ng
Contact: The Director/CEO

FORESTRY RESEARCH INSTITUE OF NIGERIA (FRIN)
Address: Forestry Hills, Jericho G.R.A., Ibadan
Tel: (02) 2414441, 2414022, 2414073
Fax: (02) 2410515
E-mail: dfrin@skannet.com
Website: www.frin-ng.com
Contact: The Director/CEO

GEOLOGICAL SURVEY OF NIGERIA
Address: 1 & 2, Aliyu Makama Road, Kaduna
Tel: (062) 232857

HYDRAULIC EQUIPMENT DEVELOPMENT INSTITUTE (HEDI-K)
Address: Opp., Kumbotso L.G. Secretariat, Kumbotso Town, Kano State
Tel: (064) 641260, 634027
Contact: The Director/CEO

INSTITUTE FOR AGRICULTURAL RESEARCH (IAR)
Address: Ahmadu Bello University Campus, Sokoto Road, Samaru, Zaria, Kaduna State
Tel: (069) 551355, 550681, 550563
Fax: (069) 550563
E-mail: director@iar.abuzaria
Contact: The Director/CEO

INSTITUTE FOR PEACE & CONFLICT RESOLUTION (IPCR) (The Presidency)
Address: Plot 496, Abogo Largema Street, off Constitution Avenue Central Business District, Garki, Abuja
Tel: (09) 5239458 **Fax:** (09) 4130637
Contact: The Director-General/CEO

INSTITUTE OF AGRICULTURAL RESEARCH & TRAINING (IAR & T)
Address: Moor Plantation, Abeokuta Road, Apata, Ibadan
Tel: (02) 2312523, 2312692, 2312574
Fax: (02) 2312567
E-mail: drart@infoweb.abs.net
Contact: The Director/CEO

LAKE CHAD RESEARCH INSTITUTE (LCRI)
Address: Km. 5, Gamboru/Ngala Road, Maiduguri
Tel: (076) 233075, 231188
E-mail: lcri@infoweb.abs.net
Contact: The Director/CEO

MICHAEL IMOUDU INSTITUE FOR LABOUR STUDIES
Address: Olunlade Village, Km. 7, Ajase-Ipo Road, Ilorin
Tel: (031) 223108, 220652 **Fax:** (031) 223108
E-mail: minils@minils.org
Contact: The Director/CEO

NATIONAL ANIMAL PRODUCTION RESEARCH INSTITUTE (NAPRI)
Address: Shika, c/o Ahmadu Bello University, Zaria
Tel: (069) 550596
Contact: The Director/CEO

NATIONAL CENTRE FOR AGRICULTURAL MECHANISATION
Address: Km. 20, Ilorin-Lokoja Highway, Idiofian, Ilorin
Tel: (031) 224831, 224836
E-mail: ncam@skannet.com
Contact: The Director/CEO

NATIONAL CENTRE FOR ECONOMIC MANAGEMENT AND ADMINISTRAITON (NCEMA)
Address: 1-3, Oba Akinyele Avenue, off Rotimi Williams Avenue, Old Bodija Estate, Ibadan
Tel: (02) 8100063, 8100079, 8103265
Fax: (02) 8100079
E-mail: dg@ncema.gov.ng
Website: www.ncema.gov.ng
Contact: The Director-General/CEO

NATIONAL CENTRE FOR ENERGY RESEARCH & DEVELOPMENT, NSUKKA (NCERD)
Address: Unversity of Nigeria Campus, Nsukka, Enugu State
Tel/Fax: (042) 771853
E-mail: misunn@aol.com
Contact: The Director/CEO

NATIONAL CENTRE FOR GENETIC RESEARCH & BIOTECHNOLOGY (NACGRAB)
Address: Moor Plantation, Abeokuta Road, Apata, Ibadan
Tel: (02) 2312622 **Fax:** (02) 2312601
E-mail: nacgrab@ibadan.skannet.com
Contact: The Director

NATIONAL CENTRE FOR REMOTE SENSING
Address: Km. 11, Jos-Bukuru Expressway, Bukuru, Jos
Tel: (073) 280554, 281196, 280578
Fax: (073) 280578
E-mail: ncrs@infoweb.abs.net
Contact: The Director/CEO

NATIONAL CENTRE FOR TECHNOLOGY MANAGEMENT (NACETEM)
Address: Obafemi Awolowo University Campus, Ile-Ife, Osun State
Tel: (036) 233833, * (02) 2413002
Tel/Fax: (036) 231245
E-mail: ssanni@nacetem.rinaf.net.ng
E-mail: ssanni@nacetem.oauife.edu.ng
Website: www.oauife.edu.ng/nacetem
Contact: The Executive Director/CEO

NATIONAL CEREALS RESEARCH INSTITUTE (NCRI)
Address: Badeggi, Niger State
Tel: (066) 461233

NATIONAL EDUCATIONAL TECHNOLOGY CENTRE (NETC)
Address: Km.5, Kaduna-Zaria Expressway, Rigachikun, Kaduna
Tel: (062) 313973, 312720
E-mail: netsc@yahoo.com
Contact: The Director/CEO

NATIONAL ENGINEERING DESIGN DEVELOPMENT CENTRE
Address: 150, Igwe Nwafor Orizu Road, Otolo, Nnewi, Anambra State.
Tel: (046) 463539
Contact: The Centre Manager

NATIONAL FILM INSTITUTE
Address: 6, Alh. Badamosi Road, off Murtala Mohammed Way, Bukuru Bye-Pass, Jos
Tel: (073) 463625 **Fax:** (073) 463122
Contact: The Director

NATIONAL INSTITUTE FOR EDUCATIONAL PLANNING AND ADMINISTRATION (NIEPA)
Address: Km. 3, Laje Road, off Ondo-Ore Road, Ondo
Tel: (034) 244992, 243449, 242762 **Fax:** (034) 243449
E-mail: tajayi@skannet.com.ng
Contact: The DirectorCEO

NATIONAL INSTITUTE FOR FRESHWATER FISHERIES RESEARCH (NIFFR)
Address: P.M.B. 6006, New Bussa, Niger State
Tel: (031) 670444, ,670240, 670241
Contact: The Director/CEO

NATIONAL INSTITUTE FOR HORTICULTURAL RESEARCH (NIHORT)
Address: Idi-Ishin, Jericho, Ibadan
Tel: (02) 2412230, 2412899, 2412501
Fax: (02) 2412230
E-mail: nihort@infoweb.net
Contact: The Director/CEO

NATIONAL INSTITUTE FOR HOSPITALITY & TOURISM
Address: Baguada Lake, Kano
Tel/Fax: (064) 632560, 632562
E-mail: nihotour@samdav.com
Contact: The Director/CEO

NATIONAL INSTITUTE FOR NIGERIAN LANGUAGES (NINLAN)
Address: 53, New Umuahia Road, off Ikot-Ekpene Road, Ogbor Hill, Aba
Tel: (082) 223138, 220649, 228311, 228311, 228312, 228313
Website: ninlan.edu.org
Contact: The Director

NATIONAL INSTITUTE FOR PHARMACEUTICAL RESEARCH AND DEVELOPMENT (NIPRD)
Address: Idu Industrial Area, Idu, Garki, Abuja
Tel: (09) 5239098, 5239088, 5231602
Fax: (09) 5231043
E-mail: dgniprd@yahoo.com
E-mail: magford@skannet.com
Contact: The Director/CEO

NATIONAL INSTITUTE FOR POLICY AND STRATEGIC STUDIES (NIPSS)
Address: Kuru, P.M.B. 2024, Bukuru, Plateau State
Tel: (073) 280730, 280741, 280742 **Fax:** (073) 280740
E-mail: dg@nipss.org.ng
Website: www.nipss.org.ng
Contact: The Director-General/CEO

NATIONAL INSTITUTE FOR SPORTS
Address: National Stadium Complex, Surulere, Lagos
Tel: (01) 4703036, 5454869 **Fax:** (01) 5454869
E-mail: nisports-ng@yahoo.com
Contact: The Director/CEO

NATIONAL MATHEMATICAL CENTRE
Address: Along Abuja-Lokoja Road, Kwali, FCT, Garki, Abuja
Tel: (09) 5230618
E-mail: info@nmc.edu.ng
E-mail: info@nmc.skannet.com
Contact: The Director/CEO

NATIONAL METALLURGICAL DEVELOPMENT CENTRE
Address: BPG 179, Zaria Road, Jos
Tel: (073) 613267, 613264, 613271
Fax: (073) 613266
* Plot 214, Fort Lammy Street, off Cotonou Crescent, Zone 6, Wuse, Abuja
Tel: (09) 523243-5 (3 L)
Contact: The Project Director/CEO

NATIONAL RESEARCH INSTITUTE FOR CHEMICAL TECHNOLOGY (NARICT)
Address: Km. 4, Old Kano Road, Basawa, Zaria, Kaduna State
Tel: (069) 330510, 334503
Fax: (069) 334835
E-mail: narict@inet-global.com
Contact: The Director/CEO

NATIONAL ROOT CROPS RESEARCH INSTITUTE (NRCRI)
Address: Umudike, Umuahia
Tel: (082) 440237, 440471
Contact: The Director/CEO

NATIONAL TEACHERS INSTITUTE (NTI)
Address: Kaduna-Zaria Expressway,Rigachikun, after Kaduna International Trade Fair Complex, Kaduna
Tel: (062) 316972, 319982 **Fax:** (062) 319982
E-mail: ntikd@skannet.com
E-mail: ntikad@inet.global.com
Contact: The Director/CEO

NATIONAL VETERINARY RESEARCH INSTITUTE (NVRI)
Address: Kaduna Vom, Vom Plateau State
Tel: (073) 281452, 281453
Contact: The Director/CEO

NATIONAL WATER RESOURCES INSTITUTE (NWRI)
Address: Mando Road, Kaduna
Tel: (062) 317900, 316196, 316195, 316195, 316108, 317897
Fax: (062) 317897
E-mail: waterins@skannet.com
Contact: The Director/CEO

NIGERIAN BUILDING & ROAD RESEARCH INSTITUTE (NBRRI)
Address: Plot 335, Gabes Street, Zone 2, Wuse, Abuja
Tel: (09) 5237467, 5237466
Fax: (09) 5237466
* 15, Awolowo Road, Ikoyi, Lagos
Contact: The Director-General/CEO

NIGERIAN INSTITUTE FOR OCEANOGRAPHY & MARINE RESEARCH (NIOMR)
Address: 3, Wilmot Point, off Ahmadu Bello Way, Victoria Island, Lagos
Tel: (01) 2617530, 615175, 617540
E-mail: niomr@hyperia.com
Contact: The Director/CEO

NIGERIAN INSTITUTE FOR OIL-PALM RESEARCH (NIFOR)
Address: Off Benin-Owo Road, Benin City
Tel: (052) 440150-1 (2 L)
* Uselu-Lagos Road, Benin City
Tel: (052) 602485
Contact: The Director/CEO

NIGERIAN INSTITUTE FOR TRYPANOSOMIASIS RESEARCH (NITR)
Address: 1, Surame Road, Kaduna
Tel: (062) 248075, 248075, 241255, 241265, 216041
Fax: (062) 248075
E-mail: nitr-kaduna@yahoo.com
Contact: The Director/CEO

NIGERIAN INSTITUTE FOR ADVANCED LEGAL STUDIES (NAILS)
Address: University of Lagos Campus, Akoka, Yaba, Lagos
Tel/Fax: (01) 4976077
E-mail: nials-abuja@mlstn.com
* Supreme Court Complex, Three Arms Zone, Abuja
Tel: (09) 2346504 **Fax:** (09) 2346505
E-mail: nials-abuja@mlstn.com
Contact: The Director-General/CEO

NIGERIAN INSTITUTE OF INTERNATIONAL AFFAIRS (NIIA)
Address: 13/15, Kofo Abayomi Street, Victoria Island, Lagos
Tel: (01) 2615606-7 (2 L), 615608-10 (3 L)
Fax: (01) 2611360
E-mail: dg@niianigeria.org
* Plot 431A, Kigoma Street, off Olusegun Obasanjo Way, opp. Abuja Club, Zone 1, Wuse, Abuja
Tel: (09) 5238713
Contact: The Director-General/CEO

NIGERIAN INSTITUTE OF MEDICAL RESEARCH (NIMR)
Address: Medical Compound, 6, Edmond Crescent, off Murtala Mohammed Way, Yaba, Lagos
Tel: (01) 7744723, 4705945 **Fax:** (01) 862965
E-mail: nimr@home.metrong.com
E-mail: nimr@supernet300.com
Website: www.nimr-ng.org
Contact: The Director-General/CEO

NIGERIAN INSTITUTE OF SOCIAL & ECONOMIC RESEARCH (NISER)
Address: NISER Campus, Oyo Road, Ojoo, Ibadan
Tel: (02) 8102904 **Fax:** (02) 8101194
E-mail: dg@niser.org.ng
Website: www.niser.org
Contact: The Director-General/CEO

NIGERIAN INSTITUTE OF TRANSPORT TECHNOLOGY (NITT)
Address: Basawa/Old Kano Road, Palladan, Zaria
Tel: (069) 334095, 334358 **Fax:** (069) 332943
E-mail: nittrc@infoweb.abs.net
* NITT Guest House, 9, African Church Close, off Coker Road, Ilupeju, Lagos.
Tel: (01) 4712343 **Fax:** (01) 4970223
* Plot 45, Ubiaja Crescent, near CBN Senior Staff Quarters, Garki Village, Abuja.
Tel: (09) 2344306
Contact: The Director-General/CEO

NIGERIAN STORED PRODUCTS RESEARCH INSTITUTE (NSPRI)
Address: Km. 3, Asa Dam Road, Ilorin
Tel: (031) 222143, 228274, 223912
Fax: (031) 228274, 225805
* 34, Barikisu Iyede St, off Unilag Road, Yaba, Lagos
Contact: The Director/CEO

PROJECTS DEVELOPMENT INSTITUTE (PRODA)
Address: Km. 12, off Enugu/Abakaliki Expressway, Enugu
Tel: (042) 457691
E-mail: proda@rmrdc.nig.com
Contact: The Director-General/CEO

RUBBER RESEARCH INSTITUTE OF NIGERIA (RRIN)
Address: Iyanomo, Edo State, Benin City
Tel: (052) 254625
Contact: The Director/CEO

SCIENTIFIC EQUIPMENT DEVELOPMENT INSTITUTE, ENUGU (SEDI-E)
Address: 20, Valley Crescent, near Government House, Independence Layout, Enugu
Tel/Fax: (042) 455040
Contact: The Director-General/CEO

SCIENTIFIC EQUIPMENT DEVELOPMENT INSTITUTE, MINNA (SEDI-M)
Address: Tagwai Dam Road, Chanchaga, Minna
Tel: (066) 223872, 224907
Contact: The Director-General/CEO

TECHNOLOGY BUSINESS INCUBATION CENTRES
Address: Dept. of Technology Acquisition & Assessment, Federal Ministry of Science & Technology, Abuja
Tel: (09) 5235763
* 4, Balogun Street, opp. Pen Cinema, Agege, Lagos
Tel: (01) 4926453-6 (4 L) **Fax:** (01) 4926454
E-mail: tibic@micro.com.ng
Contact: The Director-General/CEO

FEDERAL GOVERNMENT-OWNED COMMERCIAL ENTERPRISES

AJAOKUTA STEEL COMPANY LIMITED
Business: Production of Steel Billets, Rods, Bars and Sheets
Address: Steel City, Ajaokuta, Kogi State
Tel: (058) 400700, 400540
* c/o Federal Ministry of Power and Steel, Federal Secretariat Phase 1 (2nd Floor, Rm 283), Ikoyi, Lagos
Contact: The Managing Director/CEO

ALUMINIUM SMELTER COMPANY OF NIGERIA LIMITED
Business: Smelting of Alminium & Production of Ingots
Address: Ikot Abasi, Akwa Ibom State
Tel: (087) 775534, 775840, 775750, 775749, 77839
Fax: (087) 775841
* Total House, Plot 247, Herbert Macaulay Way, Central Business District, Abuja
Tel/Fax: (09) 2347753-4 (2 L)
Contact: The Managing Director/CEO

BANK OF INDUSTRY LIMITED (BOI)
Business: Development and Industrial Trade Banking
Address: Intercontinental Bank Building (1st Floor), Plot 207, 4th Avenue, Cadastral Zone AO, off Herbert Macaulay Way, Central Business District, Garki, Abuja
Tel: (09) 2346574, 2346579; **Fax:** (09) 2346578
BOI House (10th Floor), 63/71, Broad Street, Lagos
Tel: (01) 2663495, 2663539, 2663470
Fax: (01) 2665286, 2666733
Contact: The Managing Director/CEO

DEFENCE INDUSTRIES CORPORATION OF NIGERIA (DICON)
Address: 45, Ahmadu Bello Way, Kaduna
Tel: (062) 249530-2 (3L), 249525, 249526 **Fax:** (062) 249532
Contact: The Director-General/CEO

DELTA STEEL COMPANY LIMITED
Address: Ovwian-Aladja, Warri
Tel: (053) 621004, 621006; **Fax:** (053) 621012
* c/o Federal Ministry of Power and Steel, Federal Secretariat Phase 1 (1st Floor, Rm 112), Ikoyi, Lagos
Tel: (01) 681454
Contact: The Director-General/CEO

ELECTRICITY METER COMPANY NIGERIA LIMITED
Address: Plot 30/32, Chikaji Industrial Area, Zaria
Tel: (069) 334747, 335243, 331705 **Fax:** (069) 334185
E-mail: emcon@skannet.com
* c/o NEPA Headquarters Annex, (4th Floor, Room S), 19A, Awolowo Road, Ikoyi, Lagos
Tel/Fax: (01) 2672624

ELEME PETROCHEMICALS COMPANY LIMITED (EPCL)
Business: Refining of Petroleum & Production of Petrochemicals
Address: East-West Road, Eleme, near Port Harcourt
Tel: (084) 239316, 239317; **Tel/Fax:** (087) 772020
Contact: The Director-General/CEO

FEDERAL MORTGAGE FINANCE LIMITED
Business: Mortgage Finance Services
Address: Plot 700, Tafawa Balewa Way, Area 8, Garki, Abuja
Tel: (09) 2341358, 2345813, 2342682, 2343251, 2345792
Fax: (09) 2341358, 2342682
E-mail: fmfl@hotmail.com
Contact: The Managing Director/CEO

FEDERAL SUPERPHOSPHATE FERTILIZER COMPANY LTD
Address: 4, Nasarrawa Road, Kaduna South Ind. Area, Kaduna
Tel: (062) 232130, 231005, 231050
Contact: The Managing Director/CEO

HYSON NIGERIA LIMITED
Address: Plot 460, Lobito Crescent, off Adetokunbo Ademola Crescent, Wuse II, Abuja
Tel: (09) 4134023, 4134515 **Fax:** (09) 4139503
* Cosharis Plaza (3rd Floor), 68A, Adeola Odeku Street, Victoria Island, Lagos
Contact: The Managing Director/CEO

INTEGRATED DATA SERVICES LIMITED (IDSL)
Business: Pocessing of Petroleum Geology & Siesmic Data
Address: 36, Ogba Road, Oko Village, Benin City
Tel: (052) 258809, 254451, 254632, 257401, 256591, 253114

* NNPC Office, Oju- Olobun Close,
Victoria Island, Lagos.
Tel: (01) 2670710, 2670781
Contact: The Managing Director/CEO

IWOPIN PULP AND PAPER COMPANY LIMITED
Business: Production of Pulp and Paper
Address: Iwopin, Ijebu Waterside, off Sagamu/Benin Expressway, Iwopin, Ogun State
Tel: (090) 404628, 404616
* Katia Garden, Plot 1676, Oladele Olashore Street, Victoria Island, Lagos
Tel: (01) 2615761, 265756, 2615759, 26211165
Fax: (01) 2615754, 2621115

JOS STEEL ROLLING COMPANY LIMITED
Business: Rolling of Steel Billets to Rods and Bars
Address: Azi Nyako Road, off Ahmed Nasreddin Road, Industrial Layout, Jos
Tel: (073) 463408, 463491, 463446, 462964
Fax: (073) 463344

KADUNA REFINING AND PETROCHEMICALS COMPANY LIMITED (KRPC)
Business: Refining of Petroleum & Production of Petrochemicals
Address: Km. 16, Kachia Road, Kaduna
Tel: (062) 514453, 513771, 516212, 513979
Fax: (062) 517200, 514382, 515697
E-mail: mdkrpc_office@yahoo.co.uk

KATSINA STEEL ROLLING COMPANY LIMITED
Business: Rolling of Steel Billets to Rods and Bars
Address: Shehu Yar'Adua Way, Katsina
Tel: (065) 430050, 430815, 4320178, 430640
Fax: (065) 430953
E-mail: katsteel@hotmail.com

LEASING COMPANY OF NIGERIA LIMITED
Address: Plot 740, Aminu Kano Crescent, Wuse II, Abuja
Tel/Fax: (09) 4139406
E-mail: lecon@operamail.com
Website: www.leconng.com
* Former Intel Building (1st Floor), Plot 474, Trans-Amadi Industrial Layout, Port Harcourt

NATIONAL CLEARING & FORWARDING AGENCY (NACFA)
Address: 3, Creek Road, Apapa, Lagos
Tel: (01) 5876275, 5874576, 5878562, 5457172, 5878625
Fax: (01) 5878626
E-mail: nacfa@hyperia.com
* Shippers Plaza, Michael Okpara Street, Zone 5, Wuse, Garki, Abuja
* 5, Industrial Road, Port Harcourt
Tel: (084) 333821, 333429

NATIONAL ELECTRIC POWER AUTHORITY (NEPA)
Business: Generation and Distribution of Electric Power
Address: Plot 441, Zambezi Crescent, off Aguiyi Ironsi Street, Maitama District, Garki, Abuja
Tel: (09) 4135550, 4135650, 4135606, 4135504, 4135529
Fax: (09) 4135501, 4135501
E-mail: mdnepa@alpha.linkserve.com
Website: www.nepanigeria.org

* Ibrahim Babangida Way/Loma-Mansa Street, Zone 4, Wuse, Abuja
Tel: (09) 5234134, 5231938, 5231629 **Fax:** (09) 5231262

NATIONAL ENGINEERING AND TECHNICAL COMPANY LIMITED (NETCO)
Address: Stallion House (11th & 12th Floors), 2, Ajose Adeogun Street, Victoria Island, Lagos
Tel: (01) 2611232, 2647301 **Fax:** (01) 2611230
E-mail: info@netco.com.ng
Website: www.netco.com.ng

NATIONAL FERTILIZER COMPANY OF NIGERIA LIMITED (NAFCON) (In Receiever Mnagership - March 2005)
Address: NAFCON Fertilizer Complex, Onne, Rivers State
Tel: (084) 820480-95 (16 L)
* 15, Sowemimo Street, Ikeja G.R.A., Lagos
Tel: (01) 4975471
* Plot 870, Area 11, Garki, Abuja

NATIONAL IRON ORE MINING COMPANY LTD (NIOMCO)
Business: Mining of Iron-Ore & other Solid Minerals for Steel Production
Address: Km. 15, Okene-Lokoja Road, Itakpe, Kogi State
Tel: (058) 500215, 500140 **Fax:** (058) 2348684
Plot 287, S.L. Akintola Boulevard, off Ahmadu Bello Way, Garki II, Abuja. **Tel:** (09) 2348684
Contact: The Managing Director/CEO

NATIONAL PETROLEUM INVESTMENTS MANAGEMENT SERVICES (NAPIMS)
Business: Petroleum Investments Management Servives
Address: 13, Oju-Olobun Close, Victoria Island, Close, Victoria Island, Lagos
Tel: (01) 2670770-8 (9 L)

NEW NIGERIAN NEWSPAPERS LIMITED
Business: Newspaper Publishing
Address: Ahmadu Bello Way, Kaduna
Tel: (062) 243365, 245220, 245221, 243312
Fax: (062) 213778, 214719, 214389

NICON HOTELS LIMITED.
Business: Hospitality, Hotel Services
Address: Plot 557, Port Harcourt Crescent, off Gimbiya Street, off Ahmadu Bello Way, Garki II, Garki, Abuja
Tel: (09) 3140151-2 (2 L) **Fax:** (09) 3140153
E-mail: nhl@niconhotels.com.ng
* Eleganza Biro Plaza (9th Floor), Plot 643, Adeyemo Alakija Street, Victoria Island, Lagos
Tel: (01) 611214 **Fax:** (01) 611215

NICON INSURANCE CORPORATION
Business: Insurance Services
Address: NICON Plaza, Plot 242, Muhammadu Buhari Way, Central Business District, Abuja
Tel: (09) 5237120-9 (10 L), 2345051-2 (2 L)
Fax: (09) 5231726
E-mail: infodesk@niconinsurance.com.ng
E-mail: nicon30@aol.com

NIGERDOCK NIGERIA LIMITED
Business: Ship Repair and Maintenance Services, Drydocking.

Address: Snake Island Dockyard, off Tin Can Island Expressway, Apapa, Lagos
Tel: (01) 2615347 **Fax:** (01) 2646538-9 (2 L)
* Plot 457, Asokoro, near German Embassy, Abuja
Tel: (09) 3146414-5 (2 L)
Contact: The Managing Director/CEO

NIGERIA LNG LIMITED
Business: Gathering, Refining, Sales & Exportation of Liquified Natural (Petroleum) Gas
Address: C & C Tower, Plot 1684, Sanusi Fafunwa Street, Victoria Island, Lagos
Tel: (01) 2624190-4 (5 L), 2624556, 2617305
Fax: (01) 2617146
Website: www.nigerialng.com
Contact: The Managing Director/CEO

NIGERIA MACHINE TOOLS LIMITED
Business: Production of Machine Tools
Address: Km. 8, New Ikirun Road, Osogbo
Tel: (035) 242500-3 (4 L), 243915 **Fax:** (035) 242915
E-mail: nmt@infoweb.abs.net
Contact: The Managing Director/CEO

NIGERIA REINSURANCE CORPORATION
Business: Reinsurance Services
Address: UAC Commercial Complex, Plot 272/273, off Third Avenue, Central Business District, Garki, Abuja
Tel: (09) 5234105, 5234674, 5236970, 5238603
Fax: (09) 5234105
E-mail: mails@nigeriare.com
Contact: The Managing Director/CEO

NIGERIA UNITY LINE PLC
Business: Ocean Liners, Shipping Services, Dry Cargo Carriers
Address: 34, Creek Road, Apapa, Lagos
Tel: (01) 5804808 **Fax:** (01) 5804807
E-mail: nul@hyperia.com
Contact: The Managing Director/CEO

NIGERIAN AGRICULTURAL, CO-OPERATIVE & RURAL DEVELOPMENT BANK LIMITED (NACRDB)
Business: Banking Services
Address: Yakubu Gowon Way, Kaduna
Tel: (062) 245501-3, 245017, 245011 **Fax:** (062) 210611
* North-Central, Plot 2A, Herbert Macaulay Way, Zone 6, Wuse, Abuja
Contact: The Managing Director/CEO

NIGERIAN AGRICULTURAL INSURANCE CORPORATION
Address: Plot 590, off Independence Avenue (South), Cadastral Zone AO, Central Business Area, Garki, Abuja
Tel: (09) 2342071, 2342806, 2342820
Fax: (09) 2342071, 2342820
Contact: The Managing Director/CEO

NIGERIAN AVIATION HANDLING COMPANY LTD (NAHCO)
Address: NAHCO House, Murtala Muhammed International Airport, Ikeja, Lagos
Tel: (01) 4936345, 4937272 **Fax:** (01) 4970053
* Nnamdi Azikiwe International Airport, Abuja
Tel: (09) 8100023
Contact: The Managing Director/CEO

NIGERIAN COAL CORPORATION
Business: Coal Mining
Address: 29, Okpara Avenue, Enugu
Tel: (042) 225148, 255314, 255325
Fax: (042) 257340
* 11B, Mississippi Stret, Maitama District, Abuja
Tel: (09) 4137492, 4137493
Contact: The Managing Director/CEO

NIGERIAN EXPORT-IMPORT BANK (NEXIM)
Business: Import and Export Trade Banking Services
Address: Plot 795, IBB Drive, 8th Street, off Independence Avenue, Central Business District, Garki, Abuja
Tel: (09) 2346141-7 (7 L) **Fax:** (09) 2346151
E-mail: neximabj@neximbank.com.ng
Website: www.nexmbank.com
Contact: The Managing Director/CEO

NIGERIAN FILM CORPORATION
Business: Production of Films, Cinematography Services
Address: 218T, Liberty Dam Road, Jos
Tel: (073) 463519, 416444, 461455
Fax: (073) 461233
E-mail: mdnfc@jos.rcl.nig.com
* Sky Memorial Complex, Michael Okpara Street, Zone 5, Wuse, Abuja
Contact: The Managing Director/CEO

NIGERIAN GAS COMPANY LIMITED (NGC)
Business: Management and Sales of National Petroleum Gas
Address: 1, Odin Road, Ekpan, Warri
Tel: (053) 254262, 254261, 252461, 252471, 252328, 252224
Fax: (053) 252233, 252461, 252012
E-mail: helpngc@nnpc.com.ng
* Plot 76, Yaounde Street, Zone 6, Wuse, Garki, Abuja

NIGERIAN MINING CORPORATION
Business: Solid Mineral Mining
Address: Federal Secretariat (7th Floor), Jos
Tel: (073) 462867, 465245, 464344
Fax: (073) 462867
E-mail: nmcjos@yahoo.co.uk
Contact: The Managing Director/CEO

NIGERIAN NATIONAL PETROLEUM CORPORATION (NNPC)
Business: Regulation of all Petroleum Industry activities (Upstream & Downstream), Joint Venture Exploration & Production of Oil and Gas
Address: NNPC Tower, Herbert Macaulay Way, Central Business District, Garki, Abuja
Tel: (09) 2348200-19 (20 L)
Website: www.nnpc-publicaffairs.com
* 13, Oju-Olobun Close, Victoria Island, Close, Victoria Island, Lagos
Tel: (01) 2670770, 2670711, 2670780, 2694765
Fax: (01) 2602008
Contact: The Group Managing Director/CEO

NIGERIAN NEWSPRINT MANUFACTURING COMPANY LTD
Business: Production of Newsprint from Pulp
Address: Oku Iboku Town, Itu L.G.A., Akwa Ibom State
Tel: (085) 203699
Contact: The Managing Director/CEO

NIGERIAN PETROLEUM DEVELOPMENT COMPANY LIMITED (NPDC)
Business: Exploration and Production Oil and Gas
Address: 62, Sapele Road, Benin City
Tel: (052) 251900, 251907, 251867
Fax: (052) 259514, 255497
E-mail: e.ayoola@nnpc.com.ng
Contact: The Managing Director/CEO

NIGERIAN RAILWAY CORPORATION
Business: Management of Rail Transportation, Trian Engines and Wagons Owners
Address: Railway Compound, off Moshood Abiola Road, Ebute-Metta, Lagos
Tel: (01) 5456279, 5457460, 7747320
Fax: (01) 5831367
* Plot 739, Panama Street, Cadastral Zone A6, off IBB Way, Ministers Hill, Maitama District, Abuja
* Ebute-Metta Junction, Alagomeji-Yaba, Lagos
Tel: (01) 833377
Contact: The Managing Director/CEO

NIGERIAN TELECOMMUNICATIONS LIMITED (NITEL)
Business: National Telecommunications Services; Fixed, Mobile & GSM Telephony Services.
Address: 2, Bissau Street, off Herbert Macaulay Way, Zone 6, Wuse, Garki, Abuja
Tel: (09) 5233022-31 (10 L), 5237601-2 (2 L)
Fax: (09) 5230091, 5230252
* 2, Kingsway Road, Falomo, Ikoyi, Lagos
Contact: The Managing Director/CEO

NIGERIAN TELEVISION AUTHORITY (NTA)
Business: Nationwide Television Broadcasting
Address: Television House, off Obafemi Awolowo Street, Area 11, Garki, Abuja
Tel: (09) 2346906, 2346907
Fax: (09) 2345914, 611623
E-mail: nta2cha5@nigol.net.ng
* NTA2 Channel 5, Lagos, Ahmadu Bello Way, Victoria Island, Lagos
Tel: (01) 615153, 612291, 615045, 615094
Contact: The Director-General

OSHOGBO STEEL ROLLING COMPANY LIMITED
Business: Rolling of Steel Billets to Rods and Bars
Address: Km. 8, New Ikirun Road, Dagbolu, Osogbo
Tel: (035) 241331, 241332, 243332
Fax: (035) 241330
E-mail: oshogbosteel@infoweb.abs.net
Contact: The Managing Director/CEO

PIPELINES AND PRODUCTS MARKETING COMPANY LIMITED (PPMC)
Business: National and Regiional Distribution of Petroleum and Refined Petroleum Products & Natural Gas
Address: Plot 622, Eket Close, off Tafawa Balewa Way, Area 8, Garki, Abuja
Tel: (09) 2346882, 2342522
Fax: (09) 2346882
E-mail: info@ppmc.com.ng
Website: www.ppmc.com.ng
Contact: The Managing Director/CEO

PORT HARCOURT REFINING COMPANY LIMITED (PHRC)
Business: Refining of Petroleum
Address: Alesa Eleme, Port Harcourt.
Tel: (084) 236420-39 (20 L), 235585, * (087) 771990
Fax: (084) 236431, * (087) 771994
E-mail: phrc@phca.linkserve.com
* 13, Oju-Olobun Close, Victoria Island, Close, Victoria Island, Lagos
Contact: The Managing Director/CEO

SAVANNAH SUGAR COMPANY LIMITED
Business: Production of Refined Cane Sugar
Address: Numan, Adamawa Street
Tel: (075) 625707, 625517, 625970, 625971, 624646
Fax: (075) 625517
* Plot 2009, Bissau Street, off Herbert Macaulay Way, Zone 6, Wuse, Abuja
Tel: (09) 5231298, 232956
Contact: The Managing Director/CEO

TAFAWA BALEWA SQUARE INVESTMENTS LIMITED
Business: Management of Tafawa Balewa Square Properties & Spaces
Address: Tafawa Balewa Square Complex, Race Course, Lagos
Tel: (01) 2630175, 2631907 **Fax:** (01) 2633933
E-mail: tbsil@infoweb.abs.net
Contact: The Managing Director/CEO

THE DAILY TIMES OF NIGERIA PLC.
Business: Publishing of Newspapers and Periodicals
Address: Lateef Jakande Road, Agidingbi, Ikeja, Lagos
Tel: (01) 4977280-4 (5 L) **Fax:** (01) 4977283
E-mail: info@dailytimesofnigeria.com
Website: www.dailytimesofnigeria.com
Contact: The Managing Director/CEO

THE NIGERIAN SECURITY PRINTING AND MINTING COMPANY LIMITED (NSPMC)
Business: Currency Minting and Printing Secured Materials
Address: Plot 862, New FCDA Secretariat Road, Area 11, Garki, Abuja
Tel: (09) 2341102, 2341749, 2342965, 2342880
Fax: (09) 2342753
E-mail: nspmc@nspmc.com.ng
Website: www.nspmc.com.ng
Contact: The Managing Director/CEO

URBAN DEVELOPMENT BANK OF NIGERIA PLC.
Business: Development Banking Services
Address: Sokode Crescent, off Michael Okpara Street, Zone 6, Wuse, Garki, Abuja
Tel: (09) 5233655, 5233657, 5233659 **Fax:** (09) 5233414
E-mail: udbabj@yahoo.com
Contact: The Managing Director/CEO

WARRI REFINING AND PETROCHEMICALS COMPANY LIMITED (WRPC)
Business: Refining of Petroleum & Production of Petrochemicals
Address: Ekpan, Warri, Effurun, Warri
Tel: (053) 254160-3 (4 Lines), 252535, 250812, 253701, 252006 **Fax:** (053) 252535
* 13, Oju-Olobun Close, Victoria Island, Lagos
Contact: The Managing Director/CEO

MILITARY/PARA-MILITARY ORGANISATIONS

Armed Forces:

DEFENCE HEADQUARTERS
Address: Defence Headquarters, Plot 1092, Muhammadu Buhari Way, opp. Agura Hotel, Area 7, Garki, Abuja
Tel: (09) 2340142, 2340149
Fax: (09) 2340911
* Defence Headquarters Annex, 1/3, Moloney Street, Onikan, Lagos
Tel: (01) 2634444, 2646642-3 (2 L)
Fax: (01) 2646642
Contact: The Chief of Defence Staff

NIGERIAN ARMY (NA)
Address: Plot 1092, Muhammadu Buhari Way, opp. Agura Hotel, Area 7, Garki, Abuja
Tel: (09) 2348958
* Army Headquarters Annex, Ministry of Defence Premises, 1/3, Moloney Street, Onikan, Lagos
Tel: (01) 2631969
Contact: The Chief of Army Staff

NIGERIAN NAVY (NN)
Address: Plot 1092, Muhammadu Buhari Way, opp. Agura Hotel, Area 7, Garki, Abuja
Tel: (09) 2349625 **Fax:** (09) 2343373
* Naval Headquarters Annex, Minstry of Defence Premises, 1/3, Moloney Street, Onikan, Lagos
Tel: (01) 2630947
Contact: The Chief of Naval Staff

NIGERIAN AIRFORCE (NAF)
Address: Plot 1092, Muhammadu Buhari Way, opp. Agura Hotel, Area 7, Garki, Abuja
Tel: (09) 2349625
* Lagos Liason Office, 1, Kofo Abayomi Street, Victoria Island, Lagos.
Tel: (01) 2611418
Contact: The Chief of Air Staff

NATIONAL WAR COLLEGE (NWC)
Address: Herbert Macaulay Way (North), Central Business District, Garki, Abuja
Tel: (09) 2345923, 2345947, 2340545, 2340544
Fax: (09) 2345930
Contact: The Commandant

NIGERIAN DEFENCE ACADEMY (NDA)
Address: Kaduna-Zaria Road, Jaji, Kaduna
Tel: (062) 211426
Contact: The Commandant

Para-Military Services:

NIGERIAN CUSTOMS SERVICE (NCS)
Address: Customs Headquarters, 3-7, Abidjan Street, off Sultan Abubakar Way, Zone 3, Wuse, Garki, Abuja
Tel: (09) 5236387-9 (3 L), 5236394, 5234680, 5234689
Fax: (09) 5236394, 5234690
* Zonal Co-ordinator's Office, Harvey Rd, Yaba, Lagos
Tel: (01) 5455281, 4705576
Contact: The Comptroller-General/CEO

NIGERIAN IMMIGRATION SERVICE (NIS)
Address: Federal Ministry of Internal Affairs, Block F, Old Federal Secretariat, Area 1, Garki, Abuja
Tel: (09) 2343369, 2341934-6 (3 L), 2341298, 2349128
Fax: (09) 2342029
* Alagbon Close, Ikoyi, Lagos. **Tel:** (01) 2692850
Contact: The Comptroller-General/CEO

NIGERIA POLICE
Address: Louise Edet House, Sehu Shagari Way, Central Business District, Garki, Abuja
Tel: (09) 2340756, 2340867; **Fax:** (09) 2340867
E-mail: fpro@nigeriapolice.org
Website: www.nigeriapolice.org
Contact: The Inspector-General/CEO

NIGERIA PRISONS SERVICE
Address: Prisons Service Headquarters, Block E, Old Federal Secretariat, Area 1, Garki, Abuja
Tel: (09) 2341709, 2340425, 2344224, 2341316, 234135
Fax: (09) 2344634, 2340425, 2340429
* Zonal Headquarters, Alagbon Close, off Ikoyi Road, Ikoyi, Lagos
Contact: The Comptroller-General/CEO

FEDERAL HOSPITALS

AHMADU BELLO UNIVERSITY TEACHING HOSPITALS, ZARIA
Address: P.M.B. 06, Shika-Zaria
Tel: (069) 550098, 551399, 550458; **Fax:** (069) 555001
E-mail: macoabuth@yahoo.com

AMINU KANO TEACHING HOSPITAL, KANO
Address: Zaria Road, Kano
Tel: (064) 666537, 666568, 668236
E-mail: enquire@akth.org
Website: www.akth.org

FEDERAL MEDICAL CENTRE, ABAKALIKI
Address: P.M.B. 102, Abakaliki
Tel: (043) 20069, 21628
E-mail: fedmedai@infoweb.abs.net

FEDERAL MEDICAL CENTRE, ABEOKUTA
Address: Bisi Onabanjo Way, Idi-Ara, Sapon, Abeokuta
Tel: (039) 240407, 244449, 244439; **Fax:** (039) 241020
E-mail: md-fmca@skannet.com
E-mail: cmac-fmca@skannet.com

FEDERAL MEDICAL CENTRE, ADO-EKITI
Address: Ido-Ekiti

FEDERAL MEDICAL CENTRE, ASABA
Address: Hospital Road, West End, Asaba
Tel: (056) 281483, 280548, 281901; **Fax:** (056) 281483
E-mail: fmcasaba@hotmail.com
E-mail: fmcasaba@yahoo.co.uk

FEDERAL MEDICAL CENTRE, AZARE
Address: 5, S ule Katagun Road, Bauchi State
Tel: (071) 20380

FEDERAL MEDICAL CENTRE, BIDA
Address: Efu Etsuyis, Bida, Niger State
Tel: (066) 461074, 4631021 **Fax:** (066) 460075

FEDERAL MEDICAL CENTRE, GOMBE
Address: Along Ashaka Road, Gombe
Tel: (072) 223410, 223029, 223064, 223909
Fax: (072) 223411
E-mail: gmb-medcentre@hotmail.com

FEDERAL MEDICAL CENTRE, GUSAU
Address: Old General Hospital, Sani Abacha Way, Gusau
Tel: (063) 200025, 20067, 204724 **Fax:** (063) 204725

FEDERAL MEDICAL CENTRE, JALINGO
Address: Jankada Road, Jalingo
Tel: (079) 223792, 23292

FEDERAL MEDICAL CENTRE, KATSINA
Address: Murtala Muhammed Way, Katsina
Tel: (065) 434970 **Fax:** (065) 434971

FEDERAL MEDICAL CENTRE, KEFFI
Address: Old Akwanja Road, Keffi, Nasarawa State
Tel: (047) 62020, 62095

FEDERAL MEDICAL CENTRE, MAKURDI
Address: Hospital Road, Makurdi
Tel: (044) 533254, 533133, 532427, 558853, 532240, 53200
Fax: (044) 533133

FEDERAL MEDICAL CENTRE, OWERRI
Address: Orlu Road, Owerri
Tel: (083) 232738

FEDERAL MEDICAL CENTRE, OWO
Address: Ajasin Road, Owo, Ondo State
Tel: (051) 41865, 41536 **Fax:** (051) 41381

FEDERAL MEDICAL CENTRE, UMUAHIA
Address: Aba Road, Umuahia
Tel: (088) 221456, 220981, 220982

FEDERAL MEDICAL CENTRE, UYO
Address: Ediene Ikot Obio Imo, Uyo
Tel: (085) 203249, 204313 **Fax:** (085) 201674
E-mail: fedmeduyo@alpha.linkserve.com

FEDERAL MEDICAL CENTRE, YENOGOA
Address: P.M.B. 502, Yenagoa

FEDERAL MEDICAL CENTRE, YOLA
Address: Hospital Road, Yola
Tel: (075) 624005, 625604 **Fax:** (075) 626995

FEDERAL NEUROPSYCHIATRIC HOSPITAL, ENUGU
Address: Chime Avenue, New Haven, Enugu
Tel: (042) 250579, 523098, 253165, 250125
Fax: (042) 254454

FEDERAL NEUROPSYCHIATRIC HOSPITAL, KADUNA
Address: Bamawa, Kaduna South, Kaduna
Tel/Fax: (076) 237308-10 (10 L), 230001

FEDERAL NEUROPSYCHIATRIC HOSPITAL, MAIDUGURI
Address: Federal Low-Cost Housing Estate, Baga Road, Maiduguri
Tel/Fax: (076) 235112, 235204

FEDERAL NEUROPSYCHIATRIC HOSPITAL, SOKOTO
Address: Gwadabawa, Kware Town, Sokoto
Tel: (060) 236809, 230968 **Fax:** (060) 230968

FEDERAL PSYCHIATRIC HOSPITAL, CALABAR
Address: Calabar Road, Calabar
Tel: (087) 232266, 232125 **Fax:** (087) 236208
E-mail: fphcal@alpha.linkserve.com
Website: www.fphcalabar.org

GWAGWALADA SPECIALIST HOSPITAL, ABUJA
Address: Gwagwalada, via Abuja, Federal Capital Territory

JOS UNIVERSITY TEACHING HOSPITAL
Address: P.M.B. 2076, Jos
Tel: (073) 4502269-9 (4 L) **Fax:** (073) 455038
Contact: The Public Relations Officer

LAGOS UNIVERSITY TEACHING HOSPITAL
Address: Idi-Araba Surulere, Lagos
Tel: (01) 5453760-74 (15 L) **Fax:** (01) 5849582
E-mail: luth-1-hospital@onebox.com

NATIONAL EYE CENTRE
Address: off Nnamdi Azikiwe Way, Kaduna
Tel: (062) 313956, 315026, 314934, 314935
Fax: (062) 313956
E-mail: cpozems@infoweb.abs.net
E-mail: cpozems@hotmail.com

NATIONAL HOSPITAL, ABUJA
Address: Plot 132, Central Business District, Phase II, Garki, Abuja
Tel: (09) 2342687, 2342689, 2341013, 2341328
Fax: (09) 2342632
E-mail: cmd@microaccess.com
E-mail: nathosp.cmd@nitel.com

NATIONAL ORTHOPAEDIC HOSPITAL, DALA-KANO
Address: Kofar Ruwa Road, Dala, Kano
Tel: (064) 640003-6 (4 L), 633807 **Fax:** (064) 646217
E-mail: nohdala@infoweb.abs.net

NATIONAL ORTHOPAEDIC HOSPITAL, ENUGU
Address: Abakaliki Road, Abakpa-Nike, Enugu
Tel: (042) 558244, 559877, 559885 **Fax:** (042) 557805
E-mail: nohemd@anpa.net.ng

NATIONAL ORTHOPAEDIC HOSPITAL, IGBOBI-LAGOS
Address: Ikorodu Road, Igbobi, Yaba, Lagos
Tel: (01) 821290, 7743359, 4935221, 4935222, 821147, 821027, 821270
E-mail: noh@nihigbobi.org

NNAMDI AZIKIWE UNIVERSITY TEACHING HOSPITAL, NNEWI
Address: P.M.B. 5025, Nnewi, Anambra State
Tel: (046) 463661, 463662 **Fax:** (046) 460124

E-mail: nauth@infoweb.abs.net
E-mail: nauthnnewi@hotmail.com

OBAFEMI AWOLOWO UNIVERSITY TEACHING HOSPITALS COMPLEX, ILE-IFE
Address: State Hospital, Ilesa Road, Ile-Ife, Osun State
Tel: (036) 230271-2 (2 L) **Fax:** (036) 230141
E-mail: hospital@oauthc.oauife.edu.ng

OTIBHOR OKHAE TEACHING HOSPITAL, IRRUA
Address: Irrua, Edo State
Tel: (057) 97450, 97441, 97449 **Fax:** (057) 97440

PSYCHIATRIC HOSPITAL, ARO
Address: Aro, Abeokuta
Tel: (039) 245250-4 (5 L) **Fax:** (039) 241778
E-mail: neuro@infoweb.abs.net
Contact: The Medical Director/CEO

PSYCHIATRIC HOSPITAL, USELU, BENIN-CITY
Address: New Lagos Road, Uselu, Benin City
Tel: (052) 255439, 255460, 252419 **Fax:** (052) 250596
E-mail: psy_uselu@micro.com.ng

PSYCHIATRIC HOSPITAL, YABA
Address: Murtala Mohammed Way, opp. Yaba Bus Terminus, Sabo-Yaba, Lagos
Tel: (01) 7743174 **Fax:** (01) 861817
E-mail: phylagos@yahoo.com
E-mail: phylagos@hotmail.com

UNIVERSITY COLLEGE HOSPITAL, IBADAN
Address: Elizabeth Road, Total Garden, Ibadan
Tel: (02) 2410088, 2410109, 2410270, 2413503, 2411967
Fax: (02) 2413545
E-mail: uchib@infoweb.abs.net

UNIVERSITY OF BENIN TEACHING HOSPITAL
Address: Benin-Lagos Road, Ugbowo, Benin City
Tel: (052) 600418, 600969, 600765, 602884, 600394, 600046
Fax: (052) 600418
E-mail: aob@infoweb.abs.net

UNIVERSITY OF CALABAR TEACHING HOSPITAL
Address: P.M.B. 1278, Calabar
Tel: (087) 232055, 232408-9 (2 L), 232053
Fax: (087) 232094

UNIVERSITY OF ILORIN TEACHING HOSPITAL
Address: Lagos Road, Ilorin
Tel: (031) 222076-9 (4 L), 220020; **Fax:** (031) 220020
E-mail: cmdilorin@skannet.com

UNIVERSITY OF MAIDUGURI TEACHING HOSPITAL
Address: Along Bama Road, Maiduguri
Tel: (076) 232501, 231300, 232451, 232426
Fax: (076) 232375
E-mail: umth-cmd@dnetsystem.net

UNIVERSITY OF NIGERIA TEACHING HOSPITAL, ENUGU
Address: P.M.B. 01129, Enugu
Tel: (042) 252022, 252172, 252573; **Fax:** (042) 252665
E-mail: cdunth@infoweb.abs.net

UNIVERSITY OF PORT HARCOURT TEACHING HOSPITAL
Address: P.M.B. 7163, Port Harcourt
Tel: (084) 330589, 238923, 301040-4 (5 L)
Fax: (084) 238923

USMAN DAN FODIO UNIVERSITY TEACHING HOSPITAL, SOKOTO
Address: 1, Garba Nadama Road, Sokoto
Tel: (060) 232546, 230254, 239604-8 (5 L)
Fax: (060) 231514, 231060
E-mail: uduthcmd@skannet.com.ng
E-mail: udthmis@wwlkad.com

FEDERAL UNIVERSITIES/POSTGRADUATE INSTITUTIONS

ABUBAKAR TAFAWA BALEWA UNIVERSITY, BAUCHI
Address: Dass Road, Bauchi
Tel: (077) 542964, 542065, 542092, 543500
Fax: (077) 542065
E-mail: vc@atbu.edu.ng
E-mail: vc@atbunet.org
Website: www.atbunet.org

AHMADU BELLO UNIVERSITY, ZARIA
Address: Sokoto Road, Samaru-Zaria
Tel: (069) 550583, 551144, 551294, 550691
Fax: (069) 550022
E-mail: vc@abu.edu.ng
* 1, Kujore Street, Ilupeju, Lagos

BAYERO UNIVERSITY, KANO
Address: Gwarzo Road, Kano
Tel: (064) 666023 **Fax:** (064) 665904
E-mail: registrar@buk.edu.ng

FEDERAL UNIVERSITY OF TECHNOLOGY, AKURE
Address: Along Akure-Ilesa Road, Akure
Tel: (034) 243490-4 (5 L), 242190
Fax: (034) 240450, 242190, 243744
E-mail: root@futa.oauife.edu.ng.

FEDERAL UNIVERSITY OF TECHNOLOGY, MINNA
Address: Bosso, Minna
Tel: (066) 222887, 224305, 222397
Fax: (066) 222422
E-mail: futmx@skannet.com

FEDERAL UNIVERSITY OF TECHNOLOGY, OWERRI
Address: FUTO Permanet Site, Ihiagwa, Owerri
Tel: (083) 233228, 232025, 230974, 234726
Fax: (083) 233228
E-mail: vc@futo.edu.ng

FEDERAL UNIVERSITY OF TECHNOLOGY, YOLA
Address: P.M.B. 2076, Yola
Tel: (075) 625426, 624532, 625532, 625459
Fax: (075) 624416
E-mail: vc@futy.edu.ng

NNAMDI AZIKIWE UNIVERSITY, AWKA
Address: P.M.B. 5025, Awka
Tel: (048) 550018, 553053; **Fax:** (048) 553061
Website: www.unizik.edu.ng

NATIONAL POSTGRADUATE MEDICAL COLLEGE
Address: Km. 26, Lagos-Badagry Expresway, Ijanikin, Lagos
Tel: (01) 7743240
* Block 3, Plot 835, Umuahia Close, near NTA, Area 11, Garki, Abuja

NIGERIAN ACADEMY OF SCIENCE
Address: NSPRI House, 32/36, Barikisu Iyede Street, off Unilag Road, Abule-Oja, Yaba
Tel: (080) 33083114, 37879351
E-mail: nascience@aol.com
* c/o Institute of Basic Research, 4A, Limpopo St, FHA, Maitama, Abuja.
Tel/Fax: (09) 41337599

NIGERIAN LAW SCHOOL
Address: Bwari F.C.T., Garki, Abuja
Tel: (09) 8500937, 8500694, 8500956
E-mail: lawschoolorg@yahoo.co.uk
E-mail: jkjegede@hotmail.com

OBAFEMI AWOLOWO UNIVERSITY, ILE-IFE
Address: Ile-Ife, Osun State
Tel: (036) 230290-9 (10 L), 2312523, 2312861
Fax: (036) 233128, 232401, 231822
Website: www.oauife.edu.ng

UNIVERSITY OF ABUJA, ABUJA
Address: Gwagwalada, Abuja
Tel: (09) 8821972, 8821380, 8821393 **Fax:** (09) 8821605
E-mail: vc@uniabuja.edu.ng
E-mail: vc@mailhub.uniabuja.edu.ng

UNIVERSITY OF AGRICULTURE, ABEOKUTA
Address: Alabata Road, Abeokuta
Tel: (039) 245290, 245291, 240385, 240768
Fax: (039) 243045
E-mail: vc@unaab.edu.ng
Website: www.unaab.edu

UNIVERSITY OF AGRICULTURE, MAKURDI
Address: P.M.B. 2373, Makurdi
Tel: (044) 533204, 533205, 533577, 533455, 534102
Fax: (044) 531455
E-mail: funam.edu.ng

UNIVERSITY OF BENIN, BENIN
Address: Benin-Lagos Express Road, Ugbowo, Benin-City
Tel: (052) 600546, 600547, 600549, 600553, 600558
Fax: (052) 602370
E-mail: info&pr@uniben.edu.ng
Website: www.uniben.edu

UNIVERSITY OF CALABAR, CALABAR
Address: Eta Agbor Street, Calabar
Tel: (087) 232790, 234753, 234747; **Fax:** (087) 231766
E-mail: @unical.edu.ng
E-mail: vcunical@yahoo.com

UNIVERSITY OF IBADAN, IBADAN
Address: Oyo Road, Ibadan
Tel: (02) 8101100-19 (20 L), 8102070-4 9(5 L)
Fax: (02) 8101100-19 (20 L), 8103118
E-mail: registrar@ul.edu.ng

UNIVERSITY OF ILORIN, ILORIN
Address: Tanke Road, Ilorin
Tel: (031) 225299, 221552, 221554, 221873, 221911
Fax: (031) 222561, 221593
E-mail: uniIlorin.edu.ng

UNIVERSITY OF JOS, JOS
Address: P.M.B. 2084, Jos
Tel: (073) 610936, 612513, 454089
Fax: (073) 612513, 610514
E-mail: unijos.edu.ng

UNIVERSITY OF LAGOS, AKOKA-LAGOS
Address: Akoka, Yaba, Lagos
Tel: (01) 5454891-2 (2 L), 493837-9 (3 L)
Fax: (01) 822644
E-mail: @unilag.edu.ng
E-mail: library@rcl.nig.com
Website: www.unilag.edu

UNIVERSITY OF MAIDUGURI, MAIDUGURI
Address: Bama Road, Maiduguri
Tel: (076) 231730, 231900, 232150
Fax: (076) 236314, 231639
E-mail: unimaid.edu.ng

UNIVERSITY OF NIGERIA, NSUKKA
Address: Nsukka, Enugu State
Tel: (042) 771911, 771920, 771500; **Fax:** (042) 770644
E-mail: misunn@aol.com

UNIVERSITY OF PORT HARCOURT, PORT HARCOURT
Address: Choba, Port Harcourt
Tel: (084) 230889, 230902; **Fax:** (084) 230903
E-mail: uniport@alpha.linkserve.com

UNIVERSITY OF UYO, UYO
Address: P.M.B. 1017, Uyo
Tel: (085) 201111, 202694, 202693
Fax: (085) 202694
E-mail: root@uniuyo.edu.ng

USMAN DANFODIO UNIVERSITY, SOKOTO
Address: P.M.B. 2346, Sokoto
Tel: (060) 235519, 232366, 234092
Fax: (060) 235519, 234052, 236610
E-mail: @udusok.edu.ng

FEDERAL VOCATIONAL COLLEGES AND SCHOOLS

FEDERAL COLLEGE OF AGRICULTURE, AKURE
Address: Ado-Owo Road, Akure
Tel: (034) 240892, 240891
Fax: (034) 240891

FEDERAL COLLEGE OF AGRICULTURE, IBADAN
Address: Moor Plantation, Abeokuta Road, Apata, Ibadan
Tel: (02) 2312070

FEDERAL COLLEGE OF AGRICULTURE, UMUDIKE
Address: Umudike, P.M.B. 7008, Umuahia
Tel: (088) 220498

FEDERAL COLLEGE OF ANIMAL HEALTH & PRODUCTION TECHNOLOGY, IBADAN
Address: Moor Plantation, Abeokuta Road, Apata, Ibadan
Tel/Fax: (02) 2317857
E-mail: drart@infoweb.abs.net

FEDERAL COLLEGE OF ANIMAL HEALTH & PRODUCTION TECHNOLOGY, VOM
Address: P.M.B. 01, Vom, Plateau State

FEDERAL COLLEGE OF FISHERIES & MARINE TECHNOLOGY
Address: Off Ahmadu Bello Way, Victoria Island, Lagos
Tel: (01) 2620159, 2620160, 2625588, 2625578, 2622197, 2620195; **Fax:** (01) 2620160
E-mail: fcfmt@pinetinformatics.net

FEDERAL COLLEGE OF FOREST MECHANISATION
Address: Afaka, Kaduna
Tel: (062) 246556

FEDERAL COLLEGE OF FORESTRY, IBADAN
Address: Jericho Hill, Jericho Aleshinloye, Dugbe, Ibadan
Tel: (02) 2411035; **Fax:** (02) 2414843
E-mail: dfrin@skannet.com
Contact: The Administrative Officer

FEDERAL COLLEGE OF FORESTRY, JOS
Address: P.M.B. 2019, Jos
Tel: (073) 611056, 612616; **Fax:** (073) 611056
E-mail: fcfjos@infoweb.abs.net

FEDERAL COLLEGE OF FRESHWATER FISHERIES TECHNOLOGY, BAGA
Address: Kukawa, Borno State

FEDERAL COLLEGE OF FRESHWATER FISHERIES TECHNOLOGY, NEW BUSSA
Address: P.M.B. 1500, New Busa, Niger State
Tel: (031) 670513

FEDERAL COLLEGE OF LAND RESOURCES TECHNOLOGY KURU
Address: Bukuru-Vom Road, Kuru, Jos
Tel: (073) 281260-2 (3 L)

FEDERAL COLLEGE OF VETERINARY AND MEDICAL LABORATORY TECHNOLOGY
Address: Vom, P.M.B. 01, Vom, Plateau State
Tel: (073) 280061, 281320, 281321

FEDERAL COLLEGE OF WILDLIFE MANAGEMENT
Address: P.M.B. 268, New Busa, Niger State
Tel: (031) 670447

FEDERAL SCHOOL OF DENTAL TECHNOLOGY & THERAPY, ENUGU
Address: Trans-Ekulu, Enugu
Tel: (042) 553673 **Fax:** (042) 555870

FEDERAL SCHOOL OF MEDICAL LABORATORY TECHNOLOGY, JOS
Address: Jos University Teaching Hospital, Murtala Mohammed Way, Jos
Tel: (073) 454736

FEDERAL SCHOOL OF PHYSIOTHERAPY, KANO
Address: Aminu Kano Way/Gowon Dutse Road, Kano
Tel: (064) 631659

FEDERAL SCHOOL OF RADIOGRAPHY, LAGOS
Address: 2/4, Taylor Drive,Medical Compound, off Edmund Crescent, Yaba, Lagos
Tel: (01) 862355

FEDERAL SCHOOL OF SURVEYING, OYO
Address: Ogbomoso Road, Oyo
Tel: (038) 240455, 240255, 240823, 240617
Fax: (038) 240255
E-mail: gilab@fssoyo.anpa.net.ng

MARITIME ACADEMY OF NIGERIA, ORON
Address: P.M.B. 1089, Oron, Akwa Ibom State
Tel: (087) 235559, 237802, 441303 **Fax:** (087) 441303
* Outer Marina, CMS Bus-Stop, Lagos
Tel: (01) 2630245 **Fax:** (01) 2666972
* Banex Plaza, Plot 750, Aminu Kano Crescent, Cadastral Zone A7, Wuse II, Abuja
Tel: (09) 5239648 **Fax:** (09) 5239685

METALLURGICAL TRAINING INSTITUTE, ONITSHA
Address: Km. 6/7, Onitsha-Owerri Road, Onitsha
Tel: (046) 217430, 216215; **Fax:** (046) 216215

NIGERIA FRENCH LANGUAGE VILLAGE
Address: Ajara-Dokoh, Badagry, Km. 50, Lagos-Badagry Expressway, Badagry, Lagos State
Tel: (01) 2882914, 732643, 732471, 732146, 7733506, 2882915, 2881488, 2883160 **Fax:** (01) 2882914
E-mail: nflvconsult@yahoo.com

NIGERIA ARABIC LANGUAGE VILLAGE, NGALA
Address: P.O. Box 38, Ngala, Borno State
Tel: (076) 232000 **Fax:** (076) 342350

NIGERIAN COLLEGE OF AVIATION TECHNOLOGY, ZARIA
Address: Zaria Aerodrome, Palladan-Samaru Road, Zaria, Kaduna State
Tel: (069) 332021-2 (2 L), 330233
Fax: (069) 334756 334754

PETROLEUM TRAINING INSTITUTE
Address: PTI Road, by Jeffia Junction, Effurun, Delta State
Tel: (053) 250785, 251541 **Fax:** (053) 251541
E-mail: pti@alpha.linkserve.com
* Department of Petroleum Resources (DPR), 7, Kofo Abayomi Street, Victoria Island, Lagos
Tel: (01) 2612320, 2616869, 2618228, 262398

NIGERIAN ECONOMIC ORGANISATIONS:

MANUFACTURERS ASSOCIATION OF NIGERIA
NIGERIAN ECONOMIC SUMMIT GROUP LTD/Gte
NIGERIAN EMPLOYERS' CONSULTATIVE ASSOCIATION
THE NIGERIAN STOCK EXCHANGE

NIGERIAN BUSINESS/TRADE ASSOCIATION, SOCIETIES AND GROUP:

ASSOC. OF ADVERTISING PRACTITONERS OF NIGERIA
ASSOC. OF BUREAUX de CHANGE OPERATORS OF NIGERIA
ASSOCIATION OF NIGERIAN EXPORTERS
ASSOC. OF NIGERIAN LICENSED CUSTOMS AGENTS
ASSOC. OF TELECOMMUNICATIONS CO. OF NIGERIA
BROADCASTING ORGANISATIONS OF NIGERIA
CO-OPERATIVE FEDERATION OF NIGERIA
COCOA ASSOCIATION OF NIGERIA
COMPUTER ASSOCIATION OF NIGERIA
EQUIPMENT LEASING ASSOC. OF NIGERIA LTD/Gte
FISHERIES SOCIETY OF NIGERIA
FEDERATION OF CONSTRUCTION INDUSTRY
INDEPENDENT PETROLEUM MARKETERS ASSOC. OF NIG.
INSTITUTE OF DIRECTORS, NIGERIA
INSTITUTE OF PUBLIC ANALYSTS OF NIGERIA
JOINT DOCK LABOUR INDUSTRIAL COUNCIL
MONEY MARKET ASSOCIATION OF NIGERIA
MORTGAGE BANKING ASSOCIATION OF NIGERIA
NATIONAL ASSOC. OF NIGERIAN TRAVEL AGENCIES
NATIONAL COUNCIL OF MANAGING DIRECTOR OF LICENSED CUSTOMS AGENTS
NEWSPAPER PROPRIETORS' ASSOC. OF NIGERIA
NIGERIA OLYMPIC COMMITTEE
NIGERIAN ASSOC. OF SMALL & MEDIUM ENTERPRISES
NIGERIAN ASSOC. OF SMALL-SCALE INDUSTRIALISTS
NIGERIAN CORPORATION OF INSURANCE BROKERS
NIGERIAN INSURERS ASSOCIATION
NIGERIAN ROAD FEDERATION
NIGERIAN SHIPPING COMPANIES ASSOCIATION
OUTDOOR ADVERTISING ASSOC. OF NIGERIA

NIGERIAN PROFESSIONAL/CHARTERED INSTITUTES, ASSOCIATIONS, SOCIETIES, REGISTRATION COUNCILS AND BOARDS:

ADVERTISING PRACTITIONERS COUNCIL OF NIGERIA
ARCHITECTS REGISTRATION COUNCIL OF NIGERIA
ASSOC. OF CONSULTING ENGINEERS OF NIGERIA
ASSOC. OF GENERAL & PRIVATE MEDICAL PRACTITION-ERS OF NIGERIA
ASSOC. OF NATIONAL ACCOUNTANTS OF NIGERIA
ASSOC. OF RADIOGRAPHERS OF NIGERIA
CHARTERED INSTITUTE OF ADMINISTRATION
CHARTERED INSTITUTE OF ARBITRTORS (NIGERIA)
CHARTERED INSTITUTE OF LOCAL GOVERNMENT & PUBLIC ADMINISTRATION OF NIGERIA
CHARTERED INSTITUTE OF MARKETING OF NIGERIA
CHARTERED INSTITUTE OF STOCKBROCKERS OF NIG.
CHARTERED INSTITUTE OF TAXATION OF NIGERIA
CHARTERED INSURANCE INSTITUTE OF NIGERIA
COMPUTER PROFESSIONALS REGISTRATION COUNCIL
COUNCIL FOR THE REGULATION OF ENGINEERING OF NIG.
COUNCIL OF LEGAL EDUCATION
COUNCIL OF REGISTERED BUILDERS OF NIGERIA
ESTATE SURVEYORS & VALUERS REGISTRATION BOARD OF NIGERIA
INSTITUTE OF CHARTERED ACCOUNTANTS OF NIGERIA
INSTITUTE OF CHARTERED SECRETARIES & ADMINIS-TRATORS OF NIGERIA
INSTITUTE OF LOSS ADJUSTERS OF NIGERIA
INSTITUTE OF MEDICAL LABORATORY SCIENCE & TECHNOLOGY OF NIGERIA
INSTITUTE OF PERSONNEL MANAGEMENT OF NIGERIA
MEDICAL & DENTAL COUNCIL OF NIGERIA
NATIONAL ASSOC. OF AIRCRAFT PILOT & ENGINEERS
NIGERIAN ASSOC. OF GENERAL PRACTICE PHARMACISTS
NIGERIAN BAR ASSOCIATION
NIGERIAN INSTITUTE OF ARCHITECTS
NIGERIAN INSTITUTE OF BUILDING
NIGERIAN INSTITUTE OF INDUSTRIAL MANAGEMENT
NIGERIAN INSTITUTE OF JOURNALISM
NIGERIAN INSTITUTE OF MANAGEMENT
NIGERIAN INSTITUTE OF MARKETING
NIGERIAN INSTITUTE OF PUBLIC RELATIONS
NIGERIAN INSTITUTE OF QUANTITY SURVEYORS
NIGERIAN INSTITUTN OF ESTATE SURVEYORS & VALUERS
NIGERIAN INSTITUTION OF SURVEYORS
NIGERIAN MEDICAL ASSOCIATION
NIGERIAN OPTOMETRIC ASSOCIATION
NIGERIAN SOCIETY OF CHEMICAL ENGINEERS
NIGERIAN SOCIETY OF ENGINEERS
NURSING & MIDWIFERY COUNCIL OF NIGERIA
OPTOMETRISTS & DISPENSING OPTICIANS BOARD
PHARMACEUTICAL SOCIETY OF NIGERIA
PHARMACISTS COUNCIL OF NIGERIA
QUANTITY SURVEYORS REGISTRATION BOARD OF NIG.
RADIOGRAPHERS REGISTRATION BOARD OF NIGERIA
SOCIETY OF PETROLEUM ENGINEERS (NIGERIA COUNCIL
SURVEYORS COUNCIL OF NIGERIA
TEACHERS REGISTRATION COUNCIL OF NIGERIA
VETERINARY COUNCIL OF NIGERIA

INTERNATIONAL AGENCIES & ORGANISATIONS IN NIGERIA:

A.U. SCIENTIFIC, TECHNICAL & RESEARCH COMMISSION
AFRICAN IRON & STEEL ASSOCIATION
AFRICAN REGIONAL CENTRE FOR ENGINEERING DESIGN & MANUFACTURING
AFRICAN REGIONAL CENTRE FOR SPACE SCIENCE & TECHNOLOGY EDUCATION
AFRICAN REINSURANCE CORPORATION
ALLIANCE FRANCAISE, LAGOS
COCOA PRODUCERS ALLIANCE
DELEGATION OF GERMAN INDUSTRY & COMMERCE FOR WEST AFRICA
ECONOMIC COMMUNITY WEST AFRICA STATES
FOOD & AGRICULTURE ORGANISATION (U.N.)
GERMAN AGENCY FOR TECHNICAL CO-OPERATION
GOETHE-INSTITUT, GERMAN CULTURAL CENTRE
INTERNATIONAL CIVIL AVIATION ORGANISATION
INTERNATIONAL COMMITTEE OF THE RED CROSS

INTERNATIONAL INSTITUTE OF TROPICAL AGRICULTURE
INTERNATIONAL LABOUR ORGANISATION (U. N.)
INTERNATIONAL LIVESTOCK RESEARCH INSTITUTE
INTERNATIONAL ORGANISATION FOR MIGRATION (U. N.)
JAPAN EXTERNAL TRADE ORGANISATION
JAPAN INTERNATIONAL CO-OPERATION AGENCY
PAN-AFRICAN ASSOCIATION FOR CO-OPERATION
PAN AFRICAN NEWS AGENCY
PORT MANAGEMT ASSOC. OF WEST & CENTRAL AFRICA
REGIONAL CENTRE FOR TRAINING IN AEROSPACE SURVEYS (U.N. ECON. COMM. FOR AFRICA)
REGIONAL PROGRAMME FOR TECHNOLGY MANAGEMENT
SOCIETY FOR FAMILY HEALTH
THE BRITISH COUNCIL
THE FORD FOUNDATION OFFICE FOR WEST AFRICA
THE WEST AFRICAN EXAMINATION COUNCIL
THE WORLD BANK GROUP (NIGERIA COUNTRY OFFICE)
TRADE MISSION OF THE ROC (TAIWAN) IN NIGERIA
TRADE REPRESENTATION OF THE RUSSIAN FEDERATION IN NIGERIA
UNITED NATIONS CHILDREN FUND
UNITED NATIONS DEVELOPMENT FUND FOR WOMEN (ANGLOPHONE WEST AFRICA)
UNITED NATIONS DEVELOPMENT PROGRAMME
UNITED NATIONS EDCATIONAL, SCIENTIFIC & CULTURAL ORGANISATION
UNITED NATIONS HIGH COMMISSION FOR REGUGEES
UNITED NATIONS INDUSTRIAL DEVELOPMENT ORGANISATION
UNITED NATIONS INFORMATION CENTRE
UNITED NATIONS OFFICE FOR DRUG CONTROL & CRIME PREVENTION
UNITED NATIONS POPULATION FUND
UNITED STATES AGENCY FOR INTERNATIONAL DEV'T
WEST AFRICAN BANKERS ASSOC. (NIGERIA CHAPTER)
WEST AFRICAN MANAGEMENT DEVELOPMENT INSTITUTES NETWORK
WEST AFRICAN POSTGRADUATE MEDICAL COLLEGE
WORLD HEALTH ORGANISATION (NIGERIAN REP.)
WORLD TRADE CENTRE OF NIGERIA LTD/Gte

BILATERAL ASSOCIATION & CHAMBERS OF COMMERCE

FRANCO - NIGERIAN CHAMBER OF COMMERCE & IND.
NIGERIA - ASEAN CHAMBER OF COMMERCE
NIGERIA - BRITAIN ASSOCIATION
NIGERIA - JAPAN ASSOCIATION
NIGERIAN - AMERICAN CHAMBER OF COMMERCE
NIGERIAN - BELGIAN CHAMBER OF COMMERCE
NIGERIAN - BELGIAN COMMERCIAL INFORMATION & DOCUMENTATION CENTRE
NIGERIAN - BRAZILIAN CHAMBER OF COMMERCE
NIGERIAN - BRITISH CHAMBER OF COMMERCE
NIGERIAN - DANISH CHAMBER OF COMMERCE
NIGERIAN - GERMAN CHAMBER OF COMMERCE
NIGERIAN - HUNGARIAN CHAMBER OF COMMERCE
NIGERIAN - IVIORIEN CHAMBER OF COMMERCE
NIGERIAN - KOREAN FRIENDSHIP ASSOCIATION
NIGERIAN - NETHERLANDS CHAMBER OF COMMERCE
NIGERIAN - NORDIC CHAMBER OF COMMERCE
NIGERIAN -SOUTH AFRICAN CHAMBER OF COMMERCE

NIGERIAN ECONOMIC ORGANISATIONS:

MANUFACTURERS ASSOCIATION OF NIGERIA (MAN)
Address: 77, Obafemi Awolowo Way, Ikeja, Lagos
Tel: (01) 4974240-1 (2 L), 4974244-5 (2 L), 4974248
Fax: (01) 4974247
E-mail: man@manassoc.org
* Plot 144, Trans Amadi Ind. Layout, Port Harcourt
Tel: (084) 239670-1 (2 L)
* 9, Beirut Road, Bompai, Kano
Tel: (064) 645474
* 1, Keffi Close, Kachia Rd, Kaduna South, Kaduna
Tel: (062) 237235

NIGERIAN ECONOMIC SUMMIT GROUP LTD/Gte (NESG)
Address: ICON House, (8th Floor), Plot 999F, Idejo/Danmole Street, Victoria Island, Lagos
Tel: (01) 2632963, 4702287-8 (2 L) **Fax:** (01) 2636356
E-mail: nesg@hyperia.com

NIGERIAN EMPLOYERS' CONSULTATIVE ASSOCIATION (NECA)
Address: Elephant Cement House, (6th Floor), ASSBIFI Road, Ikeja Central Business District, Alausa, Ikeja, Lagos
Tel: (01) 7742734, 7746352 **Fax:** (01) 4963172
E-mail: neca@necang.com
Website: www.necang.com

THE NIGERIAN STOCK EXCHANGE
Address: Stock Exchange House (8th, 9th & 11th Floors), 2/4, Customs Street, Lagos
Tel: (01) 2660287, 2660305, 2660335
Fax: (01) 2668291, 2668729
E-mail: nse@linkserve.com.ng
Website: www.nse.com.ng
* Labour House (4th Floor), Central District, Abuja
Tel: (09) 2349368, 2349150 **Fax:** (09) 2349150
* 10, Ikwerre Road, Port Harcourt
Tel: (084) 234977
* Old Hadejia Road, opp. Golf Course, Kano
Tel: (064) 625612 **Fax:** (064) 638057
* UBA Building, 3, Yakubu Gowon Way, Kaduna
Tel: (062) 240992, 249822

NIGERIAN BUSINESS/TRADE ASSOCIATION, SOCIETIES AND GROUP:

ASSOCIATION OF ADVERTISING PRACTITONERS OF NIGERIA (APCON)
Address: 18, Amore Street, off Toyin Street, Ikeja, Lagos
Tel: (01) 4712056-7 (2 L), 4964653
E-mail: aapnmail@hyperia.com

ASSOCIATION OF BUREAUX de CHANGE OPERATORS OF NIGERIA (ABCON)
Address: 27, Obafemi Awolowo Way, Ikeja, Lagos
Tel: (01) 7735355 **Fax:** (01) 4970361

ASSOCIATION OF NIGERIAN EXPORTERS (ANE)
Address: 41, Chingola Street, off Yaounde Street, Wuse Zone 6, Abuja
Tel/Fax: (09) 5233489

ASSOCIATION OF NIGERIAN LICENSED CUSTOMS AGENTS (ANCLA)
Address: Kariko Towers, 9, Wharf Road, Apapa, Lagos
Tel: (01) 5871703-4 (2 L), 5871764, 5871766-7 (2 L)

ASSOCIATION OF TELECOMMUNICATIONS COMPANIES OF NIGERIA (ATCON)
Address: ICON House (1st Floor), Plot 999F, Idejo/Danmole Street, off Adeola Odeku St, Victoria Island, Lagos
Tel: (01) 3201001, 3201014, 4971968, 5872798
Fax: (01) 2645153, 3201015
E-mail: atcon_ng@yahoo.com
atvcon@hyperia.com
Website: www.atcononline.org

BROADCASTING ORGANISATIONS OF NIGERIA (BON)
Address: Radio House (7th Floor), Herbert Macaulay Way (South), Garki, Abuja
Tel/Fax: (09) 2342146

CO-OPERATIVE FEDERATION OF NIGERIA LIMITED
Address: Quarters 479, Fajimi Street, Agodi G.R.A., Ibadan
Tel/Fax: (02) 711276
E-mail: coopnigeria@yahoo.com

COCOA ASSOCIATION OF NIGERIA
Address: Co-operative House, Ilesha-Benin Expreesway, Akure
Tel: (034) 243208, 244487 **Fax:** (034) 243208

COMPUTER ASSOCIATION OF NIGERIA (COAN)
Address: 190, Ikorodu Road, Palmgroove, Lagos
Tel: (01) 4811091, 7744600 **Fax:** (01) 4811091
E-mail: enquiries@coan.org

EQUIPMENT LEASING ASSOCIATION OF NIGERIA LTD/Gte
Address: Plot 294, Gbagada Expressway, Gbagada Phase II, Lagos
Tel: (01) 5553149, 7740473 **Fax:** (01) 5553149
E-mail: elanigeria@yahoo.com

FEDERATION OF CONSTRUCTION INDUSTRY
Address: Construction Hose, 18, Adeyemo Alakija Street, Victoria Island, Lagos
Tel: (01) 2616564, 616567 **Fax:** (01) 2616564

FISHERIES SOCIETY OF NIGERIA (FISON)
Address: Development House (3rd Floor), 21, Wharf Road, Apapa, Lagos
Tel: (01) 5452938, 5870888 **Fax:** (01) 5870888
E-mail: fison2k1@yahoo.com

INDEPENDENT PETROLEUM MARKETERS ASSOIATION OF NIGERIA (IPMAN)
Address: 28, Mojidi Street, off Toyin Street, Ikeja, Lagos
Tel/Fax: (01) 4936934

INSTITUTE OF DIRECTORS, NIGERIA (IoD)
Address: 48, Bayo Kuku Street, off Alfred Rewane Road, Ikoyi, Lagos
Tel: (01) 2673402, 7740920
Fax: (01) 2673402
E-mail: iodnig@infoweb.abs.net
Website: www.iod-nigeria.com

INSTITUTE OF LOSS ADJUSTERS OF NIGERIA (ILAN)
Address: ILAN House, 2, Fagbile Street, off Ojuelegba Road, Surulere, Lagos
Tel: (01) 840367

INSTITUTE OF PUBLIC ANALYSTS OF NIGERIA (IPAN)
Address: Federal Secretariat, Phase 2 (10th Floor), Ikoyi, Lagos
Tel: (01) 7743958

JOINT DOCK LABOUR INDUSTRIAL COUNCIL (JODLIC)
Address: 1, Alfred Rewane (Kingway) Road, Ikoyi, Lagos
Tel: (01) 2673396, 7749547

MONEY MARKET ASSOCIATION OF NIGERIA
Address: Plot 1398B, Tiamiyu Savage St, Victoria Island, Lagos
Tel: (01) 2620492-3 (2 L)
E-mail: mmanhq@moneymarketng.com
Website: www.moneymarketng.com

MORTGAGE BANKING ASSOCIATION OF NIGERIA (MBAN
Address: Madasa House, 31/33, Kakawa Street, Lagos
Tel: (01) 2646085, 3200212 **Fax:** (01) 3200217

NATIONAL ASSOCIATION OF NIGERIAN TRAVEL AGENCIES (NANTA)
Address: 52A, Ikorodu Road, Fadeyi, Lagos
Tel: (01) 7732876
E-mail: nantanig@yahoo.co.uk

NATIONAL COUNCIL OF MANAGING DIRECTOR OF LICENSED CUSTOMS AGENTS (NCMDLCA)
Address: Shamrock House, 10, Apapa-Oshodi Expressway, opp. Ibru Jetty, Apapa, Lagos
Tel: (01) 4712512, 4805470, 7754447

NEWSPAPER PROPRIETORS' ASSOCIATION OF NIGERIA (NPAN)
Address: 8, Maryland Crescent, Maryland Estate, Maryland, Ikeja, Lagos
Tel: (01) 4704089, 4960616 **Fax:** (01) 4960616
E-mail: npanp@yahoo.com

NIGERIA OLYMPIC COMMITTEE (NOC)
Address: NOC Building, National Stadium Complex, Surulere, Lagos
Tel: (01) 5850529, 5850530
E-mail: noc-ngr@hyperia.com

NIGERIAN ASSOCIATION OF SMALL & MEDIUM ENTERPRISES (NASME)
Address: BOI House (3rd Floor), 63/71, Broad Street, Lagos
Tel: (01) 2640682, 2665427 Fax: (01) 2648682
E-mail: nasme@nigerianet.com

NIGERIAN ASSOCIATION OF SMALL-SCALE INDUSTRIALISTS (NASSI)
Address: Lagos Small-Scale Industrial Estate, Fatai Atere Way, Matori, Mushin, Lagos
Tel: (01) 4522620

NIGERIAN CORPORATION OF INSURANCE BROKERS (NCIB)
Address: NCIB House, 58, Moleye Street, Alagomeji-Yaba, Lagos
Tel: (01) 4705633, 863021, 863459, 864079
Fax: (01) 864079
E-mail: ncib01@hotmail.com

NIGERIAN INSURERS ASSOCIATION (NIA)
Address: NIA House, 42, Saka Tinubu St, Victoria Island, Lagos
Tel: (01) 7743813, 616371 Fax: (01) 2631460
E-mail: nia@infoweb.abs.net

NIGERIAN ROAD FEDERATION
Address: 15, Awolowo Road, S.W., Ikoyi, Lagos
Tel: (01) 2600520 Fax: (01) 2630431

NIGERIAN SHIPPING COMPANIES ASSOCIATION
Address: 41, Itapeju Street, Apapa, Lagos
Tel: (01) 5870781, 5872916 Fax: (01) 5872916
E-mail: nscanig@linkserve.com

OUTDOOR ADVERTISING ASSOCIATION OF NIGERIA (OAAN)
Address: 1, Oyetola Idow Street, off Sura Mogaji Street, off Coker Street, Ilupeju, Lagos
Tel: (01) 4931916, 2880446
E-mail: oaan@infoweb.abs.net

NIGERIAN PROFESSIONAL/CHARTERED INSTITUTES, ASSOCIATIONS, SOCIETIES, REGISTRATION COUNCILS AND BOARDS:

ADVERTISING PRACTITIONERS COUNCIL OF NIGERIA
Address: APCON House, National Theatre Annex, Iganmu, Lagos
Tel: (01) 7733308
E-mail: apcon89@hotmail.com

ARCHITECTS REGISTRATION COUNCIL OF NIGERIA (ARCON)
Address: House 1A & B, Dolphin Housing Scheme, beh. Federal Secretariat Phase 11, Ikoyi, Lagos
Tel: (01) 2691476
E-mail: arcon@skannet.com

ASSOCIATION OF CONSULTING ENGINEERS OF NIGERIA (ACEN)
Address: Crusader House (5th Floor), 16A, Commercial Avenue, Sabo, Yaba, Lagos
Tel: (01) 77478910
E-mail: acen@acenigeria.org
Website: www.acenigeria.org

ASSOIATION OF GENERAL & PRIVATE MEDICAL PRACTITIONERS OF NIGERIA (AGPMPN)
Address: 9, Sam Shonibare Street, Lawanson, Surulere, Lagos
Tel: (01) 4701552
E-mail: info@agpmpn.org
Website: www.agpmpn

ASSOCIATON OF NATIONAL ACCOUNTANTS OF NIGERIA (ANAN)
Address: 248, Herbert Macaulay Street, Yaba, Lagos
Tel: (01) 863369, 863837, 866317

E-mail: ananorg@yahoo.com
Website: www.geocities.com/ananorg/ananpage.htm

ASSOCIATION OF RADIOGRAPHERS OF NIGERIA
Address: 2/4, Taylor Drive, Medical Compound, Yaba, Lagos

CHARTERED INSTITUTE OF ADMINISTRATION
Address: 4, Bode Thomas Street, Surulere, Lagos
Tel: (01) 5851395, 5851596, 5852240, 7740564
E-mail: cioa@linkserve.com

CHARTERED INSTITUTE OF ARBITRTORS (NIGERIA)
Address: 52, Upper Drive, Palmgroove Estate, off Ikorodu Road, Lagos
Tel/Fax: (01) 820885

CHARTERED INSTITUTE OF LOCAL GOVERNMENT & PUBLIC ADMINISTRATION OF NIGERIA
Address: 28, Kano Street, Ebute-Metta Lagos
Tel: (01) 8042788, 4926741 **Fax:** (01) 2645144

CHARTERED INSTITUTE OF MARKETING OF NIGERIA (CIMN)
Address: 1, Osinbajo Close, beh. 256, Ikorodu Road, Obanikoro, Lagos
Tel: (01) 4933671-2 (2 L) **Fax:** (01) 4933671
E-mail: cimnig@hotmail.com
cimnig@yahoo.com
Website: www.cimn.8m.com

CHARTERED INSTITUTE OF STOCKBROCKERS (CIS)
Address: Stock Exchange Building (Level 15), 2/4, Customs Street, Lagos Island, Lagos
Tel: (01) 2661049, 2663146, 2663921 **Fax:** (01) 2660986
E-mail: cis@nova.net.ng
Website: www.nigerianstockbrokers.com

CHARTERED INSTITUTE OF TAXATION OF NIGERIA
Address: Olabode House (4th Floor), 215/217, Ikorodu Road, Ilupeju, Lagos
Tel: (01) 4935054, 7741273 **Fax:** (01) 4935059
E-mail: citn@citn.org
Website: www.citn.org

CHARTERED INSURANCE INSTITUTE OF NIGERIA (CIIN)
Address: 27, Lagos Street, Ebute-Metta, Lagos
Tel: (01) 4705512, 5871453 **Fax:** (01) 4705512

COMPUTER PROFESSIONALS REGISTRATION COUNCIL OF NIGERIA
Address: 51, Norman Williams Street, S. W., Ikoyi, Lagos
Tel: (01) 2670823, 4805294, 7735186

COUNCIL FOR THE REGULATION OF ENGINEERING OF NIGERIA (COREN)
Address: Plot 466, Lobito Crescent off Adetokunbo Ademola Crescent, Wuse 11, Abuja
Tel: (09) 4130178, 4138891 **Fax:** (09) 4138891
* 29, Onikoyi Cresc, off Alexander Ave., Ikoyi, Lagos
Tel: (01) 2673476

COUNCIL OF LEGAL EDUCATION
Address: Bwari, Federal Capital Territory (F. C. T.)
Tel: (09) 8500694, 8500937, 8500956
E-mail: lawschoolorg@yahoo.co.uk

COUNCIL OF REGISTERED BUILDERS OF NIGERIA (CORBON)
Address: Eric Moore Towers Complex, Games Village, off Bode Thomas Street, Surulere, Lagos
Tel: (01) 2880503, 832742
E-mail: builderegistered@yahoo.com
corbonigeria@yahoo.com
* DAP Block 3 (1st Floor, Room 13), off NITEL Call Office, Area 3, Garki, Abuja
Tel: (09) 2341063

ESTATE SURVEYORS & VALUERS REGISTRATION BOARD OF NIGERIA (ESVARBON)
Address: Flats 2A & B, Old Dolphin Scheme, beh. Ikoyi Towers Formation, off Oba Adeyinka Oyekan Avenue, Ikoyi, Lagos
Tel: (01) 2880409, 688978
E-mail: esvarbon@infoweb.abs.net
* DAP Block B, Suite 15, off NITEL Call Office, Area 3, Garki, Abuja
Tel: (09) 2347541

INSTITUTE OF CHARTERED ACCOUNTANTS OF NIGERIA (ICAN)
Address: Plot PC 16, Idowu Taylor St, Victoria Island, Lagos
Tel: (01) 2614235, 2617638, 2622394 **Fax:** (01) 2610304
E-mail: info.ican@ican.org.ng
Website: www.ican.org.ng

INSTITUTE OF CHARTERED SECRETARIES & ADMINISTRATORS OF NIGERIA (ICSAN)
Address: Elephant Cement Way, by Elephant Cement Building, Central Business District, Alausa, Ikeja, Lagos
Tel: (01) 4967070, 4712396 **Fax:** (01) 4967070
E-mail: icsan@hyperia.net

INSTITUTE OF MEDICAL LABORATORY SCIENCE & TECHNOLOGY OF NIGERIA
Address: 8, Harvey Rd, off Herbert Macaulay Rd, Yaba, Lagos
Tel: (01) 863368, 5870565, 7745280 **Fax:** (01) 863368

INSTITUTE OF PERSONNEL MANAGEMENT OF NIGERIA (IPMN)
Address: IPM House, IPM Avenue, off Obafemi Awolowo Way, Central BusinessDistrict, Alausa, Ikeja, Lagos
Tel: (01) 4936547, 494779, 7736134-5 (2L)
E-mail: ipmn@nova.net.ng

MEDICAL & DENTAL COUNCIL OF NIGERIA (MDCN)
Address: Federal Secretariat, Phase 1 (8th Floor), Ikoyi, Lagos
Tel: (01) 680765, 680779, 680786 **Fax:** (01) 617667
E-mail: medcouncil@yahoo.com
* Plot 835, Block 3, Umuahia Close, off Emeka Anyaoku Street, Area 11, Garki, Abuja
Tel: (09) 2346538-9 (2 L)
* 6, North Road, Kaduna

NATIONAL ASSOCIATION OF AIRCRAFT PILOT & ENGINEERS (NAAPE)
Address: 2, Atinuke Olabanji Street, off Unity Rd, Ikeja, Lagos

Tel: (01) 4938485
E-mail: naape@hotmail.com

NIGERIAN ASSOCIATION OF GENERAL PRACTICE PHARMACISTS (NAGPP)
Address: 52A, Ikorodu Road, Fadeyi, Lagos
Tel/Fax: (01) 7747024

NIGERIAN BAR ASSOCIATION (NBA)
Address: Plot 121, Adeola Hopewell St, Victoria Island, Lagos
Tel: (01) 4618287, 4707432 **Fax:** (01) 4618287
E-mail: nba@intracom.net.ng
Website: www.nba.org.ng

NIGERIAN INSTITUTE OF ARCHITECTS (NIA)
Address: J. K. Randle Memorial Hall, 2, Island Club Road, opp. ECOWAS Lagos Office, Onikan, Lagos
Tel: (01) 2637483, 4706003
E-mail: niarc@skannet.com

NIGERIAN INSTITUTE OF BUILDING
Address: 45, Opebi Road, Ikeja, Lagos
Tel: (01) 4930411
E-mail: niob_nat@yahoo.com
Website: www.niobnat.org

NIGERIAN INSTITUTE OF INDUSTRIAL MANAGEMENT
Address: Industrial Management Centre, 8B, Onipinla Lane, off Adeniyi Jones Avenue, Ikeja, Lagos
Tel: (01) 4920560, 4926637
E-mail: niim@techemail.com
Website: www.niim-educ.org

NIGERIAN INSTITUTE OF JOURNALISM (NIJ)
Address: Lateef Jakande House, 8/14, Ijaiye Rd, Ogba, Lagos
Tel: (01) 4704648, 921031-2 (2L)

NIGERIAN INSTITUTE OF MANAGEMENT (NIM)
Address: Management House, Plot 22, Idowu Taylor Street, Victoria Island, Lagos
Tel: (01) 2615105, 216203, 4715504
E-mail: nim@rcl.ng.com
Website: www.nim-ng.org
* Plot 604, Lingu Crescent, off Aminu Kano Crescent, beh. ETB Centre & Iluobe Petrol Station, Wuse 11, Abuja
E-mail: nimabuja@yahoo.com
* 140, Aba-Owerri Road, Aba
Tel: (082) 232598
E-mail: nimeast@abianigpost

NIGERIAN INSTITUTE OF MARKETING (NIMARK)
Address: 25, Eric Moore Close, off Eric Moore Road, Surulere, Lagos
Tel: (01) 4701411

NIGERIAN INSTITUTE OF PUBLIC RELATIONS (NIPR)
Address: 39, Sobo Arobiodu Street, G.R.A., Ikeja, Lagos
Tel: (01) 4965213, 4975441, 4975443 **Fax:** (01) 4975444
Website: www.nipr.org

NIGERIAN INSTITUTE OF QUANTITY SURVEYORS (NIQS)
Address: Quantity Surveyors' Housre, 17/19, Idowu Taylor Street, Victoria Island, Lagos
Tel: (01) 4618723, 4701429, 616390
E-mail: niqs@infoweb,abs.net
Website: www.niqs.org

NIGERIAN INSTITUTION OF ESTATE SURVEYORS & VALUERS (NIESV)
Address: Flat 2B, Old Dolphin Scheme, beh. Federal Secretariat, Phase 11, off Adeyinka Oyekan Avenue, Ikoyi, Lagos
Tel: (01) 2673131, 2694435 **Fax:** (01) 2694314
E-mail: niesv@nova.net.ng
Website: www.niesv.org

NIGERIAN INSTITUTION OF SURVEYORS
Address: Plot PC 1, Engineering Close, off Idowu Taylor Street, Victoria Island, Lagos
Tel: (01) 615734
E-mail: nisng@yahoo.com
Website: www.nisng.org

NIGERIAN MEDICAL ASSOCIATION (NMA)
Address: 74, Adeniyi Jones Avenue, Ikeja, Lagos
Tel: (01) 4801569, 4936854 **Faz:** (01) 4936854
E-mail: nigerianma@hotmail.com
Website: www.nigerianma.org

NIGERIAN OPTOMETRIC ASSOCIATION
Address: 62, Bode Thomas Street, Surulere, Lagos
Tel: (01) 5455025

NIGERIAN SOCIETY OF CHEMICAL ENGINEERS
Address: 100, Oregun Road, Oregun, Ikeja, Lagos
Tel/Fax: (01) 4979615
E-mail: nsche@beta.linkserve.com

NIGERIAN SOCIETY OF ENGINEERS (NSE)
Address: 1, Engineering Close, off Idowu Taylor Street, Victoria Island, Lagos
Tel: (01) 2610743, 2617315, 2617349
Fax: (01) 2617315
E-mail: nsehq@infoweb.abs.net
nsehqr@linkserve.com
Website: www.nse.org
* 10, Damaturu Close, opp. 92, Third Avenue, Gwarimpa Fed. Min. of Housing Estate, Abuja

NURSING & MIDWIFERY COUNCIL OF NIGERIA
Address: Gwagwalada Specialist Hos[pital, Gwagwalada, F.C.T
* 6, Mobolaji Bank-Anthony Way, Maryland, Ikeja, Lagos
Tel: (01) 7746248

OPTOMETRISTS & DISPENSING OPTICIANS BOARD OF NIGERIA
Address: 2, Bode Thomas Street, Srlere, Lagos
Tel: (01) 5455025, 7742483 **Fax:** (01) 5455025
E-mail: odobnig@yahoo.com

PHARMACEUTICAL SOCIETY OF NIGERIA (PSN)
Address: 32, Faramobi Ajike Street, Anthony Village, Lagos
Tel: (01) 4701069
E-mail: psn1927@yahoo.com

PHARMACISTS COUNCIL OF NIGERIA (PCN)
Address: Medical Compound, off Edmund Crescent, off Murtala Mohammed Way, Yaba, Lagos
Tel: (01) 7740894
* Plot 8 & 9, Idu Industrial Area, Abuja

QUANTITY SURVEYORS REGISTRATION BOARD OF NIGERIA
Address: Plot 11, Yaounde Street, Wuse Zone 6, Abuja
Tel/Fax: (09) 5238870
* 147, Broad Street, Lagos

RADIOGRAPHERS REGISTRATION BOARD OF NIGERIA
Address: Federal Secretariat Complex (10th Floor), Ikoyi, Lagos

SOCIETY OF PETROLEUM ENGINEERS (SPE) (Nigeria Council)
Address: NOA Building, 4, Moscow Road, opp. Port Harcourt L.G. Office, Port Harcourt
Tel: (084) 231138
* 47A, Femi Okunnu Estate, Lekki Peninsula, Lagos

SURVEYORS COUNCIL OF NIGERIA (SURCON)
Address: Ilubinrin/Olowu Bus-Stop, by Third Mainland Bridge, near Obalende, Lagos
Tel: (01) 2634528
* Block 3 (1st Floor, Suite 14), Urban Mass Building, Area 3, Garki, Abuja

TEACHERS REGISTRATION COUNCIL OF NIGERIA
Address: Plot 567, Aminu Kano Crescent, Wuse 11, Abuja
Tel: (09) 5231439, 5239206 **Fax:** (09) 5238072

VETERINARY COUNCIL OF NIGERIA
Address: Plot 434, Zambezi Crescent, off Aguiyi Ironsi Street, Maitama Distrct, Abuja
Tel: (09) 4132253- 4 (2 L), 4135975 **Fax:** (09) 4132253
* Vet Council Building, beh. Nat. Veterinary Research Institute (NVRI), Vom, Plateau State

INTERNATIONAL AGENCIES & ORGANISATIONS IN NIGERIA:

A.U. SCIENTIFIC, TECHNICAL & RESEARCH COMMISSION
Address: NPA Building, 26/28, Marina, Lagos
Tel: (01) 2633289, 2633359, 2633430

AFRICAN IRON & STEEL ASSOCIATION (AISA)
Address: 19B, Sez Crescent, Ibrahim Abacha Estate, off Ladi Kwali Way, Wuse Zone 4, Abuja
Tel: (09) 5232135, 5233170 **Fax:** (09) 5233275
E-mail: afristeel@yahoo.com

AFRICAN REGIONAL CENTRE FOR ENGINEERING DESIGN & MANUFACTURING (ARCEDEM)
Address: Km. 9, Ibadan-Iwo Road, Wofun Village, Ibadan
Tel: (02) 2411972, 2413746, 8101124 **Fax:** (02) 8101124

AFRICAN REGIONAL CENTRE FOR SPACE SCIENCE & TECHNOLOGY EDUCATION (English)
Address: Obafemi Awolowo University, Ile-Ife
Tel: (036) 231893

AFRICAN REINSURANCE CORPORATION (Africa-Re)
Address: Africa-Re House (8th Floor), Plot 1679, Karimu Ikotun Street, Victoria Island, Lagos
Tel: (01) 2626660-2 (3L), 2663323
Fax: (01) 2626664, 2663282
E-mail: info@africa-re.com
Website: www.africa-re.com

ALLIANCE FRANCAISE, LAGOS
Address: 2,Aromire Road, off Alfred Rewane Road, opp. Ikoyi Hotel, Ikoyi, Lagos
Tel: (01) 2692035, 269235 **Fax:** (01) 2694181
E-mail: alliancelagos@maisondefrance-ng.com
Website: www.maisondefrance-ng.com

COCOA PRODUCERS ALLIANCE
Address: Western House (11th Floor), 8/10 Broad Street, Lagos
Tel: (01) 2630210, 2635574 **Fax:** (01) 2635684
E-mail: copal@alpha.linkserve.com

DELEGATION OF GERMAN INDUSTRY & COMMERCE FOR WEST AFRICA
Address: 6F, Walter Carrington Crescent, Victoria Island, Lagos
Tel: (01) 2619751-2 (2 L), 2626165
Fax: (01) 2619752
E-mail: ahk_info@nova.net.ng
Website: www.ahk_los_ng.de

ECONOMIC COMMUNITY WEST AFRICA STATES (ECOWAS)
Address: ECOWAS Secretariat & Conference Centre, 60, Yakubu Gowon Crescent, Asokoro District, Abuja
Tel: (09) 3147641, 3147427-9 (3 L), 3147647-9 (3 L)
Fax: (09) 3143005, 3147646
E-mail: info@ecowas.int
Website: www.ecowas.int
* 6, Island Club Road, Onikan, Lagos
Tel: (01) 2600720-9 (10 L), 2635975
Fax: (01) 2636822, 2637052

FOOD & AGRICULTURE ORGANISATION OF THE UNITED NATIONS (FAO)
Address: 3, Oguda Close, off Lake Chad Crescent, Maitama District, Abuja
Tel: (09) 4137546-7 (2 L)
Fax: (09) 4137544
E-mail: fao-nga@field.fao.org

GERMAN AGENCY FOR TECHNICAL CO-OPERATION (GTZ)
Address: Plot 954A, Idejo Street, Victoria Island, Lagos
Tel: (01) 3200750, 613570, 613574, 618542
Fax: (01) 3200750, 613570, 618542
E-mail: gtzlagos@infoweb.abs.net

GOETHE-INSTITUT, GERMAN CULTURAL CENTRE, LAGOS
Address: 10, Ozumba Mbadiwe Street, opp. 1004 Estate, Victoria Island, Lagos
Tel: (01) 2610717, 7746888 **Fax:** (01) 2617916
E-mail: gilagsek@infoweb.abs.net

INTERNATIONAL CIVIL AVIATION ORGANISATION
Address: Nigerian College of Aviation Technology, Zaria
Tel: (069) 332021-2 (2L)

INTERNATIONAL COMMITTEE OF THE RED CROSS (ICRC)
Address: 11, Eko Akete Close, off St. Gregory's Road, by The Police Women Barracks, Obalende, Lagos
Tel: (01) 2690082, 2691881 **Fax:** (01) 2692425
E-mail: redcross@infoweb.abs.net

INTERNATIONAL INSTITUTE OF TROPICAL AGRICULTURE (IITA)
Address: Oyo Road, Idi-Ose, Ibadan
Tel: (02) 2412626 **Fax:** (02) 2412221
E-mail: iita@cgiar.org
Website: www.iita.org
* IITA Kano Station, Sabo Bakin Zuwo Road, Kano
Tel: (064) 624046, 645350, 645351, 645353
Fax: (064) 645352
E-mail: iita-kano@cgiar.org
* IITA High Rainfall Station, Onne, Port Harcourt

INTERNATIONAL LABOUR ORGANISATION (ILO) (UNITED NATIONS)
Address: Glass House (5th Floor), 188, Awolowo Road, S. W., Ikoyi, Lagos
Tel: (01) 2693916-7 (2 L) **Fax:** (01) 2690717
E-mail: lagos@ilo.org

INTERNATIONAL LIVESTOCK RESEARCH INSTITUTE (ILRI)
Address: IITA Compound, Oyo Road, Idi-Ose, Ibadan
Tel: (02) 2412626 **Fax:** (02) 2412221, 2412974
E-mail: ilri-ibadan@cgiar.org
Website: www.ilri.org

INTERNATIONAL ORGANISATION FOR MIGRATION (UNITED NATIONS)
Address: United Nations Compound, 11, Oyinkan Abayomi Drive, Ikoyi, Lagos
Tel: (01) 2692006 **Fax:** (01) 2690885
Website: www.iom.com

JAPAN EXTERNAL TRADE ORGANISATION (JETRO)
Address: 4A, Kofo Abayomi Street, Victoria Island, Lagos
Tel: (01) 2613751, 615777
E-mail: jetrola@micro.com.ng

JAPAN INTERNATIONAL CO-OPERATION AGENCY
Address: AP Plaza, Plot 1074, Adetokunbo Ademola Crescent, Wuse 11, Abuja
Tel: (09) 5232869 **Fax:** (09) 5235431

PAN-AFRICAN ASSOCIATION FOR CO-OPERATION (PAPC)
Address: 12, Park Lane, Apapa, Lagos
Tel: (01) 5874108, 5877977, 7737609
Fax: (01) 5874108
E-mail: papc@afriports.org
pmpawca@infoweb.abs.net
Website: www.afriports.org

PAN AFRICAN NEWS AGENCY (PANA)
Address: Block A (9th Floor, Flat 16), Eko Court, Kofo Abayomi Street, Victoria Island, Lagos
Tel: (01) 7744373
E-mail: panafrican@hyperia.com
Website: www.panapress.com

PORT MANAGEMT ASSOC. OF WEST & CENTRAL AFRICA
Address: 12, Park Lane, Apapa, Lagos
Tel: (01) 5874108, 5877978, 7737609 **Fax:** (01) 5874108
E-mail: secgen@pmawca-agpaoc.org
pmawca@infoweb.abs.net
Website: www.pmawca-agpaoc.org

REGIONAL CENTRE FOR TRAINING IN AEROSPACE SURVEYS (UNITED NATIONS ECONOMIC COMMISSION FOR AFRICA)
Address: Obafemi Awolowo University, Ile-Ife
Tel: (036) 230050, 230225 **Fax:** (036) 230481
E-mail: rectas@oauife.edu.ng
Website: www.uneca.org/rectas

REGIONAL PROGRAMME FOR TECHNOLGY MANAGEMENT (REPTEM)
Address: 32-38, Barikisu Iyede Street, off Unilag Road, Onitiri-Yaba, Lagos
Tel: (01) 861929, 7744896 **Fax:** (01) 862059

SOCIETY FOR FAMILY HEALTH (SFH)
Address: PlOT 2380, Manka Close, beh. Heritage House, off Sultan Abubakar Way, Wuse Zone 3, Abuja
Tel: (09) 6702969
E-mail: info@sfhnigeria.com
* Awaye House (2nd Floor, Suites 5 & 6), Lagos-Badagry Expressway (Coker Bus-Stop), Orile Iganmu, Lagos
Tel: (01) 7730508-9 (2 L), 7742745, 7744522, 7747045
Fax: (01) 7742745
* Dan'amarya House, 12, Maiduguri Road, Hotoro G. R. A., Kano
Tel: (064) 644298

THE BRITISH COUNCIL (NIGERIA)
Address: Plot 2935, Ibrahim Badamosi Babangida Way, Maitma District, Abuja
Tel: (09) 4137870-7 (8 L) **Fax:** (09) 4130902
E-mail: abuja.info@ng.britishcouncil.org
Website: www.britishcouncil.org/nigeria
* 11, Alfred Rewane (Kingsway) Road, Ikoyi, Lagos
Tel: (01) 2615047, 2692188-92 (5 L) **Fax:** (01) 2692193
* 10, Emir's Palace Road, Kano
Tel: (064) 636620, 643489, 643861, 646652
Fax: (064) 632500
E-mail: kano.info@ng.britishcouncil.org
* The British High Commission (Information Centre), Plot 300, Olusegun Obasanjo Way, G. R. A., Phase 11, Port Harcourt
Tel: (084) 237173, 231776 **Fax:** (084) 237172
E-mail: portharcourt.info@ng.britishcouncil.org

THE FORD FOUNDATION OFFICE FOR WEST AFRICA
Address: AIB Plaza (Level 6), Akin Adesola Street, Victoria Island, Lagos
Tel: (01) 2623971-2 (2L)
E-mail: ford-lagos@fordfound.org

THE WEST AFRICAN EXAMINATION COUNCIL
Address: 21, Hussey Street, Yaba, Lagos
Tel: (01) 5453910, 800190-7 (8 L) **Fax:** (01) 5453911
* Test Development Division, Ijaiye Road, Ogba,

Ikeja, Lagos
Tel: (01) 4924106, 4924266

THE WORLD BANK GROUP (NIGERIA COUNTRY OFFICE)
Address: Plot 433, Yakubu Gowon Crescent, opp. ECOWAS Secretariat, Asokoro District, Abuja
Tel: (09) 3145269-74 (6 L) **Fax:** (09) 3145267-8 (2 L)
E-mail: iabuja@worldbank.org
Website: www.worldbank.org
www.worldbank.org/afr/nigeria

TRADE MISSION OF THE ROC (TAIWAN) IN NIGERIA)
Address: Plot 3175, Katsina-Ala Street, Cadastral Zone 6, off Yedseram Street, off IBB Way, Maitama, Abuja
Tel: (09) 4138321-2 (2 L) **Fax:** (09) 4138326
E-mail: rocvis@beta.linkserve.com

TRADE REPRESENTATION OF THE RUSSIAN FEDERATION IN NIGERIA
Address: Plots 5-8, Molade Okoya-Thomas Street, off Younis Bashorun Street, Victoria Island, Lagos
Tel: (01) 612024, 615977, 617119 **Fax:** (01) 618790

UNITED NATIONS CHILDREN FUND (UNICEF)
Address: 30, Oyekan Abayomi Drive, Ikoyi, Lagos
Tel: (01) 2690276-80 (5 L) **Fax:** (01) 2690276
* 14B, Lugard Avenue, off Alfred Rewane (Kingsway) Road, Ikoyi, Lagos
* 53, Yakubu Avenue, G. R. A., Kaduna
Tel: (062) 240114-5 (2 L), 244243, 246346
Fax: (062) 244694

UNITED NATIONS DEVELOPMENT FUND FOR WOMEN (Anglophone West Africa)
Address: 11, Oyekan Abayomi Drive, Ikoyi, Lagos
Tel: (01) 2692006 **Fax:** (01) 2690885
E-mail: unifem.staff@undp.org

UNITED NATIONS DEVELOPMENT PROGRAMME (UNDP)
Address: 11, Oyekan Abayomi Drive, Ikoyi, Lagos
Tel: (01) 2692141-3 (3 L) **Fax:** (01) 2691746
E-mail: registry.ng@undp.org
Website: www.undp.org.ng
* Co-operative Bank Building, Plot 2789, Aguiyi Ironsi Street, Maitama District, Abuja
Tel: (09) 4132088-90 (3L) **Fax:** (09) 4132110

UNITED NATIONS EDCATIONAL, SCIENTIFIC & CULTURAL ORGANISATION (UNESCO)
Address: Plot 777, Bouake Street, off Rabat Street, Wuse Zone 6, Abuja
Tel: (09) 5237088 **Fax:** (09) 5238094
E-mail: abuja@unesco.org

UNITED NATIONS HIGH COMMISSION FOR REGUGEES (UNHCR)
Address: 13, Awolowo Road, Ikoyi, Lagos
Tel: (01) 2693298 **Fax:** (09) 2692745
E-mail: nigla@unhcr.ch

UNITED NATIONS INDUSTRIAL DEVELOPMENT ORGANISATION (UNIDO)
Address: 11, Oyekan Abayomi Drive, Ikoyi, Lagos
Tel: (01) 2692141-3 (3 L), 2692707
Fax: (01) 2691746, 2692707
Website: www.unido.org

UNITED NATIONS INFORMATION CENTRE
Address: 17, Alfred Rewane (Kingsway) Road, Ikoyi, Lagos
Tel: (01) 2693758, 2694886 **Fax:** (01) 2691934
E-mail: uniclag@unicnig.org

UNITED NATIONS OFFICE FOR DRUG CONTROL & CRIME PREVENTION (ODCCP)
Address: 11, Oyekan Abayomi Drive, Ikoyi, Lagos
Tel: (01) 2692141-3 (3 L) **Fax:** (01) 2696281
E-mail: undcpstaff.ng@undp.org
Website: www.undcp.org/adhoc/nigeria

UNITED NATIONS POPULATION FUND (UNFPA)
Address: 11, Oyekan Abayomi Drive, Ikoyi, Lagos
Tel: (01) 2692141-3 (3 L), 2693108
Fax: (01) 2690531
Website: www.unfpa.org

UNITED STATES AGENCY FOR INTERNATIONAL DEVELOPMENT (USAID/Nigeria)
Address: Metro Plaza (3rd Floor), Zakari Maimalari Street, opp. National War College, Central Business District, Abuja
Tel: (09) 4138374-7 (4 L), 2342175, 2342189, 2342364, 2343048, 3143185, 6702215
Fax: (09) 2342930
* 18A/B, Temple Road, off Alfred Rewane (Kingsway) Road, Ikoyi, Lagos
TeL: (01) 2600020, 2600023, 2670359, 2670363, 3205271
Fax: (01) 2600023

WEST AFRICAN BANKERS ASSOCIATION (Nigeria Chapter)
Address: c/o Banking Spervision Department, Central Bank of Nigeria, Tinubu Square, Lagos
Tel: (01) 2640794, 2660908, 2660915, 2660925 (Ext. 22166)
Fax: (01) 2640794
E-mail: wabanigeria@yahoo.com

WEST AFRICAN MANAGEMENT DEVELOPMENT INSTITUTES NETWORK (WAMDEVIN)
Address: c/o Adminstrative Staff College of Nigeria (ASCON), Topo-Badagry, Lagos State
Tel: (01) 732292, 7737054 **Fax:** (01) 732415

WEST AFRICAN POSTGRADUATE MEDICAL COLLEGE (WAPMC)
Address: 6, Taylor Drive, Medical Compound, off Edmund Crescent, Yaba, Lagos
Tel: (01) 4710872, 861313, 862324
Fax: (01) 862324
E-mail: wapmc-lagos@yahoo.com

WORLD HEALTH ORGANISATION (WHO) (Nigerian Representation)
Address: 443, Herbert Macaulay Road, Yaba, Lagos
Tel: (01) 5453662-3 (2 L), 7737092-3 (2 L)
E-mail: admin@who-nigeria.org
Website: www.who-nigeria.org

WORLD TRADE CENTRE OF NIGERIA LTD/Gte
Address: Western House (8th Floor), 8/10, Broad Street, Lagos
Tel: (01) 2635276, 2647279 **Fax:** (01) 2647279
E-mail: wtcn@metrong.com

BILATERAL ASSOCIATIONS & CHAMBERS OF COMMERCE

FRANCO - NIGERIAN CHAMBER OF COMMERCE & INDUSTRY (FNCCI)
Address: E. P. N. L. Building (3rd Floor), 35, Kofo Abayomi Street, Victoria Island, Lagos
Tel: (01) 2621423-4 (2 L) **Fax:** (01) 2621422
E-mail: fncci@nova.net.ng
Website: www.ccife.org/nigeria

NIGERIA - ASEAN CHAMBER OF COMMERCE
Address: Block B (Suite), Falomo Shopping Complex, Falomo, Ikoyi, Lagos
Tel/Fax: (01) 2690428

NIGERIA - BRITAIN ASSOCIATION
Address: c/o British Council, 11, Alfred Rewane (Kingsway) Road, Ikoyi, Lagos
Tel: (01) 4811161

NIGERIA - JAPAN ASSOCIATION
Address: Ebani House, 149/153, Broad Street, Lagos
Tel: (01) 2661744, 2668552 **Fax:** (01) 2660830
E-mail: nigeria-japanasso@yahoo.co.uk

NIGERIAN - AMERICAN CHAMBER OF COMMERCE (NACC)
Address: I, Alfred Rewane (Kingsway) Road, Ikoyi, Lagos
Tel: (01) 2692088, 2693041
E-mail: nacc@alpha.linkserve.com

NIGERIAN - BELGIAN CHAMBER OF COMMERCE
Address: 23, Sinari Daranijo Street, off Younis Bashorun Street, off Ajose Adeogun Street, Victoria Island, Lagos
Tel: (01) 7743650
E-mail: nigbel@mailcity.com

NIGERIAN - BELGIAN COMMERCIAL INFORMATION & DOCUMENTATION CENTRE (NBCIDC)
Address: Plot 276, Ajose Adeogun St, Victoria Island, Lagos
Tel: (01) 2623045, 4705034 **Fax:** (01) 2611672
E-mail: nbcidc@hyperia.com

NIGERIAN - BRAZILIAN CHAMBER OF COMMERCE
Address: Western House (6th Floor), 8/10, Broad Street, Lagos
Tel: (01) 2665757 **Fax:** (01) 2660957
E-mail: nigbrazchambers@hyperia.net

NIGERIAN - BRITISH CHAMBER OF COMMERCE (NBCC)
Address: Ebani House (Ground Floor), 149/153, Broad Street, Lagos
Tel: (01) 2641266, 2660298 **Fax:** (01) 2660298
E-mail: nbcc@infoweb.abs.net
Website: www.n-bcc.org.uk

NIGERIAN - DANISH CHAMBER OF COMMERCE
Address: 16, Aerodrome Road, off Wharf Road, Apapa, Lagos
Tel: (01) 5875952, 7747160 **Fax:** (01) 5875952
E-mail: chamberdanig@netsape.net

NIGERIAN - GERMAN CHAMBER OF COMMERCE
Address: 22,Musa Yar'adua Crescent, off Idowu Martins Street, Victoria Island, Lagos
Tel: (01) (01) 2623984-5 (2 L) **Fax:** (01) 5875952
E-mail: ngbc@linkserve.com

NIGERIAN - HUNGARIAN CHAMBER OF COMMERCE
Address: 190, Ikorodu Road, Onipanu, Lagos
Tel: (01) 2880241, 820171 **Fax:** (01) 2880241
E-mail: nhci@yahoo.com
nhcci@hotmail.com

NIGERIAN - IVIORIEN CHAMBER OF COMMERCE
Address: Prince's Court (Suite 2A), Ahmed Onibudo Street, Victoria Island, Lagos
Tel: (01) 2622571 **Fax:** (01) 2621588
E-mail: nigeriancommerce@yahoo.com

NIGERIAN - KOREAN FRIENDSHIP ASSOCIATION
Address: Kajola House (5th Floor), 62/64, Campbell Street, Lagos
Tel: (01) 2635401, 2635714

NIGERIAN - NETHERLANDS CHAMBER OF COMMERCE
Address: Regency Suites (Suite 204), 17, Ahmed Onibudo Street, Victoria Island, Lagos
Tel/Fax: (01) 614619
E-mail: nncc78@yahoo.co.uk

NIGERIAN - NORDIC CHAMBER OF COMMERCE
Address: McIver House (Suite 13), 61, Marina, Lagos
Tel: (01) 2621539 **Fax:** (01) 2621542
E-mail: nncia@marina.nigpost.com

NIGERIAN - SOUTH AFRICAN CHAMBER OF COMMERCE
Address: 24, Norman Williams Street, S. W., Ikoyi, Lagos
Tel: (01) 4811529, 684685 **Fax:** (01) 684685
E-mail: n_sacc@yahoo.com
n_sacc@linkserve.com
Website: www.n_sacc.org

A & C INTERNATIONAL SERVICES LIMITED
Business: Building Materials & Sanitary Wares Imporation
Address: 46, Burma Road, Apapa, Lagos
Tel: (01) 5455477-8 (2L) **Fax:** (01) 5871025
* Block 5 (Shop 14/15), Agric. Market, Badagry Expressway, Coker, Orile, Lagos
Tel: (01) 7743485
Contact: Arc. Chiedozie Udeze - MD/CEO

A & H INDUSTRIES LIMITED
Business: Paper Converters;Tissue Paper Manufacture
Address: Plot 100, Sharanda Ind. Estate, Phase II Kano
Tel: (064) 640630, 633960, 637383, 660001
Fax: (064) 640080
Contact: Alhaji A. P. Hamoud - MD/CEO

A - Z COMPUTER WORLD LIMITED
Business: Computer Sales,Repairs and Training Software Development, Networking and Data Security
Address: 32, Ezekiel Street, P.O.Box 2428, Ikeja, Lagos
Tel: (01) 4931465
Contact: Mr O. A. Edu - CEO.

A - Z PETROLEUM PRODUCTS LIMITED
Business: Blending & Marketing of Lubricants, Oil Servicing
Address: Intercontinental Plaza (2nd Floor), Plot 999C, Danmole Street,off Idejo St, Victoria Island, Lagos
Tel: (01) 613465, 617714, 2622993, 4815985
Fax: (01) 2622983
E-mail: chicason@infoweb.abs.net
* Akwuru Industrial Estate, Umudim, Nnewi
Tel: (046) 460173, 460648, 462913-7 (5L)
(046) 460972, 462929
Contact: Chief (Sir) Alexander C. Okafor - Chairman/CEO

A DIFFERENT WORLD LIMITED
Business: Baby and Mothercare Items Stores
Address: 65A Opebi Road, Ikeja, Lagos.
Tel/Fax: (01) 4936023
Contact: Mrs Omolewa Ogunlesi - MD/CEO

A. IDRIS & COMPANY
Business: Estate Surveyors and Valuers, Property Managers
Address: 20A Bank Road, Kaduna
Tel: (062) 211300

A. A. MAITANGARAN & SONS LIMITED
Business: Marketing of Textile Materials, Bureau de Change
Address: Maitangaran Shopping Complex, 4, Fagge Ta Kudu Road, Kano
Tel: (064) 634962, 646806
E-mail: aamaitan@hotmail.com
Contact: Alhaji Rabiu Ali - MD/CEO

A. A. MUDALLABI ABDULLAHI & SONS LIMITED
Business: Trading, Manufacturing of Plastic Containers and Wares, Vegetable Oil Extraction.
Address: 29E Ado Bayero Road, Kano
Tel: (064) 649140, 645766, 634467, 635484, 08044120562
Fax: (064) 635483
* Plot 13, Sharada Industrial Estate, Kano
* 1, Zango Road, Dakata, Kano
Contact: Alhaji Abdulmudallabi Abdullahi - Chairman/CEO

A. A. PAPER & STATIONERY COMPANY LIMITED
Business: Importation, Sales and Distribution of Paper Cards, Boards and Stationeries
Address: A.A Plaza, 4, Araromi Street (Okesuna Bus-Stop), Shomolu, Lagos
Tel: (01) 4971726, 5820629 **Fax:** (01) 4971726
* Local Government Shop 4, Watch Tower, Shomolu, Lagos
Tel: (01) 4705322, 4972715, 5820629
Contact: Mr. S. A. Adekoya - Chairman/CEO

A. A. A. STOCKBROKERS LIMITED
Business: Stockbroking
Address: Gidan Niger, 3A Ahmadu Bello way/Yakubu Gowon Way P.M.B 2414, Kaduna
Tel/Fax: (062) 247106, 08033204803
* Tofa House (3rd Floor), Plot 770, Central Business District, Abuja
Tel: (09) 5235193, 08033112686 **Fax:** (09) 5235184
* West Pavillion, Entrance 5 (1st Floor), Suite 28/35B, Tafawa Balewa Square Complex, Lagos
Tel: (01) 2630107, 08033045928
Contact: Mr. Jacob C. Kaduma - MD/CEO

A. B. ALHASSAN CO. (INSURANCE BROKERS) LIMITED
Business: Insurance Brokers
Address: 38, Beirut Road, Kano
Tel: (064) 639019, 08033146960
E-mail: abalhassan@ecnx.net
Contact: Alh. A. B. Alhassn - Chairman/CEO

A. B CHAMI & COMPANY LIMITED
Business: Perfumery and General Merchants
Address: Plot PL 628, Industrial Layout, Old Airport Road, Jos
Tel: (073) 464624, 464739, 463075
Fax: (073) 460525, 461379, 453720
E-mail: ybchami@chamigroup.com; abc.co.ltd@chamigroup.com
* opp Monday Market Street, Maiduguri
Contact: Mr. Ali Yahya Barakat Chami - MD/CEO

A. B. MANU LIMITED
Business: Transportation; Road Haulage Services
Address: 18, Iju Road Agege, Lagos
Tel: (01) 4920553
Contact: Alh. A. Baba Manu - Chairman/CEO.

A. C. OKOCHA MOTORS LIMITED
Business: Sales and Distribution. Servicing of Automobiles.
Address: 61, Rasaq Balogun Street, Western Avenue (Alaka Bus-Stop), Surulere, Lagos
Tel: (01) 5850026-7 (2 L) 5844774
Fax: (01) 5844774
* 4/5 (Plot 796) Ahmadu Bello Way, opposite Funmilayo Ransome Kuti Road, Garki, Abuja
Tel: (09) 2348712-6 (5L) **Fax:** (09) 2348714
Contact: Chief Andrew C. Okocha JP - Chairman/CEO

A. C. M. OF NIGERIA LIMITED
Business: Oil Industry and General Engineering Services
Address: Plot 177-180, Trans - Amadi Ind. Layout, Port Harcourt
Tel: (084) 331563, 334198, 335051
Contact: Mrs. Biodun Ojutalayo - MD/CEO

A. G LEVENTIS (NIGERIA) PLC
Business: Conglomerate - Sales & Service of Commercial/ Passenger Vehicles, Motorcycles, Agricultural & Construction Equipment, and Industrial Machinery; Real Estate & Property Development/Management; Investment.
Address: Iddo House, Iddo, Lagos
Tel: (01) 7740844, 7747602, 7748339
Fax: (01) 7748073
Contact: Dr. S. Constantinidis - MD/CEO

A. G. FERRERO COMPANY LIMITED
Business: Building and Civil Engineering Contractors
Address: Plot E, Makera Road, Kaduna South, Kaduna
Tel: (062) 232676, 231812 **Fax:** (062) 234760
* Plot 419, Lobito Crescent, off Adetokunbo Ademola Crescent, Wuse 11, Abuja
Tel: (09) 4135872 **Fax:** (09) 4136621
* Plot 3A, Tukur Road, Nassarawa, Kano
Tel: (064) 646194 **Fax:** (064) 648046

A. G. SANGOSANYA & COMPANY
Business: Estate Surveyors and Valuers, Real Estate Consultancy and Project Management.
Address: Alphon House (3rd Floor Suite), 50/52 Toyin Street, Ikeja, Lagos
Tel: (01) 4937312, 4937295
Contact: Mr A. G. Sangosanya - Managing Partner

A. G. S BARMA LIMITED
Business: Transportation - Road Haulage; General Contractors. Auto Repairs.
Address: Plot 20, Block M, Ilasamaja Industrial Scheme Oshodi-Apapa Expressway, Lagos
Tel: (01) 4520432, 4521876, 7743903
Fax: (01) 4520432, 7743903
E-mail: agsbarma@infoweb.abs.net
* 4, Balogun Square, Lagos
Tel: (01) 2662168 **Fax:** (01) 4520432
Contact: Dr. S. A. Barma - Chairman/CEO

A. J. K NIGERIA LIMITED
Business: Transportation - Road Haulage Services
Address: 99, Tafawa Balewa Road, P.O.Box 1055, Kano
Tel: (064) 642243 **Fax:** (064) 646649
Contact: Mr A. J. Harriott - MD/CEO

A. M. H. ENTERPRISES LIMITED
Business: Sales of Welding Machines & Electrodes, Carboline Paints and other Industrial Consumables
Address: Plot 110, Trans-Amadi Ind.Layout, Port Harcout
Tel: (084) 231493, 232395 **Fax:** (084) 235675
E-mail: amh@phca.linkserve.com
Contact: Mr T. A. Habib - MD/CEO

A. N. EJEAGWU & SONS IMITED
Business: Manufacturing and Marketing of Toilet Rolls, Jumbo Reels and Paper Napkins.
Address: Plot 1N/61, Harbour Industrial Layout, Onitsha.
Tel: (046) 411951
* 109, Upper Iweka Road, Onitsha
Tel: (046) 413881
Contact: Chief (Dr) A. N. Ejeagwu - MD/CEO

A. S. A. NAGERO & SONS LIMITED
Business: Haulages Services
Address: C3, Naibawa Zaria Road, Kano
Tel: (064) 662555, 666845
Contact: Alh. Sale Ali Nagero - MD/CEO

A.V. I. SERVICES LIMITED
Business: Car Hire Services, Gift Shops.
Address: Sheraton Lagos Hotel Annex, Opebi Link Road, off Mobolaji Bank Anthony Way, Ikeja Lagos
Tel: (01) 4978660-9 (10L) Ext 8715 & 8019
Fax: (01) 4970321-2 (2 L)
Contact: Mrs E. Ibru - MD/CEO
Mr. O. Urhiafe - GM

A. Y. COMPUTER NETWORK LIMITED
Business: Sales & Service of Computers and Accessories
Address: Plot 915, Monrovia Street, off Aminu Kano Crescent, Wuse 11, Abuja
Tel: (09) 4133768-9 (2L) **Fax:** (09) 4133769
Contact: Aih. A. Y. Gombe - Chairman/CEO

AADE INDUSTRIAL & INVESTMENTS COMPANY LIMITED
Business: Sales, of Generators, Industrial Chemicals, Printing Paper and General Merchandise.
Address: Km 16, 385, Ikorodu Road, opp. Ojota New Motor Park, Ojota Lagos
Tel: (01) 4973785-6 (2L), 4977537, 2880505, 715461, 08023077677, 08023077679, 08023077680
Fax: (01) 4973786, 4974667, 4977839
E-mail: aasisgrp@alpha.linkserve.com
Contact: Mr. O. A. Adesanya - GM/CEO

AB JOSEF INTERNATIONAL & COMPANY LIMITED
Business: Engineering Services, Procurement, General Contractors
Address: Plot 20 East-West Road, off Oil Mill Market, Rumuokurushi, Port-Harcout
Tel/Fax: (084) 611891
E-mail: abjosef@phca.linkserve.com

AB PETERS (NIGERIA) LIMITED
Business: Building, Civil, Electrical and Mechanical and Air Conditioning/Refrigeration Engineers
Address: BD 17T, Bwandang Gyel, Bukuru-Rayfield Rd, Jos
Tel: (073) 280608, 280345 **Fax:** (073) 453291

AB TECHNOLOGIES (NIGERIA) LIMITED
Business: Computer Systems Consultancy Services, Procurement, Maintenance and Corporate Tranining Services, Systems Development and Evaluation.
Address: 33 Saji Ayangade Street, Anthony Village, Lagos
Tel: (01) 4975617 **Fax:** (01) 4974052
E-mail: abtech@hyperia.com
Contact: Mr Osmond Van Martey - Director/GM

ABA TEXTILE MILLS PLC
Business: Manufacturing of African Fancy Print Clothes
Address: Industrial Layout, Aba, Abia State
Tel: (082) 220607, 220711 **Fax:** (082) 220522
* 10A, Oba Nle-Aro Avenue, Ilupeju, Lagos
* Churchgate Tower, Afribank Street, Victoria Island, Lagos.
Tel: (01) 2620480-4 (5 L)

E-mail: agroy@churchgate.com
Contact: Mr. P. Sengupta - GM.

ABB ELECTRICAL SYSTEMS LIMITED
Business: Engineering, Design, Manufacturing, Supply, Installation, Commissioning & After-Sales Service of Low Voltage (LV) & Medium Voltage (MV) Switchgears, Feeders Pillars & Electrical Panels
Address: 46, Industrial Avenue, Ilupeju Ind. Estate, Lagos.
Tel: (01) 4932858, 4934023-4 (2L), 4937347
Fax: (01) 4932859, 4937329, 5875100
E-mail: abbng@abb.com.ng
Website: www.abb.com/ng
* Total Building (1st Floor) Herbert Macaulay Way, Central Area, Abuja
Tel: (09) 2346796, 2346797, 2346808 -3 **Fax:** (09) 2340047
* ABB Camp, Awkunanaw, Enugu.
Tel: (042) 451604
Contact: Mr. W. Pfeiffer - MD/CEO

ABB LUMMUS GLOBAL NIGERIA LIMITED
Business: Oil Industry Services and Consultancy
Address: Consortium House (5th Floor), Plot 1682, Sanusi Fafunwa Street, Victoria Island, Lagos
Tel: (01) 2624159, 2624160, 2624161 **Fax:** (01) 2624162

ABB POWERLINES LIMITED
Business: Design, Supply & Construction of Overhead Transmission Lines (33KV -400KV), Radio/ Telecommunication and GSM Installation Engineering, Roofing, Water Engineering
Address: 1, Awosika Street, off Oba Akran Avenue, Ikeja Industrial Area, Ikeja, Lagos
Tel: (01) 4972301, 4973014 **Fax:** (01) 4972301
Website: www.abb.com/ng

ABBNG LIMITED
Business: Design, Supply, Engineering & After Sales Technical Support of 132KV Transmission Lines, Substations, 33KV Outdoor Switchyards and 11KV Rural Electrification; Assembly of Switchgears/Feeder Pillars; Powerline Carier Network Engineering; Oil, Gas and Petrlchemicals Contracting Services.
Address: 46, Industrial Avenue, Ilupeju Imdstrial Estate, Ilupeju, Lagos
Tel: (01) 4937374-8 (2L), 4962187, 4966894
Fax: (01) 4937329
E-mail: abbng@ng-abb.com
Website: www.abb.com/ng

ABBEY BUILDING SOCIETY LIMITED
Business: Mortgage Finance Services
Address: 19, Warehouse Road, Apapa, Lagos
Tel: (01) 5873740, 5871493, 7911025
Contact: Mrs R. A. Okwechime - MD/CEO

ABBEY SPECIAL JEWELLERS LIMITED
Business: Jewellers and Goldsmiths; Engravers; Miners and Mining Consultant, .
Address: 15, New Balogun Street, off Ayonuga Street Ikorodu Road, Fadeyi, Lagos
Tel: (01) 5821005, 5820998, 08033066863
Contact: Alh. Ibrahim - MD/CEO

ABBEY TRAVELS & TOURS (NIGERIA) LIMITED
Business: Travel Agency, Tour Operators
Address: 30, Ajasa Street, Onikan, Lagos
Tel: (01) 2630954, 2631612 **Fax:** (01) 2647145
Contact: Mrs Abiodun Ojutalayo - MD/CEO

ABBSTAL LIMITED
Business: Packaging & Household Products Manufacturing
Address: Motorways Avenue, opposite Seven-Up Factory Oregun Alausa, Lagos
Tel: (01) 4934145-6 (2L), 7736783 **Fax:** (01) 4934149

ABDULAI & AWOMOLO CONSTRUCTION COMPANY LTD
Business: Building Construction
Address: Providence Court, Oremeji Ajibade Bus Stop, Mokola, Ibadan
Tel: (02) 8101356
Contact: Mr. Dotun Awomolo - Joint CEO
Mr. Tunde Abdulai - Joint CEO

ABDULKERIM KADIRI & COMPANY
Business: Chartered Accontants; Auditing, Taxation, Finance & Management Consultancy Services
Address: 90, Akpakpava Street, Benin City
Tel/Fax: (052) 258139, 08023424533
E-mail: kadkeram@yahoo.com
* 722 Road, A Close, House 1, Festac Town, Lagos
Tel: (01) 5885922
* Aguiyi Ironsi Cantonment Shopping Complex (Suite D37), Asokoro, Abuja
Tel: (09) 3142921-2 (2L

ABEKOGOLD LIMITED
Business: Watchmakers, Jewellers, Ind.Timers, Engravers
Address: 150, Broad Street, Lagos Island, Lagos
Tel: (01) 2641384-5 (2L) **Fax:** (01) 2641384
E-mail: abekogold@infoweb.abs.net
* Le Meridien Hotel, Plot 903, Tafawa Balewa Way, Area 11, Garki, Abuja
Contact: Mr Tunji Adeyemo - Chairman/CEO

ABEOKUTA COMMERCIAL AND INDUSTRIAL CO. LTD
Business: Manufacture of Foam Products & Soap, Distribution of Industrial Machineries, Lanterns, Chemicals for Soap & Foam Production
Address: Bolaji Adekunle Street/Joseph Ewuoso Street, Asero Industrial Estate, Sapon Abeokuta
Tel: (039) 230980, 242774, 243293 **Fax:** (039) 244509
Contact: Chief J. A. Ola Ewuoso - MD/CEO

ABERDEEN ENERGY (W. A) LIMITED (OAL)
Business: Oil, Water, Marine, Industrial & Explosion Proof Electrical Engineers
Address: Ibru Jetty Compound, c/o Marca Depot, Ibafon , Apapa - Oshodi Expressway, Lagos
Tel: (01) 5870000 **Fax:** (01) 7595379
E-mail: oalflameproof@hotmail.com

ABEX EXPRESS PARCEL SERVICE
Business: Direct Express Delivery of Parcels and Documents
Address: 52C, Ikorodu Road Fadeyi, Lagos
Tel: (01) 4714895-6 (2L), 4733935, 8115124, 7741326, 08022243436, 08033283480

Fax: (01) 5821325
E-mail: abex@yahoo.com
Website: www.abex-ng.com
Contact: Mr. Frank U. Nneji - Group Exec. Chairman
Mr. Michael D. Olabajo - GM/CEO

ABG COMMUNICATIONS LIMITED
Business: Sales & Service of Satellite Sysrems, Computers, Communication & Security Equipment; Internet Service Provider; Television Production & Broadcasting, Security Consultancy
Address: ABG Avenue, Road D3, Unguwar Muazu Expressway, P.O.Box 502 Kaduna
Tel: (062) 244501, 245385, 415946, 415944
Fax: (062) 237557, 245950
E-mail: abg@micro.com.ng
* Shop 53-57, Federal Palace Hotel Shopping Complex, Ahmadu BelloWay, Victoria Island, Lagos
Tel: (01) 613495
* Shop 17, Wuse Shopping Complex, Wuse Zone 3, Abuja.
Tel: (09) 5235251
Contact: Alh. (Engr) Mohammed Bawa - MD/CEO

ABIKOL INTERNATIONAL LIMITED
Business: Property Development and Construction, Estate Surveyors & Valuers
Address: Eko Court Complex (Block C, Suite 6 Annex), Kofo Abayomi Street, Victoria Island Lagos.
Tel: (01) 2620959, 2610513, 7749678, 08033082287
Fax: (01) 2610513
E-mail: kolakoms@metrong.com
* Goodness Place (3rd Floor, Suite 4B2), Plot 627, Sokode Crescent/Herbert Macaulay Way, Berger Junction, Wuse Zone 5, Abuja.
Tel: (09) 5239912, 08037019801
Contact: Chief Kola Akomolade - Chairman/CEO

ABIOK PUBLICITY LIMITED
Business: Outdoor Advertising Agency
Address: 308, Agege Motor Rd, Challenge, Mushin, Lagos
Tel: (01) 4520213, 4523340 **Fax:** (01) 4521998
E-mail: abiok@hyperia.com
Contact: Alh. K. Olasode - MD/CEO

ABIOLA BOOKSHOPS LIMITED
Business: Sales and Distribution of Books and Stationery
Address: Zulikha Wuraola House, 362, Herbert Macaulay Street, Yaba, Lagos
Tel: (01) 7741270
* 12, Yaounde Street, Wuse Zone 6, Abuja.
Tel: (09) 5231750
*Airways Building, 26 Ahamdu Bello Way, Kaduna
Tel: (062) 235632
* 6, Allen Avenue, Ikeja, Lagos. **Tel:** (01) 4970945
* Old Bank Bus-Stop, Ojoo, Ibadan. (02) 8102384
* 5, Ibrahim Taiwo Street, Kano. **Tel:** (064) 630536
Contact: Mr S. A. A Abiola - MD/CEO

ABJ CONSOLIDATED NIGERIA LIMITED
Business: Distribution and Sales of Medical/Laboratory Equipment and Consumables
Address: Jimade House, 2, Ojuelegba Road, Yaba, Lagos
Tel: (01) 5456478, 7734559, 08023125951, 08033144986, 08033917775, 08042136718 **Fax:** (01) 5456478
E-mail: abjconsolidated@yahoo.com
Contact: Mr Bona C. Nlemadin - MD/CEO

ABNL LIMITED
Business: Supply & Service of Oilfield Equipment; Consultancy
Address: 10, Norman Williams Street, S.W. Ikoyi Lagos
Tel: (01) 2693527, 2673518 **Fax:** (01) 2693527
E-mail: abnllagos@aol.com
* 19, Benjamin Okpara Stret, off Olu Obasanjo Road, Port Harcourt
E-mail: abnlph@aol.com
Tel: (084) 871253 **Fax:** (084) 236037
* 5A, Franklin Atake Close, G. R. A., Warri
Tel: (053) 255366, 256004
E-mail: abnlwri@aol.com
Contact: Mr Andy Boyo - Chairman/CEO

ABSAF GROUP OF COMPANIES
Business: Supply of Oil Pipes, Equipment and Chemicals. Freight Handling and Management, Shipping.
Address: 2, Road 2, Circular Road, Presidential Estate, P.M.B 5132, Port-Harcourt
Tel/Fax: (084) 230729
E-mail: absaf@micro.com.ng
* Old WASA Building, 21, Warehouse Road, Apapa, Lagos
Tel/Fax: (01) 5455609
Contact: Alhaji M. B Abdullahi - Chairman/CEO

ABUEDE INDUSTRIES NIGERIA LIMITED
Business: Sculpting, Marble & Terrazo Works, Swimming Pool Construction and Decorations, Borehole Engineering Services
Address: 539, Agege Motor Road, Ladipo , Ikeja, Lagos
Tel: (01) 4937586, 08023000725, 08036100725
Contact: Chief P. O. K. Abuede - MD/CEO

ABUJA (CAPITAL) MOTORS LIMITED
Business: Sales & Service of Motor Vehicles - Cars, Buses, Tractors and Earth-moving Equipment
Address: Leventis Close, off Olusegun Obasanjo Way, Central Business District, Abuja
Tel: (09) 5239087, 6703904, 6719054
Fax: (09) 5239087, 3142369
Contact: Mr. Ahmed Mantey - Exec. Director/CEO

ABUJA CLINICS LIMITED
Business: Medical Services
Address: Plot 1261, Amazon Street, Minister's Hill, Maitama, Abuja
Tel: (09) 4137020
* Plot 1014, Jos Street, Area 3, Garki, Abuja
Tel: (09) 2342299, 2344599

ABUJA SECURITIES & COMMODITY EXCHANGE PLC
Business: Securities and Commodity Trading
Address: Plot 397, Muhammadu Buhari Way, Central Business District, Abuja
Tel: (09) 2341969, 6710828 **Fax:** (09) 2347196
* ICON House (7th Floor), Plot 999f, Idejo/ Danmole Street, Victoria Island, Lagos

ABUJA SHERATON HOTEL & TOWERS
Business: Hotel Services
Address: Ladi Kwali Way, P.M.B 143, Maitama, Abuja
Tel: (09) 5238101-30 (30L), 5230225-44 (20L)
Fax: (09) 5231570-1 (2L)

ABULICO NIGERIA LIMITED
Business: Electrical - Power Distribution System Engineering
Address: ZA 23, Kachia Road, opp. Queen Amina College, P.O.Box 1294, Kaduna
Tel: (062) 231166

ABUMET NIGERIA LIMITED
Business: Fabrication of Aluminium Products - Windows, Doors, Partitions etc
Address: Plot 306, Idu Industrial Area, Idu, Abuja
Tel: (09) 5210827-9 (3L) **Fax:** (09) 4132831, 5210827
Contact: Mr. Markus Truninger - GM/CEO

ACADEMY PRESS PLC
Business: Industrial & Commercial Printing
Address: 28/32, Industrial Avenue, Ilupeju Industrial Estate, Ilupeju, Lagos.
Tel: (01) 4977700-4 (5L), 7730527, 8042842
Fax: (01) 4970294, 4930449, 2616702
E-mail: applc@academy.com
Website: www.academypreesplc.com
Contact: Alh. B. A. Idris Animashaun - Exec. Chairman

ACADEMY PRESS BUSINESS FORMS LIMITED
Business: Printing of Office & Computer Stationery, Security and Business Forms
Address: 28/32, Industrial Avenue, Ilupeju Industrial Estate, Ilupeju, P.O.Box 3445, Lagos
Tel: (01) 4970190, 4970195, 4977700-4 (5L), 8042842
Fax: (01) 4970294, 8047927
E-mail: academy@micro.com.ng
* Wadata Plaza, Plot 1247, Aminu Kano Crescent, Wuse 11, Abuja
Tel: (09) 6708969
Contact: Mr David Akoro - Finance/Admin. Manager

ACB INTERNATIONAL BANK PLC
Business: Commercial Banking
Address: ACB House, 106/108, Broad Street, Lagos
Tel: (01) 2660170 **Fax:** (01) 2660742
Contact: Mr John Udeka - MD/CEO

ACCAT (NIGERIA) LIMITED
Business: Communication Equipment Distribution and Sales
Address: 39, Creek Road, Apapa, Lagos.
Tel: (01) 5870458, 5878813-4 (2L) **Fax:** (01) 5870458
E-mail: sales@accat.com
Website: www.accat.com
Contact: Mr Peter Sinnot - MD/CEO

ACCENTURE
Business: Management and Technology Consultants
Address: Chartered Bank Building (4th Floor), Plot 1712, Idejo St, off Adeola Odeku St, Victoria Island, Lagos
Tel: (01) 2626929. 3200299. 2672780 **Fax:** (01) 2626933
E-mail: accenture-lagos@accenture.com
Website: www.accenture.com/nigeria

ACCELON NIGERIA LIMITED
Business: Direct Satellite-based Internet Access Service Providers
Address: 3B, Ligali Ayorinde Street, Victoria Island, Lagos
Tel: (01) 2709932, 08023209131 Fax: (01) 2705781
E-mail: info@acclonafrica.com
Website: www.accelonafrica.com

ACCESS BANK NIGERIA PLC
Business: Commercial Banking
Address: Plot 1665, Oyin Jolayemi St, Victoria Island, Lagos
Tel: (01) 2626273 - 6 (4L), 2641571 - 2(2L), 4617666-7(2L), 3201889 - 92(4L)
E-mail: info@accessbankplc.com
Contact: Mr Aigboje Aig-Imoukhuede - MD/CEO
Mr Dele Oyawa - Head (External Affairs)

ACCESSPORT NIGERIA LIMITED
Business: Shipping, Freight Forwarding, Haulage Services, Trading, Export
Address: 7A, Creek Road, Apapa, Lagos
Tel: (01) 5452409, 5454086, 08033094731
Fax: (01) 5878207
* 6, Old Aba Road, 1st Artillery, Rumuogba, Port Harcourt
Tel: (084) 610187 **Fax:** (084) 610172
Contact: Mr Gani-Alli Shobande

ACCLAIM HOME SAVINGS & LOANS LIMITED
Business: Mortgage Finance; Management Advisory Services
Address: 3A, Adebayo Mokuolu St, Anthony Village, Lagos
Tel: (01) 3422830-9 (10L), 7741931, 7755521
Fax: (01) 3422830
E-mail: acclaim@akitorch.net
Website: www.acclaimnigeria.net
* The Millenium Court (6th Floor), Ogun State House, Plot 24, 4th Avenue, Cadastral Zone, Central Business District Abuja
Contact: Mr Victor O. Akinmoluwa - Vice Chairman/CEO

ACCORD IMPEX LIMITED
Business: Rubber Footwear Manufacture and Marketing
Address: 3. Emmanuel Alayande Road, Oluyole Industrial Estate, Ring Road, Ibadan
Tel: (02) 2314865

ACCORD SAVINGS & LOANS LIMITED
Business: Mortage Finance Services
Address: 2, Aromire Avenue, Off Obafemi Awolowo Way Ikeja, Lagos
Tel: (01) 4936913 **Fax:** (01) 4972076, 5557507
E-mail: accordsl@intracom.net.ng
Contact: Mr. Adeoye A. Mapaderun - Chairman/CEO

ACCOUNTING SOLUTIONS
Business: Consulting and IT Training, Software Implementation and System Design, Manpower Recruitment
Address: 27, Macarthy Street, Onikan, Lagos
Tel: (01) 2634193, 2634233, 2634148, 2600295
Fax: (01) 2634148
E-mail: info@accountingsolutions.com.ng
Website: www.accountingsolutions.com.ng
Contact: Mrs. Olubukola Boyo - MD/CEO

ACCREDITED TRUST & AUTOMOBILE LIMITED
Business: Distribution, Sales and Service of Automobiles.
Address: 31, Sanusi Fafunwa Street, Victoria Island, Lagos
Tel: (01) 2625012, 4703185 **Fax:** (01) 2625012
Contact: Chief C. A. Ejimkonye - Chairman/CEO

ACCURATE INSURANCE BROKERS LIMITED
Business: Insurance Brokers
Address: 45, Adeboyejo Street, Ijeshatedo, Surulere, Lagos
Tel: (090) 403466
Contact: Chief Arole Akeem Adeleke Fancy - Chairman/CEO

ACE VISION LIMITED
Business: Financial Consultancy Services
Address: CSS Bookshop House (12th Floor), 50/52, Broad Street, Lagos
Tel: (01) 2667202, 8042381
E-mail: acevision@yahoo.co.uk
Contact: Mr Sam Obijiaku - MD/CEO

ACELAND INDUSTRIES LIMITED
Business: Manufacturers and Marketers of Paints, Coloured Cement, Marble and Terrazzo Products
Address: 38/44, Ojekunle Street, Papa Ajao, Mushin, Lagos
Tel: (01) 2905523, 4527471, 4803455, 7745523, 8115236, 08023195400-3 (3L), 08034040110
Fax: (01) 4527471
E-mail: acelandindltd@yahoo.com
* 35, Adam Street, Orioke, Ejigbo, Lagos
Tel: (01) 2905523
Contact: Mr. A. S. M. Nwoye - MD/CEO

ACEN INSURANCE COMPANY LIMITED
Business: Non-Life Insurance
Address: Elephant House Plaza (3rd Floor), 239/241, Ikorodu Road, Ilupeju, Lagos
Tel: (01) 4938691-4 (4L), 4970113, 4970712, 7731683
Fax: (01) 4938694
E-mail: acenico@infoweb.abs.net; acenico@aceninsurance.com
Website: www.aceinsurance.com
Contact: Mr. B. O. Oshadiya - MD/CEO

ACHINMECK NIGERIA LIMITED
Business: Water Engineering Services, Sales & Maintenance of Pumps, Consltancy
Address: 6, charity Road, New Oko-Oba, Abule-Egba Bus-Stop, Agege, Lagos.
Tel: (01) 2880691 **Fax:** (01) 4930419
E-mail: achinmeck@hotmail.com
* Plot 479, T. Balewa Way, Area 3, Garki, Abuja
Tel: (09) 2344947
* 18, Aggrey Road, Port Harcourt
Tel: (084) 233538
Contact: Engr Akin Oladejo - MD/CEO

ACHUS-ARIN LIMITED
Business: Fire Safety Engineering & Consultancy Services
Address: Safety House, U. 8, Katsina Road/Ahmadu Bello Way, Kaduna
Tel: (062) 215690, 241663, 247653 **Fax:** (062) 247653
E-mail: achus@skannet.com
* Noble Commercial Complex (1st Floor), Moshood Abiola Rd, opp. UTC, Area 10, Garki, Abuja
Tel: (09) 2342045, 08023083945

ACME BUILDERS LIMITED
Business: Building & Civil Engineering, Furniture Manufacturers, Interior Decorators, Steel & Metal Fabrication
Address: Acme House, Plot 23, Block A, Acme Road, Ogba Industrial Estate, Ikeja, Lagos.
Tel: (01) 4926206, 4707386, 08023236448, 08055365689
Contact: Mr Terrence I. Lawal - Group MD/CEO

ACORN PETROLEUM NIGERIA LIMITED
Business: Marketing of Petroleum Products
Address: Acorn Service Station, Oworonshoki, Ogudu Phsae 11, Lagos
Tel: (01) 4731353, 7736174
E-mail: acornpet@infoweb.abs.net
Contact: Engr. B. A. Kalesanwo - GM

ACOUNS NIGERIA LIMITED
Business: Distribution of Medical and Laboratory Diagnostic Equipment, Disposables & Reagents
Address: 17, Norman Williams Street, S. W., Ikoyi, Lagos
Tel: (01) 2673920, 2695454, 08037177254, 08056463385
Fax: (01) 2693150
E-mail: a.acons@micro.com.ng
Contact: Mrs Adunni Udu - MD/CEO

ACT NETWORKS LIMITED
Business: Sales & Maintenance of Communication Systems - Microwave Radios & VSAT Services
Address: ICON House (5th Floor), Plot 999F, Ideji/Danmole Streets, Victoria Island, Lagos
Tel: (01) 2611277, 3204604-5 (2L), 3204615
Fax: (01) 3204604
E-mail: actnl@nigol.net.ng
Contact: Mr Joshua Mukan - MD/CEO

ACTI-TECH LIMITED
Business: Sales & Engineering Services in Information Technology, Information Dissemination and Business Systems
Address: Plot 687A, Aminu Kano Crecscent, Wuse II, Abuja
Tel: (09) 5238937, 5241528-9 (2L), 08023112 00, 08033154235
Fax: (09) 5236842
E-mail: enquiries@actitech.net
actitech@linkserve.com
actitech@nova.net.ng
Website: www.actitech.net
Contact: Mr Peter Madu - MD/CEO

ACTIVE HEALTH MANAGERS LIMITED
Business: Health Maintenance Organization
Address: 86A, Isale Eko Avenue, Dolphin Estate, off Osborne Road, Lagos
Tel: (01) 2690363, 2696485 **Fax:** (01) 2696485
E-mail: ahmcare@infoweb.abs.net
* Plot 1065, Abaji Close, off Oyo Street, Area 2, Garki, Abuja
Tel/Fax: (09) 2347750
Contact: Prof. Umaru Shehu, CFR - Chairman
Mr. Alex Obi Okoli - MD

ADAMAC GROUP OF COMPANIES
Business: Conglomerate Oil & Gas Industry, Banking, Insurance, Engineering, Construction Services
Address: 2, East-West Road, Rumuodara, Port Harcourt
Tel: (084) 234024, 237168 **Fax:** (084) 231192

ADAMAC INDUSTRIES LIMITED
Business: Processing of Fats and Oils
Address: Plot 90, Rivoc Road, Tans-Amadi Indstrial Layout, Port Harcourt
Tel: (084) 485857

ADAMAWA INVESTMENT & PROPERTY DEVELOPMENT COMPANY LIMITED
Business: Investment Promotion, Property Development and Consultancy.
Address: Investment House, 42, Galadima Aminu Way, Jimeta-Yola
Tel: (075) 625105, 624665 **Fax:** (075) 627121
Contact: Alh. Usman Ardo Jada - GM/CEO

ADAMAWA PRESS LIMITED
Business: Newspaper Publishing, Printing.
Address: Behind Federal Secretariat, off Yola Road, P.M.B 2280, Yola
Tel/Fax: (075) 624211
Contact: Sahabo Mahdi - GM/CEO

ADAOBI NIGERIA LIMITED
Business: Manufacturing of Polythene Bags and Sheets, Processing of Solid Mineral Chemicals, Internet Service Providers
Address: Umuakpara Town, Km $11^1/_2$, Old Aba-Owerri Road Osisioma Industrial Layout, P.O.Box 702, Aba
Tel: (082) 440590, 441814, 08037409932
Fax: (082) 441814
* 59, Market Road, Aba
Tel: (082) 440590, 232058, 233653
* 70, Ayinde Adeleye St, off Toyin St, Ikeja, Lagos
Tel: (01) 4970549, 08034734222
Contact: Nze A. O. Ndubuisi - Chairman/CEO

ADATA INVESTMENTS LIMITED
Business: Investment Services and Trading
Address: 10, Balarabe Musa Crescent, Victoria Island, Lagos
Tel: (01) 2624357, 2619424, 7742291 **Fax:** (01) 2626830
Contact: Mr Tomi Okorodudu - MD/CEO

ADDAX PETROLEUM DEVELOPMENT (NIGERIA) LIMITED
Business: Petroleum Prospecting & Production
Address: 10, Bishop Aboyade Cole St, Victoria Island Lagos
Tel: (01) 2610631, 2614277, 2613238, 2613334, 2617787, 2626515, 2625820-1 (2L)
Fax: (01) 2616816, 2621915
Contact: C. D Mancini - MD/CEO

ADDIS ENGINEERING LIMITED
Business: Engineering and Manufacturing of Food Processing Equipment and Low-cost Vehicles
Address: 26, Abimbola Street, Isolo Industrial Estate, Lagos
Tel: (01) 4527483, 4523397, 522853, 08042134681
E-mail: addis@hyperia.com
Contact: Engr. O. Olowu - Chairman/CEO

ADE KOMOLAFE (NIGERIA) LIMITED
Business: Customs-Lincensed Clearing Agency, Shipping, Cargo and Freight Handling and Management
Address: Ade Komolafe Commercial House, 62, Oregun Road, Ikeja, Lagos
* NAHCO/FAAN Complex (Room 210), Cargo Section, M/ M International Airport, Ikeja, Lagos
Tel: (01) 7742487
Contact: Otunba Raheem Ade Komolafe - Chairman/CEO

ADE LANZI STYL NIGERIA LIMITED
Business: Designers & Interior Decorators, Sales of Furnishing Materials, Vertical & Venetian Blinds
Address: 261, Herbert Macaulay St, Alagomeji-Yaba, Lagos
Tel: (01) 7732215, 864648, 860296, 08023019057, 08033044500
E-mail: adelanzi@yahoo.com
* Lozumba Commercial Complex (Suite 007), Area 10, Garki, Abuja
Tel: (09) 2347370
Contact: Mr Adeyemi Adenipebi - MD/CEO

ADEBOLA SOBANJO & COMPANY
Business: Chartered Accountants, Auditing, Taxation & Management Consultancy Services
Address: Ajebo House (1st Floor), 24/26, Macarthy Street, Onikan, Lagos
Tel: (01) 2634382, 7916474, 8042032, 08022907640
Fax: (01) 2634382
E-mail: adebolasobanjo@hotmail.com
* Garki II Cornershops (Suite 29), Garki, Abuja
Contact: Dr Adebola O. Olubanjo - Mnanaging Partner

ADEBAYO HOROLOGICAL COMPANY LIMITED
Business: Distribution, Sales and Service of Watches
Address: 27, Tapa Street, Epetedo, Lagos Island, Lagos
Tel: (01) 2636672, 2636677, 2631015 **Fax:** (01) 2694128
E-mail: hobayo@hyperia.com
* 4, Odogbolu Road, Aiyepe, Ogun State
Tel: (037) 320190
Contact: Mutiat Adebayo - GM

ADEBOWALE GROUP OF COMPANIES
Business: Conglomerate - Sales of Electrical and Electronics Domestic Applicances, Furniture. Real Estate
Address: 150, Ikorodu Road, Onipanu, Lagos
Tel: (01) 4938266, 4938267 **Fax:** (01) 4938266, 4964626
* 46, Isaac John Street, G.R.A, Ikeja, Lagos
Tel: (01) 4938266, 4964626 **Fax:** (01) 4964626
E-mail: aei@adebowalegroup.com
Website: www.adebowalegroup.com
Contact: Chief Amzat Beyioku Adebowale, OON - Chairman

ADEBOWALE SUPERSTORES LIMITED
Business: Importation, Wholesales & Retail of Electrical and Electronics Household Applicances, Information Technology Equipment and Furniture
Address: 23, Opebi Road, Ikeja, Lagos
Tel: (01) 4979960-2 (3L), 5557965, 08033046243
Fax: (01) 4979962
E-mail: sales@adebowalesuperstores.com
Website: www.adebowalesuperstores.com
Contact: Prince Bode Adebowale - MD/CEO

ADECCO NIGERIA LIMITED
Business: Recruitment Consultancy Services
Address: Eleganza Biro Plaza (8th Floor), Plot 634, Adeyemo Alakija Street, Victoria Island, Lagos
Tel: (01) 2702926, 7737717 **Fax:** (01) 2702927
E-mail: info@adecconigeria.com
Website: www.adecconigeria.com
Contact: Bopo Ogundipe - Country Manager

ADEFILA & PARTNERS
Business: Estate Surveyor & Valuers, Real Estate Development & Management Consultancy Services
Address: Elder Dempster Building (8th Floor), 47, Marina, Lagos Island, Lagos
Tel: (01) 2641621, 2663604, 2667230 **Fax:** (01) 2667229
E-mail: adepartners@cyberspace.net.ng
* Plot 2942, Aguiyi Ironsi Street, Maitama, Abuja
Tel: (09) 4130636, 4130737
* 28, Forces Avenue, Old G.R.A, Port Harcourt
Tel: (084) 235212, 485834
Contact: Mr. Kola Adefila - Partner

ADEGBEMILE, AGANGAN, AKINLOSOLU & COMPANY
Business: Estate Surveying and Valuation Services
Address: 35C, Adetokunbo Ademola St, Victoria Island, Lagos
Tel: (01) 2622566, 2622570, 2621622-3 (2L)
Fax: (01) 2621620
Contact: Mr. O. A. Adeniyi - Partner

ADE-IFE TECHNICAL COMPANY LIMITED
Business: Sales, Installation and Service of Refrigerators, Airconditioners, and Cold Rooms. Tool Dealers, Property Developers.
Address: 171, Borno Way, Ebute-Metta, Lagos
Tel: (01) 8125806, 8182502, 08033017674
E-mail: adeifetech@yahoo.com
* Shops 9-14 & 99, New Extension, Area 7 Shopping Centre, Garki Abuja.
Tel: (09) 2348105
Contact: Sunday Adekunle Ifelaja - Chairman

ADE-JOY NIGERIA LIMITED
Business: Clearing & Forwarding Agency, Airfreight, Import & Export Trading, Warehousing & Transportation, General Contractors
Address: Block C (Room 203), NPA Agencies Building, Tin Can Island, Lagos
Tel: (01) 5455726, 4701117, 08033087176
Fax: (01) 5455726
E-mail: adejoy@infoweb.abs.net
Contact: Mr Ernest Adeji - MD/CEO

ADEJUMO FAM (NIGERIA) LIMITED
Business: Sales of Chemicals & Dyestuff, Antiseptic Disinfectants, Pharmaceuticals Products, Industrial Floor-Cleaning Machines & General Goods
Address: 6, Gab Jinadu Street, Off Alh. Adejumo Avenue, Ilupeju Industrial Estate, Ilupeju
Tel: (01) 4972549 **Fax:** (01) 4972548, 4972549
Contact: L. A. Adejumo - MD/CEO

ADENIYI OSUNKOJO ASSOCIATES
Business: Estate Surveyors & Valuers, Property Managers
Address: 24, Obafemi Awolowo Way, Ikeja, Lagos
Tel: (01) 4723015,
Contact: Mr. J. A. Osunkojo - Principal Partner

ADEODU TECHNICAL SERVICES LIMITED
Business: Security Safes and Fire-proof Cabinets Sales and Service; Security Consultants
Address: 23 Oguntolu Street Shomolu, Lagos
Tel: (01) 4715442, 4974989, 5820032 **Fax:** (01) 5820032
* 263, Herbert Macaulay Street, Yaba, Lagos
Tel: (01) 4720866
Contact: Mr. S. Malumi - GM (Marketing)

ADEOLA ODUTOLA INDUSTRIES PLC
Business: Retreading of Tyres. Rubber & Oil Palm Plantation. Biscuit Production
Address: Adeola Odutola Industrial Estate, Old Lagos Road, Ijebu - Ode, Ogun State
Tel: (037) 432322
E-mail: odutolaind@skannet.com
Contact: Chief F. B Osibo - MD/CEO

ADEP INTERNATIONAL VENTURES LIMITED
Business: Marketing of Gas and Oil
Address: 1 (Plot 999), Oju-Olobun Close, off Bishop Oluwole Street, Victoria Island, Lagos
Tel: (01) 2618586, 2613098 **Fax:** (01) 619846
E-mail: adeprinter@hotmail.com
* 11B, Igboukwu Street, D/Line, Port Harcourt
Tel: (084) 239401, 330213
Contact: Mrs. Nike Adebayo-Makinde - MD/CEO

ADESOYE HOLDINGS LIMITED
Business: Conglomerate - Brewers, Biscuit Producers, Estate Valuers and Agents, Printers, etc
Address: 19, Inuwa Abdulkadir Rd, Kakuri Ind Area, Kaduna
Tel: (062) 232184, 233490
* Ajasepo Road, P O Box 289, Ijagbo - Offa
Tel: (031) 801681, 801048
Contact: Chief Emmanuel O. Adesoye - Exec. Chairman

ADEXSON NIGERIA COMPANY LIMITED
Business: Sales of Steel Plates and Float Glass, Manufacturing of Toilet Rolls, Building Material Merchants
Address: Adexson House, LASU-Iba Road, Akesan, Lagos
Tel: (01) 4707184, 2882965, 7731722, 7752077
Fax: (01) 2882965
Contact: Prince (Dr) Adebare Adeyemo - Chairman/CEO

AD-FABAK HOLDINGS LIMITED
Business: Architectural Ironmongers, Locks and Accessories
Address: 4, Ola Ayeni St, off Simbiat Abiola Rd, Ikeja Lagos
Tel/Fax: (01) 4960549, 497083, 08033047952
E-mail: adfabak@infoweb.abs.net
* Plot 184, Taiwo Ishola Street, Omole Resident Layout, Ojudu, Ikeja, Lagos
Contact: Mr A. A. Adeoye - Chairman/CEO

ADGOZO LIMITED
Business: Outdoor Advertising
Address: 5, O'Connor Street, Onitsha
Tel: (046) 412754, 413703, 08033126897
E-mail: adgozo@yahoo.com

ADHAMA TEXTILES & GARMENT INDUSTRIES LIMITED
Business: Knittng and Dyeing of Textiles.
Address: 171, Mission Road, Bompai, Kano
Tel: (064) 647164, 647178, 637178, 08033112215
Contact: Alhaji Audu Adhama - MD/CEO

ADIG PLASTICS LIMITED
Business: Manufacturing, Distribution and Marketing of Plastic Packaging Products
Address: Plot 19, Block C, Amuwo-Odofin Industrial Estate, off Festac Link Road, Amuwo-Odofin, Lagos
Tel: (01) 7740445 **Fax:** (01) 5804552
E-mail: adig@beta.linkserve.com
Contact: Mr P. O. Adigwe - MD/CEO

ADIMEX VENTURES LIMITED
Business: Sales of Oilfield Chemicals, Degreasers & Cleaners, Industrial/Engineering Tools & Machinery, Water Pumps, Filter Media, Ozone Generators and UV Sterilizers, Water Treatment Services
Address: 91, Adeniyi Jone Avenue, Ikeja, Lagos
Tel: (01) 8042567, 4972877 **Fax:** (01) 4972877
Contact: Mr. Akin Olumodimu - MD/CEO.

ADLAD GROUP
Business: Freight Forwarding; Farming; Trading; Sale of Non-Contact Meters, Waste-Management Vehicles, Industrial Chemicals and Electric Equipment; Oil Industry Services.
Address: 12, Olofin Rd, Off Warehouse Road, Apapa, Lagos
Tel: (01) 5872444, 5873422, 5450296 **Fax:** (01) 5872625
E-mail: adlad@infoweb.abs.net
Website: www.adladgroup.com
Contact: Prince Aderemi A. Olukuntuyi - MD/CEO

ADLER PRODUCTS LIMITED
Business: Manufacturing, Importation and Marketing of Pharmaceutical Products
Address: 35, Mobolaji Johnson Avenue, Oregun Industrial Estate, Ikeja, Lagos
Tel: (01) 4973717, 4973718 **Fax:** (01) 4960852
* 32, Oduyemi Street, Anifowoshe, Ikeja, Lagos

ADMIRAL MARINE SHIPPING NIGERIA LIMITED
Business: Shipping Services, Clearing & Forwarding
Address: 16, Railway Close, D-Line, Port Harcourt
Tel: (084) 232213
E-mail: admiralshipping2004@yahoo.com

ADMIRALTY FLEET LIMITED
Business: Property Development and Management
Addreess: Admiralty House, 99, Olu Obasanjo Road P.O.Box 8165, Federal Secretariat, Port Harcourt.
Tel: (084) 238291
Contact: Rear Admiral F. B. I Porbeni - Exec. Chairman

ADMIX COMMUNICATIONS LIMITED
Business: Advertising and Marketing Communications.
Address: 30, Aba Johnson Crescent , off Adeniyi Jones Avenue, Ikeja, Lagos
Tel: (01) 4971470, 4811700 **Fax:** (01) 4971470
E-mail: admix@beta.linkserve.com
Contact: Mr Dayo O. Oruwari - MD/CEO

ADOKA HOLDINGS LIMITED
Business: Farming, Flour Milling.
Address: 28/30, Bukuru Bye-Pass, P.O.Box 6822, Anglo-Jos
Tel: (073) 465109, 462550 **Fax:** (073) 463850
Contact: Major-Gen. G. O. Ejiga (Rtd) - Chairman/CEO

ADPEAK EXPOSURES LIMITED
Business: Outdoor Advertising
Address: 24, John Olugbo Street, off Toyin Street/Mojidi Street, Ikeja, Lagos
Tel: (01) 4970943, 4978175, 0803323835
E-mail: adpeak@yahoo.com
Website: www.discompaging.com
Contact: Mr Abiodun F. Odeyemi - MD/CEO.

ADPURE (NIGERIA) LIMITED
Business: Advertising and Marketing Communications
Address: 9, Joseph Gomwalk Road, Opp, Polo Ground, Jos
Tel: (073) 453560, 457611, 458602 **Fax:** (073) 458492
E-mail: adpure@wave.net
Contact: Barr. Solomon Ewuga - Chairman/CEO

ADSPACE COMMUNICATIONS LIMITED
Business: Outdoor Advertising Agency, Printing Services, Corporate Gift Items
Address: 38, Layi Oyekanmi St, Papa Ajao, Mushin Lagos.
Tel: (01) 4529350, 4525851, 0802319344, 08033027105
Fax: (01) 4525851
Contact: Chief S. O. Makinde - Chairman/CEO

ADSTRAT COMMUNICATIONS LIMITED
Business: Brand Management Consultants
Address: 43B, Oyedele Ognniyi Street, Anthony, Lagos.
Tel: (01) 8119830-1 (2L) **Fax:** (01) 4938315
Contact: Mr Charles O'Tudor - Principal Consultant

ADSWITCH PLC
Business: Manufacturing of Electric Switch-Gear & Fittings
Address: 1, Metu Uzodike Street, Off Nnobi Road, Okpuno, Otolo, Anambra State.
Tel: (046) 460606, 462244 **Fax:** (046) 462244. 462186
* 202/204, Ikorodu Road, Palmgrove, Lagos
Tel: (01) 825992 **Fax:** (01) 4521253
* Garki Village Cornershops (Suite 41), Samuel Ladoke Akintola Boulevard, Abuja
Tel: (09) 2348112, 2344804
Contact: Engr. G. C. Nzewi - MD/CEO

ADVANCED BUSINESS TECHNOLOGIES LIMITED
Business: Sales of Computers, Offices Eqipments, Note-Conting Machines & VSAT
Address: 8, Creek Road, Apapa, Lagos
Tel: (01) 5450689, 5450703, 5877600, 5451013, 7745284
Fax: (01) 5878472
E-mail: abt@intercommoep.com
itercomm@intercommoep.com
help@intercommoep.com
Website: www.intercommoep.com
Contact: Mr. Patrick George - MD/CEO

ADVANCED DIGITAL TECHNOLOGY NIGERIA LIMITED
Business: IT Equipment & Computer Hardware Sales, Web Designing and Hosting, Cyber Cafe Services

Address: 9, Sumbo Jibowu Street, off Ribadu Road off Awolowo Road S.W. Ikoyi, Lagos
Tel: (01) 4805041, 0803300076
E-mail: generalmail@adtech 1.com
Website: www.adtech 1.com
Contact: Mr. Micheal Damisa - Chairman/CEO

ADVANCED INTERNATIONAL MERCHANTS LIMITED
Business: Sales of Industrial Filter for Breweries, Distilleries and Beverage Drinks Manufacturers
Address: 22 Oduyemi Street, Anifowoshe, Ikeja, Lagos
Tel: (01) 4976126-7 (2L) **Fax:** (01) 4976128
E-mail: aiml@linkserve.com.ng
* 51, Akanro Street, of Apapa-Oshodi Expressway Ilasamaja, Mushin, Lagos
Tel: (01) 4520001, 520809 **Fax:** (01) 4527399
* 13, Geodetic Road, near Shell Office, Rumuamasi, Port Harcourt
Tel: (084) 488338, 231809 **Fax:** (084) 232039

ADVANCED MICRO COMPUTER SYSTEMS LIMITED
Business: Assembling, Sales, Maintenance & Networking Computers and Accessories.
Address: 11, Ali Akilu Road, P.O.Box 2162, Kaduna
Tel: (062) 243464, 243565, 08023278068
Fax: (062) 243564
E-mail: ams@wwlkad.com
Website: www.ams.com
Contact: Mr Daniel Omale - Chairman/CEO

ADVANCED PROTECTION TECHNOLOGIES NIGERIA LTD
Business: Information Technology, Power Protection and Telecommunication
Address: 11, Alh Kanike Close, off Awolowo Rd, Ikoyi,Lagos
Tel: (01) 267190, 2672017, 2692030, 4741831, 08022905086, 08023140275
Fax: (01) 2692030
E-mail: afrosys@excite.com
switec2000@yahoo.com
apt-ng@excite.com
Contact: Chief S. N. Anyanwu - Chairman/CEO

ADVANCED SOFTWARE SYSTEMS LIMITED
Business: Software Development, Maintenance of Computer Hardwares, IT Training & Consultancy
Address: 30, Bourdillon Road, Ikoyi,Lagos
Tel: (01) 2691610, 2691612, 08034743396
E-mail: assl88@hotmail.com

ADVENT COMMUNICATIONS LIMITED
Business: Advertising, Marketing, Public Relations, Publishing
Address: 27, Sabiu Ajose Street, Off Bode Thomas Street, Surulere Lagos.
Tel: (01) 837870, 848485. 4710906 **Fax:** (01) 5850053
Contact: Mr. Willy Iyiegbuniwe - Chairman

ADVERTISING TECHNIQUES LIMITED
Business: Advertising Services, Marketing Communication
Address: 111, Adeniyi Jones Avenue, Ikeja Industrial Estate, Ikeja, Lagos.
Tel/Fax: (01) 4970284, 4975736, 4817173 **Fax:** (01) 4975739
E-mail: alt@infoweb.abs.net
Contact: Mr. Michael O. Nwaobi - MD/CEO

AEI (NIGERIA) LIMITED
Business: Shipping, Clearing & Forwarding, Packing and Removals, Transportation and Warehousing
Address: 1, Adeola Ajayi Crescent, Off Interntional Airport Road, Mafoluku-Oshodi, Lagos.
Tel: (01) 4965175, 4966662, 7749430
Fax: (01) 4966662, 2691031
E-mail: aeilos@linserve.com.ng
Contact: Mr Adolphus Okebugwu - CEO

AERIAL & SATELLITE RESOURCES LIMITED
Business: Aerial Photography and Satellite Imagery Acquisition, Geographic Information Systems Consultancy Services, Sales of GIS Software/Hardware, Training in Remote Sensing & GIS
Address: 2, Buffalo House (2nd Floor), 2, Allen Avenue Ikeja, Lagos.
Tel: (01) 5557691-5 (5L) **Fax:** (01) 4934594
E-mail: info@aerialisat.com
Website: www.aerialsat.com
Contact: Capt Augustine Okon - Chairman/CEO.

AERO CONTRACTORS COMPANY OF NIGERIA LIMITED
Business: Aircraft Charter, Airline Service
Address: General Aviation Terminal, Murtala Mohammed Airport, Ikeja, Lagos
Tel: (01) 4979122-4 (3L), 4962570, 4961340, 7749723
Fax: (01) 4971973
E-mail: aero@acn.aero
Website: www.acn.aero
Contact: Mr. Eduard J. M. Van Dam - MD/CEO

AEROCONTROL LIMITED
Business: Aviation Finance and Consultancy
Address: 14, Allen Avenue Ikeja, Lagos
Tel: (01) 4967586, 4964015, 4971104 **Fax:** (01) 4964015
E-mail: aerocontrol@hyperia.com
Contact: Capt. W. B. Noelle - MD/CEO

AEROMARITME GROUP OF COMPANIES
Business: Aeromaritime Services & Leasing, Shipping & Stevedoring, Clearing & Forwarding, Warehousing, Oil Base Services, National Carriers & Liner Operator.
Address: Maritime House, Kirikiri Lighter Terminal Phase 1, Oshodi-Apapa Expressway, Kirikiri Wharf, Lagos.
Tel: (01) 5872491, 5872582, 5871684, 5873561, 5874026, 5876603
Fax: (01) 5876335, 5877376, 5873450
E-mail: aerogroup@infoweb.abs.net
* Investment House, 3, Grace Avenue, Elelewo, Port Harcourt.
Tel: (084) 332934, 239428, 238005, 612480-2 (3L)
Fax: (084) 238006.
Contact: Chief Victor I. Odili - Chairman/CEO

AEROSPACE SYSTEMS (NIGERIA) LIMITED
Business: Aviation and Allied Technical Services, Expansion and Development of Existing Airports
Address: 24/28, Strachan Street (1st Floor), Lagos Is., Lagos.
Tel: (01) 2635892 **Fax:** (01) 2635892, 2631422
E-mail: olusolaobh@excite.com
Contact: Dr. Yemisi Olusola - MD/CEO

AES NIGERIA BARGE LIMITED
Business: Electrical Power Generation
Address: Yinka Folawiyo Plaza (7th Floor), 38, Warehouse Road, Apapa
Tel: (01) 5450287, 5453637, 5878208 **Fax:** (01) 5450301
* Egbin Thermal Station, Egbin, Lagos State
Tel: 08034020370, 08034020373
Contact: Mr Dennis Skipper - Project Manager/CEO

AFCOTT NIGERIA PLC
Business: Farming & Agro Processing
Address: Plot 122/132, Oshodi-Apapa Expressway, Lagos
Tel: (01) 4527257, 4527841.
* Mayoine Project, Ngurore - Yola, Adamawa state
Tel: (075) 626973 - 4 (2L)
Contact: Mr. G. D Chanrai - MD/CEO

AFEMA CHEMICAL INDUSTRIES LIMITED
Business: Manufacturers of Industrial Chemicals, Antiseptics & Disinfectants, Descaling Agent, Degreasers, Agro Chemicals, Industrial & Liquid Detergents, Sanitizers, Candles and Cosmetics
Address: Afema House, Apapa-Oshodi Expressway, (near Sanya Bus Stop) Amuwo Odofin, Lagos
Tel: (01) 4963505, 835322. 837682 **Fax:** (01) 4963505
Contact: Chief G. O. Egabor, JP - Chairman/CEO

AFFORDABLE CARS LIMITED
Business: Automobile Sales and Service
Address: 89, Opebi Road, Ikeja, Lagos
Tel: (01) 4970706, 4967085, 4700764 **Fax:** (01) 4967085
E-mail: affordable@workmail.com
Contact: Mr Biola Ayeni - MD/CEO.

AFLON NIGERIA PLC
Business: Manufacture and Marketing of Yarn
Address: 48, Marina, Lagos
* Plot 122/132, Apapa-Oshodi Expressway, Iyana Isolo, Lagos
Tel: (01) 523989, 525277, 4525267, 4525279
E-mail: yam_marketing@afprint.com

AFN BROKERS LIMITED
Business: Insurance Brokers, Audit and Consultancy.
Address: 7, Ajao Rd, off Adeniyi Jones Avenue, Ikeja, Lagos
Tel: (01) 4965513, 4972475, 4930210 **Fax:** (01) 4972476
E-mail: afnbrokers@linkserve.com
Contact: Mr J. O. Alabi - MD/CEO

AFPLY NIGERIA LIMITED
Business: Wood, Plywood and Particle Board Manufacturing and Laminating, Pharmaceuticals Importation; Export of Wood Products and Commodities
Address: 15/17, Kopek Road off Fatai Atere Way, Matori Industrial Estate, Mushin, Lagos
Tel: (01) 4525919 **Fax:** (01) 2612655
Contact: Mr J. O. Pase - Admin Manager

AFPRINT NIGERIA PLC
Business: Cultivation of Cotton,, Production & Sales of Edible Oil,Yarn and Cloth; Export of Textile & Agricultural Products.
Address: Plot 122-132, Apapa Expressway, Isolo, Lagos
Tel: (01) 4522189, 4522051, 4522964, 4522375, 4525267, 4520361, 4523909
Fax: (01) 4523909
* 24/30, Abebe Village Road, Iganmu, Lagos
Tel: (01) 5850873, 5850486, 5832659
Contact: Mr. D. P. Chanrai - MD/CEO

AFPROHAND NIGERIA LIMITED
Business: Independent Television Producers.
Address: 4, Remilekun St, Ogunlana Drive, Surulere, Lagos.
Tel: (01) 5851110, 5851106, 834554, 841901, 4701753
Fax: (01) 5851110
Contact: Mr. Seun Sonoiki - MD/CEO

AFRAB-CHEM LIMITED
Business: Pharmaceutical Production
Address: 22, Abimbola St, Isolo Ind.Estate, Isolo, Lagos
Tel: (01) 4522571, 4522777 **Fax:** (01) 4520328
Contact: Chief M. A. Shahin - Chairman./CEO

AFREENET LIMITED
Business: Systems Integration and Networking.
Address: 1B Molade Okoya-Thomas St, Victoria Is., Lagos
Tel: (01) 2646874
E-mail: info@afreenet.com
lagos@afreenet.com
Contact: Mr S. Ike Nwagbo - President/CEO

AFREX VENTURES LIMITED
Business: Groundwater Development Services and Consultancy, Borehole Drilling and Maintenance.
Address: Buffalo House, 2 Allen Avenue, Ikeja, Lagos
Tel: (01) 4931132, 4936081, 08023138651
Fax: (01) 4931132
E-mail: afrex@mail.nigol.net.ng
Contact: Mr Cornelius O. Tay - Exec. Chairman

AFRI HOTEL LIMITED
Business: Hospitality Services, Conferenc Centre
Address: Plot 281, Herbert Macaulay Way, Central Business District, Garki, Abuja
Tel: (09) 2343003, 2342873, 2349723-7 (5L)
Fax: (09) 2343003, 2342873
E-mail: afrihotel@hotmail.com
afrihotel@rosecom.net

AFRI-AIR INTERNATIONAL LIMITED
Business: Aircraft Charter Services
Address: DANA Complex, General Aviation Terminal, Murtala Mohammed Airport, Ikeja, Lagos
Tel: (01) 4978751, 4702449 **Fax:** (01) 4978751
E-mail: afriair@alpha.linkserve.com
Contact: Mr Ibrahim Idrissa - GM

AFRIBANK NIGERIA PLC
Business: Conglomerate - Banking & Financial Services.
Address: Afribank Plaza, 51/55, Broad Street, Lagos
Tel: (01) 2662301, 2662608 2662490, 2660569, 2641566, 2662480, 2645132, 2646970
Fax: (01) 2666327, 2664890
E-mail: info@afribank.net
Website: www.afribank.net
afribank.moneynett.com

* Afribank House, 3, Kaura Namoda Street, Off Tafawa Balewa Way, Area 3, Garki, Abuja.

Tel: (09) 2343935, 2343257, 2343844, 2343898, 2342680, 2342681
Fax: (09) 2342979
Contact: Alh. Kashim M Njidda - GMD/CEO
Mr. Lanre Alabi - Head (Corporate Affairs)

AFRIBANK ESTATE COMPANY LIMITED
Business: Real Estate, Facilities and Property Development, Management and Agency.
Address: 4, Adekunle Odunlami Crescent, off Aina George Street, Ilupeju Lagos
Tel/Fax: (01) 8124398, 8129273, 7742577
E-mail: afribankestate@yahoo.com
Website: www.afribank.net
Contact: Mr A. O. Olufon - MD/CEO

AFRIBANK INSURANCE BROKERS LIMITED
Business: Insurance Brokers
Address: 94 Broad Street (6th Floor) Lagos
Tel: (01) 2662550, 2662570, 2666649, 2666795
Fax: (01) 2662550
E-mail: afribankins@nove.net.ng
* 40, Okporo Road, Port Harcourt
* 3B Tamandu Road, Nassarawa G.R.A. Kano
* Kaura Namoda Street, off Tafawa Balewa Way, Area 3, Garki Abuja
Contact: Mr Pascal E. Egerue - MD/CEO

AFRIBANK INTERNATIONAL LTD (MERCHANT BANKERS)
Business: Merchant Banking
Address: Plot PC, 28, Afribank Street, Victoria Island, Lagos
Tel: (01) 2616089, 2616090, 2614644, 2166255
Fax: (01) 2616028
E-mail: ailhq@hyperia.com
* Afribank Plaza, 51/55, Broad Street, Lagos
* Akintola Williams House, Michael Okpara Street, Wuse Zone 7, Abuja.
Tel: (09) 5239523, 5239474 **Fax:** (09) 5239244
* Plot 15, Trans-Amadi Ind. Layout, Port Harcourt
Tel: (084) 238068, 238069, 238070 **Fax:** (084) 238072
Contact: Mr. Francis A. Odunlami - MD/CEO

AFRIBANK TRUST & INVESTMENTS LIMITED
Business: Stockbroking, Financial Services.
Address: 94, Broad Street (7th Floor), Lagos
Tel: (01) 2646961, 2663551 **Fax:** (01) 2646961
Contact: Mr Ben I. Nwoji - MD/CEO

AFRICA OILFIELD SERVICES LIMITED
Business: Oilfield Engineering Services
Address: Plot 272, Trans-Amadi Ind.Layout, Port Harcout
Tel: (084) 230283-4 (2L), 238817
Fax: (084) 238687, 238812
* First Zenith Height Building (Flat 661), 4, Cooper Road, Ikoyi, Lagos
Tel: (01) 2694229, 2696113
Contact: Mr David Simpson - MD/CEO

AFRICA ONLINE NIGERIA LIMITED
Business: Internet Service Provider
Address: Chartered Bank Building (6th Floor), 19, Martins Street, Lagos Island, Lagos.
Tel: (01) 2666473, 2641913 **Fax:** (01) 2666359
E-mail: funsho@panaol.com
Contact: Mr. Funsho Olamigoke - MD/CEO

AFRICA PORT SERVICES LIMITED
Business: Shipping, Clearing & Forwarding
Address: Plot G2, Moshood Abiola Way, Iganmu, Lagos
Tel: (01) 5850677, 5456155

AFRICA SHIPPING LIMITED
Business: Freight Forwarding, Clearing, Import and Export
Address: 54A, Kofo Abayomi Street, Victoria Island, Lagos
Tel: (01) 2626767, 2617357, 7748900 **Fax:** (01) 2617367
E-mail: africashipping@hyperia.com
Website: www.afrishipping-tradeamerica.com
Contact: Mrs Toyin Ogunmola Ubah - MD/CEO

AFRICAN ALLIANCE INSURANCE COMPANY LIMITED
Business: Life Assurance (Individual & Group) and Pensions
Address: 112, Broad Street, Lagos
Tel: (01) 2664300, 2664373, 2664398, 2664419
Fax: (01) 2660943
E-mail: info@africanallianceinsurance.com
Website: www.africanallianceinsurance.com
Contact: Mr. Opeoluwa Oredugba - MD/CEO

AFRICAN BROADCAST NETWORK
Business: Television Programming, Radio Broadcasting
Address: 49, Adeknle Fajuyi Way, G.R.A., Ikeja, Lagos
Tel: (01) 4971305, 7740520, 08023261380
Fax: (01) 4971305
E-mail: abn@mwebafrica.com
africanbarter@hyperia.com
Website: www.africanbroadcast.com
Contact: Mr. Yeside Oriyomi - GM/COO

AFRICAN DEVELOPMENT CONSULTING GROUP LIMITED
Business: Statistical/Research-based Consultancy, Industry Studies and Economic Information Services, Contract Research and Training/Seminars
Address: C & C Towers (8th Floor), Plot 1684, Sanusi Fafunwa Street, Victoria Island, Lagos
Tel: (01) 3201389, 3201390
Contact: Mr. Collins Uweribe - Head (Marketing/Sales)

AFRICAN DEVELOPMENT INSURANCE COMPANY LTD
Business: Life and Non-Life Insurance, Risk Management
Address: ADIC House, 78, Etim Inyang Crescent, Victoria Island, Lagos.
Tel: (01) 2624202-3(2L), 4702802 **Fax:** (01) 2624204
E-mail: adic@hyperia.com
adic@cybaaspace.com
Contact: Chief (Mrs) S. C. Oladipo - Co. Sec./Legal Adviser

AFRICAN EXPRESS BANK PLC
Business: Commercial Banking
Address: Plot 230, Idowu Martins St, Victoria Island, Lagos
Tel: (01) 2611250-2 (3L), 3200029-30 (2L), 4617662-4(3L), 7749719, 2700309
E-mail: customerservices@afexbank,com
Website: www.africanexpressbankplc.com
Contact: Mr Basil A. Onugu - MD/CEO

AFRICAN FARMS LIMITED
Business: Agro-Allied Business, Feed Processing, Livestock and Cotton Farming, Trading
Address: Block D, Flat 1, Eko Court Complex, Kofo Abayomi Street, Victoria Island, Lagos.
Tel: (01) 2618163, 2615346 **Fax:** (01) 2614894
Contact: Sam Iwuajoku - MD/CEO

AFRICAN GENERAL INSURANCE BROKERS LIMITED
Business: Insurance Brokers
Address: A.G.I.B. House, 32 Balogun Street, Lagos
Tel: (01) 2641302, 2660370 **Fax:** (01) 2663269
E-mail: agib@hotmail.com
* Plot 821, Obafemi Awolowo Way, Area 11, Garki, Abuja.
Tel: (09) 23455760
* 21 Hospital Road, Ikot Abasi, Akwa Ibom State
Tel: (085) 801204
Contact: Mrs S. O. Oladnjoye - MD/CEO

AFRICAN INSURANCE BROKERS LIMITED
Business: Insurance Broking and Consultancy
Address: 25, Boyle Street (1st Floor) Onikan, Lagos
Tel: (01) 2647786, 2647202 **Fax:** (01) 2692666
E-mail: aibbrokers@intracom.net.ng
* 3, Kanta Road, Kaduna
Tel: (062) 242943
* 135C, Aba Road, St John's, Port Harcourt
Tel: (084) 232013
Contact: Mr Peter C. Utulu - GM/CEO.

AFRICAN INTERNATIONAL BANK LIMITED
Business: Commercial Banking
Address: Gidan Ibrahim Dabo, 18, Ibrahim Taiwo Road, Kano
Tel: (064) 637847, 640451, 648259 **Fax:** (064) 636049
E-mail: business@aib.com.ng
* AIB Plaza, AIB Terrace, Akin Adesola Street, Victoria Island, Lagos
Tel: (01) 2620262-4(3L), 2620283-5(3L)
Fax: (01) 2620262, 2620270
* 112, Broad Street, Lagos
Tel: (01) 2664549, 2665614
Contact: Alh. Ibrahim Ahmed Kofa - Ag. MD/CEO

AFRICAN NEWSPAPER OF NIGERIA PLC
Business: Newspaper Publishing (THE TRIBUNE)
Address: Imalefalafia Street, Oke-Ado, Ibadan
Tel: (02) 310886, 310000 **Fax:** (02) 317573
E-mail: tribune@hyperia.com
Contact: Pastor Segun Olatunji - MD/Editor-in Chief

AFRICAN PACKAGING COMPANY LIMITED
Business: Manufacture of Aluminium Collapsible Tubes
Address: 20, Oba Akran Avenue, Ikeja, Lagos.
Tel: (01) 4971346 **Fax:** (01) 4976661
Contact: Mr . D. N. Sabarwa - Group MD/CEO

AFRICAN PAINTS (NIGERIA) PLC
Business: Manufacturing and Marketing of Paints
Address: Plot 51, Morison Crescent, Oregun Industrial Estate, Alausa, Lagos.
Tel: (01) 5557618-9 (2L) **Fax:** (01) 4963241
Contact: Prince O. R. Ladigbolu - MD

AFRICAN PETROLEUM PLC
Business: Marketing of Refined Petroleum Products, Blending of Lubricating Oils
Address: AP House 54/56, Broad Street, Lagos
Tel: (01) 2600050-7 (8L) **Fax:** (01) 2635290, 2634341
E-mail: aplagos@applcng.com
* 1, AP-National Road, Apapa, Lagos
Tel: (01) 5451227-8(2L), 5453086-7(2L), 5876826, 5870745
* 11, Moscow Road, Port Harcourt
Tel: (084) 236100-1(2L), 233340
* 33, Ali Akilu Road, Kaduna
Tel: (062) 236958-9 (2L), 233907
* Club Road, Kano
Tel: (064) 639581-2 (2L), 647052
Contact: Mr. Peter Eloka Okocha OON - Chairman
Mr. Abdullai Sule - MD/CEO

AFRICAN PRUDENTIAL INSURANCE COMPANY LIMITED
Business: Insurance
Address: Church House, 29, Marina, Lagos
Tel: (01) 2600180-2 (3L), 2664435 **Fax:** (01) 2635838
* 83, Ojuelegba Road, Surulere Lagos
Tel: (01) 836599, 08033254138
* 14, Supreme Shopping Centre, near Aso Guest Inn, Garki 11, Abuja. **Tel:** 08033156179
* 57, Old Market Road, Onitsha
Tel: (046) 216705
Contact: Mr O. E. Nwokocha - MD/CEO

AFRICAN SAFETY INSURANCE COMPANY LIMITED
Business: Non-Life Insurance
Address: 18, Okpara Avenue, P.O.Bix 3490, Enugu
Tel: (042) 255278, 259588
* 26, Abibu Oki Street, Marina Lagos
Tel: (01) 2644005
* 128, Ikwerere Road, Port Harcourt
* 2, Iboku Street, Old Market, Onitsha.
Tel: (046) 215766
* 119, Azikiwe Road, Aba.
Tel: (082) 223004
Contact: Ojie H. A. Nzepuome - MDO

AFRICAN SAFARI HOTEL, ABUJA
Business: Hospitality Services
Address: Plot 3226, off Aminu Kano Crescent, Zone A6, Maitama District, Abuja
Tel: (09) 2341365, 2341881

AFRICAN STEAMSHIP COMPANY NIGERIA LIMITED
Business: Shipping Agency, Air & Sea Freight Forwardimg, Gropage Export
Address: 34, Wharf Road, Apapa, Lagos
Tel: (01) 5803140-2 (3L), 5803410-2 (3L)
Fax: (01) 5871528
* 121, Custom Road, Port Harcourt
Tel: (084) 23710
Contact: Mrs Shirley Cook - GM

AFRICAN STEEL MILLS (NIGERIA) LIMITED
Business: Production of Steel Building Materials
Address: Plot 337, Ikorodu Industrial Estate, Odogunyan, Ikorodu, Lagos State
Tel: (01) 7741549 **Fax:** (01) 5450918, 5870916

AFRICAN TELECOMMUNICATIONS NETWORK LIMITED
Business: Telecommunications, Sales and Service of Digital Wireless Radio Communication Equipment.
Address: 10, Balarabe Musa Crescent, Victoria Island, Lagos
Tel: (01) 2619424, 2624357, 7744540, 7742291
Fax: (01) 2626830
E-mail: biz@atnl.com.ng
Contact: Mr Tomi Okorodudu - ED (Operations)

AFRICAN TEXTILES MANUFACTURERS LIMITED
Business: Manufacturing of Textile Goods
Address: 53, Fagge Takudu, Kano
Tel: (064) 632336, 642512-3 (2L), 647559
Fax: (064) 635572, 635671
E-mail: atmltd@ecnex.net
* Suhail Akar Lane, opp. Coca Cola Bottling Plant, Challawa Industrial Estate, Kano
* 4, Caulcrick Crescent, Apapa, Lagos
Tel: (01) 5455495
Contact: Mr. Suhail Akar - Chairman/CEO

AFRICAN UNIVERSITIES PRESS LIMITED
Business: Publishing of Educational & Literature Books
Address: 1st Road, Oluyole Industrial Estate, Scheme II, after Methodist High School, Lagos-Ibadan Expressway Link, Ibadan
Tel: (02) 2317208 **Fax:** (02) 2317909
E-mail: auppbl@infoweb.abs.net
Contact: Dr E. A. M Leigl - MD/CEO

AFRICAN WINGS (TRAVELS) LIMITED
Businees: Travel Agency, Tour Operators
Address: Lautai House, 5C, Wudil Road, Nassarawa, Kano
Tel: (064) 631745, 632420, 649623, 08037869682, 08044117534
Fax: (064) 631745
E-mail: africanwingstravels@hotmail.com
* Plot 2222, SFAX Close, Wuse Zone 4, Abuja
Tel: (09) 5232818, 5234075, 08037870193
Fax: (09) 5234075

AFRICANA-FEP PUBLISHERS LIMITED
Business: Publishing Books
Address: Book House Trust, 1, Africana-Fep Drive, Onitsha.
Tel: (046) 210669
* 4, Industrial Avenue, Ilupeju, Lagos
Tel: (01) 4731241
Contact: Mr R. O. Ekpeh - MD.

AFRIJET AIRLINES LIMITED
Business: Airline and Cargo Operations
Address: NAHCO Complex, Murtala Mohammed International Airport, P.O.Box 6413, Ikeja, Lagos
Tel: (01) 2882860, 4933484, 4933861, 7747800
Fax: (01) 4933483, 2882860
E-mail: afrijet@yahoo.com
afrijet@supernet300.com
Website: www.afrijet.com
Contact: Dr H. O. Demuren - MD/CEO.

AFRIKANA INVESTMENTS LIMITED
Business: Sales of Musical Equipment, Public-Address Systems and Electronic Appliances.
Address: 56/58 Iweka Road, Onitsha
Tel: (046) 411918
Contact: Mr Phillip Iheanacho - Chairman/CEO.

AFRILINKS NIGERIA LIMITED
Business: Sales and Maintenance of IT Products, Office Automation and Telecommunication Equipment.
Address: Lafayette Mall, Plot 1436, Sanusi Fafunwa Street, Victoria Island, Lagos
Tel: (01) 2625543, 3200566, 7753553, 08033000601
Fax: (01) 2625543
E-mail: afrilinks@intracom5.com
Website: www.afrilinks.com
Contact: Vivian Raliat Malik - Product Manager

AFRIONE LIMITED
Business: Provision of Internet Services & International Phone Services, Pre-Paid International Phone Cards Operators
Address: 15, Ahmadu Bello Way, Jos
Tel: (073) 450451 **Fax:** (073) 450452
Contact: Mr Matthew Udanoh - MD/CEO

AFRI-OVIS INSURANCE BROKERS LIMITED
Business: Insurance Broking
Address: 55, Kakawa Street, Lagos
Tel: (01) 2635659, 2634909, 2631658
Contact: Mr Iyawa Philip - MD/CEO

AFRI-PROJECTS CONSORTIUM
Business: General Consultancy Services
Address: Plot 2198, off IBB Way, Wuse Zone 4, Abuja
Tel: (09) 5237200-4 (5L) **Fax:** (09) 5237197
E-mail: apc@linkserve.com.ng

AFRIQUE SECURITIES & FINANCE LIMITED
Business: Stockbroking
Address: Investment House (3rd Floor), 27/29 Ali Akilu Road, Kaduna.
Tel: (062) 247621 **Fax:** (062) 215715
* Suite 5A, Tafawa Balewa Square Complex, Onikan Lagos.
Tel: (01) 2637288 **Fax:** (01) 2633093

AFRI-VENTURES NIGERIA LIMITED
Business: Livestock Farming
Address: Stallion House (4th Floor), 2, Ajose Adeogun Street, Victoria Island Lagos
Tel: (01) 4704769

AFRO SYSTEMS & TECHNOLOGY LIMITED
Business: IT Products and Systems Sales and Installation
Address: 1, Alhaji Kanike Close, off Awolowo Road, Ikoyi
Tel: (01) 2692030, 2671906, 2672017
E-mail: afrosys@excite.com
apt-ng@excite.com
* 22A Suez Crescent, Ibrahim Abacha Housing Estate, Wuse Zone 4, Abuja
* 10, Emekuku Street D-line, Port Harcourt
Contact: Chief S. N. Anyanwu - Chairman/CEO

AFROCAT (NIGERIA) COMPANY LIMITED
Business: Sales, Refurbishing & Service of Heavy Industrial

Equipment, Industrial Engineering Services, Transport & Haulage Services
Address: Km 5, Ekenwan Road, Benin City.
Tel: (052) 251446 **Fax:** (052) 259246
Contact: Mr. A. Iyamu - Chairman/CEO

AFROCOMMERCE (W.A) LIMITED
Business: Sales & Service of Industrial Technical Goods, Forklift Trucks, Machine Tools, Lubricants, Generators and Transformers
Address: 16, Commercial Road, Apapa, Lagos
Tel: (01) 5871391, 5871536, 5457939, 08033101722
Fax: (01) 5451513
E-mail: afrocom@alpha.linkserve.com
* Plot 468, Adetokunbo Ademola Crescent, Cadastral Zone A8, Wuse II, Abuja
* Plot 270, Trans-Amadi Ind, Layout, Port Harcourt
Tel: (084) 232400
Contact: Mr. Boyan Olovanov - MD/CEO

AFRO-EQUIP NIGERIA LIMITED
Business: Sales, Refurbishing and Service of Heavy-Duty Industrial and Earth-Moving Equipment, Industrial Engineering Services
Address: 1, 3 & 5, Osimiri Street, off Km 5, Enugu-Onitsha Expressway G.R.A. P.O.Box 2222, Enugu
Tel: (042) 253366, 257090 **Fax:** (042) 259701
E-mail: osimiri@infoweb.abs.net
Contact: Dr N. O. Jombo-Ofo -MD/CEO.

AFROMEDIA NIGERIA LIMITED
Business: Advertising Services
Address: Km 21, Badagry Expressway, Ajangbadi, Lagos
Tel: (01) 7741799, 7749039 **Fax:** (01) 7590480
E-mail: email@afromedianig.com
Contact: Mr. J. S. Olaghere - Chairman/MD

AFROMEDIA PLASTICS & ENGINEERING LIMITED
Business: Plastic Manufacturing
Address: Km 21, Badagry Expressway, Ajangbadi, Lagos
Tel: (01) 7741799, 7749039
Contact: Mr Akin Ire Olopade - Ag. MD/CEO

AFROTEC TECHNICAL SERVICES (NIGERIA) LIMITED
Business: Sales and Service of Construction and Building Equipment, Sales of Spare
Address: 21/23, Abimbola Street, Isolo Industrial Estate, Isolo, Oshodi Lagos
Tel/Fax: (01) 4811975
E-mail: afrotecindustries@skannet.com
afrotecindustries@linkserve.com
Contact: Mr. Gbenga Runsewe - ED/CEO

AFTRADE (NIGERIA) LIMITED
Business: Distribution of Plastic Raw Materials, Domestic Plastic Wares and Finished Goods
Address: 10/12, Industrial Estate Street, off Town Planning Way, Ilupeju, Lagos.
Tel: (01) 4971944, 4971922, 4930167 **Fax:** (01) 2618848
E-mail: aftrade@micro.com.ng
* 10, Faith Road, off Unity Road, Kano
* 19B, Ozubulu Road, off Port Harcourt Road, Aba
Contact: MR. R. S. Gwalani - Chairman/MD/CEO

AGATHA'S INTERIOR DESIGNS LIMITED
Business: Interior Designing and Decor. Services; Office and Home Furniture Sales
Address: 106 Awolowo Road S.W. Ikoyi Lagos
Tel: (01) 2690375, 8049346 **Fax:** (01) 2690375
E-mail: agathas@nova.net.ng
* 11, Gana Street, Maitama District, Abuja
Tel: (09) 6713066, 08042125489
Contact: Mrs Agatha Eric Udorie - CEO

AGBARA ESTATES LIMITED
Business: Real Estate Development and Management.
Address: Motorways Centre (3rd Floor), 1, Motorways Avenue, opp Seven-Up Factory, Oregun, Lagos
Tel: (01) 4722192
* Igbesa Road, South Industrial Zone, Agbara Estate, Agbara, Ogun State.
Tel: (01) 712320, 4713362 **Fax:** (01) 2622551
Contact: Mr. O. A. Odebunmi - MD/CEO

AGBODYKE INDUSTRIES LIMITED
Business: Importation of Automobile Spare Parts; General Contractors
Address: Ancestors House, 58, Onitsha Road, Nnewi, Anambra State
Tel: (046) 460383 **Fax:** (046) 460942
Contact: Mr Kene Onyedika Agbodike - Exec. Director

AGCOMEX LIMITED
Business: Distribution and Installation of Transformers
Address: 2A, Bauchi Road, Apapa Lagos
Tel/Fax: (01) 5878119
E-mail: agcomex@nigerianet.com
Contact: Mr H. P. Bogerd - MD/CEO

AGELEX PRINTERS LIMITED
Business: Printing, Publishing, Packaging and Advertising
Address: 32, Bankole Street, Apongbon, Lagos
Tel: (01) 2662600
E-mail: agelex@onebox.com
* 6B Odanye Close, off James Oluleye Street, off Adeniyi Jones Avenue, Ikeja, Lagos
Contact: Mr Okorosi Ikenna - MD/CEO

AGILITY & BROTHERS ENTERPRISES NIGERIA LIMITED
Business: Importation, of Paints and Industrial Chemicals
Address: 222, Ikwerre Road, Diobu, Port Harcourt
Tel: (084) 238369, 570612, 570673
Contact: Chief Jude Nwagbo - MD/CEO

AGOFURE NIGERIA LIMITED
Business: Transportation, Courier Srvices, Retail Stores
Address: 154, P. T. I. Road, Effurun, Warri
Tel: (053) 254839, 257275, 257688, 08046103025
Contact: Mr Godwin O. Agofure - Chairman/CEO

AGIP ENERGY & NATURAL RESOURCES LIMITED
Business: Oilfield Engineering Services, Production of Oil from Offshore Concession
Address: Agip House, PC, 23, Engineering Close, off Idowu Taylor Street, Victoria Island, Lagos.
Tel: (01) 2621600-9
Contact: Mr. S. Palma

AGIPNIGERIA PLC

Business: Marketing & Distribution of Petroleum Products Blending & Sales of Lubricants, Manufacture & Marketing of Insecticides & Deodorants.
Address: Agip House, PC, 23, Engineering Close, Victoria Island, Lagos
Tel: (01) 2613862, 2613884, 2621107
Fax: (01) 2614930, 2615111
* Plot 509, Olusegun Obasanjo Way, Wuse Zone 3, Abuja.
Tel: (09) 5231569
Contact: Mr. Salvatore Recupero - MD/CEO

AGRIC DIVISION (Div. of Dizengoff West Africa (Nig.) Ltd)

Business: Manufacturers' Representatives in Agricultural Machineries, Agro Chemicals, Irrigation Equipment, Poultry and Livestock
Address: 28, Creek Road, Apapa, Lagos
Tel: (01) 5872346, 5874217, 5875549, 7749615
Fax: (01) 5874021
E-mail: dizengoff@dizengoff.com
Website: www.dizengoff.com
* Plot 108, Adetokunbo Ademola Crescent, Cadastral Zone A8, Wuse II, Abuja
Tel: (09) 4131240-1 (2L), 4139558
* 58C, Tafawa Balewa Road, Kano
Tel: (064) 645015

AGRIC INTERNATIONAL TECHNOLOGY & TRADE (NIGERIA) LIMITED (AGRITED)

Business: Agro-Allied & Poultry Services, Premix Production
Address: Plot 897B, Balarabe Musa Crescent, off Samuel Manuwa Street, Victoria Island, Lagos
Tel: (01) 2615932, 2620909, 2624482 **Fax:** (01) 619893
E-mail: mishlat@nigol.net.ng
* 1A, Queen Amina Road, Angwanrimi, G. R. A, Kaduna
Tel: (062) 245252

AGRIC SERVICES NIGERIA LIMITED

Business: Construction of Cold Rooms, Sales and Installation of Suspended Acoustic Ceilings, Window Blinds and Security Doors
Address: 1, Ashanti Road, P.O.Box 808, Apapa, Lagos
Tel: (01) 5875509, 5872392 **Fax:** (01) 5875382
E-mail: csa@cyberspace.net.ng

AGRICULTRAL PRODUCT PROCESSING MILL LIMITED

Business: Milling and Refining of Vegetable Oil
Address: 151/152, Club Road, Kano
Tel: (064) 630808, 630854, 0803786320
Fax: (064) 630808
Contact: Alh. Sani Aminu Kofa - ED(Admin/Finance)/CEO

AGRO ALLIED DEVELOPMENT ENTERPRISES LIMITED

Business: Exporting of Cocoa Products (Butter, Powder & Liquor) Solid Minerals & Agricultural Products, Importation of Frozen Fish, Agricultural Equipment & Machinery & Chemicals.
Address: 12B, Akin Olugbade Street, off Idowu Martins Street, Victoria Island, Lagos.
Tel: (01) 2627818, 2627897, 616298, 08023222789
Fax: (01) 2618365
* 4/5 Happy Home Avenue, Kirikiri Industrial Layout, Apapa, Lagos
Tel: (01) 7730529, 7740633, 7752323, 7752424, 7755060, 5878467 **Fax:** (01) 5875251
E-mail: aadel@beta.linkserve.com
* Plot 477, Arusha Crescent, off Nouakchott Street Wuse Zone 1, Abuja
Contact: Mr. Suresh Puri - Chairman/CEO

AGRO-COMMODITIES HANDLING SERVICES LIMITED

Business: Agricultural Commodities Handling, Warehousing and Transportation.
Address: Plot 13, Block G, Oshodi Ind. Scheme, Oshodi-Isolo Expressway (Charity Bus-Stop) Oshodi, Lagos
Tel: (01) 4527787, 4521806
E-mail: agrocomm@linkserve.com
* 100, Oyemekun Road, Akure.
Tel: (034) 243727

AGRO-INDUSTRIES & DEVELOPMENT SCHEME LIMITED

Business: Land Reclamation and Dewatering Services, Agro-Industrial Developers & Consultants, Plant Hire
Address: 4, Warehouse Road, P.O.Box 187, Apapa, Lagos
Tel: (01) 5870995, 5870118, 5874971, 5876372
Fax: (01) 5870949
E-mail: morpol@linkserve.com.ng
Contact: Alh. Ibrahim Abdurrahman - MD/CEO

AGROMAR (NIGERIA) LIMITED

Business: Fish and General Sea food Importation
Address: 57/59, Osolo Way, off International Airport Road, Aswani Area, Ajao Estate, Isolo, Lagos
Tel/Fax: (01) 4523378
E-mail: agromar@micro.com.ng
* Sagamu/Ijebu-Ode Road, Odogbolu, Ogun State
Tel/Fax (037) 320629
Contact: Chief R. T. Bakare - Chairman/MD/CEO

AGUAGEM DENTAL CLINIC LIMITED

Business: Dental Care Services
Address: Fabac Centr, 3B, Ligali Ayorinde Street, Victoria Island, Lagos
Tel: (01) 2620976, 2626376
Contact: V. A. da Costa - Dental Surgeon

AGUATECNICA COMPANY LIMITED

Business: Construction of Swimming Pools, Sales of Swimming Pool Equipment and Allied Products, Water Treatment Chemicals, Industrial and Oilfield Chemicals, and Pharmaceuticals Products
Address: 2, Ola Ayinde Street, Ikeja, Lagos.
Tel: (01) 4936981, 4974312, 4971681, 4962149
Fax: (01) 4936982
* 1st Artillery Junction, Port Harcourt
Tel: (084) 612817
Contact: Mr. John Ifenso Okpala - Chairman/CEO

AGUBAS NIGERIA LIMITED

Business: Industrial & Management Consulting, Feasibility Studies, Finance Sourcing & Export Promotion, Fabrication of Industrial Machinery.
Address: 55, Western Avenue, Ojuelegba, Lagos
Tel/Fax: (01) 5851043

E-mail: agubas@alpha.linkserve.com
Contact: Dr Chidi Ezeaguba - Chairman/CEO.

AGURA HOTEL, ABUJA
Business: Hospitality Services
Address: Moshood Abiola Road, Area 7, Garki, Abuja.
Tel: (09) 2341753-60 (8L), 2342000 **Fax:** (09) 2342750
E-mail: agurahotels@yahoo.com
Website: www.agurahotel.com
Contact: Prince Daniel Kanu - CEO

AGUSTO & COMPANY LIMITED
Business: Credit Rating Agency, Business Information Services, Training
Address: 57, Marina, Lagos.
Tel: (01) 2643571-4 (4L), 2643572, 2643574-5 (2L)
Fax: (01) 2643576
E-mail: info@augusto.com
Website: www.augusto.com
Contact: Mrs Vivien Shobo - MD/CEO

AHMED ZAKARI & COMPANY
Business: Chartered Accountants
Address: African Alliance Building (5th Floor) Sani Abacha Way, Kano
Tel: (064) 645400, 646447, 647888, 08023095804, 08037019128
Fax: (064) 647888
Contact: Alh. Ahmed Zakari - Principal Partner

AIA INTERNATIONAL GROUP
Business: Sales & Maintenance of Electrical & Telecommnication Equipment
Address: Wadata House (3rd Floor), Plot 1247, Aminu Kano Crescent, Wuse II, Abuja
Tel: (09) 5234272-3 (2L)
E-mail: sunny-hitest@yahoo.com
Contact: Mr Sunny A. Arusuraire - Chairman/CEO

AICETEC NIGERIA LIMITED
Business: Measurement, Instrumentation and Control Engineering and Services
Address: 6, Shiro Street, off Ikorodu Road, Fadeyi, Lagos
Tel: (01) 4705939, 7738307 **Fax:** (01) 862050
E-mail: aiceteclcmeter@yahoo.com

AIICO INSURANCE PLC
Business: All classes of Insurance
Address: AIICO Plaza, Plot PC 12, Afribank Street, Victoria Island, Lagos
Tel: (01) 2610651, 2612472, 2612527, 2613568, 2614049, 2614669, 2615395, 2618481
Fax: (01) 2617433
E-mail: info@aiicoplc.com
Website: www.aiicoplc.com
Contact: Mr. Jon Michael C. Quirk - MD/CEO
Mr. Charles A. Okhavhe - Co. Sec./Legal Adviser

AIKON ENGINEERING LIMITED
Business: Oilfield Engineering Services, Procurement and Calibration, Equipment/Vehicle Leasing and Services, Sales of Diamond/Tricome Drilling Bits
Address: Km 5, East-West Road, Rumuodara, Port Harcourt.
Tel: (084) 611965, 612936, 613249 **Fax:** (084) 611948
E-mail: aikon@aikon-ng.com
Contact: Engr Chris Ujah - Chairman/MD/CEO

AIL SECURITIES LIMITED
Business: Stockbroking and Portfolio Management.
Address: 94, Broad Street (5th Floor), Lagos.
Tel: (01) 2644131, 2663223, 2660518, 8154432
* Afribank House, 3, Kaura Namoda Street, Area 3, Garki Abuja.
Tel: (09) 2342634
* Afribank House, Afribank Plc Kaduna Main Branch, Kaduna.
* Plot 15, Trans-Amadi Ind. Layout, Port Harcourt
Tel: (084) 238068-71 (4 L)
Contact: Mr Jubril Isa - MD/CEO

AIM GROUP
Business: Multi-Disciplinary Engineering Consultancy Services. Real Estate Development, Confectionery Production, Petroleum Products Marketing, Radio Broadcasting Services
Address: AIM Plaza, Plot 267A, Etim Inyang Crescent, Victoria Island Annex, Lagos
Tel: (01) 2614838, 2614848 **Fax:** (01) 2614779, 2616636
E-mail: aimlagos@hyperia.com
Website: www.aimgroup.nu
* AIM Centre, Plot 592, Ibrahim Babangida Drive South City Centre, Garki, Abuja.
Tel: (09) 2340057, 2340065 **Fax:** (09) 2340065
E-mail: aima@infoweb.abs.net
Contact: Engr. Amin I. Moussalli - MD

AINONISE (NIGERIA) LIMITED
Business: Sales &Installation of Kitchen Equipment & Systems
Address: 7, Saka Jojo St, off Idejo St, Victoria Island, Lagos
Tel: (01) 615591, 615112, 2620314, 4706942
Fax: (01) 2620314
E-mail: aino@cyberspace.net.ng

AIR AFRIQUE (NIGERIA)
Business: International Airline Service
Address: 24A, Amodu Tijani Street, off Sanusi Fafunwa Street, Victoria Island, Lagos.
Tel: (01) 2621891, 2621892, 2616405, 2616467
Fax: (01) 2621893
Contact: Mr. Codjia Guy - GM

AIR FRANCE (NIGERIA)
Business: International Airline Services
Address: ICON House, (4th Floor), Plot 999f, Idejo/Danmole Street Victoria Island Lagos
Tel: (01) 4610461, 4612345, 7740701 (Airport); 7740702 (Cargo), 08034612345
Fax: (01) 2617959
E-mail: mail.los@airfrance.fr
loscargo@airfrance.fr
* Plot 1267, Ahmad Bello Way, Garki, Abuja
Tel: (09) 3147419-20 (2L)
* Eastern Garden House 1, Ogbunabali Layout/ Aba Road, Port Harcourt.
Tel: (084) 231917, 486901-2 (2L) **Fax:** (084) 238106
Contact: Mr. Pierre de Saint-Albin - GM

AIR GABON (NIGERIA)
Business: International Airline Services
Address: Big Leaf Hous, 7, (Plot 1664), Oyin Jolayemi Street, Victoria Island, Lagos
Tel: (01) 2624902, 08033006598 **Fax:** (01) 2624903
Contact: Mr Rehouma Mohamed - GM.

AIR INDIA (NIGERIA)
Business: International Airline Services
Address: 16/16A, Tafawa Balewa Square Complex, Lagos
Tel: (01) 2635418 **Fax:** (01) 2635481
E-mail: airindialagos@hotmail.com
Website: www.airindia.com
Contact: Mr P. B Mistry - GM (Nigeria, Central & W. Africa)

AIR LIQUIDE NIGERIA PLC
Business: Manufacture of Industrial Gases & Medical Oxygen, Sales of Welding Equipment
Address: Plot 232A, Adeola Odeku St, Victoria Island, Lagos
Tel: (01) 2617704, 613983 **Fax:** (01) 2622258
* 104/106, Ladipo Street, Mushin, Lagos
Tel: (01) 4521875, 4523937, 523594, 7746445
Fax: (01) 4521251
* Plot 108, Trans-Amadi Industrial Layout, Port Harcourt
Tel: (084) 238064-6 (3L), 230301, 230695
* Plot 2036, Cadastral Zone A2, Abuja
* 71A, Airport Road Warri
Contact: Mr. Jean Yves Faudou - MD/CEO

AIR SEA FREIGHTERS LIMITED
Business: Shipping, Freight Clearing and Forwarding, Transportation, Cargo Brokers & Superintendents, Stevedoring and Consultancy
Address: 213, Aba Road, opposite Shell Residential Area Port Harcourt
Tel: (084) 612582-3 (2L), 08033428463 **Fax:** (084) 610592
* 2C, Forcados Road, Apapa, Lagos
Tel: (01) 5453905
Contact: Sir Enoch A Iwueze - Chairman/CEO

AIR SEPARATION (NIGERIA) LIMITED
Business: Manufacturers of Industrial & Medical Oxygen, Sales of 'AirSep PSA Oxygen-Generating Systems'
Address: Plot 7A, Block C, Acme Road, Ogba Industrial Estate, Lagos.
Tel: (01) 4923834, 4925862, 4925000 **Fax:** (01) 4925000
E-mail: airsep@alpha.linkserve.com
* Cross River House, 42, Bishop Oluwole Street, Victoria Island, Lagos.
Tel: (01) 3201408
Contact: Engr. Sosan A Akpieyi - GM /CEO

AIRBORNE EXPRESS NIGERIA LIMITED
Bsiness: Courier, Freight & Cargo Services
Address: Airborne Plaza, 28, Aromire Avenue, off Adeniyi Jones Avenue, Ikeja, Lagos
Tel: (01) 4938148, 4972647, 4742285
Website: www.airborneexpress.com

AIRCOM NIGERIA LIMITED
Business: Sales, Installation, and Maintenance of Telecommunication Systems and Office Automation
Address: Kingsway Building (1st Floor), 51, Marina Lagos
Tel: (01) 2663370, 2641452-3 (2 L) **Fax:** (01) 2667338
* Aircom Plaza, 57A, Adeniyi Jones Avenue
Contact: Mr. Yemi Idowu - MD/CEO

AIRCRAFT, AVIONICS, PARTS & SUPPORT LIMITED
Bsiness: Military & Commercial Aircraft Maintenance & Consultancy
Address: 17, Sowemimo Street, G.R.A., Ikeja, Lagos
Tel: (01) 4934518-9 (2L) **Fax:** (01) 4934518
E-mail: aapsakm@cyberspace.net.ng
* 121, Ikeja Close, off Oyo Street, off Moshood Abiola Road, Area 2, Section 1, Garki, Abuja
Contact: Mr J. A. Badejo - GM

AIRFLOW ENGINEERING WORKS LIMITED
Business: Manufacturing and Installation of Airconditioning Products, Electrical and Plumbing Installation, Engineering Facilities Maintenance.
Address: 25/27, Oke-Aro Road, By Taju-Bello B/Stop, Iju-Agege, Lagos
Tel: (01) 7741497, 7745171, 7929763
Fax: (01) 7741497, 4930634
E-mail: airflowng@alpha.linkserve.com
airflowng@nova.net.ng
* Yashua Plaza (Suite 35), beh. AP Plaza, Adetokunbo Ademola Crescent, Wuse II, Abuja
Tel: (09) 6703683, 08022907647
Contact: Mr. Sola Giwa - MD/CEO

AIRLINE SERVICES LIMITED
Business: In-Flight Operations, Lounge & Bar Operation, Contract Catering, Warehousing
Address: 13B, Bishop Oluwole Street, Victoria Island, Lagos
E-mail: info@airlineserve.com
* Murtala Mohammed Airport, Ikeja, Lagos
Tel: (01) 2618657, 7749652 **Fax:** (01) 4975129
Contact: Mr Colin M. Waterton - MD/CEO

AIRTEL NIGERIA LIMITED
Business: Distribution, Sales & Service of Mobile Phones, GSM Services Agency
Address: Plot 224, Etim Inyang Crescent, off Muri Okunola Street, Victoria Island, Lagos
Tel: (01) 461960-6 (2L), 08022912311 **Fax:** (01) 4619607
E-mail: info@airtelng.com
Website: www.airtelng.com

AIRWAVE HOTELS NIGERIA LIMITED
Business: Hospitality Services
Address: Plot 13/527, Durban Street, Cadastral Zone A8, off Adetokunbo Ademola Crescent, Wuse II, Abuja
Tel: (09) 5240149, 5240151
Contact: Dr I. Iwuh - Chairman/CEO

AJANAKU GROUP OF HOSPITALS
Business: Medical and Health-Related Services
Address: 20, Sura Mogaji St, off Coker Road, Ilupeju, Lagos
Tel: (01) 4960418

AJAOKUTA STEEL COMPANY LIMITED
Business: Mining and Processing of Iron Ore into Steel
Address: Steel City, P.M.B 1000, Ajaokuta, Kogi State

Tel: (058) 400221, 400432 **Fax:** (058) 400150
E-mail: ascomdce@hyperia.com
* Federal Secretariat Phase II (2nd Floor, Rm 283), Ikoyi, Lagos
Tel: (01) 2670756
* Metallurgical Training Institute, Km 6/7, Onitsha-Owerri Road, Onitsha
Tel: (046) 217430, 08033379989
Contact: I. D. Mohammed - Manager (Public Relations)

AJAYI MEMORIAL HOSPITAL LIMITED
Business: Provision of Medical Services
Address: 159, Moshood Abiola Way, Ebute Metta, Lagos.
Tel: (01) 5830131, 08023131700, 08033008328
Contact: Mrs. P. A. Ajayi - Exec. Director/CEO

AJE & BAWORA (NIGERIA) LIMITED
Business: Warehousing and Transportation, Exporters, Clearing and Forwarding, Consultancy
Address: Plot 57, Akanbi Onitiri Close, Eric Moore Rd, Lagos
Tel: (01) 7744208, 4812055, 08023703377, 08033059703
Contact: Mr. E. E. O. Bali - Chairman/CEO

AJELENJE NIGERIA LIMITED
Business: Clearing and Forwarding, Food Processing, Distribtuion of Car Paints and Additives, General Contractors, Newspaper Publishing
Address: 46, Sadiku Street, Olodi-Apapa, Lagos
Tel: (01) 5450300, 08033060896 **Fax:** (01) 5450289
E-mail: ajelenje@ajelenjegroup.com
Contact: Mr Katsina U. O. Uzor - Chairman/CEO

AJOKE STORES LIMITED
Business: Importation and Marketing of Food Commodities, Dairies and Domestic Appliances
Address: 22, Tijani Ashogbon Street, Bariga Lagos
Tel: (01) 7744349,.4974678, 820580, 825749
* 41, John/Oke-Arin Street, Lagos Island, Lagos
Tel: (01) 2642559, 2642743, 2665647
Contact: Mrs M. A. Okusanya - Chairman/CEO.

AKAROLO GROUP OF COMPANIES
Business: Building & Civil Engineering, Importers, Security Services, Real Estate Development.
Address: Plot 36, Trans-Amadi Industrial Layout, P.O.Box 128, Port Harcourt.
Tel: (084) 231665, 335740 **Fax:** (084) 231665
Contact: Chief A. W. Akarolo - Chairman/CEO
Chief (Mrs) P. N. Akarolo - MD

AKBAK ENGINEERING & TECHNICAL SERVICES INC.
Business: Importation & Sales of Valves and Flow-Control Equipment and Accessories
Address: 13, Raymond Njoku Street, S.W. Ikoyi, Lagos
Tel: (01) 2695491, 2695492 **Fax:** (01) 2691669
E-mail: sales@tyco-nigeria.com
* 380, Ikorodu Road, Maryland, Ikeja Lagos
Tel: (01) 4962172, 4971907, 4716355 **Fax:** (01) 4930903

AKER NIGERIA LIMITED (Aker Maritime)
Business: Maritime Services, Drilling and Construction, Oil Industry Consultancy Services.
Address: Aker Road, Rumuolumeni, Port Harcourt
Tel: (084) 239271, 239273, 571711, 571715
Contact: Mr F. O. Agu - Admin/Personal Manager..

AKIN IBIYODE & COMPANY
Business: Estae Surveyors & Valuers, Property & Project Management, Estate Agency
Address: 64, Iwo Road, Ibadan
Tel: (02) 8104459, 8108144, 08023379496, 08023387059, 08023445494, 08033272618, 08055223031
E-mail: ibiyode@infoweb.abs.net
Contact: Chief Akin Ibiyode - Principal Partner

AKIN OLAIFA & COMPANY
Business: Estae Surveyors & Valuers, Property & Project Management, Estate Agency
Address: 92, Oyemekun Road, Akure
Tel: (034) 243695
* Aduke House (3rd Floor), 1, Adeola Adeoye, Street, off Toyin /Olowu Streets, Ikeja, Lagos
Tel: (01) 4974709, 4975376

AKINSOMI & PARTNERS
Business: Estae Surveyors & Valuers, Real Estate Developmemt & Management, Estate Agency
Address: New Niger House Annex (4th Floor), 3, Tinubu Street, Lagos Island, Lagos
Tel: (01) 2667229, 2667231, 08023467804
Fax: (01) 2668059
E-mail: ayoakinsomi@infoweb.abs.net
* Bensima House (Suite C4), Plot 2942, Aguiyi Ironsi Street, Maitama District, Abuja
Tel: (09) 4130636, 4130737
Contact: Mr Ayo Akinsomi - Principal Partner

AKINTOLA WILLIAMS, DELOITTE & TOUCHE
Business: Chartered Accountants, Management & Taxation Consultancy Services, Company Secretarial Services, Receivership/Special Corporate Services
Address: 235, Ikorodu Road, Lagos
Tel: (01) 4930720-4 (5L) **Fax:** (01) 4978736
Contact: Mr Victor G. Hammond - Chairman/CEO

AKITORCH SECURITIES LIMITED
Business: Portfolio and Funds Management, Capital Market Operations
Address: 3A Adebayo Mokuolu Street, Anthony, Lagos
Tel: (01) 3422830-9 (10L), 7741931, 7755521
Fax: (01) 3422830
E-mail: info@akitorch.net
Website: www.akitorch.net
Contact: Mr Victor O. Akinmoluwa - MD/CEO.

AKKAD GROUP OF COMPANIES
Business: Trading, Manufacturing, Investments
Address: Plot 104/105, Sharada Ind. Esate, Phase II, Kano
Tel: (064) 660024, 662186, 666391 **Fax:** (064) 662136
E-mail: akkadgroup@ecnx.net
* 38E, Marine Road, Apapa G.R.A., Lagos
Contact: Alh. Mohammed L. Akkad - Chairman/CEO

AKKAD TANNING COMPANY LIMITED
Business: Hide & Skins Tanning, Exportation
Address: Sharada Industrial Estate, Kano

Tel: (064) 630025, 630030, 634389 **Fax:** (064) 634136
Contact: Alh. Mohammed L. Akkad - Chairman

AKKLAIM TELECOMMS LIMITED
Business: Telecommunication Service Provider
Address: 7, Norman Williams St, South-West Ikoyi, Lagos
Tel: (01) 2624213-4 (2L), 2695387, 7595000, 7590759
Fax: (01) 2624214
* Plot 567, Durban Street, off Adetokunbo Ademola Crescent, Wuse II, Abuja.
Tel: (09) 5237344, 5238444 **Fax:** (09) 5237347
*2B, Agudama Avenue, D-Line, Port Harcourt
Tel: (084) 237500, 234101 **Fax:** (084) 230678
E-mail: akklaim@alpha.linkserve.com
Contact: Mrs. Halita Aliyu - MD/CEO

AKOWHO SERVICES LIMITED
Business: Engineering (Mechanical & Electrical); Welding & Hydrotesting Works; Instrumentation; Oil Pipeline Maintenance; Supply of Industrial Spare Parts.
Address: 1, Ovonomo St, off Okere-Ugborikoko Road, Warri.
Tel: (053) 253633, 251074 **Fax:** (053) 251074
Contact: Chief Paul O. Ideh - Chairman/CEO.

AKPAKA ASSOCIATES LIMITED
Business: Importers & Exporters, General Commerce
Address: 132, Azikiwe Road, P.O.Box 20606, Aba
Tel: (082) 233771, 301290, 08046104422
Fax: (082) 231516
E-mail: akpakaassociates@yahoo.com
* Shop C53, Niger 1, Trad Fair Complex, Lagos
Tel: (01) 8048688
* E-137, Abacha Line, Sabon Gari Market, Kano
Tel: (064) 649204
Contact: Mr. Alphonsus O. Akpaka - MD/CEO

AKRON (NIGERIA) LIMITED
Business: Importation and Distribution of Diary Foods and Commodities, Real Estate Developers
Address: 86A, Allen Avenue Ikeja, Lagos
Tel: (01) 4936291, 4936293, 4936310-1 (2L), 7915844
Fax: (01) 2617258, 4971672
E-mail: AkronNigeria@aol.com
Contact: Mr. G. T. Dalamal - Chairman/CEO

AKROSAMIK INVESTMENTS LIMITED
Business: Clearing & Forwarding Agency, Transportation, Oilfield Equipment Procurement and Supply
Address: 7, Ajoke Akinbami St, off Unity Road, Ikeja, Lagos.
Tel: (01) 4975778, 4807265, 7746232, 8164502
Fax: (01) 4975778
E-mail: akrosam@infoweb.abs.net
* 59, Western Avenue Ojuelegba, Surulere, Lagos
Tel: (01) 4807265, 7746232
Contact: Mr. Samuel Akpan - Chairman/CEO

AKSA GENERATORS (WEST AFRICA) LIMITED
Business: Assembly, Sales & Maintenance of Generators
Address: 90, Kudirat Abiola Way, beh. Philips Factory, Oregun, Lagos
Tel: (01) 4813121, 08033026880 Fax: (01) 3205681
E-mail: aksanigria@yahoo.com
Contact: Mr Mutlu Sevmil - Chairman/CEO

AKU INTERNATIONAL (NIGERIA) LIMITED
Business: Importation of General Goods, Manufacturing
Address: 9/10, Ojike Lane, Aba
Tel: (082) 221151, 220707 **Fax:** (082) 234050
* 37B, Modele St, off Tejuosho St, Surulere, Lagos.
Tel: (01) 832592
Contact: Chief Kalu K. Onuma - Chairman/MD/CEO

AKU-ROGERS LIMITED
Business: Sole Importer & Distributor of WYNN's Car Care Products, Sale of Auto Spare Parts
Address: 115, Borno Way, Ebute-Metta, Lagos
Tel: (01) 8185385, 08033339923
Contact: Mr. Romanus N. Onyene - Chairman/CEO

AKWA IBOM PROPERTY & INVESTMENTS COMPANY LTD
Business: Development Finance & Investment Services
Address: Hosing Estate, Abak Road, Uyo
Tel: (085) 201298

AKWIWU MOTORS LIMITED
Business: Road Haulage (Goods & Heavy Equipment); Shipping, Clearing and Forwarding; Tyre and Spare Parts Imporation; Automobile Maintenance
Address: 24, Ado Avenue, Apapa, Lagos
Tel: (01) 5451473-4(3L), 5870542 **Fax:** (01) 5451473
E-mail: micl@nigol.net.ng
*108, Refnery Road, Ekpan, Warri.
Tel: (053) 254130
Contact: Mr. O. N. Akwiwu - MD/CEO

AL'RASHEED GROUP
Business: Electrical Home Appliances, Footwear Sales, Foods and Commodities Trade.
Address: 26, Oladipo Kuku St, off Allen Ave, Ikeja, Lagos.
Tel: (01) 4937205, 4971840, 08023005916, 08033037150
Contact: Abdul Rasheed Agunbiade - Group CEO

ALAGBE & PARTNERS
Business: Estate Surveyors & Valuers
Address: 2, Muazu Mohammed Road, opp. New Central Post Office, Minna
* Edo House (1st Floor, Suite 12B), Plot 1225, Bishop Oluwole Street, Victoria Island, Lagos
Tel: (01) 3200372, 8149737, 08023071137

ALAN UNIVERSAL GROUP
Business: Oil & Gas Field Development, Drilling & Workover Services; Marketing of Crude Oil & Petroleum Products; International Business Finance
Address: Great Nigeria House, 47/57, Martins Street, Lagos
Tel: (01) 2644547, 4744092, 08033032696
Fax: (01) 2660024
E-mail: alanni@linkserve.com
Contact: Mr. Anthony Alani - Chairman/CEO

ALAR LIMITED
Business: Manufacture of Aluminium & Steel Roofing/ Cladding, Translucent Sheets, Guttaint Roofing/ Cladding & Special Fibre Products
Address: Plot 26, Oregun Rd, Oregun Ind Estate, Ikeja, Lagos
Tel: (01) 967296, 967987
* G.M.P. Compound, Plot 490 (7), Wuse II, CAD

Zone A8, Wuse Abuja.
Tel: (09) 5236203
Contact: Mr. J. Franklin - Project Co-ordinator

ALARM CENTRE LIMITED
Business: Security Escort Services, Distress- Call Monitoring, Sales of Security and Surveillance Systems
Address: 17A, Fola Osibo Street, off Road 14, Lekki Phase 1, Lekki, Lagos
Tel: (01) 5555858, 5555859, 08023519679, 08034051887
* 12, Waziri Ibrahim Crescent, off Elsie Femi-Pearse Street, Victoria Island, Lagos.
Tel: (01) 2615852, 7744200, 7749659, 7753606, 3200453, 3205198
E-mail: cctvnig@beta.linkserve.com
Contact: Engr. H. Obi - MD/CEO

ALBA CLINICS & MEDICAL CENTRE LIMITED
Business: Medical & Health Care Services
Address: 25, Constitution Road, Kaduna.
Tel: (062) 241234-5 (2L) **Fax:** (062) 249388
Contact: Senator (Dr.) Olu A Alabi - Chairman/Chf Med. Dir

ALBA NIGERIA LIMITED
Business: Environmental Management and Engineering Services, Oil Spill Control.
Address: 40, Norman Williams Street, S.W. Ikoyi
Tel: (01) 2693139 - 42 (4L) **Fax:** (01) 2693570, 2693565
E-mail: info@albanigria.com
alba_ltd@yahoo.com
Contact: Joy Laniyan - MD/CEO

ALBA PETROLEUM & CHEMICAL INDUSTRIES LIMITED
Business: Detergent and Soap Manufacturers and Marketers
Address: 46, Aba-Owerri Road, P.O.Box 695, Aba
Tel: (082) 221478, 224992
Contact: Chief Albert N. Ibeanu - MD/CEO

AL-BASHA RESTAURANT & TAKE-AWAY
Business: 126, Awolowo Road, S. W., Ikoyi, Lagos
Tel: (01) 2692971, 7754400, 08023155731
Fax: (01) 4615961
* Plot 643, Sassandra Street, off Usuma Street, Maitama District, Abuja
Tel: (09) 4138038-9 (2L)
Contact: Mr Ali Fawaz - Chairman

ALBANS INTERNATIONAL (NIGERIA) LIMITED
Business: Oilfield Marine Engineering Services, Marine Transportation, Consultancy.
Address: 67, Ogbunabali Road, P. O. Box 8090, Port Harcourt.
Tel: (084) 236976, 332284
* 9, Bakpa Johnson Street, P.O.Box 1894, Warri
Tel: (053) 233691
Contact: Chief. G. M. Olele - Chairman

ALBARKA AIR PLC
Business: Airline Services
Address: 8A Udi Street Off Aso Drive, Maitama, Abuja
Tel: (09) 5233554,5232619, 5233576 **Fax:** (09) 5233576
E-mail: albarkaair@skannet.com
Contact: Brig. Gen. Buba Marwa (rtd) - Chief Steward
Capt. D. S. A. Tarfa - MD

ALBERDIN ENERGY SERVICES LIMITED
Business: Oil Well Drilling and Support Services (Well Testing, Casing & Tubular Running, Drilling, Waste & Environmental Services)
Address: Alberdin House, Plot 133H, Trans-Amadi Industrial Layout, P.O.Box 6795, Port Harcourt
Tel/Fax: (084) 234210, 08023054467, 08023384380, 08033107811 Fax: (084) 234210
E-mail: alberdin@phca.linkserve.com
Contact: Mr. Albert O. Umuze - MD/CEO

AL-BRETT INTERNATIONAL LIMITED
Business: Stockist of Promotional & Corporate Gift Items; Engraving & Colour Transfer, Screen Printing.
Address: Eleganza Biro Plaza (8th Floor), Plot 634, Adeyemo Alakija Street, Victoria Island, Lagos
Tel: (01) 2702966, 4801262, 7752552, 08033000399
Fax: (01) 2705957
E-mail: albrett@yahoo.com
mails@albrettnigeria.com
Website: www.albrettnigeria.com
* 27, Bode Thomas Street, Surulere, Lagos
Tel: (01) 4803919, 5850166, 7764636 **Fax:** (01) 5835971
Contact: Chief Albert King Iyorah - Chairman/CEO

ALCATEL NIGERIA LIMITED
Business: Global Telecommunications and Internet Service Provision and Support.
Address: 23, Idejo Street, Victoria Island, Lagos
Tel: (01) 3204510-9 (10L)
* 10, Usuma Street, Maitama, Abuja.
Tel: (09) 41302920 - 2 (3L) **Fax:** (09) 4137500
E-mail: alcatnig@premiernetng.net
Website: www.alcatel.com
* Plot 1046, Adetokunbo Ademola Street, Victoria Island, Lagos
Tel: (01) 2614434, 2623930 **Fax:** (01) 2623878
Contact: Mr. G. Mazzotti

ALCON NIGERIA LIMITED
Business: Engineering Construction Services and Steel Works for Oil & Gas Industry
Address: 22, Chief Nwuke Street, Plot 17, Trans-Amadi Industrial Layout, Port Harcourt
Tel: (084) 235699

AL-DAWOOD TOURS & TRAVELS LIMITED
Business: Travel Agency, Tour Operations & Promotions
Address: Eleganza Biro Plaza (6th Floor, Suite 6C), Plot 634, Adeyemo Alakija Street, Victoria Island, Lagos
Tel: (01) 2702972, 7748979, 08033024837
Fax: (01) 2702971
E-mail: aldawoodtours@hotmail.com
Website: www.aldawoodgroup.com
Contact: Mrs Bola Labinjo - MD/CEO

ALDER CONSULTING LIMITED
Business: Professional & Business Services, Marketing Communications and Public Relations Consultancy
Address: 1, Ajose Adeogun Street, Victoria Island, Lagos
Tel: (01) 2705408-9 (2L), 3200282, 4705865
Fax: (01) 3200282
E-mail: alder@alder-consulting.com

ALFA GROUP OF COMPANIES
Business: Aluminium Fabrication (Doors, Windows, Curtain Walls, Partitioning, Structural Glazing, Display Units, Showcases, Vehicle Bodies); Exhibition Services (Shell Schemes, Design & Construction of Personalized Stands, Event Management, Furniture Hire); Mnaufacturing of Mosquito Net & Textile, Importation of Insecticides, Writing Pens, Corporate Gifts and Stationery
Address: ALFACO House, Plot E, Ikosi Road, Oregun Industrial Estate, Ikeja, Lagos
Tel: (01) 4971350-1 (2L), 08023339515, 08034040404, 08036056000 **Fax:** (01) 5557979
E-mail: info@groupalfa.com
Website: www.groupalfa.com

ALFA LABORATORIES LIMITED
Business: Quality Assurance Consultancy; Raw Materials & Finished Products Analysis & Evaluation; Cargo Superintendence; Product/Process Formulation; Environmental Services
Address: 11B, Amuwo-Odofin Industrial Estate, Apapa Expressway, Amuwo-Odofin, Lagos
Tel: (01) 7742022, 8124472, 08023003707, 08055228436
Fax: (01) 5893342
E-mail: alfalabi@hotmail.com
Contact: Mr. D. A. Akoh - Chairman
Mr. Musa James - Admin. Manager

ALFAM INSURANCE BROKERS LIMITED
Business: Insurance Brokers, Life & Pensions Consultants
Address: 20, Berkely Street, Onikan, Lagos.
Tel: (01) 2602669, 2632217, 08023029618
Fax: (01) 2632217
E-mail: alfam@infoweb.abs.net
Contact: Mr. S. T. A Yusuf - MD/CEO

ALFRED JAMES PETROLEUM LIMITED
Business: Oil & Gas Exploration and Production
Address: Yinka Folawiyo Plaza (3rd Floor) 38 Warehouse Road, Apapa, Lagos.
Tel: (01) 5450436 - 40 (5L)

ALGARITA TRADING COMPANY LIMITED
Business: Manufacturing of Blankets
Address: Km 18, Hadejia Road, Kano
Tel: (064) 311204
Contact: Mr C. A. Jaafar - MD/CEO

ALH. AMINU AHMED & COMPANY LIMITED
Business: Import & Export, General Merchandise
Address: 28E, Ado Bayero Road, P.O.Box 2585, Kano
Tel: (064) 645174 **Fax:** (064) 649919
Contact: Alh. Aminu Ahmed Maiturare - Chairman

ALH. J. SULEIMAN & SONS (NIGERIA) LIMITED
Business: Electronic Appliances, Office Equipment and General Goods Importation and Sales
Address: J1, Ahmadu Bello Way, P.O.Box 1503, Kaduna
Tel: (062) 242184, 242981, 240413 **Fax:** (062) 242981
* N2 & J6, Ahmadu Bello Way, Kaduna
Tel: (062) 240413
* Block C, Phase 2, Herbert Macaulay Way, By Michael Okpara Street, Wuse Zone 5, Abuja
Tel: (09) 5235660, 5213464
Contact: Alh. Jibrin Suleiman Egu - Chairman/CEO

ALH. SABIU TANKO & COMPANY (NIGERIA) LIMITED
Business: Importers and Exporters; General Merchandising
Address: 24E, Ado Bayero Road/M. Mohammed Way, Kano
Tel: (064) 648601 **Fax:** (064) 635944
Contact: Alh. Sabiu Tanko - Chairman
Alh. Nura Sabiu - MD/CEO

ALH. SULEIMAN RIBADU COMPANY LIMITED
Business: General Merchandising
Address: 96, Mohammed Mustapha Way, Jimeta-Yola
Tel: (075) 625620
Contact: Alh. Suleiman Ribadu - Chairman/CEO

ALH. YAHAYA UMARU & COMPANY LIMITED
Business: Civil Engineering, Quarrying, Spinning & Wearing.
Address: Bank Road, opp Yankari Savings & Loans, Gombe.
Tel: (072) 220206, 220223
* 22, Unity Road, Fagge Ta Kudu, Kano
Tel: (064) 644504, 647867
* 4, Calcrick Road, Apapa Lagos
Tel: (01) 5874280
Contact: Alh. Musa Yahaya - MD/CEO

ALIBAN GROUP LIMITED
Business: Airconditioning & Refrigeration; Trading; Sales of Corporate Gift Items, Special Purpose Vehicles, Eye-Care & Optical Products
Address: 348, Ikorodu Road, Maryland, Lagos.
Tel: (01) 4966257, 4966929, 960890, 935636
Fax: (01) 4966257

ALIBERT PRODUCTS (NIGERIA) LIMITED
Business: Manufacture of Furniture
Address: 1-5, Isolo Road, Egbe, Alimosho L.G.A. Lagos
Tel: (01) 5873838, 2645189, 4701925, 5875277, 4703485
Fax: (01) 5877849
32, Burma Road, Apapa, Lagos
E-mail: alibert@hyperia.com
Contact: Chief Majed Ali Taan - MD/CEO

ALIDOT NIGERIA LIMITED
Business: Manufacturing of Polyprophylene Woven Bags
Address: Km 4, Lokoja - Ajaokuta Road, P.O.Box 144 Lokoja
Tel: (058) 220322; *Lagos (01) 2691208

ALINCO STEEL & METAL CONSTRUCTION COMPANY LTD
Business: Steel Fabrication and Construction, Marketing of Petroleum Products, Manufacture of Paints
Address: Km. 27, Abeokuta Expressway, Ijaiye-Ojokoro, Agege, Lagos
Tel: (01) 4921447, 7741351 **Fax:** (01) 4922749
Contact: Alh. A. Adeniji - Chairman
Miss Fausat Adeniji - CEO

ALIND (NIGERIA) LIMITED
Business: Manufacturing of Electric Cables and Conductors
Address: Plot 22 & 23, Industrial Estate, Bauchi
Tel/Fax: (077) 543687
Contact: Dr. Ahmad Mai Abba - GM/CEO

ALITALIA (NIGERIA)
Business: International Airline Service
Address: Churchgate Towers (3rd Floors), Plot PC. 30, Afribank Street, Victoria Island, Lagos
Tel: (01) 2611559 - 60 (2L), 2618106, 2610024
Fax: (01) 2610435
* Central Busines District, Abuja
Tel: (09) 2348433
Contact: Trevor Henry - General Manager
Michelle Pagnelli - District Manager

ALKEM NIGERIA LIMITED
Business: Production of Polyester Staple Fibre
Address: Block D, Plot 4, Amuwo-Odofin Industrial Estate, Apapa-Oshodi Expressway, Lagos
Tel: (01) 5802255-9 (5 L), 7742890
Fax: (01) 2611391, 5802259
E-mail: alkem@linkserve.com.com
Contact: Air Vice Mar. Ishaya Aboi Shekari (rtd.) - Chairman
Mr. Igbal Sadruddin Hirji - MD/CEO

ALKO LIMITED
Business: Telecommunications, Industrial Insulation and Pipe Works, Environmental Engineering Services
Address: 12, Oremeji Street, (2nd Floor) Off Simbiat Abiola Road, Ikeja, Lagos
Tel: (01) 4975576 **Fax:** (01) 4974082
E-mail: alko-ltd@yahoo.com
Contact: Mr. Alex U. Ejumedia - MD/CEO

ALL AFRICA TRAVELS LIMITED
Business: Travel Agency
Address: 2F, Sani Abacha Way, Kano
Tel: (064) 642127, 634866 **Fax:** (064) 642127
E-mail: allafricatrvl@yahoo.com
Contact: Alh. Ibrahim Umar - MD/CEO

ALL BUSINESS FURNITURE COMPANY
Business: Manufacture & Marketing of Business Furniture.
Address: 90, Adeniyi Jones Avenue, Ikeja, Lagos.
Tel: (01) 4935472, 7733438 **Fax:** (01) 4930470
E-mail: caroncgroupcontrol@yahoo.com
* 284B, Ajose Adeogun St, Victoria Island, Lagos
* 4 Olu Akijiyan Street, Ejigbo, Lagos
Contact: Mr. Chris A. Alabi - Chairman/CEO
Mr. R. O. Odende - Mgr (Business Dev/Planning)

ALL CROWN INVESTMENT SERVICES LIMITED
Business: Company Registrars
Address: 24/26, Macarthy Street, Onikan, Lagos
Tel: (01) 2647567
Contact: Otunba M. A. Hassan - Chairman/CEO

ALL MANAGEMENT SERVICES COMPANY LTD (AMSCO)
Business: Leasing, Repair and Service of Automobiles and Machineries, Sales of Automobile
Address: 206, Apapa Road, Ijora, Lagos
Tel: (01) 5451939
Contact: Major Gen. M. Magoro (rtd.) - Chairman
Mr. E. Valcke - MD/CEO

ALL SEASONS INDUSTRIES LIMITED
Business: Manufacture of Aluminium Roofing Sheets
Address: Plot 3 & 4, Otta Industrial Estate, Km 7, Idiroko Road (beh. Honda), Otta, Ogun State
Tel: (039) 722299
Contact: Engr. A. Ayoola - Chairman/CEO

ALL SEASONS MEDIACOM LIMITED
Business: Media Consultants
Address: 50, Adekunle Fajuyi Way, Ikeja, Lagos.
Tel: (01) 4938978-9 (2L), 4934435, 4932697, 7740521
Fax: (01) 4932697
E-mail: mediacom@pinet.com.ng
mediacom@hyperia.com
Contact: Dr. Ken O. Ikpe - GM/CEO

ALL STATES BUREAU DE CHANGE LIMITED
Business: Bureau de Change Services
Address: Blocks 88/89, Federal Palace Hotel Complex, Ahmadu Bello Way, Victoria Island, Lagos.
Tel: (01) 2629289, 2611645, 08037176550, 08033087259
Fax: (01) 2629289
* 24 , Cornership, Addis Ababa Crescent, Zone 4, Wuse, Abuja.
Contact: Alh. Musbau M. Mustapha - Chairman/CEO

ALL STATES GROUP OF COMPANIES
Business: Travel Agency, Car Hire and Tour Operations, Holiday Resort (Zuma Rock Nigeria Village)
Address: Plot 915, Alexandria Crescent, off Aminu Kano Crescent, Wuse II, Abuja
Tel: (09) 4132177, 4130405, 6701213, (080) 33076356
Fax: (09) 4131914
E-mail: allstatesng@yahoo.com
Contact: Alh. Munzali A. Dantata - Chairman/CEO
Mr. Cornel A. Agim - Group Gen. Manager

ALL TECHNOLOGY LIMITED
Business: Sales, Installation and Maintenance of Computers Design; & Local/Wide Area Networking
Address: 22, Norman Williams Street, S.W; Ikoyi, Lagos
Tel: (01) 2696237, 2673166 **Fax:** (01) 2696237, 683242
E-mail: alltech@hyperia.com
Website: www.alltechng.com
* Plot 735, Kade Street, Off Aminu Kano Crescent, Wusu 11, Abuja.
Tel: (09) 4133276
* 24B, Otigba Street, Off Obafemi Awolowo Way, Ikeja, Lagos.
Tel: (01) 4711097, 4933491
Contact: Engr. Kenechukwu Ikedife - MD/CEO

ALLIANCE & GENERAL INSURANCE COMPANY LIMITED
Business: All Classes of Insurance including LIfe
Address: Allied Bank Building, 155/161, Broad Street, Lagos
Tel: (01) 2660678, 2669825, 2642864, 2642860, 2669450
Fax: (01) 2661406, 2669450
E-mail: aginsure@ag-insurance.com
* 4B, Mobolaji Bank Anthony Way, Maryland, Ikeja, Lagos.
Tel: (01) 4932072
* Plot 2087, Ndande Court, Wuse Zone 5, Abuja
Tel: (09) 5231210
Contact: Lt. Gen. Ipoola Alani Akinrinade (rtd.) - Chairman
Mr. Gordon Cameron-Dick - MD/CEO

FOOD FOR THOUGHT
Try Quality for CHANGE
go for
Uncle Ben's® BRAND Rice
Uncle Ben's
USA
Rice
Vitamins/Mineral Enriched
Requires no washing
Needs no sorting
Swells up to 4 times
Faster cooking
Tastes so much better
NOW AVAILABLE IN
TAMPERPROOF BAGS
Exclusively Distributed in Nigeria by
Allied Merchants & Brokers Ltd.
1/3, Warehouse Rd., P. O. Box 4075 Apapa, Lagos, Nigeria.
Tel/Fax: (01) 5453609, 5453610
E-mail amb@alpha.linkserve.com
Also Available at FAREAST MERCANTILE CO LTD. 15, Martins Street, Lagos.

ALLIANCE CAPITAL MANAGEMENT COMPANY LIMITED
Business: Stockbroking, Asset Management, Research & Advisory Services
Address: New Africa House (13th & 14th Floors), 31, Marina, Lagos Island, Lagos
Tel: (01) 2642927, 2669962, 08033288059, 080366747718
E-mail: acml2005@usa.com
alliancecapital@yahoo.co.uk
Contact: Mr. Edward Diete-Koki - MD/CEO

ALLIANCE INTERNATIONAL (NIGERIA) LIMITED
Business: Production of Galvanised & Corrugated Roofing Sheets, Plastic & Polyethylene Products, Shoe Sole & Footwear Accessories, Bakery Products & Confectioneries
Address: 45, Olufemi Rd, off Ognlana Drive, Surulere, Lagos
Tel: (01) 830180, 836239, 08033343437 **Fax:** (01) 836239
E-mail: alinco@marina.nipost.com.ng
* 46, Limca Road, Nkpor, Onitsha
Tel: (090) 500652
Contact: Chief J. E. Muoghalu - Chairman/CEO

ALLIED BOND STANDARD COMPANY LIMITED
Business: General Imports, Sales of Whirlpools and Sanitary wares, Stationery Manufacturers
Address: Allied Bond House (1st Floor), 26, Lagos-Badagry Expressway, Odunade Bus-Stop, Lagos
Tel: (01) 5851717, 5450378 **Fax:** (01) 5851718
Contact: Chrisitian O. Iregbu - GM

ALLIED COMPUTERS LIMITED
Business: Marketing and Serving of Computers & Peripherals
Address: 227, Ikorodu Road, Anthony, Lagos
Tel: (01) 4971623, 4930592-3 (2L), 4704195, 7731066
Fax: (01) 4971623
E-mail: alliedcom@alliedcomputers.com.ng
Contact: Mr. Biodun R. Balogun - MD/CEO

ALLIED HOME APPLIANCES LIMITED
Business: Sales of Electrical & Electronic Home Appliances
Address: 18B, Creek Road, Apapa, Lagos
Tel: (01) 5872653, 5451654
* Elpina Plaza, Plot 642C, Akin Adesola Street, Victoria Island, Lagos
Tel: (01) 2616919, 2617222, 08034030475
* 7A, Azikiwe Road, Port Harcourt
Tel: (084) 236063-4 (2L) **Fax:** (084) 236065

ALLIED TECHNOL SYSTEM LIMITED
Business: Sales of Fragrances and Flavours
Address: 1, Cocosheen Close, by Ikeja Medical Centre, beh. Alade Market, off Allen Avenue, Ikeja, Lagos
Tel: (01) 4963357, 4973629, 4726874
E-mail: ablesell@nova.net.ng
* 56, Port Harcourt Road, Aba
Tel: (082) 225333

ALLIED MERCHANTS & BROKERS LIMITED
Business: Importation and Marketing of **Uncle Ben's** Long Grain Rice, **McCormick** Spices and Other Food-Seasoning Products
Address: 1/3, Warehouse Road, Apapa, Lagos
Tel: (01) 5453609, 5453610 **Fax:** (01) 5453610
E-mail: amb@alpha.linkserve.com
Contact: Mrs. Owanari Bob-Manuel Duke - Chairman/CEO
Mr. Henry Vwamhi - GM

ALLIED TECHNOLOGIES & DIVERSIFIED SERVICES LTD
Business: Structured Cabling and LAN Installation, Collaboration, Messaging & Intranet Development, WAN Installation and Equipment Supplies, Maintenance Services, Microsoft Software Legalisation and Licensing, Software Development, Web Development/Hosting, Software Integration, e-Commerce
Address: 7, Oyin Jolayemi Street, Victoria Island, Lagos
Tel/Fax: (01) 2618903, 3200105, 2617267
E-mail: info@allied-technologies.com
Website: www.allied-technologies.com
Contact: Mr. Chukwuma Ofoche - MD/CEO
Mr. Abiodun Adisa - Marketing Director

ALLIED TRUST INSURANCE BROKERS LIMITED
Business: Insurance Brokers
Address: 6, Tiamiyu Street, Mende, Maryland, Lagos
Tel: (01) 4936940, 4938294, 4961881, 4703151
Fax: (01) 4938294
E-mail: alltrust@beta.linkserve.com
Contact: Mr. Olatunde A. Odunsi - MD/CEO

ALLOT NIGERIA LIMITED
Business: Civil Engineering Consultants
Address: Ebani House, 149/153, Broad Street, Lagos
Tel: (01) 2662073 **Fax:** (01) 2662073, 2691212
E-mail: allot@nova.net.ng
Contact: Engr. (Chief) A. O. Akideinde - Chairman/CEO

ALLROUND AUTOMOBILE ASSISTANCE LIMITED
Business: Support Services to Registered Motorist (Technical & Towing Assistance on Broken-Down Vehicles), Maintenance & Repairs of Vehicles, Rentals & Leasing of Vehicles
Address: 264, Ikorodu Road, Obanikoro, Lagos
Tel: (01) 8048850, 8174796, 08023366787
E-mail: info@allroundautomobile.com
Website: www.allroundautomobile.com
Contact: High Chief Bayo Akinnola - Chairman
Mr. Uyi O. Asaolu - Chief Operating Officer

ALLSTATES TRUST BANK PLC
Business: Comprehensive Universal Banking Services
Address: ALLSTATES Centre, Plot 1675, Oyin Jolayemi Street, Victoria Island, Lagos
Tel: (01) 2647031-5 (5L), 2617303, 2625840 -5 (6L), 4618445-50 (6L)
Fax: (01) 2612206
E-mail: enquiry@allstates.com.ng
Website: www.allstates.com.ng
Contact: Mr. Ebibomo Timitimi - MD/CEO

ALMAS TRADING LIMITED
Business: Sales, Installations and Service of Long Range Cordless Telephones, Sales of Mats and Blankets, Household Appliances & Cement Bags, General Trading, Import & Export
Address: Plot 4, Apapa-Oshodi Expressway, near Guardian Newspapers, Isolo, Lagos

Tel: (01) 4523927, 4522456, 08034007575
Fax: (01) 4526139
E-mail: almasltd@yahoo.com
almas@starnet.net.ng
Website: www.almasltd.com
* 21, Nabada Badamosi Road, Kano
Tel: (064) 634459, 312055
Contact: Mr. Khaled Moussallati - MD/CEO

AL-MIFTAH TELECOMMUNICATION LIMITED
Business: Sales & Repairs of Mobile Phones & Accessories
Address: 19, Saka Tinubu Street, Victoria Island, Lagos
Tel: (01) 4701825, 8181505
* Plot 169, Aminu Kano Crescent, opp. Banex Plaza, Wuse II, Abuja
Tel: (09) 4132189, (08023142036, 08034000128
Contact: Mr. Jafaru Abdullahi - MD/CEO

ALO ALUMINIUM MANUFACTURING COMPANY LIMITED
Business: Production of Long-Span Aluminium Roofing Sheets an Accessories
Address: East-West Road, Rumuokoro, Port Harcourt
Tel: (084) 770174, 770211, 08033165629
Fax: (084) 556088
* Enugu - Abakaliki Road, Opp. Mobil Station, off Port Harcourt Expressway, Enugu
Tel: (042) 556088, 559898
* Km 1, Nkpor-Umuoji Road, Nkpor, Onitsha
Tel: (046) 251540, (090) 501092
Contact: Sir Alex O. Ani - CEO

ALOLIS GEO-SCIENCES NIGERIA LIMITED
Business: Oil & Gas Industry Consultancy Services
Address: 18, Adeleke Street, off Allen Avenue, Ikeja, Lagos
Tel: (01) 4964079, 618933 **Fax:** (01) 2625055
E-mail: oia@infoweb.abs.net
Contact: Chief Olatunde I. Aluko - Chairman/CEO
Mr. Nelson O. Bienlonwu - ED

ALPH DESIGNERS (NIGERIA) LIMITED
Business: Sales of Security and Fire-fighting Equipment, Architechtural Ironmongers, Building Materials Merchants, Import & Export.
Address: 19, Idahosa Ojo-Osagie Street, beh. Aiyetoro Primary School, Aguda Surulere, Lagos
Tel: (01) 836662, 2882683 **Fax:** (01) 2882683
E-mail: alpha@infoweb.abs.net
Contact: Chief A. C. Nwimo - Chairman/CEO

ALPHA & BETA MERCHANTS COMPANY LIMITED
Business: Transport, Import & Export, Customs Licensed Agents, General Merchandising
Address: 295/296, Apapa Wharf Road, Apapa, Lagos
Tel: (01) 5450052, 5451243, 5451590 **Fax:** (01) 5451243
Contact: Alh. Mohammad K. Zailani - MD/CEO

ALPHA BROKERS LIMITED
Business: Insurance & Reinsurance Broking, Pensions & Financial Planning Consultancy
Address: 75, Chime Avenue, New Haven, Enugu
Tel: (042) 253155, 257721 **Fax:** (042) 253155
E-mail: cyberway@nova.net.ng
Contact: Sir. J. E. C. Ogbonna - MD/CEO

ALPHA-SI EYE CLINIC
Business: Ophthalmologists & Ophthalmic Surgeons, Optometristists
Address: 7, Western Avenue (1st Floor), Ojuelgba Roundabout, Surulere, Lagos
Tel: (01) 5850440, 4803565, 4817017, 08034881447, 08042127655
* Former Kingsway Stores Building, 12, Azikiwe Road, Port Harcourt,
Tel: (084) 330762 **Fax:** (084) 236841
Contact: Ms. T. A. Shonibare - Administrator

ALRAINE SHIPPING AGENCIES (NIGERIA) LIMITED
Business: Shipping, Chartering, Liner & Tramp Agents
Address: 28, Burma Road, Apapa, Lagos
Tel: (01) 5876692, 5877580 **Fax:** (01) 5874771, 5877251
E-mail: shipping@alrainelos.com
Contact: Mr. Niels Riechers - MD/CEO

ALREN TRADING COMPANY (L'Uomo Lifestyle Plus)
Business: Fashion & Accessories
Address: Plot 1321, Karimu Kotun St, Victoria Island, Lagos
Tel: (01) 2625787, 3200343 **Fax:** (01) 2625787
E-mail: alren@hyperia.com
* Olajuwon House, 15/17, Opebi Road, Ikeja, Lagos
Tel: (01) 5557645
* Plot 1173, Adetokunbo Ademola Crescent, near AP Plaza, Wuse II, Abuja
Tel: (09) 5235712
* CFC Building, 49, Aba Road, Port Harcourt
Tel: (084) 571644
Contact: Mr. Kennedy Aloguga - MD/CEO

ALRISK INSURANCE BROKERS LIMITED
Business: Insurance Brokers
Address: 24, Ekololu Street, Surulere Lagos.
Tel: (01) 830972, 08023521818
* Plot AA 24/25, Nisama Road, off Rabah Road G.R.A, Kaduna.
Tel: (062) 201228, 214660
Contact: Otunba Y. A. O. Giwa - GM/CEO

ALTAK INDUSTRIES LIMITED
Business: Manufacturing and Marketing of Plastic Furniture and Household Wares
Address: Km. 8, Old Lagos Road, Ibadan
Tel: (02) 2311938, 2311923 **Fax:** (02) 2311446
E-mail: altak@skannet,com
* 39, Warehouse Road, Apapa, Lagos
Tel: (01) 5871163

ALTIMAX METAL INDUSTRIES LIMITED
Business: Fabrication of Aluminium Building Product
Address: 79/81, Tejuosho Street, P.O.Box 267, Surulere Lagos
Tel: (01) 5456950, 7746062, 08023122645-6 (2L)
Contact: Chief Olusanya A. Abiola - Chairman/CEO

ALTITECH LIMITED
Business: Fabrication of Plastic, Aluminium &Illuminated Signs
Address: 41C, Commercial Avenue, Sabo Yaba Lagos.
Tel: (01) 860380
E-mail: altitech@home.panafrica.com
Contact: Mr. Davis Ezechinedu - MD/CEO

ALTRADE SECURITIES LIMITED

Business: Stockbroking, Portfolio Management, Financial Advisory Services.
Address: Todebo House (1st Floor), 127, Obafemi Awolowo Way, Ikeja Lagos.
Tel: (01) 4938215, 4973970, 3453020, 23036347, 08023037858, 08023313422 **Fax:** (01) 4973970
altrade@infoweb.abs.net
Contact: Mr. Yusuf Alhassan - MD/CEO

ALUCON BUILDING PRODUCTS LIMITED

Business: Manufacture and Supply of Aluminium Building Products (Partitioning, Ceiling, Doors & Windows)
Address: Plot 13A, Acme Rd, Ogba Ind. Estate, Ikeja, Lagos
Tel: (01) 4706666, 4926032 **Fax:** (01) 4965794
E-mail: alucon@alpha.linkserve.com
Website: www.nigeria-tours.com/alucon
Contact: Chief Ikedi Ohakim - MD/CEO

ALUFOILS NIGERIA LIMITED

Business: Manufacturing of Aluminium Foil Paper & Flexible Packagings, Lamination of Strip Foil & Tagger Foil
Address: 9, Oba Akran Avenue,Ikeja Ind.Estate, Ikeja, Lagos
Tel: (01) 4968611-5 (5 L), 08037756300
Fax: (01) 4971320
E-mail: alufoils@alpha.linkserve.com
* Km 32, Abeokuta Expressway, opp. Tax Office Alagbado, Lagos
Tel: (01) 7730279, 7756300 **Fax:** (01) 4934541, 4971320
Contact: Capt. Mukherjee - MD/CEO

ALUKATEX INVESTMENT LIMITED

Business: Food Commodities Importers, General Merchants
Address: 8, Koseh Street, Balogun Lagos
Tel: (01) 2643815 **Fax:** (01) 2663324
E-mail: ainl@infoweb.abs.net
Contact: Mr. Tony Ugochukwu - Chairman/CEO

ALUKE INTERNATIONAL COMPANY LIMITED

Business: Importation and Marketing of Satellite Communication Dishes and Equipment, Electronics and General Goods
Address: 43, Iweka Road, Onitsha
Tel: (046) 210310
* Palm Avenue Mushin, Lagos
Tel: (01) 4521868, 4522824
* A124E, Alaba International Market, Ojo, Lagos
Contact: Mr. Luke E. Aniakor - President/CEO

ALUMACO PLC

Business: Manufacturing and Marketing of Aluminium Products, Construction & Erection of Aluminium-Based Components, Allied Services
Address: 32, Creek Road, Apapa, Lagos
Tel: (01) 5803270-4 (5 L) **Fax:** (01) 5870368
E-mail: alumaco@hyperia.com
* Bolingo Hotel (Technical Floor), Central Business District, Abuja
Tel: (09) 4130205, 08023060237, 08042117266
* 9, Aba Road (2nd Floor), Port Harcourt
Tel: (084) 579854, 08033295279
Contact: Alh. (Dr) Shehu A. Musa CFR, GCON - Chairman
Mr. M. O. Lakanu - MD/CEO

ALUMINIUM CITY LIMITED

Business: Manufacture and Distribution of Aluminium Building Components & Accessories
Address: 1, Alhaji Adejumo Avenue, Ilupeju Industrial Estate, Oshodi-Expressway, Lagos
Tel: (01) 4963511, 4966742 **Fax:** (01) 4970691
E-mail: info@aluminiumicity.com
* Plot 740, Aminu Kano Crescent, Wuse 11, Abuja.
Tel: (09) 4131597, 6714895 Fax: (09) 4131597
Contact: Mr. Richard J. Willmott - ED/CEO

ALUMINIUM EXTRUSION INDUSTRIES PLC

Business: Manufacturing of Extruded Aluminium Profiles.
Address: Km. 4, Atta-Amaimo Rd, Inyishi Town, via Owerri
Tel/Fax: (083) 234412, 234427 **Fax:** (083) 234412
E-mail: alex@rcl.nig.com
* 9, Oba Akran Avenue, Ikeja, Lagos.
Tel: (01) 4971320
Contact: Mr. G. S. Bhatia - MD/CEO

ALUMINIUM FABRICATION COMPANY LIMITED (ALFACO)

Business: Fabrication of Aluminium Products
Address: ALFACO House, Plot E, Ikosi Road, Oregun Industrial Estate, Oregun, Ikeja, Lagos
Tel: (01) 4971350-1 (2L), 08023339515, 08034040404, 08036056000
E-mail: alfa@nova.net.ng
Contact: Mr. F. Jarmakani - MD/CEO

ALUMINIUM METAL TECHNOLOGIES LIMITED

Business: Fabrication of Aluminium Windows, Doors and Partitions
Address: 16/18, Obagun Avenue, off Fatai Atere Way, Matori Industrial Estate, Lagos
Tel: (01) 4528211, 4528212 **Fax:** (01) 4528211
Contact: Mr. G. O. Ominiyi - MD/CEO

ALUMINIUM PRODUCTS (NIGERIA) LIMITED

Business: Manufacturing of Aluminium Doors, Windows and Partitions
Address: 9, Maimalari Road, Bompai Industrial Estate, Kano
Tel: (064) 648108, 648042, 649032, 634180
Fax: (064) 633526
Contact: Mr Roda Fawaz - Joint M.D

ALUMINIUM ROLLING MILLS (Div of Tower Aluminium Plc)

Business: Extrusion of Aluminium Profiles, Processing of Aluminium Ingots and Scraps
Address: Otta Industrial Estate, Onipanu-Otta, Otta
Tel: (039) 722058, 722254-5 (2L), 722657, 722682
Fax: (039) 722409 (01) 4971320
E-mail: armltd@linkserve.com.ng
* Plot 9, Oba Akran Avenue, Ikeja, Lagos
Tel: (01) 4968611-5 (5L) **Fax:** (01) 4971320
E-mail: tower2@linksrve.com.ng
Contact: Mr D. N. Sabarwal - Group MD/CEO
Mr S. K. Meratra - GM

ALUMINIUM SMELTER COMPANY OF NIGERIA LIMITED (ALSCON)

Business: Production of Aluminium Ingots & Billets
Address: Ikot Abasi, P.M.B. 1054, Ikot Ibasi, Akwa Ibom State
Tel: (087) 775534, 775840, 775750, 775749, 775839

Fax: (087) 775841
* TOTAL House, Plot 247, Herbert Macaulay Way, Central Business District, Abuja
Tel: (09) 2347753-4 (2L), 2346806, 08033146397
Fax: (09) 2347753-4 (2L)
E-mail: alsonabuja@rosecom.net

ALUMINIUM TECHNOLOGY PRODUCTS PLC
Business: Fabrication & Installatin of Aluminium Roofing Sheets, Windows & Doors, Curtain Walling, Specialised Structural Glazing, Architectural Louvres, Partitioning Systems, Suspended Ceiling
Address: NAL Towers, (2nd Floor), 20, Marina, Lagos
Tel: (01) 2601370-7 (8 L); **Fax:** (01) 2632704
E-mail: altec@inofwb.abs.net
Contact: Mr. E. A. Adelakun - ED

ALWYN NIGERIA LIMITED
Business: Consultancy Services
Address: 5, Ade Ojo Street, Wemabod Estate, off Adeniyi Jones Avenue, Ikeja, Lagos
Tel: (01) 4960951, 7731515 **Fax:** (01) 4973877
E-mail: alwyn@alpha.linkserve.com
Contact: Mr Gope Bakshani - Chairman/CEO

ALZICO LIMITED
Business: Industrial Suppliers, Suppliers to Special Projects of the Petroleum and Mining Industries, Public Works Projects and Agriculture
Address: Plot 18, Jimoh Odutola Road, Iganmu Industrial Estate, Iganmu, Lagos
Tel: (01) 835211, 835823, 5834741 **Fax:** (01) 5835160

AMABROS TECHNICAL COMPANY LIMITED
Business: Sales of Power Generating Sets and Spare Parts
Address: 107, Oshodi-Apapa Expressway, near Ilasa Police Post, Ilasamaja, P.O.Box 2912, Mushin, Lagos
Tel: (01) 4520124, 4528127, 4525379, 4528636
E-mail: amabros@cyberspace.com.net
Website: www.amabros.com
* Main Neighbourhood Centre, (Suite 17) Wuse Zone 3, Abuja.
Tel: (09) 5234974
Contact: Mr Polycarp O. Asika - Chairman/CEO.

AMACO INVESTMENTS LIMITED
Business: Video Cassettes Duplication and Marketing, Film Production Financing.
Address: 51, Iweka Road, P.O.Box 152, Onitsha.
Tel: (046) 414033
E-mail: gabrielmoses@yahoo.com
* 1/3 Pound Road, Aba
Tel: (082) 230430
* 145, Nnamdi Azikiwe Street, Idumota, Lagos
Contact: Mr Gabriel M. Ezunu - MD/CEO

AMADEUS NIGERIA
Business: Global Distribution System Service Providers
Address: Maku Plaza, 109C, Awolowo Road, Ikoyi, Lagos
Tel/Fax: 01-2610817
E-mail: amadeus@amadeusng.com
Website: www.amadeus.com
Contact: Mr Olumide Idowu - Country Manager

AMAFCO ENTERPRISES LIMITED
Business: Plastics Mats Manufacturers
Address: 1A, Fagge Takudu, P.O.Box 830 Kano
Tel: (064) 630720, 633700 **Fax:** (064) 638886
* Km 16, Hadejia Road, Kano
Contact: Alh. Ahmed A. Fadlallah - Chairman/CEO.

AMAFO ENGINEERING LIMITED
Business: Electrical & Building Engineering Services, Cleaning Services, Transportation, Garment Manufacturing, Importation of Industrial Spare Parts
Address: Amafo House, 8, Apostle Famuyiwa Avenue, off Haruna Street, Ifako-Ijaiye, Lagos
Tel/Fax: (01) 4923443
* 15B, Post Office Road, Kano.
Tel: (064) 649800
* 28, Ajilosun Street, Ado Ekiti.
Tel: (030) 250572
Contact: Pastor (Engr) S. M. Adetunji - Chairman/CEO

AMAHAJ LIMITED
Business: Marketing of Furniture, Office Equipment and Safety Wears
Address: 29/31, Obafemi Awolowo Way, Ikeja, Lagos
Tel/Fax: (01) 4974631
Contact: Alh. A. Mohammed - Chairman/CEO

AMALGAMATED GROUP OF COMPANIES
Business: Investment, Property Development, Food Processing, Construction and Civil Engineering.
Address: Banex Plaza, (Suite B.S. 207-208), Plot 750, Aminu Kano Crescent, Wuse 11, Abuja
Tel: (09) 4130870 **Fax:** (09) 4130871
* 15, Alfred Rewane Road, Ikoyi, Lagos
* 17, Liberty Street, G.R.A. Benin City
Contact: Barr. Alex Adoghe - Chairman/CEO

AMALGAMATED PLASTIC INDUSTRIES LIMITED
Business: Plastic Products Manufacturing
Address: Plots 21/22, Sharada Industrial Estate Kano
Tel: (064) 665521, 665523 **Fax:** (064) 660190
E-mail: apiplastic@micro.com.ng
* 15, Idejo Street, Victoria Island, Lagos
Tel: (01) 2611172, 2614654 **Fax:** (01) 2620289
E-mail: apilagos@intracom5.com

AMANA CONSORTIUM
Business: Engineering Consultancy Services, Projects Management
Address: Plot 315B, Akin Ogunlewe Street, off Ligali Ayorinde Avenue, Victoria Island, Lagos
Tel: (01) 2613784
* 8, Nwaniba Road, Uyo, Akwa-Ibom State.
Tel: (085) 203608,
Contact: Obong (Engr) Edet J. Amana - Chairman/CEO

AMANA INSURANCE BROKERS & CONSULTANTS LTD
Business: Insurance Brokers and Consultants
Address: KL0, Ahmadu Bello Way/Jos Road, Kaduna
Tel: (062) 24115
* NIPOST Cornershops (Suite 35) Area 11, Garki, Abuja
Contact: Chief Gabriel A. Ojo - MD/CEO

AMANA PRINTING & ADVERTISING LIMITED
Business: Printing Services, Light Packaging Production
Address: 2, Club Road, opp. Golf Course, Kaduna.
Tel: (062) 216279, 217544, 240504

AMARILO INDUSTRIES LIMITED
Business: Importation of Chemicals, Home Appliances and Kitchen Equipment
Address: Universal Packaging Compound, Km. 16, Ikorodu Road, Ojota, Lagos
Tel: (090) 407040, 407060, 407373 **Fax:** (01) 2618138

AMASAYE INVESTMENT LIMITED
Business: Electrification Project Services, Sales & Service of Electronic & Electrical/Mechanical Machinery and Components, Marketing of Petroleum Products Projects Financing
Address: 6, Zoo Road/New Court Road Junction, Kano
Tel: (064) 661711 **Fax:** (01) 2641931
Contact: Alh. Ibrahim N. Danbatta - Chairman/CEO

AMAZON ENERGY LIMITED
Business: Oil & Gas Services - Engineering, Construction Underwater Marine Maintenance, Installation
Address: House of His Glory (3rd Floor), Block 94, Plot 18, Lekki-Epe Expressway, by Jazz 38 Bus-Stop, after 1st Roundabout, Lekki, Lagos
Tel: (01) 5555206-9 (4L), 08023209444 **Fax:** (01) 5555210
E-mail: amazonenergy@hyperia.com
Website: www.amazonenergy.net
Contact: Engr. Olayinka Fawehinmi - GM/CEO

AMBED INTERNATIONAL (NIGERIA) LIMITED
Business: Cargo Handling, Shipping, Plastic Manufacturing.
Address: 33, Osolo Way, off Murtala Muhammed International Airport Road, Ajao Estate, Isolo, Lagos
Tel: (01) 7742254
E-mail: ambyder@yahoo.co.uk
Contact: Mr. Ambrose O. Eke - Chairman/CEO

AMBER RESOURCES NIGERIA LMITED
Business: Building/Civil Engineering, Pipeline Corrosion and Sandblasting Services.
Address: 5A, Aerodrome Road, Apapa, Lagos
Tel: (01) 5450082, 5874255, 5874726
Fax: (01) 2694110, 2694111
* Plot 144, Trans-Amadi Ind. Layout, Port Harcourt
Tel: (084) 237528-30 (3L)

AMCO TECHNICAL ENGINEERING COMPANY LIMITED
Business: Mechanical, Electrical and Aircondition Engineering, Borehold and Water Engineering
Address: Plot 8, Block M, Abimbola Street, Isolo Industrial Estate, Isolo, Lagos
Tel: (01) 4525469, 4705725, 522400, 522508
Fax: (01) 4525469
E-mail: amcotech@infoweb.abs.net
Contact: Mr. Alony Moshe - MD/CEO

AMEKON (NIGERIA) LIMITED
Business: Telecommunication/Engineering Support Services
Address: 21A, Mobolaji Bank-Anthony Way, Ikeja, Lagos
Tel: (01) 4976466 **Fax:** (01) 4976467
E-mail: amekonltd@yahoo.com
* Plot 2105, Herbert Macaulay Way, Wuse Zone 6 Abuja.
Tel: (09) 3148724. **Fax:** (09) 3144894

AMERICAN FURNITURE GALLERIES LIMITED
Business: Import and Sales of Furniture and Furnishings
Address: 23A, Akin Adesola Street, Victoria Island, Lagos
Tel: (01) 2618776, 2615909, 2624712, 7740185, 5450500, 5871190 **Fax:** (01) 2615909, 5450530
E-mail: afg@j4group.com
sales@afgalleries.com
Website: www.afgalleries.com
* D10, Falomo Shopping Complex, Ikoyi, Lagos
Tel: (01) 2670853
* NICON Hilton Hotel, Maitama, Abuja
Tel: (09) 4137188
Contact: Mr. S. Jarmakani - MD/CEO

AMESI COMMERCIAL ENTERPRISES LIMITED
Business: Import and Marketing of Building Materials and Food Spices; General Contractors
Address: 8, Edinburgh Road, Enugu
Tel: (042) 255360 **Fax:** (042) 258843
* 36, Ojekule Street, Papa Ajao, Mushin, Lagos
Tel: (01) 4528084, 526221 **Fax:** (01) 4934056
* 24 Issa Williams Street, Lagos
* Aba Expressway, near 1st Artillery Junction, Rumuogba Obio, Port Harcourt.
Contact: Mr. B. O. Umeozulu - Chairman/CEO

AMEXCO PHARMACEUTICAL COMPANY LIMITED
Business: Manufacture and Marketing of Pharmaceutical Products Electronic and Other Variety Items
Address: 2B, Buraimoh Street, Abule Okuta, Bariga, Lagos
Tel: (01) 820233, 7753511
Contact: Chief (Dr.) C. A. Emereole - Chairman/CEO
Mr I. G. A. Emereole - Pharmacist/Director

AMFAS ELECTRONICS LIMITED
Business: Radio Communication and Security Equipment & Systems Sales and Service
Address: 3A Olayide Benson Street, Onigbongbo, Maryland, Ikeja, Lagos
Tel: (01) 4960272
E-mail: amfas@infoweb.abs.net
Contact: Engr Mike A. Uzamere - MD/CEO

AMIN BROTHERS ENGINEERING COMPANY LIMITED
Business: Sole Distribution Partner for Foreign Manufacturers of Tools and Allied Products, Biscuits, Confectionery and *Conqueror* Paper
Address: 30A, (Plot 1291), Akin Akinsola Street, Victoria Island, Lagos
Tel: (01) 3201778-80 (3 L) **Fax:** (01) 2613667
E-mail: sales@aminbros.com
Website: www.aminbros.com
Contact: Mr. S. A. Balogun - Admin. Manager

AMINEX INDUSTRIAL MACHINES LIMITED
Business: Engineering Services, Machine Fabrication, Drilling and Mining, Consultancy Services.
Address: 46, Chime Avenue, New Haven, Enugu

Tel: (042) 251467
* 32, Mbanefo Street, New Haven, Enugu
Contact: Engr Peter Ajemba - MD/CEO

AMIR GROUP LIMITED
Business: Auto Spare Parts Imports and Sales
Address: 101/103, Enuowa Street (1st Floor), Idumota, Lagos
Tel: (01) 2665885, 2644000 **Fax:** (01) 2667663
Contact: Mr Cletus Onyemenam - Chairman

AMLYN COMPANY LIMITED
Business: Technical Procurement for Oil & Energy Sectors
Address: Ajebo House (2nd Floor), 24/26 Macarthy Street, Onikan, Lagos
Tel: (01) 2631584 **Fax:** (01) 2637855
E-mail: fmamlyn@infoweb.abs.net
Contact: Dr Sesan Ani - MD/CEO

AMNI INTERNATIONAL PETROLEUM DEVELOPMENT COMPANY LIMITED
Business: Oil & Gas Exploration and Production
Address: Plot 1377B, Tiamiyu Savage St, Victoria Island, Lagos
Tel: (01) 2621522-5 (4 L), 2610163, 2610164, 2610167
Fax: (01) 2621526
Website: www.amni-international.com
Contact: Col. Sani Bello (rtd.) - Chairman
Mr. T. O. Afolabi - MD/CEO

AMO FARM SANDERS HATCHERY LIMITED
Business: Poultry Breeding and Farming
Address: Block D, Plot 4A, Wempco Road, Ogba Industrial Scheme, Ogba, Lagos
Tel: (01) 4924438, 4924439, 4922164 **Fax:** (01) 4926009
Contact: Chief (Dr.) Amoje - MD/CEO

AMO SANDERS (NIGERIA) LIMITED
Business: Manufacturing of Animal Feeds and Concentrates
Address: Block D, Plot 4A, Wempco Road, Ogba Industrial Scheme, Ogba, Lagos
Tel: (01) 4924438, 4924439, 4922164 **Fax:** (01) 4926009
Contact: Chief (Dr.) Amoje - MD/CEO

AMSCO NIGERIA LIMITED
Business: General Merchandising
Address: Plot 9, Block A, Ilasamaja Industrial Estate, behind Itire New Garage, Itire, Lagos
Tel: (01) 4521588, 4522261
Contact: Elder O. O. Kalu - Chairman/CEO

AMSEL LIMITED
Business: Manufacture of Food and Beverages
Address: 6, Abimbola St, Isolo Industrial Estate, Isolo, Lagos
Tel: (01) 4528829, 525879 **Fax:** (01) 4528829
E-mail: amsel_nsek@yahoo.co.uk
susanproduct@yahoo.com
Contact: Chief P. J. U. Nsek - Chairman/CEO

AMT COMPUTERS LIMITED
Business: Sales and Maintenance of Computers/Accessories
Address: 30, Omodara Street, Awuse Estate, off Opebi Road, Ikeja, Lagos
Tel: (01) 9770259
Contact: Mr. Teme Amachree - MD/CEO

AMYN INVESTMENT LIMITED
Business: Stockbroking, Portfolio Management, Investment Advisory Services, Pension Fund Management.
Address: Stock Exchange House (16th Floor), 2/4 Customs Street, Lagos
Tel/Fax: (01) 2643973
E-mail: info@amyninvestment.com
Website: www.amyninvestment.com
Contact: Ms Hauwa M. Audu - MD/CEO

ANADRILL (NIGERIA) LIMITED
Business: Drilling, Logging and Related Oilfield Services
Address: Plot 33, Trans-Amadi Ind. Layout, Port Harcourt
Tel: (084) 239551, 230362, 232649, 334872
Website: www.portharcourt.geoquest.slb.com

ANALYSED DATA LIMITED
Business: Sale of Access Control & Security Systems Fire-Suppression Systems, Facility Management & Industrial Engineering Consultancy
Address: 59, Adelabu Street, Surulere, Lagos
Tel: (01) 5850283, 832973 **Fax:** (01) 5850283, 4938139
E-mail: info@anadal.com
info@advertisers.com
Website: www.anadalcom
www.advertisersforum.com
Contact: Mr Agwu Kalu - MD/CEO

ANAMBRA HOME OWNERSHIP CMPANY LIMITED
Business: Mortgage Banking Services
Address: 10, Prince (Engr) Arthur Eze Avenue, Awka.
Tel: (048) 550258, 550103, 552733 **Fax:** (048) 550258
Contact: Ms I. E. Okezie - CEO

ANAMBRA MOTOR MANUFACTURING COMPANY LTD
Business: Manufacture and Assembly of Mercedez Commercial Vehicles (Trucks and Buses)
Address: Plot 94, Younis Bashorun Street, off Ajose Adeogun Street, Victoria Island, Annex, Lagos
Tel: (01) 2612088, 2611262, 2616682 **Fax:** (01) 2612945
Contact: Chief (Engr.) Bassey E. Bassey - Chairman
Mr. Rudi Kornmayer - MD/CEO

ANAMIKE NIGERIA LIMITED
Business: Sales and Distribution of Electricity Stabilizers, Electronic Products and Musical Equipment
Address: Shop DD7, Electrical Section, Alaba International Market, Ojo, Lagos.,
Tel: (01) 4712282, 5891797, 7731631 **Fax:** (01) 5891471
Contact: Prince Mike Mberedeogu

ANATRADE LIMITED
Business: Oil & Gas Industry Procurement and Supply
Address: 26, Idowu Taylor Street, Victoria Island, Lagos
Tel: (01) 2620461-3 (3 L) **Fax:** (01) 2618435
E-mail: anatrade@beta.linkserve.com
* 69B/70, Trans-Amadi Ind. Layout, Port Harcourt
Tel: (084) 335167, 333752 **Fax:** (084) 237956
Contact: Mr. Chris Analo - Chairman/CEO

ANAZODO TRADING COMPANY LIMITED
Business: Importation and Sales of Granite, Marble Palladiana and Italian Paints

Address: 9, Fatail Irawo Street, Off Lateef Salami Street, Ajao Estate, Isolo, Lagos
Tel: (01) 4520864, 4526068, 7741206 **Fax:** (01) 4520864
E-mail: anazodo@beta.linkserve.com
Contact: Chief J. U. S. Anazodo - Chairman/CEO

ANBUS WELDSERV (NIGERIA) LIMITED
Business: Distribution and Sales of Welding Electrodes, Equipment and Consumables
Address: 69, Ladipo St, Matori Ind. Scheme, Mushin, Lagos
Tel: (01) 4523346 **Fax:** (01) 4520989
E-mail: weldserv@hyperia.com
* 9, Chief Ejims Street, off Old Aba Road, Rumuomasi, Port Harcourt
Tel: (084) 236700 * (090) 503609

ANCHOFF STRONGHOLDS LTD
Business: Clearing & Forwarding Agency
Address: 228B, Muri Okunola Street, Victoria Island, Lagos
Tel: (01) 2622314, 2622576, 2703636-7 (2L)
Fax: (01) 2622314, 2623093
* 7, Tombia Street, G.R.A. Phase II, Port Harcourt
Contact: Alh. Gidabo Idris - Chairman
Sir Emeka C. Offor (KSC) - MD/CEO

ANCHOR INSURANCE COMPANY LIMITED
Business: Insurance Business
Address: 7/13, Aka Road (2nd -4th Floor), P.M.B. 1151, Uyo.
Tel: (085) 201583, 201633, 200192, 202165
* LSDPC House (8th Floor), Nnamdi Azikiwe Street/Alli Balogun Street, Lagos
Tel: (01) 2669367, 2666612
* 12, Ikwerre Road, Diobu, Port Harcourt
Tel: (084) 350165
Contact: N. E. Ukpabio - GM/CEO

ANCHORIA INVESTMENT & SECURITIES LIMITED
Business: Stockbroking, Portfolio Management, Financial Advisory and Nominee Accounts Services.
Address: 112, Lewis Street Lafiaji Lagos.
Tel: (01) 2634166, 2634733 **Fax:** (01) 2646092
E-mail: anchoria@gacom.net; anchoria@wananet.net
Website: www.anchoria.com
* Oxford House (1st Floor), Dugbe Ibadan
Tel: (02) 2413938, 413733
* Plot 899, Gimbiya Street, Off Ahmadu Bello Way, Garki, Abuja.
Tel/Fax: (09) 3148308
Contact: Chief L. Olusola Dada - Vice Chairman/CEO

ANDCHRISTIE DENTAL CLINIC
Business: Dentistry (Prosthodontics, Orthodontics, Endodontics and Implantology)
Address: 46, Raymond Njoku Street, off Awolowo Road, S. W. Ikoyi, Lagos
Tel: (01) 2693147 **Fax:** (01) 2693149
E-mail: andchristieclinic@yahoo.co.uk
Contact: Dr. Folarin Gbadebo-Smith - Chairman
Dr. Oluyemisi Fadahunsi - Dental Surgeon

ANDOMEZ LIMITED
Business: Sales of Medical/Scientific Equipment & Chemicals
Address: 5/9 Oregun Road, Alausa, Lagos
Tel/Fax: (01) 4937793
E-mail: andomezltd@infoweb.abs.net
Contact: Chief Chimezie Ukeje - Chairman

ANDROMEDIA PRODUCTIONS LIMITED
Business: Television & Multi-Media Production, Web Designing, Production of Documentaries and Trainer Video, Video-Coverage of Events
Address: LSDPC Flats (Block A, Flat 18), 24, Adeola Odeku Street, Victoria Island, Lagos
Tel: (01) 2610684, 2880190 **Fax:** (01) 2610684
E-mail: info@yinkacraig.com
Website: www.yinkacraig.com
Contact: Mr Yinka Craig - Chairman
Mr Rotimi Bisiriyu - Production Director/CEO

ANDY MEDICAL SUPPLIES LIMITED
Business: Sales, Installation and Servicing of Medical/ Laboratory Equipment
Address: Oshodi-Apapa Expressway, opp. Diamond Spinners by NEPA, Amuwo-Odofin, Lagos
Tel: (01) 5880482
Contact: Sir Andrew Isiudumekho Ogun - Chairman/CEO

ANGEL SPINNING & DYEING LIMITED
Business: Spinning, Weaving, Dyeing & Printing of Textiles
Address: Plot 8, Sharada Industrial Area, Phase III, Kano
Tel: (064) 647140, 647930, 667304, 646141
Fax: (064) 667303
Contact: Mr. Abullatif Dayekh - MD/CEO

ANGELA PLASTICS INDUSTRIES LIMITED
Business: Manufacture of Plastics & Polythene Bags
Address: 39, Hospital Road, Tin-Can Island Expressway, Apapa Lagos.
Tel: (01) 5450209, 5872189
Contact: Mr. John Kay Nwaolisa - Chairman/CEO

ANGEL-COT NIGERIA LIMITED
Business: Cotton Ginning
Address: Plot 12B, Sharada Industrial Estate, Phase III, Kano
Tel: (064) 667300, 667301 **Fax:** (064) 667303
Contact: Abdullatif Dayekh - Director/CEO

ANGELS COMMUNICATIONS LIMITED
Business: Advertising, Public Relations, Marketing Consultancy
Address: 61, Falolu Street Surulere Lagos
Tel: (01) 5841160, 832218, 2882393 **Fax:** (01) 832218
Contact: Mr. Longley O. Evru - Chairman/MD/CEO

ANGLO NORMAN SHIPPING NIGERIA LIMITED
Business: Clearing & Forwarding, Transporation , Shipping
Address: 14, Ado Avenue, Apapa Lagos
Tel: (01) 5451110 **Fax:** (01) 5873173

ANILAD INTERNATIONAL LIMITED
Business: Distribution of Security Locks & Security Gadgets
Address: 39, Agarawu Street, off Idumagbo Avenue Lagos.
Tel: (01) 2668882, 2669901, 2664548 **Fax:** (01) 2664548
Contact: Mr. Adebowale Animashaun - Marketing Manager

ANIMAL CARE SERVICES KONSULT NIGERIA LIMITED
Business: Livestock-Production & Health Products Market-

ing, Livestock Farming, Poultry Feeds Production.
Address: 8m Adamo Kabiawu Street, Orile-Agege, Lagos
Tel: (01) 4920889, 4923597, 4924991 **Fax:** (01) 4920720
E-mail: anicare@infoweb.abs.net
* 43, New Market Road, Commercial Area, Gombe
Tel: (072) 204255
* 195 Abeokuta Expressway, Iyana Ipaja Lagos
Tel: (01) 4921778
* 9, Ibrahim Taiwo Road, Kano.
Tel: (064) 648288
Contact: Dr. Olatunde Agbato - President/CEO

ANNIG & NOWAS GROUP LIMITED
Business: Solid Minerals Mining and Processing, Petroleum Products Marketing, Import & Export.
Address: Nowas House, Trans-Ekulu/Abakpa Nike Road Junction, Trans-Ekulu, Enugu
Tel: (042) 550131, 553171 **Fax:** (042) 550131
* 9, Balogun Street Lagos.
Tel: (01) 2640827
* National Filling Station, 53, Awka Road Onitsha.
Tel: (046) 213809, 211793
Contact: Chief (Dr) E. J. Nnubia - President/CEO

ANOFENCO (NIGERIA) LIMITED
Business: Sales & Maintenance of Filmdex Cameras, Installation & Maintenance of Technical Security Systems
Address: 23, Mercy Eneh Street, Surulere, Lagos
Tel: (01) 5454410
* 4, Lugard Road, Jos
Contact: Andrew E. Agugbuem - Chairman/CEO

ANON FURNITURE COMPANY LIMITED
Business: Furniture and Furnishing Production and Sales
Address: Plot 672, Ogbomosho Street Area 8, Garki Abuja
Tel: (09) 2347256 **Fax:** (09) 2347275
E-mail: anon@infoweb.abs.net
Contact: Chief (Dr) Angus O. Nmoh - MD/CEO

ANOZIE ELECTRICAL INDUSTRIES LIMITED
Business: Sales of Electrical Equipment, Materials and Appliances
Address: 2, Shagbemi Street, Idumota, Lagos
Tel: (01) 2667814
Contact: Chief Austin Anozie - MD/CEO

ANSA SYSTEMS LIMITED
Business: Sales & Service of Computers & UPS, Information Technology Consultancy
Address: 133A, Eti Osa Street, Dolphin Estate off Osborne Road, Ikoyi Lagos
Tel: (01) 2691084, 2695273 **Fax:** (01) 2693703
E-mail: ansa@cyperspace.net.ng
Contact: J. A. Olusoga - MD/CEO

ANSBREED INVESTMENT LIMITED (Numero uno)
Business: Italian Furniture Importation and Sales
Address: 65, Karimu Kotun Street, Victoria Island, Lagos
Tel: (01) 3200075 **Fax:** (01) 3200076
E-mail: info@numero1.it
Website: www.numerouno.it
Contact: Mr. Ugo Orchini - MD/CEO

ANTHOG DECORATIONS NIGERIA LIMITED
Business: Marketing of Home & Office Furniture and Accessories, Furnishing Services
Address: 33, Norman Williams Street, S.W. Ikoyi, Lagos
Tel: (01) 2671910, 2671683 **Fax:** (01) 2671683
E-mail: anthog@nigol.net.ng
Contact: Mr. Anthony N. Ogbodu - CEO

AOL NETWORKS LIMITED
Business: Satellite Internet Services, Internet Service Provider, VSAT Connectivity Services
Address: Motorways Centre, 1, Motorways Avenue, Oregun, Ikeja, Lagos
Tel: (01) 7900680, 7900690, 08033058162, 08023376251
E-mail: info@aolnetworks.com
Website: www.aolnetworks.com
Contact: Mr. Hilary Agbaiza - Chief Executive

A-ONE (SOFISTICAT) LIMITED
Business: Fashion Design and Sales, Corporate Gifts, and Cosmetics.
Address: 4, Mobolaji Bank-Anthony Way, Maryland, P. O.Box 295, Ikeja, Lagos
Tel: (01) 961819, 967323, 4970395 **Fax:** (01) 967317
Contact: Mr. Lanre Ogunlesi - CEO

AOP-CONSULT LIMITED
Business: Civil & Mechanical Engineering Consultancy, Construction and Project Managers
Address: Development House (3rd Floor), 21, Wharf Road, Apapa Lagos
Tel: (01) 5870452, 5878487, 5453126 **Fax:** (01) 5870452
E-mail: aop@linkserve.com.ng
Contact: Engr. (Dr) R. A. Adu - Director

APAPA SECURITIES LIMITED
Business: Sales of Shipping Equipment & Materials (Engine, Deck, Safety Equipment, Marine Chemicals & Paints)
Address: 64, Calcutta Crescent, Apapa, Lagos
Tel: (01) 5876352, 5874347, 4823812
Fax: (01) 5451897, 5874347
E-mail: shoretideseastores@hyperia.com

APEX (EASTERN NIGERIA) LIMITED
Business: Manufacturing of School Exercise Books and Paper Stationeries
Address: 18, Chief Nwuke Street, Trans-Amadi Industrial Layout, Port Harcourt
Tel: (084) 237670
Contact: Mr. L. A. O. Osayemi - Chairman/CEO
Mr. O. C. Amadi-Ikpa - Admin. Manager

APEX ALUMINIUM LIMITED
Business: Manufacturing of Aluminium Products
Address: Mattonella Building, 25, Gwamma Road, off Nnmadi Azikiwe Exp/way, Badikko New Extension, Kaduna
Tel: (062) 411089

APEX PAINTS LIMITED
Business: Manufacture & Marketing of Industrial & Decorative, Marine & Wood-Finishing Paints
Address: Km 93, Abeokuta-Lagos Road, Abeokuta.

Tel: (039) 240714, 242245.
E-mail: apex@infoweb.abs.net
* 43, Ojoto Street, Mile 2, Diobu, Port Harcourt
Contact: Mr. V. Janakiraman - MD/CEO

APK EXPRESS SERVICES LIMITED
Business: Courier Services
Address: 6, Ilojo Crescent, off Ikorodu Rd, Obanikoro, Lagos
Tel: (01) 4936613, 08033818873
Contact: Chief Maxwell F. Agbagwu - MD/CEO

APEX SECURITIES LIMITED
Business: Stockbrokers
Address: Ridgeway/Station Road Corner, Enugu
Tel: (042) 253804
* 1/3, Ladipo Adeyemi St, Anthony Village, Lagos
Tel: (01) 4933788
Contact: Mr. C. V. Ndunagu - MD/CEO

APOL PETROLEUM NIGERIA LIMITED
Business: Oilfield Engineering Services, Oil Tools and Petroleum Products Supply; Marine Transportation and Leasing Services
Address: Plot 1218D, Sam Adegbite Close, Off Amodu Ojikutu Street, Victoria Island, Lagos
Tel: (01) 2644627, 2644628, 7744470, 7749129
Fax: (01) 2644627
E-mail: apolpetroleum@micro.com.ng
* 1, Paul Gbinije Close Ekpan, Warri

APPLEBY NIGERIA LIMITED
Business: Computer Systems Development & Supply; Training & Consultancy.
Address: 4, Alhaji Bashorun Street, of Norman Williams Street, S.W., Ikoyi, Lagos
Tel: (01) 686224, 2694095. 2694761 **Fax:** (01) 2694761
E–mail: appleby@beta.linkserve.com
Contact: Mrs. Folusho M. Ojelade - Director/CEO

APPLIED SERVICES LIMITED (APPSERV)
Business: IT Business Systems, Document Processing System, IT Training, Management and Professional Development, Office Systems and Products, Corporate Printing & Publishing Service
Address: 1A, Clegg Lane, off Western Avenue, opp. Federal Fire Service, beh National Station, Surulere Lagos.
Tel: (01) 5850101 **Fax:** (01) 5851864
E-mail: appserv@nigol.net.ng
Contact: Mr. O. A. Erogbogbo - MD/CEO

APPLIED-TECH MANAGEMENT CONSULTANTS LIMITED
Business: IT Management, Sales and Maintenance of Computer Systems, Design & Development of Software, Consultancy Services and Training
Address: 4, Airport Road, by Kosini Junction Warri
Tel/Fax: (053) 254875
E-mail: applied@infoweb.abs.net
Contact: Mr. Andrew F. Desi - Chairman/MD/CEO

APRICOT PLASTICS INDUSTRIES LIMITED
Business: Manufacture of Plasticware
Address: 4, Henry Carr Street, off Oba Akran Avenue Ikeja Industrial Estate, Ikeja, Lagos
Tel: (01) 4938233, 4970108, 4964429 **Fax:** (01) 4972845
* Plot 56, Sharada Industrial Estate, Phase 2 Kano
Tel: (064) 666641, 661256

APT SECURITIES & FUNDS LIMITED
Business: Stockbroking, Portfolio Management, Investment Advisory Services
Address: Church House (5th Floor), 29, Marina, Lagos Island, Lagos
Tel: (01) 2646540, 2637127, 2645379, 4747356
Fax: (01) 2646540
E-mail: aptsec@intracom.net.ng
Contact: Al.-Mujtaba Abubakar Gumi - Chairman
Kasimu Garba Kurfi - MD/CEO

APTICS LIMITED
Business: Sales of Fire, Safety and Security Equipment
Address: 18, Moloney Street, Onikan Lagos
Tel: (01) 2645100-1 (2L) **Fax:** (01) 2645102
E-mail: aptics@nova.net.ng
Contact: Mrs. Stella Obuba - MD/CEO

AQUAMARINE INVESTMENTS NIGERIA LIMITED
Business: Shipping, Freight forwarding Haulage
Address: Eleganza Plaza (Pisces Block, 2nd Floor), 1, Commercial Road, Apapa, Lagos
Tel: (01) 5458542, 7751158, 08033085488, 08023021186
Fax: (01) 5458542
E-mail: aquamarine2000@yahoo.com
Contact: Tamuno Iyowuna Orieyebaka - MD/CEO

ARAB CONTRACTORS O.A.O. NIGERIA LIMITED
Business: Building & Construction Works
Address: Plot 145, Ajose Adeogun St, Victoria Island, Lagos
Tel: (01) 2620313, 2615271 **Fax:** (01) 2616900
E-mail: arabco@cyberspace.net.ng
* Utako Main Yard, Berger Junction, Abuja
Contact: Engr. Medhat Riyad Askar - MD/CEO

ARBICO PLC
Business: Building Construction
Address: Plot D, Block 7, Industrial Crescent, Ilupeju Industrial Estate, Ilupeju Lagos.
Tel: (01) 4972261, 4961588, 4962867, 4962869
Fax: (01) 4962868
Contact: Mr. A. Makaronidis - MD/CEO

ARBITECH NIGERIA LIMITED
Business: Sales of Banking Automation, Security Doors and Polycarbonate Roofing Sheets
Address: 12, Idowu Taylor Street, Victoria Island, Lagos
Tel: (01) 610951, 08022906992, 08023200315
Fax: (01) 5558261
E-mail: arbitec@infowb.abs.net
Contact: Najm Atallah - MD/CEO

ARBITRAGE FINANCE & INVESTMENT LIMITED
Business: Investment Advisory and Financial Services Consultancy, Training.
Address: Kajola House, 62/64, Campbell Street, Lagos
Tel: (01) 2631939, 2634615
E-mail: arbitrage@nova.net.ng
Contact: Dr. Olaseni A. Bello - Chairman/CEO

ARBON LIMITED
Business: Sales of Industrial Laundry & Kitchen Equipment
Address: 20, Aba Road, Port Harcourt
Tel/Fax: (084) 232121, 234700
E-mail: arbonlimited@hotmail.com

ARC (NIGERIA) LIMITED
Business: Building and Civil Engineering Contractors, Asphalt Production, Road Surfacing Services
Address: Km 11, Lagos - Badagry Expressway, Alakija Bus Stop Lagos.
Tel: (01) 880486, 880183 **Fax:** (01) 880183
Contact: Mr. Sammy O. Adigun - M.D/CEO

ARCEE TEXTILE INDUSTRIES LIMITED
Business: Textile Lace Fabric Manufacturing
Address: Aswani Market Road, Oshodi-Apapa Expressway, Isolo, Lagos.
Tel: (01) 4502500, 4520514

ARCHARRIS ENGINEERING CONSTRUCTION LIMITED
Business: Building and Civil Engineering Service
Address: 11, Olujobi Street, Opp. Corona School, Gbagada Estate, Lagos
Tel: (01) 4975812, 4979380 **Fax:** (01) 4975812
E-mail: haibasso@linkserve.com.ng
Contact: Mrs Tonia D. Wright Igiehon

ARCHBODE ENGINEERING LIMITED
Business: Drilling of Borehole, Installation of Storage Tanks & Pumps, Construction of Water Treatment Plant
Address: 115, Iju Water Works Road, Ifako Agege
Tel: (01) 920751
Contact: Mr. Olaniyi Olubode - MD/CEO

ARCHCON NIGERIA LIMITED
Business: Architectural Designing & Planning
Address: 8, Giwa Road, Abakpa, Kaduna
Tel: (062) 238812-4 (3 L), 228805 **Fax:** (062) 238813
* 17A, Commercial Avenue, Yaba Lagos.
Tel: (01) 860086, 868306, 861730
* 2, Tafawa Balewa Road, Sokoto.
Tel: (060) 232879
Contact: Arch. S. O. Omotosho - MD/CEO

ARCHI-HIVES (Architects + Planners)
Business: Architectural Consultancy, Project Management
Address: 21, Coker Road, Ilupeju Lagos
Tel: (01) 4978421
* 76, Allen Avenue Ikeja, Lagos.
Tel: (01) 4974951
* 41 Oshuntokun Avenue, Bodija Estate, Ibadan
Contact: Arc. Femi Ayodele - Partner

ARCHITECTURAL PRODUCTS LIMITED
Business: Manufacture of Accessories of Hollowares and Roofing, Aluminium Rivets, Sheet-Metal Hinges, Currency Boxes, Tower Bolto, Zinc Alloy Casts Aluminium Accessories
Address: Km 8, Abeokuta-Lagos Road, Sapon, Abeokuta
Tel: (039) 240288, 241753, 242427 **Fax:** (039) 241753
E-mail: arco@infoweb.abs.net
Contact: Mr. A.C. Potnis - GM/CEO

ARCLAND PROPERTIES LIMITED
Business: Estate Valuers & Project Consultants
Address: Great Nigeria House, 47/57, Martins Street, Lagos
Tel: (01) 2666788
* Church House, 29, Marina, Lagos.
Conatact: Mr. Ladi Oredugba - Chairman/CEO

ARCO MARINE & OILFIELD SERVICES LIMITED
Business: Marine Transporttion, Logistics Support Solutions
Address: 42, Adetokunbo Ademola Street, V/Island, Lagos
Tel: (01) 2612159, 2611259, 2610759, 2617072
Fax: (01) 2705301, 2625548
E-mail: arcolos@alpha.linkserve.com
Website: www.arco-nigeria.com
* 69, King Perekule St, GRA Phase II, Port Harcourt
Tel: (084) 239608, 239632 **Fax:** (084) 239608
E-mail: arcoph@alpha.linkserve.com
Contact: Mr. Alfred I. Okoigun - MD/CEO

ARCO PETROCHEMICAL ENGINEERING COMPANY LTD
Business: Oilfield Engineering Services; Oilfield Equipment Sales and Service.
Address: 42, Adetokunbo Ademola St, Victoria Island, Lagos
Tel: (01) 2611259, 2612159, 2616132, 2617092
Fax: (01) 2617354, 2617096
E-mail: arcolas@alpha.linkserve.com
Website: www.arco-nigeria.com
* 69, King Perekule St GRA.Phase II, Port Harcourt.
Tel: (084) 239608, 239631
* 93, Effurun - Sapele Road, Warri
Tel: (053) 256686 - 7 (2L)
E-mail: arcowri@skannet.com
Contact: Mr. Alfred I. Okoigun - MD/CEO

ARCON ALUMINIUM NIGERIA LIMITED
Business: Manufacturing of Aluminium Roofing Sheets
Address: 13, Nnobi Road, Anambra State
Tel: (046) 463541, 463540
E-mail: arcon@infoweb.abs.net
* 57, Afikpo Street, Mile 1, Diobu, Port Harcourt
Tel: (084) 238839
Contact: Mr. Chidi Anuligo - Chairman/CEO

ARCTURUS MERCHANT TRUST LIMITED
Business: Trading, Oil & Gas Logistics, Operations of Fleet of Aluminim Tankers for Oil Industry, Telecommuncations and Real Etate
Address: Eleganza Biro Plaza (6th Floor), Plot 634, Adeyemo Alakija Street, Victoria Island, Lagos
Tel: (01) 2702918-9 (2 L), 4616730, 4612033, 7918606
Fax: (01) 4616730
E-mail: arcturusk17@yahoo.com
Contact: Mr Adeniyi Adeoye - Chairman/CEO

AREWA HOTELS (DEVELOPMENT) LIMITED
Business: Hotel Development & Management Services
Address: 24, Muhammadu Buhari Way, Kaduna
Tel: (062) 233919 **Fax:** (062) 218565
Contact: Mr. Philip A. Nyabam - MD/CEO

AREWA METAL CONTAINERS LIMITED
Business: Metal Fabrication and Structural Engineering Works, Water Engineering, Pipeline Production

and Construction Services.Production Facility Operation and Maintenance Service.
Address: 1, Mohammed Ladan Road, Kakuri Industrial Area, Kaduna South, Kaduna
Tel: (062) 232615, 231846 **Fax:** (062) 231707
E-mail: armeco@net.global.com
* c/o NIWA Dockyard, Marine Road, Lokoja
* 2, Zaire Cres, Off Mississippi St, Maitama, Abuja.
Tel/Fax: (09) 4137099
* 18 Keffi Street, Falomo, Ikoyi Lagos.
Tel: (01) 2691443 **Fax:** (01) 2694258
E-mail: safe@infoweb.abs.net
* Plot 3, Trans-Amadi Ind. Layout Port Harcourt
E-mail: pipeline@phca.linkserve.com
Contact: Alh. Isiaq F. Babatunde - MD/CEO

AREWA PHARMACEUTICALS LIMITED
Business: Pharmauceuticals Production and Marketing
Address: 13, Inuwa Abdulkadir Road, Kakuri Industrial Estate, Kaduna South, Kaduna
Tel: (062) 232303
Contact: M. T. Umar - Admin. Manager

AREWA SUITES, ABUJA
Business: Hospitality Services, Conference Facilities
Address: Off Herbert Macaulay Way, Central Business District, Garki, Abuja
Tel: (09) 5239252-3 (2L), 5233742 **Fax:** (09) 5239251

AREWA TEXTILES PLC
Business: Manufacturer of Textile Materials
Address: Kaduna South Industrial Areas, Kaduna
Tel: (062) 233032, 231481 **Fax:** (062) 233039

AREWA TILES INDUSTRIES LIMITED
Business: Terrazzo Floor Tiles, Pavement Cement - Tiles Slaba, Steps and Raisers Production.
Address: 811, Kawaji Quarters, P.O.Box 6459, Bompai, Kano
Tel: (064) 633740, 647020, 337723 **Fax:** (064) 632536
Contact: Hassan Boukarroum - Chairman/CEO

ARFO CONSTRUCTION COMPANY NIGERIA LIMITED
Business: Civil Engineering and Construction Works
Address: Plot 240C, Kofo Abayomi St Victoria Island, Lagos.
Tel: (01) 2623692-3 (2L), 2647650-1 (2L)
Fax: (01) 2647652
E-mail: arfo@hyperia.com
Website: www.arfoconstruction.com
* Plot 2001, Tafawa Balewa St, Area 7, Garki Abuja
Tel: (09) 2341007 **Fax:** (09) 2348747
* 75, Evo Road, G.R.A. Phase II, Port Harcourt
Contact: Alh. Baba Shehu Shettima - Chairman/CEO

ARIB (WEST AFRICA) LIMITED
Business: Training & Management Consultancy, Freight Forwarding, Fire Protection & Safety Engineering, Engineering Construction & Consultancy
Address: 127, Abeokuta Expressway (2nd Floor), Adealu Bus-Stop, Dopemu, Agege, Lagos
Tel: (01) 7743739, 4814440, 08023065551, 08042126300
Fax: (01) 7743739
E-mail: aribwest@hotmail.com
* IIDL Suite 08, Plot 1210, Idofian Close, off Sharon Regency Hotel Road, Zone A7, Wuse II, Abuja
Tel: (09) 2342674
Contact: Hon. (Engr.) Femi Adeniyi - Group MD

ARIBISALA PROPERTIES LIMITED
Business: Real Estate Agency/Practitioners, Developers & Mortgage Brokers
Address: Canute House (1st & 3rd Floors), 31, Campbell Street, Lagos Island, Lagos
Tel: (01) 2632269, 2630657, 2637702, 2631763, 2631758
Fax: (01) 2633835
E-mail: aribisala@gacom.net
Contact: Chief Ajibola A. Aribisala - Chairman/CEO

ARIGUNA NIGERIA LIMITED
Business: Distribution of Pharmaceuticals, Import & Export
Address: Tamburawa, Zaria Road, Kano
Tel: (064) 638764 **Fax:** (064) 639390
Contact: Alh. Abubakar Siddiq Suleiman - MD/CEO

ARIT OF AFRICA LIMITED
Business: IT Products Sales & Back-up Services
Address: 174B Murtala Mohammed Way, Yaba, Lagos.
Tel: (01) 3425235-6 (2L), 7742340
* N6/775A, Polytechnic Road, Sango, Ibadan
Tel: (02) 8101695, 8100564
Contact: Engr Olu Ogunsola - Chairman

ARIZONA CONSTRUCTION LIMITED
Business: Building Construction & Renovation; Mechanical & Electrical Engineering Contractors; Turnkey Projects
Address: 6, Chari Close, off Gana Street, by Bobo Close, Maintama District, Abuja.
Tel: (09) 4135419 **Fax:** (09) 4135429
Contact: Majeed Abou Matar - MD/CEO

ARIZONA TRADING LIMITED
Business: Photograhic Films and Accessories Marketing
Address: 1B Ozumba Mbadiwe Street, Victoria Island, Lagos
Tel: (01) 2626263-4 (2L), 7741212 **Fax:** (01) 2626265
E-mail: arizona@cyberspace.net.ng

ARK INSURANCE GROUP
Business: Insurance Broking Group
Address: Glass House, 11A Karimu Kotun St, V/I, Lagos.
Tel: (01) 2615826. 2615901, 615952-5 (4L) 615922
Fax: (01) 2615850
E-mail: ark@nova.net.ng
Website: www.nigeriaweb.com/ark
* 20 Olaeto Street, D/Line Port Harcourt
Tel: (084) 330580
* 27B, Post Office Road, Kano.
Tel: (064) 648309
Contact: Mr. N. 1. Kadiri - Director (Marketing & Admin)

ARK LIFE & PENSIONS BROKERS LIMITED
Business: Life and Pensions Insurance Broking
Address: Glass House, 11A, Karimu Kotun St, V/I, Lagos
Tel: (01) 2615826, 2615901, 615952-5 (4 L), 615922
Fax: (01) 2615850
E-mail: ark@nova.net.ng
Website: www.nigeriaweb.com/ark
Contact: Prince Francis Olu Awogboro - Chairman/CEO

ARKSEGO NIGERIA LIMITED
Business: Security Services
Address: Plot 174, Oworonsoki Expressway, Gbagada Phase 1, Lagos
Tel: (01) 4974839, 3422292, 5552922, 5820902-3 (2l)
Fax: (01) 4974839, 5552922
E-mail: arksego@hyperia.com
* Suite 38, Area 7 Cornershops, Tafawa Balewa Way Area 7B, Garki Abuja.
Tel: (09) 2341528
Contact: Mr. Segun Labiyi - MD/CEO

ARMOUR GUARDS NIGERIA LIMITED
Business: Security Services
Address: 120, Adeniyi Jones Avenue, Ikeja, Lagos
Tel: (01) 4975871, 08033046860, 08033079425
E-mail: armourguardsltd@yahoo.com
Contact: Chief Val Eze - MD/CEO

ARMTAGE NIGERIA LIMITED
Business: Sales of Building Materials, Tiles, Sanitarywares, Doors & Locks
Address: 4B, Idowu Taylor Street, Victoria Island, Lagos
Tel: (01) 3200269, 2629312, 08034040403, 08033004654
Fax: (01) 610255
E-mail: armtage@beta.linkserve.com

AROLAB NIGERIA LIMITED
Business: Supply of Material-Testing, Technical-Education, Medical Laboratory & Reprographic Equipment, Calibration of Engineering Laboratory Equipment
Address: SW8/1540, Liberty Stadium Road, Ibadan.
Tel: (02) 2315362, 2316091 **Fax:** (02) 2314216
E-mail: arolab@infoweb.abs.net
Contact: Chief Otis Okoromadu - Chairman/CEO

AROPIN-NTEDA ENTERPRISES LIMITED
Business: Manufacturing & Sales of Steel-Shelving Storage Racks, Office & Industrial Equipment, Contractors
Address: 7, Alarape Street, Oremeji, opp. Obalende Garage, Bariga, Lagos
Tel: (01) 8042303, 08023211344, 08023283866
E-mail: aropin-nteda@yahoo.com
Contact: Mr. A. A. Nofiu - Chairman/MD/CEO

ARON NIGERIA LIMITED
Business: Engineering Services, Design and Contracts
Address: 9, Lagos Street, P.O.Box 300, Ebute-Metta Lagos
Tel: (01) 867729, 867045, 5457914, 7743115, 7747729
Fax: (01) 862724
E-mail: aron2@infoweb.abs.net

ARRIBOND INTERNATIONAL LIMITED
Business: Sales of Banking (Currency) Equipment
Address: Great Nigeria House (8th Floor), 45/47, Martins Street Lagos.
Tel: (01) 2221593, 8045752
Contact: Mr. A. Aremu - GM

ARTEE INDUSTRIES LIMITED
Business: General Merchandise Import and Sales, Supermarkets and Furniture Shops Owners
Address: 47, Adeola Odeku Street, Victoria Island, Lagos.
Tel: (01) 2626180-1 (2L), 7763004 **Fax:** (01) 2626284
E-mail: feedback@arteegroup.com
Website: www.arteegroup.com

ARTHUR ANDERSEN (NIGERIA)
Business: Assurance & Business Advisory, Tax & Business Regulatory Services; Business Consultants
Address: 22A, Gerrard Road, Ikoyi Lagos
Tel: (01) 2696040-4 (5 L), 470556. 4705553-4 (2 L), 4705547, 269660-4 (5L) **Fax:** (01) 2691248
Website: www.arthurandersen.com
Contact: Mr. Oluseyi Bicersteth - Country Managing Partner

ARTHUR MBANEFO & ASSOCIATES
Business: Corporate & Financial Consultancy
Address: Ebani House, 149/153 Broad Street, Lagos
Tel: (01) 2665996, 2665998
Contact: Chief Arthur C. I. Mbanefo - Chairman/CEO

ARVEE INDUSTRIES LIMITED
Business: Manufacturing of Flexible Packaging Material
Address: Veepee Industrial Avenue, Off Km 38, Abeokuta Motor Road, Sango-Otta, Ogun State.
Tel: (039) 722209, 722212, 722104, 722301, 722051
Fax: (01) 2692051, 4973110
Contact: Chief V. P. Vaswani - Chairman
Mr. Rajan Vaswani - MD/CEO

ASA CEILINGS LIMITED
Business: Ceiling Technology Consultants, Civil Engineering Services for the Oil Industry
Address: 43, Osolo Way, Ajao Estate, Marina Lagos
Tel: (01) 4524109, 4526623, 7745116, 08033028036, 08033044969 **Fax:** (01) 4526313
E-mail: asaceilings@justice.com
Contact: Mr. Alozie Sunday Alozie - MD/CEO

ASABA ALUMINIUM COMPANY LIMITED
Busines: Manufacturing and Marketing of Aluminium Roofing & Cladding Sheets, Doors & Windows
Address: Km. 11, Asaba-Benin Expressway, Asaba.
Tel: (056) 280044, 281215, 281473 **Fax:** (056) 281215
E-mail: asalco@micro.com.ng
* Km. 14, PH-Aba Expressway, Port Harcourt.
Tel: (084) 613124, 613337 Fax: (084) 613337
* 2, Edingburgh Road, Enugu.
Tel: (042) 250131

ASAD GENERIC LABORATORIES LIMITED
Business: Production of Liquid Pharmaceutical Preparations
Address: 103, Hadejia Road, P. O. Box 932, Kano
Tel: (064) 315655, 08037050606
E-mail: asadhc@yahoo.com
Contact: Haruna Sulaiman - Chairman
Shehu Yau Saad - MD/CEO

ASADA GROUP LIMITED
Business: Quarrying, Sales of Stone Products & Tiles, Sales of Water Tanks
Address: Plot 14, Murtala Muhammed Square Extension, Independence Way, Kaduna
Tel: (062) 240672
* Sanusi Dantata House, Plot 274, Central Busi-

ness District, Garki, Abuja
Tel: (09) 2340656, 5236499 **Fax:** (09) 4136543

ASADA PLASTICS LIMITED
Business: Manufacturing of Sacks and Bags
Address: Plot 91, Sharada Industrial Estate Phase II, Kano
Tel: (064) 668188

ASCENT LIMITED
Business: Mechanical, Electrical and Power Engineering, Supply of V-Belts, Timing and Conveyor Belts, Construction and Repair of Industrial Machinery, Sales of Liquid & Gas Measurement and Control Equipment and Control Equipment
Address: 643, Abeokuta Express Road (General Bus-Stop), Ojokoro, Lagos
Tel: (01) 4926795, 4926412, 4973634, 7746364
Fax: (01) 4926795, 4926412
E-mail: ascent@infoweb.abs.net
Contact: Mr. Paul de Waart - MD/CEO

ASCON OIL COMPANY LIMITED
Business: Marketing of Petroleum Products and Industrial Chemicals, Bottling and Marketing of Liquefied Petroleum Gas
Address: 39A, Bishop Aboyade Cole St Victoria Island, Lagos
Tel: (01) 2610624 **Fax:** (01) 2610625
E-mail: asconoil@infoweb.abs.net
Contact: Engr. George I. Enenmoh - Chairman/CEO

ASCOT OIL & GAS NIGERIA LIMITED
Business: Oil & Gas
Addreess: Plot 88, RIVOC Road, Trans-Amadi Industrial Layout, Port Harcourt
Tel: (084) 237987
Contact: Mr. Ron Metcalf - CEO

ASCOTT FABRICATORS & CONSTRUCTORS NIG. LTD
Business: Oil & Gas Business
Address: Plot 88, RIVOC Road, Trans-Amadi Industrial Layout, Port Harcourt
Tel: (084) 237987, 238483 **Fax:** (084) 238483
Website: www.ascofnig.com
Contact: Mr Henry Imasekha - Chairman
Mr Sean P. Kidney - MD/CEO

ASCOTT AGENCIES LIMITED
Business: Production of Cosmetics
Address: 52, Adekunle Fajuyi Road, G.R.A Ikeja Lagos.
Tel: (01) 4939895 **Fax:** (01) 4939896
Contact: Mr. K. O. Achukwu - MD/CEO

ASD GROUP OF COMPANIES
Businesss: Motor Vehicles Distribution, Sales and Service.
Address: 15/17, Constitution Road, Kaduna
Tel: (062) 248540, 244036, 242112, 248587, 241491
Fax: (062) 248540
Contact: Alh. (Dr.) Sani Dauda - Chairman/CEO

ASEA BROWN BOVERI LIMITED
Business: Engineering, Design, Supply, Installation, Commissioning, Operation & Maintenance & Industrial & Building Systems, Rail Transportation Systems & Broadcasting Equipment
Address: 46, Industrial Avenue, Ilupeju Industrial Estate, Ilupeju, Lagos
Tel: (01) 4937347-8 (2 L), 4966894, 4962187
Fax: (01) 4937329
E-mail: abbng@abb.com.ng
* Total Building (1st Floor), Plot 247, Herbert Macaulay Way, Central Area, Abuja
Tel: (09) 2346796, 2346797, 2346800-3 (4L), 2340520-1
Fax: (09) 2340047
* ABB Camp, Awkunanaw, Enugu
Tel: (042) 451604
Contact: Mr. Wolfgang Pfeiffer - MD/CEO

ASEMOTA MOTORS LIMITED
Business: Sales & Services Peugeot Cars & Trucks
Address: 45, Alh. Tokan St, Alaka Estate, Surulere, Lagos
Tel: (01) 5830435, 5837296, 5830433 **Fax:** (01) 5830433
* Km. 6, Lagos-Badagry Expressway, Lagos
Tel: (01) 5452300
Contact: Mr. Sunny Asemota - Chairman/CEO

ASFERRO LIMITED
(Ajaokuta Steel Co/Ferrostaal AG Joint Venture)
Business: Engineering &Planning Services; Fabrication, Repair &Maintenance for all Industries, Steel Structures; Bridge Construction; Rolling Stock; Tool Manufacturing; Welding &Special Equipment; Hydro-Mechanical Equipment; Electrical & Mechanical Installation, Traning &Technical Services.
Address: P.M.B. 1000, Steel City, Ajaokuta
Tel: (058) 400522
* Plot 3323, Barada Close off Amazon Street, Maitama, Abuja.
Tel: (09) 4135251 **Fax:** (09) 4135250
E-mail: fs-abuja@alpha.linkserve.com

ASHAKACEM PLC
Business: Manufacture and Marketing of Cement Products
Address: * Ashaka works, near Gombe, Gombe State
Tel: (072) 70127-30 (4L)
* 1, Audu Bako Way, Kano
Tel: (064) 634908, 646960
* Plot 193, Jide Oki Street, off Younis Bashorun Street, Victoria Island, Lagos
Tel: (01) 2612223, 2612207, 2618293
* Plot 42/43, Karu New Town, Abuja
Tel: (09) 523596, 5235497
Contact: Engr. Muhammad M. Daggash - MD/CEO

ASHAKA SECURITY COMPANY LIMITED
Business: Security Services; Electronic Secruity Equipment Sales and Installation; Security Survey, Training
Address: 39A Festac Link Road, Amuwo Odofin, Lagos
Tel: (01) 5887363, 5887364 **Fax:** (01) 5887363
E-mail: waashaka@hotmail.com
Website: www.ascoltd.com
Contact: Mr. Jonah Ashaka - Chairman/CEO

ASH-BERT (NIGERIA) LIMITED
Business: Oil & Gas, Environmental Consultancy Services, Energy & Transport Service, Photography and Leisure Service.

Address: 196B, Awolowo Road S.W. Ikoyi, Lagos
Tel: (01) 2692749, 2672922 **Fax:** (01) 2692718
E-mail: info@ashbert.com
ashbert@hyperia.com
Website: www.ashbert.com
Contact: Mr. Albert Esiri - Chairman/CEO

ASHMOUNT INSURANCE BROKERS LIMITED
Business: Insurance Brokers
Address: 38/40 Strachan Street, Off Igbosere Road Lagos
Tel: (01) 2645093 2646814 **Fax:** (01) 263376
* Plot 139, Monrovia Street, Wuse 11, Abuja
Tel: (09) 4122331
Contact: Mr. Emmanuel Ojarikre - GM

ASI BUILDING SYSTEMS LIMITED
Business: Building Construction Engineering, Mass Concrete Systems Design.
Address: Plot PC 10, Engineering Close, Off Idowu Taylor Street, Victoria Island, Lagos
Tel: (01) 2626751,2617788, 2618022 **Fax:** (01) 2626751
E-mail: asio@lvcm.com
Website: www.asibuildsystems.com
* 8, Adetokunbo Ademola Crescent, Plot 561, Cadastral Zone A8, Wuse 11 Abuja
Tel: (09) 5235624-6 (3L) **Fax:** (09) 5235627
Contact: Mr. Mayer Lagnado - MD/CEO

ASIA PLASTIC INDUSTRY (NIGERIA) LIMITED
Business: Manufacturing of Plastic Products
Address: Km. 18, Hadejia Road, Jagana, Kano
Tel: (064) 631431, 646362, 08034080828
Fax: (064) 638185
E-mail: standard@samdav.com
Website: www.opin-nigeria.com
* 3, Ladipo Oluwole Avenue, Ikeja Industrial Estate Ikeja, Lagos
Tel: (01) 4920740, 4973596, 4964497

ASK ELECTRICAL LIMITED
Business: Electrical Engineering Services; Supply, Installation & Maintenance of High-Voltage Equipment and Transformers
Address: Bamboo Plaza (4th Floor), 6/8, New Isheri Road, Omole, Ikeja, Lagos
Tel: (01) 7757687, 4717263, 4710916, 4721452, 08033068989
* 472, Ikwere Road, Port Harcourt
Contact: Pastor Fred Odekhian - MD/CEO

ASKAR PAINTS (NIGERIA) LIMITED
Business: Manufacturing and Marketing of Paints and Chemical Products; Contract Painting
Address: Askar Paints Road (Eleyele Bus Stop), Ibadan.
Tel: (02) 2410933, 2410374 **Fax:** (02) 2410374
E-mail: askar@skannet.com
Contact: Mr. Ladipo Salako - MD/CEO

ASNL MODELS & COMMUNICATIONS LIMITED
Business: Architectural Model - Building Securities
Address: 25, Alhaja Kofoworola Crescent, Off Obafemi Awolowo Way, Ikeja, Lagos
Tel: (01) 4971153
E-mail: asnl@building.com
Contact: Mr. Sam Odia - MD/CEO

ASO MOTEL KADUNA LIMITED
Business: Hospitality Services
Address: 14, Waff Road, Kaduna
Tel: (062) 242168-9 (2L), 247389 **Fax:** (062) 242170

ASO SAVINGS & LOANS LIMITED
Business: Mortgage Finance Services
Address: 8, Ogbomoso Street, Area 8, Garki, Abuja
Tel: (09) 2345156-8 (3L) **Fax:** (09) 2345158
Contact: Charles Akin-Adaramola

ASO SOLID INSURANCE BROKERS LIMITED
Business: Insurance Broking, Pensions Management
Address: 8, Ogbomosho Street, Area 8, Garki, Abuja
Tel: (09) 2345156-8 (3 L), 2347154 **Fax:** (09) 2345158
Contact: Otunba C. A. Adaramola - Chairman
Mr. Joseph Nyam - GM/CEO

ASONNET TECHNOLOGIES LIMITED
Business: Telecommunications; Networking; Website Design, Development & Hosting; ISP; Hard & Software Solutions
Address: Mamman Kontagora House (14th Floor), 23, Marina Lagos
Tel: (01) 2601342-4 (3L) **Fax:** (01) 2601341
E-mail: linus.asonye@asonnet.zzn.com
Website: www.asonnet.com
Contact: Mr. Ibe Asonye Onwumere - Chairman/CEO

ASSAN OIL MILLS LIMITED
Business: Vegetable Oil Milling
Address: Plot 23, Sharada Industrial Estate, Phase II, Kano

ASSAY NIGERIA LIMITED
Business: Sales and Service of Bank Automation Equipment
Address: 38, Modupe Johnson Crescent, Off Adeniran Ogunsanya Street, Surulere Lagos
Tel: (01) 5851482, 832136, 4718692 **Fax:** (01) 5851482
E-mail: jojieke@usa.net
Contact: Mr. George Eke - Chairman/CEO

ASSET & LIABILITY INSURANCE COMPANY LIMITED
Business: Non-life Insurance
Address: 71, Opebi Road, Ikeja, Lagos
Tel: (01) 5451105, 4979469 **Fax:** (01) 966585
Contact: Mr. F. T. Adebayo - GM/CEO

ASSET & RESOURCES MANAGEMENT COMPANY LIMITED
Business: Asset and Portfolio Management, Investment Advisory Services
Address: 9, Bayo Kuku Road, Off Kingsway Rd, Ikoyi Lagos
Tel: (01) 2690056, 2692097, 2692971, 2692976, 2695212-3

ASSET & RETIREMENT MANAGEMENT COMPANY LTD
Business: Pension Fund Administration & Management, Consultancy Services
Address: 4, Dapo Solanke Close, off Jerry Iriabe Street, off Babatunde Anjous Street, off Admiralty Way, Lekki Peninsula Phase 1, Lekki, Lagos
Tel: (01) 2708061-3 (3L) **Fax:** (01) 2708063

E-mail: armcopension@21ctl.com
Contact: Mr. Dapo Solanke - MD/CEO

ASSET MANAGEMENT GROUP LIMITED
Business: Financial Services
Address: Foreshore Services (6th Floor), 2A, Osborne Road, Ikoyi, Lagos
Tel: (01) 2692985

ASSET PLUS SECURITIES LIMITED
Business: Stockbroking Financial Advisory Services
Address: Bookshop House (5th Floor), 50/52, Broad Street, Lagos
Tel: (01) 2645723, 2601930-4 (5L) 2645724
Fax: (01) 2630856
E-mail: info@assetplusgroup.com
securities@assetplusgroup.com
Website: www.assetplusgroup.com
* Ogun State House (2nd Floor), Plot 74, 4th Ave, Off Ahmadu Bello Way, Central Area, Garki Abuja.
Tel/Fax: (09) 5235700
Contact: Mr Wole Ogbonyomi - MD/CEO

ASSI CHEMICAL PRODUCTS LIMITED
Business: Cosmetics Production and Sales
Address: Plot 3, Billingsway, T.A. Doherty Industrial Layout, Oregun, Ikeja, Lagos.
Tel: (01) 4933530, 7741349
E-mail: acpl@beta.linkserve.com

ASSIAPLAST LIMITED
Business: Manufacturing of Footwear
Address: 6, Ibassa Road, Badagry Expressway, Ojo, Lagos
Tel: (01) 5880123 **Fax:** (01) 5870556
* Km. 12, Old Lagos Road, Ayetoro Village, Ibadan.
Tel: (02) 2314526-7 (2L)
Contact: Hani Safieddine - Chairman

ASSOCIATED AVIATION LIMITED
Business: Executive Jet Charter Services, Scheduled Passenger Flight Operation
Address: 56, Moshood Abiola Crescent, off Toyin Street, Ikeja, Lagos
Tel: (01) 4960360, 4936514, 4966185, 4966185, 4963562
Fax: (01) 4936514
E-mail: assoair@linkserve.com
Contact: Mr. Tunde Oremule - Chairman

ASSOCIATED BIOTECHNOLOGY LIMITED
Business: Marketing of Food & Beverage Chemicals & Additves, Pharmaceutical Raw Materials, Water-Treatment, Oil Processing & Prospecting Chemicals
Address: 290, Ikorodu Road, Anthony, Lagos
Tel: (01) 4974439, 8045396 **Fax:** (01) 4936656, 4971572
E-mail: abctech@alpha.linkserve.com
Contact: Nze Clarkson Iheanyi Nnadi - Chairman/CEO

ASSOCIATED BUS COMPANY LIMITED (ABC Transport)
Business: Passenger and Cargo Transportation Services
Address: 122, Wetheral Road, Owerri.
Tel: (083) 231246, 231716, 232167 **Fax:** (083) 231275
Website: www.abctransport.com
Contact: Mr. Frank Nneji - Chairman/CEO

ASSOCIATED DATA SYSTEMS LIMITED
Business: Computer Sales & Services, Software Development Marketing, Networking, Training and Consultancy
Address: Mandilas Building (6th Floor), 35, Simpson Street, Lafiaji Lagos.
Tel/Fax: (01) 2634095, 2634105
E-mail: adslagos@infoweb.abs.net
Contact: Dr. Clement O. Oshaka - MD/CEO

ASSOCIATED DISCOUNT HOUSE LIMITED
Business: Portfolio,Finance and Stock Management
Address: St Nicholas House, 6th Floor, 28A, Catholic Mission Street, Lagos.
Tel: (01) 2601970-1, 2645824, 2647883, 2647884, 7732753, 4715857 **Fax:** (01) 2647994, 2645821, 2647886
E-mail: adh@adh-ng.com
Website: www.adh.-ng.com
* Legion House, Plot C 1 & 2, Kaura Namoda Street, Area 3, Garki, Abuja.
Tel: (09) 2343972, 2347295, 090-410956
* Fleet House, 105 (Plot 349), Olu Obasanjo Road, Port Harcourt.
Tel: (084) 236361, 572297

ASSOCIATED GARAGES LIMITED
Business: Motor Vehicles Repairs, Maintenance and Refurbishing
Address: 391/398, Apapa - Oshodi Expressway, Opp Ilasa Police Post, Ilasamaja, Lagos
Tel: (01) 4528415
Contact: Engr. O. O. Akintunde - MD/CEO

ASSOCIATED GRANITE INDUSTRIES LIMITED
Business: Quarrying
Address: Gudo Quarry, Oke Saje, Abeokuta
Tel: (039) 243979, 244098 **Fax:** (039) 243979, 244650
Contact: Prof. Fola Aboaba - MD/CEO

ASSOCIATED MANUFACTURING COMPANY LIMITED
Business: Production and Marketing of Pharmaceuticals
Address: 56, Moshood Abiola Crescent, Ikeja, Lagos
Tel: (01) 4960360, 4963562, 4973700 **Fax:** (01) 4936514
* Km 14, Otta-Idiroko Road, Iju Village, Otta
Contact: Mrs Susan Oremule - MD/CEO

ASSOCIATED MATCH INDUSTRIES (NIGERIA) LIMITED
Business: Manufacture of Safety Matches & Allied Products
Address: Eleiyele Industrial Layout, (opp. Police Command), Eleiyele Road, Ibadan
Tel: (02) 2414398, 2411402, 2411016 **Fax:** (02) 2410989
* Plot 3, Chief T. A. Doherty Layout, Oregun Industrial Estate, Oregun Lagos.
Tel: (01) 4968359
Contact: Mr. A. Mehandru - MD/CEO

ASSOCIATED METAL & ALLIED LTD (ASSOMETAL GROUP)
Business: Manufacture of Enamelware
Address: Plot 1 & 2, Block XI, Industrial Estate, Wasimi, Onipanu, off Idiroko Road, Otta, Ogun State
Contact: Mr. M. H. Lee - MD/CEO

ASSOCIATED PHARMACEUTICAL PRODUCTS LIMITED
Business: Manufacturing of Pharmaceutical Products
Addresss: Plot 3, Block A, Amuwo-Odofin Industrial Estate,

Lagos Badagry Expressway,Orile Iganmu Lagos.
Tel: (01) 801390-3, (4L), 836192 **Fax:** (01) 836192
Contact: Mr M. Suleman - Admin. Manager

ASSOCIATED PHARMACEUTICALS, FOOD & CHEMICALS LIMITED
Business: Manufacture of Pharmaceuticals & Chemicals, Food Processing
Address: 4/6, Eziama High School Road, Eziama, Aba
* 152, Azikiwe Road, Aba
Tel: (082) 220645, 231131 **Fax:** (082) 220645
E-mail: starline@phca.linkserve.com
Contact: Mazi Clement Owunna - Chairman/CEO

ASSOCIATED SURVEYORS & ADJUSTERS
Business: Loss Adjusting & Claims Administration; Condition and Valuation Survey; Engineering Survey and Plant/Equipment Inspection, Risk Management, Cargo Superintendence.
Address: 2/4, Bauchi Road, Off Bombay Crescent, Apapa, Lagos
Tel: (01) 5804558, 5870381 **Fax:** (01) 5804558
Contact: Chief (Engr) F. E. O. Jackson Cole - MD/CEO

ASSOCIATED TELECOMS & ELECTRONICS CO NIG. LTD
Business: Radio Communication Equipment & Accessories
Address: 90, Aba Road, Port Harcourt
Tel/Fax: (084) 232383, 238378; (082) 440880
E-mail: assotel@yahoo.com
* 82, Egbede/Iloabuchi Street, Mile 2, Diobu, Port Harcourt
* F2083, Alaba International Market, Ojo Lagos
Tel: (01) 80423217 (Ext. 257)

ASSURANCE BANK NIGERIA LIMITED
Business: Commercial Banking
Address: Abibu-Oki Court, 19, Abibu-Oki Street, Lagos
Tel: (01) 2642012, 2642029 **Fax:** (01) 2660342
E-mail: assurancebank@assurancebank.com
Contact: Alh. Mohammed T. Umaru - Ag. MD/CEO

ASTAC NIGERIA LIMITED
Business: Traffic Lights Installation and Management
Address: 41, Oduduwa Way, Ikeja GRA, Ikeja, Lagos
Tel/Fax: (01) 4963662, 4970069, 4970071, 4971609
E-mail: office@astac-nigeria.com
Website: www.astac-nigeria.com
* Plot 199, Fort Lammy Street, Opp Sharon Hotel, Wuse Zone 6, Abuja.
Tel/Fax: (09) 52344073-4 (2L)

ASTRA INSTRUMENTS LIMITED
Business: Sales and Installation of Laboratory & Medical Equipment, Scientific Instruments, Analytical Reagents and Chemicals
Address: 111, Okigwe Road, P.O.Box 20609, Aba.
Tel/Fax: (082) 232870
E-mail: astrainstrument@micro.com.ng
* Alphon House, 50/52, Toyin Street, Ikeja Lagos.
Tel: (01) 4935990-1 (2L) **Fax:** (01) 4935991
* 76, Mubi Road, P.O.Box 1098, Jimeta Yola.
Tel: (075) 624805 **Fax:** (075) 626693
Contact: Mr. Uchenna A. Okpara - Chairman/CEO

ASTRAL WATERS LIMITED
Business: Bottled Drinking Water Dispensing Equipment Marketing
Address: 58, Akanbi Onitiri Close, Off Eric Moore Road, Surulere, Lagos
Tel: (01) 4705335, 4706066, 5802600-6 (7L)
Fax: (01) 5456114, 5842163
E-mail: astral@hyperia.com
Contact: Mr. K. N. Sanghv - Head (Sales)

ASTROMATIC NIGERIA LIMITED
Business: Airconditioning and Refrigeration Applicances & Equipment Marketing
Address: 3, Dabiri close, Off Remilekun Street Off Ogunlana Drive, P.O. Box 5223, Surulere, Lagos.
Tel: (01) 5830789, 5851938, 830739 **Fax:** (01) 5830739
E-mail: astromatic@infoweb.abs.net

AT & S INVESTMENTS LIMITED
Business: Engineering Services, Fire & Safety Services, Procurement of Goods & Equipment, Marine & Energy Services, Financial & Investment Advisory Services
Address: Eleganza Building (3rd Floor), 15B, Joseph Street, Lagos Island, Lagos
Tel: (01) 7740138, 2636008, 08023039010, 08036694783, 08042132651 **Fax:** (01) 2635891
E-mail: atslimited@yahoo.com
Contact: Mr. Akin Oluwole - MD/CEO

ATILAB NIGERIA LIMITED
Business: Pharmaceutical Products Production and Marketing, Sales of Medical Equipment and Consumables
Address: Plot 25, Block C, Oluyole Industrial Estate Extension, Off Ring Road, Ibadan
Tel: (02) 2315518, 08033282903, 08033357663
* 20A, N.U.D, Road, Oke-Ijeun, Sapon, Abeokuta
Contact: Mr G. M. Abiodun - Chairmamn/CEO.

ATLANTIC CARPETS (NIGERIA) LIMITED
Business: Manufacturing of Carpets, Rugs & Velvet Upholstery
Address: Km. 8, New Iwo Road Olodo, Ibadan
Tel: (02) 711582-3 (2 L), 8106969, 8104134, 08055134315, 08055310620 **Fax:** (02) 8100838
E-mail: seyiamao@skannet.com
Contact: Chief J. O. Amao - Chairman/CEO

ATLANTIC HOTEL, UYO
Business: Hospitality & Catering Services
Address: 6, Atakpo Street, off Nwaniba Road, Uyo
Tel: (085) 200754, 204412

ATLANTIC INSURANCE BROKERS LIMITED
Business: Insurance Brokers, Risk Management Consultants
Address: 13, Ladipo Oluwole Avenue, Off Adeniyi Jones Avenue, Ikeja
Tel: (01) 4975160, 7753074
Contact: Mr. Sola A. Akingbade - MD/CEO

ATLANTIC INSURANCE COMPANY LIMITED
Business: Insurance - General Business and Special Risk
Address: Adebola House, 40, Opebi Road, Ikeja, Lagos
Tel: (01) 4966028, 4976600-4 (5L) **Fax:** (01) 4930639

E-mail: atlanticinsure@infoweb.abs.net
* Foto House, Plot 479, Tafawa Balewa Way, Area 3, Garki, Abuja.
Tel: (09) 2344947
* Foto House 18, Aggrey Road Port Harcourt.
Tel: (084) 233538
Contact: Mr. Clement O. Atere - MD/CEO

ATLANTIC INTERNATIONAL VENTURES LIMITED
Business: Freight Forwarding, Shipping Agents, Cargo Consolidation, Warehousing, Transport
Address: Eleganza Plaza (Libra Block, 2nd Floor), Aerodrome Road, Apapa, Lagos
Tel: (01) 5453070, 5876725 **Fax:** (01) 5876725
E-mail: aivl@hotmail.com
Contact: Mr. Vincent O. Ikekeregor - Chairman/CEO

ATLANTIC MARINE & OILFIELD SERVICES LIMITED
Business: Offshore & Oilfield Corrosion Control; Subsea Diving Inspection, Installation & Survey; Supply of Oilfield Tools and Equipment.
Address: 14, Alhaji Kanike Close, S.W; Ikoyi,Lagos
Tel: (01) 2694058 **Fax:** (01) 2692072
E-mail: atlanticmarine@nova.net.ng
* 23 Aggrey Road, Port Harcourt. **Tel:** (084) 232064
Contact: Mr. Humphrey Okposo - MD/CEO

ATLANTIC MARINE & PETROLEUM MANAGEMENT LTD
Business: Ship owners & Mangers, Tanker Chartering, Oil & Gas Services (Offshore), Marketing of Petroleum Products, Bunkering, Marine Consultants.
Address: Eleganza Plaza (Virgo Block Right Wing, 2nd Floor) 1, Commercial Road, Apapa, Lagos
Tel: (01) 5451025, 5455480 **Fax:** (01) 5450412
E-mail: oceantrends@hotmail.com
Contact: Mr. Babatunde A. Kayode - MD/CEO

ATLANTIC MEDITERRANEAN OIL SERVICES CO. LTD
Business: Oilfield Engineering Services, Pipeline Inspection Services, Quality Assurance and Control
Address: 14/15, Chief Nwuke Street, Trans-Amadi Industrial Layout, Port Harcourt.
Tel: (084) 233004, 233647

ATLANTIC MERIDEAN LIMITED
Business: Oil Services
Address: Plot 33A/B, Adetokunbo Ademola St, V/I, Lagos
Tel: (01) 2611893 **Fax:** (01) 2610073
Contact: Mr. Charles Momoh - MD/CEO

ATLANTIC TEXTILE MANUFACTURING COMPANY LTD
Business: Manufacture of Textile Piece Goods
Address: State Highway, Ilupeju Ind.Estate, Ilupeju, Lagos
Tel: (01) 4791370-5 (6L)
Contact: Mr. Friedrick Ludwig Hinklemann - MD/CEO

ATLAS PAINTS LIMITED
Business: Paints Manufacturing, Machineries Fabrication, Interior Decoration, Home Renovation & Painting, Roof Maintenance/Leakages
Address: 15, Idem Etim Family Square, Abiakpo Ikot Essien, Ikot Ekpene
Contact: Mr. Svetlana I. Idio - Financial Director

ATLAS PETROLEUM INTERNATIONAL LIMITED
Business: Exploration & Production of Hydrocarbon
Address: 4, Akin-Olugbade Street, Victoria Island, Lagos
Tel: (01) 2612566, 2623471 **Fax:** (01) 2615689
Contact: Mr Chike Okoye - MD/CEO

ATS TRAVEL NIGERIA LIMITED
Business: Airline Booking, Hotel Reservation, Airport Services, Holiday & Safaris,Car Hire Service
Address: 4, Alhaji Bashorun Street, off Norman Williams Street, S. W. Ikoyi, Lagos
Tel: (01) 686224, 2694095, 2694761 **Fax:** (01) 2694761
E-mail: atstravels@beta.linkserve.com
Contact: Mr Taiwo Charles Ojelade - Chairman/CEO

AUDIT CONTROL & EXPERTISE (NIGERIA) LIMITED (ACE)
Business: Collateral Management; Credit Support; Cargo Superintendents & Surveyors; Warehouse Agents
Address: 10A, Fabac Close, off Ligali Ayorinde Street, Victoria Island, Lagos
Tel: (01) 2618798, 613509, 3204115 **Fax:** (01) 3204115
E-mail: acenig@hyperia.com
Website: www.ace-group.net
Contact: Mr. Akin Akintunde - GM (Mktg & Credit Support)

AUGIAS ENVIRONMENTAL & CONSULTING SERVICES LTD
Business: Environmental Management & Pest Control Services, Laboratory Services, Supply of Laboratory Equipment and Consumable
Address: Plot PC 10, Engineering Close, off Idowu Taylor Street, Victoria Island, Lagos
Tel: (01) 2617788, 2618022, 2618320, 2626751, 4619019
Fax: (01) 2626751, 4619011
E-mail: augias@hyperia.com;
angias@aol.com
Contact: Dr. Richard Vanderhoof - MD/CEO

AUGUST VENTURES LIMITED
Business: Sales of Banking Equipment and Automation
Address: 61, Iwaya Road, Onike, Yaba, Lagos
Tel/Fax: (01) 4925093

AUGUST TRUCKS & HAULAGE COMPANY LIMITED
Business: Haulage Services
Address: 29, Abimbola Street, Isolo Ind. Estate, Isolo, Lagos
Tel: (01) 4528888, 4528009, 7745858, 4523766, 08033357220, 08033015786 **Fax:** (01) 4529013
E-mail: vanvliet@infoweb.abs.net
Contact: Mr. Dayo Adetunmbi - Chairman/CEO

AULIC NIGERIA LIMITED
Business: Sales of Vulcanizing Equipment and Materials Alignment and Balancing Machines
Address: 12, Amusement Park Complex, Randle Road, Apapa, Lagos.
Tel: (01) 5870741 **Fax:** (01) 5450026-7(2L)
Website: www.auliclimited.com
* Exodus Block (Shop 73) ASPMDA Plaza, Lagos International Trade Fair Complex, Ojo, Lagos
Tel: (01) 2885004, 3208229
* 42, Olu Obasanjo Road, Port Harcourt
Tel: (084) 333082
Contact: Chief N. Nzeh - Chairman/CEO

AULT & WIBORG (NIGERIA) LIMITED
Business: Manufacture of Printing Inks, Graphic Supplies
Address: Km 38, Abeokuta Express Road, off Lynson Chemical Avenue, Sango Otta, Ogun State
Tel: (039) 722445-7 (3L)
Contact: Chief Patrick E.Williams - Chairman/CEO

AURA WEST AFRICA LIMITED
Business: Automobile Sales and Service
Address: 38 Kofo Abayomi Street, Victoria Island, Lagos
Tel: (01) 7740421 **Fax:** (01) 2622596
* Plot 3/4, Abebe Village Road/Eric Moore Road Iganmu Industrial Estate, Surulere, Lagos
Contact: Mr. G. S. Malile - MD/CEO.

AUREOL SERVICES LIMITED
Business: Sales and Installation of Ventilation Hygiene and Pest Control Equipment
Address: 191, Igbosere Road, 2nd Floor, Lagos
Tel: (01) 2634662, 2635256

AUSKEN INTERNATIONAL (NIGERIA) LIMITED
Business: Importation of Exquisite Furniture, Lightining Fittings & Lamps, Manufacture of Furniture
Address: Ausken House, 86A, Olojo Drive,Ojo, Lagos
Tel: (01) 880724, 885259
* 144, Lagos-Badagry Expressway, Agboju, Lagos
Tel: (01) 885259
* 150, Olojo Drive,Ojo Town, Lagos
* Shop H11, H19 & F2042, Alaba Int'l Mkt, Lagos
Contact: Chief Augustine Okoli - Chairman/CEO

AUSTIN & ASSOCIATES LIMITED
Business: Insurance Broking & Arbitration
Address: 55, Western Avenue, Surulere, Lagos
Tel/Fax: (01) 841277
Contact: Chief Austin O. Obiora - Chairman/CEO

AUSTIN SHERIF LIMITED
Business: Sales and Service of Equipment for Petroleum Marketing and Automotive Service.
Address: 26, Fatai Atere Way, Opp Obagun Avenue, Plot 6, Block A, Matori Industrial Scheme, Oshodi Lagos
Tel/Fax: (01) 4520641
Contact: Mr. A. A. Adebiyi - MD/CEO

AUSTOMA ENTERPRISES NIGERIA LIMITED
Business: Marketing of Petroleum Products, Engineering Services
Address: Km 4, Otukpo Road, Opp. Radio Benue, Makurdi
Tel: (044) 533070, 533636 **Fax:** (044) 533636
E-mail: austoma@infoweb.abs.net
* Plot 178, Ahmadu Bello Way, Wuse 11, Abuja
Tel: (09) 5237094 **Fax:** (09) 5234942
Contact: Chief A. O. Ezekwesili - Chairman/CEO

AUSTON REED INTERNATIONAL LIMITED
Business: Distribution of Roller Bearings, Mechanical Seals Packing, Industry Tools & Equipment, Oil-Servicing Equipment & Spares
Address: 68, Adeniyi Jones Avenue (2nd Floor), Ikeja Lagos
Tel: (01) 4970460, 4936337, 8042075 **Fax:** (01) 4936339
E-mail: austonreed@yahoo.com
Contact: Dr (Mrs) Comfort Tonkumoh - MD/CEO

AUTO AFFAIRS
Business: Sales of Motor Vehicles, Distribution of DUNLOP Tyres and Tubes
Address: 4/6, Mobolaji Bank-Anthony Way, Onigbongbo Maryland, Ikeja, Lagos
Tel: (01) 8914950
E-mail: autoaffairs@linkserve.com.ng
Contact: Mr. A. Rotimi - Chairman/CEO

AUTO COMPONENTS LIMITED
Business: Manufacture of Motor Vehicle Spare Parts
Address: Plot 3, Block IV, Otta Industrial Estate, Km 6, Idiroko Road, Otta, Ogun State .
Tel: (039) 722417, 722464
Fax: (01) 5872518, 5877201, (039) 722417
Contact: Mr. C. O. Majekodunmi - GM

AUTO TRADE NIGERIA LIMITED
Business: Import, Assembly & Marketing of Motorcycles
Address: 40, Church Road, Sabon Gari, Kano
Tel: (064) 649344, 316995
Contact: Mr. Charles Uba - MD/CEO

AUTO HAUL NIGERIA LIMITED
Business: Car-Care Products Sales
Address: 58, Kayode Street Off Ijaiye Road, Ogba, Lagos
Tel: (01) 4923764

AUTO SYMBOL NIGERIA LIMITED
Business: Sales and Maintenance of Cars and Accessories
Address: 80, Adeniran Ogunsanya Street, Surulere, Lagos.
Tel: (01) 834929
Contact: Chief Kingsley Ufere - Chairman/CEO

AUTOMANIA (NIGERIA) LIMITED
Business: Organisers of The Annual Lagos Motor Fair
Address: 21B, Bush Street, Okupe Estate, Maryland
Tel: (01) 4977855, 4976354, 4970052 **Fax:** (01) 4970052
E-mail: pwheels@infoweb.abs.net
Website: www.automanialagos.com
Contact: Mr. Olufemi Osilaja - ED

AUTOMATED PROCESS LIMITED
Business: Sales and Service of Industrial Process Control and Analytical Instrumentation and Equipment.
Address: 32, Lagos-Abeokuta Expressway, near Cement Bus-Stop, Dopemu, Agege, Lagos
Tel: (01) 4926869, 08023043105/9 **Fax:** (01) 4937992
E-mail: automated_process@yahoo.com
Contact: Mr. Ubi Kalu Udi - MD/CEO

AUTOMOBILE MANUFACTURERS COMPANY LIMITED
Business: Sales of Automobiles and Motorclycles
Address: 206, Moshood Abiola Way, Ijora Lagos
Tel: (01) 5451939
Contact: Mr. E. M. H. Valcke - MD/CEO

AUTOMOTIVE PARTS INDUSTRY LIMITED
Business: Manufacturing of Auto Spare Parts and Accessories, General Engineering Services
Address: 24, Niger Street, P.O.Box 5012, Kano
Tel: (064) 639288, 649271 **Fax:** (064) 634965
Contact: Mr. H. Korth - MD/CEO

AUTOMOTO SERVICES LIMITED
Business: Automobile Maintenance and Servicing
Address: 19, Burma Road, P.O.Box 1023, Apapa, Lagos
Tel: (01) 5878388, 5450373 **Fax:** (01) 5878388
Contact: Mr. Walid Ziade - GM/CEO

AV.COM/gws EASTEND AUDIOVIZ
Business: Audio-Visual Programming & Content Providers, Television & Radio Programme/Commercial Production
Address: 1 (Plot 322B), Daranijo Close, off Abisogun Leigh Street, behind Zenith Bank, Ogba, Ikeja, Lagos
Tel: (01) 4740951, 4740952, 08023057955, 08023156896, 08033036996
E-mail: audio_viz@yahoo.com
Contact: Mr. Jaiye Ojo - MD/CEO

AVANCE SYSTEMS LIMITED
Business: Software Consulting, Training and Service
Address: 5, Akinyemi Crescent, Off Fatai Atere Way, Matori Mushin, Lagos
Tel: (01) 4526200, 7920299, 08033030935, 08033923517
Fax: (01) 526251, 3201033
E-mail: info@avancesystems.com
Website: www.avancesystems.com
Contact: Mr. Richard Shasanya - Chairman/CEO

AVC FUND LIMITED
Business: Portfolio/Fund Managers, Financial Advisers
Address: Plot 71B, Molade Okoya-Thomas Street, Victoria Island Annex, Lagos
Tel: (01) 2611012, 2614828 **Fax:** (01) 2621350
* ASEI World Centre, 57, Aba Road, Port Harcourt
Tel: (084) 237623-6 (4L)
Contact: Mr. Preye B. Zuobai - MD/CEO

AVENTIS PASTEUR LIMITED
Business: Production, Distribution and Sales of Vaccines
Address: Plot 634, Adeyemo Alakija Street, Eleganza Biro Plaza, (7th Floor), Victoria Island, Lagos
Tel: (01) 2620121, 2647150 **Fax:** (01) 2620121
Website: www.aventispastuer.comff
Contact: Mr. Jean-Baptiste Daurat - MD/CEO
Mr. Frank Chambrier - GM (Sales and Marketing)

AVERY NIGERIA LIMITED
Business: Sales and Services of Weighing Equipment & Scales, and Power Protection Equipment, Date-coding of Products
Address: Obasa Road, off Oba Akran Avenue, Ikeja Industrial Estate, Lagos
Tel: (01) 4963627, 4963657 **Fax:** (01) 4963627
E-mail: averynig@beta.linkserve.com
* 280, Trans-Amadi Ind. Layout, Port Harcourt
Tel: (084) 335896

AVIL SERVICES LIMITED
Business: General Merchandising, Contracts
Address: 28/30, Bukuru Bye-Pass, P. O. Box 6822, Jos
Tel: (073) 465109, 462550 **Fax:** (073) 463850
E-mail: avil@bwave.net
Contact: Major Gen. G. O. Ejiga (rtd.) - Chairman/CEO
Mr. Jerry Alechenu - Ag. Snr. Manager

AVIATION DEVELOPMENT COMPANY PLC (ADC Airlines)
Business: Airlines & Airfreight Services
Address: 84, Opebi Road, Ikeja, Lagos
Tel: (01) 4965750, 4962657, 4962230, 4933666, 4936221
Fax: (01) 4970086
E-mail: adc@adcairlines.com
Contact: Capt. Mfon E. Udom - MD/CEO

AVIATION LOGISTICS & MANAGEMENT LIMITED
Business: Aviation Services, Airline Consultancy Services
Address: Marble House (2nd Floor), 1, Alfred Rewane (Kingsway) Road, Falomo, Ikoyi
Tel: (01) 7757480

AVON CROWN CAPS & CONTAINERS (NIGERIA) PLC
Business: Manufacturer & Sales of Crowncaps, Metal Containers, Screw caps, Aerosol Components, Roll-on Pilfer-Proof Caps, Tinlets, Metal Printing
Address: 22, Musa Yar'Adua Street, Victoria Island, Lagos
Tel: (01) 2612786, 2611433 **Fax:** (01) 2618604, 2619624
E-mail: avon@linkserve.com.ng
* Km 38, Lagos-Abeokuta Road, Sango Otta.
Tel: (039) 722229-30(2L), 7222162
Contact: Mr. S. R. Ramchandani - MD/CEO

AVSATEL COMMUNICATIONS LIMITED
Business: Radio & Satellite Communication Equipment Sales and Engineering, Training
Address: 1, Osmenyi River Clos, off Lake Chad Crescent, off IBB Way, Maitama, Abuja.
Tel: (09) 4135350, 4136760 * (01) 7751885
Fax: (09) 4136761
E-mail: avsatelm4@eikmail.com
Contact: Engr. Obi Ogbunugafor - GM(Commercial)

AW CONSULTANTS LIMITED
Business: Management Consultancy Services
Address: 7, Town Planning way, Ilupeju, Lagos
Tel: (01) 4970020-1 (2L), 4970214, 4960442
Fax: (01) 4970023, 4978736
E-mail: akintola.williams@logosmail.sprint.com
Contact: Mr. Victor G. Hammond - Chairman/MD

AWAYE HOLDINGS LIMITED
Business: Property Development and Warehousing.
Address: Awaye House, Awaye Industrial Estate, Awaye Coker, Badagry Expressway, Orile, Iganmu, Lagos
Tel: (01) 4701931, 5851368 **Fax:** (01) 2647010
E-mail: forti9@hotmail.com
Contact: Mr. Wole O. Madariola Jr - MD/CEO

AWML INTERNATIONAL LIMITED
(Formerly Atlantic Waste Managemenet Ltd)
Business: Environmental Impact Assessment and Auditing, Post Impact Assessment, Effluent Monitoring, Biodegradation/Bioaccumulation Studies, Air Quality Studies, Oil Waste Management, Pollution Control & Laboratory Analytical Services)
Address: Plot 58, Akanbi Onitiri Close (3rd Floor, Right Wing), off Eric Moore Road, Surulere, Lagos
Tel: (01) 833094, 4807687 **Fax:** (01) 833094
* 35, Nembe Street, Rumuibekwe Housing Estate, Off Port Harcourt - Aba Road, Port Harcourt

Tel: (084) 612800
* Plot 161, 30th Street, Delta Property Dev. Authority Housing Estate, Effurun, Warri
Contact: Mr. Emeka Ugwu - Oju - Chairman
Dr. J. Nwankwo - MD/CEO

AWK-PRINT LIMITED
Business: Paper Printing and Packaging
Address: Metal House, Plot 6, Cocoa Industries Road, Ogba Industrial Estate, Ikeja, Lagos
Tel: (01) 4922252, 4922253 **Fax:** (01) 4922249
Contact: Mr. Chiji Agbo - Chairman/CEO

AWUTOLO INDUSTRIES LIMITED
Business: Importation of Educational Materials and Food Commodity; Manufacture of Plastic Products,Toilet Paper, Stationery and Tapes
Address: Ugonnia House, 40, Awka Road, Onitsha
Tel: (046) 216844, 216921, 411249
E-mail: awutolo@alpha.linkserve.com
Contact: Chief E. A. Okafor - Chairman/CEO

AXIS INFORMATION SYSTEMS LIMITED
Business: Information Technology Services, Sales of Anti-Virus & Internet-Security Softwares, Network and Communications. Application Softwares.
Address: Elephant Cement House (3rd Floor D Wing) ASSBIFI Road, Central Bus.District, Alausa Lagos
Tel: (01) 8043173, 7745080-9 (10L) (Ext 8300)
Fax: (01) 8048029
E-mail: axis@infoweb.abs.net
Contact: Mr Olufemi J. Adefemiwa - MD/CEO

AXIS INSURANCE BROKERS LIMITED
Business: Insurance Brokers
Address: 161, Herbert Macaulay St, Adekunle Yaba, Lagos
Tel: (01) 867445 **Fax:** 01) 862192
Contact: Mr E. E. Omiunu - MD/CEO

AYH INVESTMENT LIMITED
Business: Bureau de Change Services, General Contractors
Address: 36, Breadfruit Street, Balogun, Lagos Island, Lagos
Tel: (01) 2641885, 08033482323-4 (2 L)
Contact: Yau Haruna - CEO

AYMAN ENTERPRISES LIMITED
Business: Hair Weave-on and Braids Manufacturing
Address: 12/18, Akinyemi Cres, off Fatai Atere Way, Lagos
Tel: (01) 4525985, 4528600

AZUMA BOTTLING COMPANY LIMITED
Business: Bottling of Carbonated Soft Drinks
Address: Commercial Area, P.M.B 113, Gombe
Tel: (072) 220630, 220423
Contact: Alhaja Aishatu A. Hashidu - MD/CEO

AZUBROS COMMERCIAL ENTERPRISES NIGERIA LTD
Business: Import, Assembly & Marketing of Motorcycles
Address: 29/30, Niger Road, Sabon Gari, Kano
Tel: (064) 641756, 647323, 08037044661
* 62/63, Lagos Crescent, Garki, II Shopping Complex, Garki, Abuja
Contact: Mr. Azuka Morah - Chairman/CEO

B. B. MICHAEL & COMPANY LIMITED
Business: Sales of Pharmaceutical Products, Manufacturing of Hospital Furniture, Sales & Maintenance of Medical & Laboratory Equipment
Address: 1, Itire Road, Surulere, Lagos
Tel: (01) 8048538, 8047239, 7744345
Contact: Engr. Dele Bialose - MD/CEO

B. OLOJO PHARMACEUTICAL LIMITED.
Business: Hospital Engineering Services, Sales & Services of Hospital Equipment, Pharmaceutical Services
Address: 110, Murtala Mohammed Way, Kano
Tel: (064) 641675

B. STABILINI & COMPANY LIMITED.
Business: Building and Civil Engineering Contractors
Address: Railway Avenue, Kakuri, Kaduna
Tel: (062) 231405, 231423, 232772 **Fax:** (062) 231405

B.C. IFEGBO & ASSOCIATES LIMITED
Business: Paper Coverters, Import & Export
Address: 25, New Market Road, Onitsha
Tel: (046) 411720
Contact: Mr. Boniface C. Ifegbo - ChairmanCEO

B. C. MADIEBO & COMPANY LIMITED.
Business: Insurance Brokers and Pension Consultants
Address: Plot 133, Block B, Sinari Daranijo Street, Victoria Island Annex, Lagos.
Tel/Fax: (01) 2623847
Savannah Bank Building, 3, Waff Road, Kaduna
Tel: (062) 215534
Contact: Mr. A. O. Okonkwo - MD/CEO

B. M. COMPUTER SERVICES NIGERIA LIMITED
Business: Computer Training, Consultancy, Sales & Service
Address: 300, Ikorodu Road (Anthony Bus-Stop), Lagos
Tel: (01) 4936055, 08023043414
E-mail: bmcomputerschool@hotmail.com
Contact: Major Gen. M. Magoro (rtd) - Chairman
Dr. Bode Olajumoke - MD/CEO

B. N. NATSON COMPANY LIMITED
Business: Manufacture of Toothbrushes & Industrial Fan Belts
Address: Zone, D, Block 7 (Shop 122) ASPMDA Complex, International Trade Fair Complex, Lagos-Badagry Expressway, Abule-Osun Ojo, Lagos.
Tel: (01) 3208173
* 26, Church Street (1st Floor), Idumota, Lagos
Tel: (01) 2668597 **Fax:** (01) 2667192
Contact: Mr. B. N. Atueyi - MD/CEO

B. T. MICROXPERTS LIMITED
Business: Sales of Computers and Accessories, Networking and Structured Cabling, Training
Address: 7, Toyin Street, Ikeja Lagos
Tel: (01) 4931804, 4937687, 4975332 **Fax:** (01) 4931804
E-mail: btmicro@infoweb.abs.net
Contact: Mr. Bola Adegboro - CEO

BABA PLASTICS LIMITED
Business: Manufacturing and Marketing of Plastic Footwear
Address: 15/16B, Post Office Road, Kano

Tel: (064) 631941, 643282 **Fax:** (064) 643282
Contact: Alh. Zubairu Baba - Chairman/MD

BABINGTON ASHAYE & COMPANY
Business: Auditing Consultancy, Tax Consultancy and Insolvency Practitioners
Address: Speedway House, 21, Araromi Street, off Moloney Street, Onikan Lagos
Tel: (01) 2634491, 2637638 **Fax:** (01) 2631279
E-mail: babington@nigol.net.ng
Contact: Prince Ade Babington-Ashaye - Chairman/MD

BABS ANIMASHAUN HOLDINGS LIMITED
Business: Finance and Investment Consultants, Transporters
Address: 191, Babs Animashaun Road, Lagos
Tel: (01) 5850660 **Fax:** (01) 5850658
Contact: Chief Babs A. Animashaun - Chairman/CEO

BACAD FINANCE & INVESTMENT COMPANY LIMITED
Business: Stockbroking, Portfolio Management, Financial Advisory Services,
Address: Management House (2nd Floor, Suites 13 & 14), Plot 22, Idowu Taylor Street, Victoria Island, Lagos
Tel: (01) 4617747 **Fax:** (01) 2618649, 4617747
E-mail: bacadinvest@yahoo.com
Contact: Mr. Kola Alagbada - GM/CEO

BACOM COMMUNICATIONS LIMITED
Business: Sales of Telecommunication Equipment & Computers , Internet Services Provision, VSAT, Networking, Pre-Paid Call-Card Operations
Address: Plot 285, Akin-Olugbade Street, off Idowu Martins Street, Victoria Island, Lagos.
Tel: (01) 2620185, 2616035, 3201825 **Fax:** (01) 2616273
E-mail: bacom@bacomonline.com
Website: www.bacomonline.com
Contact: Engr. Femi Adeoti - Chairman/MD

BAFANI ENGINEERING COMPANY LIMITED
Business: Electrical, Electronic & Mechanical Engineering Consultancy/Contracting, Sales & Service of Elevators
Address: 175, Ikorodu Road, Onipanu Lagos
Tel: (01) 7741687, 825456, 822816 **Fax:** (01) 821589
E-mail: bafanieng@hotmail.com

BAFLINE NIGERIA LIMITED.
Business: Clearing and Forwarding Agency
Address: Eleganza Plaza (Aquarius Block, 1st Floor), 1, Commercial Road,Apapa, Lagos
Tel: (01) 5873204
Contact: Mr. Adekola Michael - Chairman/CEO

BAGAUDA TEXTILE MILLS LIMITED
Business: Manufacture of Textile Products
Address: 58, Ibrahim Taiwo Road, Kano
Tel: (064) 635930, 634313 **Fax:** (064) 649935
Contact: Alh. Isiyaku Rabiu - Executive Chairman

BAICO INSURANCE PLC
Business: General Insurance Business & Life Insurance
Address: Baico Plaza, 12, Abibu-Oki Street, Lagos
Tel: (01) 2641200-6 (7L) **Fax:** (01) 2641193
E-mail: baico@intracom.net.ng
Contact: Mr. Oluwagbolaga Adeyanju - MD/CEO

BAID TECHNICAL SERVICES COMPANY LIMITED.
Business: Sales of Radio Communication Equipment and Accessories
Address: 43, Aba Road, Port Harcourt
Tel: (084) 571409 **Fax:** (084) 233858
E-mail: obiora@baidtechserv.com
Contact: Engr. Obiora Ezenwukwa - MD/CEO

BAJABURE INDUSTRIAL COMPLEX LIMITED
Business: Manufacturing and Marketing of Foam Products and Polythene Bags/Sheetings
Address: Mubi Road, P. O. Box 506, Yola
Tel: (075) 624008, 624097 **Fax:** (075) 625224
E-mail: nimafoam@gmx.com
* Plot 3153, off Osun Crescent, Cadastral Zone 6, Maitama, Abuja. **Tel:** (09) 4135072
E-mail: bellogroup@gmx.net

BAJIS LIMITED.
Business: General Merchandising
Address: 27/28, Sani Buhari Triangle, Zoo Road, Kano
Tel: (064) 668154, 668155 **Fax:** (064) 668155
Contact: Alh. Baba Buhari Sani - Chairman/CEO

BAKER HUGHES NIGERIA LIMITED.
Business: Oil Drilling Services, Supply of Drilling Chemicals and Completion Fluids, Treatment of Cuttings
Address: Plot 268, Trans-Amadi Ind. Layout, Port Harcourt
Tel: (084) 237944, 234683 **Fax:** (084) 237944
Contact: Mr. Ricky Landrum - MD/CEO

BAKER NIGERIA LIMITED
Business: Servicing Oil Wells, Supply of Equipment & Chemicals for Oil Exploration and Production
Address: * Plot 1676, Oladele Olashore Street, Victoria Island, Lagos
Tel: (01) 2622121, 2619864, 263554, 2623765, 2623766
Fax: (01) 2614068, 2623555
* Plot 74, Trans-Amadi Ind. Layout, Port Harcourt
* Edewor Shopping Centre,Warri-Sapele Road, Effurun, Warri
Tel: (053) 252191, 254227, 254228, 255653
Fax: (053) 251804
Contact: Mr. Rolf Arne Haukelid - MD/CEO

BAKERS WORLD LIMITED
Business: Baking of Cakes, Sales of Cake Decoratig Materials, Production of Icing Sugar, Browning and Glucose Syrup
Address: 54, Allen Avenue, Ikeja, Lagos
Tel/Fax: (01) 4979477, 4970288
Contact: Princess A. Adefulu-Efunnuga - Chairman/CEO

BAKFAJ INTERNATIONAL NIGERIA LIMITED
Business: Clearing and Forwarding, Shipping, Import Procurement, Insurance Brokers, Haulage Operations,
Address: 6, Aimasiko Street, off Afariogun Street, International Airport Road, Apakun-Oshodi, Lagos.
Tel: (01) 4931178, 7743181 **Fax:** (01) 4938159
E-mail: info@bakfaj.com

corp.biz.information@bakfaj.com
Website: www.bakfaj.com
Contact: Alh. Fatai A. Abudul-Azeez - MD/CEO

BALLAST HAM NIGERIA (formerly Ham Dredging Nig Ltd)
Business: Dredging and Maintenance of Harbour, Land Reclamation, Coastal and Embankment Protection, Offshore Services, Irrigation Works etc.
Address: 7, Eletu Ogabi Street, off Adeola Odeku Street, Victoria Island, Lagos
Tel: (01) 2617731, 2617732, 3200725
Fax: (01) 2617733, 3200067
E-mail: hamdredging.nig@linkserve.com.ng
Website: www.hamdredging.com
* Amadi-Ama Yard, Eastern Bye-Pass, Through NLNG, Port Harcourt
Tel: (087) 771553, 771776 **Fax:** (087) 770976
Contact: Engr. B. A. O. Fisher - Chairman
Mr. M. P. Meijers - MD/CEO

BALLY PLASTIC & FOOTWEAR INDUSTRIES (NIGERIA) LTD
Business: Manufacturing and Marketing of Plastic Footwear
Address: Tudun-Murtala, Dakata Industrial Estate, Bompai
Tel: (064) 636627, 649585, 649453 **Fax:** (064) 634872
E-mail: ballyplasticd@intracom5.com

BALKON NIGERIA LIMITED
Business: Import & Export Trading
Address: 4, Ezejiofor Street, Abakaliki
Tel: (043) 220788, 08033139747 **Fax:** (043) 300132
E-mail: balkonltd@yahoo.co.uk
* 46B, Abeokuta Street, Anifowoshe, Ikeja, Lagos
Tel: (01) 3450496

BALOG TECHNOLOGIES LIMITED
Business: Sales and Maintenance of Computers & Radio Communication Systems, Security Equipment
Address: 21, Kodesoh Street, Ikeja, Lagos.
Tel: (01) 2881520, 4931561, 4718993, 4718705, 4979480
Fax: (01) 4931561
E-mail: balog@infoweb.abs.net

BALUFON ANIMAL FEEDS LIMITED
Business: Manufacturing of Animal Feeds and Concentrates
Address: Sagamu-Benin Expressway, Sagamu, Ogun State
Tel: (037) 640043 **Fax:** (037) 640041
E-mail: balufon@infoweb.abs.net

BALTON ENGINEERING (Div. of Dizengoff (W. A.) Nig Ltd.)
Business: Supply, Installation & Maintenance of Airconditioners, Generators & Transformers
Address: 28, Creek Road, Apapa, Lagos
Tel: (01) 5875780, 5872352, 7749614 **Fax:** (01) 5874021
E-mail: dizngoff@dizengoff.com
* Plot 108, Adetokunbo Ademola Crescent, Cadastral Zone A8, Wuse II, Abuja
Tel: (09) 4131240-1 (2L), 4139558 **Fax:** (09) 4131242

BAMFORDS INTERNATIONAL NIGERIA LIMITED
Business: Sales of Agricultural Machinery, Foundry and Casting Works
Address: Rayfield Industrial Estate, Jos
Tel: (073) 280903, 280908 **Fax:** (073) 280457

BAMIS COMPANY LIMITED
Business: Importation and Marketing of Electronic Audio-visual, Electronic Appliances and General Goods
Address: A119C, Alaba International Market, Ojo, Lagos
Tel: (01) 5554045, 5554351, 5893446, 08033255833
* 127, Nnamdi Azikiwe Street, Idumota, Lagos
Tel: (01) 2644849, 2644623, 2662400
Contact: Mr Bartholomew Ibeanu - Chairman/CEO

BANARLY (NIGERIA) LIMITED
Business: Trawling, Seafood Exports and Local Sale
Address: Plot C, Oba Ganiyu Adesanya Way, Otto, Lagos
Tel: (01) 5802875-9 (5 L), 7730233
Fax: (01) 5802876-7 (2 L)
E-mail: md@banarly.com
Website: www.banarly.com
Contact: Mr Paul De Petter - MD

BANEX GROUP LIMITED
Business: Conglomerate (Manufacturing, Export, Real Estate, Hospitality, Finance & Trading)
Address: 15/17, Abimbola Street, Isolo Industrial Estate, Isolo, Lagos
Tel: (01) 4525244, 4525247, 4527037, 4527047
Fax: (01) 4527047
E-mail: banex@micro.com.ng
* Banex Plaza, Plot 750, Aminu Kano Crescent Cadastral Zone A7, Wuse II, Abuja
Tel: (09) 4136420-5 (5L)
* 57, Ikorodu Road, Fadeyi, Lagos
Tel: (01) 820645, 824324
* Banex Plaza, Plot J, Park Road, Agbedo Market Extension, Nnewi.
Tel: (046) 460246, 463683
Contact: Rev. (Dr) Victor O. Mbanisi - Chairman/CEO

BANEX PLAZA HOTEL, ABUJA
Business: Hospitality & Catering Services
Address: Plot 750, Aminu Kano Crescent, Wuse II, Abuja
Tel: (09) 4136420-5 (6L), 08037020612
Fax: (09) 4136423
E-mail: banexph@yahoo.com
Contact: Rev. (Dr) Victor Mbanisi - Chairman
Mr. Felix Amadi - MD/CEO

BANG & OLUFSEN NIGERIA LIMITED
Business: Sales and Service of Electronic Hifi Systems
Address: 89, Awolowo Road, S. W. Ikoyi Lagos
Tel: (01) 2647933, 2631937 **Fax:** (01) 2631937
E-mail: sales.bo@nova.net.ng
Website: www.bang-olufsen.com
Contact: Mr. Benson Uwatse - MD/CEO

BANILUX GROUP OF COMPANIES
Business: Importation & Sales of Cars, Telecommunications, Printing Services
Address: 127, Herbert Macaulay St.Ebute-Metta, Lagos
Tel: (01) 4975379, 4975377, 4972466, 5453626, 5454807
Fax: (01) 4975378
* Plot 477, Airport Road, opp.New Wuse Market, Central Business District, Abuja.
Tel: (09) 5230045
Contact: Mrs M. O. Akinwale - Chairman/CEO

BANIT INVESTMENT LIMITED
Business: Distribution of Electric-Power Control, Distribution & Utilization Equipment.
Address: 3/5, Adeyemo Alakija Street, Victoria Island, Lagos
Tel: (01) 7755607, 616835 **Fax:** (01) 2615511
E-mail: banitinvest@yahoo.com
Contact: Mr Babalola Adeniyi - Chairman/MD

BANK OF INDUSTRY LIMITED
Business: Development Banking
Address: BOI House, 63/71, Broad Street, Lagos
Tel: (01) 2663495, 2663539, 2663470
Fax: (01) 2667074, 2665286
E-mail: info@boi.ng.com
Website: www.boi.ng.com
* Bank of the North Building, Plot 785, Herbert Macaulay Way, Central Business District, Abuja
Tel: (09) 2341395, 2349450 **Fax:** (09) 2349378
Contact: Dr Lawrence Osa-Afiana - MD/CEO

BANK OF THE NORTH LIMITED
Business: Commercial Banking
Address: Ahmadu Bello House, 2, Zaria Road, Kano
Tel: (064) 660290-9 (10L), 663608, 667033, 667692
Fax: (064) 661361
* Plot 1230B, Bar Beach Side, Ahmadu Bello way, Victoria Island, Lagos
Tel: (01) 2616193, 2616699, 2612675
Contact: Alh. B. B Mohammed - Prin. Manager (Public Rel.)

BANK OF THE NORTH TRUSTEES LIMITED
Business: Funds & Pension Fund Mnangement, Trusteeship,
Address: 5A/6A, Sani Abacha Way Kano
Tel/Fax: (064) 633177
E-mail: trustees@bankofthenorth.com
Contact: Alh. S. Iro - GM

BANKSWAY INTERNATIONAL LIMITED
Business: Supply of Photographic Materials and Equipment
Address: 86, Shipeolu Street, Palmgroove, Lagos
Tel: (01) 7740768, 820091, 826961, 4975651
Fax: (01) 7740768, 4975651
E-mail: banksway@infoweb.abs.net

BANTOKS NIGERIA LIMITED
Business: Sales and Installation of Building Partitioning Productss Ceilings, Blinds, Furniture and Carpets.
Address: Eleganza Plaza (Aries Block), Apapa, Lagos
Tel: (01) 4703741, 5871470-1 (2L)

BANUSO FISHERIES LIMITED
Business: Importation and Marketing of Frozen Foods and Fish, Trawling, Rental of Cold-Storage Facilities
Address: Oshodi-Apapa Expressway (Coconut Bus-Stop), Ibafon Tin Can Island, Apapa
Tel: (01) 4703603, 5455585
Contact: Mr. L. A. Ajenifuja - MD/CEO

BAO GROUP OF COMPANIES
Business: Sales and Service of Motor Vehicles and Spare Parts, Commodities and Crude Oil Brokerage
Address: 14/16, Boyle Street, Onikan, Lagos
Tel: (01) 2632116, 2632972, 2631653 **Fax:** (01) 2631820
E-mail: bao-motors@yahoo.com
Contact: Prince B. A. Osho - Chairman/CEO

BAP SERVICES LIMITED
Business: Sales and Service of Vehicles
Address: 18, Aba Road, Port Harcourt
Tel: (084) 233491, 230433 **Fax:** (084) 233491
E-mail: arbonlimited@hotmail.com
Contact: Mr. B. Okon - MD/CEO

BARAKA PRESS & PUBLISHERS LIMITED
Business: Printing and Lithographic Services; Publishing
Address: 5, Ahmadu Bello Way Kaduna
Tel: (062) 240174
E-mail: joseli@infoweb.abs.net
Contact: Mr. D. J. Ekpikhe - Executive Director/CEO\

BARBWILLOMS LIMITED
Business: Advertising, Design and Construction of Exhibitions and Trade Shows
Address: 72, Opebi Road, Ikeja, Lagos.
Tel/Fax: (01) 4973443
E-mail: barbwilloms@infoweb.abs.net
Contact: Mr. W. Omigbe - MD/CEO

BAREWA PHARMACEUTICAL LTD
Business: Manufacture, Distribution and Packaging of Drugs
Address: 1-5, Olugbo Close (by Oremeta Bus-Stop), Shasha Road, Akowonjo, Dopemu Lagos
Contact: Mr. Kola G. Okunola - Chairman/MD

BARIN EPEGA & COMPANY
Business: Estate Surveyors and Valuers, Chartered Surveyors
Address: 80, Norman Williams Street, S. W. Ikoyi
Tel: (01) 2692205, 2691762, 2673485 **Fax:** (01) 2673485
E-mail: bepega@hyperia.com
Contact: Mr. Barin Epega - Principal Partner

BARNAX ENGINEERING COMPANY (NIGERIA) LIMITED
Business: Sales and Service of Diesel Generators
Address: 172A, Aba Road, Port Harcourt
Tel: (084) 331176, 335349, 334175
* Plot 1644, Oko-Awo Close, Victoria Island, Lagos
Tel: (01) 614145 **Fax:** (01) 614268

BARNES DIAGNOSTIC & HEART CENTRE
Business: Medical & Cardiac Diagnostic Services
Address: Plot 292H, Ajose Adeogun St, Victoria Is, Lagos
Tel: (01) 4610395, 4616644, 2611093, 2627994, 08033020925 **Fax:** (01) 2693179
E-mail: barneshospital@cyberspace.net.ng
Contact: Dr. I. C. Monu - MD/CEO

BAROID OF NIGERIA LIMITED
Business: Oilfield Services, Sales of Drilling Fluids
Address: c/o Halliburton Energy Services Nigeria Ltd., 90, Ajose Adeogun Street/Younis Bashorun Street, Victoria Island Lagos
Tel: (01) 2620765-8 (4 L) **Fax:** (01) 2616632

BARRI ELEVATORS NIGERIA LIMITED
Busness: Installation and Maintenance of Lifts, Escalators, Trollivators, Hoists and Auto Conveyors

Address: 1, Alh. Rafiu Street, off International Airport Road, Mafoluku-Oshodi, Lagos.
Tel: (01) 4975828, 4961024, 7741706 **Fax:** (01) 4961024
Contact: Prince M. A. Arimoro - Chairman/CEO

BASIC INFORMATION & COMMUNICATION SYSTEMS LIMITED
Business: Integrated IT Training Solutions, NIIT Licensee
Address: 68, Adetokunbo Ademola Crescnt, Wuse II, Abuja
Tel: (09) 5234318, 5234336, 08035922353, 08033207768
Fax: (09) 5234336
E-mail: abuja@niitng.com
Contact: Mr. Shaka Momoh - Chairman

BASF (NIGERIA) LIMITED
Business: Sales & Provision of Technical Services for Pigments, Chemicals, Plastics and Plant Protection Products
Address: Etiebets Place (4th Floor), 21, Mobolaji Bank-Anthony Way, Ikeja, Lagos
Tel: (01) 4976451, 4976452, 4977860 **Fax:** (01) 4976453
Contact: Mr. Bernd Fries - MD/CEO

BASIC COMMERCE & FINANCE (NIGERIA) LIMITED
Business: Bureau de Change, Import and Export, Real Estate
Address: 134, Awolowo Road, S. W, Ikoyi, Lagos
Tel/Fax: (01) 2692327
E-mail: basic@infoweb.abs.net
Contact: Chief (Dr.) Chukwuemeka P. Ezeife - Chairman/CEO

BASILMAN & COMPANY (NIGERIA) LIMITED
Business: Engineering Construction, Procurement, Marine Support Services
Address: 19, Trans-Amadi Rd, Rumuobiakani, Port Harcourt
Tel: (084) 236894, 335081 **Fax:** (084) 236894
E-mail: basilman@infoweb.abs.net
Contact: Mr. Basil M. Njoku - MD/CEO

BASSCOM NIGERIA LIMITED
Business: Low-Voltage Security Systems (Access Control, Fire, CCTV), Information Technology and Communications Products
Address: 31, Igbosere Road, Lagos
Tel: (01) 2635260, 2646634 **Fax:** (01) 2646634
E-mail: basscommlg@aol.com
Contact: Mr. Dimeji Matesun - MD/CEO

BATE COSSE LIMITED
Business: Advertising, Marketing Communications
Address: 26, Sobo Arobiodu Street, GRA, Ikeja, Lagos
Tel: (01) 4968292, 4970981-2 (2L) **Fax:** (01) 4930968
E-mail: cosse@micro.com.ng
Contact: Mr Funmi Onabolu - MD/CEO

BATEX NIGERIA LIMITED
Business: Quality Control, NDT & Drill Pipe Inspection Services, Manpower & Industrial Supplies
Address: 164, P. T. I. Road, Ohimor Lane, off Ughelli Road/ P.T.I. Road Junction, Warri
Tel: (053) 252544
Contact: Mr. Julius Aroyewun - MD/CEO

BATHLEY INFORMATION DEVICES LIMITED
Business: Sales and Maintenance of Computers and Power Protection Equipment
Address: 1, Mercy Eneli St, off Alh. Masha St, Surulere, Lagos
Tel: (01) 5850017, 5851885 **Fax:** (01) 5850017
E-mail: bidpc@beta.linkserve.com
Contact: Mr. G. A. Okoh - MD/CEO

BATTERY MANUFACTURING COMPANY (NIGERIA) LTD
Business: Manufacturing and Marketing of Dry-Cell Batteries
Address: WAHUM Compound, 3, Adeniyi Jones Avenue, Ikeja Industrial Estate Ikeja, Lagos
Tel: (01) 4978770-4 (5L) **Fax:** (01) 4528689

BAUCHI FERTILIZER BLENDING COMPANY LIMITED
Business: Blending and Production of Fertilizers
Address: Plot 2, Railway Road, Industrial Estate, Bauchi
Tel/Fax: (077) 543488
Contact: Alh. Inuwa Dattijo - GM/CEO

BAUCHI HOTELS LIMITED.
Business: Hospitality and Catering Services
Address: Jos Road, P. O. Box 395, Bauchi
Tel: (077) 543815-20 (6L), 543590-7 (8 L), 542840
Fax: (077) 543596
Contact: Ade David Ajiboye - Asst. GM/CEO

BAUCHI MEAT PRODUCT COMPANY LIMITED
Business: Processing of Corned Beef and Fresh Meat
Address: Railway Road, Industrial Area, Bauchi
Tel: (077) 540834, 540835, 543086 **Fax:** (077) 540834
Contact: Abubakar Mohammed Bibi - MD/CEO

BAUCHI PUBLISHING & PRINTING COMPANY LIMITED
Business: Newspaper Publishing, Printing Services
Address: 8A, Adamu Jumba Road, Bauchi
Tel/Fax: (077) 542264, 542803
E-mail: bppc@micro.com.ng
Contact: Alh. Aminu Mohammed Dan Bauchi - MD/CEO

BAUCHI STATE AGRICULTURAL SUPPLY COMPANY LTD
Business: Distribution and Sales of Agricultural Chemicals and Materials
Address: Gidan Gona, Dass Road, P. M. B. 1567, Bauchi
Tel: (077) 543423

BAUCHI STATE INVESTMENT & PROPERTY DEVELOPMENT COMPANY LIMITED
Business: Project Promotion & Supervision (Manufacturing, Agro-Allied Business, Property Dev., Commerce)
Address: 37, Abdulkadir Ahmed Road, P.M.B. 0162, Bauchi
Tel: (077) 542956, 542922, 542917, 542445
Fax: (077) 542956
Contact: Alh. Mustapha Mahe - Ag. MD/CEO

BAYKAM VENTURES LIMITED
Business: Sales of Printing Papers and Boards
Address: 65, Ladipo Street, Mushin, Lagos
Tel: (01) 4526091, 4525177, 4528258, 4521813
Contact: Mrs. Oludayo Abdul - ED (Admin.)

BAYWOOD CONTINENTAL LIMITED
Business: Engineering Construction and Technical Oilfield Services, Procurement
Address: 334, Ikorodu Rd (Idiroko B/Stop), Maryland, Lagos

Tel: (01) 4968393, 4704703 **Fax:** (01) 4968393, 4970646
E-mail: info@baywoodcontinental.com
Website: www.baywoodcontinental.com
* 8, Chief Mgba Street, Harmony Way, Rumurolu-Woji, Port Harcourt.
Tel: (084) 571170
E-mail: baywood@phca.linkserve.com

BAZEE NIGERIA LIMITED
Business: Manufacturing of Vertical Blind & Furniture, Water Engineers
Address: 240, Herbert Macaulay St, Alagomeji, Yaba, Lagos
Tel: (01) 5454129, 863632, 861984 **Fax:** (01) 5454129
E-mail: bazee@hyperia.com
Website: www.vertiscapes.com
Contact: Mr. Obodechine I. Nwaokolo - Chairman/MD

BBc CONSULTING LIMITED
Business: Human Resource and Management Consultancy
Address: 199, Ikorodu Road, Obanikoro, Lagos
Tel: (01) 4977941-4 (4L) **Fax:** (01) 4977940
E-mail: bbccharter@micro.com.ng
MG House, Plot 1921, Dalaba St, Wuse Zone 5 Abuja
Contact: Chief D. O. Alasoadura - Managing Partner

BCN PLC
Business: Manufacturing and Marketing of Pharmaceutical & Cosmetic Products
Address: Plot 22/23, Chief T. A. Doherty Layout, Oregun Industrial Estate, Oregun, Ikeja, Lagos
Contact: Mr. Wole Sarumi - MD/CEO

BDO OFO CONSULTING
Business: Management and Accounting Consultancy
Address: Elephant Cement House (5th Floor), Aluasa, Lagos
Tel/Fax: (01) 2221015, 4729187, 4922943, 4922952, 4922960
E-mail: ofopro-advisors@cyberspace.net.ng
ofopro-advisors@bdo.com.ng
bdoofo@mweb.com
Contact: Mr M. A. Adigun - Managing Partner

BEACHGROVE SECURITIES & INVESTMENT CO. LTD
Business: Stockbroking
Address: 70B, Apapa Road, Ebute-Metta (West), Lagos
Tel: (01) 831583, 5851980
Contact: Mr. Mukaila A. Alogba - MD/CEO

BEAMCO NIGERIA LIMITED
Business: Sales of Iron; Constrction and Engineering
Address: 1, Oniru Street Apapa, Lagos
Tel: (01) 5450000-1 (2L), 7745425 **Fax:** (01) 5450000
Email: beamcola@linkserve.com.ng

BEARING SERVICES LIMITED
Business: Marketers of Ball & Roller Bearings, Mechanical Power Transmission Products and Industrial Spare Parts, Construction, Repair and Maintenance of Belt & Roller Conveyors and Bucket Elevators
Address: 142-146, Oshodi-Apapa Expressway, beside Concord Press, Isolo, Lagos
Tel: (01) 521086, 521427 **Fax:** (01) 4528762
E-mail: daid@beta.linkserve.com
Contact: Mr. Adewale Olagunju - Asst. GM

BEAVER SECURITIES LIMITED
Business: Stockbroking, Commodity Trading, Financial Advisory Services
Address: 18B, Idowu Taylor Street, Victoria Island, Lagos.
Tel: (01) 2613406, 2635338, 2635371 **Fax:** (01) 2631299
* Plot 146, Lusaka Road, Wuse Zone 6, Abuja
Tel: (09) 5234756
Contact: Mr. Charles A. Irojah - MD/CEO

BEBEJI OIL AND ALLIED PRODUCTS LIMITED
Business: Processing and Production of Edible Oils
Address: 123, Maganda Road, Bompai Ind. Estate, Kano
Tel: (064) 645993, 633176
Contact: Alh. Tajuddeen A. Dantata - MD/CEO

BECHTEL (NIGERIA) LIMITED
Business: Building, Civil Mechanical & Electrical Engineers, Erosin Control
Address: 2/4, Onitsha Crescent, Independence Layout, Enugu
Tel/Fax: (042) 456106
Contact: Engr. Chidozie Odiatu Chiejina - Chairman/MD

BEDMATE NIGERIA INTERNATIONAL ENTERPRISES COMPANY LIMITED
Business: Importation & Marketing of Furniture and Accessories for Homes and Offices
Address: Adebola House, 38, Opebi Road, Ikeja, Lagos
Tel: (01) 4734793, 7762489, 08034033889, 08037206022, 08034747211, 08035687372 **Fax:** (01) 3450139
E-mail: bedmatenig@yahoo.com
Contact: Mr. James Chi - Chairman/CEO

BEE DRILLING SERVICES LIMITED
Business: Borehole Drilling, Water Distribution, Tank Construction and Soil Investigation
Address: Plot 6, East-West Rd Rumukwurushi, P/ Harcourt.
Tel: (084) 611348, 08033091161 **Fax:** (084) 235597
Contact: Engr. Ben. I. Iloabachie - Chairman/MD

BEES COMPANY LIMITED
Business: Manufacturing & Sales of Electrical Transformers, Sales of Electrical Materials & Equipment, Electrical Engineering Services and Building Contractors, Paper Converters, Bakers & Confectioners
Address: 6, Scotty Asuen Way, off Km. 6, Sapele Road, P. O. Box 1751, Benin City
Tel: (052) 255687, 256848 **Fax:** (052) 257438
Contact: Chief B. Ezekwere - Chairman/CEO

BEENTHING INVESTMENT LIMITED
Business: Customs Licensed Agents, Transit Cargo Handlers, Freight Forwarders, General Contractors
Address: 3, Tex Olawale Crescent, Coconut Bus Stop, Apapa, Lagos
Tel: (01) 7758467, 08022239108
E-mail: Bintin2000@yahoo.com
* Agents Office Complex, beside Co-operative Bank, Seme Border, Badagry.
Tel: 08033473786
Contact: Alh. Mikky Ola Okunola - MD/CEO

BELLAN ASSOCIATES LIMITED
Business: Consultancy Services, Networking, Corporate

Training, System Support Services, Software Development, Web Hosting & Design, Sales and Supply of Computers
Address: Plot PC. 10, Engineering Close, off Idowu Taylor Street, Victoria Island, Lagos
Tel: (01) 4703648, 611784, 616914 **Fax:** (01) 616914
E-mail: bellan@micro.com.ng
Contact: Chief R. N. Animadu - Chairman

BEL IMPEX LIMITED
Business: Production of Cellotapes, Toiletries & Tissue Paper
Address: Plot 6, Kudirat Abiola Way (Clay Bus-Stop), Oregun, Ikeja, Lagos
Tel: (01) 7745232, 7763560, 5557761-3 (3 L), 08035607080
E-mail: riado@nova.net.ng

BELLO & COMPANY
Business: Estate Surveyors & Valuers, Real Estate Development and Management
Address: Plot 10A, Kigoma St, Wuse Zone 7, Garki Abuja.
Tel: (09) 5233150, 5233250 **Fax:** (09) 5233150
E-mail: bello@cyberspace.net.ng

BELLVIEW AIRLINES LIMITED
Business: Air Transportation
Address: Belview Plaza, 66B, Opebi Street, Ikeja
Tel: (01) 4931731-5 (5L), 4977715, 4970061
E-mail: bellview@bellview.com.ng
* Murtala Mohammed International Airport (Rm. 2035), Ikeja, Lagos
* Plot 270, Ozumba Mbadiwe Ave, V/Island, Lagos
* St Gabriel House (Bwing), 22 Warehouse Road, Apapa, Lagos.
Tel: (01) 5452316-8 (3 L)
Contact: Mr. Kayode O. Odukoya - MD/CEO

BELLVIEW TRAVELS LIMITED
Business: Travel Agency, Aviation Services
Address: Waterfront Plaza, Plot 270, Ozumba Mbadiwe Avenue, Victoria Island, Lagos.
Tel: (01) 4977715, 4970061, 4931731-5 (5L)

BELOXXI & COMPANY LIMITED
Business: Marketing of Biscuits and Confectionery
Address: 31, Ekolulu Street, off Itire Road, Surulere, Lagos
Tel: (01) 5848995 **Fax:** (01) 5851620
E-mail: beloxxi@hyperia.com
Contact: Mr. Obi Ezeude - President/CEO

BEL-PAPYRUS LIMITED
Business: Manufacture and Marketing of Crepe Tissue Jumbo Rolls, Toilet Tissue, Sanitary Pads, Paper Napkins & Facial Tissue
Address: Block 6, Kudirat Abiola Way, Oregun Industrial Estate Ikeja, Lagos
Tel: (01) 7745232, 7763560, 4964319, 4960948, 4968078
Fax: (01) 2619609
E-mail: riado@nova.net.ng
Contact: Mr. Gabriel G. Boulos - MD/CEO

BELTECO ENGINEERING LIMITED
Business: Building and Civil Engineering Works
Address: 248, Murtala Mohammed Way, Ebute Metta, Lagos
Tel: (01) 862570, 864555, 862815 **Fax:** (01) 862815
E-mail: beltecoengineering@yahoo.com
Contact: Mr. Benson Ojor Usiagwu - Chairman/CEO

BELTON LINK LIMITED
Business: Sales of Furniture/Furnishings, Interior Decoration
Address: 34, Adeniran Ogunsanya Street, Surulere, Lagos
Tel: (01) 7761655, 5455018, 8110067, 08033064048, 08033054171
Contact: Mr. Dotun Aboaba - MD/CEO

BEMAR DMP LIMITED
Business: General Steel Works, Construction of Boreholes and Water-Treatment Plants, Concrete Works
Address: 9A, Lisabi Road, Apapa G.R.A., Lagos
Tel: (01) 5871148, 5874461, 7749216 **Fax:** (01) 5874461
E-mail: bemar@micro.com.ng
*Plot 1, Acme Road, Ogba Ind. Estate, Ikeja, Lagos
Tel: (01) 921074, 7753685
Contact: Dieudonne Petit - MD/CEO

BEMIL NIGERIA LIMITED
Business: Comprehensive Security Services, Installation and Service of Security Systems, Funeral Services, Catering & Rental Services
Address: 1, Bemil Road, off Isheri Road, Ojodu-Abiodun, Ojodu Ikeja, Lagos
Tel: (01) 7740311, 7740356, 2630619, 2630415
Fax: (01) 2630797, 2630088
E-mail: bemilojodu@bemil.com.ng
Website: www.bemil.com.ng
* Bookshop House, 50/52, Broad Street, Lagos
Tel/Fax: (01) 2664136
E-mail: bemillagos@bemil.com.ng
Contact: Omo'ba Jide Martins - Chairman/CEO

BEMS LIMITED
Business: Airfreight and Shipping Services, Customs Brokerage, Courier Services, Consolidation, Warehousing
Address: 83B, Marine Road, Apapa G.R.A., Lagos.
Tel/Fax: (01) 5877321, 5451177, 5874800
E-mail: bems@micro.com.ng

BEN-AD LIMITED
Business: Billboard Signwriting, Outdoor Advertising and Promotions
Address: 31A, Atanda Alonge Street, Oworonsoki, Lagos
Tel: (01) 8042228, 08033017571, 08023090050, 08023534152
Contact: Chief Olufemi Ajayi - Chairman/CEO
Mr. Lekan Bakare - Outdoor Manager

BEN HOLDINGS LIMITED
Business: Importation & Sales of Musical Equipment and Public Address Systems, Motor-Vehicle Parts and Bible, Manufacture of Plastic Containers
Address: The Music House, Plot 12A, Aminu Jinadu Close, off Jimoh Odutola Street, off Eric Moore Road, Iganmu, Lagos
Tel: (01) 5832995, 5836571, 5850706, 7742607
Fax: (01) 5850706
Contact: Prince Ben Ukadike - Chairman/CE

BENBO GAMES VILLAGE HOTELS LIMITED
Business: Hospitality Services, Technical Facilities for Sports Training
Address: Ojeta, Abraka, Delta State
Tel: (054) 66132, 66133
* Apata, Ibadan. **Tel:** (02) 2315588, 2316244

BENCHMARK COMPUTER SOLUTIONS LIMITED
Business: Sales & Service of Computers & Accessories, Software Development, Training
Address: 175, Ikorodu Road, Onipanu, Shomolu, Lagos
Tel: (01) 824114
Contact: Idowu Odujinrin - MD/CEO

BENCHMARK TECHNOLOGIES LIMITED
Business: Sales, Maintenance and Service of Computer Hardware and Accesories, Networking Solutions
Address: Quantity Surveyors House (Ground Floor), 17/19, Idowu Taylor Street, Victoria Island, Lagos.
Tel: (01) 2620991, 2622822 **Fax:** (01) 2620992
E-mail: benchmark@hyperia.com
Website: www.benchmarkng.com
Contact: Mr. O .Oyeniyi - Chairman

BENCOD PRESS LIMITED
Business: Commercial Printing and Packaging, Designing and Production of Exercise Books
Address: Km. 3, Badagry Expressway (by Alafia Bus Stop), Iganmu, Lagos
Tel: (01) 7741364
Contact: Chief B. C. Odigboh - Chairman/CEO

BENCOV CONSTRUCTION COMPANY LIMITED
Business: Building & Civil Engineering Contractors
Address: Km. 6, Old Aba-Owerri Road, Osisioma Industrial Layout, Aba.
Tel: (082) 350068
Contact: Chief Vincent Ofolabe - MD/CEO

BENDEL BREWERY PLC
Business: Brewing of Alcoholic & Non-Alcoholic Beverages
Address: Oregbeni Estate, Benin-Agbor Road, Benin City
Tel: (052) 254285 **Fax:** (052) 250472

BENDEL FEED AND FLOUR MILLS LIMITED
Business: Milling of Flour, Production of Livestock Feeds
Address: Km 100, Benin-Auchi Road, Ewu, Edo State
Tel: (057) 97321, 97322, 97323
* Former Cocoa Board Premises, 24, Ladipo Oluwole St, off Oba Akran Avenue, Ikeja, Lagos.
Tel: (01) 4960584, 4960571

BENDEL INSURANCE PLC
Business: Insurance
Address: 167, Sapele Road, Benin City
Tel: (052) 253227, 259598, 253184 **Fax:** (052) 253184
Contact: Mr. Alfred Daudu - G M/CEO

BENDEL NEWSPAPER COMPANY LIMITED
Business: Printing Services, Newspaper Publishing, Media Consultancy Services
Address: 24, Airport Road, Benin City
Tel: (052) 257531 **Fax:** (052) 257492

BENDEL WOOD INDUSTRY LIMITED
Business: Chemical Preservation of Transmission Poles and Cross-Arms, Wood Milling, Fabrication
Address: Plot 741, Adeola Hopewell St Victoria Island, Lagos
Tel: (01) 2612383, 2622919 **Fax:** (01) 2621146
E-mail: bwil@igi-insurers.com
Website: www.igi-insurers.com
* Ekehuan/Ogba Water Works Road, Benin City.
Tel/Fax: (052) 255578
Contact: Mr. I. O. Ayinde - GM/CEO

BENEFICIAL HEALTH PLANS LIMITED
Business: Managed Health Services
Address: 34, Town Planning Way, Ilupeju, Lagos
Tel: (01) 4701255, 4704062 **Fax:** (01) 2635285
E-mail: bhp-info@yahoo.com
Contact: Prof. T. A. J. Ogunbiyi - Chairman

BENEFIT LOSS ADJUSTERS LIMITED
Business: Loss Adjusting, Risk Surveying, Marine Cargo, Superintendents, Recovery Agent
Address: 61, Tejuoso Street, Surulere, Lagos.
Tel: (01) 837917, 841171, 7748811
Contact: Mr. Tayo Okewole - CEO

BENEK ENGINEERING COMPANY LIMITED
Business: Oilfield & General Engineering Services; Oil & Gas Supplies; Equipment Leasing, Dredging Operations, Borehole Drillling & Maintenance
Address: Km. 4, East-West Road, Obio, Port Harcourt
Tel: (084) 612226, 612685, 612733, 612709
Fax: (084) 612179
E-mail: benek@phca.linkserve.com
Contact: Engr. Uche B. Ekekwe - Chairman/CEO

BENEVOLENT LOSS ADJUSTERS LIMITED
Business: Loss Adjusting
Address: Ireti Hospital Building (4th Floor), 161, Herbert Macaulay Street, Yaba, Lagos.
Tel: (01) 863269
Contact: Mr. J. D. Olawoye - MD/CEO

BENGAS INDUSTRIES (NIGERIA) LIMITED
Business: Manufacturing and Marketing of Gas Cookers, PVC Pipes and Plastics, Tissue Papers and Pens
Address: 33/35, Agarawu St, Idumota, Lagos Island, Lagos
Tel: (01) 2668318 **Fax:** (01) 2664896
E-mail: bengasbech@yahoo.com
bengasbech@hotmail.com
Contact: Chief B. O. Ichiebuka - Chairman/CEO

BENHOUSE BUILDING SOCIETY LIMITED
Business: Mortgage Banking Services
Address: 41, Railway Bye-Pass, Makurdi
Tel: (044) 533024

BENIGAN FORWARDERS LIMITED
Business: Clearing & Forwarding, Warehousing
Address: Plot 1, NPA New Port Gate Complex, Expressway Junction, Warri
Tel: (053) 253127, 254654 **Fax:** (053) 253654
E-mail: benigan@seanitt.com
Contact: Mr. Ben O. U. Nwachukwu - Chairman

BENJACK TRANSWORLD AGENCIES LIMITED
Business: Telecommunication, Civil Construction Works; Procurement; Clearing and Forwarding
Address: Plot 329A, Olu Obasanjo Road, G.R.A., Phase II Port Harcourt
Tel: (084) 239041, 571003
E-mail: benjacktrans@hotmail.com
Contact: Mr Benjamin Ejiogu - MD/CEO

BENJAMIN BLACK & COMPANY LIMITED
Business: Media Brokerage, Outdoor Advertising Agency
Address: 1, Hagley Road, Jibowu, Lagos
Tel: (01) 2881819, 861217, 867776, 08023130926
Fax: (01) 2881820
E-mail: benjaminblack2000@yahoo.co.uk
Contact: Mr. Dapo Adelegan - MD/CEO

BENJAMIN FOSTER & COMPANY LIMITED
Business: Subscription Management for Professional and Business Publications.
Address: ED Building (5th Floor), 47, Marina Lagos.
Tel: (01) 2662950 **Fax:** (01) 7597064
E-mail: benjaminfosterltd@yahoo.com
* 34, Onne Road, G.R.A. Phase II, Port Harcourt
Tel: (084) 234784
Contact: Mr. F. U. C. Ordor - MD/CEO

BENLOCK NIGERIA LIMITED
Business: Importation of Trucks, Industrial Machines, Earth-moving Equipment, Generators, Transformers, Crane-Hiring Services, Sewage Contractors
Address: 143, Badagry Expressway (Pako Bus-Stop), Agboju-Amuwo, Festac Town, Lagos
Tel: (01) 5890474, 5890032, 2881311
Fax: (01) 5890474, 2881311
* 56, Agulu Street, Old Motor Spare Parts Market, Amafor Nkpor, Onitsha.
Tel: (046) 211915, 214814
* Zone C, Block 6, ASPMDA Plaza, Trade Fair Complex, Badagry Expressway, Ojo, Lagos

BENMAX CABLES LIMITED
Business: Manufacturing of Electrical Cables and Wires
Address: Plot IN/123, Emene Ind. Layout Extension, Enugu.
Tel: (042) 559392, 451775 **Fax:** (042) 451775
Contact: Chief (Engr.) B. C. Okwo - Chairman/CEO.

BENNETT INDUSTRIES LIMITED
Business: Manufacture and Supply of Light Fittings and Fixtures. Supply and Installation of Suspended Ceilings, Acoustic and Thermal Products
Address: Plot D, Ikosi Road, Oregun Industrial Estate.
Tel: (01) 4964843 **Fax:** (01) 4976286
E-mail: bennaziki@beta.linkserve.com
Contact: Mr. R. I. Odiah - Chairman/CEO

BEN-NICE LIMITED
Business: Drycleaning & Laundry Services
Address: Drycleaning Plaza, 21, Adetola Street (Cele Bus-Stop) Aguda, Surulere, Lagos
Tel: (01) 7911367, 5851175, 7764101, 08033304962
E-mail: bennice@infoweb.abs.net
Contact: Mr. Benedict Ifezue - Chairman/CEO

BENOD INTERNATIONAL LIMITED
Business: Central Airconditioning Works
Address: 99, Adeniyi Jones Avenue, Ikeja, Lagos
Tel: (01) 7730654, 7753105, 2880138, 4744917, 08023017065, 08023017079 **Fax:** (01) 4938303
E-mail: brunton@alpha.linkserve.com
sales@benod.com
Contact: Mr. David Brunton - MD/CEO

BENTOS PHARMACEUTICAL PRODUCTS LIMITED.
Business: Manufacturing of Pharmaceutical Products
Address: Km. 8, Old Lagos Road, Ibadan.
Tel: (02) 2318293, 2318941 **Fax:** (02) 2313508
E-mail: bentos@skannet.com
bentos@bentospharm.com

BENUE BREWERY LIMITED.
Business: Brewing and Bottling of Beer
Address: Km. 5, Gboko Road, Makurdi
Tel: (044) 533350, 532629 **Fax:** (044) 532980, 533231
E-mail: benbrew@alpha.linkserve.com
Contact: Mr. S .G. Garba - MD/CEO

BENUE CEMENT COMPANY PLC
Business: Production and Sales of Portland Cement
Address: Km 72, Makurdi-Gboko Road, Tse-Kucha, Benue State
* Plot 306, Adeola Odeku St, Victoria Island, Lagos
Tel: (01) 2610766, 2610615, 2610771 **Fax:** (01) 2610766
* Plot 468, Lobi Crescent, Wuse II, Abuja
Tel: (09) 5230771
Contact: Engr. Moses I. Aende - Ag. MD/CEO

BENUE HOTELS LIMITED
Business: Hospitality Services
Address: 5/7, Ahmadu Bello Way, Makurdi
Tel: (044) 5322178
Contact: Mr. J. Kwaghgba - GM/CEO

BENUE INVESTMENT & PROPERTY COMPANY LIMITED
Business: Investment Promotion, Development Financing, Property Development and Management
Address: Km. 4, Yohanna Madaki Road, Makurdi
Tel: (044) 533159, 533509 **Fax:** (044) 533159
E-mail: benueinvestment@yahoo.com

BENUE PRINTING & PUBLISHING CORPORATION
Business: Newspaper Publishing, Commercial Printing
Address: Otukpo Road, Makurdi
Tel: (044) 532875
Contact: Mr Innocent Uvah - GM/CEO

BENWILS CELLULAR CONSULTANTS LIMITED
Business: Sales of Communication Equipment and Computers GSM & Mobile Phones and Accessories
Address: 12, Ogui Road, opp. Guaranty Trust Bank, Enugu.
Tel: (042) 257800, 255200, 08033118808
Fax: (042) 255200
E-mail: benwils@benwils.com
Website: www.benwilscellular.com
* 28, Ogunlana Drive, Surulere, Lagos
Tel: (01) 5850688
Contact: Mr. Mac C. Benito Ozigbo - MD/CEO

BEOKON NIGERIA LIMITED
Business: Sales of Car-Body Repair Products Cosmetics, Automobile Batteries and General Goods
Address: 52/54, James Roberton Street, Surulere, Lagos
Tel: (01) 7744702 **Fax:** (01) 2644447
E-mail: beokon@hyperia.com
* Zone D, Block 8, Shops 20 & 23, ASPAMDA Plaza, Trade Fair Complex, Ojo, Lagos.
Tel: (01) 3208292
Contact: Sir Bertram Orji Okoye - Chairman/CEO

BERGMANNE NIGERIA LIMITED
Business: Construction Services
Address: 161B, Raufu Taylor Close, off Idejo Street, Victoria Island, Lagos
Tel: (01) 4722568, 2701228
E-mail: bergmanne@hyperia.com
Contact: Mr. Gbolahan Animashaun - Chief Executive

BERGER PAINTS NIGERIA PLC
Business: Manufacture of Paints, Coatings & Allied Products
Address: Plot 142, Oba Akran Avenue, Ikeja Industrial Estate, Ikeja, Lagos
Tel: (01) 4976982-4 (3L), 4976980 **Fax:** (01) 4977078
E-mail: berger@hyperia.com
Website: www.bergerpaints.com.ng
* Plot 70, Trans-Amadi Ind. Layout, Port Harcourt
Contact: Mr. Adebowale A Thompson - MD/CEO

BERLIAC GROUP
Business: Manufacturing of Long-Span Aluminium & Galvanized Plain-Iron Roofing Sheets, Sales of Building Materials and Gaskets
Address: Plot 523, Agege Motor Road (Alasia Bus-Stop), Shogunle, Oshodi, Lagos
Tel: (01) 4932393, 3934113 **Fax:** (01) 4934111
E-mail: berliac@skannet.com
berliac@micro.com.ng

BERNADOS PHARMACEUTICALS LIMITED
Business: Sales of Pharmaceuticals, Surgical and Dental Items, Pharmaceutical Redistributing
Address: 65, Ishaga Rd, opp. LUTH 2nd Gate Surulere Lagos
Tel: (01) 4528933, 4528705
E-mail: bernados@skannet.com
* 3, Carr Lane, off Issa Williams Street, Lagos
Tel: (01) 2644572, 2644520-1 (2L)
* Plot 40, Cornershops, opp. Rockview Hotel, Adetokunbo Ademola Crescent, Wuse II, Abuja
Tel: (09) 4133213, 4133214 **Fax:** (09) 4133213
Contact: Pharm. (Dr.) Sola Omiwade - Chairman/CEO

BERTIE-JOHN (NIGERIA) PRINTERS LIMITED
Business: Commercial Printing
Address: 36, Okesuna Street, Somolu, Lagos
Tel: (01) 823674, 5457919 **Fax:** (01) 5457919
*46A, Market St, (Abiodun B/Stop) Somolu, Lagos
Contact: Mr. Albert O. Oyenuga - Chairman/CEO

BERTOLA MACHINE-TOOLS LIMITED
Business: Machines and Tools Merchandising, General Engineering Services, Servicing of Oil Companies
Address: Bertola House, 296, Ikorodu Road, Anthony Lagos
Tel: (01) 4965323, 4933538 **Fax:** (01) 4966352
E-mail: bertola@alpha.linkserve.com
* 32, Trans-Amadi Industrial Road, Port Harcourt
Tel: (084) 230383 **Fax:** (084) 230384
E-mail: bert@alpha.linkserve.com
Contact: Mr. Albert I. Inyang - Chairman/CEO

BEST ALUMINIUM MANUFACTURING COMPANY LIMITED
Business: Manufacturing of Longspan Aluminium Roofing Sheets and Cookware
Address: 30/32, Anyika Street, Ozalla Layout, Awada, near ABS Television, Onitsha
Tel: (046) 411625, 411399, 413794, 414459
* 85, Aba Road, Port Harcourt
Tel: (084) 233758-9 (2L), 233757 **Fax:** (084) 233757
E-mail: bamco@phca.linkserve.com
best@skannet.com
Contact: Chief P. N. Nweke - MD/CEO

BEST BAGS LIMITED
Business: Manufacturing of Polythene Bags and Sheetings
Address: Plot 52, Sharada Industrial Estate Phase II, Kano
Tel: (064) 666396-7 (2L)
Contact: Mr. Hong Yu Leung - Chairman/CEO

BEST FOODS GLOBAL (NIGERIA) LIMITED
Business: Sales of Foods and Grocery, Home/Office Delivery Services, Slaughtering, Processing and Marketing of Cows, Chicken, Goat and Pork
Address: 15A, Maduike Street, off Raymond Njoku Street, S.W. Ikoyi, Lagos
Tel: (01) 2672737, 2696356, 2673014
Fax: (01) 2672169, 2692387
E-mail: bestfoodsglobal@yahoo.com
Contact: Mr. E. I. Ijewere - Chairman/CEO

BEST LAND & SEA SERVICES LIMITED
Business: Servicing of Oil Wells, Supply of Equipment and Chemicals for Oil Exploration and Production
Address: NAL-Comet House, 4, Hinderer Road, Apapa G.R.A., Lagos
Tel: (01) 7740143 **Fax:** (01) 5453214
E-mail: comet@micro.com.ng
* Plot 41, Trans-Amadi Ind. Layout, Port Harcourt
Tel: (084) 235111, 335540 **Fax:** (084) 236768
E-mail: bls@phca.linkserve.com
Contact: Mr. Dauda Y. Danjuma - MD/CEO

BEST STORE LIMITED
Business: General Trading and Importation, Warehousing and Exportation of Agricultural Products
Address: Plot 1303A, Akin Adesola St Victoria Island, Lagos
Tel: (01) 2622232, 2622259, 2615505
Fax: (01) 613402, 2619487
E-mail: primlak@hyperia.com
* Plot 4, Block E, Amuwo-Odofin Industrial Layout, Suru-Alaba, Orile-Iganmu, Lagos
Tel: (01) 7756660, 5836017 **Fax:** (01) 5832250
Contact: Otunba A. O. Adewunmi - Chairman
Mr Anil R Hemnani - CEO

BESTLINE NIGERIA LIMITED
Business: Sales of Welding Equipment and Products

Address: 15, Hospital Road, off Oti Carpets Apapa-Oshodi Expressway (Warehouse B/S), Olodi, Apapa Lagos
Tel: (01) 5454519, 5876814, 7741305 **Fax:** (01) 5451368
E-mail: bestline@infoweb.abs.net

BESTMAN AZIA COMPANY (NIGERIA) LIMITED
Business: Marketing of Luggage Carriers and Travel Goods
Address: Urban Renewal Shopping Complex (Block B, 1st Floor), opp. Wema Bank, Nnamdi Azikiwe Street, Tinubu Square, Lagos
Tel: (01) 2660899, 2665335, 2644929
* B63, Old Abeokuta Motor Road, Agege, Lagos.
Tel: (01) 4921082, 4923353

BESTWORTH ASSET & TRUST LIMITED
Business: Stockbroking, Portfolio &Assets Management, Advisory Services,
Address: Great Nigeria House (5th Floor), 47/57, Martins Street, Lagos.
Tel: (01) 2641380, 2646476
Contact: Mr. Sola Adeniyi - MD/CEO

BETA ADAM PLASTICS LIMITED
Business: Manufacturing of Household Plastic Products and Industrial Plastic-Packaging Products
Address: Iddo House, Iddo, Lagos
Tel: (01) 7740844, 7747602, 7748339
Fax: (01) 7748073, 2618285

BETA COMPUTERS LIMITED
Business: Sales of Computer Hardware, Computer Maintenance, Networking, Desktop Publishing, Training
Address: 20, Adebola Street, off Adeniran Ogunsanya Street, Surulere, Lagos
Tel: (01) 5834178, 5847564, 4700051-2 (2 L)
Fax: (01) 5841266
E-mail: info@beta-computers.com
* 6, Tombia Street, off Aba Road, G.R.A. Phase I, Port Harcourt
Tel: (084) 239521, 238752, 237889 **Fax:** (084) 237889
E-mail: bclph@phca.linkserve.com
Contact: Mr. Will E. Anyaegbunam - MD/CEO

BETA GLASS PLC
Business: Manfacture & Sales of Hollow glass Containers, Lantern globes, and Table Wares
Address: Iddo House, Iddo, Lagos
Tel: (01) 867315 (DL), 80020-9 (10L) (Ext. 2158, 2180);
Fax: (01) 863671
* Delta Plant; Km. 17, Warri-Patani Road, Agbarho-Ughelli, Delta State.
Tel: (053) 251072
* Guinea Plant, Km. 32, Lagos-Badagry Express Road, Agbara Industrial Estate, Ogun State
Tel: (01) 7740911, 7747662 **Fax:** (01) 2883047
Contact: Dr. S. Constantinidis - MD

BETA T.S.G. (NIGERIA) LIMITED
Business: Manufacturing of Automotive Safety Glass and Architectural & Decorative Glass
Address: Iwo Road, near West African Batteries, Ibadan
Tel: (02) 8104637, 8108053;
* Abuja - (09) 5211994
* Port Harcourt - (084) 231725
* Lagos - (01) 7748339, 7740844 **Fax:** (02) 8108053
Contact: Mr. C. Patriarcheas - MD/CEO

BETAN HOLDINGS LIMITED
Business: Distribution and Marketing of Digital Satellite, AudioReceivers, Consultancy Services
Address: 79, Ogunlana Drive, Surulere, Lagos
Tel: (01) 5840458, 5843194, 7752664
Fax: (01) 5843194, 5849824
E-mail: betan@cybaaspace.net.ng
betan@micro.com.ng
Contact: Chief Anthony Obinwa

BETCY GROUP OF COMPANIES
Business: Civil/Structural, Electrical, Mechanical & Water Engineering Contractors, Marketing of Wines and Vehicles, Television Productions, Corporate Promotion and Advertising, Sales of Medical Equipment
Address: Becty House, Block, 14, Plot 241, Amuwo-Odofin/ Festac Access Road, off Oshodi-Apapa Expressway, Amuwo-Odofin, Lagos.
Tel: (01) 5890552, 5890553, 7746755 **Fax:** (01) 5882969
E-mail: betcygp@gacom.net
betcygp@nigol.net.ng
Contact: Dr. Ausbeth Nnamdi Ajagu - Chairman/CEO

BETRAM NIGERIA LIMITED
Business: Marketing of Papers , Boards; Glass & Ceramics
Address: 6A, Mainland Way, Dolphin Estate, Ikoyi, Lagos
Tel: (01) 2691291, 2696119 **Fax:** (01) 2696119, 619857
E-mail: betram@hyperia.com
Contact: Mr. J. R. Bondioli - Chairman/CEO

BETTA
(British Educcational Training & Technical Association)
Business: Educational Counselling & Advisory Services
Address: 33, Ogundana St, off Allen Avenue, Ikeja, Lagos
Tel: (01) 4973897, 4717887, 4712088, 08033436350
Fax: (01) 4967233
E-mail: bettalag@yahoo.com
* 18, Okoroji Street, D-Line, Port Harcourt
Tel: (084) 484174
Contact: Mr. Bayo Balogun - Director

BETTA METHODS (NIGERIA) LIMITED
Business: Sales of Traffic-Control Equipment and Products
Address: 4/6, Oil Mill Street (next to Lion Building), off Catholic Mission Street, Lagos Island, Lagos.
Tel: (01) 2634493, 263434
Contact: Mr. Gbola Sarumi - MD/CEO

BETTER FOODS LIMITED
Business: Production & Import of Food-Beverages Drinks
Address: 12B, Idowu Martins Street, Victoria Island, Lagos
Tel: (01) 2616103

BETTER LIVING LIMITED
Business: Furniture Making, Sales of Accessories
Address: Plot 1676 Oladele Olashore St Victoria Island Lagos
Tel: (01) 2615196 **Fax:** (01) 3200388
Contact: Engr. (Chief, Dr.) D. O. Ekesi - Chairman

BEVERLY COPS & SECURITY SERVICES LIMITED
Business: Security and Consultancy, Sales and Installation of Security Equipment
Address: Plot 151, Younis Bashorun Street, off Ajose Adeogun, Victoria Island Annex, Lagos
Tel: (01) 262934, 3200615 **Fax:** (01) 2621173
Contact: Dr. E. I. Kachikwu - Chairman/CEO

BEVISTA & COMPANY LIMITED
Business: Fashion Sales
Address: 16, Opebi Road, Opebi, Ikeja, Lagos
Tel: (01) 4937178, 8042672 **Fax:** (01) 4937178
E-mail: bevista@infoweb.abs.net

BFCL ASSETS & SECURITIES LIMITED
Business: Stockbroking, Leasing, Contracts
Address: UBA House (5th Floor), 57, Marina Lagos
Tel: (01) 2644017, 2642949, 7738525 **Fax:** (01) 2644017
E-mail: bfcl@bfcl.com
Contact: Mr. Simpson E. Okoro - MD/CEO

BGL LTD
Business: Corporate Finance & Wealth Management, Issuing House, Financial Advisory Services
Address: Plot 1061B, Abagbon Close, off Ologun Agbaje Street, Lagos.
Tel: (01) 2623141, 2623257, 2672799, 2672820, 612340, 4810529 **Fax:** (01) 2623258
E-mail: info@bglltd.com
info@ibglltd.com
Website: www.bglltd.com
Contact: Mr Albert E Okumagba - MD/CEO

BHI LIMITED (Baker Hughes Inteq)
Business: Drilling, Evaluation and Maintenance of Oil Wells
Address: Plot 175, Trans-Amadi Ind. Layout, Port Harcourt
Tel: (084) 238884, 238394 **Fax:** (084) 236086
Contact: Mr. Danny J. Holder - MD/CEO

BHN PLC
Business: Sales and Service of Earth-Moving Equipment & Machinery, Generators, Escort Motorcycles, Buses Refurbishment of Heavy Equipment
Address: 13/15, Wharf Road, Apapa, Lagos.
Tel: (01) 5877000, 5453057, 5453058 **Fax:** (01) 5451398
Contact: Mr Sajen G Aswani - MD/CEO

BHOJSONS & COMPANY (NIGERIA) PLC
Business: Conglomerate, Trading
Address: 29C, Kofo Abayomi Street, Victoria Island, Lagos
Tel: (01) 2618322, 2615994
E-mail: bhojsons@linkserve.com.ng
* 51, Docemo Street, Idumota, Lagos
Tel: (01) 2662181, 2663155, 2661488 **Fax:** (01) 4930958
Contact: Mr. D. M. Dalamal - Group MD.

BHOJRAJ INDUSTRIES PLC
Business: Manufacturing of Textile Piece Goods
Address: Plot B, Block 1, Industrial Avenue, Ilupeju Industrial Estate, Ilupeju, Lagos.
Tel: (01) 4930960, 7737482-4 (3L) **Fax:** (01) 4930959
* Plot C, Block IX, State Highway, Ilupeju Industrial Estate, Ilupeju, Lagos.
Tel: (01) 4960944, 4972268-9 (2L), 497582-3 (2L)
E-mail: biltexsec@bhojrajchanrai.com
Contact: Mr. B. B. Chanrai - Chairman
Mr. M. R. Sadhwani - Group MD/CEO

BHOJWANI BROS (NIGERIA) LIMITED
Business: Sales of Motor Vehicles
Address: 9, Alh. Bashorun Street, S. W. Ikoyi, Lagos
Tel: (01) 2694358, 2693894 **Fax:** (01) 2694149
* 1, Ahmadu Bello Way (Entry via 3, Eleke Crescent), Victoria Island, Lagos.

BIASOWL NIGERIA LIMITED
Business: Manufacturing and Sale of Paints
Address: 22, Adekunle Street, Isolo, Lagos.
Tel: (01) 521658, 4528485, 4711271 **Fax:** (01) 4528485
Contact: Prince Bayo Otulana - Chairman/CEO

BIC SECURITIES LIMITED
Business: Stockbroking
Address: c/o Benue Investment & Property Company Ltd. Km. 4, Old Oturkpo Road, Makurdi.
Tel: (044) 533159, 533509 **Fax:** (044) 533509
Contact: Mr. J. Andzenge - MD/CEO

BICU & SONS LIMITED
Business: Marketing of Cosmetics
Address: 12, Balogun Street (West), Lagos
Tel: (01) 2660107, 2669531, 2669079
Fax: (01) 5878824, 2665341
E-mail: bicu@micro.com.ng
Contact: Chief (Mrs) C C Nwazojie - CEO

BIDAT SPORTS WEAR COMPANY LIMITED
Business: Manufacture of Sports Wear and Related Apparel; Sports Promotional and Advert Materials
Address: 43, Town Planning Way, Ilupeju, Lagos
Tel/Fax: (01) 4962943
E-mail: bidat@linkserve.com.ng
Contact: A. A. Buraimoh-Ademuyewo - Chairman/CEO

BIE-USHA (WEST AFRICA) LIMITED
Business: Corrosion Control, Operation & Maintenance of Pipelines and Production Facilities, Civil & Mechanical Engineering, Manpower Mobilisation
Address: 201B, Port Harcourt/Aba Expressway, Rumuola Junction, Port Harcourt
Tel: (084) 236749, 333254, 08033397924
E-mail: bie_usha@hotmail.com
Website: www.bie-usha.com
Contact: Engr. B. J. Chapp-Jumbo - Chairman/CEO

BIFEX CONSULTANTS LIMITED
Business: Multi-Discipline Consultancy Services
Address: 86A, Isale Eko Avenue, Dolphin Estate, Ikoyi, Lagos
Tel: (01) 2690363, 680417 **Fax:** (01) 2695459
E-mail: bifex@hyperia.com
Website: www.bifex.com
Contact: Dr Ndi Onuekwusi - MD/CEO

BIG TREAT CONFECTIONERIES LIMITED
Business: Production and Sales of Confectionery
Address: 5, Opebi Road, Ikeja, Lagos.

Tel: (01) 4937396
* 58, Awolowo Road, S. W. Ikoyi, Lagos.
Tel: (01) 2694656
* 32, Adeniran Ogunsanya Street, Surulere, Lagos
* Yemosa Shopping Mall, Akowonjo Road, Egbeda, Lagos.
Contact: Pamale Wu - MD/CEO

BILFINGER BERGER GAS & OIL SERVICES NIGERIA LTD
Business: Oilfield Engineering Services
Address: Ijora Causeway, Ijora, Lagos
Tel: (01) 802473-4 (2L), 5831649
E-mail: lagos_office@BBGOS.com
* 133, Old Aba Road, opp. Mini-Okoro Police Station, Port Harcourt.
Tel: (084) 61018, 611673

BILL + BROTHERS LIMITED
Business: Distribution of Various Manufactured Goods, Marketing of Pure-Water Distillers, Importation of Pharmaceutical Products and Auto-Care Kits
Address: LSDPC Alaka Shopping Complex (Suites 9 & 11), Western Avenue, Alaka, Surulere, Lagos
Tel: (01) 5850159, 7752519 **Fax:** (01) 5834297
E-mail: bill@hyperia.com
Contact: Mr Bill Nkemdirim - Chairman
Mrs Agnes U Nkemdirim - MD/CEO

BILLAND CHEMICALS & PAINT INDUSTRIES LIMITED
Business: Manufacture of Industrial and Decorative Paints
Address: 29/30, Alh Haruna Street, off College Road, Ifako, Agege, Lagos
Tel: (01) 4920033, 4921527, 4921656 **Fax:** (01) 4920033
Contact: Mr B. O. U. Anozie - Chairman/CEO

BILLING COST ASSOCIATES
Business: Quantity Surveying, Consultancy, Project Management, Construction Claims Consultancy
Address: 15, Macarthy Street (1st Floor), Onikan, Lagos
Tel: (01) 2637461, 2634194, 08023396844
Fax: (01) 2600445
E-mail: nbillings@beta.linkserve.com
Website: www.billingsng.com
Contact: A. A. Ijogun - Managing Partner

BIMBY LADS LIMITED
Business: Production & Sales of Hats and Accessoriess.
Address: 54, Queen's Street, Alagomeji, Yaba, Lagos
Tel: (01) 865132, 866938 **Fax:** (01) 269263
E-mail: bimbylads.com
Website: www.bimbylads.com
Contact: Mrs. Bimbo Sofeso - Chairman/CEO

BIMDOC FARMS INTERNATIONAL
Business: Fish Farming, Production of Fingerlings and Feeds
Address: beh Yanaty Flour Mills, by Yekini Adeojo Mosque, Boluwaji Area, Iwo Road Expressway, Ibadan
Tel: (02) 2311482, 2319598, 08034705151
Contact: Mr. Bimbo Oluwayose - Chairman/CEO

BIMKOL NIGERIA LIMITED
Business: Building & Civil Engineering Contractors
Address: 84/86, Aba Road, Port Harcourt
Tel: (084) 234556, 238339
E-mail: okolo@infoweb.abs.net
* 28, King George V Road, Onikan, Lagos.
Tel: (01) 2631736

BINARY FUNCTIONS LIMITED
Business: Sales and Maitenance of Computer Hardware, Computer, Engineering and Training
Address: Ikeja Shopping Plaza (Suite 303), Sir Mobolaji Bank-Anthony Way, Ikeja, Lagos.
Tel: (01) 4973930
* Cornershop 33, Area 7, Garki, Abuja
Tel: (09) 2346875
Contact: Mr. Ayodeji O. Omoyeni - MD/CEO

BINDALO AGRICULTURAL & INDUSTRIAL COMPANY LTD
Business: Sales of Agricultural Machines, Engines and Industrial Equipment
Address: 70, Cardoso Street, Awodi-Ora Estate, Ajegunle, Apapa, Lagos.
Tel: (01) 5451093, 5875863
* 34, Bridge Street, Idumota, Lagos.
Contact: Chief A. A. Abiodun - MD/CEO

BINEZ HOTELS LIMITED
Business: Hospitality and Catering Services
Address: 5/7, Nwaogu Street, Aba.
Tel: (082) 222941, 225267 **Fax:** (082) 440030
Contact: Nze (Dr.) C. O. Maduako - Chairman/CEO

BINT & PRATHEL LIMITED
Business: Oil & Gas Services, Equipment/Material Procurement, Manpower Supply and Resources Management for the Oil & Gas Industry
Address: Plot 932, Idejo St (Suite B2), Victoria Island, Lagos
Tel: (01) 7741307, 3204545 **Fax:** (01) 3204545
E-mail: binprat@infoweb.abs.net
Contact: Mr. E. B. Odunlami - Chairman/CEO

BIO-INGREDIENTS LIMITED
Business: Marketing of Animal Feed Additives and Supplements
Address: 23B, Olarewaju Street, Oregun, Ikeja, Lagos
Tel/Fax: (01) 4931656, 4931657, 08023014873
E-mail: montizen@alpha.linkserve.com
Contact: Mr. George Ejiogu

BIO-ORGANICS NUTRIENT SYSTEMS LIMITED
Business: Human Nutrition Divisio n (Fortification of Foods and Beverages with Vitamins and Mineral Premixes, and Supply of Nutraceuticals), Animal Nutrition Division (Local Production of Vitamins and Mineral Premixes for the Livestock Industry, and Veterinary Medicaments)
Address: Plot 893, Isheri Road, by Ojodu Bus-Stop, Ojodu-Ikeja, Lagos
Tel: (01) 4700189, 4925511, 7748310 **Fax:** (01) 4925511
E-mail: bio@hyperial.com
Contact: Dr. Uzoma Kenny Acholon - Chairman/CEO

BIO-ROYAL HOSPITAL LIMITED
Business: Medical Care and Medical Diagnostic Service
Address: Plot 190, Okene Street/Jebba Close, Area 2, Section

2, Garki, Abuja
Tel: (09) 2342440, 08023127733 **Fax:** (09) 2342458
E-mail: bioroyal@yahoo.com
Contact: Dr. Frank Odafen -Chairman/Chief Medical Director

BIODUN ODELEYE & COMPANY
Business: Estate Surveyors and Valuers, Property Development and Management, Real Estate Consultants
Address: 14, Opebi Road, Ikeja, Lagos
Tel: (01) 4966467, 08022236541 **Fax:** (01) 4966467
E-mail: odeleye@infoweb.abs.net
* Nouakchott Street (Suite 46, off Olusegun Obasanjo Way, Wuse Zone 1, Wuse, Abuja.
Tel: (09) 5238153-4 (2L) **Fax:** (09) 5238154
Contact: Mr. Biodun Odeleye - Principal Partner

BIOMEDICAL SERVICES COMPANY LIMITED
Business: Manufacturing & Marketing of Intravenous Fluids, Dialysis Concentrates, Irrigation Fluids & Oral Rehydration Salt (ORS)
Address: 1, Ohimege Road, Industrial Estate, Ilorin.
Tel: (031) 220625, 222614 **Fax:** (031) 225785

BIOTEC LABORATORIES LIMITED
Business: Manufacturing of Pharmaceuticals and Chemicals
Address: Biotec House, Bauchi Ring Road, Jos.
Tel: (073) 610521 **Fax:** (073) 610609
E-mail: biotec@hyperia.com
* 3, Bank Road, Ikoyi, Lagos
Tel: (01) 680059 **Fax:** (01) 2695606

BIOTECH AUDIO VISUALS (NIGERIA) LIMITED
Business: Sales and Maintenance of Audio-Visual Teaching and Multimedia Presentation Equipment, Marketing of Corporate Promotion Materials, Leather Products, Office Equipment, Computer Systems & Accessories, Engineering Hand Tools
Address: 82, Mobolaji Bank-Anthony Way beside Customs Federal Operations Unit, Ikeja, Lagos.
Tel: (01) 4937829, 4936676
Fax: (01) 4934545
E-mail: biotech@beta.linkserve.com
Contact: Mr. Steve Onyemaechi - Chairman/CEO

BISCORDINT TRAVEL AGENCY LIMITED
Business: Travel Agency
Address: 28, Musa Yar'Adua Street, Victoria Island, Lagos.
Tel: (01) 2617778, 614578, 614577, 614517
Fax: (01) 2617778
Contact: Brigadier Gen. M. O. Johnson (rtd) - Chairman
Mrs R T Johnson - MD

BISHOPSGATE INTERNATIONAL (NIGERIA) LIMITED
Business: Sales and Services of Security Equipment
Address: Apalagada House, 24/26, Moloney Street, Onikan, Lagos
Tel: (01) 2636039, 2637703, 2630718, 2631049
Fax: (01) 2637732
E-mail: binl@alpha.linkserve.com
Contact: Mr. R. S. Mays - Chairman/CEO

BISSO NIGERIA LIMITED
Business: Publishing of Christian Literature, Distribution & Sales of Christiana Books
Address: 32A, Aba Johnson Crescent, off Adeniyi Jones Avenue, Ikeja, Lagos.
Tel/Fax: (01) 4938270
E-mail: bisso@alpha.linkserve.com
Contact: Mrs. Adebisi Olagoke - MD/CEO

BITCOM SYSTEMS (NIGERIA) LIMITED
Business: Sales, Installation and Repairs of Computers, Hardware Engineering, Network Design & Implementation, Software Development & Support, Multichannel e-Business Service Provider
Address: Marble House (7th Floor), 1, Alfred Rewane Road (formerly Kingsway Road), Ikoyi, Lagos
Tel: (01) 4705501, 2696786, 2696775 **Fax:** (01) 2696786
Contact: Biodunn Omoniyi - MD/CEO

BI-TRAXAXXENT COMPANY LIMITED
Business: Information Technology Solutions Provider; Training; Sales of Computer Hardware and Software; Networking; Telecommunications Equipment
Address: Plot 12, Block 88, Otunba Adedoyin Ogunmbe Crescent, Lekki Phase 1, Lekki, Lgaos
Tel: (01) 2706212, 2706214, 2706215, 2706122-3 (2 L)
Fax: (01) 2706215
E-mail: info@bi-traxaxxent.com
Website: www.bi-traxaxxent.com
Contact: Mr. Adedayo O. Afolabi - MD/CEO

BITTS TRAVEL & TOURS LIMITED
Business: Travel & Tour Agency, Holiday Packaging
Address: Falomo Shopping Centre (Suite E7), Awolowo Road, S. W. Ikoyi, Lagos
Tel: (01) 2696095, 2691337, 687813
E-mail: bittstravel@hotmail.com
* Zuma Shopping Mall (Suite B2), Ndola Square, off Michael Okpara Street, Wuse Zone 5, Abuja.
Contact: Chief (Mrs.) Opral M. Benson - Chairman
Mr Richard U. Okpoko - MD/CEO

BITUMEN MARKETING COMPANY (WEST AFRICA) LTD
Business: Marketing of Bitumen
Address: Plot 566, Admiral Oduwaye Street, Omole Estate Phase II, Ikeja, Lagos
Tel: (01) 4714101, 08023132495 **Fax:** (01) 7734334
E-mail: bitumen@bmcwa.com
bmc(wa)@yahoo.com

BJ SERVICES COMPANY NIGERIA LIMITED
Business: Oilfield Engineering Services
Address: Plot 470, Trans-Amadi Ind. Layout, Port Harcourt
Tel: (084) 232968, 232963, 237934
Tel/Fax: (084) 232967, 237935
Contact: Chief Alex Duduyemi - Chairman

B-JAY'S HOTEL
Business: Hotel and Catering Services
Address: 24, Samuel Manuwa Services (by 2nd Gate, 1004 Flats), Victoria Island, Lagos.
Tel: (01) 2622902, 2623706-8 (3L), 7746900-1 (2L), 2880429, 2880461 **Fax:** (01) 2622903
E-mail: bjays@alpha.linkserve.com
Contact: Ms. Abimbola Johnson - Chairman/CEO

BKI BUILDING & CIVIL ENGINEERING COMPANY LIMITED
Business: Building and Civil Engineering Contractors
Address: 62, Maganda Road, Bompai Industrial Estate Kano
Tel: (064) 632769, 632751, 648600
Contact: Mr. Bogialla Terry - MD/CEO

BLACK HORSE PLASTIC INDUSTRIES LIMITED
Business: Manufacturing of Plastic Chairs and Household Plastic wares
Address: Km. 12, Old Lagos Road, Ibadan.
Tel: (02) 2310302, 2314512 **Fax:** (02) 2318562
* 18, Emekuku Street, off Kaduna St, Port Harcourt
Contact: Mr. Hani Safieddine - Group Chairman
Mr Suheil Mudayhli - Group MD

BLACK MOUNTAINS LIMITED
Business: International Procurement of Agricultural Inputs of World Bank-Financed Projects
Address: 60, Adekunle Fajuyi Way, G.R.A., Ikeja, Lagos.
Tel: (01) 4935571 **Fax:** (01) 4935572
E-mail: bkmount@infoweb.abs.net
blackmountainsltd@yahoo.com
Contact: Mr. Kenny E. Idedevbo - Chairman/CEO

BLACKIE THOMAS NIGERIA LIMITED
Business: Laundry & Drycleaning, Industrial & Office Cleaning, Christian Bookshop
Address: 43, Airport Road, Effurun, P. O. Box 2198, Warri
Tel: (053) 253396
E-mail: blackiethomas@yahoo.com
Contact: Engr. J. O. Arubayi - Chairman/CEO

B-LINE COMMUNICATIONS LIMITED
Business: General Contracting
Address: 54, Town Planning Way, Ilupeju, Lagos
Tel: (01) 4701243, 7749537, 08023204513, 08022342345
Fax: (01) 5850018
Contact: Dr. (Prince) D. Okonkwo - Chairman

BLISS INFORMATION & COMMUNICATION SYSTEMS LTD
Business: IT Training, NIIT Licensee
Address: Plot 1094, Kolda Link, off Adetokunbo Ademola Crescent, Wuse II, Abuja.
Tel: (09) 5234318, 5234336, 5235560-1 (2L)
E-mail: wuse@niitng.com
niitabuja@linkserve.com

BLUE CHIP EXPRESS LIMITED
Business: Domestic & International Courier, Overseas Procurement and Cargo Servives
Address: 284, Ikorodu Road Anthony Lagos.
Tel: (01) 4930815 **Tel/Fax:** (01) 4970054
E-mail: bluechipexpress@hotmail.com
Website: www.bluechipexpress.net
Contact: Chief N. O. Adebiyi - MD/CEO

BLUE FUNNEL NIGERIA LIMITED
Business: Ship & Ocean Liner Agents
Address: 34, Wharf Road, Lagos
Tel: (01) 5803140-4, (5L), 5803410-4 (5L), 5803410
Fax: (01) 5871526, 5871560
E-mail: blue.funnelsales@alpha.linkserve.com
Contact: Gloria J. Wilhelm - Liner Manager

BLUE STAR SERVICES COMPANY LIMITED
Business: Management Services, Sales of Rice, Iron Rods & Cotton
Address: Marble House, 1 Alfred Rewane Road,Ikoyi, Lagos
Tel: (01) 2695108, 2695109, 2695110
Fax: (01) 2695009, 2965316
E-mail: dangote@dangote-group.com
* 32, Irede Road, opp. Trade Fair Complex, Abule-Oshun, Lagos-Badagry Expressway, Ojo, Lagos.

BLUEBERRY TECHNOLOGIES
Business: Internet Information Services for Real Estate Business
Address: 15, Obafemi Awolowo Way, Ikeja, Lagos
Tel: (01) 4922681, 8045837 **Fax:** (01) 7597251
E-mail: blueberry@infoweb.abs.net
Website: www.bluecores.com
Contact: Mr. Kolawole Olambiwonnu - Chairman/CEO

BLUEBIRD COMMUNICATIONS LIMITED
Business: Marketing Communications Services
Address: 22, Okunola Aina Street, Mende, Maryland, Lagos.
Tel: (01) 4961098, 4960193, 08023143710-1 (2L)
Fax: (01) 4960193
E-mail: bluebird@beta.linkserve.com
Contact: Mr Kunle Ogunmefun - MD/CEO

BLUE-CHIP COMMUNICATIONS LIMITED
Business: Sales & Installation of Commnication Equipment
Address: Plot 247B, Muri Okunola Street, off Ajose Adeogun Street, Victoria Island, Lagos
Tel: (01) 5558257, 8119455 **Fax:** (01) 4616162
Website: www.bluechipcomms.com

BMA NIGERIA LIMITED
Business: Civil Engineering Construction, Building, Mechanical & Electrical Engineering Consultancy
Address: 7, Bolo Street, D-Line, Port Harcourt
Tel: (084) 231062, 239015, 08033016799, 08033106321
Fax: (084) 230162
Contact: M. B. Ajala - Chairman/CEO

BNL ENGINEERING & CONSTRUCTION LIMITED
Business: Building Construction, Civil Engineering & Design
Address: Plot 564 & 565, Block D, Airport Road, Central Area, Garki, Abuja.
Tel: (09) 5239883-4 (2L), 4136615, 6121011
Fax: (09) 4136614, 6121671
E-mail: bnl@bouygues-constrction.com
*Plot 232A Adeola Odeku St Victoria Island, Lagos
Tel: (01) 2613590, 2619724 **Fax:** (01) 2615113
Contact: Mr. Christian Teutsch - MD/CEO

BOBBY INDUSTRIES LIMITED
Business: Production of Industrial Starch
Address: 75, Subaru Oje St, Caaso B/Stop, Alagbado, Lagos.
Tel: (01) 4936315, 4970486
Contact: Mr. Falayi E. Babatunde - MD/CEO

BOC GASES NIGERIA PLC
Business: Manufacture of Industrial, Special & Medical Gases, Assembly & Distribution of Medical & Welding Equipment

Address: Plots 1-3, Block H, Oshodi Industrial Estate, Oshodi Lagos.
Tel: (01) 4521326, 4523630, 4523659 **Fax:** (01) 4525865
* Mcdermott Road, Warri. **Tel:** (053) 250959
* 3, Kachia Road, Kaduna. **Tel:** (062) 232577
* Plot 94, Trans-Amadi Industrial Layout, RIVOC Road, Port Harcourt. **Tel:** (084) 572923
Contact: Mr. Johnson A. Idowu - MD/CEO

BODE ADEDIJI PARTNERSHIP
Business: Estate Surveying and Valuation, Real Estate Research and Construction, Property Consultants
Address: 43, Sinari Daranijo St, off Younis Bashorun St, Lagos
Tel: (01) 2622256, 2614382, 2622267. 2622269, 2622128
Fax: (01) 2622128
E-mail: bapestate@hyperia.com
Contact: Mr. Bode Adediji - Group Executive Chairman

BOD-GEE VENTURES NIGERIA LIMITED
Business: Engineering and Telecommunications
Address: 46, Adetokunbo Ademola St, Victoria Island, Lagos
Tel: (01) 2623682, 7747195 **Fax:** (01) 2623682
E-mail: bod-gee@beta.linkserve.com
Contact: Navy Cdre Olabode I. George (rtd) - Chairman/CEO

BOF DESIGN GALLERY LIMITED
Business: Manufacturing and Marketing of Furniture
Address: Orosi House (Ground Floor), 28, Forces Avenue, G.R.A Port Harcourt.
Tel: (084) 232049
* 24, Babs Animashaun Street, Surulere, Lagos.
Tel: (01) 5873720
* Abuja Sheraton Hotel (Suite 158/160), Wuse Zone 4, Abuja. **Tel:** (09) 6028408

BOFF & COMPANY INSURANCE BROKERS LIMITED
Business: Insurance Broking
Address: Great Nigeria House (2nd Floor), 8, Obafemi Awolowo Road, Oke-Ado, Ibadan
Tel: (02) 2313942, 2318175, 2310849 **Fax:** (02) 2312169
E-mail: boff.co@linkserve.com.ng
boff@skannet.com
Contact: Chief Babajide Olatunde-Agbeja - MD/CEO

BOGO SACKS NIGERIA LIMITED
Business: Manufacturing of Polyropylene Woven Sacks
Address: Km. 10, Hadejia Road, Kano.
Tel: (064) 649966, 630858 **Fax:** (064) 649966
Contact: Mr. Jamal Ammouri - Chairman/CEO

BOI-TEAC (NIGERIA) LIMITED
Business: Telecommunication Equipment Sales and Servicing
Address: 36, Airport Road, near Delta Palace Hotel, Warri
Tel/Fax: (053) 250876
* 23, Burma Road, Apapa, Lagos
* 29, Mbonu Street, D-Line, Port Harcourt
Contact: Mr. Ben O. Igwebuike - Chairman/CEO

BOLA ONABADEJO & COMPANY
Business: Estate Surveying and Valuation, Development, Management and Sales of Property; Agency and Consultancy Services
Address: 13, Ogundana St, off Allen Avenue, Ikeja, Lagos
Tel: (01) 4972215 - 6(2L) **Fax:** (01) 4972216
E-mail: bolaonas@hotmail.com
Website: www.niesv.org/boc.com
* Plot 122, Ikeja Crescent, Area 2, Section 1, P.O.Box 583, Garki, Abuja
Tel: (09) 2342374
Contact: Otunba B. O.Onabadejo - Managing Partner/CEO

BOLAMARK ENGINEERING LIMITED
Business: Electrical Contracting, Sales of Electrical Goods, Manufacturing of Low-Voltage Panels & Switchgears
Address: 10, Abebe Village Road, Iganmu, Lagos.
Tel: (01) 5850087, 5831806, 5845918 **Fax:** (01) 5831130
E-mail: bolamark@pinet.com.ng
Contact: Alh. F. B. Azeez - Chairman/CEO

BOLAX NIGERIA LIMITED
Business: Sales of Veterinary Drugs and Agro Chemicals
Address: 6, Kolawole Odunsi St, Unity Road, Ikeja, Lagos.
Tel: (01) 4962708, 4967408 **Fax:** (01) 4936875
E-mail: bolax@cyberspace.net.ng

BOLINGO HOTEL & TOWERS PLC
Business: Hospitality Services
Address: Independence Avenue, Garki Area 10, Abuja.
Tel: (09) 2344701-11 (11L) **Fax:** (09) 2344710
E-mail: bolingohotel@yahoo.com
Contact: Chief J. U. Igweh - Chairman/CEO

BOLORI BROTHERS & COMPANY LIMITED
Business: General Merchandising, Distributive Trade
Address: 18, Gumsu Road, P. O. Box 38, Maiduguri
Tel: (076) 232597, 233347
Contact: Alh. Bukar Bolori - Chairman
Alh. A. R. Yusuf - Marketing/Admin. Manager

BOLTON NIGERIA LIMITED
Business: Sales and Procurement of Oilfield Tools, Construction of Cold Rooms
Address: 114, Aba Road, Port Harcourt.
Tel/Fax: (084) 237704
* 7, Grace Bill Road, Eket.
Tel: (085) 701797
Contact: Mr Bola Ogunjinmi - Chairman/CEO

BOLU, TOKUN & COMPANY
Business: Estate Surveying and Valuation.
Address: 49, Lawson Street (1st Floor), off Moloney Street, Onikan, Lagos.
Tel: (01) 2633860, 2646635 **Fax:** (01) 2646635
E-mail: bolutokun@hyperia.com
Contact: Mr. Olugbenga Tokun - Principal Partner

BON TECHNICAL LIMITED
Business: Sales and Service of Security Equipment
Address: 280, Murtala Mohammed Way, Yaba, Lagos
Tel: (01) 864040, 7744245 **Fax:** (01) 860111
Contact: Mr. B. O. Nkwo - MD/CEO

BON VOYAGE TRAVEL AGENCY (NIGERIA) LIMITED
Business: Travel Agency, Tours & Pilgrimage Operations
Address: 57, A. J. Marinho Drive, Kuramo Waterfront,

P. O. Box 73459, Victoria Island, Lagos
Tel: (01) 4618874, 4618875, 08023010430, 08023525000
E-mail: bonvoyage@theobech.com

BONAMA NIGERIA LIMITED
Business: Sales of Audo-Visual Products, Training Equipment, Public Address Systems, Presentation and Communication Aids, Stands and Trolleys
Address: 61, Allen Avenue, Ikeja, Lagos.
Tel: (01) 4972381, 4938622 **Fax:** (01) 4938622
E-mail: bonama@infoweb.abs.net
* Goodness Plaza (1st Floor), Plot 627, Sokode Crescent, opp. Federal Inland Revenue, Wuse Zone 5, Abuja.
Tel: (09) 5239704, 5239708
Contact: Mr. Chris Okere - Chairman/CEO

BOND BANK LIMITED
Business: Universal Banking Services
Address: 3, Akin Adesola Street, Victoria Island, Lagos
Tel: (01) 2627760-9 (10L) **Fax:** (01) 2627598
E-mail: bondbank@bondbankng.com
Website: www.bondbankng.com

BOND CHEMICAL INDUSTRIES LIMITED
Business: Manufacturing of Pharmaceutical Products
Address: Bond House (1st Floor), 22A, Alafia Street, off Isolo Road, Mushin, Lagos
Tel: (01) 4522975, 4521014
E-mail: bonchem@infoweb.abs.net

BONIMAS NIGERIA LIMITED
Business: General Merchants, Marketing of Petroleum Products, Transportation, Agro-Allied Business
Address: 55, Azikiwe Road, P. O. Box 2035, Aba
Tel: (082) 234689 **Fax:** (082) 232883
E-mail: bonimas@phca.linkserve.com
Contact: Chief B. O. Mbachu - Chairman/CEO

BONNY ALLIED INDUSTRIES LIMITED
Business: Importation of Bulk Cement, Bagging and Marketing of ROCK Brand of Cement
Address: Cement House, Akpajo Junction, Eleme Road, Port Harcourt
Tel: (084) 571841, 571913
* Federal Ocean Terminal, Onne via Eleme, Rivers State. **Tel:** (082) 440625

BOOF AFRICA INSURANCE BROKERS LIMITED
Business: Insurance Broking
Address: 26, Montgomery Road, opp. All Saints Church Yaba, Lagos
Tel: (01) 5850271, 5850272, 860947 **Fax:** (01) 4527632
E-mail: boof@infoweb.abs.net
* 6, Zaria Road, Garki II, Abuja
Tel: (09) 2345953 **Fax:** (09) 2345954
* 3, Worlu Street, opp Sedco Forex, off Olu Obasanjo Road, Port Harcourt
Tel: (084) 231433, 232121, 332121
* 14, Kudeti Avenue, Onireke, Ibadan
Tel: (02) 2411120
Contact: Dr. Bode Olajumoke - Chairman
Mr B Olumide Fatogun - MD/CEO

BOOK SERVICES (WEST AFRICA) LIMITED
Business: Development, Networking, Furnishing and Computerization of Libraries, Book Procurement, Library Security and Book Protection
Address: 11, Ademola Street, off Awolowo Road, S. W. Ikoyi, Lagos
Tel: (01) 2694535, 2691749 **Fax:** (01) 2691749
E-mail: bookserwa@bookserv.com
Website: www.bookserv.com
* Bobsar Office Complex (Suite C9), off Ahmadu Bello Way, Garki II, Abuja

BOOKWORM LIMITED
Business: Retail of Books and Allied Products, Book Services
Address: Eko Hotel Shopping Complex (Unit 6), 1, Ajose Adeogun Street, Victoria Island, Lagos
Tel: (01) 3200606, 08023089323, 08037154293
Fax: (01) 3200606
E-mail: bookworm@nova.net.ng
* The Russel Centre (Shop F15), Plot 2425, Herbert Macaulay Way, Zone 4, Wuse, Abuja
Contact: Mr. Kunle Akinkugbe - Chairman
Mrs. Adeola Adewunmi - MD/CEO

BORG & HESS MOTORS LIMITED
Business: Sales & Service of Motor Vehicles
Address: Isaacstan Close, 1st Gate Bus-Stop, off Wempco Road, Ogba Industrial Scheme, Lagos
Tel: (01) 4808056, 5557557, 08023103781

BORINI PRONO & COMPANY (NIGERIA) LIMITED
Business: Civil Engineering & Building Contractors
Address: 7/9, Burma Road, Apapa, Lagos.
Tel: (01) 5876087, 5875751 **Fax:** (01) 5871397
* 18, Ahmed Talib Avenue, Kaduna
Tel: (062) 231864, 232270 **Fax:** (062) 232270
Contact: Mr. A. Prono - MD/CEO

BORNO ALUMINIUM COMPANY LIMITED
Business: Manufacturing of Aluminium Roofing & Cladding
Address: 9/12, Galadima Road, Maiduguri
Tel: (076) 233993, 235218
Fax: (076) 235218
E-mail: bacc@infoweb.com.ng
* Total Filling Station (Suite 5), Sultan Abubakar Way, Wuse Zone 5, Abuja
Tel: (09) 5238506

BORNO INVESTMENT COMPANY LIMITED
Business: Development Finance Institution
Address: 10, Nguru Road, P. M. B. 1023, Maiduguru
Tel: (076) 231703, 231295, 231998, 08043160150
Fax: (076) 231703
Contact: Alh. Mohammed Sanusi Liman - MD/CEO

BORODO & COMPANY (NIGERIA) LIMITED
Business: Sales of Car-Security System, Fire-Fighting Equipment and Satellite Communication Dishes
Address: 16, Beirut Road, Kano
Tel: (064) 649026, 630793, 630795, 08034567877
Fax: (064) 630793
E-mail: borodo@mail.com
Contact: Alh. Bashir M. Borodo - Chairman/CEO

BOSKEL NIGERIA LIMITED
Business: Thermal Process Engineering, Sales of Smokeless Flares & Burners and Waste Incinerators
Address: 37, Nembe Rd, Rumuibekwe Estate, Port Harcourt
Tel/Fax: (084) 612352, 612353
E-mail: boskel@aol.com

BOTNIC METALCRAFT (NIGERIA) LIMITED
Business: Metal Fabrication (Wrought Iron Gates, Iron Chairs & Tables, Fence Railings and Balcony Railings)
Address: A/4, Lagos State Small-Scale Industrial Estate, Fatai Atere Way, Matori, Mushin, Lagos.
Tel: (01) 4526397, 4520854, 4522581 **Fax:** (01) 4526397
E-mail: botnic99@yahoo.com
Website: www.botnic-metalcraft.com
Contact: Engr. 'Biodun Johnson - Chairman/CEO

BOULOS ENTERPRISES LIMITED
Business: Marketing of SUZUKI Motorcycles, Generators & Outboard Engines, Domestic Plastics, Toilet Tissues, Water Heaters, Water Pumps, Fuel Filters & Gas Cookers
Address: Plot 10, Block D, Acme Road, Ogba Industrial Scheme, Ikeja, Lagos.
Tel: (01) 5557972-4 (3L) **Fax:** (01) 2619609, 5557971
E-mail: boulos@micro.com.ng
Contact: Mr. Gabriel G. Boulos - MD/CEO

BOURDEX TELECOMMUNICATION LIMITED
Business: Manufacturing, Trading, Telecommunications, Financial Services, Importation of General Goods, Estate Developers
Address: 1,First Ave,Ubani Ukaoma Layout, Ogbor Hill, Aba
Tel: (082) 440082-9 (8L), 440000, 440898
Fax: (082) 440094
* 100, Awolowo Road, S W, Ikoyi, Lagos
Tel: (01) 2693205, 2693609 **Fax:** (01) 2615974
Contact: Chief David Ogba Onuoha - Chairman/CEO

BOUSSALLE GROUP LIMITED
Business: Engineering, General Contracting and Merchandising, Stock & Property Brokerage, Oil & Marine Services, Financial Consultancy, Haulage, Real Estate Development, Telecommunications & Interior Decoration
Address: Boussale House, 50, Bornu Crescent, Apapa,Lagos
Tel: (01) 5453620, 5453621 **Fax:** (01) 5453622
E-mail: bousalle@infoweb.abs.net
*Plot 620, Ihiala Close, Area 8, Garki, Abuja
*8 Abobiri Crescent, off Harbour Rd, Port Harcourt
Contact: Chief S. B. O. Ugwoebu - Chairman/CEO

BOWCLOSE NIGERIA LIMITED
Business: Importation and Sales of Animal-Pet Foods
Address: 83B, Marine Road, Apapa, G.R.A., Lagos.
Tel: (01) 5451177, 5877321, 4818128, 7915946

BOWSPRING INDUSTRIES LIMITED
Business: Distribution and Sales of Pharmaceutical Products
Address: 19, Ogunu Road, Warri
Tel/Fax: (053) 255504
E-mail: bowspharm@infoweb.abs.net
Contact: Engr. Enoch Nwobi - Chairman/CEO

BOX OFFICE NIGERIA LIMITED
Business: Sales of Personal-Wear Fashion Items
Address: Metro Park, 31, Isaac John St, G.R.A., Ikeja, Lagos
Tel: (01) 4975966, 7741588
* Asokoro Shopping Mall, Plot 1552, T. Y. Danjuma Street, Asokoro, Abuja
Tel: (09) 3149028, 08033081484
Contact: Mr. Blaise Igbonwelundu - MD/CEO

BOYLE-STREET CONSULTING LIMITED
Business: Organisational Consulting, In-House Training and Open Programmes, Recruitment
Address: 12, Boyle Street (1st Floor, Suite 2), Onikan, Lagos.
Tel: (01) 2632525, 2637968, 08033020057, 08034022967, 08037876478 **Fax:** (01) 2631231
E-mail: boylecon@skannet.com
boylecob@hyperia.com
Contact: Mr. Dapo Oyewumi - MD/CEO

BRAINWAVE LIMITED
Business: Internet Service Provider, Internet Cafe, Telephony, Web Hosting and Domain Name Regisitration, VSAT Procurement & Installation
Address: 2, Tafawa Balewa Street, P.O.Box 13141, Jos
Tel: (073) 454221, 08033551984 **Fax:** (073) 450091
E-mail: bestman@bwave.net
Website: www.bwave.net
Contact: Mr. Bestman Uwadia - MD/CEO

BOYSON (NIGERIA) LIMITED
Business: Security Services
Address: 1, Gafari Balogun Street Opebi, Ikeja, Lagos
Tel: (01) 935195
Contact: Dr. Nnamdi Okonkwo - MD/CEO

BRACON WIRE & CABLE (NIGERIA) LIMITED
Business: Manufacturing of Electrical Wires & Cables
Address: Km 34, Lagos- Abeokuta Expressway, Anije Bus-Stop, Lagos
Tel: (01) 4523665, 7740782

BRAINPOWER LIMITED
Business: Newsletter Publishing
Address: Plot 932, Idejo Street, Victoria Island, Lagos.
Tel: (01) 3210819, 7755365
E-mail: udogie@yahoo.com
Contact: Mr. Martin E. Udogie - MD/CEO

BRAITHWAITE WATER RESOURCES (NIGERIA) LIMITED
Business: Supply and Installation of Pressed Steel Sectional Water Storage Tanks/Tower/Pipework/Pumps
Address: Tractor & Equipment Premises, Billingsway, Oregun Industrial Estate, Oregun Ikeja, Lagos
Tel: (01) 4703134, 4930430-3 (4 L) **Fax:** (01) 4964499
Contact: Mr. Evan Bode Thomas - MD/CEO

BRAND SUPPORT SERVICES LIMITED
Business: Publishing of Marketing Journals
Address: Plot 44, Oki-Balogun Street, Magodo G. R. A., Shangisha, Lagos
Tel: (01) 5557872, 7743381, 4735219, 08034705218, 08037133377
Contact: Mr. Tokunbo Modupe - MD/CEO

BRANDS & PRODUCTS ENTERPRISES
Business: Publishing of Marketing Trade Journal
Address: 8B, Adenubi Close, off Allen Avenue, by Oshopey Plaza, Ikeja, Lagos
Tel: (01) 4933160, 4813852, 8905451, 8905447, 8905450, 08033163233
Contact: Mr. Adebola Familoni - Executive Director

BRANDS INTERNATIONAL COMPANY LIMITED
Business: Trading, Project Development & Management, Manufacturer's Representative, Publishing
Address: 43, Town Planning Way, Ilupeju Ind. Estate, Lagos.
Tel/Fax: (01) 4926943
Contact: Mr A A Buraimoh-Ademuyewo - Chairman/CEO

BRAS MOTORS LIMITED
Business: Marketing of Automobiles, Car Rentals
Address: 30A Adetokunbo Ademola StVictoriaIsland,Lagos.
Tel: (01) 2623932, 610988,7746666 **Fax:** (01) 8047905
Contact: Mr. Abayomi Sonuga - Chairman/CEO

BRAWAL LINES NIGERIA LIMITED
Business: Shipping, Warehousing, Terminal Operatios
Address: Maritime House, Kirikiri Lighter Terminal Phase 1, Oshodi-Apapa Expressway, Apapa, Lagos.
Tel: (01) 5872491, 5872582, 5873561, 5871684
Fax: (01) 5876355, 5877376, 5873450
E-mail: aerogrup@infoweb.abs.net
* Investment House, 3, Grace, Avenue Elelenwo, P.M.B. 6061, Port Harcourt
Tel: (084) 332934, 239428, 238005, 612480 (3L)
Fax: (084) 238006
* Shed 3, Fed. Lighter Terminal, Onne, P/ Harcourt.
Tel: (084) 820033
Contact: Chief Victor I. Odili - Chairman/CEO

BRAWAL SHIPPING (NIGERIA) LIMITED
Business: Clearing , Forwarding, Shipping Services, Oilbase
Address: Maritime House, Kirikiri Wharf Terminal Phase 1, Oshodi Expressway, Kirikiri Wharf, Apapa, Lagos.
Tel: (01) 5872491, 5872582, 5873561, 5871659, 5876603
Fax: (01) 5876355, 5873450
E-mail: aerogroup@infoweb.abs.net
* Investment House, 3,Grace, Avenue, Elelenwo, Port Harcourt
Contact: Chief Victor I. Odili - Chairman/CEO

BREDERO SHAW (NIGERIA) LIMITED
Business: Oil & Gas Pipeline Coating Services, Supply of FBE/P.E Pipecoating and Concrete Weight Coating
Address: Plot 239D, Kofo Abayomi St, Victoria Island, Lagos
Tel: (01) 2616643 **Fax:** (01) 2622148
Website: www.brederoprice.com
Contact: Mr. Stuart Mclennan - Lagos Office

BREWTECH NIGERIA LIMITED
Business: Consultancy and Engineering Services to Brewing, Beverage-Producing & Plastic Industries
Address: 1, Brewtech Street, off Adenekan Street, Okota Estate, Isolo, Lagos.
Tel: (01) 524702, 524615, 524671, 524543, 2882507
Fax: (01) 2882507, 524702
Contact: Mr Jobst Meier zu Biesen - MD/CEO

BRIAN MUNRO LIMITED
Business: Manufacturing of Consumer Goods, Nutritional and Pharmaceutical Products
Address: 25, Ize Iyamu Street, Oregun Industrial Estate, Oregun, Ikeja, Lagos.
Tel: (01) 4972379, 4972380, 7745676 **Fax:** (01) 4972380
E-mail: bmoffice@rumon-nigeria.com
Contact: Ms. Lizzy Iroha - Marketing Services Manager

BRICK HOUSE CONSTRUCTION COMPANY LIMITED
Business: Architectural & Building Construction Servies
Address: 6, Tiamiyu Street, Mende, Maryland, Lagos
Tel: (01) 4703151, 4938294 **Fax:** (01) 4938294
E-mail: brickhse@alpha.linkserve.com

BRICKFIELD CONCERNS LIMITED
Business: Property Development and Estate Management, Logistic Support Services, Petroleum Marketing, Pest Control and Environmental Services
Address: 7, Oyin Jolayemi Street, Victoria Island, Lagos
Tel: (01) 2621906, 2623487 **Fax:** (01) 2621906
Contact: Mr. M. N. Nwaokolo-Oba - MD/CEO

BRIGHT MOTORS LIMITED
Business: Sales and Service of Motor Cars
Address: 9B, Adeola Odeku Street, Victoria Island, Lagos.
Tel: (01) 613815
Contact: Chief Johnson Anumudu - Chairman/CEO

BRIGHTWAY INTERNATIONAL (NIGERIA) LIMITED
Business: Importation, Marketing and Distribution of Diary Products and General Merchandise
Address: 63/78, Lawanson Street, Surulere, Lagos.
Tel: (01) 5851146, 5851526, 5851227, 2660713, 2666030
Fax: (01) 5850211
E-mail: brightwayint@yahoo.com

BRIGHTWAYS INSURANCE BROKERS LIMITED
Business: Insurance Broking
Address: 2, Rasaq Okoya Lane, off Igbosere Road, Lagos
Tel: (01) 2632674, 2635719 **Fax:** (01) 2635719
Contact: Mr. Kayode Odusegun - GM/CEO

BRILA BROADCASTING SERVICES LIMITED (88.9 Brila FM)
Business: Sports Consultancy, Sports Events Marketing, Sponshorship Advisory Services, Programmes Production for Radio and Television, Printing Press and Audio-Visual Studios, Broadcasting
Address: Eleganza Biro Plaza (10th Floor), Plot 634, Adeyemo Alakija Street, Victoria Island, P. O. Box 75504, Victoria Island, Lagos
Tel: (01) 2702948, 4812119, 4734333 **Fax:** (01) 2702948
E-mail: info@brila.net
Website: www.brila.net
Contact: Mr. Larry Izamoje - Chairman/CEO

BRISCOEatlascopco (Div of R.T.Briscoe Nig Plc)
Business: Sales and Service of "Atlascopo" Stationary & Portable Air Compressors, Electric Generators
Address: 16/18, Fatai Atere Way, Matori Industrial Scheme, Oshodi, Lagos.
Tel: (01) 4522175, 4520564, 4523201, 4524497, 4524560

4524579, 7741751 **Fax:** (01) 4524519, 4522943
E-mail: name@rtb.com.ng
* 105, Olusegun Obasanjo Way, Central Business District, Abuja.
* 17, Azikiwe Road, Port Harcourt
Tel: (084) 238115, 238116, 335685 **Fax:** (084) 238116
Contact: Mr. Jens Erik Mollenbach - Group MD/CEO

BRISCOEmobile (Div of R.T.Briscoe Nig Plc)
Business: Distribution, Marketing, Sales & Service of GSM Phones & Accessories, Communication
Address: 18, Fatai Atere Way, Matori Industrial Estate, Mushin, Lagos
Tel: (01) 4520564, 4522175, 4524560
Fax: (01) 4524519, 4522943
E-mail: mobile@rtb.com.ng
* 105, Olusegun Obasanjo Way, opp. Leventis Stores, Central Business District, Abuja
Tel: (09) 2349224, 2349225
* 17A, Azikiwe Road, Port Harcourt
Tel: (084) 238115, 335685, 238116, 08033062429
Fax: (084) 238116
* 6, Saka Tinubu Street, Victoria Island Lagos
Contact: Mr. Olumide Olugbile - CEO

BRISCOEmotors (Div of R.T.Briscoe Nig Plc)
Business: Distribution, Sales and Service of Toyota Vehicles and Spare Parts
Address: 16/18, Fatai Atere Way, Matori Industrial Scheme, Oshodi, Lagos
Tel: (01) 4520564, 4522175, 4524560, 7741752
Fax: (01) 4524519
E-mail: sales@rtb.com.ng
services@rtb.com.ng
Contact: Mr. Jens Erik Mollenbach - MD/CEO

BRISTOL HOTEL
Business: Hotel and Catering Services
Address: 18, Oba-Elegushi Road (Club Road), Ikoyi, Lagos.
* 8, Martins Street, off Broad Street, Lagos.
Tel: (01) 2661204, 2661207, 2661296 **Fax:** (01) 2661296
Contact: Mr. O. J. S. Attah - GM

BRISTOW HELICOPTERS (NIGERIA) LIMITED
Business: Air Charters, Air Transportation (Aeroplanes & Helicopters), Support Services to Oil Exploration/ Production Activities)
Address: General Aviation Terminal, Murtala Mohammed Airport, Ikeja, Lagos.
Tel: (01) 4961070, 4962610 **Fax:** (01) 4961501
Contact: Capt. F. D. Layton - MD/CEO

BRITISH AIRWAYS (NIGERIA)
Business: International Airline Service
Address: 3/5 Oyinkan Abayomi Drive, Waterfront, Ikoyi, Lagos
Tel: (01) 4978660-9 (10 L), 4970311
* Corporation Building, Aba Road, Port Harcourt
Tel: (084) 331986, 238351, 334600
* NICON Hilton Hotel, Maitama, Abuja
Tel: (09) 4139610, 4139608
Website: www.british-airways.com/nigeria
Contact: Mr. Andy Stern - GM

BRITISH-AMERICAN TOBACCO COMPANY (NIGERIA) LTD
Businees: Production of Cigarette and Tobacco Products
Address: PC 35, Idowu Taylor Street, Victoria Island, Lagos
Tel: (01) 2625770-4 (5L), 4617500-4 (5L), 4617104
Fax: (01) 2625780, 3201801, 4617514
* 2, Tobacco Road, Muchia, Zaria, Kaduna State.
Tel: (069) 333421-5 (5L)
* BAT Factory, Ibadan-Lagos Expressway, near Toll Gate, Ibadan.
* Oyo House (2nd Floor), Ralph Shodeinde St, off Ahmadu Bello Way, Central District, Abuja.
Tel: (09) 2348647, 6702168 **Fax:** (09) 2348651
Contact: Mr Richard Hodgson - MD/CEO
Mr Kehinde Johnson - Corporate Affairs Director

BROAD BANK OF NIGERIA LIMITED
Business: Commercial Banking
Address: Plot 1668, Oyin Jolayemi St, Victoria Island, Lagos
Tel: (01) 3200096, 3200097, 3200099, 3200100, 7740800, 7745384
E-mail: broadbank@hyperia.com
Website: www.broadbankng,com
Contact: Mr Austen Obigwe - MD/CEO

BROADCROWN WEST AFRICA LIMITED
Business: Sales, Installation, Maintenance & Service of Generations, Sales of Generator Parts
Address: 2, Kudirat Abiola Way, Alausa, Ikeja, Lagos
Tel: (01) 4822576-7 (2 L), 08034079759
E-mail: broadcrownwa@hotmail.com
Website: www.broadcrown.com

BROADEDGE SECURITIES LIMITED
Business: Stockbroking
Address: Unity House (4th Floor), 37, Marina, Lagos
Tel: (01) 2666435, 2666438 **Fax:** (01) 2666435
Contact: Mr. Lekan Otesile - MD/CEO.

BROADLINE SERVICES LIMITED
Business: Courier Services, Cargo Operations, Clearing and Forwarding, Consolidators and Airline Agents
Address: 18A Simbiat Abiola Road, Ikeja, Lagos
Tel: (01) 4936151, 4960297, 3450497, 08023134792, 08037181923 **Fax:** (01) 4930419
E-mail: blineexp@yahoo.com
Website: www.broadlineexpress.com
Contact: E. Oluwole Adeyemi - MD/CEO.

BROADLINK AVIATION & CARGO SERVICES LIMITED
Business: Cargo Services. Airline Agents
Address: Akron House, 86A, Allen Avenue, Ikeja, Lagos
Tel: (01) 4935429, 7743254, 4708331
E-mail: broadlink@beta.linkserve.com
broadlink@onebox.com
* 20, Lewis Street, Lagos Island, Lagos
Tel: (01) 2637520
Contact: Capt. Mike Omokore - MD/CEO

BROMLEY LIMITED
Business: Financial Advisory/Consultancy Services
Address: Fortune Towers, 27, Adeyemo Alakija Street (7th Floor), Victoria Island, Lagos
Tel: (01) 2610458-9(2L) **Fax:** (01) 2610456

E-mail: info@bromleycorp.com
Contact: Mr. Henry Efe Imasekha - Chairman/CEO
Mr. Blessing Irubor - Accountant

BROSSETTE (NIGERIA) LIMITED
Business: Fabrication and Fixing of Aluminium Door & Windows, Distribution of Industrial Equipment;Consultancy/Contracts in Hydraulic & Irrigation Systems, Fabrication of Shelters
Address: 311, Apapa Road, Lagos
Tel: (01) 5803310, 5803311, 5803312, 5803313
Fax: (01) 5875374
Contact: Mr. Jean-Pierre Lamarque - MD/CEO

BRUME SANKEY MEDICAL LIMITED
Business: Sales and Maintenance of Medical & Laboratory Equipment
Address: 10, Stephen Osibote Close, off Oludegun Street, Ire-Akari Estate Road, Okota Layout, Isolo, Lagos
Tel: (01) 4523026, 4524276 **Fax:** (01) 4521277, 4526422
E-mail: sankey@infoweb.abs.net
Contact: Mr. Vincent O. Sankey - Chairman/CEO

BRUNELLI CONSTRUCTION COMPANY NIGERIA LIMITED
Business: Piling, Railway, Civil Engineering and Building Contractors. Manufacture of Precast Spun Concrete Poles to NEPA Specifications
Address: Km. 3, Lagos-Badagry Expressway, By Alafia Bus-Stop, Orile-Iganmu, Lagos
Tel: (01) 7741803
Contact: Alh. A..S..A. Dantata - Chairman
Engr. Dante Piccolo Brunelli - MD/CEO

BTAS COMMUNICATIONS LIMITED
Business: Advertising and Public Relations
Address: 59, Aba Johnson Crescent, off Adeniyi Jones Avenue, Ikeja, Lagos
Tel: (01) 4926102, 4961837, 2904091 **Fax:** (01) 4961837
E-mail: btas@beta.linkserve.com
Contact: Mr Bola Oludairo - MD/CEO

BTN (NIGERIA) LIMITED
Business: Sales and Service of Telecommunication Systems
Address: 23, Festival Road, Victoria Island, Lagos
Tel: (01) 2647133, 2647137 **Fax:** (01) 2647133
E-mail: btntelecom@nigol.net.ng
Contact: Engr. Y. A. Raji - MD/CEO

BUA INTERNATIONAL LIMITED
Business: General Merchandising, Manufacturing, General Imports (Rice, Sugar, Fertiliser, Cement)
Address: 58, Ibrahim Taiwo Road, Kano
Tel: (064) 645930, 634313, 649935
E-mail: rabiu@bua.com.ng
* 22B, Creek Road, Apapa, Lagos
Tel: (01) 5451584, 5878087, 5876260 **Fax:** (01) 5876110
E-mail: bua@bua.com.ng
Website: www.bua.com.ng
Contact: Khalifa Isiyaku Rabiu - Chairman
Alh. Abdulsamad Rabiu - President/CEO

BUCKLES LIMITED
Business: Sales of Shoes and Leather Accessories
Address: Lafayette Mall (Suite 3), Plot 1436, Sanusi Fafunwa Street, Victoria Island, Lagos
Tel: (01) 3200192 **Fax:** (01) 5450688
E-mail: osben@linkserve.com.ng
* 34, Awolowo Road, Ikoyi, Lagos
Tel: (01) 2670283; Fax: (01) 5450688
* Suite B22, McLewis Plaza, Wuse II, Abuja
* Buckles Plaza, 7, Babbe Street, D-Line, by Matinique Restaurant, off Aba Road/Mbonu St, Port Harcourt.
Tel: (084) 232360
Contact: Mr. Ben-Willy Owuapu - MD/CEO.

BUFAMBRA INDUSTRIES LIMITED
Business: Importers and Distributors of Batteries, Fire Extinguishers and Security Devices for Cars, Distribution and Sales of Skin Care Products
Address: ASPAMDA Plaza, Trade Fair Comples, Lagos-Badagry Expressway, Abule-Osun, Ojo, Lagos
Tel: (01) 2664809 **Fax:** (01) 2882319
* Glass House, 21, Oregun Road, Ikeja, Lagos
Contact: Chief Franklin Okeke - Chairman/CEO

BUG BUSTERS LIMITED
Business: Pest Management, Environmental Services; Marketing of Pest-Control Equipment
Address: 53, Bode Thomas Road, off Shyllon Street, Palmgrove, Shomolu, Lagos
Tel: (01) 8042761, 08023005258
E-mail: bugbusters_ltd@yahoo.com
Contact: Mr. Kayode Odubogun - MD/CEO

BUHARI PROPERTIES & INVESTMENTS
Business: Real Estate Development and Management
Address: Gidan Buhari, 12/13, Zoo Road, P. O. Box 778, Kano
Contact: Alh. Buhari Sani - MD/CEO

BUILDERS' MALL LIMITED
Business: Manufacturing & Installation of Security Doors
Address: 16, Aromire Avenue, off Adeniyi Jones Avenue, Ikeja, Lagos
Tel: (01) 49337490
E-mail: buildersmall@cyberspace.net.ng
buildersmall@hotmail.com
Contact: Arc. Melie Nwankwo - Chairman/CEO.

BUILDING & TECHNICAL INFORMATION CONSULTANTS
Building: Architectural Consultancy; Software & Hardware Consultancy
Address: Princess Plaza, 2, Araromi Street, off Moloney Street, Onikan, Lagos
Tel: (01) 2647140, 2647148 **Fax:** (01) 2647140
E-mail: btic@nova.com.ng
Contact: Arc. Paul Taiwo Aina - Managing Partner/CEO.

BUILDING DEVELOPMENT & CONSTRUCTION LIMITED
Business: Building and Civil Engineering Contractors
Address: CSS Bookshop House (5th Floor), 50/52, Broad Street, Lagos Island, Lagos
Tel: (01) 2645723, 2645724 **Fax:** (01) 2630858

BUILDING SERVICES PRODUCTS LIMITED
Building: Sales and Service of Building Industry Products

Address: D4, Alh. Masha Street, Surulere, Lagos
Tel: (01) 5847953, 837871, 7743818 **Fax:** (01) 5849730
* Delec House, Km. 4, Apapa-Oshodi Expressway (Sanya Bus-Stop), Lagos
* Plot 418, Bamako Street, Wuse Zone 1, Abuja
Tel: (09) 5238492
Contact: Mr. O. A. Odoh-Tadafe - MD/CEO.

BUILDING STOCK LIMITED
Building: Real Estate Investment, Property Brokerage
Address: House D17, H.F.P. Way, Dolphin Estate, Ikoyi, Lagos
Tel: (01) 2696197, 2691249 **Fax:** (01) 2696197
E-mail: buildstock@infoweb.abs.net
* UNIC Insurance Building Plot 1046, Ahmadu Bello Way, Garki II, Wuse, Abuja
Tel/Fax: (09) 3140942, 3140943
E-mail: blgstock@infoweb.abs.net

BUILDWELL PLANTS & EQUIPMENT INDUSTRIES LTD
Building: Building Construction, Heavy Equipment Haulage, Hire and Lease of Heavy Duty Equipment
Address: 41, Hospital Road, opposite Ibru Warehouse, Apapa-Isolo Expressway, Olodi-Apapa, Lagos
Tel: (01) 5454491-2 (2 L), 5450145 **Fax:** (01) 5450227
E-mail: buildwell@hyperia.com
*Plot 309,Trans-Amadi Phase II Layout, PHarcourt.
Tel: (084) 238094-5 (2 L)
Contact: Chief R. A. Habib - Chairman/CEO.

BULET INTERNATIONAL (NIGERIA) LIMITED
Business: Civil Engineering, Building Construction Contractors and Consultants
Address: Plot 4, Shehu Shagari Way, Central Business District, Garki, Abuja.
Tel: (09) 2344180, 5233139 **Fax:** (09) 2347063
E-mail: buletng@metrong.com
Contact: Mr. Pavel Zarev - MD/CEO

BULKSHIP (NIGERIA) LIMITED
Business: Ship-Owners, Operators of Dry Bulk Cargo,
Address: 22. Creek Road, Apapa, Lagos
Tel: (01) 5877573, 5877451, 5450473, 5877316
Fax: (01) 5877638
E-mail: bulkship@oan.com.ng
*c/o OAN Overseas Agency Nigeria Limited Km. 4, Refinery Road, off St. Peter's Church, opp Ekpan Police Station, Effurun, Warri.
Tel: (053) 252524
Contact: Mr J. J. Bonmarchand - MD

BUKMOT LIMITED
Business: Sales & Repairs of ID Card Printers and Accessories, Production of Plastic ID Cards
Address: 89, Palm Avenue, Mushin, Lagos
Tel: (01) 4715314, 4721340, 08033056755
E-mail: bukmot@yahoo.com
Contact: Mr. Olubukola Ladipo - Chairman/CEO

BUNDI (NIGERIA) LIMITED
Business: Importation of Textiles and General Goods
Address: 117, Cameroun Road, Aba
Tel: (082) 232646
Contact: Chief Robert Udeaga - Chairman/MD/CEO.

BUNIT (NIGERIA) LIMITED
Business: Manufacturing of Portable Accommodation
Address: 3, Church Street (2nd Floor), off Olowu Street, Ikeja, Lagos
Tel: (01) 4748136, 4937031 **Fax:** (01) 4937031

BUOSHISHI HOLDINGS LIMITED
Business: Sales of Hospital Equipment and Diagnostic Reagents, Civil & Electrical Engineering, Printing Services, Travel Agency, General Contractors
Address: Intercity Bank Building (1st Floor), 89E, Ibrahim Taiwo Road, Kano
Tel: (064) 639194, 639195 **Fax:** (064) 630400
Contact: Alh. Y. A. Mohammed - Exec. Chairman/Group MD

BUREAU GROUP LIMITED
Business: Maritime Consultancy, Secured Commnications, Real Estate Developers & Managers, Printing, General Contractors
Address: 15, Ola Ayinde Street, off Mobolaji Bank-Anthony Way, Ikeja, Lagos
Tel: (01) 4936730, 4975354, 08033210348, 08023004028
Fax: (01) 4975354
E-mail: fomene@infoweb.com.ng
Contact: Dr. O. W. Omene - Chairman/CEO

BUREAU VERITAS NIGERIA LIMITED
Business: Cargo & Industrial Inspection Services, Consultancy Services
Address: 25, Glover Road, Ikoyi, Lgos
Tel: (01) 2692614-15 (2L), 2695248-39 (2L)
Fax: (01) 2693827, 2693157
* Plot A48, Birabi St, GRA Phase 1, Port Harcourt
Tel: (084) 256157
* Block 7, Aba Close, Garki Area 8, Abuja
Tel: (09) 2343238
Contact: Mr Gerard Lematre - MD/CEO

BURTOMLINE LIMITED
Businees: Marketing Communication, Advertising, Public Relations and Allied Services
Address: 3, John Olugbo Street, off Unity Road, Ikeja, Lagos
Tel: (01) 4713900, 7761289, 08033067079
E-mail: BURTOMLINE@yahoo.com
Contact: Mr Dele Daramola - MD/CEO

BUSINESS COMPUTERS & INFORMATION SYSTEMS LTD
Business: Sales of Computers, Telecommunication Equipment & Accessories;.Networking; Training
Address: Plot 14, Old Aba Road, by Shell Residential Area, off Aba/Port Harcourt Expressway, Rumukurusi Junction, Port Harcourt
Tel: (084) 611897, 610686, 613034 **Fax:** (084) 613033
E-mail: bcis@bcisnet.com
Website: www.bcisnet.net
*1B, Tinuade St, off Allen Avenues, Ikeja, Lagos
Tel: (01) 4932169
Contact: Mr. I. T. D. Braide - MD/CEO

BUSINESS CONTRACTING LIMITED
Business: Building & Civil Engineering and Construction, Real Estate Development and Management
Address: Maritime House, 4, Burma Road, Apapa, Lagos

Tel: (01) 5872918, 5451645 **Fax:** (01) 5451645
E-mail: bcllagos@hyperia.com
* Plot 186, A4 Deeper Life Road, off Shehu Shagari Road, Asokoro, Abuja
Tel: (09) 3141787, 3141788 **Fax:** (09) 3141784
* Block 9, NEMI Estate, 11, Abuloma Road, Port Harcourt
Tel: (090) 503328

BUSINESS EDUCATION EXAMINATION COUNCIL
Business: Manpower Development and Training, Professional Examination Administration
Address: Kingsway Building (2nd Floor), 74/78, Kofo Abayomi Avenue, Apapa, Lagos
Tel: (01) 5803221, 5874254, 5874256, 5878179, 4931545
Fax: (01) 4931545, 5878179
E-mail: beectraining@alpha.linkserve.com
Contact: Prof. D. Abdulkadir - Chairman
Mr Mike O Okereke - President/CEO

BUSINESS VENTURES LIMITED
Business: Marketers of Petroleum Products (Buvel Oil)
Address: 222, Murtala Muhammed Way, Benin City
Tel: (052) 250590
Contact: Prince Kennedy Okoeguale - MD/CEO

BUSINESSDAY MEDIA LIMITED
Business: Publishing of Business Newspaper
Address: Plot 247, Amuwo-Festac Link Road, off Oshodi-Apapa Expressway, Amuwo-Odofin, Lagos
Tel: (01) 3454500-3 (4 L), 4701845, 3205954, 3205953, 08023000008
Fax: (01) 3454510
E-mail: mail@businessdayonline.com
Website: www.businessdayonline.com
* 1, Owena Street, off Suez Crescent, Ibrahim Abacha Estate, Zone 4, Wuse, Abuja
Tel: (09) 5231869 **Fax:** (09) 5231862
Contact: Prof. Pat Utomi - Chairman
Mr. Frank Aigbogun - CEO

BUSSDOR COMPANY LIMITED
Business: Civil Engineering & Procurement Services, Sales of Chemicals and Analytical Equipment.
Address: 2, Aba Road, Port Harcourt
Tel: (084) 234053, 236972 **Fax:** (084) 239925
E-mail: bussdor@infoweb.abs.net
* Close 21, House 10, Satellite Town, Lagos
Tel: (01) 880986
Contact: Oscar Igokwe (JP) - Chairman/CEO.

BUTLER NIGERIA LIMITED
Business: Sales and Supply of Petroleum Products and Engineering Systems
Address: 2, Gabaro Close, Victoria Island, Lagos
Tel/Fax: (01) 2624377, 3201619, 2610670
E-mail: butler@nova.net.ng
Contact: Major-Gen. M. M. Magoro (rtd.) - Chairman

BVM FURNITURE LIMITED
Business: Marketing of Furniture
Address: 78, Awolowo Road, S.W., Ikoyi, Lagos
Tel: (01) 2671616, 08033027885, 090-801269

C & A PRINTS NIGERIA LIMITED
Business: Printing Services
Address: 4, Ilupeju Bye-pass, Ilupeju, Lagos
Tel/Fax: (01) 4970103, 5550295-7 (3L) **Fax:** (01) 4970103
E-mail: candaprint@hyperia.com
Contact: Mr. Kayode Apara - GM/CEO

C & C CONSTRUCTION COMPANY LIMITED
Business: Construction, Building and Civil Engineering
Address: C & C Towers, Plot 1684, Sanusi Fafunwa Street, Victoria Island, Lagos
Tel: (01) 2620793-4 (2 L) **Fax:** (01) 2611307
E-mail: ccmain@hyperia.com
Contact: Mr. Ronald R. Chagoury - Chairman/CEO.

C & D PAVING BLOCKS
Business: Manufacture and Sales of Paving Blocks
Address: Gate No. 2, Tincan Island Port Apapa, Lagos
Tel: (01) 5453295, 5450094 **Fax:** (01) 5871024
* Opp. Jabi Forest, Old Life Camp Road, Abuja.
Tel/Fax: (09) 5230836

C & I LEASING PLC
Business: Equipment Leasing, Capacity Utilization Financing, Invoice Discounting, Purchase Order, Project & Other Assets-Backed Financing Hertz Car Rentals
Address: 12, Keffi Street, Obalende, Lagos
Tel: (01) 2693978-80 (3L), 3205010-20
Fax: (01) 2693977
E-mail: c&ileasing@linkserve.com.ng
*13, Geodetic Road, Near Shell Industrial Area, Port Harcourt.
Tel/Fax: (084) 230652
E-mail: ci@infoweb.abs.net
Contact: Mr. Chukwuemeka Ndu - MD/CEO.

C. C & M LIMITED
Business: Importation (Stockfish), Exportation (Cotton Seeds, Cashew Nuts etc.)
Address: Mclver House (Suites 13 & 14), 61, Marina, Lagos
Tel: (01) 2640024, 2641194, 2621541
Fax: (01) 2641195, 2621542
E-mail: ccm@infoweb.abs.net
Contact: Mrs. C. H. Abba Gana - Chairman/CEO.

C. JOE KANNON INTERNATIONAL LIMITED
Business: Sales of Generators and Auto Spare Parts
Address: Zone A, Block 11 (Shops 62-65), ASPMDA Plaza, Trade Fair Complex, Badagry Expressway, Lagos.
Tel: (01) 3208497, 7748879
Contact: Chief Joseph Onyebuchi - Chairman/CEO

C. WOERMANN (NIGERIA) LIMITED
Business: Sales of Generators, Power Tools, Industrial and Agricultural Equipment, Sanitary Ware and Motor-Vehicle Spare Parts
Address: 6, Badejo Kalesanwo Street, Matori Industrial Estate, Mushin, Lagos
Tel: (01) 4526324, 7730904 **Fax:** (01) 4526324
E-mail: cwnl.mb@nova.net.ng

C. ZARD & COMPANY LIMITED
Business: Sales of Agrochemical Products and Lawnmowers.

Spraying Technology and Crop Protection
Address: 184, Adeniji Adele Road, opposite Pelewura Market, Idumagbo, Lagos Island, Lagos
Tel: (01) 8044832, 2667586, 2667588, 2667590
* Plot 511, Obafemi Awolowo Way, Jabi, Abuja
Tel: (09) 2341908
Contact: Mr. G. A. Akle - Chairman/CEO.

C. F. CANUTE LIMITED
Business: Importation of Safety Boots & Related Equipment
Address: 6, Toyin Street, Ikeja, Lagos
Tel: (01) 4974199, 4977297, 0802301938, 08033128257, 08033168836, 08033898415 **Fax:** (01) 4935991
E-mail: cfcanutenig@hotmail.com

C. G. C. NIGERIA LIMITED
Business: Engineering and Construction Services
Address: 3A, Ali Akilu Road, Kaduna
Tel: (062) 242465, 234839, 235571 **Fax:** (062) 23571

C. H. F. HERON NIGERIA LIMITED
Business: Importation and Marketing of Briefcases, Travel Goods and Domestic Cookers
Address: 39, Warehouse Road, Apapa, Lagos
Tel: (01) 5452916, 5873591 **Fax:** (01) 5873591
E-mail: chf@micro.com.ng

C. J. MARTINS (WEST AFRICA) LIMITED
Business: Sales of Office Equipment and Business Systems
Address: Neighbourhood Shopping Centre (Suites A8/A9), Wuse Zone 3, Garki, Abuja
Tel: (09) 5236210, 08033066991, 08037864441
* 1A, Omoku Street, D-Line, Port Harcourt
Tel: (084) 572163
Contact: Prince C. J. Martins Ekwe - Chairman/CEO.

C. J. TERMINAL & STEVEDORES LIMITED
Business: Terminal Operators & Stevedoring, Export Packaging & Crating, Heavy Trucking, Bonded Warehouse Operations, Towing and Marine Salvage Operations, Pollution Control, Diving Services
Address: Jaros Base, Km. 2, Iwofe/College of Education Road, Rumuepirikom, Port Harcourt
Tel: (084) 238926, 236338; (082) 440057
Fax: (084) 239339; (082) 440057
* National Maritime Authority Annex, 2B, Burma Road, Apapa, Lagos.
Tel/Fax: (01) 5878252, 4811645

C. M. A. LIMITED
Business: Freight Forwarding and Shipping , Human Husbandry, Haulage
Address: Engineering Centre, 1, Engineering Close, off Idowu Taylor Street, Victoria Island, Lagos
Tel: (01) 2618349, 7730292 **Fax:** (01) 2618349
E-mail: cma@mdob.net
* 11, Manila Pepple Street, D-Line, Port Harcourt
Tel: (084) 235555
Contact: Ambassador Chris Chukwu - Chairman

C. N. OKOLI INVESMENT COMPANY NIGERIA LIMITED
Business: Transporters, Saw-Millers, Importers and General Contractors
Address: 15A, Iganmu Road, Ladipo B/Stop, Amukoko, Lagos
Tel: (01) 5451339, 5872763, 2882435
* 48/50, Balogun Street, Idumota, Lagos
Tel: (01) 2660301, 2667155
Contact: Chief C. N. Okoli - Chairman

C. N. ORAJI'S CRAFT CENTRE LIMITED
Business: Woodcraft
Address: 112, Awka Road, Onitsha
Tel: (046) 41346, 08023148511
Contact: Chief C. N. Oraji - Chairman/CEO

C. S. A NIGERIA LIMITED
Business: Interior Design & Decoration Services, Installation of Security Doors, French Doors, Ceiling Tiles and Danpalon Canopy
Address: 9, Warehouse Road, Apapa, Lagos
Tel: (01) 5872016, 5872017 **Fax:** (01) 5872018
E-mail: csa@skannet.com
* 1, Inani Estate, Maitama District, Abuja
Tel/Fax: (09) 4130922, 4134316

C. U. LAMAC MERCHANDISE (NIGERIA) LIMITED
Business: Sales and Maintenance of Water Pumps
Address: 202 ()ld 102), Oshodi-Apapa Expressway, opposite Ibalex Limited, Ilasamaja, Lagos
Tel: (01) 7730206
* Block 6 (Suite 4), Agric Market, Badagry Expressway, (Odun-Ade Bus-Stop), Lagos
Tel: (01) 7744490

CA CONSULTANTS LIMITED
Business: Consulting Engineers (Mechanical, Electrical & Piping)
Address: Bookshop House (5th Floor), 50/52, Broad Street, Lagos Island, Lagos
Tel: (01) 2646293, 2646744, 2646845 **Fax:** (01) 2646627
E-mail: cacons@linkserve.com.ng
Website: www.cacons.com
Contact: Engr. C. A. Akindayomi - MD/CEO

CABLE & SATELLITE COMMUNICATIONS LIMITED
Business: Broadcast and Telecommunication Services, Electrical and Electronics
Address: 3rd Avenue, E Close, House 14, Festac Town, Lagos
Tel: (01) 5892132, 5891075, 5887601 **Fax:** (01) 5891075
E-mail: casanig@hotmail.com
Contact: Engr. Anthony O. Osedume - Chairman/CEO

CABLE MISSION TELEVISION NETWORK
Business: Satellite Cable TV Re-Broadcasting Services
Address: 202, Aba Rd, by Rumoola Junction, Port Harcourt
Tel: (084) 232466, 232467, 230849, 08032034028
Fax: (084) 230849
Website: www.cmtvonline.com
Contact: Mr. Godfrey N. Ohuabunwa - MD/CEO

CACHE HOMES LIMITED
Business: Furnishing, Sales, Supply and Renovation of Furniture. General Contractors
Address: 56, Norman Williams Street, S.W. Ikoyi, Lagos
Tel: (01) 2673430, 2696442 **Fax:** (01) 2673430
* 7, Orimolode Crescent, off Adeniyi Jones

Avenue, Ikeja, Lagos
Contact: Chief Jerry Ibekwe - MD/CEO.

CACHEZ GROUP
Business: Construction and Civil Engineering, Turnkey Projects, Property Development and Management
Address: Plot 913, Alexandria Crescent, beside Whiz Oil Station, off Aminu Kano Crescent, Wuse II, Abuja
Tel: (09) 4134450, 4139882, 4138993 **Fax:** (09) 4134451
E-mail: cachez@hotmail.co

CADBURY NIGERIA PLC
Business: Manufacturing & Marketing of Foods, Food Drinks and Confectionery Products
Address: Lateef Jakande Road, Agidingbi, Ikeja, Lagos
Tel: (01) 4975390-9 (10L) **Fax:** (01) 2645590
E-mail: cnplc@cadburynigeria.com.
Website: www.cadburynigeria.com
Contact: Mr. Olubunmi Olusola - MD/CEO.
Mr. Gbenga Adebija - Corporate Affairs Manager

CADVANTAGE LIMITED
Business: Computer-Aided-Design Consultancy Services
Address: CSS Bookshop House (12th Floor), 50/52, Broad Street, Marina, Lagos
Tel: (01) 2645147, 2647943 **Fax:** (01) 2647943
E-mail: info@cadvantageonline.com
cadvantage@yahoo.com
Website: www. cadvantageonline.com

CAKASA (NIGERIA) COMPANY LIMITED
Business: Oil Industry Engineering, Procurement and Construction
Address: 96, Palm Avenue, Mushin, Lagos
Tel: (01) 4522955, 523225, 526477, 526157
Fax: (01) 4522887, 4528283
E-mail: cnchq@nigol.net.com
* 14, Emekuku Street, Oromineke Layout, D/Line, Port Harcourt
Tel: (084) 335575, 3344201 **Tel/Fax:** (084) 231175
* Corner Plot 3, Addis Ababa Crescent, Wuse Zone 4, near Sheraton Hotel, Abuja
Tel: (09) 5234788
Contact: Alh. M.S.A. Yunus - Chairman
Engr. Hyacinth U. F. Enuha - MD/CEO

CALAG CAPITAL & CONSULTING LIMITED
Business: Financial & Investment Consultancy Services
Address: Eleganza Biro Plaza (4th Floor), Plot 634, Adeyemo Alakija Street, Victoria Island, Lagos
Tel: (01) 2702928, 08033163344

CALLNET TELECOMMUNICATIONS LIMITED
Business: Sales of Telecommunication Equipment and Systems, Telecommunication Service Providers
Address: Oshopey Plaza (3rd Floor), 17/19, Allen Avenue, Ikeja, Lagos
Tel: (01) 4938777, 4935141 **Fax:** (01) 4938777
E-mail: sales@cllnetng.com
Contact: Mr. Charles C. Nwachuku - Chairman/CEO.

CALTA CONSTRUCTION (NIGERIA) LIMITED
Business: Oilfield Construction Engineering Services
Address: Africa Re-House, Plot 1679, Karimu Kotun Street, Victoria Island, Lagos
Tel: (01) 2626697, 2626698

CALYX SECURITIES LIMITED
Business: Stockbroking, Portfolio Management, Investment Advisory Services
Address: CSS Bookshop House (13th Floor), 50/52, Broad Street, Lagos
Tel: (01) 2665207, 2633960 **Fax:** (01) 2665207
E-mail: calyx@infoweb.abs.net
Contact: Air Vice Marshal Joe Ehigie (rtd) - Chairman
Mr. Wale Onigbode - MD/CEO

CAMCO NIGERIA LIMITED
Business: Oilfied Engineering Services and Equipment Supply
Address: 18A, Thompson Avenue, Ikoyi , Lagos.
Tel: (01) 2692100
* Trans-Amadi Industrial layout, Port Harcourt
Tel: (084) 333178, 234725, 232824, 234953

CALTEX LIMITED
Business: Real Estate Consultancy & Agency
Address: Sura Shopping Complex (Block A2-9, Suite 292), Simpson Street, Lagos Island, Lagos
Tel: (01) 2646005, 2646006, 08033064805
Fax: (01) 2646006
E-mail: kolaallen@yahoo.com
Contact: Mrs. Titilayo Odukoya - MD/CEO

CAMEL STAR LIMITED
Business: Manufacturing of Polyprolene Mats and Sacks
Address: 10A, Dantata Road, Kano
Tel/Fax: (064) 640928, 08037021362
Contact: Nasiru Mohammed - GM/CEO

CAMELA PURE VEGETABLE OIL COMPANY LIMITED
Business: Processing of Palm-Kernel Oil to Edible Vegetable Oil
Address: C1/24, Industrial Layout, Onitsha Road, Owerri
Tel: (087) 772503, (090) 500516, 501988,
E-mail: camelaoil@yahoo.co.uk
Contact: Chief Kingsley Okechukwu Ikoro - Chairman/CEO

CAMEROON AIRLINES (NIGERIA)
Business: International Airline Service
Address: 16, Oko-Awo Close, off Adetokunbo Ademola Street. Victoria Island, Lagos.
Tel: (01) 2614993, 2703608-10 (3L), 7745729
* M. M. International Airport, Ikeja, Lagos
Tel: (01) 7741281

CAMPAIGN + CONCEPTS LIMITED
Business: Advertising, Marketing & Public Relations Agency
Address: Elephant House (4th Floor), 229/241, Ikorodu Road, Ilupeju, Lagos.
Tel: (01) 5550291-2 (2L), 8160483, 08033001929, 08033024722 **Fax:** (01) 5550291
Website: www.campainandconcepts.com
Contact: Mrs Imelda Faleye - MD/CEO

CAMPAIGN PALACE LIMITED
Business: Advertising, Marketing and Advertising Research
Address: 39, Isaac John Street, G.R.A., Ikeja, Lagos.

Tel: (01) 4977880, 7918786 **Fax:** (01) 4977880
E-mail: campaign003@yahoo.co.uk
Contact: Mr. Ade Akinde - MD/CEO

CAMPAIGN SERVICES LIMITED
Business: Advertising, Public Relations and Marketing
Address: 26, Ogunlana Drive, Surulere, Lagos.
Tel: (01) 5835275, 08023063531 **Fax:** (01) 5835275
E-mail: campaingservices@linkserve.com
Contact: Mr. Remi Adeneye - MD/CEO

CAN INDUSTRIES (WEST AFRICA) LIMITED
Business: Importation, Production and Sales of Auto Paints and General Merchandise
Address: 24A, Modebe Avenue, Onitsha
Tel: (046) 210273, 216751, 412520, 08022252934
Fax: (046) 216751
Contact: Sir C. N. C. Nwafor - Chairmn/CEO

CANDID COMMUNICATIONS LIMITED
Business: Advertising
Address: 21, Maduagwu Moronu Street, Surulere, Lagos
Tel: (01) 2880490, 802620-4 (5L)
E-mail: candid@nigercompass.com
Contact: Mr. Bath Okigbo - MD/CEO

CANDID LOSS ADJUSTERS LIMITED
Business: Loss Adjusting, Cargo Superintendents/Surveyors, Marine Loss Recoveries, Aviation, Oil & Engineering Claims
Address: 48, Falomo Street, Surulere, Lagos.
Tel/Fax: (01) 823070
Contact: Mr. C. O. Ujah - Chairman
Mr. Chris E. Nlemoha - MD/CEO

CANNES LIMITED
Business: Freight Forwarding Services
Address: 2A, Raymond, Njoku Street, S. W. Ikoyi, Lagos
Tel: (01) 2694935, 2671789, 08023042222, (090) 401470
Fax: (01) 2694935
E-mail: spacedy@cyberspace.net.ng
Contact: Mr. C. J. Okekearu - MD/CEO

CAPERNAUM VENTURES LIMITED
Business: Distribution and Sales of Electrical Power Distribution, Control & Protection Equipment
Address: Plot 1, Trans-Amadi Ind. Layout, Port Harcourt
Tel: (084) 234308, (082) 440441, 4400885
Fax: (084) 610784
E-mail: cap.trust@pdq.net

CAPHI NIGERIA LIMITED
Business: Manufacturing of Pharmaceutical Plastic Bottles, Containers and Healthcare Plastic Products
Address: 22, Abimbola Street, Isolo Ind. Estate, Isolo, Lagos.
Tel: (01) 4525426
Contact: Chief G. L. Obe - Chairman

CAPIMPEX NIGERIA LIMITED
Busniess: Manufacturing of Interlocking Paving Stones; Sales of Beverage Drinks, Tools & Allied Products
Address: 35, Adeniran Ogunsanya Street, Suruler, Lagos.
Tel: (01) 5451784, 7752792, 5878361, 7740464, 08033008967 **Fax:** (01) 5451784
E-mail: capimpex@yahoo.com
Contact: Mr. S. A. Olumba - Chairman/CEO

CAPITAL AIRLINES LIMITED
Business: Airline Services
Address: 56A, Isaac John Street, G.R.A. Ikeja, Lagos
Tel: (01) 4973826-7 (2 L) **Fax:** (01) 4973827
E-mail: capitalnigeria@aol.com
Contact: Capt. Ernest I. Bell-Gam - MD/CEO

CAPITAL ALLIANCE NIGERIA LIMITED
Business: Private Equity Investment Services
Address: Octagon Towers (5th Floor), 13, A. J. Marinbo Drive, Victoria Island Annex, Lagos
Tel: (01) 3205187-7 (2 L) 4707392-3 (2 L), 2625238
Fax: (01) 2625238
E-mail: capitalalliance@can-aca.com
Contact: Mr. Okechukwu Enelamah - MD/CEO

CAPITAL ASSETS LIMITED
Business: Stockbrokers, Issuing House, Portfolio Managers
Address: Great Nigeria House (1st Floor), 47/57, Martins Street, Lagos.
Tel: (01) 2663476, 2669231 **Fax:** (01) 2663476
E-mail: capas@infoweb.abs.net
Contact: Mr. Muritala Ariyo Olushekun - MD/CEO

CAPITAL BANCORP LIMITED
Business: Stockbroking, Corporate Finance and Equipment Leasing
Address: Eleganza Building (11th Floor), 15B, Wesley/ Joseph Street, Lagos.
Tel: (01) 2600705-9 (5 L) 2647674-5 (2 L)
Fax: (01) 2631283
* 35, Aba Road, Port Harcourt.
Tel: (084) 230753
Contact: Mr. M. O. K. Williams - Chairman
Mr. Olutola O. Mobolurin - MD/CEO

CAPITAL BANK INTERNATIONAL LIMITED
Business: Commercial Banking
Address: Plot 146B, Ligali Ayorinde St,Victoria Island, Lagos
Tel: (01) 2625700-6 (6L), 2625710-4 (5L), 2625720-6 (7L)
Fax: (01) 2625699
E-mail: info@capbankint.com
Contact: Mr. Omatseyin A. Ayida - MD/CEO

CAPITAL EXPRESS INSURANCE COMPANY LIMITED
Business: Life Assurance, Pension and Investment Business
Address: Crusade House, 23/25, Martins Street, Lagos.
Tel: (01) 2660590, 2641519 **Fax:** (01) 2664526
E-mail: capex@infoweb.abs.net
* FMBN Building (3rd Floor), 1, Adekunle Fajuyi Road, Dugbe, Ibadan.
Tel: (02) 2410890, 2414626
* Plot 3B, Accelerated Development District, Herbert Macaulay Way, Wuse, Abuja
Contact: Otunba B. A. Adenuga - Chairman
Mr. Tony Aletor - MD/CEO

CAPITAL EXPRESS SECURITIES LIMITED
Business: Stockbroking, Porfolio & Asset Management,

Investment Advisory Services
Address: Crusader House , 23/25, Martins Street, Lagos.
Tel: (01) 2641519,2660590 **Fax:** (01) 2664526
E-mail: capex@infoweb.abs.net
Contact: Otunba B. A. Adenuga - Chairman
Mr. Tony Aletor - MD/CEO

CAPITAL HOTELS PLC
Business: Hotel & Catering Services
Address: Ladi Kwali way, Central Area, Maitana, Abuja
Tel: (09) 5230225-44 (20 L) **Fax:** (09) 5231570-1 (2 L)
E-mail: sales-abuja@sheraton.com
Contact: Mr. A. K. Alhassan - Director of Sales

CAPITAL HOSPITAL & MATERNITY LIMITED
Business: Medical Services
Address: Plot 472, Ibrahim Babangida Way, by Adetokunbo Ademola Crescent, Wuse II, Abuja
Tel: (09) 5230217, 5230332, 5230622
Contact: Dr. B. C. Oputa - Medical Director

CAPITAL OIL PLC
Business: Marketing of Petroleum Products and Chemicals
Address: Plot 18, Adeniyi Jones Avenue, Ikeja, Lagos.
Tel: (01) 4965148 **Fax:** (01) 4923275
Contact: Alh. (Dr.) S. A. Bello - Chairman
Engr. A. A. Adenekan - President/CEO

CAPITAL PARTNERS LIMITED
Business: Business Advisory Services to Financial Institutions, Investment Advisory Services
Address: AIB Plaza (5th Floor), AIB Terrace, Akin Adesola Street, Victoria Island, Lagos.
Tel: (01) 2623891-2 (2 L) **Fax:** (01) 2623893
E-mail: capitalpartners@linkserve.com.ng
Contact: Mr. Cyril Chukwumah - MD/CEO

CAPITAL RESOURCES CONSORTIUM
Business: Financial Consultancy Services
Address: 130, Lewis Street, Lafiaji, Lagos.
Tel: (01) 2646039
E-mail: caprecom@nova.net.ng
Contact: Mr. Ken Pela - MD/CEO

CAPITAL SECURITY & SURVEILLANCE LIMITED
Business: Security Guards Services, Security Training and Consultancy Services, Supply of Security Systems and Equipment, Bullion Transportation Services
Address: 43, Toyin Street, Ikeja, Lagos
Tel: (01) 4931210 **Fax:** (01) 4932551
E-mail: capitalsecuritysurveillance@hotmail.com
Contact: Mr. Chijoke Okoronko - Chairman/CEO

CAPITAL TECHNOLOGY SOLUTIONS LIMITED
Business: IT and Telecommunication Consultancy, Equipment Supply
Address: Plot 999, Oju Olobun Close off Bishop Oluwole Street, Victoria Island, Lagos
Tel: (01) 2672823, 611718, 611734 **Fax:** (01) 2672824
E-mail: capitaltech@btinternet.com
Website: www.capitaltech-group.com
Contact: Apostle Hayford I. Alile - Chairman
Mr. Nosa Afe - CEO/Consultant

CAPITAL TRUST BROKERS LIMITED
Business: Stockbroking, Portfolio & Investment Management
Address: Unity House (4th Floor), 37, Marina, Lagos
Tel: (01) 2664938, 2664742, 2664933, 2664729
Fax: (01) 2664938
E-mail: ctb@beta.linkserve.com
Contact: Otunba Adekunle Ojora, OFR, JP - Chairman
Mr. M. A. Adefila - MD/CEO

CAPPA AND D'ALBERTO PLC
Business: Building & Civil Engineering Contractors
Address: 72, Campbell Street, Lagos Island, Lagos
Tel: (01) 2645169-73 (5 L) **Fax:** (01) 2633794
* 82, Okesuna Street, Lagos Island, Lagos
Tel: (01) 2631872
Contact: Mr. F. Fianotti - MD/CEO

CAPPA HOLDINGS LIMITED
Business: Plumbing Services, Sales, Installation and Maintenance of Hydromassage Bath and Sanitary Wares
Address: 23A, Karimu Kotun Street, Victoria Island Lagos
Tel: (01) 2624965, 2624966 **Fax:** (01) 2624967
E-mail: cappaholdings@hyperia.com
Contact: Mr. Anthony Cappa Anaeto - Chairman/CEO

CAPRI-MARTINS FINANCE LIMITED
Business: Financial Services
Address: Plot 290, Ajose Adeogun St, Victoria Island, Lagos
Tel: (01) 2615280 **Fax:** (01) 2622846
Contact: Chief E. M. Egwuenu - Chairman/CEO

CAPS FEED LIMITED
Business: Production of Poultry Feeds, Marketing and Poultry Feed Ingredients & Consultancy Services
Address: Old Ife Road (Ola-Ogun Bus Stop), Ibadan
Tel: (02) 8100993, 8109269, 8109270
Contact: Dr. J. N. Pension-Smith - Chairman/CEO

CAR LINK LIMITED
Business: Automobiles Marketing
Address: Plot 641, Akin Adesola St, Victoria Island, Lagos
Tel: (01) 2613184, 4703954 **Fax:** (01) 2616824
E-mail: carlink@cll.com.ng
* 23A, Adeyemo Alakija St, Victoria Island, Lagos
Tel: (01) 618726, 611237, 616063
* 169, Aba Road, Port Harcourt.
Tel: (084) 233660
* 58B, Isaac John Street, Ikeja, G.R.A., Lagos
Tel: (01) 7755448
Contact: Mr. Bube Okorodudu - Chairman/CEO

CARAT ALUMINIUM LIMITED
Business: Fabrication and Installation of Aluminium Building Products (Windows, Doors, Roofing etc)
Address: 14, Olaribiro Street, behind Ecobank, off Allen Avenue, Ikeja, Lagos.
Tel: (01) 4935102, 7741311 **Fax:** (01) 4935102
E-mail: carat@alpha.linkserve.com
Contact: Olatunde Biobaku - Chairman/CEO

CARDCENTRE LIMITED
Business: Licensed GSM (SIM & Recharge) & Bank (Debit & Smart) Card Producrs

Address: 8, Louis Solomon Close, Victoria Island, Lagos
Tel: (01) 2700070-5 (6 L) **Fax:** (01) 2700079

CARDINAL CONCEPTS ADVERTISING LIMITED
Business: Advertising, Marketing Communications, Public Relations, Events Management, Production of P.O.S. and Promotional Materials
Address: 1A, Aina George Street, off Coker Road Roundabout, Ilupeju, Lagos
Tel/Fax:: (01) 4975803
E-mail: okeycardinal@yahoo.com
okeycardinal@hyperia.com
Contact: Mr. Okey P. Onyia - MD/CEO

CARGO INSPECTION & FREIGHT LIMITED
Business: Cargo Superintendents and Marine Surveyors, Analytical & Testing Laboratory, Marine Bulk Oil Surveyors, Ship Broker and Agent
Address: 46, Burma Road, Apapa, Lagos.
Tel: (01) 5451862 **Fax:** (01) 5871591
E-mail: cargoinsp@infoweb.abs.net
Website: www.cargoinspect.com
Contact: Mr. C. N. Nwankiti - Chairman/CEO

CARGO MARKETING INTERNATIONAL LIMITED
Business: Clearing and Forwarding, IATA Cargo Agency, General Cargo Handling, Exporting and Importing
Address: 28, Alh. Ogunsolu Street, Onilekere-Cement Bus Stop, off Lagos-Abeokuta Expressway, Lagos
Tel: (01) 4922402, 4925585, 4925582, 4960529, 4963319, 4965842, 4962018, 4965070
Fax: (01) 4922402, 4963319, 4925585, 4925582
E-mail: cmilagos@cminingeria.com
Website: www.cminigeria.com
* 220, Block A4, NAHCO Shed Phase I, M.M. International Airport, Ikeja, Lagos.
Tel: (01) 7748587, 4960529
Contact: Mr. Rasaki Oseni - Chairman/CEO

CARGO VISION NIGERIA LIMITED
Business: Customs Bonded-Terminal Operators, Warehousing, Clearing and Forwarding
Address: Plot 9, Southern Oregun Industrial Estate, opp. Old Toll Gate, near 7UP Factory, Oregun, Ikeja, Lagos
Tel: (01) 4931434-5 (2 L) 7741986-7 (2 L), 5557483
E-mail: cargovisionng@hyperia.com
Website: www.cargovisionng.com
Contact: Otunba (Dr.) Olugbenga Ayileka - MD/CEO

CARIBBEAN FINANCE LIMITED
Business: Portfolio Management, Investment Advisers, Loans & Advances, Hire-Purchase Financing and Equipment Leasing
Address: 8, Obafemi Awolowo Road, Oke-Ado, Ibadan.
Tel: (02) 2313413 **Fax:** (02) 2316860
Contact: Dr. E. O. Yewande - Executive President

CARLDOM INTERCONTINENTAL AGENCIES LIMITED
Business: Clearing & Forwarding, Shipping & Warehousing
Address: 7, Kofo Abayomi Avenue, Apapa, Lagos
Tel: (01) 5452204, 5451407 **Fax:** (01) 5451402
* 30, Uyo Street, Port Harcourt
Contact: Chief A. M. Georgewill - Chairman/CEO

CARLIN CONCEPT INTERNATIONAL LIMITED
Business: Sales of Industrial Environmental Machines, Pressure Washing Machines, Cleaning Chemicals
Address: 94, Opebi Road, Ikeja, Lagos
Tel: (01) 8046551, 4978863, 08023063444, 08042136711
Fax: (01) 4978863
E-mail: carlindulevo@aol.com

CARNCO FOODS (NIGERIA) LIMITED
Business: Manufacture of Diary Products
Address: Km 3.5, Lagos-Badagry Expressway, Alaba-Suru, behind Eleganza Building, Lagos
Tel: (01) 7740868, 7740878, 5852349-50 (2L)
Fax: (01) 2617270, 2622819
Contact: Mr. Arvind. Nagpaul - MD/CEO

CARONC HOLDINGS LIMITED
Business: Manufacture of Business Furniture, Sales of Power Generators and Security Fencing Wires
Address: 90, Adeniyi Jones Avenue, Ikeja, Lagos.
Tel: (01) 4935472, 7733438, 08023390737, 08034151219
Fax: (01) 4930470
E-mail: caroncgroupcontrol@yahoo.com
* 284B, Ajose Adeogun St, Victoria Island, Lagos
* 4 Olu Akijiyan Street, Ejigbo, Lagos
Contact: Mr. Chris A. Alabi - Chairman/CEO
Mr. R. O. Odende - Mgr (Business Dev/Planning)

CARONC INVESTMENT LIMITED
Business Investments-Oil Palm Estate, Banking, Educational Institutions, Manufacturing, Trading
Address: 90, Adeniyi Jones Avenue, Ikeja, Lagos.
Tel: (01) 4935472, 7733438 **Fax:** (01) 4930470
E-mail: caroncgroupcontrol@yahoo.com
Contact: Mr. Chris A. Alabi - Chairman/CEO

CARRIER INSURANCE BROKERS LIMITED
Business: Insurance Broking & Consultancy
Address: 13, Maduagwu Moronu Street, off Ibezim Obiajulu Street, off Adelabu Street, Surulere, Lagos
Tel: (01) 5846149, 833702, 2882067, 5455752
Fax: (01) 5455752
E-mail: carrier@infoweb.abs.net
* Assia House, Plot 2087, Herbert Macaulay Way (North), Wuse Zone 5, Abuja.
Tel: (09) 5239610
Contact: Mr. O. Oshiafi - Chairman
Mr. Richard Akinwale - Asst. GM/CEO

CASAC NIGERIA LIMITED
Business: Information Technology (IT) Consultancy, Equipment Purchase, Structured Cabling, Software Acquisition and Installation, Application Development and Training
Address: 1, Montgomery Road, Yaba, Lagos
Tel: (01) 7742503, 866899, 865795 **Fax:** (01) 866889
E-mail: casac@beta.linkserve.com
Contact: Mr. Olisamedua Uwaechia - Chairman/CEO

CASCHE NIGERIA LIMITED
Business: Shipping & Ports Operations, Total Security Solution, Services to Oil & Gas Industry
Address: 13, Randle Road, Apapa, Lagos

Tel: (01) 5454380, 5872400 **Fax:** (01) 5878021
E-mail: casche@infoweb.abs.net
Contact: Mr. Chris A. Alabi - Chairman/CEO

CASH 'N' CARRY (NIGERIA) LIMITED
Business: Trading in Electronic and Household Appliances
Address: Kingsway Building, 51, Marina, Lagos.
Tel: (01) 2660785, 2661133, 2662907 **Fax:** (01) 2690598
* 78/84, Kofo Abayomi Street, Apapa, Lagos
* 28, Kodesoh Street, Ikeja, Lagos
* Conakry Street, Zone 3, Wuse, Abuja
Tel: (090 6713070-2 (2L)
Contact: Mr. Kan R. Chatlani - GM/CEO

CASH FLOW LIMITED
Business: Export of Agricultural Products, Trade Finance
Address: 11, Allen Avenue, Ikeja, Lagos
Tel: (01) 4931585, 4971834 **Fax:** (01) 4971834
Contact: Mr. Charles C. Ibe - MD/CEO

CASHCRAFT ASSET MANAGEMENT. LIMITED
Business: Stockbroking, Pension Funds Management
Address: Foreshore Towers, 2A, Osborne Rd, Ikoyi, Lagos
Tel: (01) 2694287-9 (3 L), 2696764, 08023050195, 08033036430, 08033080687 **Fax:** (01) 2694289
E-mail: lagos@cashcraft.com
Website: www.cashcraft.com
* Chanrai Building, 13, Aba Road, Port Harcourt
Tel: (084) 234952, 487129, 08023060203, 08023060192
E-mail: portharcourt@cashcraft.com
* Aisha House, Plot 2087, Herbert Macaulay Way (North), Wuse Zone 5, Wuse Abuja
Tel: (09) 5232218, 5232947 **Fax:** (09) 5232947
E-mail: abuja@cashcraft.com
Contact: Otunba J. A. O. Ogunfuwa - Chairman
Mr. Deolu Ireyomi - MD/CEO

CASHLINK FINANCE & INVESTMENT PLC
Business: Trade Financing, Equipment Leasing, Car Rental, Foreign Exchange Trading, Consltancy Services
Address: Plot 23B, Adeola Odeku St, Victoria Island, Lagos
Tel: (01) 2620376-7 (2 L), 2620379, 3200366-7 (2L)
Fax: (01) 2620379, 3200188
E-mail: info@cashlinkplc.com
Website: www.cashlinkplc.com
Contact: Air Cdre Dan Suleiman (rtd) - Chairman
Mr. Tayo Soetan - MD/CEO

CASHVILLE INVESTMENT & SECURITIES LIMITED
Business: Stockbroking
Address: NIM Building (2nd Floor), 22, Idowu Taylor Stree, Victoria Island, Lagos
Tel: (01) 2626295 -6 (2l), 4739100, 4745353
Fax: (01) 2626295
E-mail: info@cashvillegroup.com
Contact: Esther Balogun - Head (Administration)

CASMAN LIMITED
Business: Clearing and Forwarding
Address: 13, Commercial Road, Apapa, Lagos
Tel: (01) 5875291 54514632
Contact: Chief Chiji Agbo - Chairman
Mr. I. O. Ugwu - MD/CEO

CASTARIO LIMITED
Business: Fashion Sales Outlets, Production of Uniforms
Address: 13, Ademola Street, off Awolowo Road, S. W. Ikoyi, Lagos
Tel/Fax: (01) 2692101
E-mail: castario@infoweb.abs.net
* 8, Sanni Adewole Street, off Breadfrit St, Lagos
Tel: (010 2667397, 2669819 **Fax:** (01) 2669771

CASTILLA LIMITED
Business: Importation and Sales of Furniture
Address: 66, Awolowo Road, S. W. Ikoyi, Lagos
Tel: (01) 2672107
* 15, Agoro Odiyan Street, off Adeola Odeku Street, Victoria Island, Lagos.
Tel: (01) 4703647
* 141, Ahamdu Bello Way, Victoria Island, Lagos.
Tel: (01) 2672107, 4703647, 4708046

CASTLAT GROUP OF COMPANIES
Business: Sales & Service of Electric Generators & Airconditioners, Mining, Freight Management
Address: Plot 1-3, Amuwo-Odofin Park Estate Oshodi-Apapa Expressway, Ijesha B/Stop, Lagos
Tel: (01) 4520595, 4520527, 7743631, 08022908458, 08023017691, 08033064064, 08033204357
Fax: (01) 7745947
* Block 1, Plot 516, Sultan Abubakar Way, TMQ, Wuse Zone 2, Abuja.
Tel: (09) 5237447-8 (2L), 08023069620, 08033254101
* 6A, Aba Road, Port Harcourt.
Tel: (084) 231228, 08023069634
Contact: Prince C. Abiodun. Latunde - Chairman/CEO

CATEC NIGERIA LIMITED
Business: Architectural, Civil & Electrical/Electronic Engineering, Information Technology & Networking Consulting, Production of Table Water
Address: Plot 6, East-West Road, Rumukwurushi, Port Harcourt
Tel: (084) 611348, 08033104355
Contact: Engr. Ben. I. Iloabachie - Chairman/CEO

CATHAY PACIFIC AIRWAYS
Business: International Airline Service
Address: Plot 1661, Oyin Jolayemi St, Victoria Island, Lagos
Tel: (01) 2626223, 3200665, 7746431
Fax: (01) 2626224, 3200664
E-mail: cathlos@yahoo.co.uk
Contact: Rev (Dr) Edward Benson - GM

CATLAND INTERNATIONAL LOSS ADJUSTERS LIMITED
Business: Loss Adjusting, Risk Surveying, Engineering Surveying, Marine & Aviation Consultancy
Address: 2, Olaide Tomori Street, off Simbiat Abiola Road, Ikeja, Lagos
Tel: (01) 4973003, 8134282, 08022914693, 08023369349
E-mail: catlandadjusters@yahoo.co.uk
Contact: Mr. S. F. Olatunbosun - MD/CEO

CAUTIOUS INSURANCE BROKERS LIMITED
Business: Insurance Broking
Address: 254, Herbert Macaulay St, Alagomeji, Yaba, Lagos

Tel: (01) 865736, 860970, 08022913292, 08023664301, 08037232064 **Fax:** (01) 860640
Contact: Mr. Shamsideen O. Salako - MD/CEO

CAVENISH PETROLEUM NIGERIA LIMITED
Business: Oil Exploration and Production
Address: 22, Adeleke Adedoyin St, Victoria Island, Lagos
Tel: (01) 2623343, 2647072 **Fax:** (01) 2623343
Contact: Alh. Gambo Gubio - MD/CEO

CAZOGIE TRAVELS & TOURS LIMITED
Business: Travel Agency and Tour Operators
Address: Stay Fit Plaza, Opp. 1004 Flats, 6/8, Ozumba Mbadiwe Avenue, Victoria Island, Lagos
Tel: (01) 2620595, 613758 **Fax:** (01) 2620595
E-mail: cazogie@gacom.net
* Plot 991-992, 4th Avenue, Central Business District, Abuja
Contact: Mrs. Carol Ogunbufunmi - MD/CEO

CCC CONSTRUCTION NIGERIA LIMITED
Business: Highways & Roads Construction, Mechanical & Electrical Engineering Services
Address: Plot 2836, Danube Close, off IBB Way, Maitama, Abuja
Tel: (09) 4132195, 4132613 **Fax:** (090 4132196
E-mail: ccng@microaccess.com
Contact: Mr Jamil Awaida - CEO

CCECC NIGERIA LIMITED
Business: Construction and Civil Engineering Services
Address: Airport Road, beh. Dantata Quarry, 2nd Junction, off Galadima Village, Abuja
Tel: (09) 5242023, 5242123 **Fax:** (09) 5240300, 5242153
E-mail: ccecc-nigeria@access.com.cn

CEASAR'S PALACE HOTEL
Business: Hotel and Restaurant Business
Address: 72, Kofo Abayomi Avenue, Apapa, Lagos
Tel: (01) 5872785
Contact: Mr. Cheriff Fawaz - MD/CEO

CECIL-DOLTON NIGERIA LIMITED
Business: Sales of Mobile-Phone Handsets and Accessories
Address: 30/32, Creek Road, Apapa, Lagos
Tel: (01) 5877613, 5453098 **Fax:** (01) 5453098
Contact: Chief A. O. Obioha - Chairman/CEO

CDH HOME & OFFICE INTERIORS
Business: Sales of Home & Office Furniture
Address: 21B, Idowu Martins Street, Victoria Island, Lagos
Tel: (01) 7741913, 2614818, 08042100209
* Poly Plaza (Suite B4), beside AP Plaza, Adetokunbo Ademola Crescent, Wuse II, Abuja
Tel: 08042100290

CE BROKER (NIGERIA) LIMITED
Business: Importation & Sales of Computers & Accessories
Address: Oshopey Plaza, 17/19, Allen Avenue, Ikeja, Lagos
Tel: (01) 3205716, 08023300705
E-mail: info@cebroker.ch
Website: www.cebroker.ch
Contact: Mr. Adeyemi J. Anise - MD/CEO

CEE BEN NIGERIA LIMITED
Business: Installation of Telecommunication Terminals, Sales of Mobile Phones and Accessories
Address: 3/5, Adeyemo Alakija Street, Victoria Island, Lagos
Tel: (01) 2610655, 2909891, 4932050, 08033067854
Fax: (01) 2610655
E-mail: ceeben@hyperia.com
* Plot 2219, Constantine Street (Shop 307), Wuse Zone 4, Abuja.
Tel: (09) 5232345
Contact: Prince John Afam Nnaji - MD/CEO

CEETADEL COMPUTERS LIMITED
Business: Sales of Computer Hardware, Software and Accessories, Maintenance and Traning
Address: 56, Bornu Crescent, Apapa, Lagos
Tel: (01) 5876468, 5876367, 08033281905
Fax: (01) 5873169
E-mail: ajamy@cyberspace.net.ng
Contact: Alh. Mohammed Adjarho Oyibo - Chairman/CEO

CELEBRITY LEISURE TRAVELS LIMITED
Business: Travel Agency, Organisation of Tours
Address: 7, Anthony Village Road, off Ikorodu Road, Lagos
Tel: (01) 4971699, 4733331, 08023451222, 08023512025
Fax: (01) 4971699

CELL COMMUNICATIONS LIMITED
Business: Fixed-Wireless Telephone Service Provider (PTO)
Address: 33, Saka Tinubu Street, Victoria Island, Lagos
Tel: (01) 2901111, 2900000, 2900122, 2900121
Fax: (01) 2900000
E-mail: cellcom@bacomonline.com
Contact: Mr. Patrick T. Chidolue - Chairman/CEO

CELLOPACK INDUSTRIES LIMITED
Business: Manufacturing of Polythene Bags and Plastic Bottles for Pharmaceutical Products & Juices
Address: Plot 42, Sharada Industrial Estate Phase III, Kano
Tel: (064) 664701, 664702 **Fax:** (064) 665887
* 75, Payne Avenue, Apapa, Lagos
Tel: (01) 5872530 **Fax:** (01) 5871160
Contact: Capt. S. Shahani - MD/CEO

CELLULAR SERVICE LOGISTICS (NIGERIA) LIMITED
Business: Sales & Service of Cellular Phones, Spare Parts & Accessories, Cellular Units & Terminals
Address: Plot 8, Kofo Abayomi Street, Victoria Island, Lagos
Tel: (01) 2620632, 2700230-1 (2 L)
E-mail: info@cslnigeria.com
Website: www.cslafrica.com
* Plot 4, Queen Idia St, Zone A4, Asokoro, Abuja
Tel/Fax: (09) 3143409
Contact: Ronnie Garland - MD/CEO

CELPAS INDUSTRIES NIGERIA LIMITED
Business: Manufacturing of Coolers, Garden Furniture, Industrial & Domestic Plastic Products
Address: 27A, Fatai Atere Way, Matori Industrial Estate, Mushin, Lagos
Tel: (01) 4527314, 4522738, 4520374, 7761188, 7767148
Fax: (01) 4520374, 4522738, 4827314
E-mail: celphas@alpha.linkserve..com

CELTRON NIGERIA LIMITED
Business: Global Marketing Communications, Advertising, Event Management and Promotions
Address: 1, Hagley Road, off Jibowu Road, Yaba, Lagos
Tel: (01) 2881819, 861217, 867776 **Fax:** (01) 2881820
E-mail: enquiries@madeinnigeria.co.uk
Website: www.madeinnigeria.co.uk
Contact: Mr. Adedapo Adelegan - Chairman/CEO

CEM NIGERIA LIMITED
Business: Civil Electrical Mechanical Engineering Services
Address: 39, Niger Street, P. O. Box 1218, Kano
Tel: (064) 638238, 638235, 08023277777, 08034500007
Fax: (064) 638238
E-mail: cemnigltd@yahoo.com
Contact: Mr. Charles El-Daueihy - MD/CEO

CEMENT COMPANY OF NORTHERN NIGERIA PLC
Business: Manufacture & Marketing of Portland Cement
Address: Km. 10, Kalambaina Road, Sokoto
Tel: (060) 236887, 230338 **Fax:** (060) 234805
* 5, Park Lane, Apapa, Lagos
Tel: (01) 5872479, 965446, 965420 **Fax:** (01) 5872479
Contact: Engr. Ibrahim A. Gobir - MD/CEO.

CENTO GROUP OF COMPANIES
Business: Manufacturing of Automobile Accessories, Spare Parts, Auto Batteries and Travelling Bags
Address: Nkwo Akwu Village, Umudim, Anambra State
Tel: (046) 460976, 460454 **Fax:** (046) 460069
E-mail: cento@infoweb.abs.net
Contact: Mr. I. S. N. Okafor - Chairman/CEO

CENTRAL AUTO DISTRIBUTION & ASSEMBLY NIGERIA LIMITED
Business: Importation., Assembly, Marketing & Distribution for Motor Vehicles
Address: Plot 1682, Sanusi Fafunwa Street, V. Island, Lagos
Tel: (01) 4616408 -10 (3 L) **Fax:** (01) 4616410
E-mail: cadaltd@yahoo.com
* 10, Aerodrome Road, Apapa, Lagos
Tel: (01) 5874737, 5870641

CENTRAL BAGS MANUFACTURING CO. NIGERIA LTD
Business: Manufacture of Polypropylene Woven Sacks
Address: 10, Akanbi Onitiri Close, off Eric Moore Road, Iganmu Industrial Estate, Iganmu, Lagos
Tel: (01) 5831952, 5833421, 833685 **Fax:** (01) 2611348
E-mail: cbmc@infoweb.abs.net
Contact: Chief Mike Umeh - Chairman/CEO

CENTRAL DYNAMICS LIMITED
Business: Sales of Radio Communication Equipment, Telecommunication, Instrumentation and Electronics
Address: 14, Hospital Road, Port Harcourt
Tel/Fax: (084) 239421
E-mail: cdynamics2000@yahoo.co.uk
Contact: Mr. Otonye Inko-Tariah - MD/CEO

CENTRAL ESTATES COMPANY LIMITED
Business: Real Estate Agency, Investment & Consultancy, Sale, Leasing & Repairs of Heavy-Duty Construction Machinery, Borehole Drilling & Construction
Address: Western House (2nd Floor, Suite 10), 8/10, Broad Street, Lagos Island, Lagos
Tel: (01) 8132932, 2647514, 4723269, 0802302223, 08023049373, 08033483122, 08055402922,
Fax: (01) 2647514, 4723269
E-mail: cecl@nova.net.ng
Website: www.cecl-ng.com
Contact: Mr. Femi Ogunro - Chairman
Mr. Akinseyinde J. Ogunrinde - MD/CEO

CENTRAL HOTEL, KANO
Business: Hotel and Catering Services
Address: 1, Bompai Road, Kano
Tel: (064) 630000-9 (10 L), 08033477340
Fax: (064) 630008
Contact: Alh. Bashir Ibrahim - GM/CEO.

CENTRAL INSURANCE COMPANY LIMITED
Business: All Classes of Insurance
Address: Bookshop House (9th Floor) 50/52, Broad St Lagos
Tel: (01) 2646794-6 (3L), 2632396 **Fax:** (01) 2646792
* Plot 1304, Mogadishu St, Wuse Zone 4, Abuja
Tel: (09) 5239932, 5239941
Contact: Mr. Sim O. Okeke - MD/CEO.

CENTRAL SECURITIES CLEARING SYSTEM LIMITED
Business: Computerised Depository Clearing, Settlement and Delivery System for Transactions in Shares listed on the Nigerian Stock Exchange
Address: The Stock Exhange House (1st & 11th Floors), 2/4, Customs Street, Marina, Lagos
Tel: (01) 2664075, 2643007, 2643139, 2666660
Fax: (01) 2643007, 2664058
E-mail: cscs@alpha.linkserve.com
cscs@supernet300.com
Contact: Apostle (Dr.) H. I. Alile, OFR - Chairman
Mr. Onyewuchi C. Asinobi - MD/CEO

CENTRE-LINE CONSTRUCTION NIGERIA LIMITED
Business: Building Construction and Civil Engineering
Address: 26A, Adetokunbo Ademola St, Victoria Island, Lagos
Tel: (01) 2622499 **Fax:** (01) 2624663
* 9, Vaal Street, off IBB Way, Maitama, Abuja
Tel: (09) 4138388

CENTRE-POINT BANK PLC
Business: Investment Banking
Address: Plot 497, Abogo Largema Street, off Constitution Avenue, Central Business District, Abuja.
Tel: (09) 6701082-9 (8L)
* ICON House, Plot 999F, Idejo/Danmole Street, Victoria Island, Lagos
Tel: (01) 2662624-7 (4L) **Fax:** (01) 2665001
* NIDB Building, 1, Asa Road/Constitution Crescent, Aba.
Tel: (082) 231766
* AISSA House, Plot 2087, Herbert Macaulay Street, Wuse Zone 5, Abuja
Tel: (09) 5238758 **Fax:** (09) 5238759
* UNIC House, 39, New Market Road, Onitsha
Tel: (046) 214113, 217517 **Fax:** (046) 215444
* NICON House, 5, Customs Street, Lagos
Contact: Chief Dennis Onyemaechi Odife - Chairman/CEO

CENTRE-POINT INVESTMENTS LIMITED
Business: Issuing House, Stockbroking and Securities Dealing, Investment Advisory Services
Address: NICON House, 5, Customs St, Lagos Island, Lagos
Tel: (01) 2643177, 2662629, 2669913 **Fax:** (01) 2643177
* Aissa House, Plot 2087, Herbert Macaulay Way (North), Wuse Zone 5, Abuja
Tel: (09) 5238758 **Fax:** (09) 5238759
Contact: Mr. J. I. Odife - MD/CEO

CENTRE-POINT SECURITIES LIMITED
Business: Share Registration Services, Financial Advisory Services, Debt/Financing
Address: NICON House (4th Floor), 5, Customs Street, off Marina, Lagos
Tel: (01) 2662629, 4707092 **Fax:** (01) 2669108
E-mail: cpsl@nova.net.ng
Website: www.centrepointbank.com
Contact: Mrs R. A Aragho - MD/CEO

CENTRESPREAD FCB LIMITED
Business: Advertising, Publicity & Marketing, Communication, Consultancy, Public Relations
Address: 3, Sawyer Crescent, Anthony/Gbagada Road, By Corona Nursery School, Lagos
Tel: (01) 4974627, 4977480, 5550347 Fax: (01) 4930316
E-mail: info@centrespread.net
Contact: Mr. Kolawole Ayanwale - MD/CEO

CENTURION NETWORKS LIMITED
Business: Operations of Pre-Paid Phone Cards
Address: 38/40, Strachan Street, off Igbosere Road, Lagos
Tel: (01) 2646150, 2637825, 2636966
Fax: (01) 2630065, 2634172

CENTURY 21 SYSTEMS LIMITED
Business: Advertising, Public Relations, Publishing, Management Consultancy, Television &Film Production
Address: 7/9, Itire Road, Surulere, Lagos
Tel/Fax: (01) 3209478, 7743404, 08033050267
E-mail: century21s2@yahoo.com
Website: www.century21lagos.com
* 41, Diya Street, Gbagada Estate, Lagos
Contact: Kenneth Odusola Stevenson - President/Joint CEO

CENTURY DYES & CHEMICALS LIMITED
Business: Manufacture of Dyestuffs and Pigments
Address: Churchgate Towers, Plot PC, 30, Afribank Street, Victoria Island, Lagos
Tel: (01) 2620532, 2620533, 2620550
Fax: (01) 2620326, 2620420
* Km. 33, Lagos-Badagry Expressway (Churchgate Bus-Stop), Ologe, Agbara, Ogun State
Tel: (01) 7740671, **Fax:** (01) 2620531
E-mail: pchcdc@churchgate.com
Contact: Mr. B. Mahtani - Chairman/CEO

CENTURY MEDIA LIMITED
Business: Publishing of Newspapers
Address: 217/219, Moshood Abiola Way, Iganmu, Lagos
Tel: (01) 4723021, 7911032 **Fax:** (01) 7730294
E-mail: centurymedia@hyperia.com
Website: www.newage-online.com
* Plot 718, Block 8, Minna St, Area 8, Garki, Abuja
Tel/Fax: (09) 2349715, 2341046
Contact: Mr. Sully Abu - Publisher/Editor-in-Chief

CENTURY OIL SERVICES LIMITED
Business: Oilfield Drilling Services, Supply of Drilling Chemicals and Fluids
Address: 5, Idowu Taylor Street, Victoria Island, Lagos
Tel: (01) 611831, 618258, 619624
Contact: Air Vice Marshal A.D. Bello (rtd.) - CEO.
Dr. S. Bello - MD

CENTURY POLYESTER PLC
Business: Manufacture of Polyester Staple Fibre and Non-Woven Products (Matresses, Sheetings etc.)
Address: Plot 64, Ikorodu Industrial Estate, Ikorodu, Lagos
Tel: (01) 7780264, 7780327, 7780495, 7780623, 7780920, 7780599, 7780429, 7780848
Fax: (01) 7780951
Contact: Lt. Gen. M. I. Wushishi (rtd.) - Chairman
Mr. S. W. Dalamal - MD/CEO

CENTURY SECURITIES LIMITED
Business: Stockbroking, Investment Advisors, Portfolio Management, Money Market Activities
Address: UTC Building, 27, Wharf Road, Apapa, Lagos
Tel: (01) 5871597, 5872827
Contact: Chief (Dr.) Ime E. Ebong - Chairman
Mr. Ola Iranloye - MD/CEO

CENTURY SHOES & ALLIED PRODUCTS NIGERIA LTD
Business: Manufacture of Footwear
Address: 19-23, Okoduwa Street, Kirikiri Industrial Estate, Apapa, Lagos
Tel: (01) 5454729, 7742811
Contact: M. S. Fawaz - Chairman/CEO.

CENTURY TECHNOLOGY LIMITED
Business: Procurement Services for the Oil & Gas Industry, Pipeline/Mechanical Construction, Cathodic Protection and Inspection Services
Address: 116, Awolowo Road, S.W. Ikoyi, Lagos
Tel: (01) 2693337, 2691534 **Fax:** (01) 2693338
E-mail: centurytechnology@hyperia.com
* Plot 127, Trans-Amadi Layout, Port Harcourt
Tel/Fax: (084) 234705
E-mail: centuryph30@hotmail.com
Contact: Engr. Orji Okereke - MD/CEO

CEOTI LIMITED
Business: Oilfield Engineering Services
Address: Plot PC, 10, Engineering Close, off Idowu Taylor Street, Victoria Island, Lagos
Tel: (01) 2623618 **Fax:** (01) 2623617
E-mail: ceoti@hyperia.com
Contact: Mr. Charles O. Thomas - Chairman/CEO.

CEPCO COMMUNICATION SYSTEMS LIMITED
Business: Assembly, Sales, Installation, Service of Digital Transmission Systems, CCTV Monitoring & Communication Equipment. Sales, Service of Computers, Water Treatment & Dispensing Equipment; IT Networking and Training.

Address: Plot 173, Oshodi-Oworonshoki Expressway, Gbagada Estate Phase I, Lagos
Tel: (01) 4932534, 550195, 7743022 Fax: (01) 5550196
E-mail: cepco@cepcosysrems.com
Contact: Dr. Charles Evi Parker - MD/CEO.

CERAMIC MANUFACTURING NIGERIA PLC
Business: Manufacture of Ceramic Sanitary Wares
Address: Plot 5, Challawa Industrial Estate, Kano
Tel: (064) 624724
Contact: Alh. Mahmud Salihu Umoru - Chairman

CES NIGERIA LIMITED
Business: Sales of Laboratory/Medical Equipment/Reagents
Address: 10, Boyle Street (Suite 2), Onikan, Lagos
Tel: (01) 2645035 **Fax:** (01) 2631231
E-mail: cesintl@aol.com
agoll@alpha.linkserve.com
* 12, Azikiwe Road/Forces Avenue (Agoll Suite), Old G.R.A., Port Harcourt.
Tel/Fax: (084) 236037, 236111

CFAO NIGERIA PLC
Business: Conglomerate
Address: 19, Bayo Kuku Street (formerly Waring Road), off Alfred Rewane Road (formerly Kingsway Road), Ikoyi, Lagos
Tel: (01) 2664230, 2662050, 2662129, 2660321
Fax: (01) 2665320, 2663985
E-mail: cfao@hotmail.com
Contact: Mr Jeremy de Brabant - MD/CEO.
Mr S. A. Faderin - Dep. MD.

CFAO MOTORS (Div. of CFAO Nig. Plc)
Business: Distribution and Maintenace of Commercial Vehicles, Passenger Cars & Accessories
Address: 4A, Ijora Causeway, Ijora
Tel: (01) 2880695, 5878450-3 (4L), 7743455, 7746102
Fax: (01) 3205721
E-mail: motorsng@cfao.com
* Plot 568, M Okpara Street, Wuse Zone 11, Abuja.
Tel: (09) 5232913, 5232918
* 2A, Aba Road, Port Harcourt
Tel: (084) 332242, 332522
Contact: Mr. R. Grant - MD/CEO.

CFAO STRUCTEC (Div. of CFAO Nig. Plc)
Business: Water Pumps, Storage, Treatment & Proofing. Site Equipment, Building Materials
Address: Plot 2 & 4, Block D, Amuwo-Odofin Industrial Scheme, Apapa-Oshodi Expressway, Lagos
Tel: (01) 801730-8 (9L), 5847709 **Fax:** (01) 5801739
* Plot 568, M Okpara Street, Wuse Zone 11, Abuja.
Tel: (09) 5232913, 5232918
* 8, Azikiwe Road, Port Harcourt
Tel: (084) 231885, 236140-2 (3L)
Contact: Alh. A. R. Manzuma - GM.

CFAO TECHNOLOGIES (formerly Electro-Hall Nig. Ltd) (Div. of CFAO Nig. Plc)
Business: Distribution & Maintenance of Domestic Appliance & Office Equipment
Address: 1, Aerodrome Road, Apapa, Lagos
Tel: (01) 5803940-9 (10L), 7752098 Fax: (01) 5803949
* Plot 568, M Okpara Street, Wuse, Zone 11, Abuja
* 4, Aba Road, Port Harcourt
Contact: Mr. J. P. Genoud - MD/CEO.

CFC FURNITURE COMPANY (WEST AFRICA) LIMITED
Business: Manufacture & Marketing of Furniture
Address: 334/336, Agege Motor Road, Mushin, Lagos
Tel: (01) 4520724, 4521975
* 49, Aba Road, Port Harcourt
Tel: (084) 332195, 330743
Contact: Chief A.G. Sabbagh - MD/CEO.

CHALLENGER INVESTMENT CO. NIGERIA LTD (Wrangler)
Business: Fashion Sales Outlets
Address: 67, Adeniran Ogunsanya Street, Surulere, Lagos
Tel: (01) 7746792, 08023245843
E-mail: wrangler@linkserve.com
Website: www.wrangler-ci.com
* 7, Allen Avenue, Ikeja, Lagos
Tel: (01) 4938410, 08034078269
* 9B, Adeola Odeku Street, Victoria Island, Lagos
Tel: (01) 5558053
Contact: Mr. Promise Chinekwe - Manager

CHAMICORP LIMITED
Business: Transportation (Haulage)
Address: 109, Maganda Road, Bompai Ind. Estate, Kano
Tel: (064) 645771, 648044, 648077 **Fax:** (064) 645771
E-mail: chamicorp@hotmail.com
Contact: Mr. Khaled B. Chami - MD/CEO

CHAMPION ALUMINIUM METAL COMPANY LIMITED
Business: Fabrication of Aluminium Doors, Windows, Partitions
Address: 73, Old Bukuru Road, Bukuru Low-Cost Junction, Nyango Gyel, Jos
Tel: (073) 280732
Contact: Mr. Stephen Miner - MD/CEO.

CHAMPION BREWERIES PLC
Business: Brewing of Alcoholic Beverages
Address: Industrial Layout, Aka/Nung Udoe Road, Aka Offiot, Uyo
Tel: (085) 200892, 201822, 203925, 204765, 204859.

CHAMPION NEWSPAPERS LIMITED
Business: Journalism & Publishing
Address: Champion House, 156/158, Oshodi-Apapa Expressway, Isolo Industrial Estate, Ilasamaja, Lagos
Tel: (01) 4525807, 4525840, 4525983
Fax: (01) 4520424, 4524421
E-mail: letters@champion-news.com
Website: www.champion-news.com
* Block 4 (Flat 10), Katagum Street, opposite NYSC Headquarters, Area 3, Garki, Abuja
Tel: (09) 2349830 **Fax:** (09) 2349831
Contact: Mr. Emma Agu - MD/Editor-in-Chief

CHAMS NIGERIA LIMITED
Business: Production of Computerised ID Cards & Smartcards, Networking, Wireless Communication; Sales, Maintenance & Maintenance & Repairs of Computers; Sales & Rental of Projectors

Address: 8, Louis Solomon Close, off Ahmadu Bello Way, Victoria Island, Lagos
Tel: (01) 2700070-5 (6L), 4619801-2 (3L)
Fax: (01) 2700079
E-mail: md@chams.com
Website: www.chams.com
Contact: Mr Tnji Aladekomo - MD/CEO

CHANCHANGI AIRLINES (NIGERIA) LIMITED
Business: Airline and Airfreight Services
Address: CV 4, Makera Road, Kakuri, Kaduna
Tel: (062) 231778, 232144, 232555, 232777, 236442, 233857, 236442, 249949, 08033030814
Fax: (062) 231010
E-mail: chanchan@wwlkad.com
* M. Mohammed Airport (Terminal 2), Ikeja, Lagos.
Tel: (01) 4939744, 4939755, 4978226, 7744660
Fax: (01) 4939744, 4978226

CHANGE MANAGEMENT ASSOCIATES LIMITED
Business: Human Resources & Management Cosultancy
Address: Societe Bancaire Building (2nd Floor), Plot 1683, Sanusi Fafunwa Street, Victoria Island, Lagos
Tel: (01) 618177-8 (2 L), 2625059 **Fax:** (01) 3200110
E-mail: cma@infoweb.abs.net
Contact: Mr. Tokie Cardoso - MD/CEO

CHANNEL IT (NIGERIA) LIMITED
Business: Marketing & Distribution of Dell Computers
Address: Plot 1434, Amodu Tijani Street, off Sanusi Fafunwa Street, Victoria Island, Lagos
Tel: (01) 4616716-8 (3 L)
E-mail: info@channelit.net

CHANNEL OIL & PETROLEUM LIMITED
Business: Oil-Field Services
Address: Eleganza Biro Plaza (5th Floor), Plot 634, Adeyemo Alakija Street, Victoria Island, Lagos
Tel: (01) 2702962 **Fax:** (01) 2702967
E-mail: channelpetco@yahoo.com
Contact: Mr. Ebuwa Arigbe - GM/CEO

CHANNEL TECHNOLOGIES LIMITED
Business: Telecommunications Solutions & Service Provider, Sales of GSM Phones & Accessories
Address: 68, Adeniyi Jones Avenue, Ikeja, Lagos
Tel: (01) 7901174, 8120700
Website: www.channeltechnologies.net
Contact: Mr. Bonny Obieze - Chairman/CEO

CHANNELS INCORPORATED LIMITED
Business: Television Broadcast; News & Events Marketing
Address: Kresta Laurel Complex, 376, Ikorodu Road, Maryland, Ikeja, Lagos
Tel: (01) 4934271, 4934272, 4701980 **Fax:** (01) 4934271
Contact: Mr. John Momoh - Chairman/CEO.

CHARDON INDUSTRIES LIMITED
Business: Marketing of Non-Alcoholic Wines
Address: 26, Issa Williams Street, off Broad Street Apongbon, Lagos Island, Lagos
Tel: (01) 2660172, 2667236, 2640049
Contact: Mr. Charles Odunukwe - MD/CEO

CHARELLA NIGERIA LIMITED
Business: Outdoor Advertising, Adveritising Production, Gifts and Promotional Items
Address: 23, Fatai Atere way, Matori Industrial Estate, Mushin, Lagos
Tel: (01) 4528632, 4521089, 8151752 **Fax:** (01) 4521089
E-mail: charella@yahoo.com
charellaltd@yahoo.com
Contact: Mr. Charles Chijide - MD/CEO

CHARIS OPTICIANS LIMITED
Business: Manufacture of Optical Lenses, Optical Services
Address: 26, Broad Street, Lagos Island, Lagos
Tel: (01) 2637037, 2637707 **Fax:** (01) 2636623
E-mail: charisopticians@yahoo.com
* 103, Allen Avenue, Ikeja, Lagos.
Tel: (01) 4935199
* 11, Trans-Amadi Industrial Layout, Port Harcourt
Tel: (084) 230834, 230839 Fax: (084) 230834

CHARLES ADEBIYI & COMPANY
Business: Estate Surveyors, Agents & Valuers, Project & Property Managers, Auctioneering, Continuous Professional Development (CPD) Services
Address: 27, Kakawa Street (1st Floor), Marina, Lagos
Tel: (01) 2647644, 2634281 **Fax:** (01) 2634110, 2634167
* Idowu House, 79/81, Obafemi Awolowo Way, Ikeja, Lagos.
Tel: (01) 4971904, 4971906
Contact: Chief Charles O. Adebiyi - MD/CEO

CHARLES-FLORY LIMITED
Business: Market Consultancy Services, Radio/Television Commercial Production, Advert Placement Monitoring Services, Public Relations, Campaign & Outdoor Services.
Address: 8, Sere Cose, off Coker Road, Ilupeju, Lagos
Tel: (01) 4965354
Contact: Mrs Bunmi Abanishe - MD/CEO

CHARTERED ALUMINIUM SYSTEMS LIMITED
Business: Manufacture, Sales and Installation of Longspan Aluminium Roofs, Windows and Doors, Partitions, Curtain Wallings, etc.
Address: 134, Happy Home Avenue, Kirikiri Industrial Layout, via Mazamaza, Lagos
Tel: (01) 4701339, 4711559, 7732010, 7732009, 08033063994 **Fax:** (01) 2880100
* 9, Obidaya Street, Nnewichi, Nnewi.
Tel: (046) 460544, 462881, 462882
Fax: (046) 461655
* Idu Industrial Layout, Abuja.
Tel: (09) 5239206, 6701113
Contact: Mr. John N. Ajene - Chairman/CEO

CHARPMAN EXPRESS LIMITED
Business: Licensed Customs Agency, Import & Export Consultancy
Address: 6, Industry Road, NPA Wharf, Port Harcourt
Tel: (084) 571781, 0803313210, * (087) 771472
Fax: (084) 571781
* 248, Kirikiri Road, Olodi-Apapa, Lagos
Tel: (080) 33229074

CHARTERED BANK LIMITED
Business: Commercial Banking
Address: Plot 1712, Idejo Street, Victoria Island, Lagos
Tel: (01) 2620380-9 (10 L) **Fax:** (01) 2615094, 2615096
E-mail: info@charterbank.com
Contact: Mr. Odunayo Olagundoye - MD/CEO

CHARTERED LOSS ADJUSTERS LIMITED
Business: Loss Adjusting, Pre-Insurance Surveying
Address: Great Nigeria House (11th Floor), 47/57, Martins Street, Lagos
Tel: (01) 2663816, 2640666 **Fax:** (01) 2640666
Contact: Mr. Darllington C. N. Mgbojikwe - Chairman/CEO

CHARVET NIGERIA LIMITED
Business: Building Civil and Water Engineering, Turnkey Prefab Facilities for Accommodation & Site Office
Address: Hassan Steel Building, Plot 7, Block H, Oshodi Indl Estate, Apapa-Oshodi Expressway, Oshodi, Lagos
Tel: (01) 7741419, 7745720, 522123, 4966233
Fax: (01) 4966233
E-mail: charvet@hyperia.com
linarita@hyperia.com
Contact: A. Abou Hassan - MD/CEO

CHASE EXECUTIVE BUSINESS SERVICES LIMITED
Business: Provision of Serviced Offices, Conference/Meeting Room Facilities
Address: Fortune Towers (9th Floor), 27/29, Adeyemo Alakija Street, Victoria Island, Lagos.
Tel: (01) 2626115, 3200194 **Fax:** (01) 2703372
E-mail: nquiris@chaseexecutive.com

CHASE INSURANCE BROKERS LIMITED
Business: Insurance Broking and Pensions Consultancy
Address: Corporate Ideals House, 72, Bode Thomas Street, Surulere, Lagos
Tel: (01) 801800-4 (5 L), 5851577, 5851536
Fax: (01) 5851577
Contact: Mr. Ikechukwu Obiorah - Chairman
Mr. Bolarinwa T. Joel - GM/CEO

CHASLIT CHEMICAL INDUSTRIES LIMITED
Business: Importation of Industrial & Agricultural Chemicals
Address: 70, Aba-Owerri Road, Aba
Tel: (082) 224172, 225734
* 194/195, Faulks Road, Aba
Contact: Chief Charles Njoku - MD/CEO

CHASTE PROJECT GROUPE
Business: Construction & Civil Engineering Projects Realisation, Functions Enhancing Systems & Products, Specific Industrial Equipment, Oil & Gas Services
Address: 75, D'Alberto Rd, Palm Groove Estte Ilupeju, Lagos
Tel: (01) 7741963,. 4967032; **Fax:** (01) 4967032
E-mail: haccess@nigol.net.ng
Website: www.chastergroupe.com
Contact: Mr. Harry Odey - MD/CEO

CHELIS BOOKAZINE LIMITED
Business: Sales & Distribution of Books, Cards and Stationery, Library Development, School Supplies
Address: 3, Remilekun St, Ogunlana Drive, Surulere, Lagos
Tel: (01) 5837212, 7742241 **Fax:** (01) 5850732, 5832374
E-mail: chelbooks@cyberspace.net.ng
Contact: Mr. A. N. Udoji - MD/CEO

CHELLARAMS PLC
Business: Conglomerate, Manufacturing, Distributive Trade, Farming, Property Development
Address: 2, Goriola St, off Adeola Odeku St, V/ Island, Lagos
Tel: (01) 262453-5 (3 L), 262457, 2623459, 2623461
Fax: (01) 2623458, 2623460
E-mail: kc@linkserve.com.ng
Website: www.chellaramsplc.com
* 100/104, Murtala Road Mohammed Way, Kano
Tel: (064) 637647, 631637
* 9, Trans-Amadi Industrial Layout, Port Harcourt
Tel: (084) 235976, 232460
Contact: Mr. M. T. Chellaram - Chairman

CHELLCO INDUSTRIES LIMITED
Business: Manufacturing of Blankets
Address: A1/E2, Kudenda Industrial Estate, Kaduna
Tel: (062) 232275
* SRC Industries Ltd, Tundun-Wada Light Industrial Layout, Nnamdi Azikiwe Expressway, Kaduna,
Tel: (062) 415938, 413586 **Fax:** (062) 415937
E-mail: srcindu@inet-global.com
Contact: Mr. Chakra Borty - MD/CEO

CHELSEA HOTELS LIMITED
Business: Hospitality
Address: Plot 389, Cadastral Zone AO, Central Area, by Muhammadu Buhari Way, Abuja
Tel: (09) 2349080-98 (19 L) **Fax:** (09) 2349074
E-mail: chelseahotel@mlstn.com
Contact: Chief Patrick Chidolue - Chairman/CEO

CHEMBIAN HERITAGE SUITES LIMITED
Business: Hospitality Services
Address: Plot 1538, Justice Sowemimo St, Asokoro, Abuja
Tel: (09) 3148135

CHEMCOM INDUSTRIES LIMITED
Business: Manufacturers & Importers of Industrial Chemicals
Address: Plot PC, 12, Afibank Street, Victoria Island, Lagos
Tel: (01) 2620339, 2620340, 7742397
Fax: (01) 2613064, 2622093
E-mail: chemcom@infoweb.abs.net
Contact: Mr. Murli Mirchandani - MD/CEO

CHEMIC LIMITED
Business: Spinning of Yarn
Address: 125, Bello Road, P.O.Box 657, Kano
Tel: (064) 649244, 635604
Contact: Mr. Mario Jose - MD/CEO

CHEMICAL & ALLIED PRODUCTS PLC
Business: Manufacturing & Marketing of Paints, Industrial, Agrochemicals & Pharmaceuticals Chemicals
Address: 2, Adeniyi Jones Avenue, Ikeja Ind. Estate, Lagos
Tel: (01) 4972766, 4972450 **Fax:** (01) 4937891
* Oluyole Industrial Estate, off Ring Road, Ibadan
Tel: (02) 23114858, 2312008
Contact: Mr. S. S. Solanke - MD/CEO

CHEMICAL & WIRE MANUFACTURING NIGERIA LTD
Business: Manufacture of Foam Products; Sales of Chemicals
Address: Jagal Road, off Ikosi Road, Oregun Industrial Estate, Oregun, Lagos
Tel: (01) 4964651, 4961382 **Fax:** (01) 4960371
Contact: Mr. Wael Jarmakani - MD/CEO

CHEMIRON INTERNATIONAL LIMITED
Business: Manufacturing of Pharmaceutical Products
Address: Plot 1405, Adetokunbo Ademola Street, V/I, Lagos
Tel: (01) 7743660, 2882976, 4925235, 4925235, 4925556, 7730201, 4925635 **Fax:** (01) 4925556
E-mail: chemironogba@hyperia.com
Contact: Mr. Suresh Jobanputra - Chairman
Mr. Debnath - Marketing Manager

CHEMLAP NIGERIA LIMITED
Business: Production and Marketing of various Classes of Synthetic Resins for Paints, Adhesives Textiles
Address: Chief Adaelu Road, off Km. 5, Old Aba-Owerri Road, Osisioma Industrial Layout, Aba
Tel: (082) 350095, 350096, 350097
* 621, Lagos-Abeokuta Expressway, Danjuma Garage, Ijaiye Ojokoro, Agege, Lagos
Tel: (01) 4922971, 4924238
Contact: Mr. E. O. Adaelu - Chairman/CEO

CHEMO-PHARMA LABORATORIES LIMITED
Business: Manufacturing of Pharmaceutical Products
Address: 10A, Olanrewaju St, Oregun Ind Estate, Ikeja,Lagos
Tel: (01) 4936718
Contact: Mrs. I. O. Adeyemi - Exec. Director/CEO

CHEMSTAR PAINT INDUSTRY (NIGERIA) LIMITED
Business: Manufacturing of Paints and Varnishes
Address: 6, Obasa Road,off Oba Akran Avenue, Ikeja, Lagos
Tel: (01) 7744066, 7755612
E-mail: finecoatpaints@yahoo.com
Contact: Mr. Remi Awode - MD/CEO

CHESS COMPUTER SOLUTIONS LIMITED
Business: Sale & Service of Computers
Address: 111, Ogunlana Surulere, Lagos
Tel: (01) 4702894
E-mail: chess@nigercompass.com
* 24B, Otigba Street, off Obafemi Awolowo Way, Ikeja, Lagos.
Tel: 08023120705
Contact: Mr. Emeka Ochuba - Chairman/CEO

CHESTERFIELD RESOURCES LIMITED
Business: Sales of Furniture and Furnishings
Address: Chesterfield House, 97, Awolowo Road, S. W. Ikoyi, Lagos
Tel: (01) 2695457, 2695373 **Fax:** (01) 2695373
* 47, Allen Avenue, Ikeja, Lagos
Tel: (01) 4975980, 4975979 **Fax:** (01) 4975980
* Plot 511, Herbert Macaulay Way, Wuse Zone 4, Abuja. **Tel:** (09) 5232206
* 13, Gana Street, Maitama District, Abuja
Tel: (09) 4138648, 4138648 **Fax:** (09) 4138648
* 59, Woji Street, G.R.A., Phase II, Port Harcourt
Tel: (084) 233043

CHEVRONTEXACO NIGERIA LIMITED
Business: Exploration & Production of Crude Oil & Gas
Address: 2, Chevron Drive, Lekki Peninsula, Lagos
Tel: (01) 2600600 **Fax:** (01) 2600395
Website: www.chevron.com
* 46, Trans-Amadi Industrial Layout, Port Harcourt
* Km 4, Warri Port Expressway, Warri
Contact: Mr. Jay R. Pryor - Chairman/MD
Mr Femi Odumabo - GM (Govt/Public Affairs)

CHEZPAQ LIMITED
Business: Sales of Security Equipment & Systems and Long-Range Cordless Telephone Sets, Telecommunication Services
Address: 22, Alhaja Kofoworola Crescent, off Obafemi Awolowo Way, Ikeja, Lagos
Tel: (01) 4937053, 4938533; **Fax:** (01) 4977021
E-mail: chezpaq@infoweb.abs.net
Contact: Maxwel Mark - Chairman/CEO

CHI PHARMACEUTICALS LIMITED
Business: Importation, Distribution and Marketing of Pharmaceuticasl Products
Address: Plot 20, Chief Benson Anorue Street, Ajao Estate, Apakun-Oshodi, Lagos.
Tel: (01) 4520626-32 (7 L), 4520592, 7740383, 45220965
Fax: (01) 4520980, 4975280
E-mail: chipharma@clicktgi.com
Website: www.clicktgi.com
Contact: Mr. C. G. Vink - Chairman/CEO

CHIBEK OILTOOLS LIMITED
Business: Supply and Maintenance of Petroleum Testing/ Analytical Instruments
Address: 11, Allen Avenue, Ikeja, Lagos
Tel/Fax: (01) 4971834, 4931585
E-mail: office@chibek.com
Website: www.chibek.com
Contact: Mr Charles Ibe - GM/CEO

CHIBEX INTERBIZ AGENCY (NIGERIA) LIMITED
Business: Importer of Automobile Spare Parts & Accessories
Address: B6/18, New Auto Parts Market, Nkpor via Onitsha
Contact: Mr. Chibuzor W. Okolo - Chairman/CEO

CHIBUEZE CHEMIST LIMITED
Business: Importation and Sales of Pharmaceutical Products
Address: 15, Limca Road Nkpor, Onitsha
Tel: (046) 412937
E-mail: chibuezechem@hotmail.com
Contact: Chief G. O. Chibueze - Chairman/CEO

CHIC AFRIQUE BEAUTY COMPANY LIMITED
Business: Manufacture of Cosmetics and Fragrances, Beauty Training Institute
Address: 3, Thorburn Avenue, Sabo-Yaba, Lagos
Tel: (01) 5455266 **Fax:** (01) 2693627
E-mail: opra@hyperia.com
Contact: Chief (Mrs.) Opral Mason Benson - Chairman/CEO

CHICAGO MERCHANDISING COMPANY LIMITED (CMC Interiors)
Business: Manufacturing, Importation and Sales of Furniture,

Furnishings and Accessories
Address: Plot CL. 2, Ikosi Road, Opp. Steelways, Oregun, Ikeja, Lagos
Tel: (01) 7749789, 08022905238 **Fax:** (01) 4934884
E-mail: yinkaosobu@usa.net
* Plot 470, Aminu Kano Crescent, Wuse II, Abuja
Tel: (09) 5231328
Contact: Yinka Osobu - Chairman
Ms. Ayo Delumo - MD/CEO

CHICASON GROUP OF COMPANIES
Business: Conglomerate (Manufacturing, Lubricant Refining, Trading & Contracting)
Address: Rimco Drive, Chicason Avenue, Akwa-Uru Industrial Estate, Umudim, Nnem, Anambra State
Tel: (046) 460173, 460648, 462913-7 (5 L)
Fax: (046) 460972, 462929
* Intercontinental Plaza (2nd Floor), Plot 999C, Danmole St, off Idejo St, Victoria Island, Lagos
Tel: (01) 613465, 617714 **Fax:** (01) 2622983
* A-Z Gas Plant, Idu Industrial Estate, Idu FCT
Contact: Chief (Sir) A C Okafor - Chairman/CEO
Mr. Mike Oji - Executive Assistant to CEO

CHIEME GROUP OF COMPANIES
Business: Manufacturing & Marketing of Auto Parts and Accessories, General contractors, Import & Export
Address: 33, St. Michael's Road, Aba
Tel: (082) 222330, 225456 **Fax:** (082) 228316
E-mail: chieme@phca.linkserve.com
Website: www.chieme.com
Contact: Chief (Sir) Francis C. Chukwuonye - Chairman/CEO

CHIFY (NIGERIA) LIMITED
Business: Oilfield Engineering Services
Address: Plot 216, Trans-Amadi Industrial Layout Phase II, by Ordinance Junction, Port Harcourt
Tel/Fax: (084) 237614

CHILEX SECURITY PRODUCTS LIMITED
Business: Supply of Ironmongery Products and Assorted High-Security Locks, Master Key Systems, Electrical Locks, Door-Closers, Key-Duplicating Machines and Blanks and Security Gadgets
Address: 12, Olowu Street, Ikeja, Lagos
Tel: (01) 4965005, 4932551 **Fax:** (01) 4965005
* 213, Port Harcourt, Aba
* Banex Shopping Plaza (Suite BS 115) Aminu Kano Crescent, Zone A7, Wuse II, Abuja
Contact: Mazi Mannix A. Ihueze - Chairman/CEO

CHIMEX UNITED COMPANY LIMITED
Business: Importation and Marketing of Gas Lighters and General Merchandise
Address: 2, Pedro Street, off 7, Docemo St, Idumota, Lagos
Tel: (01) 2640101, 2661438, 7746122
E-mail: chimex99@alpha.linkserve.com
Contact: Nze Chimezie Osuala - Chairman/CEO

CHINA CIVIL ENGINEERING CONSTRUCTION CORPORATION
Business: Civil & Transport Engineering, Building Services
Address: Plot 564 & 565, Block B, Airport Road, Central Area Garki, Abuja
Tel: (09) 2341105, 2347430
* Railway Compound, 46, Nnamdi Azikiwe Drive, Ebute-Metta, Lagos
Tel/Fax: (01) 5850712, 5851905, 7743142
E-mail: cceccnr@alpha.linkserve.com

CHIMONS GAS LIMITED
Business: Marketing of Petroleum Products, Engineering Construction & Consultancy, Oil & Gas Services
Address: Fortune Towers (6th Floor), 27/29, Adeyemo Alakija Street, Victoria Island, Lagos
Tel: (01) 2623561-3 (3 L), 2620085, 08036060555
Fax: (01) 2620086
E-mail: chimons@chimons.com
Contact: Engr. Chibuike Achigbu - Chairman/CEO

CHINA HARBOUR ENGINEERING COMPANY LIMITED
Business: Construction and Civil Engineering
Address: Intercontinental Plaza (5th Floor), Plot 999C, Danmole St, off Idejo Street, Victoria Island, Lagos
Tel: (01) 2623015, 2622991 **Fax:** (01) 2622991
Contact: Engr. Zhu Gang - MD/CEO

CHINA JOINT PARIS (C.J.S.) LIMITED
Business: Processing & Bottling of Table Water
Address: 21, Nababa Badamasi Rd, Bompai Ind. Estate, Kano
Tel: (064) 634295, 634193 **Fax:** (064) 634807
E-mail: alma@starnet.net.ng
Contact: Mr. Tariq Mossallati - MD/CEO

CHINEDU NWOSU & COMPANY
Business: Estate Surveyors & Valuers, Estate Agency & Property Development, Feasibility & Viability Appraisals, Project Development & Management, Rating Consultancy
Address: Coscharis Plaza (3rd Floor), 68A, Adeola Odeku Street, Victoria Island, Lagos
Tel: (01) 2624325, 08033343529, 08033234902
* Zone 6 Cornershops Complex (Suite 20), Sudan Street, Wuse Zone 6, Abuja
Tel: (09) 6708277, 5235239, 08044129769
Contact: Mr. A. Chinedu Nwosu - Principal Partner

CHIPS, BITS & BYTES LIMITED
Business: Sales & Repairs of Computer Systems, System Integration & Networking, Software Development
Address: 24, Aromire Avenue, Ikeja, Lagos
Tel: (01) 77442144, 4933459, 4932157, 4967992
Fax: (01) 4932157
E-mail: cbbl@hyperia.com
Contact: Mr. Tunji Ola - MD/CEO

CHISCO GROUP OF COMPANIES
Business: Transporter, Import & Export, Courier & Air Services, General Merchandising
Address: 6/8, Market Street, Oyingbo, Lagos
Tel: (01) 2880536, 7749594, 7749520, 7749419, 863537, 867191, 867691, 862983 **Fax:** (01) 2880536
E-mail: chisco@hyperia.com
* Plot 176, Utako Life Camp Road, Berger, Abuja
* 29 & 36, Ikwerre Road, Port Harcourt
Contact: Chief (Dr.) Chidi Anyaegbu - Chairman/CEO

CHIYODA NIGERIA LIMITED
Business: Design, Construction and Maintenance of Petro-chemical Plants and Refineries
Address: AIICO Plaza, Plot PC. 12, Afribank St, V/I, Lagos
Tel: (01) 2613219

CHIZECK CHEMICAL COMPANY LIMITED
Business: Manufacturers of Hair-Care Products
Address: Benson Akinyele Street, off Ejigbo Road, Oke-Afa, Isolo, Lagos
Tel: (01) 7740946
Contact: Mr. I. C. Chibzor - MD/CEO

CHOFFAN COMMUNICATIONS LIMITED
Business: Communications, VSAT Services, Networking
Address: 228B, Muri Okunola Street, Victoria Island, Lagos
Tel: (01) 2622314, 2622576, 2703636-7 (2 L)
Fax: (01) 2622314, 2623093
E-mail: chrometech@hyperia.com
chromeoil@hyperia.com
Contact: Alh. Gidado Idris - Chairman
Sir Emeka C. Offor (KSC) - MD/CEO

CHOCOLATE ROYAL LIMITED
Business: Manufacture of Foods and Cofectionery
Address: 267A, Etim Inyang Crescent, Victoria Island, Annex, Lagos
Tel: (01) 2623055, 2623056 **Fax:** (01) 2614779

CHOICE FINISHING & FURNISHING LIMITED
Business: Sale of Leather, Home & Office Furniture, Marble & Granite Works, Sales/Installation of Vitrified Tiles, Doors & Frames
Address: Plot 642F, Akin Adesola St, Victoria Island, Lagos
Tel: (01) 2617479, 2621939, 7752631 **Fax:** (01) 2621938
* 8, Mobolaji Bank-Anthony way, Ikeja, Lagos
* Plot 536, Adetokunbo Ademola Crescent, Wuse II, Abuja.
Tel: (09) 5238774, 08023003840 **Fax:** (09) 5238781
Contact: Mr. Chinedu Chigbu - Chairman/CEO

CHOIZCOM LIMITED
Business: Sales of Internet Telephony Equipment
Address: 10, Toyin Street, Ikeja, Lagos
Tel: (01) 4937813, 4932459, 7747521 **Fax:** (01) 4932459
E-mail: choizcom@yahoo.com
Website: www.chioz.net

CHRIS EJIK GROUP OF COMPANIES LIMITED
Business: Sales of Power Generation, Distribution & Supply Equipment, Agricultural Equipment and Agro-Allied Chemicals, Beauty PharmaceuticalProducts
Address: 3, Oje-Imianvan Rd, off Oregun Road, Ikeja, Lagos
Tel: (01) 4938181, 4964758 **Fax:** (01) 4972155
E-mail: chris-ejik@hyperia.com
Website: www.chrisejik.com

CHRIS ERNEST (NIGERIA) LIMITED
Business: Clearing & Forwarding Agents, Import & Export, Transportation and Warehousing Services
Address: 8, Adesina Street, Ijeshatedo, Lagos
Tel: (01) 5846713, 835691-2 (2 L), 08033211611
Fax: (01) 3206320
E-mail: xrisernest@yahoo.com
Contact: Sir. Chibu Ernest - MD/CEO

CHRIS IMPEX LIMITED
Business: Importation of Cement Aluminium Products, Electronic, Steel Products & Security Equipment
Address: 50, Modupe Johnson Crescent, off Adeniran Ogunsanya Street, Surulere, Lagos
Tel: (01) 834717 **Fax:** (01) 4922249
E-mail: chrisimpexltd@yahoo.com
Contact: Mr. Chris Mofunanya - MD/CEO

CHRISLINK INTERNATIONAL LIMITED
Business: Sales & Maintenance of Computers & Accessories
Address: 99B, Obafemi Awolowo Way, Ikeja, Lagos
Tel: (01) 4974639
Contact: Chief Chris Nwalor -MD/CEO

CHRISMATEL HOLDINGS LIMITED
Business: Shipping, Container Terminal Operations, Pharmacueticals & Fruit-drinks Production, Oil & Gas Business, Insurance, Leasing and Finance
Address: 8, Akanbi Onitiri Close, off Eric Moore Road, Iganmu Industrial Estate, Surulere, Lagos
Tel: (01) 2646746, 2646748, 2646071, 5454140-2 (3 L), 5456070-3 (4 L), 5456074
Fax: (01) 5456071, 2646066, 5454143-4 (2 L)
E-mail: chrismatel@hyperia.com
Website: www.chrismatel.com
Contact: Mr. Peter Eloka Okocha OON - Chairman/CEO

CHRISMATEL SHIPPING COMPANY (NIGERIA) LIMITED
Business: Clearing & Forwarding, Shipping, Ship Chandling, Warehousing, Customs Bonded-Terminal Operators, Transportation and Stevedoring
Address: 8, Akanbi Onitiri Close, off Eric Moore Road, Iganmu Industrial Estate, Surulere, Lagos
Tel: (01) 2646746, 2646748, 2646071, 5454140-2 (3 L), 5456070-3 (4 L), 5456074
Fax: (01) 5456071, 2646066, 5454143-4 (2 L)
E-mail: chrismatel@hyperia.com
Website: www.chrismatel.com
* BLock 121, NAHCO Shed (Cargo Section), M.M.International Airport, Ikeja, Lagos
* General Post Office Building, Station Road, Port Harcourt
Tel: (084) 235093-4 (2 L)
Contact: Mr. Peter Eloka Okocha OON - Chairman
Mr Babatope Ogungbemile - MD/CEO

CHRISROCK INDUSTRIES LIMITED
Business: Manufacturing and Marketing of Security Doors, Panels and Flush Doors, Mouldings and Kitchen Units, Wood Processing
Address: 7, Ladipo Oluwole Street, off Adeniyi Jones Avenue, Ikeja, Lagos
Tel: (01) 4924309

CHRISTELLA CHEMICAL WORKS LIMITED
Business: Manufacture of Intravenous Infusions, Hospital and Chemical Works, Manufacture of Scientific Chemical Equipment and Pharmaceuticals
Address: 102, St. Finbarr's College Rd, Akoka, Yaba, Lagos

Tel/Fax: (01) 823005
Contact: Dr. Peter K. E. Idundun - Chairman/CEO

CHRISTLIEB PLC
Business: Manufacture & Distribution of Pharmaceuticals, Cosmetics & Toiletries, Icing Sugar & Glucose & Plastic Bottles
Address: 39, Creek Road, Apapa, Lagos
Tel: (01) 5452731 **Fax:** (01) 5872781
Contact: J B Arogunmati - Group MD/CEO

CHRISTON INVESTMENT LIMITED
Business: Sales and Maintenance of Generator Spare Parts and Machinery Filters
Address: 36, Oregun Road, Oregun, Ikeja, Lagos
Tel: (01) 7742393, 4932636
Contact: Mr. Chris Ojo-Emovon - Chairman/CEO

CHRISTOVAL INDUSTRIAL COMPANY LIMITED
Business: Manufacturing & Importation of Petrochemical Products (HDPE, LDPE, PP, Polythene)
Address: 31E, Madueke St, opp.Afex Bank, Odoakpu, Onitsha
Tel: (046) 411168, 413930
Contact: Mr. Ignatius I. Okechukwu - Chairman/CEO

CHROME AIR SERVICES LIMITED
Business: Charter Airline Services; Maintenance of Aircraft
Address: Plot 228, Muri Okunola St, Victoria Island, Lagos
Tel: (01) 7746067 **Fax:** (01) 2622314
E-mail: chromeoil@hyperia.com
Contact: Sir Emeka C. Offor - (KSC) - MD/CEO

CHROME ENVIRONMENTAL & ENGINEERING SERVICES LIMITED
Business: Environmetal Consultancy Services
Address: 228B, Muri Okunola Street, Victoria Island, Lagos
Tel: (01) 2622314, 2622576 **Fax:** (01) 2622314, 2623093
E-mail: chrometech@hyperia.com
chromeoil@hyperia.com
* Bungalow 1, Crystal Palace Estate, NNPC Housing Complex Road, Edjeba, Warri
* 7, Tombia Street, G.R.A., Phase II, Port Harcourt
Contact: Sir Emeka C. Offor (KSC) - MD/CEO

CHROME OIL SERVICES LIMITED
Business: Oilfield Engineering & Consultancy Services, Electrical, Mechanical, Civil and Building Works
Address: 228B, Muri Okunola Street, Victori Island, Lagos
Tel: (01) 2622314, 2622576 **Fax:** (01) 2623093, 2622314
E-mail: chrometech@hyperia.com
chromeoil@hyperia.com
* 7, Tombia Road, G.R.A., Port Harcourt
Contact: Sir Emeka C. Offor, KSC - MD/CEO

CHROME SURVEY LIMITED
Business: Dredging Operations and Land Reclamation
Address: 228B, Muri Okunola Street, Victoria Island, Lagos
Tel: (01) 2622314, 2622576, 2703636-7 (2 L)
Fax: (01) 2622314, 2623093
E-mail: chrometech@hyperia.com
chromeoil@hyperia.com
Contact: Alh. Gidabo Idris - Chairman
Sir Emeka C. Offor (KSC) - MD/CEO

CHUKABEN AGENCIES NIGERIA LIMITED
Business: Clearing and Forwarding Agency
Address: 10, Industrial Road, Olodi-Apapa, Lagos
Tel: (01) 5877566, 7748228 **Fax:** (01) 5877566
Contact: Mr. Benett Anumudu - Chairman/CEO

CHUKACON GROUP
Business: Import & Export Trading, Freight Forwarders
Address: Eagle Bank House, 12, Idumagbo Avenue, Idumota, Lagos
Tel: (01) 2640537, 2662663
E-mail: cgl@chkacongroup.com
sales@chukacongroup.com
Website: www.chukacongroup.com
* Block 1 (No 5), Lagos Island L G. Plaza, Oroyinyin Street, Idumota, Lagos
Tel: (080) 23444048

CHUKPEE INTERNATIONAL LIMITED
Business: Sales of Information Products & Accessories, Sales & Installation of Office Equipment
Address: 10, Adepele Street, off Medical Road, Ikeja, Lagos
Tel: (01) 4933910, 08033087010, 08033025290
Fax: (01) 4933910
* Abuja Shopping Mall (Suite D10), Zone 3, Wuse, Abuja
Tel: (09) 5230725, 08034727038, 08023304955
Fax: (01) 5230725

CHUKWU DI TRANSPORT SERVICES (NIGERIA) LIMITED
Business: Passenger Transportation Services
Address: Km. 4, Onitsha-Owerri Road, Onitsha
Tel: (046) 482152, 08022243110
Contact: L. N. Akpawusi - Chairman/CEO

CHURCHBELLS PHARMACEUTICALS (NIGERIA) LIMITED
Business: Manufacturing, Importation and Distribution of Pharmaceutical Products
Address: 22/24, Creek Road, Apapa, Lagos
Tel: (01) 5455873, 5871510 **Fax:** (01) 5455873
E-mail: churchbells@micro.com.ng
Website: www.churchbells-inc.com
* 12A, Dennis Osadebe Street, Aso Rock Villa, Asokoro, Abuja.
Tel: (09) 3140864
Contact: Mr. Etim Oyosoro - MD/CEO.

CHURCHGATE NIGERIA LIMITED
Business: Trading and Merchandising, Importation and Marketing of Rice, Sugar and other Commodities
Address: Churchgate Tower (8th Floor), Plot PC. 30, Afribank Street, Victoria Island, Lagos
Tel: (01) 2620532, 2620533 **Fax:** (01) 2620326
E-mail: gaitonde@churchgate.com
Website: www.churchgate.com
Contact: Mr. Ratan Mahtani - Chairman

CHURCHIS VENTURES LIMITED
Business: Sales, Installation, Maintenance & Engineering of Telecommunication Equipment
Address: 69, H. Macaulay St/Jebba St, Ebute-Metta, Lagos
Tel: (01) 866845, 868176 **Fax:** (01) 5890219, 866845
Contact: Mr. Uche B. Iloka - MD/CEO

CHUTZPAH INTERNATIONAL LIMITED
Business: Manufacturing & Sales of Furniture, Interior Decoration & Landscaping Services, Importation & Sales of General Merchandise
Address: 18, King George V Street (Suites 5, 12 & 13), Onikan, Lagos
Tel: (01) 2636310, 7730062, 08033050333, 08023135610
Fax: (01) 4615203
E-mail: info@chutzpaths.com
Website: www.chutzpahs.com
Contact: Ms. Angela Agidi - MD/CEO

CHYZOB ENTERPRISES LIMITED
Business: Real Estate, General Contractors, Import & Export, Telecommunications
Address: 168, Awolowo Road, S.W. Ikoyi, Lagos
Tel: (01) 2694545, 2691086, 2693715 **Fax:** (01) 2695544
E-mail: chyzobcomms@yahoo.com
Contact: Dr. Obioha N. Ugoji - Chairman/President

CIBI NIGERIA LIMITED
Business: Importation and Sales of Granite Tiles and Slabs; Engraving Services
Address: Plot F3, Cibi Road, Mando Light Ind. Area, off N. Azikiwe Expressway, behi New Panteka, Kaduna
Tel: (062) 319908 **Fax:** (062) 318901
E-mail: cibi@skannet.com
nuhuwya@skannet.com
* Area 11 Cornershops, near FCDA, Ahmadu Bello Way, Area 11, Garki, Abuja.
Tel: (09) 3140765
* 116, Ikorodu Road, Palmgrove, Lagos
Contact: Arc. Nuhu S. Wya - Chairman/CEO.

CICA NIGERIA LIMITED
Business: Sales and Service of Forklifts, Generators, Water Pumps and Photocopier Papers
Address: 1, Davies Street, off Marina, Lagos
Tel: (01) 2662050, 2660321, 2662129, 2665256
Fax: (01) 2665320
* 11, Sapara Williams Street, off Ladipo Oluwole Avenue, Ikeja Industrial Estate, Ikeja, Lagos
Tel: (01) 4931952-4 (3 L), 8042387 **Fax:** (01) 4931955
E-mail: cica@cyberspace.net.ng
Contact: Pastor B. O. Ajidagba - GM/CEO

CICO HOLDINGS LIMITED
Business: Manufacturing and Marketing of PVC Roofing Materials & Pressure Pipes, Polyethylene & Polypropylene Bags
Address: Plot 84, Trans-Amadi Ind. Layout, Port Harcourt
Tel: (084) 237607, 232614, 235075 **Fax:** (084) 237608
E-mail: cico@phca.linkserve.com
Contact: Mr. R. Chu - Chairman/CEO

CIKA GROUP OF COMPANIES
Business: Manufacturing of Pharmaceutical Products, Importaton of Pharmaceutical Raw Material, Surgical Equipment & Sundries; Book Publishing, Power & Energy, Building & Construction
Address: Plot 23, Block 2, Thinkers Corner, Enugu
Tel: (042) 555236, 559489 **Fax:** (042) 559489
Contact: Prince Chris C. Atuegwu - Chairman/CEO

CIKASON WEST AFRICA LIMITED
Business: Industrialists, Import & Export, Manufacturer's Representatives, General Merchandising
Address: Block A (1st Floor, Shop 5), Urban Shopping Complex, near Rita Lori Hotel, Nnamdi Azikiwe Street, Lagos
Tel: (01) 2660022 **Fax:** (01) 2663996

CINCON INTERNATIONAL COMPANY LIMITED
Business: Sales of Medical and Health Products
Address: 49, Ashogbon Street, Isale-Eko, Idumota, Lagos
Tel: (01) 2667381, 2666336 **Fax:** (01) 2667381, 2623985
Contact: Mr. Celestine C. Izugha - MD/CEO

CINEKRAFT INDEPENDENT FILM & ASSOICIATES
Business: Television/Film Production, Equipment Rental and Crew Hire
Address: 7, Adeniyi Jakande Close, off Adeniran Ogunsanya Street, Surulere, Lagos
Tel: (01) 831104, 830709 **Fax:** (01) 831104
E-mail: cinekraft@nova.net.ng
cinekraft@usa.net
Contact: Mr. Adewale Fanu - MD/CEO

CINO NIGERIA LIMITED
Business: Design, Sales and Leasing of Pump Operating Systems; Depot Process Layout & Design; Installation of Water & Sewage Treatment Plants; Cathodic Protection, Environmental Impact Assessment
Address: 14/16, Oladipo Kuku St, Allen Avenue, Ikeja, Lagos
Tel: (01) 4976543 **Fax:** (01) 4972550
E-mail: cino@alpha.linkserve.com
* 4, Chief Nwuke Street, off BEWAC Junction, Trans-Amadi Industrial Layout, Port Harcourt
Tel: (234-84) 232773
E-mail: cino@phca.linkserve.com

CINSERE SEWING MACHINES INDUSTRIES CO. LTD
Business: Assembly and Sales of Sewing Machines, Importation of Motorcycle Parts and Pharmaceuticals
Address: 6/8, Badejo Kalesanwo Streeet, Matori Industrial Estate, Mushin, Lagos
Tel: (01) 520872, 523065 **Fax:** (01) 526851
Contact: Chief J. A. Babatayo - Chairman/CEO

CISCON NIGERIA LIMITED
Business: Oilfield Services, Fabrication of Machines and Parts, Sales of Oilfield Equipment
Address: Km. 14, P. Harcourt-Aba Expressway, Port Harcourt
Tel: (084) 612082-3 (2 L), 612273 **Fax:** (084) 612080
E-mail: cison@alpha.linkserve.com

CITEC INTERNATIONAL ESTATES LIMITED
Business: Property & Real Estate Development and Managment
Address: CITEC House, Plot 2434, Ganges Street, off Alvan Ikok Way, Maitama, Abuja
Tel: (09) 4138262, 4138871, 4132490
Fax: (09) 4138263
E-mail: citec-international@linkserve.com
citecestates@linkserve.com
Website: www.citec-international.com

CITECO TECHNICAL COMPANY LIMITED
Business: Clearing Services, Engineering Services, Fabrication of Tyres, Repair of Conveyor Belts
Address: CITECO Towers, Plot 7, New Secretariat Road, Agidingbi, Ikeja, Lagos
Tel: (01) 4922048, 4924407, 7741965, 7751867
Fax: (01) 4961301
Contact: Elder Olu Ogunlude - President/CEO

CITI COMMUNICATIONS LIMITED
Business: Telecoms Engineering/Internet Services, Sales, Installation and Maintenance of Computers and Office Communication Systems, Information Technology Training & Consultancy
Address: 8B, Wetheral Road, Owerri
Tel: (083) 234710, 232505 **Fax:** (083) 230596
Contact: Engr. Boniface M. Osunkwo - Chairman/CEO

CITI PROPS LIMITED
Business: Real Estate Development and Managment
Address: 130, Lewis Street, Lafiaji, Lagos
Tel: (01) 7754715, 2646039
E-mail: citipros@yahoo.com
Contact: Mr. Ejiofor Ezekwe - Chairman

CITIBANK NIGERIA
Business: Commercial Banking
Address: Commerce House, 1, Idowu Taylor Street, Victoria Island, Lagos
Tel: (01) 262000-9 (10L), 2622024-32 (9L)
Fax: (01) 2618916, 2621404
Contact: Mr. Arit Usmani - MD/CEO
Mr Diran Olojo - Public Affairs Officer

CITILADS INSURANCE BROKERS LIMITED
Business: Insurance Broking
Address: 57, Awoyokun Street, Onipanu, Lagos
Tel: (01) 821260
Contact: Mr Tunde Sode - MD/CEO

CITILINK GROUP
Business: Sale of Information Technology Products, Finance and Network Security Consultancy Services
Address: Regency Suite (Ground Floor), 17, Ahmed Onibudo Street, Victoria Island, Lagos
Tel: (01) 2625063, 2624409, 4702394 **Fax:** (01) 2624409
Contact: Mr Osita Odife - MD/CEO

CITITRUST INVESTMENT LIMITED
Business: Ship Chartering, Shipping, Investments.
Address: Cititrust Plaza (9th Floor), 9/11, Catholic Mission Street, Lagos
Tel: (01) 2635631, 2645380, 2635880 **Fax:** (01) 2664165
E-mail: clubs@infoweb.abs.net

CITIZENS INTERNATIONAL BANK LIMITED
Business: Commercial Banking
Address: Plot 130, Ahmadu Bello Way, Victoria Island, Lagos
Tel: (01) 2623780-7 (8L)
Fax: (01) 2615138
Website: www.citizensbank.org
Contact: Mr. Chika C. Mbonu - MD/CEO
Mr Tony Ndiulor - Head(Corporate Affairs)

CITIZENS INVESTMENT & SECURITIES LIMITED
Business: Financial Services, Portfolio Management, Warehousing Services. Advisory Services
Address: 23A, Akin Adesola Street, Victoria Island, Lagos
Tel: (01) 2621174, 611199, 611199, 611167
Fax: (01) 2621175
Contact: Mr. I. C. Ilozumba - MD/CEO

CITRACO INDUSTRIES LIMITED
Business: Manufacturing Import & Export
Address: 252B, Aba-Owerri Road, Aba
Tel: (082) 350039, 350040
Contact: Chief C. I. Ogugua - Chairman/CEO

CITY BUSINESS COMPUTERS LIMITED
Business: Distribution of Computer Hardware, Software Applications and Peripherals, Computer Consultancy Services
Address: 8, Obanta Road, Apapa G.R.A., Lagos
Tel: (01) 54533085, 5453112 **Fax:** (01) 2667898
E-mail: cbc@linkserve.com.ng
Contact: Mr. Gbade Alabi - MD/CEO

CITY EXPRESS BANK PLC
Business: Commercial Banking
Address: City Express Bank House, Plot 1637, Adetokunbo Ademola Street, Victoria Island, Lagos
Tel: (01) 2622454-8 (5L), 3201472-4 (3L)
Fax: (01) 2619024, 2622464
E-mail: inbank@industrialbank.com.ng
E-mail: ceb@cityexpress.com
Website: www.cityexpressbank.com
* 1E, Bello Road, Kano
Tel: (064) 642749, 635065, 646048 **Fax:** (064) 645048
* AP Plaza, Adetokunbo Ademola Crescent, Wuse II, Abuja
Tel: (09) 5235140, 5234396 **Fax:** (09) 5233293
* Admiralty Building, Plot 202, Olu Obasanjo Road, Port Harcourt
Tel: (084) 2341429
Contact: Mrs. Olusola E. Adeoti - MD/CEO

CITY EXPRESS PROPERTIES LIMITED
Business: Real Estate Development & Management
Address: City Express Bank House, Plot 1637, Adetokunbo Ademola Street, Victoria Island, Lagos
Tel: (01) 2622454-8 (5 L), 3201472-4 (3 L), 08023159343, 08023221885, 08023212850

CITY FINANCE & SECURITIES LIMITED
Business: Stockbroking, Investment Advisory Services, Portfolio Management, Trade & Import Financing
Address: City Express Bank Building (1st Floor), Plot 1637, Adetokunbo Ademola St, Victoria Island, Lagos
Tel: (01) 461897, 2622454-7 (4L), 2616752, 3201473-5 (3L)
Fax: (01) 2619024, 2622464
E-mail: indbank@industrialbank.com.ng
Contact: Prince (Dr.) Samuel Adedoyin - Chairman
Mrs. Sola Adeoti - Managing Director

CITY INVESTMENT MANAGEMENT LIMITED
Business: Stockbroking, Portfolio Manageemnt, Corporate Business Consultants, Investment Advisory

Services, Issuig House
Address: 20, Bombay Crescent, Apapa, Lagos
Tel: (01) 5872675, 5872677 **Fax:** (01) 5876157
Contact: Mr. Kayode B. Sonaike - Chairman/CEO

CITY LOSS ADJUSTERS (NIGERIA) LIMITED
Business: Loss Adjusting, Risk Surveying and Valuations
Address: Como House, 9, Western Avenue, opp. U.B.A., Ojuelegba Roundabout, Surulere, Lagos
Tel: (01) 4700245, 77446948, 08033063979
Fax: (01) 58511798
E-mail: citylossadjuster@yahoo.com
* 68, Mbonu Street, D/Line, Port Harcourt
Contact: Chief R. O. Okpara - Chairman/CEO

CITY MESSENGERS NIGERIA LIMITED
Business: Express Courier Services
Address: Nurses House (2nd Floor), Plot PC, 43, Afribank Street, Victoria Island, Lagos
Tel: (01) 3200330, 2624409, 614601, 614046, 613809, 7758390
E-mail: citymessengers@yahoo.com
Contact: Mr. Nick O . Odife - Chairman/CEO

CITY SECURITIES LIMITED
Business: Corporate Finance and Capital Market Operations, Stockbroking and Nominee Services, Money & Commercial Market Operations, Registrars.
Address: Primrose Tower, 17A, Tinubu Street, Lagos
Tel: (01) 2665944-53 (10 L), 2641293
Fax: (01) 2665126, 2668833
E-mail: research@csl-group.com
Website: www.csl-group.com
* UAC Complex (Ground Floor), Plot 272 & 273, Central Business District, Abuja
Tel: (09) 5237910, 5237908-9 (2 L) **Fax:** (09) 5237918
* 282A, Port Harcourt/Aba Expressway (1st Floor), G.R.A. Phase II, Port Harcourt
Tel: (084) 237773-4 (3 L), 236533 **Fax:** (084) 237773
Contact: Mr M T Akporowho - Exec.Director/CEO

CITY TRAVELS & TOURS NIGERIA LIMITED
Business: Travel Agency, Packaging & Operations of Tours and School Excursions
Address: Plot 1681, Sanusi Fafunwa St, Victoria Is, Lagos
Tel: (01) 2621896, 7746947, 7752542, 08032001666
Fax: (01) 2627733
E-mail: citytravels2@yahoo.com
E-mail: citytravel@vgccl.net
* Verdict Plaza (Shop 209), Plot 1059, Adetokunbo Ademola Crescent, Wuse II, Abuja
Tel: (09) 5232792, 6700969, 08033061094
Contact: Chief (Mrs.) F. O. Lad-Ojomo - MD/CEO

CITY TRUST INSURERS LIMITED
(formerly Olympia Insurance Nigeria Ltd)
Business: Non-Life Insurance
Address: Lamlat House, 270, Ikorodu Rd, Obanikoro, Lagos
Tel: (01) 7743112 **Fax:** (01) 4934218
Contact: Mr. William Ossai Ezeogu - MD/CEO

CITY UNION INSURANCE COMPANY LIMITED
Business: Courier Services
Address: 65, Old Yaba Road, Ebute-Metta (East), Lagos
Tel: (01) 613809, 614601, 865879
Contact: Mr. Anthony Ekwensi - MD/CEO

CITY-CODE SAVINGS & LOANS LIMITED
Business: Mortgage Financing
Address: 6, Davies Street, off Marina, Lagos Island, Lagos
Tel: (01) 2641355, 2662568. 2666794 **Fax:** (01) 2662568
E-mail: ctilagos@hyperia.com
* Pabod Building, 1, Azikiwe Road, Port Harcourt
Contact: Mr. Ebilate Mac-Yoroki - MD/CEO

CITY-CODE TRUST & INVESTMENT COMPANY LIMITED
Business: Stockbroking, Issuing House, Porfolio Management, Investment Advisors
Address: 6, Davies Street (3rd Floor), off Marina, Lagos
Tel: (01) 266469, 2662568, 2641355 **Fax:** (01) 266794
E-mail: ctlagos@hyperia.com
* 15, Blantyre Street, off Ademola Adetokunbo Crescent, Wuse II, Abuja.
Tel: (09) 5234146
* 1, Azikiwe Road, Port Harcourt.
Tel: (084) 237971
Contact: Rear Admiral Nelson Soroh (rtd) - Chairman

CIV-DATUM LIMITED
Business: Engineering Construction
Address: 34, Sunmola Street, Okupe Estate, Mende, Maryland, Lagos
Tel: 08033484886
Contact: Engr. Eddy Atumonyogo - Chairman/CEO

CIVILETIS NIGERIA LIMITED
Business: Sales, Services & Support of Printing Presses & Machines, Lithographic Equipment, Digital Colour-Separation Systems, Printing Accesories & Consumables
Address: 27A, Fatai Atere Way, Matori Industrial Estate, Mushin, Lagos
Tel: (01) 4529314 **Fax:** (01) 4522803
E-mail: civiletis@nova.net.ng
Contact: Mr. Bayo D. Okpaku - President/CEO

CIV-STRUCT ASSOCIATES
Business: Civil and Structural Engineering Consultancy Services, Project Management
Address: 126, Lewis Street, Marina, Lagos
Tel: (01) 2630936, 2635448 **Fax:** (01) 2635448
E-mail: civstruc@linkserve.com.ng
Contact: Engr. T. O. A. Bamgbopa - Partner

CLAIMSWATCH INTERNATIONAL LOSS ADJUSTERS LTD
Business: Loss Adjusting, Cargo Superintendent, Valuer, General Surveying and Claims Consultancy
Address: 127, Ojuelegba Road, Surulere, Lagos
Tel: (01) 5850061, 8311726 **Fax:** (01) 5850061
Contact: Mr. Tom Mensah - MD/CEO

CLAIR RESOURCE LIMITED
Business: Fitness, Recreation, Sports, Tourism & Culture
Address: Universal Fitness Centre Place, 1, Palace Drive, Federal Palace Hotel Complex, Ahmadu Bello Way, Victoria Island Lagos

Tel: (01) 2612689, 612689 **Fax:** (01) 2617265
Contact: Mr. Emmanuel O. Okereke - Chairman/CEO

CLARKSON, EDU & COMPANY LIMITED
Business: Incorporated Insurance & Reinsurance Brokers, Pension & Acturial Consultants
Address: 33, Alh. Tokan Street, Alaka Estate, off Western Avenue, Surulere, Lagos
Tel: (01) 5833182, 5831586, 5851371, 5842056
Fax: (01) 5834065
* 27, Aba Road, Port Harcourt.
Tel: (084) 238763
Contact: Chief B. Edu - Chairman

CLASSIC BEVERAGES NIGERIA LIMITED
Business: Production of Soft Drinks and Table Water
Address: Plot 9A, Block E, Amuwo-Odofin Ind Estate, Apapa - Oshodi Expressway, Mile 2, Lagos
Tel: (01) 7743696 **Fax:** (01) 7912613
E-mail: classicbev@hotmail.com
classic.beverages@jotna.com
Contact: Dimitris Papadapoulos - MD/CEO

CLASSIC INSURANCE BROKERS LIMITED
Business: Insurance Broking
Address: Yinka Folawiyo Plaza (8th Floor), 38, Yinka Folawiyo Avenue, Apapa, Lagos
Tel: (01) 5450436-40 (5 L), 5450220 **Fax:** (01) 5450204
Contact: Deacon P A Ajagunna - GM/CEO

CLAY INDUSTRY NIGERIA LIMITED
Business: Manufacture of Structural Clay Products
Address: Oregun Road, Oregun Ind. Estate, Ikeja, Lagos
Tel: (01) 4972405, 4972516
Contact: Mr. U. Bernardi - Director

CLAYBORNE TRADING COMPANY LIMITED
Business: Importation and Marketing of Textiles, Polyurethane and PVC Artificial Leather
Address: 6, Ojike Lane, Aba
Tel/Fax: (082) 220625
E-mail: clayborne52@yahoo.com
Contact: Mr. O. E. Onuma - MD/CEO

CLEAN TOWN LIMITED
Business: Environmental, Sanitary/Public Health Consultancy & Contracting
Address: Neighbourhood Centre (Suite 12), Adetokunbo Ademola Crescent, Wuse II, Abuja
Tel: (09) 4132421, 4132422 **Fax:** (09) 4132421
* 53, Airport Road, Kano
Tel: (064) 631893, 635493

CLEANAQUA AFRICA LIMITED
Business: Water Engineering Services, Distribution and Marketing of Water-Purification Equipment
Address: 18, Club Road, Ikoyi, Lagos
Tel: (01) 2693018, 2693467 **Fax:** (01) 2962705
E-mail: eurafric@hyperia.com

CLEAR IMPRESSIONS LIMITED
Business: Colour Separation, Printing and Light Packaging
Address: Plot 54, Sharada Industrial Estate Phase I, Kano
Tel: (064) 663640 **Fax:** (064) 666420
E-mail: clearimpressions@homstead.com
clearimp@hotmail.com
Contact: Alh. Iro Ibrahim Yahaya - MD/CEO

CLEARSIGHT NIGERIA LIMITED
Business: Promotional & Gift Items, Trophies, Awards & Plaques
Address: 6, Ilupeju Bye-Pass, Ilupeju, Lagos
Tel: (01) 4721259, 08023221722
E-mail: clearsight_nig@yahoo.com
Website: www.clearsightltd.com
Contact: Mr. Chukwuma Dan-Chigwal - GM/CEO

CLEAR VIEW OPTICS LIMITED
Business: Eye Clinic, Optical & Optomertric Services
Address: 5, Ribadu Road, S. W. Ikoyi, Lagos
Tel: (01) 2694547, 2673789 **Fax:** (01) 2692278
Contact: Dr. (Mrs) Uche Mbah - Consultant

CLEARLINE INTERNATIONAL LIMITED
Business: Health Insurance Underwriting Medical Equipment Procurement, Overseas Treatment Consultancy
Address: The Penthose, 20, Sobande St, Akoka, Yaba, Lagos
Tel: (01) 7741092, 4704558, 823653
E-mail: clear@linkserve.com.ng
Contact: Alh. Umaru A. Shinkafi - Chairman
Dr. Segun Ogundimu - MD/CEO

CLEARVIEW INVESTMENT COMPANY LIMITED
Business: Stockbroking
Address: NCR Building (6th Floor), 6, Broad Street, Lagos
Tel: (01) 2637820
Contact: Mr. Olu Odejimi - MD/CEO

CLEM-BOLD (NIGERIA) LIMITED
Business: Manufacturing, Export & Import of General Merchandise
Address: 9, Ring Road Challenge, Ibadan
Tel: (02) 2315432 **Fax:** (02) 2313820
Contact: Mr. C. B. Daramola - Chairman/CEO

CLEM EZE & COMPANY
Business: Estate Surveyors & Valuers, Real Estate Development, Property Management
Address: Plot 602, Ringim Close, by Tafawa Balewa Way, Area 7, Garki, Abuja
Tel: (09) 2345778-9 (2L) **Fax:** (09) 2345798
Website: www.clemeze.com
Contact: Chief Clem Eze - Principal Partner/CEO

CLEMCO INDUSTRIES LIMITED
Business: Trading, Manufacturing of Plastic Products
Address: Plot 30, Babs Animashaun Street, Surulere, Lagos
Tel: (01) 48040000, 4800001, 4805512, 4803470
Fax: (01) 5850018, 5850019
E-mail; clemco@alpha.linkserve.com
* Km. 10, Owerri Road, Near Rojenny, Oba, Onitsha
Tel: (046) 463010, 461366, 461370
Contact: Chief (Sir) C. A. Okonkwo - ChairmanCEO

CLEMESSY NIGERIA LIMITED
Business: Electrical Automation and Telecommunications,

High and Low Voltage Installations, Monitoring and Technical Management of Projects
Address: Plot 182A, Kofo Abayomi St, Victoria Island, Lagos
Tel: (01) 2617977, 611485, 616469

CLIENTS INTERNATIONAL LIMITED
Business: Courier Services
Address: 3, Biaduo Street, off Keffi Street, S. W. Ikoyi, Lagos
Tel: (01) 267717, 2672718 **Fax:** (01) 2694532
E-mail: clients@siotel.com
Contact: Mr. Tony Alumba - Chairman
Mr. Walter Baker - MD/CEO

CLIMAX INSURANCE BROKERS LIMITED
Business: Insurance Broking
Address: 200, Sapele Road, Benin City
Contact: Chief Ifeanyi Araraume - Chairman

CLINA-LABS NIGERIA LIMITED
Business: Medical Laboratory Services
Address: 8, Tafawa Balewa Square Complex, Lagos
Tel: (01) 2633614
E-mail: clinalab@hyperia.com
* 43, Calcutta Crescent, Apapa, Lagos.
Tel: (01) 5875362

CLONE CONCEPTS LIMITED
Business: Sales of Computers; Consultancy & Training
Address: 59, Adeniran Ogunsanya Street, Surulere, Lagos
Tel: (01) 832382, 5850341, 5850493 **Fax:** (01) 5850493
Contact: Ndubueze E. Nwana - MD/CEO.

CLOVERLEAF SHIPPING LIMITED
Business: Shipping Services (Ship Agency & Chartering)
Address: TAS Plaza, 1, Warehouse Road, Apapa, Lagos
Tel: (01) 5870333, 5871303, 5872979, 7740694
Fax: (01) 5871303
E-mail: cloverleaf@hyperia.com
info@cloverleafshipping.com
Website: www.cloverleafshipping.com
* 14, Khana Street, D-Line, Port Harcourt
Tel: (084) 236825, 238973 **Fax:** (084) 236825
E-mail: cloverleaf@phca.linkserve.com

CLOVIC NIGERIA LIMITED
Business: Water Engineering Services
Address: Plot 9, Block C, Ilasamaja Industrial Scheme, 196, Oshodi-Apapa Expressway, Ilasamaja, Lagos
Tel: (01) 4526858
E-mail: clovic@beta.linkserve.com

CMC CONNECT LAGOS
Business: Perception & Events Management, Media Relations
Address: 19, Town Planning Way Ilupeju, Lagos
Tel: (01) 4966621, 7745389 **Fax:** (01) 4966621
Contact: Mr Yomi Badejo-Okusanya - MD/CEO

CMC INTERNATIONAL LIMITED
Business: Confidential Due Diligence/Credit Report and Business Information Services
Address: 6, Ajele Street, off Campbell Street,Lagos
Tel: (01) 2645845-7(3L) **Fax:** (01) 2645844
E-mail: cmc@cmcint.com
Website: www.cmcint.com
Contact: Mr. Emmanuel I. Ijewere - Chairman
Dr Chris M E Onalo - MD/CEO

CNEICO (NIGERIA) LIMITED
Business: Importation of and Sales of Diesel Generating Sets, Machine Tools and General Goods
Address: Plot 8, Block E, Amuwo-Odofin Industrial Layout, Badagry Expressway, Mile 2, Amuwo-Odofin, Lagos
Tel: (01) 5875241, 5851424 **Fax:** (01) 5851424
E-mail: cneico@beta.linkserve.com
cneico@hyperia.com

CO-LINK INVESTMENT MANAGEMENT COMPANY LTD
Business: Financing of L.P.O., Investment Management
Address: Oluwatobi House (3rd Floor), 71, Allen Avenue, Ikeja, Lagos
Tel: (01) 4932202, 4933221 **Fax:** (01) 4933221
E-mail: colink@beta.linkserve.com

CO-OPERATIVE BANK PLC
Business: Commercial Banking
Address: Oba Adebimpe Road, Ibadan.
Tel: (02) 2410026, 2411034, 2411336, 2412294, 2412496, 2414411, 2414941, 2415711, 2414850
Fax: (02) 2414284
E-mail: md@coopbank.com.ng
* 30, Marina, Lagos
Tel: (01) 2663127, 2664205, 2667928, 2668828
Contact: Mr. Ariyo A. Ajaja - MD/CEO
Mr. Phil Aragbada - Head (Corp. Affairs)

CO-OPERATIVE DEVELOPMENT BANK PLC
Business: Commercial Banking
Address: 105, Oron Road, Uyo.
Tel: (085) 200821, 201540, 202833, 203449, 204373, 204573
* 1A, Ligali Ayorinde Avenue, beh. Mobil House, Victoria Island, Lagos
Tel: (01) 2600811-3(3L), 2600815, 2600818, 2635816, 2637069, 2637326, 2646171 **Fax:** (01) 2637069
E-mail: cdb@intracom.net.ng
Contact: Mr. Johnnie J. Udofa - MD/CEO

CO-OPERATIVE SUPPLY ASSOCIATION LIMITED
Business: Sales of Agro-Chemicals, Hardware, Building Materials and Grocery
Address: 129, Railway Siding, Magazine Rd, Dugbe Ibadan
Tel: (02) 2413055, 415921 **Fax:** (02) 2413055
Contact: Pastor F. O. Adegbulugbe - MD/CEO

COASTAL BOTTLERS LIMITED
Business: Bottling and Marketing of Carbonated Drinks
Address: Plot 12A, Amuwo-Odofin Industrial Estate, Apapa-Oshodi Expressway, Mile 2, Festac Town, Lagos
Tel/Fax: (01) 7742311
Contact: Mr. G. A. Koledoye - MD/CEO

COASTAL SERVICES (NIGERIA) LIMITED
Business: Clearing and Forwarding, Transportation, Travel Agency
Address: Umarco House, 5, Creek Road, Apapa, Lagos
Tel: (01) 5870528, 5872885, 5874882, 5870519

Fax: (01) 5876197
* 11/13, First Aluminium Road, Trans-Amadi Industrial Layout, Port Harcourt
Contact: Chief 'Bode Akindele - Chairman/CEO

COATES BROTHERS (WEST AFRICA) LIMITED
Business: Manufacturing of Printing Inks and Can Coatings, Roller Recovery
Address: Lateef Jakande Road (opposite Cadbury), Agindingbi, Ikeja, Lagos
Tel: (01) 4920337, 4926699, 7732069 **Fax:** (01) 4922081
E-mail: coates@infoweb.abs.net
Contact: Mr. F. O. A. Ohiwerei - Chairman

COATS WEST AFRICAN TREAD COMPANY LIMITED
Business: Manufacture and Supply of Industrial & Domestic Thread and Twines
Address: 17, Burma Road, Apapa, Lagos
Tel: (01) 5875788, 5874209, 5874739 **Fax:** (01) 587866
Contact: Mr. Manoj Agarwal - CEO

COBAL INSURANCE BROKERS LIMITED
Business: Insurance Broking
Address: 20, Olukole Street, off Olufemi Road, off Ogunlana Drive, Surulere, Lagos
Tel: (01) 832612
Contact: Ade Okunlade - GM/CEO

COBRANET LIMITED
Business: Internet Service Provider, Networking, LAN/WAN/ VPN Solutions Provider
Address: Plot 8, Rafiu Babatunde Street, off Admiralty Way, Lekki Phase I, Lagos
Tel: (01) 5555656-9 (4L) **Fax:** (01) 5555660
E-mail: info@cobranet.org
Website: www.cobranet.org
Contact: Mr. Tony A. Abboud - MD/CEO

COCA-COLA NIGERIA LIMITED
Business: Production of Concentractes & Beverage Bases for the Coca-Cola Range of Soft Drinks
Address: Pemberton Place, 16, Gerrad Road, Ikoyi, Lagos
Tel: (01) 2695686-4 (11L) **Fax:** (01) 2695695
Contact: Mr. Olaolu Akinkugbe - Public Affairs Director

COCOA INDUSTRIES LIMITED
Business: Processing of Cocoa Beans into Cocoa Products (Butter, Cakes, Liquor & Powder); Manufacture of Chocolate Food-Beverage Drink, Third-Party Cocoa Processing
Address: 1, Cocoa Industries Road, Ikeja Ind Estate, Lagos
Tel: (01) 4925080, 4925070, 4923991, 4924355
Fax: (01) 4926383
E-mail: cocoaindustries@linkserve.com
Contact: Mr. R. O. Agbaje - MD/CEO.

COGEMAT NIGERIA LIMITED
Business: Supply and Installation of Aluminium Building Products
Address: Plot K9, Apapa Expressway, Iyana-Isolo, Lagos
Tel: (01) 4524388, 7744720 **Fax:** (01) 4524843
Contact: Chief T. O. Akinkugbe - Chairman
Mr. A. J. M. Trebuchere - MD/CEO

COLBON INDUSTRIES LIMITED
Business: Importation and Marketing of Photo-Finishing Materials, Photo Finishing Services
Address: 17, Ezeiweka Road, Awada Layout, Onitsha
Tel: (046) 413798, 411551

COLBYCO NIGERIA LIMITED
Business: Importation and Marketing of Cosmetics
Address: TAS Plaza, 1, Warehouse Road, Apapa, Lagos
Tel: (01) 5455735, 5874481

COLEMAN TECHNICAL INDUSTRIES LIMITED
Business: Manufacture of Electrical Wires and Cables
Address: 28, Badejo Kalesanwo Street, Matori Industrial Estate, Mushin, Lagos
Tel: (01) 4522817 **Fax:** (01) 4522849
Contact: Otunba S.K. Onafowokan - Chairman
Website: www.co-link-invest.com

COLLECTIBLES
Business: Sales of Fashion Wears and Footwear Accessories, Designers of Textile Products
Address: 36, Adeniran Ogunsanya Street, Surulere, Lagos
Tel: (01) 5830800
E-mail: collectibles@hyperia.com
collectibles@cyberspace.net.ng
Website: www.collectibles-ng.com
*223, Adetokunbo Ademola Cr, Wuse II, Abuja.
Tel: 08033083706
* 29, Rumuola Rd, Port Harcourt.
Tel: (084) 571346
* 31A, Toyin Street, Ikeja, Lagos.
* 54, Allen Avenue, Ikeja, Lagos.
Tel: (01) 4933337
Contact: Joyce Daniels - GM

COLLOSSIANS INTERNATIONAL (NIGERIA) LIMITED
Business: Clearing & Forwarding Agency, Warehousing & Transport Services, Maritime Consultancy, Import & Export Trading, General Contract Finance
Address 8, Funsho Ajayi Street, off Oladimeji Street, Aguda, Surulere, Lagos
Tel: (01) 5851648, 835961, 08023173882, 08033342330
Fax: (01) 5851648
* 8, Iron Avenue, Aguda, Surulere, Lagos
Contact: Mr. Ifeanyi Okafor - MD/CEO

COLODENSE NIGERIA PLC
Business: Manufacturing of Flexible Packaging Materials
Address: Plot C12/1, Shagamu Road, Agbara Industrial Estate, Km. 32, Lagos-Badagry Expressway, Agbara, Ogun State
Tel: (01) 712106, 712010, 712129, 712048, 712022, 7749976 **Fax:** (01) 712010
Contact: Chief Victor I. Odili - Chairman
Mr Gray B. Kleinert - MD/CEO

COLOUR IMAGE PUBLICITY LIMITED
Business: Outdoor Advertising Agency, Media Representatives, Silkscreen Printing and Signwriting
Address: 3, Little Road, Sabo-Yaba, Lagos
Tel: (01) 863218, 865992, 864307, 4703315
E-mail: colourimagepublicitylimited@yahoo.com

COLOURS IN AFRICA
Business: Sales of Gift Items
Address: Plot 283A, Akin Olugbade St Victoria Island, Lagos
Tel/Fax: (01) 2625754
E-mail: colours@hyperia.com
* 9, Lagos Road, off Aba Expressway, Rumuomasi, Port Harcourt.

COLUMBIA INTERNATIONAL LIMITED
Business: Table Salt Processing, Textiles Trading
Address: Plot 1303A, Akin Adesola St Victoria Island, Lagos
Tel: (01) 2615505, 2622232, 2622259 **Fax:** (01) 2619487
E-mail: primlaks@hyperia.com
* 16, Burma Road, Apapa, Lagos.
Tel: (01) 5453822 **Fax:** (01) 5455498
* Shed E/6, NPA, Apapa Wharf, Apapa, Lagos.
Tel: (01) 5453805
Contact: B. C. P. Gowda - MD/CEO.

COLVIA SECURITIES LIMITED
Business: Stockbroking, Portfolio Management, Investment Advisory Services, Treasury Bills
Address: Stock Exchange House (14th Floor), 2/4, Customs Street, off Marina, Lagos
Tel: (01) 2630428, 2645167
E-mail: colvia_securities_ltd@hotmail.com
Website: www.colviasecurities.com
Contact: Mr Collins O Igbinovia - MD/CEO.

COLXIMATE INSURANCE BROKERS LIMITED
Business: Insurance Broking
Address: 2, Mobolaji Bank-Anthony Way, Maryland, Lagos
Tel: (01) 4979348
E-mail: colximate@yahoo.com
Website: www.africacoop.net/colximate
Contact: Mrs. Olufunke A. Adenusi - MD/CEO.

COMAG STEEL & CONSTRUCTION COMPANY LIMITED
Business: Importation and Marketing of Building Materials; Steel Stockist & Supplier
Address: Comag Group House, Km. 16, Port Harcourt-Aba Expressway, beside Mobil Base , Port Harcourt
Tel: (084) 611920, 611936 **Fax:** (084) 611890
Contact: Chief Cosmas Agu - Chairman/CEO

COMATEL INDUSTRIES LIMITED
Business: Manufacturing of Industrial Safety Footwear, Fire Services and Procurement
Address: 1, Adebayo Akande Street, off Oregun Road, by Dunlop Bus-Stop, Oregun, Ikeja, Lagos
Tel: (01) 4967885, 7750525 **Fax:** (01) 4967885
E-mail: ammartstar@nova.net.ng
Contact: Mr. Mayowa Adekoya - Chairman/CEO

COMBINATION INDUSTRIES LIMITED
Business: Manufacture of Extruded Corn Snacks (Cheeseballs, Cheezy Tastee Snacks)
Address: Plot D18 - D19, Close 2, Broadway Street, Calabar Free Trade Zone, Calabar
Tel: (087) 210210, 210015 **Fax:** (087) 210024
E-mail: info@combinationindustries.com
Website: www.combinationindustries.com
Contact: Mr. Nik G. Mirpuri - MD/CEO

COMBINED BUSINESS LIMITED (PAKTEL)
Business: Telecommunications, Importation and Sales of Industrial Chemicals and General commodities.
Address: St. Gabriel House (Wing B, 2nd Floor), 22, Warehouse Road, Apapa, Lagos
Tel: (01) 5450996, 5453365 **Fax:** (01) 5451690
Contact: Alh. Mohammed M Rabiu - MD/CEO

COMBINED CHEMICAL COMPANY LIMITED
Business: Sales of Industrial Chemicals
Address: Olayinka House, 368, Ikorodu Road, Maryland, Ikeja, Lagos
Tel/Fax: (039) 722319, 722320

COMERINT (NIGERIA) LIMITED
Business: Corporate and Industrial Services (Engineering and Procurement)
Address: 9B (Plot 820), Samuel Manuwa Street, Victoria Island, Lagos
Tel: (01) 2614535, 2614530 **Fax:** (01) 2617436
Contact: Alh. Magaji M. Inuwa - Chairman

COMET AIRLINES LIMITED
Business: Airline Services (Passenger & Cargo)
Address: 27, Joel Ogunnaike St, Ikeja, G.R.A., Ikeja, Lagos
Tel: (01) 4934971-3 (3 L) **Fax:** (01) 4934971
E-mail: cornair@hotmail.com
Contact: Capt. A. K. Inogbo - MD/CEO

COMET SHIPPING AGENCIES NIGERIA LIMITED
Business: Shipping Agency
Address: 4, Hinderer Road, Apapa G.R.A., Apapa, Lagos
Tel: (01) 2634284, 2645201, 2645594, 5874926, 7740143
Fax: (01) 5453214
Plot 278, Trans-Amadi Ind. Layout, Port Harcourt
Contact: Mr Musa Danjuma - Chairman/CEO

COMEX LIMITED
Business: Advertising, Marketing and Public Relations
Address: 13, Tafawa Balewa Crescent, off Adeniran Ogunsanya Street, Surulere, Lagos
Tel: (01) 835487, 844330 **Fax:** (01) 5850215
E-mail: comex@skannet.com
Contact: Mr. Lanre Folorunsho - Chairman/CEO.

COMFAX NIGERIA LIMITED.
Business: Sales of Satellite Communication Equipment
Address: 1, Adele Road, off Warehouse Road, Apapa, Lagos
Tel: (01) 5878183 **Fax:** (01) 5450479

COMFORT ROYALE HOTEL, ABUJA
Business: Hospitality Services
Address: Plot 1033, Takum Close, off Ahmadu Bello Way, by Assemblies of God Church, Garki II, Garki, Abuja
Tel: (09) 3148377-83 (7L) **Fax:** (09) 3148384
Contact: Ms. Ekaete Umo - Personnel & Admin. Manager

COMMEDOR NIGERIA LIMITED
Business: Manufacturing of Aluminium Doors and Windows; Distribution of Building & Construction Materials
Address: 13, Commercial Area, Bukuru Bye-Pass, Jos
Tel/Fax: (073) 462447
Contact: Alh. Sanusi Mato - MD/CEO

COMMERCIAL & SCIENTIFIC COMPUTING NIGERIA LTD
Business: Consultancy, IT Services (Structured Cabling, Networking, Hardware Sales & Maintenance, Software Development, Support & Training)
Address: 2B, Adewunmi Ind. Estate, Oregun Rd, Ikeja, Lagos
Tel: (01) 4937340, 4938098, 4938099 **Fax:** (01) 4937340
E-mail: csc@cscng.com
csc@infoweb.abs.net
Contact: Mr. Lucky P. C.Ajieh - GM

COMMERCIAL GIVE 'N' TAKE (NIGERIA) LIMITED
Business: Sales of Electronic Products and Home Appliances
Address: 158, Broad Street, Marina, Lagos
Tel: (01) 2665776, 2669614-15 (2 L) **Fax:** (01) 2665144
Contact: Mr. Richard Ajayi

COMMERCIAL MARINE INSURANCE BROKERS LIMITED
Business: Insurance Broking
Address: Churchgate Towers, Plot PC. 30, Afribank Street, Victoria Island, Lagos
Tel: (01) 2619163, 2619831-3 (3 L) **Fax:** (01) 2619163
E-mail: pchmib@churchgate.com
* Plot 1118, A4, Kwame Nkrumah Crescent, Asokoro District, Wuse, Abuja
Tel: (09) 3140167-8 (2 L)
Contact: Mr. Y. O. Lawal - GM/CEO.

COMMERCIAL MEDICINE STORES LIMITED
Business: Sales of Pharmaceuticals
Address: 23, Nnamdi Azikiwe Street, Tinubu, Lagos
Tel/Fax: (01) 2660662
Contact: Chief D. B. Hunponu-Wusu - Chairman/CEO.

COMMODITIES SUPPORT SERVICE LIMITED
Business: Warehousing, Inspection, Certification and Freighting of Commodities for Exporters
Address: Gefin House, 106/108, Oshodi-Apapa Expressway, Oshodi Industrial Estate, Isolo, Lagos
Tel: (01) 4701540, 7747323, 4528934 **Fax:** (01) 4528934
E-mail: cssl@micro.com.ng

COMMON INTEREST COMMUNICATIONS LIMITED
Business: Newspaper Publishing:
Address: FUNMEC House, Plot 70B, ACME Road, Ogba Ikeja, Lagos
Tel: (01) 8044113, 4922743 **Fax:** (01) 4922743
E-mail: nationalinterest@email.com
Contact: Mr. Ide Eguabor - CEO/Editor-in-Chief

COMMUNICATION TRENDS LIMITED
Business: Internet Services Providers, Cable Television & Digital Satellite Communication Services
Address: CTL Emporium, Plot 57, Woji Road, G.R.A. II, Port Harcourt
Tel: (084) 236754 -5 (2 L), 237808 **Fax:** (084) 237809
E-mail: comtrends@supernet300.com
Website: www.supernet300.com
* Plot 1221, Aminu Kano Crescent, Wuse II, Abuja
Tel: (09) 4139921-3 (3 L)
Contact: Engr. Uzo Udemba - Chairman/CEO

COMMUNICATION WAYS & MEANS LIMITED
Business: Sales of Data Security Systems, Networks and Database
Address: 15, Biaduo St, off Keffi Street, S. W. Ikoyi, Lagos
Tel: (01) 2693165, 685752 **Fax:** (01) 2694909
E-mail: cwm@infoweb.asb.net

COMMUNICATIONS ASSOCIATES OF NIGERIA LIMITED
Business: Sales and Installation of Telecommunication Equipment, External Line Plants, Maintenance of PABX's and Radio Equipment, Microwave Links, Satellite Equipment, Local & Wide-Area Networks
Address: 6/10, Industrial Crescent, Ilupeju, Lagos
Tel: (01) 4972946, 4936586 **Fax:** (01) 4933240
E-mail: comsac.nig@alpha.linkserve.com
Contact: Chief N. O. Idowu - Chairman

COMMUNICATOR NIGERIA LIMITED
Business: Public Relations Consultancy, Advertising
Address: 8, Shode Street, Ijeshatedo, Lagos
Tel: (01) 520036, 521051, 520052
Contact: Chief (Sir) Alex Akinyele - Chairman/CEO

COMPACK FINANCE & SECURITIES LIMITED
Business: Business Financing and Vehicle Leasing
Address: 33, New Market Road, Onitsha
Tel: (046) 410351, 410620
* ED Building (8th Floor), 47, Marina, Lagos
Contact: Chief (Sir) C. N. C. Nwafor (JP) - Chairman

COMPASS SHIPPING NIGERIA LIMITED
Business: Shipping, Clearing & Forwarding Agency, Construction Fabrication, Stevedoring
Address: 12, Payne Crescent, Apapa, Lagos
Tel: (01) 5453608, 5458958, 5458957, 08033190581
Fax: (01) 5453608
E-mail: compass@infoweb.abs.net
compasship@beta.linkserve.com
compasoil@beta.linkserve.com
Contact: Mr. Austine Umole - GM

COMPENSATIONS (NIGERIA) LIMITED
Business: Bakery Equipment Manufacturing and Sales
Address: Plot 8, Cocoa Industries Road, Ogba Industrial Estate, Ikeja, Lagos
Tel: (01) 4960571, 4960584 **Fax:** (01) 4936971

COMPETENT INSURANCE BROKERS LIMITED
Business: Insurance Broking
Address: 25, Nnamdi Azikiwe Street, Tinubu, Lagos
Tel: (01) 2643606
Contact: Mrs. I. O. Adeyemi - Chairman

COMPLETE BUSINESS MACHINE (NIGERIA) LIMITED
Business: Sales, Installation and Maintenance of Computers, Consultancy Services, Training
Address: 59, Campbell Street, Lagos Island, Lagos
Tel: (01) 2633191 **Fax:** (01) 2631137
E-mail: cbm@home.metrong.com
* 42A, Trans-Amadi Rd, Rumuobiakani, P Harcourt
Contact: Engr. Ayo Oyaronbi - Chairman/CEO

COMPLETE COMMUNICATIONS LIMITED
Business: Publishing of Sports Magazines and Sports Dailies
Address: Plot 3, Alhaji Adenekan Street, Okota, Isolo, Lagos

Tel/Fax: (01) 4528556, 4524220
E-mail: completesports@hyperia.net
Contact: Chief Femi Olukanmi - Chairman

COMPLETE COMPUTER & TECHNOLOGY LIMITED
Business: Sales, Installation & Maintenance of Computers, IT Consultancy
Address: 73, Akpakpava Street, Benin City
Tel: (052) 255051, 252922 **Fax:** (052) 252922
E-mail: cctlimited@yahoo.com
Contact: Mr. Galit Adeyosoye - MD/CEO

COMPLETE NETWORKS NIGERIA LIMITED
Business: Network Solutions
Address: Plot 269A, Muri Okunola St, Victoria Island, Lagos
Tel: (01) 2626277-8 (2 L) **Fax:** (01) 2626278
E-mail: info@completenetworks-ng.com
Website: www.completenetworks-ng.com
Contact: Mr. Charles Onuba - Chairman/CEO

COMPLETE PROJECTS ENGINEERING CONSORTIUM LTD
Business: Construction Engineering, Projects Development, Agriculture & Food Industry, Oil & Gas Business
Address: 12, Oremeji Street, off Medical Road, Ikeja, Lagos
Tel: (01) 4978452, 4977173, 4975576 **Fax:** (01) 4978452
E-mail: mails@cpecltd.net
cpeclted2003@yahoo.com
* 5, Azikiwe Road, Port Harcourt
Contact: Engr. C. U. A. Olugu - Chairman/CEO

COMPLETE SUCCESS PUBLICATIONS LIMITED
Business: Publication of Magazines, Seminars & Workshops, Presentation of Awards
Address: 3, Shasha Road, Akowonjo Roundabout, opp. NEPA Office, Agege, Lagos
Tel: (01) 7733729, 08023186368
E-mail: completesccessus@yahoo.com
Contact: Mr. Osa Osunde - Chairman
Mr. Mike Akhigbe-Agge - Managing Editor/CEO

COMPREHENSIVE PROJECT MANAGEMENT SERVICES LTD
Business: Project Management, Training, Engineering Consultancy
Address: Kresta Laurel Complex (3rd Floor), 376, Ikorodu Road, Maryland, Ikeja, Lagos
Tel: (01) 4933141-2 (2 L) **Fax:** (01) 4933140
E-mail: cpms@alpha.linkserve.com
Contact: Engr. Kadri A Adeola - MD

COMPULEB NIGERIA LIMITED
Business: Sales of Computer Parts & Accessories
Address: Plot 10, Block D, Acme Road, Ogba Industrial Estate Ikeja, Lagos
Tel: (01) 5557764 - 9 (6L), 8042080
Fax: (01) 5558504, 4923550
E-mail: sales@compuleb-ng.com
Website: www.compuleb-ng.com
Contact: Mr. Karim G. Boulos - Chairman/MD

COMPUNET SYSTEM LIMITED
Business: Sales, Installation & Maintenance of Computers and Telecommunication Equipment, Networking
Address: 4A, Oke-Fia Street, opp. Akinola Chemist & Supermarket, Oshogbo
Tel: (035) 240741, 420795, 2422778 **Fax:** (035) 240741
E-mail: compunet@infoweb.abs.net

COMPUSCOPE VENTURES LIMITED
Business: Sales, Supply and Repairs of Computer Hardware and Software Programmes, Software Development and Engineering, I.T. Consultancy Services and Training, Digital Image Processing
Address: 63, Simpson Street, Adekunle-Yaba, Lagos
Tel: (01) 5457523, 7741529, 862910, 861677
Fax: (01) 2631102
E-mail: compuscope@hyperia.com
Contact: Mr. O. O. Awolesi - MD

COMPUSOLVE INTERNATIONAL LIMITED
Business: Document Management, Sales of Electronic Records Management Systems and Service of Computers, Networking, Corporate Training & Research, Software Applications and Development, Intranet/Internet Services
Address: 27, Yesufu Sanusi Street, off Adeniran Ogunsanya Street, Surulere, Lagos
Tel: (01) 5454811
* Ibro Hotel (Suite 1B), Wuse Zone 6, Abuja
Tel: (09) 5237409 **Fax:** (09) 5237407
E-mail: compusolve@metrong.com
Contact: Mr. Bunmi Akinyemi - Chairman
Mr. Femi O. Davis - MD/CEO

COMPUTER & INFORMATION MANAGEMENT CENTRE LTD
Business: Information Technology Training, Development of Software, Sales of Computer Hardware
Address: 142, Adekunle Fajuyi Road, opp. Alafia Hospital Adamasingba, Ibadan
Tel/Fax: (02) 2413531
E-mail: coinmac@skannet.com
Contact: Mr. Ayo Salami - Chairman/CEO

COMPUTER DESIGNS SYSTEMS SERVICES LIMITED
Business: Autocad Dealers, Traning and Autocad Bureau Services, Sales and Maintenance of IT Products
Address: Plot 188, Shittu Animashaun Street, Gbagada Estate Phase II, Gbagada, Lagos
Tel/Fax: (01) 3422815, 3422759
E-mail: cdss@home.metrong.com
Contact: Engr. Peter A. O. Fisher - Chairman/CEO

COMPUTER POWERHOUSE INTERNATIONAL LIMITED
Business: IT Training, Software Development, Computer Sales/Service, Networking and Systems Integration
Address: 80, Allen Avenue, Ikeja, Lagos
Tel: (01) 4967890-1 (2 L), 4939188 **Fax:** (01) 4939189
E-mail: sales@cpiltd.com
Website: www.cpiltd.com
Contact: Chief Olu Adegbite - Chairman
Mr. Kayode Elusoji - MD/CEO

COMPUTER SOLUTIONS LIMITED
Business: Sales and Maintenance of Computers, Communications Equipment and Business Machines
Address: 8, Alli Street, Tinubu Square, Lagos
Tel: (01) 2631618, 2634619, 4708415, 4702491

Fax: (01) 2646084
E-mail: computersoln@hotmail.com
kennyawe71@hotmail.com
Contact: Mr. Kenny T. Awe - Chairman/CEO

COMPUTER SPECIALITIES & TECHNOLOGIES LIMITED
Business: Computer Sales, Networking and Training
Address: 11, Falolu Road, Surulere, Lagos
Tel: (01) 5842839, 835353 **Fax:** (01) 5842839
E-mail: ct12ng@nova.net.ng
ct1usa@aol.com
Contact: Mr. Paul I. Nnaoji - Chairman/CEO

COMPUTER SYSTEMS ASSOCIATES (NIGERIA) LIMITED
Business: Information Technology Solutions Provider (Development Marketing and Support of Business & Banking Application Software), Product Development, Consultancy
Address: Yinka Folawiyo Plaza (5th Floor), 38, Warehouse Road, Apapa, Lagos
Tel: (01) 5454050-4 (5 L) **Fax:** (01) 5870420
E-mail: frontdesk@csasystems.com
Contact: Mr. Simeon C. Agu - Chairman/CEO

COMPUTER WAREHOUSE LIMITED
Business: Information Technology Services Conglomerate (Reselling, Service and Maintenance of Hardware, Sales and Implementation of Software, Communications, Networking Connectivity)
Address: 20, Adelabu Street, Surulere, Lagos
Tel: (01) 5847343, 2880485, 774368, 836589
Fax: (01) 5849367, 5852168
E-mail: cwl@cwlgroup.com
Website: www.cwlgroup.com
* 5th Floor, Octagon Building, 13A, Marinho Drive, Victoria Island Annex, Lagos.
Tel: (01) 3200803-5 (3L), 4700220, 7744368
* Plot 8, Abeokuta Street, Area 8, Garki, Abuja
Tel: (09) 2346446
E-mail: cwgabuja@mlstn.com
* 11A, Igbodo Street, Old G.R.A., Port Harcourt
Tel: (084) 231257
Contact: Mr. Austin Okere - MD/CEO

COMPUTE-RITE SYSTEMS LIMITED
Business: IT Solutions; Systems Integration & Networking; Software Development & Project Management, Computer Sales & Maintenance; Training
Address: Eleganza Building (3rd Floor), 15B, Joseph Street, Lagos Island, Lagos
Tel: (01) 2634520, 2634287 **Fax:** (01) 2634520
E-mail: comprite@linkserve.com.ng
Website: www.cmpute-rite.com
Contact: Mr. Kolawole O. Ogunlana - Chairman/CEO

COMPUTERPORT LIMITED
Business: Online Sales of Information Technology Products
Address: 4, Obanikoro St, off Ikorodu Rd, Obanikoro Lagos
Tel: (01) 4979501, 5550801-5 (5L)
E-mail: sales@computerport.biz
Website: www.computerport.biz
Contact: Mr. Biodun Marquis - MD/CEO

COMTEL SYSTEMS LIMITED
Business: Information Technology Solutions Provider
Address: 27/29, Adeyemo Alakija St Victoria Island, Lagos
Tel: (01) 2623561-3 (3 L) **Fax:** (01) 2620086
E-mail: info@comtel-Ltd.com
Website: www.comtel-Ltd.com
Contact: Engr C. Achigbu - Chairman

CON ENGINEERING NIGERIA LIMITED
Business: Electrical, Civil & Mechanical Engineering Services, Turnkey Projects, Distribution of ABB Low-Voltage Products
Address: Plot 519, Cadastral Zone AO, Central Business District, Abuja
Tel: (09) 2345805, 2345733, 08033141098, 08044184355, 08044184354, 08055234204, 08055234205, 08055055371, 08055055374
Fax: (09) 2346452
E-mail: conengineering2003@yahoo.com
Contact: Ichie G. O. Okoye - MD/CEO

CONAIR CARGO SERVICES LIMITED
Business: Clearing and Forwarding Agency, Shipping and Airfreight Services, Road Haulage, Warehousing
Address: 7C, Murtala Mohammed Way, Kano
Tel: (064) 632816, 648784, 6344491 **Fax:** (064) 648784
E-mail: conair-cargo@yahoo.com
* 1, Azikiwe Road, Port Harcourt.
Tel: (084) 331808
Contact: Chief Sunmonu S. Asani - Chairman/CEO

CONCEITO MOTORS (NIGERIA) LIMITED
Business: Importation of Volvo Trucks and Luxury Buses
Address: Plot 31, Ize-Iyamu Street, Oregun Industrial Estate, Ikeja, Lagos
Tel/Fax: (01) 4939501
E-mail: cmotors@micro.com.ng
Contact: Mr. Carlos L. Barella - Chairman/CEO

CONCEPT UNIT LIMITED
Business: Advertising Communications
Address: 77, Samuel Adedoyin St, Victoria Island Annex, Lagos
Tel: (01) 2619071, 4702467 **Fax:** (01) 5850321, 5455515
E-mail: lereawo@yahoo.com
Contact: Aduralere M. Awokoya - Chairman/CEO

CONCRETE TECHNOLOGY INDUSTRY LIMITED
Business: Concrete Designing & Surfacing
Address: 5B, Oko-Awo Street, Victoria Island, Lagos
Tel: (01) 2624541, 4934555 **Fax:** (01) 2624542, 4934556
Contact: Mr. Morrison Okunbor - MD/CEO

CONCEPT COMPUTER NIGERIA LIMITED
Business: Software Development & Marketing, Sale/Service of Computer Hardware & Accessories, Computer Training & Networking, Website Design & Management Consultancy
Address: 32, Montgometry Road, Sabo-Yaba, Lagos
Tel: (01) 3425221, 5878852, 868294, 860084, 08033087154. 08034544643
E-mail: conceptcom@infoweb.abs.net
conceptcomputers@yahoo.com
Contact: Chief I. B. Ochonogor - Chairman/CEO

CONFIDENCE INSURANCE PLC
Business: Non-Life Insurance (including Special Risks)
Address: Confidence Insurance House, Plot 3, Alagbaka Junction, Ado/Owo Road, Akure
Tel: (034) 240148, 240924, 240609 **Fax:** (034) 240609
E-mail: confidenceinsurance@intracom.net.ng
* Great Nigeria House (6th Floor), 47/57, Martins Street, Lagos
Tel: (01) 2665085, 2669668
* 3B, Herbert Macaulay Way, Wuse Zone 6, Abuja
Tel: (09) 5242317, 08037253101, 08034526556
Contact: Mr. A. Adebayo - Chairman
Dr. F. C. A. Akanbi - MD/CEO

CONFLUENCE INSURANCE BROKERS LIMITED
Business: Insurance Broking
Address: UTC Shopping Complex, off Moshood Abiola Road, Area 10, Garki, Abuja
Tel: (09) 2342317, 2342373 **Fax:** (09) 2342373
Contact: Mal. Bala Ocholi - Chairman

CONIAH SYSTEMS SUPPORT LIMITED
Business: Computer Engineering Service, Sales and Rentals of IT Products, Networking
Address: 5, Ogundana Street, off Allen Avenue, Ikeja, Lagos
Tel: (01) 4931015
E-mail: coniah@nova.net.ng

CONIC GROUP OF COMPANIES
Business: Telecommunications, Advertising, Auto Sales, Construction
Address: Km. 8, Old Lagos/Ijebu-Ode Road, Opere Village, Podo, Ibadan
Tel: (02) 2318105, 2318106
Contact: Alh Wahid Hassan - Chairman/CEO

CONNECTIONS TRAVEL & TOURS LIMITED
Business: Travel Agency, Tour Operations
Address: 38, Kofo Abayomi Street, Victoria Island, Lagos
Tel: (01) 2624573, 2624574, 2624258, 261873
Fax: (01) 2624258
Contact: Mr. Clement Femi Laniyan - Chairman/CEO

CONNECTIVITY RESOURCES LIMITED
Business: Web-Based Consultancy Services
Address: The Phoneserve Centre, 65/67, Shipeolu Street, Palmgrove, Lagos
Tel: (01) 7731836
E-mail: phoneserve@connectivitiyresources.com
Website: www.connectivityresources.com
Contact: Dr. Kola Russel Ojo - Chairman

CONOCO ENERGY NIGERIA LIMITED
Business: Oilfield Engineering and Drilling Services
Address: 252E, Muri Okunola Street, Victoria Island, Lagos
Tel: (01) 2622226, 2622248
Contact: Mr. Mardond Rymond - MD/CEO

CONOIL PLC
(formerly National Oil & Chemical Marketing Plc)
Business: Marketing of Refined Petroleum Products, Manufacture & Marketing of Lubricants, Industrial & Household Chemicals
Address: 38/39, Marina, Lagos
Tel: (01) 2665880-5 (6L), 2662226, 2662270, 2665960
*Apapa Installation, National/AP Road, New Naval Base, Apapa, Lagos
Tel: (01) 5451674-5 (2L), 5451680, 5451684, 5872907, 5873453, 5874377, 4718668, 4718778
* Aerosol Plant, Kachia Road, Kaduna
Tel: (062) 512564, 512758, 513041, 513243
* Bitumen Plant, Reclamation Road, Port Harcourt
Tel: (084) 2230414, 230697, 232366-7(2L), 232369
* Edewor Shopping Centre, 50, Effurun-Warri Road, Warri.
Tel: (053) 253081, 252340, 253465
Contact: Dr. Mike Adenuga (Jr) - Chairman
Mr. Owen Adesina Tychus - MD/CEO

CONOIL PRODUCING NIGERIA LIMITED
Business: Exploration & Production of Oil
Address: Plot 289, Ajose Adeogun St, Victoria Island, Lagos
Tel: (01) 2616282, 2623509
Contact: Otunba Mike Adenuga, Jnr. - Chairman
Mr. Ebi Omatsola - MD/CEO

CONSOLIDATED ACE LIMITED
Business: Development and Marketing of Software
Address: Unity House (17th Floor), 37, Marina, Lagos
Tel/Fax: (01) 2666098
E-mail: ceeaceltd@hotmail.com
Contact: Mr. Olugbenga Ojerinola - Chairman/CEO

CONSOLIDATED BREWERIES PLC
Business: Production of Alcoholic & Malt Beverage Drinks
Address: Iddo House (4th Floor), Iddo, Lagos
Tel: (01) 7740661-3 (3 L) **Fax:** (01) 2880560
* Awo Omamma Brewery, Km 24, Owerri-Onitsha Road, Awo Omamma, Imo State
Tel: (083) 232765, 232941 **Fax:** (083) 230796
* Ijebu Ode Brewery Imagbon Town, Epe Road, Ijebu Ode, Ogun State
Tel: (037) 432221, 431405, 430166 **Fax:** (037) 432922
Contact: Mr. J. M. A. Poizat - MD/CEO
Mr. Omoruyi Omoigui - Corp. Services Manager

CONSOLIDATED DISCOUNTS LIMITED
Business: Securities Trading
Address: Eagle House (10th, 11th & 12th Floors), 38/39, Marina, Lagos
Tel: (01) 2644281-4 (4 L) 2644271-9 (9L)
Fax: (01) 2644285, 2662385, 2644280
E-mail: cdl@cdlnigeria.com
Website: www.cdlnigeria.com
* Afribank House (2nd Floor), Kaura Namoda Street, Area 3, Garki, Abuja
Tel: (09) 2341696-7(2L),'
Contact: Mr. Samuel I Ayininuola - MD/CEO
Mrs. L. M. Cloud-Ennin - Head (Corp. Servives)

CONSOLIDATED FOOD & BEVERAGES LIMITED
Business: Manufacturing of Food-Seasoning Cubes, Tea, Semolina, Maize Grit, Milk and Margarine
Address: 4, Commercial Road, Apapa, Lagos
Tel: (01) 5452050-2 (3 L), 5452059, 5451719
Fax: (01) 5452054, 2664781, 5878480

E-mail: info@doyin.net
Website: www.doyin.net
Contact: Prince (Dr) Samuel Adedoyin - Chairman/CEO

CONSOLIDATED INVESTMENTS LIMITED
Business: Stockbroking, Portfolio Management, Investment Advisory Services, Financial Analysts
Address: Plot 1232, Bishop Oluwole Street, Lagos
Tel: (01) 614463, 615382, 2880248, 4717565
Fax: (01) 2880248
E-mail: consil@linkserve.com.ng
Contact: Mr. Mustapha Zibiri-Aliu - MD/CEO

CONSOLIDATED MANAGEMENT CONSULTANTS LIMITED
Business: Project Management & Business Reactivation, Management Training &Information Technology Consulting, Financial &Management Consultancy
Address: 46, Opebi Road, Ikeja, Lagos
Tel/Fax: (01) 4930631
E-mail: cmcl-gcs@hyperia.com
cmcl-it@hyperia.com

CONSOLIDATED OIL LIMITED
Business: Exploration and Production of Oil and Gas
Address: Plot 289, Ajose Adeogun St, Victoria Island, Lagos
Contact: Mr. Ebi Omatsola - MD/CEO

CONSOLIDATED RESOURCES LIMITED
Business: Stockbroking, Portfolio Management, Investment Advisory Services, Financial Analysts
Address: CSS Bookshop House (8th Floor), 50/52, Broad Street, Lagos
Tel: (01) 2646768 **Fax:** (01) 2646769

CONSOLIDATED RISK INSURERS LIMITED
Business: Non-Life Insurance
Address: Plot 33D, Bishop Aboyade Cole St, V/Island, Lagos
* 266, Ikorodu Road, Obanikoro, Lagos
Tel: (01) 8159072, 8129251, 7918424, 7918425, 4618222-5 (4L), 08033043974, 08033024171, 08033829519
Fax: (01) 493211, 4618380
E-mail: cri@cybaaspace.net
* Metro Plaza (Annex A), Central Business District, Abuja
Tel: (080) 33578107
Contact: Dr. Layi Fatona - Chairman
Mr. Eddie Efekoha - MD/CEO

CONSOLIDATED TIN MINES LIMITED
Business: Mining and Processing of Solid Minerals, Consultancy Services
Address: Barkin-Ladi Road, Jos
Tel: (073) 280585, 280224
Contact: Mr. F. M. Ikwueme - MD/CEO

CONSTRUCTION PRODUCTS NIGERIA LIMITED
Business: Engineering Construction and Supplies, Construction of Water Supply Schemes, Borehole Drilling and Development, Building and Civil Engineering Construction, Supply and Installation of Pumps, Generators, Irrigation Gates and Water-Treatment Plants, Electro-Mechanical Installation
Address: De-Crown House, Plot 6 & 6, Block E, Town Planning Road, opp. N.C.I. Building, Oluyole Main Estate, Ring Road, Ibadan
Tel: (02) 2318946, 2318947-9 (3 L) **Fax:** (02) 2318946
E-mail: de-crown@ibadan.skannet.com
Contact: Engr. J. B. O. Adewunmi - MD/CEO

CONSTRUMAT NIGERIA LIMITED
Business: Sales of Ceramic Tiles, Sanitary Wares, Marble Tiles, Vitrified Tiles, Wooden Doors and other Building Materials
Address: C71, Amuwo-Odofin Industrial Estate, by Festac Link Road, off Oshodi Expressway, Lagos
Tel: (01) 8042616, 4706633 **Fax:** (01) 8047858
E-mail: construmat@hyperia.com
Contact: Mr. Taofik Abdallah - Chairman

CONSULTANCY IN AFRICA SERVICES LIMITED
Business: Management and Financial Consultancy Services
Address: Africa-Re Building, Plot1679, Karimu Kotun Street, Victoria Island, Lagos
Tel: (01) 2626663 **Fax:** (01) 2626676
E-mail: casltd@infoweb.abs.net
Website: www.consultancyinafrica.com
Contact: Mr. Abiodun Kester Eke - MD/CEO

CONSUMER INVESTMENTS LIMITED
Business: Funds Management, Loans & Advances, Equipment Leasing, Financial Advisory Services
Address: 7, Adetokunbo Ademola Crescent, Wuse II, Abuja
Tel: (09) 5235146-8 (3L), 5237020 **Fax:** (09) 5235149
E-mail: consumer @consumer-investments.com
consumerinvestments@hotmail.com

CONTACT INTERNATIONAL NIGERIA LIMITED
Business: Shipping, Import & Export, Customs Agents
Address: 9, Calcutta Crescent, Apapa, Lagos
Tel: (01) 5451298 **Fax:** (01) 5457247
E-mail: contacty2k@hotmail.com
Contact: Chief I. K. D. Mbulu - MD/CEO

CONTACT LINK LIMITED
Business: Window-Treatment Systems; Cleaning Services
Address: 34, Opebi Road, Ikeja, Lagos
Tel: (01) 4930880, 4930919 **Fax:** (01) 4930880
E-mail: contactlink@hotmail.com
Contact: Jane Chima - MD/CEO

CONTACT MARKETING SERVICES LIMITED
Business: Marketing Consultancy, Direct Marketing, Provision of Temporary Sales Force, Events Marketing and Trade Marketing
Address: Plot 149, Ekundayo, Babaniji Street, off Fatai Irawo Street, Ajao Estate, Lagos
Tel: (01) 4526199, 7743625 **Fax:** (01) 4526199
E-mail: cmsl@alpha.linkserve.com
Contact: Mr. Chris I. Ogbechie - MD/CEO

CONTECH NIGERIA LIMITED
Business: Manufacturing of Plastic Packaging Products
Address: 7, Modupe Olajumoke Street, off Obafemi Awolowo way, Ikeja, Lagos
Tel: (01) 4960354, 4964738, 4970232, 4970233
Fax: (01) 4970232, 4970233

CONTINENTAL BROKERS LIMITED
Business: Insurance Broking
Address: 266, Herbert Macaulay St, Alagomeji, Yaba Lagos
Tel: (01) 867254, 863941
Contact: Mr. Ben Mbonu - MD/CEO

CONTINENTAL CEMENT LIMITED
Business: Production and Marketing of Portland Cement.
Address: Polo House, 2 Tin-Can Island Port Road, Tin-Can Complex, Apapa, Lagos.
Tel: (01) 5873971-3 (3L), 5873773, 5973975
Fax: (01) 5873976
E-mail: conticem@mail.com
* Marble House, 1 Alfred Rewane Rd, Ikoyi, Lagos
Tel: (01) 2695108, 2695109, 2695110
Fax: (01) 2695009 2695316
E-mail: dangote@dangote-group.com

CONTINENTAL FEEDERS (NIGERIA) LIMITED
Business: Cold Storage & Food Preservation Facilities, Warehousing, Importation Dairy Products
Address: 20, Olayiwola Street, Oregun, Ikeja, Lagos
Tel: (01) 4961128, 4967034 **Fax:** (01) 4931946
E-mail: cfnl@nova.net.ng
Contact: Mr. A. M. Jarmakan - Chairman

CONTINENTAL INDUSTRIAL GASES LIMITED.
Business: Manufacturing of Industrial and Medical Gases
Address: 4, Onafeko Street, Akoka, Yaba, Lagos
Contact: Chief R. A. Olowu - MD/CEO

CONTINENTAL INSURANCE BROKERS LIMITED
Business: Insurance Broking
Address: 266, Herbert Macaulay St, Alagomeji, Yaba, Lagos
Tel: (01) 867254, 863941
Contact: Mr. Ben Mbonu - MD/CEO

CONTINENTAL LOSS ADJUSTERS (NIGERIA) LIMITED.
Business: Loss Adjusting, Risk Surveying
Address: Tisco House, 23, Association Ave, Ilupeju, Lagos
Tel: (01) 4968448
Contact: Chief T. O. Idowu - MD/CEO

CONTINENTAL OCEAN PORTS NIGERIA LIMITED
Business: Importation and Marketing of Fishing Materials
Address: 14/16, Sokoto Road, Onitsha
Tel: (046) 212728
Contact: Mr. Joshua O. Mbanugo - Chairman/CEO

CONTINENTAL PLASTIC (WEST AFRICA) LIMITED.
Business: Manufacturing and Marketing of Plastic Products
Address: 23/25, Continental Plastic Road, off Km. 5, Aba-Owerri Road, Aba
Tel: (082) 440222, 350033, 350034
Fax: (082) 440222, 350028
Contact: Mazi A. C. Eneogwu - MD/CEO

CONTINENTAL REINSURANCE COMPANY LIMITED
Business: Reinsurance Business (Life and Non-Life)
Address: Reinsurance House (11th Floor), 46, Marina Lagos
Tel: (01) 2665350, 2665354, 2665368 **Fax:** (01) 2665370
E-mail: crc@rcl.nig.com
Contact: Mr. A. Adejumo - MD/CEO

CONTINENTAL SHIPYARD LIMITED
Business: Ship Repairs and Maintenance, Construction of Navigational Buoys and Steel Strutures, Off Shore Construction and Procurement
Address: Apapa Dockyard, Apapa, Lagos
Tel: (01) 5452874-7 (4 L) **Fax:** (01) 5451611
E-mail: cls@micro.com.ng
Website: www.csl-apapa.com

CONTINENTAL TRUST BANK LIMITED
Business: Commercial Banking
Address: Plot 697, Amodu Tijani St, Victoria Island, Lagos
Tel: (01) 2624030-32 (3L) **Fax:** (01) 2620860
E-mail: enquiries@continental-bank.com
Website: www.continental-bank.com
* 86B, Olu Obasanjo Road, Port Harcourt
Tel: (084) 230666, 230667, 230669, 230672, (090) 503347
* Plots 1142/1143, Adetokunbo Ademola Crescent, Cadastrial Zone A8, Wuse II, Abuja.
Contact: Mr. Ike Nwabuoku - MD/CEO.

CONTRANSAR INTERNATIONAL NIGERIA LIMITED
Business: Dredging and Land Reclamation
Address: 8B, Adekunle Fajuyi Way, Ikeja G.R.A., Lagos
Tel: (01) 4968644, 4930185 **Fax:** (01) 4968644
E-mail: contransar@infoweb.abs.net
Contact: Engr. Ebosie Ezeoke - Chairman/CEO.

CONTRANSIMEX NIGERIA LIMITED
Business: Civil Engineering and Construction
Address: 8, Adekunle Fajuyi Road, Ikeja G.R.A., Ikeja, Lagos
Tel: (01) 4968644, 4930185, (090) 502913

CONTROLLED PLASTICS LIMITED
Business: Manufacturing of Plastic Containers and Bags
Address: Km. 8, Hadejia Road, Kano
Tel: (064) 312661

CONVEYANCER (NIGERIA) LIMITED
Business: Sales of Forklift Trucks and Rams, Materials-Handling Equipment, Cranes, Excavators, Hand Pallet Trucks and Trolleys, Generator Sets and Hot Water Cleaners; Precision Engineering Services
Address: 64, Eric Moore Rd, Iganmu Ind Estate, S/L, Lagos
Tel: (01) 4826181, 7742278, 837025, 08033220784
Fax: (01) 5452384, 833563
E-mail: dodco@linkserve.com.ng
Contact: Senator David Dafinone - Chairman
Engr. Francis Redemi - GM

CONYBIRD NIGERIA LIMITED
Business: Sales and Engineering of Computers and Office Automation; Consultancy Services
Address: 8, Tokunbo Alli Street, off Toyin St, Ikeja, Lagos
Tel: (01) 4961215, 4966536, 4978504 **Fax:** (01) 4930945
E-mail: conybrid@infoweb.abs.net
* 29, Olowu Street, Ikeja, Lagos
* Plot 0081, Aba Close, Area 8, Garki, Abuja
Contact: Mr. Akinbola E. Olamilokun - MD/CEO.

COOMY AUTOMOBILES LIMITED
Business: Sales and Service of Automobiles
Address: 9A, Adeola Odeku Street, Victoria Island, Lagos

Tel: (01) 7786929, 08033047196
Contact: Mr. Collins Masadey - MD/CEO

COOL PENNY (NIGERIA) LIMITED
Business: Hotel & Catering Services, Printing & Packaging, General Merchandising
Address: 16/18, Industrial Road, Olodi - Apapa, Lagos
Tel: (01) 5450268, 7744528, 5450253, 08033312780, 08033235425 **Fax:** (01) 5450268
E-mail: ezeeva@yahoo.com
Contact: Dr. Obasi Chukwunenye - Chairman/CEO

COOP BUILDING SOCIETY LIMITED
Business: Mortgage Banking
Address: 15, Seventh Day Adventist Road, Oke Bola, Ibadan
Tel: (02) 2315178, 2315184 **Fax:** (02) 2315191
E-mail: coopbuilding@skannet.com

COOP COCOA PRODUCTS LIMITED
Business: Processing, Sale & Exportation of Cocoa
Address: Coop House, Ilesa-Benin Expressway, Akure
Tel: (034) 240844, 242681, 242192
E-mail: coopcocoa@gannetcity.net

COOPER CAMERON CORPORATION NIGERIA LIMITED
Business: Supply and Service of Oil and Gas Equipment
Address: Plot 45, Trans-Amadi Ind. Layout, Port Harcourt
Tel: (084) 231605, 2311264, 232187 **Fax:** (084) 239112
Contact: Mr. Peter Maude - MD/CEO

COOPER FLEMING STOCKBROKERS LIMITED
Business: Stockbroking, Portfolio Management, Investment Advisory Services, Fund Management
Address: Churchgate Towers (8th Floor), Plot PC. 30, Afribank Street, Victoria Island, Lagos
Tel: (01) 2619831-3 (3 L), 2620550, 2620554, 2621281
Fax: (01) 2619833, 2620420
E-mail: pchcfs@churchgate.com
Contact: Mr. B. Mahtani - Chairman

CO-OPERATIVE SUPPLY ASSCIATION LIMITED
Business: Sales of Agro-Chemicals, Hardware, Building Materials and Grocery
Address: 129, Railway Siding, Magazine Road, Ibadan
Tel: (02) 2413055, 2411864, 08037262062, 08034723838, 34723839 **Fax:** (02) 2413055
Contact: Pastor F. O. Adegbulugbe - MD/CEO

COPAC NIGERIA LIMITED
Business: Manufacturing of Healthcare Products
Address: Plot 6, Block K, Isolo Industrial Scheme, Apapa-Oshodi Expressway, Isolo, Lagos
Tel: (01) 4526669, 4526039

COPIERS NIGERIA LIMITED
Business: Suppliers of Drawing Office, Art, Graphic, Engineering, Surveying and Cartographic Materials, Manufacturing of Plan-Printing Papers
Address: 6, Razak Okoya Lane (formerly Cow Lane), off Igbosere Road, Lagos
Tel: (01) 2630489, 2634625 **Fax:** (01) 2630489
Contact: copiersltd@hotmail.com
Contact: Mrs A. A. Anibaba - MD/CEO

COPLUC NIGERIA LIMITED
Business: Procurement and Supplies to Oil and Gas Industry
Address: 150, Obafemi Awolowo Way, Ikeja, Lagos
Tel: (01) 4965638, 4960558 **Fax:** (01) 4965638
Contact: Rose C. Haywood - MD/CEO

COPPERS' LODGE NIGERIA LIMITED
Business: Sales and Services of Broadcasting Equipment
Address: 29, Norman Williams Street, S. W. Ikoyi, Lagos
Tel: (01) 2672860, 2671466
E-mail: copperslodge@hyperia.com
Contact: Squadron Ldr B. Martins (rtd) - Chairman/CEO

COPYCAT LIMITED
Business: Sales, Supply & Maintenance of Office Equipment
Address: 15, Hospital/Orlu Road, Owerri
Tel: (083) 234367 **Fax:** (083) 232161
* 34, Aba Road, Port Harcourt
Contact: Nze Judie-Ik Ogamba - GM/CEO

CORAL INTERNATIONAL INSURANCE COMPANY LIMITED
Business: Non-Life Insurance
Address: Tower Fernandez (Suites 3, 4 & 5), 1-9, Berkley Street, Onikan, Lagos
Tel: (01) 2637159, 2637661, 2645305, 2637679
Fax: (01) 2637679
E-mail: coral@micro.com.ng
Contact: Mr. Andy Azike - MD/CEO

CORELAB NIGERIA LIMITED
Business: Oilfield Services
Address: Plot 66, Trans-Amadi Ind. Layout, Port Harcourt
Tel: (084) 239116, 230483, 233569 **Fax:** (084) 239117
E-mail: corelab@hyperia.com

CORMART (NIGERIA) LIMITED
Business: Importation & Marketing of Industrial Chemicals
Address: Plot 20, Chief Benson Anorue Street, Ajao Estate, Apakun-Oshodi, Lagos
Tel: (01) 4520965, 4520877, 4520987, 4520592
Fax: (01) 4520980

CORNERSTONE BUILDING SOCIETY LIMITED
Business: Mortgage Banking Services
Address: 71, Adeniyi Jones Avenue, Ikeja, Lagos
Tel: (01) 4972451, 4972452, 8042306 **Fax:** (01) 4972451
Contact: Mr. Bode Ogunlusi - G M/CEO

CORNERSTONE CONSTRUCTION (NIGERIA) LIMITED
Business: Housing Estate Development; Building & Civil Engineering
Address: 3, Ope-Oredugba Close, off Mobolaji Bank-Anthony Way, Abule Onigbagbo Bus-Stop, Ikeja, Lagos
Tel: (01) 4975563, 4704110, 4931697 **Fax:** (01) 4975563
E-mail: csconstr@gacom.net
Contact: Mr. Lanre Okupe - MD/CEO

CORNERSTONE INSURANCE PLC
Business: General Insurance
Address: 136, Lewis Street, Lagos Island, Lagos
Tel: (01) 2636140, 2631832, 2632863 **Fax:** (01) 2633079
E-mail: marketing@cornerstone.com.ng

Website: www@cornerstone.com.ng
Contact: Mr Jacob Erhabor - MD/CEO
Mr Kenny Borisade - DGM (Business Dev. Group)

CORNERSTONE TRUSTEES LIMITED
Business: Trust and Financial Services, Equipment Leasing
Address: 31, Moloney Street, opp. Kam Selem Building, Obalende, Lagos
Tel: (01) 2632708, 2633499, 2636140, 2631832
Fax: (01) 2633079, 2633112
E-mail: enquiries@cornerstoneplc.com
Contact: Mr. Dominic Ichaba - GM/CEO

CORONA PLASTIC INDUSTRIES LIMITED
Business: Manufacturing and Marketing of Plastic Products
Address: 1, Ajibade Oke Street, behind King Carpet, off Asa Afariogun Street, Ajao Estate,Isolo, Lagos
Tel: (01) 7749633, 775915 **Fax:** (01) 2690198
E-mail: coronaindustries@aol.com
Contact: Mr. Bharat G. Assomull - Director

CORPORATE CITIZENS INSURANCE BROKERS LIMITED
Business: Insurance Broking & Risk Management Consultancy
Address: Plot 130, Ahmadu Bello Way, Victoria Island, Lagos
Tel: (01) 2621901, 612540 **Fax:** (01) 2621901
E-mail: ccib@hyperia.com
Contact: Mrs. Adesola O. Williams - GM/CEO

CORPORATE CLOTHIERS LIMITED
Business: Fashion Designing, Boutique
Address: 79, Opebi Road, Ikeja, Lagos
Tel: (01) 4937987, 4709745
* Great Nigeria House (Suite 1, 8th Floor), 47/57, Martins Street, Lagos
Tel: (01) 2668695
Contact: Mr. Ayo Aremu - Chairman

CORPORATE DIAMOND SECURITIES & INVESTMENTS LTD
Business: Capital Market Operations (Registrars, Portfolio Managers, Investment Advisers), Financial, Communication and Marketing Consultants
Address: Waterfront Plaza, First Avenue, opp. Mr. Biggs, Festac Town, Lagos
Tel: (01) 5890248
E-mail: cordsil@onebox.com
Contact: Chief C. A. Mosindi - Chairman/CEO

CORPORATE GUARDS LIMITED
Business: Security Services & Consultancy, Sales and Installation of Security Equipment
Address: 28A, Adetokunbo Ademola St,Victoria Island, Lagos
Tel: (01) 7748463, 2881906, 2644919 **Fax:** (01) 2644919
E-mail: cguards@micro.com.ng
* 18, Odum Close, Access Bank Bus - Stop, Trans-Amadi Industrial Layout, Port Harcourt
* c/o Plot 1499, IBB Way, Ministers' Hill, Maitama, Abuja.
Tel: (09)2346490-4 (5 L)
Contact: Mr. Wande Akinboboye - Chairman/CEO

CORPORATE HEADFITTERS LIMITED
Business: Manufacturing and Sale of Hats, Headgears, Hat Materials & Accessories
Address: 17, Maitama Sule Street, off Awolowo Road, S. W. Ikoyi, Lagos
Tel: (01) 2671339, 2670963, 4701326., 08023027242
Fax: (01) 2671339
E-mail: corpheadfitters@yahoo.com
Contact: Mrs. Eme O. Akenzua - MD/CEO

CORPORATE IDEALS INSURANCE COMPANY LIMITED
Business: General Insurance, Special Risk & Life Assurance
Address: 72, Bode Thomas Street, Surulere, Lagos
Tel: (01) 5851577, 5851536, 8010800-4 (5 L)
Fax: (01) 5851577
Contact: Mr. Okey A. Obiorah - Exec. Vice Chairman

CORPORATE MEDIA LIMITED
Business: Outdoor Advertising
Address: Elephant Cement Housee (6th Floor), ASSBIFI Rd, Central Business District, Alausa, Ikeja, Lagos
Tel: (01) 3451166

CORPORATE PICTURES LIMITED
Business: Producers and Marketers of Motion-Film Pictures
Address: 4, Edidi Lane, Idumota, Lagos
* 25, Kayode St, off Ikorodu Road, Onipanu, Lagos
Contact: Mr. Abdulai Abdulrasaki - MD/CEO

CORPORATE PRESS SERVICES INCORPORATED
Business: Corporate Communications, Public Relations & Advertising, Market Research & Consultancy Services, Events Management & Organisation, Printing & Packaging, Publishing & Allied Services
Address: White House, 23, Folawewo Close,off Allen Avenue, Ikeja, Lagos
Tel: (01) 4937174, 4972006, 4972009 **Fax:** (01) 4972007
E-mail: corporatepress@imperialunion.com
corporate-press@worldwemail.com
* 6B, Trans-Amadi Ind. Layout, Port Harcourt
Tel: (084) 233132 **Fax:** (084) 233481
Contact: Dr. Emmanuel Ibeziako - Chairman/CEO

COSCHARIS GROUP
Business: Importers, Exporters, Manufacturers, Manufacturer's Representatives, Agents, Distributors, Dealers in Auto-Care Products, Agricultural Products, Medical Equipment
Address: * Coscharis Plaza, 68A, Adeola Odeku Street, Victoria Island, Lagos
Tel: (01) 2624310-18 (9 L) **Fax:** (01) 2624319, 2624320
E-mail: bmw-rover@coscharis.com
Website: www.coscharis.com
* 1-7, Coscharis Street, off Alahun Osumba Street, Kirikiri Town, Maza-Maza, Lagos
Tel: (01) 5880511, 5884368, 5890418
Fax: (01) 5880511, 5885158
Contact: Mr. Cosmas M. Maduka - President/CEO

COSCHARIS AUTO INDUSTRIES LIMITED
Business: Manufacturing of Chains for Motorcycles and Bicycles, and Nails
Address: 1-7, Coscharis Street, Kirikiri Industrial Estate, Maza-Maza, Lagos
Tel: (01) 5881031, 5884259, 7745133

Fax: (01) 5885158, 2880339
Contact: Mr. Cosmas M. Maduka - President/CEO

COSCHARIS FINANCE & INVESTMENT LIMITED
Business: Money Market Operations, Funds Management Services, Export Operations
Address: 1-7, Coscharis Street, Kirikiri Industrial Estate, Maza-Maza, Lagos
Tel: (01) 7745906, 2624318-25 (8L), 5881031
Fax: (01) 5885158
E-mail: exports@coscharis.com
Website: www.coscharis.com
Contact: Mr. Cosmas M. Maduka -Executive President/CEO\

COSCHARIS MEDICALS & FOODS LIMITED
Business: Importation & Sales of Medical Equipment and Processed Foods (including Purified Table Water)
Address: 1-7, Coscharis Street, Kirikiri Industrial Estate, Maza-Maza, Lagos
Tel: (01) 7744478, 3205054 **Fax:** (01) 3205055
E-mail: legal@coscharis.com
imports@coscharis.com
Website: www.coscharis.com
Contact: Dr. Cosmos M. Maduka - Chairman
Mr. Charles I. Akujobi - MD/CEO

COSCHARIS MOTORS LIMITED
Business: Sales of Motor Vehicles and Spare Parts, Maintenance and Repairs, Manufacturer's Representative (BMW and ROVER Vehicles)
Address: Coscharis Plaza, 68A, Adeola Odeku Street, Lagos
Tel: (01) 2624310, 2624314, 2624316, 2624315
Fax: (01) 2624319
E-mail: info@coscharis.com
bmw-rover@coscharis.com
Website: www.coscharis.com
* Plot 591, Aminu Kano Crescent, off Ahmadu Bello Way, Wuse II, Abuja.
Tel: (09) 4136450, 4139114.
* 50, Trans-Amadi Industrial Layout, by Nkpoju Junction, Port Harcourt
Contact: Mr. Cosmas M. Maduka - President/CEO

COSCHARIS TECHNOLOGIES LIMITED
Business: Sales, Supply and Maintenance of Computers, Software Development, System Assembling and Intergration IT Training
Address: Coscharis Plaza, 68A, Adeola Odeku Street, Lagos
Tel: (01) 2610801-2 (2 L), 2624323, 3201497
Fax: (01) 2624319
E-mail: costech@infoweb.abs.net
* 27, Obafemi Awolowo Way, Ikeja, Lagos.
Tel: (01) 4934703, 4973531, 4973533, 4710366
* 29, Ogunlana Drive, Surulere, Lagos.
Tel: (01) 5850883, 5458236
* Plot 591, Aminu Kano Crescent, Wuse II, Abuja
E-mail: costech@micro.com.ng
Contact: Mr. Cosmas M. Maduka - Executive President

COSEC SERVICES LIMITED
Business: Company Secretarial Services
Address: Ebani House, 62, Marina, Lagos
Tel: (01) 2669892, 2665534, 2661462
Fax: (01) 2662709, 2640742
E-mail: eyng@linkserve.com.ng
Contact: Chief William O. Oziabor - Chairman/CEO

COSKOLI VENTURES NIG. LIMITED
Business: Importation and Exportation of General Goods, General Contractors and Suppliers
Address: 7, Ikorodu Road, Maryland, Ikeja, Lagos
Tel/Fax: (01) 4931972
E-mail: maardec@infoweb.abs.net
Contact: Mr. Cosmas I. B. Okoli - Chairman/CEO

COSMIC FOAM & CHEMICAL INDUSTRIES NIGERIA LTD
Business: Manufacturing and Marketing of Foam Products, Sales of Industrial Chemicals
Address: 3, Independence Road, Bompai, Kano
Tel: (064) 638443, 6322919
Contact: Mr. Cosmas Chukwuma - Chairman
Mr. Promise Nduji - MD/CEO

COSMIC INSURANCE BROKERS LIMITED
Business: Insurance Broking
Address: Bloc 1, (1st Floor), M.K.O. Abiola Gardens, Central Business District, Alausa, Lagos
Tel: (01) 4707801, 7748778 **Fax:** (01) 4974844
E-mail: cosmic.insurance@skannet.com
Contact: Air Vice Marshal Bayo Lawal, mni (rtd) - Chairman

COSMOS CHEMICALS LIMITED
Business: Manufacturing of Black Soap and Canwood
Address: All Seasons Plaza (Amethyst Block, Suite 7), Lateef Jakande Road, Agidingbi, Ikeja, Lagos
Tel/Fax: (01) 2881994
Contact: Mr. Biola Ogunrinde - MD/CEO

COSMOS FISHING COMPANY LIMITED
Business: Fishing and Shrimping
Address: Plot 1303A, Akin Adesola St, Victoria Island, Lagos
Tel: (01) 2622232, 2622259, 2615505
Fax: (01) 2619487
E-mail: primlaks@hyperia.com
Contact: Mr. Manjit R;. Sadarangani - MD/CEO

COSMOS TECHNOLOGIES LIMITED
Business: Corporate Internet & E-Commerce Solutions.
Address: CSS Bookshop House (14th Floor), 50/52, Broad Street, Lagos
Tel: (01) 2646574, 2646890 **Fax:** (01) 2601206
E-mail: mails@cosmotech.com
Website: www.cosmotech.com
www.naira.net
Contact: Mr. Ade Adekanmbi - Business Dev. Manager

COSMOS TRADE NIGERIA LIMITED
Business: Total Sales & Support of Ice-Cream Business (Machines, Powder, Slush Machines)
Address: 6, Ilupeju Bye-Pass, Ilupeju Lagos
Tel: (01) 4717217, 4932683, 08023222530
Fax: (01) 4932683
E-mail: cosmos@hyperia.com
* 11, Bende Street, Rumuomasi, Port Harcourt
Tel: (084) 484920
Contact: Mr. Tunji Olaniyi - MD/CEO

COSMOT NIGERIA LIMITED
Business: Manufacture of Cosmetics Products, Plastics, Packaging and Sleeves
Address: 9, Happy Home Avenue, Kirikiri Ind. Estate, Lagos
Tel: (01) 5454224, 7744867 **Fax:** (01) 5453129
E-mail: cosmotcnl@yahoo.com
Contact: Mr. Bassam Hanaoui - Chairman/CEO

COSOKOLI VENTURES NIGERIA LIMITED
Business: Import & Export, General Contractors & Suppliers, Transporters, Clearing & Forwarding Agency
Address: 7, Ikorodu Road, Maryland, Ikeja, Lagos
Tel: (01) 4931972, 08033008999 **Fax:** (01) 4931972
E-mail: maardec@yahoo.com
Contact: Mr. Cosmos I. B. Okoli - Chairman/CEO

COSPAM (NIGERIA) LIMITED
Business: Production and Refurbishment of Fire-Fighting Vehicles, Sales of Agricutural Machinery and Fire-fighting Equipment
Address: Fireoff House, 17, Nise Street, Uwani, Enugu
Tel: (042) 256720, 250950

COST CARE PARNERSHIP
Business: Chartered Quantity Surveyors, Construction Cost Consultants
Address: 29, Isaac John Street, (2nd Floor), off Ikorodu Road, Igbobi, Lagos

COST MODEL ASSOCIATES
Business: Quantity Surveyors and Project Managers
Address: 20, Oweh Street, Fadeyi Lagos
Tel: (01) 7747654, 867994 **Fax:** (01) 7747654
* Plot 10A, Kigoma Street, Wuse Zone 7, Abuja
* 30, Isato Street, Irona, Ado-Ekiti.
Tel: (030) 251502
Contact: I. J. Oyebade - Principal Partner

COST PEAK CONSULT
Business: Quantity Surveying, Design Cost Planning, Estate & Project Management
Address: Acme House (2nd Floor), Acme Road, Ogba Industrial Estate, Ikeja, Lagos
Tel: (01) 8114392, 08033077396, 08055639443
E-mail: costpeak@yahoo.com
Contact: Mr. Joel Chiedo Nwachukwu - Principal Partner

COSTAIN (WEST AFRICA) PLC
Business: Building & Civil Engineering Contractors, Furniture Manufacturers
Address: 174, Western Avenue, Iganmu, Lagos
Tel: (01) 5801870-4 (5 L) **Fax:** (01) 5801879
* Costain Life-Camp, Festival Road, Garki Area 10, Abuja.
Tel: (09) 5232066
Contact: Chief N. C. Jibunoh - Chairman/CEO

COSTEC CONSULTANTS
Business: Quantity Surveying, Construction Economist, Project Management
Address: 72, Queen's Street, Sabo-Yaba, Lagos
Tel: (01) 3425186, 08033007382, 08023116427
Fax: (01) 3425186
E-mail: costec@infoweb.abs.net
* Block 12, Area 1, Section 2, Garki, beh NYSC Office, Garki, Abuja
Tel: (09) 2342208
* 22, Udom St, beh. NITEL, D-Line, Port Harcourt
Tel: (084) 236636, 230336

COST-LINK ASSOCIATES
Business: Quantity Surveyors and Certified Cost Engineers
Address: 28, Gbolade Adebanjo Street, off Coker Road, Ilupeju, Lagos
Tel: (01) 4965406, 8045020 **Fax:** (01) 4965406
E-mail: cost-link@hyperia.com
Contact: Mr. Tony Ndah - Principal Partner

COTECNA INSPECTION LIMITED
Business: Inspection Services
Address: Marble House (4th Floor), 1 Alfred Rewane Road, Ikoyi, Lagos
Tel: (01) 2690323, 2692648-9 (2L) 2696301-4 (4L)
Fax: (01) 2690985

COT-SYN NIGERIA LIMITED
Business: Manufacturing of Fabrics and Garments
Address: Plot 35/36, Iganmu Industrial Estate, Imam Dauda Street, off Eric Moore Road, Surulere, Lagos
Tel: (01) 5830487, 5864575, 7747105
Fax: (01) 5831314, 5834549
*Plot A1, Block IX, Ilupeju Industrial Estate, Lagos
Tel: (01) 960949, 964612

COUNTERS TRUST SECURITIES LIMITED
Business: Stockbroking, Financial Advisory Services, Issuing House, Corporate Finance
Address: 1/5, Odunlami Street, Lagos
Tel: (01) 26401061-9 (10L) **Fax:** (01) 2640171
E-mail: info@counterstrust.com
Website: www.counterstruct.com
Contact: Mr. Dan Agbor - Chairman

COUNTRY & CITY INSURANCE BROKERS LIMITED
Business: Insurance Broking and Consultancy
Address: 14, Queen's Street, Alagomeji-Yaba, Lagos
Tel/Fax: (01) 866334
Contact: Mr. Tunde Onanuga - Chairman

COUNTRY HOME REAL ESTATE COMPANY
Business: Estate Surveyors, Integrated Property Consultants
Address: WAPIC House (Country Home Suite), 119, Awolowo Road, S. W. Ikoyi, Lagos
Tel: (01) 2694529, 2670355
* McLewis Complex (2nd Floor), Ibrahim Babangida Way, Wuse II, Abuja.
Tel: (09) 5237744
Contact: Mr. E. Bassey Udosen - Managing Partner

COUNTRYWIDE AFFORDABLE ESTATES PLC
Business: Building and Management of Industrialised Housing Units
Address: Plot 170B, Gbagada Estate Phase I, Gbagada-Oworonsoki Expressway, Gbagada, Lagos
Tel: (01) 2882616, 3422212
Contact: Mr. Soji Okusanya - GM/CEO

COUNTY HOSPITAL LIMITED
Business: Healthcare Delivery Services
Address: 41-45, Isheri Road, Aguda-Ogba, Agege, Lagos
Tel: (01) 4921987
Contact: Dr (Chief) A. B. Craig - Chairman/Medical Director

COURDEAU NIGERIA LIMITED
Business: Catering Services, Hotel Management, Furniture Production
Address: C & C Towers, Plot 1684, Sanusi Fafunwa Street, Victoria Island, Lagos
Contact: Mr. Joseph Chidiac - Chairman/CEO

COURIERMASTERS INTERNATIONAL
Business: Courier Services
Address: 33, Ikorodu Road, Jibowu, Yaba, Lagos
Tel: (01) 4734963, 4706576, 7755546, 08023428314
E-mail: cmi@limkserve.com
Website: www.abc.com
Contact: Mrs. Uche Obi - MD/CEO

COUTINHO CARO & COMPANY (NIGERIA) LIMITED
Business: Power Supply, Engineering and Industrial Plants, Construction, Refractories, Industrial Consumables, Machineries and Equipment, Project Management, Trading and After-Sales Services
Address: 30/32, Creek Road, Apapa, Lagos
Tel: (01) 5870907, 5877602, 5877621, 2882550
Fax: (01) 5877621
E-mail: coutinhonig@hyperia.com

COWADAY FOODS LIMITED
Business: Sales of Livestock, Seafoods, Groceries, Beef Chicken etc, Cold-Storage Facilities
Address: 1, Onowu Anatogu Street, Woliwo, Onitsha
Tel: (046) 2144247, 215503
Contact: Mrs. Okeoma Nwangwu - MD/CEO

CPEC LIMITED
Business: Sales and Installation of Industrial Plants
Address: 12, Oremeji Street, Ikeja, Lagos
Tel: (01) 4977173, 4978452, 4806453, 090-408838, 08033203423, 08033203425, 08033203501
E-mail: cpecltd2003@yahoo.com

COVENANT ENTERPRISES SOLUTIONS LIMITED
Business: Sale, Implementatation, Training & Support for Accounting and Business Management Software
Address: Olatunji House (2nd Floor), 299, Ikorodu Road, Maryland, Lagos
Tel: (01) 8112147, 4960575, 4934160, 08056123008
E-mail: covenant@intracom.net.ng
Website: www.ceasolutions.net
Contact: Mr. Lanre Carew - MD/CEO

CPI-MOORE (NIGERIA) LIMITED
Business: Manufacture of Computer Stationery, Printing and Sales of Business Forms and Security Documents, Sales of Printing Equipment & Allied Products, Sticky Labels and Lineflow
Address: 374, Ikorodu Road, Maryland, Ikeja, Lagos
Tel: (01) 4938331 **Fax:** (01) 4938329
Contact: Mr. O. O. Osinsanya - Chairman/CEO

CPL INDUSTRIES LIMITED
Business: Manufacture and Marketing of Personal Products, Cosmetics, Pharmaceuticals and Plastic Containers
Address: 381/383, Agege Motor Road (Ilupeju Bye-Pass), Mushin, Lagos
Tel: (01) 521044, 523914 **Fax:** (01) 523914
Contact: Prince Albert A. Awofisayo - Chairman/CEO

CPU TECHNOLOGY (NIGERIA) LIMITED
Business: Computer Sales & Repairs, Training, Network Installation & Business Center/Internet Services
Address: 22, Yaya Abatan Street, Ogba-Aguda, Ikeja, Lagos
Tel: (01) 4925959
E-mail: cupunigeria@aol.com
Contact: Mr. Garald Okereke - Bus. Dev. Manager

CRANE CONSTRUCTION LIMITED
Business: Building and Civil Engineering Services
Address: 79, Awolowo Road, S.W., Ikoyi, Lagos
Tel: (01) 2672411, 2672554 **Fax:** (01) 2670653

CREATIVE PLUS LIMITED
Business: Advertising, Marketing
Address: 5, Ilupeju Bye-Pass, Ilupeju, Lagos
Tel: (01) 4960557, 4960579, 4966633 **Fax:** (01) 4960557
Contact: Mr. Niyi Alonge - Chairman/CEO

CREATIVITYLAND LIMITED
Business: Sales of Educational Toys
Address: Plot 1412, Ahmadu Bello Way, opp. Bar Beach, Victoria Island, Lagos
Tel: (01) 4711276
E-mail: creativitykids@aol.com
Contact: Mr. Ben Odukwe - Chairman
Mrs. Bimbo Adetola - GM

CREDIT SWIFT LIMITED
Business: Finance and Trust Services, Portfolio Management, Investment Consultants, Structured Lease Financing, International Trade Financing
Address: Foreshore Towers (1st Floor), 2A, Osborne Road, Ikoyi, Lagos
Tel: (01) 2695230 **Fax:** (01) 2670053
E-mail: creditswift@nova.net.ng
Contact: Mr. F. O. Coker - GM/CEO

CREMOTRADE COMPANY LIMITED
Business: Construction, Building and Civil Engineering
Address: Plot 5A, Kudenda Industrial Layout, Western Bye-Pass, Nnamdi Azikiwe Expressway, Kaduna
Tel: (062) 236780
E-mail: cremotrade@cyberspace.net.ng
Contact: Mr. Guido Firetti - MD/CEO

CRESEADA INTERNATIONAL LIMITED
Business: Shipping, Clearing and Forwarding, Warehousing, Transporting; Container Terminal Operators
Address: Plot 1, Block G, Oshodi Ind. Layout, Isolo-Oshodi Expressway (Toyota Bus - Stop), Isolo, Lagos
Tel: (01) 4523903, 45238171, 45298937
Fax: (01) 4524659, 4528874
E-mail: creseda@hyperia.com
Contact: Mr. M. A. Ayinde - Chairman/CEO

CRESTWOOD HOLDINGS LIMITED
Business: Travel Agency
Address: 88, Ajose Adeogun Street, Victoria Island, Lagos
Tel: (01) 2624171, 2624172, 619832, 619833

CRISP INTERNATIONAL LIMITED
Business: Clearing and Forwarding Agency, Transportation, Warehousing, Travel Agency
Address: 6, Kachia Road, Kaduna South, Kaduna
Tel: (062) 232357, 234396 **Fax:** (062) 232357
E-mail: crisp@skannet.com
Website: www.crisp.inter.com
* 27, Kudaisi Street, off Tin Can Island Expressway, Olodi, Apapa, Lagos
* 8, Nsukka Street, by Garki Hotels, Garki II, Abuja
Tel: (090) 8011421
* 8A, Aba Rd/Lagos Street, opp. Airforce Secondary School, Rumumasi, Diobu, Port Harcourt
Contact: Mr. Steve Ikechi Amadi - MD/CEO

CRISP LEISURE TRAVELS & TOURS LTD
Business: Travel Agency
Address: Falomo Shopping Centre (Suite A-7B), Awolowo Road, Falomo, Ikoyi, Lagos
Tel: (01) 2671552, 2672439, 2693127, 2693835, 08023101715 **Fax:** (01) 2693835
E-mail: crisptravels@excite.com
* Zuma Shopping Mall (Suite B9), Ndola Square, off Michael Okpara Street, Wuse Zone 5, Abuja
Tel: (09) 5232542, 5237697 **Fax:** (09) 5232542
Contact: Engr. Jaiye Balogun - Chairman/CEO

CRITICAL RESCUE INTERNATIONAL (NIGERIA)
Business: Advanced 24-Hour Emergency Medical Services, Medical Transportation, Medihelp Telephonic Service, Rescue Services
Address: 42, Isaac John Street, G. R. A., Ikeja, Lagos
Tel: (01) 4936684 **Fax:** (01) 4960482
Contact: Chief (Dr) E. A. O. Shonekan, CBE. - Chairman
Michelle Gerard - Client Liaison Manager

CRITTALL-HOPE NIGERIA LIMITED
Business: Aluminium & Steel Product Fabrication
Address: 330/332, Agege Motor Road, Challenge, Mushin, Lagos
Tel: (01) 4520691, 4520790, 4520825-6 (2L), 4521155-7(2L
Fax: (01) 4520891
E-mail: chnl@crittal-hope.com
* 30B, Agudama St, Aba Rd, Port Harcourt
Tel: (084) 578804, 08023083613, 08023132907
* Kachia Road, Kaduna
Tel: (062) 231654, 232699 **Fax:** (062) 231309
Contact: Alh. I. A. Bello - MD/CEO

CROCODILE MACHETES NIGERIA LIMITED
Business: Manufacturing of Machetes and Domestic Knives
Address: Plot 29, Trans-Amadi Industrial Layout, opp. First Aluminuum Nigeria Plc, Port Harcourt
Tel: (084) 301190-4 (5 L)
Contact: Mr. A. I. Iwuoha - MD/CEO

CROSS COUNTRY LIMITED
Business: Road Passenger-Transportation Services
Address: Murtala Muhammed Way, near Yaba Bus-Stop, opp Presbyterian Church, Yaba, Lagos
Tel: (01) 5821581, 7764000

CROSS MARINE SERVICES LIMITED
Business: Shipping Agency
Address: 28, Burma Road, Apapa, Lagos
Tel: (01) 5872266, 5871375, 5872931 **Fax:** (01) 5873294
E-mail: crossmarine@ng.dti.bollore.com
* 3-4, Trans-Amadi Estate, Port Harcourt
Tel: (084) 236959 **Fax:** (084) 237196
Contact: Alh. A. A. Banda - Chairman
Mr. Niels Riechers - MD/CEO

CROSS SOAP INDUSTRY NIGERIA LIMITED
Business: Manufacturing of Laundry Soap
Address: 6, Michael Shosanya Street, off Olajide Avenue, Liasu Road, Egbe, Lagos
Tel: (01) 8045468

CROSSAIDS LIMITED
Business: Pump Assembly, Construction and Repairs of Cooling Towers, Sales and Servicing of Metering Pumps, Water and Waste-Water Treatment
Address: 66, Modupe Johnson Crescent, off Adeniran Ogunsanya Street, Surulere, Lagos
Tel/Fax: (01) 5850984
* Caspian House, Polytechnic-Sango Road, Ibadan
Tel: (02) 411744
* 12A, Alkalawa Street, off Ibrahim Taiwo Road, Tudun Wada, Kaduna
* 13, Worukwo Street, off Wokogoloma Street, Oroworukwo, Diobu, Port Harcourt
Contact: Mr. B. B. Majekodunmi - Operations Manager

CROSSWORLD SECURITIES LIMITED
Business: Portfolio Management, Corporate Finance, Stockbroking, Investment Advisory Services Lease Finance , Pension Fund Management
Address: 2/4, Cutoms Stret, off Tinubu Squre, Lagos
Tel: (01) 2666604, , 2664078, 2668580, 2667757, 7740599
Fax: (01) 2668580
E-mail: cwsl@metrong.com
Website: www.crossworldsec.com
Contact: Mr. Olu Abyomi Sanya - MD/CEO

CROWN COURIER SERVICES LIMITED
Business: Courier, Cargo and Bulk Delivery Services
Address: 3A, Allen Lane off Allen Avenue, Lagos
Tel/Fax: (01) 4961487
Contact: Mr. Gabriel Odueyi - MD/CEO

CROWN DRINKS LIMITED
Business: Production and Sales of Fruit and Juice Drinks
Address: 322, Ikorodu Road, Anthony Lagos
Tel: (01) 4936054, 4936846, 7743176 **Fax:** (01) 4939150
Contact: Chief Michael Ade Ojo - Chairman

CROWN FLOUR MILLS LIMITED
Business: Flour Milling
Address: Plot 53, Malu Siding Road, c/o 20, North Avenue, Apapa, Lagos
Tel: (01) 5450094, 5450088, 5873721, 5453721, 5453294,

5875378 **Fax:** (01) 5871024
E-mail: tncancfm@rcl.nig.com
Contact: Chief Maan Lababidi - MD/CEO

CROWN INSURANCE BROKERS LIMITED
Business: Insurance Broking and Risk Management
Address: 8, Creek Road, Apapa, Lagos
Tel: (01) 5872121, 5870842
Contact: Mr. Felix O. Amadi - MD/CEO

CROWN REALITIES PLC
Business: Property & Hotel Development
Address: 8A, Lalupon Close, off Keffi Street, S. W. Ikoyi
Tel: (01) 2694570-2 (3 L) **Fax:** (01) 2694573
E-mail: info@crownrealities.com
Website: www.crownrealities.com
Contact: Prof. Kunle Ade Wahab - Chairman

CROWN TRUST LIMITED
Business: Civil & Irrigation Engineering, Manufacturing of Tarpaulin Carpets and Leather Products, Production of Palm Oil
Address: Crown Trust Building, Dugbe Ibadan
Tel: (02) 2413685, 2411606 **Fax:** (02) 2411361
Contact: Chief M. F. Fagbohun - Chairman/CEO

CROWNRISE FINANCE & INVESTMENTS PLC
Business: Financial Services
Address: 202/204, Ikorodu Rd, (2nd Floor), Palmgrove, Lagos
Tel: (01) 8042679, 822167
Contact: Mr. Olalekan R. Sebioniga - Chairman

CRUSADER INSURANCE (NIGERIA) PLC
Business: All Classes of Insurance
Address: Crusader House, 23/25, Martins Street, Lagos
Tel: (01) 2662717, 266507, 2669008, 2667324, 2668840, 2662644, 2668864 **Fax:** (01) 2660751
Contact: Dr. Femiu Oyetunji - MD/CEO

CRUSADER TRUSTEES LIMITED
Business: Trusteeship
Address: Crusader House, 23/25, Martins Street, Lagos
Tel: (01) 2662717, 2661507, 2668389 **Fax:** (01) 2660751
E-mail: crusader@crusader.com.ng
Contact: Mr. Olutola Mobolurin - Chairman
Mr. Emwanta O. Ehigiato - GM

CRUSHED ROCK INDUSTRIES NIGERIA LIMITED
Business: Crushing and Sale of Rocks
Address: Km 16, P. Harcourt/Aba Expressway, Port Harcourt
Tel: (084) 610338, (082) 440076
Contact: Chief Evan Enwerem - Chairman
Mr. Edwin Ikott - GM

CRYSTAL GLASS (NIGERIA) LIMITED
Business: Manufacturing of Safety Glass & Mirrors, Glass Processing
Address: 153/155, Old Ojo Road, Kuje-Amuwo off Lagos-Badagry Expressway, Lagos
Tel: (01) 5885360, 5885027, 4701729
Fax: (01) 5885287, 5885027
E-mail: crystalglass@hyperia.com
Contact: Mr. John Aluya - Chairman/CEO

CRYSTAL PALACE HOTEL, ABUJA
Business: Hospitality & Catering Services, Conference Facilities
Address: Plot 687, Port Harcourt Crescent, off Gimbiya Street, off Ahmadu Bello Way, Garki II, P. O. Box 6560, Garki, Abuja
Tel: (09) 3140033-6 (4 L) **Fax:** (09) 3140034
E-mail: crystal@yahoo.com

CRYSTAL TRUST INSURANCE BROKERS LIMITED
Business: Insurance and Re-insurance Broking
Address: 16, Akinhanmi Street, off Western Avenue, by Mosalasi Bus-Stop, Lagos
Tel/Fax: (01) 5454979
E-mail: ctibltd@yahoo.com
Contact: Gen. (Dr.) Yakubu Gowon (rtd) - Chairman
Mrs. Ekeoma E. Ezeibe - MD/CEO

CSA PRODUCTIONS LIMITED
Business: Television Sport & Events Marketing, Corporate Incentives; Publications, Promotions, Consultancy
Address: 40, Ladipo Labinjo Crescent, off Akinsemoyin Street, off Bode Thomas Street, Lagos
Tel: (01) 5850888, 5851685, 4702323 **Fax:** (01) 7595697
E-mail: csa@micro.com.ng
Website: www.sportafrikana.com
Contact: Dr Henry O. Nzekwu - MD/CEO

CSL STOCKBROKERS LIMITED
Business: Securities Trading, Investment Advisors, Portfolio Management, Equities Research and Underwriting
Address: Primrose Tower (4th Floor), 17A, Tinubu St, Lagos
Tel: (01) 2665945-53 (9 L), 2641293 **Fax:** (01) 2665126
E-mail: research@csl-group.com
Website: www.csl-group.com
* Plot 282A, Port Harcourt/Aba Expressway (1st Floor), G.R.A. Phase II, Port Harcourt
Contact: Otunba Michael O. Balogun, CON - Chairman
Mr. Mike T. Akporowho - Chief Operating Officer

CSS BOOKSHOPS LIMITED
Business: Importation, Distribution and Sales of Christian Books and Literature, Education and General Books, Office Equipment & Stationery, Printing and Publishing
Address: Bookshop House, 50/52, Broad Street, Lagos
Tel: (01) 2637023, 2633010, 2633081 **Fax:** (01) 2637089
E-mail: cssbookships@skannet.com.ng
* 15, Broad Street, Lagos. **Tel:** (01) 2633151
* 50, Hospital Rd, Port Harcourt. **Tel:** (084) 233633
Contact: Chief T. A. Akinyele, OON - Chairman
Mr. Kola Olaitan - Ag. MD/CEO

CT & ASSOCIATES LIMITED
Business: Advertising, Public Relations, Press Relations
Address: Buffalo House, 2, Allen Avenue, Ikeja, Lagos
Tel/Fax: (01) 4931132, 4936081
E-mail: ctay@nigol.net.ng
Contact: Mr. Cornelius O. Tay - Chairman/CEO

CTI INSURANCE BROKERS LIMITED
Business: Insurance Broking
Address: Bookshop House (12th Floor), 50/52, Broad Street,

Lagos Island, Lagos
Tel: (01) 2645621, 2645623, 2645624 **Fax:** (01) 2645622
Contact: Mr. Popoola O. David - GM/CEO

CTN EXPRESS LIMITED
Business: Courier and Cargo Services
Address: Chisco Transport Nigeria Limited, 6, Ikorodu Road, Jibowu, Yaba, Shomolu, Lagos
Tel: (01) 7749419

CUMBERLAND HOTEL
Business: Hospitality Services
Address: 2/4, Adeola Odeku Street, Victoria Island, Lagos
Tel: (01) 2629245-7 (3 L) **Fax:** (01) 2629566
E-mail: cumberlandhotel@hotmail.com

CURTAIN WORLD INCORPORATED
Business: Importation and Marketing of Curtain Fabrics, Rails and Accessories, Interior and Exteriors Decoration and Design
Address: 39, Awka Road, Onitsha
Tel: (046) 413865, 410966 **Fax:** (046) 413865
Contact: Chief I. G. Igboanua - Chairman/CEO

CUSAL INDUSTRIES LIMITED
Business: Sales of Agricultural Equipmet and Tractors, Science Equipment and Industrial Chemicals, Importers and Exporters
Address: 87, Ogui Road, Enugu North L.G.A., Enugu
Tel: (042) 252328 **Fax:** (042) 258600
Contact: Chief Sam O. Anyamele - Exec. Chairman

CUSTEVE INDUSTRIES NIGERIA LIMITED
Business: Manufacturing of Stationery, Importation and Marketing of General Goods
Address: 13, New Market Rooad, Onitsha
Tel: (046) 411468 **Fax:** (046) 410129
E-mail: custeve@excite.com
Contact: Mr. Chika Steve Obi - Chairman

CUSTODIAN & ALLIED INSURANCE LIMITED
Business: Insurance
Address: 43, Campbell Street, Lagos Island, Lagos
Tel: (01) 2634690, 2645784-6 (3 L) **Fax:** (01) 2634676
E-mail: custodian@hyperia.com
Website: www.ppsltd.com/custodian
* 24, Campbell Street (8th Floor), Lagos
Tel: (01) 2632423, 2636566
* Plot 516, Block 1, Sultan Abubakar Way, Wuse Zone 2, Abuja.
Tel: (09) 5237209, 5239219
* 172A, Aba Road, Port Harcourt.
Tel: (084) 231697
Contact: Mr. O. B. Oshin - MD/CEO

CUTIX PLC
Business: Manufacture & Marketing of Wires & Cables
Address: 17, Osita Onyejianya Street, Anuka, Otolo, Nnewi Anambra State
Tel: (046) 460789, 460170
* 17, Olutosin Ajayi St, Ajao Estate, Isolo, Lagos
Tel/Fax: (01) 4521253, 7918827
* Suite 41, Row 2, Garki Village Corner Shop, Samuel Ladoke Akintola Crescent, Garki Abuja
Conact: Engr. Ajulu Uzodike - Chairman/CEO

CUTLER-HAMMER NIGERIA LIMITED
Business: Manufacturing of Industrial Control & Power Distribution Systems
Address: Plot 10, Block B, Ilasamaja Industrial Scheme, Apapa-Oshodi Expressway (Itire Junction), Lagos
Tel: (01) 7748639
E-mail: ching@micro.com.ng
Contact: Mr. L. Ladipo - MD/CEO

C-WAY DRINKING WATER SCIENCE & TECHNOLOGY COMPANY NIGERIA LIMITED
Business: Importation, Marketing and Distribution of Water Purification and Dispensing Systems
Address: 1, Abebe Village Road, off Eric Moore Road, Iganmu Industrial Estate, Surulere, Lagos
Tel: (01) 5852261, 7756242, 7743036-7 (2 L)
E-mail: cwaywater@hotmail.com

CYBELE COSMETICS LIMITED
Business: Manufacturing of Cosmetics and Perfumes
Address: 98/100, Ladipo Street, Matori Industrial Estate, Mushin, Lagos
Tel: (01) 4521051, 4521147, 4520036, 4529151-3 (3 L)
Fax: (01) 4526809
E-mail: cybele@micro.com.ng

CYBERSPACE LIMITED
Business: Provision of Internet Services
Address: 1, Olosa St off Karimu Kotun St, Victoria Is., Lagos
Tel: (01) 2624288 **Fax:** (01) 2624287
E-mail: info@cyberspace.net.ng
info@cybaaspace.com
Website: www.cybaasapce.com
Contact: Chief P. O. K. Okanigbe - Chairman

D.E.R LIMITED
Business: Publishing of Newspaper, Directories, Journals
Address: 13, James Robertson Street, Surulere, Lagos
Tel: (01) 830930, 4714291, 08033484201
Fax: (01) 610203
E-mail: thecountry2001@yahoo.com
* Plot 185, Bissau Street, Wuse Zone 6, Abuja
Tel: (09) 5239755
Contact: Chief Ikechi Emenike - Chairman/CEO

D.P.C. MANUFACTURING LIMITED
Business: Manufacturing and Marketing of Rubber Footwear
Address: 8, Mai-Malari Road, Bompai Ind. Estate, Kano
Tel: (064) 642383

D.S.D. (NIGERIA) LIMITED
Business: Construction (Steel), Mechanical, Electrical and Civil Engineering
Address: 5, Forcados Road, Apapa G.R.A., Apapa, Lagos
Tel: (01) 5452113, 5453080 **Fax:** (01) 5874385
E-mail: dsdltd@alpha.linkserve.com
Contact: W. Weipert - Exec. Manager/CEO

D'LORD, MASELI & PARTNERS
Business: Land Resources Solutions Providers

Address: 82, Cornershop, by Bataiya, Plaza, opp. Corporate Affairs Commission, Area 11, Garki, Abuja
Tel: (09) 3148243
E-mail: dmaseli1@hotmail.com
Contact: Mr. David Maseli - Principal Partner

D'ROVANS HOTEL LIMITED
Business: Hospitality and Catering Services, Conference and Recreation Facilities
Address: Francis Aiyegbeni Close, Ring Road, Ibadan
Tel: (02) 2312907-8 (2 L), 2313617-8 (2 L), 08023319565, 08037171988 **Fax:** (02) 2318371
Contact: Chief Francis Aiyegbeni - Chairman/CEO

D-POLAN LIMITED
Business: Oilfield Services, Construction & Fabrication, Labour Procurement, Sales of Generators, Vehicles, Tyres Batteries and Airconditioners,
Address: Block A-5 (Suite 79), Sura Mall, Simpson Street, Lagos Island, Lagos
Tel: (01) 3202118, 08023175411, 08056182217
Fax: (01) 3202118
E-mail: dpolan27@yahoo.com
Contact: Otunba Paul Oladapo Oladele - Chairman

DAAR COMMUNICATIONS LIMITED
Business: International Radio, Television Broadcasting & Information Services
Address: Communications Village, AIT Road, off Abeokuta Expressway, Ilapo Village, Alagbado, Lagos
Tel: (01) 2644814-6 (3L) **Fax:** (01) 2644817
*Plot 99, Moshood Abiola Rd, Area 2, Garki, Abuja
Tel: (09) 2347572 **Fax:** (09) 2347242
Contact: Dr. Ailogho Raymond Dokpesi - Chairman
Mr. Ladi Lawal - Chief Operating Officer

DAAYAD CAR & ACCESSORIES LIMITED (formerly Doyin Motors Ltd)
Business: Sales and Service of Motor Vehicles.
Address: Doyin Motors House, Plot 27, Iganmu Industrial Estate, Orile, Iganmu, Lagos
Tel: (01) 4704447, 4707192, 7741436 **Fax:** (01) 5851690
* 8, Samuel Manuwa Street, Victoria Island, Lagos
Tel: (01) 5558075, 5558154 **Fax:** (01) 5558075
* Plot 277, Trans Amadi Ind. Layout, Port Harcourt
Tel: (084) 231149, 572708
E-mail: doyinmotors@hyperia.com
Website: www.peacegategroup.com
Contact: Mr. Ayorinde Adedoyin - Chairman/CEO

DABENO ENTERPRISES LIMITED
Business: Production of Mats & Poly Products; Recycling
Address: 10, Dantata Road, Bompai Industrial Estate, Kano
Tel: (084) 649107
Contact: Hesine Yasim - Chairman/CEO

DABMOL NIGERIA LIMITED
Business: Importation & Sales of Information Technology Products, Sales of Office Equipment, Networking
Address: 15, Oremeji St, off Simbiat Abiola Rd, Ikeja, Lagos
Tel: (01) 4934840, 8044439, 08042135100
Fax: (01) 4934840
Contact: Mr. David D .Aigbokhai - MD/CEO

DADDO INDUSTRIES LIMITED
Business: Manufacturers of Drums and Metal Containers
Address: 13A, Eletu Ogabi Street, off Adeola Odeku Street, Victoria Island, Lagos
Tel: (01) 2613758, 2613956 **Fax:** (01) 2610610
E-mail: daddo@linkserve.com.ng
Contact: Alh. B. M.Tukur - Chairman
Engr. P. O. Ogunbitan - GM

DADDO MARITIME SERVICES LIMITED
Business: Shipping Services, Clearing and Forwarding, Ship Agents, Managers and Charterers, Road Haulage
Address: Kariko Towers, 9, Wharf Road, Apapa, Lagos
Tel: (01) 5457312, 5457314, 5871748-51 (4L)
Fax: (01) 2610610
E-mail: dmsoperations@daddoggrop.com
* 33, Tombia Street, G.R.A. Phase II, Port Harcourt
Tel: (084) 239311 **Fax:** (084) 233924
Contact: Mr. Mahmud Tukur - MD/CEO

DADE SADARE CONSULTANTS (DSC)
Business: IT & Management Technology Consultants
Address: 191, Herbert Macaulay Street, opp. Police Station, Adekunle, Yaba, Lagos
Tel: (01) 7917579
E-mail: itadvice@dsconsultants.ws
Website: www.dsconsultants.ws
Contact: Dr. Dade Sadare - Principal Consultant/CEO

DAEWOO MOTOR SERVICES (NIGERIA) LIMITED
Business: Sales, Distribution, Repairs, Service & Maintenance of Daewoo Motor Vehicles & Spare Parts
Address: Plot 5, Block A, Amuwo-Odofin Industrial Scheme, Oshodi Expressway, Amuwo-Odofin, Lagos
Tel: (01) 5802720-9 (10L), 5832874, 4705574
Tel/Fax: (01) 7742590 **Fax:** (01) 5835440
* Daewoo Nigeria Limited, Plot 1608, Adeola Hopewell Street, Victoria Island, Lagos
* 43, Okporo Road, Artillery Junction, Rumuogba, Port Harcourt. **Tel/Fax:** (084) 440074
Contact: Mr. Hong Seon Cho - MD/CEO

DAEWOO NIGERIA LIMITED
Business: Conglomerate
Address: Plot 1608, Adeola Hopwell St Victoria Island Lagos
Tel: (01) 2622111, 2622112, 2617108-9 (2L), 2616957
Fax: (01) 2622110
Contact: Mr. S. Y. Lee - MD/CEO

DAFINONE CONSULTING LIMITED
Business: Supply, Installation and Maintenance of Accounting Software; Consultancy Services
Address: CEDDI Towers, 16, Wharf Road, Apapa, Lagos
Tel: (01) 5451863-7 (5 L), 48223495-6 **Fax:** (01) 5452384
E-mail: sage@dafinone.com
Contact: Senator D. O. Dafinone - Chairman

DAGASTEEL INTERNATIONAL LIMITED
Business: Petrochemical & Oil Services
Address: Nurses House (3rd Floor), Plot PC 43, Afribank Street, Victoria Island, Lagos
Tel: (01) 7754853, 2627578
E-mail: dagasteel@infoweb.abs.net

DAID NIGERIA LIMITED
Business: Sales of Mechanical Power Transmission Products
Address: Plot 2, Block J, Limca Way, Isolo Industrial Estate, Oshodi-Apapa Expressway, Isolo, Lagos
Tel: (01) 4528722-3 (2 L), 4521561 **Fax:** (01) 4528762
E-mail: daid@beta.linkserve.com
services@daid.net
* 2, Creek Road, Apapa, Lagos
Tel: (01) 5450349, 5451621 **Fax:** (01) 5450348
Contact: Mr. Olu Adeleye - Chairman/CEO.

DAILY-NEED INDUSTRIES LIMITED
Business: Manufacture and Marketing of Pharmaceuticals, Dental Care Products and Cosmetics
Address: 24, Orogiri Street, off Idoluwo St, Marina, Lagos
Tel: (01) 2642034, 7739387 **Fax:** (01) 3205013
E-mail: dailyneed@hyperia.com
Contact: Otunba Oyin Jolayemi - Chairman/CEO.

DAJO OIL LIMITED
Business: Distribution and Marketing of Petroleum Products
Address: 13, Alh. Bashorun Street, off Norman Williams Street, S.W. Ikoyi, Lagos
Tel: (01) 2692057, 2694016 **Fax:** (01) 2694443
*Plot 47, Wuse II, opp.Rockview Hotel,Garki,Abuja
Tel: (09) 4130052, 4130215 **Fax:** (09) 4130051
Contact: Deacon Domingo Obende - Chairman/CEO

DAKAL SERVICES LIMITED
Business: Economic & Financial Consultancy Services, Financial Brokerage & Intermediation; Stockbrokerage & Capital Issues; LPO Financing
Address: Prince's Court (Suite IG), 37, Ahmed Onibudo Street, Victoria Island, Lagos
Tel: (01) 2885960, 3200532 **Fax:** (01) 2885960
Contact: Dr. Kalu I. Kalu - Chairman/CEO.

DAKOVA FASHIONS
Business: Fashion Designing
Address: 82, Brickfield Street, off Moshood Abiola Way, Ebute-Metta, Lagos
Tel: (080) 2318810
E-mail: dakovastudio@yahoo.com
Contact: Mr. David Kolawole Vanghan - MD/CEO

DALA AGRICULTURAL & ALLIED PRODUCTS LIMITED
Business: Agro-Allied Business
Address: 53, Fagge Takudu, Kano
Tel: (064) 632336, 647559, 642512-3 **Fax:** (064) 635572
Contact: Suhail Akar - Chairman/CEO

DALA BUILDING SOCIETY LIMITED
Business: Mortgage Banking
Address: 1, Danhausa Road, Nassarawa G.R.A., Kano
Tel: (064) 647455, 08023101860, 08023105111
E-mail: dbsbank@hotmail.com
Contact: Mr. Abdul-Nasser Abdu - GM/CEO

DALA FOODS NIGERIA LIMITED
Business: Production of Tea and Food-Beverage Drinks
Address: Plot 85, Sharada Industrial Estate Phase III, Kano
Tel: (064) 660999, 664311 **Fax:** (064) 664311
Contact: Alh. A. L. Madugu - CEO

DALEWARES LIMITED
Business: Importation and Marketing of Graphic Screen-Printing & Heat Transfer Equipment
Address: 46, Oyekan Road, Surulere, Lagos
Tel: (01) 4719589, 5456704
E-mail: dalewares@gacom.net

DALEX COMPANY LIMITED
Business: Building & Engineering Services; Sales of Note-Counting Machines, Digital Copiers & Printers
Address: 78, Adeniyi Jones Avenue, Ikeja, Lagos
Tel: (01) 4936251, 4939032, 8044508.
Fax: (01) 4936251, 4939032
E-mail: dalex@alpha.linkserve.com
* Bataya Plaza (Annex E, Suite 10), Plot 1271, Area 2, Garki Abuja
Contact: Mr. O. B. A. Obadina - Chairman/CEO.

DALLAS BAKERY & CONFECTIONERIES INDUSTRIES LTD
Business: Baking and Confectioning
Address: 67, Kofo Abayomi Avenue, Apapa, Lagos
Tel: (01) 5452312
Contact: Mr. Hussain H. Soufan - MD/CEO

DALMACO INTERNATIONAL NIGERIA LIMITED
Business: Importation and Sales of Auto & Motorcycle Spare Parts/Accessories and General Merchandise
Address: 175, Nnamdi Azikiwe Street, Idumota, Lagos
Tel: (01) 3208249
E-mail: damatex@beta.linkserve.com

DALTRADE NIGERIA LIMITED
Business: Manufacturing and Distributionof Building Materials and Workshop Equipment
Address: 16, Ilupeju Bye-Pass, Ilupeju, Lagos
Tel: (01) 4966769, 4522140, 8042200 **Fax:** (01) 2691832
E-mail: daltrade@nova.net.ng
Website: www.daltradenigeria.com
* DCC Ventures, Plot 525, Obafemi Awolowo Road, Jabi District, Wuse, Abuja.
Tel/Fax: (09) 5239657
* DCC Ventures, Link Advertising Building, beside Crushed Rock Ltd., Km. 16, Port Harcourt/Aba Expressway, Rumuokwurusi, Port Harcourt
Tel/Fax: (084) 571626
Contact: Pastor A. Odunaiya - Chairman
Mr. Salwomir Panta - MD/CEO

DAMATEX OVERSEAS INDUSTRIES LIMITED
Business: Sales of Computer Parts & Accessories and Telecommunications Products
Address: 5, Oremeji St, off Simbiat Abiola Road, Ikeja, Lagos
Tel: (01) 4937175-6 (2 L), 7748168, 08032030211
Fax: (01) 5850969
E-mail: dcmomah@yahoo.com
Contact: Mr. Dan C. Momah - Chairman/CEO

DAMOG NIGERIA LIMITED
Business: Security Guard Services, Sales of Security Systems and Equipment, Consultancy Services
Address: Guinness Co-operative Building, 111, Iju Road, Jungle Bus-Stop, Ifako-Agege, Lagos
Tel: (01) 921297

DAN DOLLARS GROUP LIMITED
Business: Transportation Services, Marketing of Petroleum Products
Address: 266, Port Harcourt Road, Aba
Tel: (082) 440179, 440181 **Fax:** (082) 440179
Contact: Chief Dan Okemuo - MD/CEO

DAN DUKO GROUP OF COMPANIES LIMITED
Business: Importation of Automotive Batteries and General Merchandise
Address: 27, Ademola St, off Awolowo Rd, S.W. Ikoyi, Lagos
Tel: (01) 2672565, 2672567 **Fax:** (01) 2672565
E-mail: danieldo@infoweb.abs.net
* Cornershop 17, oppoite Garki General Hospital, Area 7B, Garki, Abuja.
Tel: (09) 2342968, 2344461
Contact: Sir Daniel Uchendu - Chairman/CEO.

DAN ODIETE & COMPANY
Business: Estate Surveyours & Valuers, Plant & Machinery Valuers, Development Consultants, Feasibility Analysts
Address: Shelter Investment House, 118, Akpakpava Street, Benin City
Tel: (052) 250260, 254301, 258085, 08023351290
* Unity House (9th Floor), 37, Marina, Lagos
Tel: (01) 2668849
Contact: Dr. Dan Odiete - Principal Consultant/CEO.

DANA GROUP
Business: Manufacturing of Pharmaceutical Products, Table Water and Plastics
Address: Wema Towers, 54, Marina Lagos
Tel: (01) 2666118, 2666283, 2663645
Fax: (01) 26411871, 2663645
E-mail: contact@danagroup.net
* Dana House, 8A, Olubadan Industry Estate, off New Ife Road, Ibadan
Tel: (01) 8100456, 716556
* Dana House, Shiroro Dam Road, Minna.
Tel: (090) 801845
* 113, Maganda Road, Zaria Avenue, Kano
Tel: (064) 631551 **Fax:** (064) 631552
Contact: Mr. Jacky Hathiramani - MD/CEO

DANAA SHIPPING COMPANY LIMITED
Business: Shipping Agency, Freighting, Clearing, Forwarding
Address: 39, Adele Road, Apapa, Lagos
Tel: (01) 5877493, 7754264 **Fax:** (01) 5451527

DANAKAN GROUP OF COMPANIES
Business: Engineering Construction, Petroleum & Energy Consultants; Distributive & International Trade
Address: PC 14, Ahmed Onibudo St, Victoria Island, Lagos
Tel: (01) 618730-31 (2L), 7743784
Contact: Chief E. D. Akan - Chairman/CEO.

DANBA ENERGY LIMITED
Business: Refining of Crude Petroleum, Petrochemicals, Oil Trading, Oilfield Engineering, Power Production
Address: 7, Walter Carrington Crescent, Victoria Island, Lagos
Tel: (01) 4616330, 4721951, 08037866166
E-mail: danbanigeria@hotmail.com

DANBARE TRAVEL AGENCY LIMITED
Business: Travel Agency
Address: 19C, Murtala Muhammed Way, Kano
Tel: (064) 631786, 641116, 311783, 310294, 642061
Fax: (064) 641116
E-mail: danbaretraveel2000@hotmail.com
* Mangal Plaza (Unit 24), Wuse Zone 1 Cornershops, Abuja
Tel: (09) 5234733, 08044183427, 08033357894
Contact: Alh. Nasidi Yahaya Suleiman - Chairman/CEO

DANBRITE COMPANY NIGERIA LIMITED
Business: Electrical & Water Engineers, Contractors, Building Materials Merchants
Address: 19, Lagos-Badagry Expressway, opp Zenith International Bank, Orile-Iganmu, Lagos
Tel: (01) 4705058, 7731893
E-mail: danbrite@37.com
Contact: Chief D. U. Udo-Anagor - Chairman/CEO

DANCO MANNYON INDUSTRIES LIMITED
Business: Printing of Labels, Calendars & Packaging, Plastic Products Manufacturing, Technical Engineering
Address: Km. 5, Onitsha-Owerri Road, Onitsha
Tel: 08037036241, (090) 502562
Contact: Chief (Dr) Sir D. C. Okafor - Chairman/CEO

DANDICKINS LIMITED
Business: Sales of Welding Consumables, Technical Equipment, General Hardware & Metallurgical Equipment
Address: 30, Commercial Road, Apapa, Lagos
Tel: (01) 5804544, 08034047906 **Fax:** (01) 5804544
Contact: Chief Daniel E. Dike - Chairman/CEO

DANELEC LIMITED
Business: Electrical/Electronic Engineering & Construction
Address: Plot 278, Trans-Amadi Ind Layout, Port Harcourt
Tel: (084) 233285, 08023103982 **Fax:** (084) 239282
E-mail: danelec@linkserve.com.ng
* Plot 593, Birnin Kebbi Crescent, Abuja
Tel: (09) 2349719
Contact: Mr. P. I. Carrodano - MD/CEO

DANFODIO CONSTRUCTION & COMMERCIAL CO. LTD
Business: Engineering Construction and Consultancy
Address: F2, Sani Abacha Way, Kano
Tel: (064) 640596 **Fax:** (064) 640786
Contact: Mr. Isam'eel Mohammed Ishaq - Chairman/CEO

DANGOTE GROUP
Business: Conglomerate
Address: Marble House, 1A, Alfred Rewane Road, Falomo, P.M.B. 40032, Falomo, Ikoyi, Lagos
Tel: (01) 2695108, 2695109, 2695110
Fax: (01) 2695009, 2965316
E-mail: dangote@dangote-group.com
* 13B, Jigawa Road, Kano.
Tel: (064) 647994-5 (2L)
* 2/3, Maimalari Road, Bompai Ind. Estate, Kano.
Tel: (064) 639037, 639479, 647990
* Plot 143, Olu Obasanjo Way, Port Harcourt
Tel: (084) 236324-5 (2L)
Contact: Alh. Aliko Dangote OON - President/CE

DANGOTE AGRO SACKS LIMITED
Business: Production & Marketing of Polypropylene Woven/ Laminated Socks
Address: Marble House, 1, Alfred Rewane Rd, Ikoyi, Lagos
Tel: (01) 2695009, 2695108, 2695109, 2695110
Fax: (01) 681472, 2695316
E-mail: dangote@dangote-group.com
Contact: Alh. Aliko Dangote OON - President/CEO

DANGOTE CHEMICALS LIMITED
Business: Production of Industrial Chemicals
Address: Marble House, 1 Alfred Rewane Road, Ikoyi, Lagos
Tel: (01) 2695108, 2695109, 2695110
Fax: (01) 2695009, 2965316
E-mail: dangote@dangote-group.com

DANGOTE FARMS LIMITED
Business: Agro-Allied Business
Address: Dangote Ginning Company Premises, Kankara, Kankara L.G.A., Katsina State
*Marble House, 1 Alfred Rewane Road, Ikoyi, Lagos
Tel: (01) 2695108, 2695109, 2695110
Fax: (01) 2695009, 2695316
E-mail: dangote@dangote-groupco

DANGOTE GENERAL TEXTILES PRODUCTS LIMITED
Business: Manufacturing and Markteting of Yarn, Grey Shirting and African Prints
Address: Marble House, 1 Alfred Rewane Rd, Ikoyi, Lagos
Tel: (01), 2695108, 2695109, 2695110
Fax: (01) 2695009 2695316
E-mail: dangote@dangote-group.com
Contact: Alh. Aliko Dangote OON - President/CEO

DANGOTE HOLDINGS LIMITED
Business: Food Processing and Production, Marketers
Address: 1A, Alfred Rewane Road, Falomo, Ikoyi, Lagos
Tel: (01) 2695009, 2695108, 2695109, 2695275, 2695110
Fax: (01) 2695009, 2695316
E-mail: dangote@dangote-group.com
Contact: Alh. Sani Dangote - Chairman/CEO

DANGOTE INDUSTRIES LIMITED
Business: Production & Packaging of Cement, Sugar & Spaghetti; Milling of Flour, Refining of Salt
Address: Marble House, 1 Alfred Rewane Road, Ikoyi, Lagos
Tel: (01) 2695108, 2695109, 2695110
Fax: (01) 2695009, 2965316
E-mail: dangote@dangote-group.com
Contact: Alh. Aliko Dangote OON - President/CEO

DANGOTE TRANSPORT AND LEASING CO. LIMITED
Business: Road Haulage and Leasing Services
Address: Polo House, 1 Tin Can Is.Port Rd, Apapa, Lagos
Tel: (01) 5873971-2 (2L), 5873773, 5973975
Fax: (01) 5873976
E-mail: conticem@mail.com
Contact: Alh. Aliko Dangote OON - President/CEO

DANICO (WEST AFRICA) LIMITED
Business: Food Manufacturing
Address: Km. 38, Lagos-Abeokuta Expressway, Sango-Ota
Tel/Fax: (039) 722194, 722207, 4750701
E-mail: danico@hyperia.com
Contact: Mr Jan Halfdan Madsen - MD/CEO

DANIEL TRAVELS AGENCY LIMITED
Business: Travel Agency
Address: 38/40, Burna Road, Apapa, Lagos
Tel: (01) 5453338, 5873312
Contact: Mr Khali - MD/CEO

DANIMEX COMMUNICATIONS (NIGERIA) LIMITED
Business: Distribution, Sales, Installatioin and Service of Communication Equipment
Address: Elephant Cement House (2nd Floor), ASSBIFI Rd, Central Business District, Alausa, Ikeja, Lagos
Tel: (01) 3203336, 3203372
E-mail: danimex@infoweb.abs.net
Website: www.danimex.com
Contact: Mr Egon Bruun - MD/CEO

DANISAT NIGERIA LIMITED (formerly Addnet Ltd)
Business: Telrcommunication Servives - THURAYA Global Satellite Telephony Service Provider
Address: GT House, 3/5, Boyle Street, Onikan, Lagos
Tel: (01) 2637723, 2645152, 4800669, 08033175294, 080372000050 **Fax:** (01) 2645153
E-mail: sales@addnet-nigeria.com
* Metro Plaza, Plot 99/992, Zakari Miamalari Street, Central Area, Abuja
Tel: (09) 5230004, 5230613, 5230623, 08033495811
Contact: Mr. Peter Post - MD/CEO

DANLON ASSOCIATES LIMITED
Business: Company Formation & Secretarial Services, Industrial Set-Up and Management, Contract Manufacturing, Import Opportunities and Export Marketing, Turn-Around Management
Address: 26, Ilupeju Road, off Tinubu Road, Ilupeju, Lagos
Tel: (01) 821335, 7746548 **Fax:** (01) 821589
E-mail: danlon.b@rcl.nig.com
Contact: Mr. D. L. Oni - Chairman/CEO

DANMAN PLASTICS & PACKAGING INDUSTRIES LIMITED
Business: Manufacturing of Conduit/Pressure/Drainage Pipes, Water Hoses, Plastic-Packaging Products and PVC Compounds for Shoes
Address: 21, Kopek Road, off Fatai Atere Way, Matori Estate, Mushin, Lagos
Tel: (01) 4527896, 7741525 **Fax:** (01) 4527896
E-mail: dppil@hotmail.com
Contact: Engr. Sanjay Bathija - MD/CEO

DANNIC HOTELS LIMITED
Business: Hospitality Services
Address: 3, Edem Close, Upper Chime Avenue, New Haven, Enugu
Tel: (042) 454234
* Plot 33, Circular Road, Presidential Estate, G.R.A., Port Harcourt
Tel: (084) 236919

DANSA FOODS LIMITED
Business: Food Processing and Production, Marketers
Address: Polo House, 1 Tin Can Is.Port Rd, Apapa, Lagos

Tel: (01) 5873971-2 (2L), 5873773 **Fax:** (01) 5873976
E-mail: dansa_foods@yahoo.com
dangote@dangote-group.com
Contact: Alh. Sani Dangote - Chairman/CEO

DANSPITAL NIGERIA LIMITED
Business: Medical and Laboratory Equipment and Reagents
Address: 7, Ola Ayinde Street, Ikeja, Lagos
Tel: (01) 4964348

DANSY INDUSTRIES (NIGERIA) LIMITED
Business: Manufacture of Household/Industrial Plastics
Address: 9, Samuel Anibaba Street, Ketu, Lagos
Tel: (090) 402613 **Fax:** (01) 618307
Contact: Chief R. O. Ezenwa - Chairman

DANTATA ORGANISATION LIMITED
Business: Conglomerate (Fertilizer Processing, Crude Oil Exploration and Marketing, Vegetable Oil Production etc)
Address: 66/67, Murtala Muhammed way, Kano
Tel: (064) 630692, 633834, 635952-5 (4 L), 636232, 639939, 647778 **Fax:** (064) 633834, 639939, 639942
Website: www.aminuadamu.com
* 11, Festival Road, Victoria Island, V/I, Lagos
Tel: (01) 2615115, 2615838 **Fax:** (01) 2616077
* Independence Road, Bampai, Kano
Contact: Alh. Tajudeen Aminu Dantata - Group MD

DANTATA & SAWOE CONSTRUCTION COMPANY (NIGERIA) LIMITED
Business: Building and Civil Engineering Contractors
Address: Outer Southern Expressway, Abuja
Tel: (09) 2340301, 2342214 **Fax:** (09) 2342213
E-mail: dansaw@alpha.linkserve.com
* 77, Club Road, Kano
Tel: (064) 633008, 647021 **Fax:** (064) 640988
* 20, Babatunde Ladeja St, off Isheri Road, Lagos.
Tel: (090) 400339 **Fax:** (01) 4970236

DAR EL FIKR NIGERIA LIMITED
Business: Publishing of Industrial, Arabic & Islamic Books Exportation of Agricultural Products
Address: 46, Mallam Aminu Kano way, Kano
Tel: (064) 638648, 631345, 638647 **Fax:** (064) 631345
Contact: Alh. A. Y. Muhyideen - MD/CEO

DARA MEDICAL CLINICS
Business: Medical & Health Care, Medical Diagnostic Services
Address: Plot 202, Bacita Close, off Plateau Street, Area 2, Section 2, Garki, Abuja
Tel: (09) 2345031, 2340077
E-mail: daramed@yahoo.com
Contact: Dr. Edet M. Umana - Medical Director

DARAKON RESOURCES LIMITED
Business: Autocad Design Drafting, Digital Scanning, Project Management & Inspection, Design Engineering
Address: Block 4 (1st Floor), Edewor Shopping Centre, Warri/Sapele Road, P.O.Box 3783, Warri
Tel: (053) 251548, 320013, 08022903897, 08023250167
E-mail: darakan@skannet.com
Contact: Engr. (Dr.) D. K. Uko - Chairman/CEO

DARCHIWORK GROUP
Business: Architectural Consultants, Project Management
Address: * 1, Alh. Sadiku Street, off Alh. Lateef Jakande Road, Agidingbi, Ikeja, Lagos
Tel: (01) 4920788
* 48, Opebi Road, Ikeja, Lagos
Tel: (01) 4964461, 932333
Contact: Arc. (Dr.) Dele Adeyemi - Principal Partner

DAREUFET INTERCON INVESTMENT LIMITED
Business: Electrical, Instrumentation, Mechanical & Civil Engineering Services for the Oil & Gas Industry
Address: 154, P.T.I. Road, Effurun, Warri
Tel: (053) 253333, 255282, 230419, 08046108732
Fax: (053) 255282
E-mail: darufet@yahoo.co.uk
Contact: Chief D. O. Okorare - Chairman/CEO

DARLEZ NIGERIA LIMITED
Business: Sales and Service of Laboratory, Hospital and Research Equipment, Reagents and Consumables, Laboratory Furniture and Fittings. Power Conditioners for Sensitive Laboratory Instruments.
Address: Plot 604, Lingu Crescent, off Aminu Kano Cres, beh. Iluobe Filling Station, Wuse II, Abuja
Tel: (09) 5238250, 5238227, 5237269 **Fax:** (09) 5237269
E-mail: darlezabj@hotmail.com
Contact: Mr. Eze D. Ajoku - Chairman/CEO

DASAB AIRLINES LIMITED
Business: Passenger/Cargo Airline Services, Aircraft Charter
Address: Plot 983, Ahmadu Bello Way, opp. Legislative Quarters, Apo, P.M.B. 610, Garki, Abuja
Tel/Fax: (09) 2311063
Contact: Dr. Titus Oludare Babayemi - Chairman/CEO

DASAT NETWORK SYSTEMS LIMITED
Business: Electrical and Communications Systems Engineers
Address: 9, Babatunde St, Ogunlana Drive, Surulere, Lagos
Tel/Fax: (01) 2882483, 4805473, 5456327
E-mail: dasat@nova.net.ng
Contact: Engr. A. Emole - MD/CEO

DASCO ENGINEERING INDUSTRIES (NIGERIA) LIMITED
Business: Electro-Galvanising, Manufacturing of Gravure Printing Cylinders, Various Electroplating Services
Address: Plot 2, Block D, Apapa-Oshodi Expressway, opp Afprint (next to NEPA), Isolo, Lagos
Tel: (01) 4520716, 4523773
E-mail: dasco@dascochrome.com

DAT MERCHANT INVESTMENTS LIMITED
Business: Shipping, Airfreight, Clearing & Forwarding, Haulage Services, Supply of Chemicals, Oil and Oil-Related Products, Tools and Equipment for Industrial Use, Sale of Agricultural Equipment
Address: 25/55, Oluwaleyimu St, Allen Avenue, Ikeja, Lagos
Tel: (01) 4936250, 4938033, 960380 **Fax:** (01) 4936250
Contact: Mr. Sanusi T. Ademola - GM

DATA & TELECOMMUNICATIONS (NIGERIA) LIMITED
Business: Computer Consulting, Software Development, Sysetms Sales and Maintenance, Networking,

Training and Professional Development, Electronic Document Management Systems
Address: 64, Ogunlana Drive, Surulere, Lagos
Tel: (01) 5831613, 830610, 831613 **Fax:** (01) 5831613
E-mail: dandt@infoweb.abs.net
Contact: Mr. Okey J. Arinze - MD/CEO

DATA PROCESSING MAINTENANCE AND SERVICES LIMITED (DPMS LTD)
Business: Marketing, Installation, Support and Maintenane of IBM Equipment, Provision of Information Technology Solution
Address: 40, Macarthy Street, Onikan, Lagos
Tel: (01) 2630371, 2632739, 2633869, 2633969, 2634453, 2634473, 2636288 **Fax:** (01) 2633622, 2637980
E-mail: hq@dpmsnigeria.com
dpms@micro.com.ng
* Niger Ins. House, PLot 1207, Obafemi Awolowo Way, off Tafawa Balewa way, Garki Area 8, Abuja.
Tel: (09) 2342106, 2342109
* 44, Trans-Amadi Industrial Layout, Port Harcourt
Tel: (084) 233877
Contact: Mr. Patrick Honrnecker - MD/CEO

DATA SCIENCES NIGERIA LIMITED
Business: Sales and Maintenance of IT Systems
Address: Etiebet's Place, 21, Mobolaji Bank Anthony Way, Ikeja, Lagos
Tel: (01) 4962125, 49676481 **Fax:** (01) 4971290
E-mail: info@datasciences.com
* Obodex House, 225, Ikorodu Rd, Ilupeju, Lagos
Tel: (01) 4933369, 4936273, 4971270, 4971290, 4978570
Fax: (01) 4971290, 4978570
Contact: Mr. Ladi Ogunneye -MD/CEO

DATA FUNCTIONS NIGERIA LIMITED
Business: Sales of Information Technology Products
Address: 132, Bode Thomas Street, Surulere, Lagos
Tel: (01) 5454503, 7744808, 4740834 **Fax:** (01) 2672191
E-mail: datanigltd@yahoo.com
* 19B, Oginigba Road, opp. West African Glass Ind Plc, Trans-Amadi Ind. Layout, Port Harcourt
Tel: (084) 237389

DATACOM EXPRESS
Business: Wireless Communication Services & Solutions, Sales of Wireless Products, Sales & Deployment of Voice Solution, Telecommunication Consultancy
Address: 26, Commercial Avenue (2nd Floor), Yaba, Lagos
Tel: (01) 4705931, 4717532, 08023431975
Fax: (01) 3425179
E-mail: sales@datacommexpress.com
info@datacommexpress.com
Website: www.datacommexpress.com
Contact: Adegboyega Ogunrayewa - MD/CEO

DATAFLEX NIGERIA LIMITED
Business: Information Technology & Power Solution Providers, Distribution of UPS, Sales of IT Systems
Address: Plot 227B, Muri Okunola St, Victoria Island, Lagos
Tel: (01) 2625095-8 (4 L), 2620837 **Fax:** (01) 2625099
E-mail: dataflex@infoweb.abs.net
Contact: Mr. Andy Nwani - Chairman/CEO

DATAMATICS COMPANY (NIGERIA) LIMITED
Business: Sales and Maintenance of Copiers, Computers and Office Automation
Address: 4/6, Mobolaji Bank-Anthony Street, formerly Oil Mill Street, off Broad Street, Lagos
Tel: (01) 263334, 2646882 **Fax:** (01) 2634493
E-mail: datamatics2000@yahoo.com
* Erisco Bonpet Plaza, Plot 2357, Duala Street, Wuse Zone 5, Abuja.
Tel: (09) 5236390
Contact: Mr. Gbola Sarumi - MD/CEO

DATANET INTERNATIONAL LIMITED
Business: Internet Services
Address: 24B, Isaac John Street, Ikeja, G.R.A., Lagos
Tel: (01) 4975931, 4974747, 4975949 **Fax:** (01) 4975945
E-mail: info@datanetinternational.net
Website: www.datanetinternational.net

DATANET SYSTEMS LIMITED
Business: Sales, Maintenance and Repairs of Computers, Software Development, Training
Address: 61/32H, Bauchi Road, Jos
Tel: (073) 456569, 455198 **Fax:** (073) 456569
E-mail: datanet@yahoo.com
Contact: Engr. Sani M. Mansur - MD/CEO

DATAPRO LIMITED
Business: Trade Development, Rating & Confirming House
Address: Great Nigeria House (5th Floor), 47/57, Martins Street, Lagos
Tel: (01) 2660106, 2661782, 08033069114, 08033091467, 0805416135 **Fax:** (01) 2660106
E-mail: datapro@imwebafrica.com
Website: www.datapronigeria.com
Contact: Mr. Abimbola A. A. Adeseyoju, Snr - Chairman

DATASOURCE LIMITED
Business: Sales of Information Technology Products, Networking, Internet Services
Address: 45A, Saka Tinubu Street, Victoria Island, Lagos
Tel: (01) 7746333, 2610653, 2611135 **Fax:** (01) 2610633
E-mail: datasource45@aol.com
enquiry@datasourcelimited.com
Website: www.datasourcelimited.com
Contact: Mr. Stanley Ekezie - MD/CEO

DATAWATCH NIGERIA LIMITED
Business: Internet Service, Sales of Computers, Networking
Address: Jere Street, off Funmilayo Ransome-Kuti Road, Garki II, Abuja
Tel: (09) 2343810, 08033346068 **Fax:** (09) 2634493
E-mail: sabajibril@yahoo.com
Contact: Engr. Saba Jibril - MD/CEO

DATEC INTERNATIONAL (NIGERIA) LIMITED
Business: Sales of Electronic Security and Surveillance Systems, Office Interior Decor & Furniture
Address: 3, Gerrard Road, Ikoyi, Lagos
Tel: (01) 2691029 **Fax:** (01) 2693419
* NICON Hilton Hotel (Level 01), Maitama, Abuja
Tel: (09) 4135163, 4136651
Contact: Chief (Dr.) Okon Mfon Amana - Chairman

DATLEX (NIGERIA) LIMITED
Business: Sales of Office & Security Equipment & Machines
Address: Glass House, 4, Adelabu Street, Surulere, Lagos
Tel: (01) 2880170, 5851640 **Fax:** (01) 5851640
E-mail: datflex@yahoo.com
* Plot 1001, Adetokunbo Ademola Crescent, Wuse II, Abuja
Tel: (09) 4130681-2 (2L), 4135932, 08033057384, 08033071697 **Fax:** (09) 4135932
E-mail: datlex@yahoo.com
Contact: Mr Tunde Ajiniran - MD/CEO

DATUM CONSTRUCTION (NIGERIA) LIMITED
Business: Construction and Civil Engineering Contractors
Address: 94, Kachia Road, Kakuri, Kaduna
Tel: (062) 255050, 232993, 233480 **Fax:** 235518, 235166
* 5, Gana Street, Maitama District, Abuja
Tel/Fax: (09) 4134753, 4134754
* 24A, Cameroon Road (Flat 6), Ikoyi, Lagos
* Ranco Estate (House 5), Olu Obasanjo Road, Port Harcourt. **Tel/Fax:** (084) 231197

DAULA HOTEL, KANO
Business: Hospitality Services
Address: 150, Murtala Mohammed Way, Kano
Tel: (064) 640010-6 (7 L) **Fax:** (064) 640017
Contact: Alh. Zakari Ibrahim Bagwai - Chairman

DAVANDY FINANCE & SECURITIES LIMITED
Business: Stockbroking, Capital Market Operations
Address: 9, Chamley Street, Calabar
Tel: (087) 235442, 234016 **Fax:** (087) 232953
E-mail: davandy@phca.linkserve.com
* Re-Insurance Building, 46, Marina, Lagos
Tel: (01) 4728962, 08023149781

DAVCO INTERNATIONAL (NIGERIA) LIMITED
Business: Enviromental Protection and Waste Management Consultants Oil Industry Pollution Control Services,Marketing of Bio-Remediation Chemicals and Bio-Polymers
Address: 7, Adewunmi Abudu Street, off Osolo Way, Ajao Estate, Lagos
Tel: (01) 4523337, 4520294 **Fax:** (01) 4520294
E-mail: adolphus@linkserve.com.ng
Contact: Chief A. O. Okebugwu - MD/CEO

DAVELT (NIGERIA) LIMITED
Business: Property Developers & Managers, Estate Agents
Address: Plot 1025 (590F), Adetokunbo Ademola Crescent, Wuse II, Abuja
Tel: (09) 5238661 **Fax:** (09) 5231661
Contact: Chief C. K. Uganden - Chairman/CEO

DAVE-MAY GROUP
Business: Manufacturers, Importation and Exportation of General Merchandise
Address: 90, Fred McEwen Street (2nd Floor), beside Shitta House, Lagos Island, Lagos
Tel: (01) 2664640, 4811085
* 9, Old Market Road, opp. Christ Church, Onitsha
Tel: (046) 410445, 4121699
Contact: Chief Dan Onyebu - MD/CEO

DAVID LABORATORIES LIMITED
Business: Manfacturing and Distribution of Pharmaceuticals Products and Medical Consumables
Address: 9, Ajasa Street, Onikan Lagos
Tel/Fax: (01) 2630768
* C4/75, Owerri Industrial Layout, Owerri
Tel: (083) 234839, 233777
Contact: Mr. C. O. I. Joseph (SAN) - Chairman

DAVOF TRADING COMPANY (NIGERIA) LIMITED
Business: Agrictural Produce Merchandise, Import and Export and Service of Electricty Generators
Address: 90, Awolowo Road S.W. Ikoyi, Lagos
Tel: (01) 2692758, 2670789 **Fax:** (01) 2692758
E-mail: koda@infoweb.abs.net
Contact: Mr. Roelof Wonter Poel - Chairman

DAVRO (NIGERIA) LIMITED
Business: Fisheries, Fishing and Shrimping
Address: 19, Rhodes Crescent, Apapa, Lagos
Tel: (01) 5453320, 5453045 **Fax:** (01) 5874223
E-mail: davro@linkserve.com.ng
Contact: Mopamoba K. Jones - Office Manager

DAVORE INDUSTRIES PLC
Business: Manufacturing of Interlocking Paving Stones and Wall Tiles
Address: 7, Ladipo Oluwole Street, off Adeniyi Jones Avenue, Ikeja, Lagos
Tel: (01) 4967052, 08033043127
Contact: Mrs. Ebunoluwa Oyenuga - MD/CEO

DAWN FUNCTIONS NIGERIA LIMITED
Business: Integrated Marketing Communications (Advertising, Public Relations, Events & Media Relations Management and Consulting)
Address: 84, Nza Street, Independence Layout, Enugu
Tel: (042) 455098, 454267 **Fax:** (042) 456194
E-mail: dawnmail@infoweb.abs.net
Contact: Mr. Okechukwu Nwadinobi - Chairman/CEO

DAX TECHNOLOGY NIGERIA LIMITED
Business: Sales of GSM Handsets and Accessories, Sales & Service of Computers, Information Technology Products Distribution & Services
Address: 8A, Saka Tinubu Street, Victoria Island, Lagos
Tel: (01) 2700388, 4817224, 8045360, 08023073499, 08033120827, 08034749384 **Fax:** (01) 4931891
E-mail: daxtechnology@yahoo.com
nnamdi19@yahoo.com
Website: www.daxtech.20m.com
Contact: Mr. Longinus Ozoagu - GM

DAYAKAS NIGERIA LIMITED
Business: Sales, Installation and Repairs of Power Transformers and Distribution Transformers
Address: Plot 14, Oshodi-Expressway, Lagos
Tel: (01) 8044464, 4968121 **Fax:** (01) 4968121
E-mail: dayakas@infoweb.abs.net
Contact: Mr. Adedayo Akande - Chairman/CEO

DAYSPRING HOTEL, ABUJA
Business: Hospitality & Catering Services, Conference

Facilities, Business Centre
Address: Plot 2382, Juba Street, Wuse Zone 6, Abuja
Tel: (09) 5238714-5 (2 L) **Fax:** (09) 5238817
E-mail: enquiry@dayspringhotel.com
dayspringhotel@yahoo.com
Website: www.dayspringhotel.com

DAZEINE PRESS LIMITED
Business: Lithographic Printers, Publishers of Journals, Newspaper and Magazine, Manufacturers of Exercise Books, Stationery Suppliers
Address: 21B, Lateef Jakande Road, Agidingbi, Ikeja, Lagos
Tel: (01) 4750642, 08023261267 **Fax:** (01) 4923665
Contact: Mr. Tunde Pimno - GM

DAZZ MOTORS LIMITED
Business: Sales and Distribution of Motor Vehicles
Address: 34, Adetokunbo Ademola St, Victoria Island, Lagos
Tel: (01) 2618247, 7441284, 7752022, 08022236726, 08033134243 **Fax:** (01) 2618247
E-mail: dazzmotors@hyperia.com
Contact: Mr. Emmanuel Jack - Chairman/CEO

DBL SECURITIES LIMITED
Business: Registrar, Investment Advisors, Capital & Money Market Operations
Address: 16, Norman Williams Street, S. W. Ikoyi, Lagos
Tel: (01) 2695444, 2695446, 2695696, 2695617
Fax: (01) 2695446, 2695617
E-mail: dblsecurities@hyperia.com
Contact: Engr. Michael I. Ufoeze - Chairman

DBN LIMITED
Business: TV Broadcasting, Entertainment and Production of Programmes, Sports Marketing
Address: 65, Awolowo Road, S. W. Ikoyi, Lagos
Tel: (01) 2690051-2 (2L), 7740289-90 **Fax:** (01) 2693888
Contact: Mr. Osa Sonny Adun - President/CEO

DBSL SECURITIES LIMITED
Business: Stockbroking, Porfolio Management, Investment Advisory Services
Address: 56, Norman Williams Street, S. W. Ikoyi, Lagos
Tel: (01) 2673407 **Fax:** (01) 2695013
E-mail: dominium@linkserve.com.ng

DCC SATELLITE & NETWORKS LIMITED
Business: Computer Communications, Local and Wide Area Networking, Systems Integration
Address: Plot 10, Block 54A, off Adebayo Doherty Road, off Admiralty Way, Lekki Phase I, Lagos
Tel: (01) 270998, 2706065, 4721306 **Fax:** (01) 2705998
E-mail: dcc@cwlgroup.com
Website: www.cwlgroup.com
Contact: Mr Philip Obioha - MD/CEO

DDB CASERS LIMITED
Business: Advertising, Marketing Communications and Events Management, Printing
Address: 1, Joel Ogunnaike Street, Ikeja, G.R.A., Lagos
Tel: (01) 4936587, 4936588 **Fax:** (01) 4936587
E-mail: casers@infoweb.abs.net
Contact: Mr. Enyi Odigbo - MD/CEO

DDS MINES LIMITED
Business: Mining and Processing of Solid Minerals.
Address: 18, Utonkon Road, Jos
Tel: (073) 450623, 451200 **Fax:** (073) 450624

DE HAASTRUP COMMUNICATION NIGERIA LIMITED
Business: Telecommunication Service Providers, Software Engineering, E-information Services
Address: 24B, Isaac John Street, G.R.A. Ikeja, Lagos
Tel: (01) 4711924, 7733784
E-mail: info@dclsolutions.net
Website: www.dclsolutions.net

DE PETRACO LEASING COMPANY LIMITED
Business: Leasing of Vehicles, Marine Vessels, Generators, and Household Equipment
Address: Glover Memorial Hall Building, 4, Customs Street, off Marina, Lagos Island, Lagos
Tel: (01) 4739955, 7947595, 08023186525
E-mail: depetracoleasingco@yahoo.com
* Manila House, 27, Harbour Road, Port Harcourt
Tel: (084) 484082
Contact: Mr. D. D. Peterside - MD/CEO

DE NATUMAS INTERCONTINENTAL FREIGHT AGENCY LTD
Business: Shipping, Clearing and Forwarding Agency, Cargo Handling and Consolidating
Address: 7, McNeil Street, Sabo, Yaba, Lgos
Tel: (01) 863950, 867662, 7743008
Fax: (01) 863950, 5457916
Contact: Chief (Dr.) John O. Nwatu - Chairman/CEO

DE PONY INDUSTRIES LIMITED
Business: Fan Assembling, Wood Processing
Address: 2, Dockyard Road, Apapa Lagos
Tel: (01) 8042024, 8042443 **Fax:** (01) 5450358
Contact: Mr. Tony Lee - GM/CEO

DEAGBO INDUSTRIES (NIGERIA) LIMITED
Business: Manufacturing of Table Mineral Water
Address: Plumbing House, Km. 5, New Ife Road, Adegbayi, Ibadan
Tel: (02) 8104567
Contact: Chief I. A. Akinpade - Chairman/CEO

DE-ABEGA INTERNATIONAL LIMITED
Business: Surveying of Pipeline & Flowline Roules, Land/ Cadastral Surveying and Geodetic Surveying, Swamp & Offshore Surveying
Address: 119, Jakpa Road, P.O.Box 1728, Effurun, Warri,
Tel: (053) 257197 **Fax:** (053) 258169
E-mail: deabega@infoweb.com.ng
* Block 325 (Flat 3), LBIC Housing Estate, Mile 2, Lagos
Tel: (01) 886177

DEALERS WAREHOUSE LIMITED
Business: Distribution of Computer Systems, Accessories and Peripherals
Address: 80/82, Opebi Road, Ikeja, Lagos
Tel: (01) 4965367, 4970229, 4705561 **Fax:** (01) 4970228
E-mail: dealers@linkserve.com.ng
Contact: Mr. Uche Nwanguma - MD/CEO

DEAP CAPITAL MANAGEMENT & TRUST LIMITED
Business: Management of Funds & Portfolio, Pension Funds and Project, Financial Advisory Services
Address: St. Nicholas House (14th Floor), 6, Catholic Mission Street, Lagos Island, Lagos
Tel: (01) 4725793-4 (2 L), 261651, 4751756-7(2 L)
Fax: (01) 2669254
E-mail: info@deapcaptrust.com
Website: www.deapcaptrust.com
Contact: Mr. Emmanuel I. Ugboh - MD/CEO

DEBIS (NIGERIA) LIMITED
Business: Computer Sales & Services, Consultancy Services, Education and Training, Internet Bureau Services
Address: 110, Obafemi Awolowo Way, Ikeja, Lagos
Tel: (01) 4705561, 4817213, 7734243, 08033255383
E-mail: info@debiscomputer.com
* 3B, Herbert Macaulay Way, Wuse Zone 5, Wuse, Abuja
Tel: (09) 5236847, 5236848 **Fax:** (09) 5236848
* Phase I Shopping Complex, University Road, Gwagwalada, F.C.T.
Tel: (09) 8822072
Contact: Dr. L..A. Odeyemi - Chairman/CEO.

DEBO INDUSTRIES LIMITED
Business: Manufacturing of Deep Freezers, Refrigerators, Airconditioners and Milling Machines
Address: Plot 6, Block H, Oshodi Industrial Scheme, Lagos
Tel: (01) 522894, 524246, 524402, 4524238, 4520510, 4520115 **Fax:** (01) 4523351
Contact: Chief Amzat Beyioku Adebowale, OON - Chairman

DEBUK (NIGERIA) LIMITED
Business: Clearing and Freight Forwarding
Address: 23, Jaiyeola Ajatta Street, beh. Lasal Hotel, off Fatai Irawo St, Ajao Estate, Apakun-Oshodi, Lagos
Tel: (01) 4528049, 7734582 **Fax:** (01) 4528049
E-mail: debuknig@infoweb.abs.net
* c/o Rosyic International Agencies, Restaurant Lane 2, Cargo Complex, Port Harcourt International Airport, Omagwa, Rivers State
Tel: (084) 231926, 08022232129 **Fax:** (084) 230238
Contact: Mr. Dele Osunsanya - Chairman/CEO.

DE-CANON INVESTMENT LIMITED
Business: Investment Banking, Capital Market Operations
Address: Wesley House (4th Floor), 21/22, Marina, Lagos
Tel: (01) 2647273, 2668058, 2632830 **Fax:** (01) 2647291
E-mail: ngof.dil@decanon.com
Contact: Dr. Fred Offodile - Chairman
Mr. Uchenna Obodoekwe - MD/CEO

DECENT BAG INDUSTRIES LIMITED
Business: Manufacturing of Poly Bags
Address: Km. 11, Hadejia Road, Gunduwawa, Kano
Tel: (064) 646041 **Fax:** (064) 638185
E-mail: info@decent-polybag.com
Website: www.decent-polybag.com
Contact: Miss Bonnie Lau - MD/CEO

DECISION SUPPORT CONSULTANCY LIMITED
Business: Marketing & Social Research Services
Address: Tosil House, 53, Opebi Road, Ikeja, Lagos
Tel: (01) 4931945 **Fax:** (01) 4936195
E-mail: decisionsupport@yahoo.com
Contact: Ms. Joy A. Uyanwune -MD/ CEO

DECO-ART FURNITURE LIMITED
Business: Manufacturing and Sales of Furniture
Address: Plot 785, Paiko Road, Tunga, Minna
Tel: (066) 220247, 221780
Contact: Arc. Sunday Yakubu Ajenajeyi - Chairman

DECROSS LIMITED
Business: Audio & Tapes Mastering/Duplication, Transfer of 1/4 Master Tapes from Analogue to Digital Formats, Compact Disc Writing and Duplication.
Address: Decross House, Abigail Oyindamola Close, off Km. 1, Ijoko Road, Sango Ota Ogun State
Tel: (039) 722341, 722426 **Fax:** (039) 722426
E-mail: decross@pinet.com.ng
Contact: Evang. (Dr.) Ebenezer Obey-Fabiyi - Chairman

DE-CROWN (WEST AFRICA) LIMITED
Business: Multi-Discipline Engineering Consultancy Services, Project Management
Address: 3, Zuma Close, Udi St, Aso Drive, Maitama, Abuja
Tel/Fax: (09) 5234734
* De-Crown House, Plots 6 & 7, Block E, Town Planning Rd, OluyoleMain Estate,Ring Rd, Ibadan
Tel: (02) 2318946-8 (3L) **Fax:** (02) 2318946
Contact: Engr. (Dr) J. B. O. Adewumi

DEEBEE COMPANY LIMITED
Business: Wine and Fruit Juice Manufacturing
Address: The Winery, Erunwon-Isonyin Road, Ilupa, Isonyin, Ogun State
Tel/Fax: (037) 431813
E-mail: deebee@alpha.linkserve.com
Contact: Dr. Dolapo B. A. Ogutaga - Chairman/CEO

DEEKAY & SONS NIGERIA LIMITED
Business: Importation and Marketing of General Merchandise
Address: Plot 239C, Kofo Abayomi St, Victoria Island, Lagos
Tel: (01) 2626906-8 (3 L), 08023024496
Fax: (01) 2626846

DEFENCE INDUSTRY CORPORATION OF NIGERIA
Business: Manufacture of Small Arms & Ammunition. Production of Salt
Address: 45, Ahmadu Bello Way, Kaduna
Tel: (062) 249530, 24531, 249532, 249525, 249526
Fax: (062) 249532

DE-FRIENDSHIP CATERING SERVICES LIMITED
Business: Hotel Ownership and Management, Hospitality and Catering Services
Address: 17/19, Niger Street, Kano
Tel: (064) 639350, 639352, 639353, 647496
Fax: (064) 639358
Contact: Alh. Abdullahi Aliyu - Chairman/CEO

DEFUNTOKS INTERNATIONAL TRAVELS LIMITED
Business: Travel Agency
Address: Iponri Shopping Centre (Suite 277/24B), Iponri,

Surulere, Lagos
Tel: (01) 5831398, 5832250, 5837775, 846857, 835557, 08023150155, 08037181104 **Fax:** (01) 5831398
E-mail: defuntokstravels@hotmail.com

DEGOAL INVESTMENT LIMITED
Business: Assembling, Sales and Servicing of Computers, Office Equipment and Telecoms Systems
Address: Aduke House (1st Floor), 1, Adeola Adeoye Street, off OLowu/Toyin Street, Ikeja, Lagos
Tel: (01) 4936389, 4934578 **Fax:** (01) 4934579
E-mail: degoal@infoweb.abs.net
Contact: Mr. Dele Adeoye - Chairman/CEO

DEGREMONT NIGERIA LIMITED
Business: Water Treatment Engineering Services
Address: 10, Elsie Femi-Pearse Street (2nd Floor), V/I, Lagos
Tel: (01) 2623472
E-mail: ondeo_degremont@yahoo.com
Contact: Dr. S. E. Olaoye - Chairman/CEO

DE-KOMPASS VENTURES LIMITED
Business: Importation of Auto Trucks and Spare Parts
Address: 19A, Child Avenue, off Liverpool Rd Apapa, Lagos
Tel: (01) 7741555, 5871912 **Fax:** (01) 5871912
E-mail: snfman@metrong.com
* Plot 5, Block M, Abimbola Street, Isolo, Lagos

DEKIT CONSTRUCTION LIMITED
Business: Building & Civil Engineering Contractors
Address: Plot 148B, Gana Street, Maitama District, Abuja
Tel: (09) 6702658 **Fax:** (09) 4130605
E-mail: dekitconstruction@hotmail.com
Website: www.dekitconstruction.com
Contact: Arc. Dele Olagunju - Chairman/CEO

DELATTRE BEZONS (NIGERIA) LIMITED
Business: Oilfield Engineering Services, Construction and Mechanical Engineering
Address: Plot 184A/B, Moshood Olugbani Street Victoria Island Annex, Lagos
Tel: (01) 2623881, 2623882 **Fax:** (01) 2623880
E-mail: contact@delattre-bezons.com
* Plot 107, Trans Amadi Ind. Layout, Port Harcourt
Tel/Fax: (084) 232502, 238837
* Km 2, Refining Road, Warri
Tel: (053) 320437
Contact: Engr. (Chief) Dr. A. A. Adejumo - Chairman

DELE DINA & COMPANY
Business: Chartered Accountants, Auditing, Taxation Services
Address: 47A, Itafaji Road, off Corporation Drive, Dolphin Estate, Ikoyi, Lagos
Tel: (01) 2694214

DELE GROUP INTERNATIONAL LIMITED
Business: Shipping and Freight Forwarding, Import and Export, Contracting and Merchandising
Address: Development House (7th Floor), 21/23, Wharf Road, Apapa, Lagos
Tel/Fax: (01) 5878551
Contact: Mr. Samuel Oludele Ogundeji - Chairman/CEO

DELI FOODS NIGERIA LIMITED
Business: Manufacturing of Biscuits and Confectionery
Address: Plot 14, Block B, Ilasamaja Industrial Scheme, Isolo-Apapa Expressway, Ilasamaja, Lagos
Tel: (01) 4523615, 4522121, 7740228, 7740227
Fax: (01) 4523615, 7740207
E-mail: delifoods@hotmail.com
Contact: Mr. Youseef Fattal - Chairman/CEO

DELMAN GROUP OF COMPANIES
Business: Transportation of Petroleum Products, Bottling of L.P.G. Gas, Manufacture of Paints
Address: 18, Lewis Street, Lafiaji, Lagos
Tel: (01) 2647571, 2647572 **Fax:** (01) 2647572
Contact: Alh. Lukman Adeyemi Adebiyi - Chairman/CEO

DELMAR PETROLEUM COMPANY LIMITED
Business: Oilfield Engineering Services
Address: 25B, Rumuola Road, Port Harcort
Tel: (084) 231581, 236885
* 21A, Liverpool Road, Apapa, Lagos
Tel: (01) 5870214

DELOITTE & TOUCHE MANAGEMENT SOLUTIONS
Business: Management and Business Consultancy Services
Address: 1, Town Planning Way, Ilupeju, Lagos
Tel: (01) 4935810, 4930720-4 (5 L)
Fax: (01) 4970023, 4978736
E-mail: info@awdeloitte.com
Website: www.deloitte.com
Contact: Mr. Victor G. Hammond - Chairman/MD

DE-LORDS SECURITIES LIMITED
Business: Stockbroking
Address: Eleganza Building (9th Floor), 15B, Joseph Street, off Broad Street, Lagos
Tel: (01) 2634889, 2634893 **Fax:** (01) 2634893
E-mail: de-lords@mail.com
Contact: Mrs. C. O. Ajayi - Chairman/CEO

DE-LOUIS TECHNOLOGIES LIMITED
Business: Sales, Installation and Maintenance of Fire, Safety and Security Systems, Consultancy, Training and Guard Services
Address: 7, Association Avenue, Ilupeju, Lagos
Tel: (01) 4931102
Contact: Louise Ihuka Otele - MD/CEO

DELTA BROTHERS LIMITED
Business: Shipping, Clearing and Forwarding
Address: 22/24, Calcutta Crescent, Apapa, Lagos
Tel: (01) 587300
E-mail: deltabrothers@hyperia.com
Contact: Mr Peter Edukugha - Chairman/CEO

DELTA BUILDING SOCIETY COMPANY
Business: Mortgage Banking
Address: 126B, Nnebisi Road, Asaba
Tel: (056) 280642, 282268

DELTA COLOUR PRODUCTION NIGERIA LIMITED
Business: Printing Services, Production of Corporate Gifts
Address: Plot 12, Latson Azeez Crescent, Onipetesi

Industrial Estate, Agege, Lagos
Tel: (01) 4921839, 4926596

DELTA MANUFACTURING COMPANY LIMITED
Business: Manufacture of Industrial Plastic Packaging
Address: Plot 9, Block E, Badejo Kalesanwo Street, Matori Industrial Estate, Matori, Mushin, Lagos
Tel: (01) 4520349, 4523413 **Fax:** (01) 4527938
E-mail: info@deltanigeria.com
Website: www.deltanigeria.com
Contact: Mr. C. D. Papanastasiou - Chairman/CEO.

DELTA MARINE SHIPPING COMPANY LIMITED
Business: Shipping and Maritime Servcies
Address: 25B, Rumuola Road, Port Harcourt
Tel: (084) 231581, 236885

DELTA OIL & GAS (NIGERIA) LIMITED
Business: Marketing and Transportation (Sea & Road) of Petroleum Products, Petroleum Consultancy
Address: 70, Raymond Njoku Street, S. W. Ikoyi, Lagos
Tel: (01) 4614033, 4614034 **Fax:** (01) 2672214
E-mail: deltaoil@vgccl.net
Contact: Mr. Fred Agbeyegbe - Chairman/CEO

DELTA PACKAGING COMPANY LIMITED
Business: Manufacturing of Polypropylene Woven Sacks for Flour, Feeds and Produce
Address: Ogorode Industrial Estate, Sapele, Delta State
Tel: (054) 342628, 341036, 342102, 341363, 08035844767, 08035350545 **Fax:** (054) 342422
E-mail: lifesapale@infoweb.abs.net
Contact: Mr. Donald Spencer - MD/CEO

DELTA STEEL COMPANY LIMITED
Business: Steel Production, Manuafacturing of Steel and Allied Products, Gas Production
Address: Ovwian-Aladja, Warri
Tel: (053) 621001-10 (10L), 08033800244
Fax: (053) 621012
* 19B, Suez Crescent, Ibrahim Abacha Estate, off Ladi Kwali Way, Wuse Zone 4, Abuja
Tel/Fax: 5240319, 08033003617
Contact: Engr Anthony A. Madagua - MD/CEO

DELTATEL COMMUNICATIONS LIMITED
Business: Sales and Service of Telecommunication Equipment and Systems
Address: Murphis Plaza, 27, Sanusi Fafunwa Street, Victoria Island, Lagos
Tel: (01) 2624343, 2623335, 4701035 **Fax:** (01) 2623498
E-mail: deltatel@mail.com

DELUXE COLOUR PRODUCTIONS LIMITED
Business: Outdoor Advertising
Address: 10, Omiaro Street, Iwaya, Yaba, Lagos
Tel: (01) 8146277, 863759, 861509 **Fax:** (01) 863756
E-mail: deluxeemarkings@yahoo.com
Contact: Otunba O. O. Selesi - MD/CEO

DEMOLA DAWODU & ASSOCIATES
Business: Chartered Surveyors, Estate Surveyors and Valuers
Address: 168, Awolowo Road, S .W. Ikoyi, Lagos
Tel: (01) 8042559, 5831831, 5835432
E-mail: demoladawodu@metrong.com

DENCA SERVICES LIMITED
Business: Clearing and Forwarding, Transporting and General Merchansing
Address: 37, Alh. Yusuf Adebayo St, Olodi, Apapa, Lagos
Tel: (01) 5450163, 4801242, 7741319, 7759302
Fax: (01) 5455369
E-mail: denca@micro.com.ng
Contact: Mr. Dennis Okafor - Chairman/CEO

DENHAM MANAGEMENT LIMITED
Business: Portfolio Management, Investment Advisors
Address: New Africa House (17th Floor), 31, Marina, Lagos
Tel: (01) 2644641, 2664445, 2661763 **Fax:** (01) 2661763
E-mail: info@denham-management.com
Website: www.denham-management.com
Contact: Mr Gamaliel Onosode (Jr) - MD/CEO

DEN-HARRIS & COMPANY LIMITED
Business: Marketing of Office Machines and Equipment
Address: 284, Herbert Macaulay, Sabo-Yaba, Lagos
Tel: (01) 862368, 868810, 865824, 7911849, 4730666, 08056181501 **Fax:** (01) 862368
E-mail: dighrs@yahoo.com
Contact: Mr. Denis Ifeanyi Ogamba - Chairman/CEO

DENKI WIRE & CABLE (NIGERIA) LIMITED
Business: Manufacturing of Electric Wire & Cable
Address: Olufoam Industrial Estate, Km. 1, Akure-Ife Expressway, P.O.Box 727, Akure
Tel: (034) 241347

DENLYN NIGERIA LIMITED
Business: Marine and Special Transport Service, Fashion Designing and Garment Manufacturing
Address: 27, Ribadu Road, S. W.l Ikoyi, Lagos
Tel: (01) 2693607 **Fax:** (01) 2695202

DENSINE INDUSTRIES (WEST AFRICA) LIMITED
Business: Sales of Musical Instrument, Household Appliances
Address: 16, Alh. Okin Street, Ojo, Lagos
Tel: (01) 5884687, 5892571, 5891388
Fax: (01) 5884687, 5892571
E-mail: densine@beta.linkserve.com
densine@micro.com.ng
Contact: Chief Dennis Adindu Okafor - Chairman/CEO

DENSON PAPER MILL LIMITED
Business: Paper Conversion, Production of Exercise Books and Stationery, Sheeting of Paper Reels
Address: 12, New Market Road, Onitsha
Tel: (046) 488467
E-mail: denson@infoweb.abs.net
Contact: Chief D. E. Okatta - Chairman/CEO

DENVER PETROLEUM SERVICES LIMITED
Business: Petrochemical Industry Services, Procurement and Maintenance of Oilfield Service Equipment and Products, Sales of Pumps for Petroleum Products
Address: 380, Ikorodu Road, Mende, Maryland, Ikeja, Lagos

Tel: (01) 4971907, 4962172 **Fax:** (01) 4930930
E-mail: sales@dpsltd.com
dpsl@hyperia.com

DEO MAKRO LIMITED
Business: Transportation Engineering (Airports Development; Civil & Defence Communication Engineering), Communication & Environmental Engineering
Address: 27, Kakawa Street, off Broad Street, Lagos
Tel/Fax: (01) 2645125, 7730881
E-mail: deomakro@micro.com.ng
* Plot 684, Agadez Crescent, off Aminu Kano Crescent, Wuse II, Abuja.
Tel: (09) 5233820
Contact: Engr. J. A. Adenle - MD/CEO

DEPENDABLE SECURITIES LIMITED
Business: Stockbroking
Address: Stock Exchange House (2nd Floor), 2/4, Customs Street, off Marina, Lagos
Tel: (01) 2665580, 2644875, 2668537, 8045412
Fax: (01) 2668537
E-mail: info@dependablesec.com
Contact: Mr. C. S. U. Anyanwu - MD/CEO

DEPENDABLE SYSTEMS NIGERIA LIMITED
Business: Sales of Computers, Training in Computer Engineering, Supply and Maintenance of Office Automation Equipment
Address: Maryland Shopping Complex (Suite BC 40-42), along Ikorodu Road, Maryland, Lagos
E-mail: dependeable_sys@yahoo.com
Contact: Engr. Ola F. Bakare - Chairman/CEO

DER KURIER (AIR ACTION COURIER)
Business: Courier Services (Mails, Parcels and Cargo), Customs Brokerage
Address: 26/28, Oshodi-Apapa Expressway, opposite BOC Gases, by Charity Bus-Stop, Oshodi, Lagos
Tel: (01) 7742254, 4700147
E-mail: derkurieaac@linkserve.com
derkurieaac@atelo.com
Website: www.airaction.com
* Cornershops (Suite 273/274), Garki II, Abuja
Tel: (09) 2348817
* 4, Agudama Street, D/Line, Port Harcourt
Tel: (084) 231271
Contact: Air Vice Marshal Canice Uwenwaliri - Chairman
Mr. Ambrose Eke - MD/CEO.

DERIN (NIGERIA) LIMITED
Business: Sales & Servicing of Computers & Communications Systems; Training & Consultancy
Address: Commercial House, 19/21, Commercial Avenue, Sabo-Yaba, Lagos
Tel: (01) 864373, 866981 **Fax:** (01) 864373
E-mail: acadesida@derincomputers.com
tunji-esan@yahoo.co.uk
Contact: Prince Abiodun C. Adesida - Chairman/CEO.

DEROS MARITIME LIMITED.
Business: Shipping Agency, Clearing & Forwarding, Sea & Air Freighting, Warehousing & Transportation, Cargo Consolidation, Tramp Vessels, Bulk Cargo
Address: 3, Ibikunle Akitoye Street, Apapa, Lagos
Tel: (01) 5870089, 5871234, 5871236 **Fax:** (01) 5455324
E-mail: derosmaritime@hypeira.com
Contact: Mrs. Mopelola A. Rosiji - Chairman/CEO.

DEROTECH INTERNATIONAL LTD.
Business: Fertilizer Distribution, Sales of Chemicals, Procurement Services
Address: 103, Allen Avenue (5th Floor), Ikeja, Lagos
Tel/Fax: (01) 4965751
E-mail: b_derotech@yahoo.com
Contact: Captain Haastrup - Chairman
Mr. Yusuf Bello - Operations Manager

DE-SEARS PHARMACEUTICALS & CHEMICALS LIMITED
Business: Importation, Distribution and Marketing of Pharmaceutical & Health Care Products
Address: 29, Isaac John Street, off Ikorodu Road, Fadeyi-Igbobi, Lagos
Tel: (01) 2665388, 2665054, 7741459
Contact: Chief Nnamdi Nwigwe - Chairman/CEO

DESIGN OPTIONS LIMITED
Business: Sales of Rugs and Furnishings, Interior Decoration Services, Project Management
Address: Plot 292C, Ajose Adeogun St, Victoria Is., Lagos
Tel: (01) 5558093, 2615711, 08033082853
E-mail: d.options@beta.linkserve.com
do.mgt@beta.linkserve.com
* 13, King George V Road, Onikan, Lagos

DESTINY INSURANCE COMPANY LIMITED
Business: Insurance
Address: Reinsurance House (12th Floor), 46, Marina, Lagos
Tel: (01) 2668936, 2663722, 2669206, 4718348, 4718349
* 190, Aba Road, Rumuola Junction, Port Harcourt
Tel: (084) 331747
Contact: Chief (Dr.) C. E. Igbokwe - Chairman
Mr. S. A. Imarachi - MD/CEO.

DE-UNITED FOOD INDUSTRIES LIMITED
Business: Food Processing, Production of Noodles
Address: 11B, Osborne Road, Ikoyi, Lagos
Tel: (01) 2693368-9 (2 L) **Fax:** (01) 2692491
* Km. 4, Idiroko Road, Otta, Ogun State
Tel: (039) 722264-6 (3 L)
Contact: Mr. Haresh Aswani - Chairman/MD.

DEUTAG NIGERIA LIMITED
Business: Oilfield Drilling and Work-Over Operations
Address: Km. 16, P. Harcourt/Aba Expressway, Port Harcourt
Tel: (084) 611619, 611757 **Fax:** (084) 611632
E-mail: deutag.nigeria@deutag.com
Contact: Chief H. Idisi - Chairman
Mr. John George Joyce - MD/CEO.

DEUX PROJECT LIMITED
Business: Deisgn, Building and Equipment of Hospitals and Laboratories; Provision of Hospital, Laboratory and Scientific Equipment, After-Sales Support
Address: 261A, Corporation Drive, Dolphin Estate, Ikoyi, Lagos
Tel: (01) 2694220, 2694033 * Abuja - (09) 5236585

Fax: (01) 2694248
E-mail: deuxprj@phca.linkserve.com
Contact: Dr. Tunji Olowolafe - Chairman/CEO.

DEVCOM BANK LIMITED
Business: Commercial Banking
Address: 18, Oko-Awo Close, off Adetokunbo Ademola Street, Victoria Island, Lagos
Tel: (01) 2610206-8 (3L), 2615148, 2615732, 2615734, 2613157 **Fax:** (01) 2612615
Contact: Dr. Mike Adenuga, Jnr - Chainman
Mr. Zachariah Jacob - MD/CEO

DEVCOM SECURITIES LIMITED
Business: Stockbroking, Portfolio Management, Investment Advisory Services, Issuing House Activities, Insurance Agency
Address: 18A, Oko-Awo Close, Victoria Island, Lagos
Tel: (01) 2619569, 2613157, 2615148, 2615031, 2615734
Fax: (01) 614652
Contact: Mr. Niyi Adewunmi - Chairman
Mr. J. O. Ariyo - MD/CEO

DEVELOP OFFICE PRODUCTS LIMITED
Business: Importation, Sales and Service of Office Automation & Business Machines
Address: Oluwatobi House, 71, Allen Avenue, Ikeja, Lagos
Tel: (01) 8042747, 4970517, 4701687 **Fax:** (01) 4970517
Website: www.develop.de
* Abuja Shopping Mall (Suite B18), Wuse Zone 3, Abuja.
Tel: (09) 523585
* 92, Aba Road, Port Harcourt.
Tel: (084) 231052
Contact: Mr. Peter Okonji - National Sales Manager

DEVELOPMENT FINANCE & INVESTMENT COMPANY LTD
Business: Development Finance Institution, Equipment Leasing, Feasibility Studies
Address: Plot 15, Commissioners' Quarters, Concorde Street, off Port Harcourt Road, Owerri
Tel: (083) 231981, 231937
Contact: Mr. C. O. Mbonu - Ag. GM/CEO

DEVICES & TECHNIQUES LIMITED
Business: Computer and Telecommunication (Equipment Procurement, Engineering & Maintenance, Configuration & Programming; Sales and Consultancy)
Address: 122, Elekahia Road, Port Harcourt
Tel: (084) 236929, 238444 **Fax:** (084) 238444, 578360
E-mail: devices@infoweb.abs.net
Contact: Engr. Alex Mbaekwe - MD/CEO.

DEXDEE FOUNTAINS LIMITED
Business: Construction, Property Development, Installation and Maintenance of Water Fountains & Falls
Address: 63, Allen Avenue, Ikeja, Lagos
Tel: (01) 4931944, 4734307, 7738250, 08033066901
Fax: (01) 4975041
E-mail: dextroc@hyperia.com
* Plot 2942, Aguiyi Ironsi Street, Maitama, Abuja
Tel: (09) 4132099 **Fax:** (09) 4132100
Contact: Engr. Desmond Odiase - Chairman/CEO

DEZACHI CONSTRUCTION LIMITED
Business: Architects and Builders
Address: 21, Lucina Joseph Street, off Adeniran Ogunsanya Street, Surulere, Lagos
Tel: (01) 4701842, 08033259835
E-mail: dezachi@infoweb.abs.net
Contact: Mr. Ambrose Okuhor - MD/CEO

DEZERN NIGERIA LIMITED
Business: Manufacturing of Lubricants and Resins
Address: 87, Ogui Road, Enugu
Tel: (042) 255366, 251474 **Fax:** (042) 255366
E-mail: dezern@infoweb.abs.net
Contact: Engr. N. I. Enekwa - Chairman/CEO.

DGC AFRICA NETWORK SERVICES LIMITED
Business: Operations of Pre-Paid Telephone Cards, Pre-Paid Dial-Up Internet Services, Broadband, Wireless Internet Solutions, Web Design, Software Design
Address: 13B, Isaac John Street, G.R.A., Ikeja, Lagos
Tel: (01) 3420059 - 60 (2 L), 7765965, 4961210
Fax: (01) 3420061
E-mail: info@dgcafrica.com
Website: www.dcgafrica.com
Contact: Dr. Femi Majekodunmi - Chairman
Mr. Wahaab Abdallah - MD/CEO

DHL INTERNATIONAL (NIGERIA) LIMITED
Business: Air Express Services
Address: DHL House, Oshodi-Isolo Expressway/Int'l Airport Road Junction, Isolo, Lagos
Tel: (01) 4501000, 4501999 **Fax:** (01) 4501001, 4501222
* 609, Dambata Close, by Tafawa Balewa Way, Garki Area 7, Abuja
Tel: (09) 5238555, 5238600
* Plot 156/157, Trans-Amadi Industrial Layout, Port Harcourt
Tel: (084) 230472-3 (2L), 232595, 232397
Contact: Mr. Richard P. K. Seaver - MD/CEO
Mr Aigbe Olotu - Zonal Finance Manager.

DIAMOND BANK LIMITED
Business: Commercial Banking
Address: Plot 1261, Adeola Hopewell Street, Victoria Island, Lagos
Tel: (01) 2620740-7 (8L) **Fax:** (01) 2619728
E-mail: info@diamondbank.com
Contact: Mr Emeka Onwuka - MD/CEO

DIAMOND BICYCLE INDUSTRIES LIMITED
Business: Importation, Assembly & Marketing of Bicycles
Address: Eleganza Plaza (Gemini Block, 2nd Floor), 1, Commercial Road, Apapa, Lagos
Tel: (01) 5804740-4 (5 L), 5451660
* 26, Niger Street, opp. Gidan Goldie, Kano
Tel: (064) 639030, 647380

DIAMOND FOODS LIMITED
Business: Production of Various Brands of Biscuits
Address: Modondola Group, 15, Creek Road, Apapa, Lagos
Tel: (01) 5450810 **Fax:** (01) 5450789
* Km 17, Old Ijebu-Ibadan Road, Alomaja, Ibadan
Contact: Chief Bode Akindele - Chairman

DIAMOND FOREVER MARITIME SERVICES LIMITED
Business: Clearing & Forwarding Agency
Address: 15, Okwei Street, Onitsha
Tel: (046) 251841, 413270, 08033108530, 08033271918, 08033232431, 08033402780
* 14B, Industry Road, Port Harcourt
Tel: (084) 4821490, 08033108530, 08033402780

DIAMOND SPINNERS LIMITED
Business: Production of Yarn
Address: Plot 9, Block E, Amuwo-Odofin Industrial Estte, Apapa-Oshodi Expressway, Amuwo-Odofin, Lagos
Tel: (01) 5837905, 5843909, 7740266

DIAMOND TOBACCO PROCESSING COMPANY LIMITED
Business: Tobacco Processing & Rehandling
Address: 24B, Limca Road, Nkpor, Onitsha
Tel: (046) 413974 **Fax:** (046) 413289
Contact: Chief B. C. Igwealor - Chairman

DIDI MUSEUM
Business: Exhibition and Sales of Art Works and Painting
Address: 175, Akin Adesola Street, Victoria Island, Lagos
Tel: (01) 7747898, 08023141630
Contact: Ifi Robin Chidubem - Exhibition Co-ordinator

DIGICOM TRENDS LIMITED
Business: Sales of Computers, Telecommunication Equipment
Address: 103, Obafemi Awolowo Way, Ikeja, Lagos
Tel: (01) 4971671, 7755087 **Fax:** (01) 4971671
E-mail: digicom@infoweb.abs.net
Contact: Mr. A. O. Olanrewaju - Chairman/CEO

DIGIPRINTS INTERNATIONAL LIMITED
Business: Digital Wide-Format Printing, Signages, Vehicle Branding, Direct-Image Paper Printing, Event branding & Organisation
Address: Plot 17, Kudirat Abiola Way (Clay Bus-Stop), opp. Household of God Church, Oregun, Ikeja, Lagos
Tel: (01) 4975569, 4961667, 7900887, 0803449444
Fax: (01) 4975569
E-mail: twehbe@hotmail.com
Website: www.digiprintinternational.com
Contact: Mr Talal Wehbe - Chairman/CEO

DIGITRUST (NIGERIA) LIMITED
Business: Computer Assembling, Sales and Maintenance, Network Installation, Consultancy Services
Address: 9, Olufemi Rd, off Ogunlana Drive, Surulere, Lagos
Tel: (01) 5836282, 848417 **Fax:** (01) 5836282
E-mail: digitrust@infoweb.abs.net
Contact: Mr. Emma E. Chukwu - Chairman/CEO

DIKE OBIALO & COMPANY
Business: Estate Surveyors & Valuers
Address: 132, Azikiwe Road, P. O. Box 3670, Aba
Tel: (082) 234889, 08035411004
* 3, Macaulay Street, Umuahia
Contact: Dr. E. D. Obialor - Principal Partner

DIL/MALTEX (NIGERIA) PLC
Business: Bottling of Non-Alchoholic Malt Drink
Address: 19, Bayo Kuku Street, Ikoyi, Lagos
Tel: (01) 2660312, 2662050, 2662129, 2664230
* Plot C12/3, Shagamu Road, Agbara Indstrial Estate, off Km 32, Lagos- Badagry Expressway, Agbara, Ogun State
Tel: (01) 712460-1 (2 L), 712481, 7740891
Fax: (01) 712483
Contact: Chief B. O. Benson (SAN) - Chairman
Mr. A. Beyls - MD/CEO

DILIC HOTELS LIMITED
Business: Hospitality & Catering Services, Conference Facilities
Address: Plot 1123, Adetokunbo Ademola Crescent, Wuse II, Abuja
Tel: (09) 4134850-2 (3 L) **Fax:** (09) 4134853

DIMARS INDUSTRIES LIMITED
Business: Haulage Services
Address: Plot 2/3, T. A. Doherty Industrial Layout, Kudirat Abiola Way, Ikeja, Lagos
Tel: (01) 4934395, 080230012
Contact: Mrs. Beatrice Achilike - Chairman

DIMENSIONS CEILING PRODUCTS LIMITED
Business: Importation, Sales and Installation of Suspended Ceilings and Insulation Systems; Importation
Address: 109, Tafawa Balewa Crescent, off Adeniran Ogunsanya Street, Surulere, Lagos
Tel: (01) 5834090, 08034001362, 08037203407
Contact: Engr. P. N. B. Erinne - Chairman/CEO.

DINTA RISK & INSURANCE BROKERS LIMITED
Business: International Risk & Insurance Management
Address: 19, Opebi Road, Ikeja, Lagos
Tel: (01) 4973805, 4719608, 08033228278
Fax: (01) 4970556
E-mail: dinta@nigerianet.com
Contact: Mr. Ejindu Ijekpa - Snr. Superintendent

DIOSCON GROUP NIGERIA LIMITED
Business: Hotel and Catering Services, Engineering Services
Address: 24, Moshood Abiola Way, Ebute-Metta, Lagos
Tel: (01) 831437, 08034091432, 08037401996, 08055445674
E-mail: dioscongroup@onebox.com
dioscon overseas@yahoo.com
Contact: Chief Dan. Ik. Ojukwu - Chairman/CEO

DIPLOMAT TRAVELS & TOURISM AGENCY
Business: Travel Agency, Tour Operators, Packaging of Conference & Seminars
Address: News Engineering Plaza Plot 511, Herbert Macaulay way, Wuse Zone 4, Abuja
Tel: (09) 5233770, 08037006676 **Fax:** (09) 5241147
E-mail: diptrata@yahoo.com
Contact: Mr. Akor Otobo - MD/CEO

DIRECT MARKETING COMMUNICATIONS LIMITED
Business: Marketing, Promotions and Advertisig
Address: 41, Isaac John Road, Ikeja, G.R.A., Lagos
Tel: (01) 4971424
E-mail: dmcnig@metrong.com
Contact: Mr. Ron Boon - Chairman/CEO

DIRECT ON PC LIMITED

Business: Broadband Internet Service Provider, Virtual Private Network, VoIP Solutions, Mailing Solutions, Firewall, Solutions, Network Consultancy, Sales of IT Products, Integration and IT Planning
Address: Plot B, Block 1, Industrial Avenue, Ilupeju, Lagos
Tel: (01) 7737400-4 (5 L), 08037758243, 08037758224, 08037758245, 08037758001, 08037758005
Fax: (01) 4930958
E-mail: info@directonpc.com
Website: www.directonpc.com
* Plot 696, Agadez Crescent, off Aminu Kano Crescent, Wuse II, Abja
Tel: (09) 6711754, 08037758250
E-mail: infoabuja@directonpc.com
* 124, Woji Road, G.R.A. Phase II, Port Harcourt
Tel: (084) 488251, 08022904393
E-mail: infoph@directonpc.com

DISC COMMUNICATIONS LIMITED

Business: Sales, Installation and Service of Wireless Telephone Systems, Paging Systems and Terminals, Internet Services
Address: Lateef Jakande Road, Agidingbi, Ikeja, Lagos
Tel: (01) 3450000, 3450009, 3453070, 3453080
Fax: (01) 3450004
E-mail: discom@discompaging.com
Website: www.discompaging.com
* 603, Dambatta Close, Area 7, Garki, Abuja
Tel: (09) 2346490 (5 L)
* 2B, Railway Close, D-Line, behind NITEL Garrison, Port Harcourt.
Tel: (084) 236050 (9 L)
Contact: Engr. A. G. M. Banjo - MD/CEO

DIYA, FATIMILEHIN & COMPANY

Business: Estate Surveyors & Valuers, Property Develpment & Management, Real Estate Agency
Address: Property Plaza, Plot 237B, Muri Okunola Street, Victoria Island, Lagos
Tel: (01) 2623951-4 (4L), 615673 **Fax:** (01) 2623959
E-mail: diyafat@infoweb.abs.net
Website: www.diya-fatimilehin.com
* 3, Lokoja Street, Garki Area 8, Garki, Abuja
Tel: (09) 2344486, 2345586
E-mail: abuja@diya-fatimilehin.com
Contact: Mr. G. Fatimilehin - Founding Partner
Mr. M. K. Diya - Founding Partner

DIZENGOFF WEST AFRICA (NIGERIA) LIMITED

Business: Sales and Maintenance of Telecommunication Equipment and Systems
Address: 28, Creek Road, Apapa, Lagos
Tel: (01) 5874387, 5875990, 7749613 **Fax:** (01) 5874021
E-mail: dizengoff@cyberspace.net.ng
Website: www.dizengoff.com
Contact: Prof. J. K. Duncan - Chairman
Mr. David Wyn - Ricketts - MD/CEO

DIZPHARM (NIGERIA) LIMITED

Business: Importation and Manufacture of Human Drugs, Veterinary Drugs and Feed Additives
Address: 13, Creek Road, Apapa, Lagos
Tel: (01) 5875179, 5874082, 5871944 **Fax:** (01) 5875437
E-mail: dizpharm@hyperia.com
Contact: Mrs. M. Dekel - MD/CEO

DKA REALTY LIMITED

Business: Real Estate Consultancy & Management
Address: YMCA Building (1st Floor), 77, Awolowo Road, S. W. Ikoyi, Lagos
Tel: (01) 2707272-3 (2 L), 8114027, 08033574888
E-mail: donald@dkarealty.com
Website: www.dkarealty.com
Contact: Mr. Donald Kunle Afun - MD/CEO

DKK & ASSOCIATES LIMITED

Business: Advertising and Marketing Communications
Address: 2, Bode Thomas Street, off Bode Thomas Road, off Ikorodu Road, Onipanu, Lagos
Tel: (01) 4709628, 7740784, 8129537
E-mail: dkkltd@mwebafrica.com
Contact: Mr. Kolawole Ayanwale - Chairman

DN MEYER PLC

Business: Manufacture & Marketing of Paints
Address: Plot 34, Oregun Industrial Estate, Mobolaji Johnson Avenue, (Formerly Secretariat Road), Alausa, Ikeja, Lagos
Tel: (01) 4931256-8 (3L), 7740590 **Fax:** (01) 4933802
E-mail: info@meyerpaints.com
Website: www.meyerpaints.com
Contact: Mr. M. J. Yinusa - MD/CEO.
Mr. B. A. Lawal - Business Dev. Controller

DOBLINK KREDIT & COMMERCE LIMITED

Business: Procurement of Pharmaceutical & Industrial Raw Materials
Address: 18/20, Commercial Road, Apapa, Lagos
Tel: (01) 5870411 **Fax:** (01) 5455438
E-mail: doblink@hyperia.com
Contact: Mr. D. O.Browns - Chairman/CEO

DOF NIGERIA INSTITUTES LIMITED

Business: Hospitality-Profession Training, Fashion & Textile Design Training, IT Training
Address: 43, Oritshe Street., Off Obafemi Awolowo Way (Balogun Bus-Stop), Ikeja, Lagos
Tel: (01) 7741530, 08056304606
* 10, Lord Emmanuel Drive, Rumuomasi, PHarcourt
Tel: (080) 23104007

DOFAS TECHNICAL NIGERIA LIMITED

Business: Sales of Water Dispensers, Sanitary Ware, Electrical Equipment and General Merchandise
Address: Block 8 Extension (1st Floor, Suites 3-6), Agric Market, Badagry Expressway, Coker, Orile, Lagos
Tel: (01) 2881316, 5451902, 5452171, 7740728, 08023139311 **Fax:** (01) 5451902
E-mail: dofas@infoweb.abs.net
Contact: Mr. Athan Onwuekweikpe - Manager

DOHAGRO LIMITED

Business: Merchandising, Transportation, Import & Export, Timicom Telecommunications Limited
Address: A2, Billingsway, Oregun Ind. Estate, Ikeja, Lagos

Tel: (01) 4932985, 4933241, 7743555 **Fax:** (01) 4933241
E-mail: dain@siotel.com
Website: www.timicom.com.ng
Contact: Mr. Deji Doherty - Group Chairman/CEO.

DOKU & SONS ENTERPRISES NIGERIA LIMITED
Business: Clearing and Forwarding Agency, Transport Services, General Contractors
Address: 6, Oniru Street, Apapa, Lagos
Tel: (01) 5452675, 5877491, 5872466 **Fax:** (01) 5872466
Contact: Mr. Godfrey I. Bobmanuel - Chairman/CEO.

DOLBIC FINANCE LIMITED
Business: Loans & Advances, L.P.O. & Project Financing
Address: Crankshaft House (2nd Floor), 4, Limca Road, Nkpor, Onitsha
Tel: (046) 485176
Contact: Dr. Ikechukwu E. Ugwu - GM/CEO

DOLLY BUSINESS MACHINES LIMITED
Business: Sales of Office Automation Products
Address: Eleganza Plaza (Aries Block, Ground Floor), Apapa, Lagos
Tel: (01) 4703741, 5871470-1 (2 L)

DOLMECH ENGINEERING NIGERIA LIMITED
Business: Mechanical, Airconditioning, Ventilation Engineering Services, Fabrication Engineering Services, Processing and Marketing of Timber Logs
Address: 228A, Murtala Mohammed Way, Yaba, Lagos
Tel: (01) 861590, 862099, 08023263587
Contact: Mr. L. A. Mukoro - Chairman/CEO.

DOLPHIN OTIS INVESTMENTS LIMITED
Business: Sales & Service of Computers & Office Equipment
Address: 8, Sawyer St, off Bamgbose Street, Tinubu, Lagos
Tel: (01) 2601595, 2645533, 4708645, 5556162, 08033226275 **Fax:** (01) 2601595
Contact: Mr. Adolphus Otigba - MD/CEO

DOLPHIN STUDIOS
Business: Computer Graphic and Printing, Post-Production Editing, Equipment Rental, Industrial Photography, Audio Recording
Address: 29, Itire Road, Surulere, Lagos
Tel: (01) 5850605, 08033277235, 08033328388
Fax: (01) 833537
Contact: Chief Emeka Ogoh - MD/CEO

DOLPHINE FISHERIES LIMITED
Business: Deep-Sea Fishing and Shrimping
Address: 11, Barth Road, G.R.A. Sokoto.
* D.T.V. Jetty, Ibafon, Oshodi-Apapa Expressway, Tin-Can Island, Apapa, Lagos
Tel: (01) 5450085, 5877296, 7752239, 7752241
Fax: (01) 5877296
Contact: Alh. Abubakar Koko - Chairman
Mr. Yuan Xiao Guang - MD

DOMART GROUP OF COMPANIES LIMITED
Business: Real Estate Development, Petroleum Marketing & Haulage Services, Printing and Manufacturing
Address: 5, Funsho Martins St,Parkview Estate, Ikoyi, Lagos
Tel: (01) 7732405, 680053, 2672009 **Fax:** (01) 2672009
E-mail: info@goldenparkestate.com
Website: www.goldenparkestate.com
Contact: Air Vice Marshal O. G. Martins (rtd) - Pres/CEO

DOMAX INTERNATIONAL LIMITED
Business: Electrical Distribuition & Control Engineers, Contractors and Equipment Stockists, Manfacturing of Electrical Panels.
Address: 84/86, Ladipo Street, Matori, Mushin, Lagos
Tel: (01) 4520153, 7745313, 8128150, 08023144090, 08033002543, 08033091999, 08033722174
Fax: (01) 4520153
E-mail: domax@infoweb.abs.net
Website: www.domaxinternational.com
Contact: Mr E. I. Ezeoke - Director/CEO

DOMINE WATERDRILL ENGINEERING & GEOTECH SERVICES LIMITED
Business: Drilling of Boreholes, Sales of Generators
Address: 3, Shehu Laminu Way, by JAMB Office, Maiduguri
Tel: (076) 235339 **Fax:** (076) 235394
Contact: Abubakar Alkali - Chairman/CEO

DOMINION TRUST LIMITED
Business: Finance and Investment
Address: Great Nigeria House (11th Floor), 47/57, Martins Street, Lagos
Tel: (01) 2669185, 2668372, 2644630, 2642458, 4707250
Fax: (01) 2668898
E-mail: dominion@alpha.linkserve.com
Contact: Princess Adenike A. Adeniran - Chairman/CEO

DOMINIUM BUILDING SOCIETY LIMITED
Business: Mortage Banking and Financial Services
Address: 58, Norman Williams Street, S. W. Ikoyi, Lagos
Tel: (01) 2695013, 2690651, 2671610-1 (2L), 2673408, 2673406, 2693388 **Fax:** (01) 2695013
E-mail: dominium@linkserve.com
Contact: Dr. John C. Nnadi - Chairman/CEO

DOMINO DEVELOPMENT LIMITED.
Business: General Merchandising
Address: Yada Giwa Road, Gadata-Zang Road, Gadata Industrial Layout, Waje District, Kano
Tel: (064) 630791 **Fax:** (064) 632891
Contact: Mr George Akle - MD/CEO

DOMINO STORES LIMITED
Business: Supermarkets, Wholesales Distribution of Groceries, Property Development, Fast Foods
Address: 13, Commercial Avenue, Yaba, Lagos
Tel: (01) 4739947 **Fax:** (01) 3425277
* 1, Harbour Road, Apapa, Lagos
Contact: Mr. Michael L. Murray-Bruce - Chairman/CEO

DON LANFORD & COMPANY LIMITED
Business: Sales of Security-Identification Systems and Staff Attendance Systems
Address: 7A, Herbert Macaulay Crescent, Lagos
Tel: (01) 4971866, 8043626
E-mail: donlangfor@infoweb.abs.net
Contact: Chief Joju Fadiaro - Chairman

DONGFENG INVESTMENT (NIGERIA) LIMITED
Business: Sales of Automatic Liquid-Filling Machinery, Manufacture of Plastic Moulds
Address: Plot 2, Lateef Jakande Road, off Wempco Road, Agidingbi, Ikeja, Lagos
Tel: (01) 7763608, 4728933, 5557332, 08033776823
Fax: (01) 5557801, 5557332
Contact: Mr. Peng Xi Guang - MD/CEO

DON-CHARLES (NIGERIA) LIMITED
Business: Secrurity Services and Systems
Address: 152, Obafemi Awolowo Way, Ikeja, Lagos
Tel: (01) 4970472, 7740828
Contact: Mr. Don Ikemefuna - MD/CEO

DONE MOTORS & AUTO SERVICES NIGERIA LIMITED
Business: Sales of Automobiles
Address: 37, Opebi Road, Ikeja, Lagos
Tel: (01) 4933651, 4933652
* Km 16, Enugu-Abakaliki Expressway, Emene, Enugu. **Tel:** (042) 556667-8 (2L)
Contact: Chief Dan Ekwevi - Chairman/CEO

DONMARINE AND TRADING LIMITED.
Business: Ship Managers and Owners' Representatives, Clearing and Forwarding, Supply of Boats, and Tug Boats, Warehousing, Procurement, Marine Consultancy, Supply of Petroleum Products, Trading, Documentation
Address: Block A, Plot 4, Apapa-Oshodi Expressway, by Daewoo Autoland, Amuwo-Odofin, Lagos
Tel: (090) 406339
E-mail: donmarine@hotmail.com

DONNATEC ENGINEERING COMPANY LIMITED
Business: Engineering and Technical Services, Sales of Technical Equipment, Pumping Machines, Electric Products and Generators
Address: 108, Herbert Macaulay Street, Ebute-Metta, Lagos
Tel: (01) 8042856, 7758429, 08033860991
Fax: (01) 8047913
Contact: Sir Jonathan O. Shodimu - Chairman

DOR-E ENGINEERING COMPANY LIMITED
Business: Borehole & Water Engineering, Irrigation Engineering, Construction of Dams
Address: Plot 8, Block M, Abimbola Street, Isolo Industrial Estate, Isolo, Lagos
Tel: (01) 452549, 4527416, 4707525
Contact: Mr. Alony Moshe - MD/CEO
Engr. Shalom Freiberg - Exec. Director

DORCHESTER PROPERTY MANAGEMENT & LEASING COMPANY LIMITED
Business: Leasing & Management of Serviced Properties, Real Estate Agency
Address: 3, Norman Williams Street, S. W. Ikoyi, Lagos
Tel: (01) 2671369, 2671370, 2694588, 08033275525, 23349707, 33216844, 23349737
E-mail: dpmalcltd@hotmail.com
dpmalcltd@yahoo.co.uk
Contact: Mr. Babatunde Shonekan - MD/CEO

DORI CONSTRUCTION & ENGINEEERING (NIGERIA) LTD
Business: Road & Building Construction, Civil & Mechanical Engineering Services
Address: Plot 897B, Balarabe Musa Cresc, V/Island, Lagos
Tel: (01) 2615932, 4618661, 2620909 **Fax:** (01) 4618981
* Port Harcourt **Tel:** (084) 613125
E-mail: doring@vgccl.net
Contact: Col. Lawan Gwadabe (rtd.) - Chairman
Mr. Chaim Zach - MD/CEO

DORMAN LONG & AMALGAMATED ENGINEERING LTD
Business: Civil/Structural Steel Engineering, Steel Works, Storage Tanks, Pressure Vessels and Process Equipment for the Oil and Gas Industries, Conventional Process Industries, Cement Plants and Agro-Allied Industries, Turnkey Projects
Address: 12/14, Agege Motor Road, Idi-Oro, Mushin, Lagos
Tel: (01) 4529029, 45290277, 7748357 **Fax:** (01) 4529027
E-mail: dlae@hyperia.com
Website: www.dormanlongeng.com
* UTC Plc Compound, 16, Azikiwe Road, Port Harcourt.
Tel: (084) 233707 **Fax:** (084) 233704
* UTC Plcs Compound 27, Sapele Road, Warri
Tel: (053) 252088
Contact: Air Vice-Marshal Usman Mu'azu (rtd) - Chairman
Mr. G. F. E. Ravelli - MD/CEO

DORNIER AVIATION NIGERIA AIEP LIMITED
Business: General Aviation Services, Aircraft Componenet Maintenance Aircraft Production
Address: General Aviation Service Centre, Old Kaduna Airport, Kawo Kaduna
Tel: (062) 236676, 233391, 238843, 238844
Fax: (062) 237325
E-mail: danaing@aol.com
* 15, Lusaka Street, Wuse Zone 6, Abuja
Tel: (09) 5232955
* Dornier Aviation, New Exit Road, Gen. Aviation Terminal, Murtala Muhammed Airport, Ikeja, Lagos
Tel: (01) 4966252, 4978752 (3 L), 4978750
Contact: Mr. Klauls Gloege - MD/CEO
Mall. Bashir Chedi - PR Manager

DOSU FATOKUN & COMPANY
Business: Estate Surveyors and Valuers, Property and Asset Valuation, Estate Agency, Property Management and Development, Project Consultancy
Address: 3, Club Arcade Annexe, Tafawa Balewa Square Complex, Lagos
Tel: (01) 2630782, 2637081 **Fax:** (01) 2630782
E-mail: dosufatokun@hyperia.com
Website: www.nigeriacommerc.com/fatokun.htm
Contact: Chief (Hon.) T. O. Fatokun - Managing Partner

DOUBLE ZERO CHINESE RESTAURANT LIMITED
Business: Restaurant, Outdoor Catering Services
Address: Excelsior Hotel (Ground Floor), 3-15, Ede Street, Apapa, Lagos
Tel: (01) 5455503 **Tel/Fax:** (01) 5875137, 5455599
E-mail: ewong@nova.net.ng
Contact: Mr. Edward Wong - MD/CEO

DOULATRAM'S (NIGERIA) LIMITED
Business: Distributive Trading, Manufacture of Textiles and Plastics
Address: 9, Olorogun Street, Idumagbo, Lagos
Tel: (01) 2661662, 2665759, 2662267, 2666840, 2666528, 2641436, 2641440 **Fax:** (01) 2668051
E-mail: dnl@linkserve.com.ng

DOUMICOM INTERNATIONAL LIMITED
Business: Civil Engineering Contractors
Address: Play 99, Rivoc Road, Trans-Amadi Industrial Layout, Port Harcourt
Tel: (080) 37254098

DOWELL (NIGERIA) LIMITED
Business: Oilfield Engineering Service
Address: Plot 161, Trans-Amadi Industrial Layout, Port Harcourt
Tel: (084) 237952, 237951, 237879
Website: www.porthacourt.dowell.slb.com
* NPA Compound, Warri.
Tel: (053) 232127

DOYIN INDUSTRIES LIMITED
Business: Manufacturing of Toothpaste, Petroleum Jelly, Medicaments and Cosmetics
Address: 4, Commercial Road, Apapa, Lagos
Tel: (01) 5452050-2 (3 L) **Fax:** (01) 5452054, 5878480
E-mail: info@doyin.net
doyin@hyperia.com
Website: www.doyin.net
* Plot 9, Block C, Amuwo-Odofin Ind. Scheme, off Lagos-Badagry Expressway, Coker, Lagos
*Loma-Mansa St, near NEPA, Wuse Zone 4, Abuja
Tel: (09) 4131141
* Wateco Building, SW7/43, Oke-Bola, Ibadan
Tel: (02) 2310485
* 25A, New Bridge Road, beside Ugo Foam, North Bank, Makurdi
Contact: Prince (Dr.) S. Adedoyin - Chairman/CEO

DOYIN PHARMACEUTICALS (NIGERIA) LIMITED
Business: Manufacturing of Pharmaceutical Products
Address: 4, Commercial Road, Apapa, Lagos
Tel: (01) 5451719, 5452050-2 (3 L), 5451718
Fax: (01) 5452054, 5878480, 2664781
* Km. 2, Lagos-Badagry Expressway, Opp. Alaba-Suru Market, Lagos
Tel: (01) 837534, 4701400
Contact: Prince (Dr.) Samuel Adedoyin - Chairman/CEO

DOZZY OIL AND GAS LIMITED
Business: Blending and Marketing of Lubricants, Re-Filling of Gas Cylinders, Marketing of Petroleum Fuels
Address: Plot 10/12, Niger Bridgehead Ind. Layout, Onitsha
Tel: (046) 414396, 218007, 218008 **Fax:** (090) 502062
* 3, Orofin Street, Maza-Maza Bus-Stop, Badagry Expressway, Amuwo, Lagos.
Tel: (01) 5892295
* 16C, Court/Middle Road, Sabon-Gari, Kano
* 37, Trans-Amadi Industrial Layout, Rumuobiakani, Port Harcourt
Contact: Chief (Dr.) D. N. Chukwudozie -Chairman/CEO

DR ABIMBOLA AWOLIYI MEMORIAL HOSPITAL CONSULTANTS LIMITED.
Business: Healthcare Delivery Services, Importation of Medical Equipment, Manufacture of Pharmaceuticals Products, Organisation of Medical Workshops
Address: 183, Bamgbose Street, Marina, Lagos
Tel: (01) 2630915, 2630916, 2631520
Contact: Dr. E. A. O. Bucknor - Chairman

DRAGETANOS CONSTRUCTION (NIGERIA) LIMITED
Business: Construction and Civil Engineering
Address: 19A, Idejo Street, Victoria Island, Lagos
Tel: (01) 618614, 2880798, 2620358-9 (2 L)
Fax: (01) 2620508
E-mail: dcnl@hyperia.com
* 8, Adetokunbo Ademola Crescent, Plot 861, Cadastral Zone A8, Wuse II, Garki Abuja
Tel: (09) 5235624-7 (4 L) **Fax:** (09) 5235625

DRAKE & SCULL (NIGERIA) LIMITED
Business: Airconditioning, Electrical/Mechanical Engineering
Address: 12, Ali Akilu Road, Kaduna
Tel: (062) 241412, 242620 **Fax:** (062) 241412
E-mail: drake@skannet.com
* 2, Olufunmilola Okikiola Street, off Toyin Street, Ikeja, Lagos
Tel/Fax: (01) 4971178
E-mail: dsnlagos@yahoo.com
Contact: Engr O. B. Lasisi - MD/CEO

DREDGING INTERNATIONAL SERVICES NIGERIA LIMITED
Business: Oilfield Engineering Services, Dredging and Land Reclamation
Address: 35A, Kingsway Road, Ikoyi, Lagos
Tel: (01) 2636486, 2633643

DREK COMPANY LIMITED
Business: Electrical/Mechanical Engineering, Fire Protection Services, Installation of Access Control Equipment
Address: 29, Association Avenue, Ilupeju, Lagos
Tel/Fax: (01) 4962790
E-mail: firemuse@infoweb.abs.net
Contact: Engr David A Nwamara - Chairman/CEO

DRESSER-RAND NIGERIA LIMITED
Business: Oilfield Engineering Services
Address: 2, Reclamation Road, Port Harcout
Tel: (084) 333145, 332200

DRILLOG PETRO-DYNAMICS LIMITED
Business: Oilfield Engineering Services (Directional Drilling, Measurement-while-Drilling, Borehole Surveys)
Address: Plot C, Trans-Amadi Ind. Layout, Port Harcourt
Tel: (084) 237237, 237195, 237186, 233719, 237190
Fax: (084) 232350
E-mail: drillpet@ph.rcl.nig.com
Contact: (Ugo) O. R. Ekezie - MD/CEO

DROCHESSY LIMITED
Business: Distribution and Marketing of Chain Saws
Address: 97, Port Harcourt Road, Fegge, Onitsha
Tel: (046) 218047, 214792 **Fax:** (064) 218047
* 40, Oyadiran Estate, Sabo-Yaba, Lagos

DRUG AND HEALTHCARE LIMITED.
Business: Importation and Supply of Industrial (Chemicals) Raw Materials, Laboratory Reagents, Laboratory Equipment and Pharmaceuticals
Address: 60, M.M. International Airport Rd, Oshodi, Lagos
Tel/Fax: (01) 4936756, 7914531, 08033005181
E-mail: drughealthcare@hotmail.com
Contact: Mr. U. U. Chijoke - Chairman/CEO

DRUGFIELD PHARMACEUTICALS LIMITED
Business: Manufacturing of Pharmaceutical Products
Address: Lynson Chemical Avenue, Km. 38, Lagos-Abeokuta Expresway, Sango-Otta, Ogun State
Tel: (039) 720602, 721236-7 (2L)

DRURY INDUSTRIES LIMITED
Business: Manufacturing of Aluminium Sulphate, Sulphuric Acid and Fertilizers
Address: Plot 1405, Adetokunbo Ademola Street, V/I, Lagos
Tel: (01) 2615048, 2613518 **Fax:** (01) 2618340
* Plots 9 & 18, OPIC Industrial Estate, Agbara
Contact: Mr. Suresh Jobanputra - MD/CEO

DSC PUBLICATIONS LIMITED
Business: Publishing of Law Books and Reports
Address: 203, Ikorodu Road (Obanikoro Bus-Stop), Lagos
Tel: (01) 4976695 **Fax:** (01) 616172
E-mail: dsc@nova.net.ng
Contact: Mr. Ayodeji Sasegbo - Chairman/CEO

DSV PIPETRONIX LIMITED
Business: Oilfield Engineering, Supply of Oilfield Equipment
Address: Plot 144B, Olabode George Street, Victoria Island Annex, Lagos
Tel: (01) 2611247, 2626227, 2626228

DTD SERVICES NIGERIA LIMITED
Business: Provision of Logistics and Support Services to Foreign Investors
Address: Yinka Folawiyo Plaza (3rd Floor), 38, Warehouse Road, Apapa, Lagos
Tel: (01) 5450283, 5878208, 5453384

DTT SERVICES LIMITED
Business: Company Secretarial Services
Address: 1, Town Planning Way, Ilupeju, Lagos
Tel: (01) 4930720, 4931471 **Fax:** (01) 4970023

DUBI (NIGERIA) COMPANY LIMITED
Business: Oilfield Engineering Services
Address: Km. 16, P. Harcourt/Aba Expressway, Port Harcourt
Tel/Fax: (084) 612525, 612594
E-mail: dubi@phca.linkserve.com
* Camp 22, Kpohraror Estate, 75, Airport Rd, Warri
* 11, Eleruwa Street, Wemabod Estate, Ikeja, Lagos
Contact: Mr. Ifeanyi Ogbechie - Chairman/CEO

DUBRI OIL COMPANY LIMITED
Business: Exploration and Production of Crude Oil and Gas
Address: 13A, A. J. Marinho Drive, off Ajose Adeogun Street, Victoria Island Annex, Lagos
Tel: (01) 2625220 **Fax:** (01) 7740458
Contact: Dr. U. J. Itsueli - Chairman/CEO

DUCAT LIMITED (formerly Fujikura Nig. Ltd)
Business: Telecommunication Engineering, Sales, Installation and Maintenance of Telecoms Equipment
Address: Plot 8, Block G, Ladipo St, Matori, Mushin, Lagos
Tel: (01) 525249 **Fax:** (01) 525257
Contact: Mr. J. O. Omosun - GM/CEO

DUEMAN CHEMICALS LIMITED
Business: Manufacturing of Colourants
Address: Km. 5, Nkpor-Umuoji Road, Umuoji, Anambra State
Tel: (046) 412702, 412134, 08033255502
E-mail: avemaria@metrong.com
Contact: Chief E. N. Orakwue - Chairman

DuMEC INTERNATIONAL MARKETING COMPANY LTD
Business: Marketing of Herbal Products and Nutraceuticals
Address: 63, Allen Avenue, Ikeja, Lagos
Tel: (01) 4934342, 4934375, 7911354 **Fax:** (01) 4934375
Contact: Mr. Daniel Umeakunne - MD/CEO

DUMEZ (NIGERIA) PLC
Business: Building and Civil Engineering Contractors
Address: Dumez House, 7/11, Sir Mobolaji Bank Anthony Street, (Formerly Oil Mill Street), Lagos
Tel: (01) 2600450- (4 L), 263430 **Fax:** (01) 263390
Contact: Engr. Andre Kamel - MD/CEO

DUMSON NIGERIA LIMITED
Business: Water Boreholes, Pumps, Treatment Plants, Storage Tanks and Distribution Network.
Address: 13, Osolo Way, off M.M. International Airport Road, Ajao Estate, Apakun-Oshodi, Lagos
Tel: (01) 7742429, 4521393 **Fax:** (01) 4521393
E-mail: dumsoltd@yahoo.com
Contact: Mr. Mba Onwuka - MD/CEO

DUNCAN MARITIME NIGERIA LIMITED
Business: Freight Consolidators, Bonded Container Warehouse, Clearing, Forwarding, Groupage, General Cargo Procurement, Documentationa and Haulage
Address: 41, Adeniyi Jones Crescent, off Oba Akran Road, Ikeja, Lagos
Tel: (01) 4936961, 4974697 **Fax:** (01) 4936961
* Duncan Bond Terminal, Block A, Plot 4, Amuwo-Odofin Ind. Estate, Oshodi Expressway, Lagos.
Tel: (01) 5456151-2(2L)
* Wuse Shopping Complex (Suite 14C), Wuse Zone 3, Abuja. **Tel:** (09) 5236236
* 1A, Airport Road, Kano. **Tel:** (064) 626704
E-mail: duncan@alpha.linkserve.com,
Website: www.duncaninternational.com
Contact: Mr. Godfrey Shitgurum - Chairman/CEO

DUNLOP NIGERIA PLC
Business: Manufacture and Sales of Vechicle Tyres and Tubes, Floor Tiles, Carpets, Adhesive and Industrial Rubber Components
Address: Plot 23, Oba Akran Avenue, Ikeja, Lagos
Tel: (01) 4978910-19 (10L), 4962666-7 (2 L)
Fax: (01) 4964734, 2622063
E-mail: info@!dunlopng.com
Website: www.dunlopng.com
Contact: Mr. Jabez Dayo Lawuyi - Group MD/CEO

DUPRE INTERNATIONAL NIGERIA LIMITED
Business: Supply and Maintenance/Repairs of Valves, Line Pipe and Fittings, Oilfield Engineering Services
Address: Plot 47, Trans-Amadi Ind. Layout, Port Harcourt
Tel/Fax: (084) 234845
E-mail: portdin@hyperia.com
Website: www.cap-resources.com
Contact: Mr. Stanley Ukaga - Chairman/MD

DURACLEAN CHEMICALS & ALLIED PRODUCTS LIMITED
Business: Production of Paints, Wood Printers and Chemicals
Address: 5, Vori Close, off Acme Road, Ogba Industrial Estate, Ikeja, Lagos
Tel: (01) 4960854, 4964666, 4974777, 4976293, 4702555
Fax: (01) 4974777
E- mail: duraclean@micro.com.ng
duraclean@linkserve.com
Contact: Chief F. M. Emeya - Chairman/CEO

DURACLEAN SERVICES (NIGERIA) LIMITED
Business: General Cleaning Services, Pest Control and Fumigation, Refuse Collection, Landscaping, Paints Manufacturing
Address: 15, Atinuke Olabanji St off Unity Rd, Ikeja, Lagos
Tel: (01) 4974777, 4964666, 4960854 **Fax:** (01) 4976293
E-mail: duraclean@micro.com.ng
* 9, Gnassingbe Eyadema Street, Asokoro, Abuja
Tel: (09) 5230747, 3140973, 3147107
Contact: Chief F. M. Emeya - Chairman/CEO

DURACLEAN SPECIALISTS NIGERIA LIMITED
Business: Office and Industrial Cleaning Services, Pest Control, Cleaning Management Consultancy
Address: 45, J.D. Gomwalk Rd, opp PRTV Admin. Office, Jos
Tel: (073) 455814, 455107 **Fax:** (073) 455107
* Wuse Zone 3 Shopping Complex (Suite E39), Garki, Abuja
E-mail: duracleanspecialists@yahoo.com
Contact: AbdulAziz Badamasi - MD/CEO

DURAPLAST NIGERIA INDUSTRIES LIMITED
Business: Manufacture of UPVC Pressure Pipes, Sewer Pipes, Fittings Crates, Pipe-Laying Services & Fabrication
Address: Plot 47, Oregun Industrial Estate, Ikeja, Lagos
Tel: (01) 4963915 **Fax:** (01) 2880455
Contact: Chief T. A. Balogun - Chairman/CEO

DURO SOLEYE HOSPITALS
Business: Medical Services, Occupationals Health Therapy, Dental and Optical Services
Address: 34, Allen Avenue, Ikeja, Lagos
Tel: (01) 4960410, 4970808, 4961849 **Fax:** (01) 4961849
E-mail: dsh@linkserve.com
* Health-Aid Ltd., 23, Allen Avenue, Ikeja, Lagos
Tel/Fax: (01) 4961849
Contact: Chief J. D. Soleye - Chairman

DUSTMEN CLEANING SERVICES LIMITED
Business: Pest Control and Contract Cleaning Service
Address: 99, Clegg Street, Western Avenue, Surulere, Lagos
Tel: (01) 5842216, 830488 **Fax:** (01) 5842216
E-mail: safetech@infoweb.abs.net
Contact: Mr. Gabe N. Ginigeme -Chairman/CEO

DUTEE INSURANCE BROKERS LIMITED
Business: Insurance and Re-insurance Broking, Life and Pension Consultancy
Address: 7, Unity Road, Ikeja, Lagos
Tel: (01) 4975729 **Fax:** (01) 4966716
E-mail: dutee@wannanet.net
Contact: Chief S. O. Akinwale - Chairman

DUTSI LABORATORY ENGINEERING LIMITED
Business: Design, Sales, Installation and Maintenance of Laboratory Furniture, Scientific Equipment and Kitchen Furniture/Fittings
Address: 8/10, Oweh Street, off Ikorodu Road, Fadeyi, Lagos
Tel: (01) 862001, 864834, 866393, 7742568
Fax: (01) 862001
E-mail: dutsilab@yahoo.com
Contact: Mr Segun Balogun - Chairman/CEO

DVC LIMITED
Business: Automotive Chemicals, Autocare Products and Fluids Marketers
Address: 7/9, Ayanlu St, off Ire-Akari Estate Rd, Isolo, Lagos
Tel: (01) 4523189, 4523709, 4529329, 4733350, 5556368
Fax: (01) 4523189, 4523709
E-mail: dvcltd@alpha.linkserve.com
Contact: Chief (Dr.) D. V. C. Obi - Chairman/CEO

DYECHEM NIGERIA LIMITED
Business: Sales of Industrial Chemicals and Dyestuffs
Address: 5, Ade Ojo Street, Wemabod Estate, off Adeniyi Jones Avenue, Ikeja, Lagos
Tel: (01) 4973877, 7781515, 7752990 **Fax:** (01) 4960951
* Plot 1, 2 and 4, Block 10, Ota Industrial Estate, Ota, Ogun State
Tel: (039) 720450, (01) 7744070 **Fax:** (039) 722492
E-mail: dyechem@linkserve.com.ng
dyechem@hotmail.com
Conact: Gope Bakshani - Chairman

DYKES INSURANCE BROKERS LIMITED
Business: Insurance Broking
Address: 29, Olonode Street, Alagomeji, Yaba, Lagos
Tel: (01) 4734278, 4803871, 7731341, 860567
E-mail: dib@hyperia.net
* Point Block (6th Floor), Rivers State Secretariat Complex, Port Harcourt.
Tel: (084) 239603, 08033012043
Contact: H.R.M. King Alfred P. Diete-Spiff -Chairman
Mr. E. S. Tekenah - MD/CEO

DYNAMIC INDUSTRIES LIMITED
Business: Manufacture of Polythene Bags & Plastic Products
Address: Aswani Textile Premises, Oshodi-Apapa Expressway, Isolo, Lagos
Tel: (01) 7751860, 7763773, 4521190, 4521192

DYNAMIC PORTFOLIO LIMITED
Business: Stockbroking, Investment Advisors; Portfolio, Leasing and Fund Managers, Issuing House
Address: Dynamic House (Ground Floor), 20, Campbell Street, Lagos Island, Lagos
Tel: (01) 2669386
Contact: Chief Anoli Guobadia - Chairman

DYNAMIC PHARMACEUTICALS NIGERIA LIMITED
Business: Importation of Pharmaceuticals & Related Products
Address: 221, Apapa Road, Iganmu, Lagos
Tel: (01) 5801010-4 (5 L) **Fax:** (01) 5832123
E-mail: mega@linkserve.com.ng
Contact: Mr. Vijay Naidu - MD/CEO

DYS TROCCA VALSESIA & COMPANY LIMITED (DTV & CO LTD)
Business: Building and Civil Engineering Contractors
Address: Oshodi-Apapa, Expressway, Ibafon, Kirikiri, Lagos
Tel: (01) 5876891, 5872174, 7732198 **Fax:** (01) 5870886
Contact: Mrs. D. A. Alakija - Chairman
Dott. V. Marvelli - MD/CEO

E & J INTERNATIONAL LIMITED
Business: Marketing of Medical, Laboratory & Scientific Equipment, Medical Advisory Services
Address: 112, Obafemi Awolowo Way (Suite 6), Ikeja, Lagos
Tel: (01) 4977207, 4931485, 4819094, 08023225021-2 (2 L) 08033014224-7 (4 L),
E-mail: ejintern@infoweb.abs.net
info@e&jinternationalltd.com
Website: www.e&jinternationalltd.com
* Grajam House, 92/94, East-West Road, Rumuodara, Port Harcourt
Tel: (084) 578261
Contact: Mr. John C. Ogenyi - Chairman

E. CLEMFAN (WEST AFRICA) COMPANY LIMITED
Business: Distribution and Sales of Airconditioners
Address: Jawa House, 6/7, Abimbola Street, Isolo Industrial Estate, Isolo, Lagos
Tel: (01) 7749658 **Fax:** (01) 4520498
E-mail: act@micro.com.ng
* 1, A.C.T. Street, Km 16, Aba Road, Port Harcourt
Tel: (084) 613366-7 (2L) **Fax:** (084) 613357

E. D. & F. MAN (NIGERIA) LIMITED
Business: Importation of Sugar and Ric, Exportation of Ginger, Cocoa and Cocoa Products
Address: 5/7, Kopek Road, off Fatai Atere Way, Matori Industrial Estate, Mushin, Lagos
Tel: (01) 7744741-2 (2 L), 7748057-8 (2 L), 7745160
Fax: (01) 7744743
Contact: Mr. Richard Morgan - MD/CEO

E. DUMS MERCHANDISE COMPANY LIMITED
Business: Marketing of Fans and Electrical Appliances
Address: Oceanic Bank Building (3rd Floor), 55, Idumagbo Avenue, Idumota, Lagos
Tel: (01) 2664842, 2632649, 2642894 **Fax:** (01) 2667327
E-mail: edums@infoweb.abs.net

E. EKESONS BROTHERS NIGERIA LIMITED
Business: Transportation, Motorcycle Distribution and Sales
Address: 31, Ikorodu Road, Jibowu, Yaba, Lagos
Tel: (01) 861120, 5874153
Contact: Chief E. N. Ojukwu - Chairman/CEO.

E. A. ABIMBOLA & COMPANY LIMITED
Business: Manufacturers of Disposable Cups and Plates, Conduit Pipes, Ebonite Strips and Junction Bowls, Take-Away Boxes and Aluminium Profile Gasket
Address: Plot 13, Block D, Fatai Atere Way, Matori Estate, Mushin, Lagos
Tel: (01) 524869, 524865, 4524018, 4524230, 08023417295, 08033200945, 08033200955
Fax: (01) 4524018, 4524230
Contact: Chief E. A. Abimbola - Chairman/CEO.

E. B. M. SYSTEMS NIGERIA LIMITED
Business: Fabrication of Aluminium Structures, Doors, Windows and Partitions
Address: 1, Pacific Close, off Oregun Road, Olushosun Village, Ikeja, Lagos
Tel: (01) 4974328, 4935510, 4721398, 08033002286
Fax: (01) 4977511
Contact: Mr. David Atias - Director

EAGLE ALUMINIUM INDUSTRIES LIMITED
Business: Manufacture & Installation of Longspan Aluminium Roofing Profiles
Address: Plot 30, Idu Industrial Area, Idu, Abuja
Tel: (09) 6700738, 5230834-6 (3 L), 08033289410, 08033737099
Contact: Prince Linus Ukachukwu - Chairman
C. E. Ogbonnaya - GM

EAGLE BANK LIMITED
Business: Commercial Banking
Address: 22, Akin Adesola Street, Victoria Island, Lagos
Tel: (01) 2623071, 2623073-5 (3 L), 615484
Fax: (01) 2623072
E-mail: eaglebank@hyperia.com
Contact: Mr Abdulkadir Idris - MD/CEO

EAGLE CONSTRUCTION LIMITED
Business: Building & Civil Engineering Contractors
Address: 20B, Wase Road, Jos
Tel/Fax: (073) 464119, 465565
* Plot 1179, Cadastral Zone B6, Mabushi, off Nnamdi Azikiwe Expressway, Wuse II, Abuja
Tel: (09) 5234199, 5238946 **Fax:** (09) 5232002.
E-mail: ecl@tiscali.it
Contact: Alh. Mahdi Mohammed Abubakar - Chairman
Mr. G. Micheletti - MD/CEO.

EAGLE PACKAGE PRINTING LIMITED
Business: Manufacturer of Printed Light Packaging Cartons, Labels, Wrappers, Films, Laminates & Shopping Bags
Address: Plot 9/10, Block VI, Industrial Estate, off Idiroko Rad, Otta, Ogun State
Tel: (039) 722294-6 (3L) **Fax:** (039) 722297
E-mail: eaglepack@alpha.linkserve.com
* Oasis Headquarters, Km. 16, Ikorodu Road, opposite Ojota Motor Park, Lagos
Tel: (01) 4977535, 4977537 **Fax:** (01) 4977539
Contact: Chief O. Oriade - MD/CEO

EAGLE PAINTS NIGERIA LIMITED
Business: Manufacturing of Paints
Address: 5, Lateef Jakande, Road, Agidingbi, Ikeja, Lagos
Tel: (01) 4920559, 4920057, 4925200, 3453390, 7941327
E-mail: eaglepaint@supernet300.com
Contact: Mr. T. A. Disu - Chairman/CEO

EAGLE TRANSPORT COMPANY LIMITED
Business: Road Transport Service
Address: 44, Dawson Road, Benin City
Tel: (052) 254188
* Plot 696, Utako District, behind Arab Contractors, Abuja
* 15, Aba Road, Port Harcourt
* 72, Effurun/Sapele Road, Effurun, Delta State

EAS AIRLINES LIMITED (Executive Airline Services)
Business: Executive Aircraft Charter, Scheduled Domestic Passenger Operations, Aviation Consultants
Address: 29, Adeniyi Jones Avenue, Ikeja, Lagos
Tel: (01) 4937816, 4975016, 4975017, 4975019
Fax: (01) 4965736, 4975020
E-mail: easair@easng.com
* General Aviation Terminal, Murtala Mohammed Airport, Ikeja, Lagos
Tel: (01) 4931852, 4934150, 4937598, 08023123165
* Plot 2357, Douala Street, Wuse Zone 5, Abuja
Tel: (09) 5235656, 5239398
Contact: Capt. I. I. Wada - MD/CEO
Mrs Hannah Koloko - Marketing/PR Officer

EASITECH PROJECTS (NIGERIA) LIMITED
Business: Precision Engineering Works, Fabrication & Remoulding of Industrial Spare Parts
Address: 11, Abeokuta St, Anifowoshe Area, Ikeja, Lagos
Tel: (01) 4977121
Contact: Engr. E. C. Asiegbu - Chairman/CEO.

EAST WEST COAST MARINE SERVICES LIMITED
Business: Ship Managers, Ship Agents, Marine Consultants
Address: Maritime Complex, 34, Creek Road, Apapa, Lagos
Tel: (01) 7741106 **Fax:** (01) 5453731, 5870127
Contact: Capt. S. A. Omoteso - MD/CEO

EASTERN BULKCEM COMPANY LIMITED
Business: Production of Cement, Manufacturing of Cement Paper-Bags, Marine Services
Address: Rumuolumeni, Port Harcourt
Tel: (084) 239334, 231509, 236927, 2339190, 232322, 232923
Fax: (084) 239334
Website: www.eaglecement.com
Block 2 (Flat 5) 11, Awolowo Rd, S.W. Ikoyi, Lagos
Tel: (01) 2691114, 2694684 **Fax:** (01) 2691114
Contact: Captain (Dr.) I. A. Haastrup - Chairman
Mr. Vincent Nehikhare - MD/CEO

EASTERN DISTILLERIES & FOOD INDUSTRIES LIMITED
Business: Manufacturing & Distilling of Spirits and Wines
Address: Plot 9, Eziachi Street, by 4, Atani Road, Harbour Industrial Layout, Ogbaru, Onitsha
Tel: (046) 216978
E-mail: eastern@infoweb.abs.net
Contact: Chief Oranu C. Chidume - Chairman/CEO

EASTERN STAINLESS STEEL LIMITED (E S S LTD)
Business: Importation of Computers and Building Materials
Address: 3rd, Avenue, C Close, House 12, Festac Town, Lagos
Tel/Fax: (01) 4806818, 5890524
E-mail: essben@hotmail.com
Contact: Mr. Ben Atueyi - Chairman/CEO

EASTERN WROUGHT IRON LIMITED
Business: Manufacturing and Marketing of Wrought Iron Products (Storage Tanks, Hospital Equipment, School Furniture) and Foam Products
Address: Plot 47, Trans-Amadi Ind. Layout, Port Harcourt
Tel: (084) 231253, 234922 **Fax:** (084) 234922
E-mail: cbeke@skannet.com
Contact: Hon. Charles Beke - Chairman/CEO.

EASY EMPEROR AGENCIES LIMITED
Business: Clearing, Freight Forwarding and Customs Brokerage, Logistics
Address: 205, Ikorodu Road, Obanikoro, Lagos
Tel: (01) 8124253, 7741017 **Fax:** (01) 4968115
E-mail: easyemperor@linkserve.com
www.easyemperor.com
Contact: Mr. Isaac A. Odunewu - MD/CEO

EASY-LINK AVIATION LIMITED
Business: Domestic Airline Operations
Address: Enugu Airport, Enugu
Tel: (042) 552779

EAUXWELL NIGERIA LIMITED
Business: Waste & Waste-Water Engineers, Water Engineering Equipment, Pumps & Accessories Stockists
Address: Plot 123, Joel Ogunaike Street, Ikeja, Lagos
Tel/Fax: (01) 4976059
E-mail: eaux@hyperia.com
Contact: Engr. Edwin Enwegbara - MD/CEO

EBELOSE CHEMICALS LIMITED
Business: Sales of Industrial Chemicals and Paints
Address: 321, Port Harcourt/Aba Expressway, Port Harcourt,
Tel: (084) 612640, 612819, 610782 **Fax:** (084) 612819
E-mail: info@izziorganisation.com
Contact: Chief Omohuyi L. Izzi (JP) - Chairman/CEO

EBENEZER IKEYINA & PARTNERS
Business: Estate Surveyors and Valuers, Property and Assets Valuation; Feasibility/Viability Appraisals, Project Management, Building Refurbishment
Address: 13, Awoniyi Elemo Street, off Osolo Way, Ajao Estate, Isolo, Lagos
Tel: (01) 2901931, 08023137101, 08034752840
E-mail: ikeyina@yahoo.com
Contact: Senator Ebenezer C. Ikeyina - Snr Partner

EBICE HOSES LIMITED
Business: Sales & Repairs of Hoses and Fittings, Installation of Fluid Dynamic Systems, Consultancy Services
Address: 42, T.O.S. Benson (formerly Commercial) Avenue, Sabo-Yaba, Lagos
Tel: (01) 861145, 863570, 865811, 7743584
Fax: (01) 3425254
Contact: Sir E. C. Emechebe - Chairman

EBIMO NIGERIA LIMITED
Business: Building, Civil & Structural Engineering Contractors
Address: 15/17, Oromenike Street, D-Line, Port Harcourt
Tel: (084) 334280
* Biogbolo-Yenagoa, Bayelsa State
Contact: Mr. Mark Kuro Amakoromo - Chairman/CEO.

EBONY & COMPANY LIMITED
Business: Funeral Undertakers, Manufacture of Caskets and Furniture, General Contractor
Address: 7, Igbosere Road, Lagos
Tel: (01) 2646393, 2636242, 2632501, 2601076, 2601077, 08023428809, 08033070527, 08033219892, 08033353556, 08033545293 **Fax:** (01) 2636242
E-mail: ebony@nigerianet.com
Website: www.ebonylimited.com
Contact: Mr. Harrison Dehinde Omojuwa - Chairman/CEO.

EBONY PAINTS LIMITED
Business: Manufacturing of Paints and Allied Products
Address: 48, Zik Avenue, Uwani, Enugu
Tel: (042) 453406
* 52-60, Ebony Paints Road, Awkunanaw, Enugu
Tel: (042) 453406, 08033387072
Contact: Prince Uche Den Chukwu - Chairman/CEO

EBUN INDUSTRIES LIMITED
Business: Cocoa Processing, Cocoa-Related Consultancy
Address: 104, Obafemi Awolowo Way, Ikeja, Lagos
Tel: (01) 4936885, 4965863 **Fax:** (01) 4933806
E-mail: info@ebun.com
Website: www.ebun.com
* 113, Iju Road, Ifako-Agege, Lagos
Tel: (01) 4924092-3 (2 L), 4924624
Contact: Mr. Ayo Bakare - MD/CEO.

EBUNSO NIGERIA LIMITED
Business: Manufacturing, Sales & Service of Engineering Equipment
Address: Amiliba Road, Okofia, Otolo, Anambra State
Tel/Fax: (046) 460905
Contact: Engr. (Dr.) S. E. Chukwujekwu - Chairman/CEO.

EBUNY SHIPPING AGENICIES LIMITED
Business: Shipping, Cargo Clearing & Forwarding.
Address: 12, Oyewunmi Close, off Falolu St, Surulere, Lagos
Tel: (01) 5850014, 5850987, 2646748, 837040
Fax: (01) 2646066
E-mail: ebunyshipping@nova.net.ng
Contact: Mr. Ebuni Okocha - MD/CEO

ECAD DESIGN GROUP LIMITED
Business: Architectural Design & Planning
Address: 62, Awolowo Road (3rd Floor), S.W. Ikoyi, Lagos
Tel: (01) 2691519, 2672102, 2694201 **Fax:** (01) 2694201
E-mail: ecad@infoweb.abs.net
Contact: Mr. Ade Laoye - Chairman

ECAS TELECOMMUNICATIONS & SYSTEMS LIMITED
Business: Telecommunication Systems Engineeringt
Address: Plot 213B, Muri Okunola St, Victoria Island, lagos
Tel: (01) 4616960-2 (3 L) **Fax:** (01) 2703627
E-mail: ecas@21ctl.com
* Plot 522, Usuma St, off Gana St, Maitama, Abuja.
Tel: (09) 4132061 **Fax:** (09) 4132062
Contact: Mr. Izchak Weiss - MD/CEO

ECNEL LIMITED
Business: Commercial Printing, Surveying & Mapping, CAD Services Management
Address: 20, Bende Street, Rumuomasi, Port Harcourt
Tel: (084) 238367, 231687, 488022 **Fax:** (084) 231687
E-mail: info@iecnel.com
Website: www.ecnel.com
Contact: Mr Emmanuel Ezeano - MD/CEO

ECO-BUILDING SYSTEMS NIGERIA LIMITED
Business: Building Construction, Manufacturing of Panelised Homes and Buildings
Address: 10A, Anifowoshe Street, Victoria Island, Lagos
Tel: (01) 2623062, 2617144, 2618579, 4701754
Fax: (01) 2622254
E-mail: fymak@infoweb.abs.net
* Plot 1028, Ruvuma Street, off Yesderam Street, off IBB Way, Maitama, Abuja
Tel/Fax: (09) 4132326, 4137965
Contact: Mr. Maduka Nwakwesi - Chairman

ECO-CONSULT LIMITED
Business: Consultancy Services
Address: NCWS House (3rd Floor), Plot PC. 14, Ahmed Onibudo Street, Victoria Island, Lagos
Tel: (01) 2617215, 4618489 **Fax:** (01) 618146

ECO-PILLAR INSURANCE BROKERS LIMITED
Business: Insurance Broking, Life & Pensions Consultancy
Address: 3, Sylvia Crescent, off Anthony Road, off Ikorodu Road, Anthony Village, Lagos
Tel: (01) 4977059, 4979290
Contact: Mr. O. A. Onabolu - Chairman

ECOBANK NIGERIA LIMITED
Business: Commercial Banking
Address: 2, Adeogun Street, Victoria Island, Lagos
Tel: (01) 2612953-7 (5L), 2620910-4 (5L), 2626710-17 (8L), 2626638-44 (7L) **Fax:** (01) 2616568, 2620920
E-mail: ecobank@linkserve.com.ng
Contact: Mr. Disun Holloway - MD/CEO.
Dede Dori-Yebori - Head (Corporate Affairs Unit)

ECWA PRODUCTIONS LIMITED
Business: Printing Services
Address: 10, Kano Road, Jos
Tel: (073) 457624
E-mail: ecwa@alpha.linkserve.com
Contact: Mr. Daniel J. Anyip - GM

ECWA RURAL DEVELOPMENT LIMITED
Business: Production of Livestock Feeds, Livestock Farming, Manufacturing of Agricultural Implements
Address: Km. 2, Dan Mangu Road, off Yelwa Club Junction, Bukuru, Plateau State
Tel: (073) 280952, 280942, 281035 **Fax:** (073) 280952
Contact: Mr. Stephen Gado - MD/CEO

EDDY MOORE MARBLE & FURNISHING LIMITED
Business: Importation and Marketing of Marble & Granite, Furniture, Swimming Pools and Water Fountains
Address: 36, Aromire Avenue, by 50, Adeniyi Jones Avenue, Ikeja, Lagos
Tel: (01) 4975515, 0803029277 **Fax:** (01), 4939538
E-mail: eddymoore@infoweb.abs.net
Contact: Mr. Ini Umoren - Chairman/CEO

EDEGBE MOTORS COMPANY LIMITED
Business: Passenger Transportation Services
Address: 245, Ugbowo-Lagos Road, Ugbowo, Benin City
Tel: (052) 600189, 600318, 600411, 602055
Fax: (052) 600411
* Plot 325, Adeyemo Adakpa Street, Omole Phase 1, Ikeja, Lagos
Tel: (01) 7746007 (090) 403946
Contact: Chief Idahosa D. Edegbe - Chairman/CEO

EDEWOR INTERNATIONAL LIMITED
Business: Industrial Projects, Property Development, Mining
Address: Edewor Shopping Centre, Effurun, Warri
Tel: (053) 250054, 250622 **Fax:** (053) 250054
* Edewor White House, J21, Oduduwa Way, GRA, Ikeja, Lagos
Tel: (01) 4961811, 4961845, 4961850
Contact: Chief James O. Edewor - Chairman/CEO

EDIC CHEMICALS & ALLIED DISTRIBUTIONS LIMITED
Business: Importation, Distribution & Sales of Industrial Chemicals and Pharmaceutical Products
Address: 61, Coker Road, Ilupeju, Lagos
Tel: (01) 8043564, 4934827, 4821335, 08023103335
Fax: (01) 4934828
E-mail: edic@nova.net.ng
Contact: Mr Evans M. Okeke - GM

EDILCENTRE (NIGERIA) LIMITED
Business: Marketers of Building Equipment and Materials
Address: Oshodi-Apapa Expressway (Westminster Bus-Stop), Ibafon, Kirikiri, Lagos
Tel: (01) 5450670, 5450682 **Fax:** (01) 5450909
E-mail: edilcent@infoweb.abs.net

EDISON AUTO INDUSTRIES LIMITED
Business: Marketers of Building Equipment and Materials
Address: Plot 1, Umunne Ind Estate, Edoji, Uruagu, Nnewi
Tel: (046) 462298
Contact: Mr. Edwin Obichebendu - Chairman/CEO

EDNEL NIGERIA LIMITED
Business: Production & Sales of Corporate Gift Items
Address: 11, Ogui Road, Enugu
Tel/Fax: (042) 255115
Contact: Engr. Chuba Nwokoro - MD/CEO

EDO PHARMACEUTICALS COMPANYS LIMITED
Business: Manufacturing of Pharmaceutical Products
Address: 188, Sapele Road, P.M.B. 1130, Benin City
Tel: (052) 252902

EDO LINE TRANSPORT LIMITED
Business: Passenger Transportation , Courier Services
Address: 22, James Watt Road, Benin City
Tel: (052) 257454, 256185, 250942

EDO STATE INVESTMENT COMPANY LIMITED
Business: Investment Management & Financial Advisors, Commodity Trading, Management Consultancy Services, Project Financing, Loans & Equity Investment, Human Resources Development/ Training, Portfolio Management, Haulage Services
Address: 3rd Floor, NNB Building, Ring Road, Benin City
Tel (052) 250162
E-mail: ESinvest@edostateofnigeria.gov.ng
* Edo House, Plot 1225, Ahmadu Bello Way, Victoria Island, Lagos
Tel: (01) 2610984:
Contact: Mr. Edward Owie - MD/CEO

EDO TEXTILE MILLS LIMITED
Business: Manufacturing of Textile Products
Address: 100, Edo Textile Mill Road, Benin City
Tel: (052) 250256, 251091 **Fax:** (052) 251091
Contact: Mr. Augustus Eribo - MD/CEO

EDO TRANSPORT SERVICE LIMITED
Business: Passenger Transportation, Courier Services
Address: 22, James Watt Road, P.M.B. 1046, Benin City
Tel: (052) 257454, 256185, 250942
Contact: Chief (Dr.) Godwin Edosa (JP) - MD/CEO
Hon. Oludele Odion Enahoro - AGM.

EDP AUDIT & SECURITY ASSOCIATES
Business: Information Systems Audiotors, Information Technology Consulting & Research, Computer Auditing, Software Development
Address: Limson Road, off Isheri Road, Ojodu, Lagos
Tel: (01) 2221558, 4702732, 4807742 **Fax:** (01) 2221558
E-mail: solution@edp.com.ng
*23, Senanga St, off Accra St, Wuse Zone 5, Abuja
Tel: (09) 5230791, 5230591 **Fax:** (01) 5230591
Contact: Mr. Chris C. Ekeigwe - Managing Consultant

EDYSMART (NIGERIA) LIMITED
Business: Manufacturers of Cosmetics & Hair Care Products
Address: 33, Ayo Alabi Street, Fadunsi Bus-Stop, Oke-Ira, Ogba, Lagos
Tel: (01) 4925837, 921858

EFOSA EXPRESS LIMITED
Business: Road Passenger - Transportation Services
Address: 4, Urubi Street, Iyaro, Benin City
Tel: (052) 251990
Contact: Engr. Isaac I. Uhunmwagho - Chairman/CEO

EFT INSURANCE BROKERS LIMITED
Business: Insurance Broking
Address: 80, Allen Avenue, Ikeja, Lagos
Tel: (01) 4931882, 4931881 **Fax:** (01) 4931882
Contact: Mr. Tunde Olayemi - GM/CEO

EGHIEMAI INDUSTRIES LIMITED
Business: Production of Baking Ingredients /Processed Foods
Address: Plot 36, Yakoyo Road, Ojodu, Lagos
Tel: (01) 8043294
Contact: Mrs. H. E. Oghuma - MD/CEO

EGUNJOBI ADEGBITE & COMPANY
Business: Chartered Accountants, Auditing & Investment, Tax Advisory Services
Address: 9, Turton Street, Sabo-Yaba, Lagos
Tel: (01) 7744149, 4731475, 08023434144
E-mail: egunade2004@yahoo.com
* 18/19, Ahmadu Bello Way, Kaduna

EGYPT AIR (NIGERIA)
Business: International Airline Services, Tourism Services
Address: UBA Trustee House, 22B, Idowu Taylor Street, Victoria Island, Lagos
Tel: (01) 2613329, 2620087 **Fax:** (01) 2624407
Contact: Mr. Mohsen Ayoub - GM

EIB BUILDING SOCIETY LIMITED
Business: Mortgage Banking Services
Address: TISCO Plaza, Central Business District, Alausa, Ikeja, Lagos
Tel: (01) 4706466, 4932567, 7763230
Contact: Mr A. B. Cole - MD/CEO

EIB INTERNATIONAL BANK PLC (formerly Eko Int. Bank Plc)
Business: Commercial Banking
Address: Plot 5, Ikeja Commercial Scheme, Alausa, Lagos
Tel: (01) 4932513, 4932583, 4702330, 4702471, 4632567
E-mail: ekobank@ekobank.com
coporateeib@ekobank.com
Website: www.ekobank.com
* Ikeja Plaza, M. Bank-Anthony Way, Ikeja, Lagos.
Tel: (01) 4970475-6 (2L)
* 34, Creek Road, Apapa, Lagos.
Tel: (01) 5877125, 5877918
* Plot 618, Tafawa Balewa Way, Garki, Abuja.
Tel: (09) 2347125, 2347134
* Plot 270, Trans-Amadi Ind. Layout, Port Harcourt
Tel: (084) 237551-3 (3L)

EIB TRUSTEES LIMITED
Business: Trustee Services, Funds Mnanagement
Address: Tisco Plaza (1st Floor), Plot 6, Central Business District, Alausa, Ikeja, Lagos
Tel: (01) 4934369, 7731546, 7921306 **Fax:** (01) 4934369
Contact: Mr G. D. N. Feyi - MD/CEO

EIL TELECOM LIMITED
Business: Sales, Installation and Maintenance of Telecommunication Terminal Equipment, Consultancy, Training
Address: 7C, Oduduwa Way, Ikeja G.R.A., Lagos
Tel: (01) 4979321-2 (2 L), 4968485-6 (2 L), 08034007267
Fax: (01) 4968486
E-mail: eil@cyberspace.net.ng
Website: www.eiltelecom.com
* Plot 2177, Lama Mansa St, Wuse Zone 4, Abuja.
Tel: (09) 5234651
Contact: Mrs. Nkoli E. Moka - MD/CEO

EJIX MARITIME LIMITED
Business: Freight Forwarding, Clearing, Ship Agency, Export and Import, Haulage and Warehousing
Address: T.D.T. Photo Plaza, 51, Kofo Abayomi Avenue, Apapa, Lagos
Tel: (01) 5450206, 5452061, 7742102 **Fax:** (01) 5450196
E-mail: ejix@cyberspace.net.ng
Contact: Mr. Kris C. Keme - Chairman/CEO.

EKENE DILI CHUKWU GROUP OF COMPANIES
Business: Transportation and Haulage Services
Address: 1, Ilodibe Road, Awada Layout, Onitsha
Tel: (046) 210452, 211213, 410346, 481820
Contact: Chief (Dr.) Augustine E. Ilodibe - Exec. Chairman

EKEOBA & EMIOWELE PARTNERSHIP
Business: Quantity Surveying, Construction Cost Consultancy, Project Management, Facilities Management
Address: 12, Gbaja Street, Surulere, Lagos
Tel: (01) 5454282, 08033272762
E-mail: eep23401@yahoo.com
Contact: Chief I. E. Ekeoba - Principal Partner

EKERE ASSOCIATES
Business: Estate Surveyors & Valuers, Real Estate Agents & Development Consultants
Address: 12B, Khana St, off Olu Obasanjo Rd, Port Harcourt
Tel: (084) 238729, 235363 **Fax:** (084) 231771

EKILOS ENGINEERING COMPANY NIGERIA LIMITED
Business: Construction, Installation and Maintenance of Swimming Pools, Sales of Swimming Pool Equipment and Chemicals
Address: Km. 3, Lagos-Badagry Expressway, Alafia Bus-Stop, opp. Unipetrol Filling Station, Coker, Lagos
Tel: (01) 7744817, 58511426, 842007 (090) 412932
Fax: (01) 5851426
* 63, Ogbunabali Road, Port Harcourt
Contact: Mr. E. O. Nweke - Chairman/CEO.

EKLIPPS TELEPHONE SYSTEMS LIMITED
Business: Sales, Installation and Maintenance of Telecommunication Equipments
Address: Eklipps House, 83, Adeniyi Jones Av, Ikeja, Lagos
Tel: (01) 4977564, 4930790, 4930791, 4968379, 4710581
Fax: (01) 4968379
*14, Adetokunbo Ademola St, Victoria Island Lagos
Tel: (01) 2610525-6, 610891, 610893
Website: www.eklipps.com
Contact: Mr. Akintunde Shodipe - Chairman/CEO

EKO HOTELS LIMITED
Business: Hotel and Restaurant Owners and Managers - Eko Hotel & Suites, Kuramo Lodge, Oceanview Restaurants, Eko Hotel Shopping Complex
Address: Kuramo Waters, Plot 1415, Adetokunbo Ademola Street, Victoria Island, Lagos
Tel: (01) 2624600-19 (20L), 08034020112
Fax: (01) 2615205, 2618083
E-mail: azammarieh@ekohotels.com
Contact: Mr. Antoine A Zammarieh - MD/CEO

EKO HOTEL AND SUITES
Business: Hospitality Services and Hotel Business (5-Star)
Address: Kuramo Waters, Plot 1415, Adetokunbo Ademola Street, Victoria Island, Lagos
Tel: (01) 2624600-19 (20L), 2614444, 2620076, 2614836
Fax: (01) 2615205, 2618083
E-mail: reservation@ekohotels.com
Contact: Mr. Alain Chatel - GM.

EKO NOMINEES LIMITED
Business: Company Sercretarial/Corporate Advisory Services
Address: Plot 252E, Muri Okunola Street, Victoria Is, Lagos
Tel: (01) 2703100, 3203100 **Fax:** (01) 3203101
E-mail: enquiry@ng.pwc.com
Website: www.pwc.com/ng
Contact: Mr.Adebimpe Balogun - MD/CEO

EKO TRANSPORT SERVICES LIMITED
Business: Metropolitan Transportation Services
Address: LSTC Building (1st Floor), Plot 2, Block E, Ilupeju Indl Estate, State Highway, Oshodi B/Stop, Lagos
Tel: (01) 7745380 **Fax:** (01) 2694149

EKOCHIN LIMITED
Business: Medical Consultancy and Diagnostic Services
Address: 50, Kano Street, Ogbete, Enugu
Tel: (042) 552050
Contact: Dr. K. O. O. Ochin-Ekochin - Chairman/Director

EKOCORP PLC
Business: Healthcare Delivery
Address: 31, Mobolaji Bank-Anthony Way, Ikeja, Lagos
Tel: (01) 4978800-9 (10 L) **Fax:** (01) 4960159
Contact: Dr. Alex Chuma Eneli - Joint Chief Medical Director
Dr. Sonny F. Kuku - Joint Chief Medical Director

EKULO GROUP OF COMPANIES
Business: Manufacturing of Cosmetics, Merchandising
Address: Plot 1401B, Tiamiyu Savage St, Victoria Is., Lagos
Tel: (01) 2626510-2 (3 L) **Fax:** (01) 2626363, 2626343
E-mail: ekulo@infoweb.abs.net
Contact: Chief (Sir) E. C. Okonkwo - Chairman/CEO

EKWENIBE & SONS TRADING COMPANY LIMITED
Business: General Merchandising & Importation of Goods, Manufacturing & Assembling, Haulage, Agro-Allied Business
Address: 14A, Old Cemetry Road, P.O.Box 384, Onitsha
Tel: (046) 211157, 210901, 410934, 08023208072, 08033089252, 08034546449
Fax: (046) 410934, * (042) 259229
E-mail: estconig@yahoo.com
Contact: Chief (Dr.) C.A. Ekwenibe - Chairman/CEO

EL & KAY NIGERIA LIMITED
Business: Production and Sales of Corporate Gifts & Awards, Printing Services, General Supplies
Address: 15, Adeshiyan Street, Ilupeju, Lagos
Tel: (01) 820676
Contact: Mr. Abdullateef O. Na'Allah - Chairman/CEO.

EL-AMIN BAKERY & CONFECTIONERY LIMITED
Business: Bakery, Confectionery & Food Processing
Address: Plot 32, Wushishi Road, High Ind. Estate, Minna
Tel: (066) 22224

EL-BEZALEEL CONSULTS LIMITED
Business: Commercial and Project Engineers, Distribution of Gas-Fixed Airconditioners, Lightning Arrestors, Cathodic Protection and Batteries
Address: Topaz Plaza, Km. 14, Lekki-Epe Expressway, Idado New Road Bus-Stop, before Chevron Office, Lagos
Tel: (01) 8044260, 7730370
Fax: (01) 2694642, 685252, 8047994, 7730370
E-mail: bezaleeel@infoweb.abs.net
Contact: Evang. (Engr.) C. Osagiator-Obude - MD/CEO

ELBE PHARMA LIMITED
Business: Import & Export, Distribution of Pharmaceuticals
Address: 4, Akanbi Danmola Street, Ikoyi, Lagos
Tel: (01) 8179648, 4706030, 7927093, 7731473
Contact: Mr. Uchenna Obiakor - MD/CEO

ELCHEM LIMITED
Business: Importation of Auto Care Products and General Merchandise; Process & Manufacturing Engineers, Chemical Laboratories, Distilling
Address: 9, Moses Ike Street, Tedi Village, off Badagry Expressway, Ojo, Lagos
Tel: (01) 4707833, 4708947
E-mail: elchem@siotel.com

ELCO CONTRACTING NIGERIA LIMITED
Business: Assembly & Installation of Airconditioners, Sales & Service of Transformers
Address: Plot 32, Billingsway, off Mobolaji Johnson Avenue, Oregun Industrial Estate, Ikeja, Lagos
Tel/Fax: (090) 403071
* Plot 642B, Adeyemo Alakija S, Victoria Is, Lagos
Tel: (01) 2622775, 2621890 **Fax:** (01) 2621890
Contact: Mr. B. Lanciano - MD/CEO.

ELDORADO (NIGERIA) LIMITED
Business: Fabrication of Steel Structures, Tanks, Trailers and Pipes, Civil Works
Address: 27, Henry Carr Street, Ikeja Ind. Estate, Ikeja, Lagos
Tel: (01) 4974706-7 (2 L) **Fax:** (01) 4961738

ELECTRA SIGNS LIMITED
Business: Neon & Metal Signs Producers
Address: 34, Warehouse Road, Apapa, Lagos
Tel: (01) 5452948, 5451610
Contact: Mr. J. O Moemeke - MD/CEO.

ELECTRA TECHNICAL COMPANY LIMITED
Business: Electrical Engineering Contractors, Installation and Maintenance of Airconditioners
Address: 34, Warehouse Road, Apapa, Lagos
Tel: (01) 5452948
Contact: Mr F. A Thomas - GM/CEO

ELECTRICARE LIMITED
Business: Marketing of Luminary Lightnings for Projects, Electrical & Electronic Appliances, Telecommunication & IT Equipment (incl. GSM), Personal & Corporate Safety and Security Equipment; Lotteries Ticketing and Subscription Agents
Address: Electricare House, 385, Herbert Macaulay Street, Yaba, Lagos
Tel: (01) 860273, 2880242, 7742744, 4703499, 08033016890 **Fax:** (01) 860256, 860273
E-mail: electricare@hotmail.com
Website: www.firstelect.com
Contact: Dr. Herbert A. B. Ajayi - Chairman/CEO.

ELECTRICITY METER COMPANY NIGERIA LIMITED
Business: Assembling of Electricity Meters & Circuit Breakers
Address: Plot 30/32, Chikaji Industrial Area, Zaria
Tel: (069) 334747, 335243, 334827, 331705
Fax: (069) 334185
E-mail: emcon@skannet.com
*NEPA Hq Annex, 19A, Awolowo Rd, Ikoyi, Lagos
Contact: Engr. Shehu Ahmed Karaye - MD/CEO

ELECTRO TRUST (NIGERIA) LIMITED
Business: Distribution & Sales of Electronic Appliances & Merchandise
Address: H121, Alaba Int'l Market, Ojo-Alaba, Lagos
Tel: (01) 4805893, 5554416, 5890402 **Fax:** (01) 5890402
E-mail: electrotrust@hyperia.com
Contact: Chief Chike Ejimofor - Chairman/CEO.

ELECTRONIC CONNECTIONS LIMITED
Business: Internet & Pre-Paid Phone Services Providers,
Address: 8A, Race Course Road, P.O.Box 572, Kano
Tel: (064) 311470-3 (4 L), 08037865001
Fax: (064) 42056
E-mail: info@ecnx.net
Website: www.ecnx.net
Contact: Jihad N Jaafar - MD/CEO

ELECTRONIC LEARNING SYSTEM LIMITED
Business: IT Management and Sales of Learning Aids
Address: 63, Kudirat Abiola (Oregun) Road, Ikeja, Lagos
Tel: (01) 4968655, 4933189, 4939477
E-mail: enquiry@els.bz
Website: www.els.bz
* Eleganza Biro Plaza, Suite 4 (4th Floor), Adeyemo Alakija Street, Victoria Island, Lagos
Tel: (01) 2702924, 2702934, 7736997
Contact: Mary Fasola - MD/CEO

ELEGANZA GROUP OF COMPANIES
Business: Conglomerate
Address: 3/5, Ikoyi Crescent, Ikoyi, Lagos
E-mail: eleganza@cyberspace.net.ng
* Eleganza Industries Ltd, Plot 33, Mobolaji Johnson Way, Oregun Industrial Estate, Ikeja, Lagos
Tel: (01) 4977699, 7738817, 7741240 **Fax:** (01) 4977691
Contact: Alh. (Dr.) Rasaki Okoya - Exec. Chairman/MD

ELEGANZA BALL-POINT PEN INDSTRIES
Business: Manufacturing of Ball-Point Pens
Address: Eleganza Complex, Lagos-Badagry Expressway, Alaba, Orile-Iganmu, Lagos
Tel: (01) 7731131, 5851202

ELEGANZA BIG COOLER & BUCKET INDUSTRIES LTD
Business: Production of Storage Containers for Domestic use
Address: Plot 52/53, Akanbi Onitiri Close, off Eric Moore Road, Iganmu Industrial Estate, Surulere, Lagos
Tel: (01) 2902452, 4702670

ELEGANZA CERAMIC & COOLER INDUSTRIES LIMITED
Business: Manufacture of Ceramic Household Goods
Address: 79, Asa Afariogun Street, Ajao Estate, Apakun, Isolo, Lagos
Tel: (01) 4521970, 4527403 **Fax:** (01) 4521970
Contact: Alh. (Dr.) Rasaq Akanni Okoya - Chairman/CEO.
Mrs. Sade Okoya - Dep. MD

ELEGANZA INDUSTRIES LIMITED
Business: Manufacture of Ball-Point Pens & Household Goods
Address: Plot 33, Mobolaji Johnson Avenue, Oregun, Lagos
Tel: (01) 4977691, 4977699, 4977705
Fax: (01) 4977697, 4977695
E-mail: eleganza@linkserve.com.ng
Contact: Alh. (Dr.) Rasaq Akanni Okoya - Chairman/CEO.
Alhaja Ajoke Okoya - MD

ELEKTRIM NIGERIA LIMITED
Business: Rural Electrification, Electrical and Mechanical Installations, Electrical Motor/Machines Repairs
Address: Western House (17th Floor), 8/10, Broad Street, Marina, Lagos
Tel/Fax: (01) 2634370, 08036885555
E-mail: elektrim1@yahoo.com
Contact: Chief (Dr.) H. O. Osomo - Chairman/CEO.

ELEKTRINT (NIGERIA) LIMITED
Business: Electrical and Mechanical Engineering Services
Address: Plot II, Gbagada Industrial Estate, Oworonshoki-Apapa Expressway, Gbagada, Lagos
Tel: (01) 7741582, 7742297 **Fax:** (01) 7741582
E-mail: elektrintlagos@yahoo.co.uk
* Plot 362, Niamey St, Wuse Zone 2, Garki, Abuja
Tel: (09) 5231161 **Fax:** (09) 5231543
E-mail: elektrintabuja@hotmail.com
* 6 (Plot 20), Nkpogu Crescent, off Trans-Amadi Industrial Layout, Port Harcourt
Tel: (084) 570023, 485870 **Fax:** (084) 230361
Contact: Mr. Roberto Finco - MD/CEO.

ELEME PETROCHEMICALS COMPANY LIMITED
Business: Refining of Crude Oil into Petrochemicals and Oil-Based Raw Materials
Address: Eleme Petrochemicals Complex, East-West Road, Port Harcourt
Tel: (084) 235416, 231916, 239318-9 (2 L), 234669, 08022240360, 08033405196
Fax: (084) 235749, 239316
* 13, Ojo-Olobun Close, off Bishop Oluwole Street, Victoria Island, Lagos.
Tel: (01) 613007
Contact: Engr. Austen O. Oniwon - MD/CEO

ELEPHANT GROUP LIMITED
Business: Exportation of Commodities, Importation of Cement and Sugar; Haulage, Oil Service & Construction
Address: 21, Opebi Road (3rd Floor), Ikeja, Lagos
Tel: (01) 4966920, 49303 86, 7751723-4 (2L), 08055414265
Fax: (01) 4930386
E-mail: info@elephantgroupltd.com
Website: www.elephantgroupltd.com
Contact: Mr. Tunji Owoeye - MD/CEO.

ELESON INDUSTRIES NIGERIA LIMITED
Business: Importation and Sales of Industrial Chemicals
Address: 46, New Market Road, Onitsha
Tel: (046) 412712, 08046112023
E-mail: elesonltd@yahoo.com
Contact: Mr. G. O. Eleigwe - Chairman/CEO.

ELEVATOR TECHNOLOGIES NIGERIA LIMITED
Business: Supply, Installation & Maintenance of Lifts, Escalators, Moving Walks, Cleaning Cradle etc.
Address: 227, Ikorodu Road, Ilupeju, Lagos
Tel/Fax: (01) 4968266, 7911687
E-mail: elevator@cyberspace.net.ng
Contact: Engr. Adewale Balogun - GM/CEO

ELGAR (NIGERIA) LIMITED
Business: Electrical, Electronics and Instrumentation Engineering, Sale & Service of Testing Equipment
Address: 5, Mercy Eneli St, Alh. Masha Rd, Surulere, Lagos
Tel: (01) 2902643, 5842667, 836140 **Fax:** (01) 5842667
E-mail: info@elgarnig.com
Contact: Engr. Ayo Bankole - Chairman/CEO

ELICO INDUSTRIES LIMITED
Business: Foam Manufacturing
Address: 3/5, Elico Street, off Igbede Road, Sabo-Oniba, after Alaba International Market, Ojo-Alaba, Lagos
Tel/Fax: (01) 5846116, 08033033998, 08033033858
E-mail: elicofoam@yahoo.com
Contact: Prince E. O. Omogbehin - Chairman/CEO

ELIMI MOTORS NIGERIA LIMITED
Business: Sales & Service of Motor Vehicles
Address: 4, Saka Tinubu Street, Victoria Island, Lagos
Tel: (01) 3201806, 3201807
E-mail: elim@yahoo.com
Contact: Rev. Chukwuemeka Ngubo - Chairman/CEO

ELITE TEXTILE INDUSTRIES (NIGERIA) LIMITED
Business: Production of Lace Textile Materials
Address: Plot 7, Block H, Limca Way, Isolo, Lagos
Tel: (01) 4520008, 4521060 Fax: (01) 4521027

ELIZADE NIGERIA LIMITED
Business: Marketing, Servicing & Repairs of Automobiles
Address: Elizade - Toyota Plaza, 322A, Ikorodu Road, Anthony Village, Ikeja, Lagos
Tel: (01) 4702101, 4717226, 4936054, 4936845-6 (2L), 7743168, 7743176, 08022904151, 08023144577, 08033052380 **Fax:** (01) 4936829, 4939150
E-mail: elizade@elizade.com
* Block A, Plot 24, Acme Road, Ogba Industrial Estate, Ikeja, Lagos.
Tel: (01) 4920943, 4921882, 4707682 **Fax:** (01) 4922060
* Plot 158, Gimbiya Street, off Ahmadu Bello Way, Area 11, Garki, Abuja.
Tel/Fax: (09) 3142272-3 (2L)
* Plot 14/15, Chief Nwuke Street, Trans-Amadi Industrial Layout, Port Harcourt.
Tel/Fax: (084) 233847
Contact: Chief (Dr.) M. Ade Ojo - Chairman/CEO
Mr. Olu Tikolo - Director (Marketing)

ELMAC ASSURANCE (NIGERIA) LIMITED
Business: Insurance
Address: Alaga House, 172, Herbert Macaulay Street, Ebute-Metta, Lagos
Tel: (01) 800070-9 (10L), 4701915-6 (2L), 5455945-7 (3L)
Fax: (01) 5455948-9
E-mail: elmac@elmacassurance.com
Website: www.elmacassurance.com
Contact: Mr. Adeyemi Soladoye - MD/CEO.

ELO-PEE WORLDWIDE TELEVISION LIMITED
Business: Production of Television Programmes, Broadcast Edit Studio, Trade Promotion, Events Management and Media Consultancy, Publishing
Address: Plot 2396, Addis Ababa Crescent, Wuse Zone 4, Garki, Abuja
Tel: (09) 5237667, 5237855 **Fax:** (09) 5237855
E-mail: elosia@elopee.com
Website: www.elopee.com
Contact: Mr. Peter Elosia - Chairman/CEO.

ELPINA ASSOCIATES LIMITED
Business: Assembly and Sales of Airconditioners, Refrigerators, Freezeers, Laundry Units, Cookers, Microwave Ovens and Hifi Sets
Address: 188, Creek Road, Apapa, Lagos
Tel: (01) 5451654, 5872653 **Fax:** (01) 5451654
* 71, Azikiwe Road, Port Harcourt
Tel: (084) 236063, 236064
Contact: Mr. Louis Ezeigwe - Chairman/CEO.

EL-RUFAI & PARTNERS LIMITED
Business: Quantity Surveyors, Project Management, Environmental Management Services
Address: Plot 1164, Sirasso Crescent, off Aminu Kano Crescent, Wuse 11, Abuja
Tel: (09) 4133853, 4137161 **Fax:** (09) 4137160
E-mail: elrufai@linkserve.com.ng
* 54A, Abosede Kuboye Crescent, off Imam Dauda Road, off Eric Moore Road, Surulere, Lagos
Tel: (01) 5836524, 4705001 **Fax:** (01) 5836524
Contact: Mal. Hassain A. Dikko - Chairman/CEO

EMACONPRINT LIMITED
Business: Printing Services
Address: 1, Ogundare Awise Street, Soliyi Estate, Gbagada, Lagos
Tel: (01) 7740793
E-mail: emacprint@yahoo.com
Contact: Omo-Oba Sam A. Ogundogba - Chairman/CEO

EMBASSY DRYCLEANING & LAUNDRY SERVICE LIMITED
Business: Drycleaning and Laundry Services
Address: 7, Olayinka Bamgbose Street, off Unity Road, by Toyin Street Junction, Ikeja, Lagos
Tel: (01) 4937577, 8129568
E-mail: embassydrycleaners91@yahoo.com
Contact: Chief Leo Okoye - Chairman
Mr. Mike Afam Etiobi - MD/CEO

EMBEE & PARTNERS NIGERIA LIMITED
Business: Engineering & Consulting Services
Address: Plot 934, off Aminu Kano Crescent, Wuse II, Abuja
Tel/Fax: (09) 4138702, 08033277077
E-mail: embee@rosecom.net
Contact: Engr. Nnoka Mbanefo - MD/CEO

EMCAST WORKS LIMITED
Business: Precision Casting and Monogramming Services, Screen Printing and Transfer Printing
Address: 11, Ajumobi Olorunmoje Street, off Acme Road (1st Gate Bus-Stop), Agidingbi Ikeja, Lagos
Tel: (01) 4705956, 08023141960, 08023141963
E-mail: idisystems@nova.net.ng
Contact: Mr. A. J. Idiakhoa - MD/CEO

EME TECHNICAL COMPANY LIMITED
Business: Water Drilling, Sales of Safety Materials, Machines

Pipes and Technical Equipment, Leasing of Trucks
Address: Km. 14, P.Harcourt/Aba Expressway, Port Harcourt
Tel: (084) 610333, 610316 **Fax:** (084) 610316
E-mail: emetech@infoweb.abs.net
Contact: Mr. Emmanuel Eme - Chairman/CEO

EMEKA ONUORAH & COMPANY
Business: Chartered Surveyors & Valuers, Estate Agents
Address: 7, Biaduo Street, off Keffi Street, S. W. Ikoyi Lagos
Tel: (01) 2695260, 2691172, 08042154909
Contact: Mr. Emeka Onuborah - Principal Partner

EMENITE LIMITED
Business: Manufacturing and Marketing of Fibre Roofing Sheets and Ceiling Boards
Address: 7, Old Abakaliki Road, Emene, Enugu
Tel: (042) 552597, 555256, 557052, 559295
Fax: (042) 554273
E-mail: emenite@infoweb.abs.net
Contact: Mr. W. Mcinnes - MD/CEO
Engr. B. N. Osakwe - Commercial Manager.

EMERALD AGENCIES LIMITED
Business: Travel Agency, Bureau de Change Services
Address: 8, Okpara Avenue, Enugu
Tel: (042) 257523, 257563, 08037105428
* Falomo Shopping Centre (Unit A9), Awolowo Road, Falomo, Ikoyi, Lagos
Tel: (01) 2671107, 2671108 **Fax:** (01) 2681107

EMERALD INSURANCE BROKERS LIMITED
Business: Insurance Broking and Consultancy Services
Address: 35, Town Planning Way, Ilupeju, Lagos
Tel: (01) 4960234, 4935631, 08023179701, 08023416056
Fax: (01) 4935631
E-mail: emerald@rcl.nig.com
Contact: Mr. Henry Olusegun Ewumi - MD/CEO

EMESPO J. CONTINENTAL LIMITED
Business: General Merchants, Auto Spare Parts Dealers
Address: Zone A, Block 1, Shops 20-23, ASPMDA Plaza, Trade Fair Complex, Badagry Exp.way, Ojo, Lagos
Tel: (01) 3208147 **Fax:** (01) 3208146
E-mail: pat-com@excite.com
Contact: Mr. Patrick Okafor - MD/CEO

EMI CAPITAL RESOURCES LIMITED
Business: Stockbroking, Issuing House, Financial Advisors
Address: 45A, Campbell Street, Lagos Island, Lagos
Tel: (01) 2637552, 2631844, 2630971 **Fax:** (01) 2631844
E-mail: emiltd@emi-capital.com
Contact: Mr. Edwin T. Ikhinmwin - MD/CEO

EMI SYSTEMS LIMITED
Business: Sales of Security Equipment, Security Consultancy & Management, Security Training
Address: 4A, Lawrence Road, off Glover Road Roundabout, Ikoyi, Lagos
Tel: (01) 4615480, 2673098-9 (2 L), 08023297203, 08033027255 **Fax:** (01) 4615148, 2670137
E-mail: sales@emi-systems.com
Website: www.emi-systems.com
Contact: Mr. Yehuda Mesika - MD/CEO

EMIC VENTURES LIMITED
Business: Sales of Water Purification Systems
Address: 110, Ikwerre Road, Mile 2, Diobu, Port Harcourt
Tel/Fax: (084) 572055, 08033132136, 08033259655, 08036705641
E-mail: mightypureuv@yahoo.com
Contact: Chief Iwu M. Ogbu - Chairman/CEO

EMILY MILLIONAIRE COSMETICS INDUSTRIES LIMITED
Business: Manufacturing of Cosmetic Products
Address: Olumba Olumba Olu Close, off Ojodu Abiodun Rd, Berger Bus-Stop, Ojodu, Ikeja, Lagos
Tel: (01) 2640472, 2640473, 2644612, 08022241578
Contact: Apostle Joe Brown Agu - MD/CEO

EMINENT COMMUNICATIONS LIMITED
Business: Advertising and Public Relations Consultancy
Address: 14, Ezekiel Street, off Olayinka Bamgbose Street, off Toyin Street, Ikeja, Lagos
Tel: (01) 7739078, 8044674, 8044676, 8115255, 2903291
E-mail: eminent@eminentcomm.com
Contact: Mr. Sesan Ogunro - Chairman/CEO

EMINENT INSURANCE BROKERS COMPANY LIMITED
Business: Insurance Broking
Address: 61, Tejuosho Street, Surulere, Lagos
Tel: (01) 837917, 841171, 7748811
Contact: Mr. Fatai A. Sulaimon - GM/CEO

EMMA SAINT GEORGE GROUP LIMITED
Business: Water Treatment Services, Manufacture of Costmetics, Computer Sales and Service, Spring Water Production
Address: 110, Opebi Road, Ikeja, Lagos
Tel/Fax: (01) 4937010
Contact: Saint George A. Ekeh - Chairman/CEO

EMI-INTERNATIONAL SYSTEMS LIMITED
Business: Fixed Wireless Telephone Operator
Address: Intercontinental Plaza (3rd Floor), Plot 999C, Danmole Street, Victoria Island, Lagos
Tel: (01) 2881000-2 (3 L), 08034727331
Fax: (01) 2881004
E-mail: emis@mwebafrica.com
Website: www.emis.com
Contact: Chief Joe-Billy Ekwunife - Chairman
Mr. Emeka J. Onwuegbzia - MD/CEO

EMIRATES (NIGERIA)
Business: International Airline Services
Address: Churchgate Towers, Plot PC 30, Afribank Street, Victoria Island, Lagos
Tel: (01) 2617759, 2617738, 2611665, 2617752

EMMANUEL ELECTRONICS LIMITED
Business: Design of Telecommunication Systems, Sales of Radio Communication Equipment for Marine, Aviation and Land Mobile Use, Sub Assembly of Modems and Rural Telephone Systems
Address: 31, Kofo Abayomi Avenue, Apapa, Lagos
Tel: (01) 5872798, 8048465 **Fax:** (01) 5877107
E-mail: electronics@linkserve.com.ng
Contact: Chief E. A. Ukpong - Chairman/CEO

EMMYSON NIGERIA LIMITED
Business: Sales of Industrial and Agricultural Chemicals
Address: 200, Awolowo Road, S. W. Ikoyi, Lagos
Tel: (01) 2690674, 2693966 **Fax:** (01) 2692206, 2692236

EMO-TIMEX LIMITED
Business: Sales & Installation of Transformers, Feeder Pillars and Electrical Equipment
Address: 7, Okunola Martins Close, off Okotie Eboh Street, off Awolowo Road, S. W. Ikoyi, Lagos
Tel/Fax: (01) 2691898, 2691005
E-mail: emotimex@beta.linkserve.com
Contact: Mrs. Conka Matlieva - Chairman
Mr. Naum Kitanoski - Dep. Chairman/CEO

EMPIRE GROUP LIMITED
Business: Investments, Management Consultancy
Address: Plot 935, Azores Street, off Aminu Kano Crescent, Wuse II, Abuja
Tel: (09) 6701483, 4132387, 08037870428
Fax: (09) 4132387
* 13, Macarthy Street (2nd Floor), Onikan, Lagos
Tel: (01) 2647206, 2630219 **Fax:** (01) 2630219
E-mail: abuja@empire-group-grp.com
Contact: Yahyah Ali - Chairman
Haruna Mohammed Sambo - MD/CEO

EMPIRE GROUP OF COMPANIES
Business: Manufacturing of Carpets & Rugs, Hospitality Services, Import & Export
Address: Plot 187, Aguiyi Ironsi Layout, Umuahia
Tel: (088) 220685, 220689, (082) 441904
E-mail: empire@infoweb.abs.net
Contact: Chief (Sir) Empire N. Kanu - Chairman/CEO

EMPIRE SECURITIES LIMITED
Business: Stockbroking and Dealing
Address: 13, Macarthy Street (2nd Floor), Onikan, Lagos
Tel: (01) 2647206, 2630219 **Fax:** (01) 2630219
E-mail: empiresec@yahoo.com
Contact: Mr. Bodunde Rafiu Tiamiyu - Ag. MD/CEO

EMS/SPEEDPOST
Business: Express Courier Services
Address: 8, Mobolaji Bank-Anthony Way, Ikeja, Lagos
Tel: (01) 2906334, 4979147-8 (2L), 4801449-50 (2L), 4801826, 4823605, 08023317053 **Fax:** (01) 4979148
E-mail: gmems@emsng.com
Website: www.emsng.com
Contact: Mr. Adedamola Osuntuyi - GM/CEO

EMY HOLDINGS NIGERIA LIMITED
Business: Manufacturing of Cosmetics and Pharmaceuticals
Address: Choki Laboratories (Cee Sheen), First Avenue, Independence Layout, Enugu
Tel: (042) 458930 **Fax:** (042) 450730
E-mail: emy@infoweb.abs.net
Contact: Prince Chukwuemeka I. Onyesoh - Chairman/CEO.

EMZOR PHARMACEUTICAL INDUSTRIES LIMITED
Business: Manufacturing of Pharmaceutical Products
Address: Plot 3C, Block A, Ilupeju Extension Scheme 11, Aswani Market Road, Isolo, Lagos
Tel: (01) 4532570, 4523721, 4527160, 7763863, 08023149878 **Fax:** (01) 4525288
E-mail: emzor@hyperia.com
Website: www.emzorpharma.com

ENCEE ENTERPRISES NIGERIA LIMITED
Business: Importation of Bicycles, Industrial Chemicals, Textile Printing Machinery Spares & Chemicals, and Rotary Screens
Address: 7, Civic Centre Road, Kano
Tel: (064) 646430, 649650 **Fax:** (064) 649610
E-mail: encee@ecnx.net
bajaj@compuserve.com
* 20, Ogunlowo St, off Awolowo Way, Ikeja,Lagos.
Tel: (01) 4932189, 7751948
Contact: Mr. V. K. Bajaj - Chairman/CEO.

ENCOMIUM VENTURES LIMITED
Business: Publishing of Magazines
Address: Encomium's Place, May 14 House, 23, Thomas Salako Street, off Ogba-Ijaiye Road, Ikeja, Lagos
Tel: (01) 4705675, 08023032710
Contact: Mr. Kunle Bakare - MD/CEO

ENCRISTO PHARMACEUTICAL INDUSTRIES LIMITED
Business: Manufacturing and Sale of Pharmaceuticals
Address: 8, Second Avenue, Independence Layout, Enugu
Tel: (042) 457095, 451512 **Fax:** (042) 451512
E-mail: encristo@linkserve.com.ng
Contact: Chief I. O. Meregini - Chairman/CEO

ENDY GENERAL PRODUCTS ;LIMITED
Business: Sales of Industrial Equipment, Bakery
Address: 185, Akowonjo Road, Dopemu, Agege, Lagos
Tel: (01) 4750644, 4923354, 4925523 **Fax:** (01) 4925523
E-mail: enprob@yahoo.com
Contact: Mr N. O. Adewusi - MD/CEO

ENERGIE NIGERIA LIMITED
Business: Importation of Generators, Sanitary Wares, Marble Tiles and Ceramic Tiles; Construction Contractors
Address: 96, Awolowo Road, S.W. Ikoyi, Lagos
Tel: (01) 2694705-6 (2 L), 2690998 **Fax:** (01) 2694677
Contact: Mr. Talal A. R. Sayegh - Director/CEO

ENERGO NIGERIA LIMITED
Business: Oilfield Procurement and Supplies, Generation of Electricity
Address: Plot 269B, Kofo Abayomi St, Victoria Island, Lagos
Tel: (01) 2620497, 2620498 **Fax:** (01) 618160
E-mail: energo@cyberspace.net.ng
* Plot 699, Amin Kano Crescent, Wuse 11, Abuja
Tel: (09) 5231006, 5237159 Fax: (09) 5231006.

ENERGY COMPANY NIGERIA LIMITED
Business: Independent Electricity-Power Producers (Generation, Transmission & Distribution)
Address: All Seasons Plaza (Amethyst Block, 2nd Floor), 24, Lateef Jakande Street, Agindingbi, Ikeja, Lagos
Tel: (01) 4925818, 2882130, 8043986, 08023341726
E-mail: encom@encon-ng.com
Contact: Engr. A. Ayoola - Chairman/CEO
Engr E. A. Ajagbe - MD

ENERGY FOODS COMPANY LIMITED
Business: Manufacturing of Biscuits and Confectioneries
Address: 9, Obafemi Awolowo Road, Dugbe, Ibadan
Tel: (02) 2412120, 2413305 **Fax:** (02) 2410811
* 95, Aba Road, Port Harcourt
Contact: Mr. W. M. Zard - MD/CEO

ENGINEERING & TECHNICAL CO. (NIGERIA) LTD (ETCO)
Business: Electrical Engineering; Airconditioning & Plumbing Services; Sales & Service of Fire-Fighting and Telecommunication Equipment
Address: 14, Creek Road, Apapa, Lagos
Tel: (01) 5804070-9(10L), 5871541, 5876658
Fax: (01) 5877826, 5450013
E-mail: etco_office@etco-nigeria.com
Contact: Mr. I. Weiss - Charman/CEO

ENITONA NIGERIA LIMITED
Business: Hospitality Services, Catering Services
Address: 8, Margaret Avenue, P.O.Box 108, Aba
Tel: (082) 222601, 222200, 08035472144
E-mail: enitona@yahoo.com
Contact: Sir Richard Nnamani - Chairman/CEO

ENKAY PLASTICS LIMITED
Business: Manufacture of Expanded Polystyrene and Plastics
Address: 146,Gbolade Adebanjo Street, Ilupeju, Lagos
* Km. 38, Abeokuta Motor Road, Sango Otta.
Tel: (039) 720678, 721786, 722223, 722324
Fax: (039) 720786, 722324
Contact: Mr. K. V. Vaswani - MD/CEO

ENOSCO LIMITED
Business: Mechanical/Structural Engineering, Shore Protection and Land Reclamation, Building and Civil Engineering Services
Address: 310, Aba Expressway, Rumukurushi, Port Harcourt
Tel: (084) 610080, 610508, 08023251887
Contact: Chief Akpan Enoh - Chairman/CEO

ENPEE INDUSTRIES PLC
Business: Manufacturing & Marketing of Textile Products Weaving, Dyeing; Printing & Embroidery of Cloth
Address: Plot K & L, Block 1, Industrial Avenue, Ilupeju Industrial Estate, Ilupeju, Lagos
Tel: (01) 4968340-2 (3L), 4968398 **Fax:** (01) 498342
E-mail: enpee@linkserve.com.ng
Contact: Mr. Naraindа P. Kirpalani - MD/CEO

ENPLAN GROUP
Business: Engineering Consultancy and Planning Services, Project Management
Address: 18, Johnson Street, Ilupeju, Lagos
Tel/Fax: (01) 4960961
E-mail: eg.lagos@linkserve.com.ng
eg.kt@linkserve.com.ng
eg-inc@compuserve.com
Contact: Engr. F. A. Sonuga - Partner

ENTERPRISE INFORMATION TECHNOLOGIES LIMITED
Business: Sales and Support of IT Systems, Networking, Consultancy and Project Management, Training
Address: NICON House (5th Floor), 5, Customs Street, off Marina, Lagos
Tel: (01) 2660791, 2667856, 2643256 **Fax:** (01) 2662022
E-mail: eit-helpdesk@hyperia.com
eitnig@hyperia.com

ENTERPRISE STOCKBROKERS PLC
Business: Stockbroking, Issuing House, Funds Management
Address: 85, Ogunlana Drive, Surulere, Lagos
Tel: (01) 5851173, 835285 **Fax:** (01) 5851173
E-mail: enter@rcl.nig.com
Contact: Mr. Sylvester A. Abamba - Chief Operating Officer

ENVIRON WASTE NIGERIA LIMITED
Business: Environmental Srvey, Protection & Management Services, Geophysical Surveying & Engineering
Address: 28, Forces Avene, Old GRA, Port Harcourt
Tel: (084) 232212
E-mail: environ@phca.linkserve.com

ENVIRONMENTAL INFORMATION FACTOR LIMITED
Business: Automatic Vehicle-Location Technology
Address: 14, Raufu Williams Crescent, off Adelabu Street, Surulere, Lagos
Tel: (01) 5456812, 7745353 **Fax:** (01) 5456812
E-mail: eif@micro.com.ng

ENVIRONMENTAL RESOURCES MANAGERS LIMITED
Business: Consultancy Services (Environmetal Studies, Pollution Control, Waste Management, General Laboratory Analytical and Toxicity Services
Address: Plot 107A, Imam Abibu Adetoro Street, Lagos
Tel: (01) 2625897, 7746028 **Fax:** (01) 2695122
E-mail: erml2@linkserve.com.ng
info@erml.net
Website: www.erml.com
* Plot 5, 38th St, Bendel Estate, Ugborikoko, Warri
Tel: (053) 255631
Contact: Mr. Victor O. Imevbore - MD/CEO

ENVOY OIL INDUSTRIES LIMITED
Business: Crushsing of Palm Kernel, Refining Palm Kernel Oil to Vegetable Oil
Address: 1, Ekwuluobia St/120, Upper Iweka Road, Onitsha
Tel: (046) 213239, 213358, 217359, 480269, 08034050112, 08046112265 **Fax:** (046) 413297
E-mail: envoil@infoweb.abs.net
* Plots IN/115, 117 & 118, Bridge-Head Industrial Layout, off Atani Road, Ogbaru, Onitsha
Contact: Chief (Sir) L. M. Ojimba - Chairman/CEO

EPEGA & COMPANY
Business: Chartered Surveyors, Estate Surveyors and Valuers
Address: 19, Norman Williams Street, S.W. Ikoyi, Lagos
Tel: (01) 269256, 686234, 685345, 4740661, 08033068397
Contact: Dr. Benjamin O. Epega - Principal Partner

EPESOK PAPER MILL LIMITED
Business: Manufacture of Tissue Paper (Jumbo Reels), Conversion of Tissue Paper to Toilet Rolls, Serviette Paper, Napkins etc., Slitting Services
Address: Plot Y, Mobolaji Johnson Avenue, Oregun Industrial Estate, Alausa
Tel: (01) 4966774, 4966775, 7740371-2 (2L)

Fax: (01) 4967528, 2647747
Contact: Chief M. O. Obagun - Chairman/CEO

EPIC DYNAMICS PLC
Business: Manufacture of Fibreglass Products
Address: Plot C 40, Alakoso Avenue, New Amuwo-Odofin Industrial Estate, Lagos
Tel: (01) 4730900, 482443, 7743419 **Fax:** (01) 5454239
E-mail: epic@hyperia.com
Contact: Mr. Godfrey Ogwu - Chairman/CEO

EPIC INVESTMENT TRUST LIMITED
Business: Stockbroking, Investment Advisory Services
Address: OPIC Plaza (Suite 314), Mobolaji Bank Anthony Way, Ikeja, Lagos
Tel: (01) 2903763, 08037270677
E-mail: epicng@hotmail.com
Contact: Chief J. O. Olowo-Okere - MD/CEO

EPIDATA CONSULTING LIMITED
Business: Training for Certification in Applied Information Technology
Address: 39, Oshuntokun Avenue, Old Bodija Estate, Ibadan
Tel: (02) 8101812, 08023134519, 08033251511
Fax: (02) 8104709, 8105371
E-mail: epidata@skannet.com
Contact: Mr. Olubi Johnson - Chairman/CEO

EPXON OIL PRODUCING COMPANY LIMITED
Business: Oil Tanker & Marine Support Services, Oil Traders
Address: Plot 15, Udi Street, Osborne Estate, Osborne Road, Ikoyi, Lagos
Tel: (01) 2673802, 2613634, 2673358 **Fax:** (01) 26473802
E-mail: onyungmillennium@aol.com
Contact: Dr. O. E. Onyun - Chairman/CEO

EQUATOR FINANCE & SECURITIES LIMITED
Business: Stockbroking
Address: BAICO Plaza, 12, Abibu Oki Street, off Marina, Lagos Island, Lagos
Tel: (01) 2667359, 2667398, 2640756
E-mail: eqasec@infoweb.abs.net
Contact: Mr A. A. Kolawole - GM

EQUIFAX COMPUTERS & OFFICE EQUIPMENT LIMITED
Business: Sales of Computer Hardware and Software, Network Integrations, Systems Support and Hardware, Training
Address: Elegant Twins Building (1st Floor), 41, Ogunlana Drive, Surulere, Lagos
Tel: (01) 5834125, 7734523 **Fax:** (01) 5834125, 7761728
E-mail: info@equifaxcomputer.com
Website: www.equifaxcomputers.com
Contact: Mr. Augustine O. Ugbaja - Chairman/CEO

EQUINOX ASSETS MANAGEMENT LIMITED
Business: Research; Financial & Management Consultancy; Portfolio Managers and Investment Advisors
Address: 16A, Commercial Avenue, Sabo-Yaba, Lagos
Tel/Fax: (01) 3425157
E-mail: equinox@theobech.com
Website: www.equinoxasset.com
Contact: Mr. Nick Opara-Ndudu - MD/CEO

EQUINOX INTERNATIONAL RESOURCES LIMITED
Business: Sales of Furniture & Soap, Bureau de Change
Address: 71, Awolowo Road, S. W. Ikoyi, Lagos
Tel: (01) 8043509, 2672170-1 (2 L) Fax: (01) 4977621
E-mail: info@equinoxresources.com
Website: www.equinoxresources.com
* 16, Amore Street, off Toyin Street, Ikeja, Lagos
Tel: (01) 4974512, 4934814 **Fax:** (01) 4974512
Contact: Mr Obinna P. Ezeuko - MD/CEO

EQUITIES & STRATEGIES NIGERIA LIMITED
Business: Business and Management Consultancy Services
Address: Cross River State Liasion Office Premises, 42, Bishop Oluwole Street, Victoria Island, Lagos
Tel: (01) 2611003; 7748472 **Fax:** (01) 2611003
E-mail: equities&strategies@email.com
Contact: Mr. Niyi Oyedele - Chairman
Mr. Kola Adebayo - CEO

EQUITORIAL TRUST BANK LIMITED
Business: Commercial Banking
Address: Plot 1092, Adeola Odeku St, Victoria Island, Lagos
Tel: (01) 2624021-5 (5L), 2625391-5 (5L), 2623576-80 (5L), 3201595, 3201609 **Fax:** (01) 2619124, 2611052.
E-mail: infotech@etb.com.ng
Website: www.etb.com.ng
Contact: Mr. Ike Oraekwuotu - CEO
Mr Onyekachi Nwosu - Manager (Corp. Affairs)

EQUITY & TRUST LIMITED
Business: Hire Purchase and Equipment Leasing
Address: New Africa House (4th Floor), 31, Marina, Lagos
Tel: (01) 2644127-8 (2L), 2667083, 2668876
Fax: (01) 2667818
E-mail: equitrust@hyperia.com
Contact: Mr J. M. A Igbon - MD/CEO

EQUITY BANK OF NIGERIA LIMITED
Business: Commercial Banking
Address: Kingsway House, 107/113, Broad Street, Lagos
Tel: (01) 2665142, 2666183, 2665160, 2664420, 2643607-8 (2L), 2643596 **Fax:** (01) 2668567
E-mail: ebnheadoffice@equity-bank.com.ng
Contact: Mr. Akin Ajayi - MD/CEO
Mr. Yemi Adeniran - Head (Corporate Affairs)

EQUITY INDEMNITY INSURANCE COMPANY LIMITED
Business: Insurance
Address: Eleganza House (15th Floor), 15B, Joseph St Lagos
Tel: (01) 2637802, 2637337, 2637845, 2634904, 2647345, 2635861, 2634936 **Fax:** (01) 2637479
E-mail: equity@infoweb.abs.net
* Tofa House (1st Floor), Plot 770, Central Business District Abuja.
Tel: (09) 2346123
* 9, Trans-Amadi Industrial Layout, Port Harcourt
Tel: (084) 239552, 239563, 236114 **Fax:** (084) 236115
Contact: Mr. I. A. Balogun - MD/CEO

EQUITY LIFE INSURANCE COMPANY LIMITED
Business: Insurance
Address: Eleganza House (12th Floor), 15B, Josepeh Street, off Broad Street, Lagos

Tel: (01) 2637802, 2637337, 2634936, 2635861, 2636800
Fax: (01) 2637479
E-mail: equilife@infoweb.asb.net
* 9, Trans-Amadi Industrial Layout, Port Harcourt
Tel: (084) 239552, 239563, 236114 **Fax:** (084) 236115
E-mail: equityph@infoweb.abs.net
* Tofa's House (1st Floor), Plot 770, Central Business District, Abuja
Contact: Mrs. 'Seyi Ifaturoti - MD/CEO

EQUITY LOSS ADJUSTERS LIMITED
Business: Loss Adjusting, Marine and Aviation Surveys
Address: 13, Bashiru Oweh Street, off Medical Road, Lagos
Tel/Fax: (01) 4977183, 08033078314
Contact: Mr. Babatunde Fadun - CEO

EQUITY MANAGEMENT CONSULTANTS
Business: Managemeng Consultancy & Financial Services
Address: 9, Turton Street, Sabo-Yaba, Lagos
Tel: (01) 7744149, 4731475, 08023434144
* NW/352, Adekunle Fajuyi Road, Ekotedo, Ibadan
Tel: (022) 415273

EQUITY SERVICES LIMITED
Business: Company Secretarial &, Corporate Consultancy
Address: Jimade House, 2, Ojuelegba Road, Yaba, Lagos
Tel: (01) 861868, 8042948

EQUITY TRUST LOSS ADJUSTERS LIMITED
Business: Loss Adjusters, Marine & Aviation Surveyors
Address; 17, Murtala Mohammed International Airport Road, Ajao Estate, Apakun-Oshodi, Lagos
Tel: (01) 4527028-9(2L) **Fax:** (01) 4527026

ERADA CLINIC LIMITED
Business: Medical Services
Address: Plot 875, Oshogbo Close, off Emeka Anyaoku Street, Area 11, Garki, Abuja
Tel: (09) 2344406, 08023126762
E-mail: erada1116@yahoo.com
Contact: Dr. Eric Umeh - Medical Director

ERIJOY HOTELS NIGERIA LIMITED
Business: Hospitality Services, Conference Facilities
Address: Plot 5, Trans-Amadi Industrial Layout, Rumuobiakani, Port Harcourt
Tel: (084) 486170 **Fax:** (084) 571849
Contact: Chief E. B. Aso - Chairman/CEO

ERNST & YOUNG CONSULTING LIMITED
Business: Audit & Assurance Business Services, Taxation Consultancy, Management Consultancy, Company Secretarial Services
Address: Eboni House, 62, Marina, Lagos Island, Lagos
Tel: (01) 2661462, 2662833, 2662881, 2665534
Fax: (01) 2640742
E-mail: eyng@linkserve.com.ng
* Turaki Ali House (1st Floor, Bay 4), 3, Kanta Road, Kaduna
Tel: (062) 240034
* Plot 8B, Sani Abacha Road, GRA,. Phase III, Port Harcourt
Contact: Mr. Eddie O. Osakwe - MD/CEO

ESCO SUPERSTORES LIMITED
Business: Supermarkets, Importation of Diary Products
Address: Esco Plaza, 21, Udu Road, Warri
Tel: (053) 250614, 250699, 253358, 250913
Fax: (053) 250699
* 7, Ekunola Street, off Ago Palace Way, Okota, Isolo, Lagos.
Tel: (01) 5556225
Contact: Mr. Lucky Jerry Esigie - Chairman/CEO

ESENARD INSURNACE BROKERS LIMITED
Business: Insurance Broking and Consultacy Services
Address: 40, Aba Road, Port Harcourt
Tel: (084) 232545, 230442 *Abuja-(09) 3140545
Fax: (084) 232545
E-mail: esenard@phca.linkserve.com

ESE-TECH (NIGERIA) LIMITED
Business: Electrical and Mechanical Engineering Services
Address: 82, Allen Avenue (3rd Floor), Ikeja, Lagos
Tel: (01) 4976448 **Fax:** (01) 4979295
E-mail: esetech@yahoo.com
* Plot 9, Yaounde Street, by Sudan Street, Wuse Zone 6, Abuja
Contact: Mr. O. S. Esegine - Asst. GM/CEO

ESL SECURITIES LIMITED
Business: Financial Services, Stockbroking, Registrars
Address: Cowrie House (3rd Floor), 27/29, Adeyemo Alakija Street Victoria Island, Lagos
Tel: (01) 2612983, 2612986 **Fax:** (01) 2612983
E-mail: ecosec@hyperia.com
Contact: Prof. T. A. J. Ogunbiyi- Chairman
Mr. Uddin Amin - CEO

ESO & ASSOCIATES
Business: Estate Surveyors & Valuers, Property Development & Management, Estate Agency
Address: 1, Esa Close, off Oduduwa Crescent, Ikeja G.R.A., Ikeja, Lagos
Tel: (01) 4964450, 08023040038
E-mail: Ileso@yahoo.com
Contact: Rev. L. L. Eso - Principal Partner

ESSEM INTERNATIONAL LIMITED
Business: Distribution, Marketing and Sales of Cosmetics, Beauty Products and Pharmaceuticals
Address: Eleganza Road, (Libra Block, 2nd Floor, Right Wing), 1, Commercial Road, Apapa, Lagos
Tel: (01) 5451043
E-mail: essem@cyberspace.net.ng
Contact: Mr. M. Venugopal - GM/CEO

ESSENTIAL MARINE OIL SERVICES LIMITED
Business: Procurement and Supply of Oilfied Servicing Equipment, Dredging
Address: Elephant Cement House (5th Floor, Wing D), ASSBIFI Road, Central Business District, Alausa Ikeja, Lagos
Tel: (01) 2882588, 7756238 **Fax:** (01) 2882588
E-mail: essential@onebox.com
Website: www.e-marine.com
Contact: Mr. Akin Adesomoju - Chairman/CEO

Eternit Decorative Ceiling Tiles
Complement any periodic style.
* Beautiful
* Restful patterns
* Durable
* Decorative
Eternit
CERTIFIED
Eternit Limited
Eternit Lasts For you
The masters of roofing and ceiling sheets technology.
Factory & Head Office: 102, Sapele-Warri Road, P.O. Box 483, Sapele, Delta State. Tel: (054) 341311, 341405. E-mail: eternit@infoweb.abs.net
Aba Depot: Old Aba-Owerri Road, Osisioma, Aba, Abia State. Tel: 082 - 350231 * Abuja Depot: Old Dumez Yard, Kaduna/Lokoja, Road, F.C.T., Abuja. Tel: 090 - 806425
an Etex group company

ESSENTIALS LIMITED
Business: Corporate Promotions, Total Marketing Support Services, Manufacturing & Supply of Diaries, Awards, Corporate & Promotional Gift Items
Address: Plot 6, Aina Eleko Street, Onigbongbo, Maryland, Ikeja, Lagos
Tel: (01) 4960850, 7738678, 4973204 **Fax:** (01) 4973204
E-mail: essentials@infoweb.abs.net

ESSENTIAL SEA FOODS LIMITED
Business: Importation and Marketing of Frozen Seafoods
Address: Plot 1673, Oyin Olayemi St, Victoria Island, Lagos
Tel/Fax: (01) 2623716
E-mail: essenti@infoweb.abs.net

ESSO EXPLORATION & PRODUCTION (NIGERIA) LIMITED
Business: Crude Oil and Gas Exploration and Production
Address: Mobil House, Lekki Expressway, Victoria Is, Lagos
Tel: (01) 2622740-3 (4 L) **Fax:** (01) 2622744
Contact: Mr. D. Carr - MD/CEO

ESTATE DRUGS LIMITED
Business: Distribution, Supply and Sales of Pharmaceuticals and Disposable Medical Products.,
Address: Ebani House, 149/153, Broad Street, Lagos
Tel: (01) 2643713-4 (2L) **Fax:** (01) 2663888
E-mail: tejieji@yahoo.com
Contact: Mr. Tony C. Ejieji - Chairman/CEO

ESTATE LINKS LIMITED
Business: International Real Estate Consultancy
Address: WAPIC Building (2nd Floor), 119, Awolowo Road, S. W., Ikoyi, Lagos
Tel: (01) 2671564, 2901905, 4615729, 7911134
Fax: (01) 4614829
E-mail: ooestatelinks@hotmail.com
Website: www.estatelinks.net
Contact: Mr. Olugbenga Olaniyan - Chairman/CEO

ESTEC GROUPE LIMITED
Business: Sales & Service of Electric/Electronic Prepayment Meters, Electronic Security & Surveillance Devices
Address: NPS Trust Building (Top Floor), 2, Akinyemi Way, Ring Road, Ibadan
Tel: (02) 2316006, 08033295359
E-mail: estecgroup@webmail.co.za
Contact: Dr Isaac Muyiwa Ojo - MD/CEO

ESTENDO POWER PRODUCTS COMPANY LIMITED
Business: Sales & Maintenance of Electricity Generators
Address: 300, Apapa Rd (Airways Bus-Stop), Apapa, Lagos
Tel/Fax: (01) 5451820, 5876206
E-mail: estendo@cybaaspace.net
*Shop B61, Alaba International Market, Ojo, Lagos
Tel: (01) 5554133

ET & T INVESTMENTS COMPANY LIMITED
Business: Stockbroking, Asset & Portfolio Management, Project Finance Promotion & Management, Market Research & Feasibilty Studies, Advisory Services
Address: 99, Obafemi Awolowo Way (Suite 22), Ikeja, Lagos
Tel: (01) 4739695, 4977843, 08033004910
Fax: (01) 4977843
E-mail: ett@gacom.net
Website: www.etandtonline@.com
Contact: Mr Etim O. Onwionu-Okor - MD/CEO

ETERNA OIL & GAS PLC
Business: Manufacture and Marketing of CASTROL Lubricants and Petroleum Products
Address: 241, Igbosere Road, Lagos
Tel: (01) 2613265, 2635617, 2636266, 2646203
Fax: (01) 2633516
* Plot 168, Trans-Amadi Ind Layout, Port Harcourt.
Tel: (084) 239607

ETERNIT LIMITED
Business: Manufacturing of Fibre - Cement Roofing, Ceiling Materials and Concrete Roofing Tiles
Address: 102, Sapele - Warri Road, Sapele, Delta State
Tel: (054) 341311, 341405 **Fax:** (054) 341406
* Old Dumez Yard, Kaduna-Lokoja Road, FCT
Tel: 090-806425

ETHIOPE PUBLISHING CORPORATION
Business: Publishing
Address: Ring Road, beside Oredo L.G., Benin City
Tel: (052) 253036
E-mail: ethiopepublishing@yahoo.com

ETHIOPIAN AIRLINES (NIGERIA)
Business: International Airline Services
Address: 3, Idowu Taylor Street, Victoria Island, Lagos
Tel: (01) 7744711-2 (2L) **Fax:** (01) 4616297
E-mail: losam@ethiopianairlines.com
* Murtala Mohammed Int;l Airport, Ikeja, Lagos
Tel: (01) 7744710, 7751921, 7751923

ETN DISCOUNT NETWORK NIGERIA LIMITED
Business: Provision & Enlisting of ETN (European Travel Network) Discount Card Services
Address: 24A, Apapa Lane, Dolphin Estate Phase II, Ikoyi, Lagos
Tel: (01) 2690221, 2691719, 2671331 **Fax:** (01) 2695647
E-mail: info.ng@etn.org
Website: www.etn.nl
* 8, Badejoko Shopping Complex, Idi-Ape, Bashorun, Ibadan.
Tel: (02) 715211, 714136
Contact: Prof. Aba S. Sagoe - Chairman
Mr. Adekolapo Ademola - MD/CEO

ETTEH ARO & PARTNERS
Business: Consulting Civil and Structural Engineers
Address : Lawrence Arokodare House, 35, Oshutokun Avenue, Old Bodija, Ibadan
Tel: (01) 2413983; **Fax:** (01) 8100357
E-mail: etteh@steineng.net
* 14, Godwin Okigbo Street, Surulere, Lagos
Tel: (01) 5841884
* Plot 510, Olussegun Obasanjo way, Wuse Zone I, Abuja.
Tel: (09) 5231845
* 5, Port Harcourt/Aba Expressway, Port Harcourt
Tel: (084) 332835
Contact: Rev. (Engr.) Etteh I. Etteh (OFR) - Principal Partne

ETUDO & COMPANY
Business: Estate Surveyors and Valuers
Address: 126, Lewis Street, Lafiaji, Lagos
Tel: (01) 2635835, 2633596
* Pont Block (Basement), State Secretariat Complex Forces Avenue, Port Harcourt.
Tel: (084) 239243
Contact: Mr. E. L. Etudo - Principal Partner

EUCLID COMMUNICATIONS LIMITED
Business: Advertising and Public Relations Agency
Address: 217/219, Ikorodu Road, Obanikoro, Lagos
Tel/Fax: (01) 4716377, 4971736
Contact: Mr. Gori Ogunyemi - Chairman/CEO

EUNACO INDUSTRIES LIMITED
Business: Manufacture of Refractory Bricks and Mortar, Importation of Various Engineering and Technical Equipment & Spares
Address: 8, Hill View, Independence Layout, Enugu
Tel: (042) 457951 **Fax:** (042) 457774
Contact: Engr. Nathaniel N. Obinwa - Exec. Chairman

EUNACO REFRACTORIES LIMITED
Business: Sales of Industrial Machinery, Equipment, Adhesives and Lubricants
Address: 2/4, Unity Close, off Ladipo Street (by Minaj Press), Matori Industrial Estate, Mushin, Lagos
Tel: (01) 4520143
E-mail: eunaco@hotmail.com

EUNIBROWN (WEST AFRICA) LIMITED
Business: Sales of Generators
Address: Eunibrown House, 195, Ikorodu Road, Palmgrove, Lagos
Tel: (01) 5454962, 821690 **Fax:** (01) 822762
E-mail: eunibrag@gacom.net

EURAFRIC OIL & COASTAL SERVICES LIMITED
Business: Marketing & Distribution of Petroleum Products, Energy Services
Address: 24B, A.J. Marinho Drive, Victoria Island, Lagos
Tel: (01) 4617870, 4617890 **Fax:** (01) 4617870 (Ext. 102)
E-mail: anthony@koochicommunications.com
eurafic@nova.net.ng
Contact: Rear Admiral G. Ndubuisi Kanu (rtd.) - Chairman
Capt. Anthony O. Onoh - MD/CEO

EUREKA METALS LIMITED
Business: Manufacture of Building Materials (Nails, BRC Welded Mesh, Barbed Wire, Chainlink Fencing, Binding Wire etc.)
Address: Plot 130A, Akin Adesola St, Victoria Island, Lagos
Tel: (01) 2622232, 2622259, 2615505 **Fax:** (01) 2619487
E-mail: primlaks@hyperia.com
* Cocoa Board Warehouse (Gate 5), Ladipo Oluwole Street, Ikeja, Lagos
Tel: (01) 7763429, 7919506 **Fax:** (01) 4978644
E-mail: eurekametals@wannanet.net
Contact: Mr. S. Kar - MD/CEO

EURO SPORTS WEAR NIGERIA LIMITED
Business: Manufacture of Garments and Sports Wear
Address: Plot 9/11, Segun Irefin Street, (Synagogue B/Stop), Ikotun Egbe, Lagos
Tel: (01) 4936648 **Fax:** (01) 4936665
Contact: Mrs. E. Fakhry - MD/CEO

EUROCOLOR
Business: Colour Processing and Photo-Finishing
Address: 8, Oshodi-Apapa Expressway, Oshodi-Oke, Lagos
Tel: (01) 4975187
* 59, Obafemi Awolowo Way, Ikeja, Lagos
* 196, Herbert Macaulay St Adekunle, Yaba, Lagos
* 198, IBB Way, Katsina
Tel: (065) 432316

EURO-AFRICA LOGISTICS LIMITED
Business: Supply of Oil Tools & Equipment
Address: 3, Bethel Close, East-West Road, Rumuodara, Port Harcourt
Tel: (084) 485173, 611692, 08023119565, 08046105414
Fax: (084) 611692
E-mail: euro.africa@onebox.com
Contact: Mr Victor Enyidede - Chairman/CEO

EURO-TECH ALUMINIUM LIMITED
Business: Aluminium Roofing and Cladding Contractor
Address: H.F. Schroeder Compound, Plot 3, Block D, Apapa-Oshodi Expressway, Amuwo-Odofin Industrial Estate, Mile 2, Lagos
Tel: (01) 2881114, 7753152 **Fax:** (01) 2881114
Contact: Mr. Guido Helfenstein - Chairman/CEO

EUROBANC SAVINGS & LOANS LIMITED
Business: Mortgage Banking Service
Address: 8, Fure Avenue, Hotoro G.R.A. off CBN Rd, Kano
Tel: (064) 668337, 668338, 08044119551
Fax: (064) 668339
E-mail: abdulsalaam@yahoo.com
Contact: Ambassador Babagana Kingibe - Chairman
Alh. Abdulsalam Mohammed - MD/CEO

EUROBASE CONSULTS LIMITED
Business: Integrated Oilfield Services, Supply of Oil-Drilling Equipment & Chemicals, General Import & Export
Address: 29, Saka Tinubu Street, Victoria Island, Lagos
Tel: (01) 2615873, 611559, 611560 **Fax:** (01) 2615873
E-mail: eurobase@hyperia.com
Website: www.eurogroup.com
Contact: Mr. Don Obi - Chairman/CEO

EUROBRIDGE INDUSTRIES LIMITED
Business: Importation, Distribution and Marketing of Industrial Raw Materials (Foods and Beverages Flavours, Fragrance and Oils), Sales of Paint Raw Materials, Cosmetics and Allied Chemicals, Waxes and Jelly Oleochemicals etc.
Address: 34/36, Burma Road, (Ground Floor), Apapa, Lagos
Tel: (01) 5877656, 5451141 **Fax:** (01) 5451141
Contact: Mr. R. M. S. Farrant - Chairman/CEO

EUROCOM SECURITIES LIMITED
Business: Stockbroking, Investment Advisory Services
Address: Stock Exchange House (18th Floor), 2/4, Customs Street, off Marina, Lagos Island, Lagos

Tel: (01) 2664700, 2641726
Contact: Mr. Uchenna Ogbu - MD/CEO

EUROLINK NIGERIA LIMITED
Business: Manufacturing and Marketing of Pharmaceuticals, Chemicals, Hospital Equipments, Agro-Chemicals & Equipments, and Veterinary Drugs; Trading; General Contractor
Address: Plot PL, 7364, Anglo Jos New Industrial Area, Zarmaganda, of Yakubu Gowon Way, Jos
Tel: (073) 463665, 08034081116
Contact: Major Gen. Garba A. Mohammed (rtd) - Chairman
Alh. A. M. Nasir - MD/CEO

EUROPEAN ALL FREIGHT LIMITED
Business: Freight Forwarding, Curier Services, Clearing, Haulage, Import & Export
Address: 3, M. M International Airport Road, Isolo, Lagos
Tel: (01) 2229960, 3205139, 4520916, 4527796
Fax: (01) 3205138, 4520917
E-mail: eaflos@linkserve.com
Contact: Mr B. A. Jimoh - Chairman/CEO

EUROPRODUCTS LIMITED
Business: Manufacturing of Foam Products
Address: 4/5, Ahmed Talib Avenue/Textile Road, Kakuri Industrial Estate, Kaduna South, Kaduna
Tel: (062) 230728, 230729

EVA RUBBER & PLASTIC PRODUCTS NIGERIA LIMITED
Business: Manufacture of Rubber and Plastic Products
Address: Km. 10, Hadejia Road, Kano
Tel: (064) 645414
Contact: Mr. M. D. Tahir - MD/CEO

EVANS BROTHERS (NIGERIA PUBISHERS) LIMITED
Business: Publishing (Educational and General Books
Address: Jericho Road, Ibadan
Tel: (02) 2414394, 2414287, 2413708 **Fax:** (02) 2410757
E-mail: evans@skannet.com
* 44, Hakeem Balogun Street, Agidingbi
* 23, Ajao Road, Ikeja, Lagos
Contact: Mr. Gbenro Adegbola - MD/CEO
Mr. Wale Oluniawo - GM (Marketing and Sales)

EVANS MEDICAL PLC
Business: Manufacture and Marketing of Pharmaceutical and Nutraceutical Products
Address: Agbara Industrial Estate, off Km. 32, Lagos-Badagry Expressway, Agbara, Ogun State.
Tel: (01) 7740595, 7749178, 2882929, 2883192
Fax: (01) 2882788, 712124
Contact: Mr. Kiran Virat - MD/CEO

EVEN-EZRA NIGERIA LIMITED
Business: Fishing and Trawling, Audio-Visual Productions, Boutique/Tailoring Services, Technical/Sales Service Centre, Seafoods and Bakery, Security and Surveillance Equipment
Address: 1, Yeshayahu Lasode Crescent, Maroko Sandfilled, Victoria Island, Lagos
Tel: (01) 2611927, 611916, 611367 **Fax:** (01) 2614608
Contact: Engr. Isaiah Olufemi A. Lasode - Chairman/CEO

EVERLEAD COMMUNICATIONS LIMITED
Business: Sales of Computer, Mobile Phone and Accessories
Address: 202, Awolowo Road, S.W. Ikoyi, Lagos
Tel: (01) 2694319, 2670898, 2671314, 08022237999, 08022908516 **Fax:** (01) 2671313
E-mail: mails@everlead.net
Website: www.gsm-warehouse.com
Contact: Mr. Marcy Okwor - MD/CEO

EXCEL ENERGY SERVICES LIMITED
Business: Oil and Gas Engineering Services
Address: Plot 1618, Raufu Taylor Close (2nd Floor), off Idejo Street, Victoria Island, Lagos
Tel: (01) 3200885, 3200887 **Fax:** (01) 3200886
E-mail: info@excelenergyservices.com

EXCEL SECURITIES LIMITED
Business: Stockbroking, Company Secretarial Services
Address: UBN Building, 6, Ijora Causeway, Ijora, Lagos
Tel: (01) 5850752, 5871210, 5851897, 7733329
Fax: (01) 5850752
E-mail: excel@nigtel.com
Contact: Mr. J. E. Iriabe (JP) - Chairman/CEO

EXCELSIOR HOTEL LIMITED
Business: Hotel and Catering Services
Address: 3-15, Ede Street, Apapa, Lagos
Tel: (01) 5803680-2 (3 L), 5876095 **Fax:** (01) 5875002
E-mail: excelsior@infoweb.abs.net
Contact: Mr. Youssef F. Bohasali - MD/CEO

EXCLUSIVE INTERNATIONAL LIMITED
Business: Manufacturing of Furniture, Supermarket, Contract
Address: 200, Sapele Road, Benin City
Tel: (052) 251074, 251124, 08023404143
Contact: Barr. (Mrs.) Gladys Araraume - MD/CEO

EXCLUSIVE INTERIORS (NIGERIA) LIMITED
Business: Production, Importation, Distribution and Sales of Furniture, General Furnishing
Address: 34, Toyin Street, Ikeja, Lagos
Tel: (01) 4937897, 4977826 **Fax:** (01) 4937897
* 70, Wellington Bassey Road, Uyo
Contact: Chief Okon U. Bassey - Chairman

EXECUTIVE GUARDS LIMITED
Business: Security Guard Services, Training, Sales of Security Equipment, Consultancy
Address: 2, Ibrahim Taiwo Road, G R A, Jos
Tel/Fax: (073) 450208, 08034732147
Contact: Chief Edinen Usoroh - MD/CEO

EXOTIC CARS LIMITED
Business: Sales of Automobiles; Engineering Services
Address: 39, Rasaq, Balogun Street, Western Avenue, Surulere, Lagos
Tel: (01) 5850109, 08023161430
Contact: Mr. Vince Okey Agu - Chairman/CEO

EXP. MOMENTUM (NIGERIA) LIMITED
Business: Marketing, Promotions and Advertising
Address: 41, Isaac John Street, G.R.A. Ikeja, Lagos
Tel: (01) 4971424, 4972791

E-mail: dmcnig@metrong.com
Contact: Ron Boon - Chairman/CEO
Justin Howard - MD

EXPERT AVIATION AGENCY NIGERIA LIMITED
Business: Freight Consolidation, Clearing and Forwarding, Travel Agency, Car Hire Serives, Aviation Consultancy Services
Address: Concord Airline Premises, opp, Unipetrol Filling Station, General Aviation Terminal, Murtala Muhammed Airport, Lagos
Tel: (01) 4975988, 4935478, 08022234315
Fax: (01) 4975988
* Hajj Camp (Suite 123), NAHCO Area, Murtala Muhammed Airport, Ikeja, Lagos
Contact: Mr. Emmnauel A. Ajayi - Chairman/CEO

EXPLICIT
(formerly Explicit Communications Ltd)
Business: Advertising, Marketing and Public Relations
Address: 71, Adebayo Mokuolu St, Anthony Village, Lagos
Tel: (01) 4930868, 5550660, 08023139957
E-mail: explicitinfo@explicit-ng.com
Website: www.explicit-ng.com
Contact: Mr. Olatunde Thani - Chairman/CEO

EXPO SHIPPING LINE (NIGERIA) LIMITED
Business: Shipping, Ship Management, Chartering & Agency Oil Trading
Address: 69, Payne Crescent, Apapa, Lagos
Tel: (01) 5873253, 5873185
Fax: (01) 5876857, 2619690
E-mail: expoship@aol.com
marineser@aol.com
Contact: Mr. Toufic Abdallah - Chairman/CEO

EXPOMA NIGERIA LIMITED
Business: Telecommunucation Engineering, Consultancy Services, General Merchandising
Address: Plot 213, Muri Okunola St, Victoria Island, Lagos
Tel: (01) 2622453, 2882415
Contact: Major Gen Abubakar Waziri (rtd) - Chairman
Mr. B. Seriboh - Manager (Admin. & Finance)

EXPRESS DISCOUNT LIMITED
Business: Security Trading, Discount House, Funds Managing
Address: Marine View Plaza, 60, Marina, Lagos
Tel: (01) 2641650-5 (5L), 2641660-7 (8L, Dealing)
Fax: (01) 2641656, 2641673
E-mail: edl@expdisc.com
Website: www.expdisc.com
* Oyo House, Plot 77, 4th Avenue, off Ahmadu Bello Way, Central Business District, Abuja
Tel: (09) 2348580 **Fax:** (09) 2348581
E-mail: edl-abuja@expdisc.com
Contact: Mr. M. Kwesi Sagoe - MD/CEO

EXPRESS FISHERIES LIMITED
Business: Deep-Sea Fishing; Merchandising; Import and Export; Entertainment
Address: 295, Ikorodu Road, Maryland, Lagos
Tel: (01) 520608, 961529
Contact: Dr. Kunle Balogun - Chairman/CEO

EXPRESS PETROLEUM & GAS COMPANY LIMITED
Business: Exploration and Production of Crude Oil and Gas
Address: 11, Festival Road, Victoria Island, Lagos
Tel: (01) 2615115, 2616077, 2615838 **Fax:** (01) 2616077
* 66/67, Murtala Mohammed Way, Kano
Tel: (064) 634671, 639942 **Fax:** (064) 632060

EXPRESS PORTFOLIO SERVICES LIMITED
Business: Stockbroking, Portfolio Management, Investment Advisory Services
Address: BOI House (6th Floor), 18, Waff Road, Kaduna
Tel: (062) 241384-5 (2 L) **Fax:** (062) 241385
Contact: Alh. Abdul Wahab A. Ibraheem - Chairman
Mr. Solomon L .Boro - MD/CEO

EXPRESS SECURITY INSURANCE BROKERS LIMITED
Business: Insurance Broking and Consultancy Service
Address: 20, Association Avenue (2nd Floor), Ilupeju, Lagos
Tel : (01) 4935862 **Fax:** (01) 4935863
* behind Lara Hotels, Gaa Akanbi Area, Ilorin
Tel: (031) 23659
E-mail: excurity@yahoo.com
Contact: Mr. Omotayo Dada - -MD/CEO

EXQUISITE INDUSTRIES (NIGERIA) LIMITED
Business: Importation of Stockfish Fingers and Natural Fish Flavours, Frozen and Dried Fish, Exporters of Agricultural Produce, Clearing and Forwarding
Address: 19, Milverton Avenue, Aba, Abia State
Tel: (082) 220635 **Fax:** (082) 221707
* 22, Itapeju Street, Apapa, Lagos
* Shop 24, Kingsway Building 51, Marina, Lagos
Tel/Fax: (01) 5874490, 2664833
E-mail: nnkalu@infoweb.abs.net
Contact: Chief Kalu Nnana Kalu - Chairman/CEO

EYEWARE LIMITED
Business: Manufacture of Optical Lenses
Address: Matilda House, 5, Owodunni Street off Amore St, off Toyin Street, Ikeja, Lagos
Tel: (01) 4971329, 4934822, 4806827, 7735263, 7915470
Fax: (01) 4971329
E-mail: eyeware@hotmail.com
Contact: Dr. (Mrs.) Oyinlola Ilo - Chairman/CEO

EYIS RESOURCES LIMITED
Business: Clearing & Forwarding Agency
Address: 25, Alh. Kareem Akande Street, off Apapa-Oshodi Expressway, Olodi-Apapa, Lagos
Tel: (01) 4712512, 7927451
Contact: Mr. Lucky Amiwero - MD/CEO

EZERA INTERNATIONAL GROUP OF COMPANIES
Business: Importation of General Merchandise, Industrialists, Agro-Allied Business
Address: 105, Azikiwe Road, Aba
Tel: (082) 221118 **Fax:** (082) 220545, 221118
E-mail: ezeraintem@infowb.abs.net
Contact: Chief (Dr.) N. O. Nwojo - Chairman/CEO

EZIOBI MOTORS NIGERIA LIMITED
Business: Importation and Sales of Auto Spare Parts
Address: A4/A5, Zone 13, Main Market, Anambra State

Tel: (046) 462318, 462529 **Fax:** (046) 460868
* 42A, Agoro Street, Idumota, Lagos
Contact: Mr. Sunday Eziobiora - Chairman/CEO

F & C SECURITIES LIMITED
Business: Stockbroking
Address: 17B, Bishop Aboyade Cole St, Victoria Is, Lagos
Tel: (01) 2621307, 2620722, 7747122 **Fax:** (01) 2620839
E-mail: fcsl@infoweb.abs.net
Contact: Mr. Rasheed Alimi - MD/CEO

F & F GROUP
Business: Sales & Maintenance of Banking and Office Automation Products
Address: Unity House (Ground Floor), 37, Marina, Lagos
Tel: (01) 2600505-8 (4 L) **Fax:** (01) 2600509
E-mail: f_and_f@infowe.abs.net
Contact: Mr. B. O. Onamusi - Chairman/CEO

F & G INTERNATIONAL NIGERIA LIMITED
Business: Production of Chemicals and Mineral Products
Address: F & G House, 7, Ade Akinsanya Avenue, off Town Planning Way, Ilupeju, Lagos
Tel: (01) 4977268, 4975923, 7745193, 08033344661
Fax: (01) 2668128
E-mail: oakwood@infoweb.abs.net
* Industrial Road, by Century Polyester Plc, Lagos State Ind. Estate, Odongunyan, Ikorodu, Lagos
Contact: Otunba F. I. Ajayi - Chairman/CEO

F & K SECURITY EQUIPMENT & SYSTEM LIMITED
Business: Sale and Maintenance of Security Equipment
Address: 122, Ogunlana Drive, Surulere, Lagos
Tel: (01) 5850154, 7742710 **Fax:** (01) 5850154
E-mail: fotofab@infoweb.abs.net
fandksecurityequipment@infoweb.abs.net
* 6, Sudan Street, Wuse Zone 6, Abuja.
Tel/Fax: (09) 5235319
* 1, Rumuola Rd, Port Harcourt.
Tel: (084) 238059
Contact: Chief Fab K. Uche - Chairman/CEO

F F & T LIMITED
Business: Management Consultants, Book Distribution
Address: Plot 38, Kofo Abayomi St, Victoria Island, Lagos
Tel: (01) 2625828, 2610430, 2625969, 612232, 2700054, 08023430961 **Fax:** (01) 2624704
E-mail: ifp@nova.net.ng
Contact: Prof. B. O. Nwabueze, SAN - Chairman
Mr. Felix N. Akpe - MD/CEO

F. A. ONWUACHU ENTERPRISES LIMITED
Business: Importers, Industrialists, Transporters, Manufacturer's Representatives and General Merchants
Address: 21, Modebe Avenue, Onitsha
Tel: (046) 211399, 212516, 411082, 08033248868
Contact: Chief F. A. Onwuachu - Chairman/CEO

F. A. O. PHILLIPS & ASSOCIATES
Business: Mechanical & Electrical Engineering Consultancy
Address: 22, Ogunlana Drive, Surulere, Lagos
Tel: (01) 4705214, 4710658, 833645, 08034020505
Fax: (01) 7916292
E-mail: foopaces@yahoo.com
Contact: Engr Foluseke A. O. Phillips - Principal Consultant

F. G ONYENWE MOTORS NIGERIA LIMITED
Business: Transportation Services
Address: 112, Upper Iweka Road, Onitsha
Tel: (046) 460704, 412735

F. G. N. OKOYE & SONS GROUP LIMITED
Business: Conglomerate
Address: FEGNO Hosue 2, Felix Chuks Okeye Crescent, off Presidential Road, Independence Layout, Enugu
Tel: (042) 457761, 453973, 458190, 458191
Fax: (042) 459148, 452813
* 21/22, Marina, Lagos
Tel: (01) 2632800 **Fax:** (01) 2631499
* Gwagwalada Industrial Layout, Abuja
* 10/11, Lagos Street, Kano.
Tel: (046) 620020
Contact: Mrs. Joy O. Okeke - Group Legal Adviser

F. K. CONSTRUCTION COMPANY LIMITED
Business: Building and Civil Engineering
Address: 10, Miller Rd, off Club Rd, Bompai Ind.Estate, Kano
Tel: (064) 631574, 632001 **Fax:** (064) 632001
* 10, Makoko Road, Yaba, Lagos.
Tel: (01) 863653
* Plot 218, Shehu Shagari Way, Abuja
Tel: (09) 2347080 **Fax:** (09) 2347081
* 1, Ohiamini Road, D-Line, Port Harcourt
Tel: (084) 232197
Contact: Mr F. Khouri - MD/CEO

FABROS ENTERPRISES (WEST AFRICA) LIMITED
Business: Distribution and Sales of Electric Transformers, Generators, Welding Machines, Armoured Cables & Submersible Pumps
Address: 11, Emekuku Street, D-Line, Port Harcourt
Tel: (084) 239088, 08023243525
E-mail: fabrosgroup@yahoo.com
* 2, Mustapha Ojora Close, off Badagry Expressway, Lagos
Tel: (01) 7744459
* Area 11 Shopping Centre, Garki, Abuja
Tel: (09) 3148228
Contact: Engr Fred Anagwu - Chairman/CEO

FACILITY PRODUCTS (NIGERIA) LIMITED
Business: Manufacuturing of Plastic Products
Address: Plot 68, Ikorodu Industrial Estate, Odogunyan, Ikorodu Town, Lagos State
Tel: (01) 7743076, 7741760, 7781353
Fax: (01) 2881288
* 5B, Inuwa Wada Lane, off Civic Centre Rd, Kano
Tel/Fax: (064) 633966

FAFINC NIGERIA LIMITED
Business: Financial Services, Manufacturing
Address: Plot 13, Acme Road, Ogba Ind. Estate, Ikeja, Lagos
Tel: (01) 4925708, 8043113 **Fax:** (01) 4925708
E-mail: fafinc@cyberspace.net.ng
Contact: Alh. (Dr.) Shehu Musa, CFR - Chairman
Mr. Fidel C. Anujuo - MD/CEO

FAGBOHUN & COMPANY LIMITED
Business: Tailoring and Fashion Designing
Address: 3, Awolowo Road, Oke Bola, Ibadan
Tel: (02) 2412354, 0803304961
* 1, Bank Lane, Town Planning Way, Ilupeju, Lagos.
Tel: (01) 4735561
E-mail: wole.fagbohun@skannet.com
Contact: Mr. Wole Fagbohun - Chairman/CEO

FAGET NIGERIA LIMITED
Business: Ship Owners and Operators
Address: 8, Ibiere Crescent, off Kofo Abayomi Avenue, Apapa, Lagos
Tel: (01) 5804050-9 (10 L), 5872648 **Fax:** (01) 5876704
* 25, Mbonu Street, D/Line Diobu, Port Harcourt
Tel: (084) 232334
E-mail: canice@nigol.net.ng
E-mail: ceetoh@usa.net
Contact: Chief Canice Etoh - MD/CEO

FAIR BOND GROUP OF COMPANIES
Business: Banking and Office Automation, Pharmaceuticals, Luxury Apartments, Real Estate, Produce Export, Oil Services and Crude Oil Export, Information Technology Solutions and Networking, Advisory Services, Financing
Address: Edo House, Plot 1225, Ahmadu Bello Way, Bar Beach, Victoria Island, Lagos
Tel: (01) 2620174-5 (2 L), 2621381, 26621383, 2621384
Fax: (01) 2621386
Contact: Mr. Kenneth S. Odongbanro - Chairman/CEO

FAIR DEAL INSURANCE BROKERS LIMITED
Business: Insurance Broking
Address: 24, Ekololu Street, Surulere, Lagos
Tel: (01) 5836468, 08023154620, 08023198573
E-mail: fairdealinscebrokersltd@yahoo.com
Contact: Mrs. J. O. Ajetunmobi-Ayeni -- MD/CEO

FAIRLAWN TECHNOLOGIES LIMITED
Business: Wireless Internet Service Provider
Address: Crusader House (12th Floor), 16A, Commercial Avenue, Sabo-Yaba, Lagos
E-mail: chrisemka@wavecircuit.com
Tel: (01) 3425337-8 (2L)
Contact: Mr. Chris C. Ekeanyanwu - MD/CEO

FAIRWINDS (NIGERIA) LIMITED
Business: Marketing of Lubricants and Petroleum Products
Address: 19, Oyekan St, off Bombay Crescent, Apapa, Lagos
Tel: (01) 5455393, 7745369, 08033561645
Fax: (01) 5455392
E-mail: fairlub@yahoo.com
Contact: Mrs. Olajumoke Oyaghua - CEO

FAITH CITY HOSPITAL LIMITED
Business: Hospital & Medical Services, Supply of Medical Equipment & Consumables
Address: 16, Asa Afariogun Street, off Osolo Way, Ajao Estate, Lagos
Tel: (01) 4804001
* 2B, Oko-Awo Close, off Karimu Kotun Street, Victoria Island, Lagos
Tel: (01) 3200189, 2705612, 08023201234
Contact: Dr. Austine O. Ebhomielen - Chief Medical Director

FALACOL GROUP OF COMPANIES
Business: Manufacturing of Pharmaceutical Products, Medical Services, Building and Civil Engineering
Address: 72, Sani Abacha Way (formerly Airport Rd), Kano
Tel: (064) 647075, 648989, 669401 **Fax:** (064) 632171
* Km. 14, Hadejia Road, Kano
Contact: Mr. A. Farouk Labaran - Chairman/CEO

FALCON CHEMICALS LIMITED
Business: Manufacturing and Consulting Chemist
Address: 2, Amusa Oloyede Street, off Tokunbo Alli Street, off Toyin Street, Ikeja, Lagos
Tel: (01) 4971751, 4968635, 08023291849
Fax: (01) 4971751
* Km. 42, Lagos-Abeokuta Express Road, Ijako-Otta, Ogun State
Contact: Chief Francis B. Adefarati - Chairman/CEO

FALCON COMPUTERS LIMITED
Business: IT Training and Certification Consultancy, Sales, Repairs and Maintenance of Computers
Address: Re-Insurance House (5th Floor), 46, Marina, Lagos
Tel: (01) 2669235, 2666775 **Fax:** (01) 2665014, 2666775
E-mail: falcon@infoweb.abs.net
Contact: Mr. Davis F. Mirilla - President/CEO

FALCON PETROLEUM LIMITED
Business: Re-Engineering for Natural Gas Utilisation (Equipment Conversion and Reticulation Services), NDT Inspection and Corrosion Management Services, Construction of Tanks, Pipelines/Flowlines, Engineering and Environmental Consultants
Address: former DPR Building (3rd Floor), 44, Eric Moor Road, Surulere, Lagos
Tel: (01) 5870700, 5870710, 4803054, 080330088117, 08056012767 **Fax:** (01) 5870700
E-mail: falconpetro@hyperia.com
info@fp.com
Website: www.fp.com
Contact: Chief C. A. Okonkwo - Chairman
Dr. Joe Ezigbo - MD/CEO

FALCON SECURITIES LIMITED
Business: Stockbroking
Address: New Africa House (9th Floor), 31, Marina, Lagos
Tel: (01) 2661498, 2663286
Contact: Mr. Peter U. Ololo - MD/CEO

FALMA ORGANICS LIMITED
Business: Importation of Pharmaceutical Products
Address: 38/40, Burma Road, Apapa, Lagos
Tel: (01) 5875000, 5871378, 7912114 **Fax:** (01) 5871378
E-mail: falmaorganics@linkserve.com.ng
Contact: Mr. T. M. Mathai - MD/CEO

FAMAD PLC
Business : Manufacture & Marketing of Assorted Footwear, Processing of Crumb Rubber
Address: Km. 15, Ikorodu Road, Ojota, Lagos
Tel: (01) 4968421-3 (3 L), 7929483 **Fax:** (01) 2222031

E-mail: famad@infoweb.abs.net
Contact: Chief(Mrs.) O. O. Olaknrin, OFR - Chairman
Mr. M.O. Ajado - Technical Director

FAME PUBLICATIONS LIMITED
Business: Magazine Publishing, Event Packaging
Address: 16, Eleruwa Street, Wemabod Estate, off Ajao Road, off Adeniyi Jones Avenue, Ikeja, Lagos
Tel: (01) 4961080
E-mail: fameweekly@hotmail.com
* NIPOST Complex (Suite 52),Area 10, Garki, Abuja
Tel: (09) 8500451
Contact: Mr. Afolabi Odeyemi - Exec. Editor
Mr. S. Obazie - A.G.M. (Operations)

FAMFA OIL LIMITED
Business: Oil and Gas Exploration and Production
Address: 290A, Ajose Adeogun St, Victoria Island, Lagos
Tel: (01) 7744421, 7747979, 7747980 Fax: (01) 5558090
E-mail: admin@famfa.com
Website: www.famfa.com

FAMILY FOODS LIMITED
Business: Sales of Industrial Baking Equipment, Bakery
Address: 185, Akowonjo Road, Dopemu, Agege, Lagos
Tel: (01) 4923354, 4925523 **Fax:** (01) 4925523
E-mail: egpro@infoweb.abs.net
* 1, Reggie Close, Abule Egba, Agege, Lagos
Tel: (01) 4925523

FAN MILK PLC
Business: Production of Diary & Allied Products
Address: Eleiyele Industrial Layout, Ibadan
Tel: (02) 2412032, 2411021, 2413264-5 (2L)
Fax: (02) 2412743
E-mail: fanmilk@skannet.com
* Challawa Industrial Estate, P.O.Box 6683, Kano
* 102, Obafemi Awolowo Way, Ikeja, Lagos
Tel: (02) 4971813
Contact: Mr. K. H. Rassmussen - MD/CEO
Mr. O. A. Alabi - GM (Marketing)

FANO SHIPPING AGENCIES LIMITED
Business: Shipping, Clearing & Forwarding
Address: 34, Aggrey Road, Port Harcourt
Tel: (084) 232944
* 30/32, Creek Road, Apapa, Lagos
Tel: (01) 5871857, 5450715 **Fax:** (01) 5457874
Contact: Chief Damian Emeka Obianigwe - Chairman/CEO

FANTASYLAND
Business: Entertainment, Receptions, Rentals
Address: 11, Bayo Kuku St/Kingsway Road, Ikoyi, Lagos
Tel: (01) 2693592, 2673424 **Fax:** (01) 2693592

FAOLA REPROGRAPHICS NIGERIA LIMITED
Business: Sales, Supply and Maintenance of Microfilms ad Microfilm Equipment, Bureau Service for Micro-Reproduction of Documents
Address: 14A, Oshodi-Apapa Expressway, Oshodi Lagos
Tel: (01) 4973384, 4976248-9 (2L) **Fax:** (01) 4973348
E-mail: faola@micro.com.ng
Contact: Mr. D. A. Faola - Chairman/CEO

FAR EAST TECHNICAL NIGERIA LIMITED
Business: Sales of Generators and Spare Parts, Repairs, Service and Maintenance
Address: 3A, Degema Close off Park Lane, Apapa, G.R.A. Lagos
Tel: (01) 5450045, 5871551, 5873978, 5873980
Fax: (01) 5871551
E-mail: fareasttechnical@linkserve.com
Contact: Alh. M. Ahmed - Chairman
Mr. Eta Saha - MD/CEO

FARADAY NIGERIA LIMITED
Business: Manufacturing and Marketing of Eductional Materials/Teaching Aids, Supply and Installation of Laboratory Equipment, Fixtures and Fittings
Address: 9, Tobun Street, Onike, Yaba, Lagos
Tel: (01) 7900986
* 45, Community Road, Akoka, Yaba, Lagos
Tel: (01) 823743, 0802410150
Contact: Alhaja Abolaji Tiamiyu - Chairman
Alh. Babatunde Abdul - MD/CEO

FAREAST MERCHANTILE COMPANY LIMITED
Business: Importation of Food Products, Domestic & Industrial Appliances; General Merchandising
Address: Plot 721 (House 1), Adetokunbo Ademola Street, Victoria Island, Lagos
Tel: (01) 2612933, 2610381- 8(8L) *Abuja-(09) 5232855
Fax: (01) 2619438
* 61, Enu-Owa Street, (1st Floor), Lagos
Tel: (01) 2666758, 2664393
* 19, Martins Street, Lagos.
Tel: (01) 2662125, 2643760
Contact: Mr. B. Sundor

FARMEX MEYER LIMITED
Business: Manufacture of Pharmaceuticals
Address: Km. 38, Lagos-Abeokuta Road, Sango Ota,
Tel: (039) 722201-3 (3 L) **Fax:** (039) 722203
Contact: Mr. P. S. Lalvani - MD/CEO

FAS AGRO INDUSTRIAL COMPANY LIMITED
Business: Manufacture of Polypropylene Bags and Laminated Shopping Bags
Address: 27, Burma Road, Apapa, Lagos
Tel: (01) 5874996, 5452108, 5874988, 5452107
Fax: (01) 5452105, 5452107
Contact: Alh. Muazu Abbas - Chairman
Mr. Reda Fawaz - MD/CEO.

FASTSPREAD COMMUNICATIONS LIMITED
Business: Outdoor Advertising, Fabrication of Plastic & Aluminium Illminated Services
Address: 41C, Commercial Avenue, Sabo-Yaba, Lagos
Tel: (01) 860380, 8172489, 08033303797
E-mail: fspreadcom@yahoo.com
Contact: Mr. Samuel O .Joshua - MD/CEO

FATA TANNERIES
(Export Processing Factory)
Business: Tanning of Hides & Skins
Address: Plot 53, Challawa Industrial Estate, Kano
Contact: Mr. Y. Vicinoni - MD/CEO

FATBOL OJIKUTU NIGERIA LIMITED
Business: Importation and Marketing of Woven Lining Materials and General Merchandise, Exportation of Agricultural Commodities, General Contractors
Address: 90, Fred McEwen Street, off Martins Street, Lagos
Tel: (01) 4716324, 8129420 **Fax:** (01) 2665530
Contact: Alh. F. O. Ojikutu - Chairman/CEO

FATE FOUNDATION
Business: Entreprenerial Development, Training
Address: Water House (1st Floor), Lagos State Water Cooperation Building, Ijora Causeway, Lagos
Tel: (01) 4706836-40 (5L), 4744237, 08036708806
* 279, Aba-Port Harcort Road, opp Rivon Clinic, First Artillery, Port Harcourt

FATGBEMS (NIGERIA) LIMITED
Business: Marketing of Tyres and Petroleum Products
Address: Ibadan Road, Car Wash, Adatan, Abeokuta
Tel: (039) 245080, 244233, 08033161343
* 47, En-Owa Street, Idumota, Lagos
Tel: (01) 2660583
Contact: Alh. Fatai A. O. Gbemisola - Chairman/CEO.

FAVOURITES LIMITED
Business: Fast-Food Outlets, Outdoor Catering Services
Address: 75, Bode Thomas Street/Adeniran Ogunsanya Street, opposite Mr. Biggs' Surulere, Lagos
Tel: (01) 5456133, 5456134
* Akanbi Place, 73B, Opebi Road, Ikeja, Lagos

FB ASSET MANAGEMENT LIMITED
Business: Portfolio Management, Corporate Finance, Investment Advisory Services, Equipment Leasing, Pension Funds Management, Property Development, Management and Support Servics
Address: 12, Agoro Odiyan Street, off Adeola Odeku Street, Victoria Island, Lagos
Tel: (01) 2610626-7 (2 L) **Fax:** (01) 2610628
E-mail: fbasst2001@yahoo.com
* Fortune Bank Building (2nd Floor), 1, Isaac Boro Park, Old G.R.A. Port Harcourt
Tel: (084) 236021-2 (2 L)
Contact: Mr. G. A. B. Owope - GM/CEO

FBCO LIMITED
(Div. of FBTC Group)
Business: Importation & Sales of Heavy-Duty Construction Trucks and Equipment
Address: Otto Wolff Complex, Cardoso Street, beh. Julius Berger Yard, Ajegunle, Apapa, Lagos
Tel: (01) 8042369, 7750824, 08033024824, 08033085572
Fax: (01) 8042469

FBN (MERCHANTS BANKERS) LIMITED
Business: Merchant Banking
Address: 9/11, Macarthy Street, Onikan, Lagos
Tel: (01) 2600880-9 (10L) **Fax:** (01) 2633600, 2630709
E-mail: fbnmb@fbnmb.com
Website: www.fbnmb.com
* Coomasie Building, Plot 777, Muhammadu Buhari Way, Abuja.
Tel: (09) 2347842-3 (2L) **Fax:** (09) 2346824
* Plot 346B, Olu Obasanjo Road, Port Harcourt
Tel: (084) 230261-3 (3L), 230251, 230253
Tel/Fax: (084) 238529
Contact: Mr. Rasheed Adewale Raji - MD/CEO.

FBN INSURANCE BROKERS LIMITED
Business: Insurance Broking & Consultancy Services
Address: Stock Exchange Building (14th Floor), 2/4, Customs Street, off Marina, Lagos
Tel: (01) 2660498, 4803586 Fax: (01) 2660140
Contact: Dr. Udo Udo-Aka - Chairman
Mr. O. O. Akinyemi - MD/CEO.

FCMB CAPITAL MARKETS
Business: Capital Market Activities
Address: Primrose Tower, 17A, Tinubu Street, off Tinubu Square, Marina, Lagos
Tel: (01) 2665944-53 (10 L) **Fax:** (01) 2665126, 2668833
E-mail: capmkts@firstcitygroup.com
Website: www.fcmb-ltd.com
* Plot 1661, Oyin Jolayemi St Victoria Island, Lagos
Tel: (01) 2625674-5 (2L), 2625860-3 (3L), 2880373-4 (2 L)
E-mail: vioffice@fcmb-ltd.com
* Plot 282A, Port Harcourt/Aba Expressway (1st Floor), G.R.A. Phase II, Port Harcourt
Tel: (084) 237772-4 (3 L) 236533 **Fax:** (084) 237773
* UAC Complex (Ground Floor), Plot 272 & 273, Central Business District, Abuja
Tel: (09) 5237910, 5237908-9 (2 L) **Fax:** (09) 5237918
Contact: Mr 'Ladi Balogn - Dep. MD

FCN INSURANCE BROKERS LIMITED
Business: Insurance Broking
Address: 99, Ognlana Drive, Surulere, Lagos
Tel: (01) 4709119, 4802078
Contact: Ogbuesi F.C. Nwokolo - Exec. Chairman

FEBI OIL (NIGERIA) LIMITED
Business: Marine Services & Consultancy, Onshore/Offshore Drilling Servics
Address: White House Plaza, 1, Sedco Road, off Udu Ferry Way, Warri
Tel: (053) 258349, 0803345340 **Fax:** (053) 2129200
E-mail: foni@febioil.com
Contact: Mr. Frank Efole - MD/CEO

FEDERAL AIRPORTS AUTHORITY OF NIGERIA (FAAN)
Business: Administration & Maintenance of Airports
Address: Murtala Muhammed Airport, Ikeja, Lagos
Tel: (01) 4970335-7 (3L), 4971129, 4971132
Fax: (01) 4970342
E-mail: md@faan.com.ng
Contact: Mr Sylvester Oputa - GM/Head (Public Affairs)

FEDERAL HOUSING AUTHORITY (FHA)
Business: Provision & Management of Federal Housing Projects
Address: Julius Nyerere Crescent, off Yakubu Gowon Cr. opp.ECOWAS Secretariat, Asokoro, Abuja
Tel: (09) 3144962, 3144964 **Fax:** (09) 3144963
* 202 Road, B Close, Festac Town, Lagos
Tel: (01) 5892489
Contact: Engr. Mustapha Ibrahim - MD/CEO
Mr. Fola Owolabi - DGM/Head - Public Relations

FEDERAL MORTGAGE BANK OF NIGERIA (FMBN)
Business: Mortgage Banking
Address: Plot 124, Moshood Abiola Road (Festival), Garki Area 2, Abuja
Tel/Fax: (09) 2344212, 2344213, 2349537
Contact: Alh. Kassim M. Bichi - MD/CEO.
Mr. Dauda A. Yusuf - Manger (Public Relations)

FEDERAL RADIO CORPORATION OF NIGERIA (FRCN)
Business: Radio Broadcasting Services, Information Dissemination, Public Enlightenment, Education and Entertainment
Address: Radio House, Herbert Macaulay Way (South), Area 10, Garki, Abuja.
Tel: (09) 2341023, 2346484, 2346487 **Fax:** (09) 2346485
E-mail: frcnhq@alpha.linkserve.com
Contact: Dr. Eddie Iroh - Director General/CEO

FEDERAL SUPERPHOSPHATE FERTILIZER COMPANY LTD
Business: Manufacture of Single Superphosphate Fertilizer
Address: 4, Nassarawa Rd, Kaduna South Ind. Area, Kaduna
Tel: (062) 233099, 234412, 370328
* Behind NEPA Power Station, Coal Wharf, Ijora-Olopa, Lagos
Contact: Engr. Abdu M. Kanti - MD/CEO
Mr. Shaldas C. Tanko - Asst. Mgr (Corp. Affairs)

FEDERATED LOSS ADJUSTERS LIMITED
Business: Loss Adjusting and Risk Surveying
Address: 18, Kaffi Street, off Obafemi Awolowo Way, Alausa- Ikeja, Lagos
Tel: (01) 4707801, 773536, 7748778, 08033037607, 08033531531 **Fax:** (01) 4974848
E-mail: fedloss@yahoo.com
* UTC Complex (Suite FF04), Area 10, Garki, Abuja
Tel: (09) 2340462 **Fax:** (09) 2342575
* 145, Ikwere Road, Port Harcourt.
Tel: (090) 402865
Contact: Mr. Kayode Oshinuga - MD/CEO

FEDERATED STEEL MILLS LIMITED
Business: Manufacturers of all Sizes of Steel Reinforcing Bars, Flat Bars & Welding Electrodes
Address: Block XI, Plot 3-10, Otta Industrial Estate, off Idiroko Road, Otta, Ogun State
Tel: (039) 722008-9 (2L), 722681, 08034733709
Fax: (090) 404508, (01) 4970011
E-mail: fedsteel@alpha.linkserve.com

FEDERATION PRODUCTS (NIGERIA) LIMITED
Business: Manufacture of Plastic Materials, Travel Goods Suitcases & Briefcases
Address: 38, Burma Road, Apapa, Lagos
Tel: (01) 875444, 877140
Contact: Otunba S. K. Onafowokan - Chairman

FedEx RED STAR EXPRESS
Business: Courier & Logistic Services
Address: 70, International Airport Road, Isolo, Lagos
Tel: (01) 4973547, 4973255, 4973309, 4705074, 4708377, 7736938
Fax: (01) 4528629, 4976612, 4528629, 4705814
E-mail: enquiries@redstar-ng.com
Website: http//:www.fedex.com
* 4, Lumumbasi Street, Wuse Zone 3, Abuja
Tel: (09) 5233360, 2349437
Contact: Mr. Isaac Orolugbagbe - MD/CEO

FEEDEX (NIGERIA) LIMITED
Business: Manufacturing of Livestock Feeds & Concentrates
Address: Plot 5A, Kudenda Industrial Area, Nnamdi Azikiwe Expressway Bye-Pass, Kaduna
Tel: (062) 230131, 235401
Contact: Alh. (Dr) Yahuza Yashe - MD/CEO

FEEZY ENGINEERING NIGERIA LIMITED
Business: Elevator Engineering
Address: 4, Olufunmilola Okikiolu Street, off Toyin Street, Ikeja, Lagos
Tel: (01) 4964650, 4742287 **Fax:** (01) 4931987, 4974556
Contact: Engr. O. O. Adeyinka - MD/CEO.

FELDEN LIMITED
Business: Importation and Sales of Broadcast Materials and Accessories, Data & Multimedia Products
Address: 3, Oje-Imianvan Street, off Oregun Rd, Ikeja, Lagos
Tel: (01) 4938181, 4964758 **Fax:** (01) 4972155
E-mail: chris-ejik@hyperia.com
Website: www.chrisejikgroup.com

FEMEB NIGERIA LIMITED
Business: Design, Production and Sales of Promotional Materials, Corporate Gifts and Awards
Address: 21, Coker Road, behind Mr. Bigg's, Ilupeju, Lagos
Tel; (01) 4972000, 4978421, 4961094 **Fax:** (01) 4972000
E-mail: femeb@infoweb.abs.net
Contact: Arc. Femi Ayodele - Chairman

FEMI JOHNSON & COMPANY LIMITED
Business: Insurance Brokerage
Address: Broking House (Exec. Suite, 9th Floor), 1, Alh. Jimoh Odutola Road, Ibadan.
Tel: (02) 2410224, 2410236, 2410238, 2410382, 2412236, 2412238, 2412279, 2412290, 2412293, 08033440141
Fax: (02) 2410941
E-mail: femijohnson@skannet.com
* New Africa House (5th Floor), 31, Marina, Lagos
Tel: (01) 2660286, 2660728, 2660757, 08033440143
Fax: (01) 2662478
* NICON Hilton Hotel (Mezzanine Floor), Abuja
Tel: (09) 4131926, 08033440128 **Fax:** (09) 4131926
* Plot 144, Trans-Amadi Ind Layout, Port Harcourt
Tel: (084) 232987, 08033440724 **Fax:** (084) 232987
Contact: Mr. C. O. Fatanmi - MD/CEO

FEMI MAJEKODUNMI ASSOCIATES LIMITED
Business: Architectural Designs
Address: St. Nicholas Building (Penthouse Suite), 6, Catholic Mission Street, Lagos Island, Lagos
Tel: (01) 2635559, 2635360, 2637113, 2637082
Fax: (01) 2632291
E-mail: fmalag@fma-arch.com
Contact: Arc. (Chief) Olufemi Majekodunmi - Exec. Chairman

FEMI POPOOLA & ASSOCIATES LIMITED
Business: Quantity Surveying, Project Management

Address: 33, Berkley St, off King George V Rd Onikan, Lagos
Tel: (01) 2634437, 2635208, 2634836 **Fax:** (01) 2635079
E-mail: femipopoola@cyberspace.net.ng
Contact: Mr. O. Popoola - Chairman/CEO

FEMINA HYGIENICAL PRODUCTS (NIGERIA) LIMITED
Business: Manufacturing of Santary Pads, Cosmetics, Paper Napkins & Toilet Tissue
Address: Plot 9E, Isolo Industrial Area, Akinwunmi Street, off Ladipo Street, Papa Ajao, Mushin, Lagos
Tel: (01) 4524964, 7732092 **Fax:** (01) 4523509
E-mail: femina@alpha.linkserve.com
* Plot 28, Trans-Amadi Ind. Layout, Port Harcourt
Tel: (084) 232082, 234018

FEMOPE LIMITED
Business: Sales of Medical Equipment and Surgical Supplies, Sexual & Reproductive Health Programme, Support for Network of NGO's, Funds Management
Address: 7, Saka Street, Mushin, Lagos
Tel: (01) 4522016, 521166, 4521456
Fax: (01) 4524088, 4522016
E-mail: femope@infoweb.abs.net
Contact: Chief I. Olufemi Moradeyo - Chairman/CEO.

FEMTRON TECHNICORP
Business: Installation, Repairs, Maintenance, Calibration, Sales & Service of Digital Electronic Weighbridges, Platform Scales & Balances, Industrial Weighing Systems & Printing of Weighing Tickets
Address: 23, Olabisi Street, beh. Real Oil Mills Ltd, Ikorodu Road, Ojota, Lagos
Tel: 08033488158, 08033031116
E-mail: isobanwa@yahoo.co.uk
Contact: Mr. Femi Shobanwa - Tech. Operations Manager

FENABROS LIMITED
Business: Importation and Distribution of Fishing Material
Address: 2, Pam Pam Lane, Odoakpu, Onitsha
Tel: (046) 210260, 217297
Contact: Chief Felix Nduaguba - Chairman/CEO.

FENCE TECHNOLOGY NIGERIA LIMITED
Business: Sales and Installation of Security Fencing Materials, Security Services
Address: Suite BC4, Maryland Shopping Complex, Maryland, Ikeja, Lagos
Tel: (01) 4937244, 4718320 **Fax:** (01) 4937244
* Lekki Road, Maroko, Victoria Island, Lagos
Contact: Engr. Sam Segun Adeyemo - Chairman/CEO.

FENGATE INSURANCE BROKERS LIMITED
Business: Life & Non-Life Insurance Broking
Address: 174B, M.Muhammed Way, Ebute-Metta, Lagos
Tel: (01) 865874, 4700977, 4734796, 7736217
Fax: (01) 862805, 3425284
E-mail: fengateins@aol.com
Contact: Mr. Lekan A. Biobaku - MD/CEO.

FENGURU NIGERIA LIMITED
Business: Importation and Sales of Industrial Chemicals, Water Treatment Chemicals & Pharmaceutical Chemicals, Supply of Oil & Gas Tools and Spare Parts, General Contractors
Address: 8, Oyekan Road, Apapa, Lagos
Tel: (01) 5870501, 5875495 **Fax:** (01) 5875495
Contact: Alh. M. K. Jada - Chairman/CEO.

FENIKOH NIGERIA LIMITED
Business: Electrical & Mechanical Engineering Services
Address: 1, Okon Crescent, off Plaza Avenue, Sango-Otta
Tel/Fax: (039) 722048, 722018

FENLAB & COMPANY (NIGERIA) LIMITED
Business: Suppliers of Cold Rooms, Commercial Refrigeration & Kitchen Equipment, Mortaries & Blood Banks
Address: Plot 29, Ysuf Maitama Sule Street, Asokoro, Abuja
Tel: (09) 3142280, 6709496, 08033140513, 08035897436
E-mail: fenlab_abuja@yahoo.com
fenlab_nigabja@yahoo.com
* 35, Fagbenro Square, off Randle Avenue, Surulere, Lagos
Tel/Fax: (01) 832168, 834334, 7735168, 8043661
E-mail: fenlab_lagos@yahoo.com
Contact: Chief Felix C. Nwabueze - MD/CEO.

FENWAY COURIER EXPRESS SERVICE (NIGERIA) LIMITED
Business: Courier Services
Address: 11, Bayo Shodipo Street, Anifowoshe, Ikeja, Lagos
Tel: (01) 4939904, 4936306, 4970894-5 (2L), 8119875
E-mail: fenway@alpha.linkserve.com
Contact: Mrs. E. A. Ogunsanlu - Chairman/CEO.

FERDINAND TECHNICAL & TRADING COMPANY LIMITED
Business: Sales of Self-Inking Stamps, Name Plates, Numbering Machines, Component Badges, Sign-Manufacturing Equipment and Company Seals
Address: 1, Ukeche Street, off Ezillo Avenue, Independence Layout, Enugu
Tel: (042) 458964 **Fax:** (042) 453322
Contact: Chief Ferdinand Nwafor - Chairman/CEO.

FERDISON HOLDINGS LIMITED
Business: Importation of Electronics, Household Appliances, Office Equipment and Pharmaceutical Products
Address: Chief Uche Ubochi Close, beh, Total Filling Station, Alaba Road, Ojo-Alaba, Lagos
Tel: (01) 2644844, 5881030, 5883104, 7740550
Fax: (01) 2644845, 2631610
E-mail: ferdison@hyperia.com
* Plot 1995, H.Macaulay Way, Wuse Zone 5,Abuja.
Tel: (09) 5230278 **Fax:** (09) 5230177
Contact: Mr Fredinard A. Uwagba - Chairman/CEO

FERROSTAAL NIGERIA LIMITED
Business: Construction and Civil Engineering
Address: 5, Forcados Road, off Oduduwa Street, off Marine Road, Apapa, Lagos
Tel: (01) 5458736-7 (2L) 5458979-80 (2L), 8116116
Fax: (01) 5458736
* Plot 3323, off Amazon Street, Maitama, Abuja
Tel: (09) 4135251, 4136875 **Fax:** (09) 4135250

FERTILIZER PROCESSING COMPANY LIMITED
Business: Manufacturing of Fertilizer
Address: Dantata House, 66/67, Murtala Mohammed Way,

P.O.Box 84, Kano
Tel: (064) 630692, 636232, 647778 **Fax:** (064) 638982
Contact: Alh. Aminu Alhassan Dantata - Chairman/CEO
Alh. Tajudeen Aminu Dantata - Group MD

FERTILIZERS & CHEMICALS LIMITED
Business: Manufacturing of NPK Fertilizers
Address: Ahmadu Doka Road, P.O.Box 8899, Kaduna
Tel: (062) 415456, 415481 **Fax:** (062) 413084, 413539
E-mail: fck@hyperia.com

FESCO ELECTROSAFETY SYSTEMS LIMITED
Business: Marketing, Supply & Installation of Safety & Secutiry Equipment, CCTV Surveillance Systems, Burglar & Fire Alarm, Fire-Fighting Equipment, Safety & Crime-Detection Gadgets
Address: 59, Akerele Street, Surulere, Lagos
Tel: (01) 2881731, 08033045499, 08055071400
*Area 7, Shopping Centre (Shop 129), Garki, Abuja
Tel: (09) 2344310
Contact: F. E. Okpara - Chairman/CEO

FESSOK INTERNATIONAL LIMITED
Business: Bottling of Table Water
Address: Lamour Industrial Estate, Abagana, Anambra State
Tel/Fax: (048) 571483

FERTECHO INDUSTRIES LIMITED
Business: Manufacuturing and Marketing of Pharmaceuticas Jars and Caps and other Plastic Products
Address: 1, Ukehe Street, off Ezilo Avenue, Independence Layout, Enugu
Tel: (042) 458964 **Fax:** (042) 453322
E-mail: fertecho2000@yahoo.com
Contact: Chief Ferdinand Nwafor - Chairman/CEO

FESTAC '77' HOTEL PLC
Business: Hotel and Catering Services, Conference Facilities
Address: Off Lagos-Badagry Expressway, near Mile 2, Amuwo-Odofin, Lagos
Tel: (01) 5884055, 5884049, 5884111 **Fax:** (01) 5884105
Contact: Mr. S. A. Oladosu - GM/CEO
Mrs. J Adetujumobi - Marketing/PR Manager

FESTUS OBAYIUWANA & COMPANY
Business: Estate Surveyors, Valuers & Agents , Chartered Surveyors & Town Planners; Development Consultants
Address: Unity House, 37, Marina, Lagos
Tel: (01) 2669488, 2640000, 2640001
Contact: Mr. Festus O. S. Obayiuwana -- MD/CEO

FHA HOMES LIMITED
Business: Mortgage Banking
Address: 54-56, 34th Crescent, Gwarinipa II Estate, Garki Abuja
Tel/Fax: (09) 5239842
* FHA Headquarters, Asokoro, Abuja
Tel: (09) 3140776
Contact: Mr. Musa Kura - GM/CEO

FHOMO NIGERIA LIMITED
Business: Construction and Civil Engineering
Address: 15, Ola Ayinde Street, off Mobolaji Bank-Anthony Way, Ikeja, Lagos
Tel: (01) 4936131, 7942794, 8124340, 8175092
E-mail: fho@infoweb.abs.net
Contact: Engr Omon F. O. Uduokhai - MD/CEO

FIDDIL NIGERIA LIMITED
Business: Logistic, Procurement, Shipping
Address: Plot 129/131, Fiddil Commercial Avenue, off Ordinance Junction, Trans-Amadi, Port Harcourt
Tel: (084) 232171, 232137 **Fax:** (084) 232173
E-mail: fiddil@yahoo.com
* 29, Palace Road, Olodi-Apapa, Lagos
* 30, Warri/Sapele Road, Warri
Tel: (053) 252059 **Fax:** (053) 253338
Contact: Mr. Felix Odili - MD/CEO

FIDEI INSURANCE BROKERS LIMITED
Business: Insurance Broking and Pensions Consultancy
Address: 33B, Unity Road, Ikeja, Lagos
Tel: (01) 7744934, 4936735 **Fax:** (01) 4934520
Contact: Mr. Oyeniyi Famoriyo - MD/CEO

FIDELITY BANK PLC
Business: Commercial Banking
Address: Savannah House (8th/10th Floors), 62/66, Broad Street, Lagos
Tel: (01) 2601960-9 (10 L) **Fax:** (01) 2636868
E-mail: fidelity@alpha.linkserve.com
Contact: Mr. Nebolisa O. Arah - MD/CEO
Mr. Emma Esinnah - Head (Corporate Affairs)

FIDELITY BOND OF NIGERIA LIMITED
Business: Insurance and Re-insurance Brokerage
Address: Elephant Cement House, ASSBIFI Road, Ikeja Central Business District, Alausa, Ikeja, Lagos
Tel: (01) 7747771, 4935296 **Fax:** (01) 4972870
E-mail: md@fidelitybond-ng.com
Contact: Mr. Adebiyi O. Olafisoye - Chairman

FIDELITY FINANCE COMPANY LIMITED
Business: Stockbroking, Securities Trading, Portfolio Management, Financial Services
Address: Niger Insurance Plaza (3rd Floor), 48/50, Odunlami Street, Lagos Island, Lagos
Tel: (01) 2636136, 2632867, 2640204, 2647380, 08022900798, 08033345399 **Fax:** (01) 2634470
E-mail: ffcl@rcl.nig.com
Website: www.fidelityfinance.com
Contact: Mr. Osa Osunde - MD/CEO

FIDELITY INTRA AFRICA LIMITED
Business: Import and Export of Commodities
Address: Prince's Court (2nd Floor, Room 2A), 37, Ahmed Onibudo Street, Victoria Island, Lagos
Tel: (01) 2622571 **Fax:** (01) 2622854
E-mail: valcommng.@lagosmailsprint.com
Contact: Umar S. Abdullahi - MD/CEO

FIDELITY UNION SECURITIES LIMITED
Business: Stockbroking, Financial Advisory Service, Insurance Intermediation
Address: 36, Adeola Hopewell Street, Victoria Island, Lagos
Tel: (01) 3200405-9 (5 L), 5558263-5 (3L), 08033071757
Fax: (01) 5558266

E-mail: fidelity@alpha.linkserve.com
Contact: Mr. Frank Onwu - MD/CEO

FIDEPAT INTERNATIONAL COMPANY LIMITED
Business: Shipping & Freight Forwarding, Logistics & Trade
Address: Plot 14, Old Aba Rd, Rumukwurushi, Port Harcourt
Tel: (084) 610369, 612284, 612886 **Fax:** (084) 612887
E-mail: fidepat@phca.linkserve.com
fidepat@yahoo.com
Contact: Amobi Anaka Luke Osuizugbe - Chairman/CEO

FIDSON HEALTHCARE LIMITED
Business: Importation and Production of Pharmaceuticals
Address: Olabode House, 215/219 & 266, Ikorodu Road, Obanikoro, Lagos
Tel: (01) 4933319, 4976171, 4706379 **Fax:** (01) 4930841
E-mail: fidson@hyperia.com
Website: www.fidson.com
* Km 38, Lagos-Abeokuta Expressway, Sango-Ota
Tel: (039) 720056 * (01) 7738233
Contact: Mr. Fidelis Ayebae - Chairman/CEO

FIELD OFF-SHORE DESIGN ENGINEERING (NIGERIA) LTD
Business: Offshore Engineering Services
Address: 24, Norman Williams Street, S.W. Ikoyi, Lagos
Tel: (01) 2694081, 2694131 **Fax:** (01) 2690284
E-mail: fode@micro.com.ng
fodelados@yahoo.com
* 14, Onne Road, G.R.A. Phase II, Port Harcourt
Tel: (084) 238690
Contact: Mr. Frank Azuogu - Chairman

FILADE MARBLE WORKS LIMITED
Business: Marble Works, Art Works
Address: Block E. D 10, Adeoyo State Hospital Road, Ring Road, Ibadan
E-mail: filade.marble@alpha.linkserve.com
Tel: (02) 2312544, 2316020, 0802422553, 08023249557
Fax: (02) 2318319
* 34, Ikorodu Road, Jibowu, Yaba, Lagos
Tel: (01) 7745092, 08023327027, 37170800
Contact: Mr. Oladipupo Filade - MD/CEO

FILMORE FURNITURE & FITTINGS LIMITED
Business: Marketing of Lighting Fittings and Office Furniture
Address: 18B, Idowu Taylor Street, Victoria Island, Lagos
Tel: (01) 2620338, 2620396 **Fax:** (01) 2620325
E-mail: filmore@metrong.com
Contact: Mr. B. T. David-West - MD/CEO

FIMCON LIMITED
Business: Manufacture of Garment Buttons, Accountrements and Decorative Accessories of Shoe, Bags and Related Industry; Engraving; Precision Stamping and Gift Items; Manufacture of Tools, Rubber Moulds and Immitation Jewellery; Electroplating and Anodizing Works; Production of Palm Kernel Oil, Cake and Sludge
Address: 2, Ladipo Oluwole Street, Ikeja, Industrial Estate, Ikeja, Lagos
Tel/Fax: (01) 4663788
E-mail: fimcon@mail.nigol.net.ng
Contact: Chief (Dr.) Sunday Dankaro, CON - Chairman

FINA WHITE HOUSE HOTELS LIMITED
Business: Hospitality Services
Address: NE. 20, Bonney Road, Kaduna
Tel: (062) 218143-4 (2l), 240979, 240862
Contact: Chief Francis Nanebunna - Chairman/CEO

FINACORP BUILDING SOCIETY LIMITED
Business: Mortgage Banking Services
Address: 14B, Anifowoshe Street of Adeola Odeku Street, Victoria Island, Lagos
Tel: (01) 2622876, 2624642, 2625327-8 (2 L)
Fax: (01) 2622867, 2618981
E-mail: finacorp@alpha.linkserve.com
Website: www.finacorpbuildingsocieity.com
* 60C, Trans-Amadi Ind. Layout, Port Harcourt
Tel: (084) 232861-3 (3 L) **Fax:** (084) 232865
Contact: Dr. Pat Utomi - Chairman
Mr. Efiong Bassey - President/CEO

FINACORP PROPERTIES LIMITED
Business: Real Estate Agents, Developers & Managers
Address: 14B, Anifowoshe Street, Victoria Island, Lagos
Tel: (01) 2622876, 2624642, 2625327-8 (2 L) 08034706199, 08023376792

FINANCE APPLICATION SYSTEMS LIMITED
Business: Software Services; Marketing and Support of Banking & Finance Application Software
Address: Amazing Grace Plaza (3rd Floor), Plot 2E-4E, Ligali Ayorinde Street, Victoria Island, Lagos
Tel: (01) 2694411, 2695924, 2696049, 4617390-4 (5L), 461950-2 (2L), 8043180, 612992, 612996
Fax: (01) 2690210, 2695924
E-mail: fasyl@linkserve.com.ng
flexcubeubs@yahoo.com
* Plot 1147, Adetokunbo Ademola Crescent, behind AP Plaza, Wuse II, Abuja
* 1, Isiokpo Close, Rumuibekwe Housing Estate, Port Harcourt
Tel: (084) 480689, 08022243345
Contact: Mr. Frank Onuzo - Chairman
Mr. Bade Aluko - MD/CEO

FINANCIAL ASSURANCE COMPANY LIMITED
Business: All Classes of Insurance
Address: 1-4, Balogun Street/Breadfruit Street, Lagos
Tel: (01) 2661637, 2640511, 2640510, 2661017
Fax: (01) 2668128
E-mail: finassure@yahoo.com
* Plot 74, Ralph Shodeind Street, opp. Fed. Min. of Finance Hqtrs, Central Business District, Abuja
Contact: Otunba (Dr.) W. O. O. Ajayi - Chairman
Mr. P.A. Olusanya - MD/CEO

FINANCIAL DERIVATIVES COMPANY LIMITED
Business: Issuing House, Stockbroking
Address: 11A, Goriola Street, off Adeola Odeku Street, Victoria Island, Lagos
Tel: (01) 2614204, 2618294, 2618279
Fax: (01) 2613675
E-mail: fdc@hyperia.com
Website: www.fdc.com.ng
Contact: Mr. Bismack J. Rewane - MD/CEO

FINANCIAL EQUITIES LIMITED
Business: Stockbroking, Issuing House
Address: 188, Awolowo Road, S.W. Ikoyi, Lagos
Tel: (01) 2690402-9 (8 L) **Fax:** (01) 2692469
E-mail: jinaduk@stanbic.com
Contact: D. W. Kennedy - Chairman
Kunle Lawal Jinadu - MD/CEO

FINANCIAL TRUST COMPANY NIGERIA LIMITED
Business: Stockbroking, Investment & Portfolio Management
Address: Financial Trust House (15th Floor), 1-4, Balogun Street/Breadfruit Street, Lagos Island, Lagos
Tel: (01) 2661466, 2608040, 2665351 **Fax:** (01) 2668128
Contact: Otunba W. O. O. Ajayi - Chairman/CEO
Mr. M. G. Bakare - Manager (Stockbroking)

FINASA COMPANY LIMITED
Business: Production of Confectionery, Bakery
Address: Plot 7, Block A, Amuwo-Odofin Industrial Estate, Apapa-Oshodi Expressway (Coker Bus-Stop), Amuwo-Odofin, Lagos
Tel: (01) 7758130, 08033186861
E-mail: nira@linkserve.com

FINCO ENGINEERS
Business: Engineering Consultancy Services (Electrical, Mechanical & Industrial)
Address: 14, Ikorodu Road, Jibowu, Yaba
Tel: (01) 861080, 860920, 7740847 **Fax:** (01) 861839
Contact: Engr. (Prof.) V.A. Akinsete - Principal Partner
Engr. O. Adeyinka - Principal Partner

FINE ALUMINIUM LIMITED
Business: Manufacturing and Marketing of Aluminium and Other Metal Building Materials
Address: 9, Ahmed Talib Avenue, Industrial Estate, Kaduna South, Kaduna
Tel: (062) 231719, 232704, 237433 **Fax:** (062) 230552
Contact: Muhammed Dikko Ladan - Chairman

FINE CHEMICALS NIGERIA LIMITED
Business: Manufacture of Textile Pigment Emulsions, Printing Inks, Metal Coatings, Colourants for Paints and Detergents, and Shoe Lacquers
Address: 22, Musa Yar'Adua Street, Victoria Island, Lagos
Tel: (01) 2611433, 2612786 **Fax:** (01) 2619624, 2618604
Contact: Mr. S. B. Akande - Chairman
Mr. P. R. Ramchandani - MD/CEO

FINEPRO MANUFACTURING COMPANY LIMITED
Business: Manufacturing & Marketing of Agro Chemical and Control Products
Address: 17, Dosumu Street, off Bodrin Street, Mafoluku-Oja, Oshodi, Lagos
Tel: (01) 4725559, 4931776, 4974728, 08033027717
Fax: (01) 4931776
E-mail: finepro@mail.com
Contact: Chief G. O. Oruh - Chairman/CEO

FINIDEL NIGERIA LIMITED
Business: Importer of Cookware, Kitchenware & Lightings, Corporate Gift Items
Address: Suite 27A, Tafawa Balewa Square Complex, Lagos
Tel: (01) 2636763, 08023186078, 08023229252
Fax: (01) 2637356
E-mail: finidel@hyperia.com
Website: www.finidel.com
Contact: Mrs. Fikayo Tunde - Ojo - MD/CEO

FININVEST ASSOCIATES NIGERIA LIMITED
Business: Financial Investment Services
Address: 21/25, Broad Street, Lagos Island, Lagos
Tel: (01) 2669565, 4706766, 08033051318
Fax: (01) 2616779

FINISHING MARBLE PRODUCTS COMPANY NIGERIA LTD
Business: Sales of Marble, Granite and Accessories, Mable Works, Furniture Sales
Address: 12, Adeyemi Bero Crescent, off State Highway, Ilupeju, Apapa, Lagos
Tel: (01) 4979329, 4934481, 4717351, 7756590
Fax: (01) 4934481
Contact: Mr. Franco Gassani - Chairman/CEO

FINLAB NIGERIA LIMITED
Business: Supply, Installation and Maintenance of Laboratory Equipment, Furniture, Fittings, Chemicals and Glassware; Sale of Audio-Visual Equipment, Material Testing Equipment and Engineering Tools, Hospital Equipment and Consumables
Address: 1, Sylvia Crescent, off Anthony Village Road, off Ikorodu Road (Anthony Bus-Stop), Anthony Village, Lagos
Tel: (01) 4968200, 4977303, 7735876, 7736512, 08033056626 **Fax:** (01) 4979056
E-mail: finlab@finlabng.com
finlab@hyperia.com
Website: www.finlabng.com
* Iluobe Petroleum Plaza (Suite 2B), Aminu Kano Crescent/Kashim Ibrahim Way, Wuse 11, Abuja
Tel/Fax: (09) 6708169, 08033765202
Contact: Mr. Uzo M. Nwaije - Chairman/CEO

FINNIH MEDICAL CENTRE
Business: Medical & Healthcare Services
Address: 42, Oduduwa Crescent, G.R.A., Ikeja, Lagos
Tel: (01) 4965613, 08033068661
E-mail: fmci@hotmail.com
Contact: Dr. (Mrs.) Oreoluwa Awokoya - Director

FIRE EQUITY & GENERAL INSURANCE COMPANY LTD
Business: Insurance
Address: 72, Adetokunbo Ademola Street, Victoria Is., Lagos
Tel: (01) 2629158 **Fax:** (01) 2629167
E-mail: fegic@yahoo.com
Contact: Mr. Alex Ibru - Chairman
Mr. B. O. Banjo - MD/CEO

FIRE RISK ENGINEERING LIMITED
Business: Sales & Maintenance of Fire-Fighting Equipment, Fire Safety Engineering, Fire Consultancy & Training, Sales of Photoluminescent Signs and Anti-Slip Materials
Address: Block A (Flat 29), Eko Court Complex, Kofo Abayomi Street, Victoria Island, Lagos
Tel: (01) 4722991, 4819306, 2622217, 08023006250

Fax: (01) 2622217
E-mail: firerisk@hyperia.com
* 49, Aba Road, Port Harcourt
Tel: (084) 239791, 335106 **Fax:** (084) 239791

FIRESTOP INTERNATIONAL LIMITED
Business: Marketing of Fire-Fighting Equipment
Address: 1, Balogun Street, off Kudirat Abiola Way, Alausa, Ikeja, Lagos
Tel: (01) 4970965, 7741288, 08037165408
Contact: Mr. S. A. Hassan - Chairman

FIREWORKS INVESTMENTS LIMITED
Business: Sales, Installation & Maintenance of Fire-Fighting, Safety & Security Equipment & Accessories
Address: Vessel House, Plot 135, Trans-Amadi Industrial Layout, opp. Michelin, Oginigba, Port Harcourt
Tel: (084) 233852
Contact: Mr. Chima Okparanta - CEO

FIRST ALUMINIUM NIGERIA PLC
Business: Manufacture of Aluminium Coils, Sheets, Circles and Collapsible Tubes
Address: 2, Akilo Street, Ogba Industrial Estate, Ikeja, Lagos
Tel: (01) 4922202, 4922205, 4922207 **Fax:** (01) 4922206
E-mail: info@firstaluminium.com
* Packaging Division, 2, Akilo Street, Ogba Industrial Estate, Ikeja, Lagos
Tel: (01) 4922172-3 (2L)
E-mail: firstpak@infoweb.abs.net
* Rolling Mill Complex, 19/21, Onitsha Street, Trans-Amadi Industrial Layout, Port Harcourt
Tel: (084) 239758-60 (3L)
E-mail: info@fanphc.com
Contact: Mr. Michael E. Parsey - MD/CEO

FIRST ATLANTIC BANK PLC
Business: Universal Banking
Address: 4/6, Adetokunbo Ademola Street, Victoria Island Lagos
Tel: (01) 2622472-8 (9l) Fax: (01) 2622497
E-mail: info@firstatlanticbank.com
Website: www.firstatlanticbank.com
www.flashmecash.com
Contact: Mr Okey Nwosu - MD/CEO
Mr. Bayo Adelabi - Group Head (Control Group)

FIRST ATLANTIC SECURITIES LIMITED
Business: Stockbroking, Capital Market Operations, Financing, Insurance Broking and Consultancy
Address: BAICO Plaza (10th Floor, Right Wing), 12, Abibu-Oki Street, Lagos Island, Lagos
Tel: (01) 2665542, 2664275, 4701532 **Fax:** (01) 2664275
E-mail: firstatlansec@hyperia.com
Contact: Mr. Charles Chukwuemeka Eze - Chairman
Mr. Eugene E. Ezenwa - GM/CEO

FIRST BANK OF NIGERIA PLC
Business: Commercial Banking
Address: Samuel Asabia House, 35, Marina, Lagos
Tel: (01) 2665900-19 (20L) **Fax:** (01) 2669073, 2665939
E-mail: fbn@firstbank-nig.com.ng
Website: www.firstbank-nig.com.ng
www.firstbank.com
www.firstbank.org
www.firstbank.net
Contact: Mr. Jacob Moyo Ajekigbe - MD/CEO
Mr. Toyin Abayomi - Banjo - Head (Corp Affairs)

FIRST CAPITAL SAVINGS & LOANS LIMITED
Business: Mortgage Banking
Address: 37, Murtala Mohammed Way, Jos
Tel: (073) 453181, 458138 **Fax:** (073) 458137
E-mail: firstcapital@rosecom.net
Contact: Mrs. Juliana M. Mafwil - GM/CEO

FIRST CHARTERED INSURANCE COMPANY LIMITED
Business: Insurance
Address: 55, Bishop Oluwole Street, Victoria Island, Lagos
Tel: (01) 2610341-3 (3 L), 2611211, 2611227
Fax: (01) 2611210
E-mail: fcic@infoweb.abs.net
Website: www.firstcharteredins.com
Contact: Mr Gbenga Olakolu - MD/CEO

FIRST CITY ASSET MANAGEMENT LIMITED
Business: Investment Advisors, Asset Managers
Address: Primrose Towers (4th Floor), 17A, Tinubu Street, Lagos Island, Lagos
Tel: (01) 2665944-53 (10 L) (Ext. 330)

FIRST CITY ESTATE LIMITED
Business: Real Estate Development & Management
Address: 19A, Adeola Odeku Street, Victoria Island, Lagos
Tel: (01) 2620515, 7942068
Contact: Mr Humphrey Anumudu - Chairman/CEO

FIRST CITY MONUMENT BANK LIMITED
Business: Universal Banking
Address: PRIMROSE Tower, 17A, Tinubu Street, Lagos
Tel: (01) 2665944-53 (10L), 2665864, 2640614
Fax: (01) 2665126, 2668833
E-mail: caf@firstcitygroup.com
Website: www.firstcitygroup.com
www.fcmb-ltd.com
* UAC Commercial Complex, Plot 272 & 273, Central Business District, Abuja
Tel: (09) 5237908-10 (3L), 5237910 **Fax:** (09) 5237918
E-mail: abujaoffice@fcmb-ltd.com
* Plot 282A, Port Harcourt-Aba Express Road, GRA Phase II, Port Harcourt
Tel: (084) 237772, 237774, 236533 **Fax:** (084) 237773
E-mail: phoffice@fcmb-ltd.com
* African Alliance Building, F1, Airport Rd, Kano
Tel: (064) 646510. 646411, 631766, 644965, 631767
Fax: (064) 646511
E-mail: kanooffice@fcmb-ltd.com
Contact: Dr. Jonathan A. D. Long - MD
Mr. Olufemi Adebiyi - Head (Corporate Affairs)

FIRST CITY-TRANSITS PLC
Business: Metropolitan Road Transportation Services
Address: Royal Building (2nd Floor), Apapa-Oshodi Expressway (Jakande Bus-Stop), Mile 2 Oke, Amuwo-Odofin, Lagos
Tel: (01) 482958., 4828894, 08023199875

FIRST CLASS BOOKS NIGEREIA LIMITED
Business: Sales of Encyclopaedia, Business Books and Motivational Book Procurement Services, Library & Bookshop Consultancy Services, Organisation of Seminars
Address: 9B, Adeola Odeku Street, Victoria Island, Lagos
Tel: (01) 2611904, 2700039, 2629878, 08023087089, 08033067201 **Fax:** (01) 2700548
E-mail: firstclassbooks@hotmail.com

FIRST CONSULTANTS HOSPITAL
Business: Medical Consultancy Services
Address: 16/24, Ikoyi Road, Obalende, Ikoyi, Lagos
Tel: (01) 2691166, 2691162-5 (4 L), 2690243-7 (5 L), 688343-5 (3 L), 680761, 680702

FIRST DIRECT MARKETING LIMITED
Business: Direct Marketing (Below-the-Line Marketing)
Address: Ivory Music House (3rd Floor), IPM Avenue, Central Business District, Alausa, Lagos
Tel: (01) 7911213 **Fax:** (01) 2221548
E-mail: info@firstd.com
Website: www.firstd.com
Contact: Mr. 'Lolu Akinwunmi - Chairman/CEO

FIRST DOLPHIN TRAVELS LIMITED
Business: Travel Agency, Tour Organisation & Operations
Address: Federal Palac Hotel (Suite 458), Ahmadu Bello Way, Victoria Island, Lagos
Tel: (01) 2614967, 2614927, 262114, 2626112, 08023133348, 08023201577 **Fax:** (01) 226114
E-mail: firstdolphin@hyperia.com
Contact: Dr. (Mrs.) T. Gbadebo - Managing Director

FIRST DOMINICAN HOSPITAL
Business: Health Care & Medical Services
Address: 27, Alhaji Masha Road, (By Masha B/Stop), Surulere, Lagos
Tel: (01) 835876
Contact: Dr. Egbuna Okafor-Mbah - Chief Medical Director

FIRST DOMINION INSURANCE BROKERS LIMITED
Business: Insurance Broking
Address: 6, Lake Street, off Broad Street, Lagos
Tel: (01) 2641354 **Fax:** (01) 2662143
* 4, Lumumbashi Streeet, Wuse Zone 3, Abuja
Tel: (09) 5231566
* NUJ House, Ankpa Quarters Road, Makurdi
Tel: (09) 533922
Contact: Mr. S. A. Afolabi - MD/CEO

FIRST EKIMOGUN NIGERIA LIMITED
Business: Laundry and Drycleaning Services, Industrial Cleaning and Fumigation Services
Address: 17, Soloki Street, off Adetola Street, Aguda Surulere, Lagos
Tel: (01) 5847974, 08023134693
Contact: Alh. (Chief) I. B. Yusuf - Chairman/CEO

FIRST EQUITY SECURITIES LIMITED
Business: Stockbroking
Address: Stock Exchange House (22nd Floor), 2/4, Customs Street, Lagos Island, Lagos
Tel: (01) 2640634 **Fax:** (01) 2666871
E-mail: firstequitysecurities@yahoo.com

FIRST FINANCE & TRUST LIMITED
Business: Financial Planning & Management Consultancy
Address: Plot 38, Kofo Abayomi St, Victoria Island, Lagos
Tel: (01) 613557, 612232, 2610430, 2625828
Fax: (01) 617565
E-mail: ifp@nova.net.ng
Contact: Prof. B. O. Nwabueze, SAN - Chairman
Mr. Felix N. Akpe - MD/CEO.

FIRST FOUNDATION MEDICAL COMPANY LIMITED
Business: Medical Engineering, Sales and Service Medical Equipment, Manufacturer's Representative
Address: First Foundation Place, 36, Opebi Rd, Ikeja, Lagos
Tel: (01) 4973726, 4973724, 4973725 **Fax:** (01) 4973727
Contact: Dr. Tosin Ajayi - MD/CEO.

FIRST FUNDS LIMITED (Sub. of First Bank of Nig. Plc)
Business: SMIEIS (Small & Medium industries Equity Investment Scheme) Management Services. Investments and Financial Advisory Services5
Address: BULL Plaza (old Eagle House), 38/39, Marina, Lagos.
Tel: (01) 2665211, 2665214 **Fax:** (01) 2665250
E-mail: kayodeayeni@aol.com
Contact: Mr. Kayode Ayeni - MD/CEO

FIRST GRANT NIGERIA LIMITED
Business: Investments, Conglomerate
Address: Plot 281, Gbagada-Oworonshoki Expressway, Gbagada, Lagos
Tel: (01) 5551030, 7740575, 7746000
Fax: (01) 2643930, 5551030
Contact: Mr. S. Y. Akeju - Chairman/CEO

FIRST INTERSTATE MERCHANT BANK PLC
Business: Merchant Banking
Address: Kingsway Building Complex, 2/4, Davies Street off Marina, Lagos
Tel: (01) 2666446, 2600500-4 (5 L) **Fax:** (01) 2668273
E-mail: fimb@fimbnig.com
merchant@fimb.metrong.com
Contact: Prof. A. L. Mabogunje - Chairman
Mr. Adelupo Aderemi - MD/CEO

FIRST LINK NIGERIA LIMITED
Business: Sales and Installation of Telecommunication (G.S.M) Systems and Security Equipment, Production of Computerised Identity Cards
Address: 8A, Kasumu Ekemode Street, off Saka Tinubu Street, Lagos
Tel: (01) 2623236, 2900244, 2907866, 08033823378
Contact: Mr. Akinyemi Moses Akinkunmi - Chairman/CEO

FIRST MARINE AND ENGINEERING SERVICE LIMITED
Business: Shipping, Clearing and Forwarding, Contracting
Address: NITP Franklin Akinyemi House (3rd Floor), Plot PC 10, Engineering Close, off Idowu Taylor Street, Victoria Island, Lagos
Tel: (01) 5454542-3 (2 L) **Fax:** (01) 5454541
E-mail: firstmarine@micro.com.ng
* 6A/B, Woji Road, G.R.A. Phase II, Port Harcourt

Tel: (084) 231425, 232616 **Fax:** (084) 238536, 239280
Contact: Prince Joseph T. Penawou - Chairman/CEO

FIRST MOTORS LIMITED
Business: Importation and Sales of Motor Vehicles
Address: 21, Adeola Odeku Street, Victoria Island, Lagos
Tel: (01) 2622642, 2620515 **Fax:** (01) 2620515
* 11, Imani Estate, Shehu Shagari Way, Maitama District, Abuja.
Tel: (09) 4132848
* 178, Aba Road, Port Harcourt.
Tel: (084) 238535
E-mail: firstmotors@intracom5.com
Contact: Mr. Humphrey Anumudu - Chairman/CEO

FIRST PLASTICS LIMITED
Business: Manufacture of PVC Pressure Pipes, Related Produucts and Household Plasticware
Address: Plot 26/26B, Sharada Ind. Estate Phase 1, Kano
Tel: (064) 66803, 319165
Contact: Alh. Mukhtar Ahmad - Vice Chairman/CEO

FIRST REGISTRARS (NIGERIA) LIMITED
Business: Registrars and Company Secretarial Services
Address: Plot 2, Abebe Village Road, Iganmu, Lagos
Tel: (01) 7743309, 5851418 **Fax:** (01) 5850552
* Coomasie House, Plot 777, Mohammadu Buhari Way, Central Business District, Abuja
Tel: (09) 6706140

FIRST RESEARCH NIGERIA LIMITED
Business: Market & Social Research, Opinion Polling
Address: 24, Wilmer Street, off Town Planning Way, Ilupeju, Lagos
Tel: (01) 4937421, 2641166, 2641167
E-mail: rinl@rcl.nig.com
* 114, Tenant Road, Aba
* SW7/758, Oshibodun Street near CAC Miracle Centre, Challenge, Ibadan
Contact: Mr. Chris A. Dogbuje - Chairman
Mr. K.A.R. Kegbe - MD/CEO

FIRST RIVERS HOSPITALS LIMITED
Business: Health Care & Medical Services
Address: 250, Port Harcourt/Aba Expressway, or 7/9, Old Aba Road, Rumuomasi, Port Harcourt
Tel: (084) 238405, 233367, 08033096444
E-mail: drsola-frh@phca.linkserve.com

FIRST SECURITIES DISCOUNT HOUSE LIMITED
Business: Trading In Money-Market Securities
Address: Niger House (6th & 7th Floors), 1/5, Odunlami Street, Lagos Island, Lagos
Tel: (01) 2640160-9 (10L), 2640150-9 (10L), 2640175-6 (2L
Fax: (01) 2640173-4 (2 L)
E-mail: info@fsdh-ltd.com
fsdh@fsdh-ltd.com
Website: www.fsdhp-ltd.com
Contact: Mr. Hakeem Belo-Osagie - Chairman
Mr. Rilwan N. Belo-Osagie - MD/CEO

FIRST SOURCE TRAVEL & TOURS LIMITED
Business: Travel Agency
Address: Kingsway Building (Suite 5), 51, Marina, Lagos
Tel: (01) 2643377, 08023251012, 0802304008, 08023251016, 08033789938
Fax: (01) 2640349
E-mail: firstsource@infoweb.abs.net
Contact: Mrs. E. O. Nkpubre - MD/CEO

FIRST STANDARD TRAVELS & TOURS LIMITED
Business: Travel Agency
Address: Kingsway Building (Suite 27), 51, Marina, Lagos
Tel: (01) 2643377, 2640349 **Fax:** (01) 2640349
E-mail: firstand@infoweb.abs.net
Contact: Mrs. E. O. Nkpubre - MD/CEO

FIRST SPINNERS LIMITED
Business: Spinning of Yarn
Address: Plot 66, Ikorodu Industrial Estate, Odogunyan, Ikorodu, Lagos State
Tel: (01) 7740672

FIRST STOCKBROKERS LIMITED
Business: Stockbroking
Address: Plot 38, Kofo Abayomi St, Victoria Island, Lagos
Tel: (01) 2625979, 2700053, 08055607148
Fax: (01) 2624704
E-mail: info@ifpng.com
Website: www.ifpng.com
Contact: Mr. F. N. Akpe - Chairman

FIRST TRUSTEES NIGERIA LIMITED
Business: Trusteeship, Portfolio Management, Pension Funds, Management, Advisory Services
Address: A.G. Leventis Building, 42/43, Marina, Lagos
Tel: (01) 2634801, 2634780, 2647438, 2646472, 2646474, 2634563, 4702621 **Fax:** (01) 2647438
E-mail: ftnl@first-trustees.com
Website: www.first-trustees.com
* Ahmadu Coomassie House, Plot 777, M.Buhari Way, Central Business District, Abuja
Tel: (09) 2348598 **Fax:** (09) 2348597
Contact: Oba Otudeko - Chairman
Nsikak T. Ekure - MD/CEO

FIRST VENTURES LIMITED
Business: Import and Export, Marketing of Petroleum Products, Re-Filling of Gas Cylinders
Address: Plots 26 & 26B, Sharada Ind.Estate Phase I, Kano
Tel/Fax: (064) 668036, 669455
Contact: Alh. Aliu Mahmood Galadanchi - MD/CEO

FIRST-LINK INSURANCE BROKERS LIMITED
Business: Insurance Broking and Pensions Consultancy
Address: 34, Okesuna Street (1st Floor), off Hawley Street, off Lewis Street, Lafiaji, Lagos.
Tel: (01) 2647525

FIRSTHOUSE LIMITED
Business: Sales and Service of Computers and Peripherals
Address: 47, Faramobi Ajike Street, Anthony Village, Lagos
Tel: (01) 4936045, 7741976 **Fax:** (01) 4936045
E-mail: firsthouse@nova.net.ng
* 51, Adeniran Ogunsanya Street, Surulere, Lagos
Contact: Mr. Oluseyi Faseyiku - MD/CEO

FIS SECURITIES LIMITED
Business: Capital Market Operations, Stockbroking, Corporate Finance, Portfolio Management, Issuing House
Address: 2, Macarthy Street, Onikan, Lagos
Tel: (01) 2635253, 2634059 **Fax:** (01) 2634555
E-mail: fis@infoweb.abs.net
fis@nova.net.ng
Contact: Mr. H. O. G. Otiti - MD/CEO

FITTING FINISHES LIMITED
Business: Importation and Distribution of Furnishing and Finishing Products for Homes and Offices
Address: 1,Oyefeso Ave., Ikorodu Road, Obanikoro, Lagos
Tel: (01) 4974135, 4976296, 4936007, 7750804, 4974136
08033032615, 080333032955
E-mail: fittingfinishes@nova.net.ng
Contact: Mr Taiwo Odutola - MD/CEO

FIVE ANCHORS GROUP (NIGERIA) LIMITED
Business: Shipping Services, Maritime Services
Address: 13, Creek Road, Apapa, Lagos
Tel: (01) 5878262, 5878278, 5877500 **Fax:** (01) 5875957

FIVE STAR TRAVEL LIMITED/BTI-Nigeria
Business: Global Travel Management
Address: 28C, Adetokunbo Ademola St,Victoria Island, Lagos
Tel: (01) 2625920-5 (6 L) **Fax:** (01) 2628929
E-mail: 5starlos@compuserve.com
Contact: Major Gen. (Dr.) Henry Adefope (rtd) - Chairman
Mr. Olufemi Adefope - MD/CEO

FIXWELL NIGERIA LIMITED
Business: Manufacturing and Marketing of Automotive Rubber Parts, Glass-Packing Fingers and Industrial Machinery Rubber Parts Repair of Conveyor Belts, Production/Machining of Machinery Spares
Address: 2, Ashanke Layout, beside Yanathy Flour Mills, Lagos-Ibadan-Ilorin Expressway, Ibadan
Tel/Fax: (02) 2311178
Contact: Elder Anthony O. Kehinde - Chairman/CEO

FLA RISK SURVEYS LIMITED
Business: Cargo Superintendence, Hull Survey and Valuation, Marine Loss Recovery, Marine Survey
Address: 48, Falolu Street, off Akerele Road, Surulere, Lagos
Tel/Fax: (01) 5455226, 7733750, 7734454, 08033314874, 08037208840 **Fax:** (01) 5455226
Contact: Mr. Chris Nlemoha - MD/CEO

FLAME PETROLEUM & GAS COMPANY LIMITED
Business: Marketing of Petroleum Products & Cooking Gas
Address: Plot 151, Younis Bashorun Street, off Ajose Adeogun Street, Lagos
Tel: (01) 4705208-9 (2 L), 2621173, 2705280
Fax: (01) 2621173
Contact: Dr. E. I. Kachikwu - Chairman/CEO

FLAMINGO (NIGERIA) LIMITED
Business: Restaurant and Bar Services, Outdoor Catering
Address: 10, Kofo Abayomi Street, Victoria Island, Lagos
Tel: (01) 2610387, 2622225, 2629017
Fax: (01) 2629016
Contact: Mr. Budhrani - Chairman/MD

FLEMING INTERNATIONAL AGENCIES LIMITED
Business: Customs Licensed Agents, Freight Handling
Address: 56/58, Opebi Road, Ikeja, Lagos
Tel: (01) 4975987, 2901912, 08033076487
Contact: Mr. Fleming O. Momodu - Chairman/CEO

FLO COMPUTERS LIMITED
Business: Sales of Computers & Accessories, Assembling & Installation of Computers, Programming
Address: 9, Otigba Street, Computer Village, Ikeja, Lagos
Tel: (01) 7737898, 0803325801
E-mail: flocomputers @yahoo.com
Website: www.flocomputer.com
Contact: Princess (Mrs.) A. Adesulupe - Chairman/CEO

FLOOP NIGERIA LIMITED
Business: General Merchandising
Address: 12 Abraham Adesanya (Douala) Rd, Apapa, Lagos
Tel: (01) 5870324, 5871005, 5804102 **Fax:** (01) 5458990
E-mail: floop_2001@yahoo.co.uk
Contact: Mr. Tahiru - Opute - MD/CEO

FLOOROSIL CLEANING SERVICES LIMITED
Business: Office/Industrial Cleaning and Pest Control Servies
Address: 25, Association Avenue, Ilupeju, Lagos
Tel: (01) 8112905, 08023067791, 08033076557
E-mail: floorsil@yahoo.co.uk
* The Millennium Court, Ogun State House, Plot 74, Ralph Sodeinde Street, Central Area, Abuja
Tel: (09) 2348805
Contact: Mr. Bola Odukoya - Chairman/CEO

FLORA TRUWORTHS ENTERPRISES LIMITED
Business: Importation of Cosmetics and Hair Care Products
Address: 35, Breadfruit Street, Lagos
Tel: (01) 2660246, 2660487, 2666686
Fax: (01) 2666222
E-mail: floratruworths@micro.com.ng
Contact: Chief (Mrs.) Flora Nwazojie - MD/CEO

FLORIDA BOOKSHOP LIMITED
Business: Importation and Sale of Books
Address: 5, Association Avenue, Ilupeju, Lagos
Tel: (01) 4975789, 4963483
E-mail: natufomadufloridabk@yahoo.com
Contact: Chief N. O. Ufomadu - Chairman/CEO

FLORIN TECHNOLOGIES LIMITED
Business: Sales of Computers; Consultancy; Training
Address: 5, Otigba St, Obafemi Awolowo Way, Ikeja, Lagos
Tel: (01) 4710252, 08023036526, 08033046133
E-mail: sales@florintech.com
Website: www.florintech.com
Contact: Mrs. Fadekemi Akintoye - GM

FLOUR MILLS OF NIGERIA PLC
Business: Milling of Grains into Flour, Macaroni, Spaghetti, Grits and Their Offals; Operation of Bulk Cement Handling Facility; Sale of Bulk and Bagged Cement
Address: 2, Old Dock Road, Apapa, Lagos
Tel: (01) 5453960-9 (10L), 5803370-9(10 L)
Fax: (01) 5870395, 5871602
Contact: Chief E. A. Ukpabi - MD/CEO

FLOW PRECISION LIMITED

Business: Calibration, Pressure Testing and Non-Destructive Testing Services
Address: Eleganza Plaza (Virgo Block, 1st Floor), 1, Commercial Road, Apapa, Lagos
Tel: (01) 5457143, 804894, 0803017261, 08033043002
E-mail: flow_precision@yahoo.com
Contact: Mr. Chimezirim Nkwocha - MD/CEO

FLUOR DANIEL NIGERIA LIMITED

Business: Oil Industry Consultancy Services
Address: Octagon House (3rd Floor), 13, A.J.Marinho Drive, Victoria Island Annex, Lagos
Tel/Fax: (01) 2626718, 2625233

FLUREX INDUSTRIES (NIGERIA) LIMITED

Business: Manufacture of Spirits and Wines
Address: Flurex House, 6A, Bisi Oluwole Crescent (Igbala), Km., 38, Abeokuta Road, Sango Otta, Ogun State
Tel: (01) 4937724, 4937724
E-mail: flurex@cyberspace.net.ng
129B, Oba Ladejobi Street, Ikeja, G.R.A., Lagos
Tel: (01) 4934907, 4937724
Contact: Mr. Jerry Ariomovuohoma - President

FLYING DOVE LIMITED

Business: Distribution, Marketing and Service of SONY Electronics Products
Address: Plot 1089A, Adeola Odeku St Victoria Island Lagos
Tel: (01) 2618793, 7740107 **Fax:** (01) 2622393
* 34/38, Burma Road, Apapa
Tel: (01) 5876474, 5876479, 5876476

FLYING EAGLE SHIPPING LIMITED

Business: Clearing, Forwarding, Import, Export, Warehousing
Address: 2, Okanlawon Ajayi Street, end of Alh. Masha Road, Surulere, Lagos
Tel: (01) 4818844, 4725021, 08033212868, 08056632292
E-mail: flyingeagle@infoweb.abs.net
Website: www.flyingeagle.8k.com
Contact: Mr. Elvis Nwuju - MD/CEO

FMA ARCHITECTS LIMITED

Business: Architectural Designs
Address: St. Nicholas Building (Penthouse Suite), Catholic Mission Street, Lagos Island, Lagos
Tel: (01) 2635359, 2635360, 2637113, 2637082
Fax: (01) 2632291
E-mail: fma@fma-arc.com
Contact: Arc. (Chief) Olufemi Majekodunmi - Exec. Chairman
Arc. Olumoroti Delana - MD/CEO

FMC NIGERIA LIMITED

Business: Facilities Management Services for Corporate Bodies and Institutions
Address: 19, Bola Ajibola Street, off Community Road, off Allen Avenue, Ikeja, Lagos
Tel: (01) 4930326
E-mail: fmc@metrong.com
Contact: Arc. Dipo Adebo - Chairman/CEO

FOBAC EQUIPMENT MANUFACTURING COMPANY LTD

Business: Manufacturing of Hospital and School Furniture, Supply, Repair and Refurbishing of Medical and Science Equipment, Turnkey Projects
Address: 2, Akindele Coker Street, off Liasu Road (Ile Iwe Bus- Stop), Egbe, Lagos
Tel: (01) 2885273, 7745279, 8174138, 08023102452, 08033370448 **Fax:** (01) 2885273
E-mail: fobac2001@yahoo.com
Contact: Chief Akindele A. Coker - Chairman/CEO

FOLA OYEKAN & ASSOCIATES

Business: Estate Surveyors & Valuers, Property Brokerage, Management & Valuation, Real Estate Consultancy
Address: Lennards Building (2nd Floor), 14/16, Abibu-Oki Street, off Broad Street, Lagos
Tel: (01) 2660289, 2663665, 2660270, 08023029212, 08035529333 **Fax:** (01) 2660270
E-mail: foyekan@cyberspace.net.ng
* 21, Aba Road, (First Floor), Port Harcourt
Tel: (084) 579970, 08036685172
Contact: Mr. Kehinde Ademakinwa - Managing Partner

FOLAWIYO FARMS LIMITED

Business: Farming, Integrated Agricultural Production
Address: Yinka Folawiyo Plaza, 38, Yinka Folawiyo Avenue, Apapa, Lagos
Tel: (01) 5451402, 5876532, 5450436 (5 L)
Fax: (01) 5450204, 5450274
* Iloro, P.O.Box 658, Oyo, Oyo State
Tel: (038) 230884, 230889
Contact: Alh. Chief (Dr.) W. I. Folawiyo, OFR - Chairman
Alh. T. B Folawiyo - Group Exec. Director

FOLAWIYO FISHERIES LIMITED

Business: Fishing and Shrimping
Address: 38, Yinka Folawiyo Avenue, Apapa, Lagos
Tel: (01) 5451402 **Fax:** (01) 5450204
E-mail: info@yinkafolawiyo.org
Website: www.yinkafolawiyo.org
Contact: Alh. (Chief) W. I. Folawiyo, OFR - Exec. Chairman
Alh. T. B. Folawiyo - Group Exec. Director

FOLBEN NIGERIA LIMITED

Business: Building and Civil Engineering, Oil Industry Construction Services, Manufacturing and Marketing of Occupational Safety Footwear
Address: 29, Mobolaji Bank-Anthony Way, Ikeja, Lagos
Tel: (01) 4973426, 4975061, 08023433352, 08033108758
E-mail: folben2000@yahoo.com
* 1A, Emmanuel Street, off Mobolaji Bank-Anthony Way, Maryland, Ikeja, Lagos
Tel: (01) 4932025, 4938043
Contact: Mr. R. F. Olowookere - Chairman/CEO

FOLD NIGERIA LIMITED

Business: Sales of Catering Equipment, Hygiene-Enhancing and Sanitary Wares
Address: 7, Akinhanmi Street, Surulere, Lagos
Tel/Fax: (01) 5846601, 830649, 4709959, 8144720
E-mail: fold@cyberspace.net.ng

FOLHAM NIGERIA LIMITED

Business: Outdoor Advertising
Address: 32, Asiri-Abo Street, Isolo, Lagos

Tel: (01) 4521957, 4703457
Contact: Chief H. A. Olamuyiwa - Chairman/CEO

FOLIO CONSTRUCTION LIMITED
Business: Building Construction
Address: 2A, Maduike Street, S.W. Ikoyi, Lagos
Tel: (01) 2672578, 4703927
Contact: Mr. Folahan Olumide - MD/CEO

FOLU SECURITIES & FINANCE LIMITED
Business: Trade Financing, Leasing, Money-Market Operations, Loan Syndication, Financial Advisory Services, Asset Management
Address: UBA Trustees (2nd Floor), 22B, Idowu Taylor Street, Victoria Island, Lagos
Tel: (01) 4705765, 2624510, 2625792 **Fax:** (01) 2625792
Contact: Chief Bode Sunmonu - MD/CEO

FOMENE MARITIME INTERNATIONAL LIMITED
Business: Maritime Consultancy, Shipping Management
Address: 15, Ola Ayinde Street, off Mobolaji Bank-Anthony Way, Ikeja, Lagos
Tel: (01) 4936730, 4937148 **Fax:** (01) 4936730
Contact: Dr. Odafe Wilson Omene - Chairman/CEO

FOOTWEAR SERVICES LIMITED
Business: Shoe Repairs and Manufacturing of Shoe Soles
Address: 71, Opebi Road, Ikeja, Lagos
Tel: (01) 4967825, 4966585
E-mail: 3008wear@infoweb.abs.net
Contact: Chief T. A. Williams - Chairman/CEO

FOOD CONCEPTS & ENTERTAINMENT LIMITED
Business: Operation of Fast-Food Outlets (Chicken Licken & St. Elmos)
Address: Xerox House, 12/14, Fatai Atere Way, Matori Industrial Estate, Mushin, Lagos
Tel: (01) 3205839
* 60A, Adeola Odeku Street, Victoria Island, Lagos
Tel: (01) 2700169
* 37A, Opebi Road, Ikeja, Lagos

FOREMOST CATERERS LIMITED
Business: Industrial Catering Services, Outdoor Catering, Fast-Food Outlets and Restaurants
Address: The Kitchen Towers, Plot 3, Block F, Omole Junction, Ogba, Lagos
Tel: (01) 4926769, 4704222, 4923642
E-mail: thekitchen@linkserve.net
Contact: Mr. Afolabi Babalola, MON - Chairman
Chief Fola Omolayo - MD/CEO

FORESIGHT INSURANCE BROKERS LIMITED
Business: Insurance Broking
Address: Goodwill House (2nd Floor, Suite 5), 278, Ikorodu Road, Obanikoro, Lagos
Tel: (01) 4932268, 4932400 **Fax:** (01) 4932268
E-mail: dudu@infoweb.abs.net
E-mail: bolatsi@infoweb.abs.net
* 36, Abeokuta Street, D-Line, Port Harcourt
Tel: (084) 232878
Contact: Mr. Sam Amuka - Chairman
Mr. B. O. Dudu - MD/CEO

FORESIGHT SECURITIES & INVESTMENT LIMITED
Business: Capital Market Operations, Stockbroking, Issuing House, Portfolio Management
Address: New Niger House Annex (2nd Floor), 3/4, Tinubu Street, Lagos Island, Lagos
Tel: (01) 2641043, 2664310, 7749455
E-mail: foresight@nigerianet.com
Website: www.foresightsecurities.com
Contact: Prof. M. Ayo Ajomo - Chairman
Mr. B. A. Ogbebor - Dep. Chairman/CEO

FOREST CITY LIMITED
Business: Importation of Generators and Spare Parts
Address: 118, Awolowo Road, S.W. Ikoyi, Lagos
Tel: (01) 2692934, 2691952, 08023122763
Fax: (01) 2692934, 2691952
E-mail: forestcity@compuserve.com

FOREVER LIVING PRODUCTS NIGERIA LIMITED
Business: Importation of Herbal Beauty and Health Products
Address: Speedwriting House, 16, Ajanaku St, off Salvation Road, Awuse Estate, Opebi Road, Ikeja, Lagos
Tel: (01) 4967937, 4937824, 7404096 **Fax:** (01) 4936851
Website: www.foreverliving.com

FORMOSA BOTTLING COMPANY LIMITED
Business: Bottling of Sparkling Fruit Juice Drinks, Soft Drink (LULU Brand), Health/Table Water; Production of PET Preforms, Bottles, Caps and Plastic Products.
Address: 6E, Idejo Street, Victoria Island, Lagos
Tel: (01) 2625115-8(3L), 2621198 **Fax:** (01) 5456286
E-mail: Sales-formosa@Microcom.com
Plot 2, Block A, Amuwo-Odofin Industrial Scheme, Apapa-Oshodi Expressway, Lagos
Tel: (01) 5456285-7(3L), 7750673-5(3L), 7752868
Contact: Mr. Frank Lin - MD/CEO

FORSTER WHEELER NIGERIA LIMITED
Business: Oil Industry Services, Construction, Engineering
Address: 12A, Akin Olugbade Street, off Adeola Odeku Street, Victoria Island, Lagos
Tel: (01) 2610073

FORTE ASSET MANAGEMENT LIMITED
Business: Stockbroking
Address: NICON House (1st Floor), 5, Customs Street, off Marina, Lagos
Tel: (01) 2642878, 2643213-4 (2L) **Fax:** (01) 2642878
E-mail: stockbrokers@forteasset.com
Website: www.forteassetmgt.com
Contact: Mr. Tunji Oba - MD/CEO

FORTHRIGHT SECURITIES & INVESTMENTS LIMITED
Business: Stockbroking, Portfolio Management, Investment Advisory Services
Address: Chartered Bank Building (3rd Floor), 19, Martins Street, Marina, Lagos
Tel: (01) 2644981, 2644913 **Fax:** (01) 2644805
E-mail: forthrightsec@yahoo.com
Contact: Mr. Johnson T. Faromoju - MD/CEO

FORTIFIERS PROTECTION SERVICES LIMITED
Business: Private Guard, VIP/Executive & Personal Protection

Services, Facilities Protection, Sales of Security Equipment & Self-Defence Products, Consultancy
Address: Awaye House (Suite 10), Lagos-Badagry Expressway, Coker, Lagos
Tel: (01) 4701931, 4803228, 4824329, 08033044774
Fax: (01) 7946458
E-mail: forti9@hotmail.com
Website: www.fps9.com
Contact: AIG Alban C. E. Ikenwa, mni (rtd) - Chairman
Mr O. Wole-Madariola II - MD/CEO

FORTSCHRITT ENGINEERS LIMITED
Business: Computer Systems Sales and Support, Network Installation, Systems Engineering and Integration
Address: 13, Bombay Crescent, off Calcutta Crescent, Apapa, Lagos
Tel: (01) 5452394-5 (2 L) **Fax:** (01) 5874210
E-mail: fortschritt@hyperia.com
Contact: Prof. A. O. Demuren
Mr. Tayo Demuren - Exec. Director/CEO

FORTUNATE CARPET LIMITED
Business: Wholesales & Retail of Carpets, Rugs & Underlay
Address: 7, Mabo Street, off Ishaga Road, Surulere, Lagos
Tel: (01) 4733830, 4738874, 08022911484
Fax: (01) 4733830
E-mail: tony@fortunatecommunication.com
* Plot 527, Sokode Crescent, Berger Junction, Wuse Zone 5, Abuja
Tel: (09) 5233627, 5230939
Contact: Mr. Tony Igbaroola - Managing Director

FORTUNE ASSURANCE COMPANY LIMITED
Business: General, Life and Special-Risk Insurance
Address: Plot 1309A, Karimu Kotun St, Victoria Is., Lagos
Tel: (01) 2623623-4 (2 L), 2610012, 3200631
Fax: (01) 2623622
E-mail: fortuneassurance@hyperia.com
Contact: Mr. Henry A. MacPepple - Chairman
Mr. Peter Monye- MD/CEO

FORTUNE EBIE & COMPANY
Business: Estate Surveyors & Valuers, Chartered Surveyors, Property Developers & Management Consultants
Address: 14, Elegbata Street, off Apongbon Street, Olowogbowo, Lagos
Tel: (01) 2669871, 2641974, 2668525 **Fax:** (01) 2640504
E-mail: spofebie@cyberspace.net.ng
spofebie@cybaaspace.com
Contact: Mr. S. P. O. Fortune Ebie - President/CEO

FORTUNE INTERNATIONAL BANK PLC
Business: Commercial Banking
Address: Plot 1703A, Adetokunbo Ademola Street, Victoria Island, Lagos
Tel: (01) 2626130-1 (2 L), 2672471-8 (8L), 7747863-4 (2L), 2620778 **Fax:** (01) 2626833, 2626789
E-mail: fb@fortunebankplc.com
Website: www.fortunebankplc.com
* Banex Plaza, Plot 750, Aminu Kano Crescent, Cadastral Zone A7, Wuse II, Abuja
Tel: (09) 4139436-8 (3 L), 4136463
Contact: Mr. Fidelis C. Tilije - MD/CEO

FORUM ADVERTISING LIMITED
Business: Avertising, Public Relations, Marketing Consultancy
Address: 41, Femi Ayantuga Crescent, off Adelabu Street, Surulere, Lagos
Tel: (01) 5843347, 834020
E-mail: forum-ad@yahoo.com
Contact: Mr. Louis Edafe Toweh - MD/CEO

FORWARD VENTURES NIGERIA LIMITED
Business: Production and Marketing of Industrial Salt
Address: Ogun-Oshun River Basin Development Authority Premises, opp. Coco-Cola, behind UTB, Lateef Jakande Road, Agindingbi, Ikeja, Lagos
Tel: (01) 4926387, 77442554 **Fax:** (01) 4926387
E-mail: forward@infoweb.abs.net
Contact: Mr. Charles Ojei

FOSAD CONSULTING LIMITED
Business: Human Resources & Managemeent Consultancy, Business Support Services
Address: Ladico House (4th Floor), Plot 1661, Oyin Jolayemi Street, Victoria Island, Lagos
Tel: (01) 4617399, 4617400 **Fax:** (01) 4616958
E-mail: fosad@skannet.com
Contact: Dr. (Mrs.) Mary Adefosudo - MD/CEO

FOTO CHRIS INTERBIZ LIMITED
Business: Sales of Laminating/Binding Machines and Accessories, and Office Equipment
Address: 13, Isale-Agbede Street, Lagos Island, Lagos
Tel: (01) 2630694
* 58, Aroloya Street, Idumota, Lagos
Contact: Mr. Christopher Onyibo - MD/CEO

FOTO KWIK INDUSTRIES LIMITED
Business: Photographic Processing & Development Laboratory Services, Sales of Cameras and Photographic Equipment
Address: 26, Ikwrre Road, Port Harcourt
Tel (084) 239063
* Rumuokwuta Roundabout, Port Harcourt
Tel: (084) 237341, 572925
Contact: Mr. Solly C. Idehen - Chairman/CEO

FOTO PIE GROUP LIMITED
Business: Sales of Computers, Photographic Materials, Office Machines and Laminating-Pouch Films
Address: 4, Idowu Lane, off Kodesoh Street, Ikeja, Lagos
Tel: (01) 4931354, 7748050 **Fax:** (01) 4931354
E-mail: fotoangels@linkserve.com.ng
Contact: Mr. Alex Ayika - Chairman/CEO

FOTOKLINIC NIGERIA LIMITED
Business: Importation and Sales of Photographic Papers, Chemicals, Equipment and other Accessories, Sales of Generating Sets
Address: 44, Ikorodu Road, Jibowu, Yaba, Lagos
Tel: (01) 2880380, 7740559, 7741914-5 (2L), 7741918, 7745323, 08023861142, 08033074772, 08033537689
Fax: (01) 2880380
Contact: Mr. Oludare Aturamu - Chairman/CEO
Mr. Oladapo Oyeniyi - GM

FOTOTEK INDUSTRIES LIMITED
Business: Photographic Printing Services
Address: Adebola House, 40, Opebi Road, Ikeja, Lagos
Tel: (01) 4976600-4 (5L)
E-mail: ess-ayholdings@cyberspace.net.ng
Contact: Alh. (Dr.) S. A. Adegunwa - Exec. Chairman
Mr. O. Olatunji - GM

FOTOMAGNET LIMITED
Business: Colour Processing and Printing Laboratory, Sales of Photographic Materials
Address: 106, Ogunlana Drive, Surulere, Lagos
Tel: (01) 4707223, 5456546, 08033195210, 08023207024
E-mail: fotomagnet@yahoo.com
Contact: Mr. Collin K. Ogbuechi- MD/CEO

FOUANI NIGERIA LIMITED
Business: Marketing & Distribution of LG Consumer Electronic Appliances, Manufacturer's Representative
Address: 11/13, Warehouse Road, Apapa, Lagos
Tel: (01) 7917391, 5873722, 5873727, 7756868, 5873730
Website: www.lgeafrica.com
Contact: Mohammad S. Fouani - MD/CEO

FOUGEROLLE NIGERIA LIMITED
Business: Building and Civil Engeineering Contractors
Address: Total House, 4, Afribank St, Victoria Island, Lagos
Tel: (01) 2622352 **Fax:** (01) 2622354
* Total House II, Plot 247, Herbert Macaulay Way, Central Business District, Abuja
Tel: (09) 2343440, 2343467 **Fax:** (09) 2349301
* Elf Building (3rd Floor), 35, Kofo Abayomi Street, Victoria Island, Lagos
Tel: (01) 2621426 **Fax:** (01) 2621427
* Plot 3-4, Trans-Amadi Ind. Layout, Port Harcourt
Tel: (084) 237961 * (087) 771031
Contact: Mr. E. A. Adewusi - Chairman
Mr. J. P. Gaultier - MD/CEO

FOUNDATION CONSTRUCTION LIMITED
Business: Piling and Civil Engineering Work
Address: 7, Eletu Ogabi Street, Victoria Island, Lagos
Tel: (01) 2621056, 2621057, 2616807 **Fax:** (01) 2616272
E-mail: initerbeton.nig@linkserve.com.ng
Contact: Mr. W. J. Wilson - MD/CEO

FOUNDATION ENGINEERING SERVICES LIMITED
Business: Geotechnical Consultancy Services
Address: 290, Herbert Macaulay Street, Sabo-Yaba, Lagos
Tel: (01) 867712, 2885079, 8173368
E-mail: feslng@yahoo.co.uk
Contact: Prince Babatunde Ajayi-Fajomodu - Tech. Director

FOUNDATION SOLID (NIGERIA) LIMITED
Business: Road Construction, Civil Engineering
Address: Plot 1141, Industrial Layout, Anglo-Jos
Tel: (073) 463749, 08037035147, 08037035148
Fax: (073) 463749
Contact: Mr. Fawaz Kassem - MD/CEO

FOUNDATION TECH LIMITED
Business: Piling Works, Foundation Engineering
Address: Plot 3162, Ibrahim Babangida Way, Maitama, Abuja
Tel: (09) 4133570-1 (2 L), 08033118184, 08055203337
Fax: (09) 4135012
Contact: Mr. Said Khalaf - Chairman
Mr. Elias Rbeiz - MD/CEO

FOUNTAIN INSURANCE BROKERS LIMITED
Business: Insurance Broking and Consultancy Services
Address: 19, Town Planning Way, Ilupeju, Lagos
Tel: (01) 4968487, 4931849, 7730411-3 (3 L)
Fax: (01) 4979309, 5553324
E-mail: broking@fountaininsurance.net
Website: www.fountaininsurance.net
* Plot 516, Sultan Abubakar Way, Wuse Zone 2, Abuja.
Tel: (09) 5234112
Contact: Mr. Eddie Efekoha - MD/CEO

FOUNTAIN SECURITIES LIMITED
Business: Stockbroking, Funds Management, Trade and Project Financing
Address: 107, Bamgbose Street, Lagos Island, Lagos
Tel: (01) 2647657, 2637964, 4802444 **Fax:** (01) 2647657
E-mail: fslsecurities@msn.com
akd@nova.net.ng
Contact: Alh. H. A. Ajani - Chairman
Chief Abiodun Kola-Daisi - MD/CEO

FOUNTAIN SPRINGVILLE ESTATE LIMITED
Business: Real Estate Development & Management
Address: Plot 10, Gabby Adeosun St, off Anthony Etukdo Avenue, off Admiralty Way, Lekki Phase 1, Lagos
Tel: (01) 5555401-2 (2 L), 08034087746, 08033012204, 08033024953 **Fax:** (01) 5555401
E-mail: aolabiyi@fountainspringville.com
Website: www.fountainspringville.com

FOUNTAIN TRUST BANK LIMITED
Business: Commercial Banking
Address: Plot 1611, Adeola Hopewell St Victoria Island Lagos
Tel: (01) 2625990, 2625987, 2614207, 3200120, 3200117-20 (4L) **Fax:** (01) 2614211
E-mail: hq@fountaintrustbank.com
Website: www.fountaintrustbank.com
* UAC Commercial Complex, Plots 272/273, off 3rd Avenue, Central Business District, Abuja
Tel: (09) 5238490, 5235906 **Fax:** (09) 5239182
E-mail: abuja@fountaintrustbank.com
* Plot 9/10, Trans-Amadi Ind.Layout, Port Harcout
Tel: (084) 230371, 236087, 230396 **Fax:** (084) 230371
E-mail: ph@fountaintrustbank.com
Contact: Dr. Adebola Adetumbi - Head (Reputation Mgt)

FOURTH DIMENSION PUBLISHING COMPANY LIMITED
Business: Publishing of Books
Address: 16, First Avenue, City Layout, Upper Chime, New Haven, Enugu
Tel: (042) 459969, 453739 **Fax:** (042) 456904, 453298
E-mail: info@fdpbooks,com
Contact: Chief (Engr.) Victor U. Nwankwo - MD/CEO.

FOURTH FORMATION (NIGERIA) LIMITED
Business: Importation and Sales of Auto Spare Parts
Address: 4, Market Rd, Main Market, Nnewi, Anambra State

Tel: (046) 460919, 461336 **Fax:** (046) 461337
E-mail: gerald@infoweb.abs.net
Contact: Chief Gerald Ozojie - Chairman/CEO.

FOWOBI ENTERPRISES LIMITED
Business: Marketing of Petroleum Products (Fuels & Gas)
Address: 106/108, Oshodi-Apapa Expressway, by Aswani Market Road, Isolo, Lagos
Tel: (01) 4522240, 4523373 **Fax:** (01) 4520954
E-mail: fowobi@fowobi.com
Contact: H.R.H. Oba A. A. Oguntayo - Chairman
Princess O. O. Laja - MD/CEO

FRAB AND COMPANY (NIGERIA) LIMITED
Business: Aluminium Fabrication, Construction of Steel Gates, Interior Design and Decoration
Address: 46, Allen Avenue, Ikeja, Lagos
Tel: (01) 4966961, 4933169 **Fax:** (01) 4933169
E-mail: frab3.f@rcl.nig.com
Contact: Engr. (Chief) F. A. Bakare - Chairman/CEO

FRAJEND INVESTMENT (NIGERIA) LIMITED
Business: Importation of Motorcycles, Automobiles & Outboard Engines, Spare Parts General Merchadise
Address: 34, Bola Street, Ebute-Metta (East), Lagos
Tel: (01) 7744637, 582061, 5821308
E-mail: frajend@infoweb.abs.net
* 48, Willoughby Street, Ebute-Metta (East), Lagos
Tel: (01) 861490

FRAMAN ENTERPRISES NIGERIA LIMITED
Business: Importation and Sales of Cosmetics, Chemicals, Oil Treatment Chemicals and Radiator Sealers
Address: 98, Docemu Street (1st Floor), Idumota, Lagos
Tel: (01) 2667135, 2640690, 2665966 **Fax:** (01) 2640829
E-mal: framan@micro.com.ng
* Plot 474, Trans-Amadi Ind. Layout, Port Harcourt
Tel: (084) 231134, 231135 **Fax:** (084) 231146
Contact: Mr. Emeka Francis Mba - MD/CEO.

FRANCHISE COMMUNICATIONS LIMITED
Business: Advertising, Public Relations Consultany
Address: 63B, Coker Road, Ilupeju, Lagos
Tel: (01) 4974915, 4976794, 7947540-1 (2L), 7745794
E-mail: info@franchise-ng.com
Contact: Mr. Don Oporuozor - MD/CEO

FRANCIS STILLWATERS NIGERIA LIMITED
Business: Outdoor Advertising, Printing, Production of Awards & Recognition Items, Designs
Address: 11, Isaac John Street, Igbobi, Fadeyi, Yaba, Lagos
Tel: (01) 4706719, 7900774
E-mail: francisstillwaters_ng@yahoo.co.uk
Contact: Mr. Taiwo Oladipo - MD/CEO

FRANCIS VAN-LARE LIMITED
Business: Sales and Repairs of Computers and Accessories, Training and Research, Desktop Publishing
Address: 5, Unity Road, Ikeja, Lagos
Tel: (01) 4963441 **Fax:** (01) 2647220
E-mail: service@fvl.com.ng
service@vanlare.com
Contact: Mr. Francis Van-Lare - Chairman/CEO.

FRANCO NIGERIA INSURANCE BROKERS & CONSULTANTS LIMITED
Business: Insurance Broking & Consultancy
Address: 52, Itolo St, off Eric Moore Road, Surulere, Lagos
Tel: (01) 5801991-4 (4 L), 4702405 **Fax:** (01) 5801990
E-mail: fienna@micro.com.ng
Website: www.franconig.com
* 68, Mbonu Street, D-Line, Port Harcourt.
Tel: (084) 331500
Contact: Chief F. C. Ozomah - Chairman/CEO

FRANEMM INDUSTRIES LIMITED
Business: Manufacturing and Marketing of Hair-Care Products and other Cosmetics
Address: 10/12, Old Otta Road, Oke-Odo, Agege, Lagos
Tel: (01) 2883229, 4702906
Contact: Mr. Francis Nwakamma - Chairman/CEO.

FRANK MARKETING COMMUNICATIONS LIMITED
Business: Outdoor Advertising and Productions
Address: 5, Oluwalogbon Street (Okesuna Bus-Stop), Shomolu, Lagos
Tel: (01) 7929424, 08033341264
Contact: Pastor Francis Sode - MD/CEO

FRANK'S COMET GROUP
Business: Electrical, Mechanical and Airconditioning Engineering, Sales and Service of Generators.
Address: Frank's Comet House, 5/7, Oregun Road, Lagos
Tel: (01) 4971257, 4971256 **Fax:** (01) 4971256
E-mail: frank-ojo@hyperia.com
Contact: Engr. Francis Ojo - CEO

FRANK'S INTERNATIONAL OILFIELD SERVICES NIG. LTD
Business: Hammer, Casing and Tubing Tong Services
Address: Plot 5, Trans-Amadi Ind., Layout, Port Harcourt
Tel: (084) 231482, 231731, 231751 **Fax:** (084) 237087
E-mail: frankswestafrica@frankswa.com
Contact: Mr. Keith Mosing - Chairman
Mr. Guy Hustinx - MD/CEO

FRANOSON MANNYON INTERNATIONAL COMPANY LTD
Business: Manufacturing of Pharmaceutical Products
Address: 2, Enugu Rd, Idemili South L.G.A., Anambra State
Tel/Fax: (046) 463944
* 176, Tenant Road, Aba.
Tel: (082) 221368, 220813
Contact: Chief F. N. Okonkwo - Chairman/CEO

FRED GAY INTERNATIONAL LIMITED
Business: Commercial Printers, Creative Designers, Light Packaging, Publishing
Address: 1, Stella Osholake Street, off International Airport Road, near Stop-Over Motel, Ajao Estate, Lagos
Tel: (01) 521795, 4522898 **Fax:** (01) 5457155
E-mail: fredgayinter@yahoo.com
E-mail: fredgay@hyperia.com
Contact: Chief G. A. Olojo - Chairman
Mr. O. A. Wright - MD/CEO

FRED REFRIGERATION & COMPANY LIMITED
Business: Refrigeration and Airconditioning Engineers
Address: Omojole House, Plot 22, Oshodi-Apapa Express-

Let's build your body
WATER TANKER
8 PALLET BOTTLE CARRIER
WHEAT CARRIER
BUS BODY ON CHASSIS
BUS BODY ON CHASSIS
BOX BODY
DROPSIDE DROPTAIL
FLATBED/CONTAINER CARRIER
TRAILER BOTTLE CARRIER (20 PALLETS)
■ FRIGOGLASS CITY-LINER (95 SEATER BUS)
Also available:
Low Loaders, Trailer Water/Fuel Tankers, Surface Tanks, Underground Tanks, Septic Tank, Produce Body, Specialised/Customised Body, Bullion Body, Tipping Trailers, Standard Tippers, Bitumen Tankers, Silos, Car Carrrier, Aviation Trailers, Mobile Workshop/ Clinics, Towing Vehicles, Troop Carrier , Dropside Droptail etc.
Made in Nigeria
FRIGOGLASS
For enquiries/order, contact:
FRIGOGLASS INDUSTRIES (NIG) LTD.
A member of the LEVENTIS GROUP
(Formerly Beta Industries Ltd)
Head Office: Iddo House, Iddo, Lagos P. O. Box 159 Lagos, Nigeria. Tel: 01-7740844, 7748339 Fax: 7748073
Plant: Frigoglass Vehicle Division, Off Oyo Rd., Moniya. P. O. Box 17056 Dugbe, Ibadan. Tel: 02-2413811, 2411699 Tel/Fax: 02-2413709
0802 346 0562, 0802 332 8357, 0802 346 8408. E-mail: betavmp@skannet.com

way, by Berliet Bus-Stop, Ilasamaja, Lagos
Tel: (01) 4521738, 4521729, 521560, 7744944
Fax: (01) 4521229, 4528181, 4521738
E-mail: fredrefrigeration@hyperia.com
Contact: Dr. Fred Omojole - MD/CEO

FREDPAK SERVICES NIGERIA LIMITED
Business: Shipping, Clearing & Forwarding
Address: 20, Oyekan Road, Apapa, Lagos
Tel: (01) 5876747

FREEDOM AIR SERVICES LTD. (FAS)
Business: Airline Services, Chartered Flight Operations
Address: 3, Dallaji Road, off Isa Kaita Road, Malili G.R.A., P. O. Box 2330, Kaduna
Tel: (062) 241850 **Fax:** (062) 243478
E-mail: operations@freedomairng.com
Website: www.freedomairng.com
• Nnamdi Azikiwe Interntional Airport, Abuja
Tel: (09) 8100200, 08023664747
Contact: Alh. Garba K. Shitu - Chairman/CEO
Capt. Mohammd Babazima - GM

FREEDOM RADIO 99.5 FM
Business: Broadcasting
Address: Plot 47, Sharada Industrial Estate, Kano
Tel: (064) 669629, 08034510750 **Fax:** (064) 666993
E-mail: muryafreedom@yahoo.com
Contact: Air Vice Marshal M. Mohammed (rtd.) - Chairman

FREEDOM DEVELOPMENT COMPANY LIMITED
Business: Mining and Processing of Solid Minerals, Production of Adhesives, Food and Beverages, Dredging and Excavation of Sand
Address: 17, Ihama Road, off Airport Rd, G.R.A, Benin City
Tel: (052) 252134, 252067
E-mail: freedomgroppu@hyperia.com
* Veepee Industrial Avenue, off Km., 38 Lagos-Abeokuta Road, Sango Otta, Ogun State
Tel: (01) 7741720, 2882307

FREEZELAND NIGERIA LIMITED
Business: Rental of Party Equipment, Hire of Cooling Van, Production of Ice Blocks, Cubes and Flakes
Address: 37, Adeyinka Street, Ilupeju, Lagos
Tel: (01) 4971618, 4933584, 7915614, 08023177760, 08042170296
Fax: (01) 4933584, 4971618
Contact: Mr. Lanre Awonuga - Chairman/CEO

FREIGHT FORWARDERS (NIGERIA) LIMITED
Business: Shipping, Clearing and Forwarding
Address: 16B, Tombia Street, G.R.A. Phase II, Port Harcourt
Tel: (084) 230271, 230274 **Fax:** (084) 230273
E-mail: ff@phca.linkserve.com
Contact: Mr. Peter A. Mojuetan - Chairman/CEO

FRENCHIES LIMITED
Business: Food Processing, Bakery, Restaurant, Fast-Food Shop
Address: 29A, Akin Adesola Street, Victoria Island, Lagos
Tel: (01) 2610096, 2647263 **Fax:** (01) 2610186
Contact: Alh. (Dr.) Hassan Adamu - Chairman
Mr. Laurent S. Costagliola - MD/CEO

FRESH AIR LIMITED
Business: Aircraft Charter Services
Address: Buffalo House, 2, Allen Avenue, Ikeja, Lagos
Tel: (01) 4979870, 5557691-5 (5L) **Fax:** (01) 4934594
Contact: Capt Augustine Okon - Chairman/CEO

FRESHFONES NIGERIA LIMITED
Business: Sales, Installation, Maintenance and Engineering of Telecommunication Equipment
Address: Stayfit Plaza, 6/8, Ozumba Mbadiwe Avenue, opp. 1004-Flats Estate, Victoria Island, Lagos
Tel: (01) 7743708, 615345 **Fax:** (01) 5890219
E-mail: churchis@alpha.linkserve.com
Contact: Mr. Uche B. Iloka - Chairman/CEO

FRIGALE NIGERIA LIMITED
Business: Sales of Computer Hardware and Accessories
Address: Ikeja, Shopping Plaza (3rd Floor, Suite B316), Mobolaji Bank-Anthony Way, Ikeja, Lagos
Tel: (01) 4937016, 08033037163 **Fax:** (01) 4937016
E-mail: frigale@theobech. com
Contact: Mr. S. Igonikon - MD/CEO

FRIGOGLASS INDUSTRIES (NIGERIA) LIMITED
Business: Construction of Vehicle Bodies-Pallet Carriers, Buses; Manufacturing of Plastic Crates, PET Preforms & Ice Boxes.
Address: Iddo House, Iddo, Lagos
Tel: (01) 7740844, 7748339, 7747602, 5454212
Fax: (01) 7748073, 2618285
E-mail: betavmp@skannet.com
* Frigoglass Vehicle Div., off Oyo Road, Moniya, Ibadan
Tel: (02) 2413811, 2411699 **Fax:** (02) 2413709
Contact: Dr. S. Constantinidis - MD/CEO

FRIGOTERMICA NIGERIA LIMITED
Business: Sales, Installation and Maintenance of Airconditioning and Refrigeration Systems, Electrical and Mechanical Engineering
Address: 3, Rumuodalu Road/Rumuola Road, Port Harcourt
Tel/Fax: (084) 332144 * (082) 440405

FRISTOTUNE NIGERIA LIMITED
Business: Outdoor Advertising, Signwriting and Printing, Marketing and Media Consultants
Address: Block C (2nd Floor, Suite 15), Fajol Plaza, Lagos-Abeokuta Expressway, Ipaja, Agege, Lagos
Tel: (01) 8175700, 08023053515
* 9A, Junction Road, (3rd Floor), Kaduna
Contact: Mr. Osa E. Obazee - Chairman/CEO

FRONTLINE FARMS LIMITED
Business: Poultry and Fish Farming, Cattle Rearing
Address: 11, Adelabu Street, Surulere, Lagos
Tel: (01) 5837349, 5802630-1 (2 L) **Fax:** (01) 5802632
E-mail: frontfarms@micro.com.ng
Contact: Chief G. N. Otobor - Chairman
Apostle S. E. K. Obrutse - MD/CEO

FROSS INVESTMENT LIMITED
Business: Sales of Packaging Machinery and Materials, Water Dispensers and Treatment/Bottling Plants, Plastic-Manufacturing Moulds and Machinery

Address: 26/28, Oshodi-Isolo Expressway (Charity Bus-Stop), Oshodi, Lagos
Tel: (01) 7741442
E-mail: orientalwaters@hotmail.com
nissipet@onebox.com
Contact: Mr. Festus Denis-Akano - Chairman/CEO

FSB INTERNATIONAL BANK PLC
Business: Commercial Banking
Address: 23, Awolowo Road, S.W. Ikoyi, Lagos
Tel: (01) 2690576-8 (3L), 2690739-45(7L)
Fax: (01) 2690397
E-mail: customerservice@fsbint.com
Website: www.fsbint.com
Contact: Alh. Bello Maccido - MD/CEO

FSG COMMUNICATIONS NIGERIA LIMITED
Business: Advertising & Marketing Services to Pharmaceutical and Medical Equipment Companies, Publishing of Medical Journals, Organisation of Seminars, Conferences, Product Launches and Medical Equipment Exhibitions:
Address: 10, Afolabi Lesi Street, Ilupeju, Lagos
Tel: (01) 4729443 **Fax:** (01) 4935855, 4960363
E-mail: brkuti@infoweb.abs.net
Contact: Dr. A. P. Balogun - Regional Oper. Co-ordinator

FSS GASES LIMITED
Business: Sales & Supply of Fire-Suppression Gas & Accessories, Provision of Technical Support to Installers & End-Users, Provision of Operational Consumables, Training, Design and Certification
Address: Xerox Building, 12/14, Fatai Atere Way, Matori Industrial Estate, Mushin, Lagos
Tel: (01) 4732205, 7945150, 08036001037
E-mail: fssgases@yahoo.com
Contact: Chief (Dr.) Dele Fajemirokun - Chairman
Mrs. Antonia Tchouambe - GM/CEO

FUGRO SURVEY NIGERIA LIMITED
Business: Oil Industry Surveying Services, Land & Marine Surveying, Mapping & Land Information Systems
Address: 8, Geodetic Road, Rumuobiakani, Port Harcourt
Tel: (084) 235095, 233991 **Fax:** (084) 233991
Contact: Alabo C. T. John-Horsefall - Chairman

FUGRO-IGN LIMITED
Business: Oil & Gas Industry Mechanical & Civil Engineering Contractors
Address: 8, Geodetic Road, Rumuobiakani, Port Harcourt
Tel: (084) 235095, 233991 **Fax:** (084) 233991
* IGN House, Ogunu Road, Warri
Tel: (053) 250799 **Fax:** (053) 265256

FUMMAN (NIGERIA) LIMITED
Business: Sales of Industrial Cooling Systems, Water-Treatment & Food-Disinfecting Chemicals; Fabrication of Tanks and Vessels
Address: Fumman House, 22, John Olugbo Street, end of Unity Road, Ikeja, Lagos
Tel: (01) 4960664, 4936374 **Fax:** (01) 4936441
E-mail: fumman@fumman.com
Contact: Mr. Lai Adeyemi - Chairman/CEO

FUMMAN AGRICULTURAL PRODUCTS INDUSTRIES LTD
Business: Processing of Fruits and Juices
Address: Fumman House, 22, John Olugbo Street, end of Unity Road, Ikeja, Lagos
Tel: (01) 4960664, 4936374 **Fax:** (01) 4936441
E-mail: fumman@fumman.com
* Ibadan-Abeokuta Road, Apata-Gangan, Ibadan
Tel: (02) 2318090
Contact: Mr Lai Adeyemi - Chairman/CEO

FUNDTECH FINANCE & INVESTMENT LIMITED
Business: Short-Term Loans, Financial Services
Address: Wiberforce House (Suite F2), 181/184, Broad Street, Marina, Lagos
Tel: (01) 2641151, 2641153 **Fax:** (01) 2641151
E-mail: fundtec@hotmail.com
Contact: Air Commodore S. E. Omeruah (rtd) - Chairman
Mr. Linus Ezugwu - GM/CEO

FUNG-TAI ENGINEERING COMPANY LIMITED
Business: Engineering & Civil Construction (Dredging, Channelisation, Pipe-Laying, Constrution of New Canals, Sweeping of Shallow/Deep Water Beds); Consultancy Services
Address: Prestige House, 10, Turtons St, Sabo-Yaba, Lagos
Tel: (01) 7745169, 863886, 2881195 (2 L)
Fax: (01) 7745169, 863866
E-mail: fungtai@micro.com.ng
Contact: Sir Isaac Chuks - Chairma/CEO

FUNLAYO ADEBO ENTERPRISES LIMITED
Business: Manufacturing of Envelopes and Exercise Books, Packaging and Full-Process Printing
Address: 2, Adu Street, behind New Country Hospital, Aguda-Ogba, Ikeja, Lagos
Tel: (01) 4920085, 8042022, 08023035431, 08035754715
E-mail: faenigltd@hotmail.com
Contact: Princess Layo Bakare Okeowo - MD/CEO

FUNTAI LIMITED
Business: Turnkey Projects, Hospital Management
Address: 33A, Bishop Oluwole Street, Victoria Island, Lagos
Tel: (01) 2610474, 5558218, 619462 **Fax:** (01) 2610011
E-mail: funtai@yahoo.com
Contact: Dr. Taiwo Ebunola Malumi - Chairman/CEO

FUNTUNA VENTURES NIGERIA LIMITED
Business: Marketing of Herbal Bodycare Products
Address: 8, Adamo Kabiawu Street, Orile Agege, Lagos
Tel: (01) 4920889, 4923597, 4924991 **Fax:** (01) 4920720
E-mail: anicare@infoweb.abs.net

FUSELINE NIGERIA LIMITED
Business: Electrical & Mechanical Engineering Services
Address: 1, Balogun St, Obafemi Awolowo Way, Ikeja, Lagos
Tel: (01) 8045296, 5557384, 473237, 08037122970, 08033861916 **Fax:** (01) 3453459
E-mail: fuselinenl@yahoo.com
* Plot 332, Mambolo Street, off Olusegun Obasanjo Way, Zone 2, Wuse, Abuja
Tel: (09) 6715805, 0802326519
Contact: Alh. S. Idris - Chairman
Mr Salaudeen Olalekan - MD/CEO

FUSL INSURANCE BROKERS LIMITED
Business: Insurance Broking
Address: 36, Adeola Hopewell Stret, Victoria Island, Lagos
Tel: (01) 5558263-5 (3 L) **Fax:** (01) 5558266
E-mail: fidelity@alpha.linkserve.com
Contact: Mr Reginald Ihejiahi - Chairman
Mr Frank Onwu - Group MD

FUTEB NIGERIA LIMITED
Business: Hiring of Tugs, Boats, Barges and Land Equipment
Address: Enerhen Waterside, off Okofie Sawmill Close, off Enerhen Road, Warri
Tel: (053) 254885, 251546
E-mail: futeb@skannet.com
Contact: Rev. (Engr) Felix Utebu - MD/CEO

FUTUNE (NIGERIA) LIMITED
Business: Construction, Building & Civil Engineering, Engineering Consultancy, Importers
Address: Plot 348, Bamako Street, Wuse Zone 1, Abuja
Tel: (09) 5237570, 5237762
E-mail: bgalkali@yahoo.co.uk
* 3, Gombole Road, G.R.A., Maiduguri
Tel: (076) 235226
Contact: Alh. BabaGana Ali Alkali - Chairman/CEO

FUTURE CONCERNS NIGERIA LIMITED
Business: Oil Industry Service Company, Distribution of Occupational Safety Accessories
Address: Imperial House, Plot 274, Ajose Adeogun Street, Victoria Island, Lagos
Tel: (01) 2620633, 2706561-3 (3L) **Fax:** (01) 3204355
E-mail: fcnl@aol.com
* Plot 37, Trans-Amadi Ind., Layout, Port Harcourt
Tel: (084) 238708
* Block 1, (Flat 1), 2nd Edewor Estate, Enerhen Road, Effurun, Warri
Tel: (053) 253014, 258011 **Fax:** (053) 258011
Contact: Engr. Anthony Uzo Oguike - Chairman/CEO

FUTURE ENTERPRISES NIGERIA LIMITED
Business: Production of Terrazo Tiles, Marble & Granite
Address: Plot 15, Sharada Industrial Estate Phase III, Kano
Tel: (064) 660490
Contact: Mr. Walid Tahir - Chairman/CEO

FUTURE TECHNOLOGY SYSTEMS LIMITED
Business: Software Development, Internet Services, Training
Address: JKK House, 229, Ikorodu Road, Ilupeju, Lagos
Tel: (01) 4931535-7 (3 L) **Fax:** (01) 4931537
E-mail: sales@ftsng.com
Website: www.ftsng.com
Contact: Mr. Tunde Yusuf - MD/CEO

FUTURE VIEW SECURITIES LIMITED
Business: Stockbrokerage, Issuing House, Financial Consultancy, Ivestment/Private Banking
Address: 161D, Raufu Taylor Close, off Idejo St, V/I, Lagos
Tel: (01) 2629856-7 (2L), 4724959, 4733570, 4822015, 08023142314, 08033524706 **Fax:** (01) 2629857
E-mail: futureview@linkserve.com
Website: www.futureview.8m.com
Contact: Mrs. E. N. Ebi - MD/CEO

FYMAK MARINE AND OIL SERVICES (NIGERIA) LIMITED
Business: Marine Vessels, Logisic Support to Oil Industry
Address: 10A, Anifowoshe Street, Victoria Island, Lagos
Tel: (01) 2623062, 2611191, 2611709
Fax: (01) 2622254, 2614470
E-mail: fymak@infoweb.abs.net
* Mobil Oil Terminal, Qua Iboe Terminal, Eket
* 17, Barracks Road, Eket, Akwa Ibom State
Contact: Dr. Maduka Nwakwesi - Chairman/CEO

G & V INSURANCE BROKERS LIMITED
Business: Insurance Broking
Address: 74, Norman Williams Street, Ikoyi, Lagos
Tel: (01) 2690813, 2671528
Contact: Mr H. N. Nnadi - GM/CEO

G & W INTERNATIONAL LIMITED
Business: Importation, Marketing and Service of SHARP Brand of Electronic/Electrical Appliances &Products
Address: Plot 1437, Sanusi Fafunwa St, Victoria Island, Lagos
Tel: (01) 2625192, 4700063, 7766869, 08033337822
Fax: (01) 2625193
E-mail: gwnig@hyperia.com
Contact: Mr. Chris Imoka - Chairman

G. CAPPA PLC
Business: Building & Civil Engineering Contractors
Address: 8, Taylor Road, Iddo, Ebute Meta, Lagos
Tel: (01) 800080-4 (5 L), 7740931, 7744810, 4701337, 4703690 **Fax:** (01) 2691815. 2694534
* Omnia House, Poot 2186, Ibrahim Babangida Way, Wuse Zone 4, Abuja.
Tel: (09) 5235466, 08033344786 **Fax:** (09) 5210104

G. A. PRODUCTIONS
Business: Events & Experimental Marketing
Address: 30B, Agodogba Ave, Parkview Estate, Ikoyi, Lagos
Tel: (01) 2695514, 2695515
E-mail: asdia@nigol.net.ng
Contact: Mr. Trevor Henning - MD/CEO

G. E. C. OBIAMALU & SONS LIMITED
Business: Importation & Distribution of Building Materials; Building Construction; Interior Decoration
Address: 75, Chime Avenue, New Haven, Enugu
Tel: (042) 255008 **Fax:** (042) 251152
E-mail: cyberway@infoweb.abs.net
Contact: Chief (Sir) G. E. C. Obiamalu - Chairman/CEO

G. E. N. P NIGERIA LIMITED
Business: Oil & Gas Engineering Services
Address: 11C, Agodogba Avenue, Park View Estate, Ikoyi, Lagos
Tel: (01) 2692258, 2692259 **Fax:** (01) 2694221
E-mail: genp@infoweb.abs.net

G. N. BISHOP INSURANCE BROKERS (NIGERIA) LIMITED
Business: Insurance Broking
Address: 174, Western Avenue (Costain), Surulere, Lagos
Tel: (01) 4712334-6 (3 L), 5852344-7 (4L), 08022232459, 0802141371 **Fax:** (01) 2619209
E-mail: glanvill@hyperia.com
Contact: Chief H. B. Chanrai - Chairman
Mr. S. O. Ottah - GM/CEO

G. N. IHEAKU & COMPANY LIMITED
Business: Importation & Distribution of General Merchandise
Address: 24, Old Market Road, Onitsha
Tel: (046) 412130, 412852, 08033323668, 08033407910
E-mail: iheakugins@infoweb.abs.net
Contact: Dr. G. N. Iheaku - Chairman/CEO

G. O. EWELUNDU LIMITED
Business: Importation and Distribution of General Merchandise; Real Estate Development
Address: 52, New Market Road, Onitsha
Tel:: (046) 411828, 0807066405 Fax: (046) 411828
E-mail: goff_gold@yahoo.com
* 1, Abagana Street, Fegge, Onitsha
Contact: Chief Godfrey Emeka Ekwelundu - Chairman/CEO

G. U. OKEKE & SONS LIMITED
Business: Transportation Services
Address: Km. 12, Onitsha-Enugu Expressway, Ogbunike via Onitsha, Anambra State
* 112, Upper Iweka Road, Onitsha
* 81A, Ikwerre Road, Mile 3, Diobu Port Harcourt
Contact: Chief G. U. Okeke -Chairman/CEO

G-EURAFRIC LIMITED
Business: Energy and Allied Services, Petroleum Products Exploration & Production, Distribution and Marketing, Maritime Consultants
Address: 24B, A.J. Marinho Drive, Victoria Island, Lagos
Tel: (01) 4617870, 4617890, 2629708, 2629709
Fax: (01) 2629709, 4617870 (Ext. 102)
E-mail: anthony@koochicommnications.com

GABIMO ENGINEERING COMPANY LIMITED
Business: Sales of Diesel Generators, Power Equipment, Agro-Produce and Commodities; Engineering Services
Address: 57,Jimoh Balogun St, off CMD Ave., Ketu, Lagos
Tel: (01) 7742559, 4965903
E-mail: gabimohold@hotmail.com
Contact: Alh. Bisi Mohammed - Chairman/CEO

GABROS GROUP OF COMPANIES
Business: Importation and Sales of Automobiles and Motorcycle Spare Parts; Hospitality Services
Address: 74, Onitsha Road, Nnewi Anambra State
Tel: (046) 460636, 460718, 460697 **Fax:** (046) 460697
E-mail: gabros@infoweb.abs.net
Contact: Chief Gabriel I. Chukwuma - Chairman/CEO

GABUMO PUBLISHING COMPANY LIMITED
Business: Printing and Publishing
Address: Gabumo House, Plot 5, North Industrial Layout, Esuk Utan, Calabar
Tel: (087) 232127, 234429, 234430
* 302B, Murtala Mohammed Way, Yaba, Lagos
Tel: (01) 861159, 860265, 4704954, 08023390432, 08033188990, 0803346666
Contact: Mr. G. E. Umoden - Chairman/CEO

GAFUNK NIGERIA LIMITED
Business: Assembly and Supply of Computer Hardware and Accessories, Supply and Installation of Software, Networking, Consultancy
Address: 7, Afisman Drive, opp. Pam Pam Hotel, Anifowoshe, Ikeja, Lagos
Tel: (01) 4704274, 4938271, 7730169, 7741951, 7744091, 08023070918 **Fax:** (01) 4938271
E-mail: sales@gafunk.com
Website: www.gafunk.com
Contact: Mr. G. A. Alimi - Chairman/CEO

GALA INDUSTRIES LIMITED
Business: Manufacture of PVC Sheetings and PVC Carpets
Address: Plot 9 & 10, Block XIII, Industrial Estate, Otta
Tel: (039) 722256-9 (4 L) **Fax:** (039) 722258, 722259
Contact: Alh. Bello Othman - Chairman
Mr. H. Cheung - MD/CEO

GALAXY TELEVISION LIMITED (Channel 27)
Business: Television Broadcasting, Production,
Address: 25, Community Road (B1 Close), off Bamisile Road, off Allen Avenue, Ikeja, Lagos
Tel: (01) 5557511, 5557512, 08037138560
E-mail: galaxy@hyperia.com
galaxynews2004@yahoo.com
Contact: Chiet Steve Ojo - Chairman/CEO

GALBA LIMITED
Business: Engineering and Technical Services, Manufacturing of Foundry Products for Industrial, Technical and Construction Use
Address: Plot 311, Trans-Amadi Ind. Layout, Port Harcourt
Tel/Fax: (084) 238965
E-mail: galba@phca.linkserve.com
* 15, Elsie Femi-Pearse Street, off Adeola Odeku Street, Victoria Island, Lagos.
Tel: (01) 614910

GALCON ENGINEERING LIMITED
Business: Builders, Civil & Structural Engineering Services, General Contractors
Address: Ladico House (4th Floor), 3 (Plot 1661), Oyin Olayemi Street, Victoria Island, Lagos
Tel: (01) 2621230 **Fax:** (01) 2614297
E-mail: galcon@beta.linkserve.com
Contact: Engr. O. O. Ogali - Chairman/CEO

GALILEO NIGERIA
Business: Electronic Global Distribution Services for the Travel Industry
Address: The Plaza, 66B, Opebi Road, Ikeja, Lagos
Tel: (01) 4931731-5 (5 L) **Fax:** (01) 4979832
E-mail: galileo@flybellview.com
Website: www.galileo.com

GALVANSING INDUSTRIES LIMITED
Business: Manufacture of Corrugated Iron Roofing Sheets, Galvanizing Services
Address: Oba Akran Avenue, Ikeja Industrial Estate, Lagos
Tel: (01) 4976430-4 (5 L), 4964756 **Fax:** (01) 4964746
Contact: Otunba B. T. Odebiyi - MD/CEO

GAMA ENGINEERING LIMITED
Business: Electrical & Electronic Engineering, Supply and Installation of Electrical, Fire-Alarm, Fire-Fighting, Security Systems and Electronic Billboards

Address: 63, Raymond Njoku Street, S. W. Ikoyi, Lagos
Tel: (01) 2693387 **Fax:** (01) 2695455
Contact: Alh. Umar F. Bashar - MD/CEO

GAMJI FERTILIZER PROCESSING COMPANY LIMITED
Business: Importation & Processing of Fertilizer
Address: 4, Mohammd Maude Street, off President's Avenue, Bompai Kano
Tel: (064) 647319, 08023104509, 08037872468, 08044115774 **Fax:** (064) 647320
E-mail: gamjifertilizer2000@yahoo.com
Website: www.france-appro.com
Contact: Mr. Lionel Martin - Chairman
Alh. Mohamed Sani Abdullahi - MD/CEO

GAMJI-TEC GROUP OF COMPANIES
Business: Manufacturing of Aluminium Building Materials
Address: 50/52, Kachia Road, Kaduna South, Kaduna
Tel: (062) 235658, 08037868714 **Fax:** (062) 235658
E-mail: gamji@yahoo.com
* Erisco Bonpet Plaza (Shop) 173, Plot 2357, Douala Street, Zone 5, Wuse, Abuja
Tel: (09) 5237299, 08037868983
Contact: Alh. M. Aliyu Yerima - MD/CEO

GAMLA NIGERIA LIMITED
Business: Supply and Installation of Scientific, Medical, Research, Surveying and Photogrammetric Equipment and Instruments
Address: Plot A39, Delta Crescent, G.R.A., Benin City
Tel: (052) 251247, 252111, 252140 **Fax:** (052) 255666
E-mail: gamla@linkserve.com.ng
* 20, New Layout, off Liberty Dam Road, Jos
Tel: (073) 460311
Contact: Mr. Nelson D. Ononye - Chairman/CEO

GANI INTERNATIONAL SERVICES & TRADING COMPANY NIGRIA LIMITED
Business: Sales and Supply of Oil Tools, Marine Products, Industrial Machinery and Engineering Equipment
Address: Plot 79, Trans-Amadi Ind. Layout, Port Harcourt
Tel: (084) 237427, 484993,08033409292, 08037110974
E-mail: ganiinternational2000@yahoo.com
Website: www.gani-services.com
Contact: Mr Godson Alexander Iheoma - Chairman/CEO

GAOXINQI NIGERIA LIMITED
Business: Sales of Telecommunication Terminal Equipment, Mobile Phones & Accessories
Address: 13B, Saka Tinubu Street, Victoria Island, Lagos
Tel: (01) 7759058, 5558661, 08033084062. 08033069685
Fax: (01) 5558661
E-mail: newepochlgs@yahoo.com
Contact: Mr O. R. Yang - Chairman
Mr Shunfeng Xu - MD/CEO

GAP PUBLICITY LIMITED
Business: Outdoor Advertising, Artistic Designs, Screen Printing
Address: 55, Sule Street, Idimangoro, Agege, Lagos
Tel: (01) 4923039 **Fax:** (01) 4926365
Contact: Mr. Babatunde Adegbite - MD/CEO

GARAGES LIMITED
Business: Sales & Repairs of Automobiles/Motor Vehicles
Address: Garages House, 43/45 (Km. 2), Lagos-Badagry Expressway, (by Alafia Bus-Stop), Orile-Iganmu
Tel: (01) 4702642, 7751594, 08033031946, 08033303753
Contact: Mr. Bayo Amusan - Chairman/CEO

GARBS ORGANISATION LIMITED
Business: Importation and Distribution of Automoble & Motorcycle Parts, Agro-Allied Business, Real Estate Development, Manufacturing of Rubber & Plastic Products • General Merchandising
Address: Garbs Building, 39, Awka Road, Onitsha
Tel/Fax: (046) 4120, 413645, 480053
Mr. Don-Iyke Onwugbenu - Group MD

GARKIDA PRESS LIMITED
Business: Commercial & Industrial Printing, Publishing, Prodction of Light Packaging, Colour Separation
Address: Plot 742, Kade Street, off Aminu Kano Crescent, Wuse II, Abuja
Tel: (09) 4138636, 4138638, 080556033047
Fax: (09) 4138386
E-mail: garkida@nipost.nipost.com.ng
Contact: Alh. Sani Garkida - Chairman/CEO

GARMENT CARE LIMITED
Business: Drycleaning and Laundry Services
Address: Plot 1088, Adeola Odeku St, Victoria Island, Lagos
Tel: (01) 3200225, 3200235, 7748017 **Fax:** (01) 2700151
E-mail: garmntcare@21ctl.com
* 23B, Isaac John Street, G.R.A.Ikeja, Lagos
Tel: (01) 2700823, 4931240, 4931420-1 (2L)
Fax: (01) 2700823
Contact: Mrs. Nana Otedola - MD/CEO

GARNET INDUSTRIES (NIGERIA) LIMITED
Business: Manufacturing and Importationi of PVC Resins, Water-Proofing Oxidised Membrance and Bitumen
Address: 1, Abimbola Shodipe Street, Western Avenue (Barracks Bus-Stop), Surulere, Lagos
Tel: (01) 5836695, 5837744, 5840791 **Fax:** (01) 5836498

GAS LINE ENGINEERING COMPANY LIMITED
Business: Oilfield Services & Contracting, General Procurement, Supply of Pipes, Equipment Leasing
Address: 277, Aba/Port Harcourt Expressway, Rumuogba, Port Harcourt,
Tel: (084) 612700, 611962, 613425 **Fax:** (084) 611959

GASHASH TANNERIES LIMITED
Business: Tannery
Address: 23, Nababa Badamasi Rd, Bompai Ind Estate, Kano
Tel: (064) 634749

GASLINK NIGERIA LIMITED
Business: Distribution & Supply of Natural Petroleum Gas for Industrial, Commercial & Transportation use
Address: 1, Motorways Avenue, opp, 7up Factory, near Old Toll Gate, Oregun Industrial Estate, Oregun, Lagos
Tel: (01) 4935708-9 (2 L), 5557909-10 **Fax:** (01) 7912295
E-mail: info@gaslink.org
Contact: Alh. Ibrahim Boyi - Ag. MD/CEO

GATEWAYBANK PLC
Business: Commercial Banking
Address: 32, Lalubu Street, Oke-Ilewo, Sapon, Abeokuta
Tel: (039) 233479, 233583
* 61, Marina, Lagos
Tel: (01) 2641831-4 (2L), 2644497, 2640525, 2640527, 4717280-2 (3L) **Fax:** (01) 2641835
E-mail: gwb@gatewaybankplc.com
Contact: Mr. Samuel O. Olatunji - MD/CEO

GATEWAY HOTELS LIMITED
Business: Hospitality and Catering Services
Address: Gateway Hotel Ota, Lagos-Abeokuta Expressway, Sango-Ota, Ogun State
Tel: (039) 722002, 722004, 722007, (01) 7730937
Fax: (039) 722007, 722377
Contact: Mr. J. O. Obajimi - GM/CEO

GATEWAY PHARMACEUTICALS COMPANY PLC
Business: Manufacturing and Marketing of Pharmaceuticals
Address: Plot 3-8, Housing Corporation Industrial Estate, Ikangba, Ijebu-Ode, Ogun State
Tel: (037) 430202, 430526 **Fax:** (037) 430526
Contact: Prof. Thomas Adeoye Lambo - Chairman
Mr. J. O. Akinbinu - MD/CEO

GATEWAY PLASTIC & PAPER PACKAGING NIGERIA LTD
Business: Manufacturing of Plastic Products & Cement Sacks
Address: Km. 9, Abeokuta-Lagos Road, Abeokuta
Tel: (039) 243795, 241625

GATEWAY PORTLAND CEMENT LIMITED
Business: Production and Packaging of Portland Cement
Address: Km. 8, Abeokuta-Lagos Road, Ibara, Abeokuta
Tel/Fax: (039) 243795, 242876
E-mail: gppnl@bacomonline.com
Contact: Dr. E. O. Odegbami - Chairman/CEO

GATIMO LIMITED (Ruff'N' Tumble)
Business: Sales of Children's Wear Fashion Items
Address: 23A Isaac John Street, G.R.A., Ikeja, Lagos
Tel: (01) 4932387, 2700817, 08033255183
Fax: (01) 4972010
E-mail: ruffntumblekids@yahoo.com
ruffntumblekids@hyperia.com
* Sandiland Arcade, Plot 230, Muri Okunola Street, Victoria Island, Lagos
Tel: (01) 5558182
Contact: Mrs. N. Ogunlesi - MD/CEO

GATOY NIGERIA COMPANY LIMITED
Business: Manufacturing of Electrical Control Equipment
Address: Block C11, Lagos State Industrial Estate, Fatai Atere Way, Matori, Mushin, Lagos
Tel: (01) 4526547, 4701226, 0802321667
Contact: Mr. Gabriel Badejo - MD/CEO

GAZAL INDUSTRIES ENTERPRISES LIMITED
Business: Manufacturing of Terrazo Floor Tiles, Pre-Cast Pavement Stone, Flush Doors and Windows
Address: 27, Kundila Road, Bompai Industrial Estate, Kano
Tel: (064) 335406, 646648, 08033609461
Contact: Alh. Baba Nabegu - Chairman/CEO

GBOLADE ODUSINA BROKERS
Business: Real Estate Consultants
Address: 64, Bornu Crescent, P.O.Box 2693, Apapa, Lagos
Tel: (01) 5871359, 4724751
E-mail: gobsky@yahoo.com

GEACAN LIMITED
Business: Importation, and Sales of Hair-Care Equipment
Address: 9, Bankole Street, Balogun, Lagos
Tel: (01) 2669765, 2663979 **Fax:** (01) 2668347

GEE DEE ENTERPRISES LIMITED
Business: Importation & Sales of Bicycles, Sewing Machines, Plastic Raw Materials and Industrial Chemicals
Address: 5/6, Sani Abacha Way, Kano
Tel/Fax: (064) 645865, 647729, 08037878144
E-mail: gobind@gee-dee.com
Contact: Mr. Mohan Mahtani - MD/CEO

GEE WILLIAMS NIGERIA LIMITED
Business: Importation, and Sales of Electronic Appliances and Electrical Parts
Address: 124, Nnamdi Azikiwe Street, Idumota, Lagos
Tel: (01) 2665958, 2641842 **Fax:** (01) 2663981
E-mail: geewilly@alpha.linkserve.com
Contact: Mr. Jonathan Umechiedo - Chairman/CEO

GEEKOS SECURITY NIGERIA LIMITED
Business: Installation of Electrical/Electronic Security Equipment; Security Consultants and Advisers
Address: Nayee House, Plot 1, Lambert Imasuen Drive, Ajao Estate, Isolo, Lagos
Tel: (01) 4528452, 4528479, 4528805-6 (2 L)
Fax: (01) 4528488
E-mail: nayee@nova.net.ng
* Plot 279A, Addis Ababa Cr, Wuse Zone 4, Abuja
Tel: (09) 5231387
Contact: Mr. Kenneth O. Gbagi - MD/CEO

GEEPEE INDUSTRIES LIMITED
Business: Manufacture of Storage Tanks, Industrial Containers, Toys and Balls
Address: Km. 38, Abeokuta Motor Road, Sango-Otta
Tel: (039) 722311, 720311, 720552 * (01) 7759430
Fax: (039) 720552, * (01) 4968280
E-mail: geepee@linkserve.com.ng
Contact: Mr. P. V. Vaswani - MD/CEO

GEETEE NIGERIA LIMITED
Business: Shipping, Clearing and Forwarding •Air Freight, Warehousing, Transportation and Oil Rig Movers
Address: 22, Oyekan Road, Apapa, Lagos
Tel: (01) 5458806, 8126641
Contact: Mr. G. Obot - Chairman/CEO

GEMCARD NIGERIA LIMITED
Business: Marketing and Support of Electronic Cards
Address: CSS Bookshop (14th Floor), 50/52, Broad Street, Lagos Island, Lagos
Tel: (01) 2643970, 2635773
Fax: (01) 2647016
Website: www.globalelectronicmoney.com
Contact: Mr. Alex Nwuba - MD/CEO

GEMINI PHARMACEUTICALS NIGERIA LIMITED
Business: Manufacture and Marketing of Pharmaceuticals
Address: Plot 13, Block A, Amuwo-Odofin Industrial Estate, Apapa-Oshodi Expressway, Amuwo-Odofin
Tel/Fax: (01) 2883056, 7901184
Contact: Mr. E. O. Ebere - MD/CEO

GEMS VENTURES NIGERIA LIMITED
Business: Importation and Distribution of Motor Vehicles Spare Parts and Accessories, Import & Export of General Merchandise
Address: 8, Gems Crescent, Nkpor, Onitsha
Contact: Mr. G. E. Ezeoke - Chairman/CEO

GENASEC NOMINEES NIGERIA LIMITED
Business: Management & Legal Consultancy Services, Company Secretarial Services
Address: Kresta Laurel Complex (4th Floor), 376, Ikorodu Road, Maryland, Ikeja, Lagos
Tel: (01) 4935391, 7744873
*Broking House, 1, Alh. Jimoh Odutola Rd, Ibadan.
Tel: (02) 2411681 **Fax:** (02) 2411683

GENERAL AGRO OIL INDUSTRIES LIMITED
Business: Crushing of Oilseeds •Refining of Vegetable Oil, Production of Palm Kernel Cakes/Pellets
Address: 109, Awolowo Road, S. W. Ikoyi, Lagos
Tel: (01) 2692132, 2694291 **Fax:** (01) 2691463
E-mail: gaoil@phca.linkserve.com
* Plot 78/79, Trans-Amadi Layout, Port Harcourt
Tel: (084) 236695, 232188, 238968, 236696
E-mail: gaoil@phca.linkserve.com
Contact: Chief N. Idowu - Chairman
Mr. T. V. Eashwar - MD/CEO

GENERAL b.m. LIMITED
Business: Importation and Sales of General Building Materials, Bathroom Suites and Accessories
Address: 12/14, Aerodrome Road, Apapa, Lagos
Tel: (01) 5875406 **Fax:** (01) 5877356
Contact: Alh. Sulaimon Onabiyi - Chairman

GENERAL ELECTRIC N. P. NIGERIA
Business: Multi-Energy Solutions (Pipeline Integrity Solutions, Turbines, Compressors, Turbo Expanders, Pumps, Valve, Fuel Dispensers)
Address: 11C, Agodogba Ave, Park View Estate, Ikoyi, Lagos
Tel: (01) 2692258, 2692259 **Fax:** (01) 2694221
* NAL Place (4th Floor), Plot 13, Trans-Amadi Industrial Layout, Port Harcourt
Te/Fax: (084) 572516
Website: www.ge.com
Contact: Mr. Adewale O. Audifferen - Chairman/MD

GENERAL COTTON MILL LIMITED
Business: Manufacturer & Sales of Textile Products
Address: Niger Bridge Industrial Layout, Onitsha
Tel: (046) 210144, 210252, 211619, 210181, 210792
Fax: (046) 210144
* Block 4A, Apapa Lane, off Corporation Drive, Dolphin Estate, Ikoyi, Lagos\
Tel: (01) 2694420 **Fax:** (01) 2694419
Contact: Mr R. N.W. Lee - MD/CEO

GENERAL DATA ENGINEERING SERVICES NIGERIA LTD
Business: Internet Service Provider
Address: 18B, Oshin Road, Kongi Layout, Bodija, Ibadan.
Tel: (02) 8105156 **Fax:** (02) 8106268
E-mail: info@skannet.com
Website: www.skannet.com
Contact: Mr Akin Akinbola - MD/CEO

GENERAL FOODS & SWEETS MANUFACTURING LIMITED (Chocolat Royal)
Business: Manufacturing of Foods, Pastries & Confectioneries, Restaurant Services
Address: 267A, Etim Inyang Crescent, Victoria Island, Lagos
Tel: (01) 2623055-6 (2L) **Fax:** (01) 2614779, 2620105

GENERAL IMPORT (Div..of CFAO Plc)
Business: Distribution of General Goods
Address: 71/72, Adeniji Adele Road, Elegbata, Lagos
Tel: (01) 2664695, 2664699 **Fax:** (01) 2641226
* Plot 568, Michael Okpara St, Wuse Zone 2, Abuja
* 12, Murtala Mohammed Way, Kano
* 8, Azikiwe Road, Port Harcourt
Contact: Chief Molade Okoya-Thomas, MFR - Chairman
Mr. C. M. Villa - MD/CEO

GENERAL METAL PRODUCTS LIMITED
Business: Manufacturing of Aluminium Curtain-Wall, Doors, Windows Partitioning & Skylights, Steel Doors and Security Doors, Office Furniture, Side-Boards and Cabinets, Office
Address: Plot 9, Block A, Amuwo-Odofin Industrial Estate, Apapa-Oshodi Expressway, Amuwo-Odofin, Lagos
Tel: (01) 5801540-4 (5L), 4705713, 4702613
Fax: (01) 5833651
E-mail: kahl.gmp@hyperia.com
*Plot 490, Bangul Street, Cadastral Zone A8, Abuja
Tel: (09) 5236102, 5235297 **Fax:** (09) 5235297
Contact: Mr Joachim Kahl - MD/CEO

GENERAL METALWARE COMPANY LIMITED
Business: Manufacture of Galvanised Metal Products and Plasticware
Address: 1, Onikoyi Road, Ikeja Ind. Estate, Ikeja, Lagos
Tel: (01) 4961200
E-mail: wempco@linkserve.com.ng
Contact: Alh. Inua Wada - Chairman
Mr. Phillip Tung - MD/CEO.

GENERAL OIL LIMITED
Business: Marketing of Refined Petroleum Products, Industrial and Household Chemicals
Address: Plot 1170, Saka Tinubu St, Victoria Island, Lagos
Tel: (01) 2616287, 2611350, 611561, 611573
Fax: (01) 613581
Contact: Mr. Olatunde A. Fajimolu - MD/CEO.

GENERAL SECURITIES & FINANCE COMPANY LIMITED
Business: Stockbroking, Financial Services, Bureau de Change Operations
Address: 1A, Hospital Avenue, G.R.A., Enugu
Tel: (042) 259503, 25976, 253927 **Fax:** (042) 259576
* Great Nigeria House (11th Floor), 47/57, Martins Street, Marina, Lagos

Tel: (01) 2664523, 2669351, 2664127 **Fax:** (01) 2664127
E-mail: gensec@alpha.linkserve.com
Contact: Chief Ezugo Dan Nwandu - Chairman/CEO

GENERAL TELECOM PLC
Business: Manufacture, Marketing & Maintenance of Telecommunication Equipment
Address: 3/5, Boyle Street, Onikan, Lagos
Tel: (01) 2601100-4 (5L), 2645530-2 (3L)
Fax: (01) 2645529, 2645153
E-mail: gt@generaltelecom.com
Website: www.generatelecom.com
* Plot 1293, Abidjan Street, off Herbert Macaulay Way (North), Wuse Zone 3, Abuja
Tel: (09) 5230613, 5230623
* 40, Railway Close, beh. NITEL, Port Harcourt
Tel: (084) 239294
Contact: Engr Karl Teller - Group MD/CEO

GENERAL TELEPHONES & ELECTRONICS LIMITED
Business: Telecommunications and Electronic Engineering
Address: 9, Estaport Avenue, Soluyi Estate, Gbagada, Lagos
Tel: (01) 5550000-9 (10 L), 5550043, 08023230652
E-mail: gteeci@nigol.net.ng
Contact: Dr. Felix Olumogba - Chairman/CEO

GENERAL TIRE WEST AFRICA LIMITED
Business: Importation of Heavy-Duty and Special Tyres
Address: 5/7, Queen's Barracks Road, Apapa, Lagos
Tel: (01) 5452559 **Fax:** (01) 5452336
E-mail: gentire@megafortune.com
gentire2@nova.net.ng
Contact: Alh. Bode Abdullai - MD/CEO

GENERATOR WAREHOUSE LIMITED
Business: Sales of Generators, Transformer and Electrical Equipment
Address: Plot 146C, Ligali Ayorinde St, Victoria Is, Lagos
Tel: (01) 3201559, 2708822 **Fax:** (01) 2708822

GENESIS SECURITIES & INVESTMENT LIMITED
Business: Stockbroking, Portfolio & Fund Management
Address: Cocoa House (9th Floor), Oba Adebimpe Road, G.P.O. Box 11265, Dugbe, Ibadan
Tel: (02) 2412323
Contact: Mr. A. B. Aluko - MD/CEO

GENESIS WORLDWIDE SHIPPING COMPANY LIMITED
Business: Ship owners, Third-Party Ship Managment, Shopping Agency, Marine Consultancy, Offshore Services and Supplies, Logistics
Address: 41, Itapeju Street, Apapa, Lagos
Tel: (01) 5451905, 5870781, 08037165974
Fax: (01) 5451906
E-mail: genesis@hyperia.com
Contact: Capt. Emmanuel Ihenacho - Chairman/CEO

GENIC VENTURES LIMITED
Business: Marketing of Street Lighting Fixtures
Address: 123, Olojo Drive, Ojo Town, Lagos
Tel: (01) 5887640 **Fax:** (01) 5891119
E-mail: ecl.genic@hyperia.com
* Wuse Shopping Plaza (Suite B2), Plot 1995, Herbert Macaulay Way, Wuse Zone 5, Abuja
Tel: (09) 5235943 **Fax:** (09) 5234421
E-mail: ecilo@eudoramail.com
Contact: Chief Chuba Ilo - Chairman/CEO

GENIENG COMMUNICATIONS LIMITED
Business: Telecommnications, Pre-Paid Phone Cards
Address: Okoi Arikpo House (1st Floor), 5, Idowu Taylor Street, Victoria Island, Lagos
Tel: (01) 2705823-4 (2 L), 08037777724
Fax: (01) 2705733
E-mail: info@genieng.com
Website: www.genieng.com
Contact: Mr Peter Edovia - MD/CEO

GENII SYSTEMS LIMITED
Business: Sales and Supply of IT Systems, Internet Services, Value-Added Network Services
Address: 11B, Olosa Street, Victoria Island, Lagos
Tel: (01) 3201721, 4619047 **Fax:** (01) 3201727
E-mail: sales@algenii.com
* 4, Oyekan St, off Akerele Street, Surulere, Lagos
Tel: (01) 5851216, 7748798, 8042830 **Fax:** (01) 5851216
Contact: Engr. Ismail Adebayo - MD/CEO

GENPROGETTI NIGERIA LIMITED
Business: Building and Construction Engineering, Commerce.
Address: 25, Aba Road, Port Harcourt
Tel: (084) 233851
E-mail: enprogetti@yahoo.com
* Plot 75B, Trans-Amadi Ind Layout, Port Harcourt
Tel: (084) 461158
Contact: Engr. N. O. Okoye - Chairman/CEO

GENTECH POWER SUPPLY NIGERIA LIMITED
Business: Sales and Service of Generators
Address: 26, Niger Street, Kano
Tel: (064) 638558 **Fax:** (064) 634500, 634510
* 2, Ayo Rosiji Crescent, G.R.A., Ikeja, Lagos
Tel: (01) 4938082, 4938082 **Fax:** (01) 4938082
* 2, Maiduguri Road, Sokoto.
Tel: (060) 230744, 233450
Contact: Alh. Muhammad M. Saidu - Chairman/CEO

GENUSS INVESTMENTS LIMITED
Business: Importation, Sales, Installation of Computers, Telecommunication and General Electronic Engineering, Consultancy and Training,
Address: 13, Adepele St, off Medical Road, Ikeja Lagos
Tel: (01) 3205183, 08034032586, 08037150776
Fax: (01) 2721602
E-mail: genussworldwide@yahoo.co.uk
Contact: Mr. Michael Nwanna - MD/CEO

GEOBI (NIGERIA) LIMITED
Business: Manufacturing; Trading and Assembly; Supply, Installation, Service and Maintenance of Electric Generating and Distribution (Generating Sets, Gas Turbines, Transformer, Switch Gears, Complete Power Sub-Stations
Address: 176, Ikorodu Road, Onipanu, Shomolu, Lagos
Tel: (01) 4976187, 4701822, 3209351 **Fax:** (01) 4976187
E-mail: geobi.ng@usa.net

* 15, Benson Anorue Street, Ajao Estate, Apakun - Oshodi, Lagos
Tel: (01) 4528584, 4527617
Contact: Mr. George N. Obioha - Chairman/CEO

GEODETIC POSITIONING SERVICES LIMITED
Business: Surveying, Offshore Engineering Surveying, Photogrammetic Consultancy, Geodetists
Address: 25B, Oyetola Idowu Street, off Coker Road, Ilupeju, P.O.Box 8353, Ikeja, Lagos
Tel: (01) 4970616, 4967433

GEOELIS CABLES LIMITED
Business: Manufacturing and Marketing of Electrical and Telecommunication Cables
Address: Nkpor Ind.Layout, Umuoji Road, Nkpor, Onitsha
Tel: (046) 611024, 211241
Contact: Chief G. C. O. Ezebube - Chairman/CEO

GEOMAINS INSURANCE BROKERS LIMITED
Business: Insurance Broking
Address: 19, Ikorodu Road, Jibowu, Yaba, Lagos
Tel: 08033026189, 08033026177
E-mail: ssa@nigol.net.ng
* 6B, Obinachi Close, Nali Estate, Port Harcourt
Contact: Mr. Olawale O. Soyinka - Gen. Manager/CEO

GEOMATICS NIGERIA LIMITED
Business: Environmental Consultancy Services, GIS/Remove Sensing Technology Implementation, Environmental Impact Assessment, Pollution Management
Address: Plot 7, off DPC Road, Agodi G.R.A., Dugbe Ibadan
Tel: (02) 8105577 **Fax:** (02) 8105623
E-mail: geomatics@informatics.com.ng
Website: www.geoniger.com

GEOMESAF & COMPANY LIMITED
Business: Sales & Service of Copiers /Duplicating Machines
Address: Plot 46, Ishawu Adewale Street, off Modupe Johnson Crescent, Surulere, Lagos
Tel: (01) 5455289-93 (5 L), 5850279, 802510-4 (5 L), 833539 **Fax:** (01) 5836909
E-mail: ssa@nigol.net.ng
* 32, Emekuku Street, D-Line, Port Harcourt
* Plot 607, Danbatta Close, Area 7, Garki, Abuja
Tel: (09) 2345727 **Fax:** (09) 2347931
Contact: Mr. S. S. O. Afemikhe - Chairman/CEO

GEONNASONS INTERNATIONAL GROUP NIGERIA LIMITED
Business: Clearing and Forwarding, Shipping Services, Manufacture of Pharmaceutical Products
Address: Plot 90, Block C, Latif Salami Street off International Airport Road, Ajao Estate, Lagos
Tel: (01) 4521032, 4524564, 4525546, 7759803, 7943012-3
Fax: (01) 4521032
E-mail: panholding@pannannah.com
Website: www.pannannah.com
Contact: Prince G. A. Nnannah - Chairman/CEO

GEOPHIL SERVICES NIGERIA LIMITED
Business: Engineering Consultancy, Contract Procurement
Address: LSDPC House (12th Floor), Nnamdi Azikiwe Street, Idumota, Lagos
Tel: (01) 2668125, 08034030508 **Fax:** (01) 2668125
E-mail: puumunnakwe@hotmail.com
Contact: Engr. (Chief) P. U. Umunnakwe - Chairman/CEO

GEORGE COHEN (NIGERIA) LIMITED
Busines: Steel Stockist, Crane Hire Services
Address: Ibru Jetty, by Coconut Bus-Stop, Oshodi-Apapa Expressway, Ibafon, Apapa, Lagos
Tel: (01) 5876477, 7919117 **Fax:** (01) 5876477
Contact: Mr. G. M. Ibru - Chairman
Mr. J. I. Ajibulu - Consultant

GEORGIO INVESTMENTS NIGERIA LIMITED
Business: Property Investment
Address: NISSCO House (Ground Floor), Plot 232A, Adeola Odeku Street, Victoria Island, Lagos
Tel: (01) 2612406
* 8A, Gana Street, Maitama, Abuja
Tel: (09) 4139176, 4136889, 4131931

GEOSANNA DIGITAL COMMUNICATIONS LIMITED
Business: Sales of Mobile Phones & Accessories
Address: 42, Bishop Oluwole Street, Victoria Island, Lagos
Tel: (01) 2629592, 2629593, 7916124, 08023316055, 08023695022, 08034731133 **Fax:** (01) 2629592

GEOSERVICES NIGERIA LIMITED
Business: Oilfield Engineering Services
Address: Plot 271, Trans-Amadi Ind., Layout, Port Harcourt
Tel: (084) 461160-4 (5L) Fax: (084) 461166
E-mail: base.geoservices@phca.linkserve.com
Contact: Mr. Robert Eregroid - MD/CEO

GERIZIM GROUP
Business: Leasing, Treasury Support, Telecommunications; Travel and Tour Agency
Address: NICON House (6th Floor, Front Wing), 5, Customs Street, off Marina, Lagos Island, Lagos
Tel: (01) 2669344, 2662071, 2634371, 2642783, 2662412
Fax: (01) 2642783
E-mail: gerizimgroup@e-mail.com
Contact: Mr. Olakunle Ajuyala - MD/CEO

GERMAINE AUTO CENTRE LIMITED
Business: Sales, Service, and Leasing of Automobiles
Address: 2nd Roundabout, Lekki-Epe Expressway, Lagos
Tel: (01) 8042181, 7748000, 7749585, 7742080, 08023143358, 4707137 **Fax:** (01) 8047815
E-mail: germaine@germaineauto.com
germaine@supernet300.com
Contact: Mr. Jerry Chukwueke - Chairman/CEO

GERMAINE HAULAGE LIMITED
Business: Road Haulauge Services
Address: Lekki Expressway (2nd Roundabout), V/Is, Lagos
Tel: (01) 8042181, 7947546, 7748000, 7749585, 4707137
Fax: (01) 8047815
E-mail: germaine@germaineauto.com
Contact: Mr. Jerry Chukwueke - Chairman/CEO

GERSH HENSHAW & COMPANY
Business: Estate Surveying & Valuation, Facility Managment
Address: 80, M.C.C. Road, P.O.Box 2881, Calabar

Tel/Fax: (087) 234010
E-mail: gershhenshaw@hotmail.com
Contact: Mr Gersham Henshaw - Principal Partner

GEZHIL LIMITED
Business: Enterprise Resource Planning, Business Consultancy and Project Management, Networking and Systems Installation
Address: 33, Ademola St off Awolowo Rd, S.W. Ikoyi, Lagos
Tel: (01) 2693593, 2672629 **Fax:** (01) 2693593
E-mail: gezhil@linkserve.com
gezhil@hyperia.com
* Pees Galleria, 2A, Osborne Road, Ikoyi, Lagos

GHANA AIRWAYS (NIGERIA)
Business: Air Transport Services
Address: 128, Awolowo Road, S.W., Ikoyi, Lagos
Tel: (01) 2695379, 2692363, 2691397 **Fax:** (01) 2692658
E-mail: ghanaairways@hyperia.com
Website: www.ghana-airway.com
* Murtala Mohammed International Airport (Rooms 1100 & 1104), Ikeja, Lagos
Tel: (01) 4931140-9 (10L) (Ext. 5026)
Contact: Mr Francis Tettey - GM

GHOTEK TECHNOLOGIES LIMITED
Business: Internet Services, Software Development, Sales and Services of Hardware, Networking
Address: 66, Campbell Street, beside Western House, Lagos
Tel: (01) 2634057, 2637068, 2646941 **Fax:** (01) 2646941
E-mail: info@ghotek.com.ng
Website: www.ghotek.com.ng
Mr Ope Odusan - Chairman/CEO

GIBRALTAR CONSTRUCTION (NIGERIA) LIMITED
Business: Project Design, Finance and Implementation, Construction of Marine Barges, Tanks, Tankers and Warehouse, General Steel and Metal Fabrication, X-Ray Welding and Pressure Testing
Address: Metal Construction Annex, Plot 1, Manna Industrial Estate, Alagbon-Metta, Km. 36, Lagos-Abeokuta Road, Otta, Ogun State
Tel: (090) 402462, 462381
E-mail: gibraltar4@hotmail.com
* 15B, Bayo Kuku Road, Ikoyi, Lagos
Tel: (01) 2693537, 2691116, 2671715, 08023159191
Contact: Mr. O. C. Okeowo - Chairman/CEO

GIBSON M. INTERLINING INDUSTRIES LIMITED
Business: Importation and Sales of Tailoring Materials
Address: 14, Nottidge Street, Onitsha
Tel: (046) 215317, 215447, 485772, 08033424315, 08037258231
Contact: Mr. Gibson M. Chukwujindu - Chairman/CEO

GIDAUNIYA INVESTMENT & SECURITIES LIMITED
Business: Stockbroking, Real Estate Development
Address: Kano Foundation Building, 15, B.U.K. Road, Kano
Tel: (064) 318561, 667844 **Fax:** (064) 667844
* Eleganza Plaza (Leo Block, 1st Floor, Left Wing), 1, Commercial Road, Apapa, Lagos
Tel: (01) 4701015, 5878649
Contact: Alh. Muhammad Aminu Dangama - MD/CEO

GIGABYTE SYSTEMS (NIGERIA) LIMITED
Business: Business Processing Re-Engineering and IT Strategic Planning, Application Software Development and Implementation; IT Consultancy and Training, Share Registration Processing
Address: 24/26, Macarthy Street, Onikan, Lagos
Tel: (01) 2630651, 2647567, 08033552693
E-mail: gigabytesystem2003@yahoo.com
gigabyte@nigtel.com
Contact: Dr. S. O. Okolie - GM/CEO

GIGAHERTZ TECHNOLOGIES LIMITED
Business: Sales of Information Technology Products
Address: Plot 239, Kofo Abayomi St, Victoria Island, Lagos
Tel: (01) 2621473, 7751910

GIGINYA HOTEL, SOKOTO
Business: Hospitality Services
Address: Bye-Pass Road, P.M.B. 2228, Sokoto
Tel: (060) 231262, 231466, 231670
Contact: Hajia Aishat Turai Suka - GM/CEO

GILCO NIGERIA LIMITED
Business: Electrical, Power Transmission and Mechanical Engineering, Supply of Power Transformers
Address: 90, Awolowo Road, Ikoyi, Lagos
Tel: (01) 877370, 2690211
Contact: Chief (Dr.) Oladele Fajemirokun - Chairman

GILMOR ENGINERING LIMITED
Business: Engineering & Construction Services
Address: 7, Usuma Street, off Gana Street, Maitama, Abuja
Tel: (09) 4138456, 4138807-9 (3 L) **Fax:** (09) 4131274
E-mail: gilmorabuja@hyperia.com

GILOLA INTERNATIONAL AGENCIES LIMITED
Business: Shipping, Ship Chartering , Integrated Logisitics Management, Onshore/Offshore Services
Address: 77A, Marine Road, Apapa G.R.A., Apapa, Lagos
Tel: (01) 5873165, 5454349, 7752608, 08033019479, 08033807072 **Fax:** (01) 5873165
E-mail: gilola@hyperia.com
Contact: Olorogun Moses Taiga - Chairman
Mr. Gilbert E. O. Ibeanusi - MD/CEO

GILT-BOND FINANCE & SECURITIES LIMITED
Business: Financial Services
Address: 28, King George V Road, Onikan, Lagos
Tel: (01) 2646211, 2637648, 2632406 **Fax:** (01) 2623406
Contact: Mr. Chibuzor M. O. Eze - Chairman/CEO

GIMNS INDUSTRIAL COMPANY LIMITED
Business: Manufacturing and Marketing of Plastic Containers, General Merchants
Address: 15, Osisioma Ind. Layout, Old Aba-Owerri Rd, Aba
Tel: (082) 220647, 226927, 227827
Contact: Chief G. N. Ndubuisi - Chairman/CEO

GINO RESOURCES LIMITED
Business: Corporate and Business Gifts Items, Sales of Heat-Transfer Printing Equipment & Materials
Address: 34, Marcarthy Street, Onikan, Lagos
Tel: (01) 4812153, 5555847, 08033070228

Fax:: (01) 4812153
E-mail: ginoreso@infoweb.abs.net
Website: www.ginoresources.com
Contact: Mr. Ginika Oduah - MD/CEO

GINPAT ALUMINIUM PRODUCTS LIMITED
Business: Fabrication of Aluminium Roofing Sheets, Doors, Windows
Address: 86, Awka Road, P.O.Box 6087, Onitsha
Tel: (046) 414731, 08023352080, 08033134565
E-mail: ginpataluminium@mailcity.com
* 79, Abeokuta Expressway, Dopemu, Lagos
Tel: (01) 4925982, 08023129288, 08033184600
Contact: Mr. Pat Okpalaeke - MD/CEO

GIORGIO DREDGING LIMITED
Business: Dredging and Construction Services, Shore Protection, Pipe-Laying Services, Land Reclamation, Constrution of Canals, Sweeping of Seabeds and Waterways
Address: 10, Park Lane, Apapa, Lagos
Tel: (01) 4722616, 5452795, 5450632, 5452796
Fax: (01) 5873753, 5451962
E-mail: giorgio@nova.net.ng
giorgio@hyperia.com
Contact: Mr. B. N. Ozoadibe - MD/CEO

GIOVANNI MARBLES LIMITED
Business: Importation and Sales of Italian Marbles, Granite, Palladiana & Paint; Cutting of Marble and Granite
Address: 9, Fatai Irawo Street, Ajao Estate, Isolo, Lagos
Tel: (01) 4520864, 4526068, 7741266, 7753780, 524125, 08023107798, 08023010164
Fax: (01) 4520864, 4526068
E-mail: giovanni@infoweb.abs.net
* 585, Agege Motor Road, Shogunle-Ikeja, Lagos
Tel: (01) 4972898-9 (2 L), 08023010164
* Lansar House, 9, Aba Road, 1st Artillery Junction, Port Harcourt.
Tel: (084) 484054, 08033024264
Contact: Mr. Davidson Anazodo - MD/CEO

GITCOBOOKS INFORMATION SERVICES
Business: Sales and Distribution of Business and Management Books; Publishing of Business Newsletter, Library Services; Printing
Address: 17, Akin Adesola Street, Victoria Island, Lagos
Tel: (01) 614313 **Fax:** (01) 2636643, 614313
E-mail: gitco@infoweb.abs.net
Contact: Mr. John-Bode Anthonio - President/CEO

GIRAFFE PLASTIC & MATS LIMITED
Business: Manufacturing of Plastic Wares & Mats
Address: 349, Umaru Babua Road, Bompai Ind Estate, Kano
Tel: (064) 633371, 635155, 333338
Contact: Hussein A. Fadlallah - MD/CEO

GIWA-OSAGIE DFK & COMPANY
Business: Auditing, Consultancy, Company Secretarial
Address: 290, Borno Way, Yaba, Lagos
Tel: (01) 7744212, 5820568 **Fax:** (01) 5820568
E-mail: goclag@linkserve.com
Contact: Alh. (Chief) R. O. V. Giwa-Osagie - Prin. Partner

GIWARITE LIMITED
Business: Manufacturing of Roofing and Ceiling Sheets
Address: Sharada Industrial Estate, Phase II, Kano
Tel: (064) 666057, 664111, 669294-5 **Fax:** (064) 666014
E-mail: giwarite@ecnx.net
* Behind KASUPA Workshop, Kakuri, Kaduna
Tel: (062) 232552

GIWO HOLDINGS LIMITED
Business: Drilling of Boreholes
Address: Giwo House, 6, Ahmadu Bello Way, Bauchi
Tel: (077) 543235, 08023533862
Contact: Engr. Garuba Bagel - MD/CEO

GLANVILL ENTHOVEN LIFE & PENSIONS CONSULTANTS LIMITED
Business: Life and Pensions Broking and Consultancy
Address: 174, Western Avenue, Costain, Surulere, Lagos
Tel: (01) 4712334-6 (3 L), 5852344-7 (4L), 08023141375
Fax: (01) 5852343
E-mail: glanvill@hyperia.com
Contact: Mrs. F. O. Onanuga - GM/CEO

GLANVILL ENTHOVEN REINSURANCE BROKERS LIMITED
Business: Reinsurance Broking
Address: 174, Western Avenue, Costain, Surulere, Lagos
Tel: (01) 4712334-6 (3 L) 5852344-7 (4L), 08023141373
Fax: (01) 5852343
E-mail: glanvill@hyperia.com
Contact: Mr. J. D. Oke - GM/CEO

GLAXO SMITHKLINE CONSUMER NIGERIA PLC
Business: Marketing of Pharmaceutical Products
Address: Km 16, Ikorodu Road, Ojota, Lagos
Tel: (01) 4938000-5 (6L) **Fax:** (01) 4938006
* Igbesa Road, Agbara Industrial Estate, Km 32, Lagos-Badagry Expressway, Agbara, Ogun State.
Tel: (01) 712212, 712313, 712298, 712399
* 49/51, Town Planning Way, Ilupeju Industrial Estate, Ilupeju, Lagos
Tel: (01) 4979091, 4979093

GLENDORA INTERNATIONAL (NIGERIA) LIMITED
Business: Sales of Books, Novels and Stationery; Publishing
Address: Block C, Shop 4, Falomo Shop Centre, Ikoyi, Lagos
Tel/Fax: (01) 2692762, 4750168, 08033161857
E-mail: sales@glendorabooks.com
Website: www.glendorabooks.com
Contact: Mr. Olakunle O. Tejuoso - MD/CEO

GLENYORK NIGERIA LIMITED
Business: Electrical and Mechanical Engineering Services
Address: Plot 684, Cadastral Zone A6, Maitama, Abuja
Tel: (09) 4137835, 4137836 **Fax:** (09) 4137836
E-mail: glenyork@nova.net.ng
* Plot 103, Medical Guild Close, off Olabode George, Victoria Island Annexe, Lagos
Tel: (01) 2610881, 2622104 **Fax:** (01) 2612071
Contact: Mr. Eyal Shatz - GM/CEO

GLITZ PETROLEUM LIMITED
Business: Oilfield Service (Drilling Support Services), Environmental Services and Supply of Chemicals

Address: 20, Association Avenue, Ilupeju, Lagos
Tel: (01) 8042697 **Fax:** (01) 4930297
E-mail: glitzpetro@yahoo.com
Contact: Prince Ernest Essien - Chairman/CEO

GLITZ RESOURCES LIMITED
Business: Sales and Maintenance of Security & Identification Systems; Computer Sales and Service
Address: 20, Association Avenue, Ilupeju, Lagos
Tel: (01) 4960740, 5553454, 08023183715, 08033027686, 08033267686 **Fax:** (01) 4933507
E-mail: glitzresources@yahoo.com
glitzpetro@yahoo.com
Contact: Prince Ernest Essien - Chairman/CEO

GLOBACOM LIMITED
Business: Full Telecommunication Service Providers (Second National Telecommuncations Carrier)
Address: 25, Saka Tinubu Street, Victoria Island, Lagos
* 21, Adeola Odeku St, V/Island, Lagos
* 44, Adeniran Ogunsanya St, Surulere, Lagos
* 2, Opebi Road, Ikeja, Lagos
* 1101, Aminu Kano Crescent, Wuse II, Abuja
* 163, Aba Road, Port Harcourt
* 97, Lagos Bye-Pass, Challenge, Ibadan
* 57, Mission Road, opp Holy Cross, Benin City
Contact: Otunba Mike Adenuga, Jr - Chairman

GLOBAL ASSET MANAGEMENT (NIGERIA) LIMITED
Business: Stockbroking, Investment Advisory Services, Portfolio Management
Address: 21, Boyle Street, (8th Floor), Onikan, Lagos
Tel: (01) 2630098, 2636793 **Fax:** (01) 2631876
E-mail: globalass@hyperia.com
Contact: Mr. Babatunde E. Sobamowo - MD/CEO

GLOBAL BANK PLC
Business: Commercial Banking
Address: Amazing Grace Plaza,Plot 2E-4E, Ligali Ayorinde Street, Victoria Island, Lagos
Tel: (01) 2626001-7 (7L) **Fax:** (01) 2626033, 2626017
E-mail: info@globalbankplc.com
Website: www.globalbankplc.com
* Plot 2107, T. Balewa Way, Area 3, Garki, Abuja.
Tel: (09) 2349036-9 (4 L) **Fax:** (09) 2349035
* 13-15, Wharf Road, Apapa, Lagos
Tel: (01) 4703806, 4703801
Contact: Mr. Yinka Obalade - MD/CEO
Mr. Harold Nzekwe - Head (Corporate Affairs)

GLOBAL BOOKSHOP LIMITED
Business: Sales & Supply of Cambridge Textbooks for O Level, GCSE & A level Examinations
Address: 49, Raymond Njoku Street, S.W. Ikoyi, Lagos
Tel: (01) 2690332, 08023145131, 08056067038
Fax: (01) 290332
E-mail: globalbooks@hyperia.co,
Contact: Mrs. Abolaji Osime - Chairman/CEO

GLOBAL COMMERCE & GENERAL ASSURANCE LIMITED
Business: General Insurance Business
Address: 8, Akanbi Onitiri Close, off Eric Moor Road, Iganmu Industrial Estate, Surulere, Lagos
Tel: (01) 4742022, 4752392
E-mail: gcgassure@micro.com.ng
Contact: Mr. Peter Eloka Okocha OON- Chairman
Mr. Joseph Izuka Mardi - MD/CEO

GLOBAL COMMUNICATIONS NETWORK LIMITED
Business: Satellite and Wireless Communications
Address: Plot 26, Admiralty Way, Lekki Estate Phase 1,Lagos
Tel: (01) 2708081-4 (4 L) **Fax:** (01) 2708082

GLOBAL CONCEPTS (WEST AFRICA) LIMITED
Business: Manufacturing and Marketing of Plastics Products
Address: Plot 78, Ikemba Layout, Akwa
Tel: (048) 552823, 552763, 552889
Contact: Mr. Everestus Ofordile - Chairman/CEO

GLOBAL COUNSELLING LIMITED
Business: Foreign-Education Services
Address: 1A, Ribadu Rd, off Awolowo Rd, S.W. Ikoyi, Lagos
Tel: (01) 2690057, 7756069, 7737566, 7734171, 4714615, 08023145124, 08033014156, 08033016651
Fax: (01) 2690057
E-mail: globalcounsel@hyperia.com
Website: www.globaleducationcounselling.com
www.globainternationalcollege.com
Contact: Mr. Theo Theodorou - Dir of Int'l Affiars/CEO
Mrs. Abolaji Osime - Director of Admissions

GLOBAL CREDIT RATING COMPANY LIMITED
Business: Credit Rating & Investment Research Services
Address: New Africa House (8th Floor), 31, Marina, Lagos Island, Lagos
Tel: (01) 2641933, 2665491
Contact: Mr. Adebisi Ajiboye - Managing Director

GLOBAL ENERGY COMPANY LIMITED
Business: Geoscientific and Engineering Services, Energy Advisory Services
Address: Plot 182B, Kofo Abayomi St, Victoria Island, Lagos
Tel: (01) 2616949, 2621297, 2626723 **Fax:** (01) 2621296
E-mail: mdo@globalenergyco.com
Website: www.globalenergyco.com
* Saros Plaza, 33A, Aba Road, Port Harcourt.
Tel/Fax: (084) 235326
18, Airport Road, Warri.
Tel: (053) 320325-6 (2L) **Fax:** (053) 320326
Contact: Mr. Joe Obiago - Chairman/CEO

GLOBAL ENVIRONMENTAL CONSULTANTS LIMITED
Business: Environmental Consultancy Services, Analytical Laboratory Services
Address: Crystal Palace Estate, NNPC Housing Complex Road, Edjeba, Warri
Tel: (053) 254193-212 (Ext. 50443), 254622
Fax: (053) 254193
* 4, Ada George Road, Rumuerikom-Rummueme, Port Harcourt
E-mail: benayade@infoweb.abs.net
Contact: Dr. B. B. Ayade - Chief Consultant/CEO

GLOBAL ENVIRONMENTAL TECHNOLOGY LIMITED
Business: Environmental Studies, Waste Management Services
Address: Stock Exchange Building (17th Floor), 2/4, Customs

Street, Marina, Lagos
Tel: (01) 2644951, 2644958, 2661402, 2661404
E-mail: globenv@rcl.nig.com
globenv@hyperia.com
* Plot 39, Trans-Amadi Ind. Layout, Port Harcourt
Contact: Apostle Hayford I. Alile - Chairman
Mr. Tayo Seriki - Chief Operating Officer

GLOBAL EXPRESS LIMITED
Business: Courier and Cargo Services
Address: 2, Murtala Mohammed International Airport Road, Mafoluku-Oshodi, Lagos
Tel: (01) 4701368, 4975178 **Fax:** (01) 2640666
E-mail: globex_ng@hotmail.com
* 27, Aba Road, Port Harcourt.
Tel: (084) 234608, 481771
* Suite A5, Plot 500, Tafawa Balewa, Way, Area 3, by Jamea Filling Station, Garki, Abuja.
Tel: (09) 2348637
Contact: Mr. Joe C. Nwosu - GM/CEO

GLOBAL GAS & REFINING LIMITED
Business: Processing of Gas
Address: Plot 39, Trans-Amadi Ind. Layout, Port Harcourt
Tel: (084) 230727, 230043. 571505 **Fax:** (084) 230727
E-mail: gerl@ph.rcl.nig.com
* Plot 932, Idejo Street, Victoria Island, Lagos.
Tel: (01) 3200210 **Fax:** (01) 3200208
Contact: Mr. Kenneth Yellowe - Chairman/CEO

GLOBAL INSURANCE BROKERS LIMITED
Business: Insurance Broking
Address: 64, Raufu Williams Crescent, Surulere, Lagos
Tel: (01) 5845894, 830331 **Fax:** (01) 5850470
E-mail: gibltd@skannet.com
Contact: Mr. Yomi Ogunyannwo - MD/CEO

GLOBAL INTERNET LIMITED
Business: Computer Consultancy; Computer Systems and Components Sales; System Integration and Networking, Training, Connectivity Solutions
Address: 52, Bode Thomas Street, Surulere, Lagos
Tel: (01) 5847979, 4702193 **Fax:** (01) 5847979
E-mail: gil@hyperia.com
Contact: Mr. P. Chuka Eleodimuo - Chairman/CEO

GLOBAL MARINE & TECHNICAL SERVICES LIMITED
Business: Maritim & Shipping Consultancy, Inspection Services, Cargo Surveying and Calibration, General Transportation Services
Address: 6, Elsie Femi-Pearse Street, off Adeola Odeku Street, Victoria Island, Lagos
Tel: (01) 4723342, 2629870, 08033789620
E-mail: gmts@yahoo.com
4, Nzimiro St Amadi Flats, Old G.R.A. Port Harcourt
Tel: (084) 573223, 08023045139
Contact: Mr. Angus O. Ozoamaka - Chairman
Mr. A. N. Victor - GM

GLOBAL INVESTMENT & SECURITIES LIMITED
Business: Stockbroking
Address: Amazing Grace Plaza, 2E-4E, Ligali Ayorinde Street, Victoria Island, Lagos
Tel: (01) 2626038, 2626034, 2626042, 2626017
Fax: (01) 2626047
E-mail: global@cyberspace.net.ng

GLOBAL MOBILE COMMUNICATIONS LIMITED
Business: Sales of Mobile/GSM Phones & Accessories
Address: 3, Obafemi Awolowo Way, opp. Ikeja L.G., Lagos
Tel: (01) 8049254, 8113358, 8124248, 08023469525, 08037260196, 08033163017
E-mail: goldencrest@yahoo.co.uk
Contact: Mr. Ben Adefeyisan - MD/CEO

GLOBAL OFFSHORE DRILLING LIMITED
Business: Deep Offshore Oilfield Drilling Services
Address: Km 14, Aba Expressway, near Eleme Junction, Port Harcourt.
Tel: (084) 231349, 231354, 231356 **Fax:** (084) 231353

GLOBAL OFFSHORE INTERNATIONAL LIMITED
Business: Oil Industry Services, Pipeline Construction and Maintenance
Address: 42, Tony Eromosele Street, Parkview Estate, Ikoyi, Lagos
Tel: (01) 2694622, 2691753 **Fax:** (01) 2695981
E-mail: busdey@globalind.com
Website: www.globalind.com

GLOBAL OUTDOOR SYSTEMS NIGERIA
Business: Outdoor Marketing Communications
Address: HFP Industrial Park, beside Ikota Shopping Complex, Victoria Garden City, Km. 22, Lekki-Epe Expressway, Ikota, Lagos
Tel: (01) 4613854, 08034023219 **Fax:** (01) 4613850
E-mail: gos@hyperia.com

GLOBAL PLASTIC INDUSTRIES (NIGERIA) LIMITED
Business: Manufacturing and Marketing of Plastic Products
Address: Plot 3D, Aswani Market Road, off Osolo Way, behind Emzor Pharmaceutical Industries, Isolo Industrial Estate, Isolo, Lagos
Tel: (01) 7743385, 4521180, 4520613 **Fax:** (01) 4522637
E-mail: globalplastic@aol.com
Contact: Mr. Anil G. Ratnani - Director

GLOBAL RISK ASSOCIATES LIMITED
Business: Insurance Broking and Consultancy Services
Address: 47, Alh. Tokan Street, off Western Avenue, near National Stadium, Surulere, Lagos
Tel: (01) 5852333-4 (2L), 08023261896 **Fax:** (01) 5851670
E-mail: info@globalriskassociates.com
* 41, Kwame Nkrumah Crescent, Asokoro, Abuja
Tel/Fax: (09) 3148300
* 47, Woju Street, D-Line, Port Harcourt
Tel: (084) 7745932, * (090) 40144
Contact: Chief O. A. Fajorin - MD/CEO

GLOBAL SEAWAY INTERNATIONAL COMPANY LIMITED
Business: Dredging, Ship Owners, Suppliers of Cargo & Tanker Vessels, Clearing & Forwarding Agents, Marine Consultants, Cement Distributors, Sand Suppliers and Fish Marketers, Supply of Earth-Moving Equipment
Address: Plot 199, Woji Road, G.R.A. Phase 2, Port Harcourt

Tel: (084) 231670, 231673 **Fax:** (084) 237449
E-mail: global.seaway@skannet.com
Contact: Prince (Capt.) F. N. Okurapko (JP) - Chairman/CEO

GLOBAL SOAP & DETERGENT INDUSTRIES LIMITED
Business: Manufacturing of Soaps, Detergents and Scouring Powder
Address: 4, Commercial Road, Apapa, Lagos
Tel: (01) 5452050-2 (3 L) **Fax:** (01) 5452054, 5878480
E-mail: info@doyin.net
Website: www.infodoyin.net
* Loma-Mansa St near NEPA, Wuse Zone 4, Abuja
Tel: (09) 4131141
Contact: Prince (Dr.) Samuel Adedoyin - Chairman
Mrs. Omolola Olobayo - Exec. Director/CEO

GLOBAL STERLING PRODUCTS LIMITED
Business: Sales of Industrial Plants & Equipment
Address: 379, Ikorodu Road, opp. Ojota New Garage, Lagos
Tel: (01) 4971393, 4972831, 7737853, 0802314812
Fax: (01) 4971392
E-mail: harness@hyperia.com

GLOBAL TRUST SAVINGS & LOANS LIMITED
Business: Mortgage Banking
Address: Plot 740, Adeola Hopewell St Victoria Island, Lagos
Tel: (01) 2614922, 617183 **Fax:** (01) 2621146, 610202
E-mail: globatrustmortgage@financier.com
Contact: Mr. Steve Elusope - MD/CEO

GLOBAL VIEW TRAVELS & TOUR LIMITED
Business: Travel Agency, Tour Operators, Car Hire Services
Address: Ultimate Plaza (2nd Floor), 122/124, Broad Street, Lagos
Tel: (01) 2665280, 08033011006 **Fax:** (01) 2665280
E-mail: globalview@yahoo.com
Contact: Mr. Godfrey Omo Elaiho - Chairman/CEO

GLOBE ENGINEERING & CONSTRUCTION COMPANY LTD
Business: Construction and Civil Engineering
Address: NCWS House, Plot PC. 14, Ahmed Onibudo Street, Victoria Island, Lagos
Tel: (01) 4618550-4 (5 L), 4618141-6 (6 L)
* VGC Shopping Complex, Victoria Garden City, Km. 22, Lagos-Epe Expressway, Lagos
Tel: (01) 4618005-6 (2 L), 4618008 **Fax:** (01) 4618007
E-mail: vgccl@nigol.net.ng

GLOBE FISHING INDUSTRIES LIMITED
Business: Fishing, Trawling; Marketing of Frozen Seafoods
Address: 13A, Ijora Causeway, Ijora, Lagos
Tel: (01) 5834199, 5836794, 5836900 **Fax:** (01) 5836900
* Plot 476, Trans-Amadi Ind. Layout, Port Harcourt
Tel: (084) 230900, 232966 **Fax:** (084) 230719
E-mail: globefish@cybaaspace.com

GLOBE MOTORS HOLDINGS (NIGERIA) LIMITED
Business: Importation, Distribution & Service of Motor Vehicles
Address: Plot 637, Akin Adesola St, Victoria Island, Lagos
Tel: (01) 2622778-9 (2 L), 2619639, 7742257, 2626207-9
Fax: (01) 2613501
E-mail: globemts@linkserve.com.ng
* 43/45, Rasaq Balogun Street, Surulere, Lagos
Tel: (01) 580990-12 (2L), 833123
* Plot 616, Eket Close, Opp. Garki General Hospital, Garki Area 8, Abuja.
Tel: (09) 2346768-9 (2 L)
* Areta Farm Estate, 178-186, Aba Expressway Road, Port Harcourt.
Tel: (084) 230606, 232340
Contact: Mr. William Anumudu - Chairman/CEO

GLOBE PACKAGING INDUSTRIES LIMITED
Business: Manufacturing of Metal Drums and Flexible Packaging Products
Address: 22A, Musa Yar'Adua Street, Victoria Island, Lagos
Tel: (01) 2612786, 2611433 **Fax:** (01) 2618604, 2619624
Contact: Mr. Samuel Babafemi Akande - Chairman
Mr. Milind Jadhav - MD/CEO

GLOBE REINSURANCE PLC
Business: Re-Insurance Business
Address: Akuro House (1st Floor), 24, Campbell St, Lagos
Tel: (01) 2601160-5 (6L) **Fax:** (01) 263127, 2634409
E-mail: globere@globereinsurance.com
Contact: Mr. A. B. Ajomale - Vice Chairman/CEO

GLOBE SHIPPING LINES LIMITED
Business: Tanker & Shipping Line Operations, Clearing and Forwarding Agency, Ship Management
Address: Eleganza Plaza (Leo Block, Right Wing, 1st Floor), 1, Commercial Road, Apapa, Lagos
Tel: (01) 5877519, 5870618, 5870622 **Fax:** (01) 5878886
E-mail: gls@infoweb.asb.net
* Supaboad Stores Building (1st Floor), 1, Nnamdi Azikiwe Road, Port Harcourt
Contact: Engr. Chris O. Okoye - Chairman
Mr. Festus Obonna - GM/CEO

GLOBE SPINNING MILLS (NIGERIA) LIMITED
Business: Manufacturing of Yarn & Threads
Address: Plot B, Block 1, Ilupeju Industrial Estate, Lagos
Tel: (01) 5837420, 5843061, 5831015, 7742926, 7756606
Fax: (01) 2614079, 4930958
E-mail: globespin@lbhojsons.net
* Plot 3, Block A, LSDPC Industrial Scheme, Apapa/Oshodi Expressway, Amuwo-Odofin, Lagos
Contact: Mr. D. M. Dalamal

GLOBE TAPE MANUFACTURING COMPANY LIMITED
Business: Manufacturing & Marketing of Adhesive Tape
Address: 6, Bankole Street, Pedro, Shomolu, Lagos
Tel: (01) 7741445-6 (2 L), 08033062616
E-mail: ogbuta@yahoo.com

GLOBECOM INTEGRATED SYSTEMS LIMITED
Business: Sales and Service of Copiers, Banking Machines, Computers and Telecommunication Equipment
Address: Lamlat House, 70, Ikorodu Road, by Mobil Filling Station, Obanikoro, Lagos
Tel: (01) 4935829, 4708454 **Fax:** (01) 4935829
E-mail: globecom76@yahoo.com
Contact: Alh. Yakubu Abdullahi - MD/CEO

GLOBESTAR ENGINEERING COMPANY NIGERIA LIMITED
Business: Oil & Gas Offshore Construction

Address: Plot 293, Akin Olugbade St, Victoria Island, Lagos
Tel: (01) 2613720, 2613800, 2619789 **Fax:** (01) 2613805
E-mail: gbs.lag@alpha.linkserve.com
* McDErmoot Road, Warri
Tel: (053) 253553, 254190 **Fax:** (053) 253408, 255003
Contact: Mr. B. Wurmser - MD/CEO

GLOCAL TRENDS LIMITED
Business: Marketing Communication Servies
Address: Unit D, 3rd Floor, Pentagon Plaza, 23, Opebi Road, Ikeja, Lagos
Tel: (01) 4972701, 7730698
Contact: Mr. Segun Ogungbangbe

GM NIGERIA LIMITED
Business: Assembly, Sales and Service of Motor Vehicles, Sales of Spare Part, Specialised Body Building
Address: 17, Creek Road, Apapa, Lagos
Tel: (01) 5803000-4 (5L) **Fax:** (01) 5872525
Contact: Mr. P. K. Ndiema - Ag MD/CEO

GMT SHIPPING NIGERIA LIMITED
Business: Shipping
Address: 22, Warehouse, Road, Apapa, Lagos
Tel: (01) 5453925-7 (3L), 5455542 **Fax:** (01) 5453928
E-mail: enquiriesgmt@gmt.com.ng
Contact: Mr. Bosco Ngan - Chairman/CEO

GOCUZ GROUP LIMITED
Business: International Trade and General Contracts, Marketing and Supply of Telecommunication & Engineering Equipment, Generators, Test Calibration and Measuring Instruments; Rural Electrification and Sub-Station Construction
Address: 14A, Karimu Kotun Street, Victoria Island, Lagos
Tel: (01) 2623502, 2623581, 2623704
Fax: (01) 2623503, 2692383
E-mail: gocuz@infoweb.abs.net
Contact: Barr. (Dr.) Obinna Uzoh - Chairman/CEO

GOD'S LITTLE TANNERY LIMITED
Business: Tanning and Processing of Leather
Address: Plot 65, Challawa Industrial Estate, Kano
Tel/Fax: (064) 660232, 636117 Fax: (064) 636117
Contact: Mr. Koffy N. Udeagha - Chairman/CEO

GODDY EDOSA MOTORS COMPANY LIMITED
Business: Road Transport Services
Address: 50B, Dawson Road, Benin City
Tel: (052) 259572
* Badagry Expressway, Mile 2, Lagos
Tel: (01) 7746164
* Agege Motor Rd, Idi Oro, Mushin, Lagos
Contact: Chief (Dr.) Godwin Edosa (JP) - Chairman/CEO

GODWIN HOPWOOD KUYE LIMITED
Business: Architectural Consultancy, Project Management
Address: 14, Modupe Street, Somolu, Lagos
Tel: (01) 4703708, 823724 **Fax:** (01) 823096
E-mail: ghkarchitects@ghk.metrong.com
* 27, Boyle Street, Onikan, Lagos
Tel: (01) 2600845-7 (3 L) **Fax:** (01) 2632660
Contact: Prof. (Arc) John Godwin - Partner

GOGINS TRAVELS LIMITED
Business: Travel Agency, General Aviation Consultancy Services, Organisation of Tours & Trade Missions
Address: 91, Ojuelegba Road, Surulere, Lagos
Tel: (01) 5850828, 5843738, 7743945 **Fax:** (01) 7743945
E-mail: gogins@hyperia.com
*3B, Herbert Macaulay Way, Wuse Zone 6, Abuja
Tel: (09) 5242275, * (080) 37871897, 37871754, 37871698
Contact: Mr. Godwin Nnamdi Anyanwu - Chairman/CEO

GOKAS NIGERIA LIMITED
Business: Sales of Pumping of Machins, Power-Generating Sets, Agricultural Tractors, Implements, Industrial Filters and Spare Parts
Address: 16A, Kudirat Abiola Way (Oregun), Ikeja, Lagos
Tel: (01) 4714473, 4931847, 08023033497, 08023100803, 08034085311 **Fax:** (01) 4931847
E-mail: gokas8@hotmail.com
Contact: Alh. D. K. Gbadamosi - Chairman/CEO

GOLD CROSS HOSPITAL
Business: Multidisciplinary Tertiary Care Hospital
Address: 6, Keffi Street, S.W. Ikoyi, Lagos
Tel: (01) 2695470, 2672902-3 (2L) **Fax:** (01) 2695670
Contact: Dr. Ladi Okuboyejo - Chairman/Medical Director

GOLD STANDARD INSURANCE BROKERS LIMITED
Business: Insurance and Re-Insurance Broking
Address: 275, Borno Way, Ebute-Metta, Lagos
Tel: (01) 4724289
Contact: Prince M.A. Akinsemoyin - MD/CEO

GOLD STANDARD INSURERS LIMITED
Business: Non-Life Insurance
Address: Great Nigeria House (13th Floor), 47/57, Martins Street, Lagos
Tel: (01) 2641136, 4827929 **Fax:** (01) 2641136
* 43, Olu Obasanjo Road, Port Harcourt
Tel: (084) 573220
* Kenaz Plaza (Suite B24), Wuse II, Abuja
Tel: (09) 5236959
Contact: Mr. Okay I. Okafor - GM/CEO

GOLDCHAINS INTERNATIONAL LIMITED
Business: Commodity Merchants; Import and Export
Address: NUJ House (Ground Floor), 3/5 Adeyemo Alakija Street, Victoria Island, Lagos
Tel/Fax: (01) 618214, 612158
E-mail: goldchainsinternational@yahoo.com
goldchainsinternational@hotmail.com
Contact: Mr. Boma S. Anga - Chairman/CEO

GOLDEN CONCEPTS INVESTMENTS LIMITED
Business: Clearing & Forwarding, Shipping & Air-Freighting
Address: Nnewi Building (2nd Floor, Right Wing, Suite1), 1/3, Creek Road, Apapa, Lagos
Tel: (01) 5455830, 08033027962 **Fax:** (01) 5455830
E-mail: goldenconcepts@yahoo.com
* 14, Wakogoloma Street, Port Harcourt
Contact: Dr. Chuma Aghanwa - Chairman/CEO

GOLDEN CROSS TECHNICAL LIMITED
Business: Sales and Maintenance of Weighing Scales and

Systems, Pumps, Airconditioners, Hardware Tools and Machines, Technical Equipment & Products
Address: Eleganza Plaza (Middle Gate House), Aerodrome Road, Apapa, Lagos
Tel: (01) 5871894, 7747801 **Fax:** (01) 5871894, 2693680
E-mail: gctl-salter@beta.linkserve.com
Website: www.salterhousewares.co.uk
Contact: Prince Olukayode Omidiya - Chairman/CEO

GOLDEN CROWN CHINESE RESTAURANTS LIMITED
Business: Restuarant
Address: 181, Ikorodu Road, Palmgrove, Lagos
Tel: (01) 5820506 **Fax:** (01) 5820507
Contact: Mr. Tony Thang - Manager

GOLDEN FERTILIZERS COMPANY LIMITED
Business: Blending and Bagging of Fertilizer
Address: 47, Eric Moore Road, Iganmu, Lagos
Tel: (01) 5454391-2 (3L), 7745301, 7749306
E-mail: goldenfertilizers@hyperia.com
* Km. 19, Kano-Zaria Rd, Gada Tamborawa, Kano
Contact: A. Plytas - Chairman
Mr. P. M. Gbadebo - Director/Plant Manager

GOLDEN GATE PARADISE NIGERIA LIMITED
Business: Restaurant Services, Banqueting and Conference Facilities; Party Catering Services
Address: Golden Gate Complex, 25B, Glover Road/Alfred Rewane (Kingsway) Road, Ikoyi, Lagos
Tel: (01) 2695337-9 (3 L), 2695346 **Fax:** (01) 2695192
Contact: Chief Solomon Adebayo Ayoku - Chairman/CEO

GOLDEN GATE PLASTICS INDUSTRIES LIMITED
Business: Manufacturing of Plastic-Packaging Products
Address: Plot 10, Block B, Ilasamaja Industrial Estate, Apapa-Oshodi Expressway, Itire Junction, Ilasamaja, Lagos
Tel: (01) 2637596, 4811106
Contact: Alh. Abdulahi Kwaku - MD/CEO

GOLDEN GUINEA BREWERIES PLC
Business: Brewing of Alcoholic and Non-Alcoholic Beverage Production of Agricultural Products
Address: Aba Road, Afara Industrial Layout, Umuahia
Tel: (088) 220055, 220086, 222616-9 (4 L), 222623, 222625
Fax: (088) 222621
Contact: Mr. I. G. Idika - MD/CEO

GOLDEN INSURANCE COMPANY LIMITED
Business: Insurance
Address: 300, Ikorodu Road, Anthony, Lagos
Tel: (01) 7745258, 4938089 **Fax:** (01) 4938089
Contact: Mr. S. A. Osasona - MD/CEO

GOLDEN INVESTMENT (WEST AFRICA) LIMITED
Business: Sales and Maintenance of Computers, Training
Address: 117, Agbani Road, Enugu
Tel: (042) 255944
E-mail: giwal@infoweb.abs.net
Contact: Mr. Emmanuel O. Oha - MD/CEO

GOLDEN SECURITIES LIMITED
Business: Stockbroking, Financial Services, Leasing, Fund Sourcing and Investment Management
Address: CSS Bookshop House (8th Floor) 50/52, Broad Street, Lagos
Tel: (01) 2631375, 2632670, 2642447 **Fax:** (01) 2632760
E-mail: golden@alpha.linkserve.com
Contact: Mr. J. S. Adebiyi - MD/CEO

GOLDEN SHIPPING COMPANY NIGERIA LIMITED
Business: Shipping Agency and Services
Address: Flour Mills Building, 2, Old Dock Rd,Apapa, Lagos
Tel: (01) 5452667, 5803370 (10 L) (Ext. 110)
Fax: (01) 5872749, 5870395, 5871602
Contact: Mr. Babatunde Amusu - Chairman
Capt. D. M. Osah - MD/CEO

GOLDENWAYS AIR SERVICES LIMITED
Business: Travel Agency
Address: 22, Niger Street, P.O.Box 346, Kano
Tel: (064) 633603, 335871 **Fax:** (064) 633497
Contact: Mal. Musa Garba - MD/CEO

GOLDLINK INSURANCE COMPANY LIMITED
Business: Insurance
Address: Westerm House (15th Floor), 8/10, Broad St, Lagos
Tel: (01) 2601070-4 (5L), 2645449-51 (3L)
Fax: (01) 2637339
E-mail: goldlink@hyperia.com
insure@goldlinkltd.com
Website: www.goldlinkinsure.com
* 80, Allen Avenue, Ikeja, Lagos
Tel: (01) 4972872, 4977376
Contact: Mr. Gbenga Afolayan - Chairman/CEO

GOLDMARK LIMITED
Business: Advertising, Public Relations, Marketing Agency
Address: 23, Oladipupo Kuku St, off Allen Ave., Ikeja, Lagos
Tel: (01) 4971903, 08023062771, 08033345645
E-mail: goldmark@yahoo.com
Contact: Chief Obi Nwagbara - Vice Chairman/CEO

GOLDSTAR PUBLISHERS (NIGERIA) LIMITED
Business: Publishing of Business & General Directories; Information Communication & Consultancy
Address: 15, Osolo Way, off International Airport Road, Ajao Estate, Isolo
Tel: (01) 7745025
Contact: Dr. Kenneth A. Ukegbu - MD/CEO

GOMAC VENTURES LIMITED
Business: Sales of Electrical Electronics, Public Address Systems, Musical Instruments and General Goods
Address: BB 19F & G, Alaba Int'l Market, Ojo Alaba, Lagos
Tel: (01) 5891170, 2883112 **Fax:** (01) 2883112, 8044028
* 2, Irewole Avenue Adj. Tastee Fried Chiken, Opebi, Allen, Ikeja.
Tel: (01) 8044453
E-mail: gomacventures@hotmail.com
Contact: Mr. Greg N. Ikonkwo Chairman/CEO

GOMBE FERTILIZER COMPANY LIMITED
Business: Blending of Fertilizer
Address: Ashaka Bye-Pass, Gombe
Tel: (072) 223262

GOMBE OIL SEED PROCESSORS LIMITED
Business: Processing of Oil Seeds
Address: Biu Road, BCJ, Gombe
Tel: (072) 220131, 220077, 220208
* 18, Iju Road, Ifako-Agege, Lagos
Contact: Alh. A. Baba Manu - Chairman/CEO

GOMBE STATE INVESTMENT & PROPERTY DEVELOPMENT COMPANY LIMITED
Business: Investment Promotion, Project Financing, Real Estate Developing
Address: NEPA Drive, adj. Bima Lodge, Gombe
Tel: (072) 223113, 222460 **Fax:** (072) 222460
E-mail: gsipc@yahoo.com
Contact: Alh. Hamza Sule Wurobokki - MD/CEO

GONAC GROUP
Busines: Wholesale Importation of Frames, Framing of Photographs and Artwork, Corporate Gifts
Address: 42, Tejuosho Street, Surulere, Lagos
Tel: (01) 835559
* 14, Agunbiade Street, Surulere, Lagos
Contact: Mrs. Ifeoma Duru - GM

GONGONI COMPANY LIMITED
Business: Manufacture of Insecticides and Air Freshners; Plastic Containers, Liquid Detergent and Public Health Products
Address: 89A, Sharada Industrial Estate Phase III, Kano
Tel: (064) 667730, 647721, 648652, 668850, 662261
Fax: (064) 640029, 668591
E-mail: gongonico@aol.com
* 1, Sapara St, Ikeja Industrial Estate, Ikeja, Lagos
Tel: (01) 4971614
* 71A, Old Market Road, Onitsha.
Tel: (046) 214617
Contact: M.A. Ghosn - MD/CEO

GOODHOMES ESTATES LIMITED
Business: Real Estate Development and Management
Address: Lamlat House, 270, Ikorodu Rd, Obanikoro, Lagos
Tel: (01) 4716112, 4934484, 0802373398
Contact: Alh. (Dr.) L. K. Jakande - Chairman
Engr. M. A. Akintan - MD/CEO

GOODWILL IMPEX INTERNATIONAL LIMITED
Business: Importation & Sales of Agric Sprayer, Building Materials and Industrial Chemicals
Address: 15, Bishop Oluwole Street, Victoria Island, Lagos
Tel: (01) 2615521, 2612043, 7754600
Fax: (01) 2614326, 2694563
E-mail: goodwillengrgroup@nova.net.ng
Contact: Mr. Anil Khurana - MD/CEO

GORI NIGERIA LIMITED
Business: Security Engineers, Sales of Security Equipment, MICR Machines, Currency Sorters
Address: 3 (Plot 1621), Danmole Street, off Idejo Street, Victoria Island, Lagos
Tel: (01) 2614975, 2610986, 2614808 **Fax:** (01) 2614808
E-mail: gori@infoweb.abs.net
Contact: Alh. Magaji Mohammed - Chairman
Mr. G. P. Malkani - MD/CEO

GOSORD SECURITIES LIMITED
Business: Stockbroking, Portfolio Management, Trade Finance, Advisory Services
Address: Stock Exchange House (12th Floor), 2/4, Customs Street, Tinubu, Lagos Island, Lagos
Tel: (01) 2661443, 2667805
Contact: Chief M. N. Ejezie - Exec. Chairman

GRACE FOUNTAINS INTERNATIONAL LIMITED
Business: Sale of Hospital/Medical, Laboratory/Scientific Equipment and Consumables, Office Equipment
Address: 13, Oremeji Street, off Medical Road, Ikeja, Lagos
Tel: (01) 4964100, 4938723, 08023096555
Contact: Dr. Ezenwo Forster Samuel - President/CEO

GRACES HATS LIMITED
Business: Milinery (Hat Making)
Address: 7B, Toyin Street, Ikeja, Lagos
Tel: (01) 4973721 **Fax:** (01) 4977021
E-mail: graces@infoweb.abs.net
Website: www.GracesHat.com
* 10, Adelabu Close, off Ola Ayinde Street, opp. Customs Training College Gate, Ikeja, Lagos
Tel: (01) 4936370, 08023135377
Contact: Mrs. Chito Mark - MD/CEO

GRAHAM BELL (NIGERIA) LIMITED
Business: Telecommunication and Electrical Engineering, Rural Electrification, Traffic Light Systems
Address: 118, Western Avenue, Iponri, Surulere, Lagos
Tel: (01) 5832891, 5851383, 830396 **Fax:** (01) 5851383
E-mail: grahambellnig@mail.pt
Contact: Dr. Marcelo Hyczy Da Costa - Chairman/CEO

GRAHAM GRANT KITCHEN SYSTEMS
Business: Design and Installation of Kitchen Cabinets Fittings and Appliances
Address: 30, G. Cappa Estate, Mobolaji Bank-Anthony Way, Ikeja, Lagos
Tel: (01) 4961477 **Fax:** (01) 4963379
E-mail: egbor@infoweb.abs.net
grahamgrantkitchen@hotmail.com

GRAMEN PETROSERVE NIGERIA LIMITED
Business: Civil and Structural Engineering; Pipeline and Flowline Construction, Maintenance of Oil Gas Facilities, Oil and Gas Consultancy Services
Address: Plot 200, Trans-Amadi Industrial Layout, Off Ordiance Junction, Port Harcourt
Tel: (084) 236651, 235709, 08022235090-7 (8L)
Fax: (084) 235709
E-mail: gramenpetroserve@yahoo.com
Contact: Mr J. A. Aghedo - Chairman/CEO

GRAND CEREALS & OIL MILLS LIMITED
Business: Manufacturing of Cereals, Animal & Poultry Feeds Processing of Vegetable Oils
Address: Km. 17, Zawan Roundabout, Bukuru, Jos
Tel: (073) 280314-7 (4 L) **Fax:** (073) 280014
E-mail: gcoml@cyberspace.net.ng
* 32, Commercial Road, Apapa, Lagos
TeL (01) 5454513, 5455605 **Fax:** (01) 5451276, 5455605
Contact: Mr. J. I. D. Dada - MD/CEO

GRAND FOUNDRY & ENGINEERING WORKS LIMITED (formerly Canplas Ltd)

Business: Manufacturer of Castings, Components and Spares, Steel Fabrication, Sales and Service of Pharmaceutical & Packaging Machines
Address: 1, Mobolaji Bank-Anthony Way, opp. Ikeja Post Office, Ikeja, Lagos
Tel: (01) 4936984, 4936042, 4936983 **Fax:** (01) 4937001
E-mail: canplas@infoweb.abs.net
Contact: Major Gen. Mohammed Magoro (rtd.) - Chairman
Mr Peter Menezes - MD/CEO

GRAND HOTEL, ASABA

Business: Hospitality Services, Convention Centre & Resort
Address: Nnebisi Road, Asaba
Tel: (056) 282030-49 (20 L) **Fax:** (056) 280661
E-mail: grandhotel@siotel.com
Website: www.grandhotelasaba.com
Contact: Chief S. I. Odogwu - Chairman
Chief Francis Nwajei - MD/CEO

GRAND METROPOLITAN ASSOCIATES LIMITED

Business: Insurance Loss Adjusting, Claims Consultancy, Recovery Agents
Address: House of Gold, 100, Apapa-Oshodi Expressway (Cele Bus-Stop), Lagos
Tel: (01) 5556173-4 (2L), 08023003024
E-mail: granmet@metrong.com
Contact: Chief Nwakibie P. O. Egbuniwe - Chairman/CEO

GRAND OLYMPUS (NIGERIA) LIMITED

Business: Marketing of Sports Goods and Equipment
Address: 76, Ojuelegba Road, Surulere, Lagos
Tel: (01) 5851052, 5851784 **Fax:** (01) 5840899
E-mail: grand_olympus@hotmail.com
Contact: Mr. Patrick N. Ubajaka - MD/CEO

GRAND PRODUCTS COMPANY LIMITED

Business: Sales of Electrical Home/Commercial Appliances
Address: 28, Wharf Road, Apapa, Lagos
Tel: (01) 5871725-7 (3 L), 5453644, 5451445, 5451065, 5453655, 7762634, 7768589 **Fax:** (01) 5453200
E-mail: gpcl@grandproducts.org
Website: www.grandproducts.org
* 25, Aba Road, Port Harcourt
Tel/Fax: (084) 237016-7 (2 L), 237027, 237027, 239483, 331421
Contact: Chief G. C. Nweze - Chairman/CEO

GRAND SUMMIT GROUP INTERNATIONAL LIMITED

Business: Real Estate Agents & Consultants, International Property Consultants
Address: Grand Summit Villa, Plot 27, Block 60, Theophilus Orji Street, Lekki Peninsula Phase I, Lagos
Tel: (01) 2706036, 08023544323 **Fax:** (01) 2706037
E-mail: enquiries@grand-summit.com
info@grand-summit.com
Website: www.grand-summit.com

GRANDBOND FINANCE LIMITED

Business: Financial Services
Address: 8A, Ibiyinka Olorunnimbe Close, off Amodu Ojikut Street, Victoria Island, Lagos
Tel: (01) 4616432, 7916620 **Fax:** (01) 4616432
Contact: Mr. Jacob Olusanya - Chairman
Adebimpe Uchebenu - MD/CEO

GRANIMARBLE INDUSTRY LIMITED

Business: Cutting, Polishing & Sales of Marble & Granite.
Address: 6, Queen's Barracks Road, Lagos
Tel: (01) 5878359 **Fax:** (01) 5878807
Contact: Mr. Raza Ali - GM/CEO

GRANT ADVERTISING NIGERIA LIMITED

Business: Advertising, Media Agency
Address: 61, Oduduwa Crescent, Ikeja, G.R.A., Lagos
Tel: (01) 4975272
Contact: Bashorun J. K. Randle - Chairman
Mr. J. O. Oloyede - MD/CEO

GRANT PROPERTIES LIMITED

Business: Property Development and Management
Address: Abimbola House, Goshen Beach Estate, beh. UPDC Estate, Lekki, Lagos
Tel: (01) 2708019-21 (3L) **Fax:** (01) 2708022
Contact: Rev. Olajide Awosedo - Chairman/CEO

GRAPHIC PROJECTS LIMITED

Business: Outdoor Advertising and Production
Address: 12, Olatunde Onimole St, Aguda, Surulere, Lagos
Tel/Fax: (01) 4728710, 5851968, 08033259161, 08022242547
E-mail: grapro@yahoo.com
* 24, Awka Road, opp. Gen. Hospital, Onitsha
Tel: (046) 214057, 412167
Contact: Prince Emeka Okezie - Chairman/CEO

GRAPHICORP LIMITED

Business: Production of Signs
Address: 83B, Allen Avenue, behind Afribank, Ikeja, Lagos
Tel: (01) 4718858-9 (2L), 08023043500, 08023094060
Fax: (01) 3453435
E-mail: graphiccorp@signindustry.net
graphiccorp@graphiccorp.com
Website: www.graphicorp.net
Contact: Mr. Uzo Ojimadu - MD/CEO

GRAPHITEK VENTURES LIMITED

Business: Monogramming and Transfer-Printing, Embroidery
Address: 379, Ikorodu Road, opp. Ojota New Garage, Lagos
Tel: (01) 4971828, 7738429, 08033037959
E-mail: graphitek@micro.com.ng

GRAYDAN INDUSTRIES NIGERIA LIMITED

Business: Sales of Fireproof Safes and Business Equipment
Address: 15, M/M Int'l Airport Road, Ajao Estate, Lagos
Tel: (01) 522682, 2642321, 2669551, 2662862, 4701570, 4702462 **Fax:** (01) 2669383
Contact: Mr. Godwin O. O. Mbatu - MD/CEO

GRAYLINK FLEXFREIGHT SERVICES NIGERIA LIMITED

Business: Air Express Services
Address: Glass House, 7A, Asa-Afariogun St, off Osolo Way, off M/M Int'l Airport Rd, Ajao Estate, Lagos
Tel: (01) 4528616, 4528432, 4700025 **Fax:** (01) 4528616
E-mail: graylink@gacom.net
Contact: Chief I. N. Okoye - Chairman
Mr. Mike Onwurah - MD/CEO

GREAT AFRICA TRUST LIMITED
Business: Equipent Leasing, Raw Materials Procurement, Financial Advisory Services, Stockbroking
Address: Kajola House (3rd Floor), 62/64, Campbell Street, Lagos Island, Lagos
Tel: (01) 2647191-2 (2 L) **Fax:** (01) 2637892
Contact: Mr. R.A. Ogunkoya - AGM. (Operations)

GREAT NIGERIA INSURANCE COMPANY LIMITED
Business: All Classes of Insurance
Address: 8, Omo-Osagie St, off Awolowo Rd, Ikoyi, Lagos
Tel: (01) 2695805, 2670430 **Fax:** (01) 2693483, 2670422
E-mail: greatinsure@beezlink.com
Website: www.greatinsure-ng.com
Contact: Mr M A Siyanbola - MD/CEO
Mr. Akintunde Diya - Corp. Affairs Manager

GREAT NORTHERN TANNING COMPANY LIMITED
Business: Leather Production
Address: 22, Nababa Badamosi Road, Bompai Industrial Estate, Kano
Tel: (064) 638158, 634969 **Fax:** (064) 638158
Contact: Alh. Aliyu Nabegu - Chairman
Alh. Ibrahim Yelwa -MD/CEO

GREATGATE INVESTMENTS LIMITED
Business: Building and Civil Engineering Construction, Producer of Longspan Aluminium Roofing Sheets, Doors and Windows, Real Estate Development
Address: 7, Oguta Road, Onitsha
Tel: (046) 214139, 213749, 08033475633
Contact: Dr. T. O. Anosike - Chairman/CEO

GREEN PALACE HOTELS LIMITED
Business: Hospitality Services
Address: 9B, Bargery Road, Nassarawa G.R.A., Kano
Tel: (064) 647526 **Fax:** (064) 646542

GREENGATE & COMPANY LIMITED
Business: Advertising and Corporate Promotions
Address: 127, Old Ojo Road, Amuwo, Lagos
Tel: (01) 8822049, 7749447
Contact: Chief 'Labi Ishola-Lemomu - MD/CEO

GREENLAND PUBLICITY LIMITED
Business: Outdoor Advertising Agency
Address: 5A, Ezekiel Street, off Toyin Street, Ikeja, Lagos
Tel: (01) 4935800, 08023096421, 08034033802
* 2, Subairu Street, Ladipo Estate, Shogunle, Lagos
Tel: (01) 4963746
Contact: Mr. Bidemi Adebiyi - Chairman/CEO

GREENWICH TRUST LIMITED
Business: Stockbroking, Issuing House, Financial Advisory Services, Management Consultancy
Address: Plot 168, Oyin Jolayemi Street, Victoria Is., Lagos
Tel: (01) 4619261-2 (2L) **Fax:** (01) 4619260
E-mail: greenwich@greenwich-trust.com
Website: www.greenwich-trust.com
Contact: Mr. Kayode Falowo - Chairman/MD

GREMA MOHAMMED GROUP OF COMPANIES
Business: Conglomerate
Address: 50, Burma Road, Apapa, Lagos
Tel: (01) 5876065, 5877449, 5877101, 5877180
Fax: (01) 5872574
Contact: Alh. Grema Mohammed - Chairman/CEO

GRENIC NIGERIA LIMITED
Business: Property Development and Management
Address: Great Nigeria House (22nd Floor), 47/57, Martins Street, Lagos Island, Lagos
Tel: (01) 2664313, 2662288, 2667108, 2668019, 2663036
Contact: Otunba M. A. Jobi-Fele - Chairman

GRENIGAS LIMITED
Business: Bottling & Distribution of Liquefied Petroleum Gas, Sales and Installation of Kitchen Applicances
Address: 1, Adeyemi Bero Crescent, off State Highway, Ilupeju Industrial Estate, Ilupeju, Lagos
Tel: (01) 4973711, 080332331266 **Fax:** (01) 4971993
Contact: Chief E. A. Aguele - Chairman/CEO

GREY DE KOUROUN NIGERIA LIMITED
Business: Manufacture of Perfumes and Cosmetics
Address: 23, Happy Home Avenue, Kirikiri Ind.Estate, Lagos
Tel: (01) 5872113, 5873112, 7740635 **Fax:** (01) 5873112
Contact: Mr. Joseph - MD/CEO

GRINAKR-LTA CONSTRUCTION NIGERIA LIMITED
Business: Building & Civil Engineering Contractors
Address: Plot 234B, Muri Okunola Str, Victoria Island, Lagos
Tel: (01) 2703050-7 (8 L) **Fax:** (01) 2703058
E-mail: grinakre-lta_nigeria@21ctl.com
Website: www.grinaker-ltd.co

GRITCO NIGERIA LIMITED
Business: Sales of Abrasive and Blasting Products, Paint-Spraying Equipment and Spares
Address: 6, Forces Avenue, Old G.R.A., Port Harcourt
Tel/Fax: (084) 235139, 236652 Fax: (01) 236652
E-mail: gritco.phca.ng@africamail.com
Contact: Chief Chris Stanley - Chairman

GRIZI (NIGERIA) LIMITED
Business: Manufacturing of Wood, Metal, Chrome and Moulded Upholstery Furniture, Kitchen Cabinet, Solid and Bullet-Proof Doors; Chroming and Electroplating Services
Address: Adewunmi Estate, Oregun Road, Oregun, Lagos
Tel: (01) 4977420, 4936254, 4937339 **Fax:** (01) 4937339

GROUP AFRICA LIMITED
Business: Direct Advertising Services
Address: 19, Park View Estate, off Gerrard Road, Ikoyi, Lagos
Tel: (01) 2695514, 2695515

GROUP ENTERPRISES NIGERIA LIMITED
Business: Manufacturing of Foam Products, Trading.
Address: 2, C. Uba Close, Niger Bridge Ind. Layout, Onitsha
Tel: (046) 210458, 211548 480414 * (082) 446311
Fax: (046) 212323, 212809
E-mail: pollyfoam@yahoo.com
* 28, New Bridge Road, North Bank, Makurdi
Contact: Chief Christopher O. Uba - Chairman
Chief Evarist Uba - MD/CEO

GROUP FOUR COMPANY OF NIGERIA LIMITED

Business: Sales and Installation of Industrial and Domestic Kitchen Appliances and Laundry Machines
Address: 9/11, Gbajumo Street, beh. Union Bank Building (Balogun Branch), Marina, Lagos
Tel/Fax: (01) 2664642, 0803337776
E-mail: geefourcentre@yahoo.com
Contact: Mr. John O. Sonekan - MD/CEO.

GROUP PRECISION INDUSTRY LIMITED

Business: Oil Industry Services (Cathodic Protection & General Corrosion Control)
Address: 4F, Airport Road, Effurun, Warri
Tel/Fax: (053) 250908
E-mail: precision@alpha.linkserve.com
Contact: Chief (Dr.) H.W. Okposo - Chairman/CEO.

GRUBB CONSOLIDATION LIMITED

Business: Marketing of Foods & Chocolate-Confectionery Products, Manufacturer's Representative
Address: 26, Henry Carr Road, Ikeja Ind. Estate, Ikeja, Lagos
Tel: (01) 4701996 **Fax:** (01) 5455232
E-mail: grubb@eudoramail.com
Contact: Mr. Emmanuel Osilama Imhagwe - MD/CEO.

GRUNZ LINK LIMITED

Business: Sales of Computers and Office Equipment, Training
Address: 20, Enugu Road, G.R.A., Onitsha
Tel: (046) 410792, 412115, 08033214914
E-mail: mails@grunzlink.com
* 32, Olufemi Road, off Ogunlana Drive, S/L, Lagos
Tel: (01) 5844986, 8033243752
Contact: Engr. Uche Ubajaka - Chairman/CEO.

GS TELECOM NIGERIA LIMITED

Business: Sales and Service of Satellite & Telecommunication Equipment
Address: 46, Saka Tinubu Street, Victoria Island, Lagos
Tel: (01) 2624700 **Fax:** (01) 2622172
E-mail: info@gstelecom.com
* Plot 213, Trans-Amadi Ind.Layout, Port Harcourt
Tel: (084) 233841
* Plot 844E, Komoe St, off Limpopo St, Cadastral Zone A6, Maitama, Abuja.
Tel: (09) 4137520
Contact: Mr. Steve Chapman - MD/CEO

GTI CAPITAL LIMITED

Business: Stockbroking, Portfolio Management, Investment Advisory Services
Address: Stock Exchange House (20th Floor), 2/4, Customs Street, off Marina, Lagos Island, Lagos
Tel: (01) 2643476, 2668756 **Fax:** (01) 2643476
E-mail: gticap@yahoo.com
Contact: Dr. Bode Olajumoke - Chairman

GUARANTY AIR SERVICES LIMITED

Business: Travel Agency
Address: 99, Ibrahim Taiwo Road, Kano
Tel: (064) 638370, 647151, 08034734467
Fax: (064) 648316
E-mail: guaranty1000@yahoo.c om
Contact: Alh. Ismail Almajir - Chairman/CEO

GUARANTY TRUST BANK PLC

Business: Commercial Banking
Address: Plural House, Plot 1669, Oyin Jolayemi Street, Victoria Island, Lagos
Tel: (01) 2622650-69 (20L)
Fax: (01) 2622698, 2622699, 2622570
E-mail: corpaff@gtb.com.ng
Website: www.gtb.com.ng
Contact: Mr. Olutayo Aderinokun - MD/CEO.

GUARDIAN EXPRESS BANK PLC

Business: Commercial and Investment Banking
Address: 5A, Elsie Femi-Pearse Street, off Adeola Odeku Street, Victoria Island, Lagos
Tel: (01) 3201393-7 (5L)
E-mail: enquiry@guardianexpressbank.com
Website: www.guardianexpressbank.com
* Plot 1057, Cadastral Zone A8, Adetokunbo Ademola Crescent, Wuse II, Abuja
Contact: Mr. Nnamdi Anammah - MD/CEO.

GUARDIAN INTERNATIONAL BROKERS LIMITED

Business: Insurance Broking
Address: 169, Ikorodu Road, Onipanu, Lagos
Tel: (01) 822564
Contact: Mr. T. A. Quadri - Chairman/CEO.

GUARDIAN PRESS LIMITED

Business: Newspaper & Magazine Publishing, Printing Press
Address: Rutam House, Oshodi Expressway, Isolo, Lagos
Tel: (01) 4524080, 4524111, 4529183, 4529184
Fax: (01) 4522027, 4524481, 4524826, 4528414, 4528416
Contact: Mrs Maiden A Ibru - CEO.

GUARDIAN TRUST INSURANCE COMPANY LIMITED

Business: Underwriting of all Classes of Insurance
Address: 39A, Saka Tinubu Street, Victoria Island, Lagos
Tel: (01) 2625682, 2625684-5 (2 L) **Fax:** (01) 2880599
E-mail: gti@hyperia.com
* 30, Aba Road, Port Harcourt.
Tel: (084) 232620
* Chicken House Estate, Plot 472, Adetokunbo Ademola Crescent, by IBB Way, Wuse II, Abuja
Tel: (09) 5232454, 5232499
Contact: Chief Leo-Stan Ekeh - Chaiman

GUARDIAN TRUST SAVINGS & LOAN LIMITED

Business: Mortgage Finance Services
Address: 31, Ademola Street, S.W. Ikoyi, Lagos
Tel: (01) 2694540
Contact: Mr. Adedapo A. Soluade - Chairman/CEO.

GUARDSMARK NIGERIA LIMITEDLIMITED

Business: Security Services
Address: 100, Brickfield Road, off Moshood Abiola Way, Ebute-Metta, Lagos
Tel: (01) 4715092, 4810577, 5834533
Fax: (01) 5834533
E-mail: gdmk@cyberspace.net.ng
* B.302, Erisco Bonpet Plaza, Plot 2357, Douala St, H.Macaulay Way (North), Wuse Zone 5, Abuja
Tel: (09) 5231507, 6716086
Contact: Chief K. I. Ibirogba - MD/CEO

GUBABI & COMPANY LIMITED
Business: Sales and Service of Security Equipment, Electronic and Office Equipment
Address: 25, Fashoro Street, Surulere, Lagos
Tel: (01) 5837479, 5454504-6 (3 L), 8149955
Fax: (01) 5837591, 5882382
* Shop 60/61, opp Sheraton Hotel, Wuse Zone 4, Abuja.
Tel: (09) 5232497
Contact: Chief Goziem Chibeze - Chairman/CEO

GUBABI ROYALE HOTEL
Business: Hospitality Services
Address: Plot 2359, Sokode Crescent, off Michael Okpara Street, Zone 5, Wuse, Abuja
Tel: (09) 5242401-3 (3 L), 5240885-6 (2 L)
Fax: (09) 5240321
Contact: Chief Chibeze Goziem Chibeze - Chairman/CEO

GUFFANTI (NIGERIA) PLC
Business: Building and Civil Engineering Contractors
Address: 493/495, Agege Motor Road, Oshodi, Lagos
Tel: (01) 4964863 **Fax:** (01) 4978296
E-mail: guffanti@hyperia.com
Contact: Alh. Hassan Hadejia - Chaiman

GUINEA INSURANCE PLC
Business: Insurance
Address: Wema Towers (12th Floor), 54, Marina, Lagos
Tel: (01) 2664693, 2665201, 2660630, 2666674, 2660701
Fax: (01) 2668258
Contact: Sir Emeka Offor - Chairman
Mr. Paul A. Okafor - MD/CEO.

GUINNESS NIGERIA PLC
Business: Brewing of Guiness Foreign Stout, Lager Beer & Non-Alcoholic Malt Drink
Address: 24, Oba Akran Avenue, Ikeja Ind. Estate, Lagos
Tel: (01) 2709100, 4971560-9 (10L), 4976420-9 (10L), 4976721-4 (4L), 4970564
Fax: (01) 2709338, 4970560
* Benin-Asaba Road, Oregbeni Industrial Estate, Ikpoba Hill, Benin City
Tel: (052) 255608-9 (2L), 255598, 258616, 258630-1 (2L), 258583, 251059, 250851, 600629-31 (3L)
Fax: (052) 242129
* Aba Brewery
Tel: (082) 222157, 224828, 224845, 224957, 225108, 225772, 227298, 227535 **Fax:** (082) 226736
Contact: Chief Keith T. Richard - MD/CEO.
Mr B. A. Savage - Corp. Affairs Director

GULF AGENCY & SHIPPING (NIGERIA) LIMITED
Business: Shipping Agency, Clearing and Forwarding, Ship Supplies, Manning Agency
Address: 33A, Marine Road, Apapa G R A, Lagos
Tel: (01) 5804290-4 (5 L), 5450700, 5454429, 5877335
Fax: (01) 5450699
Contact: Capt. B. Svanholm - MD/CEO.

GULF BANK OF NIGERIA PLC
Business: Commercial Banking
Address: Gulf Bank House, PC. 42, Afribank Street, Victoria Island, Lagos
Tel: (01) 2600370-7 (8L) **Fax:** (01) 2601003
E-mail: explore@gulfbank.net
Website: www.gulfbank.net
Contact: Mr. Kayode Oluwa - Corp. Affairs Manager

GULFLINK LIMITED
Business: Transporters (Goods, Petroleum and Equipment)
Address: Plot 125, Trans-Amadi Ind. Layout, Port Harcourt
Tel: (084) 237894 **Fax:** (084) 237895
E-mail: gulflink@phca.linkserve.com
Contact: Mr. Fouad Allam - Chairman/CEO.

GUSAU HOTEL LIMITED
Business: Hospitality and Catering Services
Address: Samaru/Zaria Road, opposite Zamfara State Water Board, Gusau
Tel: (063) 200396, 200160, 200727, 200995
Fax: (063) 200127
Contact: Mr. Sanusi Lawal Jobe - GM/CEO.

GUSTO INTEGRATED LIMITED
Business: Trading, Import & Export, Contracting, Hualage, Fisheries, Sales of Electroni Appliances, Children's Products, General Household Items, Furniture and Gym Equipment
Address: Plot 4, Akinde Industrial Layout, off Abeokuta Expressway, Ajegunle, Lagos
Tel: (01) 4924027, 4924028, 7744738
Fax: (01) 4924027, 4922701
Contact: Mr. Shaka A. Momoh - Chairman

GUVIRA NIGERIA LIMITED
Business: Importation and Distribution of Electric Shields, Fuses, Switchgears and Accessories
Address: Sony Centre, Adeola Odeku St, Victoria Is., Lagos
Tel: (01) 7740107, 2618793
E-mail: flyingdove@microm.com.ng
Contact: Mr. A. Jain - MD/CEO.

GUY SARIES LIMITED
Business: Advertising, Public Relations, Marketing Agency
Address: Sheraton Lagos Hotel & Towes Annex, Opebi Link Road, Ikeja, Lagos
Tel: (01) 4978660-9 (10 L) (Ext. 8083, 8856, 8687)
Contact: Mr. Goodie M. Ibru - Chairman
Mr. Charles C. Inomah - MD/CEO

GZ MOTORS LIMITED
Business: Importation, Sales & Service of Heavy-Duty Automobile Trucks, Sales of Tyres
Address: Plot 10A, Block B, Ilasamaja Industrial Estate, Apapa-Oshodi Expressway, Ilasamaja, Lagos
Tel: (01) 7738930, 4526931, 4524557, 08023439821, 08036511510 **Fax:** (01) 4526931
* Plot 1778, Ligali Ayorinde Street, by Moshood Olugbani St, Victoria Island, Lagos
Tel: (01) 2618064, 7749380, 2614377 **Fax:** (01) 2614377

H. PIERSON ASSOCIATES LIMITED
Business: Financial Training and Consulting Services
Address: Pot 833, Festival Road, (Alh. Babatunde Jose Street), Victoria Island, Lagos

Tel: (01) 2617332, 2620989, 2612434 **Fax:** (01) 2620988
E-mail: hpierson@alpha.linkserve.com
Contact: Eileen C. Shaiyen - Managing Consultant/CEO

H. B. M. GENERAL SUPPLIES LIMITED
Business: Importation of Generators, Refrigerant Gases, Blank Audio Tapes, Agricultural Water Pumps and Multipurpose Engines
Address: 15, Biaduo Street, off Keffi St, S.W. Ikoyi, Lagos
Tel: (01) 2671208, 2671211 **Fax:** (01) 2671210
E-mail: hbm@linkserve.com.ng
Contact: Alh. Sule Katagum - Chairman
Mr. Rajeev Sitlani - MD/CEO

H. F. SCHROEDER (WEST AFRICA) LIMITED
Business: Repair & Rewinding of Electric Motors & Generators, Refurbishment of Transformers, Repair of Compressors, Manufacturing of Carbon Brushes, Rural Electrification and Electrical Installations
Address: Apapa-Oshodi Expressway, Amuwo-Odofin, Lagos
Tel: (01) 7741658, 2880764, 5456958 **Fax:** (01) 2880764
E-mail: info@hfschroeder.com
lagos@hfschroeder.com
* Plot 477, Trans-Amadi Ind. Layout, Port Harcourt
Tel: (084) 233382
* Plot 1105, Awolowo Road, beh. United Parcel Service, Area 11, Garki, Abuja.
Tel: (09) 2349393
Contact: Col. J. D. Dungs (rtd) - Chairman
Mr. Paul Haenni - GM/CEO

H. F. P. ENGINEERING (NIGERIA) LIMITED
Business: Building and Civil Engineering Contractor
Address: Plot P.C. 14A, Ahmed Onibudo Street, Victoria Island, Lagos
Tel: (01) 4618141-6(5L), 4618550, 4618567
Fax: (01) 4618114, 4618150
E-mail: chai@alpha.linkserve.com
Website: www.globesa.com
* H.F.P. Central Operations Yard, Ikota Industrial Area, Epe Expressway, Ikota, Lagos State
Contact: Mr. Yaakov Chai - Group MD/CEO
Mr. Kingsley Omojola - GM. Admin.

H_2O INTERNATIONAL NIGERIA LIMITED
Business: Sales of Water Purification Equipment & Products
Address: 10A, Anifowoshe Street, off Adeola Odeku Street, Victoria Island, Lagos
Tel: (01) 2622254, 2614470, 2611191, 2611709, 2623062, 4702908, 08033257321 **Fax:** (01) 2614470, 2622254
E-mail: hls@infoweb.asb.net
Contact: Dr. (Mrs.) Ify Maduka-Nwakwesi - Chairman/CEO

HAASTRUP LINE (WEST AFRICA) LIMITED
Business: Shipping Agency
Address: Haastrup Jetty, Rumuolumeni, Port Harcourt
Tel/Fax: (084) 235165
Contact: Capt. I. A. Haastrup - Chairman/CEO

HABIB NIGERIA BANK LIMITED
Business: Commercial Banking
Address: Gen. Shehu Musa Yar'Aua House, 7/9, Bank Road, Kaduna
Tel: (062) 245140-9 (10 L)
Fax: (062) 244584, 245272, 240174
E-mail: info@habib-bank.com.ng
* 1, Manuwa/Keffi Street, S.W. Ikoyi, Lagos
Tel: (01) 2691550-9 (10L) **Fax:** (01) 2690123, 2690139
E-mail: coadmin@habib-bank.com
Contact: Mr. Abdulfatai Akin Kekere-Ekun - MD/CEO
Alh. Ado Danjuma - DGM. (Exec Asst to MD)

HABIBU ENGINEERING NIGERIA LIMITED
Business: Building and Civil Engineering Contractors
Address: Plot 17, Murtala Mohammed Expressway, Katampe Junction, Abuja
Tel: (09) 4135923, 5239580, 6702817, 08033072272
Fax: (09) 2221031, 4135918
* 8, Maduike Street, off Raymond Njoku Street, S.W. Ikoyi, Lagos.
Tel: (01) 2694881, 2691100-1 (2L)
Fax: (01) 2694881-2 (2L)
Contact: F. A. Agha - Chairman/CEO

HAC INTERNATIONAL NIGERIA LIMITED
Business: Manufacture of Louvre Frames and Metal Fittings
Address: 19, Egbeyemi Road, Ilupeju, Lagos
Tel: (01) 4971836, 7739218 **Fax:** (01) 4971836
E-mail: hacint@hyperia.com
Contact: Chief O. K. Alli - Chairman

HACKETT NIGERIA LIMITED
Business: Oil Industry Services, Telecommnications
Address: Foreshore Tower (3rd Floor), 2A, Osborn Road, Ikoyi, Lagos
Tel: (01) 2691266, 2693225
E-mail: Ibeloosagie@yahoo.com
Contact: Lateef Belo-Osagie - Exec. Director

HACO INDUSTRIES LIMITED
Business: Manufacturing & Exportation of Medicated Infantcare, Cosmetics and Toiletery Products
Address: Ladipo Oluwole Avenue, Ikeja Industrial Estate, Ikeja, Lagos
Tel: (01) 4976572, 4976575
E-mail: haco@linkserve.com
Contact: Mr. C.U. Azike - Chairman/CEO

HADACON INTERNATIONAL LIMITED
Business: Sales, Installation and Repairs of Telecommunication Equipment, Telecommunication Systems Engineering, Computer Networking and Supplies
Address: UBA Building (3rd Floor, Suite 301), Yakubu Gowon Way, Kaduna
Tel: (062) 243317, 314916 **Fax:** (062) 243317
E-mail: hadacon@skannet.com
Contact: Engr. (Dr.) Abubakar Adama - MD/CEO

HADEMEC LIMITED
Business: Electrical and Plumbing Installation, Installation and Maintenance of Airconditioners
Address: 10A, Tinubu Rd, Palmgrove Estate, Ilupeju, Lagos
Tel: (01) 4933115 **Fax:** (01) 4977796
E-mail: hademec@micro.com.ng
Contact: Engr. (Chief) A. A. Lasebikan - Chairman/CEO

HADJI BASHY NIGERIA LIMITED
Business: Manufacturing of Binding Wire & Nails, Sales of Iron Rod
Address: 138, Abeokuta Expressway (Araromi Bus-Stop), P.O.Box 3084, Agege, Lagos
Tel: (01) 4922840, 4922521, 7751760, 7758183, 7757250, 7755254 **Fax:** (01) 4922840
Contact: Mr. Hakeem Bamigbola - MD/CEO

HAFA LIMITED
Business: Import & Export, General Merchandising
Address: 5B, Burman Road, Apapa, Lagos
Tel: (01) 5877951, 5871867 **Fax:** (01) 5878358
E-mail: hafa@micro.com.ng

HAFFAR INDUSTRIAL COMPANY LIMITED
Business: Manufacturing of Sewing and Embroidery Threads, Spinning of Acrylic Yarn
Address: 359/361, Agege Motor Road, Challenge, Mushin
Tel: (01) 4521163, 4520719, 4521091, 4523809
Fax: (01) 4521035, 4521406
E-mail: haffar@cyberspace.net.ng
Contact: Mr. F. F. Haffar - Exec. Director

HAGENE ASSOCIATES LIMITED
Business: Importation and Sales of Sanitary Wares and Hydromassage Equipment
Address: Block 4 (1st Floor, Suites 10/11), Agric Market, Lagos-Badagry Expressway, Coker, Lagos
Tel: (01) 7742145, 4702304, 4702307, 08033045851, 08033088375
Contact: Mr. Uche Hyginus Obiukwu - MD/CEO

HAKASH & COMPANY LIMITED
Business: Insurance Broking
Address: Hakash House, 22, Moleye Street, Alagomeji, Yaba, Lagos
Tel: (01) 865161, 866032, 865320, 4715677
* 4, Hospital Road, Port Harcourt
Tel: (084) 237369
Contact: Chief R. H. Akanni-Shelle - MD/CEO

HALCON ENGINEERING ASSOCIATES LIMITED
Business: Building Construction and Civil Engineering
Address: Km. 8, Abakaliki Road, Airport Junction, Enugu
Tel: (042) 551418
Contact: Engr. J. O. Onyemelukwe - Chairman/CEO

HALI BROTHERS LIMITED
Business: Marketing of Petroleum Products, Farming, Hotel Services, Sales of Motor Vehicles
Address: 1, Sallatu Estate, Malumfashi, Kaduna, State
Tel: (065) 80012, 620853
* 638, Haliru Gwagwaruwa,Kano
Contact: Hahiru Abdullahi - MD/CEO

HALILCO NIGERIA LIMITED
Business: Sales & Maintenance of Computers; Networking
Address: 26, Beirut Road, Kano
Tel/Fax: (064) 639150, 08037877595
E-mail: rabih-nor@yahoo.com
Contact: Hussein Ali Fadlallah - Chairman
Rabih Nour-Eldine - MD/CEO

HALLIBURTON ENERGY SERVICES NIGERIA LIMITED
Business: Oilfield Services
Address: Plot 90, Ajose Adeogun St, Victoria Island, Lagos
Tel: (01) 2620765-8 (4 L), 2620820-4 (5L)
Fax: (01) 2620769, 2616632
Website: www.hallburton.com
* Plot 158, Trans-Amadi Ind. Layout, Port Harcourt
Tel: (084) 571975-8 (5L)
* MCC Yard, off Enerhen Road, Warri.
Tel: (053) 250248, 253195
Contact: Mr Johan Bakker - Director

HALLMARK ASSURANCE PLC
Business: Insurance Underwriting
Address: City Express Bank House (3rd Floor), Plot 1637, Adetokunbo Ademola Street, Victoria Is., Lagos
Tel: (01) 2627620-1 (2L), 2627638-9 (2L)
Fax: (01) 2627622
* Plot 5B, Okigwe Road, opp. Govt College, Owerri
Tel: (083) 231012, 234306, 234055
Contact: Mr V. N. Nlebemuo - MD/CEO

HALLMARK BANK PLC
Business: Commercial Banking
Address: UTC Building, 137/139, Broad Street, Lagos
Tel: (01) 2640353-6 (4L), 2640553-5 (3L), 2640363, 2643313, 2663929
Fax: (01) 2640356, 2640553
E-mail: info@hallmarkbankplc.com
infohba@hallmark.com
Website: www.hallmarkbankplc.com
www.hallmark.com.ng
Contact: Mr. Marc Wabara - Chairman/CEO
Mr Eze Okorocha - Head(Legal & Corp Affairs)

HALLMARK HOMES LIMITED
Business: Mortgage Banking, Savings and Loans, Developmnt of Housing Estates
Address: 58B, Adeola Odeku Street, Victoria Island, Lagos
Tel: (01) 3200564 **Fax:** (01) 3200563
Contact: Mr. Marc I. Wabara - Chairman
Mr. Victor T. R. Halliday - MD/CEO

HALLMARK PAPER PRODUCTS PLC
Business: Paper Conversion, Manufacture of Paper Products, Business Forms and Computer Stationery, Sales of Paper and Boards
Address: 99, Palm Avenue, Mushin, Lagos
Tel: (01) 4527602, 4527603 **Fax:** (01) 4520951
Contact: Mr. D. O. Adeliyi - Chairman/CEO

HALOGEN SECURITY COMPANY LIMITED
Business: Security Guard Services, Supply and Installation of Security Gadgets , Protocol/Escort Services, 24-Hour Armed Reaction Service, Consultancy
Address: 49, Adekunle Fajuyi Road, Ikeja, G.R.A. Lagos
Tel: (01) 4742585, 4971750, 7743290
Fax: (01) 2881448, 4975234
E-mail: halogen@hyperia.com
info@halogensecurity.com
Website: www.halogensecurity.com
Contact: Mr. Biodun Shobanjo - Chairman
Capt. Ayodeji A. Bamgbose (rtd) - GM/CEO

HALSTON ENERGY LIMITED
Business: Service Provider to the Oil & Gas Sector
Address: Plot 161B, Raufu Taylor Clos, off Idejo Street, P.O.Box 70927, Victoria Island, Lagos
Tel: (01) 3204243, 4619855 **Fax:** (01) 3204243
E-mail: info@halstonenergy.com
Contact: Miss Mosun Shobo - MD/CEO

HAMADA CARPETS NIGERIA LIMITED
Business: Manufacturing and Marketing of Carpets
Address: 25A, Rabah Road, Kaduna
Tel: (062) 238761, 238762
Contact: Alh. Murtala Shehu Yar'Adua - Chairman
Mr. W. Halawi - MD/CEO

HAMADAH SHIPPING SERVICES LIMITED
Business: Shipping, Clearing and Forwarding Agency
Address: Eleganza Plaza (Cancer Block, 1st Floor), 1, Commercial Road, Apapa, Lagos
Tel: (01) 5874746, 5874110, 5874451
Fax: (01) 5876887, 5876326
E-mail: hamadah@linkserve.com.ng
hamadah@yahoo.com
Contact: Alh. Bala Shagari - Chairman
Chief T. A. Okonkwo - MD/CEO

HAMBLESIDE NIGERIA LIMITED
Business: Supply of Corporate Gifts and Printing Equipment
Address: 28/32, Industrial Avenue, Ilupeju, Lagos
Tel: (01) 4930449, 08023109767, 0023263156
E-mail: hamblesidengr@yahoo.com
Website: www.hambleside.co.uk
Contact: Mr Tunde Alade Animashaun - Chairman

HAMDALA HOTEL, KADUNA
Business: Hoteliers; Hospitality Services
Address: 26, Muhammadu Buhari Way, Kaduna
Tel: (062) 235440-7 (8L) **Fax:** (062) 235449
E-mail: kadhot@inet-global.com
Contact: Mal. Abayomi Oyelola - MD/CEO

HAMILTON HAMMER & COMPANY LIMITED
Business: Issuing House, Financial Advisory Services, Stockbroking
Address: Niger House (5th Floor), 1/5, Odunlami St Lagos
Tel: (01) 2640710-14 (5 L) **Fax:** (01) 2640709
E-mail: hh@hamiltonhammer.com
Contact: Mr. Olufemi A. Akinsnya - Chairman/CEO

HAMSTANG NIGERIA LIMITED
Business: Shipping Agents, Ship Charterers and Brokers, Clearing & Forwarding
Address: Eleganza Plaza (Libra Block, 1st Floor), 1, Aerodrome Road, Apapa, Lagos
Tel: (01) 5452973, 5872967 **Fax:** (01) 5451048, 5875964
E-mail: hamstang@alpha.linkserve.com
Contact: Mrs. C. Aliyu - Chairman

HAMMOUD & SAIDI INTERNATIONAL (NIGERIA) LIMITED
Business: Building & Civil Engineering Construction, Electrical/Instrumentation and Process Control, Logistics and International Supply, Furnishing
Address: Plot 570, Ndola Square, off Michael Okpara Street, Wuse Zone 5, Abuja
Tel: (09) 5238942, 5233687, 08033594766, 08044180447,
Fax: (09) 5235946
Contact: Mr. Tarik Hammoud - MD/CEO

HAMZAS HOLDINGS LIMITED
Business : Conglomerate (Industrialist, Construction, Financial Consultancy Services, Shipping, Road Transport & Airline Services, Import & Export, Farming
Address: 19/21, Kofo Abayomi Avenue, Apapa, Lagos
Tel: (01) 5453631, 5870450, 5870975, 08023326484, 08042149140 **Fax:** (01) 5451790, 264083, 2646084
E-mail: hamza_hd@yahoo.com
Contact: Alh. (Dr.) Garba N Hamza - Group Exec. Chairman
Alh. Mohammed N Hamza - Group MD/CEO

HANACO NIGERIA LIMITED
Business: Importation, Distribution and Sales of Electronics, Office Equipment and General Goods
Address: Hanaco Plaza, 113, Ikorodu Road, Fadeyi, Lagos
Tel: (01) 7741417, 8044846 **Fax:** (01) 2662348
* 122, Nnamdi Azikiwe Street, Idumota, Lagos
Tel: (01) 2662348, 2664967
Contact: Chief H. N. Anaekwe - Chairman/CEO

HANCOCK OGUNDIYA & PARTNERS
Business: Consulting Civil/Structural Engineers; Project Managers
Address: 24/28, Strachan Street (4th Floor), Lafiaji, Lagos
Tel: (01) 2637519, 2636112 **Fax:** (01) 2636112
E-mail: hancock@hyperia.com
Contact: Engr. O. O. Oluyemi - Partner

HANI SAFIEDINE INVESTMENTS LIMITED
Business: Haulage, Manufacture of Household/Industrial Plastics & Furniture, Perfumes, Cosmetics, Footwear
Address: Km. 12, Old Lagos Road, Ibadan
Tel: (02) 2310302, 2314512, 2314700
* 359/361, Old Ojo Road, Lagos-Badagry Expressway, Satellite Town, Lagos
Tel: (01) 5890484, 5880524, 5880123, 5880393, 7738162, 7740403 **Fax:** (01) 261874
Contact: Alh. Souheil Mudeihi - Group MD
Mr. Narayanan Vasudevan - Group GM

HANNAHSGATE LIMITED
Business: Publishing and Information Management, .Cargo Handling, Import, Export, Agricultural Produce and Solid Mineral Consultancy Services
Address: 5, Adelabu Close, off Ola Ayinde Street,opp. Customs Training College Gate, Ikeja, Lagos
Tel: (01) 4971377, 7221830, 08023235100, 08054466664
E-mail: hannahsgate@yahoo.com
Contact: Mr. Daniel I. Omoruyi - MD/CEO

HANSEATIC INTERNATIONAL LIMITED
Business: Lumbering and Wood Processing
Address: 43, Ladipo Oluwole Road, Apapa, G.R.A., Lagos
Tel: (01) 4823387, 5450074, 5453054

HAPEL (NIGERIA) LIMITED
Business: Civil Engineering, Building & Road Construction
Address: Plot C 14/15, Old Airport Road, Emene, Enugu

Tel: (042) 553873, 552054, 558272 **Fax:** (042) 553873
E-mail: hapel@hapel.org
hapelng@yahoo.co.uk
* 81B, Oduduwa Crescent, Ikeja G R A, Lagos
Tel: (01) 4963993, 4967486
Contact: Chief E. N. Nwokoro - Chairman/CEO

HAPPY HOME FURNITURE LIMITED
Business: Manufacturing of Office & Domestic Furniture
Address: Plot 172, Happyhome Avenue, New Kirikiri Industrial Estate, Lagos
Tel: (01) 5454706, 7740563, 08033293429
Fax: (01) 5871755
* Adetokunbo Ademola Crescent, Wuse II, Abuja.
Tel: (09) 5238592
Contact: Mr. F. A. Monkarem - MD/CEO

HARBURY NIGERIA LIMITED
Business: Importation and Marketing of Commodities and Food-Beverage Drinks
Address: 15, Warehouse Road, Apapa, Lagos
Tel: (01) 5455869, 5872734, 5873414, 5876530
Fax: (01) 5455869, 5876530
E-mail: harbury@hotmail.com
Contact: Mr. Terence Vince - MD/CEO

HARDEEP (NIGERIA) LIMITED
Business: Marketing of Plastic Raw Materials; Manufacturers of Plastic Storage Tanks and Household Products, PET Containers and Bottles
Address: Plot 2, Lateef Jakande Rd, Agidingbi, Ikeja, Lagos
Tel: (01) 7742002, 4922382 **Fax:** (01) 2611747
* 154, Inuwa Wada Rd, beh I. Taiwo Rd, Kano
Tel: (064) 649824, 646584, 631162
E-mail: hardeepning@aol.com

HARDEL & ENIC GROUP OF COMPANIES
Business: Conglomerate - Construction, Manufacturing, Aviation, Publishing, Farming, Sports, Real Estate
Address: Oriental Plaza, Ugwu Orji, Okigwe Road, Owerri
Tel: (083) 230236, 230755, 232698, 08037210108
Fax: (083) 230236
Contact: Chief (Dr.) E. C. Iwuanyanwu, MFR -Chairman/CEO

HARDIS & DROMEDAS LIMITED
Business: Manufacturing and Marketing of Hygiene Products, Disinfectants and Bleach
Address: Off Old Airport Road, Emene Ind. Layout, Enugu
Tel: (042) 554640, 553047
* 19, Itire Road, Surulere, Lagos
Tel: (01) 8161973, 08033275142 **Fax:** (01) 8161973
E-mail: hardis@infoweb.abs.net
Website: www.hardis&co.com
Contact: Dr. Chike Obidigbo - Chairman/CEO

HARIESCOCAN & ASSOCIATES LIMITED
Business: Building and Civil Engineering Contractor, Mining Interior Decorators
Address: 80, Lafia Road, North Bank, Makurdi
Tel: (044) 531295, 531161 **Fax:** (044) 531295
* 24, Otigba Street, off Awolowo Way, Ikeja, Lagos
Tel: (01) 4976757
Contact: Engr. (Dr.) Charles I. Onwurah - Chairman/CEO

HARLINK INVESTMENTS LIMITED
Business: Shipping, Clearing & Forwarding, Warehousing , Transportation, Export Services
Address: 25, Warehouse Road, Apapa, Lagos
Tel: (01) 5455430, 5457035
E-mail: harlink@harlink.com
Website: www.harlink.com

HARMATTAN TANNERY LIMITED
Business: Tannery
Address: Challawa Industrial Estate, Kano
Tel: (064) 632744, 645373, 648832, 08033275657, 08033561055 **Fax:** (064) 645373, 648832
Contact: Alh. Mustapha U. Mashood - Dep. GM

HARMONIA HOTELS LIMITED
Business: Hospitality Services
Address: Plot 896, Gimbiya Crescent, Garki, Abja
Tel: (09) 3143201-4 (4 L), 08055123910
Fax: (09) 3143205
Contact: Chief (Sir) Dr. Pius O. Muoghalu - Chairman/CEO

HARMONY HOUSE FURNITURE COMPANY LIMITED
Business: Manufacturing and Marketing of Furniture
Address: 389, Agege Motor Road, near Cappa Bus-Stop, Mushin, Lagos
Tel: (01) 523039, 08023423466, 08037189510, 08037219965
Contact: Mr. Femi Ajanaku - Chairman

HARMONY PROJECTS LIMITED
Business: Agroveterinary Services & Products, Pest Control Services; Construction and Supplies; Livestock Farming; Environmental Services
Address: 225 (98), Lagos-Badagry Expressway, Church Bus-Stop, opp Festac Town, Kuje-Amuwo, Lagos
Tel: (01) 4743383, 08033065713, 08033267577
E-mail: harmryprojects@yahoo.com
Contact: Dr. Chidi Ogboso - MD/CEO

HARMONY TRUST & INVESTMENT COMPANY LIMITED
Business: IT Training & Testing, Sales & Maintenance of Computers, Web and Application Development
Address: Plot 15E, Muri Okunola St, Victoria Island, Lagos
Tel: (01) 4619666, 2883141, 2622126, 2622287, 08034028655 **Fax:** (01) 4619666
E-mail: harmonycomp@yahoo.com
enquiry@harmonytrust.com
Website: www.harmonytrust.com
Contact: Mrs. Betty Obieri - MD/CEO

HARRIMAN & COMPANY
Business: Chartered Surveyors,Property Consultants, Valuers
Address: 27/29, King George V Road, Onikan, Lagos
Tel: (01) 2632290, 2630918, 2632433, 2637129, 4816811, 08033003264, 08033016282 **Fax:** (01) 2634475
* 8, Awolowo Avenue, Old Bodija Estate, Ibadan
Tel: (02) 8100078, 8103747, 8104550
Contact: Chief Hope Harriman - Chairman
Mrs. J. O. Akinyode - Managing Surveyor

HARRIS & JONES INSURANCE BROKERS LIMITED
Business: Insurance Broking

Address: 122, Murtala Mohammed Way, Ebute Metta, Lagos
Tel: (01) 8043902, 7740474, 08023221883
Contact: Chief E. O. Fagbemi - Vice Chairman/CEO

HARRITEX GROUP
Business: Import & Export, Ocean & Airfreight, Maritime Service, Ship/Cargo Charters, Consultancy
Address: 20, Birabi Street, G.R.A. Phase 1, Port Harcourt
Tel: (084) 233902
Contact: Chief Henry Njoku - Chairman/CEO

HARRYMAG VENTURES LIMITED
Business: Sales and Service of Industrial, Kitchen, Laundry & Bakery Equipment
Address: 78, Allen Avenue, Ikeja, Lagos
Tel: (01) 4930738, 5891280, 7745152 **Fax:** (01) 4930738
E-mail: harrymag@beta.linkserve.com
* Mac Lewis Plaza, Plot 799, Blantyre Street, off Adetokunbo Ademola Crescent, Wuse II, Abuja
Tel: (09) 5233176, 6700008
Contact: Barr. Harrison Nwadike - Chairman/CEO

HART INDUSTRIES LIMITED
Business: Manufacturing of Water-Storage Poly Tanks
Address: Plot 20, Challawa Industrial Estate, Kano

HARVARD FOODS LIMITED
Business: Manufacturing of Sweets and Confectionery
Address: Ring Rood (7up Bus-Stop), Oluyole Industrial Estate, Ibadan
Tel: (02) 2310195, 2315758, 2310633
Contact: Mr. S. J. Nassar - Chairman/CEO

HARVARD INTERNATIONAL INSURANCE BROKERS LTD
Business: Insurance Broking
Address: 6, Gab Jinadu Street, off State Highway, Ilupeju Ind. Estate (beh. Poly Products), Ilupeju Lagos
Tel: (01) 4962396, 4720685 **Fax:** (01) 4962396
Contact: Alh. M. A. Ghanni - MD/CEO

HARVARD TRUST SAVINGS & LOANS LIMITED
Business: Mortgage Banking, Property Services
Address: 2, Red Cross Way, Ogbete Main Market, , Enugu
Tel: (042) 2599313, 259303, 08033398743, 08033398745 08033399008 **Fax:** (042) 259349
E-mail: htsl@infowe.abs.net
Contact: Engr. Chris Okoye - Chairman
Mr. V. C. Opara - GM

HARVEST INVESTMENT COMPANY LIMITED
Business: Financial Consultants, LPO/Contract Financing
Address: Mamman Kontagoro House (12th Floor), 23, Marina, Lagos Island, Lagos
Tel: (01) 2641503
E-mail: hicbicam@infoweb.abs.net

HARVEY VENTURES LIMITED
Business: Oil & Gas Services (Production) Facility Maintenance, Offshore Procurement Services), Building & Civil Engineering Construction, Merchandising, Real Estate Development
Address: Bankers House (3rd Floor), Plot PC. 19, Adeola Hopewell Street, Victoria Island, Lagos
Tel: (01) 3200166, 08023100174, 08033042792,
Fax: (01) 3200166
E-mail: morelgroup@linkserve.com
Website: www.morelgroup.net
Contact: Olorogun Lucky Oghene-Omoru (JP) - Chairman

HAS BRICKWORKS COMPANY LIMITED
Business: Manufacturers of Vibrated Concrete Products and Building Materials, Property Developers
Address: 111, Adeniyi Jones Avenue, Ikeja, Lagos
Tel: (01) 4936645, 08023326563, 08055232575
Contact: Mr. Omolayo Akinniranye - MD/CEO.

HASKONING ENGINEERING CONSULTANTS NIGERIA LTD
Business: Consulting Engineers, Project Managers
Address: 98A, Lamido Crescent, Kano
Tel: (064) 644122, 644961 **Fax:** (064) 633515
E-mail: haskoning@micro.com.ng
Contact: Alh. A. Rufai - Chairman

HASSAN PLASTICS INDUSTRIES LIMITED
Business: Manufacture of Plastic Household & Industrial Items & Polythene Bags
Address: 1, Maimalari Road, Bompai Industrial Estate, Kano
Tel: (064) 632348, 642348 **Fax:** (064) 632536
Contact: Mr Z. R. Boukarroum - MD/CEO

HASSAN STEEL PRODUCTS (NIGERIA) LIMITED
Business: Manufacturing of Chair-Base, Steel Windows & Doors, Aluminium Building Products
Address: Plot 7, Block H, Oshodi Industrial Scheme, Isolo-Oshodi Expressway, Oshodi, Lagos
Tel: (01) 521582, 522123, 4962583, 4963110
Contact: Mr. Walid Abou-Hassan - GM/CEO.

HAT EMPORIUM
Business: Design and Marketing of Hats
Address: Shop 203, Alade Market, Allen Avenue, Ikeja, Lagos
* 5/7, Suru Bolaji Street, Balogun, Lagos
* Shop G 158, Mammy Market, Falomo, Ikoyi, Lagos
* 2B, Old Aba Road, opp. Mini Okoro Police Station, Port Harcourt

HAVANA SPECIALIST HOSPITAL LIMITED
Business: Medical and Health Care Services
Address: 115, Akerele Extension (Tesilimi Fatusi Street), Surulere, Lagos
Tel: (01) 4705300, 2881416, 2881719, 08027272727
Contact: Chief (Dr.) G. C. E. Okeke - Joint Medical Director

HAVILAH CONSULT LIMITED
Business: Industrial and Management Consultancy Services, Architects, Civil Engineers and Builders
Address: Oshopey Plaza (3rd Floor, Jolayo Suites), 17/19, Allen Avenue, Ikeja, Lagos
Tel: (01) 2901379, 08033019794
E-mail: havilah@hyperia.com
* 10, Unity Road, Ikeja, Lagos
Tel: (01) 8157710, 08023068258
* Banex Plaza (Suite BE 9), Plot 750, Aminu Kano Crescent, Wuse II, Abuja.
Tel: (090) 406059
Contact: Engr. Tunde Ekpekurede - Chairman/CEO.

HAVILLA WOOD INDUSTRIES LIMITED
Business: Processing of Wood, Manufacturing of Furniture
Address: The Wonder Place, Plot 938, Havilla Road, Azores Street, off Aminu Kano Crescent, Wuse II, Abuja
Tel: (09) 5235410, 4139472 (090) 405648
E-mail: havilla@infoweb.abs.net

HAY, BARRY, ODUNSI & ASSOCIATES
Business: Structural and Civil Engineering Consultants
Address: Lapal House (1st Floor), 235, Igbosere Road, Lagos
Tel: (01) 2631480 **Fax:** (01) 2630135
E-mail: hbolagos@infoweb,abs.net
Contact: Mr. M. S. Frost - Chairman/CEO.

HCN TECHNOLOGIES LIMITED
Business: Software Developement & Marketing, Consultancy & Training, Networking, Internet Services and E-Business Solutions
Address: IT Villa, 27, Adeleke Street, off Allen Avenue/ Tinuade Street, Ikeja, Lagos
Tel: (01) 8042996, 4972140, 4972139
E-mail: enquiry@hentechnologies.com
Website: www.hcntechnologies.com
* 32, Beirut Road, Kano
Tel: (064) 639406 **Fax:** (064) 639409

HCP WATER SERVICES LIMITED
Business: Borehole Drilling, Water Engineering Services
Address: 5, Jide Taiwo Street, Ojodu, Lagos
Tel: (01) 4702277, 08033446653 **Fax:** (01) 4977940
E-mail: hcpwaterservices@onebox.com
Contact: Mr. Kayode S. Badejo - GM/CEO

HDF & SONS LIMITED
Business: Agro-Allied, Tannery & Industrial Chemicals Sales
Address: 24, Unity Road, Kano
Tel: (064) 642764, 637656 **Fax:** (064) 637656
E-mail: hdfson@hotmail.com
Contact: Hassan H. Fawaz - Chairman

HEADWORKS LIMITED
Business: Retail and Wholesales of Hats
Address: K-One Plaza, 8, Ola-Ayinde Street, off Mobolaji Bank-Anthony Way/Toyin Street, Ikeja, Lagos
Tel: (01) 7900806, 4933696, 08033045826
* 2, Khana Lane, off Olu Obasanjo Way, Port Harcourt
Tel: (084) 571100
* Russel Centre (2nd Floor, Suite S5), Plot 2425, Herbert Macaulay Way, Zone 4, Wuse Abuja
Tel: 08023011047
Contact: Mr Mayen Effiong - Chairman/CEO

HEALTH ASSURANCE CONSULTANTS
Business: Health Insurance Consultants
Address: 2, Maroni Road, Palmgrove Estate, Lagos
Tel: (01) 4701813, 7747150 **Fax:** (01) 7596062
E-mail: hac@skannet.com

HEALTH FOREVER PRODUCTS LIMITED
Business: Formulation and Sales of Herbal Medications
Address: 7, Dipeolu Street, off Obafemi Awolowo Way, Ikeja, Lagos
Tel: (01) 4970845-6 (2L), 4704093, 4709749
E-mail: bfl@infoweb.abs.net
Website: www.jubi-formula.com

HEALTHCARE COMMUNICATIONS LIMITED
Business: Publishing, Medical Services and Supplies
Address: 3, Anike Apena Street, off Mobolaji Bank-Anthony Way, Ikeja, Lagos
Tel: (01) 4926601, 4967929
Contact: Dr. Bola Olaosebikan - Publisher/CEO

HEALTHCARE INTERNATIONAL NIGERIA LIMITED
Business: Health Management Organisation (HMO)
Address: 5, Customs Street,off Marina, Lagos Island, Lagos
Tel: (01) 2643695, 4705701 **Fax:** (01) 2666801
E-mail: info@healthcare-ng.com
Website: www.healthcare-ng.com
Contact: Mr Tunde Awosika - GM/CEO

HEALTHY LIVING SERVICES LIMITED
Business: Health Enhancement Services & Products, Health Club and Fitness Centre
Address: 64B, Anifowoshe Street, off Adeola Odeku Street, Victoria Island, Lagos
Tel: (01) 2611191, 2611709, 2614470, 2623062, 2622254, 4702902, 08033257321 **Fax:** (01) 2614470, 2622254
E-mail: hls@infoweb.abs.net
* Plot 1028, Ruvuma Street, off Ibrahim Babangida Way, Maitama, Abuja
Tel: (09) 4132326
Contact: Dr. (Mrs.) I. I. Nwakwesi - Chairman/CEO

HEARTBEAT INVESTMENTS LIMITED
Business: Stockbroking, Investment Advisory Services
Address: Wesley House (7th Floor), 21/22, Marina, Lagos
Tel: 2645124, 2645174 **Fax:** 2645308
E-mail: heartbinv@cyberspace.net
heartbinv@cyberspace.com
Website: www.heartbinv.com
Contact: Senator Musa S. Matori - Chairman
Cletus Osazee Imasuen - MD/CEO

HEARTLINK VENTURES LIMITED
Business: Employment Agency, Printing & Publishing, Internet Training and Media Consultants, Thrift Collection and Financing
Address: 51, Jubril Martins St, Lawanson, Surulere, Lagos
Tel: (01) 5851735, 4714922, 08023072254, 08033254220,
Fax: (01) 5851735
E-mail: heartlinkng@yahoo.co.uk
heartlinkng@excite.com
Website: www.heartlink-ng.com
* Plot 39, Nyanya Phase I, opposite Caliben Clinics, Nyanya, Abuja
Contact: Mrs. Anne Kemi Ladipo-Otegbade - MD/CEO

HEAVEN'S GATE INVESTMENTS LIMITED
Business: Sales of Musical & Sound Reproduction Equipment and Amplifers
Address: 4, Kofo Abayomi Street (41st Floor), Apapa, Lagos
Tel: (01) 5457746 **Fax:** (01) 5457544
E-mail: heavensgate@infoweb.abs.net

HEIDELBERG NIGERIA LIMITED
Business: Sales, Supply and After-Sales Support of Complete Printing-Equipment Systems and Consumables
Address: Heidelberg House, 38/40, Association Avenue, Ilupeju, Lagos
Tel: (01) 7746782, 4932394, 525073 **Fax:** (01) 4520636
E-mail: hnl@heidelberg-ng.com
Contact: Mr. Holger Garbrecht - Chairman
Mr. Jakob Bejer - MD/CEO.

HEINEMANN EDUCATIONAL BOOKS (NIGERIA) PLC
Business: Publishing of School, University & General Books
Address: 1, Ighodaro Road, Jericho, Ibadan
Tel: (02) 2410747, 2410943, 2411213, 2412268, 2413096
Fax: (02) 2411089, 2413237
E-mail: info@heinemannbooks.com
heinemannbooks@yahoo.com
Website: www.heinemannbooks.com
* 4, Ilupeju Bye-Pass, Lagos.
Tel: (01) 4970103
Contact: Mr. Ayo Ojeniyi - MD/CEO.

HELPDESK TECHNOLOGIES NIGERIA LIMITED
Business: Sales & Repairs of Computers, Networking, Internet Services
Address: Areta Plaza, 178, Aba Road, Port Harcourt
Tel: (084) 57144, 239227, 08023149352, 08033024024, 08033147357
E-mail: phc@helpdesk-net.net
sales@helpdesk-net.net
Website: www.helpdesk.-net.net
Contact: Engr. Teddy Ezeike - Chairman/CEO

HEN-FAG NIGERIA LIMITED
Business: Sales of Photographic Processing Equipment
Address: 9, Breadfruit Street, Lagos Island, Lagos
Tel: (01) 2642513, 4713683 **Fax:** (01) 2642513
Contact: Mr. H. Akinwunmi - Chairman/CEO

HENKEL CHEMICALS NIGERIA LIMITED
Business: Manufacture of Industrial Adhesives, Industrial Detergents, Textile Auxilliaries, Glue for Furniture and Consumer Products
Address: Plot 7, Block K, Apapa Expressway, Isolo, Lagos
Tel: (01) 4520015, 4520031, 4520060, 4522869
Fax: (01) 4520024
* AU 11, Gamagira Road, Angwa Sanui Tudun Wada, Kaduna.
Tel: (062) 238248
* 220, Airport Road, Geri-Alimi, Ilorin
Tel: (031) 221419
Contact: Alh. Baba Abubakar - Chairman/CEO

HENLEY INDUSTRIES (NIGERIA) LIMITED
Business: Manufacture of Sodium Silicate and Crystalline Glassware
Address: Plot 1405, Adetokunbo Ademola Street, opp. Eko Hotel, Victoria Island, Lagos
Tel: (01) 2615048, 2613518 **Fax:** (01) 2613518
* Plot C21/6, Anioma Road, Agbara Ind. Estate, Lagos-Badagry Express Road, Agbara Ogun State
Contact: Mr. T. E. M. Ifet - Chairman
Mr. Suresh Jobanputra - MD/CEO

HENRY STEPHENS GROUP OF COMPANIES
Business: Conglomerate, Agricultural Construction & Material Handling, Equipment Sales & Service
Address: * 90, Awolowo Road, Ikoyi, Lagos
Tel: (01) 2690211, 2671720 **Fax:** (01) 2690758
* 2, Ilupeju Bye-Pass, Ilupeju, Lagos
Tel: (01) 5553316, 08023222483, 08033489300
Fax: (01) 2690758
Contact: Chief (Dr.) Oladele Fajemirokun - Chairman/CEO

HENSEN TRUST LIMITED
Business: Engineering, Maintenance Services, Sales, Maintenane and Repair of Fire Suppression Systems and Equipment
Address: 20C, Akin Ogunlewe Street, off Ligali Ayorinde Street, Victoria Island, Lagos
Tel: (01) 2626352-4 (3L), 2705188 **Fax:** (01) 2626351
E-mail: hensen@hensengroup.com
Website: www.hensengroup.com
Contact: D. O. Ngerem - MD/CEO

HENSMOR GROUP OF COMPANIES
Business: Customs Licensed Agents, Shipping, Deep-Sea Fishing and Farming, Engineering, Plastic Manufacturing, Petroleum Exploration and Marketing, Bureau de Change
Address: Okoi Arikpo House, 5, Idowu Taylor Street, Victoria Island, Lagos
Tel: (01) 2625199, 2621364, 2693418 **Fax:** (01) 2625198
E-mail: hensmor@infoweb.abs.net
Contact: Prince (Dr.) H .H. Omorodion - Chairman/CEO

HENVACO LIMITED
Business: Sales and Service of Office Equipment
Address: 262, Herbert Macaulay St, Alagomeji, Yaba, Lagos
Tel: (01) 7744598, 4527886, 4528236, 08033108929
* Shop 1, Neighbourhood Centre, Wuse Zone 3, Abuja
Tel: (09) 5235444
Contact: Chief Henry Mgbechi Nlewedim - Chairman/CEO

HEPTAGON VENTURES LIMITED
Business: Sales of Printing Equipment and Graphic Materials, Trading, Medical Diagnostic Services, Digital Colour Separation
Address: 3, George Alade Lane, Fola-Agoro, Somolu, Lagos
Tel/Fax: (01) 4976680, 4977845, 08023033533, 08023138980
E-mail: heptagon@nova.net.ng
heptagon@hotmail.com
Contact: Mr. Adeniran Adedeji - National Sales Director

HERBERT ONODINGENE & PARTNERS
Business: Estate Surveyors & Valuers, Estate Agency, Real Estate, Facility & Property Management.
Address: Engineering Centre (4th Floor), Plot PC.1, Engineering Close, Victoria Island, Lagos
Tel: (01) 5558561, 2622260, 7767787, 08023045261, 08033559196
E-mail: hebno@yahoo.com
* McLewis Plaza (Suite A24), IBB Way/Blantyre Street, Wuse II, Abuja
Tel: (080) 23045261
Contact: Mr. Herbert Onodingene - Principal Partner

HERE & THERE TELEVISION
Business: Cable Television & General Broadcasting Services, Satellite Communications, Audio/Visual Productions, Marketing & Distribution of Films
Address: Here & There Broadcasting Complex, 226, Obafemi Awolowo Way, Oke-Odo, Ibadan
Tel: (02) 2318553, 2318556, 08023382404
Fax: (02) 2318556
E-mail: httv@infoweb.abs.net
Contact: Mr. Abayomi A. Davies - Chairman/CEO

HERITAGE ASSURANCE COMPANY LIMITED
Business: Non-Life Insurance Business
Address: 27A, Bishop Oluwole Street, Victoria Island, Lagos
Tel: (01) 7744507, 2624237, 2629168-9 (2L)
Website: www.heritageassurance.com
Contact: Mr. K. V. Aderinokun - Chairman

HERITAGE COURTS & INNS
Business: Hospitality Services
Address: 187, Moshood Olugbani Street, off Ligali Ayorinde Street, Victoria Island Annex, Lagos
Tel/Fax: (01) 2614949, 2619501, 3200134, 4619460, 4619834-5
E-mail: ecog@infoweb.abs.net

HERITAGE INVESTMENTS & SECURITIES LIMITED
Business: Stockbroking, Registrars, Issuing House, Nominal Transfer
Address: 5, Ademola Street, S.W. Ikoyi, Lagos
Tel: (01) 2695563-4 (2L), 08033018530, 08033250974, 08033250976, 08033251104 **Fax:** (01) 2695564
* Plot 242, Muhammadu Buhari Way, Central Business District, Abuja
Tel: (09) 6702221, 6702275,6702469 **Fax:** (09) 2347105
Contact: Alh. Issa Yahaya Zarewa - Chairman/CEO

HERITAGE INVESTMENTS LIMITED
Business: Supply of Oilfield Equipment
Address: Western House (7th Floor), 8/10, Broad St, Lagos
Tel: (01) 26003300-9 (10 L) **Fax:** (01) 2637598
E-mail: uuu@infoweb.abs.net
Contact: Prof. U. U. Uche - Chairman/CEO.

HERITAGE PUBLISHING LIMITED
Business: Commercial and Industrial Printing Services, Manufacturing of Light Packaging, Colour Separation Services
Address: Plot 636A, Sultan Abubakar Way, Wuse Zone 3, Abuja
Tel: (09) 5233927 **Fax:** (09) 5233926

HEROES FURNITURE LIMITED
Business: Sales of Furniture, Furnishings, Corporate Gift Items
Address: Km 3, Lekki Expressway, Lekki Peninsula, Lagos
Tel: (01) 7732063, 7757693, 5555359, 4803609
E-mail: heroes@hotmail.com
* 33, Akin Adesola Street, Victoria Island, Lagos
Tel: (01) 2621528, 2624413 **Fax:** (01) 2621528
*13,Adetokunbo Ademola Crescent,Wuse II,Abuja
Tel: (09) 5238847
* 199, Evo Road, G.R.A. Phase II, Port Harcourt
Tel: (084) 238117, 571615
Contact: Mrs. Rita Emerhor - MD/CEO.

HEROES OF FAITH NIGERIA LIMITED
Business: Marketing of Business Gift Items
Address: Nega Plaza Centry 21 Mall (2nd Floor), 14, Idowu Martins Street, Victoria Island, Lagos
Tel: (01) 4718385, 7731704, 08034700201
E-mail: heroesnig@yahoo.com

HERTZ CAR RENTAL (NIGERIA)
Business: Car Rentals
Address: 12, Keffi Street, Ikoyi, Lagos
Tel: (01) 2691099, 2691144, 2693978-80 (2L), 32050167 (2L) **Fax:** (01) 2691099
Website: www.hertzcarrentalnigeria.com
Contact: Mrs P. A. Otrofanowei - GM/CEO

HEXA CONSULT NIGERIA LIMITED
Business: General Contractors, Importer and Exporter.
Address: 42, .M. K. O. Abiola Way, Garki, Abuja
Tel: (09) 2341947, 08023092884, 08037273258, 08055245523
Contact: Alh. Yussuf Abdul-Ra'uf - Chairman/CEO

HIGH PERFORMANCE DISTRIBUTION NIGERIA LIMITED
Business: Distributution, Marketing and Wholesale of HP Informaton Technology Products
Address: Consortium House (1st Floor), Plot 1682, Sanusi Fafunwa Street, Victoria Island, lagos
Tel: (01) 7754577, 7755901, 2616614, 2610842, 2610838
Fax: (01) 2616614
* 50, Isaac John Street, Ikeja G R A, Lagos
Tel/Fax: (01) 4978115-7 (3L), 08033042824

HIGH-GRADE TECHNOLOGIES LIMITED
Business: Sales and Service of Computers, Printer Accessories, Manufacturer's Representative
Address: 89, Allen Avenue, Ikeja, Lagos
Tel: (01) 4934639, 4805944, 08033080572
E-mail: genicom@infoweb.abs.net
Contact: Mr. J. Azike - MD/CEO.

HIGH-POINT (Div. of Artee Ind. Ltd)
Business: Distribution of Sales of Footwear
Address: Plot 226, Musa Yar'Adua Street, off Idowu Martins Street, Victoria Island, Lagos
Tel: (01) 2625507-8 (2 L)
* Plot 740, Aminu Kano Crescent, Wuse II, Abuja
Tel: (09) 4135892-5 (4 L)

HIGHGATE INSURANCE BROKERS LIMITED
Business: Insurance Broking
Address: CEDDI Towers, 16, Wharf Road, Apapa, Lagos
Tel: (01) 5878180, 58041653, 5451990, 5878158
Fax: (01) 5452384
E-mail: highgate@beta.linkserve.com
* 68, Ogbia (Mbonu) Street, D-Line, Port Harcourt
Tel: (084) 237728
* Millenium Court (Ceddi Suite), Ogun State House, 4th Avenue, Cadastral Zone AO, Abuja
Contact: Senator D. O. Dafinone - Chairman
Mr. E. A. Ilori - GM/CEO

HIGHLIGHT NIGERIA LIMITED
Business: Conglomerate, Import & Export Trading, General

Merchandising
Address: 28E, Aminu Ahmed, P.O.Box 2585, Kano
Tel: (064) 649919, 645174, 08023088102
Fax: (064) 649919
Contact: Alh. Abdulkadir Ahmed - MD/CEO

HIGHWAY MANAGERS LIMITED
Business: Waste Management Services
Address: 2, Moshood Abiola Road, Oyingbo Bus-Stop, Ebute-Metta, Lagos
Tel: (01) 7753642-5 (3L), 4718203, 4718205
E-mail: highwaymanager@yahoo.com
Contact: Snr. Evang J. S. O Odunmbaku - Chairman/CEO.

HILL STATION HOTEL LIMITED
Business: Hospitality Services
Address: 10, Tudun-Wada Road, Jos
Tel: (073) 455300-2 (3 L), 455396, 454817, 452808.
Fax: (073) 455399
Contact: Major L. Ugboh (rtd.) - Chairman
Mr. A. Nuhu - GM/CEO

HIMMA FREIGHT LIMITED
Business: Shipping and Airfreight Services, Clearing and Forwarding, Warehouse and Transportation
Address: Plot 1, Kudaisi St, Olodi-Apapa, off Apapa-Oshodi Expressway (Warehouse Bus-Stop), Apapa, Lagos
Tel: (01) 5873255, 7732439 **Fax:** (01) 5450846
Contact: Chief T. O. Olubaji - Chairman/CEO

HINCKLEY GROUP
Business: Sales & Service of Iinformation Technology Products and Telecommunication Equipment
Address: 70, Evo Road, G.R.A. Phase II, Port Harcourt
Tel: (084) 234543, 572790
E-mail: hinckey@hinckleyassociates.com

HIRE PACIFIC INTERNATIONAL LIMITED
Business: Manufacturing and Sales of Security Doors and Furniture; General Contractors
Address: Plot 745, Kade Street, off Aminu Kano Crescent, Wuse II, Garki, Abuja.
Tel: (09) 4138764, 4138877-8 (2 L) **Fax:** (09) 4139294
*Plot 200B, Muri Okunola St, Victoria Island, Lagos
Tel: (01) 2612305, 2622068
Contact: Mr. Rafi Edry - MD/CEO

HITECH (NIGERIA) LIMITED
Business: Sales & Service of Banking Security Systems & Products
Address: 272, Ikorodu Road, Obanikoro, Lagos
Tel: (01) 5550274, 5550471, 7737904, 7737909
Fax: (01) 5550472
E-mail: hitech@rcl.nig.com
Contact: Dr. O. S. Kamanu - Chairman/CEO

HIUNA ELECTRONICS NIGERIA LIMITED
Business: Importation of Electronics, Electrical Materials & Equipment, Electrical &Mechanical Plants and Materials, Defence Hardwares & Accoutrement
Address: 35, Ribadu Road, S.W. Ikoyi, Lagos
Tel/Fax: (01) 2691256, 2690680
Contact: Prince H. I. Unachuwu - Chairman/CEO

HIYCO PLASTIC LIMITED
Business: Manufacturing of Plastic Kettles & Jugs
Address: Plot 63, Sharada Industrial Estate Phase 1, Kano
Tel: (064) 630672, 644797 **Fax:** (064) 648839
Contact: Alh. Hadi Ibrahim Yahaya - MD/CEO

HLB Z. O. OSOSANYA & COMPANY
Business: Chartered Accountants, Auditing & Investigation, Taxation Services
Address: Gloria House, off Alaafin Avenue, Oluyole Industrial Estate, Ibadan

HNB TRUSTEES LIMITED
Business: Capital Market Operations, Fund and Assets Management, Financial Services, Trustees, Leases
Address: Old Niger House, 163/165, Broad Street, Lagos
Tel: (01) 2669312, 4705444 **Fax:** (01) 2669611
E-mail: habibtrust@hyperia.com
* Plot 349, Olusegun Obasanjo Way, Wuse Zone 1, Abuja.
Tel/Fax: (09) 6716072
Contact: Mr. Dipo Akintonde - MD/CEO

HOESCH PIPE MILLS (NIGERIA) LIMITED
Business: Manufacturers of Galvanised & Black Pipes, Galvanised Bucket, Asbestos Products and Building Materials
Address: Henry Carr St, Ikeja Industrial Estate, Ikeja, Lagos
Tel: (01) 4974221-5 (5L), **Fax:** (01) 4937318
E-mail: hoesch@linkserve.com.ng
Contact: S. M. Patel - GM (Steel)
P. O. Ogbolu - Personnel/Admin. Manager

HOGG ROBINSON NIGERIA LIMITED
Business: Insurance Brokage
Address: 225, Ikorodu Road, Ilupeju, Lagos
Tel: (01) 4971360-3 (4L), 7749280-6 (4L)
Fax: (01) 4979590-2 (3L)
E-mail: hm@hogg.nig.com
Contact: Mr. E. A. Oyetoyan - Ag. GM

HOLBORN NIGERIA LIMITED
Business: Manufacturing of Textile Products
Address: Tundun Murtala, Bompai Industrial Estate, Kano
Tel: (064) 648032, 646896, 630923
Fax: (064) 638410
E-mail: holburn@intracom5.com
Contact: Mr. C. A. Jafal - MD/CEO

HOLD COMPUTERS & COMMUNICATIONS LIMITED
Business: Sales of Computers & Communication Equipment, Software Engineering, IT Training Services
Address: 24, Mohammadu Buhari Way, Kaduna
Tel: (062) 243334, 248231

HOLD-TRADE DRILLING COMPANY (NIGERIA) LIMITED
Business: Water Engineering Service
Address: 109, Opebi Road, Ikeja, Lagos
Tel/Fax: (01) 7746709, 8134053, 08023019319, 08033432487
E-mail: water@holdtradedrilling.com
Website: www.holdtradedrilling.com
Contact: Alh. A. A. Tahir - Chairman
Mr. S. A. Fadeyi - MD/CEO

HOLE 19 INVESTMENTS LIMITED
Business: Promotion & Marketing of Golf Equipment and Accessories, Gold Tournament Management, Corporate Incentives, Individual & Corporate Gift Items; Distribution of GSM Phones
Address: Plot 1089, Adeola Odeku St, Victoria Island, Lagos
Tel: (01) 4617221-2 (2L), 08034006354 **Fax:** (01) 2625341
E-mail: hole19@rcl.nig.com
Contact: Mr. Yaakov Chai - Chairman
Mr 'Dremi Ajidahun - MD/CEO

HOLGATE HAULAGE LIMITED
Business: Transportation of Goods, Importation and Sales of Trucks, Poultry Farming ,General Contractors
Address: Old Airport Road, after Jos Steel Rolling Mill, Industrial Area, Jos
Tel: (073) 464007, 465728 **Fax:** (073) 462728
Contact: Mr. Haruna Maitala - Chairman/CEO

HOLMAN BROTHERS (NIGERIA) LIMITED
Business: Sales and Service of Large Construction Equipment, Air Compressors, Drilling Equipment, Hydraulic Drill Rigs, Cranes and Draglines, Fire Extinguishers, Welding Equipment, Water Pumps, Generator Chains and Sprockets, Agricultural Tractors & Implements, Water/Geological Mobile Drill Rigs, Dumpers
Address: 26, Burma Road, Apapa, Lagos
Tel: (01) 5877057 **Fax:** (01) 5451629
E-mail: holman@beta.linkserve.com
Contact: Chief B. B. A. Verr - Chairman
Mr Nick Husk - MD/CEO

HOLT LEASING (Div. of John Holt Plc)
Business: Leasing of Cars, Generators, Airconditioners & Fire Extinguishers
Address: 25, Creek Road, Apapa, Lagos
Tel: (01) 5871531 **Fax:** (01) 5873726, 5876604, 5872232
* Warri-Sapele Road, Effurun, Warri.
Tel: (053) 25376, 252633
* 17, Azikiwe Road, Port Harcourt
Tel: (084) 334864, 236545, 333689, 330830
Fax: (084) 331721
* Nicon Noga Hilton Hotel, Abuja
Tel: (09) 5232838, 52318811 (Ext. 6372)

HOLT VENTURES (Div. of John Holt Plc)
Business: Marketing & Distribution of Consumer Items (Edibles, Electronic and Electrical Products); Warehousing and Merchandise Distribution Services; Manufacture of Cosmetics & Baby-Care Products
Address: Plot 3/4 Adewunmi Industrial Estate, Oregun Road, Ikeja, Lagos
Tel: (01) 4900180-4 (5L)
* Plot K & L, Ladipo Oluwole Street, Ikeja Industrial Estate, Ikeja, Lagos
Tel: (01) 4976570 **Fax:** (01) 4976572, 4976575

HOLY TRINITY HOSPITAL LIMITED
Business: Medical and HealthCare Delivery Services
Address: 110B, Obafemi Awolowo Way, Ikeja, Lagos
Tel: (01) 4961067, 4933728, 4933727
Contact: Chief (Mrs.) W. A. Awosika - Chairman

HOMAN ENGINEERING COMPANY LIMITED
Business: Oilfield Engineering & Steel Construction Services
Address: Plot 273, Trans-Amadi Ind., Layout, Port Harcourt
Tel: (084) 233424 **Fax:** (084) 238033

HOMAN INDUSTRIES LIMITED
Business: Manufacture of Steel and Galvanized Pipes
Address: Plot 15 & 16, Block XIII, Industrial Estate, Ogun State Housing Corporation, Idiroko Road, Otta.
Tel: (039) 722257-8 (2 L), 722610 **Fax:** (039) 722258
E-mail: homan@linkserve.com
Contact: Mr. Y. H. Leung - CEO

HOME GYM EQUIPMENT LIMITED
Business: Sports, Fitness & Health Equipment, Sport Wears, Shoes, Steambath & Sauna, Sport-Hall Floors
Address: 23, Norman Williams Street, S. W. Ikoyi, Lagos
Tel: (01) 2694403, 683220, 08033011025, 08033129089
Fax: (01) 2696088
* 73A, Opebi Rd, Ikeja, Lagos.
Tel: (01) 7734391
* Plot 751, Aminu Kano Crescent, Wuse II, Abuja
Tel: (09) 6714538, 08033188909
Contact: Mrs. Dorothy Boyd - MD/CEO

HOMELAND HOLDINGS LIMITED
Business: Sales of Electronic Sets and Appliances, Musical Instruments and Public Address Systems
Address: BB3 (I-F), Alaba Int'l Market, Ojo-Alaba, Lagos
Tel: (01) 5554590, 08033016878 **Fax:** (01) 5881694
Contact: Mr. Chris Obikobe - Chairman/CEO

HOMUS INDUSTRIES LIMITED
Business: Manufacture of PVC Pipes, Household Plastics Proplene Films and Bags and Plastics Drums
Address: Plot 2, 4, 6, 7, & 8 Block XIII, OSHC Industrial Estate, Idiroko Road, Otta, Ogun State
Tel: (01) 722256-9 (4 L) **Fax:** (039) 722259
E-mail: homan@linkserve.com
Contact: Mr. Y. H. Leung - CEO

HONDA MANUFACTURING (NIGERIA) LIMITED
Business: Manufacture and Assembly of Honda Motorcycles Power Products & Spare Parts
Address: Km 6, Ota-Idiroko Expressway, Ogun State
Tel: (039) 722431-3 (3L), (090) 405019
Fax: (039) 722431-2 (2L), (090) 405019
E-mail: hondamfg@starnet-net.ng
Contact: Mr. N Yanai - MD/CEO

HONEYWELL GROUP OF COMPANIES
Business: Conglomerate - Flour-Milling, Oil & Gas, Deep-Sea Trawling, Engineering, Investments, Real Estate
Address: 13, Agoro Odiyan Street, off Adeola Odeku Street, Victoria Island, Lagos
Tel: (01) 2610725-6 (2L), 2616227, 2620683
Fax: (01) 2616498
Website: www.honeywell-group.com
Contact: Dr. Oba Otudeko, MFR - Executive Chairman

HONEYWELL FISHERIES LIMITED
Business: Industrial Fishing (Shrimp and Fish Trawling), Processing and Exporting of Seafood

Address: 13, Agoro Odiyan Street, off Adeola Odeku Street, Victoria Island, Lagos
Tel: (01) 612557, 613153, 2616227 **Fax:** (01) 2616498
E-mail: hfl@beta.linkserve.com
Contact: Otunba Oba Otudeko, MFR - Exec. Chiarman
Mr. Kunjummen Thomas - MD

HONEYWELL FLOUR MILLS LIMITED
Business: Flour Milling
Address: 13, Agoro Odiyan Street, off Adeola Odeku Street, Victoria Island, Lagos
Tel: (01) 7740331, 612557, 613153, 2616227, 2620683, 2620684 **Fax:** (01) 7740331, 2616498
* 2nd Gate, Ashaye, Tin-Can Island Port Complex, Apapa-Oshodi Expressway, Lagos
Tel: (01) 5453679-83 (5L) **Fax:** (01) 5878308, 2616498
E-mail: hfml@honeywellflour.com
honeywellflour@micro.com.ng
Contact: Otunba Oba Otudeko, MFR - Chiarman
Mr. F. B. Odunayo - MD/CEO.

HONEYWELL OIL & GAS LIMITED
Business: Sale of Petroleum Products; Distribution of Lubricants and Chemicals; Manufacturing and Sales of Lubricants; Oil Bunkering and Marine Services; Coastal Transportation of Petroleum Products, Storage Depot/Facility for Petroleum Products, Petroleum Consultancy Services
Address: 13, Agoro Odiyan Street, off Adeola Odeku Street, Victoria Island, Lagos
Tel: (01) 2611234, 26164155, 2629490-3 (4L)
Fax: (01) 2610323, 2616498
E-mail: honeywelloil@cyberspace.net
Website: www.honeywelloil.com
* 8, Obagi Street, G.R.A. Phase I, Port Harcourt
Tel: (084) 233492, 487063
Contact: Otunba Oba Otudeko, MFR - Chiarman
Dr. Ben Attah - MD/CEO.

HONG KONG SYNTHETIC FIBRE COMPANY (NIGERIA) LTD
Business: Production of IBN, Real Wax & Super Print Textiles
Address: 158, Ilogbo Road, Otta, Ogun State
Tel: (039) 722774, 722268-9 (2 L), 722884 * (01) 2881654, 81762231 **Fax:** (039) 722269
E-mail: hksf@hotmail.com
hksf@infoweb.abs.net
hksf@skannet.com
Contact: Chief Victor S. L. Ma - MD/CEO

HONSYL MERCHANTS PLC
Business: Corporate Finance, Assets, Portfolio & Fund Managers, Forex Dealers, Leasing & Loans Syndications, Joint Venture Facilities, Oilfield Services, Management Consultancy
Address: 21, Adeboye Solanke Street, off Allen Avenue, Ikeja, Lagos
Tel: (01) 4965115, 3453536, 8179039, 08023124802
Fax: (01) 4963458
E-mail: honsyl@yahoo.com
merchants@honsylglobal.com
honsyl@nova.net.ng
Website: www.honsylglobal.com
* Plot 10, Pipeline Street, off Mini- Ezekwu, Rumuogba Estate, 1st Artillery, Port Harcourt.
Tel: (084) 334173 (090) 403253
E-mail: honsyl@yahoo.com
Contact: Alh. Mohammed Sule - Chairman
Dr. Jephter O. A. Sada - MD/CEO.

HORIZON GROUP
Business: Hospitality and Catering Services, Financial Services and Stockbroking, Mortgage Finance
Address: Plot 146, Lusaka Road, Wuse Zone 6, Abuja
Tel: (09) 5230224, 5230481
* Plot 1149, Aminu Kano Crescent, Wuse II, Abuja
Tel: (09) 4139386-9 (4 L) **Fax:** (09) 4139390
* Oluwatobi House, 71, Allen Avenue, Ikeja, Lagos
Tel: (01) 7741637, 4937637
Contact: Hon. 'Gbenga Onigbogi - Group Exec. Chairman

HORIZON FIBRES (NIGERIA) PLC
Business: Manufacturers and Exporters of Yarn
Address: 11A, Osborne Road, Ikoyi, Lagos
Tel: (01) 2693368-9 (2 L), 2693398-9 (2 L)
Fax: (01) 2692647, 2692491
* Choba Town, Port Harcourt
Tel: (084) 440728, 08033399534 **Fax:** (084) 234483

HORIZON STOCKBROKERS LIMITED
Business: Financial Services, Stockbroking
Address: Plot 146, Lusaka Road, Wuse Zone 6, Abuja
Tel: (09) 5230224, 5230481 **Fax:** (09) 5230481
* Oluwatobi House, 71, Allen Avenue, Ikeja, Lagos
Tel: (01) 5557443
Contact: Hon. Olugbenga Onigbogi - Chairman
Mr. Solomon O. Olamiju - MD/CEO

HORIZON FOCUS LIMITED
Business: Interior & Exterior Decortion and Design, Manufacturing and Marketing of Metal & Plastic Furniture, General Contractors
Address: 96, Awolowo Road, S.W. Ikoyi, Lagos
Tel: (01) 2690656, 2690998, 2692317 **Fax:** (01) 2690656
Contact: Mr. Sani Zinati - MD/CEO.

HORTICO WORKS NIGERIA LIMITED
Business: Garden Specialist, Horticultural and Landscaping Contractors, Consultancy Services, Sales &Service of Lawn Mowers &Garden Maintenance Equipment,
Address: Hortico House, Floral Acre, 69, Army Barracks Road, Ipaja, Lagos
Tel: (01) 7740517, 7741381, 4930419, 08023199350
E-mail: hortico2000@yahoo.com
Contact: Chief C. B. Bankole - Chairman/CEO

HORWATH DAFINONE
Business: Chartered Accountant, Auditing & Accounting Services, Tax Planning & Advisory Services, Financial & Management Consultancy, Installation of Computerised Accounting System
Address: Ceddi Towers, 16, Wharf Road, Apapa, Lagos
Tel: (01) 5451863-7 (5 L), 4823495-6 (2 L), 4823498-9 (2 L)
Fax: (01) 5452384
Website: www.dafinone.com
Contact: Senator D. O. Dafinone, OFR - Chairman
Mr. P. K. Bhasin - Managing Director

HOSPITAL BACKUP SERVICES LIMITED

Business: Medical Management & Consultancy Services, Supply of Medical Equipment & Products
Address: Agip Filling Station Complex, Plot 116, Isheri Road, Ojodu, Ikeja, Lagos
Tel: (01) 4705571, 4926256, 7762004, 08033282505
E-mail: hospitalback-up@metrong.com
* 29, Bello Street, off Ishaga Road, Surulere, Lagos
Tel: (01) 5850114, 7743983
* Plot 68, Area 7A Cornershops, Garki, Abuja
Tel: (09) 2347826
Contact: Mr. K..S. Ogedengbe - MD/CEO.

HOSQUIPS NIGERIA LIMITED

Business: Manufacturing of Hospital Furniture, Sales of Hospital/Medical Equipment & Ambulance
Address: 3, Bompai Road, opp. Central Hotel, Kano
Tel/Fax: (064) 644192, 648363, 08034527343
E-mail: hosquips2001@yahoo.com
Contact: Senator M.O. Oyewo - Chairman/CEO.

HOTEL & CATERING SERVICES LIMITED

Business: Hotel Management Services, Catering Services
Address: Ighogbadu Road, Warri
Tel: (053) 253225, 253208, 253087 **Fax:** (053) 253420
Contact: Chief Gordon B. McCarthy - Chairman/CEO

HOTEL BROADWAY LIMITED

Business: Hospitality, Catering, Conference Facilities
Address: Plot 796/3, Oka Akoko Crescent, off Ahmadu Bello Way, Area 3, Garki, Abuja
Tel: (09) 2347216-7 (2 L), 2348731-6 (6 L)
Fax: (09) 2347217
E-mail: hotelbroad@mlstn.com

HOTEL CONSULT LIMITED

Business: Hospitality Consultancy Services (Research & Feasibility Studies, Design & Operational Analysis, Project Management and Technical Services)
Address: Maryland Business Plaza (Suites BC 44-46), Ikorodu Road, Maryland, Ikeja, Lagos
Tel/Fax: (01) 4935999
E-mail: hcl01@consultant.com
Website: www.hotelconsultltd.com
Contact: Kunle Olushola - Exec. Director

HOTEL DE HORIZON LIMITED

Business: Hospitality & Catering Services, Conference Facilities, Subletting of Offices
Address: Plot 1149, Aminu Kano Crescent, Wuse II, Abuja
Tel: (09) 4139386-9 (4 L) **Fax:** (09) 4139390
Contact: Mrs. C. Bola Onigbogi - MD/CEO

HOTEL DORIS DEY, BENIN CITY

Business: Hospitality Services
Address: 35, Benin-Asaba Expressway, Benin City
Tel: (052) 257722, 259624 **Fax:** (052) 257354
Contact: Chief (Lady) Doris Obor - MD/CEO

HOTEL EXCEL LIMITED

Business: Hospitality & Catering Services
Address: Obada Close, off Refinery Road, P.M.B. 1199, Warri
Tel: (053) 257101-20 (20 L), 255906, 255432, 255585, 255907 **Fax:** (053) 252684
E-mail: enquiries@hotlexcelltd.com
Website: www.hotelexclltd.com
Contact: Chief M. E. Odeh (JP) - Chairman/CEO

HOTEL METROPOLE INTERNATIONAL LIMITED

Business: Hospitality Services, Hotel Management Services
Address: 19, Ogui Road, Enugu
Tel: (042) 251971, 255016, 252238 **Fax:** (042) 251971
E-mail: inter@infoweb.abs.net
Contact: Hon. (Chief) Dr. D.A. Jideofor - Chairman/CEO

HOTEL NEWCASTLE

Business: Hospitality & Catering Services
Address: Plot 11, Adebayo Mokuolu Street, off Gbagada Expressway, Anthony Village, Lagos
Tel: (01) 4971463-4 (2 L), 4971473, 4971475, 4971482
Fax: (01) 4971466, 4971480, 4971479
E-mail: hotellnc@alpha.linkserve.com

HOTEL PRESIDENTIAL LIMITED

Business: Hospitality Services
Address: Aba Expressway, Rumuola, Port Harcourt
Tel: (084) 575802-4 (3 L) **Fax:** (084) 239514
E-mail: hotelpresidential@alpha.linkserve.com

HOTEL ROSEBUD

Business: Hospitality Services
Address: Plot 685, Port Harcourt Crescent, off Ahmadu Bello Way, Area 11, Garki, Abuja
Tel: (09) 3142010-3 (4 L)

HOTEL ROYAL DAMGRETE LIMITED

Business: Hospitality Services
Address: 13/14, Factory Road, G.R.A. Umuahia
Tel: (088) 221510, 220018, 221955, 08056220310
Fax: (088) 223787
Contact: Dr Steve I. Ihedigbo - Chairman/CEO

HOTEL SUPPORT SERVICES LIMITED

Business: Hotel & Catering Management Services, Industrial Catering, Consultancy & Procurement Services
Address: 93, Allen Avenue, Ikeja, Lagos
Tel: (01) 4970003, 7737034, 7742309 **Fax:** (01) 3450720
E-mail: info@hotelsupport.com
Website: www.hotelsupport.com
* Excellence Hotel & Conference Centre Ijaiye-Isheri Road, Aguda-Ogba, Ikeja, Lagos
Tel: (01) 4922134, 4922924, 4923329, 4710779, 4710780, 4707494-5 (2 L)
E-mail: excellencehotel@hyperia.com
Contact: Mr Ayo Olowoporoku - Director/CEO

HOTEL TERMINUS COMPLEX LIMITED

Business: Hospitality, Catering Services
Address: 230-246, Azikiwe Road, P. O. Box 2608, Aba
Tel: (082) 231705, 233444, 440849
E-mail: htc@infoweb.abs.net
Contact: Chief J. D. Maduako - Chairman/CEO

HOTEL VICTORIA PALACE

Business: Hospitality Servicies, Restaurant & Catering Services, Conference & Banquet Facilities

Address: Plot 1623, Saka Jojo Street, off Idejo Street, Victoria Island, Lagos
Tel: (01) 2625901-8 (8 L) **Fax:** (01) 2625900
E-mail: hotelvp@alpha.linkserve.com

HOTSPORTS INTERNATIONAL LIMITED
Business: Sports Marketing Services
Address: 2, Olayinka Bamgbose Street (Top Floor), off Toyin/Olowu Street, Ikeja, Lagos
Tel: (01) 4930191, 08023428944

HRN TRAVEL LIMITED
Business: Travel Agency
Address: 221, Ikorodu Road, Ilupeju, Lagos
Tel: (01) 4935327-9 (3 L), 7730443 **Fax:** (01) 4935327
E-mail: hrnt@hyperia.com
Contact: Mr Justin Olabode Emmanuel - Chairman

HS DOORS LIMITED
Business: Importation & Sales of Wooden/Steel Security Doors, Production of Wooden Doors
Address: 1, Tony Oghenejode Close, off Omorinre Johnson Street, off Admiralty Way, Lekki Phase 1, Lagos
Tel: (01) 5555361-2 (2 L), 08022961960
Fax: (01) 5555360
E-mail: hsdoorsltd@yahoo.com
Contact: Mr. Tony Akpo Oghenejode - Chairman/CEO

HUFAWA ENTERPRISES LIMITED
Business: Tanning of Hides & Skins
Address: Plot 44/45, Sharada Ind. Estate Phase III, Kano
Tel: (064) 668921, 668922
Fax: (064) 666812, 669580
Contact: Mr. Mohammed Osman El-Tayeb - Chairman
Mr. Hussein Fahez Mahaloude - MD/CEO

HUGE INVESTMENT LIMITED
Business: Maritime Services, Clearing and Forwarding, Manufacturing, General Merchants
Address: 25, Adele Road, Apapa, Lagos
Tel: (01) 5877446 **Fax:** (01) 5455663
E-mail: enquiries@hugegroup.org
Website: www.hugegroup.org

HULL BLYTH NIGERIA (formerly Elder Dempster Agencies Ltd)
Business: Liner & Tanker Shipping Agency, Freight Forwarding, Commodities Export, Warehousing, Cargo Liner Services, Plant Hire, Container Repairs
Address: 34, Wharf Road, Apapa, Lagos
Tel: (01) 5803140-4 (5L), 5803410-4 (5L)
Fax: (01) 5871526
E-mail: hbntankers@hull-blyth.com
*121, Customs Street, Port Harcourt
Contact: Mr. James B. Adegboye - Finance Director

HUMAN EDGE LIMITED
Business: Human Resource Consultancy & Staffing Services
Address: 33, Adeniyi Jones Avenue, Ikeja, Lagos
Tel: (01) 4936528, 4936530, 4706332
E-mail: hedge@mwebafrica.com
Website: www.heworld.com
Contact: Mr. Folarin G. Longe - MD/CEO
Mr. A. T. Akinade - Chairman

HUMPHREY ORONSAYE & COMPANY
Business: Estate Surveying and Valuation, Feasibility Studies
Address: 1, Rasaq Okoya Lane, off Bamgbose Street, Lagos
Tel: (01) 2646212, 4750608, 08033034858, 0802111085
Fax: (01) 2646212
* 9B, Odion Road, Opp. I.C.E Warri
Tel: (053) 251926

HUNTERS PUBLICITY LIMITED
Business: Advertising & Marketing Communication Services
Address: 12, Jibowu Street, Yaba, Lagos
Tel: (01) 2885375, 4714149, 7911569 **Fax:** (01) 2880718
E-mail: hunters@supernet300.com
Website: www.hunterpublicityltd.coms
Contact: Mr. Raymond A. Kester - Chairman/CEO

HYDRIL TECHNICAL DRILLING & PRODUCTION SERVICES NIGERIA LIMITED
Business: Oilwell Drilling Services
Address: Km. 4, Effurun-Sapele Road, Effurun, Warri
Tel/Fax: (053) 252565 (Ext 44833)
E-mail: hydril@alpha.linkserve.com
* 103B, Opebi Road, Ikeja, Lagos
Tel: (01) 4932680
* Neptune Maritime Base, Aker Road, Rumuolumeni,Port Harcourt.
Tel/Fax: (084) 611201

HYDRO CONSTRUCTION & ENGINEERING COMPANY LTD
Business: Borehole Drilling, Geophysical Investigation, Water Engineering Services, Soil & Water Remediation, Spill Control etc
Address: 24, Burma Road, Apapa, Lagos
Tel: (01) 5871218, 5872722 **Fax:** (01) 5817218
E-mail: hydro@hyperia.com
Contact: Prince Patrick K Avoseh - Chairman
Mr. Stefanos Stavrou - MD/CEO

HYDRO RESOURCES INDUSTRIES LIMITED
Business: Bottling and Marketing of Natural Spring Water
Address: Plot 5, Mission Road, Umualum, Nekede, Owerri
Tel: (083) 234631, 234894, 08033427542
E-mail: rokana@infoweb.abs.net
Contact: Engr. C. C. Ugwuh - Chairman

HYDRODIVE NIGERIA LIMITED
Business: Oilfield and Marine Engineering Services, Subsea Solution Provider
Address: 19B, Festival Road, off Adetokunbo Ademola Street, Victoria Island, Lagos
Tel: (01) 2618566, 2621756, 2610732, 7749433
Fax: (01) 2618566, 2621756
E-mail: hydive@phca.linkserve.com

HYDROFLOW LIMITED
Business: Water Engineering, Hydrogeology and Geotechnics, Sales of Water Pumps & Accessories
Address: 27A, Rabah Road, P.O.Box 1487, Kaduna
Tel: (062) 248974 **Fax:** (062) 248947
Contact: Engr. Ibrahim Onimisi - MD/CEO

HYDROWORK LIMITED
Business: Water and Civil Engineering Contractors

Address: Kabir Usman Road, G.R.A., Katsina
Tel: (065) 434632, 434633 **Fax:** (065) 434081
Contact: Alh. I. M. Inuwa - Chairman
Engr.A. K. Castel - MD/CEO

HYGEIA NIGERIA LIMITED
Business: Medical & Healthcare Services, Hospital Ownership & Management (Lagoon Hospital)
Address: 11A, Idejo Street, off Adeola Odeku Street, Victoria Island, Lagos
Tel: (01) 2629284-5 (2L), 4607170-5 (6L), 7738954, 08034020280 **Fax:** (01) 5875381
* 8, Marine Road, G.R.A. Apapa, Lagos
Tel: (01) 5804063-4 (2L), 5874081, 7742187
Fax: (01) 5450119, 5875381
* 97/101, Obafemi Awolowo Way, Ikeja, Lagos
E-mail: hygeiahmo@hyperia.com
Website: www.hygeiahmo.com
Contact: Mr Kola Awokoya - Director (Mktg/Business Dev.)

HYSON NIGERIA LIMITED
Business: Logistic Services to the Oil and Gas Industry
Address: Plot 460, Lobito Crescent off Adetokunbo Ademola Crescent, Wuse II, Abuja
Tel: (09) 4134023, 4134515 **Fax:** (09) 4139503
E-mail: hyson@linkserve.com.ng
* Coscharis Plaza (3rd Floor), 65A, Adeola Odeku Street, Victoria Island, Lagos
Tel: (01) 2617736, 2618057, 2622072 **Fax:** (01) 2611183
Contact: Mr. M. S. Barkindo - MD/CEO

HYUN SUNG HYDRAULIC MACHINERY COMPANY LTD
Business: Manufacturing, Sales and Maintenance of Plastic Manufacturing Machinery
Address: 502, UDB Road, Hotoro G. R. A Ext., Tarauni, Kano
Tel: (064) 643186, 648613, 315879 **Fax:** (064) 636612
Contact: Mr. S. H. Lee - Chairman/CEO

HYUNDAI HEAVY INDUSTRIES COMPANY NIGERIA LTD
Business: Oil & Gas Industry Construction Services, Power Plants, Construction Equipment, Shipbuildimg
Address: 318, Woji Road, G R A Phase II, Port Harcourt
Tel: (084) 231305, 233194, 235989, 237478
Fax: (084) 237478, 233194 (Ext. 121)
E-mail: hhiph@hhinig.com
Website: www.hhi.co.kr
* Fortune Towers (5th Floor), 27/29, Adeyemo Alakija Street, Victoria Island, Lagos
Tel: (01) 2621399, 2626778-9 (2L) **Fax:** (01) 2621575

HYUNDAI MOTORS NIGERIA LIMITED
Business: Sales and Service of Hyundai Automobiles
Address: Akin Adesola/180, Kofo Abayomi Street, Victoria Island, Lagos
Tel: (01) 2612539, 7749444, 7749777, 7751774, 7758080, 7765556, 08034799999
E-mail: hyundainigeria@aol.com
* Plot 1, Block B. Gbagada Industral Estate, Oworonsoki Expressway, Gbagada, Lagos.
Tel: (01) 4960586, 7732661-2 (2L), 7742040, 7769457

HYWILLS GRAPHICS NIGERIA LIMITED
Business: Colour Separation
Address: 115, Ladipo Street, Mushin, Lagos
Tel: (01) 4528720, 4740906, 08023187131
E-mail: hywillsgraphics@skannet.com
Contact: Mr. William Odudu - Chairman

I.B.N NIGERIA LIMITED
Business: General Merchandising, Export Business
Address: 25B, Marine Road, G.R.A, Apapa, Lagos
Tel: (01) 5872149, 5872318 **Fax:** (01) 5872789

I.B.W. BUREAU DE CHANGE LIMITED
Business: Bureau de Change Services
Address: Lagos Airport Hotel Shopping Plaza (Shop 3), 111, Obafemi Awolowo Way, Ikeja, Lagos
Tel: (01) 4978670-9 (10 L) (Ext. 8597), 080230650117, 08033273242
E-mail: benkale2001@yahoo.com
Contact: Mrs. Mabel Amadi - Chairman/CEO

I. F. JOHNSON LIMITED
Business: Sales of Hospital Equipment, Laboraroty/Scientific Equipment and Chemicals; Manufacturing of Hospital Furniture
Address: 72, Kudirat Abiola Way, Oregun
Tel: (01) 3450522, 4701348
Fax: (01) 2661468, 7921157
E-mail: ifmedical@yahoo.com
Contact: Mrs. G. E. Okpara - Exec. Director

I. T. RESOURCES LIMITED
Business: Sales of Printers and UPS
Address: 227, Ikorodu Road, Obanikoro, Lagos
Tel: (01) 4930593, 4971623, 08023063290, 08023137735, 08033119312
Contact: Mr. Biodun Balogun - Chief Executive

I.T.I.S. SECURITIES LIMITED
Business: Stockbroking, Investment Advisors, Issuing House
Address: 9A, Raymond Njoku Street, S.W. Ikoyi, Lagos
Tel: (01) 2695382-3 (2 L) **Fax:** (01) 2695380
E-mail: itisse@anyiam-osigwe.com
* Plot 1294, Parakou Crescent, off Aminu Kano Crescent, Zone A7, Wuse II, Abuja
Tel: (09) 5238943

IAL NIGERIA LIMITED
Business: Shipping and Airfreight Services, Clearing and Forwarding Agency, Export, Warehousing
Address: 11, Creek Road, Apapa, Lagos
Tel: (01) 5450963, 5453491, 5453903
Fax: (01) 5451091, 2693041
E-mail: ial@ialnigeria.com
sales@ialnigeria.com
Website: www.alnigeria.com
* 22C, Forces Avenue, Port Harcourt.
Tel: (084) 230648
* Plot 74, Ralf Sodehinde Street, off Ahmadu Bello Way, Central Business District, Abuja
Contact: Mr. Ismail Adetola Lawal - Chairman/CEO

IBACHEM LIMITED (Ibafon Chemicals Ltd)
Business: Importation and Distribution of Chemicals, Haul-

age of Specialised Chemical, Manufacturing of Plastic Containers, Recycling of Plastic Materials, Brake Fluid Packaging
Address: Ibru Yard, Oshodi Expressway, Ibafon Apapa
Tel: (01) 5875480, 5450520, 5450525, 5450545
Fax: (01) 5450505
E-mail: ibachem@beta.linkserve.com
Contact: Olorogun M. C. O. Ibru - Chairman

IBAFON OIL LIMITED
Business: Tank Farm Operations, Marketing of Petroleum Products, Haulage & Distribution Services
Address: Ibru Yard, Oshodi-Apapa Expressway , Ibafon, near Tincan Island Port, Apapa, Lagos
Tel: (01) 5450520, 5450525, 4808105, 7767889
Fax: (01) 5450505
E-mail: ibachem@beta.linkserve.com

IBALEX NIGERIA LIMITED
Business: Importers and Wholesalers of Building Materials, Sanitary Wares, Ceramic Tiles and Marble
Address: Plot 407/413, Oshodi Expressway, Ilasamaja, Lagos
Tel: (01) 4522171, 4522979, 4523615, 7740227-8 (2L), 08034021072, 08034021074-5 (2L)
Fax: (01) 4522171
* 12B, Akin Adesola Street, Victoria Island, Lagos.
Tel: (01) 4617766-7 (2L), 08033013288
* Plot 1501, Durban St, A-6, Adetokunbo Ademola Crescent, Wuse II, Abuja.
Tel: (09) 5234908, 08037863934
Contact: Mr. Abimbola Ogunbanjo - Chairman
Mr. Youssef Fattal - MD/CEO

IBEANU BROTHERS & COMPANY LIMITED
Business: Sales of Electronic Products and Equipment, Manufacturing of Domestic Soap and Detergent, Marketers of Petroluem Products
Address: 46, Aba-Owerri Road, Umungasi, Aba
Tel: (082) 221478
Contact: Chief. A. N. Ibeanu - Chairman/CEO

IBETO GROUP LIMITED
Business: Manufacturing, Petrochemicals & Colour Processing, Community Banking, Real Estate Development Hotel Management
Address: 60-61, Igwe Orizu Rd, Otolo, Nnewi, Anambra State
Tel: (046) 460665, 460296, 460296, 460980, 460739, 462890
Fax: (046) 462894
E-mail: info@ibeto.com
ibeto@infoweb.abs.net
* 4A, Adeola Hopewell St, Victoria Island, Lagos
Tel: (01) 2616637, 2619194, 2625915-6 (2L)
Fax: (01) 2619667
E-mail: ibetolag@infoweb.abs.net
Contact: Mr. C. M. Ibeto - Exec. Chairman

IBFC AGUSTO TRAINING LIMITED
Business: Value-Based Banking & Financial Trainers
Address: Amazing Grace Plaza (3rd Floor), 2E-4E, Ligali Ayorinde Street, Victoria Island, Lagos
Tel: (01) 4704515, 4619895-6 (2 L), 2705107, 7736534, 4803890 **Fax:** (01) 4619895
E-mail: knowledge@ibfcagusto.com
Website: www.ibfcagusgto.com
Contact: Mrs. Folashade Odunaiya - Chairman
Mr. Dima N. Oruene - MD/CEO

IBIKUNLE LAWAL ORGANISATION LIMITED
Business: Property Development, Intergrated Farming, Publishing, Commercial Stores, Educational Institutions
Address: Ibikunle Lawal Plaza, Ilesha Road, Ile-Ife
Tel: (036) 231280, 233628
* Kun-faya-Koon House, 25, First Avenue, by E Close Festac Town, Lagos.
Tel: (01) 884241
Contact: Alh. (Chief) M. Ibikunle Lawal - Chairman/CEO

IBILE HOLDINGS LIMITED (Lagos State Investment Co.)
Business: Investment Promotion and Portfolio Management, Property Development and Management, Joint Venture Finance, Leasing, Trade and L.P.O Finance Net2phone Franchise
Address: Kajola Hose, 62/64, Campbell Street, Lagos
Tel: (01) 2600030-4 (5 L), 2637211 **Fax:** (01) 2637211
E-mail: ibile@beta.linkserve.com
Contact: Dr. I. A. Adewusi - MD/CEO

IBIMO INDUSTRIES LIMITED
Business: Manufacturing of Toothpicks & Aluminium Electric-Cable Clips, Importation of Chemicals forBrewed Drinks, Paints, Cosmetics, Plastic & Foam
Address: 16, Milverton Avenue, Aba
Tel: (082) 221075, 227432 Fax: (082) 221075
E-mail: ibyimo@yahoo.com
* Ogbor Hill Industrial Estate, NEAR 7Up, Aba
Tel: (082) 221075, 227432, 351676, 352272, 352274
Contact: Chief (Dr.) Engr. Iboko Imo Iboko - Chairman/CEO

IBRO HOTELS, ABUJA
Business: Hospitality Services
Address: Michael Okpara Road, Wuse Zone 5, Abuja
Tel: (09) 5233200-9 (10 L) **Fax:** (09) 5231263
Contact: Alh. Abubakar Ibrahim - MD/CEO

IBRON LIMITED
Business: Sales of Industrial Control Equipment, Components & Instrumentation, Automation of Electrical Components & Large-Scale Control Systems
Address: Ibru Complex, Oshodi Expressway, Ibafon, Lagos
Tel: (01) 5870615, 618282 **Fax:** (01) 5872476, 616622
E-mail: ibron@infoweb.abs.net

IBRU MERCHANDISE 33 LIMITED
Business: General Merchandising and Warehousing
Address: 6, Louis Solomon Close, off Ahmadu Bello Way, Victoria Island, Lagos
Tel: (01) 2610543, 2616020, 610559
* Ibru Port Complex, Oshodi-Apapa Expressway (Warehouse Bus-Stop), Ibafon, Apapa, Lagos
Tel: (01) 5803249, 5870438, 5871012, 5871564
Fax: (01) 5872476
Contact: Olorogun Oskar C. J. Ibru - MD/CEO

IBRU SEA FOODS LIMITED
Business: Fish Trawling and Marketing, Agro-Industrial Based Farming ; Irrigation Engineering

Address: Ibru Port Complex, Oshodi-Apapa Expressway (Warehouse Bus-Stop), Ibafon, Apapa, Lagos
Tel: (01) 5871012, 5872476, 08023130827
E-mail: ibron@infoweb.abs.net
emsee@infoweb.abs.net
Contact: Olorogun Oskar C. J. Ibru - Exec. Director

IBRU TRANSPORT COMPANY LIMITED
Business: Shipping and Road, Haulage Services
Address: Ibru Port Complex, Oshodi-Apapa Expressway (Warehouse Bus-Stop), Ibafon, Apapa, Lagos
Tel: (01) 5871012, 5870615, 5872476, 08023130827
Fax: (01) 5872476
Contact: Olorogun Oskar C. J. Ibru - MD/CEO

IBTC ASSET MANAGEMENT LIMITED
Business: Stockbroking, Portfoilio Management, Investment Advisory Services
Address: I.B.T.C. Place, Walter Carrington Crescent, Victoria Island, Lagos
Tel: (01) 2626520-40 (21 L) **Fax:** (01) 2626541-2 (2 L)
E-mail: IBTC@IBTCLagos.com
asstmanagement@IBTCLagos.com
Website: www.IBTCLagos.com
* Total House, Plot 247, Herbert Macaulay Way, Central Business District, Abuja
E-mail: ibtcabja@IBTCLagos.com
Tel: (09) 2348176-8 (3 L) **Fax:** (09) 2346805
* 234, Aba Road, Port Harcourt
Tel: (084) 612702, 612718, 612732, 612747
Fax: (084) 612981
E-mail: ibtcph@IBTCLagos.com
Contact: Mr. Yinka Sanni - GM/CEO

IBUKUNOLA PRINTERS (NIGERIA) LIMITED
Business: Commercial Printing and Litho Packaging
Address: 3, Wey St, off Agege Motor Rd, Olosa, Lagos
Tel: (01) 4520846, 4522993, 522428, 520992, 08023009258, 08037181886 **Fax:** (01) 4522993
* 5, Queen Elizabeth Road, Mokola, Ibadan
Tel: (02) 2412212, 2412284
Contact: Mrs. Juliana Odunayo-Ojo - Chairman
Mr. Kehinde Akinleye - GM/CEO

ICIC (DIRECTORY PUBLISHERS) LIMITED
Business: Publishing of Directories, Printing Services
Address: ICIC Buidling, 28, Taoridi Street, opp. Old Census Office, off Babs Animashaun Rd, Surulere, Lagos
Tel: (01) 5454155, 830163, 830909 **Fax:** (01) 5454156
E-mail: icicpub2002@yahoo.com
Contact: Chief Olu Adeyemi - Chairman/CEO

ICMG SECURITIES LIMITED
Business: Issuing House, Stockbroking, Financial Advisors
Address: 8B, Ademola Street, S.W. Ikoyi, Lagos
Tel: (01) 2673824, 4801352 **Fax:** (01) 2673824
E-mail: icmgsec@yahoo.com
Website: www.icmgsec.com
Contact: Mr. Akemere Mike Osime - Chairman/CEO

icoN eTECHNOLOGIES LIMITED
Business: Engineering, Communication, Telecommunication, Information Technology Services and Training
Address: 3, Oliyide Street, off Unity Road, Ikeja, Lagos
Tel: (01) 4330891, 08000432336, 08037214390
* Suite 24, Gwaripnpa Plaza, Gwarinpa, Abuja
E-mail: info@iconetechnologies.com
Website: www.iconetechnologies.com
Contact: Engr. McPaul Fide-Omojafoh - MD/CEO
Engr. Chima Uzomba - GM (Projects)

ICON MARINE SERVICES LIMITED
Business: Petrochemicals, Engineering, Marine, Oil, Gas, Logistics, Procurement and Training
Address: 3, Oliyide Street, off Unity Road, Ikeja, Lagos
Tel: (01) 4330891, 08000432336, 08037214390
* Suite 24, Gwaripnpa Plaza, Gwarinpa, Abuja
E-mail: info@iconmarine.com
Website: www.iconmarine.com
Contact: Mr. Temi I. G. Anifowoshe - Exec. Dir. (Operations)
Engr. Stanley N. Agwara - Business Dev. Manager

ICON STOCKBROKERS LIMITED
Business: Capital Market, Finance and Advisory Services
Address: N.I.D.B. House (8th Floor), 63/71, Broad St, Lagos
Tel: (01) 2663293, 2661403 **Fax:** (01) 2663293
E-mail: nwanzeec@nigol.net.ng
Contact: Mr. Peter Eloka Okocha OON - Chairman
Mr. E. Chike Nwanze - Vice Chairman/CEO

IDDO PLASTIC LIMITED
Business: Manufacturers of PVC Footwear
Address: Plot 4C, Ijora Causeway, Ijoro, Lagos
Tel: (01) 5878286, 5837026, 5453722-4 (3 L), 7903155
Fax: (01) 2627751, 5453724
E-mail: iddo@infoweb.abs.net
Contact: Mr. Harish Chulani - Chairman/CEO

IDEA KONSULT LIMITED
Business: Sales of Computers & Accessories, Training & Consultancy, Networking & VSAT Solutions
Address: Old Leventis Buidling (1st Floor), 5, Lebanon Street, Dugbe, Ibadan
Tel: (02) 2410262, 2411171, 2411488, 08023262027, 08023448964, 08033265544 **Fax:** (02) 2411488
E-mail: idea@skannet.com
ideakonsult@yahoo.com
Website: www.ideakonsult.com
Contact: Mr. Oluwole Agbaje - MD/CEO

IDEAL FLOUR MILLS LIMITED
Business: Milling of Wheat and Maize
Address: 4A, Sapara Williams Close, off Idowu Martins Street, Victoria Island, Lagos
Tel: (01) 2614575, 2618682
*Nnamdi Azikiwe St, Kudendan Ind Layout, Kaduna
Tel: (062) 232286, 233213 **Fax:** (062) 232379
Contact: Mr. Fahd El-Khouri - MD/CEO

IDEAL HOME FINISHES & FIXTURES LIMITED
Business: Sales of Lighting Fittings, Sanitary Wares and Iron Mongery; Interior Decoration Services
Address: 103, Awolowo Road, Ikoyi, Lagos
Tel: (01) 2690373-4 (2L), 2690376, 2671563, 2693870-1 (2L), **Fax:** (01) 269870-1 (2L)
Contact: Mr. Ernest I. Oji - MD/CEO

IDEAL INFOSYSTEMS (Div of Leventis Group)
Business: Distribution of Electronic Products and GSM Telephones
Address: Leventis Building, 2, Wharf Road, Apapa, Lagos
Tel: (01) 5878600-1 (2 L), 5878537, 08033017502
E-mail: idealinfogm@idealcom.net
Website: www.ideal.gr
Contact: Mr. Dennis Varivias - GM

IDEAL INSURANCE BROKERS LIMITED
Business: Insurance Broking
Address: 5, Atunwa Street, off Unity Road, Ikeja, Lagos
Tel/Fax: (01) 4975909
E-mail: idealinsure@hotmail.com
idealinsure@yahoo.com
* Abuja Shopping Mall (Suite C15), Wuse Zone 4, Abuja.
Tel: (09) 5231066
Contact: Alh. A. O. Abdulkadir - Chairman/CEO

IDEAL TRAVEL AGENCY LIMITED
Business: Travel Agency, Tour Operation
Address: Delta Hotel Building, 169, Aba Road, Port Harcourt
Tel: (084) 234219, 487444, 08037113135
E-mail: idealtravel@yahoo.com
Contact: Mr Richard Enwerem - Director/CEO

IDEAS IMC LIMITED
Business: Events Management, Corporate Promotions and Public Relations
Address: Plot 281, Gbagada Expressway, Gbagada, Lagos
Tel: (01) 7740575, 7736000, 7746000
Fax: (01) 5551030, 5551040
E-mail: ideascom@hyperia.com
Website: www.ideascom-ng.com
Contact: Mr. S. A. Akeju - Chairman/CEO

IDEKE SHIPPING LIMITED
Business: Freight Forwarding, Logistics Providers
Address: 7C, Creek Road, Apapa, Lagos
Tel: (01) 5457920-23 (4 L, 5453851-2 (2 L), 7741954
Fax: (01) 5453853, 5457923
E-mail: ideke.lagos@alpha.linkserve.com
Website: www.ideke.com
* 20, Degema Close, Rumuibekwe Housing Estate, Port Harcourt
Tel: (084) 611316, 612488
Fax: (084) 612490, 612410
E-mail: ideke.ph@phca.linkserve.com
Contact: Chief James Ezea - Chairman

IDRIS SULAIMON & ASSOCIATES
Business: Financial & Management Consultants
Address: ED House (2nd Floor), 47, Marina, Lagos
Tel: (01) 2662559 **Fax:** (01) 2662597

I-DSAM NIGERIA LIMITED
Business: Freight Forwarding
Address: Nnewi Building, 1-3, Creek Road, Apapa, Lagos
Tel: (01) 5452498, 5876334, 08033003344
Fax: (01) 5874573
E-mail: idsam2002@yahoo.com
Contact: Mr. Chima W. Idika - Chairman/CEO

IEC NIGERIA LIMITED
Business: Sales, Installation and Maintenance of Industrial Kitchen and Catering Equipment, Industrial Cold Rooms, Laundry and Drycleaning Equipment
Address: 230, Awolowo Road, S.W. Ikoyi, Lagos
Tel: (01) 2693160, 2693442, 2694596, 4615461, 7762626
Fax: (01) 2693362
E-mail: iec@cobranet.org
iec@hyperia.com
Website: www.iec.com.ng

IFESINACHI INDUSTRIES LIMITED
Business: Transporation Services
Address: 2, Ikorodu Road, Jibowu, Lagos
Tel: (01) 5455269, 861102, 863918, 08033321046
* Banex Plaza, Plot 750, Aminu Kano Crescent, Wuse II, Abuja
Contact: Prince Emeka Mamah - MD/CEO

IFEX WORLDWIDE COURIER LIMITED
Business: Courier Business
Address: 2, Ikorodu Road, Jibowu, Lagos
Tel: (01) 5821462-3 (2L), 7754808, 7911369, 7922861, 08023024491-3 (3L), 08023024500-5 (5L), 08023261090, 08023836075, 08033010855, 08035713425
E-mail: ifex@infoweb.abs.net
Contact: Prince Emekea Mamah - Chairman/CEO

IFOY NIGERIA LIMITED
Business: Import of Water Engineering Equipment and Pipes
Address: Amuwo-Odofin Shopping Complex, opp. Army Signal Hq, Badagry Expressway, Mile 2, Lagos
Tel: (01) 4702283, 08033278936
Contact: Mr. John Oy. Ezenwa - Chairman/CEO

IGNORA INVESTMENT COMPANY LIMITED
Business: Sales of Fire Extinguishers, Importers, General Merchants
Address: Trade Fair Complex, Lagos-Badagry Expressway, Abule-Osun, Ojo, Lagos
Tel: (01) 3208784
* Zone D, Block 7 (Shop 51), ASPAMDA Plaza, Trade Fair Complex, Badagry Expressway, Lagos

IGUMS INTERNATIONAL LIMITED
Business: Sales of Oilfield Services Materials, Industrial & Safety Tools, Marine, Technical & Structural Equipment, Fabrication, Instrumentation & Pipeline Engineering
Address: 148, Aba Road, Port Harcourt
Tel: (084) 233987, 612960, 613107, 0803399367
Fax: (084) 233987, 613107
E-mail: igums@yahoo.co.uk
Contact: Mr. Ignatius U. Mbachu - Chairman/CEO

IJEWERE & COMPANY
Business: Tax Consulting, Auditing & Investigation, Secretarial Services, Management Consultancy
Address: Lorunda House (1st Floor), 106/110, Lewis Street, Lagos Island, Lagos
Tel: (01) 2633494, 2635770, 2630691, 08034704077
Fax: (01) 2635770

E-mail: ijewere@infoweb.abs.net
* Afribank Nigeria Building, Plot 34, Trans-Amadi Industrial Layout, Port Harcourt
Tel: (084) 489722
Contact: E. I. Ijewere - Managing Partner

IJEWERE CONSULTING LIMITED
Business: Management Consultancy Services
Address: 106/110, Lewis Street (3rd Floor), Lafiaji, Lagos
Tel: (01) 2631958, 2630691, 2633507, 2634441
Fax: (01) 2635770
E-mail: ijewere@infoweb.abs.net
Contact: Mr. E. I. Ijewere - Chairman
Mr. F. B. Madessou - MD/CEO

IJORA TEXTILE MILLS LIMITED
Business: Manufacturers of Textile Fabrics
Address: Plot 37/39, Iganmu Industrial Estate, Eric Moore Road, Surulere, Lagos
Tel: (01) 7748843, 801860-4 (5 L), 837970
Fax: (01) 5831314, 5877280
Contact: Mr. P. B. S. Bhardwaj - Chairman

IJU INDUSTRIES LIMITED
Business: Manufacturing and Marketing of Rubber Products
Address: Garbs Motors Building, 39, Awka Road, Onitsha
* ASMPDA Plaza, Zone D, Block 1, Shop 14, Trade Fair Complex, Badagry Expressway, Lagos
Tel: (01) 3208470
Contact: Chief G. A. Onwugbenu - Chairman/CEO

IKB INDUSTRIES LIMITED
Business : Importation and Sales of Skin and Hair Care Products, General Merchandising
Address: Plot 24, Jimoh Odutola Street, off Eric Moore Road, Iganmu Industrial Estate, Surulere, Lagos
Tel: (01) 4705531, 2880261, 5837907 **Fax:** (01) 5837907
E-mail: ikb-indus@lycos.com
Contact: Chief I. K. B. Igboanugo - Chairman/CEO

IKE GOD GROUP OF COMPANIES (NIGERIA) LIMITED
Business: Sales of Electronic Appliances, Transportation
Address: 7, Adeyemo Street, by Int'l Airport Road (7-8 Bus-Stop), Mafoluku, Oshodi, Lagos
* H55 & A72B, Alaba Int'l Market, Ojo, Lagos
Tel: (01) 5892658, 7754415
114, 121 & 141, Nnamdi Azikiwe St, Idumota, Lagos
Tel: (01) 2663462
* 95, Hospital Road, Aba.
Tel: (082) 223335
* 13 & 17, Pound Road, Aba
Tel: (082) 225273

IKEJA HOTEL PLC
Business: Hotel Proprietors and Managers
Address: Federal Palace Suites Hotel, Ahmadu Bello Way, Victoria Island, Lagos
Tel: (01) 2610030, 2623116-25 (10 L)(Ext 250)
Fax: (01) 2619009, 2625815
E-mail: ihlservices@micro.com.ng
ikejahotel@micro.com.ng
Contact: Mr. Goodie M. Ibru - Chairman/CEO
Mr. I. A. Oko - Controller of Operations

IKELOMU GROUP (WEST AFRICA) LIMITED
Business: Importation, Distribution & Installation of Electrical Equipment (Distribution Transformers, Feeder Pillars, Aluminium Conductors and Insulators)
Address: 27, Abeokuta Street, Anifowoshe, Ikeja, Lagos
Tel/Fax: (01) 4960747
E-mail: ikelomu@linkserve.com
Contact: Mrs. Eby Ilomuanya - MD/CEO

ILA INDUSTRIES LIMITED
Business: Cotton Ginnery
Address: Plot 49/50, Sharad Industrial Esate Phase II, Kano
Tel: (064) 660024, 660031
Contact: Alh. Mohammed Akkad - Chairman

ILLUMINAIRE LIMITED
Business: Importation and Marketing of Furniture, Light Fittings and Accessories, Metal Craft
Address: 43C, Akin Adesola Street, Victoria Island, Lagos
Tel: (01) 2621538-9 (2 L), 2621541 **Fax:** (01) 2621542
E-mail: illum@infoweb.abs.net
* AP Commercial Complex, Plot 1186, Aguiyi Ironsi Street, Maitama District, Abuja.
Tel: (09) 4138247

ILODI GROUP OF COMPANIES
Business: Wire-Drawing Facilities, Extrusion of Plastic Granules; Cooking-Gas Refilling Plant
Address: Plot D, Bridge Head Industrial Layout, Onitsha-Asaba Expressway, near Coca-Cola, Onitsha
Tel: (046) 212602, 215092, 211510

ILUOBE OIL & MARKETING COMPANY LIMITED
Business: Marketing of Petroleum Products,
Address: 359, Uromi-Benin Road, Ivue-Uromi, Edo State
Tel: (055) 94008

IMAGE PROMOTIONS NIGERIA LIMITED
Business: Film & Television Production, Ind.Photography
Address: 3, Araromi Street, Onike, Yaba, Lagos
Tel: (01) 4701883, 8045418, 860097, 863806, 861325
E-mail: imgagepro@nova.net.ng
Contact: Shayo Holloway - MD/CEO

IMAGE TECHNOLOGIES LIMITED
Business: Sales and Maintenance of Computers and Accessories, Smart Card Technologies and Consultancy
Address: 89A, Ajose Adeogun Street, Victoria Island, Lagos
Tel: (01) 2614152, 2612965 **Fax:** (01) 2614960
E-mail: imagetech@cyberspace.net.ng
Contact: Mr. Olayinka Fisher - MD/CEO

IMAGELINK COMMUNICATIONS LIMITED
Business: Public Relations, Film and TV Production, Marketing Communications
Address: 7, Dodo Williams Close, off Razaq Balogun Street, Surulere, Lagos
Tel: (01) 4806312, 7755292, 08033224329
E-mail: magelink@beta.linserve.com
Contact: Mr. Shola Oyeneyin - Exec. Director/CEO

IMANI & SONS (NIGERIA) LIMITED
Business: Construction, Real Estate Development, Solid

Minerals Prospecting, Ranch & Resort Facilities, Mortgage Banking, Import of Building Materials
Address: Block 9, Imani Estate, Maitama District, Abuja
Tel: (09) 4133359, 4132042, 0803314217
Fax: (09) 4133358
E-mail: imani@linkserve.com
Contact: Hajia Amina Abubakar - Chairman

IMB INTERNATIONAL BANK PLC
Business: Universal Banking
Address: The IMB Plaza, 1, Akin Adesola Street, Victoria Island, Lagos
Tel: (01) 2613000, 2613652
Fax: (01) 2612216, 2616792, 2619491
E-mail: imbank@linkserve.com.ng
Website: www.imbplc.com
Contact: Mr. Edwin O. Chinye - MD/CEO

IMB MORGAN PLC
Business: Securities, Finance, Asset Management
Address: Re-insurance Building (11th Floor), 46, Marina, Lagos Island, Lagos
Tel: (01) 2669278, 2666524 **Fax:** (01) 2663369
E-mail: imbmplc@hotmail.com
• Plot 676, Port Harcourt Crescent, off Gimbiya Street, off Ahmadu Bello Way, Garki II, Abuja
Tel: (09) 3140387, 3140388 **Fax:** (09) 3141282
Contact: Mr. Sehinwa Adeusi - MD/CEO

IMB SECURITIES PLC
Business: Stockbroking, Issuing House
Address: IMB Plaza (2nd Floor), 1, Akin Adesola Street, Victoria Island, Lagos
Tel: (01) 2614741, 2614787 **Fax:** (01) 2614714
E-mail: imbsec@hotmail.com
Contact: Mr. Emmanuel I. Ugboh - MD/CEO

IMC AIRPOWER LIMITED
Business: Sales & Service of Atlascopco Air Compressors, Mining & Drilling Equipment, Generators, Forklift Trucks and Hand-Pallet Trucks
Address: 16/18, Fatai Atere Way, Matori Industrial Scheme, Oshodi, Lagos
Tel: (01) 4522175, 4520564, 4524560, 4523201, 4524497, 4524579, 7741751 **Fax:** (01) 4524519, 4522943
E-mail: name@rtb.com.ng
• 105, Olusegun Obasanjo Way, Central Business District, Abuja
Tel: (090) 801331, 801665
• 17, Azikiwe Road, Port Harcourt
Tel: (084) 238115, 238116, 335685 **Fax:** (084) 238116
Contact: Mr. Jens Erik Mollenbach - Group MD/CEO

IMMAC GROUP
Business: Sales of Automobile, Building Materials and Sanitary Wares, Real Estate Development
Address: 10, Ikorodou Road, Jibowu, Yaba, Lagos
Tel: (01) 5455037, 7737118, 865269, 866457, 867205
Fax: (01) 5455037
Contact: Mr. Kole Olatunji - Chairman/CEO

IMMUNOASSAY LABORATORIES (NIGERIA) LIMITED
Business: Medical Diagnostic Services (Hormonal, Tumor Markers and Immunological Investigations)
Address: 31, Glover Street, off Herbert Macaulay Street, Apena, Ebute-Metta, Lagos
Tel: (01) 7744106, 4808831 **Fax:** (01) 5875362, 5877509
E-mail: immuno@hyperia.com
Contact: Dr. S. F. Kuku - Chairman
Dr. P. A. Akinyanju - Director

IMO CONCORDE HOTEL LIMITED
Business: Hospitality Services
Address: Concorde Avenue, off Port Harcourt Road, Owerri
Tel: (083) 231409 **Fax:** (083) 231961

IMONIYAME HOLDINGS LIMITED
Business: Processing and Exportation of Natural Rubber, Contracting; Imports and Procurement Services
Address: 11, Adelabu Street, Surulere, Lagos
Tel: (01) 5802630-1 (2 L) **Fax:** (01) 5802632
E-mail: ihl@micro.com.ng
Contact: Apostle S. E. K. Obrutse - Exec. Chairman

IMPACTPLUS COMMUNICATIONS LIMITED
Business: Advertising, Public Relations and Marketing
Address: All Seasons Plaza (Ruby Block, Suite 8), Lateef Jakande Road, Agidingbi, Ikeja, Lagos
Tel/Fax: (01) 4922927
E-mail: impactplus@hyperia.com
Contact: Mr. Deji Doherty - Chairman
Mr. Olayiwola Afolabi - GM

IMPERIAL ALUMINIUM PRODUCTS LIMITED
Business: Fabrication and Installation of Aluminium Doors, Windows and Roofing and Specialised Items
Address: Plot 42, Oregun Road, Ikeja, Lagos
Tel: (01) 3453193, 080230443254711214
E-mail: imperialum@hotmail.com
Contact: Dr. B. O. Babalakin - Chairman
Mr. L. A. Ibrahim - MD/CEO

IMPERIAL CHINESE CUISINE LIMITED
Business: Restaurant Services
Address: Imperial Place,Plot 274, Ajose Adeogun Street, Victoria Island, Lagos
Tel: (01) 2617313, 2614225, 2617854 **Fax:** (01) 2614926
Contact: Prince K. O. Akingbade - Chairman

IMPERIAL SERVICES LIMITED
Business: Haulage, Distributor of Breweries' Products
Address: 55, Hospital Road, Aba
Tel: (082) 220667, 222784
* 240, Port Harcourt Road, Aba.
Tel: (082) 221671
Contact: Nze Emma Nwafor - MD/CEO

IMPERIAL TELECOMMUNICATIONS LIMITED
Business: Sales of Telecommunication Equipment
Address: Plot 1064, Abagbon Close, off Ologun Agbaje Street, Victoria Island, Lagos
Tel: (01) 610913, 610920, 610923, 4401010, 4402020, 4403030 **Fax:** (01) 610882

IMPERIAL TRUST INSURANCE BROKERS LIMITED
Business: Insurance Broking

Address: Imperial Place,Plot 274, Ajose Adeogun Street, Victoria Island, Lagos
Tel: (01) 2617854, 2614225 **Fax:** (01) 2614926
E-mail: igc@beta.linkserve.com
Contact: Prince K. O. Akingbade - Chairman
Mr. T. R. Olowu - MD/CEO

IMPERIAL WOODWORK INDUSTRIES LIMITED
Business: Manufacture of Doors, Wardrobes, Kitchenette and Furniture Components
Address: 45A, Campbell Street, Lagos
Tel: (01) 2636235, 2646689
Contact: Mr. John Odigie-Oyegun - Chairman
Mr. K. U. Ashien - Sales Manager

IMPEXX RESOURCES LIMITED
Business: Importation of Computers, Telecommunication Equipment and Accessories; Computer Training
Address: 2,Olu Koleoso St, off Medical Road, Ikeja, Lagos
Tel/Fax: (01) 4979266, 820826
E-mail: impexxresources@usa.net
Contact: Abdul Lateef O. Shitta-Bey - Chairman
Abdul Razaq Adekunle Adeyemi - MD/CEO

INCAR (NIGERIA) PLC
Business: Sales, Installation & Service of Generators, Agricultural Tractors and Buses, Construction of Bus Bodies, Auto Workshop, Sales of Spare Parts
Address: 10, Ijora Causeway, Ijora, Lagos
Tel: (01) 5835497, 5834212, 7740699, 08033431122
Fax: (01) 5835497, 2691784
E-mail: incar@infoweb.abs.net
Contact: Alh. (Dr.) Umaru A. Mutallah - Chairman

INCHSCAPE ARCHITECTS VO
Business: Architectural Consultancy, Project Management
Address: 16, Biaduo Street, off Keffi Street, Lagos
Tel: (01) 2694947, 2672725, 2692529, 684908
Fax: (01) 2694947
E-mail: votolorin@aol.com
Contact: Arc Victor O. Otolorin - MD/CEO

INCOMTEL NIGERIA LIMITED
Business: Sales, Installation, Service and Maintenance of Broadcast, Communication, Security and Electrical Equipment, Agricultural Tractors & Implements
Address: 87, Ogui Road, Enugu
Tel: (042) 258600, 252328, 258180 **Fax:** (042) 257991
Contact: Chief Sam O. Anyamele - Chairman/CEOO

INDEPENDENT COMMUNICATIONS NETWORK LIMITED
Business: Publishing of Newspapers and Magazines
Address: 27, Acme Road, Agidingbi, Ikeja, Lagos
Tel: (01) 4922499, 4924314, 3453865 **Fax:** (01) 4922983
E-mail: aonauga@aol.com
Website: www.icnlnews.com
Contact: Mr. Bayo Onanuga - MD/CEO
Mr. Babafemi Ojudu - Managing Editor

INDEPENDENT NEWSPAPERS LIMITED
Business: Publishing and Marketing of Newspapers
Address: Plot 7D, Block 5, Wempco Road, Ogba Industrial Estate, Ogba, Lagos
Tel: (01) 4703138-40 (3 L), 4962138, 7733489
Fax: (01) 4962136, 4962139
E-mail: info@independentng.com
Website: www.dailyindependentng.com
* Plot 15, Makeni Street, Wuse Zone 6, Abuja
Contact: Chief (Dr.) Abel K. Ubeku - Chairman
Mr. Doyin Mahmoud - Chief Operating Officer

INDEPENDENT SECURITIES LIMITED
Business: Stockbroking, Investment Management Services and Portfolio Management
Address: Leventis Building, 42/43, Marina, Lagos
Tel: (01) 2663675, 4701066, 4805642 **Fax:** (01) 2663675
E-mail: indesecltd@ihotmail.com
Contact: Remi Babalola - Director

INDEPENDENT TELEPHONE NETWORK LIMITED
Business: Telecommunication Service, Distribution and Marketing of Pre-Paid Telephone Cards
Address: 18, Isaac John Street, Ikeja, G.R.A., Ikeja, Lagos
Tel: (01) 3421020-3 (3L), 4978566 Fax: (01) 4978566
E-mail: info@itnmail.com
Contact: Chief Adebayo Akande - Chairman/CEO

INDEPENDENT TELEVISION (CHANNEL 22) & RADIO
Business: Television Broadcasting Services
Address: Glass House, Airport Road, Benin City
Tel: (052) 252119, 250242
• NEDAC Savings & Loans Building, Plot 292B, Ajose Adeogun Street, Victoria Island, Lagos
Tel: (01) 2621002
Contact: Chief (Dr.) Sir G. O. Igbinedion - Chairman/CEO

INDEV LIMITED
Business: Industrial Developoment and Promotion, Machinery Design and Manufacture, Equipment Marketing and Sales, Industrial Project Management, Power Plant Engineering, Oil and Gas Services, Project Tunaround Programme; General Engineers
Address: 24, Isaac John Street, Ikeja, G.R.A, Ikeja, Lagos
Tel: (01) 4978106 **Fax:** (01) 4978107
E-mail: indev@metrong.com
Contact: Mr. R. N. Ugbaja - Chairman
Mr. Chike Madueke - MD/CEO

INDIA BAZAAR (NIGERIA) LIMITED
Business: Import of Electronics & General Merchandise
Address: 6, Lawrence Lane, off Ereko/Martins Street, Lagos
Tel: (01) 2660059, 2662760, 2662789, 2664458, 2669298
Fax: (01) 612272
Contact: Mr Jhoney C. Daswani - MD/CEO

INDIGOID FURNISHING LIMITED
Business: Manufacturing of Furniture and Furnishings
Address: Km. 7, Hadejia Road, opp. Motor Park, Kano
Tel: (064) 661775
Contact: Mr. Ben Moronikeji - MD/CEO

INDUSTRIAL & COMMERCIAL PROJECTS (NIGERIA) LTD
Business: Sales, Supply and After-Sales Support of Surveying and Mapping Equipment and other Technical Systems; Consultancy
Address: 3, Ahmed Onibudo Street, Victoria Island, Lagos

Tel/Fax: (01) 2620838
E-mail: icpnigeria@starnet.net.ng
Contact: Mr. Werner N. Greuter - MD/CEO
Mr. Fidelis Idumebor - Head (Service Dept.)

INDUSTRIAL & FARM EQUIPMENT COMPANY LIMITED
Business: Making of Wheelbarrows, Headpans & Shovels
Address: 113, Demurin Street (Oba-Nle Aro Bus Stop), Alapere, Ketu, Lagos
Tel: (01) 2881724, 7735115, 7929828, 08033267568, 08037137955 **Fax:** (01) 2881724
E-mail: waleodunaiya@yahoo.com
Contact: Engr. G. Olawale Odunaiya - MD/CEO

INDUSTRIAL AND GENERAL INSURANCE COMPANY LTD
Business: All Classes of Insurance
Address: Plot 741, Adeola Hopewell St Victoria Island, Lagos
Tel: (01) 2613534, 2625437-42 (6L), 2622174-7(4L)
Fax: (01) 2621146, 610202
E-mail: info@igi-insurers.com
Website: www.igi-insurers.com
* opp. Unipetrol, Central Business District, Abuja
Tel: (09) 2340592, 2340583
Contact: Mr. Rotimi Fashola - Exec. Director (Marketing)
Mr. Niyi Obaremi - Snr Manager (Corp. Affairs)

INDUSTRIAL AUTOMATION (NIGERIA) LIMITED
Business: Sales of Weighing Scales and Equipment
Address: 1, Unity Road, Ikeja, Lagos
Tel: (01) 4975109 **Fax:** (01) 4937710
E-mail: ial@infoweb.abs.net

INDUSTRIAL CARTONS LIMITED
Business: Manufacture of Light Packaging, Labels, Exercise Books and Wrappers
Address: ACME Crescent, off ACME Road, Agidingbi, Ogba Industrial Area, Ikeja, Lagos
Tel: (01) 8045566, 8045577 **Fax:** (01) 3450138
E-mail: mail@icl.com.ng
Contact: Mr. Roger R. Sherlow - MD/CEO

INDUSTRIAL FLAVOURS & COLOURS LIMITED
Business: Distribution and Marketing of Industrial Flavours, Colours and Fragrance for the Pharmaceutical and Food/Beverage Industries
Address: All Seasons Plaza (Suite 3), opp. Cadbury Plc, Lateef Jakande Road, Agidingbi, Ikeja, Lagos
Tel: (01) 8042677, 7752877, 7731772
E-mail: ifcl@hyperia.com
* 1, Akokwa Street, opp. Amichi Development Union Hall, off 44B, Ngwa Road, (Suite 1), Kano
Contact: Mr. Lal Mahtani - Chairman
Mr. U. Enang - GM

INDUSTRIAL METAL PROCESSING COMPANY LIMITED
Business: Steel Processing and Merchandising
Address: Metal House, Plot 6, Cocoa Industries Road, Ogba Industrial Estate, Ikeja, Lagos
Tel: (01) 4922252, 4922253 **Fax:** (01) 4922249
E-mail: impcolimited@yahoo.couk
*Plot 282A, Trans-Amadi Ind Layout, Port Harcourt
Tel: (084) 234933
Contact: Mr. Joe E. Agbara - MD/CEO

INDUSTRIAL METALLIZING & PACKAGING CO. LTD (IMPCO)
Business: Manufacture of Packaging for Industrial, Cosmetic and Pharmaceutical Products; High Vacuum
Address: 8, Fatai Atere Way, Matori Ind. Estate, Mushin, Lagos
Tel: (01) 4521168, 4520381, 4520382, 4524508, 4524492, 08037770667 **Fax:** (01) 4526856
E-mail: impco@beta.linkserve.com
Contact: Mr. Samir Chalfoun - MD/CEO

INDUSTRIAL MINERAL PRODUCTS
(Div. of Hoesch Pipe Mills (Nig.) Ltd)
Business: Manufacturing of Fibre-Cement Roofing and Ceiling Products
Address: Henry Carr St, Ikeja Industria Estate, Ikeja, Lagos
Tel: (01) 4974221-5 (5 L); **Fax:** (01) 4937318
* Km. 38, Lagos-Abeokuta Expressway, Abule-Igbala, Sango-Ota, Ogun State
Tel: (039) 722225, 722235-8 (4L)
Contact: Chief (Dr.) J. C. Dugad - Director/CEO

INDUSTRIAL PORTS ENGINEERING SERVICES (NIG) LTD
Business: Industrial Electronic, Electrical, Hydraulic, Mechanic and Pneumatic Engineering Services
Address: 3, Sebanjo Close, Apapa, Lagos
Tel: (01) 5872943, 5870642, 7731150-1 (2L)
E-mail: genports@skannet.com.ng
Website: www.kpflohr-group.de
Contact: Mr. Klaus-Peter Flohr - MD/CEO

INDUSTRIAL PRINTING & PACKAGING LIMITED
Business: Manufacturing of Exercise Books and Paper/Board Packaging Products
Address: Plot 124, Block K, Oluyole Industrial Estate, Ring Road, Ibadan
Tel: (02) 2314355 **Fax:** (02) 2310935
Contact: Mr Joseph E. Kordahy - MD/CEO

INDUSTRIAL PROJECTS INTERNATIONAL (NIGERIA) LTD
Business: Manufacturing and Marketing of Soaps, Detergents and Sulphonic Acid
Address: 3, Oyefeso Ave, off Ikorodu Rd, Obanikoro, Lagos
Tel: (01) 4973007, 4930801 **Fax:** (01) 4976668
E-mail: headqrt@indrop-intl.com
* Km 8, Abeokuta-Lagos Road, Abeokuta
Tel: (039) 244184, 08033473639, 080421464303
E-mail: factory@indpro-intl.com
Contact: Mr. Suresh K. Gulati - Exec. Director/CEO

INDUSTRIAL TECHNOSERVE LIMITED
Business: Wholesale of Telecommunication Equipmment, GMS Phones & Accessories Real Estate, Restaurant Management & Catering Services
Address: Bishopgate Building (1st Floor), 26, Moloney Street, Onikan, Lagos
Tel: (01) 2647766, 08022234985, 08022234907
Fax: (01) 2647766
E-mail: industrialtech@lycos.com
Website: www.industrialtechnoserve.com
Contact: Mr Osagie Amusa-Eke - MD/CEO

INDUSTRIAL TRUST ENGINEERING LIMITED
Business: Oil & Gas Engineering Services
Address: 1, Oju Olobun Close, off Bishop Oluwole Street,

Victoria Island, Lagos
Tel: (01) 2613098, 2618586 **Fax:** (01) 619846
E-mail: intrusteng@usa.net
Website: www.instrusteng.com

INEH-MIC HOLDINGS LIMITED
Business: Sales of Motor Vehicles, Import of Merchandise
Address: 13, Kingsway Road, Ikoyi, Lagos
Tel: (01) 2693921, 2696072 **Fax:** (01) 2693426
* Plot 1357, Ahmadu Bello Way, Area II, Garki, Abuja
Tel: (09) 3143881-2 (2L) **Fax:** (09) 3143883
* Plot 49, Trans-Amadi Ind Layout, Port Harcourt
Tel: (084) 574054, 08033044517
Contact: Sir, Chief (Dr.) Mike Inegbese, JP - Chairman/CEO

I-NET GLOBAL SERVICES LIMITED
Business: Internet Service Provider, Communication Services
Address: 6B, Sultan Road, P.O.Box 2072, Kaduna
Tel: (062) 370391, 372125, 243002, 218794
Fax: (062) 218795

INFINITE HOLDINGS LIMITED
Business: Sales, Installation and Maintenance of Security and Telecommunication Equipment
Address: Ikeja Shopping Plaza (Suite B 431), 81, Mobolaji Bank-Anthony Way, Ikeja, Lagos
Tel/Fax: (01) 4972982
E-mail: archiinfinite@yahoo.com
Contact: Lt. Col. (Chief) O. W. Attang (rtd) - Chairman
Mr. Archibong A. Williams - MD/CEO

INFINITY COMPUTERS SYSTEMS (NIGERIA) LIMITED
Business: Sales, Supplies and Maintenance of Computer Hardware and Software, Training
Address: 38, Norman Williams Street, off Keffi Street, S. W. Ikoyi, Lagos
Tel/Fax: (01) 2696187
Contact: Hajiya Hauwa Abubakar - Chairman/CEO

INFINITY INSURANCE BROKERS LIMITED
Business: All Classes of Insurance Broking
Address: 103, Tafawa Balewa Crescent, off Adeniran Ogunsanya Street, Surulere, Lagos
Tel: (01) 4702809, 5836515
Contact: Mr. Mike Olunoiki - GM/CEO

INFINITY MERCHANTS NIGERIA LIMITED
Business: Sales of Electronics and Video Cassette, Marketing of Home-Video Films
Address: 137, Nnamdi Azikiwe Street, Idumota, Lagos
Tel: (01) 2660323, 2663793, 08023156178, 08033126473
Fax: (01) 2641860, 2660323
E-mail: dobenz@yahoo.co.uk
Contact: Mr. Dozie Emmanuel Eriobu - Chairman/CEO

INFINITY TRUST SAVINGS & LOANS LIMITED
Business: Mortgage Banking
Address: Plot 6A/769, Ahmadu Bello Way, Garki II, Abuja
Tel: (09) 6704859, 2345221, 08033467676
Fax: (09) 2345221
Contact: Engr. Adeyinka Bibilari - Chairman
Mr. Eniola Olakunri - MD/CEO

INFINITY TYPRES LIMITED
Business: Imporation and Sales of Tyres, Batteries and Sport Wheels, Motor Vehicle Wheel Services
Address: 35 (Plot 233), Adeola Odeku St, Victoria Is., Lagos
Tel: (01) 2620955-7 (3 L) **Fax:** (01) 2612388, 4619954
E-mail: infinityu@cyberspace.net.ng
* Plot 515B, Adetokunbo Ademola Crescent, Wuse II, Abuja
Tel: (09) 5234736
* 30, Trans-Amadi Ind Layout, Port Harcourt
Tel: (084) 231577-8 (2L) **Fax:** (084) 231578
Contact: Mr. A. S. Chadha - MD/CEO

INFO SOFT NIGERIA LIMITED
Business: Software Development
Address: Valley View Plaza, 99, Opebi Road, Ikeja, Lagos
Tel: (01) 4937335, 4933721, 775360
E-mail: infosoft@linkserve.com.ng
Contact: Mr. Pius Okigbo, Jnr - Chairman
Mr. Basil C. Onuoha - GM

INFORMATICS GROUP (NIGERIA)
Business: Iinformation Technology Training for Children & Adults; Professional Courses
Address: 66, Marine Road, Apapa, G.R.A., Apapa, Lagos
Tel: (01) 7755437, 5850439, 580980
E-mail: calnigeria@infomaticsgroup.com
nigeria@informaticsgroup.com
Contact: Alh. El-Nafaty - MD/CEO

INFORMATION DISPLAY EXHIBIT & SYSTEM LIMITED
Business: Sales & Hire of Audio-Visual Equipment, Staging Equipment and Display & Exhibition Systems
Address: 3, Hospital Road, opp. St Nicholas Hospital, Lagos
Tel: (01) 2636598, 2636750 **Fax:** (01) 2636674
E-mail: ideas@skannet.com
Contact: Mr. Olatokunbo O. Ogunbanjo - Chairman/CEO

INFORMATION MANAGEMENT RESOURCES NIGERIA LTD
Business: Sales of Computer Hardware, Software and Peripherals, Information Management and Technology Consultancy Services
Address: 31, Olufemi Rd, Ogunlana Drive, Surulere, Lagos
Tel: (01) 5832585, 5843871, 7901039
E-mail: info@immig.com
Contact: Dr. Remi Folorunsho - Chairman
Mr Sunday Madudu - MD/CEO

INFOSONIC COMPANY LIMITED
Business: Information Technology Training & Consultancy
Address: Bungalow 4, 1, Joel Ogunnaike Street, G.R.A., Ikeja, Lagos.
Tel: (01) 4937373, 4975174 **Fax:** (01) 4975174
E-mail: info@infosoniconline.com
Website: www.infosoniconline.com
Contact: Elizabeth Pierre - Admin. Officer

INFOWEB LIMITED
Business: Internet Service Provider
Address: NCWS House (1st Floor), PC. 14, Ahmed Onibudo Street, Victoria Island, Lagos
Tel: (01) 2623474-6 (3L), 2623496-7 (2L), 2624470-4 (5L), 2624256, 2623474

E-mail: sales@infoweb.abs.net
Contact: K. R. Simpson - MD/CEO

INLAKS COMPUTERS LIMITED
Business: Sales & Support of Computer Hardware, UPS Systems Integrators, Software Engineering, Computer Environment & Site Preparation, Consultancy, Networking & Communications
Address: NUJ Light House, 3/5, Adeyemo Alakija Street, Victoria Island, Lagos
Tel: (01) 2623516, 2621985, 611499, 4617741
Fax: (01) 2620852
E-mail: inlaks@linkserve.com.ng
Contact: Chief Sunday Adewusi - Chairman
Mr. Adelowo Adesola - MD/CEO

INLAND BANK (NIGERIA) LIMITED
Business: Banking Services.
Address: Plot 19/23, Jos Road, P.M.B. 0505, Bauchi.
Tel: (077) 541076, 541081, 542701, 542586
Fax: (077) 543401
E-mail: bauchiho@inlandbank.com
Website: www.inlandbank.com
www.inlandbank.nu
* Plot 53B, IBB Way, Wuse Zone 4, Abuja
Tel: (09) 5232730 - 1(2L), 5232745 - 6 (2L)
Fax: (09) 5233437, 5237101
* Okoi Arikpo House, 5, Idowu Taylor Street, Victoria Island, Lagos
Tel: (01) 2613190, 2614583, 2619725, 2625030 - 1(2L)
Fax: (01) 2613576, 2623528
Contact: Alh. Abubakar Maikafi - MD/CEO
Mr Nosa Igbinadolor - Corp. Affairs Manager

INLAND CONTAINERS (NIGERIA) LIMITED
Business: Shipping; Customs Bonded - Terminal Operators
Address: 46, Burma Road, Apapa, Lagos
Fax: (01) 5453929
* Abdullahi Bayero Rd, off Audu Bako Way, Kano
Tel: (064) 633682, 648409 **Fax:** (064) 633682
* Railway Avenue, off Kachia Road, Kaduna
Tel: (062) 231378, 232555 **Fax:** (062) 232555
Contact: Mr. A. I. Yusuf - GM/CEO

INLAND DOORS NIGERIA LIMITED
Business: Production of Plywood & Carved Wooden Doors
Address: 118, Akwa Road, Onitsha
Tel: (046) 415955
Contact: Mr. E. E. Ajamnia - MD/CEO

INLAND INSURANCE BROKERS LIMITED
Business: Insurance Broking and Consultancy
Address: NNIL Building, 4, Waff Road, Kaduna
Tel: (062) 240662, 247769, 08023614268
Contact: Mr. O. A. Samson - G.M. (Operations)/CEO

INNOCHRIS NIGERIA LIMITED
Business: Passenger Transportation, Sales of Motor Vehicle Spare Parts, Computer Training & Bureau Services
Address: 60, Western Avenue, Ojuelegba, Surulere, Lagos
Tel: (01) 7742574, 833942, 836799 **Fax:** (01) 834010
E-mail: innochris@beta.linkserve.com
Contact: Mr. Chris Onuoha - MD/CEO

INNOSON NIGERIA LIMITED
Business: Importation and Sales of Motorcycle CKD, Spare Parts and Accessories
Address: 20, New Market Road, Nnewi, Anambra State
Tel: (046) 460133, 460566 **Fax:** (046) 462118
E-mail: innoson@infoweb.abs.net
* 61, Herbert Macaulay Street, Ebute-Metta, Lagos
Tel: (01) 860991, 864623, 2662733
* Cornershop Shop 15, opp. General Hospital, Area 7, Garki, Abuja
Contact: Mr. Innocent Chukwuma - Chairman/CEO

INNOVATIVE SYSTEMS LIMITED
Business: Information Technology Services (Hardware, Software and Engineering)
Address: ISL House, 8, Anthony Village Rd, Anthony, Lagos
Tel: (01) 4975493, 7734599 **Fax:** (01) 4970371
E-mail: info@innovativesystemsltd.com
Website: www.innovativesystemsltd.com

INMB BANK LIMITED
Business: Universal Banking Services
Address: 42, Adeola Hopewell Street, Victoria Island, Lagos
Tel: (01) 2610052-3 (2L), 2610895, 2616562, 2621323
Fax: (01) 2622794
E-mail: mdc@indobank.com.ng
Website: www.inmb.net

INSIGHT COMMUNICATIONS LIMITED
Business: Advertising, Marketing Communications
Address: 17/19, Oduduwa Street, G.R.A. Ikeja, Lagos
Tel: (01) 4979710-15 (6L), 3420032-43 (12L), 7743157
Fax: (01) 4979716
E-mail: insight@infoweb.abs.net
Website: www.insightnigeria.com
Contact: Mr. Biodun Shobanjo - Vice Chairman/CEO

INSIGHT EYE CLINIC & OPTICAL SERVICES LIMITED
Business: Optical Services, Eye Clinic
Address: Oshopey Plaza, 17/19, Allen Avenue, Ikeja, Lagos
Tel: (01) 4937530
* Abuja Sheraton Hotel and Towers (Rooms 166), Ladi Kwali Way, Wse Zone 4, Abuja.
Tel: (09) 5230225 (Ext. 8416)
Contact: Dr. (Mrs.) D. Okereke - MD/CEO

INSTANT CLEANERS LIMITED
Business: Sales of Dry-Cleaning, Laundry and Finishing Machines; Dry-Cleaning and Laundry Services
Address: Block 1, Units 1 & 2, Industrial Estate, 3, Onike Road, Sabo-Yaba, Lagos
Tel: (01) 4742941, 08023215955
Fax: (01) 864094
Contact: Mr. B. A. S. Benson, Snr - Chairman/CEO

INSURANCE BROKERS OF NIGERIA LIMITED
Business: Insurance Broking, Risk Management Consulting
Address: IBN House, 4 A & B, Ilabere Avenue (formely Queen's Drive), Ikoyi, Lagos
Tel: (01) 2672571-4 (4 L), 2693641, 8043703-5 (3 L)
Fax: (01) 2694679
E-mail: ibnmarsh@aol.com
Contact: Mr. Prosper C. Okpue - MD/CEO

INSURANCE TECHNICAL SERVICES
Business: Loss Adjusting, Consultancy, Survey and Marine Superintendence
Address: Crusade House (1st Floor), 16A, Commercial Avenue, Sabo-Yaba, Lagos
Tel: (01) 865226, 3425304 **Fax:** (01) 3425304
Contact: Mr. Yinka Lijadu - Chairman/CEO

INTEC PRINTERS LIMITED
Business: Printing of Books, Journals, Calendars and Diaries; Electronic Colour Separations, Typesetting
Address: Km. 8, Old Lagos Road, Podo Village, Ibadan
Tel: (02) 2311678, 2313377, 2317558, 08033598907, 08033598908 **Fax:** (02) 2317558
E-mail: intec@skannet.com
Contact: Mr. Godwin Olu Abegunde - MD/CEO

INTECON PARTNERSHIP
Business: Consulting Engineers, Construction QA/QC Supervision, Project Management
Address: 16, Aperin Street, off Awolowo Avenue, Old Bodija Estate, Ibadan
Tel: (02) 8104220, 8102875, 08023375063
Fax: (02) 8102875
E-mail: intecon@intecon-ng.com

INTEGRATED APPLICATIONS ENGINEERING NIGERIA LTD
Business: Geophysical Services, Drilling Operations, Procurement
Address: 35A, Adetokunbo Ademola Street, V/Island, Lagos
Tel: (01) 2621327-8 (2 L)
Contact: Mr. Georg Mgbahurike - MD/CEO

INTEGRATED CAPITAL SERVICES LIMITED
Business: Financial Consultancy, Insurance Agency
Address: Plot 1619, Danmole Street, Victoria Island, Lagos
Tel: (01) 2616794, 2616937, 616494 **Fax:** (01) 2616794
Contact: Mr. Tunde Onafowope - GM/CEO

INTEGRATED CORPORATE SERVICES LIMITED
Business: Management and Human Resource Consultants
Address: 41, Gbolade Adbanjo Street, off Olusoji Idow Street, Association Avenue, Ilupeju, Lagos
Tel: (01) 7742211, 5552156, 5552262 **Fax:** (01) 5552262
E-mail: icslimited@hyperia.com
hmanresource@pimaweb.com

INTEGRATED DATA SERVICES LIMITED
Business: Seismic Data Acquisition, Processing and Interpretation, Petroleum/Reservoir Engineering Data Evaluation; Computer Services
Address: 36, Ogba Road, Oko Village, Benin City
Tel: (052) 258809, 254451, 254632, 257401, 256591
Fax: (052) 253325
* NNPC Towers, Herbert Macaulay Way, Central Business District, Abuja
Tel: (09) 2343115
Contact: Engr. S. U. Ekiye - MD/CEO
Engr. O. A. Okon - E. D. (Operations)

INTEGRATED DIGITAL TECHNOLOGIES LIMITED
Business: Digital Electronic and Telecommunication Service, Sales of Cellular Phone and Accessories
Address: 165, Aba Road, Port Harcourt
Tel: (084) 230323
* 23B, Ribadu Road, S. W. Ikoyi, Lagos
Tel: (01) 680155, 2695598
* 11B, Mambolo Road, Off Olu Obasanjo Way, Wuse II, Abuja.
Tel: (09) 5233362
Contact: Mr. Kenneth Owoghiri - MD/CEO

INTERGRATED DEVELOPMENT CONSULTANTS LIMITED
Business: Development & Management Consultants
Address: Turaki Ali House, 3, Kanta Road, Kaduna
Tel: (064) 247416, 247889, 246203-6 (4 L) (Ext. 3203)
Fax: (064) 247416

INTEGRATED FIBRES LIMITED
Business: Manufacturing of Synthetic Fibre and Textiles
Address: Waje District, Bompai Industrial Estate, Kano
Tel: (064) 648989, 633354, 648094 **Fax:** (064) 632904
Contact: Alh. (Dr.) Aminu Dantata - Chairman
Mr. C. A. Jaafar - MD/CEO

INTEGRATED NETWORK SOLUTIONS LIMITED
Business: Networking Solutions; Installation and Maintenance of Computers
Address: SPACO House, 27A, Macarthy St, Onikan, Lagos
Tel: (01) 2647387

INTEGRATED PRESS LIMITED
Business: Printing, Sales of Printing Materials
Address: Kingsway Building, 51/52, Marina, Lagos
* Plot 4, Block E, Isolo Industrial Estate, Apapa-Oshodi Expressway, Isolo, Lagos.
Tel: (01) 521084, 4823603
Contact: Mrs. L. A. Ocholi - MD/CEO

INTEGRATED RUBBER PRODUCTS NIGERIA PLC
Business: Manufacturing of Rubber-Related Products and Floor Tiles, Sales of Carbonless Paper
Address: 17B, McEwen Street, Sabo-Yaba, Lagos
Tel: (01) 7740500, 7749600, 7755600 **Fax:** (01) 2613248
E-mail: intrubaa@aol.com
* Km 8, opp. Ekae Amusement Park, off Benin-Sapele Road, Benin City
Tel: (052) 257429, 08033586856 **Fax:** (052) 250896
Contact: Alh. Muhtari Bello - Chairman
Mr. Anil M. R. Assomull - MD/CEO

INTEGRATED TRUST & INVESTMENTS LIMITED
Business: Stockbroking, Issue House, Funds and Portfolio Management, Trade and LPO Finance; Financial Advisory Services
Address: 17, Military Street, Onikan, Lagos
Tel: (01) 2633416, 2630063, 2631778 **Fax:** (01) 2630063
E-mail: iti@nova.net.ng
Contact: Otunba S. A. Oladunni - Chairman
Mr. Dele Lawore - MD/CEO

INTEGRATED WIRELESS TECHNOLOGIES NIGERIA LTD
Business: Telecommunications, Sales and Support of GSM Phones and Pre-paid Phone Cards
Address: The Phonexpress Place, 31, Saka Tinubu Street, Victoria Island, Lagos

Tel: (01) 2700164, 4518665, 3201481, 4705454, 4705011-4 (4L), 08032030513-6 (4L) **Fax:** (01) 4618666
E-mail: iwt@linkserve.com.ng
Contact: Mr. Opeyemi Okunoren - MD/CEO

INTEGRATION NIGERIA LIMITED
Business: Building Construction & Civil Engineering
Address: Jimade House (4th Floor), 2, Ojuelegba Road, Surulere, Lagos
Tel: (01) 8043910, 5851376, 08033314764, 08033471721
Fax: (01) 5851376
E-mail: integration@rbow.net
Contact: Lt. Gen. Salihu Ibrahim (rtd.) - Chairman
Mr. A. J. Devane - MD/CEO

INTEGRITY SYSTEMS NIGERIA LIMITED
Business: Sales of GSM Phones and Accessories, and Fixed Wireless Phones, Sales & Installation of Computers and Accessories, Computer Training
Address: 43, Kudirat Abiola Way (3rd Floor, Rear Wing), Oluyole Bus-Stop, Oregun, Ikeja, Lagos
Tel: (01) 8118836, 4719537, 497960, 7762499, 4933919, 08023377100, 08033485432 **Fax:** (01) 4933919
E-mail: integritysystems2002@yahoo.com
Contact: Mr. Prince Edobor Igbinoje - Operations Manager

INTEK GROUP LIMITED
Business: Conglomerate - Manufacturers Representative; Exporters & Importers; Whole Plant Consultants; Civil Engineering Contractors; Bottlers.
Address: 6E, Idejo Street, Victoria Island, Lagos
Tel: (01) 2621198, 2625115-8 (4 L), 7750673-5 (3 L), 7752868 **Fax:** (01) 2622838
E-mail: intekg@beta.linkserve.com
Contact: Alh. M. A. Muse - Chairman
Mr. Frank Lin - MD/CEO

INTEL TRUST LIMITED
Business: Financial Services Conglomerate
Address: Mintydale House, 13, Araromi Street,off Moloney Street, Onikan, Victoria Island, Lagos
Tel: (01) 2646771-2 (2L) **Fax:** (01) 2646770
E-mail: intertrust@yahoo.com
Contact: Mr. A. Kehinde Oniwinde - Chairman
Mr. I. Adeyemi Solarin - MD/CEO

INTELI-TECH LIMITED
Business: Sales, Supplies and Maintenance of Computer Hardware and Software, Networking; Training
Address: 15, Sinari Daranijo Street, Victoria Island, Lagos
Tel: (01) 3200735, 08033047522 **Fax:** (01) 3200735
E-mail: inteli@infoweb.abs.net
Contact: Mr. Peter Isokphehi - MD/CEO

INTELS NIGERIA LIMITED
Business: Logistic Services for Oil & Gas Industry
Address: Intels Aba Road Camp, Km 16, Port Harcourt-Aba Expressway, Port Harcourt
Tel: (084) 610521, 230921, 236193, 234212,
Fax: (084) 610520, 610552-3 (2 L), 613360
E-mail: marketing@intelservices.com
Website: www.intels.co.uk
Contact: Bashir el-Rufai - President/CEO

INTER ROOF (NIGERIA) LIMITED
Business: Civil, Corrosion and Plastic Engineering; Local/ Foreign Procurement and Supplies
Address: 13, Igbokwe Street, D-Line, Port Harcourt
Tel: (084) 335848 **Fax:** (084) 230238
E-mail: interroof2000@yahoo.com
Contact: Mr. Joseph E. Unah - MD/CEO

INTER SYSTEMS NIGERIA LIMITED
Business: Sales and Maintenance of Computers; Information Technology Consultancy
Address: Kibiya House, 11, Zoo Road, Kano
Tel: (064) 661578, 322890
E-mail: iscl_2000@yahoo.com
Contact: Sagir Muhammad - MD/CEO

INTER TRUST LIMITED
Business: Financial and Investment Consultancy Services
Address: WAPIC Building (2nd Floor), 119, Awolowo Road, S. W. Ikoyi, Lagos
Tel: (01) 2696357-8 (2 L), 2692740 **Fax:** (01) 2690592
E-mail: intertrust@wananet.net
Contact: Chief (Dr.) Chilo C. Offiah - Chairman/CEO

INTER-BAU CONSTRUCTION LIMITED
Business: Building and Civil Engineering Contractors
Address: 58A, Adeniran Ogunsanya Street, Surulere, Lagos
Tel: (01) 5835387, 7742877, 7911780 **Fax:** (01) 5837801
Contact: Sir Nath E. Okechukwu - Chairman/CEO

INTERAGRIC GROUP OF COMPANIES
Business: Information & Communication Technology Services, Sales of GSM Phones & Accessories, Medical Equipment and Consumable
Address: Plot 10, First Avenue, opp 11 Road, Junction Festac Town, Lagos
Tel: (01) 5893550, 2904049, 7918330, 08022238993, 08022238996, 08022905849 **Fax:** (01) 5893510
E-mail: interagric@yahoo.com
Contact: Chief Roger Afam Ilabor - Chairman/CEO

INTERCAP LIMITED
Business: Manufacturing of Egg-Packaging Crates
Address: Plot 8, Block K, Oluyole Industrial Estate, off Ring Road, Ibadan
Tel: (02) 2311453-4 (2L), 2318651-2 (2L)
Contact: Mr C. Zard - MD/CEO

INTERCELLULAR NIGERIA LIMITED
Business: National Fixed Wireless Telephone Services; Mobile Telephone, Internet, International Telephone Services; Iridium Satellite Phone Services
Address: UBA House, 5th Floor, Marina, Lagos
Tel: (01) 4703010-3 (4L) **Fax:** (01) 2643014, 2643013
E-mail: hq@intercellular-ng.com
Website: www.intercellular-ng.com
* 2C, Choba Street, D-Line, Port Harcourt.
Tel: (084) 573010-3 (4L)
* Millenium Court (Ground Floor), Plot 74, 4th Avenue, Central Business District, Abuja.
Tel: (09) 6703010-3 (4L)
Contact: Mr. Bashir el-Rufai - Presiden/CEO
Mr. Fidel Oluya - Director (Corp. Communication)

INTERCITY BANK PLC

Business: Commercial Banking
Address: 1, Intercity Bank Street, Plot 20, Mogadisu City Centre, off Ahmadu Bello Way, Kaduna
Tel: (062) 240344-8 (5L) **Fax:** (062) 240348
E-mail: intercity@intercity.com.ng
Website: ww.intercity.com.ng
* 32, Adetokunbo Ademola St, Victoria Is. Lagos
Tel: (01) 4707809-11 (3L), 4703566 **Fax:** (01) 2620513
* Plot 1529, Nouakchott St, Wuse Zone 1, Abuja
Tel: (09) 5231729 - 30(2L) **Fax:** (09) 5231927
Contact: Alh. Falalu Bello - Chairman
Mr. Umar S. Mairami - Head (Credit Admin. Dept)

INTERCOMM LIMITED

Business: Sales and Service of Computers, Copiers, Office Equipment & Appliances and GSM Telephones
Address: Brossette Compound, 311, Apapa Road, Lagos
Tel: (01) 5450703, 5450689, 5877600, 5451013, 7745284
Fax: (01) 5878472
E-mail: intercomm@intercommoep.com
canon@intercommoep.com
Website: www.intercommeop.com
Contact: Mr. Patrick George - MD/CEO

INTER-CONTINENTAL ASSURANCE COMPANY LIMITED

Business: Insurance
Address: Plot 1698 (C & D), Oyin Jolayemi Street, Victoria Island, Lagos
Tel: (01) 3200384, 4702131, 4811164 **Fax:** (01) 3200520
* Wuse Shopping Plaza (Suite B15), Wuse Zone 5, Abuja.
Tel: (09) 5231084
Contact: Lt. Gen M. I. Wushishi (rtd) - Chairman
Mr. R. I. Madiebo - MD/CEO

INTERCONTINENTAL BANK PLC

Business: Commercial Banking
Address: Intercontinental Plaza, Plot 999C, Danmole Street, Victoria Island, Lagos
Tel: (01) 2622940-59 (20L) **Fax:** (01) 2622981
E-mail: nimbl@nimb.com
Website: www.nimbl@nimb.com
* Union Bank House, 37, M/ Moh'd Way, Kano
Tel: (064) 630080-4 (5L)
* Plot 207, Cadastral Zone AO, Central Business District, Abuja.
Tel: (01) 2346565-6 (2L)
* 135, Olusegun Obasanjo Way, G.R.A. Phase 2, Port Harcourt.
Tel: (084) 237672 (3L)
Contact: Mr Erastus B. O Akingbola - Vice Chairman/CEO

INTERCONTINENTAL CAPITAL MARKETS LIMITED

Business: Capital Market Activities (Issuing House, Stockbroing, Asset Managerment)
Address: Wesley House, 21/22, Marina, Lagos Island, Lagos
Tel: (01) 4716278, 2647238, 2647154 **Fax:** (01) 2647154

INTERCONTINENTAL DISTILLERS LIMITED

Business: Distillers of Alcoholic Spirits and Wines
Address: Chelsea House, Plot 2, No 3, Ladipo Oluwole St, Oba Akran Avenue, Ikeja Ind., Layout, Ikeja, Lagos
Tel: (01) 4974105, 773146-1 (2L) **Fax:** (01) 4974101
Contact: Mr. Diji O. Olatoku - MD/CEO
Mr. Ambrose O. Alabi - National Sales Manage

INTERCONTINENTAL FISHING (NIGERIA) LIMITED

Business: Deep-Sea Fishing
Address: 16, Kofo Abayomi Street (Flat 2, Ground Floor), Victoria Island, Lagos
Tel: (01) 2622232, 222259, 2615505 **Fax:** (01) 2619487
E-mail: primlaks@hyperia.com
*4, Ashabi Adedire St, off Creek Rd, Apapa, Lagos
Tel: (01) 5873703, 5872690, 5872711, 5874221
Fax: (01) 5871249
Contact: Mr. A. R. Hemnani - Directorr

INTERCONTINENTAL PUBLISHERS LIMITED

Business: Publishers of "National Times" Newspapers
Address: 22, Pelewura Crescent, Apapa, Lagos
Tel: (01) 7747730, 5455847, 5455848 **Fax:** (01) 7747731
E-mail: natimes@infoweb.abs.net
Contact: Ozomma F. A. Ozobia - Exec. Director/Publisher

INTERCONTINENTAL SECURITIES LIMITED

Business: Capital Market Activities, Credit Finance, Funds Management, Financial Advisory Services
Address: Bull Plaza (16th Floor), 38/39, Marina, Lagos
Tel: (01) 2665592, 2669489 **Fax:** (01) 2667165
E-mail: isl@intersecltd.com
Website: www.intersecltd.com
Contact: Mr. Erastus B. O. Akingbola - Chairman
Mr. Oluwole O. Adeosun - MD/CEO.

INTERDRILL NIGERIA LIMITED

Business: Oilfield Engineering, Sales of Oilfield Chemicals
Address: 17, St. Mary's Hospital Road, off Airport Road, Effurun, Warri
Tel: (053) 320222, 320223 **Fax:** (053) 320223
E-mail: jamesreioux@compuserve.com
jbogwu@compuserve.com
* 163A, Sinari Daranijo Street, off Ajose Adeogun St, Victoria Island Annex, lagos.
Tel: (01) 2620695
* Jas Ebokpo House, beh. Gilbert Eke Estate, Port Harcourt
Contact: Mr. Joe Bogwu - Chairman/CEO.

INTER-FALCON SECURITY SERVICES LIMITED

Business: Provision of Security Services, Sales of Electronic/ Electrical Security Systems and Safety Equipment, Training & Consultancy
Address: 16, Burma Road, Apapa, lagos
Tel: (01) 5878751, 5878752 **Fax:** (01) 5878752
E-mail: falconguards@hotmail.com
Contact: Mr. Sola Ijitimehin - Chairman/CEO.

INTERFINISH GROUP

Business: Sales of Internet-Telephony Devices
Address: Interfinish Plaza, 66, Bode Thomas Street, Surulere, Lagos
Tel: (01) 2900209, 2902377, 4721661, 08033195215, 08033308688 **Fax:** (01) 5851979
E-mail: sales@interfinishwireless.com
Contact: Mr. Abayomi Oshikoya - Chairman/CEO.

INTERFREIGHT NIGERIA LIMITED
Business: Shipping Agency, Freight Forwarders, Marine Supply, Downstream Oil Operation
Address: 21, Warehouse Road, Apapa, Lagos
Tel: (01) 5453356-7 (2L), 08023228707 **Fax:** (01) 5452551
E-mail: interfreight@nova.net.ng
* 14, Industry Road, Port Harcourt
Tel: (084) 239617, 08033408170 **Fax:** (084) 239617
Contact: Mr. Toni Ike Ifebunandu - Chairman/CEO.

INTERGLOBAL LIMITED
Business: Importation and Sales of Computers, Communication & Security Systems
Address: Plot 489, Bangui Street, off Adetokunbo Ademola Crescent, Wuse II, Abuja
Tel: (09) 5233630 **Fax:** (09) 5233631
E-mail: nmbohammed@int-global.com.ng
Contact: Mal. Ahmed Dasuki - Chairman
Mal Nuru Mohammed - MD/CEO

INTERGLOBAL SERVICES LIMITED
Business: Importation and Marketing of Commodities (Rice, Cement, Sugar)
Address: Plot 849, Bishop Aboyade Cole St,Victoria Is.Lagos
Tel: (01) 2615284, 2615288 **Fax:** (01) 2611421
E-mail: isl@interglobal.com
Contact: Mr. Adamu Majoro - GM

INTERIOR OPTIONS LIMITED
Business: Interior Design Consultancy Services, Furniture Manufacturing and Marketing
Address: 6/8, Industrial Street, of Town Planning Way, Ilupeju Industrial Estate, Ilupeju, Lagos
Tel: (01) 4932889, 4978585, 08033011056
Fax: (01) 4978585
Contact: Mrs. Muni Shonibare - MD/CEO

INTERKEL (NIGERIA) LIMITED
Business: Builders, Civil Engineers & Designers, General Contractors
Address: WAPIC House, 119, Awolowo Road, Ikoyi, Lagos
Tel: (01) 2696414, 4700059 **Fax:** (01) 2696437
E-mail: info@interkel.com
* Plot 223, Adetokunbo Ademola Crescent, opposite AP Plaza/Ecobank, Wuse, Abuja
Tel: (09) 5239554 **Fax:** (09) 5233085
* 7, Nvuike Street, off Okpro Road, Port Harcourt.
Tel: (084) 234212, 08033018003
Contact: Engr. N. C. Agbim - MD/CEO.

INTERLAND INDUSTRIES LIMITED
Business: Bottling of Carbonated Mineral Drinks
Address: 185, Jubilee Road, Aba
Tel: (082) 231961
Contact: Chief O. U. Onwuka - MD/CEO.

INTERLAND TRANSPORT LIMITED
Business: Road Haulage
Address: Plot C. 40, Alakoso Avenue, Amuwo-Odofin Industrial Layout, off Oshodi-Apapa Expressway, Amuwo-Odofin, Lagos
Tel: (01) 4804103, 4824604, 524094 **Fax:** (01) 524094
Contact: Mr Jude O. Obi - GM/CEO.

INTERLINGUA LIMITED
Business: Bookshop
Address: NIM Building (Ground Floor), 22, Idowu Taylor Street, Victoria Island, Lagos
Tel: (01) 615797, 615105
Contact: Mr. Simpson Ekundayo - MD/CEO

INTERLINK ASSOCIATES & COMPANY LIMITED
Business: Insurance Brokerage and Pension Consultants
Address: Wilton House,77/79,Apapa Rd,Ebute-Metta, Lagos
Tel: (01) 5850936, 5833060, 8834350 **Fax:** (01) 5850663
* 1, Lokoja Street, Tafawa Balewa Road, Area 8, Garki, Abuja.
Tel: (09) 2346727

INTERLINKED TECHNOLOGIES PLC
Business: Developement, Manufacturing and Marketing of Polymeric Porcelain and Metallic Products for Electric Power Systems, Telecommunication Systems and Process Plants etc., Manufacturing of Water-Filter Candles & Units, Mechanical/Electrical Engineers and Contractors
Address: 1, Ola-Ayeni St, off Simbiat Abiola Rd, Ikeja, Lagos
Tel: (01) 4937956, 4937957, 4978454 **Fax:** (01) 4937957
E-mail: interlinked@micro.com.ng
* Plot 7B, Block C, Acme Road, Ogba Industrial Estate, Ogba, Lagos.
Tel: (01) 4921846, 4922287
Contact: Mr. Fabian C. Nnadozie - Chairman/CEO

INTERLOC NIGERIA LIMITED
Business: Supply & Installation of Broadcast Electronic Equipment and Spares
Address: 3, Osuntokun Avenue, Bodija, Ibadan
Tel: (02) 810120, 8101253 **Fax:** (02) 8105133
Contact: Mr. Debo Adewumi - Chairman/CEO

INTERMAFICO (NIGERIA) LIMITED
Business: Importation, Distribution and Sales of Priniting, Graphic and Photo Materials
Address: 7, Anuoluwapo Street, Laula, near Denis Catholic Church Bariga, Yaba, Lagos
Tel/Fax: (01) 823072, 4974780
Contact: Nze P. E. Williams - Chairman/CEO

INTERMARC CONSULTING LIMITED
Business: E-Business Consulting, E-Banking Channels Solutions (ATM's Cards and E-payments Systems)
Address: Ebani House (Marina Building, 1st Floor), 149/153, Broad Street, Lagos Island, Lagos
Tel: (01) 4721160, 2663913, 0803330690
Fax: (01) 2663913
E-mail: intermarc@linkserve.com
Website: www.intermarc-ng.com
Contact: Mrs. Ibukun Awosula - Chairman
Onajite Regha - GM/CEO

INTERMARK ASSOCIATES LIMITED
Business: Advertising and Public Relations
Address: 51, Bode Thomas Street, Palmgrove, Lagos
Tel: (01) 5878895, 821449 **Fax:** (01) 5878895
E-mail: intermark@nigerianet.com
Contact: Mr. Oliver E. Johnson - Chairman/CEO

INTERMEDIA COMMUNICATIONS LIMITED
Business: Integrated Marketing Communications
Address: 75B, Akinola Cole Crescent, off Adeniyi Jones Avenue, by Aromire Junction, Ikeja, Lagos
Tel: (01) 4707806, 3453065, 08033707247, 08033397472
Fax: (01) 3453065
E-mail: intermedicomms@yahoo.com
* Turaki Ali House, 3, Kanta Road, Kaduna
Contact: Mr. Taiwo S. Ola (Jnr.) - Chairman/CEO

INTERMATCH NIGERIA LIMITED
Business: Manufacture of Safety Matches, Splints and Allied Wood Products
Address: 15B, Ikosi Road, Oregun
Tel: (01) 4968120, 4968110, 4968111 **Fax:** (01) 4968634
Contct: Mr. Rotimi George-Taylor - Chairman/CEO.

INTERNATIONAL BEER & BEVERAGES INDUSTRIES LTD
Business: Brewing Beer and Non-Alcoholic Beverage
Address: Plot A4, C2, Kudenda Industrial Area, Nnamdi Azikiwe Expressway, Kaduna
Tel: (062) 230407, 231206, 234698, 231290
Fax: (062) 234700
E-mail: ibbi@alpha.linkserve.com

INTERNATIONAL BREWERIES PLC
Business: Brewing of Alcoholic and Malt Beverage Drinks
Address: Omi Asoro, Akure Road, Ilesha, Osun State
Tel: (036) 461500, 460150, 461600, 461020

INTERNATIONAL BROADCAST SERVICES & TRAINING LIMITED
Business: Sales, Hire and Maintenance of Broadcast Equipment, Design & Installation of Broadcast Systems, Engineering and Technical Training
Address: 77, Tafawa Balewa Crescent, off Adeniran Ogunsanya Street, Lagos
Tel: (01) 7748579 **Fax:** (01) 5455515
E-mail: intbroadserve@produxion.com
Contact: Mr. 'Remi Ogunpitan - MD/CEO.

INTERNATIONAL BUSINESS SYSTEMS LIMITED
Business: Sales of Computers and Banking Equipment
Address: 16, Bode Thomas Street, Surulere, Lagos
Tel: (01) 7743916 **Fax:** (01) 5851830, 5850928
E-mail: ibsys@metrong.com
Contact: Engr. D. E. Okon - MD/CEO

INTERNATIONAL CAPITAL MARKETS GROUP LIMITED
Business: Issuing House, Stockbroking, Financial Advisers
Address: 8B, Ademola Street, S.W. Ikoyi, Lagos
Tel/Fax: (01) 2673824
E-mail: icmgsec@micro.com.ng
Website: www.icmgsec.com
Contact: Mr. Akemere Mike Osime - Chairman/CEO.

INTERNATIONAL CAPITAL SECURITIES LIMITED
Business: Stockbroking, Investment Advisory Services
Address: 182A, Kofo Abayomi Street, Victoria Island, Lagos
Tel: (01) 2624391, 2626268, 2611402, 610195
Fax: (01) 2624392, 2626268
E-mail: intercap@rcl.nig.com
Contact: Mr. Andrew Uwuilekhue - GM/CEO.

INTERNATIONAL CARDS (NIGERIA) LIMITED
Business: Production & Marketing of Greetings Cards, Social Stationery and Calendars
Address: Plot 2 & 3, Block G, Oluyole Industrial Estate, Ring Road, Ibadan
Tel: (02) 231207, 2317745, 2317746, 2311544
Fax: (02) 2312607, 2318557

INTERNATIONAL CHARTERED INSURANCE BROKERS LTD
Business: Insurance Broking and Consultancy
Address: 47/57, Martins Street, Lagos Island, Lagos
Tel: (01) 2669167, 2669558 **Fax:** (01) 2669167
E-mail: premiumpet@hotmail.com
Contact: Chief (Mrs.) C. C. Anienwelu - MD/CEO

INTERNATIONAL CLINICS & HOSPITAL LIMITED
Business: Medical Services
Address: 40, Niger Street/2F, Sani Abacha Way, Kano
Tel: (064) 649533, 643093 **Fax:** (064) 630048
Contact: Dr. Patrick Ikhema - Medical Director

INTERNATIONAL COMPUTERS (NIGERIA) LIMITED (ICL)
Business: IT Solutions Provider and Systems Integrators
Address: St. Nicholas Building (13th & 14th Floors), 6, Catholic Mission Street, Lagos Island, Lagos
Tel: (01) 26022360-5 (6 L) **Fax:** (01) 2602358
E-mail: info@iclnig.com
support@iclnig.com
sales@iclnig.com
Contact: Dr. Remi Folorunsho - MD/CEO

INTERNATIONAL CONSULTING GROUP LIMITED
Business: Business Consultancy, Human Resources Development, Oil & Gas Engineering Service, Sourcing of Industrial Raw Materials, International Trade, IT and Telecommunications
Address: 13, Sumbo Jibowu Street, off Ribadu Road, S.W. Ikoyi, Ikoyi, Lagos
Tel: (01) 2690259-60 (2 L) **Fax:** (01) 2690259
E-mail: icgconsult@aol.com
Contact: Sir J. C. Mbanefo, KSC - Chairman/CEO.

INTERNATIONAL CONTROL SYSTEMS LIMITED
Business: Sales of Electrical Information-Technology and Communication Systems
Address: 51, Norman Williams Street, S.W. Ikoyi, Lagos
Tel: (01) 2670823-4 (2L), 8116906
Fax: (01) 2670823
E-mail: ics@webaccessng.com
ics-ltd@alpha.linkserve.com
Contact: Mr. Allwell C. Achumba - MD/CEO

INTERNATIONAL CONVERTERS OF NIGERIA LIMITED
Business: Manufacturing of Display Cartons, Labels & Flexible Packaging (inclucing Laminates)
Address: 333/335, Old Ojo Road, off Lagos-Badagry Expressway, Oluti-Amuwo, Lagos
Tel: (01) 5883308, 5884367, 8042372, 4707500
Fax: (01) 5881910
E-mail: icnl_2000@yahoo.com
icnl@bigfoot.com
Contact: Sir Michael A. Otedola - Chairman
Mr. S. N. Buxani - MD/CEO.

INTERNATIONAL DATA MANAGEMENT SERVICES LTD
Business: Information Technology & Software Development Services, Data Management & Market Research Services, Management Services and Manpower Training, Management and Computer Consultancy, Corporate Services
Address: I.D.M. Building, Oba Akran Avenue, Ikeja, Lagos
Tel: (01) 4937231, 4935200-4 (5 L) **Fax:** (01) 4935204
E-mail: idm@micro.com.ng
Contact: Chief A. O. Abudu - Chairman
Mr. Rashmi Chandaria - MD

INTERNATIONAL ENAMELWARE GROUP OF CO. LIMITED
Business: Manufacturing of Domestic Enamelware, Plastic Packaging Products and Iron Rods
Address: Km. 5, Onitsha-Owerri Road, Onitsha
Tel: (046) 270465, 270591-2 (2L) Fax: (046) 270576
E-mail: cosmos2@infoweb.abs.net
* 36, Sule Abuka Cresc., off Opebi Rd, Ikeja, Lagos
Tel: (01) 8181601 **Fax:** (01) 3450368
Contact: Mr. M. O. Agbe-Davies - A.G.M. (Ind. Relations)

INTERNATIONAL ENERGY INSURANCE COMPANY LTD
Business: Insurance
Address: Consortium House, Plot 1682, Sanusi Fafunwa Street, Victoria Island, Lagos
Tel: (01) 2624012, 2673033, 461972-4 (3L), 8132602, 8182033 **Fax:** (01) 2624012, 2673033
E-mail: globassure@micro.com.ng
Contact: Lt. Gen. Salihu Ibrahim (rtd.) - Chairman
Mr. Don O. Agbo - MD/CEO

INTERNATIONAL ENERGY SERVICES LIMITED
Business: Energy Management Services and Engineering, Procurement Consultancy and Laboratory Services
Address: Energy House, 94, Awolowo Rd, S.W. Ikoyi, Lagos
Tel: (01) 2694627-8 (2L), 08023058644 **Fax:** (01) 2692734
E-mail: ieslagos@hyperia.com
Website: www.ies-nigeria.com
* 3, Rumuokoro Street, off Aba Road, Rumuomasi, Port Harcourt
Tel: (084) 234227
Contact: Dr. Oladiran Fawibe - Chairman/CEO.

INTERNATIONAL ENVELOPES LIMITED
Business: Manufacturing of Envelopes & Stationery
Address: 22, Ajayi Road, near Excellence Hotel, Aguda-Ogba, Ikeja, Lagos
Tel: (01) 4923987, 9211888, 08033469090
E-mail: interenvelopes@nova.net.ng
* 38, Ajayi Bembe Street, Idumota, Lagos.
Tel: (01) 2669193, 08033017687
* Block E3 (Suite 1), Niger Street, Garki Model Market, Garki, Abuja
Tel: 08034061199

INTERNATIONAL EQUITABLE ASSOCIATION (COMMERCIAL & INDUSTRIAL) LIMITED
Business: Manufacture & Marketing of Fast-Moving Consumer Products
Address: 1, Nicholas Road, off Owerri Road, Umungasi, Aba
Tel: (082) 220699
Contact: Mr. Francisco Gutierrez - MD/CEO

INTERNATIONAL EXECUTIVE PLACEMENT SERVICES LTD
Business: Immigration Consultancy Services
Address: 13, Adenubi Close, off Majekodunmi Street, off Allen Avenue (by Oshopey Plaza), Ikeja, Lgaos
Tel: (01) 3450581, 8045939, 7915226, 08023023043
E-mail: iepsglobal@yahoo.com
Website: www.iepsglobalcom

INTERNATIONAL FRACTIONATION & MARGARINE PRODUCTS LIMITED
Business: Processing & Production of Vegetable Oil & Margarine
Address: 2A, Acme Road, by Akilo Road, Ogba Industrial Estate, Ikeja, Lagos
Tel: (01) 4924895, 4924997, 4925397, 4925731
E-mail: goldenoil@micro.com.ng
* 251A, Polobros Avenue, Harbour Industrial Layout, off Atani Road, Onitsha.
Contact: Mr. R. K. Mirchandani - Chairman/CEO

INTERNATIONAL GLASS INDUSTRIES LIMITED
Business: Manufacturing of Glass Containers and Packaging
Address: Churchgate Tower, Plot PC. 30, Afribank Street, Victoria Island, Lagos
Tel: (01) 2620411, 2620550, 2620413
Fax: (01) 2620420, 2620551
* New Industrial Layout, Ogbor Hill, Aba
Tel: (082) 226009, 224357 **Fax:** (082) 226009
Contact: Mr. B. Roa - GM/CEO

INTERNATIONAL INSURANCE BROKERS LIMITED
Business: Insurance Broking and Pensions Consultants
Address: 1, Beirut Road, Kano
Tel: (064) 631784, 08036085274, 08046121632
Fax: (064) 634058
Contact: Igwe Alex Nwokedi - Chairman
Chief Victor C. Areh - MD/CEO

INTERNATIONAL LEARNING SYSTEMS LIMITED
Business: IT and Business Management Training; Informatics Computer Training Franchise
Address: 170, Awolowo Road S.W. Ikoyi, Lagos
Tel: (01) 2672234-6 (3 L), 2671227-8 (2 L), 4701739, 4731268
E-mail: nigeria@informaticsgroup.com
thames_lagos@thamesfranchise.informaticsgroup.com
ics_lagos@icsfranchise.informaticsgroup.com
Website: www.informaticsgroup.com
Contact: Mrs Sekinat Olusola Yusuf - MD/CEO

INTERNATIONAL LOSS ADJUSTERS (W.A) LIMITED
Business: Loss Adjusting
Address: 221, Ikorodu Road, Ilupeju, Lagos
Tel: (01) 4705230, 4930881, 4930882
Contact: Mr. B. B. Prottey - MD/CEO

INTERNATIONAL METAL PRODUCTS LIMITED
Business: Manufacturing of Galvanised Iron Pipes
Address: Plot 15 & 16, Block XIII, Industrial Estate, Ogun State Housing Corporation, Idiroko Road, P.O. Box 608, Otta, Ogun State
Tel: (039) 722257-8 (2 L), 722610 **Fax:** (039) 722258
E-mail: homan@linkserve.com
Contact: Mr. Cheun Yanhoo - Chairman/CEO

INTERNATIONAL NETWORK COMMUNICATIONS AFRICA LIMITED (HYPERIA)
Business: Full Internet Service Provider
Address: 27, Saka Tinubu Street, Victoria Island, Lagos
Tel: (01) 2624168, 2620726, 2612474, 2610714
Fax: (01) 2620079, 2618347
E-mail: info@hyperia.com
Contact: Mr. Larry Chidi-Maha - Exec. Director

INTERNATIONAL OILFIELD SERVICES LIMITED
Business: Diving, Marine Maintenance and Scaffolding Training; Installation of Equipment
Address: Plot 20, East-West Rd, Rumuodara, Port Harcourt
Tel: (084) 613168-9 (2 L) **Fax:** (084) 231667, 613169
Website: www.iosl-nigeria.com
Contact: Mr. Henry MacPepple - Group Chairman/CEO
Mr. David Lodge - MD

INTERNATIONAL PACKAGING INDUSTRIES OF NIG. PLC
Business: Paper Conversion, Manufacturing of Paper Products
Address: 3, Obasa Road, off Oba Akran Avenue, Ikeja Industrial Estate, Ikeja, Lagos
Tel: (01) 4968199, 4712705, 8043726
Contact: Mr. B. O. Thomas - Chairman/CEO

INTERNATIONAL PLASTICS (NIGERIA) LIMITED
Business: Production of Flexible Packaging Material
Address: 4C, Ijora Causeway, Ijora, Lagos
Tel: (01) 5878286, 5453772-4 (3L), 7741507, 7760850
Fax: (01) 2627751, 5453724
E-mail: inplas@infoweb.abs.net
Contact: Mr. N. S. Kedarnath - MD/CEO

INTERNATIONAL POLYWORKS COMPANY LIMITED
Business: Manufacturing of Polypropylene Thread, Twins and Cords Hair Attachment and Ropes
Address: Command Secondary School Road, Ipaja, Lagos
Tel: (01) 7746898, 08033291782
Contact: Mr. Shakir Oluwo - GM/CEO

INTERNATIONAL STANDARD SECURITIES LIMITED
Business: Stockbroking and Investment Banking; Financial Advisory Services
Address: 144A, Association Road, Dolphin Estate, Osborne Road, Ikoyi, Lagos
Tel: (01) 2694682, 2694024 **Fax:** (01) 2694119, 2694832
E-mail: iss@linkserve.com.ng
iss@euroyellowpages.com.ng
Contact: Mr. Lere M. Ayanwola - CEO

INTERNATIONAL STARCHEM INDUSTRIES LIMITED
Business: Sales of Printing Papers & Board, Paper and Board Converts; Printing, Industrial Chemicals and Graphic Materials; Importers and Exporters.
Address: Plot 2/4, Badejo Kalesanwo Road, off Ladipo Street Matori Industrial Estate, Mushin, Lagos
Tel: (01) 4527182, 821100, 523375, 08022913445
Fax: (01) 4522908
E-mail: starchem@hyperia.com
Contact: Mr. Matthew O. Komolafe, Snr - MD/CEO

INTERNATIONAL TANNERS LIMITED
Business: Tanning of Hides and Skins
Address: Plot 72/78, Sharada Industrial Estate Phase I, Kano
Tel: (064) 665391, 665392 **Fax:** (064) 664144
Contact: Mr. M. L. Akkad - Chairman/CEO

INTERNATIONAL TECHNICAL & ENGINEERING CO. LTD
Business: Refurbishing of Heavy Machinery and Trucks, Plant Hiring, Sales of Spare Parts
Address: 8/9, Kachia Road, Kaduna South, Kaduna
Tel: (062) 231305, 237192 **Fax:** (062) 237414
E-mail: itec@wwlkad.com
Contact: Alh. A. Yusuf - MD/CEO

INTERNATIONAL TELECOMMUNICATIONS CO. LTD
Business: Sales & Service of Telecommnication Products, Telecommunication Services
Address: Nurses House (3rd Floor), Plot PC. 43, Afribank Street, Victoria Island, Lagos
Tel: (01) 2611220, 2611221 **Fax:** (01) 2611226
Website: www.itcltd.net
Contact: Alh. (Dr.) Muh'du Mainasara Gusau - Chairman
Mr. Sunil Sawlani - MD/CEO

INTERNATIONAL TEXTILES INDUSTRIES (NIGERIA) LTD
Business: Manufacturing and Marketing of Textile Products
Address: Plot 10, Block E, Isolo Ind. Estate, Isolo, Lagos
Tel: (01) 4520118, 7740673, 7745976, 7745979
Fax: (01) 4524897
E-mail: pchiti@churchgate.com
* Plot 84, Ikorodu Ind Estate, Odogunyan-Ikorodu
Tel: (01) 7740674, 7745977
Contact: Mr B. I. Mantani - Director

INTERNATIONAL TOBACCO COMPANY PLC
Business: Growing of Tobacco; Processing of Tobacco; Production of Cigarettes
Address: T & E Premises, 1, Billingsway, Oregun Industrial Estate, Oregun, Lagos
* Industrial Estate, Offa Road, Ilorin
Tel: (031) 221295-7 (3 L)
Fax: (031) 224725-6 (2 L), 224728
Contact: Alh. Aminu Wali - Chairman
Mr. Isaac L. Mowo - MD/CEO

INTERNATIONAL TOOLS LIMITED
Business: Rewindeing of AC & DC Electric Motors; Sales of Electrical & Mechanical Engineering Tools, Eqipment and Accessories
Address: 10, Abebe Village Road, near Nigerian Breweries & UBA, Iganmu, Surulere, Lagos
Tel: (01) 5454534, 5872545, 5831130 **Fax:** (01) 5850206
E-mail: epolos@infoweb.abs.net
* 69B/70, Trans-Amadi Ind., Layout, Port Harcourt
Tel: (084) 573120, 08033023504
Contact: Mr. W. H. Schommers - MD/CEO

INTERNATIONAL TROPEX COURIER SERVICES LIMITED
Business: Courier & Cargo Services
Address: 12, Mobolaji Bank-Anthony Way, Maryland,Lagos
Tel: (01) 4966897, 4966891, 4966903
Contact: Mr. Enoma Agbontaen - MD/CEO

INTERNATIONAL TRADING & CONTRACTING LIMITED
Business: Internet Service Provider, Clearing & Freight

Forwarding, Warehousing, Production of Table Water
Address: 9A, Adeola Odeku Street, Victoria Island, Lagos
Tel: (01) 5558116-9 (4 L), 5558120 **Fax:** (01) 5558116
E-mail: itcgroup@yahoo.com
Contact: Chief Emmanuel Nweke - Chairman/CEO

INTERNATIONAL TRUST BANK PLC
Business: Commercial Banking
Address: ICON House (6th Floor), Plot 999F, Idejo/Danmole Street, Victoria Island, Lagos
Tel: (01) 2625378-80 (3 L), 612829, 613674
Fax: (01) 2625756, 2622490
E-mail: itbank@linkserve.com.ng
Contact: Ambassador Hamzat Ahmadu CON - Chairman
Mr Usman Masanawa - Group Head (Credit/Mktg)

INTERNATIONAL UNIFORMS NIGERIA LIMITED
Business: Manufacturing of Uniforms, Protective Wears, Table Cloth, Napkins & Bedding; Monogramming
Address: Uniforms House, 4, Oshitelu Street, off Ola Ayeni Street, Ikeja, Lagos
Tel/Fax: (01) 4748495, 4972790
E-mail: interuniforms@nigerianet.com
Contact: Chief G. O. Egbule - Chairman/CEO

INTERNET SOLUTIONS NIGERIA LIMITED (NOVA)
Business: Internet Service Provider
Address: Eko Hotel Shopping Complex (Suite 17), 1, Ajose Adeogun Street, Victoria Island, Lagos
Tel: (01) 2615199, 2615259, 2615359, 2615559
Fax: (01) 2615559
E-mail: sales@nova.net.ng
Website: www.nova.net.ng
Contact: Mr. Rabi Jarmakani - MD/CEO

INTEROIL SERVICES LIMITED
Business: Oilfield Engineering Services; Marine Service
Address: Km 16, Port Harcourt-Aba Expressway, Port Harcourt
Tel: (084) 230921, 232888, 234214, 237716
Fax: (084) 237716
* Foreshore Towers (4th Floor), 2A, Osborne Road, Ikoyi, Lagos
Tel: (01) 2691532, 2692787, 2695154 **Fax:** (01) 2692787
Contact: Alh. M. Tukur - Chairman

INTERPAK LIMITED
Business: Manufacturing of Industrial Packaging Products, Industrial & Commercial Printing
Address: Plot 3, Block K, Oluyole Industrial Estate, Ring Road, Ibadan
Tel: (032) 2311452, 2311454

INTERPRO & SERVICES NIGERIA LIMITED
Business: Sales, Installation & Maintenance of Computers & Office Equipment, Sales of Industrial Chemicals and Safety Products for the Oil and Gas Industry
Address: 127, Ogunlana Drive, Surulere, Lagos
Tel: (01) 837362, 831685, 08023265712
Fax: (01) 837362
E-mail: infortronicsnigltd@yahoo.com
Contact: Mr A. A. Fyneface - Chairman/CEO

INTERPRODS LIMITED
Business: Sales & Service of Banking Automation Equipment
Address: Plot 281, Gbagada Expressway, Gbagada, Lagos
Tel: (01) 4971918-9 (2 L), 7740575 (DL), 2641876-7 (2L)
Fax: (01) 2643930, 2641876-7 (2L)
E-mail: interprods@hyperia.com
Contact: Mr. S. A. Akeju - Chairman/CEO

INTERPUBLIC NIGERIA LIMITED
Business: Advertising, Marketing and Public Relations
Address: 63C, Adebayo Mokuolu Street, Anthony, Lagos
Tel: (01) 5551182, 7738929
E-mail: interpub@nigol.net.ng
Contact: Mr. Sola Oluwole - Chairman/CEO

INTERSTATE SECURITIES LIMITED
Business: Stockbroking, Corporate Finance Services
Address: 14B, Keffi Street, S. W. Ikoyi, Lagos
Tel: (01) 2631600, 2646932-3 (2 L)
E-mail: interstate@micro.com.ng
Contact: Mr. R. G. Asabia - Chairman
Mr. A. O. Odunsi - MD/CEO

INTERSWITCH LIMITED
Business: Electronic Payment Solutions Provider (Transaction Switching and Payment Processing Services)
Address: Plot 1648C, Oko-Awo Close, off Karimu Kotun Street, Victoria Island, Lagos
Tel: (01) 4739101, 4616300 **Fax:** (01) 4616299
E-mail: info@interswitchng.com
Website: www.interswitchng.com
Contact: Dr. Evans Woherem - Chairman
Mr. Mitchell Elegbe - MD/CEO

INTERTEC ENGINEERING (NIGERIA) LIMITED
Business: Procurement of Specialised Materials; Maintenance and Safety Services to the Petrochemical and other Hi-Tech Industries
Address: 1A, Tiamiyu Savage Street, Victoria Island, Lagos
Tel: (01) 2624627-8 (2L), 2627915, 08023002275
Fax: (01) 2615811
E-mail: intertec@linkserve.com.ng
* 2, Temple Ejekwu Close, Rumuogba, P/Harcourt
Tel: (084) 611922-3 (2 L) **Fax:** (084) 611922
E-mail: ph-intertec@phca.linkserve.com
Contact: Mr. J. Kruttke - MD/CEO

INTERTRONIC (NIGERIA) LIMITED
Business: Sales and Maintenance of Radio and Satellite Communication Systems
Address: NISSCO House, Plot 232A, Adeola Odeku Street, Victoria Island, Lagos
Tel: (01) 2616948, 616407 **Fax:** (01) 616407
E-mail: intertronic@micro.com.ng
Contact: Chief Idris Umar-Balogun - Chairman
Mr. Jack Letanneur - MD/CEO

INTERWORLD MANAGEMENT & SERVICES LIMITED
Business: Distribution and Marketing of Books and Journals; Publishers' Representative
Address: 4, Abayomi Akinmosa Crescent, Idi-Ishin, Jericho Ibadan
Tel: (02) 2414258, 2414087 **Fax:** (02) 2414087

E-mail: omotayo@gacom.net
Contact: Mr. A. O. O. Morgan - Chairman/CEO

INTERWORLD PRODUCTS (NIGERIA) LIMITED
Business: Distribution, Sales and Marketing of BINATONE Range of Electronic and Electrical Equipment
Address: BINATONE House, 66/68, Akanro Street, Ilasamaja, Mushin, Lagos
Tel: (01) 4527965, 4523186 **Fax:** (01) 2624171
Website: www.binatone.com
* PC 10, Engineering Close, off Idowu Taylor Street, Victoria Island, Lagos.
Tel: (01) 2622209
* 94, Nnamdi Azikiwe St, Lagos.
Tel: (01) 2641485
* 23, Bello Road, Kano.
Tel: (064) 642710
Contact: Chief Alex O. Akinyele - Chairman

INTRA FISHERIES NIGERIA LIMITED
Business: Importation of Frozen Fish, Rental of Cold Storage
Address: Plot 1303A, Akin Adesola St Victoria Island, Lagos
Tel: (01) 2622259, 2615505, 2622232 **Fax:** (01) 2619487
E-mail: primlaks@hyperia.com
* Plot 1, Block M, Isolo Industrial Scheme, Ilasamaja, Lagos.
Tel: (01) 7743501, 7761938 Fax: (01) 7756660, 7768979
Contact: Mr. B. C. P. Gowda - MD/CEO

INTRACOM
Business: Internet Service Provider
Address: Plot 277A, Ajose Adeogun St, Victoria Island, Lagos
Tel: (01) 2625316-8 (3 L) **Fax:** (01) 2625315
E-mail: info@intracom5.com
info@intracom.net.ng
Contact: Mr. Adel Reda - Director
Mr. Agboola Johnson - Sales/Marketing Manager

INTRALOG LIMITED
Business: Technical Service Workshop; Sales, Installation and Maintenance of Technical Equipment
Address: Km. 14, Lekki-Epe Expressway, Ikota, Lagos
Tel: (01) 7742990 **Fax:** (01) 2614638
E-mail: splekki@compuserve.com
* Plot 330, Mike Akhigbe Drive, Trans-Amadi Ind. Layout, Port Harcourt.
Tel/Fax: (084) 239274
* Plot 494, Funmilayo Ransome-Kuti Road, Area 3, Garki, Abuja.
Tel/Fax: (09) 5239191

INTRA-NIGER INSURANCE BROKERS LIMITED
Business: Insurance Broking
Address: Western House (12th Floor), 8/10, Broad St, Lagos
Tel: (01) 2636756
Contact: Chief T. O. Balogun - Chairman/CEO

INTRASS LIMITED
Business: Pre-Shipement Inspection Consultancy Service
Address: 25, Warehouse Road (2nd Floor), Apapa, Lagos
Tel/Fax: (01) 5455579, 5455855
E-mail: intrass@hyperia.com
Contact: Mr. Femi Awogbade - MD/CEO

INVENTMEDIA LIMITED
Business: Outdoor Advertising, Lithography & Printing
Address: 10-12, Somorin Okeowo St, Ifako-Gbagada, Lagos
Tel: (01) 4707661, 5552689, 7733885, 7742843, 08037134839 **Fax:** (01) 5552841
E-mail: info@inventmedialtd.com
Website: www.nventmedialtd.com
Contact: Mr. Adekunle Adeshina - MD/CEO.

INVESTMENT ASSETS FINANCE LIMITED
Business: Portfolio Management, Financial Advisers
Address: Eleganza Plaza (Leo Block), 1, Commercial Road, Apapa, Lagos
Tel: (01) 5877082

INVESTMENT BANKING & TRUST COMPANY LTD (IBTC)
Business: Banking Services
Address: I..B.T.C. Place, Walter Carrington Crescent, Victoria Island, Lagos
Tel: (01) 2626520-40 (12L) **Fax:** (01) 2626541-2 (2L)
E-mail: IBTC@IBTClagos.com
Website: http://www.IBTClagos.com
Contact: Mrs. O. A. David-Borha - ED.

INVESTMENT COMMUNICATIONS LIMITED
Business: Television Programme Production, Spotlighting and Image Making
Address: 146, Bode Thomas Street, Surulere, Lagos
Tel: (01) 5851853, 4701366
Contact: Mr. Felix Imosili - MD/CEO.

INVESTMENT HOLDINGS LIMITED
Business: Real Estate Development and Mangement
Address: ED House (6th Floor), 47, Marina, Lagos
Tel: (01) 2660928; **Fax:** (01) 2666313
E-mail: tabins@micro.com..ng
Contact: Mrs. R. A. Braithwaite - MD/CEO

INVESTMENTS & ALLIED ASSURANCE COMPANY LTD
Business: Non-Life Assurance
Address: Block 10, Ikorodu Road, beside Seventh Day Adventist Church, Maryland, Ikeja, Yaba, Lagos
Tel: (01) 2905320, 4714855, 4970269, 7731686
Fax: (01) 4970269
Contact: Mr. Omoniyi Adeboyejo - MD/CEO

INVESTORS & TRUST COMPANY LIMITED
Business: Stockbroking, Financial Services
Address: Gottschalk House (2nd Floor), 58, Marina, Lagos
Tel: (01) 2666218 **Fax:** (01) 2641070
E-mail: invtrust@alpha.linkserve.com
Contact: Dr. R. A. Masha - MD/CEO.

IPBC NIGERIA LIMITED
Business: Supply & Installation of Fire-Fighting Systems, UPS Equipment & Stabilizers, Computer Environment Control & Site Preparation Services
Address: 6, Norman Williams Street, S.W. Ikoyi, Lagos
Tel: (01) 2671200, 2692966, 2671672-3 (2 L)
Fax: (01) 2614808
E-mail: ipbc@hyperia.com
Contact: Mr. Goodie M. Ibru - Chairman
Mr. G. P. Malkani - MD/CEO.

IPCO (NIGERIA) LIMITED
Business: Engineering Construction
Address: Edo House (4th Floor), Plot 1225, Bishop Oluwole Street, Victoria Island, Lagos
Tel: (01) 2622532-3 (2 L), 2622545, 2623660, 4617841
Fax: (01) 2625687, 2626784, 4617842
Contact: Mr P. D. Rea - MD/CEO

IPEC INDUSTRIES NIGERIA LIMITED
Business: Manufacturing of Airfreshener, Starch and Nylon
Address: 208/212, Broad Street, Lagos
Tel: (01) 2661590, 2667042 **Fax:** (01) 2643003
E-mail: ipec_industries@hotmail.com
* 4, Oyeleke Street, Alausa, Ikeja, Lagos
Tel: (01) 4931917, 4931918
Contact: Mr. M. O. Lawal - GM

ipNX NIGERIA LIMITED
Business: Infrastructure-Base Telecommunication Services
Address: 4, Balarabe Musa Cresenet, off Samuel Manuwa Road, Victoria Island, Lagos
Tel: (01) 4619943-6 (4 L) **Fax:** (01) 2614633
E-mail: info@ipnxnigeria.net
Website: www.ipnxnigeria.net
* Tractor & Equipment Premises, 30, Elf Road, Trans-Amadi, Port Harcourt
Tel: (084) 233297
* Coscharis Plaza (3rd Floor), Faskari Street, Area 3, Garki, Abuja
Contact: Engr. Isaiah A. Mohammed - Chairman
Mr. Ejovi Aror - Group MD/CEO

iPROSIT LIMITED
Business: Training, Technology Development Services, Technical Consulting, Process & Instrumentation Engineering
Address: Plot 242, Kofo Abayomi St, Victoria Island, Lagos
Tel: (01) 2611729, 2619954, 3200580-4 (5 L)
Fax: (01) 2619945
E-mail: learining@iteco.com
Website: www.iprositng.com
Contact: Mr. Tola Obigbesan - MD/CEO

IPTC (WEST AFRICA) LIMITED
Business: Technical and Industrial Consultancy Services
Address: 25, Boyle Street, Onikan, Lagos
Tel: (01) 2632714 **Fax:** (01) 2636980
Contact: Dr. J. M. Engels - Chairman/CEO.

IPWA PLC
Business: Manufacture of Paints and Lacquers
Address: Oba Akran Avenue, Ikeja Industrial Estate, Lagos
Tel: (01) 4970149, 4968155-8(4L),
Fax: (01) 4970148, 4970149
E-mail: ipwa@cyberspace.net.ng
Contact: Chief Henry O. S. Kayode - MD/CEO

IRONGATE SECURITY SERVICES LIMITED
Business: Security Services
Address: 5, Holmes Street, off Eket/Oron Road, Eket.
Tel: (085) 701748-9 (2L)
* 290, Borno Way, Yaba, Lagos.
Tel: (01) 862886, 867413.

IRS AIRLINES LIMITED (Div. of Isiyaku Rabiu & Sons Ltd)
Business: Airline Services
Address: Omnia House, 1, IBB Way, Wuse Zone 4, Abuja.
Tel: (09) 5236071, 090-809860, 08023018865, 08033114800, 08033114877, *(01) 4973122
Contact: Alh. Rabiu Isiyaku Rabiu - Chairman/CEO
Capt. Fola Akinkotun - MD/Chief Operating Officer

ISAACTAN LIMITED
Business: Manufacturing of Hygienic Tissue Paper Products
Address: Isaactan Close, Plot 16, Block D, Ogba Industrial Estate, Ikeja, Lagos
Tel: (01) 4703121, 4728221, 4807806, 4921133, 7731202
* Plot 16, Block D, Ogba Ind. Estate, Ikeja, Lagos
Tel: (01) 4703121
Contact: Major Gen. Olufemi Olutoye (rtd.) - Chairman
Elder Isaac Sunday Tapere - MD/CEO.

ISI CHIPS LIMITED
Business: Manufacturing and Marketing of Footwear
Address: 2, Unity Road, Fagge Takudu, Kano
Tel: (064) 649091, 639665, 667731-2 **Fax:** (064) 649091
E-mail: isi-chips@yahoo.com
* Plot 76, Sharada Industrial Estate Phase II, Kano
* 15, Gbajumo Street, off Breadfruit Street, Lagos
Tel: (01) 2666458
Contact: Alh. Nuhu Salisu - Chairman
Mr. Davide de Gasperin - ED

ISIJOLA OPTICAL SERVICES (NIGERIA) LIMITED
Business: Ophthalmic/Optical Services; Eye Clinic
Address: Isijola Vision House, 2, Isijola Street, off Ikorodu Road, Ilupeju, Lagos
Tel: (01) 4963034, 4963034, 08033023804
E-mail: isijola@nipost.com.ng
Contact: Dr. A. R. Isijola - Chairman/CEO.

ISIWAS NIGERIA LIMITED
Business: Sales and Servcie of UPS, Stabilizers, Security Cardkey Systems, and Fire Detection/Prevention Systems, Computer Site-Preparation Engineers
Address: 60, Surulere St, Dopemu Bus-Stop, Agege, Lagos
Tel: (01) 8112042, 08023125979, 08037175509
Fax: (01) 2317054
E-mail: isiwas@yahoo.com
Contact: Mr. Kareem Mohammed - MD/CEO.

ISIYAKU RABIU GROUP OF COMPANIES LIMITED
Business: Conglomerate (Importers, General Merchants, Industralist, & Civil Contactors)
Address: 58, Ibrahim Taiwo Road, Kano
Tel: (064) 645930, 649935 **Fax:** (064) 634313
* 10, Wharf Road, Apapa, Lagos
Tel: (01) 5452379, 5452380 **Fax:** (01) 5453754
Contact: Alh. Mohammed N. Rabiu - GMD.

ISMAIL & PARTNERS
Business: Chartered Surveyors and Valuers, Estate Managers
Address: 106/110, Lewis Street, Lafiaji, Lagos
Tel: (01) 2634917, 2630327, 2630221 **Fax:** (01) 2630241
* 25, Adeniyi Jones Avenue, Ikeja, Lagos
Tel: (01) 4973891-2 (2 L)
Contact: Otunba Tade Ismail - Principal Partner

ISN PRODUCTS NIGERIA LIMITED
Business: Marketing & Distribution of Medical & Laboratory Equipment and Health-Support Products
Address: ISN House, 143, Gbagada Expressway, Gbagada Estate Phase 1, Gbagada, Lagos
Tel: (01) 4976861, 7741438, 5550633 **Fax:** (01) 5550633

ISOGLASS INDUSTRIES LIMITED
Business: Manufacturing and Marketing of Automobile Safety Glass and Decorative Glass
Address: Plot 17, Block E, Oluyole Industrial Estate, Ibadan
Tel: (02) 2317526, 2310236-7 (2L) **Fax:** (02) 2317536
E-mail: tomtol@skannet.com
Contact: Chief (Dr.) Isaac Akinmokun CON - Chairman

ISOKO COMMUNITY BANK LIMITED
Business: Communuty Banking Services
Address: 1, Ibrahim Kefas Road, Oleh, Delta State
Tel: (048) 888419, 888457
E-mail: info@isokobank.com
Website: www.isokobank.com
Contact: Joe Arausi Esq - Chairman
Mr. Anthony O. Echewa - Manager

IT CONCEPTS LIMITED
Business: Importation, Sales, Maintenance and Repairs of Computers, Networking
Address: Plot 1661, Oyin Jolayemi St, Victoria Island, Lagos
Tel: (01) 2626303, 2626308, 7755480 **Fax:** (01) 2626303
E-mail: itconcepts@hyperia.com
Contact: Mr. Benedict E. Uzoebo - Chairman/CEO.

IT SOLUTIONS LIMITED
Business: IT Training & Certification; Internet Services and Cyber Solutions
Address: God's Grace Plaza (5th Floor), 63, Allen Avenue, Ikeja, Lagos
Tel: (01) 4977223-4 (2 L), 8151539, 08033022208, 08034716831 **Fax:** (01) 4935849
E-mail: info@itsolutions-ng.com
Website: www.itsolutions-ng.com
Contact: Col. Sani Bello (rtd.) - Chairman
Mr. Donald T. Brown - Dep MD

IT WORLD LIMITED
Business: Sales of Information Technology Products, Card Printers and Office Automation
Address: 6, Pepple Street, Ikeja, Lagos
Tel: (01) 4934489, 4934490, 7750867, 08033194384
E-mail: itworldnl@yahoo.com
Contact: Mr. Obinna Obienu - MD/CEO.

ITALIAN GRANITE & MARBLE COMPANY LIMITED
Business: Mrble and Granite Sales and Works
Address: 229, Apapa Road, Ijora, Lagos
Tel: (01) 833989, 4705278
Contact: Chief (Dr.) B.A. Adigun - Chairman
Mr. R. Panesi - MD/CEO

ITEC SOLUTIONS LIMITED
Business: Sales & Maintenance of Computers, Consultancy Services, Networking and System Integration
Address: 13A, Idowu Martins Street, Victoria Island, Lagos
Tel: (01) 2624828, 2624829 **Fax:** (01) 2624830
E-mail: itec@itecsol.com.ng
* Plot 653, Zone A8, Wuse II, Abuja
Tel: (09) 5238613, 5238614
* 42, Old Aba Rd, Artillery Junction, Port Harcourt
Tel: (084) 239269, 239270
Contact: Mr Leo Stan Ekeh - Chairman
Mrs. Chioma Ekeh - CEO

ITECO (NIGERIA) LIMITED
Business: Information Technology Consultancy Services (Enterprise Network, e-Security Solutions, Intelligent Building Systems, Managed Networks)
Address: Plot 242, Kofo Abayomi St, Victoria Island, Lagos
Tel: (01) 2611729, 2619954., 3200580-4 (5L)
Fax: (01) 2619945
E-mail: info@iteco.com
Website: www.telnetng.com
* 5, Onwuchekwa Road, Rumuomasi, Port Harcourt
Tel: (084) 233296, 233301 **Fax:** (084) 233301
* Coomassie House, Muhammadu Buhari Way, Central Business District, Abuja
Tel: (09) 6700407
Contact: Dr. B. G. Ishaku - Chairman
Mr. Ejovi Aror - MD/CEO

ITEX LIMITED
Business: Manufacturing/Marketing of World-class Office, Household and Conference/Boardroom Furniture
Address: Plot 549, Adetokunbo Ademola Cr, Wuse II, Abuja
Tel: (09) 5240633-4 (2L), 5237980 **Fax:** (09) 5236861
E-mail: itexltd@yahoo.com
Contact: Mr. Tony E. Ezekiel - Chairman/CEO
Ms. Maya Edukere - Marketing Manager

ITN-HYDROMAK LIMITED
Business: Borehole Drilling, Construction of Borehole-Based Water Supply Schemes
Address: Katsina House (1st Floor), Ralph Shodeinde Street, opp. Fed. Min. of Finance Hqters off Ahmadu Bello Way, Central Business District, Abuja
Tel: (09) 2340309, 0803314367, 08037866303
Fax: (09) 2348248
Contact: Alh. Ibrahim Ali Amin - Chairman/CEO

ITOTEC GROUP OF COMPANIES
Business: Printing and Colour Separation, Plastic Manufacturing, Transportation, Engineering, Warehousing
Address: 3/5, Francis Aghedo Close, Ojodu-Berger, Lagos
Tel: (01) 4923888, 8042657, 4701522, 08034923888
Contact: Chief Francis Aghedo - Chairman/CEO
Mr. Chris Osaze Asemota - GM

ITT NIGERIA LIMITED
Business: Telecommunication Engineering Services; Sales & Installation of Telecommunication Network Equipment
Address: Plot 1407, Adetokunbo Ademola Street, Victoria Island, Lagos
Tel: (01) 7742262, 7722265, 2620330-1 (2 L)
Fax: (01) 2620332
E-mail: alcatelittn@nova.net.ng
* Skodak HOuse, Oyo Road, Mokola, Ibadan
Tel: (02) 2410094, 2411909

ITUA PACK LIMITED
Business: Industrial Processing & Packaging, Flexographic Printing on Foils & Laminates; Engineering Services
Address: 5, Simbiat Abiola (Oregun) Road, by Radio Bus-Stop, Alausa, Ikeja, Lagos
Tel: (01) 4970860, 4965778 **Fax:** (01) 4936473
E-mail: itua@infoweb.abs.net
Contact: Mr. Augustus Itua - Chairman/CEO.

IVORY MUSIC LIMITED
Business: Manufacture and Marketing of Music Records, CD's Cassetes and Video
Address: Ivory Music House, Plot 13, Alhaja Ashabi Cole Rd, Central Business District, Alausa, Ikeja, Lagos
Tel: (01) 4968150-1 (2L) **Fax:** (01) 4968150
Contact: Mr. Bode Akinyemi - MD/CEO

IVORY PRODUCTS NIGERIA LIMITED
Business: Manufacture of Plasctic Wares and Containers
Address: 1, Henry Carr Road, Ikeja Ind. Estate, Ikeja, Lagos
Tel/Fax (01) 4960365
Contact: Otunba Adekunle Ojora - Chairman

IWEL PROPERTY BROKERS LIMITED
Business: Property Developers & Managers, Estate Agents
Address: 65, Eric Manuel Crescent, off Bode Thomas Street, Surulere, Lagos
Tel: (01) 5835853, 5832246, 7731918, 08033022237, 08033022236, 08033210765 **Fax:** (01) 5835853
E-mail: iwel@hyperia.com
iwelumo_iwelumo@yahoo.com
* Regency Suites (Suite 203), 17 (Plot 1615), Ahmed Onibudo Street, Victoria Island, Lagos
Tel: (01) 2611761, 614447, 3200177, 7731918

IWOPIN PULP & PAPER COMPANY LIMITED
Business: Manufacturing and Marketing of Bond Paper
Address: Iwopin, Ijebu Waterside, off Sagamu-Benin Expressway, Iwopin, Ogun State
Tel: (090) 404628, 404616, 404113
* Katia Gardens, Plot 1676, Oladele Olashore Street Victoria Island, Lagos
Tel: (01) 2615756, 2615759, 2621116, 2621115
Fax: (01) 2615745

IWUBA IFEDIORA & ASSOCIATES
Business: Estate Surveyors & Valuers, Property Developers
Address: A.C.B. Building (3rd Floor, Right Wing), 3/9, Ogui Road, Enugu
Tel: (042) 256551
* 55, New Market Road, Onitsha.
Tel: (046) 210930

IWUOHA BESTWAY ELECTRONICS LIMITED
Business: Importation and Marketing of Electronic Appliances; Transportation; Hospitality Services
Address: 2, Olo Street, Omagba Phase I, Opp. Enugu Park, Onitsha-Enugu Expressway, Onitsha
Tel: (046) 412050
Contact: Chief (Sir) S. I. Iwuoha - Chairman/CEO

IYAYI BROTHERS (NIGERIA) LIMITED
Business: Wood & Crumb Rubber Processing, Furniture Production; Maritime Services; Distribution and Marketing of Frozen Seafoods and Petroleum Products; Export of Agricultural Produce
Address: 6/12, Aghimien Street, off Okhoro Road, Benin City
Tel: (052) 253245, 257400, 258932, 250463, 254720, 254658, 253897 **Fax:** (052) 254037
E-mail: iyayi@infoweb.abs.net
Contact: Dr. Iyayi Efianayi JP, MFR - Chairman/CEO

IYAYI MARITIME NIGERIA LIMITED
Business: Shipping, Clearing, Forwarding, Maritime Services
Address: 6/12, Aghimien Street, off Okhoro Road, Benin City
Tel: (052) 253245, 257400, 258932, 250463, 254720, 254658
Fax: (052) 254037
E-mail: iyayi@infoweb.abs.net
* Eleganza Plaza (Leo Block, 2nd Floor), 1, Commercial Road, Apapa, Lagos.
Tel: (01) 5452277
Contact: Dr. Iyayi Efiananyi JP, MFR- Chairman/CEO

IZU CHUKWU TRANSPORT (NIGERIA) LIMITED
Business: Transport of Passenger, Haulage of Goods and Equipment
Address: Plot IN/86, Niger Bridge-Head New Layout, Onitsha
Tel: (046) 212755, 218201 Fax: (046) 214313
* 372, Murtala Mohammed Way, Yaba, Lagos
Tel: (01) 7741764, 4710215-6 (2L) **Fax:** (01) 5455721
Contact: Okaka D. C. Ubajaka - MD/CEO

IZZI INDUSTRIES LIMITED
Business: Shipping, Warehousing and Transportation
Address: 321, Aba Road, Rumukurusi, Port Harcourt
Tel: (084) 3610129, 612621, 612640, 612819

J. AJAYI PATUNOLA & COMPANY
Business: Estate Surveyors & Valuers, Plant & Machinery Valuers, Projects Development & Management
Address: Akron Building, 86A, Allen Avenue, Ikeja, Lgaos
Tel: (01) 7734224, 4742134, 4741950, 7758237, 08037136525
E-mail: japco2003@yahoo.com
* Regency Suites (Suite 005), 17, Ahmed Onibudo Street, Victoria Island, Lagos
Tel: (01) 4742134, 7734224
Contact: Dr. J. Ajayi Patunola - MD/CEO

J. AKIN- GEORGE & COMPANY LIMITED
Business: Insurance Broking
Address: 10, Bode Thomas Street, Surulere, Lagos
Tel: (01) 5834176, 7743883 **Fax:** (01) 5834176
E-mail: jakingeorge@hyperia.com
Contact: Chief J. Akin-George, OFR - Exec. Chairman
Mr. M. O. Akin-George - MD

J. IRORUN ENTERPRISES NIGERIA LIMITED
Business: Importation of Iron Roads & Bars, Wires & Nails
Address: 73, Oregun Road, Welfare Bus-Stop, Ikeja, Lagos
Tel: (01) 4934332, 4970171 **Fax:** (01) 4970171
Contact: Alh. Jamiu Irorun Ogunsola - Chairman/CEO

J. NWANKWU GROUP OF COMPANIES
Business: General Merchandising, Building Construction, Foundry and Engineering Services, Manufacturing

of Packaging, Sanitary & Plastic Products, Bottling of Carbonated Drinks, Food Processing
Address: 19, Lady Regina Nwankwu Avenue, G R.A, Onitsha
Tel: (046) 210588, 210691, 212229
* Atani Road, Bridge-Head Ind. Layout, Onitsha
Tel: (046) 212766, 212231
* Awka Ind. Layout, Old Enugu-Onitsha Rd, Awka.
Tel: (048) 550733
Contact: Chief (Dr.) Joe O. Nwankwu - Chairman/CEO

J. UDEAGBALA HOLDINGS LIMITED
Business: Importation and Marketing of Consumer Goods, Manufacturing, Farming, Real Estate Development
Address: 152, Aba-Owerri Road, Aba
Tel: (082) 350157-60 (4 L), 222950, 227888
E-mail: juhaba@alpha.linkserve.com
* 21B, Alh. Issa Williams Street, off Broad Street, Lagos Island, Lagos
Tel: (01) 2640053, 2643192 **Fax:** (01) 2665405
Contact: Ide John C. Udeagbala - Chairman/CEO

J. A. OKANDEJI & COMPANY LIMITED
Business: Building Materials Merchandising
Address: 1, Palm Avenue, Olorunshogo, Mushin, Lagos
Tel: (01) 521433, 08023663741, 08035748301
Contact: Chief J. A. Okandeji - Chairman/CEO

J. A. OLUWATUDIMU & COMPANY
Business: Estate Surveying and Valuation, Project & Property Management, Auctioneering, Real Estate Agency
Address: Wema Bank/UBA Building (2nd Floor), 52/54, Murtala Mohammed Way, Oyingbo, Lagos
Tel: (01) 7747307, 8045712
E-mail: oluwatudimu@yahoo.com
Contact: Mr. J. A. Oluwatudimu - Principal/CEO

J. D. P. CONSTRUCTION (NIGERIA) LIMITED
Business: Building and Civil Engineering Contractors
Address: Plot 792, Freetown Crescent, Wuse 11, Abuja
Tel: (09) 4139205-6 (2L) **Fax:** (09) 4139192
* 24, Kofo Abayomi Street, Victoria Island, Lagos
Tel: (01) 2613425, 2611783 **Fax:** (01) 2611795
Contact: Engr Jacob Sha'ked - MD/CEO

J. F. AVIATION & TRAVELS LIMITED
Business: Travel Agency, Organization & Operations of Tours, Car Hire Services
Address: Plot 583, U Close, 5th Avenue, Festac Town, Lagos
Tel: (01) 5880378, 4826543, 4746377, 2902561, 08033217582 **Fax:** (01) 5885370
E-mail: jfaviationtravels@hotmail.com
jftravels@intracom.com
* 42, Norman Williams Street, S. W. Ikoyi, Lagos
Tel: (01) 2673218-9 (2 L), 2902849
Contact: Modupe Taibat Adejuwon - Operations Manager

J. J. SCOT GROUP OF COMPANIES
Business: Petroleum (Oil & Gas) Services, Farming, Transportation, Cargo Freighting
Address: 131, Ajamimogha Rd, Angle Park Junction, Warri
Tel: (053) 251854, 321964-5 (2L) **Fax:** (053) 250256
E-mail: jscot@infoweb.abs.net
Contact: Mr. J. J. Scot - Chairman/CEO

J. O. ASUZU BROS & COMPANY (W.A) LIMITED
Business: Sales of Auto Spare Parts, Transformers, Electrical Wares and General Merchandise
Address: Exodus Block (Shop 5/38), ASPAMDA Plaza, Trade Fair Complex, Badagry Expressway, Lagos
Tel: (01) 3208261
E-mail: jo-asuzu@hotmail.com
Contact: Chief J. O. Asuzu - Chairman/CEO

J. T. CHANRAI & COMPANY (P.H) LIMITED
Business: General Merchandising, Improtation of Cosmetics
Address: 37/43, Enuowa Street, Idumota, Lagos
Tel: (01) 2666075, 7740137, 7730735 **Fax:** (01) 2666075
E-mail: jtc@infoweb.abs.net
Contact: Chief H. B. Chanrai - Chairman

JAASNA CITY INSURANCE BROKERS LIMITED
Business: Insurance Broking
Address: 1, Sulu Bolaji Street, off Abibu-Oki Street, behind Bristol Hotel, Lagos Island, Lagos
Tel: (01) 2668474
Contact: Chief J. A. Anumni - MD/CEO

JABROS TRADING NIGERIA LIMITED
Business: Sales of Building Materials & General Goods
Address: 20, Palmer Street, Fegge, Onitsha
Tel: (046) 212604, 217526 **Fax:** (046) 210665
Contact: Mr. Jonathan A. Ibeh - Chairman/CEO

JACLIT NIGERIA LIMITED
Business: Importation and Distribution of Ceramic Tiles, Sanitary Wares & Equipment
Address: Plot 4, Bay 4, Cocoa Industries Road, Ogba, Lagos
Tel: (01) 4924825, 7747085, 08033005082, 08033007315, 08033007341, 0803304388 **Fax:** (01) 4924825
* 11, Isheri Road, opp. Zenith Bank, Ogba, Lagos
* Haliru Dantoro Block, Abari Shopping Complex, opp. Shipper's House, Wuse Zone 5, Abuja
Tel: (09) 6708542, 08023238555, 08037230708

JACOBOD NIGERIA LIMITED
Business: Manufacturing PVC/Plastic Products, Marketing of LP-Gas, Sales & Distribution of Building Materials
Address: Km. 9, Lagos-Badagry Expressway (Alafia Bus-Stop), Lagos
Tel: (01) 7745654, 836266
E-mail: jacobod@mail.com
Contact: Pastor Israel Olorunwunmi - Chairman

JACSIL & SONS ENTERPRISES LIMITED
Business: Outdoor Advertising Agency, Printing Services, General Contractor
Address: 23, Oshineye Street, Pedro, Shomolu, Lagos
Tel: (01) 5820013, 08023269121
Contact: Mr J. O. Nwankpa - Chairman/CEO

JAESON INTERBIZ AGENCIES LIMITED
Business: Freight Forwarding, Transportation, General Contractors
Address: Nnewi Building, 1-3, Creek Road, Apapa, Lagos
Tel: (01) 5452115, 5453600 **Fax:** (01) 5452115
E-mail: jaeson@nova.net.ng
Contact: Sir James Emeka - Chairman/CEO.

JAFA FOAM PRODUCTS NIGERIA LIMITED
Business: Manufacturing and Marketing of Foam Products
Address: Km. 12, Hadejia Road, Kano
Tel: (064) 316710, 317005 (090) 807269
Contact: Alh. Mohammed Jaffal - Chairman
Alh. Nasir Skafi - MD/CEO.

JAFCO CONSTRUCTION LIMITED
Business: Building and Civil Engineering Contractors
Address: 96, Awolowo Road, S.W. Ikoyi, Lagos
Tel: (01) 2690998, 2692317, 2694704-5 (2 L)
Fax: (01) 2694677
E-mail: jafco@hotmail.com
Contact: Alh. A. Mohammed Kollere - Chairman
Mr. Talal A.R. Sayegh - MD/CEO.

JAFCO INDUSTRIES LIMITED
Business: Manufacturing and Marketing of Foam Products
Address: Kudenda Industrial Area, Nnamdi Azikiwe Expressway, Kaduna
Tel: (062) 234112-7 (6 L)
* Adam House (1st Floor), Plot 3, Block C, Amuwo-Odofin Industrial Estate, Lagos
Tel: (01) 7795836
* Jafa Foam Nigeria Ltd, Km. 12, Hadejia Rd, Kano

JAGAL NIGERIA LIMITED
Business: Building & Civil Engineering Contractors, Process & Water Engineering Services, Mechanical & Electrical Engineering, Facility Management, Turnkey Projects, Sales of Building Products
Address: Jagal House, Jagal Road, off Ikosi Road, Oregun Industrial Estate, Oregun, Ikeja, Lagos
Tel: (01) 4973390-4 (5 L) **Fax:** (01) 4973399
E-mail: enquiry@jagal.com
Website: www.jagal.com
*Jagal House, Plot 550, Usuma St, Maitama, Abuja
Tel: (09) 4133489 **Fax:** (09) 4133490
Contact: Mr. Anwar M. Jarmakani - Group Exec. Chairman
Mr. Harry Wardle - MD/CEO.

JAGAL FOODS LIMITED
Business: Restaurant Services
Address: Jagal House, Jagal Road, off Ikosi Road, Oregun, Ikeja, Lagos
Tel: (01) 4973390-4 (5 L) **Fax:** (01) 4970090
E-mail: enquiry@jagal.com
* The New Yorker (Amerian Restaurant), 15, Odudiuwa Way, G.R.A., Ikeja, Lagos
Contact: Mr. Anwar Jarmakani - Group Exec. Chairman
Mr. Donald Spencer - Group GM

JAGAL PHARMA LIMITED
Business: Manufacturing, Marketing and Distribution of Pharmaceutical & Health Care Products
Address: Jagal Road, off Ikosi Road, Oregun, Ikeja, Lagos
Tel: (01) 4973390-4 (5L) **Fax:** (01) 4965745, 4970090
Website: www.jagal.com
Contact: Mr. Anwar Jarmakani - Group Exec. Chairman
Mr. Richard Hargare - MD

JAGAL SPORTS LIMITED
Business: Marketing of Sport Wears and Equipment
Address: 2, Vanguard Avenue, off Carrara Marble, by Kirikiri Canal, Oshodi-Apapa Expressway, Mile 2, Lagos
Tel: (01) 5450510, 5450499, 5450500 **Fax:** (01) 5450530
* 23A, Akin Adesola Street, Victoria Island, Lagos
Tel: (01) 7740185
Contact: Chief Anwar Jarmakani - Chairman
Mr. Rabi Jarmakani - MD

JAGEE NIGERIA LIMITED
Business: Sales, Installatio and Maintenane of Scientif and Laboratory Equipment
Address: 13, Olaleke Taiwo Street, via Ojodu Grammar School, Ojodu, Ikeja, Lagos
Tel: (01) 4923398, 7734109, 08023383481
* 128, Adekunle Fajuyi Road, Ibadan
Tel: (02) 2410882 **Fax:** (02) 2411309
Contact: Mr Gbolade Famoriyo - MD/CEO

JAKKOS ENGINEERING LIMITED
Business: Oil & Gas Industry General Engineering & Services
Address: 9, Chief Onitana St, off Adebola St, Surulere, Lagos
Tel: (01) 5842182, 4819451, 832637 **Fax:** (01) 5849512
E-mail: jakkos@elkapyra.com
* 78/80, Aba Road, Port Harcourt.
Tel: (084) 332264
Contact: Alh. Abu Abdulkadir - Chairman
Mr. E. O. Ochi - Ag. MD/CEO.

JAKURA MARBLE INDUSTRY LIMITED
Business: Production of Marble Furniture and Structures, Production of Superfine & Fine Powders for Paints, Sweets and Livestock Concentrates
Address: Ajara Road, Marine, Lokoja
Tel: (058) 220075, 220085
* 210, Apapa Road, Ijora, Lagos

JAMATAL INDUSTRIES (NIGERIA) LIMITED
Business: Importation, Sales, Installation and Service of Fire-Fighting Equipment
Address: 45, Ogunlana Drive, Surulere, Lagos
Tel: (01) 4701954, 5851111, 08033232160
Fax: (01) 2669002, 4701954
E-mail: rayners@infoweb.abs.net
Contact: Mr. Jerry O. Anu - Chairman/CEO

JAMES CUBITT ARCHITECTS
Business: Architectural Consultancy Services, Interior Designers and Planners, Project Management
Address: Ebani House, 149/153, Broad Street, Ikoyi, Lagos
Tel: (01) 2662089, 2667480, 2665630 (D/L)
Fax: (01) 2665630, 2666398
E-mail: jca2@infoweb.abs.net
Contact: Arc. (Chief) Essien Oku - Chairman
Arc. Alan Davies - MD

JAMIL INTERNATIONAL COMPANY LIMITED
Business: Import & Export, General Merchants
Address: 98, IBB Way, Kofar Kaura, Katsina
Tel: (065) 430773, 431515 **Fax:** (065) 430805
* 27, Randle Road, Apapa, Lagos
* 327, Aminu Kano Way, Sani Mai Nagge, Goron Dutse, Kano
Contact: Alh. Amadi Kurfi - Chairman/CEO.

JAMKOL INVESTMENTS LIMITED
Business: Stockbroking, Financial Advisory Services, Portfolio Managment, Investiment Adviser
Address: Alagbon House (2nd Floor), 160/162, Broad Street, Lagos Island, lagos
Tel: (01) 2664754, 2662150 **Fax:** (01) 2662150
E-mail: jamkol@alpha.linkserve.com
Contact: Chief (Mrs) F. A. Jamodu - MD/CEO.

JANGO INTERNATIONAL COMPANY LIMITED
Business: Civil Contractors, Sales of Electrical Equipment Genrators,Transformers, Sanitary Wares
Address: 27/28, Dr Habibu M. Gwarzo Road, near Juma'a (Friday) Mosque, Hotoro Quarters, Kano
Tel: (064) 647637, 634228 **Fax:** (064) 647760
Contact: Dr Habibu Muhammed Gwarzo - Chairman/CEO

JAONI (NIGERIA) LIMITED
Business: Garment Designing & Manufacturing, Interior Decoration Services, Building & Civil Engineering
Address: 57, Hospital Road, P. O. Box 1234, Akure
Tel: (034) 241922, 241212, 08035521988, 08037209407
E-mail: jaonining@hotmail.com
Contact: Chief (Dr.) J. Ade Oni - Chief Executive

JAROS INSPECTION SERVICES LIMITED
Business: Cargo & Marine Survey, Petroleum Inspection, Tank/Metering/Instrument Calibrations, Productivity Analysis, Quality Control & Testing Services, Environmental Consultancy
Addrss: Jaros Base, Km. 2, Iwofe/College of Education Road, Rumuepirikom, Port Harcourt
Tel: (084) 238926, 236338
Fax: (084) 239339 * (082) 440057
E-mail: jarosinspection@linkserve.com
Website: www.jarosgroup.com
*NMA House Annex, 2B, Burma Rd,Apapa, Lagos
Tel/Fax: (01) 5878252, 4811645
Contact: Chief (Dr.) James O. Anigabor - Chairman/CEO.

JAROS SHIPPING LINE LIMITED
Business: Ship Catering, Ship Owners and Managers, Ship Husbandry/Agency Services
Address: Jaros Base, Km. 2, Iwofe/College of Education Road, Rumuepirikom, Port Harcourt
Tel: (084) 238926, 236338
Fax: (084) 239339 * (082) 440057
E-mail: jarosshipping@linkserve.com
Website: www.jarosgroup.com
Contact: Chief (Dr.) James O. Anigabor - Chairman/CEO.

JASPER COMMERCIAL ENTERPRISES (W.A) LIMITED
Business: Import of Agricultural Machines/Related Hardware, Water Pumps, Chainsaws & Spare Parts
Address: 33/35, Uga Street, Fegge, Onitsha
Tel/Fax: 08023291975
* 35, Osolo Way, off Murtala Muhammed International Airport Road, Ajao Estate, Isolo, Lagos
Tel/Fax: (01) 4527770, 4527769
Contact: Chief Jude I. Ezechukwu - Chairman/CEO.

JAWA INTERNATIONAL LIMITED
Business: Manufacture of Pharmaceuticals and Milk Powder, Distribution of Industrial Raw Materials, Chemicals and Textile Dyes
Address: Jawa House, 6/7, Abimbola Street, Isolo Industrial Estate, Isolo, Lagos
Tel: (01) 4529150, 4259149, 7733488 **Fax:** (01) 4529150
E-mail: jawa@alpha.linkserve.com
Contact: Mr. V. Verghese - MD/CEO

JAWACHI OILFIELD and ALLIED SERVICES NIGERIA LTD
Business: Fire, Safety & Environmental Protection Engineering and Services
Address: 144, Aba Road, (St. John's B/Stop), Port Harcourt
Tel: (084) 233815, 08023351345, 08033133914
Fax: (084) 233815
E-mail: jawachiofield@yahoo.com

JAY LABORATORIES LIMITED
Business: Manufacture of Haircare Products
Address: Plot C62, Jay Momoh Close, Amuwo-Odofin Indsutrial Estate, off Oshodi-Apapa Expressway, Amuwo-Odofin, Lagos
Contact: Mr. Jay Momoh - MD/CEO

JAYBEST INTERNATIONAL LIMITED
Business: Importation and Marketing of Office Equipment & Computer Accessories
Address: 1, Shehu Laminu Way, G.R.A. Road, opposite NITEL Complex, Maiduguri
Tel: (076) 233228, 236225 Fax: (076) 342227
E-mail: jaybest@alpha.linkserve.com
Website: www.jaybest.com

JAYKAY CARPET INDUSTRIES LIMITED
Business: Manufacturing of Carpets, Rugs & Window Blinds
Address: Plot 38/39, Sharanda Ind. Estate Phase II, Kano
Tel: (064) 648024, 645109, 664921 **Fax:** (064) 641782
E-mail: jaykaycarpets@hotmail.com
* 10, Shiro Street, off Ikorodu Road, near Agip Filling Station, Fadeyi, Lagos
Tel/Fax: (01) 7740872, 822921
* Kenaz Plaza (Suite C24), Wuse II, Abuja
Tel: (09) 5233862, 5231118
Contact: Mr. Mohit Manglani - MD/CEO.

JAYKAY PHARMACY LIMITED
Business: Manufacturing of Pharmaceutical Products, Retail of Pharmaceutical and Consumer Products
Address: 9, Randle Crescent, Apapa, lagos
Tel: (01) 5451029, 5452534, 5870464, 5870953
E-mail: jaykay@cybaaspace.net
* 32/34, Calcutta Crescent, Apapa, Lagos
Tel: (01) 5876617
Contact: Mr. Jimi Agbaje - MD/CEO.

JAZOM INTERNATIONAL (NIGERIA) LIMITED
Business: Importation of Electrical Materials; Contractors
Address: Chicago Plaza, 9A, Okwei/Moore Street, Onitsha
Tel: (046) 215532, 08036742824
Contact: Mr. Joseph O. Ikwuazom - Chairman/CEO

JD 7 LTD
Business: Marketing & Sales of Personal, Corporate and Promotional Gift Items, Monogramming, Screen

Printing, Foil & Transfer Printing, Manufacture of Unifoms, Clothing & Apparels
Address: 19A, Alh. Babatunde Jose Street (Festival Road), off Adetokunbo Ademola St, Victoria Island, Lagos
Tel: (01) 2619149, 2611302, 2622790, 08022909334
Fax: (01) 2622790
E-mail: jd7group@yahoo.co.uk
Contact: Mrs. Data E. Okorodudu - MD/CEO

JEFA TRAVELS & TOURS LIMITED
Business: Travel Agency, Tourism Services
Address: 78, Broad Street (4th Floor), Tinubu Square, Lagos
Tel: (01) 2668436, 2642016, 08033000416, 08033035612
Fax: (01) 2642016
E-mail: jefatravels@yahoo.com
Website: www.jefagroup.org
* Plot 19, Area 11 Shopping Complex (Suite 4), Ahmadu Bello Way, Area 11, Garki, Abuja
Tel: (09) 4136938, 08037019984, 08056204705
Contact: Jeff Okey Onyekaonwu - Chairman

JEFF & O'BRIEN
Business: Distribution and Marketing of Professional Resource Materials, Publisher's Representative
Address: Goodwill House, 278, Ikorodu Rd, Anthony, Lagos
Tel: (01) 2222550, 4934978, 08023049961, 08033062240
Fax: (01) 4934978
E-mail: jeff@infoweb.abs.net
Website: www.jeffandobrien.com
Contact: Mr. Pascal Odibo - Chairman/CEO

JEFS PROPERTIES PLC
Business: Civil Engineering and Building Construction, Real Estate Development, Acquisition and Procurement, Property Management
Address: Western House (16th Floor), 8/10, Broad St, Lagos
Tel: (01) 2645020, 2645021, 2630656, 08033041925
Fax: (01) 2645021
E-mail: eamedupin_co@yahoo.com
jefsplc@hotmail.com
* Plot 500, Tafawa Balewa Way, opp. Afribank Plc, Area 3, Garki, Abuja
Tel: (09) 2346784
Contact: Barr. E. A. Medupin - MD/CEO

JEKKY NIGERIA LIMITED
Business: Sales and Marketing of Computers and Office Equipment , School & Domestic Furniture
Address: 109A, Adeniyi Jones Avenue, Ikeja, Lagos
Tel: (01) 4937766, 4979226 **Fax:** (01) 4979226
E-mail: jenkinsinvest@yahoo.com

JEMI RANA
Business: Design & Marketing of African Fashion
Address: 123, Ogudu-Ojota Road, Ogudu, Lagos
Tel: (01) 5550523, 7757875, 8042014, 08034030748
* 39, Unity Road, Ikeja, Lagos
Tel: (01) 4936957, 08034105472

JENKINS INVESTMENT LIMITED
Business: Stockbroking, Financial & aianvestment Planning
Address: 12, Abibu-Oki Street, off Marina, Lagos
Tel: (01) 4702751, 2667084, 2665078 **Fax:** (01) 2667084
E-mail: jenkininvest@yahoo.com
Contact: Mr. Richard Omobogie - MD/CEO

JEROMELAIHO AND ASSOCIATES LIMITED
Business: Printing, Designing, Packaging & Colour Separation
Address: 77, Opebi Road, Ikeja, Lagos
Tel: (01) 4974638, 4707213, 4727511-2(2L)
Fax: (01) 4974061
E-mail: jealprint@infoweb.abs.net
jeromelaiho@yahoo.com
Contact: Mr. Jerome I. Elaiho - Chairman/CEO

JEROMI RADIO 95.1 FM
Business: Radio Broadcasting Services
Address: Ecobank Building, 54, Effurun/Sapele Road, Effurun, Delta State
Tel: (053) 255933
Contact: Mr. George Ugen - MD/CEO

JETA TRAVEL AGENCY LIMITED
Business: Travel Agency
Address: 110, Effurun-Warri Road, Effurun, Warri
Tel: (01) 251100, 256656
* 42, Adetokunbo Ademola St, Victoria Is., Lagos.
Tel: (01) 8043675
* Lansar House, 219, Aba Road, 1st Artillery Junction, Port Harcourt.
Tel: (084) 571293

JETLINK LIMITED
Business: Sales, Installation and Maintenance of Computers, Telecommunication, Micro-Electronics and Security Equipment, Consultancy Services
Address: 12A, Adeola Hopewell St, Victoria Island, Lagos
Tel: (01) 2621045, 616354, 616374, 4705482, 2623809
Fax: (01) 4936343, 616374
E-mail: jetlink@infoweb.abs.net
* Micro Channel Ltd., 25, Aba Road, Port Harcourt
Tel/Fax: (084) 230353 (090) 406888
* Plot 2105, Herbert Macaulay Way, Wuse Zone 6, Abuja
Tel: (09) 5233593 **Fax:** (09) 5237061
Contact: Mr. Willy Nzewi - Chairman
Mr. John Nwosu - MD/CEO

JEVANT SPENCER INTERNATIONAL COMPANY LIMITED
Business: Engineering & Oilfield Services, Procurment, Logisitics Support, Environmntal Consultancy
Address: Orosi House (1st Floor), 28, Forces Avenue, Old G.R.A., Port Harcourt
Tel: (084) 575869, 235548, 0803363264, 0805570255
Fax: (084) 235547
E-mail: jevspen@phca.linkserve.com
Contact: Mr. Thomas Masodje - Chairman/CEO

JEWEL HOTEL, GOMBE
Business: Hospitality & Catering Services
Address: opp. Government House, G.R.A.,Gombe
Tel: (072) 220204
Contact: Mrs Halima A. Mahdi - Manager

JGC NIGERIA LIMITED
Business: Engineering, Procurement, Construction and

Commissioning of Gas Plant Facilities
Address: Maku House, 109, Awolowo Road (5th Floor), S.W. Ikoyi, Lagos
Tel: (01) 2690672, 2690597 **Fax:** (01) 2690956
E-mail: jgcnig@cyberspace.net.ng
Website: www.jgc.com
* 22B, Elelenwo Rd, G.R.A. Phase I, Port Harcourt
Tel: (084) 239089 **Fax:** (084) 236745
Contact: Mr. K. Yamamato - MD/CEO

JID-BOD INDUSTRIES LIMITED
Business: Manufacture of Polyethelene & Plastics Products
Address: Plot 2, Tomori Ind. Estate, off Idiroko Road, Otta
Tel: (039) 722151, 721245
(01) 8133790, 08037222525
Contact: Hon. (Chief) E. O. Akingbade - Chairman/CEO.

JIDE TAIWO & COMPANY
Business: Chartered Estate Surveyors & Valuers, Estate Development & Managers, Real Estate Agents
Address: 136, Sinari Daranijo St Victoria Island Annex, Lagos
Tel: (01) 2625048-9(2L), 8044201, 8044231
E-mail: jidetaiwo@hyperia.com
Website: www.jidetaiwo.com
* Development House (15th Floor), 21, Wharf Road, Apapa, Lagos
Tel: (01) 5875183, 5876274, 5803131-2(2L),
Fax: (01) 5803134
E-mail: jidetaiwo@hyperia.com
Website: ww.jidetaiwo.com
* Plot 516, Block 1 (Suite 6), Sultan Abubakar Way, Wuse Zone 2, Abuja
Tel: (09) 5232704-5 (2L) **Fax:** (01) 5232892
* 25, Aba Road, Port Harcourt
Tel: (084) 239836, 330201, 08033097308
Contact: Mrs. Bimbo Soyinka - ED (Admin.)

JIMBEST AUTO SUPPLY COMPANY LIMITED
Business: Improt & Export, Dealers in Auto & Industrial Spare Parts, Manufacturer's Representative
Address: Zone A, Block 8, (Shop 1), ASPMDA Plaza, Trade Fair Complex, Badagry Expressway, Ojo, Lagos
Tel: (01) 3208453, 3208732, 8042404
Fax: (01) 3208453, 8042404
E-mail: jimbestauto@yahoo.com
Contact: Mr James C. Umeji - Chairman/CEO

JIMEX INDUSTRIES LIMITED
Business: Fabrication of Aluminium Products for Domestic and Construction Users
Address: Umuanuka Village, Otolo, Nnewi, Anambra State
Tel: (046) 460517, 463571-2 (2 L)
* 21, Seinde Callisto Crescent, Oshodi Expressway (Charity Bus-Stop), Oshodi, Lagos
Tel: (01) 4932136, 8141972
Contact: Chief J. U. Edokwu - Chairman/CEO.

JIMMY VIRGO PRESS LIMITED
Business: Printing Services, Colour Separation, Production of Promotional Gifts
Address: 33, Akinwunmi St, New Oko-Oba, Agege, Lagos
Tel: (01) 4922469, 4926324 **Fax:** (01) 4926324
Contact: Mr. Johnson A. Olujinmi - Chairman/CEO

JINIFA ALLIED LIMITED
Business: Distribution and Sales of Electronic Appliances
Address: H10, H92 & B82, Alaba International Market, Ojo-Alaba, Lagos
Tel: (01) 5554369, 7741564 **Fax:** (01) 5554365
E-mail: jinifa@infoweb.abs.net
* 38, Addis Ababa Crescent, Wuse Zone 4, Abuja
Tel: (09) 5236411, 5232091 **Fax:** (09) 5232091
Contact: Mr James I. Ezeifeoma - Chairman/CEO

JINKE MACHINERY MANUFACTURING COMPANY (NIGERIA) LIMITED
Business: Assembly, Import & Marketing of Motorcycles
Address: 397, Old Ojo Road, by Big Fish Restaurant, Abule-Ado Bus-Stop, Satellite Town, Lagos
Tel: (01) 7766149, 08023692355, 08034081600, 08033085398
E-mail: jinkemotorcycle@hotmail.com

JISACO NIGERIA LIMITED
Business: Building & Civil Engineering, Sales & Service of Construction Equipment
Address: Jisaco House, 3, Olorunfunmi Street, off Kudirat Abiola Road, beh. Phillips Factory, Ojota, Lagos
Tel/Fax: (01) 4930118
Contact: Engr. J. S. Atallah - MD/CEO

JIYODA ENGINEERING NIGERIA LIMITED
Business: Consultancy In Power System Protection, Construction and Maintenance of Protective Schemes
Address: Flat 2, Office Block I, Plot 1232, Bishop Oluwole Street, Victoria Island, Lagos
Tel: (01) 7731935, 3200622, 2883046
Fax: (01) 2646082-4 (3 L), 2883046, 3200622
Contact: Engr. A. R. A. Jimoh - MD/CEO

J-JUMAC INTERNATIONAL COMPANY LIMITED
Business: General Merchandising, Industrialists, Importation & Marketing of Travel Bags & Suitcases, UPS & Stabilizers, Computers & Telecommunication Terminal Equipment
Address: 51, Taiwo Street, off Abibu-Oki Street, off Broad Street, behind Mandilas Building, Marina, Lagos
Tel: (01) 2666851, 8043265, 08023027190, 08023394108
Fax: (01) 2880555, 8048126
Contact: Chief James Okwudili Udoh - Chairman/MD

JK INTERCONTINENTAL (NIGERIA) LIMITED
Business: Hotel & Catering Services
Address: University of Ibadan/Bodija Rd, Agbowo, Ibadan
Tel: (02) 8102221, 8103569, 8103370 **Fax:** (02) 8103370
Contact: Mr. Toufic J. Khawan - MD/CEO.

JKN LIMITED
Business: Electrical & Mechanical Engineering Construction & Services (High Voltage Transformer Substations & Transmission Lines; Electrical Piped Services & Airconditioning Installation)
Address: Plot 10, Block B, Industrial Estate, Ilasamaja, Apapa-Isolo Expressway (Itire Junction), Lagos
Tel: (01) 525864, 4522232, 4525931 **Fax:** (01) 4526090
E-mail: jkn@linkserve.com
* Plot 133, Monrovia Street, off Aminu Kano

Crescent, Cadastral Zone A7, Wuse II, Abuja *
14, Udom Street, opp. Hotel Chez Therese, D-Line, Diobu, Port Harcourt.
Tel: (084) 334179
* Km 5, NNPC Refinery Road, by AP Filling Station, Ekpan, Warri.
Tel: (053) 232666
Contact: Chief John Agboola Odeyemi - MD/CEO

JKPEEZ IMPEX COMPANY LIMITED
Business: Oilfield Supply and Services, Fire Protection Engineering, Sales of Personal Safety/Protective Equipment, Installation and Maintenance of Intruder Detection Systems on Pipelines
Address: 78A, Isale-Eko Avenue, Dolphin Estate, Ikoyi, Lagos
Tel/Fax: (01) 2693776, 7744545
E-mail: jkpeez@skannet.com
jkp-proc@metrong.com
* 16A, Trans-Amadi Rd, Ind.Layout, Port Harcourt
Tel: (084) 231796-7 (2L) **Fax:** (084) 233794
Contact: Chief P. N. Ojiaka - Chairman/CEO

JO & A MARKETING LIMITED
Business: Importation of MACK Truck Auto Spare Parts
Address: 1, Bauchi Road, Apapa, Lagos
Tel: (01) 5455535, 5878627, 4700322 **Fax:** (01) 5455534
E-mail: joa@jova.net.ng
joam2000@hotmail.com
Contact: Mr. Joel Iloh - MD/CEO

JOBIC NIGERIA LIMITED
Business: Import & Export, Distribution of Bearings, General Merchandising
Address: 4, Church Street, Idumota, Lagos
Tel: (01) 2662668, 2661263 **Fax:** (01) 2661263
E-mail: jobic@cyberspace.net.ng
Contact: Mr. Joseph Okonkwo - MD/CEO

JOBIKAN NIGERIA LIMITED
Business: Manufacture of Plastic and Rubber Products
Address: 16, Kofo Abayomi Street, Victoria Island, Lagos
Tel/Fax: (01) 2619103
* Plot 41, Oregun Industrial Estate, Ikeja, Lagos
Tel: (01) 4972711
Contact: Mr. T. S. Kang - MD/CEO.

JODAVS INTER LINKS LIMITED
Business: Improt & Export, General Merchants
Address: 151, Azikiwe Road, Aba
Tel: (082) 227877, 441503 **Fax:** (082) 231877
E-mail: jovi@beta.linkserve.com
Contact: Mr. Jovi Ukaumunna - MD/CEO

JOE AKHIGBE & ASSOCIATES
Business: Estate Surveyors & Valuers, Consultancy, Agents
Address: 19, Tinubu Street (5th Floor), Lagos Island, Lagos
Tel: (01) 2631987, 2646932, 7757869, 2646934, 08036672367 **Fax:** (01) 2646934
E-mail: joeakhigbe@xmail.com
Contact: Mr. Joseph Akhigbe - Principal Partner

JOE BEST ASSOCIATES LIMITED
Business: Importation and Marketing of Electronic Products, General Merchandising
Address: 1, Joe Best Crescent, Ajao Estate, Isolo, Lagos
Tel: (01) 4524580, 4528207, 4963920, 7740687
E-mail: joebest@cyberspace.net.ng
Contact: Sir Joe Best Okoye - Chairman/CEO.

JOE-EBOJE INTERNATIONAL AGENCIES LIMITED
Business: Shipping and Airfreight, Cargo Handling and Warehousing; Clearing and Forwarding
Address: 148, Trans-Amadi Industrial Layout, Port Harcourt
Tel: (084) 333238, 238009, 232679, 230754, 239188, 486364 **Fax:** (084) 238010
E-mail: joe-eboje@phca.linkserve.com
*Plot 3, Block D, Amuwo-Odofin Ind Estate, Lagos
Tel: (01) 4806212, 5851508, 7747900 **Fax:** (01) 5851508
E-mail: joe-eboje@hyperia.com
Contact: Dr. Joe Ehimuan JP - MD/CEO.

JOE-HAN NETWORK MARKETING LIMITED
Business: Sales & Service of Banknote-Handling and Cash-Management Technology, Integrated Document Management, Payment Transactions Solutions
Address: 20, Adeniyi Jones Avenue, Ikeja, Lagos
Tel: (01) 4972670, 4977851 **Fax:** (01) 4977851
E-mail: bim.dada@alpha.linkserve.com
jhan-networkmkt@alpha.linkserve.com
Contact: Prince Gbolahan Dada - Chairman/CEO.

JOEDONE INTERNATIONAL LIMITED
Business: Manufacturing; Real Estate Management; Real Estate, Shopping Mall & Recreational Facilities Developers; Marketing Services, Travel Agency
Adddress: 5, Okoduwa St, Kirirkiri Ind. Estate, Apapa, Lagos
Tel: (01) 5876005, 7743767, 8129410, 08023604128
Contact: Mr. Joseph N. Ofodum - Chairman/CEO

JOELEE INTERNATIONAL COMPANY LIMITED
Business: Import & Export, Contractors, Sales of Electronics, Building Materials and General Merchandise
Address: 193, Ehi Road, Aba
Tel: (082) 230065
Contact: Chief Joseph C. Ogwo - Chairman/CEO.

JOEMEDIA & COMPANY LIMITED
Business: Advertising Agency
Address: 7, Egberongbe St Ladi-Lak Bus-Stop, Bariga, Lagos
Tel: (01) 825550
Contact: Mr. J. A. Oduntan - Chairman/CEO

JOF IDEAL FAMILY FARMS LIMITED
Business: Farming, Vegetable Oil & Cashew Nuts Processing and Production, Exportation of Agricultural Commodities, Road Construction, Mining, Manufacturing of Ceramic Sanitarywares
Address: 2, Ebenezer Avenue, off Plaza Motel Road, Oke-Ijebu, Akure
Tel: (034) 244286, 244561, 244562 **Fax:** (034) 244301
E-mail: jof@rcl.nig.com
* 16/18, Oyefeso Ave, Ikorodu Rd, Obanikoro, Lagos
Tel: (01) 4976871, 4935132, 7740167
Fax: (01) 4968669, 4937163
E-mail: jof@alpha.linkserve.com
Contact: Rev. J. O. Fagboyegun - Chairmen./CEO

JOFFIN SCIENTIFIC INSTRUMENTS NIGERIA LIMITED
Business: Sales of Medical and Laboratory Equipment
Address: 58, Toyin Street, Ikeja, Lagos
Tel/Fax: (01) 4930867, 4972595
E-mail: joffin@infoweb.abs.net
Contact: Chief John E. Nwosu - Chairman/CEO

JO-GENE INTERNATIONAL LIMITED
Business: Importation of Auto Body-Filler, Lubricants & Refurbishment Products, Printing and Publishing
Address: 33, Modebe Avenue, Onitsha
Tel: (046) 213588, 217851, 08033422496, 08037105110
Fax: (046) 211420
E-mail: jogeneone@yahoo.com
Contact: Mr. Eugene C. Nwankwo - Chairman/CEO

JOHN 3V3 HATS LIMITED
Business: Mllinery (Hat Making) & Importation of Hats
Address: 17, Maitama Sule Street, off Awolowo Road, S.W. Ikoyi, Lagos.
Tel: (01) 2670963, 2671339, 4701326

JOHN AKHAMIE & COMPANY
Business: Estate Surveyors & Valuers, Plant & Machinery Valuation, Estate Agency & Property Managers
Address: Regency Suites, 17, Ahmed Onibudo Street, Victoria Island, Lagos
Tel: (01) 2624721, 4717005, 4730634, 08033195368, 08033070229, 08056277192 **Fax:** (01) 2624721
E-mail: johnakhamie@yahoo.com
* Aguiyi Ironsi Shopping Complx (Suite 37), Yakubu Gowon Way, Asokoro District, Abuja
Contact: Hadiza Akokhia - Manager

JOHN BEDOLA ENTERPRISES LIMITED
Business: Sales and Service of Bank-Note Counting Machines, Generating Sets and Office Equipment
Address: Plot 285, Gbadaga Expressway, Gbagada Phase I, Lagos
Tel: (01) 4974783, 4932423, 5820619, 7918895, 8047828
Fax: (01) 2691698
E-mail: jbedola@rcl.nig.com
jbedola@linkserve.com
Contact: Mr. Abiodun J. Adekoya - MD/CEO

JOHN HOLT PLC
Business: Conglomerate
Address: Ebani House, 149/153, Broad Street, Lagos
Tel: (01) 2611744, 2661938, 2663819 **Fax:** (01) 2660830
E-mail: mail@johnholtplc.com
* Plot 602, Ringim Close, Garki Area 7, Abuja
Tel: (09) 2340203, 2340204
Contact: Mr. Bayo Jimoh - CEO
Mr. Nosike Agokie - ED

JOHN HOLT DISTRIBUTION (Div. of John Holt Plc)
Business: Distribution of Consumer Items including Edibles, Electronics and Electrical Products, Warehousing and Merchandise Distribution Services, Manufacture of Cosmetics and Baby-Care Products
Address: John Holt Complex, Plot 3/4, Adewunmi Industrial Estate, Oregun Road, Ikeja, Lagos
Tel: (01) 4978782, 4978783, 4978784, 4967312
Fax: (01) 4976571, 4932061
Contact: Mr. James McLardy - Group MD/CEO

JOHN HOLT LEASING SERVICES (Div. of John Holt Plc)
Business: Sales & Service of Airconditioners and Fire Extinguishers, Car Rentals
Address: 25, Creek Road, Apapa, Lagos
Tel: (01) 5803430-4 (5 L) **Fax:** (01) 5877410, 5873726
Contact: Mr. John Coats - Div. CEO

JOHN HOLT SHIPPING SERVICES (Div. of John Holt Plc)
Business: Clearing, Forwarding Agency, Shipping Services
Address: 25, Creek Road, Apapa, Lagos
Tel: (01) 5803380-2 (3 L), 5875630, 5873038, 5872994, 5877883, 4976047 **Fax:** (01) 5876853, 5872994
* 16, Aba Road, Port Harcourt.
Tel/Fax: (084) 234627
Contact: Alh. A. K. Jimoh - Div. MD/CEO

JOHN HOLT TECHNICAL PRODUCTS & SERVICES (Holt Engineering) (Div. of John Holt Plc)
Business: Sales and Service of Generators, Spare Parts Sales
Address: 25, Creek Road, P.M.B. 1218, Apapa, Lagos
Tel: (01) 5803430-4 (5 L) **Fax:** (01) 5873726
* 33, Trans-Amadi Industrial Layout, Port Harcourt
Tel: (084) 333490, 332461, 332688
* c/o John Holt Distribution, Plot 602, Garki District, Zone 10, A1, Abuja
Tel: (09) 2341274, 2340203, 2340204
Contact: Mr. John Coats - Div. MD/CEO

JOHN WEST PACKAGING LIMITED
Business: Commercial Printing, Production of Light Packaging and Labels
Address: Plot 2, Block A, Acme Road, Ogba Industrial Estate, Ogba, Lagos
Tel: (01) 4925459, 921010, 921639
E-mail: johnwest@hyperia.com
johnwest2000ng@yahoo.com
Contact: Alh. (Dr.) Lateef K. Jakande - MD/CEO

JOHN WHITE INDUSTRIES LIMITED
Business: Manufacture of Fan Belts and V-Belts for Industrial Machinery.
Address: Zone D, Block 2 (Shop 4), ASPAMDA Plaza, Trade Fair Complex, Badagry Expressway, Ojo, lagos
* Ngo-Inyaba Village, Umudim, Nnewi,
Tel: (046) 460298, 460299, 460360, 460830
Contact: Mr. John Anekwe - Chairman/CEO

JOHNBULL AMAYAEVBO & COMPANY
Business: Estate Surveyor & Valuers
Address: 87, Igbosere Road (3rd Floor), Lagos
Tel: (01) 4802850, 4708360, 08023107269, 08033498466
Fax: (01) 2634505
E-mail: johnbull@nigol.net.ng
* Ploy Plaza (Suite B9), Plot 1073, Adetokunbo Ademola Crescent, Wuse II, Abuja
Tel: (09) 6703806, 08037881024

JOHNNY INDUSTRIES NIGERIA LIMITED
Business: Manufacturing of Polyethylene Bags,Sheets, LDPE Tubing Rolls, Plastic Household & Ind. Products

Address: 430, Ikorodu Road, opp. Total Petrol Station, Ojota, Lagos
Tel: (01) 4964480, 4970227, 7743435 Fax: (01) 4971099
Contact: Mr. Johnny L. Budhrani - MD/CEO

JOHNSON & JOE's CHEMIST LIMITED
Business: Distribution & Retail Sales of Pharmaceutical Products and Hospital Equipment
Address: 57, Ginuwa Road, P.O.Box 549, Warri
Tel: (053) 253311, 08023011854
Contact: Mr. Uruemu E. Ukueku - Chairman/CEO

JOHNSON PRODUCTS OF NIGERIA LIMITED
Business: Manufacturing of Cosmetics and Toiletries
Address: Plot B, Ikosi Road, Oregun Industrial Estate, Oregun, Ikeja, Lagos
Tel: (01) 4968210-2 (3L), 7744392, 8042105
Fax: (01) 2693627, 4968212
E-mail: johnsonproductsnig@yahoo.com
Contact: Chief (Mrs.) Opral Benson - Chairman
Mr. G. O. D. Olojede - MD/CEO

JOHNTRACO MOTORS LIMITED
Business: Importation & Distribution of Motorcycles, Automobile Batteries and Spare Parts
Address: 12, Herbert Macaulay Street, Ebute-Metta, Lagos
Tel: (01) 7743934, 4717983, 08034030271
Fax: (01) 7743934
Contact: Mrs. A. Nzewi - MD/CEO

JOINCROWN EXPRESS (NIGERIA) LIMITED
Business: Customs-Bonded Terminal Operators, Warehousing, Export Inspection
Address: 48, Burma Road, Apapa, Lagos
Tel: (01) 5874274, 5876925 **Fax:** (01) 5870775
Contact: Mr. Ropo Aregbesola - GM

JOINT HOLD GROUP OF COMPANIES
Business: Import & Export of General Goods
Address: 19, Bornu Crescent, Apapa, Lagos
Tel: (01) 5870671, 5874475, 08023200656
Contact: Chief Abimbla Abiodun - Chairman

JOINT KOMPUTER KOMPANY LIMITED
Business: Sales & Maintenance of Computers & Peripherals
Address: 229, Ikorodu Road, Ilupeju, Lagos
Tel: (01) 4931532-4 (3 L) **Fax:** (01) 4963143
E-mail: jkk@infoweb.abs.net
Website: www.jkknet.com
Contact: Chief O. A. Odegbami - MD/CEO

JOKAS INTERNATIONAL LIMITED
Business: Sales and Service of Banking & Office Automation Equipment and Accessories
Address: Investment House (Ground Floor), 21/25, Broad Street, Lagos Island , Lagos
Tel: (01) 2643667, 2643669, 4705309 **Fax:** (01) 2643669
E-mail: jokas@rcl.nig.com
Contact: Bshorun Kasali Alo - Chairman/CEO

JOKI (NIGERIA) LIMITED
Business: Shipping, Clearing & Forwarding, Transportation
Address: Plot 2, Oshodi-Apapa Expressway, by Beachland Estate, Apapa, Lagos
Tel: (01) 5877932, 5871481, 5873509 **Fax:** (01) 5875309
E-mail: joki@infoweb.abs.net
* 14, Industry Rd, Port Harcourt.
Tel: (084) 235949, 08033240695
Contact: Chief J. O. K. Idornigie - Chairman/CEO.

JOKKY COMPANY LIMITED
Business: Manufacturing of Fresh-Fruit Drinks
Address: 1, Chris Ogunbanjo Way, near Gateway Hotel, Imowo Roundabout, Ijebu-Ode, Ogun State
Tel: (037) 430987, 08055372922
E-mail: jokky@beta.linkserve.com
Contact: Basorun (Engr.) J. B. Buluro - Chairman/CEO

JOLA JAY NIGERIA LIMITED
Business: Sales of Motor Vehicles, Construction Services, General Contractors, Import & Export, Building Society, Supply of Oil Tools & Equipment
Address: Gateway House, 53, Murtala Muhammed International Airport Road, Ajao Estate, Lagos
Tel: (01) 4526029, 4522074, 08023214724, 08033606506, 08033558155 **Fax:** (01) 4526029
E-mail: jolajay2001@yahoo.com
Contact: Hon. Chief (Dr.) J. J. Ajatta - Exec. Chairman

JOLAG GROUP LIMITED
Business: Engineering & Computer Services; Sales of Pharmaceuticals, Medical Equipment & General Merchandise
Address: 8, Idowu Martins Street, off Adola Odeku Street, Victoria Island, Lagos
Tel: (01) 2617788, 2618022 **Fax:** (01) 4619011, 2626751
E-mail: jolag@alpha.linkserve.com
jolag@supernet300.com
* 8, Adetokunbo Ademola Crescent, Plot 561, Cadastral Zone A8, Wuse II, Abuja
Tel: (09) 5235624-6 (3 L) **Fax:** (09) 5235627
Contact: Mr. O. G. Akinsanya - Exec. Director

JOLAJ OFFICE PRODUCTS NIGERIA LIMITED
Business: Distrbution and Marketing of Writing Instruments, Office Products and Accessories
Address: Shop 78, Tafawa Balewa Square Complex, Lagos
Tel: (01) 2630627, 2632069 **Fax:** (01) 2632069
E-mail: jolaj@infoweb.abs.net
* Shop 23, Daniel Ogbaje Street, Garki Model Market, Garki, Abuja

JOLIMAIR NIGERIA LIMITED
Business: Building & Civil Engineering, Road Construction
Address: Consortium Hous (8th Floor) , Plot 1682, Sanusi Fafunwa Street, Victoria Island, Lagos
Tel: (01) 3200345, 2620502 **Fax:** (01) 2620507
E-mail: jolimair@metrong.com
* House CT5, Stallion Estate, Lobito Crescent, off Adetokunbo Ademola Crescent, Wuse II, Abuja

JOMA FROZEN FOOD PRODUCTS LIMITED
Business: Importation and Sales of Frozen Food Products
Address: 13, Refinery Road, Effurun, Warri
Tel: (053) 251468, 252264
* 77, Cementery Road, Warri
* 121B, Warri-Sapele Road, Warri

JOMBO GROUP OF COMPANIES
Business: Importation and Marketing of Stockfish
Address: Jombo Plaza (2nd Floor), 116, Cameroun Road, Aba
Tel: (082) 234512, 234087, 231583 **Fax:** (082) 234087
Contact: Chief O. Jombo - Chairman/CEO.

JONAB NIGERIA LIMITED
Business: Importation of Auto Spare Parts and Accessories
Address: Zone A, Block 12 (Shops 1 & 2), ASPMDA Plaza, Trade Fair Complex, Badagry Expressway, Ojo
Tel: (01) 3208699, 4746329, 7748823 **Fax:** (01) 7748882
Contact: Mr. Josiah N. Mgbemena - Chairman/CEO.

JONAC ENGINEERING PLANTS (NIGERIA) LIMITED
Business: Rewinding and Repairs of Electric Motors, Alternators and Transformers, Recondition and Production of Industrial Spare Partss and Moulds
Address: Plot 24, Oregun Road, off Ojota Bus-Stop, Lagos
Tel: (01) 4961201, 4972985, 4811844 **Fax:** (01) 4972985
E-mail: jonac@hyperia.com
Contact: Mr. Joseph Anayo Odobeatu - Chairman/CEO.

JONADS INSURANCE BROKERS LIMITED
Business: Insurance Broking
Address: 1B, Taiwo Road, Jos
Tel: (073) 450623, 450624, 451200 **Fax:** (073) 450624
* 268, Port Harcourt-Aba Road, Port Harcourt
Tel: (084) 480127
Contact: Mr. Wole Fatoye - MD/CEO.

JONATEX & COMPANY NIGERIA LIMITED
Business: General Merchandising and Contracting, Clearing & Forwarding Agency
Address: 1, New Market Road, Onitsha
Tel: (046) 414454, 08035534384
E-mail: jonatex@infoweb.abs.net
Contact: Chief Jonathan Umeano - Chairman/CEO.

JONES GROUP OF COMPANIES
Business: Conglomerate - Fisheries, Construction, Trading
Address: 36, Orishe Street, beh. Jabita Hotel, off Obafemi Awolow Way, Ikeja, Lagos
Tel: (01) 4936392, 4936393 **Fax:** (01) 4936392
E-mail: jonesgroup@hyperia.com
Contact: Sir J. O. Eze - Chairman/CEO.

JONES SIMPLIX & COMPANY LIMITED
Business: Insurance Broking and Pension Consultancy
Address: Great Nigeria House (19th Floor), 47/57, Martins Street, Marina, Lagos
Tel/Fax: (01) 4817883
* Inwade House (Suite 13), Plot 1331, Jere Street, off Funmilayo Ransome-Kuti Road, Zone A, Area 3, Garki, Abuja
Tel: (09) 2345219, 2348431
Contact: Mr. Bayode Samuel - MD/CEO.

JOROTOM INTERNATIONAL AGENCY (NIGERIA) LIMITED
Business: International Forwarding, Transportation, Shipping & Clearing Agency, Aircargo Agency
Address: 38, Adegbola Street, Ikeja, Lagos
Tel: (01) 4931919, 4960454 **Fax:** (01) 4967588
E-mail: jorotom@yahoo.com
jorotom@hyperia.com
* 1, Airport Road, Rupokwu, Obio-Akpor LGA, Port Harcourt

JOS FLOUR MILLS NIGERIA LIMITED
Business: Milling of Grains into Flour
Address: 1, Kurra Road, West of Mines, Jos
Tel: (073) 452880, 453258 **Fax:** (073) 455449
* Old Airport Road, Jos
Tel: (073) 461144, 461595
Contact: Mr. I. D. Sampati - Chairman/CEO.

JOS INTERNATIONAL BREWERIES PLC
Business: Brewing of Alcoholic & Non-Alcoholic Beverages
Address: 1, Brewery Road, Jos
Tel: (073) 463951-2 (2 L), 463953 **Fax:** (073) 463953
Contact: Mr. Albert T. Kattiems - Ag. Chairman
Mr. Bakko Kop Arri - ED (Technical)

JOS STEEL ROLLING COMPANY LIMITED
Business: Production of Round Steel Products
Address: Azi Nyako Road, off Ahmed Nasreddin Road, Industrial Area, Jos
Tel: (073) 463408, 463491, 463446, 462964
Fax: (073) 463344
Contact: Engr.. Mohammed B. Bello - GM/CEO.

JOS. HANSEN & SOEHNE (NIGERIA) LIMITED
Business: Water Engineering Services, Sales of Water Pumps, Sales and Machining of Spare Parts for Pumps
Address: Km. 16, Ikorodu Road, Ojota, Lagos
Tel: (01) 3453172, 4735243, 4974304, 4976936
Fax: (01) 3453172, 4976936
Contact: Mr. T. A. Braithwaite - Chairman
Mr. Hans Ripp - MD/CEO

JOSIEN HOLDINGS LIMITED
Business: Marketing of Cosmetics, Spirits & Wines
Address: 108, Western Avenue, Ojuelegba, Surulere, Lagos
Tel: (01) 833788, 834395 **Fax:** (01) 831825
Contact: Chief Joe Ogbebor - Chairman/CEO

JOSSY ELECTRONICS LIMITED
Business: Importation, Marketing & Distribution of Consumer Electronic Appliances
Address: 121, Nnamdi Azikiwe Street, Idumota, Lagos
Tel: (01) 7767703

JSH SECURITY INDUSTRIES LIMITED
Business: Sales and Safes and Security Equipment
Address: 11, Ademola St, off Awolowo Rd, S.W Ikoyi, Lagos
Tel: (01) 2671421, 2671422 **Fax:** (01) 2671422, 2692302
E-mail: jsh-nig@linkserve.com.ng
Contact: Mr. Sam Egbuchunam - MD/CEO.

JSP CORPORATE COMMUNICATIONS LIMITED
Business: Public Relations, Events Marketing, Corporate Communications
Address: 60B, Ladipo Kasumu Street, off Allen Avenue, Ikeja, Lagos
Tel: (01) 4939839, 5557734 **Fax:** (01) 4939839
E-mail: jsp@infoweb.abs.net
Contact: Mr. Phil B. Osagie - Head Consultant/CEO

JSB RESOURCES MANAGEMENT LIMITED
Business: Marketing of Computer & Accessories, IT Consultancy, Networking, Assembly & Engineering
Address: 23, Amore Street, off Toyin Street, Ikeja, Lagos
Tel: (01) 8135279, 3451319, 08023159993, 08042115345
Fax: (01) 3451319
E-mail: okeruo@lycos.com
Contact: Promise C. Nwankwo - President/CEO

JUBAILI AGROTEC LIMITED
Business: Importation & Sales of Agro-Chemicals
Address: Km. 10, Hadejia Road, Gunduwawa District, Kano
Tel: (064) 317368, 317871, 08034022526, 08034022512, 08034022513, 08034022525
E-mail: jatnigeria@jubailiagrotec.com
Website: www.jbailiagrotec.com
Contact: Mr Rajab Jubali - Chairman/CEO

JUBAILI BROS. ENGINEERING LIMITED
Business: Sales, Leasing and Servicing of Generators
Address: 111, Trans-Amadi Industrial Layout, Port Harcourt
Tel: (084) 232392-4 (3L), 461148-50 (3L)
Fax: (084) 461151
E-mail: jubaili@phca.linkserve.com
* 23, Warehouse Road, Apapa, Lagos
Tel: (01) 5453971-4 (4 L), 5450587, 5873447
Fax: (01) 5804586
E-mail: jbeapapa@jubailigroup.com
* Plot 2918, Muri Okunola St, Victoria Island, Lagos
Tel: (01) 4704656, 4706705, 3200470-2 (3 L)
Fax: (01) 3200470-2 (3 L)
* 1A, Suez Crescnt, Wuse Zone 4, Abuja
Tel: (09) 5231129 **Fax:** (09) 5234223
Contact: Mr. Ramzi Jubaili - Chairman/CEO.

JUBAILI MOUKARIM GROUP LIMITED (JMG LTD)
Business: Sales and Service of Generators; Leasing of Mobile Generators
Address: Plot 1393, Tiamiyu Savage St, Victoria Island, Lagos
Tel: (01) 2626306-7 (2L), 3200200-1(2L), 7743210
Fax: (01) 2626307
E-mail: jmg@hyperia.com
* 13, Gana Street, Maitama, Abuja
Tel: 08024040666, 08034040666
* Plot 116, Trans-Amadi Ind. Layout, Port Harcourt
Tel: (084) 484414
Contact: Mazin Al-Jubaili - MD/CEO

JUCHI NIGERIA LIMITED
Business: Oilfield Services
Address: Plot 2A, Trans-Amadi Industrial Layout, by Elekahia Railway Crossing, Port Harcout
Tel: (084) 235176, 572160
Contact: Chief Jude Ubani - MD/CEO

JUDATOM NIGERIA LIMITED
Business: Shipping, Clearing & Forwarding, Import & Export Trading, General Contractors
Address: Adesanya Shopping Plaza (1st Floor, Suite 4), 70, Obafemi Awolowo Way, Ikeja, Lagos
Tel: (01) 4822716, 4979819, 08034050697
E-mail: judatominigltd@email.com
Contact: Mr. David Juwon Eniayekan - Chairman/CEO

JUDEK NIGERIA LIMITED
Business: Importation and Sales of Motor Cars
Address: 241, Ikorodu Road, Ilupeju, Lagos
Tel: (01) 4972674, 7731076
Contact: Mr Jude Eke - Chairman/CEO

JUDIYKE INDUSTRIES LIMITED
Business: Importation and Sales of Auto Spare Parts, General Goods and Accessories
Address: 21, Hundred Foot Road, Nnewi, Anambra State
Tel: (046) 460873, 462712, 463574, 460877
Fax: (046) 462712
E-mail: judiyke@phca.linkserve.com
Contact: Chief Jude Ezenwanne - Chairman/CEO.

JUGO INVESTMENTS LIMITED
Business: Sale of Motor Vehicle Spare Parts and Accessories
Address: 5, Ashogbon Street, Idumota, Lagos
Tel: (01) 2665757, 2668346, 2665792
Fax: (01) 2660957
* Zone A-T5, ASPMDA Plaza, Trade Fair Complex, Badagry Expressway, Ojo, Lagos
Tel: (01) 3208059, 3208060
Contact: Mr. Joseph U. Okenwa - Chairman/CEO.

JUHEL (NIGERIA) LIMITED
Business: Manufacturing and Marketing of Pharmaceuticals, Marketing of Petroleum Products
Address: 55, Nkwubor Road, Emene, Enugu
* 4, Isu-Oba Close, Trans-Ekulu, Enugu
Tel: (042) 556600, 08033232035 **Fax:** (042) 558898
E-mail: juhel@infoweb.abs.net
juhel2002@hotmail.com
Contact: Dr. Ifeanyi E. Okoye - Chairman/CEO.

JUICE & GRILLADE LIMITED
Business: Catering Services, Fast-Food Outlet Operations
Address: 5, Ahmadu Bello Way, Jos
Tel: (073) 458257, 458517-8 (2L)
Fax: (073) 458518
E-mail: juice@infoweb.abs.net
Contact: Mr. Johnson Usman - GM/CEO

JULI PLC
Business: Whosesales & Retail of Pharmaceuticals and Supermarket Items
Address: 19, Kodesoh Street, Ikeja, Lagos
Tel: (01) 4961760
Contact: Mrs. J. O. A. Ogunranti - GM/Pharmacist

JUKOK INTERNATIONAL LIMITED
Business: Road Construction, Electrical & Civil Engineering
Address: 63, Nza Street, Independent Layout, Enugu
Tel: (042) 259385, 457737, (090) 500029
Contact: Mazi Kanayo C. Okoye - Group MD/CEO

JULIAND BEARINGS LIMITED
Business: Importation and Marketing of Roller Bearings
Address: 6, Remilekun Street, Ogunlana Drive, Surulere, Lagos
Tel: (01) 5850910, 4733800, 08033077450
Fax: (01) 5850910
E-mail: juliand@beta.linkserve.com
Contact: Mr Nnamdi Julius Onwuzuruike - Chairman/CEO

JULIUS BERGER NIGERIA PLC
Business: Planning, Design & Construction of Civil Engineering & Building Works
Address: Utako District, Wuse, Abuja
Tel: (09) 5233067-70 (4L), 5233632, 5233279, 6110000
Fax: (09) 5233066, 6114041, 6114043, 6114444
E-mail: jbn@julius-berger.com
Website: www.julius-berger.com
* Ijora Causeway, Ijora, Lagos
Tel: (01) 801140-4 (5L), 5801145-8 (4L)
Contact: Mr. George Mark - MD
Engr. Hans Stockhausen - Joint MD.

JUMBO NOMINEES LIMITED
Business: Importation of Chemical Raw Materials for Pharmaceuticals, Cosmetics & Foods; General Merchants
Address: 17, International Airport Road, Ajao Estate, Lagos
Tel: (01) 4522763, 7746867, 7757400 **Fax:** (01) 4522763
E-mail: jumbo@infoweb.abs.net
Contact: Mrs. Nmuta- David A. Mbamalu - CEO

JUNO FOODS LIMITED
Business: Manufacturing and Marketing of Cornflakes
Address: 25, Sanusi Fafunwa Stret, Victoria Island, Lagos
Tel: (01) 2619989, 2621950, 4700515 **Fax:** (01) 2619989
E-mail: schon@infoweb.abs.net
* Plot 3, Birabi St, G.R.A. Phase II, Port Harcourt
Contact: Senator V. K. O. Oyofo - Chairman
Mr. J. O. Solanke - GM

JUST FOOD LIMITED
Business: Distribution, Sales, Service & Repairs of Ice-Cream, Slush & Shake Machines, Flavor Burst Syrup Dispensing Machines, Grills and Ice Cream Mix; Sales of Equipment Spare Parts
Address: Plot H, Block 3, Oshodi-Oworonshoki Expressway, Ilupeju Industrial Estate, Ilupeju, Lagos
Tel: (01) 7740233, 7748429 **Fax:** (01) 4937250
E-mail: justfood_2001@hotmail.com

JUWON INVESTMENTS INTERNATIONAL LIMITED
Business: Importation, Marketing and Distribution of General Merchandise, Manufacturer's Representative
Address: 8, Strachan Street (4th Floor), off Igbosere Road, Lagos Island, Lagos
Tel: (01) 2635314, 7780269, 08023032940, 08033252646
E-mail: juwoninvest@yahoo.com

K. C. IJEWAY LIMITED
Business: Importation of Industrial & Domestic Sewing Machines and Spare Parts.
Address: 29, Louis Mbanefo Street/Zik Avenue, Onitsha
Tel/Fax: (046) 412051
E-mail: ijeway@yahoo.com
* Shop 2, Nwadiogo Park, Nyanya Market, Abuja
Contact: Mr. Kingsley C. Ijeh - MD/CEO

K. F. C. C. LIMITED
Business: Manufacturing of Furniture for Home, Kitchen, Hospital and Office Use
Address: 15, Inuwa Abdulkadir Road, Kakuri Industrial Estate, Kaduna South, Kaduna
Tel: (062) 230090 - 3(4L) **Fax:** (062) 231245, 233043

KAADAN NIGERIA LIMITED
Business: Production & Packaging of Fruit Juice
Address: Sharada Industrial Estate Phase III, Kano
Tel: (064) 667072, 08037041378, 0803703499, 08033576180

KABAYAN INTERNATIONAL SHIPPING LIMITED
Business: Shipping Agents, Ship Chandlers, Protective Agents, Marine Services
Address: 46, Calcutta Crescent, Apapa, Lagos
Tel: (01) 5452743, 5870573, 7756685, 08034050065
Fax: (01) 5875002, 5873851
E-mail: kabayan@cyberspace.net.ng
Contact: Engr. Gabby Dimude - Chairman/CEO

KABO AIR LIMITED
Business: Airline Services
Address: Plot 6773, Ashton Road, P.O. Box 3438, Kano
Tel: (064) 631480, 632762, 649915, 645172, 631355, 636870 **Fax:** (064) 632386, 630994
E-mail: kabo@ecnx.net
Contact: Capt. Saidu Mohammed - MD/CEO

KABOIL LIMITED
Business: Oilfield Engineering Services (Construction, Mechanical, Electrical & Civil Engineering)
Address: AIB Plaza, AIB Terrace, Akin Adesola Street, by Adeyemo Alakija Street, Victoria Island, Lagos
Tel: (01) 2623656, 2623657, 618166 **Fax:** (01) 2623658
Contact: Mr. D. C. Mackay - MD/CEO.

KADUNA ALUMINIUM LIMITED
Business: Aluminium Fabrication, Construction/Engineering
Address: Plot 20, Inuwa Abdulkadir Road, Kaduna South Industrial Estate, Kaduna
Tel: (062) 233037 **Fax:** (062) 230051
* 76A, Isale-Eko Avenue, Dolphin Estate, off Osborne Road, Ikoyi, Lagos
Tel: (01) 683250, 2692082 **Fax:** (01) 2692082

KADUNA EXPO INTERNATIONAL NIGERIA LIMITED
Business: Trade Fairs Organisation, Promotion & Construction
Address: 5B, Zanna Dujima Road, U/Rimi, Kaduna
Tel: (062) 237556, 237557 **Fax:** (062) 237667
Contact: Mrs. Frederique U. Nienhaus -MD/CEO

KADUNA FURNITURE & CARPETS COMPANY LIMITED
Business: Manufacturing of Furniture for Home, Hotel, Hospital, School, Laboratory and Office Use
Address: 15, Inuwa Abdulkadir Road, Kakuri South Industrial Estate, Kaduna
Tel: (062) 230090-3 (4 L) **Fax:** (062) 233043
E-mail: kfcc@agilecomp.com
Contact: Mal. Mamman Daura - Chairman

KADUNA INDUSTRIAL & FINANCE COMPANY LIMITED
Business: Development Financing
Address: Investment House (4th Floor), 27, Ali Akilu Road, Kaduna
Tel: (062) 240751, 241764, 240750, 241773
Fax: (062) 240754
E-mail: kadunainvestment@yahoo,com
Contact: Alh. Dahiru Mohammed - MD/CEO.

KADUNA REFINING & PETROCHEMICALS COMPANY LTD

Business: Refining of Crude Oil to Petroleum Products, Base Oils, Asphalt and Petrochemicals; Production of Drums and Packaging Materials for Wax
Address: Km 16, Kachia Road, Kaduna
Tel: (062) 513771, 513979, 514453, 516212
Fax: (062) 514382, 515697, 517200
E-mail: mdkrpc_office@yahoo.co.uk
Contact: Engr. Voka Mukoro - MD/CEO

KAELER TECHNICAL SERVICES LIMITED

Business: Supply of Industrial Machinery & Equipment for Plastics & Packaging, Turn-Key Projects
Address: Plot 7/9, Thomas Laniyan Street, off Ikorodu Road, by Idiroko Bus Stop, Maryland, Yaba, Lagos
Tel: (01) 4934769, 4963436, 4972765, 08022242460
Fax: (01) 4972764
E-mail: kaelerng@alpha.linkserve.com
Contact: Mr. Mike Iniedu - MD/CEO

KAFIN-KAFI NIGERIA LIMITED

Business: General Merchandising
Address: 69E, Bello Road, Kano
Tel: (064) 632392, 641715 **Fax:** (064) 643678
E-mail: kafinkafi@hotmail.com
Contact: Chief Shewak Manwani - MD/CEO

KAKAKI CHEMIST LIMITED

Business: Sales and Distribution of Pharmaceutical Products
Address: 45, Lagos Street, Ebute-Metta (East), Lagos
Tel: (01) 2885814, 7742586, 7755357, 7914238, 08033356791 **Fax:** (01) 5821443
E-mail: kakakichemistltd@yahoo.com
kakaki@infoweb.abs.net
Contact: Dr. Otunola Adeyemi - Chairman/CEO.

KAKANFO ENTERPRISES LIMITED

Business: Hospitality and Catering Services
Address: Kakanfo Inn, 1, Nihinlola Street, off Adebiyi Street, Mobil Filling Station, Ring Road, Ibadan
Tel: (02) 2311471-3 (3L), 2318603-10 (8L), 2318600-1 (2L)
Fax: (02) 2318909
E-mail: kakanfo@ibadan.skannet.com.ng
Website: www.kakanfoinn.com
Contact: Dr. Lekan Are - Chairman/CEO.

KAKAWA DISCOUNT HOUSE LIMITED

Business: Trading In Government Securities
Address: NAL Towers (10th Floor), 20, Marina, Lagos
Tel: (01) 2645480-5 (6 L), 2601516-9 (4L)
Fax: (01) 2645500, 2645501
E-mail: kdh@kakawa.com
Website: www.kakawa.com
Contact: Mrs. Bola Adesola - MD

KAL & KAY INSURANCE BROKERS COMPANY LIMITED

Business: Insurance Broking
Address: 223, Ikorodu Road, Ilupeju, Lagos
Tel: (01) 4963188, 08023129375, 08023189600
Contact: Otunba A. K. Jowosimi - MD/CEO.

KAL GROUP OF COMPANIES

Business: Manufacturing of Aluminium Building Materials
Address: Plot 20, Inuwa Abdulkadir Road, Kaduna South, Kaduna
Tel: (062) 233037, 235788, 235784, 230050, 234008
Fax: (062) 230051
* 76A, Isale Eko Avenue, Dolphin Estate, off Osborne Road, Ikoyi, Lagos

KALIFE TRAVEL BUREAU LIMITED

Business: Travel Agency
Address: Ozumba Mbadiwe Street, opposite 1004-Flats Estate, Victoria Island, Lagos
Tel: (01) 2625034, 22625033
E-mail: kalifetravel@usa.net

KANAWAT NIGERIA LIMITED

Business: Production and Marketing of Invitation, Wedding, Greeting and Complementary Cards, Stationery and School Materials
Address: 34, Acme Road, Ogba Industrial Estate, Lagos
Tel: (01) 7749000, 4923419, 4924213 **Fax:** (01) 4922540
E-mail: mikano@intracom5.com
* 62, Adeola Odeku Street, Victoria Island, Lagos
Tel: (01) 8042244, 2624007, 2624373, 3200456
Fax: (01) 2624373, 3200456
Contact: Abdul Salam Anis - GM/CEO.

KAN-DOKI LIMITED

Business: Manufacturing of Thread, Packaging Materials and Lawn Mowers, Sales of Agro-Chemicals
Address: 14E, Bello Road, Kano
Tel: (064) 648290, 648390, 6334699, 648294
Fax: (064) 633037, 645261

KANGRA INDUSTRIES LIMITED

Business: Sales of Water-Packaging & PET Blow-Moulding Machinery
Address: 5A, Vori Close, off Acme Road, Ogba Industrial Estate, Ikeja, Lagos
Tel: (01) 7741919, 7763130, 7758610, 7913130, 08033019781
E-mail: mail@kangrasnacks.com
sales@kangrasnacks.com
Contact: Mr. Dinesh Singh - MD/CEO

KANO AGRICULTURAL SUPPLY COMPANY LIMITED

Business: Supply of Agricultural Inputs, Blending of Fertilizer, Sales of Machines, Poultry & Animal Feeds
Address: KASCO House, Maiduguri Road, Kano
Tel: (064) 316440, 636592, 664270, 665595, 667106, 667256, **Fax:** (064) 661611
* 1, Nababa Badamasi Road, Dakata, Kano
Contact: Hon. Ibrahim Yusif Gama - MD/CEO

KANO DURBAR HOTEL

Business: Hospitality & Catering Services
Address: 11B, Ahmadu Bello Way, Kano
Tel: (064) 635259
Contact: Alh. Bello Maitama - MD/CEO.

KANO ELECTRODES & ALLIED PRODUCTS LIMITED

Business: Manufacturing and Marketing of Water Heaters, Kitchen Cabinets/Furniture, Wheel Barrows, Troleys and Headpanss

Address: Plot 6, Sharada Industrial Estate Phase II, Kano
Tel: (064) 661456, 660941, 668044; **Fax:** (064) 660941
E-mail: keal_861@yahoo.com
Contact: Ali Fadlallah - Chairman/CEO.

KANO KILN LIMITED
Business: Manufacturing and Marketing of Clay Products
Address: 66/67, Murtala Mohammed Way, Kano
* Plots 7, 8 & 9, Sharada Ind.Estate Phase I, Kano
Tel: (064) 667759 **Fax:** (064) 632060
Contact: Alh. (Dr.) Aminu Dantata - Chairman
Alh. Abdul Umar - CEO

KANO SACKS INDUSTRIES LIMITED
Business: Manufacturing and Marketing of Polypropylene Woven Sacks and Polyethylene Films
Address: 14, H.W. Romain Street, opposite St. Thomas Secondary School, Bompai, Kano
Tel: (064) 669561 **Fax:** (064) 643195
Contact: Arc. Musa T. Waziri - Exec. Chairman

KANO STATE INVESTMENT & PROPERTIES LIMITED
Business: Developement Finance Services, Property Development, Financial/Management Consultancy Services, Commercial Ventures
Adddress: 15, Ahmadu Bello Way/M.Muhammed Way, Kano
Tel: (064) 311253, 630032, 631457 **Fax:** (064) 630032
E-mail: ksipl@hotmail.com
ksipltdkano@hotmail.com
Contact: Alh. Isma'il Yusuf Takai - MD/CEO.

KANO SUGAR PROCESSING COMPANY LIMITED
Business: Processing and Packaging Sugar
Address: Plot 37, Sharada Industrial Estate Phase III,
Tel: (064) 669192, 667800, 634390, 661230, 660600-3 (4L)
Contact: A. N. Fadlallah - MD/CEO

KANTOMA RESORT, ABUJA
Business: Hospitality Services
Address: Block 2A, Mambolo Street, Zone 2, Wuse, Abuja
Tel: (09) 5234667-8 (2L)

KANU IROEGBU & ASSOCIATES
Business: Estate Agents, Surveyors & Valuers, Property Consultancts, Plant and Machinery Valuers
Address: 38, Kofo Abayomi Street, Victoria Island, Lagos
Tel: (01) 5558535, 8118731, 8118870, 8122090
Contact: Mr. Kanu John Iroegbu - Principal Partner

KAPEX INSURANCE BROKERS LIMITED
Business: Insurance Broking
Address: 14A, Murtala Muhammed Way, Benin City
Tel: (052) 254494, 258151
*123, Tunis Street, Wuse Zone 6, Abuja
Contact: Mr. Ifeanyi Donald Opara - Chairman/CEO

KAPITAL INSURANCE COMPANY LIMITED
Business: Insurance
Address: 116, Hadejia Road, Kano.
Tel: (064) 645666, 636614, 630661, 640156
Fax: (064) 636962
E-mail: kapitalinsurance@samdav.com
* Great Nigeria House (12th Floor), 47/57, Martins Street, Lagos.
Tel: (01) 2662417, 2641709
Contact: Engr Mohammed G. Umar - MD/CEO

KARAMU PLASTIC INDUSTRIES LIMITED
Business: Manufacture of Plastic Packaging Container, Textile Cones and Tubes
Address: Adebowale Compound, Plot 2A, Alh. Lateef Jakande Way, by Coca-Cola Plant, Agidingbi, Ikeja, Lagos
Tel: (01) 4923751, 4924639 **Fax:** (01) 4924637, 2690598

KARISTO INDUSTRIAL SYSTEMS LIMITED
Business: Manfacture of Switchgears and Electrical Appliances, Mechanical Fabrication, Electrical Engineering Contractors
Address: Km. 1.5, Aba-Umuahia Expressway, Aba
Tel: (082) 441332, 221949, *(090) 508958
E-mail: karistoswitch@yahoo.com
Contact: Engr. Emeka C. Ekwebelem - Chairman/CEO

KARLANDER NIGERIA LIMITED
Business: Ship Management
Address: 1, Adele Road, Apapa, Lagos
Tel: (01) 5455397, 5875657, 5875736
Fax: (01) 5455389, 5872169
Contact: Senator Rashidi A. Ladoja - Founder
Chief J. A. Peluola - Finance & Admin. Manager

KARRINGTON LIMITED
Business: Wide-Format Digital Printing Services
Address: 10/12, Somorin Okeowo Street, off Ketu-Oworonsoki Expressway, Ifako, Gbagada, Lagos
Tel: (01) 7733885, 7736381, 4707661, 7742843
Fax: (01) 5552841
E-mail: info@karringtonltd.com
Website: www.karringtonltd.com

KASOLUTE NIGERIA LIMITED
Business: Oil Industry Services, Directional Drilling, MWD and Surveying Services
Address: NBM Compound, Plot A1, Trans-Amadi Industrial Layout, Port Harcourt
Tel: (084) 239605, 08033425289
E-mail: kasolute@hyperia.com
Website: www.t.quadry@kasolute.com
Contact: Mr. Telle Quadry - MD/CEO

KASTEL NIGERIA LIMITED
Business: Electrical Engineering, Manufacture of Electrical Switch Boards, Supply of Electrical Equipment
Address: 20, Oshodi-Apapa Expressway, Oshodi, Lagos
Tel: (01) 4937578, 7919289 **Fax:** (01) 4968442
Contact: Mr. M. M. Eliott - Chairman
Alh. L. I. Sanusi - MD/CEO

KATCHEY COMPANY LIMITED
Business: Supply and Maintenance of Laboratory Equipment, Chemicals, Reagents and Glassware
Address: 20A, Odanye Close, off Adeniyi Jones Avenue, Ikeja, Lagos
Tel: (01) 4972629, 8042651, 4925892 **Fax:** (01) 4972629
E-mail: katchey@nigol.net.ng
Contact: Mrs. Kate Isa - MD/CEO

KATES ASSOCIATED INDUSTRIES LIMITED
Business: Manufacturing of Cosmetics and Toiletries
Address: Plot IN/76, Industrial Layout, Ogbaru, Onitsha
Tel: (046) 484683, 08033166712 **Fax:** (046) 300459
Contact: Chief Ikem Osanakpo - MD/CEO

KATSINA OIL MILL LIMITED
Business: Processing of Vegetable Oils
Address: 59, IBB Way, Katsina
Tel: (065) 430135 **Fax:** (065) 434509
Contact: Alh. Baba Buhari - Vice Chairman/CEO

KATSINA STATE INVESTMENT & PROPERTY DEVELOPMENT COMPANY LIMITED
Business: Development Finance Institution, Investment and Property Development
Address: 61, IBB Way, adjacent to Katsina Oil Mill, Katsina
Tel: (065) 432304, 432313
Contact: Alh. Bishir Gidado - MD/CEO

KATSINA STEEL ROLLING COMPANY LIMITED
Business: Steel Rolling Mill
Address: Shehu Yar'Adua Way, Katsina
Tel: (065) 430050, 430815, 430636 **Fax:** (065) 430953
E-mail: katsteel@hotmail.com
* Federal Secreatriat Phase (2nd floor, Room 232), Ikoyi, Marina, Lagos.
Tel/Fax: (01) 2691498
* Plot 225, Parakou Crescent Cadastral Zone A7, off Aminu Kano Crescent, Wuse II, Abuja
Tel/Fax: (09) 5238958
Contact: Engr. Sanusi Garba - GM/CEO
Salisu Umar - Head (Public Relations)

KAURA BISCUIT & MACARONI FACTORY LIMITED
Business: Manufacturing of Biscuits and Macaroni
Address: 12/15, Club Road, Kano
Tel: (064) 632533, 632929, 644292 **Fax:** (064) 643165
Contact: Alh. Sani Marshall - Chairman/CEO

KAVITEX MILLS LIMITED
Business: Processing and Production of Kaolin
Address: Kuru Tree Road (Gadabiu Bus-Stop), off Barkin-Ladi Road, Anglo-Jos
Tel: (073) 462370
Contact: Mr. Chris Bogwu - GM/CEO

KAYANDOT NIGERIA LIMITED
Business: Importers of General Merchandise, Sales of Bakery Products
Address: 10/12, Burma Road, Apapa, Lagos
Tel: (01) 5878764-5 (2 L), 7764516 **Fax:** (01) 5878765
Contact: Mr. Bayo Fadairo - G. M. (Administration)

KAYFEM KONSULT LIMITED
Business: Hydrological Surveys, Borehole Drilling, Water and Sewage Treatment Services; Storage Tanks and Ditribution Network Construction, Installation, and Maintenance
Address: 28, Allen Avenue, Ikeja, Lagos
Tel/Fax: (01) 4976146
E-mail: kayfem@alpha.linkserve.com
Contact: Engr. A. H. Dixon - Chairman/CEO

KAYNAL TRAVELS & TOURS LIMITED
Business: Travel Agency, Tour Operations
Address: Eleganza Building (2nd Floor), 15B, Joseph Street, off Broad Street, Lagos
Tel: (01) 2645526, 2601430, 08023017890
Fax: (01) 2601430
E-mail: kaynaltravels@yahoo.com
Contact: Mr. Oke Agboro - Chairman/CEO

KAYOK INSURANCE BROKERS LIMITED
Business: Insurance Broking and Consultancy
Address: 12, Ajigbeda St Mosalasi Bus-Stop, Surulere, Lagos
Tel: (01) 4522700, 522700 **Fax:** (01) 4522700
E-mail: kayokinsurance@hotmail.com
E-mail: batokeowo@netscapeonline.co.uk
Contact: Prince E. Kayode Okeowo - Exec. Chairman

KAYPEE FURNITURE & JOINERY COMPANY LIMITED
Business: Production of Furniture for Homes, Schools, Offices and Churches
Address: Plot 3, Block F, Oluyole Industrial Estate, off Ring Road, Ibadan
Tel: (02) 2315759, 08033033709 **Fax:** (02) 2311612
Contact: Mr Sola Adebayo - MD/CEO

KAZOGA NIGERIA LIMITED
Business: Manufacturing of Paper Products & Allied Goods
Address: NB. 4/5, Jema'a Road, Kaduna
Tel: (062) 248732, 08034081043 **Fax:** (062) 248590
E-mail: kazoga.papers@skannet.com
* 56, Palm Avenue, Mushin, Lagos
Tel: (01) 4528918, 4525329
* Cornershop Plot 28, opp. Area 7 Shopping Complex Area 7, Garki, Abuja.
Tel: (09) 2345583
Contact: Mr. C. Amuga - MD/CEO

KCA-DEUTAG (NIGERIA) LIMITED
Business: Oilfield Drilling and Work-Over Operations
Address: Km. 16, P Harcourt/Aba Expressway, Port Harcourt
Tel: (084) 611619, 611757 **Fax:** (084) 611632
E-mail: nigeria.gm@ng.kcadeutag.com
Contact: Mr. John George Joyce - MD/CEO

KE & FL LIMITED
Business: Contract Services and Marketing, Manufacture of Furniture, Flooring, Interior Design & Decoration
Address: St. Joseph's Jubilee Hall, 30, Ikoyi Road, Obalende P.O. Box 74295, Victoria Island, Lagos
Tel: (01) 2670938, 2670939 **Fax:** (01) 2670938
Contact: Prince M. A. Odedina - Chairman

KEBBI INVESTMENT COMPANY LIMITED
Business: Development Finance Institution
Address: Bauchi Rd, opp. Government Lodge, Birnin Kebbi
Tel: (068) 320683
Contact: Alh. Shehu Usman Randadli - MD/CEO

KEBBI STATE HOME SAVINGS & LOANS LIMITED
Business: Mortgage Bamking
Address: Ahmadu Bello Way, Birnin Kebbi
Tel: (068) 321986, 322211 **Fax:** (068) 321502
Contact: Alh. Abubakar Abdullahi - CEO

KEEDAK NIGERIA LIMITED
Business: Oilfield Engineering Services, Procurement of Oilfield Equipment
Address: 18, Chief Nwuke Street, Trans-Amadi Industrial Layout, Port Harcourt
Tel: (084) 237030, 239720 **Fax:** (084) 237029, 239721

KEK NIGERIA LIMITED
Business: Security Services and Consultancy; Sales and Installation of Security Systems
Address: 19, Ibadan Street, by Borno Way, Ebute-Metta (East), Yaba, Lagos
Tel: (01) 861244, 867866, 4711467 **Fax:** (01) 861244
E-mail: kek@rcl.nig.com
E-mail: kek2001@yahoo.com

KEMEBOFF LIMITED
Business: Importation, Sales and Maintenance of Fraud-Check Machines and Computer Imaging Media
Address: 62, Calcutta Crescent, Apapa, Lagos
Tel: (01) 5454036-7 (2 L), 5450697, 5452854, 4724893, 08033285248 **Fax:** (01) 5450697, 5891480
E-mail: kemeboff@alpha.linkserve.com
info@kemeboff.com
Contact: Mr. Ifeanyi B. Onwukeme - Chairman/CEO

KEMEK NIGERIA LIMITED
Business: Security Services and Consultancy; Procurement of Industrial Equipment; Commodities Franchise, Oilfield Service Equipment Suppliers and Contractors
Address: TDT Photo Plaza, 51, Kofo Abayomi Avenue, Apapa, Lagos
Tel: (01) 7742102, 5450206, 5452061 **Fax:** (01) 5450196
E-mail: kemek@cyberspace.net.ng
Contact: Mr. Kris C. Keme - Chairman/CEO

KEMENG SERVICES LIMITED
Business: Chemical and Process Engineering Services, Water Engineering Services, Marketing of Industrial Chemicals Engineering Consultancy
Address: 19, Ikorodu Road, Maryland, Ikeja, Lagos
Tel: (01) 4826213, 4933927, 08023192059, 08033041588
E-mail: kemeng@hyperia.com
Contact: Mr. Adebayo Sola Osiberu - MD/CEO

KENCHEZ NIGERIA LIMITED
Business: Stockist of Steel Materials; Equipment Leasing; Civil and Mechanical Engineering; Sales of Technical Tools and Industrial Hardware
Address: Km. 16, Port Harcourt/Aba Expressway, Obio-Akpor, Port Harcourt
Tel: (084) 611875, 611842 **Fax:** (084) 611842
E-mail: kenchezltd@hotmail.com
Contact: Chief K. C. Ezenwajiaku (JP) - Chairman/CEO

KEN-CHRISTO NIGERIA LIMITED
Business: Importation and Sales of Coloured and Super-White Cement, Terrazo Machines and Products
Address: 38, Ozomagala Street/Modebe Avenue Junction, opp. St Andrew's Anglican Church, Onitsha
Tel: (046) 212276, 217672, 211610, 08033360720
Contact: Mr. Kenneth Okeke - Chairman/MD

KENDALL SECURITIES LIMITED
Business: Stockbroking, Investment Planning & Asset-Based Financing, Financial Planning Workshops
Address: 14, Warehouse Road, Apapa, Lagos
Tel: (01) 5457584, 4820212, 08033266761
Fax: (01) 5451497
E-mail: kendall@nova.net.ng
Contact: Mr. I. N. Ananyi - MD/CEO

KENDALL TRAVELS & TOURS LIMITED
Business: Travel Agency
Address: 14, Warehouse Road, Apapa, Lagos
Tel: (01) 5451497, 585115, 5457584, 4820212
Fax: (01) 5451497
E-mail: kendall@nova.net.ng

KENDO NIGERIA LIMITED
Business: Sales of Photocopiers, Lamination & Office Equipment, Stationery & Books; Printing, Publishing; Sales and Service and Computers; IT Training
Address: S.W. 39A, New Bosso Road, Minna
Tel: (066) 222063, 222360, 221570
Contact: Chief Kenneth M. Uzoma - Chairman/CEO

KENGRAPHICS PRODUCTS LIMITED
Business: Manufacture of Business Forms, Computer Stationery and Sheet-Fed Forms
Address: 1, Agungi Rd, off Lekki Expressway, Lekki, Lagos
Tel: (01) 7747184, 8042170 **Fax:** (01) 5555366
E-mail: kplmctcl@mlstn.com
Website: www.multipleconcepts.com
* Km. 12, Onitsha-Enugu Express Road, Onitsha (System Integration & Testing Facility)
Tel: (046) 611003 **Fax:** (046) 611155
* Plot 2793, Aguiyi Ironsi Street, opp. British High Commission, Maitama District, Abuja
Tel: (09) 4138851, 4139700 **Fax:** (09) 4138851
Contact: Dr. Ken Amobi - MD/CEO

KENQUIP GROUP OF COMPANIES
Business: Oilfield Engineering, Steel Fabrication, Machine Tool-shop Services, Electrical Equipment
Address: Plot 20, Trans-Amadi Ind. Layout, Port Harcourt
Tel: (084) 232024, 235739 **Fax:** (084) 232635
E-mail: oisfa@phca.linkserve.com
Contact: Mr. Ken C. Worgu - Chairman/CEO

KENT RESOURCES LIMITED
Business: Marine Engineering Services
Address: Kent Base, Aker Rd, Rumuolumeni, Port Harcourt
Tel: (084) 232150 **Fax:** (084) 238299
E-mail: kentbase@inmarsat.francetelecom.fr
Contact: Mr. Lan Bailey - Marine Manager

KERILDBERT HOLDINGS LIMITED
Business: Import-Export Logistics - Shipping, Clearing & Forwarding, Airfreighting, Warehousing, Inland Transportation, Financing, Supply-Chain Support
Address: Prince Court (Suite 4C), 37, Ahmed Onibudo Street, Victoria Island, Lagos
Tel: (01) 2611920; 3200311, 3200179 **Fax:** (01) 2615018
E-mail: info@kerildbert.com
Contact: Mr. A.E. Ikazoboh - MD/CEO

KERLIN PRODUCTS NIGERIA LIMITED
Business: Distilling and Marketing of Wines and Spirits
Address: 10, Ilo Awela Road, Ota, Ogun State
Tel: (039) 722227, * (01) 7749110
E-mail: kerlinproducts@hotmail.com
Contact: Mr. Ebenezer A. Egbesola - Chairman/CEO

KES COMPUTER ENGINEERS LIMITED
Business: Manufacturing of Computers; Manufacturer's Representative; Mobile Computing Solutions; Information Technology Training, Software Development; Local & Wide Area Networking
Address: Silicon Village, 3/5, Town Planning Way, Ilupeju, Lagos
Tel: (01) 7742732, 7749256, 4710048, 4706029
Fax: (01) 5550402, 7749265
E-mail: kescomputers@kescomputers.com
Website: www.kescomputers.com
Contact: Mr. Kola W. Omotunde-Young - MD/CEO

KESS KARPET LIMITED
Business: Distribution and Sales of Carpets & Rug, Interior Decorators, General Contractors
Address: 127, Ikorodu Road, Fadeyi, Lagos
Tel: (01) 7744499, 7753818, 08023072034
* 9B, Adeola Odeku Street, Victoria Island, Lagos
Tel: (01) 2626625, 08023142068
Contact: Chief (Mrs.) K. Adeshina - Chairman/CEO

KEWALRAM NIGERIA LIMITED
Business: General Merchandising, Distributive Trading & Sales of Cars, Passenger & Commercial Vehicles
Address: 8A, Karimu Kotun Street, Victoria Island, Lagos
Tel: (01) 2615908, 2617103, 2613317, 2620596, 2617195, 2620328-9(2L), 7742355-6(2L) **Fax:** (01) 2615137
E-mail: customer-service@chanrai.com
Website: www.kewalramnigeria.com
* 44, Marina, Lagos.
Tel: (01) 2643671, 7742356
Contact: Mr. N. D. Chanrai - MD

KGM INDUSTRIES (NIGERIA) LIMITED
Business: Production of Industrial/Domestic Plastic Containers
Address: Block A, Plot 6, Limca Way, Isolo Industrial Scheme II, Isolo, Lagos
Tel: (01) 4520178, 4522036, 7749527 **Fax:** (01) 4527017
E-mail: kgm@hyperia.com
Contact: Mr. D. U. Melwani - MD

KHALIL & DIBBO TRANSPORT LIMITED
Business: Transport and Road Haulage Service
Address: Km 8, Old Lagos Road, Ibadan
Tel: (02) 2315096, 2315099 **Fax:** (02) 2315088
* 10, Abebe Village Road, Iganmu, Lagos
Tel: (01) 5850385, 5850233

KHEMSAFE COMPUTERS LIMITED
Business: Computer Assembling, Networking & Maintenance, Computer Cosultancy & Training, Sales & Installation of VSAT, Sales of Telecommunication Equipment, GSM Phones & Accessories
Address: 12, Constitution Road, P. O. Box 305, Kaduna
Tel: (062) 241081, 210064, 234637, 080332120028
Fax: (062) 210064
E-mail: info@khemsafe.com
Website: www.khemsafe.com
Contact: Dr. Dalhatu Tafida - Chairman
Mr. David Obiora - MD/CEO

KHUSHBU WATERS LIMITED
Business: Manufacture of PET Bottles, Containers and Jars
Address: 146, Gbolade Adebanjo Street, off Coker Road, Ilupeju, Lagos
* Km 38, Abeokuta Motor Road, Sango-Otta
Tel: (039) 721333, 721786, 722223, 722324
Fax: (039) 720786, 722324
E-mail: khushbu@hyperia.com
Contact: Mr. V. P. Vaswani - Chairman
Mr. K. V. Vaswani - CEO

KIDDIESLAND
Business: Sales of Children's Fashion
Address: Kiddiesland Shopping Mall, 21, Joel Ogunnaike Street, G.R.A., Ikeja, Lagos
Tel: (01) 4709756, 4974147 **Fax:** (01) 5837187
E-mail: yemiho@aol.com
* Elpina Plaza (Suite 6), Plot 642C, Akin Adesola Street, Victoria Island, Lagos
Tel: (01) 3200328, 4709756 **Fax:** (01) 3200328

KILOSKA VENTURES LIMITED
Business: Sales of Chalk Moulds and Raw Materials
Address: Opp. Licensing Office Premises, off Badagry Expressway, Agbara, Ogun State
Tel: (01) 5559547, 7741553, 08033340736
* 43, Yaya Abatan Street, Ijaiye-Ogba, Lagos
Contact: Engr. Rasaq Kilanko - MD/CEO

KIMBERLY RYAND LIMITED
Business: Human Resource Development Solutions Provider
Address: 11, Alh. Bashorun Street, off Norman Williams Street, S. W. Ikoyi, Lagos
Tel: (01) 2696420-1 (2 L) **Fax:** (01) 2696422

KINDELL LIMITED
Business: Sales of Corporate & Promotional Gifts & Awards
Address: 11, Ajoke Akinbami St, off Unity Rd, Ikeja, Lagos
Tel: (01) 4707150, 4937371, 4964656, 08023109321, 08033350573 **Fax:** (01) 3453155, 4937371
E-mail: kindell@micro.com.ng
kindellltd@hotmail.com

KING MANUFACTURING COMPANY LIMITED
Business: Manufacture of Carpets, Rugs and Underlays
Address: 23, Asa Afariogun Street, off Isolo Way, Ajao Estate, Apakun-Oshodi, Mushin, Lagos
Tel: (01) 4521599, 4521609, 4520750, 4523970, 7740770
Fax: (01) 4520750
E-mail: king@dalamal.com
* Prestige Fibre Ltd., Plot 2, Block E, Ogba Industrial Estate, Vori Close, off Acme Road, Ikeja, Lagos
Tel: (01) 4923415, 4925685, 4925821
Contact: Mr. Haresh Dalamal - MD/CEO

KING'S CARE HOSPITAL LIMITED
Business: Medical and Maternity Services

Address: Plot 2181, I.Babangida Way, Wuse Zone 4, Abuja
Tel: (09) 5235502, 5235504, 5235515 **Fax:** (09) 5235515
E-mail: kingscare_hospitalmail@yahoo.com
Contact: Dr. A. H. Alasa - Chairman/Medical Director/CEO

KINGS GUARDS NIGERIA LIMITED
Business: Security Guard Services
Address: 5, Ikorodu Road, Jibowu, Lagos
Tel: (01) 7742787, 08023122953, 08023127008, 08033061195 **Fax:** (01) 2693680
E-mail: kipog@infoweb.abs.net
Website: www.kingsguards.com
* Plot 689, Cadastral Zone B3, off Gidado Idris Road, by Federal Ministry of Finance Snr. Staff Quarters, Wuse, Abuja
Tel/Fax: (09) 5232843, 6702521
* 10, Eligbam Road, by Christ Embassy, off Rumuola Road, Port Harcourt.
Tel: (084) 573361, 08033107286
Contact: Chief (Dr.) Oladele Fajemirokun - Chairman
Mr. Olatunji Shittu - Director/CEO

KINGSIZE PHARMACEUTICAL COMPANY LIMITED
Business: Manufacturing of Pharmaceutical Products
Address: Km. 15, Old Enugu Road, Ogidi, Anambra State
Tel: (046) 611000
Contact: Mr. U. C. Okwuosa - Chairman/CEO

KINGSMAT COMPANY LIMITED
Business: Sales of Packaging Machineries, Borehole Drilling Equipment, UV Sterilizers, Water Filtration and Purification Systems and Water-Bottling Plants
Address: Eleganza Plaza (3rd Gate House), Aerodrome Road, Apapa, Lagos
Tel: (01) 5878268, 5878572 **Fax:** (01) 5878268
E-mail: kingsmat@yahoo.co.uk
* 123B, Rumuola Road, Port Harcourt.
Tel: (084) 441490
Contact: Chief M. C. Inyama - MD/CEO

KINLEY SECURITIES LIMITED
Business: Stockbroking, Investment Advisory Services, Portfolio Management, Issuing House
Address: Elder Demper House (2nd Floor), 47, Marina, Lagos
Tel: (01) 2664381, 2663855, 08023002458, 08023143570
Fax: (01) 2663855
E-mail: kinlesec@linkserve.com
Contact: Mr. John O. O. Akinleye - Exec. Chairman
Mr Biodun Okundalaiye - GM

KINSCO LIMITED
Business: Outdoor Advertsing. Printing and Promotions
Address: 2, Ashimowu Street, New Garage, Gbagada, Lagos
Tel: (01) 2903602, 7763124, 826501, 824975, 08033125377, 08037200770
Contact: Mr. K. O. Onyeoziri - Chairman/CEO

KIPPER PROPERTIES LIMITED
Business: Real Estate Agency & Consultancy
Address: 49, Norman Williams Street, S.W. Ikoyi, Lagos
Tel: (01) 2693250, 7946468, 7751964, 08033228250, 08037119445
Contact: Dr. Ola Peters - MD/CEO

KIWI (NIGERIA) LIMITED
Business: Manufacturing of Shoe & Body Care Products
Address: 4, Industrial Street, Ilupeju Industrial Estate, Lagos
Tel: (01) 4936639, 4962001, 4963358 **Fax:** (01) 4936629
E-mail: ngkiwi@infoweb.abs.net
Contact: Nze O. N. E. Nwaozuzu - Chairman/CEO

KIZITO NIGERIA MARITIME AGENCIES LIMITED
Business: Freight Forwarding
Address: 21, Warehouse Road, Apapa, Lagos
Tel: (01) 5874935, 5878801 **Fax:** (01) 5878801
E-mail: kizito52@yahoo.com
Contact: Kizito Anthony Uzum - Chairman/CEO

KLEENOL NIGERIA LIMITED
Business: Industrial & Office Cleaning Services, Pest Control and Fumigation Services
Address: 4, Idowu Street Karaole Estate, Ifako-Agege, Lagos
Tel: (01) 4920443, 4920749, 4920801
E-mail: kleenol@infoweb.abs.net
Contact: Chief. E. O. A. Ajibodu - Chairman/CEO

KLINK STUDIOS LIMITED
Business: Audio/Visuals, Jingle & Music Production, Non-Linear Post Production, CD Duplication & Film Production, Sales & Services of Studio Equipment
Address: 50, Tafawa Balewa Crescent, off Adeniran Ogunsanya Street, Surulere, Lagos
Tel: (01) 02722, 7924480, 08023229667
E-mail: klink@hotmail.com
klinkonline@hotmail.com
Contact: Kingsley E. Ogoro - Chairman/CEO

KLM ROYAL DUTCH AIRLINES (NIGERA)
Business: International Airline and Cargo Services
Address: Churchgate Tower, PC. 30, Afribank Street, Victoria Island, Lagos
Tel: (01) 2616656, 2619336 **Fax:** (01) 2617917
Website: www.seebuyflyklm.com
* Abuja Sheraton Hotel, Wuse Zone 4, Abuja
Tel: (09) 5239965

K-MARINE & BUSINESS NETWORK LIMITED
Business: Shipping Agency, Clearing & Freight Forwarding, Warehousing, Packaging & Relocation, Cargo Superintendence, Road Haulage, Import & Exports
Address: ANCE Building (3rd Floor), 17, Wharf Road, Apapa, Lagos
Tel: (01) 5872419, 5872421 **Fax:** (01) 5872421
E-mail: k-marine@theobech.com.ng
Contact: Alh. W. A. Kareem - Chairman/CEO

KNEIPE NIGERIA LIMITED
Business: Trading, Importation and Marketing of Diary Products, Manufacturer's Sole Agent
Address: 12, Aerodrome Road, Apapa, Lagos
Tel: (01) 5878610 **Fax:** (01) 5875822
Contact: Mr. Fawzi Karam - MD/CEO

KNIGHT CLASS NIGERIA LIMITED
Business: Manufacturing of Brewing Malt
Address: 4, Fatai Giwa Street, Olota, via Ekoro Road, off Abeokuta Express Road, Abule-Egba, Lagos

Tel: (01) 7743691, 4923984, 685737, 2672850
Fax: (01) 2672850
E-mail: knightclass@hyperia.com
Contact: Alh. Fatai Abayomi Giwa - Chairman/CEO

KNIGHT FRANK ESTATE AGENCY
Business: Estate Valuation and Consultancy, Estate Agents, Licensed Auctioneers
Address: Akuro House, 24, Campbell Street, Lagos
Tel: (01) 2600990-9 (10 L), 2631362, 2635516
Fax: (01) 2634090
E-mail: knightfrank@hyperia.com
Website: www.knightfrank.com
* 3B, Herbert Macaulay Way, Wuse Zone 5, Abuja
Tel: (09) 5233122, 5233123
Contact: Mr. O. J. A. Idudu - Chairman
Chief W. O. Olowonyo - Partnership Secretary

KNIGHTS HOLDINGS LIMITED
Business: Import and Export, Information Technology, Mining, Consultancy
Address: 36, Town Planning Way, Ilupeju, Lagos
Tel: (01) 4962870, 7747826, 7750944 **Fax:** (01) 4962870
E-mail: knights@knights.com.ng
Website: www.knights.com.ng
Contact: Otunba Abimbola Davis - Chairman/CEO

KNIGHTSBRIDGE LIMITED
Business: Oil & Gas Services, Marketing of Petroleum Products; Chartering of Vessels
Address: 234, Murtala Mohammed Way, Yaba, Lagos
Tel: (01) 7944860, 8046188 **Fax:** (01) 3425010
E-mail: info@knightbridge-ng.com
Contact: Mr. Gregory Enahoro - MD/CEO

KNORR CONSTRUCTION COMPANY (NIGERIA) LIMITED
Business: Building and Civil Engineering Construction
Address: Plot 2A, Block 2, Oshodi-Isolo Industrial Scheme, Oshodi-Mile 2 Expressway, Isolo, Lagos
Tel: (01) 522311, 524435, 523877, 4522846, 4524494
Fax: (01) 4526478, 520109
E-mail: knormotors@micro.com.ng

KODA INTERNATIONAL LIMITED
Business: Owners & Charters of Ships, Shipping Agents
Address: 11, Awonaike Crescent, off Tejuosho Street, Surulere, Lagos
Tel: (01) 5830412, 5950162, 5851483 **Fax:** (01) 5830648
E-mail: kodashipping@infoweb.abs.net
Contact: Prince Dokun Abidoye - Chairman/CEO

KODA TRADING COMPANY LIMITED
Business: Sales and Service of Construction & Building Equipment Machinery, Cranes & Hoists; Sales & Exportation of Agricultural Produce, Import & Export of General Merchandise
Address: 90, Awolowo Road, S.W. Ikoyi, Lagos
Tel: (01) 2670789, 2692758 **Fax:** (01) 2692758
E-mail: koda@infoweb.abs.net
Contact: Alh. Kola Karim - Chairman/CEO.

KOFAR-KADE NIGERIA LIMITED
Business: Sales of Carpets, Rugs and Building Materials
Address: 1E, Abdullahi Fodio Road, Canteen Area, Sokoto
Tel: (060) 231796, 232075, 234617 **Fax:** (060) 234617
E-mail: kktech@skannet.com.ng
Contact: Alh. Mu'azu Jodi - Chairman/CEO.

KOGGI INDUSTRIES LIMITED
Business: Manufacturing & Marketing of Corporate Gifts & Award Materials, Marble Works, Printing Services
Address: 30, Ayonuga St, off Ikorodu Road, Fadeyi, Lagos
Tel: (01) 4939173, 5821261, 08033041481, 08033042858
Contact: Mr. Kole Hubert-Ogunde - Chairman/CEO.

KOGI HOTELS LIMITED
Business: Hotel Development and Management
Address: Kogi Hotel & Tourism Board, 8, Lugard Road, Lokoja
Tel: (058) 220655, 221605
Contact: Mr. Jerry Agbaji, Jnr. - GM/CEO

KOGI INVESTMENT & PROPERTIES LIMITED
Business: Project Financing & Promotion, Commodity Brokerage, Warehousing, Wholesales, Import and Export, Portfolio Investment and Consultancy Services, Property Management
Address: 14, Wallance Street, Lokoja
Tel: (058) 220150

KOGUNA BARURA INSURANCE BROKERS LIMITED
Business: Insurance & Reinsurance Broking
Address: 27, Norman Williams Street, S.W. Ikoyi, Lagos
Tel: (01) 2673012, 2673013, 2692335, 680252, 680609,
Fax: (01) 2692334
E-mail: kbc@infoweb.abs.net
*Aisha House (2nd Floor), Plot 2087, Herbert Macaulay Way, Wuse Zone 5, Abuja
Tel: (09) 5211415, 08023205495
Contact: Alh. (Dr.) Mohammed H. Koguna - Chairman
Mr. E. K. Okunoren - MD/CEO

KOINONIA VENTURES LIMITED
Business: Export Consultants and Services, Exporters
Address: M.A.N. House (1st Floor), 77, Obafemi Awolowo Way, Ikeja, Lagos
Tel: (01) 4739673, 5557621, 08033065224
Fax: (01) 5557621
E-mail: koinonia@hyperia.com
Website: www.koinonia-ventures.com
Contact: Mr. Olufemi Boyede - MD/CEO

KOJACO INDUSTRIAL SUPPLIES LIMITED
Business: Sales and Maintenance of Valves and Fittings, Pumps and Compressors
Address: 12B, Udom Street, opp. Hotel Chez Therese, D-Line, Port Harcourt,
Tel: (084) 236724, 238431, 08033092659
Contact: Engr. E. O. Ahme - Chairman/CEO

KOJO MOTORS LIMITED
Business: Sales & Services of Motor Vehicles
Address: 25 & 29, Rasaq Balogun Street, via Western Avenue, Surulere, Lagos
Tel: (01) 5851572, 5851568 **Fax:** (01) 5850859
E-mail: kojomotor@yahoo.com
Contact: Mr. Franklin O. Soldier - Sales/Admin. Manager

KOLA AKOMOLEDE & COMPANY
Business: Estate Surveyors & Valuers, Estate Agents
Address: Block C (Suite 6), Eko Court Complex, Kofo Abayomi Street, Victoria Island, Lagos
Tel: (01) 2610513, 42102577
E-mail: kolakoms@metrong.com
* Plot 627, Sokode Crescent (3rd Floor, Suite B2), by Herbert Macaulay Way, Zone 5, Wuse, Abuja
Tel: (09) 5239912, 08037019801, 08044131106
Contact: Chief Kola Akomolede - Principal Partner

KOLA OLANITORI & COMPANY
Business: Estate Surveying and Valuation, Plant and Machinery Valuation, Property Development and Management, Facility Management and Project Appraisal
Address: 55B, Lawson St, off Moloney St, Onikan, Lagos
Tel: (01) 2635117, 2637835, 2645958 **Fax:** (01) 2637835
* Metal and Machines Ltd. MAOA House (1st Floor), Km. 8/9, Old Lagos Road, Ibadan
Tel: (02) 2317202, 2317422
Contact: Prince Kolawole Olanitori - Principal Partner

KOLINTON TECHNICAL INDUSTRIES LIMITED
Business: Assembly and Sales of Gas Cookers, Refrigerators and Deep Freezers
Address: 25, Abimbola Street, Isolo Industrial Estate, Lagos
Tel: (01) 4523482, 08023154167-8 (2L) **Fax:** (01) 4523494
Contact: Mr. L. A. Adewole - MD/CEO

KOLKUF INSURANCE BROKERS LIMITED
Business: Insurance Broking
Address: 7, Laboye Laleye Close, off Tafawa Balewa Crescent, off Adeniran Ogunsanya St, Surulere, Lagos
Tel: (01) 5456855

KOLORKOTE NIGERIA LIMITED
Business: Coating of Aluminium, Aluzine and G. I. Steel Coils
Address: 9, Oba Akran Avenue, Ikeja Industrial Estate,Lagos
Tel: (01) 4936247
* Plot 8, Block IV, Industrial Estate, Idiroko Road, Otta, Ogun State
Tel: (039) 722253, 722602, 722613 **Fax:** (039) 722712
E-mail: kolkot@linkserve.com.ng

KONAC INDUSTRIES LIMITED
Business: Importation and Installation of Suspended Gypsum/Plaster Boards on Wooden and Metal Profiles
Addres: 53, Western Avenuee, Ojuelegba, Surulere, Lagos
Tel: (01) 4804578, 5841221, 08033078260, 08033370211
* Abari Shopping Complex, Plot 569, Wuse Zone 5, Abuja.
Tel: (09) 5230348
Contact: Chief E. S. N. Aniakor - MD/CEO

KONTACTPOINT LIMITED
Business: Outdoor Advertising
Address: 5, African Church Close, off Tinubu Road, Ilupeju, Lagos
Tel: (01) 4968348, 4932312
Contact: Mr. Kamal Ogundeji - Chief Executive

KOOCHI COMMUNICATIONS LIMITED
Business: Broadband VSAT Internet Service & Access Provider
Address: 24B, A.J. Marinho Drive, off Younis Bashorun Street, Victoria Island, Lagos
Tel: (01) 4619151-2 (2L) **Fax:** (01) 4619151
E-mail: info@koochicommunications.com
Website: www.koochicommunications.com
* Lozumba Communication Complex (Suites 221-223), Area 10, Garki, Abuja
Tel: (09) 2345680
Contact: Mr. Kelly N. Kanu -MD/ CEO

KOPEK LIMITED
Business: Produce Merchants, Exportation of Agricultural Commodities
Address: 9, Obafemi Awolowo Road, Ibadan
Tel: (02) 2410440 **Fax:** (02) 2413839
Contact: Chief (Dr.) Raymond Zard - MD/CEO

KOPEK CONSTRUCTION LIMITED
Business: Road Construction, Sales & Delivery of Crushed Stone Aggregates and Asphalt
Address: Plots 3, 4, & 5 First Rd, Oluyole Ind. Estate, Ibadan
Tel: (02) 2312701-2 (2 L), 2315073, 2315083, 2315093
Fax: (02) 2317269
* 4, Adetokunbo Ademola Crescnt, Wuse II, Abuja
Tel: (09) 5235186
* Former Airport Hotel Premises, 1, Old Aba Road, Rumuomasi, Port Harcourt
Tel: (084) 234582

KORAMA CLOVER INDUSTRIES LIMITED
Business: Manufacturing of Paints, Wood Finishes, Protective & Industrial Coatings, Domestic & Industrial Plasticwares
Address: Km. 6, Old Aba-Owerri Rd, Osisoma Ind. Area, Aba
Tel: (082) 220581, 350101, 350102
Fax: (082) 350100, 440019
E-mail: korama@yahoo.com
cloverpaints@hotmail.com
Contact: Chief Innocent Okoroama - Chairman/CEO

KOREA MACHINERY COMPANY LIMITED
Business: Sale of Plastic Machines, Extruders, Cutting and Sealing Machines, Recycling Machines, Printing Machines, Production of Polythene Bags
Address: 2, Oregun Road, off Obafemi Awolowo Way, by Radio Bus-Stop, Alausa, Ikeja, Lagos
Tel: (01) 4978212, 7741327, 08023122390, 08037002418
Fax: (01) 4978212
* 1A, Commercial Road, Kano
Tel: (064) 315717
* 142, Limca Road, Onitsha
Contact: Mr. Park Sun-Chan - MD/CEO

KOREKT INVESTMENT LIMITED
Business: Building & Civil Engineering Construction, Electrical Engineering Services, Import & Export Trading, Property Development
Address: God First House, 54, Oyo Road, Sango, Ibadan
Tel: (02) 8104935, 08037218595 **Fax:** (02) 8104300
* 4A, Yedseram St, off IBB Way, Maitama, Abuja
Tel: (09) 4138470, 4131748
Contact: Engr. Biodun Bankole - MD/CEO

KOS WORLD NIGERIA LIMITED
Business: Sales of Personal-Wear Fashion Items, Construction Services, Sales of GSM Phones & Accessories Sales of Home Entertainment Appliances/Products
Address: The Green House, Plot 1607, Omegabank Avenue, off Adeola Hopewell Street, Victoria Island, Lagos
Tel: (01) 4703095, 4619671, 2703356, 7766173, 08037187000, 08022235454, 08033069044,
E-mail: kosgroup@vgccl.net
Website: www.kos-world.com
www.thesoundcentre.com

KOTCO LIMITED
Business: Industrial Engineering Services and Consultancy, Marketing of Petroleum Products
Address: 102, Isheri Road, Omole Estate, Ojodu, Ikeja, Lagos
Tel: (01) 7749681, 7740976, 4708397, 3453131, 2882475
* Kotco House, opp. Banex Plaza, Plot 1084, Aminu Kano Crescent, Cadastral Zone A7, Wuse II, Abuja
Tel: (09) 4139448, 4139453
Contact: Aare Kola Oyefeso - Chairman/CEO

KP BEVERAGES COMPANY LIMITED
Business: Distilling of Alcoholic Spirits & Wines
Address: Km. 15, Old Enugu Road, Ogidi, Anambra State
Tel: (046) 611623
Contact: Mr. U. C. Okwuosa - Chairman/CEO

KPMG CONSULTING LIMITED
Business: Management, Human Resources and Information Technology Consultancy Services
Address: KPMG House, 233, Ikorodu Rd, Obanikoro, Lagos
Tel: (01) 4931346-8 (3 L), 4930117, 7740432, 8044308
E-mail: nigeria@kpmg.gem.gel5.com
* Plots 239/240, Muhammadu Buhari Way, Central Business District, Abuja
Tel: (09) 5239729-30 (2 L), 5238223
Contact: Bashorun J. K. Randle - Chairman/CEO
Mr. Alfred S. Gbodimowo - Managing Partner

KPMG PROFESSIONAL SERVICES
Business: Assurance, Consulting, Financial Advisory Services, Tax & Business Regulatory Services
Address: 22A, Gerrand Road, Ikoyi, Lagos
Tel: (01) 2692635, 2694660-4 (5L), 2696040-5 (5L)
Fax: (01) 2691248
Website: www.kpmg.com

KPS LIMITED
Business: Sales of Satellite & VSAT Communication Equipment, Operation of Pre-Paid Telephone Cards, Telecommunication Consultancy, IT Training, Internet Service Provider, Web Designing
Address: 1, Abiola Segun Ajayi Street, off Etim Inyang Crescent, Victoria Island, Lagos
Tel: (01) 4618657, 08032030543
E-mail: kps02@engineer.com
kpsupport@engineer.com
info2@kpsworld.com
Website: www.kpsworld.com

KRAFT KONSULT LIMITED
Business: Design, Printing & Communication Services
Address: 39, Olukole Street, off Adegoke Street, off Alh. Masha Road, Surulere, Lagos
Tel: (01) 5845547, 4709504, 08033024189
E-mail: kraftkonsult@hyperia.com
Contact: Mr. Ede Dafinone - Chairman
Mr. Olujide Ojo - MD/CEO

KRAGHA & ASSOCIATES
Business: Oil & Gas Industry Consultancy Services
Address: Foreshore Towers (1st Floor), 2A, Osborne Road, Ikoyi, Lagos
Tel: (01) 26952245, 2673450 **Fax:** (01) 2673450
E-mail: kraghamok@yahoo.com
* 8A Close, 3rd Avenue, House 8, Federal Housing Estate, Rumueme, Port Harcourt
Contact: Mr. Moses O. Kragha - MD/CEO

KRESTA LAUREL LIMITED
Business: Sales, Installation and Maintenance of Elevators, Escalators, Cranes, Generators, Compressors and Welding Machines, Maintenance of Cradles
Address: Kresta Laurel Complex, 376, Ikorodu Road, Maryland, Ikeja, Lagos
Tel: (01) 4977172, 4977995, 4974254 **Fax:** (01) 4978346
E-mail: kresta@krestalaurel.com
kresta@alpha.linkserve.com
krestalaurel@aol.com
Website: www.krestalaurel.com
* 16, Trans-Amadi Industrial Layout, Port Harcourt
Tel/Fax: (084) 238058
* 10, Ontario Crescent, near British High Commission Residence, Maitama District, Abuja
Tel: (09) 4135015 **Fax:** (09) 4135016
Contact: Otunba (Engr.) J. O. Daniel - Founder
Engr A. Ishola - Ag. MD/CEO

KRISBOSE NIGERIA LIMITED
Business: Importers and Exporters
Address: Ebani House, 149/153, Broad Street, Lagos
Tel: (01) 2665998 **Fax:** (01) 2665996
E-mail: krisbose@cyberspace.net.ng
Contact: Mr. J. Efeyini - Chairman/CEO

KRISEL INVESTMENT LIMITED
Business: Import and Export, Manufacturers of Polythene & Plastic Product and Oxygen Gas; Construction
Address: 122, Okota Road, Isolo, Lagos
Tel: (01) 4520397, 4529118, 08033468913
E-mail: krisel@hyperia.com
Contact: Mr. Christopher Ukeje Elendu - Chairman/CEO.

KROLLENE LABORATORIES LIMITED
Business: Sales and Service of Medical and Laboratory Equipment and Chemicals
Address: 130, Bode Thomas Street, Surulere, Lagos
Tel: (01) 5851114, 5850270, 7743386, 08023073480
Fax: (01) 5850270, 7743386
E-mail: krollene@hyperia.com
Contact: Mr. Kola Olowu - MD/CEO.

KRS INVESTMENT LIMITED
Business: Bottling of Ozonised Natural Mineral Water (CASCADE), Manufacturing of PET Bottles, Sales

of Water Dispenser
Address: 52, Town Planning Way, Ilupeju, Lagos
Tel: (01) 4935980-2 (3L), 4972203 **Fax:** (01) 4935983
E-mail: crystalpet@nova.net.ng
cascade@micro.com.ng
Contact: Mr. V. K. Singh - MD/CEO

KTFB LIMITED
Business: Outdoor Advertising Agency
Address: 16, Bassie Ogamba Crescent, off Adeniran Ogunsanya Street, Surulere, Lagos
Tel: (01) 2905308, 5852233, 08023210634
Contact: Mr. Olajide Sokoya - CEO.

KUK INSURANCE BROKERS LIMITED
Business: Insurance Broking
Address: Christy House (3rd Floor), 2B, Herbert Macaulay Way, Wuse Zone 5, Abuja
Tel: (09) 5232306, 5232587, 08037009678, 08037866196
E-mail: chuzurike@hotmail.com
* 7B, Ikwerre Road, Mile 2, Diobu, Port Harcourt
Tel: (084) 332062
Contact: Mr. Chuks J. Onwuzurike - MD/CEO

KULAK TRADE & INDUSTRIES PLC
Business: Fishing, Processing & Export of Fish Products
Address: Daddo Terminal, Beachland Estate, Kirikiri Terminal Phase I, Apapa, Lagos
Tel: (01) 5877347, 7746056, 08033031308
Contact: Alh. Bamanga Tukur - Chairman
Mr Krishna Chandra Lakhotia - MD/CEO

KUNDILA FINANCE SERVICES LIMITED
Business: Stockbroking
Address: Ahmadu Dantata House (1st Floor), 1C, Beirut Road, P. O. Box 84, Kano
Tel: (064) 642195 **Fax:** (064) 648499
* 11, Festival Road, off Adetokunbo Ademola Street, Victoria Island, Lagos
Tel: (01) 2615838, 2615115
Contact: Alh. Umaru Shinkafi - Chairman
Alh. Saminu Gwadobe - MD/CEO

KUNLE OGUNBAYO & ASSOCIATES
Business: Engineering Consultancy, Project & Facilities Management, Environmental Protection Studies
Address: 12, Morris Street, Abule-Ijesha, Yaba, Lagos
Tel: (01) 7740157-8 (2 L), 5454609
Fax: (01) 3425273, 4971624
E-mail: koa@metrong.com
Website: www.koa.com.ng
* Plot 6B, Oka Akoko Street, Garki, Abuja
Tel: (09) 2341779, 2341783
Contact: Engr. I. S. Ogunbayo - Principal Partner

KUNLE-OLA ENTERPRISES (NIGERIA) LIMITED
Business: Stockist of Industrial Chemicals for Distilleries and Foam Manufacturers, Distribution of Motor Vehicles and Bicycles, Sale of Sugar
Address: Olajire House, 3, Ilupeju Bye-Pass, Ilupeju Industrial Estate, Lagos
Tel: (01) 5550925, 7746523, 7749139 **Fax:** (01) 4529395
Contact: Mr. Kunle Babalola - Chairman/CEO.

KURAMO INDUSTRIES (NIGERIA) LIMITED
Business: Manufacturing and Marketing of Healthcare Products and Household Furniture
Address: Kuramo House, Plot 6, Block K, Apapa-Oshodi Expressway, Isolo Industrial Scheme, Isolo, lagos
Tel: (01) 4701688, 4526669, 4526039, 4521798, 7758021-2
E-mail: kuramoltd@hotmail.com

KWAJAFA SECURITY & INVESTIGATION SERVICES LTD.
Business: Security Consultancy Services
Address: 56, Lusaka Street, Wuse Zone 6, Abuja
Tel: (09) 5238815 **Fax:** (09) 5234452
* 19B, Azare Crescent, off Liverpool Road, Apapa G.R.A., Lagos
Tel: 08033117929
Contact: Mr. Fulani Kwajafa (Com.of Police rtd.) - Chairman

KWARA HOTELS LIMITED
Business: Hospitality and Catering Services
Address: 9A, Ahmadu Bello Avenue, Ilorin
Tel: (031) 221490-3 (4L), 08037117295
Fax: (031) 221494

L. E. EJINKEONYE NIGERIA LIMITED
Business: Sales and Service of Motor Vehicles, Transport
Address: Plot In/112, Eziachi Street, Harbour Industrial Layout, Onitsha
Tel: (046) 217119, 08023267759, 08033164964
Contact: Chief L. E. Ejinkeonye - Chairman/CEO

L. L. NWADIKE & ASSOCIATES LIMITED
Business: Proper Converters, Printing of Exercise Books & Office Stationery, Import & Export Trading
Address: 12, New Market Road, P. O. Box 5017, Onitsha
Tel: (046) 412558, 08042117043
Contact: Sir. L. L. Nwadike (KSM) - Chairman/CEO

L. M. ERICSSON (NIGERIA) LIMITED
Business: Telecommunication Engineering Services, Sales Installation of Telecommunication Equipment
Address: 17, Walter Carrington Crescent, Victoria Island, Lagos
Tel: (01) 4616000-24 (25L) **Fax:** (01) 4616020
* 39, Usuma Street, Maitama District, Abuja
Tel: (09) 4137925-6(2L) **Fax:** (09) 4137927
* 201/203, Woji Road, Apapa, Lagos.
Tel: (084) 238829

L. N. TECHNOLOGIES LIMITED
Business: Assembly, Sales and Maintenance of Generators
Address: 9, Creek Road, Apapa, Lagos
Tel: (01) 5457816
* Ize-Iyamu St/Balogun St, opp. Papercraft, T. A. Doherty Industrial Layout, Oregun, Ikeja, Lagos

L. W. LAMBOURN (NIGERIA) LIMITED
Business: Sales, Installation, Service, Overhaul nd Refurbishment of Generators, Transformers, Switchgears and Textile Machinery, Steel Trading
Address: 23, Warehouse Road, Apapa, lagos
Tel: (01) 5452069, 5876026, 7765359, 08033014335, 08033014375, 08033199575 **Fax:** (01) 5874013
E-mail: lambourn@linkserve.com.ng
Contact: Mr. A. W. Kneafsey - MD/CEO

LA BAGUETTE LIMITED
Business: Bakery, Fast-Food Outlet Operations, Canteen Management, Outdoor Catering Services
Address: 11, Amodu Ojikutu Street, off Bishop Oluwole Street, Victoria Island, Lagos
Tel: (01) 7732248, 08037200870
* Mega Plaza, 14, Idowu Martins Street, V/I, Lagos
* 9, Warehouse Road, Apapa, Lagos

LAAS GROUP LIMITED
Business: Shipping, Clearing. Forwarding, General Contractors
Address: 206, Aba Road, Rumuola, Port Harcourt
Tel: (084) 331729, 333998, 08023122139
* 1, Francis Street, off Medical Road, Ikeja, Lagos
Contact: Chief Lawrence Ayo (JP) - Chairman

LABANA GLOBAL VENTURES LIMITED
Business: Sales of Motor Vehicles, Haulage and Sales of Petroleum Products, Real Estate Development, Export and Import, Functional Consultancy, General Merchandising, Licensed Customs Agents
Address: 295/296, Wharf Road, (2nd Floor), Apapa, Lagos
Tel: (01) 5451590, 5451243, 7741556 **Fax:** (01) 5451243
* 6, Koko Road, off Sultan Dasuki Road, Sokoto
Tel: (060) 236139, 236404
* Km. 3, Sokoto-Jega Road, Aliero, Kebbi State
Tel: (068) 321999
Contact: Alh. Abdurahman Ibrahim - Chairman
Alh. Abubakar Abba Adamu - MD/CEO

LABANELLA INDUSTRIAL LIMITED
Business: Textile Fashion Design, Interior Decoration, Sales of Shoes and Jewellery
Address: 38, Adeniran Ogunsanya Street, Surulere, Lagos
Tel: (01) 836003, 5851181, 08035756423
Contact: Mr. Adeyinka Adewumi - CEO

LABSTOCK (NIGERIA) LIMITED
Business: Distribution, Sales, Installation & Service of Scientific Instruments and Laboratory Equipment
Address: 61, Akinwunmi Street, Alagomeji - Yaba, Lagos
Tel: (01) 3425057, 3425433, 08033047925, 08033255731
E-mail: sales@labstocknigeria.com
Website: www.labstocknigeria.com
Contact: Dr. Nathan I. C. Nwachukwu - Chairman/CEO

LABYET POLARIS NIGERIA LIMITED
Business: Sales, Installation & Service of Computer Systems, Structured Cabling, Systems Maintenance & Repairs, Software Development; Training
Address: 25, Mushin Road (College Bus-Stop), opposite General Petrol Station, Isolo, Lagos
Tel: (01) 4521763, 4528960, 4520656 **Fax:** (01) 4521763
E-mail: polaris@infoweb.abs.net
Website: www.labyetpolaris.com
CTL House, opposite Banex Plaza, Plot 1221, Aminu Kano Crescent, Wuse II, Garki, Abuja
Tel: (09) 41311481
Contact: Chief O. A. Ayodele - MD/CEO

LACCOTRONICS LIMITED
Business: Importation of Electronic Systems and Appliances
Address: 132, Enuowa Street, Idumota, Lagos
Tel: (01) 2642312, 2663451, 08033188935
* 6/58, Iweka Road, Onitsha
Tel: (046) 211880 (090) 501769
Contact: Engr. Lawrence Uzoeto - Chairman/CEO.

LACOM COMMUNICATIONS LIMITED
Business: Publishing of POLICY Newsmagazine
Address: 111B, Sylvia Crescent, Anthony Village, Lagos
Tel: (01) 4701662, 4701737 **Fax:** (01) 2624271
* Plot 74, Ralph Shodeinde Street, off Ahmadu Bello Way, Central Business District, Abuja.
Tel: (09) 2348174
Contact: Mr Enitan Sanusi - Publisher/CEO.

LADGROUP LIMITED
Business: Trading, Exportation of Raw Agricultural Produce, Manufacturing, Warehousing
Address: Abimbola House, 24, Abimbola Street, Isolo Industrial Estate, Ilasamaja, Lagos
Tel: (01) 4522716, 4522113 **Fax:** (01) 4522334, 4971966
E-mail: ladgroup@supernet300.com
Contact: Prince (Dr.) B. A. Onafowokan - Exec. Chairman

LADIPO DANIEL FARMS LIMITED
Business: Agro-Allied Business
Address: Km. 32, Abeokuta Motor Road, Alagbado, Lagos
Tel: (01) 7746728, 08033812351
Contact: Snr. Apostle (Dr.) L. I. Daniel - MD/CEO

LADO LEATHER LIMITED
Business: Production of Leather Products & Corporate Gift
Address: 30, Ayonuga Street, off Ikorodu Rd, Fadeyi, Lagos
Tel: (01) 823625
Contact: Kole Hubert-Ogunde - Chairman/CEO

LAFIA HOTEL, IBADAN
Business: Hospitality and Catering Services
Address: Moor Plantation, Abeokuta Road, Apata, Ibadan
Tel: (02) 2316555, 2315720, 2313936 **Fax:** (02) 2313936
E-mail: lafiahotel@odu-a.com
Website: www.oduainvestment.com
Contact: Mr. A. A. Oladipo - MD/CEO

LAGETRONIX NIGERIA LIMITED
Business: Sales of Computers and Accessories, Networking, Storage Solution, Structured Cabling/Fibre Optics
Address: Western House (12th Floor), 8/10, Broad St, Lagos
Tel: (01) 263054.3, 2646948, 08022907805
Fax: (01) 2630996
E-mail: lagetronix@yahoo.com
Contact: Engr. Femi Adesanya - MD/CEO

LAGOON HOME SAVINGS & LOANS LIMITED
Business: Mortgage Banking and Financial Services
Address: 292A, Ajose Adeogun St, Victoria Island, Lagos
Tel: (01) 2624448, 3200212, 7743066, 7921121, 7921124
Fax: (01) 3200217
E-mail: lagoonhome@yahoo.com
Contact: Mr. Akin Adetola - MD/CEO.

LAGOS & NIGER SHIPPING AGENCIES LIMITED (LANSAL)
Business: Shipping Agency, Clearing and Forwarding Agency, Warehousing

Address: 4, Creek Road, Apapa, Lagos
Tel: (01) 5803930-4 (5 L) **Fax:** (01) 2646434
Contact: Mr. Andrew I. Wilson, OFR - Chairman
Mr. Yehuda Kotik - MD/CEO.

LAGOS AIRPORT HOTEL LIMITED
Business: Hotel Services, Conference Facilities
Address: 111, Obafemi Awolowo Way, Ikeja, Lagos
Tel: (01) 4978670-9 (10 L) **Fax:** (01) 4937573, 4970620
E-mail: laph@rcl.nig.com
Website: www.lagosairporthotel.com
Contact: Mr Niyi Badmus - MD/CEO.

LAGOS BUILDING INVESTMENT COMPANY LIMITED
Business: Mortgage Banking
Address: ASSBIFI Road, Central Business District, Elephant House Bus-Stop, Alausa, Ikeja, Lagos
Tel: (01) 4934581-5 (5 L), 7741574 **Fax:** (01) 4934580
E-mail: info@lbicltd.com
operations@lbicltd.com
Website: www.lbicltd.com
Contact: Mr Babatunde U. Jinadu - MD/CEO.

LAGOS HILTON HOTEL LIMITED
Business: Hotel Services, Banqueting & Conference Facilities
Address: 1, Hilton Drive, off Allen Avenue, Ikeja, Lagos
Tel: (01) 4739629, 4826614, 4936176-7 (2L), 4936195, 4960604, 4964947 **Fax:** (01) 4936195
Contact: Chief A. Obi Okoli - Chairman/CEO.

LAGOS HORIZON PUBLISHING COMPANY LIMITED
Business: Newspaper Publishing
Address: 1, Rev. Ogunbiyi Road, off Oba Ladejobi Road, Ikeja G.R.A., Ikeja, Lagos
Tel: (01) 4966399
Contact: Mr. Olusegun Ojo - GM/CEO.

LAGOS ISLAND CHEMIST LIMITED
Business: Sale and Distribution of Pharmaceutical Products
Address: 4, Balogun Square, Lagos
Tel: (01) 2660941, 2663857, 2661256 **Fax:** (01) 2661256
E-mail: uoo@infoweb.abs.net
Contact: Chief Nzedioranma Uche Okafor - Chairman/CEO.

LAGOS TOBACCO DISTRIBUTION COMPANY LIMITED
Business: Distribution & Marketing of General Merchandise and Tobacco Products
Address: Murhi House, Plot 45, Omole Industrial Estate, Isheri/Ogba Junction, Ogba, Lagos
Tel: (01) 4922396, 08033009591
E-mail: royallead@usa.net
Contact: Chief (Mrs.) H. I. D. Awolowo - Chairman
Mr Tunde Omotosho - CEO

LAGOS TRAVEL INN
Business: Hoel Services, Conference Facilities, Outdoor Catering Services
Address: 39, Toyin Street, Ikeja, Lagos
Tel: (01) 4970794-5 (2L), 4970785, 4975952, 7743288, 7767833
Fax: (01) 4970788
E-mail: lagos.travelinn@skannet.com
Contact: Mr Olushola Daramola - Hotel Manager

LAI SECURITY AND INVESTIGATION SERVICES LIMITED
Business: Security Services and Consultancy, Sale of Motor Vehicle Security Systems and Fire/Burglar Alarms
Address: 62, Tafawa Balewa Crescent, off Adeniran Ogunsanya Street, Surulere, Lagos
Tel: (01) 4745701, 5837137, 5456577, 08033200550, 08033202080, 08033201363 **Fax:** (01) 5456577
E-mail: lasis@infoweb.abs.net
* Plot 1205, Idofian Close, Wuse II, Abuja
Contact: Mrs. F. I. Oshodi - Chairperson
Mr. G. R. A. Sobayo - GM

LAI TAILORING SERVICES LIMITED (Lai Clothiers)
Business: Manufacturer and Exportation of Garments
Address: 26, Industrial Avenue, Ilupeju Ind. Estate, Lagos
Tel: (01) 4962225, 08033078791
E-mail: laitailoring@yahoo.com
Contact: Chief F. L. Olumegbon, MON - Chairman/CEO

LAKE CHAD GUEST PALACE, ABUJA
Business: Hospitality & Catering Services
Address: Plot 1154, Lake Chad Crescent, off Ibrahim Babangida Way, Maitama Abuja
Tel: (09) 4133864-5 (2 L) **Fax:** (09) 4132806
E-mail: lakechad@linkserve.com
Contact: Chief (Dr.) Laz Unaogu - Chairman/CEO

LAKE CONCRETE INDUSTRIES LIMITED
Business: Manufacturing and Marketing of Electric Poles, Culvert Rings, Slabs, Fence Posts and Blocks
Address: 22, Mbanugo Street, Ogbete, Enugu
Tel: (042) 251879
Contct: Chief Gogo Nwakuche - Chairman/CEO.

LAKEVAL LIMITED
Business: Library Development and Consultancy Services, Library Automation & Information Services
Address: Lapal House (4th Floor), 235, Igbosere Rd, Lagos
Tel: (01) 2601865 **Fax:** (01) 2634511
E-mail: lakeval@nova.net.ng
Contact: Mr. Emeka Arinze - Chairman/CEO

LAKHI TEXTILE INDUSTRY LIMITED
Business: Manufacturing of Textile Products
Address: 102, Maganda Rd, Bompai Industrial Estate, Kano
Tel: (064) 648024, 645109, 664921, 665289
Fax: (064) 641782
E-mail: jaykaycarpets@hotmail.com
Contact: Mr. Mohit Manglani - MD/CEO

LAKSWORTH INVESTMNTS & SECURITIES LIMITED
Business: Stockbroking, Financial & Investmenet Advisors
Address: First Bank Building (Penthouse), 23/25, Ijora Causeway, Ijora, Lagos
Tel: (01) 5453669, 08034735745, 08023366690, 08023157488
E-mail: laksworth@hotmail.com
Contact: Pastor O. R. Adesoye - MD/CEO

LAMBADA VENTURES LIMITED
Business: Import & Export, Distribution of Fashion Wears
Address: 15, Nnamdi Azikiwe Street (Shop 37), Lagos
Tel: (01) 2641582, 2660640, 4709994

* 68, Blessed Line, behind Shopping Plaza, back of Mandilas Building, off Broad Street, Lagos
Contact: Mr. Lambert Uju Obi - MD/CEO

LAMBERT INTERNATIONAL LIMITED
Business: Construction of Truck Bodies
Address: 212, Moshood Abiola Way, Ijora, Lagos
Tel: (01) 7740294, 7741603, 08033089190
Fax: (01) 7743131
E-mail: lamint@beta.linkserve.com
Contact: Comm. Lamberto Salvatori - MD/CEO

LAMBERT WILLIS & ASSOCIATES
Business: Insurance Broking and Consultancy
Address: Ashakun House (6th Floor), 13/15, Lake Street, off Broad Street, Lagos
Tel: (01) 2661419, 2664254 **Fax:** (01) 2669528
Contact: Mr. R. K. Goyal -- MD/CEO

LAMBIC TECHNICAL & GENERAL SERVICES LIMITED
Business: Sales and Maintenance of Motor Vehicles, Vehicles and Equipment Leasing, Car Rental
Address: 59, Aba Road, Trans-Amadi, Port Harcourt
Tel: (084) 238241, 244247
E-mail: lambic@phca.linkserve.com

LAMDA INSURANCE COMPANY LIMITED
Business: Non-Life Insurance
Address: 18, Moloney Street (3rd Floor), Onikan, Lagos
Tel: (01) 2630573, 2631889 **Fax:** (01) 2666580, 2668637
E-mail: lamda@cyberspace.net.ng
Contact: Ambassador J. T. F. Iyalla, OFR - Chairman
Mr. V. K. Markanda - MD/CEO

LAMID NIGERIA LIMITED
Business: Management Consultants, Business Advisors
Address: Elephant Cement House (2nd Floor, Wing B), ASSBIFI Road, Central Business District, Alausa, Ikeja, Lagos
Tel: (01) 4710788, 4743188, 4748457 **Fax:** (01) 3453183

LAMIDI AJADI & SONS NIGERIA LIMITED
Business: Importation of Tyres, Tubes and Batteries
Address: Iwo Road Roundabout/Expressway Interception, Ibadan
Tel: (02) 8105016, 8105400 **Fax:** (02) 8104833
* Block B, Space 2, Sani Kwangila Memorial Complex, Plot 518, Michael Okpara Road, opp. Elf Petrol Station, Zone 5, Wuse, Abuja
Tel: (09) 5238410, 5238414
Contact: Alh. (Chief) Lamidi Ajadi - Chairman/CEO

LAMIP INVESTMENT LIMITED
Business: Haulage, Marketing of Petroleum Products
Address: Eleganza Plaza (Virgo Block, Right Wing), 1, Commercial Road, Apapa, Lagos
Tel/Fax: (01) 5871185
E-mail: lamip2000@linkserve.com
Contact: Mr. Olajide Moses Babalola - Chairman

LAMNALCO (NIGERIA) LIMITED
Business: Marine Transportation, Terminals Management
Address: 23, Ogunu Road, Warri
Tel: (053) 520465, 252253, 253159 **Fax:** (053) 254400
E-mail: lamnig@micro.com.ng
Website: www.lamnalco.co.ae
* Plot 474, Trans-Amadi Ind. Layout, Port Harcourt
Contact: Capt. Johan Carse - GM/CEO

LAMOUR SPRING WATER LIMITED
Business: Bottling of Mineral Water
Address: Lamour Industrial Estate, Abagana, Anambra State
Tel: (048) 571483

LANCO ELECTRICAL EQUIPMENT (NIGERIA) LIMITED
Business: Sales of Transformers and Electrical Equipment
Address: Plot 642B, Adeyemo Alakija Street, opp. Guaranty Trust Bank, Victoria Island, Lagos
Tel: (01) 2620051, 2622275, 2621890, 4618562
E-mail: lanco@hyperia.com
Contact: Mr. Ben Lanciano - MD/CEO

LAND PARK HOTELS LIMITED
Business: Hospitality Services
Address: 1/3, Land Part Lane, Badagry Expressway (b/w Alafia & Coker Bus-Stop), Apapa, Lagos
Tel: (01) 7744891, 2880876, 5847507, 08033253431
Contact: Mrs. F. U. Okoye - Chairman/CEO

LANDGOLD HOLDINGS LIMITED
Business: Building and Civil Engineering Construction, Architectural Designs, Engineering and Consultancy Services; Pharmaceutical and Medical Products/Equipment; Insurance Brokerage and Bureau-de-Change; Submersible Pumps and Water Treatment Input Supplies
Address: Landgold House, 58A, Adeniran Ogunsanya Street, Surulere, Lagos
Tel: (01) 5835387, 5802200-4 (5 L), 5837801, 7742877, 7911780 **Fax:** (01) 5837801
* 2A, Suez Crescent, Wuse Zone 4, Garki, Abuja
Tel: (09) 5236801-2 (2L) **Fax:** (09) 5236802, 5236903
Contact: Chief Nath Okechukwu - Chairman/CEO

LANDGOLD INSURANCE BROKERS LIMITED
Business: Insurance Broking
Address: 63, Adeniran Ogunsanya Street, Surulere, Lagos
Tel: (01) 836996, 7749170 **Fax:** (01) 3205116, 5837801
* 2A, Suez Crescent, Wuse Zone 4, Garki Abuja
Tel: (09) 5236801, 5236803 **Fax:** (09) 5236903
Contact: Chief Nath. Okechukwu - Chairman

LANDMARK INTERNATIONAL COMPANY LIMITED
Business: LPG Haulage, Distribution & Bottling, Installation of Communication Terminals and Related Equipment, Computer Training and Maintenance
Address: 11, Sumbo Jibowu Crescent, off Ribadu Road, S. W. Ikoyi, Lagos
Tel: (01) 2670750, 2670735, 08033064311, 08033064312
Fax: (01) 2670735
E-mail: oguguo@consultant.com
Contact: Commodore A. E. Oguguo (rtd.) - Chairman/CEO

LANDMARK VIRTUAL OFFICES LIMITED
Business: Provision of Serviced Corporate Offices
Address: Africa-Re House (4th Floor), Plot 1679, Karimu

Kotun Street, Victoria Island, Lagos
Tel: (01) 2626688-9 (2 L), 08023061950, 08023165397
Fax: (01) 2626690
E-mail: ng@landmark-offices.com
Website: www.landmark-offices.com

LANDOVER COMPANY LIMITED
Business: Aviation and Oil Industry Services, Travel Agency, Aviation Publications and Consultancy
Address: 17, Simbiat Abiola Road, Ikeja, Lagos
Tel: (01) 4979780-5 (6 L) 4971247, 4971250
Fax: (01) 4937699, 4976599
E-mail: aviation@landovercompany.com
Website: www.landovercompany.com
Contact: Capt. Edward U. Boyo - MD/CEO

LANGFIELD ROYALTY MOTEL LIMITED
Business: Hospitality & Catering Services
Address: Plot 1105, Emeka Anyaoku St, Area II, Garki, Abuja
Tel: (09) 2349393, 3141223, 3142929, 08033304872
Fax: (09) 3142928
E-mail: langfieldgroup@langfieldlimited.com
Website: www.langfieldlimited.com
Contact: Col. J. D. Dungs (rtd) - Chairman/CEO

LANRE BHADMUS INDUSTRIES LIMITED
Business: Manufacturing of Car-Care & Household Products
Address: 20/22, Jimoh Farombi Drive, Ire-Akari Estate, Isolo, Lagos
Tel: (01) 4522790, 4527141-3 (3 L) **Fax:** (01) 4527144
* 26, Fagbayi (Calcutta) Crescent, Apapa, Lagos
E-mail: lanre.bhadmus@skannet.com
Contact: Mr. Lanre Bhadmus - Chairman/CEO

LANRE SABA & ASSOCIATES
Business: Architectural Design, Estate Valuers, Planners, Construction & Property Consultants
Address: 15/17, Abibu Oki Street, off Broad Street, Lagos
Tel: 08023050729, 08033041817
E-mail: talktosoji@yahoo,com
Contact: Mr. Lanre Saba - MD/CEO

LANRE SHITTU GROUP OF COMPANIES
Business: Sales of Motor Vehicles and Generators; General Merchadising; Import and Export, Sales of Industrial Chemicals
Address: 15, Alh. Tokan St, Alaka Estate, Surulere, Lagos
Tel: (01) 4708683-4 (2L), 4805336, 5850110, 801200-9 (10 L), 8311482, 08033281113
E-mail: lsmotors@rcl.nig.com
Contact: Alh. R. O. Shittu - Chairman/CEO

LANROPE (NIGERIA) LIMITED
Business: General Trading & Import; Colour-Transfer Printing
Address: 53, Adeniran Ogunsanya Street, Surulere, Lagos
Tel: (01) 5840873, 4705175 **Fax:** (01) 4971503
Contact: Mr. Oluseyi Oduntan - Chairman

LANSAR GROUP SURVEYORS & ENGINEERS
Business: Land, Sea & Air Surveying
Address: Lansar House, 219, Aba Road, Rumuogba Layout, Artillery, Port Harcourt
Tel/Fax: (084) 610178
E-mail: kcppties@infoweb.abs.net
Contact: Mr. Ikenna J. Aghaji - MD/CEO

LANTOS INSURANCE BROKERS LIMITED
Business: Insurance Broking
Address: Gidan Shehu Ahmed, 2, Bank Road, Kano
Tel: (064) 647070, 311283, 08033355151
Contact: Mr. Anthony O. Sanni - Exec. Chairman

LARO COMPUTERS LIMITED
Business: Sales, Installation & Maintenance of Computer Systems, Training & Consultancy
Address: 61/63, Old Aba Rd, Rumuobioakani, Port Harcourt
Tel: (084) 486481, 08034030441, 08033528899
E-mail: info@laronet.com
Website: www.laronet.com
* 17, Toyin Street, Ikeja, Lagos
Tel: (01) 4978053, 08034030441
Contact: Mrs. Linda N. Okpoko - CEO

LARRUTI CREATIONS NIGERIA LIMITED
Business: Fashion Outlet for Designer Products
Address: Plot 1439, Sanusi Fafunwa Street, opp. Karimu Kotun Street, Victoria Island, Lagos
Tel: (01) 2621204, 2644125
* 92, Aba Road, Port Harcourt.
Tel: (084) 230347
* Plot 750, Aminu Kano Crescent, Wuse II, Abuja
Tel: (09) 4136425, 4136422 (Ext 210)
E-mail: larrutti@hotmail.com
Contact: Mr. Leonard Anozie - Chairman/CEO

LASAL INTERNATIONAL HOTEL
Business: Hospitality Services, Outdoor Catering Services
Address: 43A, M/M International Airport Road, opp. Mafoluku Junction, Ajao Estate, Lagos
Tel: (01) 4524470, 8112656, 08033044337, 08035530375
E-mail: lasalhotel@yahoo.com
Website: www.lasalhotel.com
Contact: Mr. Segun Salami - MD/CEO

LASERGRAPHIX INVESTMENT NIGERIA LIMITED
Business: Remanufacturing of Laser Jet Toner Cartridges, Repair of Laser Printer, Sale of LCD Flat-Screen Monitors
Address: Big Leaf House (5th Floor), Plot 1663, Oyin Jolayemi Street, Victoria Island, Lagos
Tel: (01) 2612729, 2614835 **Fax:** (01) 2705101
Contact: Murphy Ifeanyichukwu Uzahue - Chairman
Uju Murphy-Uzohue - MD/CEO

LATERNA VENTURES
Business: Importation & Distribution of Christian Literature & Business Books, CDs, Training Tapes & Books
Address: 13, Oko Awo Close, off Karimu Kotun Street, Victoria Island, Lagos
Tel: (01) 2622901
E-mail: laterna@hyperia.com
remorg@linkserve.com
Website: www.laternabooks.com

LASACO ASSURANCE PLC
Business: All Clases of Insurance Business

Address: 13, Alh. Asabi Cole Street, Central Business District, Alausa, Ikeja, Lagos
Tel: (01) 4711846, 4711849-50 (2L), 08022914691-4 (4L), 08023131686, 08023191734 **Fax:** (01) 2664269
* LSDPC House (4th Floor), Nnamdi Azikiwe/Alli Balogun Street, Lagos.
Tel: (01) 2600829, 2660463, 2664269
Contact: Mr. O. O. Ladipo-Ajayi - MD/CEO
Mr. A. A. Ajibola - AGM (Marketing)

LATJOY NIGERIA LIMITED
Business: Manufacturing of Steel & Wooden Security Doors
Address: 11, Onayade Street, beside Edo Line, off Ikorodu Road, Jibowu, Lagos
Tel: (01) 822731, 08022241745-6 (2L)
* Plot 737, Aminu Kano Crescent, Wuse II, Abuja
Contact: Mr. J. O. Taiwo - Chairman/CEO

LATSON AZEEZ TECHNICAL SUPPLY COMPANY LIMITED
Business: Importation of Electric Water Pumps
Address: Plot 12, Latson Azeez Crescent, Onipetesi Ind. Estate, Agege Motor Rd (Mangoro B-Stop), Lagos
Tel: (01) 4921839, 4926596, 4936555 **Fax:** (01) 4971252
E-mail: latson@infoweb.abs.net
Contact: Alh. Azeez Lateef - Chairman/CEO

LAUTAI ENTERPRISES LIMITED
Business: General Mechandising; Import & Export; Civil Engineering Construction
Address: Lautai House, Plot C5, Wudil Road, Nassarawa Area, Kano
Tel: (064) 649791 **Fax:** (064) 648939
* BMG Plaza, Plot 2222, SFAX Close, Wuse Zone 4, Abuja
Tel: (09) 5232765 **Fax:** (09) 5234076

LAW & BUSINESS PUBLICATIONS LIMITED
Business: Publishing and Marketing of Professional Books, Consultancy Services; Training
Address: Trust Place, Niger House Annex (2nd Floor), 3/4, Tinubu Street, Lagos Island, Lagos
Tel/Fax: (01) 2641679, 2643757
E-mail: trustplace@hotmail.com
Contact: Mr. Kole Oluwajana - Chairman

LAW UNION & ROCK INSURANCE OF NIGERIA PLC
Business: All Classes of Insurance
Address: 209A & B, Muri Okunola St, Victoria Island, Lagos
Tel: (01) 2882257-8(2L), 3200488, 7733664, 7742073, 8044793, 8044795 **Fax:** (01) 3200486
E-mail: lawunion@wananet.net
info@lawunionandrock.com
Website: www.lawunionandrock.com
*14, Hughes Avenue, Alagomeji, Yaba, Lagos
Tel: (01) 7733662-3(2L), 7742074-5 (2L)
Contact: Prince Omosanya Akinyemi - MD/CEO
Mr. Benjamin S. Oke - DGM (Technical)

LAWBREED LIMITED
Business: Publishers of "The Judgement of Supreme Court of Nigeria (S.C. Reports)" and other Law Books
Address: 62A, Opebi Road, Ikeja, Lagos
Tel: (01) 4932038, 08023269565, 0802326913, 08023328208, 08033232448 **Fax:** (01) 4932038
E-mail: layibabatunde@infoweb.abs.net
lawbreed@hotmail.com

LAWRENCE OMOLE LIMITED
Business: Grain Processing (Malting), Distribution of Fertilizer and Cement
Address: B, 218, Okesa-Benin Road, Ilesa, Osun State
Tel: (036) 460237
Contact: Mr. Aderinola Omole - MD/CEO

LAWRIE GREEN EDUCATION (LGE) NIGERIA LIMITED
Business: Consultancy Services for Education in the United Kingdom
Address: Plot 15E, Muri Okunola Street, off Ajose Adeogun Street, Victoria Island, Lagos
Tel: (01) 7748948, 4616112, 2623040 **Fax:** (01) 4619859
E-mail: lge-ng@metrong.com
Contact: Dr. (Mrs.) Ogunsanya - MD/CEO

LAWSON CORPORATION
Business: Conglomerate, Property Development & Management, Brewing & Bottling
Address: Motorways Centre (3rd Floor, Wing A), 1, Motorways Avenue, opp. 7up, Alausa, Ikeja, Lagos
Tel: (01) 4722192, 4722102

LAYAL INDUSTRIES LIMITED
Business: Manufacturing and Marketing of Plastic Mats
Address: Mission Road, Bompai Industrial Estate, Kano
Tel: (064) 642163 Fax: (064) 646476
Contact: Mr S. Fadlallah - MD/CEO

LBM OVERSEAS NIGERIA LIMITED
Business: Export of Agricultural Products & Commodities
Address: 10, Liverpool Road, Apapa, Lagos
Tel: (01) 5876737, 7912374, 08055502451
Fax: (01) 5876313

Le MERIDIEN HOTEL, ABUJA
Business: Hospitality Services, Conference Facilities
Address: Plot 903, Tafawa Balewa Way, Area 11, Garki, Abuja
Tel: (09) 2342002, 2342082, 2349118 **Fax:** (09) 2341897
E-mail: info@lemeridien-abuja.com
Website: www.lemeridien-abuja.com
Contact: Mr Olivier Servet - GM
Mrs Toyin Dada - Director of Sales

Le MERIDIEN OGEYI PLACE
Business: Hospitality Services, Conference Facilities
Address: 45, Tambia Street, G.R.A. Phase II, Port Harcourt
Tel: (084) 571488, 231064 **Fax:** (084) 231138
E-mail: reservation@lemeridienphc.com
Website: www.lemeridien.com
Contact: Brigadier-Gen. Anthony S. I. Ukpo (rtd.) - Chairman

LEABROS NIGERIA LIMITED
Business: Importation & Exportation of General Goods, Manufacturing of Garments, Farming
Address: 81B, Kent Road, P. O. Box 717, Aba
Tel: (082) 230682, 234312, 234720 **Fax:** (082) 234312
E-mail: leabrosco@yahoo.com
Contact: Chief Lazarus Eke Agu - Chairman/CEO

LEAD BANK PLC
Business: Banking Services
Address: 1, Oladele Olashore Street, Victoria Island, Lagos
Tel: (01) 2620430-9 (10L) **Fax:** (01) 2614563
E-mail: info@leadbanknigeria.com
Website: www.leadbanknigeria.com
* UAC Commercial Complex, Plots 272/273, off Third Avenue, Cnetral Business District, Abuja
Tel: (09) 5239340, 5238352-3 (2L)
E-mail: leadabj@micro.com.ng
Contact: Mr. O. Abimbola Olashore - MD/CEO

LEAD SECURITIES & INVESTMENT LIMITED
Business: Stockbroking, Investment Management, Capital Issues
Address: Plot 281, Ajose Adeogun St, Victoria Island, Lagos
Tel: (01) 2622907, 2615486 **Fax:** (01) 2618424, 261456.3
E-mail: enquiries@leadbanknigeria.com
Website: www.leadbanknigeria.com
Contact: H.R.H. Oba Oladele Olashore - Chairman
Mrs Yemisi Tayo-Aboaba - Chief Operating Officer

LEADERS & COMPANY LIMITED
Business: Newspaper Publishing (ThisDay Newspaper)
Address: 35, Creek Road, Apapa, Lagos
Tel: (01) 5452730, 5871432, 5871436, 5871868, 5872807
E-mail: thisday@nova.net.ng
* Plot 1, Sector Centre B, Jabi District, Solomon Lar Way, Jabi North East, Abuja.
Tel: (09) 2342935, 2342938
Contact: Mr Nduka Obaigbena - Chairman/Editor-in-Chief

LEADING EDGE LIMITED
Business: Sales of Computers, Components and Accessories; Consultancy; Internet Solutions Provider
Address: Wesley House, 21/22, Marina, Lagos
Tel: (01) 2630247, 2645282, 2646248 **Fax:** (01) 2645283
E-mail: leadedge@infoweb.abs.net
Contact: Mr. Tony Edoror - Chairman/CEO

LEADING EDGE CONSULTANCY SERVICES LIMITED
Business: Management & Research Consultancy Services, Human Resources Management and Organisational Development
Address: 202, Awolowo Road, S.W. Ikoyi Lagos
Tel: (01) 2673537, 2673538 **Fax:** (01) 2673538
E-mail: ijeledge@infoweb.abs.net
Contact: Dr. Ije Jidenma - MD/CEO

LEADMAC PROPERTY & DEVELOPMENT COMPANY LTD
Business: Real Estate Developers, Managers & Consultants
Address: 20, Adetokunbo Ademola St, Victoria Is., Lagos.
Tel: (01) 4801612, 4704417, 4616950, 08033084465, 08033482095

LEADWAY ASSURANCE COMPANY LIMITED
Business: Insurance, Fund Management & Trusteeship
Address: Leadway Assurance House, NN 28/29, Constitution Road, Kaduna
Tel: (062) 246776, 239725 **Fax:** (062) 236838
E-mail: insure@leadway.com.ng
Website: www.leadway.com
*121/123, Western Avenue, Iponri, Surulere, Lagos
Tel: (01) 5802890-4 (5L), 5850639-41 (3L), 7749757-61(5L)
Fax: (01) 5837187, 5834169
*51, Addis Ababa Crescent, Wuse Zone 4, Abuja
Tel: (09) 5233480-1 (2L) **Fax:** (09) 5233481
Contact: Mr. Oye Hassan-Odukale - MD/CEO
Mr. Olumide Falohun -GM

LEADY-PHARMA INDUSTRIES LIMITED
Business: Manufacturing of Pharmaceutical Products
Address: Plot 3 & 4, Tomori Industrial Estate, off Idi-Iroko Road, Ota, Ogun State
Tel: (039) 722013, 721013 **Fax:** (039) 722013
E-mail: leadpharma@hotmail.com
* Plots 3 & 4, Ogun Layout, Iwo Road, Ibadan
Tel: (02) 714313, 713806
* 7, Nwobi Close, by 33, Faulks Road, Aba
Tel: (082) 234557
Contact: Mr. E. M. Odubunmi - Chairman
Mr. O. O. Adekunle - MD/CEO

LEASING COMPANY OF NIGERIA LIMITED
Business: Leasing and Trade Financing
Address: Plot 740, Aminu Kano Crescent, Wuse II, Abuja
Tel: (09) 4139563 **Fax:** (09) 4139406
E-mail: leconab@micro.com.ng
* BOI House (5th Floor), 63/71, Broad St, Lagos
Tel: (01) 2666762, 2662945 **Fax:** (01) 2666463
* Plot 474, Trans-Amadi Ind. Layout, Port Harcourt
Contact: Mrs. Roaslind Zulai Abashiya - MD/CEO

LEATHER CREATIONS LIMITED
Business: Production of Diaries and Corporate Gift Items
Address: Cocoa Board Warehouse (Block C, Gate 3), Ladipo Oluwole St, off Oba Akran Avenue, Ikeja, Lagos
Tel: (01) 4935388 **Fax:** (01) 4975280
Contact: Ms. Micky Looyens - MD/CEO

LEATHERWORLD LIMITED
Business: Sales of Leather Furniture & Home Accessories; Interior Decoration, Furnishing and Renovation
Address: 30, Raymond Njoku Street, S.W. Ikoyi, Lagos
Tel: (01) 2695723-4 (4 L) **Fax:** (01) 2691775
* Plot 326A, Aminu Kano Crescent, Cadastral Zone A7, Wuse II, Abuja
Tel/Fax: (09) 5235348, 5234655
Contact: Mrs. Bimbo Alashe-Arawole - Chairman/CEO.

LE-CAVALIER MOTEL & RESTAURANT
Business: Hospitality Services, Restaurant
Address: Plot 643, Sassandra Street, off Usuma Street, Maitama, Abuja
Tel: (09) 4138038, 4138039, 08033940142
Contact: Mr. Ali A. Fawaz - MD/CEO

LEE-NOBEC NIGERIA LIMITED
Business: Industrialists, Contactors and Road Construction Engineers, General Merchandising
Address: 26, Park Road, Aba
Tel: (082) 221575 **Fax:** (082) 224691
E-mail: leenobec@phca.linkserve.com
* Plot 629, Lingu Street, Cadastral Zone A7, Wuse II, Abuja
Contact: Chief Theo Okoye - MD/CEO

LEGACY CONSULTS LIMITED
Business: Distribution & Sales of Telecommunication Equipment, GSM Phones & Accessories
Address: NICON House, 118/120, Broad Street, Lagos
Tel: (01) 2642390, 08032030557 **Fax:** (01) 4613683
E-mail: legacyconsultslimited@yahoo.com
* Bonny Rose Shopping Mall (Suite FFI), Area 11 Cornershops, Garki, Abuja
Contact: Mr. Chike C. Orjiako - MD/CEO

LEGACY REALITIES LIMITED
Business: Real Estate Development, Management and Support Services
Address: 7A, Akin-Olugbade Street, off Idowu Martins Street, Victoria Island, Lagos
Tel: (01) 4721660, 4718857, 4619539, 4810071, 08033481253, 08035342296, 08035342299
Fax: (01) 4619538
E-mail: info@legacyrealities.com
Website: www.legacyrealities.com

LEGALTEXT PUBLISHING COMPANY LIMITED
Business: Publishing of Law Reports & Books
Address: 8, Evelyn Onwuama St, River Valley Estate (Berger Bus-Stop), Lagos-Ibadan Expressway, Lagos
Tel: (01) 3450542, 4804575, 08023614008
E-mail: legaltextl@yahoo.com
Contact: Mr Femi Falana - Editor-in-Chief/CEO

LEGEND CONSULTING
Business: Management, Financial and Tax Consultants
Address: Development House (Monzina Suite, 7th Floor), 21, Wharf Road, Apapa, Lagos
Tel: (01) 4723098, 5876719, 5452969, 08023044353
Fax: (01) 5452969
E-mail: legendkonsult41@yahoo.com
Contact: Prince Adebayo Abiodunn - Consultant/CEO.

LEKOW ASSOCIATES SERVICES LIMITED
Business: Clearing & Forwarding, Cargo Consolidation, Import & Export & Transportation
Address: 5/7, Alhaji Kofoworola Street, off Awolowo Way, (Balogun Bus-Stop), Ikeja, Lagos
Tel: (01) 4939049, 4975805, 08033022551
Fax: (01) 3453108, 4936659
E-mail: lekow@hyperia.com
Contact: Mr. Olalekan Owodunni - MD/CEO

LEKTOL INSURANCE BROKERS LIMITED
Business: Insurance Broking
Address: 2, Awaiyewaserere Close (Ground Floor), opp. Agidingbi Grammar School, off Lateef Jakande Road, Agidingbi, Ikeja, Lagos
Tel: (01) 4924459, 7929721
Contact: Mr. A.T. Odude - MD/CEO

LELA AGRO INDUSTRIES LIMITED
Business: Manufacturing of Polypropylene Woven Sacks and Polythene Shopping Bags
Address: 24, Unity Road, Kano
Tel: (064) 642672, 648056, 311073
E-mail: hdfsons@hotmail.com
Contact: Alh. Yakubu Adamu - MD/CEO

LEMANSHE MANUFACTURING & CONSULTANCY (NIG) LTD
Business: Importation and Sales of Plain & Printed PVC Shrink Labels and Sleeves for Packaging Materials
Address: Henry Stephens Compound, 2, Ilupeju Bye-Pass, near Railway Crossing, Ilupeju, Lagos
Tel: (01) 4933997, 4932342, 7745350, 7759120, 7764387
Fax: (01) 4932342, 4933997
E-mail: deveep@linkserve.com.ng
Contact: Mr. Ashok Chandni - MD/CEO

LE-MERIDIAN AIR SERVICES LIMITED
Business: Travel Agency
Address: 9, Post Office Road, Kano
Tel: (064) 632218 **Fax:** (064) 630688
Contact: Mr. J. A. Ojewunmi - MD/CEO

LENBEN MOTORS & COMPANY LIMITED
Business: Sales of Automobile and Power Products
Address: 34, Herbert Macaulay Street, Ebute-Metta, Lagos
Tel: (01) 862053, 08023339948
Contact: Mr. Benedict Okon - Chairman/CEO

LENNAP SERVICES LIMITED
Business: Company Secretarial Services
Address: Lennap House, Government Secretariat Road, Jos
Tel: (073) 464710, 460375

LENNARDS NIGERIA PLC
Business: Marketing and Distribution of Footwear & Allied Leather Products
Address: Km. 16, Ikorodu Road, Ojota, Lagos
Tel: (01) 4960170, 4963984, 4964850, 8132666, 08033448434
E-mail: lennards@beta.linkserve.com
Contact: Mr. A. A. Buraimoh-Ademuyewo - MD/CEO.

LENOIL GROUP
Business: Marketing of Petroleum Products
Address: Octagon House (3rd Floor), 13, A.J. Marinho Drive, Victoria Island Annex, Lagos
Tel: (01) 2625233, 2626718 **Fax:** (01) 7749293
E-mail: lenoil@nigol.net.ng

LENTO NIGERIA PLC
Business: Manufacturing of Aluminium Building Materials
Address: Plot 342, Jabi Life Camp Road, along Karimo Road, Jabi, Abuja
Tel: (09) 5239490, 6707294, 08033141913
Fax: (09) 4131208, 5239490
E-mail: lentoplc@hotmail.com
info@lentogroup.com
Website: www.lentogroup.com
Contact: Dr Lawrence Ojemeni Chairman/CEO

LEONIDAS ASSOCIATES LIMITED
Business: Import & Export, Dealers on Alcoholic & Non-Alcoholic Beverages, Buttons, Rivets (Haberdashery) and General Goods
Address: 10, Docemo Street, (2nd Floor), Idumota, Lagos
Tel: (01) 2669075, 2669946, 08033060057, 08042116353
Fax: (01) 2641589
E-mail: leonidas@micro.com.ng
Contact: Mr. Leo I. Chiegboka - Chairman/CEO.

NASCO

PROVIDING THE QUALITY LIFE

Corporate Headquarter: NASCO MANAGEMENT SERVICE LIMITED

Ahmed Nasreddin Road/Yakubu Gowon Way,
P. M. B. 2722, Jos
Phone (073) 463175, 463347, 463348
Telex 81127
Fax (234) 073-461554

Apapa Office
18/20, Commercial Road,
P. O. Box 261, Apapa.
Phone: (234) 01-5870945, 5870934, 5874238
Telex 21513
Fax 234-01-5871881

NASCO FIBRE PRODUCTS LIMITED
Ahmed Nasreddin Road,
P. O. Box 684, Jos, Nigeria.
Cable: JUTEMILL, Jos, Nigeria.
Phones: (073) 463333, 463334, 462615 DL, 467221 DL
Telex: 81127 NASCOS NG (JOS).

Manufacturers of Jute Bags, Hessian Cloth and Bags, Sewing Twains Carpet Backing Cloth, Carpet Underlay, Plain and Printed Carpets.

NASCO HOUSEHOLD PRODUCTS LIMITED
Yakubu Gowon Way,
P.M.B. 2243, Jos, Nigeria.
Cable DETERGENTS, Jos.
Phone: (073) 462841, 465836, 461635 DL, 464422 DL
Telex. 81127 NASCOS NG Jos.

Manufactures of Detergents, Soaps and Industrial Chemicals

NASCO BEAUTY & BODY CARE PRODUCTS
(DIVISION OF NIPCO LTD.)
Yakubu Gowon Way,
P.M.B. 2243, Jos, Nigeria.
Cable: DETERGENTS, Jos.
Phone. (073) 462841, 465836,
Telex: 81127 NASCOS NG, Jos.

Manufacturers of Cosmetics

NASCO ESTATE COMPANY (NIG.) LIMITED
P. O. Box 261 Apapa, Lagos.
Phone: (01) 880804, 880538,
Telex: 21513, NASCO NG

Estate Development NASCO TOWN - LAGOS 01 - 5875450, 5870004

NASCO MARKETING COMPANY LTD
Yakubu Gowon Way,
P. O. Box 718, Jos, Nigeria
Phone: (073) 464868, 465332, 464587, 467223
Telex: 81127 NASCOS NG
Fax: (234) 073- 460109

Involved in Product Development, Sales, Distribution, Advertising, Market Research and Sales Promotion

NASCO FOODS (NIG.) LTD
Yakubu Gowon Way,
P. O. Box 578, Jos
Cable:BISCUITS, Jos
Phone: (073) 464478, 464479, 462139, 462551, 462150 DL
Telex: 81127, NASCOS NG.

Manufacturers of Biscuits, Wafers & Cornflakes

NASCO CONFECTIONERY PRODUCTS
Ahmed Nasreddin Road,
P. O. Box 245, Jos- Nigeria
Phone: (073) 464876, 465174 DL
Telex: 81127 NASCOS NG

Manufacturers of Hard Sweets, Toffees, Table Jellies & Bubble Gum.

NASCO RICE & CEREALS
Yakubu Gowon Way
Jos

Manufacturers of Parboiled Rice, Flour and Instant Cooking Semolina

NASCO PACK LIMITED
Yakubu Gowon Way,
P. O. Box 6286, Jos, Nigeria
Cable NASPACK, Jos
Phone. (073) 462250, 462279, 462754
Fax: (234) 073-462764

Manufactures of Converters of Packaging Materials & Ladies, Offset Multicoloured Printer Labels and Cartons, Printer Cellophane, Transwarp Fil and Polythene Bags, Corrugted Boxboard Cartons, Offers a Full Design Service and Advertise on all aspect of Papel and Board Packaging

OVERSEAS CONTACT OFFICE:

NASCO
c/o Raw Mat. Limited, BP573-Zonal Franche Tanger, Morocco.
Fax 93 3893 Telex 338 75m

NASCO
P. O. Box 216-6906, Lugano Switzerland, Fax: (091) 524702,
Telex 844451 NGI CH, Tel (091) 524051

NASCO
Corso Sempione, 69 20149 - Milano Italy
Fax 02/344088, Telex 331404 1, Tel 02/3352461

Lennards Nigeria Plc

SCHOOL SHOES AND SANDALS

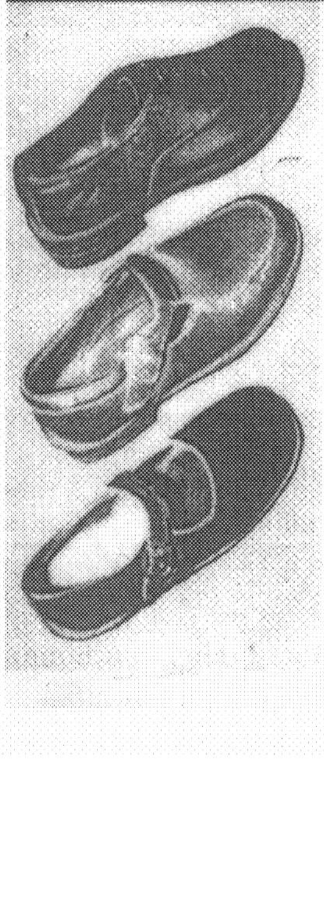

Lennards is a publicly quoted company with extensive retail network nationwide for shoes and related products

We have recently reviewed our distribution channels for school sandals and shoes which we are well known.

This development has created business opportunities suitable for the following categories:-

(A). INDEPENDENT RESELIERS
(B). DIRECT RESELIERS
(C). STOCKIST
(D). DEALERS
(E). FRANCHISEES.

We intend to appoint Limited numbers of eligible individuals/ companies on exclusive basis in towns or local government areas and will request only those with adequate financial and Accessible retail infrastructures to apply particularly for C, D, and E, above.

Kindly state the town /local government area you intend to cover and available funds for this project in your application. Resellers may not need to have retail location but will still be required to carry stock relative to their market territory.

Necessary training and marketing support will be provided for successful candidates.

Selected individuals/ companies must provide sufficient information on their ability to invest in stock

The retail prices of our product lines are highly competitive and individuals or companies with reasonable resources for initial stock purchase are encouraged to apply.

Take action in the right direction today and forward your application to start a profitable venture to the:-

Marketing Department,
Lennards Nigeria Plc, Kilometre 16, Ikorodu Road,
P.O.Box 143, Ikeja, Lagos
E-mail :lennards@beta.linkserve.com

LEOPLAST INDUSTRY LIMITED
Business: Manufacturing of Plastic Chairs and Tables
Address: Plot K, Kopek Road, off Fatai Atere Way, Matori Industrial Estate, Oshodi, Lagos
Tel: (01) 4526353, 4528977 **Fax:** (01) 4524548
E-mail: papleo@india.com
Contact: Mr Rohit Daswani - MD/CEO

LETCO FURNISHING INDUSTRIES LIMITED
Business: Production of Furniture, Sales of Carpets & Rugs, Building Construction
Address: M1, Ahmadu Bello Way, Kaduna
Tel: (062) 239456, 249458
Contact: Chief Leke Oshinowo - Chairman/CEO

LEVENTIS FOODS LIMITED
Business: Bakery; Meat Processing
Address: 2, Wharf Road, Apapa, Lagos
Tel: (01) 7741528, 5451499, 5878601
E-mail: info@leventisfoods.com
Contact: Dr Stephanos Constantinidis - MD/CEO

LEVENTIS MOTORS
Business: Sales, Service and Maintenance of Motor Vehicles, Sales of Spare Parts and HONDA Power Products
Address: 2, Wharf Road, Apapa, Lagos
Tel: (01) 5877187, 58722911, 5877007, 5873673, 5875335, 5876799 **Fax:** (01) 5877201, 5872518, 5877552
E-mail: www.leventismotors.net
Contact: Mr. John M. Fysentizidis - GM

LEVENTIS POWER SYSTEMS LIMITED
Business: Sales, Installation and Service of Generating Sets
Address: 8, Ijora Causeway, Ijora, Lagos
Tel: (01) 5837535, 5837616, 5878820-1 (2L), 5878827, 7752218, 7769296, 7769298, 8044655-6 (2L), 8044328
Fax: (01) 5878821, 5878827
E-mail: leventispower@nigerianet.com
Website: www.leventispower.com
* 49, Adeola Odeku Street, Victoria Island, Lagos
Tel/Fax: (01) 8044655-6 (2L), 8124273, 08034712387
* Abuja Capital Motors, Leventis Close, Central District, Abuja.
Tel: (09) 6706434, 08033280299
* 6, Azikiwe Road, Port Harcourt.
Tel: (084) 232531, 486275
Contact: Mr K. Schizas - GM
Mr. Daniel W. Okon - Commercial Manager

LEVERAGE HOME SAVINGS & LOANS LIMITED
Business: Mortgage Banking, Real Estate Development & Property Management
Address: 105, Nnamdi Azikiwe Street, Idumota, Lagos
Tel: (01) 2664542, 08023072368, 08055405162
E-mail: leveragehome@yahoo.com
Contact: Mr. L. T. Hassan - Ag. MD/CEO

LEVTRADE LIMITED
Business: Importation and Sales of Supermarket Products
Address: Iddo House, Iddo, Lagos
Tel: (01) 7743390 **Fax:** (01) 2618285
E-mail: levtrade@beta-leventis.com
Contact: Dr. S. Constantinidis - MD/CEO.

LEXINGTON INTERNATIONAL INSURANCE COMPANY LTD
Business: Non-Life Insurance
Address: Ebani House (3rd Floor, Rear Suites), 149/153, Broad Street, Lagos Island, Lagos
Tel: (01) 2645608-9 (2L), 2663825, 2664867
Fax: (01) 2663825
E-mail: info@lexingtoninsurer.com
Website: www.lexingtoninsurer.com
Contact: Mr. A. A. Durodola - MD/CEO

LEXYLAND LIMITED
Business: Sales of GSM Phones & Accessories, Sales of Satellite Phones and Palm-Top Mobile Computers
Address: Eko Hotel Shopping Complex (Unit 19), 1, Ajose Adeogun Street, Victoria Island, Lagos
Tel: (01) 3200999, 08023121967 **Fax:** (01) 3200999
E-mail: lexyland@yahoo.com
Contact: Mr. Akinsanya Adeleke - Chief Executive

LIAISON FRANCAIS NIGERIA LIMITED
Business: Tour Packaging, Language Classes
Address: 5, Ribadu Road off Awolowo Rd, S.W. Ikoyi, Lagos
Tel: (01) 2691831, 4701237, 08034008965, 08037155058
E-mail: femilfn@hotmail.com
Contact: Ngozi Giwa-Amu - MD/CEO

LIAS FREIGHT AGENCIES LIMITED
Business: Clearing and Forwarding, Shipping Agency
Address: 13, Egbayelo Street, Olodi-Apapa, Apapa-Oshodi Expressway (Coconut Bus-Stop), Lagos
Tel: (01) 5450430, 5872933, 5875803, 8043528, 4706967
Contact: Alh. Olushoga Elias - Chairman/CEO.

LIBERTY BANK PLC
Business: Banking Services
Address: Bello Dangote House, 31, Bishop Oluwole Street, Victoria Island, Lagos
Tel: (01) 4617410-6(7L), 2616879 **Fax:** (01) 2616873
E-mail: info@liberty-bankplc.net
Website: www.Liberty-bank-plc.com
* Plot 442, Adetokunbo Ademola Crescent, Wuse II, Abuja.
Tel: (09) 5230024, 5230126
* Plot 216B, Woji Rd, G.R.A. Phase II, Port Harcout
Tel: (084) 237094 **Fax:** (084) 237097
Contact: Mr. Lawson Omokhodion - MD/CEO.

LIBERTY INDUSTRIES LIMITED
Business: Manufacturing of Plastic Household Items, Stainless Steel and Enamelware
Address: 17, Fatai Atere Way (Plot 2, Block E), Matori Industrial Estate, Mushin, Lagos
Tel: (01) 4524158, 4527253, 4527798, 522775
Contact: Mr. R. K. Thadani - Chairman/CEO.

LIBERTY INTERNATIONAL HOTEL LIMITED
Business: Hotel Services
Address: New Layout, Lokoja
Tel: (058) 220074

LIBERTY MERCHANT SECURITIES LIMITED
Business: Financial Services, Issuing House, Stockbroking
Address: Okoi Arikpo House, 5, Idowu Taylor Street, Victoria

Island, Lagos
Tel/Fax: (01) 2626382
E-mail: lmb@infoweb.abs.net
Contact: Mr. Ifeanyi Ohazurume - Chief Operating Officer

LIBRA CAPITAL LIMITED
Business: Importation & Wholesales of Mobile/GSM Phones
Address: Great Nigeria House (16th Floor), 47/57, Martins Street, Lagos Island, Lagos
Tel: (01) 2644114, 08033255328 **Fax:** (01) 2905619
E-mail: libracorp@yahoo.com
Website: www.directdubai .com
* Lansar House (2nd Floor), Port Harcourt/Aba Expressway, 2nd Artillery, Port Harcourt
Tel: (084) 575334
* BM House (Suite 2.06/7), 1A, S. L. Akintola Boulevard, Garki II, Abuja
Tel: (09) 6717152
Contact: Mr. Ikenna Onyejiaka - Chairman/CEO

LIBRA INSURANCE BROKERS LIMITED.
Business: Insurance Broking
Address: 12, Anifowoshe Close, off Adeniran Ogunsanya Street, Surulere, Lagos
Tel: (01) 7745922
* Banex Plaza Extension (Ber 7), Plot 750, Aminu Kano Crescent, Wuse II, Abuja
Tel: (09) 5238806

LIFE BREWERIES COMPANY LIMITED
Business: Brewing/Bottling of Beer & Carbonated Beverages
Address: NCWS Building, Plot PC. 14, Ahmed Onibudo Street, Victoria Island, Lagos
Tel: (01) 2614220, 2622817
E-mail: lifebrew@hyperia.com
* 87/97, Port Harcourt Road, Fegge, Onitsha
Tel: (046) 211000, 211465, 211514, 214609, 486249, 08034071190 **Fax:** (046) 211514
Contact: Mr. A. K. Mirchandani - Chairman
Mr. R. C. Khanna - MD/CEO

LIFE FLOUR MILLS LIMITED
Business: Flour & Feed Milling from 100% US Hard Red Wheat, Polypropylene Woven Sacks Production
Address: Ogorode Road, Sapele, Delta State
Tel: (054) 341036, 341363, 342102, 342628, 08035350545, 08035844767 **Fax:** (054) 342422
E-mail: lifesapele@infoweb.abs.net
* 10A, Adetokunbo Ademola St, Victoria Is., Lagos
Tel: (01) 2611862, 613671, 611383, 2880473, 7754191, 08022921038, 08035350545 **Fax:** (01) 2616423
E-mail: lifelagos@infoweb.abs.net
* Plot 4A, Block D, Wempco Road, Ogba Industrial Scheme, Ikeja, Lagos
Tel: (01) 4926009, 7739403, 08034441950, 08035350545
Fax: (01) 4922164
E-mail: seepcgm@multilinks.com
* 23A, Kachia Road, opp. Queen Amina College, Kaduna
Tel: (062) 232917, 08023357743, 08033972347
Fax: (062) 235540
E-mail: dar3farm@yahoo.com
Contact: Mr Donald Spencer - MD/CEO

LIFE SUPPORT SYSTEMS LIMITED
Business: Medical (Dialysis) Services
Address: 1, Oba Docemo Street, Ikeja, G.R.A., Lagos
Tel: (01) 4966882, 4966916 **Fax:** (01) 4972877
E-mail: lifesupport@yahoo.com
Website: www.lifesupport-ng.com
Contact: Dr. O. B. C. Onuzo - Consultant Nephrologist/CMO

LIGHT LEVEL LIMITED
Business: Visual Communications, Branding, Sign Production
Address: 256, Herbert Macaulay Street, Yaba, Lagos
Tel: (01) 8151688
E-mail: lightlevel@nigol.net.ng
Website: www.light-level.com
Contact: Yemi Osilaja - Chairman/CEO

LIGHTHOUSE ASSET MANAGEMENT LIMITED
Business: Stockbroking, Financial Services
Address: NICON House (6th Floor), 5, Customs Street, off Marina, Lagos
Tel: (01) 2663148, 2669749, 2665598, 2665858
Fax: (01) 2669947
E-mail: info@lightasset.com
Website: www.lightasset.com
* 47, Emekuku Street, D-Line, Port Harcourt
Tel: (084) 3351147
* 1A, Monrovia Street, Wuse II, Abuja
Tel: (09) 4137125-6 (2 L), 4130453
Contact: Mr. Emmanuel A. Ocholi - Group Exec. Chairman
Mr. D. A. Enejoh - MD/CEO.

LIGHTHOUSE PETROLEUM ENGINEERING COMPANY LTD
Business: Analytical Laboratory Services for Oil & Gas Industry
Address: 6, Lighthouse Road, G.R.A., Effurun, Warri
Tel: (053) 254559, 234908

LIMCA BOTTLERS PLC
Business: Manufacture & Marketing of Assorted Soft Drinks
Address: Plot 6, Badejo Kalesanwo Street, Matori Industrial Estate, Mushin, Lagos
Tel: (01) 4524660, 4702291, 4702292 **Fax:** (01) 4524695
E-mail: limcamatori@nova.net.ng
Contact: Mr. Kushall N. Jethwani - MD/CEO

LIMITRACO INDUSTRIES LIMITED
Business: Manufacturing and Importation of Auto Parts
Address: 92, United Line, Nkwor Nnewi, Nnewi
Tel: (046) 463101, 462208 **Fax:** (046) 462208
E-mail: limitrac@infoweb.abs.net
Contact: Mr. Linus Maduagwu - Chairman

LINDIANA ENTERPRISES LIMITED
Business: Production of Furniture and Metalwood, General Contractors
Address: 3, Mai Malari Road, Bompai Industrial Estate, Kano
Tel: (064) 630502

LINETRALE OIL SUPPLY & TRADING COMPANY LIMITED
Business: Supply & Trading of Refined Petroleum Products, Supply of Equipment for Pipelines and Rigs
Address: Octagon House, 13A, A. J. Marinho Drive, Victoria Island, Lagos
Tel: (01) 4617713-4 (2L) **Fax:** (01) 4617712

E-mail: info@linetrale.com
Website: www.linetrale.com
Contact: Aramide Farri

LINKSTRIDE SECURITY SYSTEMS LIMITED
Business: Sales, Installation, Reactivation & Maintenance of Security Systems, Consultancy
Address: Plot 1661, Oyin Jolayemi Street (1st Floor), Victoria Island, Lagos
Tel: (01) 2610371, 5558469 **Fax:** (01) 5558469
E-mail: link_stride@yahoo.com
Contact: Mr. Femi Dare - MD/CEO

LINKAGE ASSURANCE COMPANY LIMITED
Business: Life, Special Risk and General Business Insurance
Address: Linkage 2000 Plaza, 25, Akin Adesola Street,Victoria Island, Lagos
Tel: (01) 2620930-1 (2 L), 3200288 **Fax:** (01) 2620933
E-mail: info@linkageassurance.com
* Plot 2306, Suez Crescent, off Herbert Macaulay Way, Cadastral Zone A2, Wuse Zone 4, Abuja
Tel: (09) 5238303
* ASEI World Centre, 57, Aba Road, Port Harocurt
Tel: (084) 2376332
Contact: Mr. Babatunde Fatayi-Williams - Chairman
Mr. L. C. Bosah - GM

LINKALL INSURANCE BROKERS LIMITED
Business: Insurance Broking
Address: 19/21, Breadfruit Street (2nd Floor), Lagos
Tel: (01) 2661970 **Fax:** (01) 2666240
* 1, Hassan Dalhatu Street, Suleja, Abuja
Tel: (09) 500034
Contact: Mr. I. L. Agboola - MD/CEO.

LINKSERVE LIMITED
Business: Provision of Full Internet Services
Address: Plot 308, Adeola Odeku St, Victoria Island, Lagos
Tel: (01) 2623900-1 (2L) **Fax:** (01) 22623906
E-mail: info@linkserve.net
Website: www.linkserve.net
* Plot 569, Durban St, off Adetokunbo Ademola Street, Wuse II, Abuja
Tel: (09) 5231821, 5231826 **Fax:** (09) 5231826
* 12, Railway Close, D-Line, Port Harcourt
Tel: (084) 230907-8 (2L) **Fax:** (084) 230909
E-mail: phca@linkserve.net
abv@linkserve.net
Contact: Mr. Chima Onyekwere - MD/CEO.
Mr. Maduka J. Emelite - Chief Operating Officer

LINKSO NIGERIA LIMITED
Business: Engineering Consultancy, Manpower Supply, Project Management & Inspection Services, Oil Industry Consultancy Services
Address: Plot 293, Akin-Olugbade St, Victoria Island, Lagos
Tel: (01) 2616615, 2622330, 611030, 611013
Fax: (01) 2623375, 2616818
E-mail: linkso@micro.com.ng
linkso@alpha.linkserve.com
Contact: Engr. Charles Osezua - Chairman/CEO
Mr. M. Mancin - MD.

LINKTEL SHIPPING LIMITED
Business: Shipping Services, Sales of Frozen Seafoods
Address: 19, Emekuku Street, D-Lines, Port Harcourt
Tel: (084) 571125, 571126, 234279, 08033714232
Fax: (084) 234279
E-mail: linktel@yahoo.com
Contact: Helen Yebufura - Admin. Manager

LINKUP LOGISTICS LIMITED
Business: Distribution of SKF Bearings
Address: All Seasons Plaza, (Shop 5), Lateef Jakande Road, opp. Cadbury Plc. Agidingbi, Ikeja, Lagos
Tel/Fax: (01) 4925818
* 12, Circular Rd, Presidential Estate, Port Harcourt
Tel: (084) 239587
Contact: Mr. F. Ijitimehin - GM/CEO.

LINK-VIC NIGERIA LIMITED
Business: Sales & Repairs of Mobile Phones & Accessories
Address: 52, Awolowo Road, S.W. Ikoyi, Lagos
Tel: (01) 2695565, 2672892, 08022908598
E-mail: linkvic@yahoo.com
* Plot 169, Aminu Kano Crescent, Wuse II, Abuja
Tel: (09) 4139354
Contact: Mr. Victor Nwosisi - MD/CEO

LINO LABORATORIES LIMITED
Business: Production of Fruit Drinks
Address: 3, Odejayi Close, Afro-Ajangbadi, Lagos
Tel: (01) 7734304

LION STOCKBROKERS LIMITED
Business: Stockbroking, Portfolio & Investment Advisory Services, Placement of Equity, Retirement Planning
Address: New Africa House (12th Floor), 31, Marina, Lagos
Tel: (01) 2646615, 08033519437 **Fax:** (01) 2633498
E-mail: lionstock@linkserve.com
* Plot 2105, H Macaulay Way, Wuse Zone 6, Abuja
Tel: (09) 5238562, 5232198
Contact: Abubakar Ibrahim Imam - MD/CEO

LINTAS LIMITED
Business: Advertising, Public Relations & Marketing Consultants
Address: 6, Sylvia Crescent, Anthony Village, Lagos
Tel: (01) 4971851-6 (6L), 5550700 **Fax:** (01) 4971857
E-mail: lintas@alpha.linkerve.com
agencymail@lowelintaslagos.com
Contact: Mr. Richard Knight - MD/CEO.

LION BANK OF NIGERIA PLC
Business: Commercial Banking
Address: 34, Ahmadu Bello Way, Jos
Tel: (073) 452223, 454214, 457614, 456275, 450778-81(4L)
Fax: (073) 454602, 450362
E-mail: lbn@lionbank-nig.com
* 121/125, Broad Street, Lagos
Tel: (01) 2662175, 2665148 Fax: (01) 2663316
Contact: Mr. John Michael Abdul - MD/CEO.

LISABI MILLS (NIGERIA) LIMITED
Business: Food Processing & Marketing
Address: 378, Ikorodu Road, Maryland, Ikeja, Lagos

Tel: (01) 2901066, 4960102, 4965744, 7730232, 08023033590
E-mail: lismil38@yahoo.com
* Lisabi House, 39, Commercial Avenue Sabo-Yaba, Lagos
Contact: Ms. J. Kayode Ladipo - MD/CEO.

LISTER FLOUR MILLS (NIGERIA) LIMITED
Business: Flour Milling
Address: Km. 8, Podo Village, Old Ibadan-Lagos Rd, Ibadan.
Tel: (02) 2311337, 2316112, 2316113. **Fax:** (02) 2318708
* 24, Ladipo Oluwole Street, off Oba Akran Avenue, Ikeja, Lagos
Tel: (01) 7733040
Contact: Alh. Azeez Arisekola Alao - Chairman/CEO

LISTER INSURANCE COMPANY LIMITED
Business: General Insurance Business
Address: Lister House (1st Floor), Plots G & H, I.C.C. Layout, Ring Road, Ibadan
Tel: (02) 2313247, 2314246
Contact: Alh. Azeez Arisekola Alao - Exec. Chairman

LITERAMED PUBLICATIONS NIGERIA LIMITED
Business: Publishing of Educational and Scientific Books; Printing; Manufacture of Corporate Gifts
Address: Lantern House, Plot 45, Oregun Industrial Estate, off Oregun Road (Alausa Bus-Stop), Ikeja, Lagos
Tel: (01) 4962512 **Fax:** (01) 4935258
E-mail: literamed@infoweb.abs.net
Contact: Otunba O. M. Lawal-Solarin - Chairman/CEO.

LITHO PACKAGES (NIGERIA) LIMITED
Business: Manufacture of Lithographic Printed Packaging Cans and Containers
Address: 1, Awosika Avenue, Ikeja Ind. Estate, Ikeja, Lagos
Tel: (01) 4961502 **Tel/Fax:** (01) 4964449, 4932550
Contact: M. O. Fashina - MD/CEO

LITHO-CHROME LIMITED
Business: Printing and Lithographic Packaging
Address: Plot 16A, Block F, Oluyole Industrial Estate, Ibadan
Tel: (02) 2313797, 2316883 **Fax:** (02) 2316873
E-mail: lithochrome@hyperia.com
E-mail: litocrom@infoweb.abs.net

LITHOTEC LIMITED
Business: Electronic Pre-Press Services, Typesetting, Digital Imaging and Proofing, Colour Separation and Photolithography
Address: 28/32, Industrial Avenue, Ilupeju, Industrial Estate, Ilupeju, Lagos
Tel: (01) 4970153, 4977700-4 (5 L), 8042305
E-mail: lithotec@cyberspace.net.ng
Contact: Mr. B. A. Idris Animashaun - Chairman
Mr. Taiwo Ogunshakin - Marketing Manager

LIVESTOCK FEEDS PLC
Business: Manufacturing and Marketing of Livestock Feeds & Veterinary Products
Address: 1, Henry Carr Street, Ikeja Ind. Estatee, Ikeja, Lagos
Tel: (01) 4933885, 4971819, 4978745, 7740210
Fax: (01) 4932541, 4971818
E-mail: lsf.infow@pinet.com.ng
* 127, Sapele Road, Benin-City
Tel: (052) 255160, 253346
* 12, Industrial Layoaut, Aba
Tel: (082) 230612, 234265
* 1, Waziri Ibrahim Crescent, Abakpam Kaduna
Tel: (062) 240361, 213419
Contact: Mr. J. K. Adesina - MD/CEO

LIVINGSPRING INVESTMENT LIMITED
Business: Stockbroking, Investment & Financial Advisors
Address: LSDPC House (4th Floor), Nnamdi Azikiwe Street, Lagos Island, Lagos
Tel: (01) 7746603, 2665640, 08023058152, 08023530456
E-mail: livingsrpinginvestment@yahoo.com
Contact: Mr. A. B. Olarenwaju - MD/CEO

LIVINGSPRING SAVINGS & LOANS LIMITED
Business: Mortgage Banking
Address: 23, Obafemi Awolowo Way, P.M.B. 4488, Oshogbo
Tel: (035) 242447, 240295

LMB STOCKBROKERS LIMITED
Business: Stockbroking, Issuing House, Investment Advisory Services
Address: Okoi Arikpo House, 5, Idowu Taylor Street, Victoria Island, Lagos
Tel/Fax: (01) 2626382
E-mail: lmb@infoweb.abs.net
Contact: Alh. Aliko Dangote - Chairman
Chief Ode S. Obla - MD/CEO

LOBATEX LIMITED
Business: Sales and Repairs of Cellular Phones, GSM Equipment and Accessories, Consultancy Services
Address: 17, Adeola Odeku Street, Victoria Island, Lagos
Tel: (01) 2621546, 2622828, 611268, 08034002659
Fax: (01) 611268
E-mail: lobatex@cyberspace.net.ng
* Plot 36, Cornershop, Nouakchott Street, near Hali Brothers, Wuse Zone 1, Abuja
Tel: (09) 5232071 (090) 806870
* Ranchers Bees Shopping Complex (Shop 35), opp. Unver. of Suya Independence Way, Kaduna
Tel: (062) 210742
Contact: Mr. Kayode J. Olabayo - Chairman/CEO

LOCKS PLUS LIMITED
Business: Supply & Installation of Security Doors & Access Control Systems, Supply of Specialised Ironmongery (Panic-Locks)
Address: Engineering House (4th Floor, Suite 406), 1, Engineering Close, off Idowu Taylor Street, Victoria Island, Lagos
Tel: (01) 4733249, 08023133053 **Fax:** (01) 2617986
E-mail: locksplus2001@yahoo.co.uk
Contact: Ifeanyi Eronini - GM/CEO

LODIGIANI NIGERIA LIMITED
Business: Building and Civil Engineering Contractors; Maintenance Services
Address: 15, Burma Road, Apapa, Ebute-Metta, Lagos
Tel/Fax: (01) 5877329

E-mail: lodigiani.nig@lodigiani.com.ng
Website: www.lodigiani.com.ng
* Lodigiani Life Camp, Abuja
Tel: (09) 5231260, 5210102
Contact: Major Gen. Amadi Rimi (rtd) - Chairman
Arc. Stefano Dela Rocca - MD/CEO

LOGIC INVESTMENT COMPANY LIMITED
Business: Production of Plastic-Packaging Containers and Melamine Wares
Address: 90, Mafoluku Road, off M.M.International Airport Road, Mafoluku, Lagos
Tel: (01) 4930800, 4933559
Contact: Mr Babarinde Makanjuola - Chairman/CEO

LOGIC SCIENCES LIMITED
Business: Sales & Services of Computer Systems & Network, Fire Alarm Systems, Security Sytems, Key Management Sytems and Guard Tour Systems
Address: 18, Ademola Street, S.W., Ikoyi, Lagos
Tel: (01) 2673413, 7744244 **Fax:** (01) 2673414
E-mail: lsl@metrong.com
Lsl@micro.com.ng
infotech@logicsciencesltd.com
Website: www.logicsciencesltd.com
* Stallion Estate (Suite A4), Lobito Crescent, Wuse II, Abuja
Tel: (09) 4138753 **Fax:** (09) 4136715
Contact: Chief Dele Fajemirokun - Chairman
Mr. Babatunde A. Akinleye - MD/CEO

LOGICTECH TERMINUS LIMITED
Business: Sales & Maintenance of Computers & Peripherals
Address: 2, Adedeji Close, off Opebi Road, Ikeja, Lagos
Tel: (01) 4961312, 4937452 **Fax:** (01) 4961312
* Shop BC 1 & BC 2, Maryland Shopping Complex, Ikorodu Road, Maryland, Lagos
Tel: (01) 4933090
Contact: Mr. Akintunde O. Komolafe - MD/CEO

LOMBARD INSURANCE COMPANY LIMITED
Business: Non-Life Insurance
Address: Ashakun House (7th Floor), 13/15, Lake Street, off Broad Street, Lagos
Tel: (01) 2662020, 2664371, 2664629 **Fax:** (01) 2669528
* 5, Beirut Road, Kano.
Tel: (064) 634092
Contact: Chief R. A. Williams - Chairman/CEO

LOMBARDY PLASTICS (NIGERIA) LIMITED
Business: Manufacture of PVC Pipes and Fittings
Address: 18, Idiroko Road, Sango-Otta, Ogun State
Tel: (039) 722336 **Fax:** (01) 4961040
Contact: Mr. V. P. Vaswani - Chairman
Mr. P. P. Vaswani - MD/CEO.

LONDO FINANCE LIMITED
Business: Business Finance and Consultancy, Venture Capital, Financial Advisors, Intenational Trade
Address: 25, Adeboye Sholanke Street, off Allen Avenue, Ikeja, Lagos
Tel: (01) 4936190 **Fax:** (01) 4970811
Contact: Chief Olusegun Durojaiye - Chairman/CEO.

LONESTAR DRILLING LIMITED
Business: Oilfield Drilling Services
Address: 37, Dafinone Way (formerly Chechester Road), Sapele, Delta State
Tel: (054) 342080, 342420, 342275, 342647
(053) 254193-212 (20L)(Ext. 50247, 50248)
Fax: (054) 342080
* Plot 1681, Olakunle Bakare Close, off Sanusi Fafunwa Street, Victoria Island, Lagos
Tel: (01) 2617483, 7747207
* 1A, Elelenwo Road, Rumukwurusi, Port Harcourt
Tel/Fax: (084) 612258, 610305
Contact: Chief Humphrey I. S. Idisi - Chairman/CEO.

LONGMAN NIGERIA PLC
Business: Publishing of Books
Address: 52, Oba Akran Avenue, Ikeja Ind. Estate, Ikeja, Lagos
Tel: (01) 4978925-9 (5L) **Fax:** (01) 4964370
E-mail: longman@infoweb.abs.net
Website: www.pearsoneduc.com
www.awl-he.co.uk
Contact: Mr. J. A. Olowoniyi - MD/CEO.

LOOKOUT COMMUNICATIONS LIMITED
Business: Outdoor Advertising and Display Communications
Address: 13, Little Road, Yaba, Lagos
Tel: (01) 4809631, 8042062 **Fax:** (01) 3425027
E-mail: lookout@alpha.linkserve.com
Contact: Mr. Obi Nnaobi - MD/CEO.

LOPA ENERGY COMPANY LIMITED
Business: Marketing of Gases - LP-Gas, Anhydrous Ammonia, etc; Fabricaiton of Pressure Vessels
Address: Plot IN/3, Emene Industrial Layout Extension, Km. 11, Enugu-Abakaliki Highway, Enugu
Tel: ()042(558871, 090) 504740 **Fax:** (042) 456539
* 8, Degema Close, Rumuibekwe Housing Estate, Port Harcourt
Tel: (084) 611273 (090) 503957
Contact: Mr. Bonnie Alloh - Chairman/CEO.

LORDMART NIGERIA LIMITED
Business: Sales & Service of Generators, Transformers, Agricultural Machinery & Airconditioners; High-Voltage Installations & Major Electrical Projects
Address: 9, Creek Road, Apapa, Lagos
Tel: (01) 5450847, 5871085, 5874881, 4705550-1 (2L)
Fax: (01) 52623084, 872315
E-mail: info@lordmart.net
lordmart@hyperia.com
* Plot 446, Lobito Crescent, Wuse II, beh. NICON Hilton Hotel, Abuja
Tel: (09) 4138138-9(2L) **Fax:** (09) 4138139
E-mail: abuja@lordmart.net
* 23, (Plot 106), Onne Rd, GRA Phase II, PHarcourt.
Tel: (084) 237244
E-mail: pho@lordmart..net
Contact: Mr. Nathan Kalaora - MD/CEO

LOTATRONICS LIMITED
Business: Sales of Airconditioners, Fans and Refrigerators
Address: 2, Ribadu Road, off Awolowo Rd, SW. Ikoyi, Lagos
Tel: (01) 2673196, 2690209 **Fax:** (01) 2690209

E-mail: lotalan@infoweb.abs.net
* AP Shopping Complex (Suite 18), opp. NICON Hilton Gate, Maitama District, Abuja
Tel: (09) 4133347, 08033140870
Contact: Mrs. Fatima I. M. Teidi - MD/CEO.

LOTEM LIMITED
Business: Manufacturing of Plastic Furniture, Sales of Plastic Raw Materials
Address: Plot CL 1, Ikosi Rd, Oregun Ind.Estate, Ikeja, Lagos
Tel/Fax: (01) 4932332, 4976678, 7917039, 08033465446
E-mail: lotem2002@hyperia.com
Contact: Mr. E. Safra - MD/CEO

LOTUS PLASTICS LIMITED
Business: Manufacturing of Industrial Packaging
Address: ICON Building (4th Floor), Plot 999F, Idejo/ Danmole Street, Victoria Island, Lagos
Tel: (01) 2622840-1 (2L), 7916456
* Agbara Industrial Estate, Km. 32, Lagos-Badagry Expressway, Agbara, Ogun State
Tel: (01) 2882999, 7735802, 7745274 **Fax:** (01) 2693785
E-mail: lotus@multilinks.com

LOUIS CARTER GROUP OF COMPANIES
Business: Manufacturing of Plastic Products, Importation and Distribution of Auto Batteries, Import & Export of General Merchandise, Trading
Address: 9, Emma Okafor Street, Akaboukwu, Nnewi
Tel: (046) 460098, 462798, 462060, 461333, 463644, 463500 **Fax:** (046) 461126
* 114, Enuowa Street, Idumota, Lagos
Tel: (01) 2668632, 2668112 **Fax:** (01) 2668632
Contact: Chief Louis I. Onwugbenu - Chairman/CEO

LOVLEEN TOYS INDUSTRIES LIMITED
Business: Manufacture of Toys & Games, Plastic Household & Industrial Items
Address: Geepee Compound, Km. 38, Lagos-Abeokuta Expressway, Sango-Otta, Ogun State
Tel: (039) 720553 * (01) 7737138, 08042134187, 08046103400 **Fax:** (039) 720552

LTC ADVERTISING LIMITED
Business: Advertising and Marketing Communications
Address: Motorways Centre, 1, Motorways Avenue, near 7-Up Factory, Alausa, Ikeja, Lagos
Tel: (01) 4712056-7 (2 L), 5557898
E-mail: ltc@ltc-jwtlagos.net
Contact: Mrs. Bola Thomas - MD/CEO

LUBCON LIMITED
Business: Manufacture and Marketing of Lubricants
Address: Pilgrims Camp Road, Adewole Ind. Layout, Ilorin
Tel: (031) 222804 **Fax:** (031) 222805
E-mail: lubconhq@micro.com.ng
* 39, Curtis Adeniyi-Jones Close, off Adeniran Ogunsanya Street, Surulere, Lagos
Tel: (01) 5850281, 5845873, 5844875 **Fax:** (01) 5845873
* 12A, Khana Street, D-Line, Port Harcourt
* Apo Mechanic Village, Abuja
Contact: Alh. Jani Ibrahim - Chairman
Chief S. O. Owojaiye - MD/CEO.

LUBESERVICES ASSOCIATES
Business: Consulting Services in Tribology, Petroleum Products Marketing, Environmental Sciences, Lubrication Engineering, Technical Publishers
Address: 4/6, Afisman Drive, off Obafemi Awolowo Way, opp. Ikeja Local Government Council, Ikeja, Lagos
Tel: (01) 4976297, 820503 **Fax:** (01) 4933460, 525219
E-mail: lubeservices@yahoo.com
Contact: Engr. Kayode Sote - Principal Partner
Engr. Yomi Collins - Managing Partner

LUBONA NIGERIA LIMITED
Business: Import & Export, Marketers of Petroleum Products, Transporters, Hotelierss, Agro-Allied Business
Address: 1, Lubona Junction, Gboko, Benue State
Tel: (044) 470777, 470313
* Plot 818, Lake Chad Crescent, off IBB Way, Maitama, Abuja.
Tel: (09) 4133740
Contact: Chief (Mrs.) L. Andohol Katsina-Alu - MD/CEO.

LUCKY FIBRES (NIGERIA) LIMITED
Business: Manufacture & Sales of Woven & Tufted Carpets & Oriental Rugs, Production of Polypropylene BCF Yarn, Ropes & Twines, Primary & Secondary Backing, Sales of Polypropylene Chips, Bopp films, Hydrogen Peroxide & Rubber Flooring
Address: 1/4, Osborne Road, Ikoyi, Lagos
Tel: (01) 2692203-4 (2L), 2696102, 2671303
Fax: (01) 2695081
E-mail: lfnikoyi@alpha.linkserve.com
* Km. 5, Itokin Road, Ikorodu, Lagos
Tel: (01) 7744128, 7746223, 7748838, 08034067213
Fax: (01) 2881789, 7781415
Contact: Mr. Harkihin Aswani - MD/CEO.

LUFTHANSA GERMAN AIRLINES (NIGERIA)
Business: International Airline Passenger & Cargo Services
Address: 150, Broad Street, Marina, Lagos
Tel: (01) 2664889, 2664430, 2660987, 2660989, 4971731, 4970722 **Fax:** (01) 2664459
E-mail: info@dlh.de
* Presidential Hotel, Port Harcourt
Tel: (084) 330634, 232014 **Fax:** (084) 330634
Contact: Mr. Michael Wurche - GM (West Africa)

LUKAB NIGERIA LIMITED
Business: Printing Services, Production of Stationeries, Publishing
Address: 22/24, Ogundele Ave,Oke-Ira, Ogba, Ikeja, Lagos.
Tel: (01) 4737111
* Plot 72B, Ozobulu Crescent, off Ubiaja Crescent, Garki II, Abuja
Tel: (09) 2347172, 2348659
Contact: Mr. John Abayomi Ode - Chairman/CEO.

LUKE & JUDE (NIGERIA) LIMITED
Business: Manufacturing of Bakery, Food-Processing & Kitchen Equipment; Sales of Industrial Machinery & Chemicals
Address: Plot 4, Luke Emmanuel Crescent, beh. Mobil Estate, Satellite Town, Ojo, Lagos
Tel: (01) 2880779, 4806472, 4826687, 08022232621

E-mail: lukeandjude@yahoo.com
* 19/20, Chukun Street, S. E. Nassarawa Residential Layout Express Road, Kaduna
Tel: (062) 230151
Contact: Mr. Luke I. Okwara - Chairman/CEO

LUSTRE VENTURES LIMITED
Business: International Procurement Services for the Oil & Gas Industry, Civil Works
Address: 114, Aba Road, Garrison, Port Harcourt
Tel: (084) 237490, 08023455377 **Fax:** (084) 237490
E-mail: lustre2t@yahoo.com
Contact: Mr. Lanre Afolabi - Chairman/CEO

LUZO LIMITED
Business: Import & Export Trading, Sales of Electrical Equipment, Power & Energy Machinery/Equipment
Address: 3, Olufemi Rd, off Ogunlana Drive, Surulere, Lagos
Tel: (01) 5851471, 5851259, 5456232-4 (3 L), 08035000444
Fax: (01) 5456234
E-mail: ekechitoe@metrong.com
Contact: Mr. Louis Okere - Chairman

LYDOLINE PAINTS LIMITED
Business: Manufacture of Paints
Address: Plot 56/58, Adeola Avenue College Road, Ifako (Estate Bus-Stop), Agege, Lagos
Tel: (01) 4920799, 4920800, 4963633 **Fax:** (01) 4920800
* Plot 29, Senegal Street, off Accra Street, Wuse Zone 5, Abuja
Contact: Chief (Sir) T. T. C. Mbakwe - Chairman

LYKA TECHNOLOGIES LIMITED
Business: Sales of Computer Systems, Information Technology & Communication Equipment and Accessories
Address: Plot 8, Akanbi Onitiri Close, off Eric Moore Road, Iganmu, Lagos
Tel: (01) 2646066
E-mail: lykatek@yahoo.com
Contact: Mr Peter Eloka Okocha, OON - Chairman
Mr. E. D. C. Ilozor - MD/CEO

LYNAC SECURITIES LIMITED
Business: Stockbroking, Portfolio Management
Address: 16, Norman Williams Street, S.W. Ikoyi, Lagos
Tel: (01) 2695617, 2695444, 2695696, 2695446
Fax: (01) 2695446
E-mail: dblsecurities@hyperia.com

M & D PRODUCTS LIMITED
Business: Trading, Distribution and Sales of Personal Protective Equipment and Safety Footwear
Address: 6, Animashaun Street, off Bode Thomas Street, Surulere, Lagos
Tel: (01) 5851740, 4706283, 831606 **Fax:** (01) 5851740
E-mail: risktech@infoweb.abs.net
Contact: Mr. Dele Adelodun - Chairman

M & I RESOURCES & ENGINEERING LIMITED
Business: Engineering Services (Water, Civil, Environmental, Mechanical, Geotechnical)
Address: Oshik House, 12A, New Bridge Road, Makurdi
Tel: (044) 533684, 534535
E-mail: miresources@yahoo.com
* 2, Odo-Ogun Close, Keffi St, S.W. Ikoyi, Lagos
Tel: (01) 2695054, 2695780
Contact: Mr. Frank Ordih - MD/CEO

M & M INSURANCE BROKERS LIMITED
Business: Insurance Broking
Address: 7, Randle Road, Apapa, Lagos
Tel: (01) 5451280
Contact: Ms. Ebeke M. Ugwu - GM/CEO

M-B AUTOMOBILE SERVICES LIMITED
Business: Sales & Service of Motor Vehicles
Address: The Mercedes-Benz Place, 145, Ogunlana Drive, Alh. Masha Roundabout, Surulere, Lagos
Tel: (01) 5835523, 5852003 **Fax:** (01) 2646712
E-mail: mdmercdexben@linkserve.com
* The Habitat, 47, Alfred Rewane (Kingsway) Road, Ikoyi, Lagos
Tel: (01) 2696690-1 (2L) **Fax:** (01) 2696691
Contact: Mr. Benson Uwatse - Chairman/CEO

M. MARTIMO NIGERIA ENTERPRISES LIMITED
Business: Distribution and Sales of Petroleum Products, Automobile Tyres and Crushed Granite
Address: 47 & 71, Benin-Agbor Rd, Ikpoba Hill, Benin City
Tel: (052) 250473, 250584

M. SALEH & COMPANY LIMITED
Business: Sales & Maintenance of Generators, Tractors, Construction Equipment, Electrical Appliances, Transformers and Agricultural Equipment
Address: 71, Aba Road, next to Park 'N' Shop, Garrison Junction, Port Harcourt
Tel: (084) 235065, 235066, 0803313022, 0033102102
Fax: (084) 235065
E-mail: m.saleh@phca.linkserve.com
Contact: Mohammed Saleh - Chairman

M. A. BELO & PARTNERS
Business: Chartered Surveyors and Project Managers
Address: 2, Oyekan Road, Sabo-Yaba, Lagos
Tel: (01) 3425282, 4702702, 4714749
E-mail: mabelopart@aol.com
Website: www.mablopartners.com

M. A. JOBITEX NIGERIA LIMITED
Business: Food Processing; Canning of Foods & Sardines
Address: 54, Adeniyi Jones Avenue, Ikeja, Lagos
Tel: (01) 4960210, 7736525-6 (2L), 8042349
Fax: (01) 4960210
Contact: Otunba Mohammed A. Jobi-Fele - Chairman/CEO

M. A. KRISHT INDUSTRIES NIGERIA LIMITED
Business: Tanning of Hides & Skins
Address: Plot 18, Sharada Industrial Estate Phase III, Kano
Tel: (064) 668531, 663627

M. B. K NIGERIA LIMITED
Business: Import and Export of Chemicals, Machinery and Steel Products
Address: N.B.A. Building, Plot 1261, Adeola Hopewell Street, Victoria Island, Lagos

Tel: (01) 2612341, 2617972, 611271, 610637
Fax: (01) 2617972
E-mail: mbklagos@hyperia.com
lagzz-inet@xm.mitsui.co.jp
Contact: Mr. E. U.Uwandu - Admin. Manager

M. C. PLASTIC LIMITED
Business: Manufacture of various Domestic Plasticware
Address: Plot 28, Sharada Industrial Estate Phase 1, Kano
Tel: (064) 318454
Contact: Mr. Nehmen Dayekh - MD/CEO

M. F. W. DREDGING & MARINE (NIGERIA) LIMITED
Business: Dredging & Land Reclamation, Marine Engineering
Address: 5, National Supply Road, off Trans-Amadi Layout, Port Harcourt
Tel: (084) 237706
Contact: Mr. Jamal A. Shahimi - MD/CEO

M. G. S GROUP LIMITED
Business: Freight Handling, Bulk Cargo Carrier, Haulage, Mraine Transportation, Terminal Operators
Address: MGS Avenue, off 24, Trans-Amadi Road, Rumuobiakani, Port Harcourt
Tel: (084) 234052, 480886, 485117, 571034
Fax: (084) 230221
E-mail: mgs@infoweb.abs.net
Website: www.marinegulf.com
Contact: Chief Ambrose Nwuzi - MD/CEO

M. I. INDUSTRIES (NIGERIA) LIMITED
Business: Importation, Marketing & Distribution of Commodities and General Merchandise
Address: Plot C89, Amuwo-Odofin Industrial Layout, Oshodi-Apapa Expressway, Amuwo-Odofin, Lagos
Tel: (01) 7730726-7 (2L) **Fax:** (01) 2691920
E-mail: miindustries@hotmail.com
Contact: Mr. Marcel Imoisili - Chairman/CEO

M. I. C. FUNERAL SERVICES
Business: Funeral Services, Embalming & Mortuary Facilities
Address: 17, Odunalmi Street, Lagos Island, Lagos
Tel: (01) 2633020, 08033160097, 08023263575
Fax: (01) 2633648
E-mail: mic_funerals@hotmail.com
Contact: Mr. Tunji Okusanya - Chairman/CEO

M. T. ENTERPRISES LIMITED
Business: Manufacturing of Furniture and Flush Doors
Address: Kawaji Quarters, Dakata Area,off Hadejia Rd, Kano
Tel: (064) 649341, 640135, 08037871009
Fax: (064) 630988, 648189
* 12C, Murtala Mohammed Way, Kano
Tel: (064) 645467
Contact: M. T. Fadlallah - Chairman

MABOL INDUSTRIES SERVICES NIGERIA LIMITED
Business: Manufacturing of Textiles
Address: 16, Chief Bension Anorue Street, Ajao Estate, Apakun-Oshodi, Lagos
Tel: (01) 4521241, 4521258, 7742220 **Fax:** (01) 4975955
E-mail: mabol_limited@hotmail.com
Contact: Chief (Mrs.) M. B. Fabiyi - MD/CEO

MABON LIMITED
Business: Oilfield Engineering Services, Oil Exploration, Geological & Geophysical Consultancy
Address: 29, Sanusi Fafunwa Street, Victoria Island, Lagos
Tel: (01) 2612382, 2624880-2 (3L) **Fax:** (01) 2624880
E-mail: mabon@nigol.net.ng
Contact: Engr. Boni Madubuyi - Chairman/CEO

MABRETA NIGERIA LIMTED
Business: Sales & Service of Electronic Products
Address: 14, Wharf Road, Apapa, Lagos
Tel: (01) 5452636, 5451099 **Fax:** (01) 5874656
Contact: Mr. Godwin Chijoke - GM/CEO

MACAW COMMUNICATIONS NGERIA LIMITED
Business: Sales of GSM Phones & Accessories
Address: Cowrie House (Top Floor), 27/29, Adeyemo Alakija Street, Victoria Island, Lagos
Tel: (01) 2610355, 2612490 **Fax:** (01) 2613221
* 72, Raymond Njoku Street, S.W., Ikoyi, Lagos
Tel: (01) 2693403, 2673679 **Fax:** (01) 2692043
E-mail: macawng@yhaoo.com
Contact: Mr. Femi Akande - Head (Mktg & Business Dev.)

MACDAVINSON INTERNATIONAL LIMITED
Business: Importation, Manufacturing and Distribution of Cosmetics and Chemicals
Address: 25B, Bankole St, off Issa Williams St, Balogun, Lagos
Tel: (01) 2661902 , 2667185, 2660969 **Fax:** (01) 2668528
Contact: Chief David Emeka Eliogu - Chairman/CEO

MACEY LIMITED
Business: Business Information Services, Network and Bandwidth Consultancy & Management; Sales & Installation of Satellite Earth Station Equipments.
Address: 11, Ogunji St, off Association Ave, Ilupeju, Lagos
* 19, Church Street, Shomolu, Lagos
Tel: (01) 4934528, 8042791, 822607, 08033078166
E-mail: maceynigeria1@hotmail.com
oladayoadeleye@hotmail.com
Contact: Mr. Oladayo Adeleye - MD/CEO

MACGREGOR & OJUTALAYO
Business: Chartered Surveyors and Valuers, Estate Surveyors and Development Consultants
Address: 19, Military Street, Onikan, Lagos Island, Lagos
Tel: (01) 2633611, 2632347, 2631738, 08033358492, 23524245 **Fax:** (01) 2647145
E-mail: ojumaco@hotmail.com
Contact: Dr. Oluyomi MacGregor - Principal Partner

MACK AMERICAN TRUCK COMPANY LIMITED
Business: Sales of MACK Trucks and Parts
Address: 26, Creek Road, Apapa, Lagos
Tel: (01) 7748757, 5803470-4 (5L) (Ext. 1063), 08022234048
E-mail: mack.nigeria@hyperia.com
Contact: Mr. Patrice Frankel - Chairman/CEO

MACMILLAN NIGERIA PUBLISHERS LIMITED
Business: Publishing (Educational Texts & General Books)
Address: 4, Industrial Avenue, Ilupeju Industrial Estate, Ilupeju, Lagos

Tel: (01) 4932135, 4962185, 4961188, 7745892-3 (2L)
Fax: (01) 4932135
E-mail: mnplagos1@hyperia.com
mnplagos2@hyperia.com
* Oluyole Industrial Estate, Scheme 2, (after Methodist High School), Lagos-Ibadan Expressway Links, Ibadan.
Tel: (02) 2316895-7 (3L) **Fax:** (02) 2310066
E-mail: macm@skannet.com
Contact: Dr. Sanya Adelekan - MD/CEO

MACRO RESOURCES INVESTMENT COMPANY LIMITED
Business: Financial and Management Consultancy Services
Address: 31, Allen Avenue, Ikeja, Lagos
Tel: (01) 4970514, 4970503 **Fax:** (01) 4970361
E-mail: jot-macro@excite.com
Contact: Mr. James Tifase - Chairmanc/CEO

MACSELL ASSOCIATES LIMITED
Business: Advertising, Public Relations and Marketing
Address: 3, Tony Oghenejode Close, off Omorinre Johnson Street, by 1st Roundabout, Lekki Phase 1, Lagos
Tel: (01) 2705975, 2880438 **Fax:** (01) 2880438
E-mail: macsellassociates@iyahoo.com
Contact: Mr. Mac Ovbiagele - Chairman/CEO

MAC-TAY TACK CONSULTING
Business: Training, Management Consultancy, Human Resource Management, Sale of Audio-Visual Aids, Performance Improvement Consultancy
Address: 5, Prince Adelowo Adedeji Street, off Admiralty Way, Lekki Peninsula Phase I, Lagos
Tel: (01) 2706003, 2706336, 4705315, 4708725, 7741016
Fax: (01) 2706002
E-mail: info@mactaytack.com
Website: www.mactaytack.com
Contact: Mr. Tayo O. Rotimi - Chairman/CEO

MAC-TONNEL (NIGERIA) LIMITED
Business: Maritime Services, Clearing and Forwarding, Shipping, Import & Export, Real Estate Agency, Palm Oil Processing
Address: Nnewi Building, 1, Creek Road, Apapa, Lagos
Tel: (01) 5804169, 5851568 **Fax:** (01) 5453243
Contact: Mr. Ugochukwu Ikem Nwabunike - MD/CEO

MADIBA (NIGERIA) LIMITED
Business: Publishing of News Magazine (AFRICA TODAY)
Address: The Roof Top (5th Floor), 24A, Campbell Street, Lagos Island, Lagos
Tel: (01) 2646374 **Fax:** (01) 2646351
E-mail: madibangr@aol.com
africatodayngr@africatoday.com
Website: www.africatoday.co.uk
www.africatoday.com
Contact: Mr. Kayode Soyinka - Chairman/CEO
Mr. Muyiwa Akintunde - Regional Editor

MADONA ORGANISATION LIMITED
Business: Building, Civil, Mechanical, Electrical & General Contractors, Oil & Gas Services, Furnishing
Address: 118, Murtala Muhammed Way, Benin City
Tel: (052) 253127, 250606 **Fax:** (052) 257678
E-mail: madona@infoweb.abs.net
Contact: Mr. Frank Omo-Amadasun - Chairman/CEO

MADSON (NIGERIA) LIMITED
Business: Clearing and Forwarding
Address: Nnewi House, 1/3, Creek Road, Apapa, Lagos
Tel: (01) 5452767, 08033012374, 08033085706
Fax: (01) 5451127
Contact: Chief Joseph Madueke - Chairman/CEO

MADUAKO TRANSPORT COMPANY LIMITED
Business: Transportation & Haulage Services, Vehicle Leasing, Cement Distributorship, Clearing & Forwarding, General Commence
Address: 1A, Factory Road, Aba
Tel: (082) 220855, 221278, 222864 **Fax:** (082) 227630
E-mail: binez@infoweb.abs.net
Contact: Nze (Dr.) Clement O. Maduako (JP) - Chairman/CEO

MADUNKA INTERNATIONAL LIMITED
Business: Distribution, Sales and Service of Motor Vehicles
Address: G22, Unguwar Kanawa/NDA Junction, off Ali Akilu Road, Kaduna
Tel: (062) 315923, 315924, 311087 **Fax:** (062) 315925
Contact: Alh. Abdullahi Haido - Chairman/CEO

MAERSK NIGERIA LIMITED
Business: Ocean Liner, Fleet Owners & Operators, Containerised & Wet Cargo Carriers
Address: Maersk House, 121, Louis Solomon Close, off Ahmadu Bello Way, Victoria Island, Lagos
Tel: (01) 2626430-49 (20L) **Fax:** (01) 2626428, 2626451
E-mail: losmng@maersk.com
ngamkt@maersk.com
Website: www.maersksealand.com
* 1, Worlu Road, off Olu Obasanjo Rd, Port Harcourt
Tel: (084) 461100 - 5 (5L) **Fax:** (084) 461113, 461108
E-mail: phcmng@maersk.com
Contact: Mr. Tom Gronnengaard Knudsen - MD
Mr. Doyin Jibodu - Sales Manager

MAFE PRINTING WORKS LIMITED
Business: Production of Industrial Paper Packages, Labels and Stationeries, Commercial Printing
Address: 124-6, Demurin Street, Ketu, Lagos
Tel: (01) 2222041, 7745882
E-mail: mpw169@yahoo.com
Contact: Mr. A. J. Mafe - Vice Chairman/CEO

MAGAZINE SUBSCRIPTIONS NIGERIA LIMITED
Business: Marketing of Local & Foreign Books/Magazines, Importation of Foreign Magazines/Books
Address: 20, Moshood Abiola Crescent, off Toyin Street, Ikeja, Lagos
Tel: (01) 4971748, 4934006, 4714973, 08023121453
Fax: (01) 4971748
E-mail: msnlonline@yahoo.com
Contact: Mr. Henry O. Emezie - Chairman/CEO

MAGCOBAR MANUFACTURING NIGERIA LIMITED
Business: Oilfield Engineering Services
Address: The Octagon (6th Floor), 13, A.J. Marinho Drive, Victoria Island Annex, Lagos

Tel: (01) 2623400, 2623545, 2618517, 2618518, 4619026-7
Fax: (01) 2615247
Contact: Otunba Adekunle Ojora - Chairman
Mr. Marc Tuminaro - MD/CEO

MAGI TRADING COMPANY LIMITED
Business: Importation & Sales of Canned Tuna Fish
Address: 45, Murtala Muhammed International Airport Road, beside Lasal Hotel, Ajao Estate, Isolo, Lagos
Tel: (01) 4528739, 08033278514

MAGIC SOFTWARE ENTERPRISES NIGERIA LIMITED
Business: Application Software Development, Sales & Maintenance Services
Address: 7B, Ahmed Onibudo Street, Victoria Island, Lagos
Tel: (01) 2620994, 2622073, 3200280 **Fax:** (01) 2623464
E-mail: magic@alpha.linkserve.com
Website: www.magic-sw.com
Contact: Ambassador Shehu Malami - Chairman
Mr. Ilan Masarana - GM

MAGNA BUILDING SOCIETY LIMITED
Business: Mortgage Banking
Address: 16, Boyle Street, Onikan, Lagos
Tel: (01) 2637349, 2637460, 2637452 **Fax:** (01) 2637452
E-mail: magna@hyperia.com
magnai@hyperia.com
* 218, Iju Water Works Road, Iju-Agege, Lagos
Tel: (01) 4921159

MAGNATRIS FINANCE & INVESTMENT LIMITED
Business: Stockbroking, Financial Services
Address: 16, Boyle Street, Onikan, Lagos
Tel: (01) 2637349, 2637452, 2637460
Fax: (01) 2637460, 2637349
E-mail: magna@hyperia.com
* 218, Iju Water Works Road, Iju-Agege, Lagos

MAGNIFICENT BUREAU DE CHANGE
Business: Bureau de Change Services
Address: Chartered Bank Building (4th Floor), 19, Martins Street, Lagos Island, Lagos
Tel: (01) 2644605-6 (2L), 08033340874
Fax: (01) 2644606
E-mail: magban@skannet.com
Contact: Abdulateef Adepetu - MD/CEO

MAGNIFICENT INTERIORS (NIGERIA) LIMITED
Business: Manufacture and Sales of Furniture
Address: 3B, Adeyemo Alakija Street, or Plot 642F, Akin Adesola Street, Victoria Island, Lagos
Tel: (01) 4619848, 4803793, 08033033709
Fax: (01) 2694078
* Plot 3B, Oluyole Industrial Estate, Ibadan
Tel: (02) 2311612, 2315759
Contact: Major Gen. R. A. Adebayo (rtd) - Chairman
Mr. Adesola Adebayo - Exec. Director/CEO

MAGNIFICENT PROPERTIES LIMITED
Business: Real Estate Brokers & Agents, Property Managers
Address: Western House (8th Floor, Suite 802), 8/10, Broad Street, Lagos Island, Lagos
Tel: (01) 2632698, 2633011, 2636381, 08023154994, 33030674 **Fax:** (01) 2636381, 5851616
* Block 107 (House 1), OAU Quarters, beh. AP Plaza, Wuse II, Abuja
Tel: (09) 5232578
Contact: Lizzy Ijeoma Ibinye - Director

MAGNIFICENT TRAVELS & TOURS LIMITED
Business: Travel and Tour Agency
Address: 160, Awolowo Road, S. W., Ikoyi, Lagos
Tel: (01) 2690312 **Fax:** (01) 2694078
E-mail: magnificent@metrong.com
Contact: Mr. Adesola Adebayo - Chairman/CEO

MAGNUM TRUST BANK PLC
Business: Commercial Banking
Address: 67, Marina, Lagos
Tel: (01) 2640140-9 (10L) **Fax:** (01) 2640061-2 (2L)
E-mail: magnum@magnum-bank.com
Website: www.magnum-bank.com
Contact: Mr. Babatunde Dabiri - MD/CEO

MAGNUM TRUST INSURANCE BROKERS LIMITED
Business: Insurance Broking (All Classes)
Address: 190, Ikorodu Road, Palmgrove, Ikeja, Lagos
Tel: (01) 7743877
* Goodness Place, Plot 627, Sokode Crescent, Wuse Zone 5, Abuja
Tel: (09) 5233864
Contact: Dr. 'Tunji Olagunju - Chairman
Mr. Bola Oyebode - MD/CEO

MAGULF NIGERIA LIMITED
Business: Importation and Marketing of Frozen Foods
Address: Plot 98, RIVOC Road, Trans-Amadi Industrial Layout, Port Harcourt
Tel: (084) 238090, 571277 * (087) 770515
Fax: (084) 238089
Contact: Chief G. O. Agbonifo - Chairman/CEO

MAHANAIM & HAVTACHA LIMITED
Business: Fashion Outlet for Men
Address: 68, Norman Williams Street, S. W. Ikoyi, Lagos
Tel: (01) 2670590, 2671606 **Fax:** (01) 2671606, 2691941
E-mail: forgiven@infoweb.abs.net
forgiven@metrong.com
Contact: Mr. David Borha - MD/CEO

MAHASSA ADVERTISING LIMITED
Business: Advertising, PR & Marketing Communications
Address: 38, Beirut Road/Civic Centre Road, Bompai Kano
Tel: (064) 630127, 644313 **Fax:** (064) 644313
* 1, Joel Ogunaike Street, Ikeja, G.R.A., Lagos
Contact: Alh. Mahmood K. Hassan - Chairman/CEO

MAHAZA COMPANY LIMITED
Business: Tannery
Address: Plot 15, Challawa Industrial Estate, Kano
Tel: (064) 642843
Website: www.nasmier.com
Contact: Hassan Mahmud - Chairman/CEO

MAIDEN SHIPPING LINES LIMITED
Business: Clearing and Forwarding Agency, Warehousing,

Haulage, Shipping Services
Address: 37, Calcutta Crescent, Apapa, Lagos
Tel: (01) 5451412
Contact: Alh. Shehu A. Musa, CFR - Chairman
Mr. Sigismund M. Coker - MD/CEO

MAIDUGURI FLOUR MILLS LIMITED
Business: Flour Milling
Address: 2, Busari Road, P.M.B. 1117, Maiduguri
Tel: (076) 232712, 232719, 08023548961
Fax: (076) 235241
Contact: Alh. Muhammad R. El-Yakub - Chairman
Alh. Adamu M. Badejo - GM/CEO

MAIJAMA'A INTERNATIONAL LIMITED
Business: Export, Engineering, Contracts, Sawmilling, Transport
Address: 1, Hospital Road, Bauchi
Tel: (077) 543301 **Fax:** (077) 541363
Contact: Alh. Sanusi Maijama - Chairman/CEO

MAIL-IN OILFIELDS SERVICES LIMITED
Business: Analytical Laboratory Services, Environmental Consultancy
Address: Plot 5, 38th Street, DDPA Housing Estate, Ugborikoko, Effurun, Warri
Tel/Fax: (053) 255631, 08023089732, 08034114004
E-mail: mail-in@linkserve.com
Contact: Mr. V. O. Imevbore - MD/CEO

MAI-NASARA & SONS LIMITED
Business: Paper Conversion, Printing Services
Address: 13A, Club Road, Kano
Tel: (064) 646333, 634170, 634141, 08044114123
Fax: (064) 646333
Contact: Alh. Nasiru Ahali Ismail - Chairman/CEO

MAINBRIDGE NETWORK LIMITED
Business: Information Technology, Telecommunication
Address: Lozumba Commercial Complex (Suite 203), opp. UTC Complex, Area 10, Garki, Abuja
Tel: (09) 2343613 **Fax:** (09) 2347770
E-mail: mbnetabuja@yahoo.com
Contact: Engr. E. C. Omeata - Chairman

MAINE VENTURES LIMITED
Business: Outdoor Advertising Services
Address: 6, Olu Aina Street, Mushin, Lagos
Tel: (01) 4520728
E-mail: maine@mail.micro.com.ng
maineoutdoor-ad@yahoo.com
Contact: Mr. M. A. Ishola - Chairman/CEO

MAINFRAME PRODUCTIONS LIMITED
Business: Production of Films & Television Motion-Pictures
Address: 16, Seinde Callisto Crescent, off Oshodi - Apapa Expressway (Charity Bus-Stop), Oshodi, Lagos
Tel: (01) 4748191
E-mail: mframe@infoweb.abs.net
tkmainframe@hotmail.com
Website: www.mainframenewproductions.com
Contact: Alh. R. A. Ladoja - Chairman
Mr. Babatunde Kelani - MD/CEO

MAINLAND HOTEL, LAGOS
Business: Hotel Services
Address: 2/4, Murtala Mohammed Way, Ebute-Metta, Lagos
Tel/Fax: (01) 7741388, 7745941, 08033068328, 08033060719
E-mail: mainlandhotel@yahoo.com

MAINLAND INSURANCE BROKERS LIMITED
Business: Insurance Broking, Pensions & Risk Management
Address: Wuraola House, 6, Coker Road, Ilupeju, Lagos
Tel: (01) 4978992, 823602 **Fax:** (01) 4978992
Contact: Senator Ali Sheriff - Chairman
Mr. Dayo Adeniyi - MD/CEO

MAINLAND TRUST LIMITED
Business: Stockbroking, Fund and Portfolio Management, Issuing House, Investment Advisers
Address: St. Peter's House (9th Floor, Chieftain Suite), 3, Ajele St, off Broad Street, Lagos Island, Lagos
Tel: (01) 2633812, 2636906, 2631024, 4700602, 4719051
Fax: (01) 2630895
E-mail: mainland@nigtel.com
Contact: Dr. S. O. Oyefesobi - Exec. Chairman

MAJOK OIL LIMITED
Business: Marketing of Petroleum Products, General Merchandising, Financial Services
Address: 28, Fola Agoro Street, Bashua-Shomolu, Lagos
Tel: (01) 821635, 933241
* 527, Agege Motor Road, Shogunle, Lagos
* 2, Ilaje Road, Bariga, Lagos
Contact: Surv. G. F. Okusanya - MD/CEO

MAJOR GAS & INDUSTRIAL LIMITED
Business: Marketing of Liquefied Petroleum Gas, Installation of LP-Gas Plants and Consultancy
Address: Plot 19, Kolex Avenue, off Asa-Afariogun Street, Ajao Estate, Apakun-Oshodi, Lagos
Tel: (01) 4521908, 4724322 **Fax:** (01) 2667815
E-mail: ani@infoweb.abs.net
Contact: Engr. Joe Anisiofor - MD/CEO

MAJOR OILS LIMITED
Business: Mareketing of Petroleum Products
Address: 52, Constitution Road, Kaduna
Tel: (062) 244755, 247688

MAKERI SMELTING COMPANY LIMITED
Business: Smelting of Tin, Lead and Bismuth
Address: 58, Yakubu Gowon Way, Jos
Tel: (073) 462777, 08033953278 **Fax:** (073) 461973
Contact: Mr. Matthew H. Ochepa - MD/CEO

MAKSAMKAY AND COMPANY LIMITED
Business: Production of Office and Household Furniture, Panel Doors, Caskets, Picture Frames and Interior Decoration Accessories
Address: 121, Ikorodu Road, Igbobi, Lagos
Tel: (01) 08033067087
Contact: Prince Similoluwa A. Odunaiya - Chairman/CEO

MAKWALLA (NIGERIA) LIMITED
Business: Importers and Exporters
Address: 11, New Market Road, Bauchi

Tel: (077) 542373, 542181, 543377
* Plot 1218F, Sam Adegbite Close, off Amodu Ojikutu Street, Victoria Island, Lagos
Tel: (01) 2614034 **Fax:** (01) 2618399
* 18, Creek Road, Apapa, Lagos
Tel: (01) 5457322
Contact: Alh. Nuru Jibrin - Chairman/CEO

MALDESA NIGERIA LIMITED
Business: Importation and Distribution of Diary Products and General Merchandise
Address: 29B, Isaac John Street, Ikeja G.R.A., Lagos
Tel: (01) 4934736 **Fax:** (01) 4939507
E-mail: maldesa@alpha.linkserve.com
Contact: Mr. Magnus A. L. De Souza - Chairman/CEO

MALDINI MARBLES LIMITED
Business: Importation and Sales of Marble, Granite, Italian Paints, P.O.P., Ceramic & Sanitary Tiles
Address: 41A, Alh. Tokan Street, Alaka Estate, by Western Avenue, near National Stadium, Surulere, Lagos
Tel: (01) 4709075, 5831994, 08033008998, 08033046200
* Maldini House, 242, Aba Road, opp. Aiforce Base, Port Harcourt.
Tel:` (084) 572403, 611154, 08023211927, 08037028032
Contact: Mr. Jones Asekhauno - GM

MAMA CASS RESTUARANTS LIMITED
Contact: Catering Services, Restaurant
Address: 2A, Ogunsiji Close, beh. Alade Market, off Allen Avenue, Ikeja, Lagos
Tel: (01) 4934601, 4937155, 08023522837
* 11, Allen Avenue, Ikeja, Lagos
Tel: (01) 4961782, 08033075029
* LSB 'B' Road, off Limpopo Road, Federal Housing Authority Estate, Maitama, Abuja
Tel: (09) 4130624, 4130626
Contact: Mrs. Charis Onabowale - Chairman/CEO

MAMBILLA SHIPPING AGENCY LIMITED
Business: Shipping Services, Freight Forwarding
Address: 18, Oyekan Road, off Bombay Road, Apapa, Lagos
Tel: (01) 5450104 **Fax:** (01) 5450105
Contact: Mr. Dayo Abdul Azeez - MD/CEO

MANAGED HEALTHCARE SERVICES LIMITED
Business: Health Maintenance Organisation
Address: 16, Obokun Street, Ilupeju, Lagos
Tel: (01) 4931629-32 (4 L) **Fax:** (01) 4931628, 8160277
E-mail: mhs@micro.com.ng
Contact: Mr. E. Ukpabio - Ag. MD/CO

MANAGEMENT INFORMATION SYSTEM COMPANY LTD
Business: Sales, Service & Maintenance of Computer Systems & Software, Test, Analytical and Measurement Instruments, Medical Equipment, Computer Consultancy
Address: 3, Gerrard Road, Ikoyi, Lagos
Tel: (01) 2693423-4(2L), 2693421, 2691307, 2691770, 2670072
Fax: (01) 2693419, 2692755
E-mail: mis@micro.com.ng
* Plot 619, Ihiala Close, off Abeokuta Street, Area 8, Garki, Abuja
Tel: (09) 2349282, 2349284, 2349285
* 7, Circular Road, Presidential Estate, GRA., Phase 2, opp. Presidential Hotel, Port Harcourt
Tel: (084) 237210, 238271 **Fax:** (084) 230035
* 3, Sixth Rd, Delta Dev. & Property Authority Estate Opp. NNPC Staff Club, Ogborikoko, Effurun, Warri
Tel: (053) 253173, 254193-212 (Ext. 44792)
Fax: (053) 254358
* 7C, Murtala Mohammed Way, Kano
Tel: (064) 644016
Contact: Chief (Dr.) Okon Mfon Amana - Chairman/CEO
Mr. B. S. Mekwunye - D.G.M (Sales & Marketing)

MANAGEMENT EDUCATION & TRAINING LIMITED (M.E.T.)
Busines: Counselling and Advisory Services on Education
Address: Plot 15, White Sands Street, off Lekki Expressway, (Elf Bus-Stop), Lekki, Lagos
Tel: (01) 2881560, 5555561, 08033025497, 08033047808
Fax: (01) 2672193
E-mail: metedu@multilinks.com
Contact: Mr. B. O. Omotosho - Chairman/CEO

MANAKSIA INDUSTRIES (NIGERIA) LIMITED
Business: Manufacturing of Metal Caps & Closures
Address: 21/23, Abimbola Street, Isolo Industrial Estate, Isolo, Lagos
Tel: (01) 4529135, 4529137 **Fax:** (01) 4529136
E-mail: manaksia@cyberspace.net.ng
Website: www.manaksia.com
Contact: Mr. K. Purkayastha - MD/CEO

MANDARA GROUP OF COMPANIES
Business: Conglomerate, General Contractors, Importers & Exporters, Hoteliers, Petroleum Products Marketers
Address: 120, Shehu Umar Garba Road, Lamisula Ward, Maiduguri
Tel: (076) 231937, 233386, 233297, 233231, 232716, 233168
* 5, Razaq Balogun Street, off Adebola Street, off Adeniran Ogunsanya Street, Surulere, Lagos
* 23, Police Barracks Road, Bompai, Kano
Tel: (064) 645863
* Opp. Standard Trust Bank, Adetokunbo Ademola Crescent, Wuse II, Abuja
Contact: Alh. (Dr.) Zanna B. U. Mandara - Chairman/CEO

MANDILAS ELECTROGAS APPLIANCES LIMITED
Business: Manufacture of Domestic Appliances, Industrial Catering and Industrial Laundry Equipment
Address: 35, Simpson Street, Lagos
Tel: (01) 2633945, 2630252, 2630266, 2634331, 2646946, 2636141, 08033226051 **Fax:** (01) 2634523
E-mail: mandilas@mandilasng.com

MANDILAS ENTERPRISES LIMITED
Business: General Merchandising, Distributive Trade, Equipment Services
Address: Mandilas Building, 35, Simpson Street, Lagos
Tel: (01) 2630252, 2630266, 2634331, 2634345, 2636141
Fax: (01) 2633045, 2634856, 2634523
E-mail: mandilas@mandilasng.com
Contact: Mr. A. B. Hadjandonis - Group GM

MANDILAS GROUP LIMITED
Business: Conglomerate
Address: Mandilas House, 96/102, Broad Street, Lagos
Tel: (01) 2663220, 2663268, 2663410 **Fax:** (01) 2662605
E-mail: mandilas@micro.com.ng
Contact: Mr. A. B. Hadjandonis - Group GM

MANDILAS MOTORS
Business: Sales and Service of Motor Vehicles
Address: 35, Simpson Street, Lagos
Tel: (01) 2634331, 2630266, 2630252, 2633015, 2633049
E-mail: mandilas@micro.com.ng

MANDILAS TRAVELS LIMITED
Business: Travel Agency
Address: 35, Simpson Street, Lagos Island, Lagos
Tel: (01) 2630284, 2634084, 2636887
Fax: (01) 2634856, 2636887
E-mail: mandilas@micro.com.ng
Contact: Mrs. T. A. Mandilas - Chairman
Mr. A. B. Hadjadonis - Group GM

MANE LIMITED
Business: Design & Manufacturing of Low-Voltage Switchgear
Address: Plot 5, Block K, Isolo Industrial Estate, by Kuramo Industries, Apapa Expressway, Isolo, Lagos
Tel: (01) 4527022-3 (2L), 4527631 **Fax:** (01) 4527632
* 6, Olu Obasanjo, Way, Port Harcourt
Tel: (084) 237839
* 56, Airport Road, Kano.
Tel: (064) 639958, 645304
Contact: Mr. A. A. Bayode - MD/CEO

MANGROVE FURNISHING COMPANY LIMITED
Business: Furnishing and Interior Decoration
Address: 18, Warehouse Road, Apapa, Lagos
Tel: (01) 5875203
Contact: Mrs. F. N. Ndupu - Chairman/CEO
Mrs. Ngozi F. Onumonu - MD

MANIFOLD COMPUTERS LIMITED
Business: Marketing and Support of Information Management Systems, IT Solution Provider
Address: 154, Ogunlana Drive, Surulere, Lagos
Tel: (01) 5830980, 5848778, 5850439, 08033158579
Fax: (01) 5830980, 2632291
E-mail: manifold@linkserve.com.ng
Contact: Mr. O. Gbemiga Delano - MD/CEO

MANINVEST SECURITIES LIMITED
Business: Stockbroking, Financial Services
Address: Africa-Re House (3rd Floor), Plot 1679, Karimu Kotun Street, Victoria Island, Lagos
Tel: (01) 2626680, 2626683, 8040310 **Fax:** (01) 3204506
Contact: Dr. J. N. Ezikpe - Chairman
Mr. Nkem Ajoku - GM/CEO

MANKRIS VENTURES LIMITED
Business: Sales & Maintenance of Computers, System Networking, Training, Consultancy
Address: 38, Allen Avenue, Ikeja, Lagos
Tel: (01) 4978468, 4974040, 3453039, 7735712
Fax: (01) 4978468
E-mail: mankris@infoweb.abs.net
* 52, Bekweri Wosu (Igboukwu) Street, off Mbonu St, D-Line, Port Harcourt.
Tel: (084) 231683
Contact: Mr. Christian K. Nwude - MD/CEO

MAN-MOUNTAIN & COMPANY LIMITED
Business: Insurance Broking
Address: 109, Borno Way, Ebute-Metta, Lagos
Tel: (01) 7733228, 7743666, 7774820
E-mail: manmountain@hyperia.com
* 52, Bekwerri Wosu Street, D-Line, Port Harcourt
Tel: (084) 239051, 238168 **Fax:** (084) 238168
* Banex Plaza (Suite 209), Plot 750, Aminu Kano Crescent, Wuse II, Abuja.
Tel: (09) 4130103, 4139432
Contact: Mr. A. A. Shoderu - Chairman/CEO

MANNY BANK NIGERIA PLC
Business: Commercial Banking
Address: 2, Adeyemo Alakija Street, Victoria Island, Lagos
Tel: (01) 2618648, 2619229, 2610211, 320010-4 (4L)
Fax: (01) 2617760
E-mail: info@mannybank.com, manny@rcl.nig.com
Website: www.mannybank.com
*Plot 2370, H Macaulay Way, Wuse Zone 6, Abuja.
Tel: (09) 5238637
E-mail: mannyabj@rcl.nig.com
* NACB Building, 96, Obasanjo Rd, Port Harcourt.
Tel: (084) 230614, 230615
E-mail: mannyph@rcl.ng.com
* Bannex Plaza, 39, New Market Road, Onitsha
Tel: (046) 214154, 217038
Contact: Dr. Jona N. Ezikpe - MD/CEO
Mr. Kelechi C. Ogbomga - Head, Corp. Affairs

MANTISSA & ONAK LIMITED
Business: Importation and Sales of Automobile Batteries
Address: Zone D, Exodus Block (Shop 7), ASPMDA Plaza, International Trade Fair Complex, Lagos-Badagry Expressway, Ojo, Lagos
Tel: (01) 3208099, 3208265
E-mail: mantissa_onak2001@yahoo.com
Contact: Mr. Tony Ikenwa

MANUCOM FISHING COMPANY LIMITED
Business: Deep-Sea Trawling for Shrimps and Fish
Address: 3, Vanguard Avenue, off Oshodi-Apapa Expressway, Kirikiri Canal, Awodi-Ora, Apapa, Lagos
Tel: (01) 5877635, 5874578, 7917799 **Fax:** (01) 5874576
E-mail: manucom@nigerianet.com
Contact: Chief Alex Duduyemi - Chairman/CEO

MANUFACTURERS DELIVERY SERVICES (MDS) (Div. of UAC of Nig. Plc)
Business: Warehousing, General Merchandise Distribution, Distribution Management
Address: Plot 32, Kudirat Abiola Way (Formerly Oregun Road), Ikeja, Lagos
Tel: (01) 8043058, 8043121, 4939300-3 (4L); 0803402156, 08033004674, 08034021257 **Fax:** (01) 4939304
E-mail: mds@uacnplc.com
Contact: Mr. J. A. Ajayi - Group MD/CEO

MANUFACTURING & MARKETING COMPANY (NIG) LTD
Business: Building of Portable Accommodation (Portakabin)
Address: Klifco Building, 28, NTA/Choba Rd, Port Harcourt
Tel: (084) 235085, 236810, 236875, 571570, 08033152409, 08033362707 **Fax:** (084) 236810
E-mail: mamco.jbf@phca.linkserve.com
Contact: Mr. J. B. Fumudoh - MD/CEO

MANUFACTURING & TECHNICAL COMPANY NIGERIA LTD
Business: Assembly of Axles and Construction of Trailers, Sales of Spare Parts
Address: 50, Burma Road, Apapa, Lagos
Tel: (01) 5877180, 5877101 **Fax:** (01) 5872574
Contact: Alh. Grema Mohammed - Chairman/CEO

MAPLE PLASTICS INDUSTRIES LIMITED
Business: Manufacturing and Marketing of Plastic Products
Address: 26, Ize-Iyamu Street, off Balogun Street, T. A. Doherty Industrial Estate, Oregun, Lagos
Tel: (01) 7742949

MAPU INVESTMENT COMPANY LIMITED
Business: Marketing of Electronic Home Applicance
Address: 96, Nnamdi Azikiwe Street, Idumota, Lagos
Tel: (01) 2640484, 2662508, 2640480 **Fax:** (01) 2644528
* H109, Alaba International Market, Ojo, Lagos

MARANATHA HOSPITAL
Business: General Medical Services
Address: 2, St. Finbar's College Road, Akoka, Yaba, Lagos
Tel: (01) 821557, 823191
* Fuyisade Diagnotic Centre, 1, Moronfolu Street, Akoka, Yaba
* Fuyisade Eye Clinic, 14, Odaliki Street, Ebute-Metta, Lagos
Contact: Dr. (Mrs.) Yinka Phillips - Medical Director

MARBELTON GROUP OF COMPANIES
Business: Importation of Industrial Coatings, Agricultural Machinery, Tools & Equipment, Herbal Remedies & Supplements, Roof Leakage-Control Services, Sales of Road-Surfacing Products
Address: Marbleton House, 31B, Gafar Animashaun Street, Victoria Island, Lagos
Tel: (01) 2621114, 2626891, 7748018 **Fax:** (01) 2617554
E-mail: mwl@marbletongroup.net
Website: www.marbletongroup.com
* McLewis Plaza (Suite 40), Plot 799, Blantyre Street, off Adetokunbo Ademola Crescent, Wuse II, Abuja
Contact: Mr. Taiwo Olaye - Chairman/CEO

MARC & MEI (NIGERIA) LIMITED
Business: Production and Marketing of Food-Seasoning & Household Electrical Appliances
Address: 42, Burma Road, Apapa, Lagos
Tel: (01) 5871094 **Fax:** (01) 5873117
Contact: Mrs. Kponton Shih Mei - MD/CEO

MARCEL PHARMACEUTICAL CHEMISTS LIMITED
Business: Importation of Pharmaceutical Products
Address: 17, Palmer Street, Fegge, Onitsha
Tel: (046) 210207, 211579, 08037144060
Contact: Chief M. O. Nwakwe - Chairman/CEO

MARCITY LIMITED
Business: Manufacture of Paints & Allied Products, Sales of Industrial Chemicals
Address: 110A, Ago Palace Way, Okota, Isolo, Lagos
Tel: (01) 4712461

MARCON GROUP OF COMPANIES
Business: Engineering Services, Marketing of Petroleum Products
Address: 88A, Opebi Road, Ikeja, Lagos
Tel: (01) 4937064, 4934395, 4937529, 08023005912
* 6, Bernard Carr St, opp. State Library, Port Harcourt
* 12, Durban Road, Wuse II, Abuja
Contact: Chief M. O. Nlemigbo - Chairman/CEO

MARHABAN INSURANCE BROKERS LIMITED
Business: Insurance Broking and Pension Consultancy
Address: 4, Lumumbashi Street, off Maputa Street/Abidjan Street, Wuse Zone 3, Abuja
Tel: (09) 5236643

MARI TRANS NIGERIA LIMITED
Business: Ship's Agency, Management and Chartering, Airfreight, Clearing & Forwarding, Warehousing
Address: 50, Burma Road, Apapa, Lagos
Tel: (01) 5877101, 5877180, 5877449 **Fax:** (01) 5872574
E-mail: maritrans@nova.net.ng
Contact: Alh. A. Mohammed Grema - Chairman/CEO

MARINA INTERNATIONAL BANK LIMITED
Business: Merchant Banking
Address: 10, Amodu Ojikutu Street, Victoria Island, Lagos
Tel: (01) 2621051-5 (5L), 2625613-7 (5L)
Fax: (01) 618978, 2610839
E-mail: marinabank@mibl.com
Contact: Dr. Jaiye Oyedotun - MD/CEO
Mrs. J. A. Agbaye - AGM (Legal & Corp. Affairs)

MARINA NOMINEES LIMITED
Business: Company Secretarial Services
Address: KPMG Nigeria, 233, Ikorodu Rd, Obanikoro, Lagos
Tel: (01) 4931245-8 (4L), 4930117, 7740219
E-mail: nigeria@kpmg.gem.ge15.com

MARINE MUTUAL SERVICES LIMITED
Business: Marine Superintendents
Address: 13, Creek Road, Apapa, Lagos
Tel: (01) 5877560, 5878267 **Fax:** (01) 5875957
Contact: Mr. Solomon Onwuka - Admin. Manager

MARINE TECHNICAL SERVICES INTERNATIONAL (NIG) LTD
Business: Marine Surveyors, Calibration, Laboratory Services
Address: GlaxoWellcome House, 41, Creek Road, Apapa, Lagos
Tel: (01) 5450509, 5450534, 5451253, 5804597
Fax: (01) 5452415
* 121, Custom Road, Port Harcourt
Contact: Mr. T. A. Braithwaite - Chairman
Mr. C. C. Nwankwo - ED. (Operations)

MARINETEC LIMITED
Business: Building, Leasing and Repairs of Aluminium Boats, Marine Transportation Services to the Oil Industry

Address: NAL Towers (2nd Floor), 20, Marina, Lagos
Tel: (01) 2601370-8 (9L), 2633004 **Fax:** (01) 2632704
E-mail: a:tec@infoweb.abs.net
* Federal Fisheries Terminal, 1, Kolokuma Street, Borokiri, Port Harcourt
Tel/Fax: (084) 331378

MARIO-JOSE ENTERPRISES LIMITED
Business: Tannery
Address: 12S, Bello Road, Kano
Tel: (064) 649244, 635604, 638177, 647006
Fax: (064) 636506
* Plot 63, Challawa Industrial Estate, Kano
Tel: (064) 649244, 635604 Fax: (064) 635604
Contact: Mr. Mario Jose - MD/CEO

MARITIME RESORT LIMITED
Business: Port and Maritime Services
Address: Eleganza Plaza (Aquarius Block, 2nd Floor), Commercial Road, Apapa, Lagos
Tel: (01) 5871512, 5871511, 08033428898, 08033733641
Contact: Mr. Peter Ofoegbu - MD/CEO

MARK IV NIGERIA LIMITED
Business: Automobile Airconditioning, Precision Engineering; Reclamation of Crankshafts etc. Maintenance of Airconditioners and Accessories
Address: Oshodi-Apapa Expressway (by Champion House), near Hassan Bus-Stop, Isolo, Lagos
Tel: (01) 4521542, 4521578, 521573 **Fax:** (01) 4521587
Contact: Mr. J. O. Okonkwo - MD/CEO

MARK ODU & COMPANY
Business: Estate Surveyors & Valuers, Property Development, Land Use Planning Consultants
Address: 53B, Akinola Cole Crescent, off Adeniyi Jones Avenue, Ikeja, Lagos
Tel: (01) 4972812
* Plot 518, Kamusi Crescent, off Aminu Kano Crescent, Wuse II, Abuja
Tel: (09) 4136755 **Fax:** (09) 4137062
Contact: Prof. (Nze) Mark Odu - Founder/Chairman

MARKET RESEARCH CONSULTANCY LIMITED
Business: Market Research (Social, Economic), Databank Management, Opinion Polls
Address: 10, Adeboye Sholanke Street, off Allen Avenue, Ikeja, Lagos
Tel: (01) 5557452, 7741758, 7901068, 7914593, 08033326079, 08037044717, 08037864271
E-mail: mrcnigeria@mrcoffice.com
mrclimited@yahoo.com
Website: www.mrcoffice.com
Contact: Mr Shola Akinnagbe - MD/CEO

MARKET TRENDS RESEARCH INTERNATIONAL
Business: Marketing Research and Consultancy Services
Address: Ibusa House, 5, Sunday Ogunyade Street, Gbagada Estate Phase II, Lagos
Tel: (01) 2880366, 5550266, 5550288, 5550573, 7750753, 08023117969, 08033322556
Fax: (01) 3202088, 3203323, 5550265
E-mail: mtrinigeria@research-intng.com
Website: www.research-intng.com
Contact: Mr. J. O. Ehbomenye - Chairman/CEO

MARKETING + MEDIA LIMITED
Business: Outdoor Advertising, Marketing & Media Advisory and Consultancy Services
Address: 3, Olufemi Rd, off Ogunlana Drive, Surulere, Lagos
Tel: (01) 5851471, 58512595456232-4 (3L), 08033461007
Fax: (01) 5851259, 5456234
E-mail: outdoor@metrong.com
* Nyanya Road, by Velvet Diamond Hotel, Abuja
Tel: 08055243686
Contact: Mr T. O. E. Ekechi - MD/CEO

MARKGREY TECHNOLOGIES
Business: Internet Service Provider, IT Training, Sales & Maintenance of Computere Hardware/Software
Address: Plot 702, Port Harcourt Crescent, off Gimbiya Stt, off Ahmadu Bello Way, Area 11, Garki, Abuja
Tel: (09) 3148571, 4139853, 08033497127
E-mail: info@markgrey.net
Website: www.markgreey.net
Contact: Chief Frank Chigbo - Chairman/CEO

MARKIS (NIGERIA) LIMITED
Business: Manufacture and Marketing of Cosmetics
Address: 7/9, Babajide Winsala St, Arifanla-Akute, Ogun State
Tel: (01) 8042366, 4707855
* 24/26, Igbariam Street, Achara Layout, Enugu
Contact: Dr. Andy Ikeokwu - MD/CEO

MARKSON CHEMICAL INDUSTRY (WEST AFRICA) LIMITED
Business: Importation, Manufacturing and Marketing of Industrial Chemicals and General Merchandise
Address: 42, Francis Street, Odoakpu, Onitsha
Tel: (046) 411218
* 13/15, Issa Williams Street, Balogun, Lagos

MARRIOT SECURITIES & INVESTMENTS LIMITED
Business: Stockbroking, Issuing House, Share Registrar Services, Finance & Portfolio Management
Address: Elder Dempster Building (3rd Floor), 47, Marina, Lagos Island, Lagos
Tel: (01) 2660936, 2661901, 2664328 **Fax:** (01) 2664328
E-mail: marriot@intracom.net.ng
Contact: Chief F. K. Bajomo - Chairman/CEO

MARSHLAND PROJECTS NIGERIA LIMITED
Business: Building & Civil Engineering Contractors, Electrical & Mechanical Engineering Services
Address: Plot 55, Trans-Amadi Ind. Layout, Port Harcourt
Tel: (084) 237339 **Fax:** (084) 237338

MARSTON BARROW FOODS LIMITED
Business: Processing and Marketing of Foods and Drinks
Address: Lynson Chemical Avenue, Km. 38, Lagos-Abeokuta Expressway, Sango-Otta, Ogun State
Tel: (039) 722199, 722303, *(01) 4966451
E-mail: marston@home.metrong.com

MART LINK ADVERTISING LIMITED
Business: Marketing Communication, Design & Printing, Public Relations, Perception Management

Address: 11, Adeboye Solake Street, off Allen Avenue, Ikeja, Lagos
Tel: (01) 4936610, 5557854, 08022904400, 08023065437, 08023379405, 08036706645, 08037270626
Fax: (01) 4936610
E-mail: martlink@skannet.com
Website: www.martlinkltd.com
Contact: Mr. Sunkanmi Ajiboye - MD/CEO

MARTCHEM INDUSTRIES NIGERIA LIMITED
Business: Manufacturing of Foam Products; Foundry
Address: 1A, Mai-Malari Rd, Bompai Industrial Estate, Kano
Tel: (064) 646747, 645906, 08023247629, 08033184018, 08037867986
Fax: (064) 646747
E-mail: martchem@yahoo.co.uk
* 27, Kunai Street, beh. Textile Labour House, off Nnamdi Azikiwe Expressway, Nasarawa Bye-Pass, Kaduna
Contact: Mr. Martins Nwaokoli - Chairman/CEO

MARTINS ELECTRONICS COMPANY LIMITED
Business: Importation and Marketing of Electronic Appliances, Safes and General Merchandise
Address: 8, Beirut Road, Kano
Tel: (064) 631493, 634569, 637548, 08036650422
* Wuse Shopping Complex (Suite 2), Wuse Zone 3, Abuja.
Tel: (09) 5233390, 5233197, 5233198
Contact: Chief Martins Okwuolisa - MD/CEO

MARUBENI NIGERIA LIMITED
Business: Liason Office of Marubeni Corporation (Japan)
Address: Plot 1652, Olosa Street, Victoria Island, Lagos
Tel: (01) 2614281, 2618993, 2621752, 2616265
Fax: (01) 2619820
E-mail: marubeni@infoweb.abs.net
Contact: Mr. T. Sato - Chairman/CEO

MASARRAH AIR SERVICES
Business: Travel Agency
Address: 6, Niger Street, Kano
Tel: (064) 316611, 330695, 634570
Fax: (064) 641604, 649346
E-mail: masarrah_air@hotmail.com
* 18, Alh. Bashorun Street, off Norman Williams Street, S. W. Ikoyi, Lagos
Tel: (01) 2690719, 682107
Contact: Fatim I. Rahi - Agency Manager

MASMA NIGERIA LIMITED
Business: Clearing & Forwarding Agency
Address: 1, Oyekan Rd, off Calcutta Crescent, Apapa, Lagos
Tel/Fax: (01) 5874356
E-mail: masmanigltd2003@yahoo.com
Contact: Mrs. Maryam Adeleke - MD/CEO

MASONS GROUP
Business: Importation and Sales of Generators
Address: 296B, Jide Oki Street, off Younis Bashorun Street, Victoria Island Annex, Lagos
Tel: (01) 8042260, 3200268 **Fax:** (01) 3200268
* Plot 4, Bay 6, Cocoa Industries Road, Ogba Industrial Estate, Ikeja, Lagos

MASPHALA COMPANY NIGERIA LIMITED
Business: Clearing & Forwarding Agency, Shipping Consultancy Services, Import & Export
Address: 33, Warehouse Road, Apapa, Lagos
Tel: (01) 7742194, 5878501, 4717652, 08033212710
Fax: (01) 5878501
E-mail: masphala@yahoo.com
Contact: Mr. Kingsley Nwanosike - MD/CEO

MASSEY UDEGBE & COMPANY
Business: Estate Surveying and Valuation, Property Development, Management, Letting & Sales, Plant & Machinery Valuation, Construction Management
Address: 2A, Montgomery Road, Yaba, Lagos
Tel: (01) 862891, 861507, 08022230823 **Fax:** (01) 862891
E-mail: mudegbe@infoweb.abs.net
Contact: Massey O. A. T. Udegbe - Chairman/Prin. Partner

MASTERPIECE LIMITED
Business: Advertising and Corporate Promotions
Address: 22, Itolo St, off Eric Moore Road, Surulere, Lagos
Tel: (01) 5846309, 842132, 08023313434
Fax: (01) 5846309
E-mail: solomasterpiece@yahoo.com
Contact: Mr. Solomon U. Oguine - MD/CEO

MASTERSOUND VENTURES LIMITED
Business: Music Production Studio, Musical Equipment Leasing & Hire
Address: Falemi House 250, Ikorodu Rd, Obanikoro, Lagos
Tel: (01) 825982 **Fax:** (01) 2633553
Contact: Chief Chris Okunowo - Chairman/CEO

MASTERSPORT INTERNATIONAL LIMITED
Business: Sports Marketing and Event Management
Address: 31B, Emina Crescent off Toyin Street, Ikeja, Lagos
Tel: (01) 7740475, 7751529, 7753187
E-mail: mastersports2000@yahoo.com
Website: www.mastersportsinternational.com
Contact: Mr. Ejiro Omonode - MD/CEO

MASTERSTROKE PACKAGES LIMITED
Business: Printing Services, Manufacturing of Light Packaging
Address: 17, Iganmu Industrial Road, Surulere, Lagos
Tel: (01) 4701975, 5846171, 7730993-4 (2L)
Fax: (01) 2881802
E-mail: masterstroke@hyperia.com
Contact: Mr. Lakin Popoola - Chairman/CEO

MAT MANUFACTURING COMPANY LIMITED
Business: Manufacture of Synthetic Mats
Address: 4, Commercial Road, Apapa, Lagos
Tel: (01) 5452050-9 (10L) **Fax:** (01) 5452054, 5878480
Contact: Prince (Dr.) Samuel Adedoyin - Chairman/CEO

MATBENY HOLDINGS LIMITED
Business: Importation of Healthcare Products; General Contracts and Supplies; Catering & Hospitality Services; Management & Financial Consultants
Address: Plot 290, Ajose Adeogun St, Victoria Island, Lagos
Tel: (01) 2615280 **Fax:** (01) 2622846
E-mail: matbeny@yahoo.com
Contact: Chief E. M. Egwuenu - Chairman/CEO

MATEF LIMITED
Business: Sales of Marble
Address: 103, Ibadan Street, Ebute-Metta (East), Lagos
Tel: (01) 5852171, 861697
Contact: Alh. Suleiman Onabiyi - Chairman/CEO

MATNA FOODS COMPANY LIMITED
Business: Manfacturing of Starch
Address: 1, Balogun Street, Oregun Ind. Estate, Ikeja, Lagos
Tel: (01) 4936356, 7757474
* BOI House, Owo Road, Akure
Tel/Fax: (034) 244713, 244883
* Km. 19, Akure-Owo Road, Owo, Ondo State.

MATERIALS MANAGEMENT SERVICES LIMITED
Business: General Consultancy Services
Address: MMS House, 159A, Isale Eko Avenue, Dolphin Estate, Ikoyi, Lagos
Tel: (01) 2694015, 2694424 **Fax:** (01) 2694424
E-mail: mms@linkserve.com.ng

MAX PROMOTIONS LIMITED
Business: Communications, Real Estate
Address: 12B, Igbodo Street, Old G.R.A., Port Harcourt
Tel: (084) 230042, 334794 **Fax:** (084) 230496
E-mail: maxpro@hyperia.com
Contact: Mr. Bobby Benson, Jnr - MD/CEO

MAXBEST GROUP OF COMPANIES LIMITED
Business: Import & Export, Industries, Estate Agents & Valuers, Property Managers, Agro-Allied Business
Address: 7, Denton Street, behind Mainland Hotel, Oyingbo, Ebute-Metta, Lagos
Tel: (01) 8178935, 08034034262
E-mail: maxbest7@yahoo.com
info@macopalltd.com
Contact: Mr. Uche Okpala - MD/CEO

MAXIFUND INVESTMENTS & SECURITIES LIMITED
Business: Stockbroking, Credit Rating, Capital Market Operations, Investment Banking, Consultancy
Address: Stock Exchange House (19th Floor), 2/4, Customs Street, off Tinubu Square, Lagos
Tel: (01) 2646064, 2632264 **Fax:** (01) 2647392
E-mail: maxifund@aol.com
Contact: Mr. O. C. K. Unegbu - MD/CEO

MAY & BAKER NIGERIA PLC
Business: Manufacturer & Distribution of Pharmaceutical Products, Vaccines, Sera & Diagnostic
Address: 3/5, Sapara St, Ikeja Industrial Estate, Ikeja, Lagos
Tel: (01) 4968130-6 (7L), 4967067, 4978199, 4960554, 4936400, 4962951 **Fax:** (01) 4962832
E-mail: info@may-baker.com.ng
Website: www.may-baker.com
* Pot F. Kawaji Quarters, Hadejia Road, Kano
Tel/Fax: (064) 645519
Contact: Mr. J. I. Odumodu - MD/CEO

MAXIVISION LASER EYE CENTRE
Business: Ophthalmic & Ophthalmological Laser-Surgery Services
Address: FABAC Close, 3B, Ligali Ayorinde Street, Victoria Island, Lagos
Tel: (01) 4619371-3 (L), 08034017880
Fax: (01) 4619374
E-mail: maxivision_bhl@yahoo.com
Contact: Dr. Rilwan Olatunji Bamgbala - Chairman
Dr. Yuri Nickolaevich Kounekine - MD/CEO

MAYFAIR BROKERS LIMITED
Business: Insurance Broking and Consultancy
Address: 4, Alara Street, Onike, Yaba, Lagos
Tel/Fax: (01) 4820186, 5836911, 7914967, 7927806-7 (2L)
E-mail: mayfairbrokers@hyperia.com
* Close 2, Presidential Housing Estate, beh. Federal Secretariat, Aba Road, Port Harcourt
Tel: (084) 334000, 234000
* 5, Sirasso Crescent, Wuze Zone 7, Abuja
Tel: (09) 5232646, 5236643, 5236815
Contact: Mr. Olatokunbo Olaofe - Chairman/CEO

MAYFIELD FARMS LIMITED
Business: Poultry Farming, Hatchery
Address: NCR Building (7th Floor), 6, Broad Street, Lagos
Tel: (01) 2646878, 2646879 **Fax:** (01) 2646879
E-mail: mayfield@home.metrong.com
Contact: Dr. Johnson Oduyemi - Group MD/CEO

MAYFIELD INVESTMENTS LIMITED
Business: Stockbroking, Portfolio Management, Investment Advisory Services
Address: NCR Building (7th Floor), 6, Broad Street, Lagos
Tel: (01) 2646878, 2646879 **Fax:** (01) 2646879
E-mail: mayfield@home.metrong.com
Contact: Dr. Johnson Olugbemi Oduyemi - Group MD/CEO

MAYOK ENGINEERING WORKS LIMITED
Business: Electricity Power Generation, Sales, Installation & Maintenance of Gas Turbines and Diesel Generators, Manufacturing of Automatic Voltage Regulators
Address: 16/18, Alufa Aminu St, Pedro, Palmgrove, Lagos
Tel: (01) 4711385, 5454987, 08023186201, 08033231707
E-mail: mayok1618@yahoo.com
Contact: Engr. (Chief/Dr.) Yomi Awodipe - Chairman/CEO

MAYOR ENGINEERING COMPANY LIMITED
Business: Manufacturing of Iron Rods, Flats and Angle Bars
Address: Plot 68, Ikorodu Industrial Estate, Odogunyan, P. O. Box 252, Ikorodu, Lagos State

MAYSSA INTERNATIONAL NIGERIA LIMITED
Business: Turnkey Engineering Managers and Contractors
Address: Plot 202B, Etim Inyang Crescent, off Muri Okunola Street, Victoria Island, Lagos
Tel: (01) 2613443, 2624475, 612006 **Fax:** (01) 4619771
E-mail: mayssa@hyperia.com
* 5, Forest Road, G.R.A., Ilorin.
Tel: (053) 222443
Contact: Mr. Eli Elias - MD/CEO

MAYWEATHER INVESTMENTS LIMITED
Business: Importation and Sales of Textile Fabrics and Photographic Materials
Address: David's Place (2nd Floor), 117, Cameroun Rd, Aba
Tel: (082) 230047, 230334 **Fax:** (082) 230047

E-mail: mayweather@phca.linkserve.com
Contact: Chief David U. Ukuku - Chairman/CEO

MAZIN ENGINEERING LIMITED
Business: Fabrication of Steel Products
Address: 20, Olayiwola Street, off Oregun Road, Oregun Industrial Estate, Oregun, Lagos
Tel: (01) 4961128, 4967034, 4965730
Fax: (01) 4931949, 4963411
E-mail: mazin@nova.net.ng
Contact: Chief. D. H. Jarmakani - MD/CEO

MAZZI NIGERIA LIMITED
Business: Management & Business Consultancy Services
Address: 21, Woji Road, off Old Aba Road, 1st Artillery, Rumuogba-Obio, Port Harcourt
Tel: (084) 575467
E-mail: mazziltd@yahoo.co.uk
Website: www.abc.com

MBC INTERNATIONAL BANK LIMITED
Business: Banking Services
Address: 16, Keffi Street, S. W. Ikoyi, Lagos
Tel: (01) 2690261-70 (9L) **Fax:** (01) 2690767
E-mail: mbc@mbc.nig.com
Website: www.mbc-nig.com
* UTC Building, 16/17, Bello Road, Bompai, Kano
Tel: (064) 633683, 648959
* 1, Agudama Street, D-Line, Port Harcourt
Tel: (084) 236000-2 **Fax:** (084) 236002
* Plot 1091, Faskari Street, Garki Area 3, Abuja
Tel: (09) 2344424
* All Season's Plaza, Suite 6 & 7, Ruby Block, Lateef Jakande Road, Agidingbi, Ikeja, Lagos
Tel: (01) 925840-1 (2L), 7740484
Contact: Mr. Raymond A. Bariou - MD/CEO
Adebola Adetunmbi - Corporate Affairs Dept

MBC SECURITIES LIMITED
Business: Stockbroking, Issuing House, Financial Advisers
Address: 4, Keffi Street, S. W. Ikoyi, Lagos
Tel: (01) 2695583, 2695586, 2692567 **Fax:** (01) 2695586
E-mail: mbcsec@hyperia.com
mbcsec@mbc-nig.com
Website: www.mbc-nig.com
* Plot 1970, Faskari Crescent, Area 3, Garki, Abuja
Tel/Fax: (09) 2342830
Contact: Chief Sunday Dankaro, CON - Chairman
TinukeOlukunle - Customer Relations Officer

MBL FINANCIAL SERVICES LIMITED
Business: Stockbroking, Financial Advisory Services
Address: 18B, Idowu Taylor Street, Victoria Island, Lagos
Tel: (01) 4714809, 4715411
* Owena House, Plot 76, 4th Avenue, off Ahmadu Bello Way, Central Business District, Abuja
Tel: (09) 2344325, 2347790, 2347791
Fax: (09) 2344326, 2344337
Contact: Mr. Oye Oyefeso - GM

MC & A LIMITED
Business: Marketing & Communications Agency
Address: 3, Shony Highway, Shonibare Estate, Maryland, Lagos
Tel: (01) 4970096, 4970097 **Fax:** (01) 4970096
E-mail: mca@hyperia.com
Contact: Mr. Victor Olaotan Johnson - MD/CEO
Mr. Busola Williams - GM

McADOG & ASSOCIATES
Business: Engineering Consultancy Services
Address: 18, Hubert Ogunade Street, Alagomeji, Yaba, Lagos
Tel: (01) 2880726, 4701928 **Fax:** (01) 2880726
E-mail: mcadog@linkserve.com.ng
Website: www.mcadog.com
* Banex Plaza (Suite BS 50), Plot 750, Aminu Kano Crescent, Zone A7, Wuse II, Abuja.
Tel/Fax: (09) 41309034-5 (2L), 5239422
Contact: Egnr. Olalekan Ogunbayo
Engr. Usman Abdulraham

McDON INTERNATIONAL LIMITED
Business: Manufacturing of Paints; Importation of Pharmaceutical Products
Address: 14/16, Lerato Avenue, Ajala Bus-Stop, Ijaiye Ojokoro, Lagos
Tel: (01) 4924945, 7748462
Contact: Mr. McDonald O. K. Matthew - President/CEO

McDONALD SCIENTIFIC EMPORIUM
Business: Sales & Installation of Laboratory Scientific Equipment & Chemicals, Furniture & Fittings, Hospital Equipment & Suppliers, Supply of Educational Equipment, Computer Services
Address: McDonald House, Plot 152, Raymond Iromaka Close, by Festac/Amuwo-Odofin Flyover Bridge, Festac, Lagos
Tel: (01) 5890950, 5890546, 8043271 **Fax:** (01) 5890950
E-mail: mcdonald@mcdonaldscientific.com
Website: www.mcdonaldscientific.com
* Bobsar Complex (Suite C8), Plot 1035, Michika Street, off Ahmadu Bello Way, Garki II, Abuja
Tel: (09) 3148563

McFORD CONSULTING LIMITED
Business: Management & Human Resources Consultants
Address: 1, Motorways Avenue, opp. 7up Factory, Alausa, Ikeja, Lagos
Tel: (01) 4935333, 4973038
E-mail: mcfold@infoweb.abs.net
Contact: Mr. Biodun Ayinde - MD/CEO

McJIN NIGERIA LIMITED
Business: Marketers of Bathroom/Shower Product. 'BETTER LIVING PRODUCT PRODUCTS' Range
Address: Suite 5, Elpina Plaza, Plot 642c Akin Adesola Street, Victoria Island, Lagos
Tel: (01) 2691504
Contact: Isioma Jennifer Nwabueke - MD/CEO

McQUINTUS LIMITED
Business: Sales & Installation of Computers and Office Automation, Engineering Services
Address: 12, Oweh Street, Jibowu, Yaba, Lagos
Tel: (01) 4708750, 7730471, 7741408, 08022243510, 08034024040 **Fax:** (01) 8047914

E-mail: mcquintus@usa.net
mcquitus@hotmail.com
* Cornershop 21, Garki village Shopping Centre, Garki, Abuja.
Tel: (09) 2346886, 2348576, 08034024041
* 8, Old Aba Road, Port Harcourt.
Tel: (084) 571562, 08033088548
Contact: Mr. Felix Chukwu - MD/CEO

MCLATEK NIGERIA LIMITED
Business: Oilfield Engineering Services
Address: Plot 146, Trans-Amadi Ind. Layout, Port Harcourt
Tel: (084) 230388, 235125
E-mail: mclatek@mclatek.com

MCXRIS INTERNATIONAL LIMITED
Business: Import & Export Trading, International Trade Consultancy, Sales of Consumer Electronic Appliances, , Commerce & Communication Representatives
Address: 21, Warehouse Road, Apapa, Lagos
Tel: (01) 5872531, 8046007 **Fax:** (01) 5872531, 5872529
E-mail: mcxris@linkserve.com.ng

MECHANICAL & ELECTRICAL CONTRACTORS NIG. LTD
Business: Electrical Installations, Repair and Maintenance, Supply and Installation of Airconditioners, Security and Communication Equipment, Plumbing, Property Maintenance & Management
Address: 14, Ajasa Street, Onikan, Lagos
Tel: (01) 2631282, 3209501 **Fax:** (01) 3209500
Contact: Mr. A. O. Young - MD/CEO

MECON INDUSTRIES LIMITED
Business: Manufacture and Marketing of Cosmetics and Industrial Chemicals
Address: Trade Fair Complex (Site 22), Lagos-Badagry Expressway, Ojo, Lagos
Tel: (01) 7746317
Contact: Mr. Michael Ezeji - Chairman/CEO

MECUS VENTURES LIMITED
Business: Importation of UPS, Computers and Accessories
Address: Adekemi Adesanya Shopping Plaza, 70, Obafemi Awolowo Way, Ikeja, Lagos
Tel: (01) 4701589 **Fax:** (01) 5851295
E-mail: mecusventuresltd@yahoo.com
* Plot 1264 (Suite 24) Muhammadu Buhari Way, zone A3, before Central Bank, Garki II, Abuja
Tel: (09) 2348925-6 (2L)
Contact: Engr. Basil N. Obishili - Chairman/CEO

MEDAC PHARMACEUTICALS LIMITED
Business: Production & Distribution of Pharmaceuticals
Address: 49, Ire-Akari Estate Road, Isolo, Lagos
Tel: (01) 521189 **Fax:** (01) 523808
E- mail: medacpham@hotmail.com
Contact: Chief L. A. Akintola - Chairman/CEO

MEDCOM NIGERIA LIMITED
Business: Sales & Installation of Telecommunication Systems & Equipment, Power-Protection Products
Address: 38A, Saka Tinubu Street, Victoria Island, Lagos
Tel: (01) 3201202-3 (2L), 3201407, 08023110043.
Fax: (01) 3201203
E-mail: medcom@cyberspace.net.ng
medcom@hyperia.com
Contact: Engr. C. A. Joseph - Chairman
Una Brooms - GM (Operations)

MEDEXIA LIMITED
Business: Medical Expenses Administration, Medical Scheme
Address: 221, Ikorodu Road, Ilupeju, Lagos
Tel: (01) 4968370-2 (3L), 7749475 **Fax:** (01) 4968373
Contact: Mr. J. O. Emmanuel - Chairman
Mr. S. O. Salami - Manager

MEDIA INTERNATIONAL LIMITED
Business: Film and Television Production, Digital Post Production, Non-Linear Editing
Address: 33, Modupe Johnson Crescent, off Adeniran Ogunsanya Street, Surulere, Lagos
Tel: (01) 4718642, 5837826, 08033108417, 08042146708
E-mail: mediant@infoweb.abs.net
Contact: Chief Olawole Babatunde Oloyede - MD/CEO

MEDIA LINK LIMITED
Business: Outdoor Advertising
Address: 6, Oyetola Idowu Street, off Sura Mogaji Street, Ilupeju, Lagos
Tel: (01) 5553312, 5553314, 7745710, 7730165
Contact: Mr. Foluso Babu Akinbobola - Chairman/CEO

MEDIA PLANNING SERVICES LIMITED
Busines: Marketing & Media-Planning Consultancy Services
Address: 1, Tafawa Balewa Crescent, off Adeniran Ogunsanya Street, Surulere, Lagos
Tel: (01) 5455206, 5850321
E-mail: mps@mpsnigeria.com
Website: www.mpsnigeria.com
Contact: Mr. Austin Enwemasor - Exec. Director/CEO

MEDIA SPACE LIMITED
Business: Outdoor Advertising
Address: 2A, Nnobi Street, Ikate, Surulere, Lagos
Tel: (01) 834923, 4817144, 08033003111
Contact: Mr. Bola Ashiru - Chairman

MEDIA TECHNIQUES NIGERIA LIMITED
Business: Publishing of Magazines
Address: 3B, Allen Lane, off Allen Avenue, Ikeja, Lagos
Tel: (01) 4974038-9 (2L), 7917074, 7947260
* 5, Mombassa Street, Wuse Zone 5, Abuja.
Tel: (09) 5235119; 6717586
* 47, Ikwerre Road, Port Harcourt
Contact: Mr. Seye Kehinde - Publisher/Editor-in-Chief

MEDIA TRUST LIMITED
Business: Newspaper Publishing, Media Consultants
Address: 22, Lusaka St, off Bissau St, Wuse Zone 6, Abuja
Tel: (09) 5238726, 5235787, 5238725 **Fax:** (09) 5238725
E-mail: dailytrust2@yahoo.co.uk
* 6, Sullubawa Close, off Katutu Road, Unguwar Sarki G.R.A., Kaduna
Tel: (062) 233734, 245916 **Fax:** (062) 242496
E-mail: mtrust1@inet-global.com

* 260C, Murtala Moh'd Way, Alagomeji, Yaba, Lagos
Tel: (01) 4707296, 861008 **Fax:** (01) 861008
Contact: Mal. Kabiru Yusuf - Editor-in-Chief/CEO

MEDIA WORLD LIMITED
Business: Media Consultancy and Advertising Services
Address: Stock Exchange House (14th Floor), 2/4, Customs Street, off Marina, Lagos
Tel: (01) 2642379 **Fax:** (01) 2642380
Contact: Dr. Ngozi Anyaegbunam - MD/CEO

MEDIAPLUS INTERNATIONAL LIMITED
Business: Advertising and Marketing Communications
Address: 117B, Itafaji Road, off Corporation Drive, Dolphin Estate, Lagos
Tel: (01) 5851237, 4701523 **Fax:** (01) 5851237
E-mail: mediaplus@nigol.net.ng
Website: ww.mediaplus-nig.com
Contact: Mr. Patrick Godwin Okebie - Chairman/CEO

MEDICAL CONSULTANT SERVICE LIMITED
Business: Medical Services, Hospital Operations, Health Scheme Consultancy
Address: Maryland Medical Centre, Maryland Crescent, Maryland, Ikeja, Lagos
Tel: (01) 4707711, 08033255533
E-mail: mdconsere@aol.com
Contact: Mr. Andrew Dada - MD/CEO

MEDICOMAT NIGERIA LIMITED
Business: Sales of Acupunture Health-Care Devices, Acupuncture Treatment
Address: 1, Igbosere Road, Lagos Island, Lagos
Tel: (01) 2646059, 08034715440, 08037140906
E-mail: medicomat_nig_ltd@yahoo.com
Website: www.medicomat-ng.com
Contact: Mr. Olugboyeega Badejo - Chairman
Mrs. Debo Anifowoshe - MD/CEO

MEDIASERVE NIGERIA LIMITED
Business: Advertising Agency
Address: 3, Banjo Street, off Tejuosho St, Surulere, Lagos
Tel: (01) 840679
Contact: Mr. A. Oyebolu - Chairman/CEO

MEDICUS INDUSTRIES LIMITED
Business: Manufacturing & Marketing of Cosmetic Products
Address: 17D, Civic Centre Road, Kano
Tel: (064) 639656 **Fax:** (064) 646980
* Plot 14, Challawa Industrial Estate, Kano

MED-IN SPECIALIST HOSPITAL
Business: Medical, Healthcare & Diagnostic Services,
Address: 1 & 3, Osogbo Street, Ogudu, Ikeja, Lagos
Tel: (01) 4961964, 7736599, 8042155, 08033052001, 08033034354, 08033086464, 08033086596
Website: www.med-in.com

MEDITERRANEAN ENGINEERING SERVICE LIMITED
Business: Oilfield Engineering Services.
Address: 59, Woji Road, G.R.A. Phase II, Port Harcourt
Tel: (084) 233043
Contact: Dr. Steve I. I. Ihedigbo - Chairman

MEDITERRANEAN SPAS & SWIMMING POOLS LIMITED
Business: Sales, Installation and Maintenance of Swimming Pools and Spas
Address: Theodolite House, 306, Ikorodu Rd, Anthony, Lagos
Tel: (01) 4935758, 08023006312, 08023116254
Contact: Pastor (Engr) Solomon Ojie - MD/CEO

MEDREICH NIGERIA LIMITED
Business: Import & Distribution of Pharmaceutical Products
Address: 8B, Fabac Close, off Ligali Ayorinde Street, Victoria Island Annex, Lagos
Tel: (01) 2614466, 4619998, 8043456
E-mail: medreichltd@yahoo.co.uk

MEGA ALUMINIUM & BUILDING SERVICES LIMITED
Business: Fabrication and Installation of Aluminium Building Products (Roofing, Doors, Windows, Partitions)
Address: 38B, Yaya Abatan Street, Ogba, Ikeja, Lagos
Tel: (01) 2905928, 3450507, 4933162, 08033451880
E-mail: megalum2000@yahoo.com
Contact: Engr. Femi Sosanya - Chairman/CEO

MEGA EQUITIES LIMITED
Business: Stockbroking, Asset & Portfolio Management, Financial Advisory & Consultancy Services
Address: Investment House Annex (5th Floor, Suite 8), 21/25, Broad Street, Lagos Island, Lagos
Tel: (01) 2669746, 2668705 **Fax:** (01) 2668705
E-mail: megaequities@hyperia.com
* Zone B, Block 3 (Shop 70), ASPAMDA Plaza, Trade Fair Complex, Badagry Expressway, Lagos
Tel: (01) 8127728

MEGA HILTON HOTELS
Business: Hospitality Services, Hospitality Management, Catering Consultancy Services
Address: 82, Refinery Road, Ekpan-Warri
Tel: (053) 32106-7 (2L), 450510-3 (3L), 08033545515
Fax: (053) 321106-7 (2L)
E-mail: info@megahilto.com
Website: www.megahilton.com
Contact: Dr. B. B. Ayade - Chairman

MEGA INVESTMENT NIGERIA LIMITED
(Mega Plaza Century 21 Mall)
Business: Sales of Household Appliances, Electronics, Office & Telecommunication Equipment, Sports & Fitness Equipment, Restaurant Services
Address: 14, Idowu Martins Street, Victoria Island, Lagos
Tel: (01) 2624624-6 (3L), 618860, 613341-2 (2L), 619942, 4616999
E-mail: megaplaza4u@hotmail.com
alon_mega@yahoo.com
Website: www.megaplaza4u.com
Contact: Mr. Alon Nelken - Chairman/CEO

MEGA SOURCE NETWORK INCORPORATED
Business: Sales & Maintenance of Computers
Address: 12B, Otigba Street, off Obafemi Awolowo Way, Ikeja, Lagos
Tel/Fax: (01) 4968122
E-mail: mega-sources@hotmail.com
Website: www.megasourcenet.com

c/o Supra Telecom, 12, Addis Ababa Crescent, Wuse Zone 4, Abuja.
Tel: (09) 5234582
c/o King's Computers, 30, Deco Road, Warri
Tel: (053) 256106
Contact: Mr. M. O. Mekuleyi - MD/CEO

MEGA TREND INVESTMENT COMPANY LIMITED
Business: Real Estate Development & Management
Address: 86, Woji Road, G.R.A. Phase II, Port Harcourt
Tel: (084) 572784, 574411, 574422 **Fax:** (084) 236075

MEGACREDITS LIMITED
Business: Stockbroking, Financing, Consultancy Services
Address: 26, Ajasa Street, Onikan, Lagos
Tel: (01) 2647407, 2647408, 2637439
Contact: Obasola Shoderu - Exec. Chairman

MEGAPROJEKT CONSORTIUM
Business: Turnkey Contracting
Address: Plot 170B, Gbagada Estate, Oworonsoki-Gbagada Expressway, Gbagada, Lagos
Tel: (01) 5552338, 7742604 **Fax:** (01) 5552212
E-mail: commerz@beta.linkserve.com
Contact: Dr. F. A. O. Alade - Chairman/CEO

MEGASCREEN LIMITED
Business: Outdoor Audiovisual Broadcasting, Advertising
Address: 3, Ade-Akinsanya Way, off Town Planning Way, Ilupeju, Lagos.
Tel: (01) 7730615, 08033078876, 08033083693
Fax: (01) 4528197

MEGASTAR TECHNICAL & CONSTRUCTION CO. LIMITED
Business: Technical Engineering and Construction Services for the Oil Industry
Address: 100, East-West Road, opp. Alo Aluminium, Rumuokoro, Port Harcourt
Tel: (084) 571485, 572034, 610434, 610899 * (082) 440554
Fax: (084) 551554
E-mail: megastar1988#yahoo.com
Contact: Arc. Harcourt B. Adukeh - MD/CEO

MEGATECH SOFTWARE LIMITED
Business: Information Technology Systems Engineering, Integration & Networking; Software Consultancy; Programming; Installation and Support Services
Address: 13, Alh. Kanike Close, off Awolowo Road, S.W. Ikoyi, Lagos
Tel: (01) 2691069, 2691073, 2670710 **Fax:** (01) 2691078
E-mail: megatech@linkserve.com.ng
Contact: Mr. Etim Amana - Chairman
Blessing Iyalla - MD/CEO

MEGATEK NIGERIA LIMITED
Business: Importation of Computers, General Merchandising
Address: 10, Ijora Causeway, Ijora, Lagos
Tel: (01) 8043134, 5804273, 7756452 **Fax:** (01) 2614298
E-mail: megatekng@yahoo.com
Contact: Mr. Maurice Khawam, Jnr. - MD/CEO

MEGER NIGERIA LIMITED
Business: Sales, Installation and Service of Jacuzzi, Italian Furniture, Lighting, Marbles/Tiles, Kitchen Cabinets, Sanitary Wares and Matching Tiles
Address: Constitution Avenue, Central Business District, Garki, Abuja
Tel/Fax: (09) 2347317
* Plot 1310, Karimu Kotun Street, V/ Island, Lagos
Tel: (01) 2610594, 7744194 **Fax:** (01) 5891294
* 26, Constitution Road, Kaduna.
Tel: (062) 236506
Contact: Chief Vincent Igwenagha - Chairman
Mr. Jude Igwe - MD/CEO

MEKIOS LIMITED
Business: Design, Manufacture & Installation of Sewage Effluent & Water Treatment Plant; Design, Fabrication and Erection of Structural Steel Works, Ware-Houses, Storage Facilities, Civil, Electrical and Mechanical Engineering Services and Consultancy
Address: 27/29, Jimoh Odutola Street, Iganmu Industrial Estate, Iganmu, Lagos
Tel: (01) 2635244, 2635128, 2633646, 2631400, 849577, 836985, 08033063106
Fax: (01) 2691891, 2692364
Contact: Chief Michael O. Obomhense - Chairman/CEO

MELAGRO EXPORTS LIMITED
Business: Exportation of Agricultural Products
Address: Plot 292C, Ajose Adeogun Street, (House B), Victoria Island, Lagos
Tel: (01) 2623368, 2623370, 2623433 **Fax:** (01) 2623369
* 3, Blind Centre Way, Matori, Oshodi, Lagos
Tel: (01) 4527128, 4527470, 4523387 **Fax:** 01) 4528111
Contact: Mr. R. Chauhan - GM

MELSONS LIMITED
Business: Importation & Sales of Electrical Appliances, Cmmodities & Products
Address: 3, Blind Centre Road, Cappa Bus-Stop Agege Motor Road, Oshodi, Lagos
Tel: (01) 4523387, 4527128, 4527470, 7743153
Fax: (01) 4522951
E-mail: headoffice@melsonsgroup.com
* 1A, Unity Road, Kano
Tel: (064) 634417
Contact: Mr. M. U. Melwani - MD/CEO

MEMMS WEST AFRICA LIMITED
Business: Paper Recycling and Conversion, Manufacturing of Paints
Address: Km. 3, Onitsha - Owerri Road, Onitsha
Tel: (046) 217168, 218974
Contact: Sir. F. O. Maduka - Chairman/CEO

MEN'S AFFAIRS LIMITED
Business: Fashion Sales Outlets for Men
Address: 33, Opebi Road, Ikeja, Lagos
Tel: (01) 4965302
* 21, Aba Road, Port Harcourt.
Tel: (084) 238553
* Iluobe Shopping Plaza, Plot 598, Kashim Ibrahim Way, Wuse II, Abuja.
Tel: (09) 5230062
Contact: Mr. Chris Iluobe - MD/CEO

MENTHOLATUM (NIGERIA) LIMITED
Business: Manufacturing and Marketing of Pharmaceuticals, Toiletries and Cosmetics
Address: Plot 50, Sharada Industrial Estate Phase I, Kano
Tel: (064) 666382, 661368 **Fax:** (064) 661368
E-mail: mustapha@ecnx.net
Contact: Alh. (Dr.) Aminu Dantata - Chairman
Alh. Umar M. Mustapha - MD/CEO

MENTOR & HOPKINS INSURANCE BROKERS LIMITED
Business: Insurance Broking
Address: 4, Alh. Salisu St, off Ikorodu Rd, Obanikoro, Lagos
Tel/Fax: (01) 4960311
Contact: Otunba S. K. Onafowokan - Chairman
Alh. A. O. Saliu - MD/CEO

MERCOV SECURITIES LIMITED
Business: Stockbroking
Address: Dolphin Shopping Plaza (1st Floor, Suite D102), Dolphin Estate, Ikoyi, Lagos
Tel: (01) 4614069, 4708128, 2694613
E-mail: mercovsec@beta.linkserve.com
Contact: Mrs. A. A. Ajayi - MD/CEO

MERCURY ENGINEERING & CONSTRUCTION CO. LIMITED
Business: Building & Civil Engineering Construction
Address: 308, Port Harcourt/Aba Expressway, Port Harcourt
Tel: (084) 612993 **Fax:** (084) 612992
E-mail: mecng@yahoo.com
Contact: Mr. Joe Beany - Chairman
Mr. Domingo Baini - MD/CEO

MERCYFAITH INSURANCE BROKERS LIMITED
Business: Insurance Broking
Address: 150, Warri/Sapele Road, Warri
Tel: (053) 252796, 252725
Contact: Mr. Lucky M. Edon - MD/CEO

MERGALLI & COMPANY NIGERIA LIMITED
Business: Construction Engineering
Address: 9, Kachia Rd,by Mr. Bigg's Kaduna South, Kaduna
Tel: (062) 231082
Contact: Mr. Mosca Marlo - MD/CEO

MERIT STEVEDORING LIMITED
(formerly Merit Shiipping Co. Nigeria Limited)
Business: Shipping, Haulage, Affreightment of Petroleum Products, Bunkering & Chandling, Clearing & Forwarding, Sales and Maintenance of Maritime Equipment and Spares, Harbour Works, Towage and Anchorage, Stevedoring, Investment
Address: Banker's House, (3rd Floor), Plot PC. 19A, Adeola Hopewell Street, Victoria Island, Lagos
Tel: (01) 2620947, 3204075, 7743920 **Fax:** (01) 3204075
E-mail: merit@hyperia.com
* Plot 143, Lusaka Street, Wuse Zone 6, Abuja
* Orosi House, 38, Forces Avenue, Port Harcourt
Contact: Dr. Edmund Daukoru - Vice Chairman
Ms Wilma Aguele - MD/CEO

MERIT VENTURES (NIGERIA) LIMITED
Business: Importation, Marketing and Distribution of Pharmaceuticals, Cosmetics and Personal Products
Address: 13/15, Issa Williams Street, off Broad Street, Lagos
Tel/Fax: (01) 2664115, 08037235131
Contact: Engr. Emma Obi-Okoye - Chairman/CEO

MERYT ADVERTISING LIMITED
Business: Advertising Agency
Address: 7, Aroyewun Street, by Ramat Bus-Stop, Ogudu G. R. A., Lagos
Tel: (01) 4976135, 4701439 **Fax:** (01) 4976135
E-mail: merytad@beta.linkserve.com
Contact: I. S. Moemeke - Chairman
R. O. C. Mgbatogu - MD/CEO

MESHICO ENTERPRISES LIMITED
Business: Industrial & Commercial Printing Services
Address: 18, Ashaolu Street, off Akilo Road, Ogba, Lagos
Tel: 08023071276
* 114/116, Igi-Olugbin Street (Awofodu Bus-Stop), Pedro-Shomolu, Lagos
Tel: (01) 5820047
Contact: Mr. Olatunji Meshioye - MD/CEO

MESO INDUSTRIES LIMITED
Business: Cargo Superintendence, Import and Export, Consultancy Services, Haulage, Manufacturing
Address: Eleganza Plaza (Libra Block, 1st Floor), Aerodrome Road, Apapa, Lagos
Tel/Fax: (01) 5450870, 5874796
E-mail: meso@nigol.net.ng
Contact: Odawe A. Muzan - MD/CEO

MESSAGE SYSTEMS LIMITED
Business: Telecommunication Service Providers
Address: 76, Awolowo Road, S. W. Ikoyi, Lagos
Tel: (01) 2695786-8 (3L) **Fax:** (01) 2695788
E-mail: messages@siotel.com
* Savannah Bank Building, 60/62, Broad St, Lagos
Contact: Chief A. O. Obioha - Chairman/CEO

MET NIGERIA LIMITED
Business: Sales and Maintenance of Pneumatic Equipment, Training, Industrial Maintenance Services
Address: 603, Agege Motor Road, Shogunle, Lagos
Tel/Fax: (01) 2885309, 7744273, 08023110111
E-mail: metpneumatics@yahoo.com
Contact: Mr. Samuel A. Ogundipe - MD/CEO

METAL FURNITURE (NIGERIA) LIMITED
Business: Manufacture of Office & Domestic Metal Furniture
Address: 1, Mobolaji Bank-Anthony Way, Ikeja, Lagos
Tel: (01) 4938371, 4938373, 4938375, 4964512, 4964544
Fax: (01) 4964674
Contact: Mr. S. O. Oyefusi - GM.

METAL SECURITY PRODUCTS LIMITED
Business: Manufacturing of Motor Vehicle Parts, Solar Water Heater, Modular Form for Building, Headpan, Shovel & Spade, Wooden Furniture, Security Locks, Agricultural Tools and Cooking Utensils
Address: Plot 45, Challawa Industrial Estate, Kano
Tel: (064) 623397, 08023104323 **Fax:** (064) 632395
Contact: Dr. Mohammed Lawal Koguna - Chairman
Mr. Kemal Isler - MD/CEO

METALUM LIMITED
Business: Manufacture of Aluminium Doors, Windows, Partitions, Curtain Walls, Roofing & Cladding
Address: Plot 5, Block D, Wempco Road, Ogba Industrial Layout, Ikeja, Lagos
Tel: (01) 4922221, 4922250, 7753997-8 (2L), 7764237
Fax: (01) 4922332
Contact: Mr. W. Stauffacher - MD/CEO

METOXIDE (NIGERIA) LIMITED
Business: Manufacturing, Importation and Marketing of Industrial Chemicals
Address: Km. 8, Abeokuta-Lagos Road, Abeokuta
Tel: (039) 240541, 243492, 243072 **Fax:** (039) 242563
E-mail: metoxide@infoweb.abs.net
Contact: Chief A. O. Abudu - Chairman
Mr. V. J. Janakiraman - MD/CEO

METRIC INSURANCE BROKERS LIMITED
Business: Insurance Broking and Pension Consultancy
Address: 58, Simpson St (Ground Floor), Ebute-Metta, Lagos
Tel: (01) 4804846, 864221, 864752 **Fax:** (01) 864221
* Zone 4 Cornershops, Wuse Zone 4, Abuja.
Tel: (09) 5238686, 6702096
Contact: Mrs. Yetunde A. Adebajo - MD/CEO

METRO CONSULTANTS
Business: Architecture & Architectural Support Services, Engineering & Construction
Address: 19, Ramat Crescent, Ogudu G.R.A., Lagos
Tel/Fax: (01) 5550186
E-mail: metrocon@beta.linkserve.com
Contact: Arc. Nnamdi Anombem - MD/CEO

METRO EYES NIGERIA LIMITED
Business: Eye Clinic, Optical Services, Manufacturing of Optical Care Products
Address: Lapal House, 235, Igbosere Rd, Lagos Island, Lagos
Tel: (01) 2636929, 2631424, 4745824, 08023410634
Fax: (01) 2635531
E-mail: metroeyes@hotmail.com
* Plot 10B, Kigoma Street, Wuse Zone 7, Abuja
Tel: (09) 5237915, 08023012067
Contact: Mrs. M. B. Oyeleye - Chairman/CEO

METRO PERIL INSURANCE BROKERS LIMITED
Business: Insurance Broking and Consultancy Services
Address: 5, Simpson Street, Lagos Island, Lagos
Tel: (01) 2635694, 7931553, 08023108636, 08023125457
Fax: (01) 2635694
Contact: Mr. E. O. Komolafe - MD/CEO

METRONEX NIGERIA LIMITED
Business: Supply of Scientific, Laboratory, Hospital & Agricultural Equipments
Address: Metronex House, 274, Effurun/Sapele Road, Effurun, P.O.Box 475, Warri
Tel: (053) 252745, 252248
Contact: Chief E. H. O. Okene - Chairman/CEO

METROPOLITAN BANK LIMITED
Business: Merchant Banking
Address: 24, Idowu Taylor Street, Victoria Island, Lagos
Tel: (01) 2612036, 3200500-4 (5L), 4617585, 4617690
Fax: (01) 2612938
E-mail: mmb@mmb-ng.com
Website: www.metropolitanbanklimited.com
* Owena House, Plot 76, 4TH Avenue, Central Business District, Garki, Abuja
Tel: (09) 2347790-1 (2L) **Fax:** (09) 2344326
Contact: Chief S. O. Bakare - Chairman
Mr. Muyiwa M. Bakare - MD/CEO

METROPOLITAN GROUP OF COMPANIES
Business: Manufacturer of Footwears, PVC & PU Soles, Polyprophylene Woven Sacks, PVC Compound, Rubber Products, Textiles & Fishing Net
Address: 7/11 (Old 16), Industrial Avenue, Ilupeju, Lagos
Tel: (01) 4968175-9, 4962197 **Fax:** (01) 4961884
E-mail: metro@infoweb.abs.net
Contact: Mr. N. G. Patel - Chairman/CEO
Mr. P. I. Vaidya - ED

METROPOLITAN MOTORS LIMITED
Business: Sales of Motor Vehicle
Address: 1, Joel Ogunnaike Street, by Mobolaji Bank-Anthony Way, opp. Lagos Country Club, G.R.A., Ikeja, Lagos
Tel: (01) 4939761-2 (2 L), 4938370, 7738970
Fax: (01) 4939761
E-mail: metromotors@hotmail.com

METROPOLITAN TRUST INSURANCE COMPANY LIMITED
Business: Non-Life Insurance
Address: 266, Ikorodu Road, Obanikoro, Lagos
Tel: (01) 4936211, 4938085 **Fax:** (01) 4936211
E-mail: metrotrust@infoweb.abs.net
* Plot 516, Sultan Abubakar Way, Wuse Zone 2, Abuja
* 24, Ikwerre Road, Port Harcourt
Contact: Alh. R. O .Yussuff - Chairman
Mr. 'Segun Balogun - MD/CEO

MEZ INDUSTRIES LIMITED
Business: Production of Industrial Chemicals for Technical, Food, Pharmaceutical & Petroleum Sectors
Address: 12, Simbiat Abiola Road Ikeja, Lagos
Tel: (01) 4972522 **Fax:** (01) 4971015
E-mail: mezindustries@yahoo.com
* 204, Aba Road, Port Harcourt
Contact: Engr. M. S. Ife - MD/CEO

MEZUE ASSOCIATES
Business: Estate Surveyors & Valuers, Estate Agents, Projects, Property & Environmental Management
Address: Old ACB Building, 9, Ogui Road, Enugu
Tel: (042) 254218 **Fax:** (042) 252087
E-mail: mezuea@infoweb.abs.net
Website: www.mezuea.com
Contact: Chief L. C. Mezue - Principal Partner/CEO

MF COMMUNICATIONS LIMITED
Business: Telecommunication Service, GSM Services
Address: 59, Campbell Street, Lagos Island, Lagos
Tel: (01) 2646286, 2636613, 4701760 **Fax:** (01) 2636613
Contact: Chief Fred Okey Nzeako - MD/CEO

MFI & ASSOCIATES LIMITED
Business: Publishing of Business Directores, Direct Marketing Services, Customised Information Services
Address: 39C, Sura Mogaji St, off Coker Rd, Ilupeju, Lagos
Tel: (01) 7748470, 08033181931, 08055184288
E-mail: mfi@infoweb.abs.net
Contact: Mr. F. R. A. Williams, Jnr - Chairman
Mrs. Layo Fajemisin Ajayi - MD/CEO

MFP LIMITED (Modern Foundry Products Ltd)
Business: Production and Installation of Satellite Dishes and DSTV Systems; Retail and Maintenance of Computer; Networking
Address: 2, Vanguard Avenue, off Carrara Marble, Kirikiri Canal, off Oshodi-Apapa Expressway, near Mile 2, Apapa, Lagos
Tel: (01) 5450313, 5872861 **Fax:** (01) 5450530
E-mail: sales@mfp.net
sales@j4group.com
info@j4group.com
Website: www.mfp.net
Contact: Dr. Franklin Adejuwon - Chairman
Mr. Hassan Nasar Jarmakani - MD/CEO

MGI ALABI EKUNDARE
Business: Chartered Accontants, Auditing & Taxation Services, Consultancy
Address: 2A, Montgomery Road, Yaba, Lagos
Tel: (01) 4822138, 866360, 861385 **Fax:** (01) 4962525
E-mail: mgie@skannet.com
Contact: Chief Alfred Bandele Alabi - Founding Partner
F. M. Ekundare - MD/CEO

M-GOLD COMMUNICATIONS LIMITED
Business: Marketing Communications
Address: 28, Aba Johnston Crescent, off Adeniyi Jones Avenue, Ikeja, Lagos
Tel: (01) 4970761, 8042183 **Fax:** (01) 4970761
E-mail: mdcomm@infoweb.abs.net
Contact: Chief Olufemi Kufo - Chairman/CEO

MIAGRO LIMITED (Formerly Niagro Ltd.)
Business: Sales of Agricultural Tractors & Equipment, Agro-Chemicals, Fertilizers and Animal Health Products
Address: 31B, Isa Kaita Rd, Unguwar Sarki G.R.A., Kaduna
Tel: (062) 249208, 373475
E-mail: miagroltd@yahoo.com
* 1A, Dakar Road, Apapa G.R.A., Lagos
Tel: (01) 5451951-1 (2L) **Fax:** (01) 5450034
Contact: Mahmood Tauhid Usman - MD/CEO

MI INDUSTRIES NIGERIA LIMITED
Business: Importation, Marketing and Distribution of Commodities and General Merchandise
Address: Plot C89, Amuwo-Odofin Industrial Layout, Oshodi-Apapa Expressway, Amuwo-Odofin, Lagos
Tel: (01) 7730726-7 (2L) **Fax:** (01) 2691920
E-mail: minndustries@hotmail.com

MICADE CONSULTANCY SERVICES
Business: Public Relations & Advertising; Publication, Conference/Seminar Planning, Commision Agency
Address: Block A. A. 28 (A), Ibadan North-East L. G. Office Complex, Agodi Ibadan
Tel: (02) 712313, 715345
Contact: Chief Yemi Akinemi, JP - Chairman/CEO

MicCOM CABLES AND WIRES LIMITED
Business: Manufacture of Electric Cables
Address: Edun-Alaran Road, Behind Ahmadiya Hospital, Ojokoro-Agege, Lagos
Tel: (01) 4922724, 4921890, 4926223 **Fax:** (01) 4924861
E-mail: miccomng@aol.com
* Plot 500, Tafawa Balewa Way, (Suite B-21), opposite Afribank, Garki Area 3, Abuja
Tel: (09) 2347756, 2347757
Contact: Engr. Michael A. Ponnle - GM

MICHAEL ADEFILA BOOKSHOPS
Business: Books Distribution and Sales, Library Consultancy
Address: 33/35, Ojuelegba Road, Surulere, Lagos
Tel: (01) 7743989, 5456556 **Fax:** (01) 2646084, 5456556
E-mail: madefila@infoweb.abs.net

MICHAEL HAMMOND ENGINEERING COMPANY LIMITED
Business: Sales, Installation & Support of Power-Protection Equipment, Security Cardkey Systems, Fire Detection & Fighting Systems, Security & Surveillance Systems, Structured Cabling, Computer Site Preparation
Address: 31, Aba Johnson Crescent, off Adeniyi Jones Avenue, Ikeja, Lagos
Tel: (01) 4974830, 4710958, 4735766, 4735984, 3209358, 08033003640, 08033003644
Fax: (01) 5557609
E-mail: mhammond@infoweb.abs.net
Contact: Mr. M. A. Elewonibi - Chairman/CEO

MICHAEL OLUSEGUN ENTERPRISES LIMITED
Business: Distribution and Sales of Carpet, Underlays, Soft Furnishing, Furniture and Lighting Products, Interior Decoration, Building Construction and Renovation, Fabrication of Aluminium Partitioning, Paint Manufacturing
Address: 167, Ikorodu Road, Onipanu, Lagos
Tel: (01) 4712167, 825496, 08023050067, 08023386204
Fax: (01) 5820575, 821509
E-mail: mikeodecor@yahoo.com
Contact: Chief Michael O. Sonaya - Chairman/CEO

MICHAEL STEVENS CONSULTING
Business: Training and Manpower Development, Financial Consulting, Auditing, Executive Search
Address: 1, Alh. Tokan Street, Alaka Estate, Surulere, Lagos
Tel: (01) 5851794, 7742512, 7915257, 830367, 08033837987 **Fax:** (01) 5851794
E-mail: msa@linkserve.com.ng
msa@cyberspace.net.ng
* Point Block (8th Floor), State Secretariat, Port Harcourt
Tel: (084) 573803
Contact: Mr. Francis O. Kudayah - Chairman/MD

MICHAKINSON (WEST AFRICA) COMPANY LIMITED
Business: Merchandise Distribution, Marketing Consultancy
Address: 71A, Agodokome Street (3rd Floor),

off Ashogbon Street, Isale-Eko, Apapa, Lagos
Tel: (01) 2644953 **Fax:** (01) 2644953, 2663944
E-mail: michakinson@yahoo.com
Contact: Mr. Michael O. Akinleye - MD/CEO

MICHANI ENTERPRISES LIMITED
Business: Property, Office and Industrial Cleaning, Pest Control Service, Laundry & Drycleaning Services, Production of REMS Custard
Address: 13, Arikewuyo St, off Majolate St, Onipanu, Lagos
Tel: (01) 5821312, 08033161272
Contact: Chief M. A. Aniyikaiye - MD/CEO

MICHELIN (NIGERIA) LIMITED
Business: Manufacture of Motor Vehicles Tyres & Tubes
Address: Plot 129-132, Trans-Amadi Industrial Layout, Port Harcourt
Tel: (084) 237555, 237557, 237560, 237562
Fax: (084) 237130
Website: www.michelin.nigeria.com
* Plot 2A, Ijora Causeway, Ijora, Lagos
Tel: (01) 5831210-6 (7L), 5831810, 5834926, 5837267
Fax: (01) 5837131, 5837237
* Total House (5th Floor), Plot 247, Herbert Macaulay Way; Central Business District, Abuja
Tel: (09) 2346512, 2346213 **Fax:** (09) 2346799
Contact: Mr. O. Amah - MD/CEO

MICHELIN TYRE SERVICES COMPANY LIMITED
Business: Sales of Vehicle Tyres & Tubes
Address: Plot 2A, Ijora Causeway, Ijora, Lagos
Tel: (01) 5801210-6(7L), 5831810, 5834926, 774720-1(2L)
Fax: (01) 5837131
* Plots 129-132, Trans-Amadi Industrial Layout, Port Harcourt.
Tel: (084) 237555, 237557 Fax: (084) 239730
* Total House (5th Floor), Plot 247, Herbert Macaulay Way, Central Business District, Abuja
Tel: (09) 2346812, 2346813 **Fax:** (09) 2346799
Contact: Mr. Gial Galhie - MD/CEO
Mr. Niyi Adekoya - Lagos Site Manager

MICHELLE BONDED TERMINAL NIGERIA LIMITED
Business: Inland Port Services, Custom-Bonded Terminal Operations, Clearing and Forwarding
Address: Plot 61, Imam Dauda St, off Eric Moore Rd, Iganmu Industrial/Commercial Scheme, Surulere, Lagos
Tel: (01) 2646748, 2646746, 2646071, 802440-4 (5L)
Fax: (01) 2646066, 5454143, 5454144, 5456071
E-Mail: chrismatel@hyperia.com
Contact: Mr. Peter Eloka Okocha OON - Chairman
Mr. Ebuni Okocha - MD/CEO

MICKMONIS MULTI-SYSTEMS & INVESTMENT CO. LTD
Business: Sales of Computers, Solar-Energy Equipment, Telecommunication Equipment
Address: 20, Ahmadu Bello Way, Jos
Tel: (073) 450819, 415834-5 (2L)
E-mail: mickmonis@yahoo.com
* Cornershop 41, Wuse Shopping Complex, Zone 6, Wuse, Abuja
Tel: (09) 5236775

MIC-MERAH GROUP LIMITED
Business: Transportation Services, Courier Services, Importation and Sales of Auto Spare Parts, Marketing of Petroleum Products, Real Estate Development, Agriculture, General Commerce
Address: E 4/7-10, New Auto Spare Parts, Nkpor, Onitsha
Tel: (046) 251528, 08033424351, 08037028447, 08037045728, 08037057087 **Fax:** (046) 250357
Contact: Chief Michael C. Emerah - Chairman/CEO

MICRO PRODUCTS INTERNATIONAL (NIGERIA) LIMITED
Business: Sales and Services of Computers, Computer Engineering, Desk-Top Publishing, Training
Address: 14, Adeniran Ogunsanya Street, Surulere, Lagos
Tel: (01) 5850038, 5850656, 4707090, 4707089, 4700688, 4706881-2 (2L) **Fax:** (01) 5850038
E-mail: micro@alpha.linkserve.com
* Chicken House Estate, Plot 472, Ibrahim Badamosi Babangida Way, Wuse II, Abuja.
Tel: (09) 5235467, 5230173
* 129, Ikenegbu Layout, Port Harcourt
Tel: 08034041989
Contact: Mr. Chris N. Anugwolu - MD/CEO

MICRO-WAREHOUSE LIMITED
Business: Distribution of IBM Computers, Workstations, Monitors, PK Electronic UPS, APC UPS, COMPAQ Computers, Typewriters, Printers & Other office Automation Equipments
Address: AIICO Plaza (1st Floor, Front Wing), Afribank Street Victoria Island, Lagos
Tel: (01) 2615471, 7740418 **Fax:** (01) 2662557
E-mail: mwhgm@beta.linkserve.com
Contact: Mr. Sam Ifeozo - MD/CEO

MICROBOSS INTERNATIONAL LIMITED
Business: Sales and Installation, Maintenance and Repairs of Computer Hardware and Software, Networking, Software Design and Development, Corporate Training, School Support Services
Address: 17, Pade Odanye Close, off Alh. Jimoh Street, off Adeniyi Jones Avenue, Ikeja, Lagos
Tel: (01) 4974487 **Fax:** (01) 4921516-7 (2L)
E-mail: mbossintl@aol.com
Contact: Mr. Babawande A. Majekodunmi - Chairman/CEO

MICROBYTE INTERNATIONAL (NIGERIA) LIMITED
Business: Networking and Systems Integration, IT Training & Consultancy, Publishing
Address: Buffalo House, 2A, Allen Avenue, Ikeja, Lagos
Tel: (01) 4930572, 4939835, 4939836, 4939837, 8116307
Fax: (01) 4939837, 8117291
E-mail: training@mcrobytenic.com.ng
Website: www.microbyteinc.com.ng
Contact: Apostle (Dr.) H. I. Alile - Chairman
Mr. Dele Ajisomo - MD/CEO

MICROCOM SYSTEMS LIMITED
Business: Internet Service Provider
Address: 8, Adeleke Adedoyin Street, off Kofo Abayomi Street, Victoria Island, Lagos
Tel: (01) 2624855-9 (5L) **Fax:** (01) 2624857
E-mail: service@micro.com.ng

Website: www.micro.com.ng
Contact: Alh. Usman Mohammed - Chairman
Mr. Raghid Kheir - MD/CEO

MICRODEVICES NIGERIA LIMITED
Business: Sales, Installation and Maintenance of Computer and Accesories, Networking
Address: Buffalo House, 2, Allen Avenue, Ikeja, Lagos
Tel: (01) 4937771, 4978025, 4700996, 08033087049
Fax: (01) 4930184
E-mail: sales@microdeviceltd.com
Website: www.microdevicesltd.com
* 9, Mbonu St, D-Line, Port Harcourt.
Tel: (084) 482905, 572447, 08023144811

MICRO-GENESIS VENTURES LIMITED
Business: Bulk Sales of Industrial Chemicals, Raw Materials, Flavours, Food Colourants, Fragrances & Perfume
Address: 10/4, Bauchi Road, (Terminus), P. O. Box 6840, Jos
Tel: (073) 453310, 610856, 08023705046, 08033307558,
Fax: (073) 611873
Contact: Mr. Mike U. T. Uwanoshiri - Chairman/CEO

MICROSOFT NIGERIA LIMITED
Busines: Computer Software Development and Consultancy
Address: Octagon Building (3rd floor), 13A, A. J. Marinho Drive, Victoria Island, Lagos
Tel: (01) 2625233, 2625239 **Fax:** (01) 2626718
E-mail: infonig@microsoft.com
Website: www.microsoft.com

MICROTECH SYSTEMS LIMITED
Business: Hardware Engineering and Network Implementation, Sales and Maintenance of Computers, Consultancy, Software Development
Address: Plot 540, off Adetokunbo Ademola Crescent, Wuse II, Abuja
Tel/Fax: (09) 5235056
E-mail: microtech@hyperia.com
Contact: Dr. M. S. Abdulrahman - Chairman
Mr. Ibrahim Y. Maiyaki - MD/CEO

MICROTEL NIGERIA LIMITED
Business: Telecommunication Services
Address: Plot 522, Durban Street, off Adetokunbo Ademola Crescent, Wuse II, Abuja
Tel: (09) 5235133, 6702256-7 (2L) **Fax:** (09) 5235133
E-mail: sales@microtelng.com
* 45, Isaac John Street, Ikeja, G.R.A., Ikeja, Lagos
Tel: (01) 4973089, 4973088 **Fax:** (01) 4973089
Contact: Alh. Ibrahim Y. Maiyaki - MD/CEO

MICROTREND LIMITED
Business: Sales and Maintenance of Computers. Hardware Engineering and Networking; Consultancy
Address: Plot 212B, Muri Okunola Street, Victoria Is., Lagos
Tel: (01) 2629049, 3204191 Fax: (01) 2703651
E-mail: info@micro-trend.com
Website: www.micro-trend.com
Contact: Mr. Muyiwa Akinbolagbe - MD/CEO

MICROVIEW NIGERIA LIMITED
Business: Sales of Computers, Networking & Connectivity Products & Accessories
Address: Obafemi Awolowo House (2nd Floor), 27/29, Obafemi Awolowo Way, Ikeja, Lagos
Tel: (01) 7736519, 4745392
E-mail: microview@hotmail.com
* 55, Ogunlana Drive, Surulere, Lagos
Tel: (01) 7749015, 5456537 **Fax:** (01) 5456537

MICROWARE LIMITED
Business: Computer Sales and Engineering, Networking, Installation, Support, Training and Maintenance Services, Software Development
Address: 52, Awolowo Road, S.W. Ikoyi, Lagos
Tel: (01) 2695676 **Fax:** (01) 2691209
E-mail: microware@globenode.com
Contact: Mr. Johnson O. Oboni - MD/CEO

MICROWORKS NIGERIA LIMITED
Business: Help-Desk Support, Procurement, Internet Service Provider, Maintenance of Hardware and Software, Toner Recycling, Bandwidth Provision Services
Address: 229, Ikorodu Road, Ilupeju, Lagos
Tel: (01) 4931538-9 (2 L) **Fax:** (01) 493558
E-mail: sales@microworksnig.com
Website: www.microworksnig.com
* Plot 1271 (Block 16), Ogbomosho Street, Area 8, Garki, Abuja
* Thompson Estate, 22, Woji Road, Port Harcourt
Tel: (084) 484661, 571873
Contact: Mr. J. O. Bankole - MD/CEO

MID MARITIME SERVICES LIMITED
Business: Marine, Shipping & Air Freight Services, Clearing & Forwarding, Container Terminal Operator, Bulk Container/Ro-Ro Operator, General Merchants, General/Bonded Warehousing Services
Address: Plot 5, Via Nigeria Ports Auth, Second Gate, opp. Crown Flour Mills., Tin-Can Island, Apapa, Lagos
Tel: (01) 5872425, 5804940-4 (5 L), 5453950, 5874786, 5877165 **Fax:** (01) 5874792
Contact: Chief Felix Omo-Izirein - Group MD/CEO

MIDAS BANK PLC
Business: Banking Services
Address: 17, Sanusi Fafunwa Str, Victoria Island Annex, Lagos
Tel: (01) 2705911-2 (2L), 3200652-6 (5L)
E-mail: midasbank@midasbank.com
Website: www.midasbank.com
Contact: Mr Femi Agbaje - MD/CEO

MIDAS STOCKBROKERS LIMITED
Business: Stockbroking, Portfolio Management, Investment Advisory Service, LPO Financing
Address: 5, Ribadu Road (2nd Floor), off Awolowo Road, S. W. Ikoyi, Lagos
Tel: (01) 2694600, 4739088, 08023186980, 08033012039
E-mail: midasstock@yahoo.com
Contact: Olorogun (Dr.) Sonny F. Kuku - Chairman
Mr. Temidayo Adetolu - GM/CEO

MIDDLE EAST AIRLINES (NIGERIA)
Business: Airline (Passenger and Cargo Services)
Address: Consortium House (1st Floor), Plot 1682, Sanusi

	Fafunwa Street, Victoria Island, Lagos
Tel:	(01) 2705141-2 (2L) **Fax:** (01) 2622594
E-mail:	solphil@hotmail.com
	* 26, Post Office Road, Kano
Tel:	(064) 631337, 634919
Contact:	Mr. F. A. Wahid - GM

MIDDLE POINT (NIGERIA) LIMITED

Business: Importation and Sales of Motor Vehicle Spare Parts, General Merchandising
Address: 2A, Raymond Njoku Street, S. W. Ikoyi, Lagos
Tel: (01) 2672287, 2672288, 2691659
Contact: Mr. Joe Obijiaku - Chairman/CEO

MIDEN SYSTEMS LIMITED

Business: Oil & Gas Services
Address: Plot 206, Muri Okunola St, Victoria Island, Lagos
Tel/Fax: (01) 611092, 2695624
E-mail: miden_b@yahoo.coms
* 49, Liberation Stadium Road, Port Harcourt

MIDIVISION LIMITED

Business: Production of Audio and Video Materials, Records, Films, Documentaries and Commercials, Rental of Audiovisual Production Equipment
Address: 4, Eric Moore Close, Eric Moore Road, S/L, Lagos
Tel: (01) 7745100, 08023003687, 08033046560
Contact: Dr. Bayo Adepetun - Chief Executive

MIDLAND GALVANISING PRODUCTS LIMITED

Business: Manufacturing of Galvanised Roofing Coils, Sheet LPG Cylinders, Gas Cooker & Water Heaters
Address: Km. 10, Abeokuta-Lagos Rd, Abeokuta, Ogun State
Tel: (039) 242552, 240129, 242583, 242839, 242910
Fax: (039) 242552, 242695
E-mail: chiefabudu@indrop-int.com
* 3, Oyefeso Avenue, Ikorodu Rd, Obanikoro, Lagos
Tel: (01) 4974050, 4974221-2 (2L), 4976122
Contact: Chief (Dr.) J. C. Dugad - MD/CEO

MIDLAND SECURITIES LIMITED

Business: Stockbroking, Finance and Investments, Issuing House, Funds Management
Address: 10, Market Street, off Abibu-Oki Street, Lagos
Tel/Fax: (01) 2666291
Contact: Mr. Lawrence N. Onochie -MD/CEO

MIDLANDS LIMITED

Business: Supply, Installation and Maintenance of Lifts; Medical Equipment; Repairs, Refurbishment and Modernisation of Lifts and Airconditioners
Address: 28, Ajao Road, Surulere, Lagos
Tel: (01) 837241, 848333 **Fax:** (01) 4971015
Contact: Major Gen. Abubakar M. Waziri (rtd.) - Chairman
Chief (Mrs.) M. M. Obiyan - MD/CEO

MIDRON INSURANCE BROKERS LIMITED

Business: Insurance Broking
Address: 156, Obafemi Awolowo Way, Ikeja, Lagos
Tel: (01) 4933351, 08023085396, 08042141026
Fax: (01) 4933351
E-mail: midinsbro@yahoo.com
Contact: Mr. Olumide O. Ifederu - MD/CEO

MIDWAY AUTOMOTIVE COMPANY LIMITED

Business: Importation & Sales of New Motorcycles, Automobile Components, Spare Parts and Accessories
Address: 4, Edo-Ezemewi Road, Nnewi, Anambra State
Tel: (046) 460133, 460566 **Fax:** (046) 462118
E-mail: innoson@infoweb.abs.net
Contact: Mr. Innocent Chukwuma - Chairman

MIGFO NIGERIA LIMITED

Business: Shipping & Freight Forwarding, Container Terminal Operation, Importers & Exporters, Estate Agents
Address: Migfo House, 17, M.M. International Airport Road, Ajao Estate, Apakun-Oshodi, Lagos
Tel: (01) 7748140, 7741542 **Fax:** (01) 7748140
E-mail: migfo@beta.linkserve.com
Contact: Chief Mike C. Nwaukoni - Chairman/CEO

MIKADO NIGERIA LIMITED

Business: Security Guards Services, Sale & Installation of Security & Access Control Systems, Fire & Burglar Alarm Systems, Sale of Flavours & Concentrates
Address: Plot 206A, Muri Okunola Str, Victoria Island, Lagos
Tel: (01) 2626834, 4616564 **Fax:** (01) 2625681
E-mail: mikado @hyperia.com
Contact: Mr. Michael O. Ojeme - Chairman/CEO

MIKANO INTERNATIONAL LIMITED

Business: Sales, Installation, Rental & Service of Generators
Address: Plot 34, Acme Road, Ogba Ind. Estate, Ikeja, Lagos
Tel: (01) 4920252, 4922540, 4923419, 4924194, 4924213, 4926860, 4926525, 5557861-7 (7L), 5557999
Fax: (01) 4922540, 5557776
E-mail: constomercare@mikano-intl.com
Website: www.mikano-intl.com
* 62, Adeola Odeku Street, Victoria Island, Lagos
Tel: (01) 2624007, 2624373, 3200456 **Fax:** (01) 2624373
* Plot 487, Adetokunbo Ademola Crescent, Wuse II, Abuja.
Tel: (09) 5233997, 5231994
Contact: Amb. (Alh.) Shehu Malami - Chairman
Mr. Nidal Karameh - MD/CEO

MIKE DAD NIGERIA LIMITED

Business: Marketing of Electronic Products, Electrical Appliances, Airconditioners, Telecommunication Equipment and Musical Instruments
Address: B 274/277, Alaba International Market, Ojo, Lagos
Tel: (01) 2631550, 5891175, 5892578, 7743585
Fax: (01) 2631637, 5890303
E-mail: mikedad@hyperia.com
Contact: Chief Mike Okeke - Chairman/CEO

MIKE OKEREKE CONSULTING LIMITED

Business: Public Relations Consultants
Address: Palm Line Building (1st Floor), 11, Wharf Road, Apapa, Lagos
Tel: (01) 5803221, 5878179, 5874254, 5874256,
Fax: (01) 4931545, 5878179
E-mail: beectraining@alpha.linkserve.com
Contact: Mr. Mike Okereke - Chairman/CEO

MILAN NIGERIA LIMITED

Business: Importation & Distribution of General Merchandise

Address: 52A, Kofo Abayomi Street, Victoria Island, Lagos
Tel: (01) 4619703-4 (2 Lines) 4619706, 2626340
Fax: (01) 4619705

MILESTONE INSURANCE BROKERS LIMITED
Business: Insurance Broking
Address: 19, Pade Odanye Close, off Adeniyi Jones Avenue, Ikeja, Lagos
Tel: (01) 4965732, 4930175, 8128722
Contact: Chief S. I. Adegbite - Chairman
Mr. H. A. Oyinlola - GM/CEO

MILESTONE INTERNET SERVICES
Buiness: Internet Service Provider, Sales of Computers, LAN, WAN and VSAT Engineering
Address: Abuja Shopping Mall (Suites C4-C6), Maputo Street, Wuse Zone 3, Abuja
Tel: (09) 5238385, 08033139180 **Fax:** (09) 5238397
E-mail: info@milestones-ng.com
Website: www.milestones-ng.com
Contact: Major Gen. S. M. Dule (rtd.) - Chairman/CEO
Mr. Dipe Adedeji - GM (Administration)

MILLENIUM TRADING COMPANY LIMITED
Business: Importation of Plasterboards and Glass Blocks
Address: 160, Awolowo Road, (1st Floor), S.W. Ikoyi, Lagos
Tel: (01) 2692429, 2695771, 2695770 **Fax:** (01) 2693034
Contact: Mr. Ladi Adelekan - MD/CEO

MILLENNIA INTERIORS
Business: Sales of Office Furnishings
Address: Guru Plaza, inside Park 'n' Shop Premises, 47B, Adeola Odeku Street, Victoria Island, Lagos
Tel: (01) 2623291-5 (5 L) **Fax:** (01) 2625502, 2623981
E-mail: enquiry@arteegroup.com
Contact: Mr. Haresh Keswani - MD/CEO

MILLENNIUM AUTOMOBILES LIMITED
Business: Sales of Motor Vehicles
Address: Akin Adesola/179A-D, Kofo Abayomi Street, Victoria Island, Lagos
Tel: (01) 4700099, 2612539, 7751774
E-mail: millennium@micro.com.ng
* Plot 581, Cadastral Zone AO, Central Business District, Abuja.
Tel: (090) 400717

MILLENNIUM HARVEST LIMITED
Business: Newspaper Publishing (FINANCIAL STANDARD)
Address: 5, Iyalla Street, Alausa, Ikeja, Lagos
Tel: (01) 4934894, 4934996, 4934891, 08034005022
E-mail: info@financialstandardnews.com
* Plot 334, Mississippi Street, Maitama, Abuja.
Tel: (09) 4139620
Contact: Weneso Orogun - Managing Editor/CEO

MILLEWY INTERNATIONAL ENTERPRISES LIMITED
Business: Colour Processing and Photo-Finishing
Address: Fotospeed I, 59, Obafemi Awolowo Way, Ikeja, Lagos
Tel: (01) 4931430
Fotospeed II, 17, Waziri Ibrahim Crescent, off Elsie Femi-Pearse Street, Victoria Island, Lagos
Tel: (01) 7741040

MINAJ PRINTERS LIMITED
Business: Commercial & Industrial Printing Services
Address: 130/132, Ladipo Street (Toyota Bus-Stop), Matori-Mushin, Lagos
Tel: (01) 4529286-7 (2L), 4529203-4 (2L), 7733933, 4751678, 08055285248 **Fax:** (01) 4528500
E-mail: minaj@minaj.net
Website: www. minaj.net
Contact: Senator (Chief) M. Ajegbo - Chairman
Mr. Alfred Akeredolu - GMD/CEO

MINAJ SYSTEMS RADIO/TELEVISION
Business: Television Broadcasting, Printing, Publishing
Address: Radiovision Plaza, Mike Ajegbo Road, P.O. Box 494, Obosi, Anambra State
Tel: (046) 413835, 411267 **Fax:** (046) 251835

MINESFIELD ENGINEERING LIMITED
Business: Casting and Fabrication of Spare Parts, Repairs of Earth-Moving Equipment, Rewinding of Electric Motors and Transformers
Address: Barkin Ladi Road, Central Stores, Bukuru, Jos
Tel: (073) 280545, 280328, 280633
Contact: Alh. M. Rimi - GM/CEO

MINET NIGERIA LIMITED
Business: Insurance Broking
Address: 266, Ikorodu Road, Obanikoro, Lagos
Tel: (01) 4968043-9 (7 L) **Fax:** (01) 4968040
*c/o Triumph Merchant Bank Plc Building, 354B, Olu Obasanjo Road, G.R.A., Port Harcourt
Contact: Olorogun M.C.O. Ibru - Chairman
Chief P. O.Otojareri- MD/CEO

MINGI SERVICES LIMITED
Business: Sales, Leasing, After-Sales Service of Automobiles and Airconditioning Equipment, Sales of Auto Spare Parts and Accessories
Address: Mingi X Building, Plot 17C, Access Road, Trans-Amadi Industrial Layout, Port Harcourt
Tel: (084) 239941, 231892, 232594 **Fax:** (084) 239362
E-mail: mingi@hyperia.com
Contact: Mrs. D. G. Audifferen-Ezike - MD/CEO

MINING & GRANITE COMPANY LIMITED
Business: Production of Dimensional Granite Stone
Address: 7, Ran Road, Bauchi
Tel: (077) 542810, 540335, 08023635085
Fax: (077) 542091
Contact: Alh. A. B. Danbappa - MD/CEO

MINL LIMITED
Business: Manufacturing of Metal Caps & Closures, Roofing Sheets and Aluminium Stucco Coils
Address: 21/23, Abimbola St, Isolo Ind Estate, Isolo, Lagos
Tel: (01) 4529135, 4529137, 4528760 **Fax:** (01) 4529136
E-mail: manakisa@cyberspace.net.ng
Website: www.manaksia.com
Contact: Mr. K. Purkayastha - MD/CEO

MINNESOTA NIGERIA LIMITED (3M)
Business: Marketing of Telecommunication Equipment, Health-Care Consumer Products, Occupational

Health/Safety Products, Tapes and Abrasives, Data Storage Materias, Audio-Visual Products and Electrical Equipment
Address: Plot 8, Block E, Apapa Expressway, Isolo, Lagos
Tel: (01) 4520590, 4521680, 4521678 **Fax:** (01) 4521491
E-mail: info@mnnig.com
*3A, Ndahbros Street, Trans-Amadi, Port Harcourt
Tel: (084) 233831, 233832 **Fax:** (084) 233832
Contact: Chief (Dr.) C. O. Ogunbanjo - Chairman
Mr. David G. Adeniran - MD/CEO

MINOR METALS & MINERALS LIMITED
Business: Processing and Sales of Solid Minerals
Address: Plot 3273, Miango Road, Dandin Kowa, Jos
Tel: (073) 460467, 460467, 461079 **Fax:** (073) 460100
E-mail: minor@jos.rcl.nig.com

MIP GINNERY LIMITED
Business: Processing of Cotton Wool
Address: opp. Rabi'a Jummat Mosque, P. O. Box 234, Gusau
Tel: (063) 200035, 200435
Contact: Alh. Abdullahi Suleiman - GM

MIPPERS INTERNATIONAL LIMITED
Business: Clearing and Forwarding, Shipping and Airfreight, Haulage and Warehousing, General Merchandising
Address: 12, Calcutta Crescent, Apapa, Lagos
Tel: (01) 5457701, 5457510, 5871036 **Fax:** (01) 5457510
E-mail: mippers@beta.linkserve.com
Contact: Chief Mike Umeh - Chairman/CEO

MISHA TRAVELS LIMITED
Business: Travel Agency
Address: Zadina Plaza, 20, Ali Akilu Road, Kaduna
Tel: (062) 248070, 242114
* EMAB Plaza (1st Floor, Suite A23), Plot 751, Aminu Kano Crescent, Wuse II, Abuja
Tel: (09) 6714761
Contact: Mrs. J. O. Abubakar - MD/CEO

MISR (NIGERIA) LIMITED
Business: Egypt Trade Representative, Import & Export
Address: 15, Martins Street (4th Floor), Lagos Island, Lagos
Tel: (01) 2660086, 2643586, 2643587 **Fax:** (01) 2630813

MISSION SECURITIES LIMITED
Business: Stockbroking and Issuing House
Address: 152/156, Broad Street, Lagos
Tel/Fax: (01) 2667727
E-mail: missionsc@wananet.com
Contact: Mr. Sam Oguntayo - MD/CEO

MITOB MOTORS LIMITED
Business: Sales and Service of Automobiles
Address: 1, Joel Ogunnaike Street, G.R.A., Ikeja, Lagos
Tel: (01) 4939761-2 (2 L) **Fax:** (01) 4939761
E-mail: mitob@alpha.linkserve.com
Contact: Mr. Olutoyin Okeowo - MD/CEO

MITSUBISHI SHOJI KAISHA (NIGERIA) LIMITED
Business: Liason Representative for Mitsubishi Corporation and its Subsidiary
Address: Metro Plaza (2nd Floor), Plot 991/992, Herbert Macaulay Way, Central Business District, Abuja
Tel: (09) 2342443 **Fax:** (09) 2341643
* Plot 1649, Olosa Street, Victoria Island, Lagos
Tel: (01) 2614480, 2612906, 2612901 **Fax:** (01) 2612901
E-mail: msknig@nigol.net.ng
Contact: Mr. Takao Fujino - MD/CEO
Mr. J. U. Ejimadu - GM

MIX & BAKE FLOUR MILL INDUSTRIES LIMITED
Business: Flour Milling
Address: 20, North Avenue, Apapa, Lagos
Tel: (01) 5873721, 5870078, 5450094, 5450088, 5872231, 5451494 **Fax:** (01) 5871024
E-mail: chiefcfm@starnet.net.ng
* 48, Airport Road, Warri.
Tel: (053) 253306, 256180, 256907
Contact: Dr. Roland Aderemi Adeleye - Chairman
Chief Maan Lababidi - MD/CEO

MMAB CABLE MANUFACTURING INDUSTRIES LIMITED
Business: Manufacfuring and Marketing of Electrical Cables and Allied Products
Address: 10, Kachia Road, Kaduna South, Kaduna
Tel: (062) 230383, 234964 **Fax:** (062) 230383

MOBIL PHONE WAREHOUSE
Business: Sales of GSM Phones & Accessories
Address: 37B, Raymond Njoku Street, S.W. Ikoyi, Lagos
Tel: (01) 2690794, 4700149, 4701200, 4617961, 4615642, 08034008971, 08034008972-3 (2 L), 08034007543
* 13, Plymouth Road, Benin City
Tel: (080) 33041012, 23466870

MOBILE SYSTEMS LIMITED
Business: Cellular Phone Vendors & Engineers, Commnity Telephony Operations, Sales of Telecommunication Equipment and Computers, Consultancy
Address: 64, Awolowo Road, S.W. Ikoyi, Lagos
Tel/Fax: (01) 2692061, 2695943, 08032030677
E-mail: torusmsl@infoweb.abs.net
Contact: Mr. Anthony C. Okoro - Chairman/CEO

MOBICELL LIMITED
Business: Sales and Repairs of Mobile Phones & Accessories
Address: 48, Bornu Crescent, Apapa, Lagos
Tel: (01) 5451012, 5878261 **Fax:** (01) 5878261
E-mail: chuka@hyperia.com
* AP Shopping Mall, opp.NICON Hilton Hotel, Maitama, Abuja.
Tel: (09) 4138544
Contact: Mr. Chuka Asiegbunam - Chairman/CEO

MOBIL OIL NIGERIA PLC
Business: Marketing of Petroleum Fuels; Manufacturing and Marketing of Automotive & Industrial Lubricants, Oils, Petroleum Jelly and Insecticides
Address: Mobil House, 1,Lekki Expressway, V/Island, Lagos
Tel: (01) 2621640, 2621660 **Fax:** (01) 2621710
* 1, Mobil Road, Apapa, Lagos
Tel: (01) 5452807, 5874015, 5877070
* 1, Reclamation Road, Port Harcourt.
Tel: (084) 237750, 237753, 334022
* 32A, Airport Road, Kano.

Tel: (064) 632566, 633169, 642343
Contact: Mr. Olumide Onakoya - Chairman/MD
Mr. Michael J. Fry - CEO
Mrs. P. N. Ojebuoboh - Manager (Public Affairs)

MOBIL PRODUCING NIGERIA UNLIMITED
Business: Exploration and Production of Hydrocarbons - Crude Oil, Condensates and Gas
Address: Mobil House, 1, Lekki Expressway, V/Island, Lagos
Tel: (01) 2621640-60 (21 L) **Fax:** (01) 2621733
* Qua Iboe Terminal, Eket, Akwa Ibom State
Contact: Mr. Mike J. Fry - Chairman/MD
Mr. Udom Inoyo - GM. (External Affairs)

MOBILE SYSTEMS LIMITED
Business: Cellular Phone Vendors and Engineers, Community Telephony Operations, Sales and Installation of Telecommunication Equipment and Computers
Address: 64, Awolowo Road, S.W. Ikoyi, Lagos
Tel/Fax: (01) 2692061, 2695943, 08032030677, 08034006659
E-mail: torusmsml@infoweb.abs.net
* 47, Opebi Road, Ikeja, Lagos
Tel: 08032030685
Contact: Mr. Anthony C. Okoro - Chairman/CEO

MOBITEL NIGERIA LIMITED
Business: Private Telephone Operator, Internet Service Provider
Address: ICON House (1st Floor), Plot 999F, Idejo Street, Victoria Island, Lagos
Tel: (01) 3204020 **Fax:** (01) 3204015, 3204018
E-mail: mobitel@hyperia.com
* Mobitel Exchange, 1, Amodu Ojikutu Street, Victoria Island, Lagos
Contact: Major-Gen. Tanko Ayuba (rtd.), mni - Chairman
Engr. Charles Alaba Joseph - President/CEO

MODANDOLA GROUP
Business: Conglomerate (Shipping, Stevedoring, Clearing & Forwarding, Manufacturing, Flour Milling, Fishing, Investment & Property Management)
Address: 15, Creek Road, Apapa, Lagos
Tel: (01) 5450810, 5450811 **Fax:** (01) 5450789
E-mail: gmt@modandola-group.com.ng
Contact: Sir (Chief) Bode Akindele, JP, KJW - Chairman
Engr. Adeoye Fowora, OON

MODANT MARINE LIMITED
Business: Building of Boats, Ships and Barges, Fleet Operators, Ship Maintenance, Supply of Pipes and Diesel for Ships and Helicopters
Address: Rumuolumeni/Iwofe, after College of Education, P.M.B. 5143, Port Harcourt
Tel: (084) 233983, 235865 **Fax:** (084) 237671
* 11B, Anifowoshe Street ,Victoria Island, Lagos
Tel: (01) 2620937, 2620938, 2610588 **Fax:** (01) 2620935
E-mail: exeho@execom.com.ng
Contact: Olorogun Moses O. Taiga - Chairman
Mr. Jean Claude Neron - Group MD/CEO

MODEL HOTELS LIMITED
Business: Hotel Development and Management
Address: Kogi Hotel & Tourism Board, 8, Lugard Road, P.M.B. 1064, Lokoja
Tel: (058) 220655, 221605
* 3, Janet Ekundayo Street, G.R.A., Lokoja

MODERN BUSINESS MACHINES (NIGERIA) LIMITED
Business: Sales, Services, Marketing and Maintenance of Computer Hardwares and Accessories
Address: 21A, Karimu Kotun Street, Victoria Island, Lagos
Tel: (01) 2361010, 2614941, 2625596-97 (2 L), 2635213
Fax: (01) 2620349
E-mail: mbm@alpha.linkserve.com
* Plot 662, Aba Close, Area 8, Garki, Abuja
Tel: (09) 2345473, 2344809, 2346303 **Fax:** (09) 2344809
* 38, Old Aba Road, Rumuomasi, Port Harcourt
Tel: (084) 239598, 239584; **Fax:** (084) 239598
Contact: Mr. Sam A. Ifeozo - MD/CEO
Engr. Chris Dadzie - Technical Director

MODERN DESIGNS & ASSOCIATES LIMITED
Business: Commercial Printing Services, Manufacturing of Light Packaging;Advertising, Publishing
Address: 6/8, Amusa Oloyede Street, by Alh. Tokunboh Alli Street, off Toyin Street, Ikeja, Lagos
Tel: (01) 4971123, 4979133, 4811039, 7744381, 8045235
Contact: Prince J. A. Odufunwa - Chairman/CEO

MODERN TELECOMMUNICATIONS (NIGERIA) LIMITED
Business: Provision of Full Internet Services, Fixed Wireless Acess and Prepaid Telephone Card
Address: 21, Ologun Agbaje Street, Victoria Island, Lagos
Tel: (01) 2624168, 2626975, 3201234, 3201200, 08033079083, 08033079084
Fax: (01) 2620079, 2626976
E-mail: info@hyperia.com
Website: www.hyperia.com
Contact: Alh. Abubakar Ahmed - Chairman
Mr. Marcle Karam - MD/CEO

MODOTELS LIMITED
Business: Hospitality Services
Address: 2, Club Road, Enugu
Tel: (042) 258870, 258871, 258000, 258867
Fax: (042) 258868

MOFALS COMMUNCATIONS LIMITED
Business: Internet Service Provider, Distribution of Information Technology Products, Sales of VSAT & other Communication Equipment, Cybercafe Operations
Address: 33, Oluwaleyimu Street, off Toyin St, Ikeja, Lagos
Tel: (01) 8151776, 4734517, 080234030810
E-mail: sales@mofals.com
Website: www.mofals.com
Contact: Alh. Ladi Sulaimon - MD/CEO

MOFAS SHIPPING LINE (NIGERIA) LIMITED
Business: Shipping, Maritime Consultancy
Address: 10, Oyekan Rd, off Bombay Crescent, Apapa, Lagos
Tel: (01) 5876011, 5457219 **Fax:** (01) 5452512
E-mail: mofas@hyperia.com
Contact: Prince E. O. Oladerehinote Olagbegi - CEO

MOG HOLDINGS LIMITED
Business: Manufacturing and Marketing of Furniture
Address: 103, Allen Avenue, Ikeja, Lagos

Tel: (01) 4931787, 4939423, 4971665,
E-mail: mogholding@infoweb.abs.net

MOGABS NIGERIA LIMITED
Business: Design & Construction of Power Sub-Stations, Transmission & Distribution Lines, Supply of High/Medium/Low Voltage Materials
Address: Plot 1341, Nkwere Crescent, beh Bobsar Shopping Complex, off Ahmadu Bello Way, Garki II, Abuja
Tel: (09) 3141431, 3141432, 08023567914, 08033145282
Fax: (09) 3141430
E-mail: mogabscontractors@yahoo.com
Contact: Chief G. U. Okonkwo - MD/CEO

MOGAMOH NIGERIA LIMITED
Business: Bureau de Change Services
Address: 77, Kofo Abayomi Avenue, Apapa, Lagos
Tel: (01) 5450443, 08055321163
Contact: Alh. Abdullahi Muhammed - MD/CEO

MOJEC INTERNATIONAL LIMITED
Business: Sales of Michelin Tyres, Paper Merchandising, Production of Calcium Carbonate for Paint and Plastic Industries
Address: 244/246, Oshodi-Apapa Expressway (by AGS Barma Ltd), Ilasamaja, Lagos
Tel: (01) 4529436, 7738393, 7745079 **Fax:** (01) 4529436
E-mail: mojecintltd@hotmail.com
mojec@infoweb.abs.net
Contact: Chief (Mrs.) A. Mojisola Abdul - Chairman/CEO

MOK GROUP OF COMPANIES
Business: Real Estate Broking & Consultancy, Property Development & Management, Sales of GSM Products, Computers & Accessories, Fabrication of Aluminium & Steel Structures, Clearing, Pest Control & Waste Management Services
Address: Iponri Shopping Centre (Suite 61B), S/lere, Lagos
Tel: (01) 4803749, 4809625, 8141598, 836496, 831570, 08023141563, 08033066822, 08033066827
E-mail: mokgroup@yahoo.com
Website: www.mokgroup.com
Contact: Mr. Emmanuel Mok - MD/CEO

MOKUOLU RUBENS & COMPANY
Business: Chartered Accountants, Accounting & Auditing, Taxation Advisory Services, Consultancy
Address: Co-operative Bank Building (7th Floor), 30, Marina, Lagos Island, Lagos
Tel: (01) 7924764, 2661195, 08023068171
Fax: (01) 2641166
E-mail: mokrubens@hyperia.net
Contact: Mr. Wale Mokuol - Chairman/Managing Director

MOLAREX HOTEL, ABUJA
Business: Hospitality Services
Address: Plot 500, Gaborone Street, off Olusegun Obasanjo Way, Wuse Zone 2, Abuja
Tel: (09) 5238451-1 (4 L)
Contact: Mr. Moses Ajuwola - Chairma/CEO

MOLTEN TRUST LIMITED
Business: Stockbroking, Investment Advisors, Portfolio Management, Share Registrar Services
Address: 135, Igbosere Road, Lagos Island, Lagos
Tel: (01) 2634417, 2634876 **Fax:** (01) 2634876
E-mail: molten135@hotmail.com
Contact: Mr. Motolani Oduwole - MD/CEO

MOMAH GABJOHN INDUSTRIAL COMPANY LIMITED
Business: Sales of Tyres & Tubes, General Merchandising
Address: 9, Bajulaiye Street, Idumota, Lagos
Tel: (01) 2661015, 2640186 Fax: (01) 2661015

MONAPLEX INDUSTRIES (NIGERIA) LIMITED
Business: Manufacture of Automotive & Industrial Plasticwares
Address: Km. 16, Ikorodu Road, Opp. Ojota New Garage, Ojota, Lagos
Tel: (01) 4978880-4 (5L), 8133000 **Fax:** (01) 4971490
E-mail: monaplex@nova.net.ng
service@monaplex.com
Website: www.monaplex.com
Contact: Mr. Abdallah A. H. Sulaiman - Chairman/CEO

MONARCH COMMUNICATIONS LIMITED
Business: Telecommunications Services
Address: 2, Agoro Odiyan Street, off Adeola Odeku Street, Victoria Island, Lagos
Tel: (01) 2629810-4 (5 L) **Fax:** (01) 2629812

MONARCH SUITES
Business: Hospitality & Catering Services
Address: 25, Church St, off Salvation Rd, Opebi, Ikeja, Lagos
Tel: (01) 8047853, 8133629, 4973290, 08034046610

MONARCH TRAVELS LIMITED
Business: Travel Agency
Address: 64, Nnamdi Azikiwe Street, Lagos
Tel: (01) 2663710, 2665034 Fax: (01) 2664715
Contact: Alh. M. A. Alebiosu - Chairman/CEO

MONIER 2000 LIMITED
Business: Indoor & Outdoor Advertising Services, Screen Printing Services
Address: Plot 984B, Saka Jojo Street, off Idejo Street, Victoria Island, Lagos
Tel: (01) 2610873, 4616498-9 (2L), 618843
Fax: (01) 2621073, 4616498
E-mail: monier2000@nova.net. ng
Website: www.monier2000.com
Contact: Mr. Samuel I. Mowo - MD/CEO

MONIER CONSTRUCTION COMPANY (NIGERIA) LIMITED
Business: Building and Civil Engineering Contractors
Address: 18/19, Abonnema Wharf Road, Port Harcourt
Tel: (084) 236350-4 (5 L), 233482 **Fax:** (084) 233482
E-mail: mcc@alpha.linkserve.com
* Plot 258, Gwelo Street, Zone 4, Wuse Abuja
Tel/Fax: (09) 5235210
Contact: Mr. Henry A. MacPepple - Chairman/CEO

MONITOR INSURANCE BROKERS LIMITED
Business: Insurance Broking
Address: 37B, St. Michael's Road, Aba
Tel: (082) 222346, 224514 **Fax:** (082) 224514

E-mail: monitorinsurance@yahoo.com
* Western House (10th Floor), 8/10, Broad St, Lagos
Tel: (01) 2633024, 2634656, 2637092 **Fax:** (01) 2631687
* 27, Aba Road, Port Harcourt
Tel: (084) 239929
Contact: Mr. Geoffrre Uzoagbara - MD/CEO

MONITOR NEWSPAPERS LIMITED
Business: Newspaper Publishing
Address: Lister House, Ring Road, Dugbe, Ibadan
Tel: (02) 2318870, 2318871, 2318546 **Fax:** (02) 2318545
* 57, Ikwerre Road, Port Harcourt
* Plot 17, Nouchott Street,Wuse Zone 1, Abuja
Contact: Evangelist Biodun Famojuro - MD/CEO

MONOGRAMM & LOGO CREATIONS LIMITED
Business: Monogramming and Creation of Logos
Address: 27/29, King George V Road, Onikan, Lagos
Tel: (01) 2632251, 2634483 **Fax:** (01) 2632251
E-mail: monogram@hyperia.com
Website: www.monogram-logo.com
Contact: Mrs. Chinwe Bildmann - Chairman/CEO

MONTAIGNE AH LIMITED
(Montaigne Place - The Spa)
Business: Health Spa, Beauty Salon and Body Care Services, Importation & Sales of Personal-Use Fashion Products, Manufacturers' Representative
Address: Plot 226B, Muri Okunola St, Victoria Island, Lagos
Tel: (01) 2705539, 2622721, 08037130408
Fax: (01) 3204200
* Clarins Place, Russell Centre, Herbert Macaulay Way, Zone 4, Wuse, Abuja
Contact: Alali Hart - MD/CEO

MONTGOMERY SECURITY VAULTS (NIGERIA) LIMITED
Business: Safe Deposit Centre
Address: 25, Montgomery Road, Yaba, Lagos
Tel: (01) 867852, 866756, 866757, 7739891
Fax: (01) 861329
Website: www.montgomeryvaults.com
Contact: Chief G. K. Animashaun - Chairman
Mr. L. O. A. Fadipe - MD/CEO

MONUMENT PLASTICS INDUSTRIES LIMITED
Business: Manfacturing of Plastic Nylon Products
Address: Plot 13A, Acme Road, Ogba Industrial Estate, Ogba, Ikeja, Lagos
Tel: (01) 4925708, 8043113 **Fax:** (01) 4925708
E-mail: fafinc@cyberspace.net.ng
Contact: Mr. Fidel C. Anujuo - Chairman/CEO

MONUMENT SECURITIES & FINANCE LIMITED
Business: Stockbroking, Investment Advisors, Portfolio Management
Address: 14C, Durbin Katsina Road, Bompai, Kano
Tel: (064) 649810, 08037878178 **Fax:** (064) 638335
E-mail: info@monsec.com
* Stock Exchange House (14th Floor), 2/4, Customs Street, off Marina, Lagos.
Tel: (01) 4700096
Contact: Air Vice Marshal Nura Imam (rtd.) - Chairman
Mr. Tersur John Kwange - MD/CEO

MONZINA COASTAL AGENCIES LIMITED
Business: Shipping, Clearing & Forwarding, Warehousing and Haulage, Cargo Security
Address: Development House (7th Floor), 21, Wharf Road, Apapa, Lagos
Tel: (01) 5452567, 5452969, 5876719, 08023115690
Fax: (01) 5452969
E-mail: monzina82@yahoo.com
monzina@linkserve.com
Contact: Chief M. Ola Okunowo - Chairman/CEO

MOODY INTERNATIONAL NIGERIA LIMITED
Business: Quality Assurance, Inspection, Expediting, Procurement, Training Certification & Personnel Services
Address: House 169 (Flat 2), Road 48, Victoria Garden City, Lekki, Lagos
Tel: (01) 4619413, 4713162 **Fax:** (01) 4619413
E-mail: moodylagos@yahoo.com
moodylagos@infoweb.abs.net
Website: www.moodyint.com
Contact: Chief Dele Fajemirokun - Chairman
Mr. Adeniyi G. Ademuson - GM

MOOREGATE LIMITED
Business: Consultants to the Solid Mineral Industry, Exploration & Mining of Solid Minerals, Supply of Equipment and Services, General Merchandising
Address: 16, Aerodrome Road, Apapa, Lagos
Tel/Fax: (01) 5450413
E-mail: mooregate26@hotmail.com
mooregate31@yahoo.com
Website: www.mooregate.com
Contact: Mr. Ikenna Nwosu - MD/CEO

MOPSON PHARMACEUTICAL LIMITED
Business: Manufacture of Pharmaceuticals, Sales of Surgical Consumables
Address: 47, Osolo Way, off International Airport Road, Ajao Estate, Apakun-Oshodi, Lagos
Tel: (01) 4523237, 4528462, 08022900833, 08022902176-7 (2L), 08023059584, 08023190336, 08033237933
Fax: (01) 4523237, 4967960
E-mail: mopson@micro.com.ng
Contact: Mr. Michael Oyebanjo Paul - Chairman/CEO

MORAGOFF ARROW INTERNATIONAL LIMITED
Business: Sales & Services of Motor Vehicle Tyres & Tubes
Address: 142, Oba Akran Avenue, Ikeja Ind Estate, Lagos
Tel: (01) 4971505, 4976139 **Fax:** (01) 4976139
E-mail: moragoff@nova.net.ng
moragoff@hotmail.com
Contact: Alh. M. S. Arowosaye - Chairman/CEO

MORE TIME CO_2 GAS PLANT LIMITED
Business: Production of Cabon Dioxide Gas and Dry-Ice, Marketing of Petroleum Products, Ice Flakes/Block
Address: 104/106, Oshodi-Apapa Expressway (Cele Bus-Stop), Isolo, Lagos
Tel: (01) 4529088, 4529081, 450888, 5556166, 7748338
Fax: (01) 4520888, 5556167
E-mail: moretimeco$_2$@yahoo.com
Website: www.moretime-ng.com
Contact: Prince Kehinde Adeniyi - Chairman/CEO

MORE TIME INFORMATION TECHNOLOGIES LIMITED

Business: Domestic VSAT Network Operations, Internet Service Provider, Sales & Installation of Telecommunications, Terminal Equipment, Cybercafe, Training
Address: 104/106, Oshodi-Apapa Expressway (Cele Bus-Stop), Isolo, Lagos
Tel: (01) 4529088, 4529081, 4520888, 7748338, 5556166
Fax: (01) 4520888, 5556167
E-mail: info@moretimeng.net
md@moretimeng.net
Website: www.moretimeng.net
Contact: Prince Kehinde Adeniyi - Chairman/CEO

MORECAB FINANCE LIMITED

Business: Financial Services
Address: 62, New Market Road, P.O. Box 4438, Onitsha
Tel: (046) 2177995

MORGAN, OMONITAN & ABE LIMITED

Business: Engineering Consultancy, Project Management
Address: 241, Igbosere Road, Lagos Island, Lagos
Tel: (01) 2631155, 2634220, 2631597 **Fax:** (01) 2634170
* Suite 9, Harper Crescent, opp. Educational Resource Centre, Wuse Zone 7, Abuja
Tel/Fax: (09) 3140788
Contact: Engr. Eric Morgan - Chairman
Engr. Oladipo Abe - MD/CEO

MORISON INDUSTRIES PLC

Business: Production of Pharmaceuticals, Cosmetics and Hygiene Products; Marketing of General Goods
Address: 2/30, Morison Crescent, off Oregun Road, (Alausa Bus-Stop), Oregun Industrial Estate, Lagos
Tel: (01) 4742573, 4967627, 7747428
Fax: (01) 3205733, 4967593
E-mail: miplc@morison-nig.com
sales.morison@morison-nig.com
Contact: Mr. Julius O. Titiloye - Chairman/CEO
Mrs. A. Olusola Popoola - MD

MORLAP GROUP OF COMPANIES

Business: Ship Owners, Charterers & Managers, Clearing & Forwarding, Mining, Farming, Money Transfer
Address: Morlap Place, 27, Abraham Adesanya (formerly Duala) Road, Apapa, Lagos
Tel: (01) 5455601-3 (3 L) **Fax:** (01) 5450464, 5872401
E-mail: morlap@alpha.linkserve.com

MORPOL ENGINEERING SERVICES LIMITED

Business: Sales of Gas Compression & Power Machinery, Field Instrumentation, Material Procurement, Electrical/ Mechanical Engineering Installation, Plant Refurblishment, Water Treatment.
Address: 4, Warehouse Road, Apapa, Lagos
Tel: (01) 5870118, 5870955, 5873201, 5454558-60 (3 L), 08033023017 **Fax:** (01) 5870949
E-mail: morpol@linkserve.com.ng
* Plot 40, Chief Wapara Street, Rumuobiakani, Port Harcourt
Tel: (084) 236340, 236344, 237084 **Fax:** (084) 237084
Contact: Alh. Ibrahim Abdurrahman - Chairman
Mr. S. D. Paulus - MD/CEO

MOS OFFICE PRODUCTS LIMITED

Business: Sales and Servicing of Office Equipment
Address: Plot 101, Oshodi-Isolo Expressway, Oshodi, Lagos
Tel/Fax: (01) 4937683
Contact: Mr. M. O. Shodeinde - Chairman/CEO

MOSAF NIGERIA LIMITED

Business: Building Construction & Civil Engineering, Oil & Gas, Fabrication Works, Designing & Procurement
Address: Plot 3348 (Suite 2A), Cadastral Zone A5, Adetokunbo Ademola Crescent, Maitama, Abuja
Tel: (09) 4131549, 4131550 **Fax:** (09) 4131551
E-mail: mosafgroup@yahoo.com
mosaf@abuja.rcl.nig.com
* 66, Ajao Raod, off Babatunde Street, off Ogunlana Street, Surulere, Lagos
Tel/Fax: (01) 5850793
Contact: Engr. (Dr.) Afam Nwama - Exec. Chairman

MOSENG NIGERIA LIMITED

Business: Iron & Steel Stockist, Supply of Industrial Raw Materials, Road Haulage, Construction Engineers
Address: Km. 1, Badagry Expressway, Orile Iganmu, Lagos
Tel: (01) 4701571, 5851582, 7744877, 08033088222
Contact: Mr. E. K. Ademosu - MD/CEO

MOTAYO FOODS & HEALTH PRODUCTS LIMITED

Business: Sales of Herbal Products, Food Supplements and Weight Management Products; Exportation of Commodities
Address: 30, Opebi Road, Ikeja, Lagos
Tel/Fax: (01) 4722221, 08034567893
E-mail: motayohealth@yahoo.com
Contact: Mrs. Morayo Fawehinmi - MD/CEO

MOTAYO HOSPITAL LIMITED

Business: Medical Services
Address: 3, Owoduni St, off Amore St, Toyin St, Ikeja, Lagos
Tel: (01) 4962846, 4964931-2 (2L), 49649314744774, 08033700616 **Fax:** (01) 4932787
E-mail: info@motayohospital.com
Website: www.motayohospital.com
Contact: Dr. Temitayo Fawehinmi - Chairman/MD

MOTEL BENIN PLAZA

Business: Hospitality Services, Catering Services
Address: 1A, Reservation Road, G.R.A., Benin City
Tel: (052) 254779, 254742, 251519, 256312
Fax: (052) 259125
E-mail: mbplaza@infoweb.abs.net
Website: www.motelbeninplaza.com
Contact: Mr Ernest Ekpenyong - GM

MOTHERCAT NIGERIA LIMITED

Business: Civil, Electrical/ Mechanical Engineering Contractors
Address: 15, Mothercat Rd, Mando Light Ind. Layout, Kaduna
Tel: (062) 314056-9 (4L) **Fax:** (062) 318383
E-mail: mcat@hyperia.com
mcat@inet-global.com
* Plot 1065, Adetokunbo Ademola Crescent, Wuse 11, Abuja
Tel: (09) 5231335 **Fax:** (09) 5231280
Contact: Mr. George N. Saliba - MD/CEO

MOTOR PARTS INDUSTRY LIMITED
Business: Sales and Service of Automobile Trucks; Spares
Address: 231, Moshood Abiola Way, Ijora, Lagos
Tel: (01) 5802290-4 (5 L)
* 109, Trans-Amadi Ind. Layout, Port Harcourt
Tel: (084) 333506
Contact: Mr. G. Carella - MD/CEO

MOTOROLA COMMUNICATIONS
Business: Distribution, Marketing & Maintenance of Radio Communication Systems, Equipment & Components
Address: 28, Creek Road, Apapa, Lagos
Tel: (01) 5871282, 5872354, 5874906 **Fax:** (01) 5874021
E-mail: dizengoff@dizengoff.com
Website: www.dizengoff.com
* Plot 108, Adetokunbo Ademola Crescent, Cadastral Zone A8, Wuse II, Abuja
Tel: (09) 4131240-2 (3L), 4139558 **Fax:** (09) 4131242

MOTORWAYS PROPERTY DEVELOPMENT COMPANY LTD
Business: Property Development and Management
Address: Motorways Centre (Penthouse B), 1, Motorways Avenue, opp. 7up Factory, Alausa, Lagos
Tel: (01) 4934145-6 (2L), 7736783 **Fax:** (01) 4934148

MOTRACO LIMITED
Business: Importation and Sales of Automobile Batteries
Address: Plot 1673, Oyin Jolayemi Street, opp. Standard Trust Bank, Victoria Island, Lagos
Tel: (01) 2700554, 08023196835 **Fax:** (01) 2623716
E-mail: essenti@infoweb.abs.net
Contact: Chief Chike Arize - Chairman/CEO

MOTU-TEC LIMITED
Business: Instrumentation & Process Control Engineering, Factory Automation
Address: 18B, Oshodi-Apapa Expressway, Oshodi, Lagos
Tel: (01) 4930350, 4934052 **Fax:** (01) 4930350, 4968121
E-mail: motutec@infoweb.abs.net
motec2000@yahoo.com
Contact: M. O. Abayomi - Chairman/CEO

MOUDACO LIMITED
Business: Sole Distributors of Mercury Mariner Outboard Engines and Mercruser Inboard Engines, Manufacturing of Pleasure Boats & Vehicle Bumpers
Address: Km. 16, Ikorodu Road, Ojota, Lagos
Tel: (01) 4974567, 4963457, 4931285, 7948663-5 (3L)
Fax: (01) 4930103, 2619477

MOUKA LIMITED
Business: Production of Foam & Spring Mattresses, Sofa-Bed, Steel Pipe Milling, Manufacture of Flat Sheets & Steel Wire Drawing & Nails, & Z-Purline
Address: Plot M, Awosika Avenue, Ikeja Industrial Estate, Ikeja, Lagos
Tel: (01) 4963309, 4962480, 4976440, 4976441, 4976442
Fax: (01) 2693310
E-mail: janah@mouka.com
Website: www.mouka.com
* Plot 24, Chief Doherty Estate, Oregun, Lagos.
Tel: (01) 4971790
Contact: Mr. Hasib F. Moukarim - MD/CEO

MOULDS (NIGERIA) LIMITED
Business: Building, Road & Civil Engineering Contractors
Address: Plot TP 24, Liberty Boulevard, Jos
Tel: (073) 465802 **Fax:** (073) 464278
E-mail: moulds@skannet.com
Contact: Engr. Samuel Olalekan Oyafemi - MD/CEO

MOUNT SINAI HOSPITAL GROUP
Business: Medical Services
Address: 177/179, Borno Way, Ebute-Metta, Lagos
Tel: (01) 4716103, 862710
Contact: Chief (Dr.) Charles Babatunde Fadipe - Chairman
Dr. Olatunde Ademola Dixon - MD/CEO

MOVI POWER SYSTEMS LIMITED
Business: Importation, Sale, Installation, Servicing & Repairs of Generators, Electrical Engineering Services
Address: 110, New Court Road, Gyadi-Gyadi, Kano
Tel: (064) 667735, 666031
Fax: (064) 666031
E-mail: movigen@yahoo.com
Contact: Mr. Philip Idemdia - Chairman/CEO

MOZED MEDICAL DIAGNOSTIC CENTRE LIMITED
Business: Medical Diagnostic Laboratory, Immuno-Assay & Ultrasound Scanning, Blood-Bank Facilities
Address: Block 5B, Godmon Estate, 2/3, Okota Road, Isolo, Lagos
Tel: (01) 4521370, 7736571, 08023399920
E-mail: mozedlab@hotmail.com
Contact: Mr. Marcus Daudu - Managing Director

MSC NIGERIA LIMITED
Business: Sales, Installation & Maintenance of 2-Way Radio Communication Equipment
Address: Elephant Cement House (3rd Floor, Wing E, Entrance B, ASSBIFI Road, Centra Business District, Alausa, Ikeja, Lagos
Tel: (01) 3203372, 08055233074

MSM MICRO DEVICES LIMITED
Business: Sales, Service and Repairs of Computer Hardware, Sale of Computer Stationery and Furniture
Address: 30/1A, Bauchi Road, Jos
Tel: (073) 456569, 455198, 08037204888
Fax: (073) 456569
E-mail: msm@yahoo.com
Contact: Engr. Sani Mansur - MD/CEO

MTN COMMUNICATIONS NIGERIA LIMITED
Business: GSM Telecommunication Service Provider
Address: Churchgate Towers (5th & 7th Floors), Plot PC. 30, Afribank Street, Victoria Island, Lagos
Tel: 08039005043
Website: www.mtnonline.com
* 16, Saka TInubu Street, Victoria Island, Lagos
* Maritime House, Berger Cement Bus Stop, Oshodi Expressway, Apapa, Lagos
* 16, Fatai Atere Way, Matori, Oshodi, Lagos
* Plot 2784, Shehu Shagari Way, Maitama, Abuja
* 330, Aba Road, Port Harcourt
Contact: Mr. Sifiso Dalengwa - MD/CEO
Mr. Afam Edozien - Chief Marketing Officer

MTS FIRST WIRELESS LIMITED
Business: Wirelss Telephony and Long Distance Telecommunication Services
Address: IMB Plaza, 1, Akin Adesola Street, V/Island, Lagos
Tel: (01) 7200070, 7200072-3 (2L), 7200097
E-mail: info@mtsfirstwireless.com
Website: www.mtsfirstwireless.com
* 12, Kudirat Abiola Way, Oregun (Alausa), Lagos
Tel: (01) 7203300, 7203319, 7203331, 7203603
Contact: Engr Richmond Kojo Aggrey - President/CEO
Mr Reuben Muoka - GM/Head, Corporate Affairs

MU'AZU INLAND TRANSPORT LIMITED
Business: Transportation Services
Address: Plot 49, Sharada Industrial Estate Phase II, Kano
Tel: (064) 665001, 667528 **Fax:** (064) 667528
Contact: Aminu Musa Baba - Chairman/CEO

MUHAMMAD & COMPANY
Business: Estate Surveyors & Valuers, Property Development & Management, Valuation & General Consultancy
Address: 24, Wharf Road (C9), P.O.Box 3770, Kaduna
Tel: (062) 241945, 248231-2 (2L), 08042156390
Contact: Hon. (Alh.) Abdullahi Muh'd Sani - Prin. Partner

MUHTARI DANGANA & COMPANY
Business: Chartered Accountants, Audit & Taxation Services
Address: 12, Bompai Road, Kano
Tel: (064) 648982, 648981
* Plot 935, Azores Street, off Aminu Kano Crescent, Wuse II, Abuja
Tel: (09) 4132590, 4132591
Contact: Alh. Muhtari Dangana - Principal Partner

MULTISECURE LIMITED
Business: Sales of Flow Meters, Pumps and Dispensers
Address: 17A, Little Road, Sabo-Yaba, Lagos
Tel: (01) 868269, 4709017, 4716384, 08023470643
E-mail: multisecure@yahoo.com
Contact: Mr. Yomi Shofoluwo - MD/CEO

MULTI-LINKS TELECOMMUNICATIONS LIMITED
Business: Digital Mobile Phone & Wireless Telephone Service Provider
Address: 231, Adeola Odeku Street, Victoria Island, Lagos
Tel: (01) 7740000, 2624430-3 (4L) **Fax:** (01) 2622452
E-mail: ccu@multi-links.com
Contact: Mr. C. K. Ramani - MD/CEO

MULTI-TAN LIMITED
Business: Tannery
Address: Plot 12, Challawa Industrial Estate, Kano
Tel: (064) 648065, 641079, 645595 **Fax:** (064) 638410
Contact: Mr. Francis Akle - MD/CEO

MULTIBANC SAVINGS & LOANS LIMITED
Business: Mortgage Banking
Address: Plot 290, Ajose Adeogun St, Victoria Island, Lagos
Tel: (01) 2615280, 2619868 **Fax:** (01) 2622846
Contact: Chief E. M. Egwuenu - Exec. Chairman

MULTICHEM INDUSTRIES LIMITED
Business: Manufacturers of Pigment Emulsions, Textile Dyestuff, Auxilliaries & Sizing Chemicals, Printing Inks & Coating, Stockist of General Chemicals and Machine Spare Parts for Textile Industries
Address: Plot D2, Israel Adebajo Close, off Ladipo Oduwole Avenue, Ikeja Industrial Estate, Ikeja, Lagos
Tel: (01) 4930447, 4936162, 7737272 **Fax:** (01) 2693746
E-mail: multikem@infoweb.abs.net
Contact: Mr. M. K. Vaswani - Chairman
Mr. Kamlesh Dani - MD

MULTICHOICE NIGERIA
Business: Subscriber Management Services - Telecast
Address: Plot 1379A, Tiamiyu Savage St, Victoria Island, Lagos
Tel: (01) 2610776, 2610779, 2622132., 2622133, 2622135, 2623340, 2626641, 2620599, 2620608
Fax: (01) 2610360, 2619429
Website: www.multichoice.com
* Nwaora Plaza, Plot 1103, Aminu Kano Crescent, off Ahmadu Bello Way, Zone A7, Wuse II, Abuja
Tel: (09) 5235304, 5235827, 5231317 **Fax:** (09) 5233678
* 10, Igbado Road, G.R.A. Port Harcourt
Tel: (084) 234344, 234350, 234355 **Fax:** (084) 234348

MULTILATERAL INSURANCE BROKERS LIMITED
Business: Insurance Broking and Consultancy
Address: Cross River House, 42, Bishop Oluwole Street, Victoria Island, Lagos
Tel: (01) 2622127, 7748472 **Fax:** (01) 2622127
E-mail: multilateral@yahoo.com
Contact: Mr. Niyi Oyedele - MD/CEO

MULTIMALT LIMITED
Business: Handling and Transportation of Bulk Cereals
Address: Berth 1, Tin Can Island, Port, Second Gate Bye-Pass, Tin Can Island, Lagos
Tel: (01) 5878780, 7749993, 7749994 **Fax:** (01) 5870715
E-mail: sobajayi@beta.linkserve.com
Contact: Chief J. Akin-George, OFR - Chairman
Mr. S. O. B. Ajayi - GM

MULTIMESH COMMUNICATION LIMITED
Business: Telecommunication & Satellite Communication Services, Information Technology Services
Address: 202, Aba Road, Rumuola, Port Harcourt
Tel: (084) 232466-7 (2L), 230849, 08032034098
Fax: (084) 230849
E-mail: multimesh@yahoo.com
Website: www.multimeshcom.com
* 3, Soji Adepegba Close, off 85, Allen Avenue, Ikeja, Lagos
Tel: (01) 4974714, 4976395
Contact: Mr. Godfrey N. Ohuabunwa - MD/CEO

MULTINATIONAL CONCEPTS LIMITED
Business: Production & Supply of Corporate Promotional Items & Diaries, Printing of Calendars, Cards, Annual Reports & other Stationery
Address: Plot 362, Oloko Crescent, off Daranijo Street, Aguda-Ogba, Ikeja, Lagos
Tel: (01) 4925529, 5557505, 7902088, 08033034196
Fax: (01) 4925529
E-mail: micl@hyperia.com
Contact: Mr. Timenyin Esuabanga - MD/CEO

MULTINATIONAL GEOSURVEYS LIMITED

Business: Petroleum Geology Surveying and Consultancy
Address: 19A, First Avenue, off Agip Road, FHA Estate, Rumuene, Port Harcourt.
Tel: (084) 235166 * (082) 440476
E-mail: mg@phc.linkserve.com
Contact: Prof. D. M. J. Fubara - Chairman
Surv. Peter Akpofure - MDCEO

MULTINATIONAL INVESTMENT & SECURITIES LIMITED

Business: Stockbroking, Investment Advisory Services, Portfolio Management, Financial Consultants
Address: Stock Exchange Building, 13th Floor, Right Wing (Teni ma Sunwon Suites), 2/4, Customs Street, Lagos Island, Lagos
Tel: (01) 2641811, 2642566, 2641969
Fax: (01) 2667215
E-mail: multibold@siotel.com
Contact: Sir J. Obasanmi Adewuyi - Chairman
Mr. Kolapo Alaka-Coker - MD/CEO

MULTINATIONAL TECHNOLOGIES LIMITED

Business: Consultancy Services (Petroleum, Energy Management, Procurement & Supplies, Surveying & Quality Control of Seismic Acquisitions)
Address: 6, Sam Adegbite Close, off Amodu Ojikutu Street, Victoria Island, Lagos
Tel: (01) 2616539, 2617771, 2610347, 2611580, 7744204
Fax: (01) 2613233, 2611580
E-mail: mel@infoweb.abs.net
Website: www.multinationalexpertise.com
*12A, Mbonu Road, D-Line, Port Harcourt
Tel/Fax: (084) 239959
E-mail: melphc@phca.linkserve.com
* 45, Upper Erejuwa Street, Warri.
Tel: (053) 251150
Contact: Mr. David A. Harper - MD/CEO

MULTIPLE CONCEPTS TELECOMMUNICATIONS CO. LTD

Business: Procurement, Installation and Maintenance of Equipment for Telecommunication, Data Communication and Computer Telephone Integration
Address: 1, Agungi Road, Lekki, off Lekki Expressway (Agungi Bus-Stop), Lagos
Tel: (01) 8042170, 7747184 **Fax:** (01) 5555366
E-mail: lagos@multipleconcepts.com
multipleconcept1976@hotmail.com
Website: www.multipleconcepts.com
* Plot 2793, Aguiyi Ironsi Street, opp. British High Commission, Maitama, Abuja
Tel: (09) 4138851, 648065
Contact: Chief Ernest Amobi - Chairman

MULTITRADE MARKETING LIMITED

Business: Stockist & Supplier of Building Materials, Hospital Equipment, Safety Equipment, Electrical Appliances Agricultural Inputs, Rice & Sugar
Address: 8A, Samuel Manuwa Street, by 2nd Gate of 1004-Flats Estate,
Tel: (01) 7749305, 2668586, 2664712, 2664525
Fax: (01) 2616452, 2694574
E-mail: kmbltd@aol.com
kmb@linkserve.com.ng

MUNAK GROUP LIMITED

Business: Power Engineering, Real Estate Management, Security Services
Address: Plot 1681, Sanusi Fafunwa St, Victoria Island, Lagos
Tel: (01) 2625837, 2624819, 7743415, 612499
Fax: (01) 2625837
E-mail: info@munakgroup.com
* Plot 857, Osogbo Close, off Emeka Anyaoku Street, Area 11, Garki, Abuja
Tel: (09) 2347283
Contact: Mr. Moses Kamanya - Chairman/CEO

MUNCHIES FAST FOOD LIMITED

Business: Operation of Convenince-Foods Outlets
Address: 33, Ahmadu Bello Way, Victoria Island, Lagos
Tel: (01) 4619154, 618911, 2882974

MUNDIAL ENTERPRISES LIMITED

Business: Sales of Corporate Gifts Items
Address: 8, Isaac John Street, G.R.A. Ikeja, Lagos
Tel: (01) 4933595, 4933850 **Fax:** (01) 4967317, 4933850
E-mail: mundial@mundialgift.com
Website: www.mundialgift.com
Contact: Mr Lanre Ogunlesi - Chairman/CEO

MURHI INTERNATIONAL COMPANY (NIGERIA) LIMITED

Business: Telecommunication Services, Independent Television Broadcasting, Mortgage Bankers, Clearing and Forwarding
Address: Plot 45, Omole Industrial Layout, Ogba/Isheri Junction, Ogba, Ikeja, Lagos
Tel: (01) 4922241, 4922304, 4706488 Fax: (01) 4926209
* Radiovision Plaza, Central Business District, Ikeja, Lagos
Tel: (01) 4706488, 4932171-3 (3L), 4972846-7 (2L)
Contact: Alh. Murhi G. Busari - Chairman/CEO

MURPHY SHIPPING & COMMERCIAL SERVICES LIMITED

Business: Shipping Agency, Warehousing, Transportation & Freight Forwarding, Global Logistics
Address: 1, Olabode Street, off International Airport Road, Apakun-Oshodi, Lagos
Tel: (01) 4525168, 4525243, 4521438 **Fax:** (01) 2880312
E-mail: murphy@linkserve.com
Website: www.murphyhou.com
Contact: Mr. B. Agbabiaka - MD/CEO

MURTY ASSOCIATES

Business: Quantity Surveying, Cost and Procurement Management, Project Management
Address: Murty House, 11, New Yidi Road, Ilorin
Tel: (031) 220851, 224368 Fax: (031) 224374
E-mail: murty@infoweb.abs.net
* Plot 07, Central Business District, Wuse, Abuja
Tel: (09) 5230952

MUSTY ELECTRICAL COMPANY LIMITED

Business: Electrical Engineering Services, Manufacture of Electric, Concrete Poles, Sales of Transformers, Aluminium Conductors and Insulators
Address: 5, Kashim Ibrahim Road, P.O. Box 2022, Maiduguri
Tel: (076) 233458, 233720
E-mail: musty-elect@usa.com

MUTUAL ALLIANCE INVESTMENT & SECURITIES LIMITED
Business: Stockbroking
Address: Charter House Annex, 199, Ikorodu Road, Obanikoro, Lagos
Tel: (01) 4933007, 5552871-3 (3 L) **Fax:** (01) 4979507
E-mail: mutasecurities@nova.net.ng
Contact: Mr. Chidi O. Ajaegbu - MD/CEO

MUTUAL ALLIANCE SAVINGS & LOANS LIMITED
Business: Mortgage Banking
Address: 209, Oron Road, P.M.B. 1235, Uyo
Tel: (085) 203150, 201103
Website: www.multualalliancebank.com

MUTUAL ASSURANCES LIMITED
Business: General Insurance Business
Address: Wesley House (3rd Floor), 21/22, Marina, Lagos
Tel: (01) 2645680-2 (3 L) **Fax:** (01) 2632909
E-mail: info@mutualassurances.com
Website: www.mutualassurances.com
Contact: Mr. Theophilus Martins - MD/CEO

MUTUAL BENEFITS ASSURANCE COMPANY PLC
Business: Non-Life & Special Risk Insurance
Address: Plot 277B, Ajose Adeogun St, Victoria Island, Lagos
Tel: (01) 2616527, 2613062, 2619811, 4619168, 7746475
Fax: (01) 4619167
E-mail: mutualbenefits@hyperia.com
* Jinifa Plaza, Plot 1014, Central Biz. District, Abuja
Tel: (09) 6707910
* 18, Mbonu Street, D-Line, Port Harcourt
Tel: (084) 571921
Contact: Mr. Akin Opeodu - Chairman
Mr. Akin Ogunbiyi - MD/CEO

MWEB NIGERIA
Business: Internet Service Provider
Address: Plot 1379, Tiamiyu Savage St, Victoria Island, Lagos
Tel: (01) 2701222, 2701333 **Fax:** (01) 2701555
E-mail: info@mwebnigeria.com
Website: www.mwebnigeria.com

MYLOID TELECOMMUNICATIONS LIMITED
Business: Telecommunication, Information Technology, Internet Service Provision
Address: 37, Saka Tinubu Street, Victoria Island, Lagos
Tel: (01) 2613222, 2624186 **Fax:** (01) 2613211
E-mail: myloid2002@yahoo.com
myloid@beta.linkserve.com
Contact: Ms. Bimbo Soremekun - MD/CEO

N. N. FEMS INDUSTRIES LIMITED
Business: Manufacturing of Haircare and Bodycare Products
Address: 9C, Wempco Road, Ogba Ind. Estate, Ikeja, Lagos
Tel: (01) 4923352, 4924787, 7742866 **Fax:** (01) 4923050
* 11, Alagbede Street, (1st Floor), beh. 35, Bread-fruit St, Lagos Island, Lagos
Tel: (01) 2663549, 2669717 **Fax:** (01) 2665631
Contact: Mr. Emmanuel Nwakanma - Chairman/CEO

N. O. JOHN GREAT (NIGERIA) LIMITED
Business: Manufacturing of Plastic Products, Importation of Automobile Spare Parts and General Gods
Address: Zone A, Block 8 (Shop 30), ASPMDA Plaza, Trade Fair Complex, Badagry Expressway, Ojo, Lagos
Tel: (01) 3208084-9 (2 L), 7748827 **Fax:** (01) 3208047
E-mail: nojohngrat@yahoo.com
Contact: Mr. John O. Nwankwor - Chairman/CEO

N'MOR AGENCIES LIMITED
Business: Shipping, Clearing & Forwarding, Warehousing, International Trade Consultancy, Haulage
Address: 23, Alh. Kareem/Owoniran Street, Olodi-Apapa, Lagos
Tel: (01) 5450669, 8043985, 08033036599, 08033292882
Fax: (01) 5450256
E-mail: nmor57@hotmail.com
Contact: Mr. Okey Enemuo - ND/CEO

NAAFCO (SCIENTIFIC SUPPLIES) LIMITED
Business: Supply of Scientific, Medical and Laboratory Equipment, Furniture and Chemicals
Address: Plot 56, Akanbi Onitiri Close, off Eric Moore Road, Iganmu Industrial Estate, Surulere, Lagos
Tel: (01) 4702837, 5832340
Fax: (01) 5837965, 2634381, 4936624
E-mail: sales@naafco.com
naafco@alpha.linkserve.com
* Plot TL 1 & 2, Badiko North, Nnamdi Azikiwe Express Bye-Pass, Kaduna.
Tel: (062) 217721, 08044125708
Contact: Mr. O. O. Sonola - MD/CEO

NABISCO PLC
Business: Production of Biscuits
Address: 4, NIWIL Close, off Oba Akran Avenue, Ikeja Industrial Estate, Ikeja, Lagos
Tel: (01) 4968215-7 (3 L)
* 5C, Civic Centre Road, Kano.
Tel: (064) 649669
* 1, Ewereaku Close, off Onitsha-Owerri Road, Upper Iweka, Onitsha.
Tel: (046) 216282

NACKOVAD HOTELS LIMITED
Business: Hospitality Services
Address: Plot 2202, Nanka Close, beh. Heritage House, off Sultan Abubakar Way, Wuse Zone 3, Abuja
Tel: (09) 5232728, 5235089, 5237070 **Fax:** (09) 5234530
E-mail: nackovad@infoweb.abs.net

NACO MOTORS LIMITED
Business: Importation of Automobile Spare Parts
Address: 57, Nnobi Street, Nnewi, Anambra State.
Tel: (046) 463959, 460018, 463971 **Fax:** (046) 463653
Contact: Mr. C. A. Nwafor - Chairman/CEO

NADINA INDUSTRIES LIMITED
Business: Importation, Distribution and Conversion of Papers and Boards
Address: 4A, Pa Olu Oshunkeye Crescent, by United Parcel Service, Gbagada Ind.Estate, Gbagada, Lagos
Tel: (01) 5550204-9 (6L) **Fax:** (01) 5550203
* Area 7 Cornershops (Shop 30), Garki, Abuja.
Tel: (09) 6700049
Contact: Mr. Oluseyi Osho - Chairman/CEO

NAHMAN CONSRUCTION COMPANY LIMITED
Business: Building and Civil Engineering Contractors
Address: 8A, Louis Solomon Close, off Ahmadu Bello Way, Victoria Island, Lagos
Tel: (01) 2610734, 2618122 **Fax:** (01) 2610753
E-mail: nabnah@aol.com
* Plot 680, Port Harcourt Cr., Area 11, Garki, Abuja
Tel: (09) 3142223-5 (3 L) **Fax:** (09) 3142788
Contact: Mr. Nabil Nahman - MD/CEO

NAIRDA LIMITED
Business: Sales, Installation and Maintenance of Mechanical, Electrical and Plumbing Systems
Address: Plot 608, Bobo Street, off Gana St, Maitama, Abuja
Tel: (09) 4130574, 4130576, 4132284, 4132289, 08036651026 **Fax:** (09) 4133602, 4137268
* 10, Burma Road, Apapa, Lagos
Tel: (01) 5873171
* 58, Alh. Balarabe Musa Crescent, off Samuel Manuwa Street, Victoria Island, Lagos
Tel: (01) 2614084, 2616685, 2618257, 2621250-5 (6L)
Fax: (01) 2618256
Contact: Hajia Misau Ibrahim - Chairman
Mr. Guy Peleg - MD/CEO

NAJICO IRON & STEEL COMPANY LIMITED
Business: Stockist and Supplier of Building, Plumbing and Electrical Materials, Transports
Address: Plot RR. 11, Junction Road, Kaduna
Tel: (062) 247772, 247822 **Fax:** (062) 247858

NAKUDU TANNERY LIMITED
Business: Tanning of Hides and Skins
Address: 23, Challawa Industrial Estate, Kano
Tel: (062) 319147, 634716
Contact: Alh. Sabo Mohammed - Chairman/CEO

NAL BANK PLC
Business: Commercial & Investment Banking Services
Address: NAL Towers, 20, Marina, Lagos
Tel: (01) 2600420-9(10L), 2600850-9(10L), 2600890-4 (5L)
Fax: (01) 2631468, 2635298
E-mail: cpbranc@nalbank.com.ng
infonal@nalbank.com.ng
Website: www.nalbank.com.ng
* Plot 990, Cadastral Zone AO, Behind Leventis Stores, Central Business District, Abuja
Tel: (09) 5239892, 5235340-2 (3L) **Fax:** (09) 5239720
* 112E, Aba Road, Port Harcourt
Tel: (084) 239002-5 (4L) **Fax:** (084) 238417
Contact: Mr. Ben Akabueze - MD/CEO
Mr. Etim E. Etim - Head (Corporate Affairs)

NAL ASSET MANAGEMENT & TRUSTEES LIMITED
Business: Asset Management, Pension Funds, Trusteeship
Address: NAL Towers, 20, Marina, Lagos
Tel: (01) 2600121-3 (3L), 2600850-9(10L), 2633636
Fax: (01) 2632284
E-mail: cpbranc@nalbank.com.ng
infonal@nalbank.com.ng
Website: www.nalbank.com.ng
Contact: Funlola Jeje - CEO
Etim E. Etim - Head (Group Corporate Affairs)

NAL INSURANCE BROKERS LIMITED
Business: Insurance Marketing
Address: NAL Towers, 20, Marina, Lagos
Tel: (01) 2633636, 4733609, 8181501, 08023128655, 08023247282 **Fax:** (01) 2633636
E-mail: insurance@nalbank.com.ng
Website: www.nalbank.com.ng
Contact: Mr Sammy D'Almeida - CEO
Mr Etim E. Etim - Head (Group Corporate Affairs)

NAL TOWERS SECURITIES LIMITED
Business: Registrar Services, Porfolio Management
Address: NAL Towers, 20, Marina, Lagos Island, Lagos
Tel: (01) 2635607, 2646582 **Fax:** (01) 2646582
E-mail: nalregistrars@nalbank.com.ng
Website: www.nalbank.com.ng
Contact: Adegboyega Babalola - CEO
Etim E. Etim - Head (Group Corporate Affairs)

NALCO/EXXON ENERGY CHEMICALS LIMITED
Business: Marketers of Oil, Water and General Control Chemicals, Apparatus and Equipment
Address: Mobil House, Room 4A27, Lekki Expressway Victoria Island, Lagos
Tel: (01) 2621640, 2621660, 2621680 Ext. 1270
E-mail: jikingston@micro.com.ng
Contact: J. L Kingston Jr. - Area Manager (West Africa)

NALEX ASSOCIATES INSURANCE BROKERS LIMITED
Business: Insurance Broking and Consultancy Services
Address: 3A, Olaide Benson Street, Maryland, Ikeja, Lagos
Tel: (01) 4978387, 7739962, 08033024753
Fax: (01) 4978387
E-mail: nalex@infoweb.abs.net
Contact: Mr. Alex Ojei - Chairman/CEO

NALMAC ALUMINIUM PRODUCTS LIMITED
Business: Sales of Alumium Roofing Sheets, Doors & Windows
Address: 71, Mbaise Road, Owerri
Tel: (083) 233029, 234706, 08033424852
Fax: (083) 233029
Contact: Sir. Mike N. Okafor (KSC) - Chairman/CEO

NAMALCO OIL MILLS LIMITED
Business: Processing and Production of Vegetable Oil
Address: Plot 101, Sharada Industrial Estate Phase II, Kano
Tel: (064) 665728, 635728
Contact: Alh. A. Gwadabe - Chairman/CEO

NAMOH INDUSTRIES NIGERIA LIMITED
Business: Manufacture of Industrial/Domestic Plastic Wares
Address: 96, Nnamdi Azikiwe Street, Lagos Island, Lagos
Tel: (01) 2663843, 2664484, 2667071 **Fax:** (01) 2661658
Contact: Mr. Ravi Babani - GM

NAMPAK NIGERIA PLC (formerly Carnaudmetalbox Nig Plc)
Business: Manufacture of Metal Containers & Crown Corks
Address: 3/7, MetalBox Road, Ogba Ind. Estate, Ikeja, Lagos
Tel: (01) 4973649, 4923765, 4923768
Fax: (01) 4923767, 4974154
E-mail: mails@crowncorknig.com
Contact: Mr. C. R. Tulsian - Operation Director
Mr. J. O. Adebayo - Sales/Marketing Controller

NANET HOTELS LIMITED
Business: Catering Services, Hotel Management and Consultancy, Confectioners
Address: NN 15, Abubakar Kigo Road, off Constitution Road, Kaduna
Tel: (062) 242696, 249639, 08033119979
Fax: (062) 249678
E-mail: nanethotel@wwlkad.net
* Lake Chad Guest Palace Hotel, Lake Chad Crescent, Maitama, Abuja
Tel: (09) 4133864-5 (2 L), 4137985 **Fax:** (09) 4132806
* Zaranda Hotel, Jos Road, Bauchi
Tel: (077) 543590-9 (10L), 543814-20 (7L)
Fax: (077) 543596
Contact: Mr. Ini Akpabio - MD/CEO

NAPAK SERVICES (NIGERIA) LIMITED
Business: Clearing and Forwarding, Removal and Packaging Services, Freight and Cargo Services, Freight Consolidation, Inland Haulage and Warehousing
Address: Plot 4, Block H, Oshodi Industrial Estate, Apapa-Oshodi Expressway, Oshodi, Lagos
Tel: (01) 4521085, 7743038, 08022243141, 08033333517
Fax: (01) 4974154
E-mail: napakservices@yahoo.co.uk
"napak"exclnapak2001@yahoo.co.uk
Contact: Mr. Adeniyi Adebakin - Chairman/CEO

NARRELI INTERNATIONAL LIMITED
Business: Real Estate Development, Project Management and Consultancy
Address: AIM Plaza, Plot 267B, Etim Inyang Crescent, Victoria Island, Annex, Lagos
Tel: (01) 2614838, 2614848, 2616191, 2616636
Fax: (01) 2614779, 2620105

NASAL INSURANCE COMPANY LIMITED
Business: Insurance (General Business and Special Risks)
Address: Reinsurance Hous (14th Floor), 46, Marina, Lagos
Tel: (01) 2643698, 2662058, 2663519, 2665780, 4736217
Fax: (01) 2665780
E-mail: nasal-insurance@siotel.com
Contact: Alh. Aliko Dangote - Group President
Mr. Frank N. Uche - GM/CEO

NASARAWA INVESTMENT & PROPERTY DEVELOPMENT COMPANY LIMITED
Business: Property/Real Estate Development, Financial Services, Stockbroking and Investment Advisory Service, Consultancy Services
Address: Investment House, 32, Jos Road, Lafia
Tel: (047) 221512., 220120
Contact: Mal. Idris Bori - MD/CEO

NASARAWA MINERALS DEVELOPMENT COMPANY LTD
Business: Mining of Solid Minerals
Address: Investment House, 32, Jos Road, Lafia
Tel: (047) 21739
Contact: Wing Cdr Isa Mohammed (rtd.) - Chairman
Mr. Ogli S. Akwe - GM/CEO

NASARAWA PUBLISHING COMPANY LIMITED
Business: Printing Services, Newspaper Publishing
Address: 11, Jos Road, opp. New State Secretariat, Lafia
Tel/Fax: (047) 20548
Contact: Muhammed Kabir Abubakar - Chairman
Mal. Rufa'i Ibrahim - CEO

NASCO GROUP (NIGERIA) LIMITED
Business: Conglomerate
Address: 1, Ahmed Nasreddin Road, Jos
Tel: (073) 463175, 463347, 463348 **Fax:** (073) 461554
E-mail: nms@nascogrp.com
Website: www.nascogrp.com
* Nigerian Shippers Council Plaza, 4, Park Lane, Apapa, Lagos.
Tel: (01) 5870004, 5870945, 5875450 **Fax:** (01) 5874238
E-mail: nascolag@alpha.linkserve.com
Contact: Mr Attia A. Nasreddin - Chairman
Alh. Ibrahim A. Sani - Group MD/CEO

NASCO FIBRE PRODUCTS LIMITED
Business: Manufacturing of Carpets and Blankets
Address: Old Airport Road, Jos
Tel: (073) 463333-4 (2L), 462615, 08034515818
Fax: (073) 461554
E-mail: nms@nascogrp.com
Website: www.nascogrp.com
Contact: Alh. Ibrahim A. Sani - Group MD/CEO

NASCO FOODS (NIGERIA) LIMITED
Business: Production of Cornflakes, Biscuits and Wafers
Address: Yakbu Gowon Way, Jos
Tel: (073) 464478, 464479 Fax: (073) 461554
E-mail: nms@nascogrp.com
Website: www.nascogrp.com
Contact: Alh. Ibrahim A. Sani - Group MD/CEO

NASCO HOUSEHOLD PRODUCTS LIMITED
Business: Manufacturing of Soap and Detergent
Address: Old Airport Rd/Yakubu Gowon Way Junction, Jos
Tel: (073) 462783 **Fax:** (073) 461554
E-mail: nms@nascogrp.com
Website: www.nascogrp.com
Contact: Alh. Ibrahim A. Sani - Group MD/CEO

NASCO MANAGEMENT SERVICES LIMITED
Business: Management Services, Consultancy
Address: Yakubu Gowon Way, Jos
Tel: (073) 453175, 453347-8 (2 L)
E-mail: nms@nascogrp.com
Website: www.nascogrp.com
* Shippers Plaza, 4, Park Lane, Apapa, Lagos.
Tel: (01) 5870004, 5870945, 5875450 **Fax:** (01) 5874238
E-mail: nascolag@alpha.linkserve.com
Contact: Alh. Ibrahim A. Sani - Group MD/CEO

NASCO PACK LIMITED
Business: Manufacturing and Marketing of Corrugated & Flexible Packaging Materials
Address: 1, Ahmed Nasreddin Road, Jos, Jos
Tel: (073) 462250
E-mail: nms@nascogrp.com
Website: www.nascogrp.com
Contact: Mr Attia A. Nasreddin - Chairman
Alh. Ibrahim A. Sani - Group MD/CEO

NASMIER NTERPRISES LIMITED
Business: Tannery
Address: 16, Umaru Babura Road, Bompai Ind. Estate, Kano
Tel: (064) 642843
Contact: Hassan Madmud - Chairman/CEO

NASSARAWA GUEST HOUSE, KANO
Business: Hospitality & Catering Services
Address: 314, Lamido Road, Kano
Tel: (064) 634668638571, 08034501789, 08034524213
Fax: (064) 644956
Contact: Alh. Bello Maitama - Chairman/CEO

NATASHA'S LIMITED
Business: General Merchandising, Supermarket
Address: Suites 6, 7, 9 & 10, Block B, Landmark Plaza, Plot 3129, Ibrahim Babangida Way, Maitama, Abuja
Tel: (09) 4132899, 08035953026
Contact: Madam Stella Akogu - MD/CEO

NATEC NIGERIA LIMITED
Business: Airline Automation and Services, Computer & Power Engineering, IT Consultancy; Supply of Airboats, Radio Communication Engineering
Address: 11, Olaribiro Street, off Allen Avenue, Ikeja, Lagos
Tel: (01) 4964181, 4936999. **Fax:** (01) 4936999
E-mail: natec@winning.com

NATELCO NIGERIA LIMITED
Business: Sales of IT Products and Telephone Systems
Address: Moragoff Arrow Compound, Plot 142, Oba Akran Avenue, Ikeja Industrial Estate, Ikeja, Lagos
Tel: (01) 4935819, 4971505 **Fax:** (01) 49716139
E-mail: natelcong@hotmail.com

NATHAN'S DRYCLEANERS
Business: Drycleaning and Laundry Services
Address: 67, Woji Road, G.R.A. Phase II, Port Harcourt
Tel: (084) 236079, 331684
* Plot 266, Kofo Abayomi St, Victoria Island, Lagos
Tel: (01) 2625919, 2626262

NATIONAL BANK OF NIGERIA LIMITED
Business: Commercial Banking
Address: 8, Idowu Taylor Street, Victoria Island, Lagos
Tel: (01) 2610027-8 (2 L), 2610033, 2610035, 2610037, 2610039, 261067, 2610054, 2610021, 2610036
Fax: (01) 2611117
Contact: Mr. Kola Ayeye - MD/CEO

NATIONAL CARGO HANDLING COMPANY LIMITED
Business: Stevedoring and Shore Handling
Address: 41, Hospital Road, off Tin Can Island Expressway, Olodi, Apapa, Lagos
Tel: (01) 54522820-4 (5 L) (Ext. 2493, 2598)
Contact: Dr. J. S. Kassa - Chairman
Chief Fabian Umunnakwe - MD/CEO

NATIONAL CLEARING & FORWARDING AGENCY (NACFA)
Business: Clearing & Forwarding Services, Travel Services
Address: 3, Creek Road, Apapa, Lagos
Tel: (01) 5876275, 5874576, 5878562, 5457172, 5878625
Fax: (01) 5878626
E-mail: nacfa@hyperia.com
Contact: Chief Bruno Abu Oshokpekhai - Chairman
Mr. Andrew Isichei - MD/CEO

NATIONAL ELECTRIC POWER AUTHORITY (NEPA)
Business: Generation, Transmission, Distribution & Marketing of Electricity to Residential, Commercial & Industrial Customers
Address: Plot 441, Zambezi Crescent, off Aguiyi Ironsi Street, Maitama District, Abuja
Tel: (09) 4135504, 4135529, 4135550, 4135606, 4135650
Fax: (09) 4135501, 4135644
E-mail: mdnepa@alpha.linkserve.com
* 24/25, Marina, Lagos.
Tel: (01) 2634299
Contact: Mal. M. Mousa-Booth - A.G.M - (Public Relations)

NATIONAL ENGINEERING & TECHNICAL CO.LTD (NETCO)
Business: Engineering, Construction Supervision, Procurement and Project Management Services
Address: Stallion House (11th & 12th Floors), 2, Ajose Adeogun Street, Victoria Island, Lagos
Tel: (01) 2611232, 2627782, 2627913, 2647301
Fax: (01) 2611230
E-mail: info@netco.com.ng
Website: www.netco.com.ng
Contact: Chief U. Okorafor - Chairman
Dr. Bunu Alibe - MD/CEO

NATIONAL FERTILIZER COMPANY OF NIGERIA LIMITED (NAFCON)
Business: Manufacture of Fertilizers
Address: NAFCON Fertilizer Complex, Onne, River State
Tel: (084) 820480-95 (16L)
* 41, Isaac John Street, GRA Ikeja, Lagos
Tel: (01) 4975471, 4978110
* Plot 870, Area II, Garki, Abuja
Tel: (09) 2342638, 2344183

NATIONAL MARITIME AUTHORITY (NMA)
Business: Regulation of Maritime Activities in Nigeria
Address: Maritime House, 4, Burma Road, Apapa, Lagos
Tel: (01) 5804800-4 (5 L), 5871673, 5872214
Fax: (01) 5450722, 5451430
E-mail: natmaritime@infoweb.abs.net
Website: www.nma-ng.com
* Plot 2891, Taraba Close, off Limpopo Street, Maitama, Wuse, Abuja
Contact: Dr. Ferdinand Agu - Director-General/CEO
Mr. Gbenga Ogunsakin - Asst Chief PRO.

NATIONAL PETROLEUM INVESTMENTS & MANAGEMENT SERVICES LIMITED (NAPIMS)
Business: Petroleum Investment & Management Services
Address: 8/10, Bayo Kuku Road, Ikoyi, Lagos
Tel: (01) 2670770, 2619355-6 (2 L), 2626216-7 (2 L)
Contact: Mr. Peter O. Chukwu - Group GM

NATIONAL RISK FUND PLC
Business: Venture Capital Financing
Address: 11, Keffi Street, S. W. Ikoyi, Lagos
Tel: (01) 2691884
Contact: Dr. A. O. Oboh - Ag. MD/CEO

NATIONAL SALT COMPANY OF NIGERIA PLC
Business: Refining & Distribution of Edible & Industrial Salt
Address: Salt City, Ijoko - Otta, Ogun State
Tel: (090) 403801
Contact: Alh. M. S. Ladan - Baki - MD/CEO
Mr. A. A. Samuel - Company Sec/Legal Adviser

NATIONAL YANKARI PARK LIMITED
Business: Tourism, Hotel Services, Travel Agency
Address: Maiduguri Bye-Pass, by Ramadan Press, Bauchi
Tel: (077) 543674, 543675

NATIONHOUSE PRESS LIMITED
Business: Commercial Printing Services
Address: Plot A3, Kudenda Industrial Area, Nnamdi Azikiwe Expressway, Kaduna
Tel: (062) 231271-2 (2L), 234206-7 (2L)
Contact: Mal. S. G. Shehu - MD/CEO

NATIONWIDE & GLOBE INSURANCE BROKERS LIMITED
Business: Insurance Broking, Life & Pension Consultancy
Address: Dantata House (1st Floor), 1, Beirut Road/Post Office Road, Kano
Tel: (064) 641035 **Fax:** (064) 644629
E-mail: nationwideglobebrokers@yahoo.com
* DMK House (2nd Floor, Suite 22), Plot 735, Kade Street, off Aminu Kano Crescent, Wuse II, Abuja
Tel: (09) 4133125
Contact: Mr. A. O. Ajayi - Chairman/CEO

NATURAL BOTTLERS COMPANY NIGERIA LIMITED
Business: Bottling of Mineral Water
Address: 6, Obasa Close, off Oba Akran Avenue, Ikeja Industrial Estate, Lagos
Tel: (01) 4703054, 4711124 **Fax:** (01) 4930419
Contact: Mr. J. D. Olujemisin - GM

NAUTILUS (NIGERIA) ENGINEERING & CONSTRUCTION LTD
Business: Oil Industry Construction & Engineering Services
Address: Okoi Arikpo House (5th Floor), 5, Idowu Taylor Street, Victoria Island, Lagos
Tel/Fax: (01) 2610809, 3200671
E-mail: osi-nnec@alpha.linkserve.com

NAVAO LIMITED
Business: Internet Services, Operation of Pre-Paid Call Cards
Address: Bookshop House (13th Floor), 50/52, Broad Street, Lagos
Tel: (01) 2633880, 2704090-2 (3L), 4820551
Fax: (01) 2704093
Contact: Mr Sola Omidiran - MD/CEO

NAYEE COMMUNICATIONS LIMITED
Business: Commercial Printing and Publishing Services
Address: Nayee House, Plot 1, Lambert Imasuen Drive, Ajao Estate, Isolo, Lagos
Tel: (01) 4528452, 4528479, 4528805 **Fax:** (01) 4528488
* 279, Addis Ababa Crescent, Wuse Zone 4, Abuja
Tel: (09) 5231387
Contact: Chief Kenneth O. Gbagi - Chairman/CEO

NBE OCEANEERING NIGERIA LIMITED
Business: Freight and Maritime Services
Address: Plot 86, East-West Road, Rumuodara Junction, Port Harcourt
Tel: (084) 571031, 611245 **Fax:** (084) 238368, 611140
E-mail: nbe@smartgroup.com
* Plot 114, Admiralty Way, Lekki Phase 1, Lagos
Contact: Chief Chris Igbojekwe - Chairman/CEO
Mr. John Ogah - Agency Manager

NBM BANK LIMITED
Business: Banking Services
Address: 228A, Awolowo Road, Ikoyi, Lagos
Tel: (01) 2690380-8 (9 L), 687017-8 (2 L), 2693257
Fax: (01) 2693256
* Plot A-1/A, Trans-Amadi Industrial Layout, Port Harcourt.
Tel: (084) 237925-7 (3L), 330520
* Medife House, Plot 2135, Herbert Macaulay Way, Wuse Zone 5, Abuja
Contact: Mr. G. Suavanet - MD/CEO
Mr. Mike Anegbode - Manager/Head (HR/Admin)

NCR (NIGERIA) PLC
Business: Sale and Service of Data Processing Equipment, IT Solutions Provider, Manufacturing and Sale of Rotary & Sheet-Fed Printing
Address: NRC House, 6, Broad Street, Lagos Island, Lagos
Tel: (01) 2601260-9 (10 L), 2633732, 2633227, 2633742
Fax: (01) 2636350, 2635950
E-mail: ncrnigeria@ncrnigeria.com
Website: www.ncrnigeria.com
* NCR Systemedia Complex, Plot 11, Block C, Ilupeju Industrial Estate, Ilupeju, Lagos
Tel: (01) 4968460-6 (7L)
Contact: Otunba Adekunle Ojora, OFR - Chairman
Mr. Syed Bader ul-Islam - MD/CEO

NEATIDY ENTERPRISES LIMITED
Business: Sales and Service of Catering & Kitchen Equipment
Address: 20, Lateef Sanni St, off Agunlejika St, off Apapa-Oshodi Expressway, Ijeshatedo, Surulere, Lagos
Tel: (01) 4827353, 5893035, 08033008012, 08033086045
Fax: (01) 4971015, 5893036
Contact: Chief M. A.Olofindayo - Chairman/CEO

NECJON INTERNATIONAL AGENCY NIGERIA LIMITED
Business: Importation of Electronic & Electrical Appliances
Address: 62/64, Iweka Road, Onitsha
Tel: (046) 212365, 217573, 480846, 08033162513
* Block 246, Electronic Section, Alaba Internation Market, Ojo, Lagos.
Tel: (01) 3295644, 7745412, 08033282861
Contact: Mr. Nnamdi W. Okwubido - Chairman/CEO

NEET (NIGERIA) LIMITED
Business: Sales & Service of Telecommunication Equipment, Office Automation Products & IT Networking
Address: Panasonic House, 43, Akin Adesola Street, Victoria Island, Lagos
Tel: (01) 2611066, 2610562, 2610878, 2619233, 613912, 616514, 616479, 08034007636 **Fax:** (01) 2691716
E-mail: neet@linkserve.com.ng
panasonic@neetnigeria.com
canon@neetnigeria.com

* Plot 612, Tafawa Balewa Way, Area 7, Garki, Abuja
Tel: (09) 2345240, 2345241, 2345242 **Fax:** (09) 2345243
* 6, Olu Obasanjo Road, Port Harcourt
Tel: (084) 230568, 230570, 230572
Contact: Dr. J. D. Awosanya - Chairman

NEGRIS LIMITED
Business: Engineering and Energy Services
Address: Victoria House, 35/37, Isheri Road, Aguda-Ogba, Ikeja, Lagos
Tel: (01) 4920353, 4920354, 4920356, 4921435-6 (2 L)
Fax: (01) 4922181
* 36, Trans-Amadi Industrial Layout, Port Harcourt
Tel: (084) 230188-9 (2 L) **Fax:** (084) 236608
* 78, Arubayi Street, off Giwa-Amu Street, Warri.
Tel: (053) 250628
Contact: Engr. Abidoye Ayoola - Group Chairman/CEO

NEIMETH INTERNATIONAL PHARMACEUTICALS PLC
Business: Manufacture of Pharmaceutical &Health Products
Address: 1, Henry Carr St Ikeja Industrial Estate, Ikeja, Lagos
Tel: (01) 4973730-4 (5 L) **Fax:** (01) 4933430, 4963866
E-mail: mails@neimeth.com.ng
Website: www.neimeth.com.ng
Contact: Maxi Sam I.Ohuabunwa, MON - Chairman/MD
Mr Okay Eni Nwaka - Corporate Affairs Manager

NEITAL SHOE & TANNERY LIMITED
Business: Tannery, Production of Shoes & Leather Items
Address: Abbatoir Road, Maiduguri
Tel: (076) 231760
Contact: Mal. Usman Tamsu - GM/CEO

NEK VIDEO LINKS LIMITED
Business: Home Video Film Production, Dubbing, Marketing & Promotion
Address: 82, Ago Palace Way, near Century Hotels, Okota
Tel: (01) 521526 **Fax:** (01) 5834392
E-mail: nek@hyperia.com
Contact: Chief Kenneth Nnebue - Chairman/CEO

NELSON PUBLISHERS LIMITED
Business: Publishing & Distribution of Educational Textbooks
Address: 8/10, Ilupeju Bye-Pass, Ilupeju, Lagos
Tel: (01) 4961452
Contact: Prof. (Chief) C. O. Taiwo - Chairman
Mr. Yinka Obatuyi - GM/CEO

NEM. INSURANCE PLC
Business: All Classes of Insurance Services
Address: 138/146, Broad Street, Lagos
Tel: (01) 2600040-5 (6 L), 2664468, 2664535, 2665258, 2665269 **Fax:** (01) 2663277
E-mail: nem@nem-insurance.com.ng
Contact: Pastor (Mrs) Helen A. Oyitso - GM/CEO

NEO STEEL COMPANY LIMITED
Business: Steel Import, Industrial Suppliers, Ship Chandlers
Address: Km. 1, Lagos-Badagry Expressway (House II), near Orile Iganmu Bus-Stop, Orile Iganmu, Lagos
Tel: (01) 7740381, 4702396, 4722379, 08023056371, 08023056377, 08023142380, 08023142386, 08034077133, 08034540401, 08037114910
Fax: (01) 5877698, 2885114
E-mail: neosteelco@yahoo.com
Contact: Mr. Augustine Nnabara - MD/CEO

NEOTERIC ELECTRONICS & TECHNOLOGY LTD (NEAT)
Business: Telecommunications, Sales of Computers
Address: 49, Aba Road, Port Harcourt
Tel: (084) 238502 **Fax:** (084) 238503
E-mail: phoffice@neat-i-t.com
Website: www.neat-i-t.com
Contact: Mr. Anthonio Lorenzo - Chairman/CEO

NEPTUNE MARITIME (NIGERIA)
Business: Maritme Services, Drilling & Construction, Oil Industry Consltancy Services
Address: Neptune Maritime Base, Aker Road, Rumolumeni, Port Harcourt
Tel: (084) 239271, 239273, 571711, 571715

NESTLE NIGERIA PLC
Business: Production and Distribution of Food Products, Production of Hydrolysed Plant Protein Mix
Address: 22-24, Industrial Avenue, Ilupeju, Industrial Estate, Ilupeju, Lagos
Tel: (01) 4978720-4 (5L), 4934131-5 (5L), 4934105-9 (5L), 4934080-4 (5L), 4932394 **Fax:** (01) 4962393
E-mail: nestle-foods.nigeria@nestle.com
* Agbara Industrial Estate, Km 32, Lagos-Badagry Expressway, Agbara, Ogun State
Tel: (01) 712007, 712323, 712353, 712362, 712377
* Km 7, Idiroko Road, Sango-Otta, Ogun State
Tel: (039) 722280, 722292
* 171/173, Aba-Owerri Road, Aba.
Tel: (082) 224964
* Plot 7112, Horoto New Layout, off Maiduguri Road, Kano.
Tel: (064) 631118 **Fax:** (064) 640428
* 8, Bank Street, Jos.
Tel: (073) 452414
Contact: Mr. Klaus P. Wachsmuth - MD/CEO
Dr. Samuel Adenekan - Corp. Relations Manager

NESTOIL LIMITED
Business: Oil Industry Services (Integrated Engineering Services, General Construction, Procurement Consultants Environmental Services)
Address: Africa-Re House (4th Floor), Plot 1679, Karimu Kotun Street, Victoria Island, Lagos
Tel: (01) 2626685-6 (2 L) **Fax:** (01) 2626687
E-mail: nestoil@infoweb.abs.net
* 27, Nzimiro Street, Amadi Flats, Old G.R.A, Port Harcourt
Tel: (084) 239933, 239956 **Fax:** (084) 256049
* Plot 19, Ontario Crescent, Maitama, Abuja
Tel: (01) 4135183 **Fax:** (01) 4135184
E-mail: nestolabuja@hyperia.com

NETARCOM NIGERIA LIMITED
Business: Sales & Installation of Radio & Satellite Communication Equipment & TV Broadcast Systems
Address: 30, Bornu Crescent, Apapa, Lagos
Tel: (01) 4702959, 5457188 Fax: (01) 5457187
E-mail: honeycrown@hyperia.com

NETCELL LIMITED
Business: Sales of GSM Telephones and Accessories
Address: Lafayette Shopping Mall (Suite 4), Plot 1436, Sanusi Fafunwa Street, Victoria Island, Lagos
Tel: (01) 3200046, 617062, 08032030737, 08034007193
Fax: (01) 3200046
E-mail: accessgate@alpha.linkserve.com
* Millenium Verdict Plaza, Plot 1059, Adetokunbo Ademola Crescent, Wuse II, Abuja
Tel: (09) 5237145-6 (2L), 08032030738-40 (3L)
Fax: (09) 5237146
* 7, Babbe Street, D-Line, Port Harcourt.
Tel: (084) 232360
Contact: Grace Adeyemi - MD/CEO

NETCODIETSMANN COMPANY LIMITED
Business: Oilfield Engineering Services
Address: Stallion House (11th & 12th Floors), 2, Ajose Adeogun Street, Victoria Island, Lagos
Tel: (01) 2611232, 2647301
Fax: (01) 2611230
E-mail: info@netco.com.ng
Website: www.netco.com.ng
Contact: Mr. Fiore Franciosa - MD/CEO

NETCONSTRUCT NIGERIA LIMITED
Business Real Estate Development & Management
Address: 19, Biodun Street (2nd Floor), off Keffi Street, S. W., Ikoyi, Lagos
Tel: (01) 4727352, 7739509, 08023608346-7 (2L)
E-mail: info@netconstructng.com
Website: www.netconstructng.com
Contact: Engr Brisan Christian - MD/CEO

NETTCOM SYSTEMS LIMITED
Business: Sales & Installation of Telecommunication Equipment
Address: 5A, Aerodrome Rd, off Wharf Rd, Apapa, Lagos
Tel: (01) 5451520, 5457022, 08033002944, 08037123173
Fax: (01) 5451520
Contact: Mr Oluwanimbe Togun - MD/CEO

NETWORK AIRLINES LIMITED
Business: Airline & Aviation Services
Address: 45, Opebi Road, opp Fototek Ltd, Ikeja, Lagos
Tel: (01) 4925988, 7947219, 08033216740, 08037210807
Fax: (01) 4925988
Contact: Capt Gbolahan O. Olushola - MD/CEO

NETWORK INSURANCE BROKERS LIMITED
Business: Insurance Broking
Address: 9, Post Office Road, Kano
Tel: (064) 642968, 645487, 08023106662
Fax: (064) 642968
Contact: Chief E. A. Fashakin - MD/CEO

NETWORK TECHNOLOGIES LIMITED
Business: Sales, Installation and Maintenance of Computer Hardware, Accessories and Office Automation
Address: 114, Obafemi Awolowo Way, Ikeja, Lagos
Tel/Fax: (01) 4931723
E-mail: network@nova.net.ng
Contact: Izundu Lawrence Maduneme - Chairman/CEO

NETWORKS (Div of Dizengoff West Africa Ltd)
Business: Sales and Maintenance of Telecommunication Equipment and Systems
Address: 28, Creek Road, Apapa, Lagos
Tel: (01) 5874217, 5875790, 5877393 **Fax:** (01) 5874021
E-mail: dizengoff@cyberspace.net.ng
Website: www.dizengoff.com
Contact: Prof. J. K. Duncan - Chairman

NETWORTH SECURITIES & FINANCE LIMITED
Business: Stockbroking
Address: E D House (4th Floor), 47, Marina, Lagos
Tel: (01) 2641349, 2641350 Fax: (01) 2641350
E-mail: networth@hyperia.com
Website: www.networthsec.com
Contact: Mr. Azu Odita - GM

NEVERFAIL INDUSTRIES LIMITED
Business: Distribution and Sales of Home Appliances
Address: 6B, Lalupon Close, off Keffi St, S.W. Ikoyi, Lagos
Tel: (01) 2691184-5 (2L) **Fax:** (01) 2691186
Contact: Mrs. Ann O. Ukpoma - MD/CEO

NEW CAPITAL PROPERTIES LIMITED
Business: Real Estate Development & Management
Address: 5A, Abubakar Gumi Rd, off Ali Akilu Rd, Kaduna
Tel: (062) 241025, 249360 **Fax:** (062) 249360

NEW CENTURY PROTECTION INSURANCE BROKERS LTD
Business: Insurance Broking & Consultancy
Address: 6, Elsie Femi-Pearse Street, off Adeola Odeku Street, Victoria Island, Lagos
Tel: (01) 2629870, 4723342, 08033789620
E-mail: newcenturypro@yahoo.com
Contact: S. Osadebe - GM/CEO

NEW COMEX TRADING COMPANY LIMITED
Business: Importation and Wholesale Distribution of Milk, Seasonings, Various Food Items, Building Materials, Plumbing Materials and Bathroom Equipment, Ceramics, Airconditioners, Fertilisers and Solar Energy Equipment
Address: 9, Olosa Street, off Adetokunbo Ademola Street, opp. Eko Hotel & Suites, Victoria Island, Lagos
Tel: (01) 2622920, 2622331, 2611328, 4619050-2 (3L)
Fax: (01) 2621836
E-mail: avy@infoweb.abs.net
Contact: Mr. E. Avy - Distribution Manager

NEW CRYSTAL COMMUNICATIONS LIMITED
Business: Outdoor Advertising Agency
Address: 226, Awka Road, opp. St Mary's Church, Onitsha
Tel: (046) 412167, 412738, 08033259306, 08033281321
E-mail: newcrystal-doz@hotmail.com
Website: www.newcrystalcommnications.com
Contact: Mr C. N. Mbanefo - MD/CEO

NEW EPOCH NIGERIA LIMITED
Business: Sales of Mobile Phones & Telephone Handsets
Address: 13, Saka Tinubu Street, Victoria Island, Lagos
Tel: (01) 5558661, 08023187355, 08033084062
E-mail: newepochlgs@yahoo.com
Contact: Mr Stephen Ifedioranma - GM (Sales & Marketing)

NEW ERA GROUP LIMITED
Business: Food Processing, Paper Converting, Health Care Services
Address: 213/215, Azikiwe Road, Aba
Tel: (01) 225520, 231728, 233607

NEW GENERATION INVESTMENTS LIMITED
Business: Manufacturing of Artificial Weave-on Braids
Address: 4A, Badejo Kalesanwo Road, Matori Industrial Estate, Mushin, Lagos
Tel: (01) 7741263, 4529386
* 28, Ikwerre Rd, Mile 1 Park, Diobu, Port Harcourt
* Plot 578, Herbert Macaulay Way/Michael Okpara Street, Wuse Zone 5, Abuja

NEW HEALTHWAY COMPANY LIMITED
Business: Manufacturing and Marketing of MOKO Pharmaceutical Products
Address: Km. 22, Badagry Expressway, Afromedia, Ajangbadi, Surulere, Lagos
Tel: (01) 7745506 **Fax:** (01) 2646437
E-mail: newhealthway@usa.net
Contact: Mr. C. I. Ezimoha - Chairman

NEW LINE INSURANCE COMPANY LIMITED
Business: General Insurance Business
Address: 13, Abraham Adesanya Road, Apapa, Lagos
Tel: (01) 5454042-3 (2 L), 5870757, 5873289
Fax: (01) 5871753
E-mail: newline@intracom.net.ng
* 24, Ikwerre Road, Port Harcourt
Contact: Senator (Chief) Olayinka O. Omilani - Chairman
Mr. S. A. Adegboyega - GM

NEW MILLENNIUM INVESTMENTS LIMITED
Business: Investment, LPO Financing, Oil & Gas Servics
Address: McIver House (Suite 5), 143/145, Broad St, Lagos
Tel: (01) 2643127, 2643134 Fax: (01) 2643134
E-mail: jaztech@hyperia.com
Contact: Dr. John Azukaego Jideonwo - Chairman/CEO

NEW NIGERIA DEVELOPMENT COMPANY LIMITED
Business: Development Finance and Holding Conglomerate.
Address: Ahmed Talib House, 18/19, Ahmadu Bello Way, Kaduna.
Tel: (062) 246200-5 (6L), 246251-5 (5L)
Fax: (062) 245482
E-mail: nndc@skannet.com
Website: www.nndcgroup.com
Contact: Lt. Gen. Garba Duba (rtd), CFR - Chairman
Alh. Abdullahi Sarki Mahmoud - Group MD/CEO

NEW NIGERIA SALT COMPANY LIMITED
Business: Refining and Marketing of Iodized Table Salt
Address: The Salt Refinery, Oghareki, Delta State.
Tel: (054) 60014
* 5, Ogbetuo Avenue, off Boundary Rd, Benin City

NEW NIGERIAN NEWSPAPERS LIMITED
Business: Newspaper Publishing and Commercial Banking
Address: Ahmadu Bello Way, Kaduna
Tel: (062) 214719, 243365, 245221, 243312
Fax: (062) 211723, 215391
Website: www.newnigerian.com
* NNN Building, 220A, Moshood Abiola Way, Ijora, Lagos
Tel/Fax: (01) 5870241 *Abuja (09) 2341925

NEW OILFIELD & ALLIED SERVICES LIMITED
Business: Surveying, Drilling and Materials Transportation, Sales & Maintenance of Oilfield Drilling & Refinery Equipment, Cathodic Protection, Corrosion Control
Address: Plot 58, Trans-Amadi Ind.Layout, Port Harcourt
Tel: (084) 238574, 239070, 239477 **Fax:** (084) 238574
E-mail: noas@phca.linkserve.com
Contact: Mr. Romesh Sharma - GM/CEO

NEW ORDER PARTNERSHIP LIMITED
Business: Architecture, Engineering, Construction
Address: NASCO House (2nd Floor), 29, Burma Road, Apapa, Lagos
Tel: (01) 5452800, 5870319, 5870327 Fax: (01) 5452800
Contact: Mr Tony Iweka - MD/CEO

NEW PLANET INSURANCE BROKERS LIMITED
Business: Insurance Broking
Address: 66, Ibidun Street, Surulere, Lagos
Tel/Fax: (01) 2881892
* Suite B 33 (2nd Floor), Abuja Shopping Mall, Zone 3, Wuse, Abuja
Contact: Mr. S. Akinsola - GM/CEO

NEW RESOURCES FINANCE & INVESTMENT CO. LTD
Business: Financial Services
Address: 327, Borno Way, Ebute-Metta, Lagos
Tel: (01) 861302
E-mail: newresources@yahoo.com
Contact: Chief Ikechukwu Wilfred Oranusi - Chairman/CEO

NEW TARZAN MOTORS LIMITED
Business: Passenger Transportation Services
Address: Km. 9, Onitsha-Enugu Expressway, Nkpor, Onitsha, Anambra State
Tel: (046) 251096, 261098
* 1, Onitsha-Owerri Road, Onitsha

NEW VENTURES TECHNICAL SERVICES LIMITED
Business: Technical Services
Address: 3, Sebanjo Close, Apapa, Lagos
Tel: (01) 7731150, 7731151
Website: wwwkpflohr-group.de
Contact: Mr. Klaus-Peter Flohr - CEO

NEW WAVE PRODUCTION LIMITED
Business: Audio & Visual Production. Entertainment Events Management and Consultancy
Address: 2, Ajidagan Street, Gbagada Estate Phase I, Lagos
Tel: (01) 4702909, 5552300, 08023035678, 08023120574, 08023185920, 08023690304, 08033252133
E-mail: newwaveproduction@hotmail.com
Contact: Mr. Charles E. Oputa - CEO

NEWBISCO LIMITED
Business: Production of Biscuits
Address: 4, NIWIL Close, off Oba Akran Avenue, Ikeja, Lagos
Tel: (01) 4968215-7 (3L) **Fax:** (01) 4968218

NEWDEVCO FINANCE SERVICES COMPANY LIMITED

Business: Financial Services
Address: NNIL Building, 4, Waff Road, Kaduna
Tel: (062) 215877, 217612, 239564 (DL)
Fax: (01) 2618363, 2636555
* Church House, 29, Marina, Lagos
Tel: (01) 2634019, ,2634076, 2647251, 2641681 (DL)
Fax: (01) 2618363, 2636555
* Medife House, Plot 2135, Wuse Zone 5, (by Wuse Main Market) Abuja.
Tel: (09) 5234257
Contact: Madu Satomi - GM/CEO

NEWMAN INVESTMENT COMPANY LIMITED

Business: Venue Letting, Events Management, Professional Training Courses, Recruitment, IT Education
Address: NCR Building (5th Floor), 6, Broad Street, Lagos
Tel: (01) 2637365, 2637348, 2635135, 2646435
Fax: (01) 2637348, 2645525
E-mail: newman@metrong.com
Contact: Mrs. Habiba Balogun - MD/CEO

NEWONE INDUSTRY (NIGERIA) LIMITED

Business: Importation of *So Klin* Detergent Powder
Address: 15, Commercial Road, Apapa, Lagos
Tel: (01) 5454099 **Fax:** (01) 5452297

NEWS ENGINEERING NIGERIA LIMITED

Business: Electrical Construction, Rural Electrification, Civil Engineering, Street Lighting
Address: Plot 2-11, Outer Northern Bye-Pass, Kubwa Express Road, opp. Gwarinpa Estate, Abuja
Tel: (09) 5240156, 6718163 **Fax:** (09) 5240157
E-mail: newsenginr@yahoo.com
Contact: Gen. Garba Duba (rtd) - Chairman
Sir. C. O. Nwaeze - MD/CEO

NEWSSTAND AGENCIES LIMITED

Business: Distribution of Newspaper, Magazines and Books
Address: 6A, Iya-Oloye Crescent, off Ikorodu Road, (Idiroko Bus-Stop), Onigbongbo, Maryland, Lagos
Tel: (01) 4936073 **Fax:** (01) 4936090
E-mail: newsstand@infoweb.abs.net

NEWSWATCH COMMUNICATIONS LIMITED

Business: Publishing of Newsmagazine, Trading
Address: 3, Billingsway (off Mobolaji Johnson Avenue), Oregun Industrial Estate, Oregun, Ikeja, Lagos
Tel: (01) 4935654, 4960950, 4723041, 7737106
Fax: (01) 4935654
E-mail: editorial.nwatch@nigol.net.ng
Website: www.newswatchngr.com
* Block 4 (Flat 2), J. S. Tarka Way, Area 3, Garki, Abuja
Tel: (09) 2341857, 2342069
* 36, Nsukka Street, Mile 1, Diobu, Port Harcourt
Tel: (084) 234375
Contact: Mr. Ray Ekpu - MD/CEO

NEXANS KABELMETAL NIGERIA PLC

Business: Manufacture of Aluminium Conductor Cables, Copper Wiring Cables, Power Cables, Telecommunication Cables, Special & Instrumentation Cables
Address: 28, Henry Carr St, Ikeja Industrial Estate, Lagos
Tel: (01) 4976080-9 (10L) **Fax:** (01) 4961315, 4930825
E-mail: crabbpeter@hotmail.com
* Bank Zone, off Tafawa Balewa Way, Garki Area 7, Abuja.
Tel: (09) 2347762 **Fax:** (09) 2347763
Contact: Mr. Narayan Moorthy - MD/CEO
Alh. Mohammed Z. Wada - GM (Sales & Mktg)

NEXEN PETROLEUM EXPLORATION & PRODUCTION NIGERIA LIMITED

Business: Petroleum Exploration & Production
Address: Octagon house (7th Floor), 13, A. J. Marinho Drive, Victoria Island, Annex, Lagos
Tel: (01) 4616464-5 (2L), 7741267, 7915049
Fax: (01) 4616467
Contact: Mr. Richard A. M. Owens - Director/President

NEXT INTERNATIONAL NIGERIA LIMITED

Business: Importers and General Merchants, Manufacturer's Representative
Address: 7, Aerodrome Road, off Wharf Road, by Eleganza Plaza, Apapa, Lagos
Tel: (01) 5453580-3 (4 L), 3209123, 3209126, 08034007443
Fax: (01) 5450110
E-mail: ndibeobi<next@mwebafrica.com
Contact: Mr Ndibe Obi - MD/CEO

NEXT. COM LIMITED

Business: Internet Service Provider
Address: 28, Sobo Arobiodu Street, Ikeja, G.R.A., Lagos
Tel: (01) 4970602, 4938500, 4938499 **Fax:** (01) 4970606
Contact: Mr. Olusegun Koya - MD/CEO

NFI INSURANCE COMPANY LIMITED
(formerly Nigerian-French Insurance Co. Ltd)

Business: Insurance
Address: 203/205, Apapa-Oshodi Expressway, Iyana-Isolo, Lagos
Tel: (01) 4520648-9 (2L), 4523209, 4524970, 4811410
Fax: (01) 4526773
E-mail: nfinigeria@linkserve.com
nigfrench@linkserve.com
Website: www.nfinigeria.com
* off Moshood Abiola Way, beh. National Cultural Centre, Area 10, Garki, Abuja
Contact: Mr. Wole Adetimehin - MD/CEO

NIC TRUSTEES LIMITED

Business: Trustee Services, Share Registratin, Loan Syndication
Address: Niger Insrance Plaza, 48/50, Odunlami Street, Lagos
Tel: (01) 2663287, 2662186
Contact: Alh. Bala Zakariya'u - Chairman
Mr. Taiwo A. Otuneye - GM/CEO

NICETOP PAPER INDUSTRIES LIMITED

Business: Kraft-Liner Paper Milling, Manufacturing and Marketing of Tissue Paper
Address: Km. 1, Kaduna-Abuja Expressway, Kaduna
Tel: (062) 233842, 233843
Fax: (062) 233236
Contact: Mr C. K. Yang - MD/CEO

NICHBEN GROUP OF COMPANIES (NIGERIA) LIMITED
Business: Manufacturing & Marketing of Pharmaceutical Products, Cosmetics, Alcholic Spirits & Wines, Plastic Products & Bottled Water, Import & Export, General Merchandising
Address: Nichben House, Plot 1610A, Alh. Masha Street, Opp. Lagos State Stadium, Surulere, Lagos
Tel: (01) 5835093, 5836709, 5834172 **Fax:** (01) 5831543
E-mail: nichphan@infoweb.abs.net
Website: www.nichbengroup.com
Contact: Chief (Dr.) Nicholas U. Onwumere - Chairman/CEO
Mr. F. E. Akubuo - GM

NICHBEN DISTILLERIES (NIGERIA) LIMITED
Business: Manufacture & Marketing of ROCKLAND Alcholic Spirits & Wines
Address: Plot 1610A, Alh. Masha Street, Opp. Lagos State Stadium, Surulere, Lagos
Tel: (01) 5835093, 5836709, 5734172 **Fax:** (01) 5831543
* Km. 25/26, Owerri-Onitsha, Road, Awo-Omamma, Oru East L.G.A. Imo State
Tel: (083) 920061-2 (2L), 920178
* 4, Ajoku Street, off Wetheral Road, Owerri
Tel: (083) 231327, 233617
Contact: Hon. Chief (Dr.) Nicholas Onwumere - Chairman

NICHBEN PHARMACEUTICAL INDUSTRIES (NIG) LIMITED
Business: Manufacturing of Pharmaceutical Products
Address: Plot 1610A, Alh. Masha Street, opp, Lagos State Stadium, Surulere, Lagos
Tel: (01) 5835093, 5836709, 5843172 **Fax:** (01) 5831543
E-mail: nichpharm@infoweb.abs.net
Contact: Hon. Chief (Dr.) Nicholas Onwumere - Chairman

NICHBEN PLASTIC INDUSTRIES (NIGERIA) LIMITED
Business: Manufacture of Plastic Products
Address: Plot 1610 A, Alh. Masha Street, Opp. Lagos State Stadium, Surulere, Lagos
Tel: (01) 5835093, 5836709, 5834172 **Fax:** (01) 5831543
* Km 25/26, Owerri-Onitsha Road, Awo-Omamma, Oru East LGS, Imo State
Tel: (083) 920061-2 (2L), 920178
* 4, Ajoku Street, off Wetheral Road, Owerri
Tel: (083) 231327, 233617
Contact: Hon. Chief (Dr.) Nicholas Onwumere - Chairman
Mr. F. E. Akubuo - GM (Headquarters)

NICHEK INSURANCE BROKERS LIMITED
Business: Insurance Broking
Address: 208/212, Broad Street, Lagos
Tel: (01) 2667462, 2663331, 2663389, 2667992
Fax: (01) 2663443
Contact: Mr. Tunde Akintajuwa - MD/CEO

NICKOK BEST INTERNATIONAL LIMITED
Business: Marketing and Sales of Beauty Products, Hair Driers and Beauty-Care Equipment
Address: Niko Best Executive Plaza, International Centre for Commerce, BBA Area, Trade Fair Complex, Lagos-Badagry Expressway, Ojo, Lagos
Tel: (01) 3206002, 3206322, 3455004, 3455255, 08033200599, 08042111888 **Fax:** (01) 3206320
Contact: Chief Nick Okeke - Chairman/CEO

NICKS NIGERIA LIMITED
Business: Marketing of Vertical & Venetian Blinds, Interior Decor, Sales of Home & Office Accessories, Design & Construction, Marble and Granite Works
Address: 7, Ibadiaran Street, Onigbongbo, Maryland, Lagos
Tel: (01) 4965209, 4965409, 8163783, 08023196167, 08033189601, 08037127923 **Fax:** (01) 4965209
Contact: Evangelist Mary I. Nick - Chairman/CEO

NICON HOTELS LIMITED
Business: Hotel Services
Address: 1, Aguiyi Ironsi Street, Maitama, Abuja
Tel: (09) 4131811-40(40L) **Fax:** (09) 413472
E-mail: nhl@niconhotels.com.ng
* Plot 557, Port Harcourt Crescent, off Gimbiya Street, Ahmadu Bello Way, Garki II, Abuja.
Tel: (09) 3140151-2 (2L) **Fax:** (09) 3140153
E-mail: nhl@niconhotels.com.ng
* Eleganza Biro Plaza (9th Floor), Plot 634, Adeyemo Alakija Street, Victoria Island, Lagos
Tel: (01) 7737934, 08023189778

NICON INSURANCE CORPORATION
Business: All Classes of Insurance
Address: NICON House, Plot 242, Muhammadu Buhari Way, Central District, Wuse, Abuja
Tel: (09) 5237120-9 (10L), 5238161-70 (10L)
Fax: (09) 5237126
E-mail: infodesk@niconinsurance.com.ng
nicon30@aol.com
Website: www.niconinsurance.com.ng
* NICON House, 5, Customs Street, Marina, Lagos
Tel: (01) 2640230-6 (7L) **Fax:** (01) 2666556

NICON TRUSTEES LIMITED
Business: Trusteeship, Share Registration, Pension Funds and Portfolio Management, Investment Advisors
Address: NICON House (2nd Floor), 5, Customs Street, off Marina, Lagos
Tel: (01) 2641523-4 (2L), 2666789 **Fax:** (01) 2641524
E-mail: nicontrustees@infoweb.abs.net
Contact: Ms. P. M. G. Soares - Chairman
Mrs F. F. Olu-Ayeni - GM/CEO

NIDB CONSULTANCY & FINANCE LIMITED
Business: Management and Economic Consultancy, Human Resources Development Services
Address: BOI House (4th Floor), 63/71, Broad Street, Lagos
Tel: (01) 2642739
Contact: Mr. A. A. Olasewere - Chairman
Engr. T. W. Ufot - MD/CEO

NIDB TRUSTEES LIMITED
Business: Financial Services, Investment Management Services and Trusteeship, Trustee Services, Pension Funds Management, Company Secretarial Services, Shares and Debenture Stock Registration, Liquidation and Insolvency Practice
Address: BOI House (4th Floor), 63/71, Broad Street, Lagos
Tel: (01) 2640762, 2640677, 2663698 **Fax:** (01) 2663698
E-mail: nidbtrust@hyperia.com
Website: www.nidtrust.com
* IBL Building (1st Floor), Plot 208, 4th Avenue,

Cadastral Zone AO, off Herbert Macaulay Way, Central Business District, Abuja
Tel: (09) 2346574, 2346579 **Fax:** (09) 2346578
Contact: Alh. A. A. Alkali, mni - Chairman
Mr. M. M. Adaba - MD/CEO

NIDOGAS COMPANY LIMITED
Business: Marketing of Liquified Petroleum Gas, Sales and Service of Industrial/Domestic Kitchen Equipments
Address: 23, Creek Road, Apapa, Lagos
Tel: (01) 2644839, 2644840, 2631221 **Fax:** (01) 2644837
* East/West Rd, Rumuoukirisi, Obio, Port Harcourt.
Tel: (084) 611536, 334475
Contact: Chief (Dr.) D. E. Awani - Chairman
Mr. J. Pogoson - MD/CEO

NIGDEL LIMITED
Business: Sales and Maintenance of Fuel Pumps
Address: 42, Adetokunbo Ademola St, Victoria Island, Lagos
Tel: (01) 2616132, 2612159, 2617072, 2611259, 2610759
Fax: (01) 2617096, 2617354
E-mail: arcolos@alpha.linkserve.com
* 69, King Perekule St, GRA Phase II, Port Harcourt
Tel: (084) 239608, 239631 **Fax:** (084) 239608
E-mail: arcoph@alpha.linkserve.com

NIGER BISCUIT COMPANY LIMITED
Business: Production of Biscuits and Confectionery
Address: 35, Creek Road, Apapa, Lagos
Tel: (01) 5803070-4 (5L) **Fax:** (01) 5875588, 5876801
Contact: Mr. B. A. Nassar - MD/CEO

NIGER CEDAR INDUSTRIES NIGERIA LIMITED
Business: Manufacture of Paints, Polishes, Woodfinishes, Wax Polish, Glue, Industrial Coatings & Adhesives
Address: 1, Cedar Road, off Kosoko Road, off Isheri Road, opp, Julius Berger Bus-Stop, Ojodu, Lagos
Tel: (01) 4701329, 7737226, 7740947 **Fax:** (01) 7740947
Contact: Engr. Silver O. Asuwata - MD/CEO

NIGER DELTA EXPLORATION & PRODUCTION PLC
Business: Exploration and Production of Crude Oil and Gas
Address: 15B, Babatunde Jose (Festival) Road, Victoria Island, Lagos
Tel: (01) 618891, 2618915 **Fax:** (01) 611361, 2618915
Contact: Dr. Layi Fatona - MD/CEO

NIGER DIVE LIMITED
Business: Diving Services, Underwater Engineering Works
Address: 18, Udu Road, Enerhen, Warri
Tel/Fax: (053) 250131
Contact: Mr. Ebere Ralph Izuogu - Chairman/CEO

NIGER HOLDINGS LIMITED
Business: Marketing of Electric Power Equipment, Furniture and Hardware
Address: Great Nigeria House, 47/57, Martins Street, Lagos
Tel: (01) 2661694, 2664426 **Fax:** (01) 2664426
E-mail: nihold2004@yahoo.com
nihold@hyperia.com
nihold@micro.com.ng
* 19/22, Eric Moore St, Wemabod Estate, Ikeja, Lagos
Contact: Chief Eric Nwobi - Chairman/CEO

NIGER HOPE ENTERPRISES NIGERIA LIMITED
Business: Building & Civil Engineering, Borehold Drilling and Servicing, Building of Water Tanks
Address: 160, Borno Way, Ebute-Metta, Surulere, Lagos
Tel: (01) 4811084, 865118
Contact: Mr. Hakeem G. Ashiru - MD/CEO

NIGER HYGIENE LIMITED
Business: Manufacturing of Plastic Containers
Address: Block M, Plot 1, Olubadan Avenue, Oluyole Industrial Estate, Ring Road, Ibadan
Tel: (02) 2314099, 2318687, 08055471878

NIGER INSURANCE PLC
Business: Insurance Business and Special Risks
Address: Niger Insurance Plaza, 48/50, Odunlami Street, Lagos Island, Lagos
Tel: (01) 2630862, 2630887, 2630928, 2632343, 2632941
Fax: (01) 2662196
E-mail: info@nigeriainsurance.com
Contact: Mr. C. C. Ehirim - Chairman
Alh. Bola Zakariya'u - MD/CEO

NIGER LINK HOTELS LIMITED
Business: Hospitality & Catering Services
Address: Plot 243/244, Molanje Street, Wuse Zone 4, Abuja
Tel: (09) 5235291-3 (3L), 08044115396, 08044115697
Fax: (09) 5231058
E-mail: nigerlinkhotels@hotmail.com
Website: www.nigerlinkhotelsng.com

NIGER MILLS COMPANY PLC
Business: Milling of Flour, Semovita and Wheat Offals
Address: Ikot Eka Edem, Murtala Mohammed Highway, P. O. Box 339, Calabar
Tel: (087) 231496, 232845

NIGER OPTICAL SERVICES COMPANY (NIGERIA) LIMITED
Business: Ownership and Management of Eye Clinics, Optical Services
Address: 39, Zik Avenue, Uwani, Enugu
Tel: (042) 258640, 259831 **Fax:** (042) 251298
* 4, Mgbemena Street, Awada Layout, Onitsha
Tel: (046) 216651
* Erisco Bonpet Plaza, Plot 2357, Herbert Macaulay Way, opp. Wuse Market, Wuse Zone 5, Abuja
Tel: (09) 5232085
* Nosco Eye & General Hospital, 2, Udi Street, Mile 1, Diobu, Port Harcourt
Contact: Chief (Dr.) Chika Goddy Monanu - Exec. Chairman
Chief (Dr.) Martin Nwafor Ezeh - MD/CEO

NIGER STATE DEVELOPMENT COMPANY LIMITED
Business: Industrial Promotion, Development Finance Institution, Stockbroking, Commerce
Address: Mu'azu Mohammed Road, Minna
Tel: (066) 220759, 221845 **Fax:** (066) 221845

NIGER-BENUE TRANSPORT COMPANY LIMITED
Business: River Transport, Inland Water Marine Logistics
Address: Plot 106B, Anifowoshe Str, Victoria Island, Lagos
Tel: (01) 2620937, 2620938, 2610588 **Fax:** (01) 2620935
* Off Warri-Aladja Expressway, Ovwian, Warri

Tel: (053) 320271, 320272 **Fax:** (053) 320272
E-mail: exeho@execon.com.ng
Contact: Ologorun Moses O. Taiga - Chairman
Mr Kenneth Beaumont - Group GM/CEO

NIGERBRAS SHIPPING LINE LIMITED
Business: Ship Owners, Ship and Container Operations
Address: 25, Warehouse Road, Apapa, Lagos
Tel: (01) 5875211, 5876710 **Fax:** (01) 5870051, 8182598
E-mail: nigeriabrass@hyperia.com
Contact: Senator Mahmud Waziri - Chairman/CEO

NIGERCHIN ELECTRICAL DEVELOPMENT COMPANY LTD
Business: Manufacture and Marketing of Electric Cables, Conductors and Related Equipment
Address: Plot 1, Ayodele Diyan Road, Ikeja Industrial Estate, Ikeja, Lagos
Tel: (01) 4964578, 4971961, 4971914, 4971912
Fax: (01) 4971913
Contact: Chief Jerome U. Udoji - Chairman
Mr. Joseph Huang - MD/CEO

NIGERCOM NETWORKS INC.
Business: IT Training, Internet Service Provider
Address: Oluwatobi House (4th Floor, Front Suite), 71, Allen Avenue, Ikeja, Lagos
Tel: (01) 3450208, 08023035915, 08033026113
E-mail: info@nigercom.com
Website: www.nigercom.com
Contact: Mr. Sunny Ofili - Chairman/CEO

NIGERDELTA SAVINGS & LOANS LIMITED
Business: Mortgage Banking Services
Address: 120, Olu Obasanjo Road, by Waterlines Junction, Port Harcourt
Tel: (084) 238862, 487141, 08033128333
Website: www.nigerdeltambank.com

NIGERDOCK NIGERIA LIMITED
Business: Ship Repairs, Shipbuilding, Offshore Construction
Address: Snake Island Dockyard, off Tin Cn Island, Expressway, Apapa, Lagos
Tel: (01) 2645347, 4701723, 7917822-5 (4L)
Fax: (01) 2645348-9 (2L)
E-mail: nigerdock@infoweb.abs.net
Website: www.nigerdock.com

NIGERGATE LIMITED
Business: Consultany (Management, Financial, Development Investment, IT, Professional Services)
Address: Katsina Hous (3rd Floor), Plot 81, Ralph Shodeinde Street, opp, Fed. Min. of Finance, off Ahmadu Bello Way, Central Business District, Abuja
Tel: (090 2343654, 2343595, 08035866747
Fax: (09) 2343654
E-mail: nigergate2003@yahoo.com
Contact: Prof. Babatunde Fafunwa - Chairman
Engr. Aliy M. Makka - MD/CEO

NIGER-GLOBAL ENGINEERING & TECHNICAL CO. LTD
Business: Engineering, Oil Industry Services, Procurement, Construction
Address: Africa-Re House, Plot 1679, Karimu Kotun Street, Victoria Island, Lagos
Tel: (01) 2626691-3 (3L) **Fax:** (01) 2626694
E-mail: nigerglobal@hotmail.com
nigerglobal@yahoo.com
Contact: Chief Hope Uzodinma - Chairman/CEO

NIGERIA ADVERTISING SERVICES LIMITED
Business: Outdoor Advertising, Media Consultants, Screen Printing, Painting and Signwriting, Printing of Posters, Printing on Vinyl & Flexies
Address: NAS House, 224, Idewu St, Olodi, Apapa, Lagos
Tel: (01) 5876949, 4710612, 08023038639, 08034041124
E-mail: nas@infoweb.abs.net
Contact: Chinyelugo A. Megafu - Chairman
Mrs. I. P. Onukwuba - MD/CEO

NIGERIA-AMERICA LINE LIMITED
Business: Shipping Services
Address: NAL-COMET House, 4, Hinderer Road, Apapa G.R.A. Apapa, Lagos
Tel: (01) 2645201, 2634284, 7740143, 5874926, 5876310
Fax: (01) 5453214, 2645594
E-mail: comet@micro.com.ng
Contact: Mr. Musa Danjuma - Chairman/CEO
Mr. P. L. Carrodano - MD

NIGERIA CLEANING SERVICES LIMITED
Business: Facility Management, Industrial & Office Cleaning Services, Pest Control, Waste Management, Swimming Pool Maintenance
Address: Cleanjohn House, 90, Ladipo Street, Matori, Mushin, Lagos
Tel: (01) 4526614, 4705563, 7740791, 08034040037
Fax: (01) 4525481
E-mail: tunjincs@cyberspace.net.ng
Contact: Mrs. M. S. Johnson - MD/CEO

NIGERIA DISTILLERIES LIMITED
Business: Manufacturing and Marketing of Wines and Spirits
Address: Km. 40, Lagos-Abeokuta Expressway, Sango-Otta, Ogun State, Lagos
Tel: (039) 722246-9 (4 L) * (01) 7743560, 7742172
Fax: (039) 722232, 722246, 722248
E-mail: ndl@ndlng.com
Contact: Mr. Olajide Oladapo Rosiji - Chairman/CEO
Mr. Anil Ahluwalia - MD

NIGERIA ENGINEERING WORKS LIMITED
Business: Manufacturing of Airconditioners, Ceiling Fans, Deep Freezers, Gas Cooker, Sheet Metal Products, Electrical Fittings, Feeder Pillars and Transformer
Address: Plot 49, Trans-Amadi Ind. Layout, Port Harcourt
Tel: (084) 238571-6 (6L), 232106, 235206, 232786, 571184
Fax: (084) 237376
E-mail: newclime@micro.com.ng
Website: www.newclime.com

NIGERIA INTER-BANK SETTLEMENT SYSTEM PLC
Business: Management of Inter-Bank Transactions
Address: BOI Building (7th Floor), Broad Street, Lagos
Tel: (01) 2640372-5 (4 L) **Fax:** (01) 2640387
E-mail: info@nibss-plc.com
Website: www.nibss-plc.com

NIGERIA INTERNATIONAL BANK LTD (Citibank Nigeria)
Business: Banking Services
Address: Commerce House, 1, Idowu Taylor Street, Victoria Island, Lagos
Tel: (01) 2622000-9 (10L), 2622024-32 (9L)
Fax: (01) 2618916, 2621404

NIGERIA KRAFT BAGS LIMITED
Business: Manufacturing of Industrial & Consumer Packaging for Cement and Allied Products
Address: Plot 38, Oregun Road (Dunlop Bus-Stop), Oregun Industrial Estate, Lagos
Tel/Fax: (01) 4963726, 4964637
E-mail: nbk@beta.linkserve.com
Contact: Mr. O. A. Osibo - MD/CEO

NIGERIA LNG LIMITED
Business: Purchase and Liquefaction of National Gas Sale of Liquefied Natural Gas
Address: C & C Towers, Plot 1684, Sanusi Fafunwa Street, Victoria Island, Lagos
Tel: (01) 2624190-4 (5 L), 2624556-60 (5L), 4617970-4 (5L)
Website: www.nigerialng.com
* LNG Plant Complex, Bonny Island, River State
Tel: (084) 232900 * (082) 440480-9 (10L)
Fax: (084) 232010
Contact: Engr. Funsho Kupolokun - Chairman
Mr. Andrew Jamiesan - MD/CEO

NIGERIA MACHINE TOOLS LIMITED
Business: Manufacturing of Machine Tools
Address: Km. 8, Ikirun Road, Osogbo, Osun State
Tel: (035) 242500-3 (4L) **Fax:** (035) 240002
E-mail: nmt@infoweb.abs.net
Contact: Mr. D. O. Makanjuola - MD/CEO

NIGERIA OIL & GAS PUBLICATION LIMITED
Business: Publishing of Petroleum-Industry Journals
Address: 24D, Adeola Odeku St (Flat 10), Victoria Is.Lagos
Tel: (01) 2610067, 613125, 617370 Fax: (01) 615537
E-mail: ogp@hyperia.com
Website: www.nigeriaoilgas.com
Contact: Mr Rasak Ogunfuyi - Managing Editor

NIGERIA ONLINE LIMITED
Business: Full Internet Service Provider
Address: Stallion House (13th Floor), 2, Ajose Adeogun Street, Victoria Island, Lagos
Tel: (01) 2624823, 5558045-6 (2L), 5558474-6 (3L)
Fax: (01) 2624823
E-mail: info@nigol.net.ng
Website: www.nigol.net.ng
Contact: Mr. Kiyoshi Seino - MD/CEO
Mr. Olaleye Alao - GM/Director

NIGERIA PIPES LIMITED
Business: Manufacturing and Marketing of PVC Pipes, Pressure Pipes and Fittings
Address: Plot 30/31A, Sharada Industrial Estate Phase I, Kano
Tel: (064) 667510, 667761
Fax: (064) 661453, 668444
E-mail: nigpipes@ecnx.net
Contact: Mr. R. Singh - MD/CEO

NIGERIA REINSURANCE CORPORATION
Business: All Classes of Reinsurance Business, Statutory Acceptance of a Compulsory 20% Cession of all Non-Life Policies Issued by Insurance Companies within Nigeria
Address: Reinsurance House, (16th, 19th & 20th Floors), 46, Marina, Lagos
Tel: (01) 2666011, 2666013, 2666019, 2666029, 2668003
Fax: (01) 2668041
* UAC Commercial Complex, Plot 272/273, off Third Avenue, Central Business District, Garki, Abuja
Tel: (09) 5234105, 5234674, 5236970, 5238603
Fax: (09) 5234105
E-mail: mails@nigeriare.com
Contact: Chief C. O. Onuoha - Chairman
Mr. T. T. Mirilla - MD/CEO

NIGERIA SUBMARINE DIVERS LIMITED
Business: General Marine Engineering Works and Services
Address: 68, Jubril Martins Street, by Lawanson Bus-Stop, Surulere, Apapa, Lagos
Tel: (01) 4705525, 834486 **Fax:** (01) 5873378
E-mail: nsdhwjv@yahoo.com
Contact: Otunba N. O. Fadayomi - Chairman

NIGERIA UNITY LINE PLC
Business: Shipowners/Operators, Ship Brokers and Charterers, General Shipping Agency, Freight Forwarding, Warehousing
Address: 34, Creek Road, Apapa, Lagos
Tel: (01) 5804808 **Fax:** (01) 5804807
E-mail: nul@hyperia.com
Contact: Chief Alabo A. Dikibo - Chairman
Rear Admiral S. B. Atukun (rtd.) - MD/CEO

NIGERIAN & OVERSEAS GAS COMPANY LIMITED (Utilgas)
Business: Sales and Supply of Liquidified Petroleum Gas (Domestic & Industrial Use, Design, Supply and Installation of Industrial Kitchen & Catering Equipment)
Address: 23, Idejo Street, off Adeola Odeku Street, Victoria Island, Lagos
Tel: (01) 2626987-8 (2 L) **Fax:** (01) 2626989
Contact: Mr. Victor Ibharalu - ED. (Personnel & Admin.)

NIGERIAN AGIP OIL COMPANY LIMITED
Business: Exporation and Production of Cude Oil & Gas
Address: Agip House, Plot PC. 23, Engineering Close, off Idowu Taylor Street, Victoria Island, Lagos
Tel: (01) 2600100-9 (10L), 2621600-9 (10L)
Fax: (01) 2622241
* New Base, Mile 4, Ikwerre Road, Port Harcourt
Tel: (084) 236400-19 (20L) **Fax:** (084) 236993
Contact: Mr. D. Spada - Chairman
Mr. A Forzoni - Vice Chairman/MD

NIGERIAN AGRICULTURAL, CO-OPERATIVE & RURAL DEVELOPMENT BANK LIMITED (NACRDB)
Business: Agricultural Credit Institution, Financing for Small & Medium Scale Enterprises, Commercial & Development Banking
Address: 1, Yakubu Gowon Way, Kaduna
Tel: (062) 245013, 245017 **Fax:** (062) 244612

* Plot 5, Block C. NERDC Road, Ikeja Central Business District, Agidingbi, Ikeja, Lagos
Tel: (01) 4922142, 4922144, 4922143
* NACRDB Building, Central Business District, P. M. B. 5041, Abuja.
Tel: (09) 2346187
Contact: Alh. Falalu Bello - MD/CEO
Alh. M. K. Rafindadi - Head(Corporate Affairs)

NIGERIAN AGRICULTURAL INSURANCE CORPORATION
Business: Agricultural and General Insurance
Address: Plot 590, off Independence Avenue (South), Cadastral Zone AO, Garki, Abuja
Tel: (09) 2342071, 2342806, 2342820
Fax: (09) 2342070, 2342820
Contact: Mr. Fola Daniel - MD/CEO
Alh. Shettima A. Bappa - ED (Finance & Admin.)

NIGERIAN AIRPORT COMMERCIAL VENTURES LIMITED
Business: Catering Services, Provision of Duty-Free-Shops, Car Hire Service, Beer Distribution
Address: M/M International Airport, Ikeja, Lagos
Tel: (01) 4903370-9 (10L) (Ext. 5222)
* Port Harcourt Airport, Omagwa via Port Harcourt
* Aminu Kano International Airport, Kano
Contact: Mr. N. R. Damasus - GM

NIGERIAN ALLIANCE ASSURANCE CORPORATION LTD
Business: Non-Life Insurance
Address: 1, Adeola Hopewell Street, Victoria Island, Lagos
Tel: (01) 2611972, 2615433, 5558556 **Fax:** (01) 5558556
Contact: Admiral Augustus A. Aikohomu (rtd.) - Chairman
Mr. Omoniyi Onifade - MD/CEO

NIGERIAN ALUMINIUM ENGINEERING COMPANY LIMITED
Business: Fabrication of Alminim Products
Address: 125, Okota Road, Okota, Isolo, Lagos
Tel: (01) 4817130, 5556206, 08033234979
Fax: (01) 5559256
Contact: Alh. M.T. Odunuga - Chairman/CEO

NIGERIAN ALUMINIUM EXTRUSIONS LIMITED
Business: Manufacture & Fabrication of Aluminium Products
Address: 125, Okota Road, Okota, Isolo, Lagos
Tel: (01) 4521426, 4524010, 4524014, 7741405
Fax: (01) 4524346
E-mail: nigalex@hyperia.com
Contact: Alh. M. T. Odunnuga - Chairman/CEO
Mrs. Jokotade Gboyega-Adebajo -ED (Marketing)

NIGERIAN-AMERICAN BANK LIMITED
Business: Banking Services
Address: Boston House, 10/12, Macarthy St, Onikan, Lagos
Tel: (01) 2600360-9 (10 L), 2601080-4 (5 L)
Fax: (01) 2631712
E-mail: nambl@micro.com.ng
* New Nigeria Building, 48/50, Ahmadu Bello Way, Kaduna.
Tel: (062) 242698
Contact: Mr. Osaro Isokpan - MD/CEO

NIGERIAN ASSOCIATED BEST FOODS LIMITED
Business: Food Processing, Production of Beverages, Fruit Juices and Ice-Cream
Address: 14, Ahmadu Bllo Way, Jos
Tel: (073) 464003, 464090, 08037037227
Fax: (073) 464090
E-mail: jonig19@aol.com
* 29, Olateju Street, Mushin, Lagos
Tel: (01) 4712444, 08023039712
Contact: Chief J. O. Onigbinde - MD/CEO

NIGERIAN AVIATION HANDLING COMPANY LIMITED
Business: Cargo (Import & Export) and Mail Handling, Passenger and Baggage Handling at International Airports in Nigeria, Ground Handling Services to Airlines, Traffic Services within Nigerian Airports, Maintenance Services
Address: NAHCO House, Murtala Muhammed International Airport, Airport, Ikeja, Lagos
Tel: (01) 4936345, 4937272, 7741161, 7741165
Fax: (01) 4970053
* Mal. Aminu Kano International Airport, Kano.
Tel: (064) 637980-1(2L)
*Port Harcourt International Airport, Port Harcourt
Tel: (084) 231928
* Nnamdi Azikiwe International Airport, Abuja.
Tel: (09) 8100023
Contact: Mr. A.G. Musa-Agbaneni - GM/Head of Mgt
Mrs Becky Igyuse - Head (Corp. Affairs)

NIGERIAN BAG MANUFACTURING COMPANY LTD
Business: Manufacturing of Woven and Laminated Polypropylene Sacks & Blown Low Density Polyethylene Sacks
Address: Plot 45, Eric Moore Road, Iganmu Industrial Estate, Iganmu, Lagos
Tel: (01) 5801650-6 (7L) **Fax:** (01) 5831533, 5831464
E-mail: petelow@bagco-ng.com
Contact: Mr. P. S. Low - MD/CEO
Mr. A. S. Ogunkoya - Commercial Director

NIGERIAN BALL-POINT PEN INDUSTRIES LIMITED
Business: Manufacturing, Marketing and Distribution of BIC Brands of Ball-Point Pens and Razors
Address: Israel Adebajo Close, off Ladipo Oluwole Street, Ikeja Industrial Estate, Ikeja, Lagos
Tel: (01) 4971067, 4964218
*CFAO Nigeria Plc, 19, Bayo Kuku Rd, Ikoyi, Lagos
Tel: (01) 2662050, 2662129 **Fax:** (01) 2665320
Contact: Mr. P. Michoux - MD/CEO
Mr. Ayodeji O. Omole - Sales/Mktg Manager

NIGERIAN BAPTIST BOOKSTORE LIMITED
Business: Religious Publications, Textbooks and Stationery
Address: Oke-Bola, Ibadan
Tel: (02) 2412841
Contact: Mr. Oyamakinde P. Oluyole - Manager

NIGERIAN BEVERAGES PRODUCTION COMPANY LIMITED
Business: Growing, Processing and Marketing of Tea
Address: Kakara Village, off Nguroje, Gembu, Mambilla, Sarduana L. G. A., Taraba State
Tel: (041) 40587
* 5, Numan Road, Yola
Tel: (075) 625191, 624387 **Fax:** (075) 624387

48, Toyin Street, Ikeja, Lagos
Tel: (01) 4966676
Contact: Alh. Ibrahim Bapetel - Chairman
Mr. Jonah A. Agyo - MD/CEO

NIGERIAN BOTTLING COMPANY PLC
Business: Bottling of Soft Drinks
Address: NBC House, Oyingbo Ebute-Metta, Lagos
Tel: (01) 2691267, 2693030 **Fax:** (01) 2691521
* Iddo House (3rd Floor), Iddo, Lagos
Tel: (01) 800220-9 (10L)
Contact: (Bashorun) A. A. Adesanya - Exec. Chairman
Mr. Marcel Martin - MD/CEO

NIGERIAN BREWERIES PLC
Business: Brewing and Marketing of Lager Beer, Stout and Non-Alcholic Malt
Address: 1, Abebe Village Road, Iganmu Industrial Estate, Iganmu, Lagos
Tel: (01) 5801340-9 (10 L)
Fax: (01) 7744227, 2646624, 5852067
E-mail: nbplc.info@heineken.nl
Website: www.nbplc.com
* 26, Elelenwa Road, G.R.A. Phase II, Port Harcourt
* 1, Joshua Nkomo Street, behind ECOWAS Secretariat, Asokoro District, Abuja
Contact: Mr. Felix O. A. Ohiwerei - Chairman
Mr. F. B. O. Odimegwu - MD/CEO

NIGERIAN CARTONS & PACKAGING MANUFACTURING COMPANY LIMITED (NICAPACO)
Business: Manufacture of Paper Packaging Materials
Address: 23, Industrial Avenue, Ilupeju Industrial Estate, Ilupeju, Lagos
Tel: (01) 4961505, 4964145, 4963944
Fax: (01) 4962425, 4970212
Contact: Mr. Anthony H. O. Shu - MD/CEO

NIGERIAN CATERERS & SUPERMARKETS LIMITED
Business: Industrial Catering & House-Keeping Services, Field Catering Services to Oil Industry Companies
Address: 132, Awolowo Road, S.W. Ikoyi, Lagos
Tel: (01) 2693629, 2691026, 2693630 **Fax:** (01) 2693632
E-mail: ncsl@hyperia.com
* 12, Chief Nwuke Street, Trans-Amadi Industrial Layout, Port Harcourt.
Tel: (084) 234118, 232037
* Odibo Estate, Effurun/Sapele Road, Warri
Tel: (053) 252887, 253749 **Fax:** (053) 251951
Contact: Mr. C. F. Aziz - Operations Manager/CEO

NIGERIAN CEMENT COMPANY PLC
Business: Manufacturing of Cement
Address: 5, Leck Avenue, Secretariat, Enugu
Tel: (042) 253829, 255794 **Fax:** (042) 253829
Contact: Chief C. C. Ogbu - CEO

NIGERIAN COAL CORPORATION
Business: Mining and Marketing of Coal
Address: 29, Okpara Avenue, Enugu
Tel: (042) 255148, 255314, 255325, 258410
Fax: (042) 257340
* 11, Nississippi Street, Maitama, Abuja
Tel: (09) 4137492, 4137493
Contact: Mr Gab Ezeani - MD/CEO

NIGERIAN CONCRETE INDUSTRIES LIMITED
Business: Production of Electric Poles, Concrete Pipes, Spun Pipes, Fencing Posts & Precast Concrete Blocks
Address: 269, Agege Motor Road, Mushin, Lagos
Tel: (01) 520782, 524756, 08034442444, 08034445444
Fax: (01) 2693410
E-mail: bilcon@intraom5.com
Contact: Mr. O. O. Sadipe - MD/CEO

NIGERIAN DOOR FABRICATION COMPANY LIMITED
Business: Manufacture of Kitchen Cabinets & Doors
Address: 6, Abimbola Street, Plot 2, Block L, Isolo Industrial Estate, Isolo, Lagos
Tel: (01) 8045886, 08023194582, 08023909106
Contact: Mr Tunde.A. Kasali - Chairman/CEO

NIGERIAN EAGLE FLOUR MILLS LIMITED
Business: Milling of Wheat and Maize Floor
Address: 4A, Sapara Williams Close, off Idowu Martins Street, Victoria Island, Lagos
Tel: (01) 2618682, 2614575 **Fax:** (01) 2612780
* Eagle Flour Road, Toll Point, Lagos-Ibadan Expressway, Ibadan
Tel: (02) 2317655-6 (2 L) **Fax:** (02) 2315872

NIGERIAN EMBROIDERY LACE MANUFACTURING CO LTD
Business: Manufacture of Embroidered Lace Textiles
Address: 48/50 (Plot B, Block 1), Industry Avenue, Ilupeju Industrial Estate, Ilupeju, Lagos
Tel: (01) 4972776, 4972777, 4963461
E-mail: som.nsfelco@bhojrajchanrai.com
Contact: Mr. M. B. Chanrai - Chairman
Mr R. Mittal - MD/CEO

NIGERIAN ENAMELWARE PLC
Business: Manufacture of Enamelware Products
Address: 1, NIWIL Close, Ikeja Ind.Estate, Ikeja, Lagos
Tel: (01) 4977616
Contact: Alh. Inuwa Wada - Chairman
Mr. Philip Tung - MD/CEO

NIGERIAN ENGINEERING & CONSTRUCTION CO. LTD
Business: Building & Civil Engineering Contractors
Address: 17A, Abdullahi Bayero Way, Nassarawa, Kano
Tel: (064) 644007, 648313, 08022255000
E-mail: slobodan_vukovic@yahoo.com
Contact: Mr Slobodan Vukovic - Chairman/CEO

NIGERIAN EXPORT -IMPORT BANK (NEXIM)
Business: Export Financing, Risk Managers and Advisers
Address: Plot 795, IBB Drive, 8th Street, off Independence Avenue, Central Business District, Garki, Abuja
Tel: 234 (9) 2346141-7 (7L), 08034089025-6 (2L), 08037850181 **Fax:** (09) 2346151
E-mail: neximabj@neximbank.com.ng
Website: www.neximbank.com
* Allied Building, 155/161, Broad Street, Lagos
Tel: (01) 2662305, 2667164 **Fax:** (01) 2641129
Contact: Dr. Samsuddeen Usman - Chairman
Dr. Rufai Omar Madaki - MD/CEO

NIGERIA FILM CORPORATION
Business: Film Production & Archiving, Post-Production Services, Consultancy & Training
Address: 218B, Liberty Dam Road, Jos
Tel: (073) 461444, 461455, 463519 Fax: (073) 461233
E-mail: mdnfc@jos.rcl.nig.com

NIGERIAN FISHING NET INDUSTRIES LIMITED
Business: Manufacture & Sale of Fishing and Trawler Nets
Address: 16, Kofo Abayomi Street (Flat 2, Ground Floor), Victoria Island, Lagos
Tel: (01) 2615505, 2622232, 2622259 **Fax:** (01) 2619487
E-mail: primlaks@hyperia.com
* Plot E, Kirikiri Industrial Estate, Alahun Osumba Street, via Maza-Maza, Lagos
Tel: (01) 7760370
Contact: Mr. C. O. Ibie - Chairman
Mr. Abhijit Sanyal - MD/CEO

NIGERIAN FORWARDERS LIMITED
Business: Clearing and Forwarding, Shipping Agency, Haulage
Address: 58, Calcutta Crescent, Apapa, Lagos
Tel: (01) 5873808, 5875287 **Fax:** (01) 5873795

NIGERIAN FOUNDRIES LIMITED
Business: Manufacturers of Cast Iron and Alloy Steel Products, Technical & After-Sales Support Services
Address: 1, Adeyemi Bero Crescent, Ilupeju Industrial Estate, Anthony/Oshodi Expressway, Lagos
Tel: (01) 4977601, 4977602, 4977604 **Fax:** (01) 4936075
E-mail: foundryng@aol.com
Website: www.nigerianfondries.com
Contact: Romeo V. Barberopoulous - Exec. Chairman

NIGERIAN GAS COMPANY LIMITED
Business: Processing, Transporting and Marketing of Natural Gas
Address: 1, Odiri Road, Ekpan, P. M. B. 1288, Warri
Tel: (053) 252012, 252224, 252328, 252471, 254261-2 (2L)
Fax: (053) 252012, 252233, 252461, 257786
E-mail hlpngc@nnpc.com.ng

NIGERIAN-GERMAN CHEMICALS PLC
Business: Production of Pharmaceuticals, Agricultural & Veterinary Medicines, Household Consumer Products, Industrial & Oil Production Chemicals.
Address: Plot 144, Oba Akran Avenue, Ikeja Industrial Estate Ikeja, Lagos
Tel: (01) 4968220-9 (10 L) **Fax:** (01) 4960482
E-mail: enquiry@ngcplc.com
Website: www.ngcplc.com
* Km 38, Lagos-Abeokuta Expressway, Sango-Otta
Tel: (039) 722219 **Fax:** (039) 722220
Contact: Mr. A. Shonekan - Exec. Vice Chairman/CEO

NIGERIAN GREEN LINES LIMITED
Business: Shipping
Address: 27, Michael Ibru Boulevard, Apapa, Lagos
Tel: (01) 5451402, 5876532 **Fax:** (01) 5450204, 5450274
E-mail: info@yinkafolawiyo.org
Website: www.yinkafolawiyo.org
Contact: Alh. (Chief) W. I. Folawiyo, CON - Chairman/CEO
Capt. S. O. Kadiri - MD

NIGERIAN INTERNATIONAL BIOGRAPHICAL CENTRE
Business: Publishers of "The New Who's Who in Nigeria"
Address: CEDDI Towers, 16, Wharf Road, Apapa, Lagos
Tel: (01) 5451869 **Fax:** (01) 5452384
E-mail: nibc@linkserve.com.ng
Contact: Senator David O. Dafinone - Chairman
Mr. Peter Ishaka - Manager Operations

NIGERIAN INTERNATIONAL SECURITIES LIMITED
Business: Stockbroking, Financial Services
Address: 3, Hospital Road (2nd Floor), opp. St. Nicholas Hospital, Lagos Island, Lagos
Tel: (01) 2645841-2 (2 L) **Fax:** (01) 2645840
E-mail: nisel@hyperia.com
Contact: Chief (Dr.) Chris O. Ogunbanjo - Chairman
Mr. Felix O. Ebosa - GM

NIGERIAN LAW PUBLICATIONS LIMITED
Business: Publishing & Sales of Law Books and Reports
Address: 90 Lewis Street, Lafiaji, Lagos Island, Lagos
Tel/Fax: (01) 4710006, 4712109, 08033152176
E-mail: ganilaw@linkserve.com
Website: www.nigeria-law-publication.com.ng
* Bobsar Building (1st Floor), Plot 1035, off Ahmadu Bello Way, Area 11, Garki, Abuja
Tel: (09) 3140836
Contact: Chief Gani Fawehinmi - Chairman/CEO

NIGERIAN LIFE & PENSION CONSULTANTS LIMITED
Business: Pensions Management & Consultancy
Address: 312, Ikorodu Road, Anthony, Lagos
Tel: (01) 4978530-4 (5 L)
E-mail: nlpc@hyperia.com
Contact: Mr. Justine Olabode Emmanuel - Chairman
Mr. E. O. Eleoramo - MD/CEO

NIGERIAN LOGGING & SUPPORT SERVICES LIMITED
Business: Oilfield Services (Logging/Geological Surveillance)
Address: 174B, Murtala Muhammed Way, Yaba, Lagos
* Plot 474, Trans-Amadi Ind.Layout, Port Harcourt
Tel/Fax: (084) 239327
E-mail: nlssphc@infoweb.abs.net
Contact: Mr. Feyi Bali - Exec. Director/CEO

NIGERIAN MARITIME SERVICES LIMITED
Business: Clearing and Forwarding, Packing and Removals, Air Freight, Warehousing and Transportation
Address: 90, Awolowo Road, Ikoyi, Lagos
Tel: (01) 2690211, 2671720 **Fax:** (01) 2690758
* 13/15, Sapele Road, Apapa, Lagos
Tel: (01) 5450275, 5875189 **Fax:** (01) 5875189
Contact: Chief (Dr.) Oladele Fajemirokun - Chairman/CEO
Mr. R. S. West-Awelewa - Asst. GM

NIGERIAN MINERAL WATER INDUSTRIES LIMITED
Business: Bottling of Carbonated Soft Drinks & Treated Water
Address: 1, Limca Road, Onitsha
Tel: (046) 215433
E-mail: limcaonitsha@nova.net.ng
Contact: Mr. S. N. C. Sampath - MD/CEO

NIGERIAN MINING CORPORATION
Business: Mining and Processing of Minerals, Quarriying

Address: Federal Secretariat (7th Floor), P.M.B. 2154, Jos
Tel: (073) 462867, 465245, 464344 **Fax:** (073) 462867
E-mail: nmcjos@yahoo.co.uk
Contact: Alh. T. O. Jimoh - MD/CEO
Mr. A. O. Onu - GM.

NIGERIAN MOBILE TELECOMMUNICATIONS LTD (M-TEL)
Business: Provision of Wireless Mobile Communication
Address: 3, M-TEL Street, Off Monrovia Street off Mal. Aminu Kano Crescent, Wuse II, Abuja
Tel: (09) 4137801-2 (2L) **Fax:** (09) 5239122
* Bar Beach, Ahmadu Bello Way, V/Island, Lagos
Tel: (01) 2645074, 2622413, 2611206 **Fax:** (01) 2622412
Contact: Alh. Ahmad Baba - G.M. (Commercial)
Mr. Umar Abdul - Hamid - PR Manager

NIGERIAN MOTORS INDUSTRIES LIMITED
Business: Marketing & Maintenance of Equipment & Vehicles
Address: 1, Davies Street, off Marina, Lagos
Tel: (01) 2660321, 2662050, 2662129 **Fax:** (01) 2665320
* Plot 1, Block D, Amuwo-Odofin Industrial Scheme, Apapa-Oshodi Expressway, Lagos
Tel: (01) 5801532-9 (8L), 7740966 **Fax:** (01) 5835268
*Plot 500, Tafawa Balewa Way, Garki Area 3, Abuja
Tel: (09) 5239799
*Plot 9, Trans-Amadi Ind. Layout, Port Harcourt
Tel: (084) 237705, 239221
Contact: Mr. J. P. Genoud - MD/CEO

NIGERIAN NATIONAL PETROLEUM CORPORATION
Business: Oil Conglomerate (Petroleum Exploration, Development & Production, Petroleum Engineering Data Processing, Petroleum Refining, Petrochemical Production, Marketing of Crude Oil, Petroleum Products and Petrochemicals, Gas Production, Distribution and Marketing)
Address: NNPC Towers, Herbert Macaulay Way, Central Business District, Garki, Abuja
Tel: (09) 2348200-19 (20 L)
Website: www.nnpc-publicaffairs.com
* 49, Moscow Road, Old G.R.A., Port Harcourt
Tel: (084) 230206
Contact: Engr. Funso Kupolokun - Group MD/CEO
Dr. Levi Ajuoloma - GM(Group Public Affairs D iv)

NIGERIAN NOMINEES LIMITED
Business: Company Secretariat Services, Company Formation & Registration, General Consultancy Services
Address: New Africa House (12th Floor), 31, Marina, Lagos
Tel: (01) 2632341, 2662297, 08033094175, 08042170267
Fax: (01) 2645069, 2662801
Contact: Mr D. O. Agbaje - Exec. Director

NIGERIAN OFFICE STATIONERY SUPPLY STORES LTD
Business: Production & Sales of Office and Social Stationery, Printing Services
Address: Adebajo House, 25, Warehouse Rd, Apapa, Lagos
Tel: (01) 5453483, 877144, 874972
Contact: O. Adekunle Adebajo - MD/CEO

NIGERIAN OIL MILLS LIMITED
Business: Manufacture and Marketing of Edible Vegetable Oil, Export of Palm Kernel Oil & Cake
Address: 80/82, Tafawa Balewa Road, Kano
Tel: (064) 632428, 647029, 632018, 634115
Fax: (064) 634677
* 10, Wharf Road, Apapa, Lagos
Tel: (01) 5803210-4 (5L), 5872255
Contact: Alh. Abdussamad Rabiu - Chairman
Mr. Harold A. Blackburne - MD/CEO

NIGERIAN PAPER CONVERTERS COMPANY LIMITED
Business: Printing, Paper Conversion & Book Production
Address: Adebajo House, 25, Warehouse, Rd, Apapa, Lagos
Tel: (01) 877144, 874972

NIGERIAN PAPER MILL LIMITED
Business: Production of Pulp from Wood, Manufacture of Paper, Clipboard, Kraft liner & Sack Kraft
Address: Jebba Town, Kwara State
Tel: (031) 400004, (01) 667423, (09) 5231754
Fax: (09) 5231892
* 38, Kofo Abayomi Street, Victoria Island, Lagos
Tel: (01) 616440, 613803 **Fax:** (01) 619400

NIGERIAN POLYVINYL CHLORIDE PRODUCTS LIMITED
Business: Manufacturing of Polyethylene Sheetings, Rolls, Bags and Printed Sacks
Address: 5E, Bello Road, near Assurance Bank, Kano
Tel: (064) 646041, 632175
Contact: Mr. J. B. Chanrai - Chairman
Mr. Mohan Thakur - GM/CEO

NIGERIAN PORTS AUTHORITY
Business: Management and Operation of Nigeria's Coastal & Inland Ports, Provision of Specific Port & Harbour Services for Nigeria's Maritime Industry
Address: NPA House, 26/28, Marina, Lagos
Tel: (01) 2600620-32 (13 L)
Fax: (01) 2636719, 2636726
E-mail: telnpa@infoweb.abs.net
Website: www.nigeriaports.com
www.aboutnpa.com
* Plot 665, Jere Street, Area A3, Garki, Abuja
Tel/Fax: (09) 2348030
Contact: Mr. Adebayo Sarumi - MD/CEO
Mr. M. N. Jiya - AGM (Marketing)

NIGERIAN PRECISION ENGRAVERS LIMITED
Business: Precision Engraving, Printing, Production of Signs, Soap Stamps, Injection Moulds, Legend Plates, Trophies, Button Badget etc
Address: 7, Ayisatu Onisemo Street (Sanya Bus Stop), Apapa-Oshodi Expressway, Lagos
Tel: (01) 5456990, 5456991
Contact: Prince Ezekietl Femi Daramola - Chairman/CEO
Prince Dele Davies - GM

NIGERIAN RAILWAY CORPORATION
Business: Rail Transport (Passenger and Freight)
Address: Railway Compound, of Moshood Abiola Road, Ebute Metta, Lagos
Tel: (01) 5456279, 5457460, 7747320
Fax: (01) 5831367
Contact: Alh. Abdulrahman Abubakar - MD/CEO
Mr. 'Wole Adeniji - Director - (Administration)

NIGERIAN ROAD CONSTRUCTION LIMITED
Business: Building & Civil Engineering Contractors
Address: 12C, Murtala Mohammed Way, Kano
Tel: (064) 6469226, 634595, 648498, 08037863016
Fax: (064) 633327, 641442
Contact: Alh. Umaru Sanda Birma - Chairman
Abdulnaer Hajaig - MD/CEO

NIGERIAN ROPES PLC
Business: Manufacturing of Fibre & Steel Wire Ropes
Address: 66/68, Eric Moore Road, Iganmu Industrial Estate, Iganmu, Lagos
Tel: (01) 5802880-4 (5 L), 4702035, 7755414
Fax: (01) 5831362
E-mail: niropes.los@alpha.linkserve.com
sales@nigerianropes.com
Contact: Alh. A. D. Mohammed - Chairman
Mr. Carlo Bertani - MD/CEO

NIGERIAN-SPANISH CEMENT COMPANY LIMITED
Business: Importation and Marketing of Cement
Address: Yinka Folawiyo Plaza, 38, Yinka Folawiyo Avenue, Apapa, Lagos
* 27, Creek Road, Apapa, Lagos
Tel: (01) 5451402 **Fax:** (01) 5450204
Contact: Alh. Chief W. I. Folawiyo, CON - Exec. Chairman

NIGERIAN-SPANISH ENGINEERING LIMITED
Business: Manufacturing of Iron Rods and Bars
Address: Plots 62-73, Sharada Industrial Estate Phase II, Kano
Tel: (064) 660506, 669378 **Fax:** (064) 668534
Contact: Mr. Masando Suzuki - Exec. Director/CEO

NIGERIAN SPINNERS & DYERS LIMITED
Business: Worsted Spinning
Address: 14E, Bello Road, Kano
Tel: (064) 648290, 648294 **Fax:** (064) 633037
* 6, Independence Road, Bompai Ind. Estate, Kano
Tel: (064) 631148, 637223
Contact: Mr George Akle - MD/CEO

NIGERIAN STOCKBROKERS LIMITED
(Sub. of NAL Bank Plc)
Business: Stockbroking, Portfolio Management, Investment Advisory Services, Nominee Account
Address: NAL Towers, 20, Marina, Lagos
Tel: (01) 2646837, 2635539, 2635843, 2600420-9 (10 L), 4754007, 4755007 **Fax:** (01) 2645477
E-mail: nsl@nalbank.com.ng
Website: www.nalbank.com.ng
*New Nigeria Building 112E Aba Rd, Port Harcourt
Tel: (084) 239002-5 (4 L) **Fax:** (084) 238417
*Plot 990, Cadastral Zone AO, behind Leventis Stores, Central Business District, Abuja
Tel: (09) 5239892, 5235390-2 (3L) **Fax:** (09) 5239720
Contact: Mr. Bosun Adekoya - MD/CEO

NIGERIAN SWEETS & CONFECTIONERY COMPANY LTD
Business: Manufacturing of Sweets and Confectionery
Address: 155, Club Road, Bompai Industrial Estate, Kano
Tel: (064) 642105, 634695 **Fax:** (064) 642099
E-mail: niccosweets@yahoo.com
Contact: El-Hadi Ibrahim - MD/CEO

NIGERIAN TECHNICAL COMPANY LIMITED
Business: Sales & Service of Motor Vehicles, Spare Parts Sales
Address: Plot 5, Block M, Abimbola Street, Isolo, Lagos
Tel: (01) 4520203
Contact: Mr. Funso Awomolo - Chairman

NIGERIAN TELECOMMUNICATIONS LIMITED (NITEL)
Business: Local & International Telecommunications Services
Address: Plot 251, Herbert Macaulay Way, Cadastral Zone A6, Central Business District, Abuja
Tel: (09) 5245000
E-mail: info@nitelnet.com
Website: www.nitelnet.com
* 3/5, Tafawa Balewa Square, Lagos
Tel: (01) 2634395, 2647597
* 44, Gerrard Road, Ikoyi, Lagos
Tel: (01) 2691446, 686155, 688078

NIGERIAN TELEVISION AUTHORITY (NTA)
Business: Television Broadcasting Services
Address: Television House, off Obafemi Awolowo Street, Garki Area 11, Garki, Abuja
Tel: (09) 2346906-7 (2L) **Fax:** (09) 2345914, 2346901
* Ahamdu Bello Way, Victoria Island, Lagos
Tel: (01) 2626099, 2672797, 614966
Fax: (01) 2626239, 611623
Contact: Dr. Tonie Iredia - Director-General/CEO
Mal. H. B. Hassan - ED (Operations & Marketing)

NIGERIAN WEAVING & PROCESSING COMPANY LIMITED
Business: Manufacturing of Textile Piece Goods
Address: Plot C, Block 1, Industrial Avenue, Ilupeju Industrial Estate, Ilupeju, Lagos
Tel: (01) 4937060, 4937043

NIGERIAN WESTMINISTER DREDGING & MARINE LTD
Business: Civil Engineering, Dredging and Pipeline Contractors
Address: Westminster House, Plot 1601, Adeola Hopewell Street, Victoria Island, Lagos
Tel: (01) 2624580, 2624581 **Fax:** (01) 2624582
Website: www.boskalis.com
* 7767, Madabi Estate, IBB Way Wuse, II, Abuja
Tel: (09) 4132893-4 (2 L)
Contact: Mr. Simeon B. Fasan - Chairman
Mr. L. Slinger - MD/CEO

NIGERIAN WIRE & CABLE PLC
Business: Manufacture and Sale of Wires and Cables for Electricity and Telecommunications
Address: Owode Industrial Estate, Km. 9, Ibadan-Abeokuta Road, Ibadan
Tel: (02) 2310610-4 (5L), 2314556 **Fax:** (02) 2318036
Contact: Dr. Busari O. Adebisi - Chairman
Mr. Olusegun M. Adeyinka - MD/CEO

NIGERIANCV.COM LIMITED
Business: Staff Recruitment Agency & Employment Conslultancy Services
Address: 21/25, Broad Street, Lagos
Tel: (01) 2661303, 4725795, 8178617, 08033357421, 08038150351-3 (3L)
E-mail: sales@nigeriancv.com
Website: www.nigeriancv.com

NIGERIANNET TECHNOLOGY SERVICES LIMITED
Business: Internet Service Provider, Software Solutions
Address: Okoi Arikpo House (2nd Floor), 5, Idowu Taylor Street, Victoria Island, Lagos
Tel: (01) 2620240-1 (2 L)
E-mail: info@nigerianet.com
Website: www.nigerianet.com
Contact: Prince Tony Momoh - Chairman
Mr. Lambert Ugorji - MD/CEO

NIGERITE LIMITED
Business: Manufacturing of Fibre-Cement Roofing & Ceiling Sheets, PVC Floor Tiles an Calcium Carbonate
Address: Oba Akra Avenue, Ikeja Ind. Estate, Ikeja, Lagos
Tel: (01) 4978900-9 (10 L), 08038885050
Fax: (01) 4936105, 4963882
E-mail: nigerite@infoweb.abs.net
Contact: Chief Ladipo Ani - Chairman
Mr. Th. Dumont - MD/CEO

NIGERMART INVESTMENT MARKET LIMITED
Business: Investment Consultant & Managers, Public Relations and Promotions Consultants
Address: Ikeja Plaza (Suite B427, 4th Floor), 81, Mobolaji Bank-Anthony Way, Ikeja, Lagos
Tel: (01) 4967691, 4710427 **Fax:** (01) 4967691
E-mail: nigermart@nipg.org
Website: www.nipg.org
Contact: Mr. Olusola O. Donye - President/CEO

NIGERNORTH LIMITED
Business: Building & Civil Engineering, Turnkey Contracts, Water Engineering
Address: Gidan Aliyu-Ndanusa, Bosso Road, Minna
Tel: (066) 222365, 224930 **Fax:** (066) 221930
E-mail: newvent@inet-global.com
nigergrp@inet-global.com
Contact: Engr. Sani Ndanusa - MD/CEO

NIGSON INDUSTRIES LIMITED
Business: Manufacturing, Importation & Exportation
Address: Plot 16, Aminu Jinadu Close, off Jimoh Odutola Street, Iganmu Industrial Estate, Lagos
Tel: (01) 5454402, 5852137, 4705831 **Fax:** (01) 5454402
E-mail: nigson@hyperia.com
Contact: Chief I. G. Nwabueze Odunukwe - Chairman/CEO

NIHOL CRANE & EQUIPMENT HIRE COMPANY LIMITED
Business: Leasing and Hiring of Cranes & Equipment
Address: 29, Abimbola Street, Isolo Ind.Estate, Isolo, Lagos
Tel: (01) 4523766, 4528888, 4528009, 7745858
Fax: (01) 4529013
E-mail: nicre@infoweb.abs.net
Contact: Mr. Dayo Adetunmbi - MD/CEO

NIIMA GINNERY LIMITED
Business: Ginning of Cotton
Address: Industrial Area, P. O. Box 16, Gussau
Tel: (063) 200529, 200918, 201660

NIIMAH GUEST PALACE LIMITED
Business: Hospitality & Catering Services
Address: Suleiman Crescent, off Lamido Crescent, Nassarawa G.R.A., Kano
Tel: (064) 642946, 644557, 647616, 08023502021, 08033432883 **Fax:** (064) 647616
E-mail: nimahguest@yahoo.com
Contact: Alh. Ahmed Usman - GM

NIIT
Business: Computer Education & Training Centre
Address: 9, Oba Akran Avenue, Ikeja, Lagos
Tel: (01) 7747994, 4935200-2 (3L)
Fax: (01) 4937231, 4935203
E-mail: ikeja@niitng.com
Website: www.niit.com

NIKE LAKE RESORT
Business: Hospitality Services, Resort
Address: Nike Town, via Enugu, Enugu
Tel: (042) 557000-19 (20 L) **Fax:** (042) 557679
E-mail: nikelake@infoweb.abs.net

NIKKI MANUFACTURING COMPANY LIMITED
Business: Manufacturing and Marketing of Biscuits
Address: Km. 1, Ogba Road, Benin City
Tel: (052) 251478, 08037402326 **Fax:** (052) 258066
E-mail: info@nikiiscuits.com
Website: www.nikibiscuits.com
Contact: Mr Nik G. Mirpuri - ED (Operations)/CEO

NIKKY AFRCANA FASHIONS NIGERIA LIMITED
Business: Fashion Designing, Fashion School
Address: Nikky Africana Plaza, 70C, Allen Ave, Ikeja, Lagos
Tel: (01) 4960846
E-mail: nikky@infoweb.abs.net
Contact: Mrs. Nike Okanlawon - Chairman

NIMADCO OIL MILLS LIMITED
Business: Milling & Refining of Vegetable Oil
Address: 15, Independence Road, Bompai Ind. Estate, Kano
Tel: (064) 634888
Contact: Alh. U. M. Gashash - MD/CEO

NIMBUS WATER SYSTEM INC.
Business: Manufacturing and Marketing of Water & Air Treatment Systems
Address: 9, Alh. Masha St/Ogunlana Drive, Surulere, Lagos
Tel: (01) 5456393, 08037232738

NIODA LIMITED
Business: Procurement, Engineering & Technical Services to the Oil & Gas Sector, Sales & Service of Electricity Generators and Agricultural Equipment
Address: 53, Oregun Rd, Oregun Industrial Area, Ikeja, Lagos
Tel: (01) 4936290, 4972454 **Fax:** (01) 4936290
E-mail: nioda@cybaaspace.com
nioada@cybaaspace.net
Contact: Mrs. R. O. Andy-Iyamah - Chairman/CEO

NIPCO PLC
Business: Procurement, Storage, Marketing & Distrbution of Petroleum Products
Address: 1 &15, Dockyard Road, Apapa, Lagos
E-mail: nipco@linkserve.com
Tel: (01) 5873184, 08023081415 **Fax:** (01) 5873184

NIPOL LIMITED
Business: Manufacturing and Marketing of Plastic Products
Address: Moor Plantation, Abeokuta Road, Apata, Ibadan
Tel: (02) 2312949, 2312918 **Fax:** (02) 2312949
Contact: Mr. O. O. Bankole - GM

NISSAN NIGERIA LIMITED
Business: Sales and Service of Nissan Motor Vehicles
Address: Apapa-Oshodi Expressway, Isolo Industrial Estate, Isolo, Lagos
Tel: (01) 4521988, 4523608 **Fax:** (01) 4521539
Contact: Dr. Massad F. Boulos - Chairman/CEO

NISSHO IWAI (NIGERIA) LIMITED
Business: Liaison & Consultancy in Oil & Gas Industry
Address: C & C Towers (7th Floor), Plot 1684, Sanusi Fafunwa Street, Victoria Island, Lagos
Tel: (01) 2613101, 2613141, 614714, 7757579, 7757581, 08033036766, 08033036775 **Fax:** (01) 2613104
E-mail: kmiki@hyperia.com
Contact: Mr. Koichi Miki - MD/CEO

NISTECH GROUP
Business: Conglomerate - Investments, Community Banking Services, Fast Food Outlets.
Address: Adegbenle House, 48, Akowonjo Road, (Bakery Bus-Stop), Egbeda, Ikeja, Lagos
Tel: (01) 4922458, 4705806
E-mail: nistech@nistechgroup.net
Website: www.nistechgroup.net

NITESHIFT COLISEUM
Business: Entertainment & Events Management
Address: 34, Salvation Road, off Opebi Road, Ikeja, Lagos
Tel: (01) 4967197, 4961381 **Fax:** (01) 4967197
E-mail: info@niteshiftcoliseum.com
Website: www.nightshiftcoliseum.com
Contact: Mr. Ken-Calebs Olumese - Guv'nor/CEO

NITOL TEXTILES MANUFACTURING CO. NIGERIA LTD
Business: Textile Manufacturing
Address: 10, Ijora Causeway, Ijora, Lagos
Tel: (01) 5451567-8 (2L), 08023099978
Contact: Mr. M. Khawam- Technical Mnanger/CEO

NITOMAC LIMITED
Business: Manufacturing of Home & Office Furniture
Address: Km. 4, Benin-Sapele Road, Benin City
Tel: (052) 250307, 252076

NITRO ATLASCO NIGERIA LIMITED
Business: Sales and Service of Construction, Mining and Quarrying Equipment, Consumables and Civil Explosives
Address: Plot K9, Apapa-Oshodi Expressway, beside Union Bank, Isolo, Lagos
Tel: (01) 4526576, 4526788 **Fax:** (01) 4525453
Contact: Mr. Yinka Akinkugbe - MD/CEO

NIVCO INTERNATIONAL LIMITED
Business: Medical Laboratory & Diagnostic Services, Pro-Life Immunoassary Laboratory, Consultancy Services, Importation, Marketing and Supply of Medical Diagnostic Equipment
Address: 277B, Ajose Adeogun St, Victoria Island, Lagos
Tel/Fax: (01) 2625422
E-mail: nivco@infoweb.abs.net
Contact: Mr. Alex Obi Okoli - Chairman/CEO

NIYAMCO PLC
Business: Production and Sale of Ethanol
Address: Jebba Road, Kwara State
Tel: (031) 641103, 641100, 6411592
* 25A, Toyin Street, Ikeja, Lagos
Tel/Fax: (01) 4970357
Contact: Aare (Dr.) Kolawole Adegbola - Chairman
Mr. Kunle Akiode - MD/CEO

NIYYA FARMS LIMITED
Business: Livestock Farming, Flour Milling
Address: TL. 3, Nnamdi Azikiwe Expressway, Western Bye-Pass, Badiko North New Extension
Tel: (062) 416286, 416270
Contact: Alh. A. D. Budah - MD/CEO

NJABA VENTURES LIMITED
Business: Importation and Sales of Ceramic Tiles, Ceiling Tiles and other Building Materials
Address: 17, Murtala Muhammed International Airport Road, Ajao Estate, Apakun-Oshodi, Lagos
Tel: (01) 4520197, 4523574, 08033059697
Fax: (01) 4520197
E-mail: njaba@beta.linkserve.com
Contact: Chief C. Osuagwa - Chairman/CEO

NNB INTERNATIONAL BANK PLC
Business: Commercial Banking
Address: 290A, Akin Olugbade Street, off Adeola Odeku Street, Victoria Island, Lagos
Tel: (01) 4619201-4 (5L), 2703321-4 (5L)
Fax: (01) 4619206
* Plot 628, Sokode Crescent, Wuse Zone 5, Abuja.
Tel: (09) 5232879, 5239728
* Plot 98, Trans-Amadi Layout, Port Harcourt.
Tel: (084) 233722, 481417
* Ring Road, Benin City.
Tel: (052) 280556, 280736
Contact: Mr. Alex Okoh - MD/CEO

NNEJI & SONS ELECTRICAL LIMITED
Business: Sale of Street Lightings and Flourescent Fittings
Address: 175, Azikiwe Road, Aba
Tel: (082) 234215, 230150, 08033167710, 08035513931
Fax: (082) 230150
E-mail: nnejisons@yahoo.com
* 41, Ojo-Giwa Street, Idumota, Lagos
Tel: (01) 2637545, 2636929
Contact: Chief (Dr.) S. N. Nneji - MD/CEO

NNIL COMMERCIAL COMPANY LIMITED
Business: Importation of Industrial & Agricultural Chemicals
Address: NNIL Building (7th Floor), 4, Muhammadu Buhari Way, Kaduna
Tel: (062) 246770, 249654, 249660 **Fax:** (062) 246770
E-mail: nnil@skannet.com
Contact: Engr. Ahmed Ibrahim - MD/CEO

NOBEL & LESLEY INSURANCE BROKERS LIMITED
Business: Insurance Broking, Pension Consultancy and Risk Management
Address: 21, Warehouse Road, Apapa, Lagos
Tel: (01) 5451382, 08037279597
* Banex Plaza (2nd Floor), Plot 750, Aminu Kano Crescent Wuse II, Abuja
Tel: (09) 4136420-5 (6L)
Contact: Mr. Felix O. Amadi - Chairman

NOBLE HEMUKA & COMPANY
Business: Estate Surveyors & Valuers
Address: 103, Forestry Road, Benin City
Tel: (052) 250639
Contact: Mr Noble Nnamdi Nemuka - Principal Partner

NOGEES SECURITY SYSTEMS, EQUIPMENT & SERVICES LTD
Business: Sales, Installation & Maintenance of Security Equipment & Systems
Address: 13, Adekunbi Crescent, off Oluwaleyimu Street, off Allen Avenue, Ikeja, Lagos
Tel: (01) 4977909
Contact: Mr. Mondi Aigbedion - MD/CEO

NOKOSING PAPER MILL LIMITED
Business: Paper Convention & Waste Paper Recycling
Address: 123/125, Ikot Ekpene Road, Ogbor Hill, Aba
Tel: (082) 223705 **Fax:** (082) 225165
Contact: Chief (Dr) Michael N.Okocha - Chairman/CEO

NOKOY INVESTMENT NIGERIA LIMITED
Business: Deep-Sea Trawling, Fishing and Shrimping
Address: First Bank Building (1st Floor, Right Wing), Imam Abibu Adetoro Street, off Ajose Adeogun Street, Victoria Island, Lagos
Tel: (01) 2613634
Contact: Dr. O. E. Onyung - Chairman/CEO

NOOREE NIGERIA LIMITED
Business: Manufacturing, Supply, Installation and Management of Polythene/Plastic Machinery
Address: Plot E3, Ikosi Rd, Oregun Ind.Estate, Ikeja, Lagos
Tel: (01) 7740261, 08033069333 **Fax:** (01) 5557817
E-mail: kisangnam@hanmail.net
* 33, Umaru Babura Street, by Gaskiya Textile Mills, Bompai, Kano.
Tel: (064) 315721, 08035866213
Contact: Mr. Ki Sang Nam - Chairman/President

NORDIC SPORT WEST AFRICA LIMITED
Business: Planning, Organisation & Set-Up of Sports Stadia, Sales, Supply & Rentals of IAAF-Certified Track & Field Sports Equipment
Address: 28, Basie Ogamba Street, off Adeniran Ogunsanya Drive, Surulere, Lagos
Tel: (01) 5851245, 08023041066, 08023069850, 08033254230, 08037027253, 08042107084, 08045049166, 08055235889, 08055245695
E-mail: nordicwestafrica@hotmail.com
* Shop Stands Area, National Stadium Complex, Surulere, Lagos
Tel: (01) 08023041066, 08045049166, 08055235889
Contact: Mr Ifeyinwa Okoye - MD/CEO

NORDY GROUP LIMITED
Business: Manufacturing of Foam Products, Hospitality Services, Farming, Sales of Motor Vehicles
Address: Plot 7A, France Road, opp. Sanigiwa Street, Kano
Tel: (064) 639510, 635845, 640688, 08044120304
* 10, Independence Rd, Bompai Ind. Estate, Kano.
Tel: (064) 645950
Contact: Chief Nnadi Atuchukwu - Group Chairman/CEO

NORFOLK PAPER & PACKAGING LIMITED
Business: Paper Conversion, Manufacturing of Stationery
Address: 1, Akinyemi Crescent, off Fatai Atere Way, Matori Industrial Estate, Mushin, Lagos
Tel: (01) 3205256, 4527627, 4722179

NORMAN INDUSTRIES LIMITED
Business: Manufacturing and Assembling of Airconditioners
Address: 35, Simpson Street, Lagos
Tel: (01) 2630252, 2633415, 2636141, 2662913
Fax: (01) 2634523
* Plot 8, Block H, Isolo Industrial Estate, Oshodi-Apapa Expreesway, by Limca Way, Isolo, Lagos
Tel: (01) 45202431, 523647 **Fax:** (01) 4523714
Contact: Mr. A. B. Hadjandonis - Group GM

NORNIT LIMITED
Business: Manufacturing of Textiles, Upholstery and Knitted Fabrics, Mosquito Netting & T-Shirt Fabrics
Address: 18, Dantata Road, Bompai Industrial Estate, Kano
Tel: (064) 632227, 648968 **Fax:** (064) 632241
Contact: Mr. G. G. Stamboulidis - MD/CEO

NORTH SOUTH OIL & INVESTMENT LIMITED
Business: Sourcing & Supply of Capital Equipment, Processing Unit, Tools Spares, Stocking of Strategic Spare Parts, Integrated Workshop Services
Address: Okoi Arikpo House, 5, Idowu Taylor Street, Victoria Island, Lagos
Tel: (01) 2613025, 2610656 **Fax:** (01) 2613025
E-mail: nsoil@infoweb.abs.net
* Caterpillar House, 19, Old Aba Road, Rumuomasi, Port Harcourt
Tel: (084) 331685
Contact: Mr Wellington Agharese - MD/CEO

NORTH-SOUTH ALUMINIUM PRODUCTS LIMITED
Business: Manufacturing of Longspan Aluminium Roofing & Cladding Sheets
Address: Km. 1, Aba-Umuahia Express Road, Aba
Tel: 08033139346, 08037027838, 08044101798
E-mail: ramesh_keshwani@yahoo.com
Contact: Mr R. K. Keswani - GM/CEO

NORTHERN BAGS MANUFACTURING COMPANY LTD
Business: Manufacturing of Woven Polypropylene Sacks
Address: Plots 47/48, Sharada Ind. Estate Phase II, Kano
Tel: (064) 661646, 669937

NORTHERN CABLE PROCESSING & MANUFACTURING COMPANY LIMITED
Business: Manufacturing and Marketing of Electric Cables and Telecommunication Cables
Address: 13, Maicibi Close, Kakuri Industrial Estate, Kaduna

Tel: (062) 231746, 232746, 234838, 237513-5 (3L)
Fax: (062) 234203
E-mail: nocaco@inet-global.com
Contact: Mr Henning Schnare - MD/CEO
Dr. Ahmadu Bello, mni - GM

NORTHERN FURNITURE INDUSTRIES LIMITED
Business: Manufacturing of Furniture & Curtain Accessories; Interior Designers & Decorators, Metal & Aluminium Works
Address: Plot 15, Sharada Industrial Estate Phase III, Kano
Tel: (064) 660490
Contact: Mr. Walid Tahir - Chairman/CEO

NORTHERN INDUSTRIES LIMITED
Business: Manufacturing of Aluminium Utensils
Address: 32, Challawa Industrial Estate, Kano
Contact: Mr. A. Yau - MD/CEO

NORTHERN NIGERIA FLOUR MILLS PLC
Business: Flour Milling
Address: 15, Mai Malari Road, Bompai Industrial Estate, Bompai, Kano
Tel: (064) 634735, 634850, 647666 **Fax:** (064) 639758
Contact: Alh. (Dr.) Aminu Alhassan Dantata, OFR - Chairman
Alh. Rabiu M. Gwarzo - MD/CEO

NORTHERN TEXTILE MANUFACTURERS LIMITED
Business: Manufacturing of Blankers, Bed Covers, Floor Dusters and Baby Shawls
Address: 5, Independence Road, Bompai Ind.Estate, Kano
Tel: (064) 630564, 630565, 636833 **Fax:** (064) 632592
Contact: Mr. M. L. Akkad - Chairman/CEO

NORTHSTAR INDUSTRIES LIMITED
Business: Manufacturing of Furniture for Offices and Homes
Address: Sharada Industrial Estate Phase I, Kano
Tel/Fax: (064) 663472
E-mail: northstarkano@yahoo.com
Website: www.northstarkano,com
Contact: Alh. Bashir O. Tofa - Chairman/CEO

NORTH-WEST COMMUNICATIONS LIMITED
Business: Operation of Pre-Paid Telephone Cards
Address: 5, Imam Abibu Adetoro Street, off Ajose Adeogun Street, Victoria Island, Lagos
Tel: (01) 2611193, 2611197, 2703616-7 (2L), 2703619, 4619791-3 (3L)
E-mail: info@northwestcommunication.com
Website: www.northwestcommunication.com
Contact: Mr Adegbemi Onakoya - ED (Admin. & Finance)

NOSAK AGENCIES LIMITED
Business: Importation and Marketing of Industrial Chemicals
Address: 116, Ogudu-Ojota Road, Ogudu G.R.A., Lagos
Tel: (01) 4968622-4 (3L), 08033024982
Fax: (01) 4964685
E-mail: nosak@nova.net.ng
* 427/433, Apapa-Oshodi Expressway, by Berliet Bus-Stop, Ilasamaja, Lagos
Tel: (01) 4700035, 7749165
* 154, Sapele Rd, after Santana Market, Benin City
Tel: (052) 257962

NOVA FINANCE & SECURITIES LIMITED
Business: Stockbroking, Financial Advisory Services, Portfolio Management
Address: Speedway House (1st Floor), 21, Araromi Street, off Macarthy Street, Onikan, Lagos
Tel: (01) 2630368, 2601407, 08023128487, 08056156194
Fax: (01) 2647040
E-mail: novafinsec@yahoo.com
* 28, Forces Avenue, Old G.R.A., Port Harcourt
Tel: (084) 487026, 08023333580
Contact: Mr. Tony E. Anenih, Jnr. - Chairman

NOVA TRADE LIMITED
Business: Importation, Sales, Servicing, Repairs & Maintenance of Airconditioners, Fridges, Freezers
Address: Trade House, Jagal Road, off Ikosi Road, Oregun Industrial Estate, Ikeja, Lagos
Tel: (01) 4964651, 7737222, 08033009966
Fax: (01) 4964964
E-mail: trade@nova,net.ng
Contact: Mr Zeid Jarmakani - Chairman/CEO

NOVACOKE BUILDERS LIMITED
Business: Building and Civil Engineering Contractors
Address: Plot 54, Akanbi Onitiri Close, off Eric Moore Road, Iganmu Industrial Estate, Iganmu, Lagos
Tel: (01) 5830934, 5456719, 5851768 **Fax:** (01) 5836323
Contact: Engr. A. Coker - MD/CEO

NOVAFOAM-CHEMICAL & WIRE MANUFACTURERS NIGERIA LIMITED
Business: Manufacture and Marketing of Foam Products, Sales of Chemicals and Furniture
Address: Trade House, Jagal Road, off Ikosi Road, Oregun Industrial Estate, Oregun, Lagos
Tel: (01) 4964651, 4961382 **Fax:** (01) 4964651
E-mail: foam@nova.net.ng
Contact: Mr. Zeid Jarmakani - Chairman/CEO

NOVAT ANIMAL HOSPITAL LIMITED
Business: Animal Care and Veterinary Services, Pest Control Services, Sales of Pet-Care Materials, Pet Breeding Consultancy, Sales and Training of Dogs
Address: Block E, LSDPC Luxury Flats, 24, Adeola Odeku Street, Victoria Island, Lagos
Tel: (01) 7744800, 08033034821
E-mail: novatanihop@yahoo.com
Contact: Dr. N. O. Funsho - Chairman/CEO

NOVEL DRUGS LIMITED
Business: Manufacturing of Pharmaceutical Products
Address: Km. 14, Ikorodu Road (Novel Drugs Bus-Stop), Owode-Onirin, Lagos
Tel: (01) 8150800, 08023323359, 08023380360
E-mail: novel@hyperia.com
novel@yahoo.com
Contact: Chief Nathaniel Ehianata-Osagie - Chairman/CEO

NOVENA MAJESTY FURNITURE INDUSTRY LIMITED
Business: Sales of Furniture and Furnishings
Address: Novenna Plaza (1st Floor), 141, Ahmadu Bello Way, Victoria Island, Lagos
Tel: (01) 2661442, 4708046, 2616101, 2617978

NOVITAS LIMITED
Business: Advertising, Public Relations & Marketing Communications, Production and Printing
Address: Oluwatobi House, 71, Allen Avenue, Ikeja, Lagos
Tel: (01) 4930285, 4930286, 7740877 **Fax:** (01) 4930286
E-mail: novitas@alpha.linkserve.com
Contact: Sesan Oyebode - MD/CEO

NPS EDUCATIONAL PUBLISHERS LIMITED
Business: Publishing of Educational and General Books
Address: Trusthouse, 2, Akinyemi Way, S.W. Ring Road, Ibadan
Tel: (02) 2316006, 08033295359, 08033700838
E-mail: npseducational@webmail.co.za
* 37, Omeagana Street, Onitsha.
Tel: (046) 213774
Contact: Dr. Isaac Muyiwa-Ojo - GM

NSL CONSULTING LIMITED
Business: Consultancy in Information Technology and Telecommunications
Address: 5, Pioneers Road, by Sebuff Plaza, Osapa-Lekki, off Lekki-Epe Expressway, Lekki Peninsula, Lagos
Tel: (01) 7747505 **Fax:** (01) 5555748
E-mail: nsl@consultant.com
Website: www.nslconsult.com
Contact: Engr. O. C. Iromantu - Chairman/CEO

NSU INTERNATIONAL COMPANY LIMITED
Business: Shipping Services, Clearing & Forwarding Agency
Address: 13, Calcutta Crescent, Apapa, Lagos
Tel: (01) 5871810, 08023121092, 08033961535, 08037258792
Contact: Sir (Chief) V. J. U. Onwu - Chairman/CEO

NTCN LIMITED
Business: Manufacturing of Carpets, Interior Decorators, General Contractors
Address: 39, Itire Rd, opp.AP Filling Station, Surulere, Lagos
Tel: (01) 5850185, 7733220, 08033121402, 08033071233, 08033329009 **Fax:** (01) 5837997
* Km. 34, Lagos-Abeokuta Expressway, beh. Texaco Filling Station, Ilo, Sango-Otta
Tel: (039) 722449, 722450
* 116, Ogbunabali Road, Port Harcourt
Tel: (084) 238737
* Wuse Shopping Complex (Shop E21), Wuse Zone 3, Abuja

NUB INTERNATIONAL BANK LIMITED
Business: Banking Services
Address: Plot 554, Adetokunbo Ademola Crescent, Wuse II, Abuja
Tel: (09) 5237050-1 (2L), 5239488, 5240723
* 29, Burma Road, Apapa, Lagos
Tel: (01) 5874290 Fax: (01) 5874091, 5874276
* Yakubu Gowon Way Near Central Bank, Kaduna
Tel: (062) 249143, 244152 **Fax:** (062) 245507

NUCHINI ENTERPRISES NIGERIA LIMITED
Business: Importation of Auto & Industrial Spare Parts
Address: 52, International Airport Road, Mafoluku, Lagos
Tel: 08033080556, 08055067622

NUCLEUS GROUP NIGERIA LIMITED
Business: Petroleum Services
Address: 3, Alabi Street, off Toyin Street, (by Alphon House), Ikeja, Lagos
Tel: (01) 4979521, 7744733, 4978618 **Fax:** (01) 4979522
E-mail: vincent@siolet.com
Contact: Mr. Vincent Abijoroh - Chairman/CEO

NUCLEUS VENTURES LIMITED
Business: Paper Merchants, Importers and Exporters, Manufacturers, Road Haulage Services
Address: Nucleus House, 21, Fatai Atere Way, Plot 1B, Block E, Matori Industrial Estate, Mushin, Lagos
Tel: (01) 4521341-4 (4 L), 4525239, 4528852-3 (2L), 5553370-4 (5L), 4745503-4 (2L)
Fax: (01) 4524718, 4525590, 5553375
E-mail: nucleus@hyperia.com
Contact: Mr. Olaide Fowosire - Chairman/CEO
Mr. Tunde Adepoju - Corporate Affairs Manager

NUDAL NIGERIA COMPANY LIMITED
Business: Manufacturing of Industrial Electrical-Control Equipment & Switch Gears
Address: 31, Shotinoye Street, Papa Ajao, Mushin, Lagos
Tel: (01) 4522658, 4521149 **Fax:** (01) 4521149
Contact: Mr. Oladunmoye Runsewe - MD/CEO

NUEL OJEI HOLDINGS LIMITED
Business: Conglomerate
Address: 362, Ikorodu Road, Maryland, Lagos
Tel: (01) 4971144-7 (4 L), 4937775-7 (3 L)
Fax: (01) 4937778
* Plot 460, Airport Rd, Central Business Area, Abuja.
Tel: (09) 5230286
Contact: Chief Nuel Ojei - Chairman/CEO

NULEC INDUSTRIES LIMITED
Business: Manufacturing & Trading
Address: 12, Ijora Causeway, Ijora, Lagos
Tel: (01) 5830310, 5834890, 5834902, 5834936
Fax: (01) 5833548, 5450424
E-mail: nulec@aol.com
nulec@multilinks.com
* Isiaka Oduntan Street, Km. 7, Shagamu/Benin Expressway, Shagamu
Contact: Mr. Aham Umunnakwem - Marketing/Sales Dept

NUMERIQUE LIMITED
Business: Sales of Electronic Components, Computer Hardware, Electronic Test Equipment, Electronic Tools and Electronic Technical Literature
Address: 11, Olufemi Str, off Ogunlana Drive, Surulere, Lagos
Tel: (01) 4826536, 5850114, 834319 **Fax:** (01) 5850114
* 29, Bello Road, off Ishaga Road, Surulere, Lagos
Tel: (01) 7735180, 7743783
E-mail: numerique@rcl.nig.com
* Plot 68, Area 7A, Cornershops, Garki, Abuja
Tel: (09) 2347826
Contact: Mr. S. Olusoga Orekoya - Chairman/CEO

NUPLAS INDUSTRIES LIMITD
Business: Manufacturing of PVC Carpets & Sheets, Rigid Foils, Leather Cloth and Blister Packs

Address: 6, Kolawole Shonibare Street, Apakun Industrial Estate, Ajao Estate, Lagos
Tel: (01) 4520195, 521093 Fax: (01) 4972370, 2622535
E-mail: nuplas@beta.linkserve.com
Contact: Mr Wahid Calcuttawala - MD/CEO

NUSRA TRAVELS & TOUR LIMITED
Business: Travel Agency and Tour Operations
Address: 15, Adeleke Street, off Allen Avenue, Ikeja, Lagos
Tel: (01) 4971644, 8047064, 08033598083
E-mail: nusratoursim@yahoo.com
Contact: Alh. Abdul Rauf Zakari - Chairman/CEO

NUTRA FOODS LIMITED
Business: Production of Chocolate and Chewing Gum Confectioneries
Address: 1, Mobolaji Johnson Avenue, Oregun Industrial Estate, Oregun, Lagos
Tel: (01) 4971451-2 (2 L) **Fax:** (01) 4971456
Contact: Farouk El-Khalil - MD/CEO

NUTRIFOOD AND BEVERAGES LIMITED
Business: Marketing of Food Drinks & Beverages
Address: 32, Awka Road, Onitsha
Tel: (046) 213308, 216374, 413308
* Valley Estate, Akowonjo, Agege, Lagos
Tel: (01) 4925141, 2643922, 2668166 **Fax:** (01) 4925141
Contact: Chief Jeffrey Uzoma - Chairman/CEO

NUTRIVITAS LIMITED
Business: Importation of Livestock Nutrition Products
Address: 9, Alh. Tokunbo Alli Street, off Toyin Street, Ikeja, Lagos
Tel: (01) 4930180, 4975759, 7757809, 08037228291
Fax: (01) 4975759
E-mail: nutrivit@infoweb.abs.net
Contact: Mr S. A. Ohwofa - MD/CO

NYAKOS NIGERIA LIMITEDLIMITED
Business: General Merchandising
Address: 191, Mohammed Mustapha Way, Nassarawa, Jimeta-Yola
Tel: (075) 625109, 625358
Contact: Alh. Isa Hammanyero - Chairman/CEO

NYCIL LIMITED
Business: Manufacture of Alkyd Resin, Adhesive Binders, Textile Finishing/Sizing Agents, Polyseter Resins, Driers and Plasticizing Agents
Address: Plot 5-8, Ogun State Housing Corporation Ind. Estate, Km. 6, Otta-Idiroko Road, Otta, Lagos
Tel: (01)7733007-8 (2L),* (039) 722274-7 (4L)
Fax: (01) 4933964, * (039) 722272
E-mail: nycil@linkserve.com
Contact: M. R. Rao - MD/CEO

NZEMAT NIGERIA LIMITED
Business: Sales of Medical Diagnostic Products, Laboratory Reagents and Chemicals
Address: 23, Adetayo Osho Street, off Fola Agoro Street, Akoka, Yaba, Lagos
Tel: (01) 5820341, 08033709476 **Fax:** (01) 2885795
Contact: Chief A. N. Odunze - MD/CEO

O' FRANK (NIGERIA) LIMITED
Business: Sales of Electronics, Import & Export, General Merchandising, Manufacture of Toilet Paper Rolls
Address: O'Frank Plaza, 113, Kirikiri Rd, Olodi, Apapa, Lagos
Tel: (01) 5871453, 871708, 877282 **Fax:** (01) 5871453
Contact: Chief Frank Crowther - Chairman/CEO

O' LA-KLEEN
Business: Office & Industrial Cleaning Services
Address: Plot 5, Prince Adelowo Adedeji St, off Admiralty Way, Lekki Phase 1, Victoria Island Extension, Lagos
Tel: (01) 2691295, 2691490, 2706210-1 (2L), 7742199
Fax: (01) 2690984
E-mail: olakleen@micro.com.ng
Website: www.o'lakleen.com
Contact: Ade Ogundeyin - MD/CEO

"O' LIX 'J' NIGERIA LIMITED
Business: Importation and Sales of Copier Papers
Address: 32, Ayinde Giwa Street, off James Robertson Street,, Surulere, Lagos
Tel: (01) 5851465, 5454864, 5870524 **Fax:** (01) 5851429
E-mail: olixj@beta.linkserve.com
* 4, Campbell Street, Lagos.
Tel: (01) 2646657
* 23, New Market Road, Onitsha.
Tel: (046) 214631
* Plot 61, Corner Shop, Area 7A, beside Cultural Centre, Garki, Abuja.
Tel: (09) 2345206-7 (2L) **Fax:** (09) 2345208
Contact: Mr Felix I. Ofodum - Chairman/CEO

O. B. BAKER LIMITED
Business: Construction, Installation and Maintenance of Swimming Pools, Water Treatment Services, Sales of Swimming Pool Equipment
Address: 20, Adeniran Ogunsanya Street, Surulere, Lagos
Tel: (01) 5848081, 5845551 **Fax:** (01) 5848081
E-mail: ob_baker@hotmail.com
Contact: Mr. Osahon Baker Osemwota - Chairman/CEO

O. M. F SECURITIES & FINANCE LIMITED
Business: Stockbrking
Address: Oasis House, 298, Ikorodu Road (Anthony Bus-Stop), Lagos
Tel: (01) 4937038, 4973145, 08033480628
Fax: (01) 4973145
E-mail: omfsec@micro.com.ng
Contact: Mr Edkan Ekong - GM/CEO

O. O. INTERNATIONAL NIGERIA LIMITED
Business: General Merchandise, Contractual Procurements
Address: 25, Asa Road, Aba
Tel: (082) 222857 Fax: (082) 221773
Contact: Chief (Dr) O. O. Okoronkwo - Chairman/CEO

O. O. P. CONSULTANTS LIMITED
Business: Construction & Architectural Consultancy
Address: Intercontinental Plaza (5th Floor), Plot 999C, Danmole Street, Victoria Island, Lagos
Tel: (01) 2623012, 611713 Fax: (01) 2622986
E-mail: oop.ng@linkserve.com
Contact: Arc. O. Odusote - Chairman/CEO

O'VIKA GROUP LIMITED
Business: Markting of Petroleum Products & General Merchandise, Project Consultancy, Oil & Gas Services, Shipping, Insurance, Property Development
Address: Waterfront Plaza, Plot 270, Ozumba Mbadiw Avenue, Victoria Island, Lagos
Tel: (01) 2621061-4 (5L) fAX: (01) 2621059
Contact: Chief Victor Aiyela - Chairman/CEO

OAK EXCLUSIVE DESIGNS LIMITED
Business: Design & Production of Shirts, Monogramming & Engraving, Heat-Transfer & Screen Printing, Customisation of Gift Items
Address: 5, Jogunosimi Street, off Obafemi Awolowo Way (Radio Bus-Stop), Alausa, Ikeja, Lagos
Tel: (01) 3453534 , 3453689, 4973370, 7734765, 08033227736 **Fax:** (01) 4973370
E-mail: sales@oak-ng.com
info@oak-ng.com
Website: www.oak-ng.com
* Plot 61, Airport Road, Warri
Tel: (053) 251319, 08023098216 **Fax:** (053) 251319

OAKWOOD NIGERIA LIMITED
Business: Sales of Corporate Gift Items, Graphic Design, General Printing & Advertising, Interior Design & Landscaping
Address: Gloriaville, 5, Ade Akinsanya Avenue (Behind Elephant House), off Town Planning Way, off Ikorodu Road, Ilupeju, Lagos
Tel: (01) 4975923, 4977268 **Fax:** (01) 2668128, 4960779
E-mail: oakwood@infoweb.abs.net
Contact: Mr. Olaleke A. Ajayi - MD/CEO

OAN OVERSEAS AGENCY NIGERIA LIMITED
Business: Maritime Services
Address: 22, Creek Road, Apapa, Lagos
Tel: (01) 5877316, 5877343, 5877451, 5877573, 5450471, 5877573 **Fax:** (01) 5871474, 5877638
E-mail: operations@oan-agency.com
* Km. 4, Refinery Rd, by. Ekpan Police Station Warri.
Tel/Fax: (053) 252524, 320285
E-mail: ops.wri@oan-agency.com
* 14, Azikiwe Road, Port Harcourt
Tel: (084) 237313, 239146, 239704 **Fax:** (084) 237313
E-mail: ops.phc@oan-agency.com

OANDO NIGERIA PLC (formerly Unipetrol Nig. Plc)
Business: Production & Marketing of Petroleum Products & Accessories (Lubricants, Greases, Insecticides), Marketing of Refined Petroleum & Gas, Bitumen
Address: Stallion House (8th-10th Floor), 2, Ajose Adeogun Street, Victoria Island, Lagos
Tel: (01) 2601290-9 (10L) **Fax:** (01) 2625480, 2633939
E-mail: info@oando.com
info@oandoplc.com
Website: www.oando.com
www.oandoplc.com
* Motorways Centre (2nd Floor), 1, Motorways Avenue, Alausa, Ikeja, Lagos.
Tel: (01) 7732173-5
* Herbert Macaulay Way, by Berger Junction, Wuse Zone 6, Abuja.
Tel: (09) 5235459 **Fax:** (09) 5235458
* Reclamation Road, Port Harcourt
Tel: (084) 230257, 235457, 235527, 239175
Fax: (084) 233370
Contact: Mr. Jubril A. Tinubu - MD/CEO
Ms. Tokunbo Dorusaro - Corp. Comm. Manager

OASIS INSURANCE COMPANY LIMITED
Business: All Classes of Insurance
Address: Oasis House, 298, Ikorodu Road, Anthony, Lagos
Tel: (01) 4932448, 4936224, 4965069
E-mail: oasisinsuranc@nova.net.ng
* Sijuwola House, 5, Dugbe Layout, Ibadan
Tel: (02) 2410431
Contact: Mr Victor O. Durojaiye - MD/CEO

OASIS SAVINGS & LOANS LIMITED
Business: Mortgage Banking Services
Address: Oasis House, 298, Ikorodu Road, Anthony, Lagos
Tel: (01) 4971186, 4968515, 4937304 **Fax:** (01) 4977082
E-mail: oasissll@micro.com.ng
Contact: Mr. Abimbola Olayinka - GM/ CEO

OBA GROUP INTERNATIONAL LIMITED
Business: Construction, Fabrication & Structural Engineering Dssign, Fabrication & Installation 0f Overhead Water Tanks, Basments & Steel Towers
Address: 34, Orhuwhorum Road, Ovwian, Warri.
Tel: (053) 256975, 621141
E-mail: obagroupltd@yahoo.com
* Plot 128, Trans-Amadi Ind. Layout, Port Harcourt
Tel: (084) 232453, 440992, 08033216816
* Abuja Shopping Mall (Suite A17), Wuse Zone 3, Abuja
Tel: (09) 5234101, 08037012418, 08037017842
Contact: Hon. (Engr.) Frederick Emiaha - Chairman/CEO

OBA PAPER PRODUCTS INDUSTRIES LIMITED
Business: Agro-Allied Business, Manufacture of *Telex* Papers, *Telex* Rolls & Carbonised Papers
Address: Moobag House, 23, Burma Road, Apapa, Lagos
Tel: (01) 5804080-4 (5L), 5877711, 5877722, 5457395
Fax: (01) 5877722

OBASANJO FARMS NIGERIA LIMITED
Business: Livestock Farming (Poultry & PiggerY); Property Development; Quarry; General Merchandising; Crop & Animal Feed Production; Plastic & Cardboard Packaging & Irrigation Equipment
Address: Agbe L'Oba House, Quarry Road, Ibara, Abeokuta
Tel: (039) 242062, 242005, 243658 **Fax:** (039) 244650
E-mail: agbeloba@hyperia.com
* Km. 5, Idiroko Road (beh Ota Gen Hospital), Otta
Tel: (039) 722420, 722536-8 (3L), 08033101691, 08033320306, 08042110498, 08055307052
E-mail: otafarm@hyperia.com

OBELAWO GROUP OF COMPANIES
Business: Manufacture of UPVC Pipes
Address: * Obelawo Estate, New Ikirun Road, Osogbo
Tel: (035) 232602, 232632 **Fax:** (035) 234273, 233317
* Plot 13, Eric Moore Road, Iganmu, Lagos
Tel: (01) 832002, 5850591

OBEV SYSTEMS LIMITED
Business: Sales, Installation & Maintnance of Education & Industrial Equipment
Address: 117A, Wetheral Road, Owerri
Tel: (083) 233802, 08037875855 **Fax:** (083) 233008
E-mail: obevltd@aol.com
Contact: Mr Evans Uhegbu - MD/CEO

OBF-HI-TEKNOLOGIES LIMITED
Business: IT Products Sales & Engineering, Telecommunication & Radio Communication Engineering, Security & Safety Systems, Consultancy Services
Address: 15, Oduyemi Street, off Obafemi Awolowo Road, Ikeja, Lagos
Tel: (01) 4975482, 4808677, 08023030009, 08023041119
Fax: (01) 4975482
E-mail: obfltd@hotmail.com
obfltd@globalwebsmaster,com
Website: www.globalwebsmaster.com
Contact: Engr. Olusegun B. Folaranmi - MD/CEO

OBI OBEMBE & ASSOCIATES
Business: Civil & Structural Engineering Consultancy
Address: Lorunda House (5th Floor), 106/110, Lewis Street, Lafiaji, Lagos
Tel: (01) 2635929, 2635190, 2631464 **Fax:** (01) 2631464
E-mail: obemebe@siotel.net
* 32, Ugbor Road, Benin City
Tel: (052) 254106
Contact: Engr. Babafemi B. Obembe - Managing Partner/CEO

OBIEFUNA MODERN BUS INDUSTRIES (NIGERIA) LIMITED
Business: Fabrication of Steel & Metal Structures (Bus Body, Tanker, Underground Tanks, Iron-Body Trucks)
Address: Mile 3, Onitsha-Owerri Road, Onitsha
Tel: (046) 486842, 08046122837
Contact: Chief B. O. Obiefuna - Chairman/CEO

OBIEKWE BROTHERS LIMITED
Business: Industrialist, Import of Electronic Appliances, Office Equipment, Domestic Appliances, Generators & Voltage Regulators, Transport Services,
Address: 82, Zik Avenue, Enugu
Tel: (042) 256269, 259920 **Fax:** (042) 259962
E-mail: obieco@infoweb.abs,net
* 110, Nnamdi Azikiwe Street, Idumota, Lagos
Tel: (01) 2666797, 2668515 **Fax:** (01) 2662465
Contact: Chief T. A. Obiekwe - Chairman/CEO

OBIGOLD INTERNATIONAL LIMITED
Busniss: Sales of Electronics and Household Appliances
Address: G16, Alaba International Market, Ojo-Alaba, Lagos
Tel: (01) 5892582, 7747780 Fax: (01) 5892582
E-mail: obigold@infoweb.abs.nt
obigold@hoymail.com
Contact: Mr Obi Emelobe - Chairman/CEO

OBIKE INDUSTRIES (NIGERIA) LIMITED
Business: Importation of Industrial Raw Materials (Fragrance & Chemicals), General Chemical Consultancy .
Address: 7, Akor Street, Near Ose Market, Onitsha
Tel: (046) 486544
E-mail: obike_ikenta@yahoo.co.uk
* 5/6, Onitsha-Owerri Road, opp Ogbanu Main Market, Onitsha
Tel: (046) 216231, 414749 Fax: (046) 414743
* 4, Opebi Road, Ikeja, Lagos.
Tel: (01) 4936974, 4937298, 4966586, 8042160
E-mail: obike@nova.nt.ng
* 69, Port Harcourt Road, Aba. **Tel:** (01) 221355
Contact: Chief (Dr) P. O. Ikenta - Chairman/CEO

OBINACO MOTORS NIGERIA LIMITED
Business: Import of Auto Spare Parts & Used Motorcycles
Address: 16, Onitsha Road, Nnewi, Anambra State
Tel: (046) 460186, 460531, 461810
Contact: Mr Obinna G. Amchukwu - Chairman/CEO

OBIRO GROUP OF COMPANIES LIMITED
Business: Trading, Import & Export, Manufacturing, Marketing and Distribtion
Address: The Lord's Plaza, 17A, Allen Avenue, Ikeja, Lagos
Tel: (01) 4930249, 4974097, 7746369, 08023613862
Fax: (01) 4930249
* Plot 221/222, Obinaocha Avenue, Orji Town Layout, Orji, Uratta, Owerri
* The Lord's Plaza II, Plot 2A, Lateef Jakande Road, Agidingbi, Ikeja, Lagos
Tel: (01) 7746369

OBIX TRUST INCORPORATED
Business: Importation of Cosmetics & Allied Products
Address: Block D (Suite 101/148), Bnue Plaza, Intrnation Centre for Commerce, BBA Area, Trade Fiar Complex, Lagos-Badagry Expressway, Ojo, Lagos
Tel: (01) 3206031, 08023021849
E-mail: obixtrust62@yahoo.com
obixtrust@hotmail.com
Contact: Mr Edwin Nnaemeka - Chairman

OBODEX NIGERIA LIMITED
Business: Manufacture & Assembly of Computer Hardware
Address: Obodex House, 235, Ikorodu Road, Ilupeju, Lagos
Tel: (01) 4936273, 4975241, 4978570, 4971270
Fax: (01) 4971290
Contact: Chief Don Etiebet - Chairman/CEO

OBUDU RANCH RESORT, OBUDU
Business: Hospitality, Hotels & Ranch Resort Management
Address: Obanliku, Cross River State.
Tel: 08035506256, Satellite +(21) 646650454
E-mail: ranch_resort@yahoo.com

OBUM LEATHERS LIMITED
Business: Sales of Home & Office Furniture
Address: 11B, Karimu Kotun Street, Victoria Island, Lagos
Tel: (01) 3200551-3 (3L) Fax: (01) 2673391
E-mail: oleathers@yahoo.com
Website: www.obumleathers.com
* 11A, Alfred Rewane Road, Ikoyi, Lagos
Tel: (01) 2673391, 2693304
* Obum Plaza, Plot 1140, Adetokunbo Ademola Crescent, Wuse II, Abuja
Tel: (09) 4133325-6 (2L)\
Contact: Chief Celestine Tagbo - Chairman/CEO
Barr. Nkacha Chinwuba - GM

OCEAN & OIL NIGERIA LIMITED

Business: Local & International Marketing of Petroleum Products, Tanker Freight Services
Address: Stallion House (5th Floor), 2, Ajose Adeogun Street, Victoria Island, Lagos
Tel: (01) 2623442-4 (3 L), 2625465-7 (3 L)
Fax: (01) 2622311
E-mail: info@oceanandoil.com.ng
Website: www.oceanandoil.com
* 21, Danube Street, off IBB Way, Maitama, Abuja
Tel: (09) 4131944-5 (2 L) **Fax:** (09) 4138869

OCEAN ENERGY NIGERIA LIMITED

Business: Exploration & Production of Crude Oil and Gas
Address: Plot 296, Ozumba Mbadiwe Str, Victoria Is. Lagos
Tel: (01)5558400-1 (2L)

OCEAN FISHERIES (NIGERIA) LIMITED

Business: Fishing & Shrimping, Exploration of Seafoods
Address: Churchgate Tower, Plot PC. 30, Afribank Street, Victoria Island, Lagos
Tel: (01) 2620550-4 (5 L), 2620410 (5 L)
Fax: (01) 2620420, 2621285
E-mail: ravi@churchgate.com
* 25, Creek Road, Apapa, Lagos
Tel: (01) 5450083, 5804680, 5804684, 5872568, 5877421
Fax: (01) 5872483
Contact: Lt. Gen. M. I. Wushish (rtd.) - Chairman
Mr. R. I. Mahtani - Director

OCEAN STEAMSHIP (NIGERIA) LIMITED

Business: Shipping Services and Consultancy
Address: 30/32, Creek Road, Apapa, Lagos
Tel/Fax: (01) 5451508
Contact: Alh. Muhammadu Maccido - Chairman
Mr. Emmanuel Akintoye-Adeniyi - Ag. MD/CEO

OCEAN TRANSPORT & SHIPPING LIMITED

Business: Clearing and Forwarding, Transport and Shipping
Address: Plot PC. 30, Afribank Street, Victoria Island, Lagos
* 25, Creek Road, Apapa, Lagos
Tel: (01) 5872644 **Fax:** (01) 5871295
Contact: Mr. B. Mahtani - Chairman

OCEAN VIEW RESTAURANTS (Div. of Eko Hotel Group)

Business: Restaurant Services
Address: Adetokunbo Ademola St, Victoria Island, Lagos
Tel: (01) 2620954, 2613555 **Fax:** (01) 2623048
Website: www.ekohotels.com
Contact: Mr. Antoine Zammarieh - MD/CEO

OCEANIC BANK INTERNATIONAL (NIGERIA) PLC

Business: Commercial Banking
Address: Herbert Macaulay Way, Wuse Zone 6, Abuja
Tel: (09) 5236388, 5237997, 5237311, 5236209, 5237997
Fax: (09) 5236085
* Water Front Plaza, Plot 270, Ozumba Mbadiwe Avenue, Victoria Island, Lagos
Tel: (01) 2622010-2 (3L), 2622157-9 (3L), 2620393, 2611489, 2610522 **Fax:** (01) 613498
E-mail: info@oceanicbanknigeria.com
Website: www.oceanicbanknigeria.com
Contact: Chief (Mrs.) C. A. O. Ibru - MD/CEO

OCEANSIDE ENGINEERING SERVICES LIMITED

Business: Oilfield Engineering Services
Address: Big Leaf House (6th Floor), 7 (Plot 1664), Oyin Jolayemi Street, Victoria Island, Lagos
Tel: (01) 4701713, 616964, 3201713

OCM NIGERIA LIMITED

Business: General Merchandise, Importers of Stockfish, Fruit Juice, Computer Consumables
Address: Plot 33D, Bishop Aboyade-Cole Street, V/I, Lagos
Tel: (01) 2624273-4 (2 L), 2622299 **Fax:** (01) 2622299

OCO INDUSTRIAL SERVICES LIMITED

Business: Sales & Leasing of Tools, Welding Equipment & Consumables, Electrodes, Air Compressors
Address: Plot 77C, Trans-Amadi Ind. Layout, Port Harcourt
Tel: (084) 230647, 08033366903, 08033393953
Fax: (084) 230608
E-mail: ocoph@oal.com
Contact: Mr. Victor Ore - MD/CEO

OCULUS PHARMACARE LIMITED

Business: Import of Pharmaceuticals & Health-Care Products
Address: Syngenta Compound, 387, Agege Motor Road, Challenge, Mushin, Lagos
Tel: (01) 4523511, 4523523, 7743119 **Fax:** (01) 4523569
E-mail: oculuspharm@metrong.com
Contact: Mr Cliff C.Nzimaka - MD/CEO

ODADIKI EYE HOSPITAL

Business: Ophthalmic, Optometric & Optical Services
Address: 7, Aba Road, Port Harcourt
Tel: (084) 231274
E-mail: odadiki_eye@yahoo.com

ODALO ENTERPRISES LIMITED

Business: Clearing & Forwarding
Address: 33, Osolo Way, off International Airport Road, Ajao Estate, Lagos
Tel: (01) 4525147, 4527695, 7743140, 08033027392
Fax: (01) 4520936
E-mail: losfelix@rclmail.com
Contact: Mr Felix Imonikhe Itoandon - Chairman/CEO

ODESCO INTERNATIONAL LIMITED

Business: Importation of Pharmaceutical Products
Address: 24, Uga Street, Fegge, Onitsha
Tel: (046) 217387
Contact: Mr. S. Okorie - Chairman/CEO

ODKA NIGERIA LIMITD

Businss: Stockist, Sales & Service of Engineering & Mechanical Equipment, Building Materials
Address: 2A, Plateau Road, Apapa,Lagos
Tel: (01) 5871975, 08023313227, 08033471606
Contact: Mr Johnson Igwe - Chairman/CEO

ODOGWU GROUP OF COMPANIES LIMITED

Business: Conglomerate - Manufacturing, Insurance, Travel Agency, Oil Marketing, Hospitality, Property Development and General Investments
Address: Group House, 4/6, Ikoyi Road, Obalende, Lagos
Tel: (01) 2691825, 2692664, 2692667 **Fax:** (01) 2692683

* 25, Boyle Street, Onikan, Lagos
Tel: (01) 2631484, 2631557 **Fax:** (01) 2634000, 2692666
Contact: Chief (Dr) Sonny Dike Odogwu - Chairman
Mr. Kenny E. Odogwu - MD/CEO

ODU'A INVESTMENT COMPANY LIMITED
Business: Holding Company, Investments
Address: Cocoa House Complex, Oba Adebimpe Road, Dugbe, Ibadan
Tel: (02) 2410869, 2414183, 2414229 **Fax:** (02) 2413000
E-mail: odua@odu-a.com
Website: www.odu'ainvestment.com
* Obafemi Awolowo House (2nd Floor), 29/31, Obafemi Awolowo Way, Ikeja, Lagos
Tel: (01) 7739060
* Great Nigeria Insurance House, Plot 94, Malanje Street, Wuse Zone 4, Abuja. **Tel:** (09) 5234217
Contact: Sir 'Remi Omotoso - Group MD/CEO
Akogun 'Lekan Alabi - Snr Manager (Corp. Affairs)

ODU'A PRINTING & PUBLISHING COMPANY LIMITED
Business: Production of School Workbooks and Stationery, Commercial Printing Services
Address: Eleyele Road, opp. Police Headquarters, Ibadan
Tel: (02) 2413310, 2410985, 2414491 **Fax:** (02) 2410985
E-mail: odua@odu-a.com
Website: www.odu'ainvestment.com
Contact: Mr. W. T. Aguntasolo - MD/CEO

ODUDU & COMPANY
Business: Estate Surveyors & Valuers, Real Estate Consultants
Address: 8/10, Sura Mogaji St, off Coker Rd, Ilupeju, Lagos
Tel: (01) 8042549, 4709308, 08033033337, 08023365105
Fax: (01) 4975629
E-mail: odudu@skannet.com
Contact: Mr. William Oruka Odudu - Principal Partner/CEO

ODUSOTE BOOKSTORES LIMITED
Business: Importation, Distribution and Sales of Educational Textbooks and Stationery
Address: 68, Obafemi Awolowo Way, Oke-Bola, Ibadan
Tel: (02) 2316451, 2315055 **Fax:** (02) 2318781
E-mail: odubooks@infoweb.abs.net
* 177, Herbert Macaulay Street, Yaba, Lagos
Tel: (01) 7746743, 8187060, 866099
Contact: Mr Femi Odusote - Chairman/CEO

OENIC INDUSTRIAL LIMITED
Business: Manufacture of Cosmetics, Grease and Lubricants, Resins and Soaps; Printing
Address: Km. 22, Badagry Expressway, Ajangbadi, Lagos
Tel: (01) 7741328, 08033029511, 08033086327
Contact: N. T. S. Obidike - Chairman/CEO

OEP INTERNATIONAL LIMITED
Business: Sales, Supply and Maintenance of Office Equipment & Products (Digital Duplicators, Binding Machines, Laminating Machines, Photocopiers, Paper Shredders and Trimmers, Cheque Writers, Digital Scan Copiers/Scanners)
Address: Old 29, Oshaga Road, by Mabo Street Junction, off Itire Road, Surulere, Lagos
Tel: (01) 8042611, 4808118, 08033084190, 08046131937
Fax: (01) 5873784
E-mail: jdidigu@yahoo.com
Contact: Mr. Joe Digigu - Chairman/CEO

OFEIMU ENGINEERING (NIGERIA) LIMITED
Business: Industrial and Marine Engineering Works
Address: Plot 6, Oshodi-Apapa Expressway, by Westminster Bus-Stop, Lagos
Tel/Fax: (01) 5453009, 080933045758, 08037225872
E-mail: ofeimuhous@yahoo.com
Contact: Engr. Sunny Ofangbomum - Chairman/CEO

OFFICE DEPOT LIMITED
Business: Marketing of Office Furniture & Accessories
Address: Plot 634, Adeyemo Alakija Street (4th Floor), Victoria Island, Lagos
Tel: (01) 2702932, 2702957, 08033016584, 08033019755
Fax: (01) 2702931
E-mail: sales@officedepotnigria.com
Website: www.officedepotnigria.com

OFFICE DEVICES LIMITED
Business: Sale & Service of Information Technology Products, Office Systems and GSM/Wireless Phones
Address: 68, Adeniyi Jones Avenue, Ikeja, Lagos
Tel: (01) 2906623, 4825184-5 (2L), 08032030778
E-mail: officedevices@yahoo.com
* 117, Allen Avenue, Ikeja, Lagos
Tel: (01) 4710584, 4970385, 8181881, 08032030780
Contact: Mr. Boni Obieze - Chairman/CEO

OFFICE WORLD NIGERIA LIMITED
Business: Sales of Office Furniture, Eqipment and Business Machines
Address: 23A, Akin Adesola Street, Victoria Island, Lagos
Tel: (01) 2615909, 2618776, 7740185, 08037890000
Contact: Mustapha Jammal - MD/CEO

OFFICETRON COMPANY LIMITED
Business: Enterprise Content Management, Networking
Address: Lofom House, 21, Mobolaji Bank-Anthony Way (Leventis Bus-Stop), Maryland, Ikeja, Lagos
Tel: (01) 4960302, 4933560-1 (2L)
Fax: (01) 4979340, 4938842
E-mail: sales@officetrn.com
Website: www.officetron.com
Contact: Mr. Niji Adelagun - MD/CEO

OFOCENT & COMPANY NIGERIA LIMITED
Business Importation & Marketing of Men's Wera Fashion
Address: Stayfit Plaza, 6/8, Ozumba Mbadiwe Street, opp. 1004-Flats Estatem Victoria Island, Lagos
Tel: (01) 2705196-7 (2L), 5558418, 08022240526, 08034037900
* 16, Opebi Road, Ikeja, Lagos
Tel: 08056125576, 08034037900

OFODUM ORJI OQUISM (W. A.) LIMITED
Business: Importer of Auto Parts, Building Materials, Tools, Agricultural, Technical & Industrial Equipment
Address: 18, Nri Street, Niger Approach Layout, Onitsha
Tel: (046) 217016, 217586, 260844
* E109 & E34, Head-Bridge Market, Onitsha

OFOMA ASSOCIATES
Business: Estate Surveyors and Valuers, Rating Consultants
Address: 193, Aba Road, Port Harcourt
Tel: (084) 480530, 08033094934, 08037080205, 08055338816 **Fax:** (084) 239214
E-mail: ofoma@infoweb.abs.net
* 17, Alh. Bashorun Street, off Norman Williams Street, S. W. Ikoyi, Lagos
Tel: (01) 4801141
* Plot 247, Monstserrado St, Wuse Zone 4, Abuja
Tel: (09) 5233700

OFOMA GROUP
Business: Importation of Tyres and Parts for Motor Vehicles & Motorcycles
Address: 156, Adeniji Adele Road, Idumota, Lagos
Tel: (01) 2644070 **Fax:** (01) 2663737
E-mail: snofoma@infoweb.abs.net
Contact: Mr. Jude C. Ofoma - MD/CEO

OFORTRACO MOTORS LIMITED
Business: Import of Motor Vehicle & Motorcycle Spare Parts
Address: 122, Owerri Road, Nnewi, Anambra State
Tel: (046) 460594., 462154, 460825 **Fax:** (046) 463573
E-mail: otcgroup@hotmail.com
otccable@infoweb.abs.net
* 19, Church Street, Idumota, Lagos
Tel: (01) 2666208
Contact: Sir D. C. Ofordeme - Chairman/CEO

OGA WILLIAMS LIMITED
Business: Advertising, Film Production, Product & Corporate Promotions, Printing Services
Address: 77, Ikorodu Road, Fadeyi, Lagos
Tel: (01) 824195, 08023671658, 08033156836
Contact: Evangelist Femi Aladegbaye - MD/CEO

OGENE HOLDINGS LIMITED
Business: Entertainment Services, Recording, Production and Promotion of Music
Address: 12, Alakija St, WAEC Area, Jibowu Yaba, Lagos
Contact: Chief (Dr.) Oliver de Coque - Chairman/CEO

OGIDI AVIATION SERVICES LIMITED
Business: Freight, Courier and Cargo Delivery Services
Address: 28, Aromire Avenue, off Adeniyi Jones Avenue, Ikeja, Lagos
Tel: (01) 4972647, 4938148-9 (2L), 08023195184, 08033327511
Fax: (01) 4938149
E-mail: ogidiaviation 1@yahoo.com
Website: www.aramex.com
www.pilotair.com
Contact: Capt. John T. Okapku (rtd.) - MD/CEO

OGINS ADVERTISING LIMITED
Business: Advertising & Marketing Communication Agency
Address: Ibusa House (3rd Floor), 5, Sunday Ogunyade Street (behind Mobil Petrol Station), Gbagada Estate Phase II, Lagos
Tel: (01) 4705364
Contact: Chief S. A. Edu - Chairman
Mr. Faith Gbagi - MD/CEO

OGO OLUWA KITAN TRADING COMPANY LIMITED
Business: Motor Vehicle Distribution; Construction; Sales of Sewing Machines and Electronics; Clearing and Forwarding; General Merchandising; Drama and Music Promotion (Records and Cassettes), Petroleum Products Marketing; Technical Services
Address: 645, Agege Motor Road, Shogunle-Ikeja, Lagos
Tel: (01) 4973144, 8118445 **Fax:** (01) 4975101
* 222, Agege Motor Rd,Atewolara-Mushin, Lagos
Tel/Fax: (01) 4521964
Contact: Chief Joseph Olayiwola Afolabi - Chairman/CEO

O-GREHAM NIGERIA LIMITED
Business: Importation of Carpets and Rugs
Address: 48B, Aba-Owerri Road, Aba
Tel: (082) 225344, 225411
Contact: Mr U. Emenike - MD/CEO

OGUBETH INDUSTRIES NIGERIA LIMITED
Business: Shipping, Transportation, Clearing & Forwarding, Warehousing
Address: Nnewi House (3rd Floor, Suite 300), 1/3, Creek Road, Apapa, Lagos
Tel: (01) 5454228, 08033134739, 08037876673
E-mail: ogubethnig@yahoo.com
Contact: Mr. Joe Ezenwa - MD/CEO

OHKMAN & DEAN LIMITED
Business: Interior Design and Decoration Services, Consultancy, Renovation of Homes and Offices, Design Building and Construction
Address: Plot 1296A, Akin Akinsola Street, Victoria Island, Lagos
Tel: (01) 2623830 **Fax:** (01) 2623830-1 (2L)
E-mail: ohkan.dean@skannet.com
Contact: Mrs. Margert Effiom - MD/CEO

OIL & INDUSTRIAL SERVICES LIMITED
Business: Oilfield Engineering Services, Steel Construction & Fabrication, Machine Shop Services
Address: Plot 98, Trans-Amadi Ind. Layout, Port Harcourt
Tel: (084) 232024, 235739 **Fax:** (084) 232635
E-mail: oisfa@alpha.linkserve.com
Contact: Mr. Ken C. Worgu - Chairman/CEO

OIL BATH NIGERIA LIMITED
Business: Marketing and Haulage of Petroleum, left Wing,
Address: Eleganza Plaza (Virgo Block, 2nd Floor, Lft Wing), 1, Commercial Road, Apapa, Lagos
Tel: (01) 5870965, 4802982, 7756894
E-mail: oilbath@yahoo.com

OIL TECH (NIGERIA) LIMITED
Business: Engineering Maintenance Servicea
Address: Plot 155, Trans-Amadi Ind. Layout, Port Harcourt
Tel: (084) 239152, 334837, 483071 **Fax:** (084) 239148
Contact: Mr. Musa Danjuma - GM

OILDATA WIRELINE SERVICES LIMITED
Business: Oilfield Engineering Services
Address: Plot 282, Trans-Amadi Ind. Layout, Port Harcourt
Tel: (084) 239398, 2314077, 571861 **Fax:** (084) 239256
* 14, Alh. Kanike Close, Awolowo Rd, Ikoyi, Lagos
Contact: Mr. Emeka Eme - MD/CEO

OILFIELD & WATERWAYS SERVICES COMPANY LIMITED
Business: Oilfield Engineering, Civil Engineering Contractors, Sales of Steel Pipes and Pumps
Address: 238, Aba Expressway, Port Harcourt
Tel: (084) 612074-6 (3 L), 613229, 08033387108
Fax: (084) 612076
Contact: Chief Emmanuel Onyejieke - Chairman/CEO

OILSCAN LIMITED
Business: Oilwell Logging and Perforation Services
Address: New 9, Airport Road, Port Harcourt
Tel: (084) 571553
Contact: Engr. Joseph Egwelle - MD/CEO

OILSERV LIMITED
Business: Pipelines and Facilities (Enginering, Procurement & Construction)
Address: 42, Nembe Road, off Aba Expressway, Rumuibekwe, Port Harcourt
Tel: (084) 610739
Website: www.oilserv-ng.com

OILTEST SERVICES NIGERIA LIMITED
Business: Oilfield Engineering Services
Address: Plot 182, Trans-Amadi Ind. Layout, Port Harcourt
Tel: (084) 230931, 235254 **Fax:** (084) 236942
Website: www.oiltestng.com
* Foreshore Towers (6th Floor), 2A, Osborne Road, Ikoyi, Lagos
Tel: (01) 2695280, 2695282 **Fax:** (01) 2695281
* EVOC Premises, off Enerhen Road, Warri
Tel: (053) 254926 **Fax:** (053) 254673

OJEMAI FARMS LIMITED
Business: Farming
Address: Plot 267, Trans-Amadi Ind. Layout, Port Harcourt
Tel: (084) 230689, 232640, 612512 **Fax:** (084) 612513
* 27, Imadiyi Street, off Etete Road, Benin City
Tel: (052) 222331, 258381
Contact: Sir. J. I. A. Arumeni Ikhide - MD/CEO

OJOKORO CEMENT INDUSTRY LIMITED
Business: Freight Forwarders
Address: Suite 23/24, Block A, N.P.A Commercial Building, Apapa Port, Lagos
Tel: (01) 5875749 **Fax:** (01) 5455807
E-mail: ojokoro@beta.linkserve.com
Contact: Chief Boniface O. Aniebonam - Chairman/CEO

OK FOODS LIMITED
Business: Production of Biscuits and Confectioneries
Address: 7A, Ilasamaja Industrial Scheme, off Apapa-Oshodi Expressway (Itire Junction), Ilasamaj, Lagos
Tel: (01) 7732483, 7732485
E-mail: ok_industries@yahoo.com
Website: www.okgroup-ng.com

OK MOBILE COMMUNICATIONS LIMITED
Business: Sales of Telecommunication Terminal Equipment
Address: 9, Aerodrome Road, Apapa, Lagos
Tel: (01) 5872295, 4816023 **Fax:** (01) 5872296
E-mail: udehold@beta.linkserve.com
Contact: Chief B. Okonkwo - Chairman/CEO

OK PLAST LIMITED
Business: Manufacturing of Plastic Products and Pens
Address: 7A, Ilasamaja Industrial Scheme, off Apapa-Oshodi Expressway (Itire Junction), Ilasamaja, Lagos
Tel: (01) 7732483, 7732485, 7753461, 08033012432
E-mail: ok_industries@yahoo.com
Website: www.okgroup-ng.com

OKAI INTEGRATED COMPANY LIMITED
Business: Sale of Lubricants, Car-Care Accessories, Textiles/ Accessories, Computer Peripherals, Household Goods and Aluminium Products
Address: 9, Agard St, off Commercial Avenue, Yaba, Lagos
Tel: (01) 4705611, 08023153240
E-mail: okainv@msn.com
Contact: Kalu Orji Kalu - Chairman/CEO
Edwyne O. Khalu - GM

OKECHINA NIGERIA LIMITED
Business: Importation and Sales of Fireproof Safes and Filling Cabinets and Business Equipment
Address: 15, Murtala Muhammed International Airport Road, Ajao Estate, Apakun-Oshodi
Tel: (01) 4701570, 4702462, 4977006, 80443296, 08022240409, 08023025937, 08023373432
Fax: (01) 4977006
E-mail: okedan@linkserve.com
* Plot 510, Olusegun Obasanjo Way (Halli Brothers), Wuse Zone 1, Abuja
Tel: (09) 5230965
* 9, Harbour Road, Port Harcourt
Contact: Mr. Godwin O. O Mbatu - Chairman/CEO

OKEMADU INTERNATIONAL LIMITED
Business: Importation of Designer Fashion Wears & Accessories
Address: 22, Allen Avenue, Ikeja, Lagos
Tel: (01) 4970064, 4937470 **Fax:** (01) 4970064
E-mail: okemadu@infoweb.abs.net
* Sherif Shopping Complex, Plot 739, Aminu Kano Crescent, Cadastral Zone A7, near Banex Plaza, Wuse II, Abuja.
Tel: (09) 4131298
* 2, Toyin Street, Ikeja, Lagos
Tel: (01) 4974999
Contact: Chief W. O. Ike - Chairman/CEO

OKIN BISCUITS LIMITED
Business: Manufacturing of Biscuits and Foam Products
Address: Ajasepo Road, Ijagbo-Offa, Kwara State
Tel: (031) 801048, 801681 **Fax:** (031) 801545
Contact: Chief C. O. Adesoye - Chairman

OKITIPUPA OIL PALM PLC
Business: Development & Management of Oil Palm Estates, Production of Palm Oil & Allied Products
Address: Marine Road, Okitipupa, Ondo State
Tel: (059) 41023, 41262, 41166-8 (3 L)

OKOLO ASSOCIATES
Business: Estate Surveyors and Valuers, Project Managment
Address: 78/80, Aba Road, Port Harcourt
Tel: (084) 238339, 234556 **Fax:** (084) 234556
E-mail: okolo@infoweb.abs.net

* 28, King George V Road, Onikan, Lagos
Tel: (01) 2631736
Contact: Dr. A. C. Okolo - Chairman/CEO

OKOLO, OKOLO & COMPANY
Business: Estate Surveyors and Valuers
Address: UNIC House, 39, New Market Road, Onitsha
Tel: (046) 411055, 08033233994, 08046101499
E-mail: okolookolo@infoweb.abs.net
* 92, Obafemi Awolowo Way, Ikeja, Lagos
Tel: (01) 4934350, 08023188863
Contact: D. C. Okolo, mni - Principal Consultant

OKOTIE & COMPANY
Business: Estate Surveyors & Valuers, Chartered Surveyors, Estate Agency and Real Estate Consultancy
Address: 55, Sapele Road, Benin City
Tel: (052) 252877
* Aisa House (2nd Floor), Plot 2087, Herbert Macaulay Way (North), Wuse Zone 5, Abuja
Tel: (09) 5236619
* 3, Kofo Abayomi Ave, (1st Floor), Apapa, Lagos
Tel: (01) 5455318

OLAM NIGERIA LIMITED
Business: Importation and Sales of Sugar and Rice, Exportation of Agro-Commodities (Cocoa, Cotton Lint, Cashew Nuts, Sesame and Sheanuts)
Address: Plot 2, Block K, Ilasamaja Industrial Estate, Apapa-Oshodi Expressway, Ilasamaja, Isolo, Lagos
Tel: (01) 4527339, 4971978, 4971979, 4973006
Fax: (01) 4528403

OLATECH BOREHOLES LIMITED
Business: Borehole Drilling & Water Treatment Services, Construction of Swimming Pool, Waterfalls and Tank Tower
Address: 543, Agege Motor Road, Ladipo Bus-Stop, Shogunle, Ikeja, Lagos
Tel: (01) 4976237, 7745205, 08023105025
Contact: Mr. Olajide Oluwadahunsi - MD/CEO

OLEJURU LIMITED
Business: Sales & Service of Office Equipment, Electronic Cash Registers, Point-of-Sales Systems, Implementation of Stock-Control Software
Address: Alphon House (1st Floor), 50/52, Toyin Street, Ikeja, Lagos
Tel: (01) 4716145, 08033042912, 08033129531
E-mail: olejuru@hotmail.com
Contact: Elder Peter Eleazu - Chairman/CEO

OLIVE FOUNDATION (NIGERIA) LIMITED
Business: Importation of Dry-Cell Battry
Address: Plot 40/42, Jimoh Odutola Street, off Eric Moore Road, Iganmu Industrial Estate, Iganmu
Tel: (01) 5833879, 5837353, 7740389, 08036708000, 08033161084 **Fax:** (01) 4962650
Contact: HRH Igwe (Dr.) G. N. C. Ezeude - Chairman/CEO

OLLIVEE NIGERIA LIMITED
Business: Importation, Packaging and Sales of Cement
Address: Irede Road, off Badagry Expressway, opp. Trade Fair Complex, Abule-Osun, Ojo, Lagos
Tel: (01) 7730298
Contact: Mr. Paul O. Akinnubi - Chairman/CEO

OLOWO TECHNICAL VENTURES & SONS (NIGERIA) LTD
Business: Marine Transportation (Tug Boats, Crew Boats, Barges), Reconditioning of Marine/Diesel Engines
Address: Edogbo Sawmill Waterside, Enerhen, Warri
Tel: (053) 253840
Contact: Engr. J. Olowo (JP) - Chairman/CEO

OLU PROFESSIONAL PHOTO COLOUR LABORATORY LTD
Business: Photographic Services & Finishing
Address: 40, Fola Agoro Street, Shomolu, Lagos
Tel: (01) 4934230, 5821179, 08022240851
Fax: (01) 4934230
E-mail: oluajix@yahoo.com
Contact: Chief Emmanuel Olu Ajisegbede - Chairman/CEO

OLUBOLA SONOIKI & PARTNERS
Business: Chartered Estate Surveyors & Valuers, Estate Agency, Property Development & Consultancy
Address: 3, McCullum Street (1st Floor), off Murtala Mohammed Way. Yaba, Lagos
Tel: (01) 8043258, 08023111985, 08033186199

OLUDEMI JAGUN, DOSUNMU & COMPANY
Business: Chartered Surveyors & Valuers, Surveyors, Estate Agency and Real Estate Consultancy
Address: 209, Herbert Macaulay Street (2nd Floor), Alagomeji, Yaba, Lagos
Tel: (01) 8042014, 860058, 866997, 867137
E-mail: jadol@nova.net.ng

OLUSOLA ADEKANOLA & COMPANY
Business: Chartered Accountants, Taxation Services, Financial & Management Consultancy, Training
Address: 4, Aderoju Street, off Alfred Olaiya Street, Opebi, Ikeja, Lagos
Tel: (01) 4968688-9 (2L), 4979230
E-mail: ihfo@oa-ng.com
Website: www.oa-ng.com
Conact: Otunba Olusola Adekanola - Managing Consultant

OLUTOLA SENBORE & COMPANY
Business: Chartered Accountants, Insolvency Services
Address: 26, King George V Road, Onikan, Lagos
Tel: (01) 2634360, 2636480
E-mail: senbore@infoweb.abs.net

OLUTOYE ESTATE DEVELOPMENT SERVICES LIMITED
Business: Real Estate Consultancy & Management
Address: 13, Adekunle Fajuyi Way, Ikeja G.R.A., Lagos
Tel: (01) 4932691, 4936702, 7731146, 08023030107, 08023070150, 08023070153, 08023223403
Fax: (01) 4973994
E-mail: tunayeni@nova.net.ng
*AP Plaza, Adetokunbo Ademola Cr. Wuse II, Abuja

OLUWA GLASS COMPANY PLC
Business: Manufacturing and Marketing of Sheet Glass
Address: Okitipupa Road, Igbokoda, Ondo State
Tel: (059) 41606

OLUWALOGBON MOTORS LIMITEDLIMITED
Business: Distribution. Sales Repair & Service of Peugeot Motor Vehicles, Sales of Spare Parts
Address: Plot A, Obafemi Awolowo Way, near Coca-Cola Factory Ikeja, Lagos
Tel: (01) 4960985, 4968195, 4966691, 4970013, 4970027, 5557540, 8189474
E-mail: oluwalogbonmotors@africamail.com
* Plot 1087B, Adeola Odeku Str, Victoria Is, Lagos
Tel: (01) 2614379, 2615887, 2624809-10 (2L), 4801576, 8189473 **Fax:** (01) 2625421
* Plot 516, Sultan Abubakar Way, TMQ, Wuse Zone 2, Abuja.
Tel: (09) 5237307-8 (2L) **Fax:** (01) 5237309
Contact: Chief S. O. Bakare - Chairman/CEO

OLYMPIC INKS LIMITED
Business: Production of Printing Inks, Additives & Varnishes
Address: 4, Dabara St, Olowogbowo, Lagos Island, Lagos
Tel: (01) 2663219, 2664877, 2640343 **Fax:** (01) 2610768
E-mail: olympic@simbaonline.net
Contact: Mr. S. A. Hathiramani - MD/CEO

Om LIMITED
Business: Manufacturing of PVC Pipes and PVC Compounds, Importation of Hand Pumps and Fittings
Address: 55, Happy Home Avenue, Kirikiri Industrial Estate, Kirikiri, via Maza-Maza, Lagos
Tel: (01) 4713319, 7742010 **Fax:** (01) 5457844
E-mail: ompipes@hotmail.com
Contact: Mr. Prabhu Chulani - GM

Om OIL INDUSTRY LIMITED
Business: Processing and Marketing of Vegetable Oil
Address: 2A, Acme Road, by Akilo Road, Ogba Industrial Estate, Ikeja, Lagos
Tel: (01) 4924895, 4924997, 4925397, 4925731, 7917744
E-mail: omoil@micro.com.ng
Contact: Mr. R. K. Mirchandani - Director/CEO

OMARS ROYAL COMPANY LIMITED
Business: Sales of LPG Storage Tanks and Accessories, Tractor Heads and Earth-Moving Equipment
Address: Km. 3, NPA Expressway, Ekpan, Warri
Tel: (053) 320336-7 (2 L), 253119

OMAS INVESTMENT & TRUST COMPANY LIMITED
Business: Stockbroking, Fund Management
Address: Agbeke House (3rd Floor), 107, Bamgbose Street, near Campos Square, Lagos Island, Lagos
Tel: (01) 2630956, 4738473, 7949793 **Fax:** (01) 2630964
E-mail: oitc@hyperia.com
Contact: Mr. M. A. O. Sadiku - MD/CEO

OMATEK VENTURES LIMITED
Business: Sales and Maintenance of Computers, Networking and Training
Address: Plot 1686B, Oladele Olashore Street, off Sanusi Fafunwa Street, Victoria Island, Lagos
Tel: (01) 3201155-6 (2 L), 7732915 **Fax:** (01) 3201149
E-mail: omatek@infoweb.abs.net
omatek@hyperia.com
Contact: Mrs. Florence Seriki - MD/CEO

OMATHA HOLDINGS NIGERIA LIMITED
Business: Manufacturing of Automotive & Industrial Filters, and Automotive Exhaust Systems, Importation of Auto Spare Parts, Rice Milling, Property Investment
Address: * 21, Iga-Udunganran Street, Idumota, Lagos
Tel: (01) 2666521, 2660730, 2666777, 7761448
* Omatha Holdings Factory Complex, 33, Omatha Drive, Uruga, Nnewi, Anambra State
Tel: (046) 460679, 462203-5 (3L)
Contact: Chief M. E. Onwugbenu - MD/CEO

Omegabank PLC
Business: Banking Services
Address: PC. 1, Engineering Close, off Idowu Taylor Street, Victoria Island, Lagos
Tel: (01) 2621971-2 (2L), 2622580
Fax: (01) 2610290-3 (4L), 2620761
E-mail: omegabank@omegabankplc.com
Website: www.omegabankplc.com
Contact: Rev. (Dr.) Segun Adegbetu - MD/CEO

OMENI GROUP LIMITED
Business: Importation of X-Ray Films & Chemicals, Pharmaceutical Products, Auto Parts and Generators
Address: 1A, Adeola Ajayi Crescent, off M.M. International Airport Road, Mafoloku-Oshodi, Lagos
Tel: (01) 4937483, 4930820
Contact: Chief (Dr.) Chriss O. Omeni - Chairman/CEO

OMICRON IMAGING TECHNOLOGY LIMITED
Business: Networking Systems, Imaging Technology/ Smartcard Systems, Large Population Data Management Systems, Document Security Systems, Anti-Fraud/Anti-Counterfiet
Address: Omicron Place, 136, Awolowo Road (1st Floor), Falomo, Ikoyi, Lagos
Tel: (01) 2691328, 4734418, 08023128196, 08023263748, 08023263668, 08023263692 **Fax:** (01) 684269
E-mail: omicron@infoweb.abs.net
Website: www.omicroncorp.com
Contact: Mr. Olusola Obasa - Vice Chairman/CEO

OMNI COMMUNICATIONS LIMITED
Business: Advertising
Address: 34, Calabar Street, off Adelabu St, Surulere, Lagos
Tel: (01) 831405, 5456154
E-mail: bizad2001@hotmail.com
Contact: Mr. George Eboakoke - MD/CEO

OMNIA NIGERIA LIMITED
Business: Manufacturing of Aluminium Doors & Windows, Sun-Breakers, Curtain Walls & Internal Partitions; Distribution of Building Materials and Machinery
Address: Plot 8, Adeyanju Daniel St, Awodi-Ora, off Oshodi-Apapa Expressway, near Mile 2, Apapa, Lagos
Tel: (01) 7901309, 7901310 **Tel/Fax:** (01) 2645215-6 (2L)
E-mail: omnia@hyperia.com
Website: www.hyperia.com
* Ominia House, Plot 2186, Ibrahim Babangida Way, Wuse Zone 4, Wuse, Abuja
Tel/Fax: (09) 5238218
Contact: Alh. (Dr.) Yinka Folawiyo, CON - Chairman
Mr. A. Bellini - MD/CEO

OMNOVISION LIMITED
Business: Eye Clinic, Manufacturing of Optical Lenses, Supply of Hospital Equipment & Consumables
Address: 4/6, Mobolaji Bank-Anthony Street (Formerly Oil Mill Street) off Broad Street, Lagos Island, Lagos
Tel: (01) 2646314, 2645321 **Fax:** (01) 2645154
E-mail: mos@linkserve.com.ng
omnivision@hyperia.com
* Plot 79, Aminu Kano Crescent, Wuse II, Abuja
Tel: (09) 6705113
Contact: Dr. (Mrs.) M. R. Adegoke - Medical Director/CEO

OMO EGBEDI & COMPANY
Business: Chartered Survyors, Estate Surveyors & Valuers, Real Estate Consultants
Address: Lapal House (2nd Floor), 235, Igbosere Rd, Lagos
Tel: (01) 2635372, 2645045, 4702506 **Fax:** (01) 2645045
E-mail: omoegbedi@yahoo.com
Contact: Mr. Gordons O. Egbedi - Principal Partner

OMOLAYOLE & ASSOCIATES
Business: Management Consultancy Services
Address: 46, Town Planning Way, Ilupeju, Lagos
Tel: (01) 4817128, 7739223, 08042106055
* 16, Aerodrome Road, Apapa, Lagos
Tel: (01) 5873072-3 (2L)
Contact: Dr. Michael O. Omolayole - Chairman

OMOSIGHO,OMORODION & PARTNERS
Business: Estate Surveyors & Valuers
Address: Supabod Stores Building (1st Floor), 1, Azikiwe Road, Port Harcourt
Tel: (084) 236543, 234856, 08022241977, 08033389655
Fax: (084) 234863
E-mail: omosigho@phca.linkserve.com
* Wuse Zone 2 Cornershops (Suite 38), opp. Holy Rosary Catholic Church, Mambolo Street, Wuse Zone 2, Abuja
Tel: (09) 5240305
Contact: H. E. Omosigho - Partner
O. P. Omorodion - Partner

OMOT FIRE PROTECTION ENGINEERING LIMITED
Business: Sales and Service of Fire Protection Systems
Address: 8, Abiodn Onitiri Avenue (Awori Bus-Stop), Abule-Egba, Lagos
Tel: (01) 8124214, 7920555
E-mail: infoomot@omotfire.com
Website: www.omotfire.com
Contact: Dr. E. O. Omotosho - Chairman/CEO

OMOT INDUSTRIES LIMITED
Business: Manufacture of Educational Toys and Games
Address: 8, Abiodn Onitiri Avenue (Awori Bus-Stop), Abule-Egba, Lagos
Tel: (01) 8124214, 7920555
Contact: Dr. H. M Omotosho - MD/CEO

OMUOJINE & ASSOCIATES
Business: Real Estate Consultancy, Valuation of Buildings, Land, Plant and Machinery, Property Management
Address: Onafeko House, 200, Igbosere Road, Lafiaji, Lagos
Tel: (01) 2633606, 2633429 **Fax:** (01) 2635881
E-mail: omuojine@infoweb.abs.net
Contact: Mr. Emma O. Omuojine - MD/CEO

ONAHSONS HOLDINGS LIMITED
Business: Project Management Consulltancy, Broadcast Engineering, Water Engineering, Oil & Gas, Telecommunications, Real Estate, Medical Equipment, Commodities, Investment
Address: Sesco House, 107B, Adeniyi Jones Avenue, Ikeja, Lagos
Tel: (01) 4924208, 4922042, 4923266 **Fax:** (01) 4922042
E-mail: onahsonsconsult@alpha.linkserve.com
Website: www.onahsonsconsult.com
* Plot 2778, Cadastral Zone A6, off Shehu Shagari Way, Maitama District, Abuja
Tel: (09) 6700114
Contact: Col. I. O. Nnonah (rtd.) - Chairman

ONAKANMI & PARTNERS
Business: Real Estate Consultancy & Agency, Valuations for All Purposes, Property Development/Management
Address: Banuso House (1st Floor), 88/92, Broad Street, Lagos
Tel: (01) 2662238, 2665214 **Fax:** (01) 2662238
* Abuja Shopping Mall (Suite C17), Maputo Street, Wuse Zone 3, Abuja
Tel: (09) 5236365
Contact: Prince Oluwole Onakanmi - Managing Partner

ONAMIK HOLDINGS LIMITED
Business: Industrialists, General Merchants
Address: Ogbuja House, 175, Cameroun Road, Aba
Tel: (082) 230929, 231803 **Fax:** (082) 231064
E-mail: onamik@phca.linkserve.com
Contact: Sir James Ogbuja O. Ikoro - Chairman/CEO

ONDO STATE DEVELOPMENT COMPANY LIMITED
Business: Development Finance Institution, Portfolio & Asset Management, Commodity Trading, Management of Cocoa and Oil-palm Plantations
Address: 7, Adekunle Ajasin Road, Akure
Tel: (034) 242017, 242248, 242307, 242594, 242857, 243273, 243538, 08035905484 **Fax:** (034) 243273
* Oba-Ile Road, Akure
Tel: (034) 240885

ONE NUMBER NIGERIA LIMITED
Business: Call-in & Web-Based Telephone Directory Service
Address: Block (Flat 1), Stallion Estate, Lobito Crescent, Wuse II, Abuja
Tel: (09) 6713003-7 (5L)
E-mail: onenumberng@yahoo.com
* Princess Plaza, 2, Araromi Street, off Moloney Street, Onikan, Lagos
Tel: (01) 2631953, 08033062255, 08039802255
Contact: Mr. Adegbe Ogbeh - Manging Partner/CEO

ONE WORLD COMMUNICATIONS LIMITED
Business: Internet Service Provider
Address: 48, Sobo Arobiodu Street, G.R.A., Ikeja, Lagos
Tel: (01) 4972708, 4976469, 4976470
E-mail: info@oneworldng.com
Website: www.oneworldng.com
Contact: Mr. Bunmi Ekundare - GM

ONE-TO-ONE NIGERIA LIMITED
Business: Direct Marketing Communications, Data Bureau Services, List Management Solutions
Address: 27A,Olatunbosun Street, Shonibare Estate, Maryland, Ikeja, Lagos
Tel: (01) 7743438, 4700093, 4709660 **Fax:** (01) 4932200
E-mail: onetoone@intra.com.net.ng
Website: www.elettershop.8m.com
Contact: Mr. Rotimi M. Olaniyan - GM/CEO

ONIBONOJE PRESS & BOOK INDUSTRY (NIGERIA) LTD
Business: Printing & Publishing
Address: Felele Layout, Ibadan
Tel: (02) 413956

ONIBUDO HOLDINGS LIMITED
Business: Oil & Gas Exploration, Shipping, Clearing & Forwarding, General Merchandising
Address: Peninsula Complex, Plot 8, Ozumba Mbadiwe Avenue, Victoria Island, Lagos
Tel: (01) 617563, 2617168, 7745656 **Fax:** (01) 2617168
E-mail: onibudoholdings@skannet.com
* 22, Bornu Street, Area 10, Garki, Abuja
Tel: (09) 2343979 **Fax:** (09) 2341626
Contact: Chief Ahmed Adisa Onibudo - Exec. Chairman

ONITSHA ALUMINIUM MANUFACTURING COMPANY LTD
Business: Manufacturing of Aluminium Cooking Utensils, Corrugation of Longspan Roofing Sheets, Fabrication of Sliding Doors and Windows
Address: 10, Akunnia Njote Street, Woliwo Layout, Onitsha
Tel: (046) 211486, 211170
* Plot 13 & 14, Ozubulu Industrial Layout, Ozubulu, Ekwusigo L.G.A., Anambra State
Contact: Chief (Dr.) C. E. Igbokwe - Chairman/CEO

ONITSHA HOLIDAY RESORT HOTELS LIMITED
Business: Hospitality Services, Night Club
Address: Onitsha-Asaba Expressway, opp. Housing Estate, Onitsha
Tel: (046) 218946
* 8, Abgu Ogbuefi Street, Woliwo, Onitsha
Tel: (046) 211013

ON-LINE TRAVELS & TOURS LIMITED
Business: Travel Agency, Travel & Tours Consultancy
Address: Woolworths Plaza (2nd Floor, Suite 204), Plot 307, Adeola Odeku Street, Victoria Island, Lagos
Tel: (01) 2626101-2 (2L), 2627758, 2627900, 08023205851, 08023209573, 08033054029 **Fax:** (01) 2626102
E-mail: online_lcc@yahoo.com
onlinetravelng@yahoo.com
Contact: Yinka Bada - MD/CEO

ONWARD FISHERIES NIGERIA LIMITED
Business: Importation of Frozen Foods, Trading
Address: 225, Apapa Road, Iganmu
Tel: (01) 7742780, 7743709, 5453834, 5453835, 5453837, 08033066924
Fax: (01) 5453834, 2630333, 2630373
E-mail: onward@cyberspace.net.ng
Contact: Alh. Sule Akande - Chairman
Mr. Abiodun Agbana - MD/CEO

ONWARD PAPER MILL LIMITED
Business: Manufacture of Paper Products, Paper Conversion
Address: Ploy Y, Mobolaji Johnson Avenue, Oregun Industrial Estate, Alausa, Ikeja, Lagos
Tel: (01) 4966774, 4966775, 4967458, 4967528, 4964586, 7740371, 7740372 **Fax:** (01) 2647747
E-mail: onward@infoweb.abs.net
* 2, Obagun Avenue, Matori Industrial Estate, Oshodi, Lagos
Tel: (01) 4522989, 4524853, 4521507, 7740378
* Plot 1111, off Aminu Kano Crescent, Beside Redeemed Christian Church, Wuse 11, Abuja
Tel: (09) 5232749, 5232757
Contact: Mr. K. O. Oniwinde - MD/CEO
Mr. M Ade Yusuf - GM (Sales Marketing)

ONWARD STATIONERY STORES LIMITED
Business: Conversion of Paper, Sales of Paper Boards and Stationery
Address: Moobag Hosue, 39, Burma Road, Apapa, Lagos
Tel: (01) 5804080-4 (5 L), 5457395, 5877711, 5877722
Fax: (01) 5877722
* Plot 1111, Onward Close, off Aminu Kano Crescent, Wuse II, Abuja
Tel: (09) 5232757, 5232749, 08033082344
Contact: Chief M. O. Obagun - Chairman
Mr. E. O. Ogunsanya - CEO

ONYEKWELU JUNIOR NIGERIA LIMITED
Business: Importation and Marketing of Auto Batteries, Tyres and General Merchandise
Address: 50, Azikiwe Road, Aba
Tel: (082) 233156
Contact: Dr. Uche Theo Onyekwelu - Chairman/CEO

OPEN LEARNING ASSOCIATES LIMITED
Business: Supply, Installation and After-Sale Support of Multimedia Projection Systems and Accessories
Address: 109, Allen Avenue (1st Floor), opp. Alade Shopping Mall, Ikeja, Lagos
Tel: (01) 4935545, 4936640, 7733804, 4723704, 08022901430, 08023275808-9 (2L), 08023416465, 08023416821, 08023444485
Fax: (01) 2646082, 2646084
E-mail: olass@alpha.linkserve.com
openlaltd@hotmail.com
Contact: Mr. A. Tunde Odumosu - MD/CEO

OPEX INSURANCE BROKERS LIMITED
Business: Insurance Broking
Address: 28, Abeokuta Street, Ebute-Metta (East), Lagos
Tel: (01) 861661, 7748294, 08033255620-1 (2L)
Contact: Mr. A. K. Akapo - MD/CEO

OPTICOM LEASING COMPANY LIMITED
Business: Equipment Leasing
Address: Niger House (8th Floor), 1/5, Odunlami Street, by Marina, Lagos Island, Lagos
Tel: (01) 2663349, 2663325, 2663349, 2662549 (Ext 1282)
Fax: (01) 2662618
E-mail: optilease@beta.linkserve.com
Manuchim Chambers, 171D, Aba Rd, Port Harcourt
Tel: (084) 232486

OPTIMA SPORTS MANAGEMENT INTERNATIONAL LTD
Business: Sports Lawyers, Consultants, Marketers ,Events and Facilities Managers, FIFA Agents
Address: Lofom Plaza (2nd Floor), 21, Mobolaji Bank-Anthony Way, Maryland, Ikeja, Lagos
Tel: (01) 4709184, 4935412, 7739484 **Fax:** (01) 4961178
E-mail: info@optima-sport.com
Website: www.optima-sports.com
Contact: Mr. Rotimi Pedro - Chairman/CEO

OPTIMAL TRAVELS & TOURS LIMITED
Business: Travel Agency
Address: 7, Club Road, Kano
Tel: (064) 314539, 08023114350 Fax: (064) 314539
Contact: Alh. Umar Yusuf Garba - MD/CEO

OPTIMUM EXPOSURES LIMITED
Business: Outdoor Advertising
Address: 11, Oduduwa Street, Ikeja, G.R.A, Ikeja, Lagos
Tel: (01) 4976457, 4976799, 4710035, 2880761
Fax: (01) 3295504
E-mail: optimumexposures@hotmail.com
optimum1_exposures@yahoo.com
Contact: Mr. Biodun Shobanjo - Chairman
Mr. Jimi Awosika - Supervisory Director

OPTIONS SECURITIES LIMITED
Business: Equipment Leasing
Address: Eleganza House (5th Floor), 15B, Joseph/Wesley Street, off Broad Street, Lagos
Tel: (01) 2668230, 2702253 **Fax:** (01) 2640306
E-mail: options_securities@yahoo.com
options@linkserve.com
Website: www.optionssecurities.com
Contact: Mr. Reuben Ogirri - MD/CEO

ORA EGBUNIKE & ASSOCIATES
Business: Estate Surveyors and Valuers, Facilities Managers
Address: Park 'N' Shop Complex (2nd Floor, Wing B), 740, Aminu Kano Crescent, Wuse II, Abuja
Tel: (09) 4137631, 4139726 **Fax:** (09) 4137685
E-mail: ora-egbunike@hyperia.com
oraegbun@infoweb.abs.net
oraegbunike@linkserve.com
Website: www.ora-egbunike.com
* Entrance B, Tafawa Balewa Square Complex (1st Floor, Suite 4B, 6B, 7B & WW 19), Lagos
Tel: (01) 2633399, 2634575, 2647919-20 (2L)
Contact: Mr. Abdulmalik Ora Egbunike - Managing Partner

ORANGE DRUGS LIMITED
Business: Importation of Pharmaceuticals and Cosmetics
Address: 66/68, Town Planning Way, Ilupeju, Lagos
Tel: (01) 4960036, 4937526, 4937528, 4933506-7 (2L), 7741197 **Fax:** (01) 4937543
E-mail: orangedl@nigol.net.ng
orangedrugslagos@yahoo.com
Contact: Mr. Tony Ezenna - Chairman/CEO
Mr. Vin E. Mgbemena - MD

ORANGE TELECOMS LIMITED
Business: Sales of Mobile Phones & Accessories
Address: 7, Saka Tinubu Street, Victoria Island, Lagos
Tel: (01) 3200768, 3200976-7(2L), 7736640, 7737418-9(2L) 08032030798, 08034004469 **Fax:** (01) 3200758
Contact: Dr. Sunny Icheke - GM

ORAZULIKE TRADING COMPANY LIMITED
Business: Steel Stockist
Address: 14A, Edinburgh Road, Ogui New Layout, Enugu
Tel: (042) 255153, 257063
*52B, Alahun Osumba Road, Maza-Maza, Kirikiri, Lagos
Tel: (01) 5893225, 7748297
Contact: Ichie Joseph O. Orazulike - Chairman/CEO

ORBITAL COMPUTERS SERVICES LIMITED
Business: Sales and Service of Computer Hardware, Peripherals and Consumables, Software Development and Marketing, Networking, Training
Address: Orbital House, 180, Awolowo Rd, S.W. Ikoyi, Lagos
Tel: (01) 2695655, 2695666 **Fax:** (01) 2695666
E-mail: orbital@nigol.net.ng
Contact: Mrs. Titi Adisa - MD/CEO

ORC FISHING & FOOD PROCESSING LIMITED
Business: Fishing, Shrimp Processing
Address: Plot 20, Chief Benson Anorue Street, Ajao Estate, Apakun-Oshodi, Lagos
Tel: (01) 4520592, 4520965, 4520877, 4520987, 7740383
Fax: (01) 4520980
E-mail: orc@clicktgi.com
Website: www.clicktgi.com
Contact: Mr. C. G. Vink - Chairman
Mr. C. Alex - MD/CEO

ORIENTAL INSURANCE COMPANY LIMITED
Business: Insurance (General Business)
Address: 5, Onitsha Road, Enugu
Tel: (042) 259003, 258313
Contact: Hon. Charles O. Ugwu - Chairman
Barr. Leonard M. Akah - MD/CEO

ORIENTAL RESOURCES LIMITED
Business: Distribution of Pharmaceuticals & Industrial Chemicals
Address: Regency Suites (1st Floor), 17, Ahmed Onibudo Street, Victoria Island, Lagos
Tel: (01) 2613788, 2641770
E-mail: multisev@infoweb.abs.net
Contact: Mr. Ugo Nwabusi - MD/CEO

ORIWU INSURANCE BROKERS LIMITED
Business: Insurance & Reinsurance Brokering, Life & Pension Consultancy
Address: 15, Shomolu Street, Onipanu, Shomolu, Lagos
Tel: (01) 5820041, 5820583, 4729976, 08023310568
* Royal Castle of Mercy Annex (Suite 3), Oba Oyefusi Close, off Lagos Road, Ikorodu
Contact: Aremo (Alh.) Adeniyi Ogunsanya - Chairman/CEO

ORPET NIGERIA LIMITED
Business: Marketing of Petroleum Products and Lubricants, Haulage Services
Address: 274, 278, Port Harcourt Road, Aba
Tel: (082) 220758, 226169, 226190 **Fax:** (082) 226007
E-mail: orpet@phca.linkserve.com
Contact: Chief J. C. Nwakpadolu - Chairman/CEO

ORPHEUS COMPANY LIMITED
Business: Importation of Musical Instruments and Equipment, Publications and Accessories; Organisation of Music Lessons, Concerts and Workshops
Address: 29, Association Avenue, Ilupeju, Lagos
Tel/Fax: (01) 4962790
E-mail: firemuse@infoweb.abs.net
Contact: Engr. David A. Nwamara - Chairman/CEO

ORRI-TECH (NIGERIA) LIMITED
Business: Electrical, Telecommunication & Mechanical Engineering Services and Contractors
Address: 21, Ebun St, off Morris St, Abule-Ijesha, Yaba, Lagos
Tel: (01) 4823686, 7742088 **Fax:** (01) 3425188
Contact: Engr Frank Atsagbede - MD/CEO

OSAGIE ESTATES LIMITED
Business: Investment in Real Estate and Hospitality
Address: 117, Akpakpava Street, Benin City
Tel: (052) 252316
Contact: Engr. Osato Edo-Osagie - MD/CEO

OSARO EGUASA & COMPANY
Business: Estate Surveyors & Valuers, Property Management & Agency, Project Management.
Address: Lapal House (Front View), 235, Igbosere Rd, Lagos
Tel: (01) 2601337, 2645096, 4823564, 08033077465
E-mail: osaroeguasa@yahoo.co.uk
Contact: Deacon Osaro Eguasa - MD/CEO

OSAS & OSEJI
Business: Estate Surveyors and Valuers
Address: CFAO Building, 8, Azikiwe Road, Port Harcourt
Tel: (084) 232673, 235587 **Fax:** (084) 235587
E-mail: osaoseji@infoweb.abs.net
* Nwaora Plaza, Plot 1103, Aminu Kano Crescent, Wuse II, Abuja
Tel: (09) 5233319, 5233322, 5237167, 5233498
Fax: (09) 5233322
* Princes Court, Plot PC 37, Ahmed Onibudo Street, Victoria Island, Lagos
Tel: (01) 7737112, 612972, 612984

OSATA SUPERMARKET & CHINESE RESTAURANT LTD
Business: Supermarket
Address: 7, Opebi Road, Ikeja, Lagos
Tel: (01) 2221560, 08033436700
Fax: (01) 2221560, 4978964
E-mail: ngosata@yahoo.com

OSCARTE NIGERIA LIMITED
Business: General Merchandising, Sales of Electrical, Mechanical, Safety and Security Equipment, Supply of Industrial Raw Materials and Spare Parts, Engineering and Construction, Telecommunication
Address: Oscarte House, 1, Moore House St, Ogui, Enugu
Tel: (042) 258043
Contact: Dr. Theo Okonkwo - Chairman/CEO

OSHOGBO STEEL ROLLING COMPANY LIMITED
Business: Steel Rolling Mill
Address: Km. 8, New Ikirun Road, Dagbolu, Oshogbo
Tel: (035) 241331, 241332, 243332 **Fax:** (035) 241330
E-mail: oshogbosteel@infoweb.abs.net
Contact: :Engr. B. A. Fasoro - GM/CEO

OSIQUIP BUSINESS AIDS LIMITED
Business: Sales and Service of Office Automation, Computers, Banking Automation Products and Security Systems; Information Technology Consultancy
Address: Palmline Building, 11, Wharf Road, Apapa, Lagos
Tel: (01) 5873088, 5873263, 5871776 **Fax:** (01) 5870156
E-mail: osifo@osiquip.com
sales@osiquip.com
tech@osiquip.com
Website: www.osiquip.com
* 3, Lokoja Street, off Ogbomosho Road, Area 8, Garki, Abuja.
Tel: (09) 2345724
Contact: Mr. F. M. O. Osifo - Chairman/CEO

OSITA OKOLI & COMPANY
Business: Estate Surveying and Valuation, Property Management, Estate Agency, Feasibility and Viability Studies, Compensation and General Consultancy
Address: Bookshop House (4th Floor), 50/52, Broad St, Lagos
Tel: (01) 2646136, 2647903 **Fax:** (01) 2647903
E-mail: osita@infoweb.abs.net
Website: www.ositaokoli.com
Contact: Mr. Emmanuel Osita Okoli - Managing Partner

OSTRA HALL & HOTEL
Business: Hospility, Hotel, Restaurant, Reception/Conference Centre Services
Address: beh. M. K. O Abiola Gardens, opp. NNPC Gas Plant, Alausa, Ikeja, Lagos
Tel: (01) 8114859, 3453362
Contact: Chief Ohio S. Ehimiaghe - Chairman/CEO

OSUNBADE, OKITI & COMPANY
Business: Chartered Accountants, Auditing, Taxation Consultancy, Company Secretarial Services
Address: 7, Maye Street, Sabo-Yaba, Lagos
Tel: (01) 4728304, 861364, 861368, 08023506055, 08033033392 **Fax:** (01) 861368
E-mail: osunbade_okiti@yahoo.com
Contact: Chief James O. Okiti - Partner

OSUNKEYE & ASSOCIATES
Business: Business & Management Consultancy Services
Address: Elephant Cement House (3rd Floor), ASSBIFI Rd, Central Business District, Alausa, Ikeja, Lagos
Tel: (01) 7747966
E-mail: oluosunkeye@yahoo.com
Contact: Chief O. Osunkeye, OON - Chairman/CEO

OSY GROUP (WEST AFRICA) LIMITED
Business: Sales of Finishing Nets and General Merchandise
Address: St. Peter's Plaza, 35, Old Market Road, Onitsha
Tel: (046) 411534, 219344 **Fax:** (046) 411534
Contact: Sir Peter Ezika - Chairman/CEO

OTI CARPETS & FURNISHING COMPANY LIMITED
Business: Marketing of Carpets, Floor-Covering and Wall-Covering Materials, Interior Decoration
Address: Plot 17, Tin-Cn Island Expressway, Apapa, Lagos

Tel: (01) 4826269, 5450481, 5450476
E-mail: oticarpets@yahoo.com
* Plot 1001, Ademola Adetokunbo Crescent, Wuse II, Abuja.
Tel: (09) 4139583, 4139471
Contact: Chief Christopher O. Oti - Chairman/CEO

OUDDY NOMINEES LIMITED
Business: Stockbroking, Invesment Advisory Services and Consultancy, Portfolio Management
Address: St. Joseph's Jubilee Hall (2nd Floor), 30, Ikoyi Road, near Obalende, Lagos
Tel: (01) 2670938, 2670939 **Fax:** (01) 2670938
Contact: Prince M. A. Odedina - Chairman

OUEC INVESTMENT LIMITED
Business: Financial Consultants and Investment Advisors
Address: Great Nigeria House (20th Floor), 47/57, Martins Street, Lagos
Tel: (01) 2660233, 4719043, 7744272 **Fax:** (01) 2660233
E-mail: ouec@infoweb.abs.net
Contact: Mr. Tony Anonyai - Managing Consultancy/CEO

OUTDOOR COMMUNICATIONS LIMITED
Business: Outdoor Advertising Agency, Printing & Publishing, Gift Supplies
Address: 4, Charity Road, New Oko-Oba Road, Abule-Egba, Lagos
Tel: (01) 4712539, 08023259789, 08023267466
Contact: Chief Ahmed Ipoola Omisore - Chairman/CEO

OUTREACH COMMUNICATIONS LIMITED
Business: Outdoor Advertising
Address: 12, Audu Bako Way, Nassarawa, Kano
Tel: (064) 646757, 08034515695, 08037865256
E-mail: outreachmedia@yahoo.com
Contact: Mr. Moses Orife - MD/CEO

OVATION COMMUNICATIONS LIMITED
Business: Publishing of Magazine (OVATION)
Address: 15A, Adekunle Fajuyi Crescent, off Olufemi Olutoye Crescent, off Adeniyi Jones Avenue, Ikeja, Lagos
Tel: (01) 7731710, 08033022045
E-mail: ovation@ghana,com
info@ovationinternational.com
Website: www.ovationinternational.com
Contact: Chief Dele Momodu - Publisher/CEO

OVE ARUP & PARTNERS NIGERIA LIMITED
Business: Structural & Civil Engineering Consultancy
Address: 25, Boyle Street, Onikan Lagos
Tel: (01) 2600520-9 (10 L) **Fax:** (01) 2630431, 2631976
Contact: Engr. C. C. Ejim

OVERLAND AIRWAYS LIMITED
Business: Airline Services, Aircraft Charter, Ticketing Service
Address: 17, Simbiat Abiola Road, Ikeja, Lagos
Tel: (01) 4979780-5 (6L), 4971247, 4971250, 08037007020, 08037007022
E-mail: cspd@overland.aero
Website: www.overland.aero
Contact: Capt. Edward Boyo - MD/CEO

OVERSEAS TECHNICAL SERVICE NIGERIA LIMITED
Business: Oilfield Services, Manpower Supply & Training, Project Management & Inspection, Non-Destructive Testing, Maintenance & Operations Services
Address: 77, Ademola S. W. Ikoyi, Lagos
Tel: (01) 2691823 **Fax:** 01) 2691484
E-mail: ots@infoweb.abs.net
* Manuchim Chambers (1st Floor), 171D, Aba Road, Port Harcourt
Tel: (084) 230103, 230105
Contact: Chief Bayo Kuku, SAN - Chairman
Mr. Derek Shelton - GM

OVUOMARORO STUDIO & GALLERY
Business: Production of Artworks, Books, Cards & Posters
Address: 41, Oloje Street, Papa-Ajao, Mushin, Lagos
Tel/Fax: (01) 4522910
E-mail: onobrak@hyperia.com
Contact: Dr. Bruce Onobrakpeya - Artistic Director/CEO

OWENA INTERNATIONAL HOTEL LIMITED
Business: Hospitality Services
Address: Igbatoro Road, Akure
Tel: (034) 241628, 243340-2 (3L) **Fax:** (034) 241628

OWODUNNI & SONS MOTORS LIMITED
Business: Importation of Motor Vehicles, Tyres & Tubes
Address: 33, Murtala Mohammed Way, Jos
Tel: (073) 452796, 453922, 454494
Contact: Alh. G. Ade Owodunni - Chairman/MD

OX4 SYSTEMS LIMITED
Business: Manufacture and Sales of Aquarium and Aquarium Accessories, Water Fountains and Glass Pulpits, Plant Hire Services, Interior and Exterior Decoration, Engineering Services and Metal Fabrication
Address: 14, Abe Street, Onipanu, Lagos
Tel: 08033436594
Contact: Mr. Olumide Odunaiya - Chairman

OXFORD SECURITIES & INVESTMENTS LIMITED
Business: Financial Services
Address: Western House (18th Floor, Suite 1802) 8/10, Broad Street, Lagos
Tel/Fax: (01) 2637720
E-mail: osilltd@hotmail.com
Contact: Mr. J. Adeleke Adefeyisan - Chairman/CEO

OXFORD SYSTEMS NIGERIA LIMITED
Business: Sales, Installation & Service of Computers and Accessories, Networking
Address: 24B, Otigba Street (Suite 15), Ikeja, Lagos
Tel: 08033462887

OXFORD TECHNOLOGIES LIMITED
Business: Sales and Maintenance of Computers; Computer, Telecommunication and Management Consultancy; Commercial Printing,
Address: 76, Mobolaji Bank-Anthony Way, beside Ikeja Shopping Plaza, Ikeja, Lagos
Tel: (01) 4967543, 4935655 **Fax:** (01) 4967543
E-mail: oxford@infoweb.abs.net
Contact: Mr. Aneto Edwin Okakpu - Chairman/CEO

OYELAMI SOETAN ADELEKE & COMPANY
Business: Chartered Accountants
Address: Kresta Laurel Complex (4th Floor), 376, Ikorodu Road, Mende, Maryland, Lagos
Tel: (01) 4935391, 4935392

OYELEKE AFOLABI & COMPANY
Business: Estate Agents, Surveyors & Valuers, Property Development & Management, Estate Consultancy
Address: 12, Simbiat Abiola Road, Ikja, Lagos
Tel: (01) 4960322, 4973599, 7746943, 08023046646, 08023154890, 08023154892 **Fax:** (01) 4973599
E-mail: gngas@yahoo.com
* 35, Awolowo Avenue, Bodija Estate, Ibadan
Tel: (02) 8100874
Contact: Chief Oye Afolabi - Managing Partner

OYO STATE FINANCIAL & INVESTMENT COMPANY LTD
Business: Investment, Cashew Plantations, Distribution of Portland Cement, Snail-Rearing and Bee-Keeping
Address: 11, Bale Oyewole Road, Jericho GRA, Dugbe, Ibadan
Tel: (02) 2412009, 241082608035531631

OZALLA PLASTICS ENTERPRISES LIMITED
Business: Manufacturing of Plastic Wares and Containers
Address: Plot P1, Pokobros Avenue, Harbour Industrial Layout, off Atani Road, Onitsha
Tel: (046) 210303, 210800, 216022, 08033230191 (048) 550765, 886695, 888171
Fax: (046) 210303 * (048) 888171
Contact: Chief (Dr.) P. A. Okonkwo - Chairman/CEO

OZDE GROUP OF COMPANIES
Business: Conglomerate - Distillers of Wine & Spirits, Agro & Agro-Allied, Trading
Address: 14, Kolawole Shonibare Street, off Lateef Salami Street, Ajao Estate, Isolo, Lagos
Tel: (01) 4524739, 522371, 528109 **Fax:** (01) 4523491
Contact: Dr. Emeka Ene - Chairman/CEO

OZED VENTURES LIMITED
Business: Sales of Water Conditioning & Disinfection Systems
Address: 9/10, Adelabu Close, opp. Customs Training College, Ola Ayinde Street, Ikeja, Lagos
Tel: (01) 4938204, 4973946, 4961642-3 (2L), 08034938204
Fax: (01) 4938204, 4971015
E-mail: ozedtechnical@metrong.com
Contact: Mr. Tony Ofoman - MD/CEO

OZIGBU ENGINEERING COMPANY LIMITED
Business: Civil & Building Engineering, Road Construction, Design & Construction of Building, Swamp Reclamation, Dredging and Sand-Filling, Equipment Leasing, Electricfication
Address: Km. 16, P. Harcourt/Aba Expressway, Port Harcourt
Tel: (082) 441237, 08033102666, 08033419126
Contact: Engr. (Chief) Paul C. Ozigbu - MD/CEO

P & J ELECTRICAL & INDUSTRIAL COMPANY LIMITED
Business: Importation and Marketing of Electrical Products
Address: 19, Moore Street, Onitsha
Tel: (046) 211913, 215456, 08033210062, 08037204855
Contact: Mr. Pius E. Okoye - Chairman/CEO.

P. CHUKS ENTERPRISES NIGERIA LIMITED
Business: Manafacturing & Marketing of Fishing Materials
Address: 2B, Sokoto Road, Onitsha
Tel: (046) 215314, 410653
Contact: Mr Paul Chukwuemeka - Chairman/CEO

P. PAIVE ASSOCIATES LIMITED
Business: Oilfield Services, Sales/Hiring of Air Compressors
Address: 37, Eboh Road, Okumagba Layout, Warri
Tel/Fax: (053) 250762, 251775
E-mail: paive.b@warri.rcl.nig.com
* 28A, Ngeche Avenue, Oginigba Trans-Amadi Industrial Layout, Port Harcourt
Tel/Fax: (084) 239104, 2239785
Contact: Prof E. Paive - Chairman/CEO.

P. B. DJEBAH & COMPANY LIMITED
Business: General Merchants, Salesof Oilfield Equipment & Tools, Hardware, Industrial & Building Materials; Iron & Steel Stockist, Import & Export
Address: Bagun House, 31, Warri Road, Effurun, Warri.
Tel: (053) 252602, 251093, 252530, 252569
Fax: (053) 2510093
E-mail: djebah.b@warri.rcl.nig.com
* 2, Davies Street, off Demurin Street, Ajelogo Market, Ketu, Lagos
Tel: (01) 4700719, 4701990, 4997325
Contact: Chief P. B. Djebah - Chairman/CEO

P. C. D. ASSOCIATES
Business: Architects, Consultants, Project Managers
Address: Plot 1364/A3, Kukawa Close/Aguleri Street, off Gimbiya Street, Area 11, Garki, Abuja
Tel: (09) 3149670, 08033120718 Fax: (09) 3148292
E-mail: pcdassociates@yahoo.co.uk
Contact: Arc. M. B. Bello - MD/CEO

P. G. H. LIMITED
Business: Construction and Civil Engineering
Address: Plot 13, Mingi Estate, Trans-Amadi Industrial Layout, Port Harcourt.
Tel: (084) 232023, 237863 **Fax:** (084) 237864
E-mail: pgh@phca.linkserve.com
Contact: Mr A. M. Zorzi - MD/CEO

P. K. OJO & COMPANY
Business: Estate Surveyors & Valuers, Facility Managers, Estate Agents, Property Consultants
Address: 13/15, Sapele Road, off Creek Road, Apapa, Lagos
Tel: (01) 5450157, 5453348, 5871951, 08023044488, 08023393683, 08034298770 **Fax:** (01) 5871951
E-mail: pkoojo@yahoo.com
* NCWS Building (2nd Floor, Suite 207), Area 11, Garki, Abuja
Tel: (09) 3140748, 08033203838
Contact: Mr P. K. Olusegun Ojo - Principal

P. N. EMERAH & SONS (NIGERIA) LIMITED
Business: Transportation; Imporation of Auto Spare Parts
Address: 52, Enugu-Onitsha Expressway, Nkpor, Onitsha
* 18, Ikorodu Road, Jibowu, Yaba, Lagos
* Opp. Polytechnic, Sango, Ibadan
Contact: Chief P. N. Emerah - Chairman/CEO

P. S. MANDRIDES PLC
Business: Production of Groundnut Oil, other Vegetable Oils & Animal Feeds; Processing, Storage & Procurement Services
Address: III, Murtala Mohammed Way, Kano
Tel: (064) 632181, 632477, 634636 **Fax:** (064) 632479
E-mail: psmkano@yahoo.com
* 72/73, Maganda Road, Kano
Contact: Mr. T. J. Frederick - Chairman/CEO.

P. W. NIGERIA LIMITED
Business: Civil Engineering & Building Contractors
Address: Plot 9, Outer Northern Expressway,Maitama, Abuja
Tel: (09) 3147961-3 (3L) **Fax:** (09) 3140088, 3140244
E-mail: pw@pwnigeria.com
Website: www.pwnigeria.com
* 9, Usuma Street, off Gana Street, opp. NICON Hilton Hotel, Maitama District, Abuja
Tel: (09) 5232898, 5230054 **Fax:** (09) 5230053
* 10/12, Ibitayo Estate, Obanta Close, Ikeja, Lagos
Tel: (01) 4936439, 4936449, 4970249
Fax: (01) 4936438, 4972384
Contact: Mr. D. Hurley - MD/CEO
Mrs. G. Akinyooye - Admin. Mgr (Lagos Office)

PACIFIC FREIGHTLINERS LIMITED
Business: Haulage Services and Transport Operators
Address: 13, Kudirat Abiola (Oregun) Road, Ojota, Lagos
Tel: (01) 4938190 **Fax:** (01) 4971273
E-mail: phl@hyperia.com
Contact: Dr. Adedeji T. Adeleke - Chairman/CEO

PACIFIC HOLDINGS LIMITED
Business: Conglomerate - Investment, Farming, Borehole Drilling, Transportation & Trading (Importation of High Tensile & Mild Steel Reinforcing Bars/Coils),
Address: 100, Kudirat Abiola (Oregun) Road, Ojota, Lagos
Tel: (01) 4971281, 4972580 **Fax:** (01) 4971273
E-mail: phl@hyperia.com
Website: www.pacificholding.ng.com
*Chief Ayoola Adeleke Ind.Estate, Ede, Osun State
Contact: Dr. Adedeji T. Adeleke - Chairman/CEO

PAL PHARMACEUTICAL INDUSTRIES LIMITED
Business: Production of Pharmaceutical Products
Address: Plot 101/102, Maganda Road, Bompai Industrial Estate, Kano
Tel: (064) 635232, 638217 **Fax:** (064) 638217
Contact: Chif Alex U. Onyido - Chairman/CEO

PALCOMMS LIMITED
Business: Advertising, Marketing Communications, Public & Media Relations, Events Marketing
Address: Pal House, 5, Ebun Street, Abule-Oja, Yaba, Lagos
Tel: (01) 7740801, 4701830 **Fax:** (01) 7740801
E-maiL pal@palcomms.com
Contact: Mr. S. Ayo Owoborode - MD/CEO

PALETTE LIMITED
Business: Importation, Sales, Installation and Maintenance of Compute Accessories and Systems
Address: Plot 1263, Adeola Odeku St, Victoria Island, Lagos
Tel: (01) 2621007, 2626404-5 (2L), 2700731, 08022909616, 08033002738 **Fax:** (01) 2621008
E-mail: palette@palettecomputers.com
sales@palettecomputers.com
Website: www.palettecomputes.com
Contact: Mr. Charles Mezu - MD/CEO.

PALM LINE AGENCIES NIGERIA LIMITED
Business: Shipping Agency, Freight Forwarding, Warehousing, Container Terminal Oprations, Plant Hiring Services, Port and Allied Service
Address: 11A, Burma Road, Apapa, Lagos
Tel: (01) 5873616, 5873618 **Fax:** (01) 5876051
E-mail: palmline@linkserv.com

PAMAQUE NIGERIA LIMITED
Business: Environmental Consultancy Services; Water, Sewage & Effluent Treatment, Water Supply & Distribution, Design, Fabrication and Construction of Metal-Plate Structure (Tanks & Vessels)
Address: 8, Iya-Oloye Crescent, Mile 8, Ikorodu Road, Onigbongbo, Lagos
Tel: (01) 4977291, 8179367 **Fax:** (01) 4967059
E-mail: pamaq@linkserve.com.ng
* 76B, Adeniyi Jones Avenue, Ikeja, Lagos
Tel: (01) 8179357, 08033072043
Contact: Engr. O. Oyefuga - MD/CEO

PAMO CLINICS
Business: Medical Services
Address: 300, Port Harcourt/Aba Expressway, Rumuomasi, Port Harcourt
Tel: (084) 579597

PAMODZI SPORTS MARKETING NIGERIA LIMITED
Business: Sports Marketing and Event Management
Address: 2, Mba Street, off Tafawa Balewa Crescent, off Adeniran Ogunsanya Street, Surulere, Lagos
Tel: (01) 5850841-2 (2 L), 7748464 **Fax:** (01) 5850842
E-mail: psm@infoweb.abs.net
Contact: Mr. Mike Itemuagbor - Exec. Chairman

PAMOL (NIGERIA) LIMITED
Business: Rubber & Oil Palm Plantations, Production and Processing of Natural Rubber and Palm Oil, Manufacture of Plastic Poducts
Address: Plantation Headquarters, Km. 15, Calabar/Ikom Highway, Calabar, Cross River State
Tel: (087) 232022, 222487 **Fax:** (087) 230769
* c/o Dunlop Nigeria Plc. Plot 23, Oba Akran Avenue, Ikeja Industrial Estate, Ikeja, Lagos
Tel: (01) 4900410-9 (10L), 4962666-7 (2L)
Fax: (01) 4964734, 2622063
E-mail: info@dunlopng.com
Website: www.dunlopng.com
Contact: Chief Bassey Edem Orok Edem - MD/CEO.

PAN AFRICAN AIRLINES (NIGERIA) LIMITED
Business: Charter Airline Services
Address: General Aviation Terminal, Murtala Mohammed Airport, Ikeja, Lagos
Tel: (01) 4931973, 4963601 **Fax:** (01) 4963798
E-mail: mdsecfw@paanltd.com
Contact: Capt. Franz Astner - MD/CO

PAN- ASIA SHIPPING AGENCY LIMITED
Business: Cargo &Freight Management, Brokage & Consolidation
Address: CAPL House (Rear Block, 1st Floor), 16, Burma Road, Apapa, Lagos
Tel: (01) 5872812, 5872813, 5872810, 08023012790
Fax: (01) 5872804
E-mail: panasia@nagusoil.com
Website: www.nagusoil.com
Contact: Mr Charles Iwara

PAN OCEAN OIL CORPORATION (NIGERIA)
Business: Crude Oil Exploration & Production
Address: The Ark Tower, Plot 17, Ligali Ayorinde Victoria Island Annex, Lagos
Tel: (01) 4616030-9(10L) **Fax:** (01) 4616075
E-mail: info@panocong.com
* Ogun Road, Warri
Tel: (053) 251263, 251271, 251930 **Fax:** (053) 252236

PAN SECURITIES LIMITED
Business: Pension Fund Management and Consultancy, Portfolio Managers, Financial & Leasing Services
Address: 3, Azikiwe Road, Port Harcourt
Tel: (084) 238553, 08034542959, 08034543039
Fax: (084) 238553
Contact: Mr. Augustine N. Nwiyordee - GM/CEO

PAN-AFRICAN INTERNATIONAL LIMITED
Business: Manufacturing of Footwear, Distribution & Sales of Safety Products and Equipment
Address: Plot 113, Trans-Amadi Ind. Layout, Port Harcourt
Tel: (084) 236799

PANA CONSULT LIMITD
Business: Estate Developers, Surveyors & Property Agents, Planning & Building Engineering
Address: 37, Cornershops, opp. Rockview Hotel, off Adetokunbo Ademola Crescent, Wuse II, Abuja
Tel: (09) 4139853, 08033147895
E-mail: palmachotels@markgrey.com
Website: www.markgrey.com
Contact: Chief Frank Chigbo - Chairman/CEO

PANA/SHARP LIMITED
Business: Sales and Maintenance of Banking & Office Automation, Computers and Telephone Systems
Address: 60, Modele St, off Tejuosho Road, Surulere, Lagos
Tel: (01) 5455278, 2880878 **Fax:** (01) 5455278
E-mal: panasharp2000@yahoo.com
* Wuse Neighbourhood Centre (Shop 5), Wuse Zone 3, Garki, Abuja.
Tel: (09) 5232187
Contact: Mr. 'Lanre Olatunde -MD/CEO.

PANABIZ INTERNATIONAL LIMITED
Business: Sales & Service of Panasonic Airconditioners, Office Automation & Telecommunication Equipment
Address: 11A, Osborne Road, Ikoyi, Lagos
Tel: (01) 2693368-9 (2L), 2693398-9 (2L)
Fax: (01) 2692491
E-mail: panabiz@panabiz.com
* Plot 446, Kontangora Close, off Jos Street, Area 3, Garki, Abjua
Tel: (09) 2346677-9 (3 L) **Fax:** (09) 2346678
* Plot 119, Trans-Amadi Ind. Layout, Port Harcourt
Tel: (084) 236856, 238773 **Fax:** (084) 238773

PANAFY LIMITED
Business: Outdoor Advertising Agency, Marketing Consultants
Address: 14B, Morris Sreet, Abule-Ijesha, Yaba, Lagos
Tel: (01) 4700228-9 (2L), 3425056 Fax: (01) 3425056
E-mail: admin@panafy.com
Contact: Mr. Terry Otuya - Chairman/CEO.

PANALPINA WORLD TRANSPORT (NIGERIA) LIMITED
Business: Shipping, Airfreight, Clearing & Forwarding, Haulage Services
Address: 4, Creek Road, Apapa, Lagos
Tel: (01) 5803440-9 (10L), 5803610-9 (10L), 2645193-6 (4L), 2645198 **Fax:** (01) 5873279, 5875333
E-mail: loscypt@los.panmail.com
Website: www.panalpina.com
Contact: Mr. M. Decker - MD/CEO

PANAM LABELS LIMITED
Business: Production, Recording, Marketing and Promotion of Music; Music Instruction
Address: 25B, Tafawa Balewa Street, Jos
Tel: (073) 461426, 450288, 08036057269, 08037023893
Fax: (073) 450091
E-mail: panam.j@bwave.net
Website: www.concerttothelord.com
Contact: Mrs. Tina Panam - MD/CEO

PANAR LIMITED
Business: Manufacturing of UPVC Pipes & Fittings and other Plastic Products
Address: 6, Elsie Femi-Pearse Street (1st Floor, Suite 4), Victoria Island, Lagos
Tel: (01) 2611482, 2615563, 2624053 **Fax:** (01) 2613139
E-mail: info@panargroup.com
* Plot 21/22, Sharada Ind.Estate Phase II, Kano
Tel: (064) 664022, 668684-5 (2L), 669113
Fax: (064) 662144
Contact: Alh. Abdullahi Bashir - Chairman
Mr Ravi Karan Daryani - MD/CEO

PANAT NIGERIA LIMITED
Business: Clearing & Forwarding, Sales of Banking Equipment
Address: 12, Agbaoku Street, off Opebi Road, Ikeja, Lagos
Tel: (01) 4971483, 4971484, 08033017330, 08033430222, 08033430239, 08033024351 **Fax:** (01) 4971485
E-mail: panat@hyperia.com
panatgeneral@hyperia.com
Contact: Prince Toye Oyinlola - Chairman/CEO.

PANITEX NIGERIA LIMITED
Business: Water Systems Engineering; Marketing and Sales of Water Pumps and Security Door Locks
Address: Block 2 (Apt. 11-12), Agric. Market, Km. 5, Badagry Expressway, Agric-Coker, Orile, Lagos
Tel: (01) 7742013, 4700941, 4700945; **Fax:** (01) 2617016
E-mail: panitex@infoweb.abs.net
* 33, Okija (Ngo) St, Mile 1, Diobu, Port Harcourt
Tel: (084) 572200
Contact: Engr. Patrick Okonkwo - Chairman/CEO.

PANNELL KERR FORSTER
Business: Management Consultants; Chartered Accountants
Address: Tapa House, 3/5, Imam Dauda Street, off Eric Moore Road, Surulere, Lagos
Tel: (01) 8042074, 8042112 **Fax:** (01) 7748366
Website: www.pkf.com

PAPERCRAFT NIGERIA LIMITED
Business: Production of Light Packaging Products, Paper Conversion, Flexo and Gravure Printing
Address: PCL House, Plot 1069, Balogun Street, Oregun Industrial Estate, Ikeja, Lagos
Tel: (01) 4975182, 7745320, 4920641
Contact: Chief B. A. Olaogun - Chairman
Mr. O. P. Bhola - MD/CEO

PAPILON INDUSTRY LIMITED
Business: Manufacturing of Plastic Products
Address: Plot K, Kopek Road, off Fatai Atere Way, Matori Industrial Estate, Oshodi, Lagos
Tel: (01) 4526353, 4528977 **Fax:** (01) 4524548
E-mail: papleo@india.com
Contact: Mr .Rohit Daswani - MD/CEO

PARADISE CITY HOTELS LIMITED
Business: Hotel Services
Address: 86/88, Atekong Dirve, P.M.B. 1336, Calabar.
Tel: (087) 225726, 225728, 221234

PARADISE TRAVELS & TOURS LIMITED
Business: Travel & Tour Agency
Address: Plot 8, Walter Carrington Crescent, V/ Island, Lagos
Tel: (01) 2625545-6 (2L), 2620621, 610101
Fax: (01) 2614861
E-mail: paradise2@nova.net.ng
Website: www.paradiseholidays.com
Contact: Mr. Khalid W. J. Zabadne - MD/CEO

PARAGON DIGITAL VISION LIMITED
Business: Wide-Format Digital Printing Servics
Address: 3, Popoola Banjoko Street, Soluyi Estate, Gbagada, Lagos
Tel: (01) 7742646, 08023610982

PARAMOUNT AIRLINES & TRAVELS SERVICES LIMITED
Business: Travel Agency, Travel and Tours Consultancy
Address: 3A, Alh. Ribadu Road, S.W. Ikoyi, Lagos
Tel: (01) 2671175, 2671176, 4743016, 08023174213, 08033456905 **Fax:** (01) 2671175
E-mail: paramounttravel@yahoo.com
Contact: AVM. A. D. Bello (rtd.) GCON, CFR -Chairman
Mr. Fatai A. Olaifa -Ag. MD/CEO

PARAMOUNT FOOD & BEVERAGE (NIGERIA) LIMITED
Business: Manufacturing of Biscuits
Address: Km. 8, Hadejia Road, Kano
Tel: (064) 633600
Contact: Alh. Tijjani Hashim (Galadiman Kano) - Chairman
Alh. Ali H. Basma - MD/CEO.

PARAMOUNT FROZEN FOOD LIMITED
Business: Imporation of Frozen Fish, Cold Storage Rental
Address: Plot 1303A, Akin Adesola Street, V/ Island, Lagos
Tel: (01) 2622232, 2622259, 2615505 **Fax:** (01) 2619487
E-mail: primalaks@hyperiacom
* Plot 5, Block E, Amuwo-Odofin Industrial Layout, Badagry Expressway, Suru-Alaba, Lagos
Tel: (01) 7743501, 7761938
Contact: Alhaja A. Amusan - Chairperson
Mr. B. C. P. Gowda - MD/CEO

PARAMOUNT TRADING & INDUSTRIES (NIGERIA) LTD
Business: Importation and Sales of Industrial Solvents, Manufacturing of PVC Hose (Plain & Braided) and PET Bottles, Productions of Table Water
Address: 22, Chief Nwobodoeze Street, Ajao Estate, Apakun-Oshodi, Lagos
Tel: (01) 4522551, 4522017, 523528, 525874
Fax: (01) 617159
E-mail: paramount@hyperia.com
Contact: Mr. Laxman H. Tulsiani - MD/CEO

PARCO ENTERPRISES (NIGERIA) LIMITED
Business: Importation and Marketing of Industrial Chemicals, Bicycles Iron and Steel Products
Address: Eleganza Plaza (Gemini Block, 2nd Floor), 1, Commercial Road, Apapa, Lagos
Tel: (01) 5804740-4 (5 L), 5875695
Fax: (01) 5450918, 5874688

PARI NIGERIA LIMITED
Business: Water Engineering Services
Address: Plot 20, East-West Rd, Rumuodara, Port Harcourt
Tel: (084) 332856, 334969 **Fax:** (084) 335578
* Allor Close, Umuoketofa Layout, Asaba
Tel: (056) 280073
* 2, Police Headquarters Layout, Calabar
Tel: (087) 225922 **Fax:** (087) 225923

PARIS BLUE NIGERIA LIMITED
Business: Manufacturing of Marketing of Computers
Address: 216, Happy Home Avenue, Kirikiri Industrial Estate, Kirikiri, Lagos
Tel: (01) 7741185, 5455322

PARK 'n' SHOP (Div of Artee Industries Ltd)
Business: Supermarket and Department Stores
Address: Block A, Eko Court Complex, Kofo Abayomi Street, Victoria Island, Lagos
Tel: (01) 2626280-1 (2L) **Fax:** (01) 2626284
E-mail: info@arteegroup.com
Website: www.arteegroup.com.ng
* Guru Plaza, 47A, Adeola Odeku Street, Victoria Island, Lagos.
Tel: (01) 2623291-5 (5L) **Fax:** (01) 2625501
* Lofam House, 21, Mobolaji Bank-Anthony Way, Maryland, Lagos.
Tel: (01) 4975046
* Plot 740, Aminu Kano Crescent Wuse II, Abuja
Tel: (09) 4135892-4 (3 L)
* 97, Aba Road, Port Harcourt.
Tel: (084) 230741-3 (3L) **Fax:** (084) 231093
Contact: Mr. Haresh T. Keswani - Chairman/CEO

PARKER DRILLING NIGERIA LIMITED
Business: Oil Drilling Services

Address: 19, Alloh Close, off Enerhen Road, Warri
Tel: (053) 250387, 251859, 252680, 254387
Fax: (053) 250387, 252680
* 72/74, Nkpogu Road, Trans-Amadi Industrial Layout, Port Harcourt
Tel/Fax: (084) 237307
Contact: Mr. Herbie Hooper - Manager (Operations)

PARKWAY RIDE & SERVICES LIMITED
Business: Entertainment and Leisure Services, Amusement Park Engineers
Address: Amusement Park, 34, Randle Road, Apapa, Lagos
Tel/Fax: (01) 5870371
Contact: Mr. Efua Mac-Arthur - MD/CEO

PARSON SCIENCE ENGINEERING COMPANY LIMITED
Business: Building & Civil Engineering and Consultancy
Address: Plot 470, Aminu Kano Crescent, Wuse II, Abuja
Tel: (09) 5232518, 5232623, 08033305153
Fax: (09) 5232623
E-mail: parsonsscience@mns.com
Contact: Col. Lawan Gwadabe (rtd) - Chairman
Mr. Sassine Sayegh - MD/CEO

PARTICIPANT PROPERTIES LIMITED
Business: Property Development and Management, Real Estate Consultancy
Address: 18B, Idowu Taylor Street,Victoria Island, Lagos
Tel: (01) 2620396, 2620338 **Fax:** (01) 2620325
E-mail: ppl@participant.com.ng
Website: www.participant.com.ng
* SPDC 1 House (2nd Floor), Plot 1154, Aminu Kano Crescent, Wuse II, Abuja
Tel: (09) 4139738-9 (2L), 6701824 **Fax:** (09) 4139744
E-mail: pplabuja@yahoo.com
Contact: Mrs. Fatima Edu - Chairperson
Mrs. Hadiza El-Rufai - MD/CEO

PARTNERSHIP INVESTMENT COMPANY LIMITED
Business: Investment Banking, Stockbroking, Issuing House
Address: 37, Ademola Street, off Awolowo Road, S.W., Ikoyi, Lagos
Tel: (01) 2694080, 2694775 **Fax:** (01) 2693737
E-mail: partnership@cyberspace.net.ng
partnership@cybaaspace.net
* NNB Buiding (4th Floor), Ring Road, Benin City
Tel: (01) 255588 **Fax:** (01) 253438
Contact: Mr. Victor O. Ogiemwonyi - MD/CEO

PARTY PLANNERS LIMITED
Business: Entertainment, Rental and Decoration, Children & Teenagers Boutique
Address: 60, Awolowo Road, S.W. Ikoyi, Lagos
Tel: (01) 2691303, 7918624, 08023145138, 08023159426, 0803014159 **Fax:** (01) 2690332
E-mail: global99@hyperia.com
osime@hyperia.com
Contact: Mrs. Abolaji Osime - Chairman/CEO

PAT OBIANWU & COMPANY
Business: Estate Surveyors, Valuers Agents, Property Development & Management, Project & Facility Management, Feasibility & Viability Studies
Address: 20, Modupe Johnson Crescent, off Adeniran Ogunsanya Street, Surulere, Lagos
Tel: (01) 5834848, 5835568, 7766420, 08033206196-7 (2L), 08022238417, 08037766420 **Fax:** (01) 5835568
E-mail: pobianwu@infoweb.abs.net
Contact: Mr. Patrick O. Obianwu - Principal Partner

PATED (NIGERIA) LIMITED
Business: Marketing of Building Materials, Granite, Marbles, Ceramic, Vitrified & Mosaic Tiles, Paints, Air conditioners, Furniture, Door, Fans, Halogen Lamps
Address: 13 (Plot 1311), Karimu Kotun Street, off Akin Adesola Street, Victoria Island, Lagos
Tel: (01) 2611704, 4703634, 7743733 **Fax:** (01) 2646788
E-mail: pated@infoweb.abs.net
* 4B, Casamance Crescent, off Herbert Macaulay Way, Sheraton Junction, Wuse Zone 3, Abuja
Tel: (09) 5230593, 5234653, 5236028, 5238507
Fax: (09) 5230591
Contact: Mr. Teddy Luttwak - Chairman/CEO

PATELENE NIGERIA LIMITED
Business: Manufacturing of Plastic Tanks
Address: 7/11, Industrial Avenue, Ilupeju Industrial Estate, Ilupeju, Lagos
Tel: (01) 4968175-9 (5 L), 4962197 **Fax:** (01) 4961884
E-mail: patelene@beta.linkserve.com
* Plot 201, Trans-Amadi Industrial Layout, Phase 11, Port Harcourt
Tel: (084) 232727, 233526 **Fax:** (084) 233526
Contact: Mr. N. G. Patel - Chairman/CEO

PATERSON ZOCHONIS INDUSTRIES PLC
Business: Manufacturing of Domestic Consumer Products, Healthcare Products and Home Appliances
Address: 45/47, Town Planning Way, Ilupeju Industrial Estate, Ilupeju, Lagos
Tel: (01) 4973460-8 (9L) **Fax:** (01) 4962076
E-mail: pzi@alpha.linkserve.com
Contact: Mr P. Varelas - CEO
Mr K. Theodorakopoulos - MD

PATIKE COMMUNICATIONS LIMITED
Business: Publishing, Advertising, Public Relations
Address: 89, Bode Thomas Street, Surulere, Lagos
Tel: (01)5847305
* Aguiyi Ironsi Shopping Complex (Suite 22), Asokoro District, Abuja.
Tel: (09) 3147885
Contact: Prof. Pat Utomi - Chairman

PATNASONIC INDUSTRIES LIMITED
Business: Property Development, Hoteliers, Communications, Wood Processing and Furniture Manufacturers
Address: Cellcom Building, Plot 374, Adetokunbo Ademola Crescent, by Rockview Hotel, Cadastral Zone A8, Wuse II, Abuja
Tel: (09) 5238691-6 (6L)
* 33, Saka Tinubu Street, Victoria Island, Lagos
Tel: (01) 2614101, 5883316, 5881847 **Fax:** (01) 2618157
* Plot 2241, Block 34, Amuwo-Odofin Residential Scheme near Mile 2, Amuwo-Odofin, Lagos
Contact: Mr. Patrick T. Chidolue - Chairman/CEO

PATOVILKI INDUSTRIAL PLANNERS LIMITED
Business: Industrial Cleaning Pest Control Services
Address: 1, Willy Ikolodo Close, beh. Mobil Filling State, Gbagada, Lagos
Tel: (01) 5552714, 5553042, 7742522, 3423042
* ECOWAS Secretariat, Yabuku Gowon Way, Asokoro District, Abuja
Tel: (09) 3147647
Contact: Chief Willy Ukadike Ikolodo - Chairman/CEO

PATPLAST NIGERIA LIMITED
Business: Production of Polypropylne Woven Sacks, PVC Compounds, PVC Pipes, PP Box Straps, Drinking Straws and Plastic Products
Address: 7-11, Industrial Avenue, Ilupeju Ind. Estate, Lagos
Tel: (01) 4968175-9 (5 L) **Fax:** (01) 4961884
E-mail: metro@infoweb.abs.net
patplast@linkserve.com.ng
Contact: Mr. N. G. Patel - MD/CEO

PAUL & PAUL CHEMISTS LIMITED
Business: Importation & Sales of Pharmaceutical Products
Address: Plot 8, Block D, Badejo Kalesanwo Street, Matori Industrial Estate, Matori, Mushin, Lagos
Tel: (01) 521318, 521329, 521341, 521349
* 8, Market Street, Lagos
Tel: (01) 2663393, 2664836
Contact: Mr. Justus O. Paul - Chairman/CEO

PAU-LOAD LIMITED
Business: Manufacturing of Furniture, Furnishing and Interior Decoration, Marketing of Petroleum Products and Chemicals, Pharmaceuticals
Address: NPA Expressway Bye-Pass, Warri
Tel: (053) 253628, 08023098396 **Fax:** (053) 253628
E-mail: tukakaltd@yahoo.com
* E5, Nnamdi Azikiwe Expressway, Kurmi Mashi Junction, Kaduna
Tel/Fax: (062) 418544, 08033108840
* Km. 15, City Gate Express Road, Abuja
Contact: Chief P. O. A. Dekpe - Chairman/CEO

PAULOSA NIGERIA LIMITED
Business: Civil Engineering; Dams & Bore Holes Construction
Address: 35, Oghosa Crescent; Benin-City
Tel: (052) 251783, 250142
Contact: Lt. Col P. O. Ogbebor (Rtd) - President/CEO

PAULSON O. EMERAH GROUP OF COMPANIES NIG. LTD
Business: Import & Export Trading, Sales of Auto Spare Parts & General Merchandise, General Contractors
Address: 8, Nwosa Lane, Nkpor, Onitsha, Anambra State
Tel: (046) 251153, 251308
E-mail: aulpe@justice.com

PAVEX INTERNATIONAL COMPANY LIMITED
Business: Supply of Agricultural Equipment, Heavy-Duty Equipment, Complete Industrial Machinery and General Merchandise
Address: 16, Burma Road, Apapa, Lagos
Tel: (01) 5871982 **Fax:** (01) 2646084
E-mail: pavex@metrong.com
Contact: Mr. R. N. Kassab - MD/CEO

PAVILON TECHNOLOGY LIMITED
Business: Design, Supply, Installation and Maintenance of Electronic Security Systems
Address: 8, Musa Yar'Adua Street, off Kofo Abayomi Street, Victoria Island, Lagos
Tel: (01) 2621314, 4619552-3 (2L) **Fax:** (01) 4619551
E-mail: pavilion@infoweb.abs.net
Contact: Mr. Oba Otudeko - Chairman
Mr. Haim Yacobi - MD/CEO

PAXS PHARMACEUTICALS LIMITED
Business: Importation & Sales of Pharmaceutical Products
Address: 80, Awka Road Onitsha
Tel: (046) 413413, 413359 08033208789
E-mail: paxspharm@yahoo.com
Contact: Mr. U. U. Apakama - Chairman/CEO

PAY-LESS INDUSTRIAL & COMMERCIAL SERVICES LTD
Business: Supermarket & Butchery; Sales of Electronics Wine & Liquor and Groceries
Address: Shakeera Plaza, 141, Ahmadu Bello Way, Victoria Island, Lagos
Tel: (01) 2616101, 2617978, 614101 **Fax:** (01) 616101
* Pay-less 1, Chevron Branch, Km. 19, Epe Express way, Lekki Peninsula, Lagos
* Pay-less 3, Shopping Mall, Plot 307, Adeola Odeku Street, Victoria Island, Lagos
Contact: Mr. Mohan Melwani - MD/CEO

PAYBACK LIMITED
Business: Sales of Computers, Electronic Appliances, Telecommunication and Security Equipment
Address: 47, Opebi Road, Ikeja, Lagos
Tel: (01) 7765134, 08023145081 **Fax:** (01) 4930007
E-mail: payback@micro.com.ng
Contact: Mr. Linus Nwosu - MD/CEO

PAYPHONE COMPANY NIGERIA LIMITED
Business: Marketing and Maintenance of Pay-Phones
Address: 1/3, Boyle Street, Onikan, Lagos
Tel: (01) 2601100-4(5L), 2645530-2(3L)
Fax: (01) 2645529
E-mail: pcnl@generaltelecom.com
Contact: Mr. K. C. Obinwanne - Sals/Marketing Manager

PBTG CONSULTING LIMITED
Business: Management & Financial Consultancy
Address: Plot 313A, Akin Ogunlewe St, Victoria Island, Lagos
Tel: (01) 2624411-2 (2L), 4803138, 08034099931
Fax: (01) 3200895
E-mail: pesley@compuserve.com
Contact: Mr. Pat Bassey - MD/CEO

PCI LIMITED
Business: Manufacturing, Distributing and Marketing of Paints, Polyester Bodyfiller and Allied Products
Address: 12, Jumoke Babalola Street, opp. Eleganza Shopping Complex, Orile-Iganmu, Lagos
Tel: (01) 7730449, 7740786 **Fax:** (01) 7740786
Contact: Mrs. M. O. K. Taiwo - Chairman/CEO

PDA WAREHOUSE
Business: Distribution and Sales of IT Products

Address: 285B, Corporation Drive Dolphin Estate, Ikoyi, Lagos
Tel: (01) 2693753, 2693754, 2393755, 08028880456
Fax: (01) 2693754
E-mail: info@pdawarehouse-ng.com
Website: www.padawarehouse-ng.com
Contact: Nkoli Oyeka - Chairman

PDS INFORMATION TECHNOLOGY INC.
Business: Sales and Support of IT Products
Address: Centage Plaza, 14, Allen Avenue, Ikeja, Lagos
Tel: (01) 4937693
E-mail: pdssoftware@netscape.net
Website: www.pdsit.com

PEACOCK CREATIONS NIGERIA LIMITED
Business: Manufacturing, Monogramming and Marketing of Corporate/Industrial Uniforms and Garment.
Address: 11, Ibiyinka Olorunnimbe Close, off Amodu Ojikutu Street off Bishop Oluwole St, Victoria Island, Lagos
Tel: (01) 7740769, 2625595
E-mail: peacockcreations2003@yahoo.com
* Peacock Plaza, Plot 662, Aba Close, off Tafawa Balewa Way, Area 8, Garki, Abuja
Tel: (09) 2346303, 2345473, 2344809 **Fax:** (09) 2344809
* MBM Plaza, 8, Old Aba Road, Rumuomasi, Port Harcourt.
Tel: (084) 239584, 239598 **Fax:** (084) 239598
Contact: Mrs. G. I. Ifeozo - MD/CEO

PEACOCK PAINTS LIMITED
Business: Manufacturing & Marketing of Paints
Address: Ikot Ekong, P.M.B. 1054, Etinan, Akwa Ibom State
Tel: (085) 204712 * (082) 440574 **Fax:** (085) 201090

PEACOCK TRAVELS & TOURS LIMITED
Business: Travel Agency, Tours & Car-Hire Services
Address: 136, Obafemi Awolowo Way, Ikeja, Lagos
Tel: (01) 4720326, 4930332, 4933371, 5557223, 7918672, 08023510864, 08023510866, 08023513817, 08033045460 **Fax:** (01) 4930332
E-mail: sales@peacocktrvelandtours.com
Website: www.peacocktrvelandtours.com

PEAK INSURANCE BROKERS LIMITED
Business: Insurance Broking
Address: 78, Broad Street (4th Floor), Tinubu Square, Lagos
Tel: (01) 2642016 **Fax:** (01) 2668436
Contact: Mr. Japhet O. Onyekaonwu - Exec. Chairman

PEAK PETROLEUM LIMITED
Business: Oilfield Services
Address: 12, Adetokunbo Ademola St, Victoria Island, Lagos
Tel: (01) 2601440-9 (10 L), 2613221 **Fax:** (01) 2612550

PEAK SECURITIES & FINANCE LIMITED
Business: Stockbroking, Portfolio Management
Address: Stock Exchange Building (22nd Floor), 2/4, Customs Street, off Marina, Lagos
Tel: (01) 8045873 **Fax:** (01) 2615465
Contact: Mr. Lawrence O. Odigwe -MD/CEO

PEBETO VENTURES LIMITED
Business: Sales & Installation of Motor Vehicles Security Systems, Hiring of House Boats, Pipeline Maintenance, Construction of Steel Structures
Address: 17, Ahmed Onibudo Street, Victoria Island, Lagos
Tel: (01) 2610002, 2610004, 7753092 **Fax:** (01) 2621440
E-mail: pebeto@theobech.com
Website: www.car-alarm.com
* 5B, Water Resource Road, Effurun, Warri
Tel: (053) 256734
Contact: Mr. Peter Eberiere Otomewo - Chairman/CEO

PECCOLO BRUNELLI ENGINEERING LIMITED
Business: Construction and Civil Engineering
Address: 9A, Dakar Road, off Oduduwa Street, off Marine Road, Apapa G.R.A., Lagos
Contact: Engr. Mocianni M. Elexandre -MD/CEO

PECUNIARY & TRUST INSURANCE BROKERS LIMITED
Business: Insuracne Broking
Address: 5, Olaide Tomori St, off Medical Road, Ikeja, Lagos
Tel: (01) 4967515, 2903640, 7737386 **Fax:** (01) 5837520
E-mail: ptibltd@yahoo.com
* Chicken House Estate (Guardian Trust Suite), Plot 472, IBB Way, Wuse II, Abuja
Tel: (09) 5232454
Contact: Mr. Samuel I. Ezearigo - MD/CEO

PEDROCCHI & COMPANY LIMITED
Business: Building & Civil Engineering Contractors
Address: 187, Sapele Road, Benin City
Tel: (052) 259458

PEFAC PAPER INDUSTRIES LIMITED
Business: Paper Conversion, Production of Toilet Tissue and Serviette
Address: Plot C, Olowogbowore Industrial Estate, Ajegunle Street, Sagamu, Ogun State
Tel: (037) 640099 **Fax:** (037) 641655
Contact: Chief E. O. Awofala - Chairman/CEO

PEKAB INTERNATIONAL NIGERIA LIMITED
Busines: Builders, Farmers, Exporters. Caterers & General Contractors
Address: 7, Edem Ekpenyong Street, Calabar
Tel: (087) 210242, 236722, 08037135667
* 53, Usuma Street, Maitama, Abuja
Tel: (09) 4130597
E-mail: ptbello@skannet.com
Contact: P. K. Bello - President/CEO

PELLEGRINI NIGERIA CATERING LIMITED
Business: Catering & Hospitality Services
Address: Plot 14, off Nkpogu Road, Trans-Amadi Industrial Layout, Port Harcourt
Tel/Fax: (084) 231748
E-mail: pelle@phca.linkserve.com
Contact: Dr. Bukar Shaibu - Chairman
Mr. Mauizio Giannotti -MD/CEO

PELLETERIA LIMITED
Business: Interior Decoration and Furnishing
Address: 39, Joel Ogunnaike Street, G.R.A., Ikeja, Lagos
Tel/Fax: (01) 4975976
Contact: Chief Victor Ogakwu - Chairman/CEO

PEMO GROUP
Business: Importation and Sales of General Merchandise
Address: Eleganza Plaza (Leo Block, 2nd Floor), 1, Commercial Road, Apapa, Lagos
Tel: (01) 5453245
Contact: Mr. P. E. Pemo - Chairman/CEO

PENEL INVESTMENTS LIMITED
Business: Distribution and Sales of Solar/Electric Lighting Lanterns and Bulbs, Oil & Gas Services
Address: Plot 932, Idejo Street, Victoria Island, Lagos
Tel: (01) 7741307, 3201405 **Fax:** (01) 3201405
Contact: Mr. E. B. Odunlami - Chairman/CEO

PENIEL APARTMENTS
Business: Management of Serviced Luxury Apartments
Address: Plot 137, Ibrahim B. Babanida Way, via Adetokunbo Ademola Crescent, Wuse II, Abuja
Tel: (09) 4130058, 4130861, 4133998 **Fax:** (09) 4130062
E-mail: penielapartments@hotmail.com
Contact: Chief (Dr) Samuel Adedoyin, CFR - Chairman/CEO

PENINSULA WATERFRONT LIMITED
Business: Hospitality
Address: Plot 8, Ozumba Mbadiwe Rd, Victoria Island, Lagos
Tel: (01) 2617168, 617563, 7745656 **Fax:** (01) 2617168
Contact: Mr. Niyi Onibudo - MD/CEO

PENSION MANAGERS NIGERIA LIMITED
Business: Pension Schemes Management
Address: 2, Tokunbo Ali Street, Ikeja, Lagos
Tel: (01) 4977929
Contact: Mr. M. U. Ekong - Chairman/CEO

PERA-BEAM LIMITED (Div. of UAC Nig. Plc)
Business: Sales, Hire, Contract Sales and Maintenance of Cooling Equipment and Appliances
Address: 6, Akinyemi Crescent Matori Industrial Estate, Lagos
Tel: (01) 4521785, 4522649, 4524457, 4523103
Fax: (01) 4522692
E-mail: perabeam@uacnplc.com
* 26, Addis-Abba Crescent, Wuse Zone 4, Abuja
Tel: (09) 5235366
Contact: Engr. O. S. Erinle - MD/CEO

PERFECT BEAUTY PRODUCTS LIMITED
Business: Manufacturing of Cosmetic & Beauty Products
Address: Plot 4, Limca Way, off Oshodi-Apapa Expressway, Isolo Industrial Estate, Isolo, Lagos
Tel: (01) 4524414

PERFECT CARE SYSTEMS LIMITED
Business: Sales and Repairs of Computers and Accessories
Address: Olatunji House, 299, Ikorodu Road, Maryland, Lagos
Tel: (01) 4933545, 8044159 **Fax:** (01) 4933545
E-mail: perfectmktn@yahoo.com
perfectcare51@hotmail.com
Contact: Mr. Gbenga Babatunde - Chairman/CEO

PERFECT INSURANCE BROKERS LIMITED
Business: Risk Managers, Life, Pension & Claims Consultants
Address: LL. 16, Ahmadu Bello Way, Kaduna
Tel: (062) 215786, 231433

PERFECT PRINTERS LIMITED
Business: Printing & Designing Services (Commercial & Industrial), Colour Separation
Address: 46, Hakeem Balogun Street, off Lateef Jakande Road, Agidingbi, Ikeja, Lagos
Tel: (01) 4930665, 08022240911, 08033195927, 08033440476 **Fax:** (01) 4930665
E-mail: perfectprintersltd@yahoo.com
Contact: Mr. Amos Edeaghe - MD/CEO

PERFECTA INVESTMENT TRUST LIMITED
Business: Financial Services, Stockbroking, Issuing House
Address: Group House, 4/6, Ikoyi Road, Obalende, Lagos
Tel: (01) 2693219, 684396
Contact: Chief (Dr.) S. I. Odogwu - Chairman
Mr. G. E. Odogwu - Exec. Director/CEO

PERFECTION SECURITIES & INVESTMENT LIMITED
Business: Stockbrokers, Financial Advisors, Receiving Agents, Portfolio Managers
Address: 3, 5 & 7, Kakawa Street, off Marina, Lagos
Tel: (01) 2643083, 08044111796 Fax: (01) 2643083

PERPETUAL ASSURANCE COMPANY LIMITED
Business: General Insurance Business and Special Risks
Address: Wuraola House (4th Floor), 82, Allen Avenue, Ikeja, Lagos
Tel: (01) 4933253, 4962069, 4978081, 2904672
Fax: (01) 4978298, 4822767
* Plot 1950, Algiers Street, opp. High Court, Wuse Zone 5, Abuja.
Tel: (09) 5232942
Contact: Mr. P. A. Daramola - MD/CEO

PERPETUAL SAVINGS & LOANS LIMITED
Business: Mortgage Finance & Banking
Address: 21, Ereko Street, Idumota, Lagos
Tel: (01) 3641331-5 (5L), 2640192 **Fax:** (01) 2641373

PERSONAL TRUST SAVINGS & LOANS LIMITED
Business: Mortage Banking Services
Address: 67, Ogunlana Drive, Surulere, Lagos
Tel: (01) 5454711, 7733584 **Fax:** (01) 5454710
E-mail: ptsl@ayserve.net
Contact: Mr. Debo Omonijo - MD/CEO

PESACO CHEMICAL INDUSTRIES LIMITED
Business: Manufacturing of Foam Products
Address: Plot P1, Pokobros Avenue, Harbour Industrial Layout, off Atani Road, Onitsha
Tel: (046) 210303, 210800, 08033230191, 08033230957
Contact: Chief (Dr.) P. A. Okonkwo - Chairman/CEO

PESTKIL (NIGERIA) LIMITED
Business: Industrial & Agricultural Pest Control Services; Importation and Distribution of Pest Control Chemicals and Equipment
Address: 149, Aba-Owerri Road, Umungasi, Aba
Tel: (082) 350448, 350452, 351240
* 200 (Mile 5), Aba Road, Rumuola Junction, Port Harcourt.
Tel: (084) 334834
Contact: Chief (Dr.) C. M. Obioha, JP - Chairman

PET JIBSON & COMPANY LIMITED
Business: Building and Civil Engineering
Address: 68, Rumuepirikom Road, along Eagle Cement Road, off Mile 4, Ikwerre Road, Port Harcourt
Tel: (084) 571009, 08033421243
E-mail: petjibson@phca.linkserve.com
* Transglobal Investment Suite, 7 (Plot 1663), Oyin Jolayemi Street, Victoria Island, Lagos
Tel: (01) 2612263, 2617908 **Fax:** (01) 2617908
* Transglobal Investment Suite, 10, Ihama Road, off Airport Road, Benin City
Tel/Fax: (052) 256521
Contact: Mr. Peter Elumelu - Chairman/CEO

PETDRILL DEVELOPMENT COMPANY LIMITED
Business: Oil & Gas Field Services, Petroleum Engineering Services, Natural Resources Development
Address: New Africa House (7th Floor), 31, Marina, Lagos
Tel: (01) 2666350, 2668635, 2668675, 2668678, 08042104407 **Fax:** (01) 2601118
* PTI Road, Effurun, Warri
Tel: (053) 254128
Contact: Chief Daniel Ogwilaya - Chairman/CEO

PETER E. VENTURES NIGERIA LIMITED
Business: Manufacturing of Hurricane Lantern, Plastic Hangers, Pharmaceutical Cups, Ploy Bags and Allied Products, General Merchandising
Address: 9/11, Isiokpo Street, Awada Layout, Onitsha
Tel: (046) 270861, 270943 **Fax:** (046) 270394
E-mail: peterv@infoweb.abs.net
Website: www.peterventure.com
Contact: Chief (Sir) Peter E. Ezemegwara - Chairman/CEO

PETER OKOLO & COMPANY
Business: Estate Surveyors & Valuers, Real Estate Agents & Developers, Feasibilty & Viability Appraisal
Address: Legion House, opp UBA, Area 3, Garki, Abuja
Tel: (09) 2340940-2 (3L), 2343242, 2343376, 08033047634, 08033086101, 08042121935 **Fax:** (09) 2340941
E-mail: peterokolo@yahoo.com
Contact: Sir Peter N. C. Okolo (KSM) - Principal Partner

PETER'S & DANIELS ENTERPRISES LIMITED
Business: Manufacturing of Plastic Packaging Products
Address: 113, Port Harcourt Road, Onitsha
Tel: (046) 215210, 08023343062, 08033237502
Fax: (046) 213286
Contact: Mr. Nduka P. Ugwuneke - Chairman/CEO

PETRA INSURANCE BROKERS LIMITED
Business: Insurance Broking and Consultancy
Address: Ade Komolafe Commercial House, 62, Oregun Road, Oregun, Ikeja, Lagos
Tel: (01) 4815431, 7738802
E-mail: petra@allnigeria.com
Contact: Mr. Kalu I. Uduma - MD/CEO

PETRALPHA LIMITED
Business: Blending and Manufacturing of Lubrication; Marketing of Petroleum Products
Address: Km. 38, Lagos-Abeokuta Expressway, Sango-Otta
Tel: (039) 721400 * (01) 7746420 **Fax:** (039) 721402

PETRANOL NIGERIA LIMITED
Business: Haulage of Petroleum Products
Address: 3B, Ribadu Rd, off Awolowo Rd, SW, Ikoyi, Lagos
Tel: (01) 2691180
E-mail: petranol@infoweb.abs.net
Contact: Biola Ogunrombi - MD/CEO

PETRO-ENERGY RESOURCES LIMITED
Business: Oilfield Engineering Services, Supply of Oilfield Tools & Equipment
Address: Princes Court (Flat 2F), 37, Ahmed Onibudo Street, Victoria Lagos
Tel: (01) 2616697, 2617164, 08023581512
Fax: (01) 2617164
E-mail: petro-energy@yahoo.com
Website: www.petro-energy.com
Contact: Mr. Effiong Ekpenyong - MD/CEO

PETROCOM SERVICES NIGERIA LIMITED
Business: Procurement & Supplies to the Oil & Gas Industry
Address: 1151A, Gabaro Close, off Amodu Ojikutu Street, Victoria Island, Lagos
Tel: (01) 2616048 **Fax:** (01) 2610288
* 1, Oluku Road, off Sapele Road, Effurun, Warri.
Tel/Fax: (053) 253386
* Plot 127, Trans-Amadi Ind Layout, Port Harcourt.
Tel: (084) 612800
Contact: Mr. Emeka Ugwu-Oju - Chairman/CEO

PETROFINA NIGERIA LIMITED
Business: Shipping Services
Address: 15A, Burma Road, Apapa, Lagos
Tel: (01) 5452108, 5874996 **Fax:** (01) 5452106
Contact: Mr. R. M. Jichi - Chairman/CEO

PETROLAND NIGERIA LIMITED
Business: Oil & Gas Integrated Services
Address: 135, Igbosere Road (Penthose Suite), Lagos
Tel: (01) 2645855, 08023065608 Fax: (01) 2645855
E-mail: petroland@lycos.com
Contact: Mr. Olubunmi Martins - MD/CEO

PETROLEIGH O.G.O. INTERNATIONAL LIMITED
Business: Oilfield Services (Equipment Supply, Products Marketing Specialized Engineering, Consultancy)
Address: 89, Awolowo Road, S. W. Ikoyi, Lagos
Tel: (01) 683817, 682649, 684876 **Fax:** (01) 2692326
E-mail: akinleigh@nova.net.ng
Contact: Mr. Edward W. A. Leigh - MD/CEO

PETROLEO BRASILEIRO NIGERIA LIMITED
Business: Exploration & Production of Crude Oil and Gas
Address: Africa-Reinsurance Building (7th Floor), Plot 1679, Karimu Kotn Street, Victoria Island, Lagos
Tel: (01) 2626703-5 (3L), 4617858

PETROLEUM PROSPECTS INTERNATIONAL LIMITED (PETROPROS)
Business: Oil and Gas Consultancy, Training
Address: 25, Sanusi Fafunwa Street, Victoria Island, Lagos
Tel: (01) 610221, 618494, 2620960 **Fax:** (01) 2620961
E-mail: petropros@aol.com
Contact: Mr. Dele Kadris - MD/CEO

PETROLOG LIMITED
Business: Hydrocation Logging, Consulting, Petroleum Engineering, Slim Hole MWD Services
Address: Edo House (2nd Floor, Suite 5-7), Plot 1225, Ahmadu Bello Way, Victoria Island, Lagos
Tel: (01) 613808, 615309, 614320 **Fax:** (01) 613807
E-mail: 112070.2031@compuserve.com
Website: www.petrologgroup.com
* 5, East-West Road, Rumuokurushi, Port Harcourt
Tel: (084) 610967-9 (3 L) **Fax:** (084) 610969
* 255, Airport Rd, Effurun, Warri.
Tel: (053) 253758
Contact: Mr. Vincent O. Ebuh - Chairman/CEO

PETROMED GROUP OF COMPANIES
Business: Marketing of Petroleum Products, Fishing & Trawling
Address: 22A & B, Oranyan Road, Apapa G.R.A., Lagos
Tel: (01) 5873606, 5450290, 5452482 Fax: (01) 5874532
E-mail: petromed@daanet.com

PETRONELLA NIGERIA LIMITED
Business: Catering & Hotel Management, Interior Decoration, Manpower Supplies, Quality Control &Inspection Services, Vehicles & Equipment Leasing
Address: 27, Nembe Street, Ruuibekwe, Port Harcourt
Tel: (084) 611640, 613099 **Fax:** (084) 611641
E-mail: petronel@infoweb.abs.net
Contact: Dr. (Engr.) Charles Tabansi - MD/CEO

PETRUS HOTELS LIMITED
Business: Hospitality Services
Address: Plot 907, Agatu Close, off Gimbiya Street, off Ahmadu Bello Way, Area 11, Garki, Abuja
Tel: (09) 3143415-9 (6L) **Fax:** (09) 3133419

PET-TIM GROUP OF COMPANIES
Business: Production of Electric Poles and Electricity Insulators, Mechanical & Electrical Engineering, Import & Export of Industrial Minerals
Address: Km. 3, Iworoko Road, Ado-Ekiti
Tel: (030) 250458, 250806, 250949

PEUGEOT AUTOMOBILE NIGERIA LIMITED
Business: Assembly of Motor Vehicles
Address: Plot 1144, Mallam Kulbi Road, Kakuri Industrial Estate, Kaduna South, Kaduna
Tel: (062) 231131-5 (5L) **Fax:** (062) 231784, 233860
E-mail: mkt@peugeotnigeria.com
* 19, Agoro Odiyan Street, Victoria Island, Lagos
Tel: (01) 2614551, 2613146, 2617448 **Fax:** (01) 2613231
Contact: Mr. Phillipe Beudet - MD/CEO

PFIZER SPECIALTIES LIMITED
Business: Marketing of Pharmaceutical Products
Address: Adeloba House, 38, Opebi Road, Ikeja, Lagos
Tel: (01) 2625366-8 (3 L) **Fax:** (01) 2625365
E-mail: robert.tade@pfizer.com
Contact: Mr. Robert Tade - Chairman/CEO
Mr. Lere Baale - Pharm. Div. Director

PGA BUILDERS' MALL
Business: Sales of Household Fittings - Shower Doors, Folding Doors, Glass Bricks, Ceiling etc
Address: 10, Durban Street, off Adetokunbo Ademola Crescent, Wuse II, Abuja
Tel: (09) 5232337-8 (2L), 5234498 **Fax:** (09) 5234401
E-mail: procon@proconafrica.com

PHAMATEX NIGERIA LIMITED
Business: Importation, Marketing and Wholesales of Pharmaceutical Products, Manufacturer's Representative
Address: 17, Simpson Street, Ebute-Metta (East), Lagos
Tel: (01) 7740193, 5455247, 4701933, 862909, 08033316589 **Fax:** (01) 5455247
E-mail: phamatex@yahoo.com
Contact: Prince C. O. Nebe - MD/CEO

PHARCHEM INDUSTRIES LIMITED
Business: Manufacturing of Pharmaceuticals Products
Address: Plot J, Industrial Street, Ilupeju Ind.Estate, Lagos
Tel: (01) 4963505, 4961004 **Fax:** (01) 4963505
E-mail: pharchem2003@yahoo.com
Contact: Chief (Dr.) G. O. Egabor (JP) - Chairman/CEO

PHARCO (PRODUCTIONS) PLC
Business: Manufacturing of Plastic Products
Address: 30/32, (Plot 9E), Akinwumi Street, Isolo Industrial Area, off Ladipo Street, Papa Ajao, Mushin, Lagos
Tel: (01) 7732092

PHARCO LABORATORIES (NIGERIA) LIMITED
Business: Manufacturing of Pharmaceutical Products
Address: Jakande Estate Gate, Egbe Rd, Oke-Afa, Isolo, Lagos
Tel: (01) 4960674, 08033056125, 08055475886
Contact: Mr. B. O. Alaka - MD/CEO

PHAREZ LIMITED
Business: Examinations, Rating, Human Development, Mergers & Acquisitions, Strategy
Address: Valley View Plaza, 99, Opebi Street, Ikeja Lagos
Tel: (01) 7916187
E-mail: consultants@pharez-limited.com
pharezfolks@yahoo.co.uk
Website: www.pharez-limited.com
Contact: Mr. Gamaliel Onosode - Chairman
Mr. Eghes Eyieyien - Managing Consultant/CEO

PHARMACIA NIGERIA LIMITED
Business: Marketing of Pharmaceutical Products
Address: Motorways Centre, 1, Motorways Avenue, opp. 7-Up Factory, Alausa, Ikeja, Lagos
Tel: (01) 7942990
E-mail: pharmacia@infoweb.abs.net
Contact: Mr. Collins Iriajen - MD/CEO

PHARMACEUTICAL & PERSONAL PRODUCTS LIMITED (Div of UAC Nig. Plc)
Business: and Marketing of Pharmaceutical and Personal-Care Products
Address: 1/3, Industrial Avenue, Ilupeju Industrial Estate, Ilupeju, Lagos
Tel: (01) 4932986-9 (4 L)
Contact: Mrs. O. A. Adetayo - MD/CEO

PHARMACEUTICAL SERVICES LIMITED
Business: Production and Marketing of Pharmaceutical

Plastic Containers & Bottles
Address: Plots 8 & 10, Lateef Jakande Rd, Agidingbi, Lagos
Tel: (01) 4921965
Contact: Mr. Lai Opayemi - Chairman/CEO

PHARMA-DEKO PLC
Business: Production and Marketing of Pharmaceutical and Consumer Products
Address: Plot C 15/3, Agbara Industrial Estate, Km. 32, Lagos-Badagry Expressway, Agbara, Ogun State
Tel: (01) 5559852, 712396, 712446
Fax: (01) 5559852, 2882014
E-mail: pharmadeko_agbara@yahoo.com
Website: www.pharmdekoplc.com
Contact: Mr. Folarin R. A Williams, Jnr - Chairman
Mr. Steve U. Osai - MD/CEO

PHARMAPLASTIC (NIGERIA) LIMITED
Business: Manufacturing of Plastic Packaging Products, Import of Pharmaceuticals and Industrial Machines
Address: 35, Mobolaji Johnson Avenue, Oregun Industrial Estate, Oregun, Lagos
Tel: (01) 4973717-8 (2L) **Fax:** (01) 4960852
* Km. 14, Abeokuta Expressway, First Bridge, Dopemu, Agege, Lagos
Tel: (01) 4922165
Contact: Mr. M. G. Nayak - MD/CEO

PHARMASERVE NIGERIA LIMITED
Business: Marketing of Pharmaceuticals & First-Aids Kits
Address: 71, Akpakpava Street, Benin City
Tel: (052) 252593
Contact: Mr. L. C. Kikanme - Chairman/CEO

PHARM-RITE NIGERIA LIMITED
Business: Sales of Pharmaceuticals, Surgicals, Industrial Chemicals, Hospital & Scientific Products
Address: Suite 6, New Look Plaza, 511 Road, Festac Town, Lagos
Tel: (01) 882776, 08023007625
E-mail: bazim_2000@yahoo.com
Contact: Mr. Charles B. Okei - Chairman/CEO

PHILIP TRIMNELL PRODUCTIONS LIMITED
Business: Industrial and Commercial Photography, Colour Separation, Television & Radio Commercials and Documentaries, Design and Printing
Address: 18, Hamed Jimoh close, off Ekolulu Street, off Itire Road, Lagos
Tel: (01) 5850797, 7754064, 08023125861, 08033055246
Contact: Mr. Philip Trimnell - MD/CEO

PHILLIPS CONSULTING LIMITED
Business: Business Consultancy Services (Strategy & Research, Change Management, Corporate Finanace, Information Systems & Security, E-Commerce, Recuitment Support, Human Capital Development, Training & Organisational Dev.)
Address: UBA House (4th floor), 57, Marina, Lagos
Tel: (01) 2665469, 2665263, 2643111 **Fax:** (01) 2665325
E-mail: info@phillipsconsulting.net
Website: www.phillipsconsulting.net
Contact: Mr. Foluso Phillips - Chairman/CEO

PHILLIPS OIL COMPANY (NIGERIA) LIMITED
Business: Exploration & Production of Oil and Gas
Address: IBTC Place, Walter Carrington Crescent, Victoria Island, Lagos
Tel: (01) 2615656, 2615667, 2622060
Fax: (01) 2615663, 2610064
Contact: Mr. Robert Smith - MD/CEO

PHILPET VENTURES LIMITED
Business: Sales and Service of Honda Motorcycles & Generators; Transportation
Address: Shop 8, Eleganza Shopping Arcade, Mobolaji Johnson Avenue, Oregun Industrial Estate, Lagos
Tel: (01) 4701764, 4708103, 5557562, 08022230341, 08023144070, 08033339704
Contact: Mr. Peter A. Obiagwu - Chairman/CEO

PHOENIX ENGINEERING & CONTRACTOR LIMITED
Business: Building , Civil, Electrical & Meechanical Engineering, Fabrication, Water Reticulation
Address: 53, Airport Road, Sabon Gari, Kano
Tel: (064) 636606, 08036665639 **Fax:** (064) 645248
Contact: Chief Sony Aloba - Chairman/CEO

PHOENIX OF NIGERIA ASSURANCE PLC
Business: Non-Life Insurance Business
Address: Phoenix Hous, Plot 26E, Abdulrahman Okene Close, off Ligali Ayorinde St, adj to Amazing Grace Plaza, Maroko Sandfill, Victorial Island, Lagos
Tel: (01) 2622106, 4701820, 7749277, 7749250
Fax: (01) 2622109
E-mail: phoenixassc@alpha.linkserve.com
Website: www.phoenixassuranceplc.com
Contact: Mr. L. O. Akamiohkhor - MD/CEO
Mr. E. O. Thomas - Head (Marketing)

PHOENIX OIL COMPANY (NIGERIA) LIMITED
Business: Exploration and Production of Oil & Gas
Address: Plot 293, Akin-Olugbade St, Victoria Island, Lagos
Tel: (01) 2618209, 2622885, 615801 **Fax:** (01) 618366
E-mail: phoenixoil@pop.metrong.com
Contact: Chief Ahmed A.Onibudo - Chairman

PHONES 'R' US NIGERIA LIMITED
Business: Sales & Repairs of Cellular Phones & Accessories
Address: Mr. Biggs' Building, 84, Ozumba Mbadiwe Street, Victoria Island, Lagos
Tel: (01) 2617261; *Abuja (090) 8044007
* Plot 219, Aba Road, Port Harcourt
Contact: Mr. Chinedu Nwokolo - MD/CEO

PHONEXPRESS DIGITAL WORLD
Business: Sales of GSM Phones & Lines, Operations of Pre-Paid International Call Cards
Address: The Phonexpress Place, 31, Saka Tinubu Street, Victoria Island, Lagos
Tel: (01) 2700164, 4618665, 08032030513-21 (9L)
Fax: (01) 4618666
Contact: Engr. O. Okunoren - MD/CEO

PHONICS HEARING CENTRE
Business: Diagnosis of Hearing Ailment, Manufacturing, Sales and Maintenance of Hearing Aids

Address: 286A,Corporation Drive,Dolphin Estate, Ikoyi, Lagos
Tel: (01) 2693339, 2693409, 7746999 **Fax:** (01) 2694041
E-mail: phonicshc@aol.com
* Investment House, 16C, Murtala Mohammed Way, by Daula Hotel Roundabout, Kano
Tel: (064) 646431, 08042116404
Contact: Mr. J. O. Olusanya - MD/CEO

PHOTO 2000 LIMITED
Business: Photographic Laboratory Processing & Development Services
Address: 11, Kofar Mazugal Rd, Gwammaja, IBB Way, Kano
Tel: (064) 639411, 644532 Fax: (064) 648131
* 4, Shendam Street, opp. Popular Club, Jos
Tel: (073) 451325
Contact: Mr. Kehinde Showole - MD/CEO

PHOTO PALACE LIMITED
Business: Photography Consultancy, Sales of Photgraphic Materials, Development and Printing of Photographic Films, Commercial Photography
Address: Adebola House, 40, Opebi Road, Ikeja, Lagos
Tel: (01) 4976600-9 (10L) **Fax:** (01) 4930890
E-mail: ess-ayholdings@cyberspace.net.ng
* 76, Ikwerre Road, Port Harcourt.
Tel: (084) 234403
*Plot 2388, H Macaulay Way, Wuse Zone 5, Abuja.
Tel: (09) 5235456
Contact: Alh. (Dr.) S. A. Adegunwa - Chairman

PI NIGERIA LIMITED
Business: Sales & Support of Softwaare, Manufacturer's Representative, Software Development, Sales & Support of Hardware, Networking
Address: 66B, Coker Road, Ilupeju, Lagos
Tel: (01) 7748385, 4704165 08033061326
E-mail: pikay@infoweb.abs.net
Contact: Mr. Kayode Onamusi - Chairman/CEO

PICCADILLY INSURANCE COMPANY LIMITED
Business: General (Non-Life) Insurance Business
Address: Great Nigeria House (9th Floor), 47/57, Martins Street, Marina, Lagos
Tel: (01) 2667552, 2662749, 2642686 **Fax:** (01) 2667552
Contact: Mr. Emmanuel Olatunji - MD/CEO

PICCOLO BRUNELLI ENGINEERING LIMITED
Business: Construction, Civil & Water Engineering, Production of Crushed Stone Aggregates & Asphalt
Address: 9A, Dakar Road, off Oduduwa Street, off Marine Road, Apapa G.R.A., Lagos
Tel: (01) 5872844 Fax: (01) 5871222
Contact: Chief (Dr) Engr. Mocenni M. Alessandro - ED

PIEDMONT PLYWOOD NIGERIA LIMITED
Business: Production of Plywood, Particle Boards and Furniture Components
Address: Ologbo Village, Km. 33, Sapele Road, Benin-City
Tel: (052) 251746, 256805
* 10/12, Abebe Village Road, Iganmu Industrial Road, Iganmu, Lagos
Tel: (01) 5852040 **Fax:** (01) 5852039
Contact: Mr. O. O. Uzzi - ED

PILOT FINANCE LIMITED
Business: Stockbroking, Corporate Finance, Bureau De Change, Travels
Address: Elephant Cement House (1st Floor, Wing E), Ikeja Central Business District, Alausa, Ikeja, Lagos
Tel: (01) 5557934, 7731014 **Fax:** (01) 4970329, 4970330
* Suite SB. 8, Cultural Centre, Area 7, Garki, Abuja
Tel: (09) 2347853
Contact: Mr. M. B. Adeisa - MD/CEO

PILROADS NIGERIA LIMITED
Business: Processing & Export of Crumb Rubber, Wood Processing, Agriculture
Address: 1, Okorotun Avenue, GRA., Benin-City
Tel: (052) 250154, 250340
Contact: Major Gen. P. I. Ademokhai (Rtd) - ED

PILSU NIGERIA LIMITED
Business: Production of Mosquito Coils and Matches
Address: Plot 19, Sharada Industrial Estate Phase III, Kano
Tel: (064) 336090, 631255, 08033890909
Contact: Mr. Sudhir Pilani - MD/CEO

PIMA SYSTEMS LIMITED
Business: Internet Service Provider
Address: Eleganza Biro Plaza (5th Floor, Suite 5), Plot 634, Adeyemo Alakija Street, Victoria Island, Lagos
Tel: (01) 5558334-5 (2L), 5558570-1 (2L), 08033134082

PINABON INDUSTRIES LIMITED
Business: Importation and Distribution of Automobile Spare Parts, Manufacturing of Brake Pads & Linings
Address: 12, Burma Road, Apapa, Lagos
Tel: (01) 5872725, 5876536 **Fax:** (01) 5870908
E-mail: pinabon@hyperia.com
* Plots 1/3, Dupe Otegbola Way, Satellite Town, Lagos.
Tel: (01) 5890021, 5872137
Contact: Mr. C. I. Ukachukwu - Chairman/CEO

PINCONSULT ASSOCIATES
Business: Civil and Structural Engineering, Industrial Project Management and Development Consultancy
Address: 33, Berkley Street, Onikan, Lagos
Tel: (01) 2633404, 2632839 **Fax:** (01) 2632839
Contact: Engr. A. B. Pinheiro - Principal Partner
Engr. A. A. Okebunkunola - Managing Partner

PINECREST SERVICES (NIGERIA) LIMITED
Business: Procurement and Installation Security & Fire-Protection Equipment, Oilfield Equipment and Parts
Address: East Pavillion (1st Floor, Suite 17B-19B), Tafawa Balewa Square Complex, Race Course, Lagos
Tel: (01) 2632589 **Fax:** (01) 2645742
E-mail: psnl.hnl@hyperia.com

PINET INFORMATICS LIMITED
Business: Internet Service Provider
Address: Western House (16th Floor), 8/10, Broad Street, Marina, Lagos
Tel: (01) 2645306 **Fax:** (01) 2631868
E-mail: info@pinet.com.ng
Website: www.pinet.com.ng
Contact: Engr. Lanre Ajayi - Chairman/CEO.

PINEWOOD INVESTMENTS LIMITED
Business: Hospitality, Farming & Agricultural Services, Real Estate Development, Telecommunication Services, Catering Services, General Merchandising
Address: 1/6, Umezuruike Close, off Orlu Road, Owerri
Tel: (083) 230135, 230958, 231376, 231411, 231680
Contact: Dr. (Chief) E. M. Umez-Eronimi - Chairman/CEO

PINKY BLUE LIMITED (MotherCare)
Business: Importation & Sales of Babies & Children's Clothings, Maternity Outfits, Toys/Accessories
Address: Elpina Plaza, Plot 642C, Akin Adesola Street, Victoria Island, Lagos
Tel: (01) 3200605, 2663729 **Fax:** (01) 2663729
E-mail: mcare-ng@hyperia.com
* Adebola Shopping Mall (Shop 6), Isaac John Street, G.R.A., Ikeja, Lagos
Tel: (01) 4726409

PINL MARINE & OIL SERVICES LIMITED
(formerly Pipeline Integrity Nig. Ltd)
Business: Inspection, Pipeline Maintenance & Construction, Plant Turn-Around, Corrosion Control /Monitoring, Geophysical & Geotechnical Survey
Address: Safetrust Centre, 18, Keffi Street, S.W. Ikoyi, Lagos
Tel: (01) 2691442-3 (2L), 2694518-9 (2L), 2694342
Fax: (01) 2694258
E-mail: pinloil&marine@pinmarine.com
* 44, King Perekule, GRA Phase 2, Port Harcourt
Tel: (084) 483113, 230685 **Fax:** (084) 230685
E-mail: pipeline@phca.linkserve.com
*2, Zaire Cresc, off Mississippi St, Maitama, Abuja
Tel: (09) 4137099
Contact: Dr. Emmanuel Egbogah - Chairman
Mr. Peter Akpofure - MD

PINNACLE INSURANCE BROKERS LIMITED
Business: Insurance Broking & Risk Managemet Consultancy
Address: Arinkandi House (3rd Floor), 1, Chief Raimi Adetokn Way, off Gbagada General Hospital Road, Gbagada, Lagos
Tel: (01) 4707686, 4803305 **Fax:** (01) 5844636
Contact: Mr. Dennis O. Nnorom - MD/CEO

PIONEER HOTELS LIMITED
Business: Hospitality & Catering Services
Address: Plot 2190, IBB Close, off Ibrahim B. Babangida Way, Wuse Zone 4, Abuja
Tel: (09)5239547-8 (2L), 5238068, 6712466
Fax: (09) 5238068
E-mail: pioneerhotels@hotmail.com
Contact: Mr. Solomon Orji - Chirman/CEO

PIONEER METAL PRODUCTS COMPANY PLC
Business: Manufacture of Galvanised Iron Roofing Sheets
Address: Oba Akran Avenue, Ikeja Industrial Estate, Lagos
Tel: (01) 4977609, 4976960-5 (6 L)
Fax: (01) 4975912, 4976960-1 (2L)
Contact: Mr. Shu Men Ho - Chairman/CEO

PIONEER SPECTRUM MINERALS NIGERIA LIMITED
Business: Mining Consultancy, Procurement of Solid Minerals
Address: 7, Dogon Karfe, Anglo-Jos
Tel/Fax: (073) 460317
E-mail: pioneerspectrum@yahoo.com

PIPC SECURITIES LIMITED
Business: Capital Market Operations and Stockbroking
Address: 39, Murtala Mohammde Way, Jos
Tel: (073) 455967, 455464 **Fax:** (073) 455867
E-mail: psecurities@pipc-nig.com
Website: www.pipc-ng.com
Contact: Mr. Luka C. Pam - MD/CEO

PIPELINES & PRODUCTS MARKETING CO. LTD (PPMC)
Business: Refined Petroleum Products Storage, Distribution and Marketing
Address: NNPC Towers (Block C), Herbert Macaulay Way, Central Business Area, Abuja
Tel: (09) 2348200-17(18L), 2008100-5(6L), 2008371-3(3L)
E-mail: info@ppmc.com.ng
Website: www.ppmc.com.ng
* Plot309, Akin Ogunlewe Street, off Ajose Adeogun Street, Victoria Island, Lagos
*9B, Trans-Amadi Industrial Layout, Port Harcourt
Tel: (084) 2368652, 238723, 238727 **Fax:** (084) 239775

PIVOT ENGINEERING COMPANY LIMITED
Business: Overhead Lines and Power Distribution, General Electrical Installation, Electric Power Generation, Renewable Energy Supply, Plumbing & General Pipe Works, Airconditioning Installaion, Water Suply and Water Treatment, Automatic Fire Detection & Control
Address: Pivot House, 6A, Acme Road, Ogba Industrial Scheme, Ikeja, Lagos
Tel: (01) 4922666, 4922855, 4923452-3 (2L), 4713878-9 (2)
Fax: (01) 4923370, 2616498
E-mail: power@pivoteng.com
Website: www.pivot-engineering.com
Contact: Mr. Dave Obray - MD/CEO

PIVOT TRUST & INVESTMENT COMPANY LIMITED
Business: Stockbroking, Investment/Trade Finance, Leasing
Address: Daily Times Building (1st Floor), 3/7, Kakawa Street, Marina, Lagos
Tel: (01) 2660084, 2663419, 2669234, 08033002855, 08035529349 **Fax:** (01) 2669234
E-mail: pivotrust@hyperia.com
Contact: Chief P. I. P. Onu - Chairman/CEO.

PLANET GRAFFIX (NIGERIA) LIMITED
Business: Colour Digital Separation and Electronic Imaging
Address: 443, Lagos-Badagry Expressway, off Alakija Bus-Stop, opposite Festac 3rd Gate, Lagos
Tel: (01) 4701279, 4748328, 7731899 **Fax:** (01) 2885323
E-mail: planetgraffix@nova.net.ng
* 113, Tafawa Balewa Crescent, off Adeniran Ogunsanya Street, Surulere, Lagos
Tel: (01) 4705902, 5840290 **Fax:** (01) 5890254
E-mail: graffix@planetearthltd.com
Contact: Mr. Simon Uchenunu - Chairman/CEO
Mr Othuke Uchenunu - GM.

PLANET DESIGNS & SIGNS LIMITED
Business: Large Format Printing - Billboards, Wall Drapes,

Vehicle & Bridge Branding, Vinpoles etc
Address: 443, Badagry Expressway(Alakija Bus-Stop), Lagos
Tel: (01) 4701279, 4748328, 7731899 **Fax:** (01) 2885323
E-mail: designs&signs@planetearthltd.com
Contact: Mr Simon Uchenunu - Chairman/CEO.
Mr. Godwin I. Ojukwu - Marketing Manager

PLANET PRESS LIMITED
Business: Direct Imaging Printing Services - Calenders, Annual Reports, Magazines, Brouchures, Books...
Address: 443, Badagry Expressway(Alakija Bus-Stop), Lagos
Tel: (01) 4701279, 4748328, 7731899 **Fax:** (01) 2885323
E-mail: press@planetearthltd.com
Contact: Mr Simon Uchenunu - Chairman/CEO
Mr. Godwin I. Ojukwu - Marketing Manager

PLANET SPORTS LIMITED
Business: Marketing of Sports Wears and Equipment
Address: 29, Commercial Avenue, Sabo-Yaba, Lagos
Tel: (01) 4702900, 863700 **Fax:** (01) 863700
E-mail: planetsports@popmetrong.com
Contact: Mr. Charles Attah - Chairman/CEO.

PLANTGERIA COMPANY LIMITED
Business: Engineeering; Sales, Installation and Maintenance of Pumps; Electrification
Address: Plot 278, Trans-Amadi Ind. Layout, Port Harcourt
Tel: (084) 233285, 236856 **Fax:** (084) 236778
E-mail: plantnigeria@phca.linkserve.com
* 4, Hinderer Road, off Oduduwa Road, G.R.A., Apapa, Lagos
Tel: (01) 2645201, 2634284, 7740143 **Fax:** (01) 5453214
E-mail: comet@micro.com.ng
Contact: Barr. Musa Danjuma - Chairman
Mr. P. L. Carrodano - MD/CEO

PLASCO SHEETS (NIGERIA) LIMITED
Business: Manufacture of PVC Leather Cloth, Plastic Sheetings and Films
Address: 18/24, Ajisegiri Street, off Agege Motor Road, Ladipo Bus-Stop, Shogunle, Lagos
Tel: (01) 4934114, 4933901
Fax: (01) 4934114
Contact: Mr. John Obichie - Dep. MD.

PLASTIC CONTAINERS & CHEMICAL SPECIALITIES LTD
Business: Production of Plastic Caps and Bottles, Construction and Repairs of Moulds, Refurbishment of Plastic-Making Machines
Address: 1, Femi Daramola Street, off Odo-Olowu Street, Ijeshatedo, Lagos
Tel: (01) 5870923 **Fax:** (01) 5870918
E-mail: passos@alpha.linkserve.com
Website: www.angel.com
www.pccsl.com
Contact: Mr. A. C. Zervous - MD/CEO.

PLASTIC PACKAGING INDUSTRIES LIMITED
Business: Manufacturing of Plastic Containers
Address: 7, Modupe Olajumoke Street, off Obafemi Awolowo Way, Ikeja, Lagos
Tel: (01) 4964738, 4960354
Fax: (01) 4970232, 4970233

PLATEAU BOTTLING COMPANY LIMITED
Business: Manufacture of Quix Soft Drinks
Address: 41/46, Liberty Boulevard, Zaravon Village, Jos
Tel: (073) 457097

PLATEAU INVESTMENT & PROPERTY DEVELOPMENT COMPANY LIMITED
Business: Investment Promotion, Development Finance Institution
Address: Murtala House, 37, Murtala Mohammed Way, Jos
Tel: (073) 454575, 454083, 457834 **Fax:** (073) 455297
E-mail: info@pipc-ng.com
Website: ww.pipc-ng.com

PLATEAU MINERALS DEVELOPMENT COMPANY LIMITED
Business: Mining, Processing of Solid Minerals, Consultancy
Address: Sarahim Plaza, Constitution Hill Road, Jos
Tel: (073) 460667

PLATEAU PUBLISHING COMPANY LIMITED
Business: Publishing
Address: 5, Joseph Gomwalk Road, Jos
Tel: (073) 455410, 454329

PLATEAU STATE TOURISM CORPORATION
Business: Marketing and Promotion of Tourism
Address: 31, Yakubu Gowon Way, Jos
Tel: (073) 465747 **Fax:** (073) 460445
E-mail: plagov@infoweb.abs.net.

PLATINUM BANK LIMITED
Business: Commercial Banking
Address: 5 (Plot 707), Adeola Hopewell Street, Victoria Island, Lagos
Tel: (01) 2621795-7 (3 L), 2613118
Website: www.platinumbanklimited.com
Contact: Prof. Pat Utomi - Chairman
Mr. Francis Atuche - MD/CEO

PLATINUM CAPITAL LIMITED
Business Financial & Invstment Services
Address: Plot 1399, Tiamiyu Savage St, Victoria Island, Lagos
Tel: (01) 2703332

PLATINUM PHARMACEUTICALS LIMITED
Business: Manufacture of Pharmaceuticals
Address: Plot PC. 30, Afribank Street, Victoria Island, Lagos
Tel: (01) 2620532, 2620534 **Fax:** (01) 2620420
Contact: Dr. C. R. Mohapatra - GM./CEO

PLATINUM TRAVEL LIMITED
Business: Travel Agency
Address: Churchgate Towers, Plot PC. 30, Afribank Street, Victoria Island, Lagos
Tel: (01) 2620550 **Fax:** (01) 2620420
E-mail: platinumtravel@churchgate.com
Contact: Mr. B. Mahtani - Chairman

PLESSEY NIGERIA LIMITED
Business: Engineering Construction
Address: Eleganza Biro Plaza (9th Floor), Plot 634, Adeyemo Alakija Street, Victoria Island, Lagos
Tel: (01) 2703640

PLUM INSURANCE BROKERS LIMITED
Business: Insurance Broking
Address: 169, Igbosere Road, Lagos Island, Lagos
Tel: (01) 2646262, 2602221 **Fax:** (01) 2602221
E-mail: plum@infoweb.abs.net

PM + CDC ASSOCIATES
Business: Architecture, Turn-Key Projects, Construction, Interior Decoration, Property Development
Address: GT House (1st Floor), 3/5, Boyle St, Onikan, Lagos
Tel: (01) 2630236, 8044613, 08033286661, 08033456670
Fax: (01) 2630236
E-mail: pmcdc@nova.net.ng
Website: www.pmcdc.com
Contact: Mr. Nelson Okuonghae -Managing Architect

PMI DIRECT LIMITED
Business: Integrated & Direct Marketing Communications
Address: 13, Jaiyeola Ajatta Street, off M/M International Road, Ajao Estate, Isolo, Lagos
Tel: (01) 4527164, 4528375, 08023092943
Fax: (01) 4528375
E-mail: contactus@pmi.com
Website: www.pmi.com
Contact: Mr. Chris I. Ogbechie - Chairman/CEO.

PODA PAINTS NIGERIA LIMITED
Business: Manufacturing and Marketing of Paints
Address: Plots 7-9, Isheri Olowora Road, Berger Area, Lagos
Tel/Fax: (01) 7747251
Contact: Engr. Osa Aibangbee - MD/CEO.

POINTVIEW TRAVELS & TOURS LIMITED
Business: Travel & Tour Agency
Address: 7, Sapara Williams Close, off Idowu Martins Street, Victoria Island, Lagos
Tel: (01) 2616588, 2621002, 2623296, 2629028, 7752313, 7764494 **Fax:** (01) 2621002
E-mail: pointviw98@yahoo.com
Contact: Mrs. Raji Bhasin - MD/CEO

POISE NIGERIA LIMITED
Business: Business-Image Consultancy Services & Training
Address: 59C, Adekunle Fajuyi Way, Ikeja G.R.A., Lagos
Tel: (01) 4974505, 7919431, 08023119769, 08023209374
E-mail: poise-tfs@yahoo.com
Contact: Mavi Isibor - Programme Director

POKO OIL MILLS (WEST AFRICA) LIMITED
Business: Production of Palm Oil, Palm Kernel Cake and Vegetable Oil
Address: Plot P1, Pokobros Avenue, off Atani Road, Harbour Industrial Layout, Onitsha
Tel: (046) 210800, 210303 * (048) 886695, 888171, 888555, 08023250112
Fax: (046) 210303 * (048) 888171
E-mail: pokobros@infoweb.abs.net
Contact: Chief (Dr.) P. A. Okonkwo - Chairman/CEO.

POKOBROS GROUP (W.A) LIMITED
Business: Manufacturing, Importers & Exporters, General Merchandising, Farming, Marketing of Petroleum Products, Agro-Allied Processing, Production of Lubricants, Transportation
Address: Plot P1, Pokobros Avenue, off Atani Road, Harbour Industrial Layout, Onitsha
Tel: (046) 210800, 210303, 216022
(048) 886695, 888171, 888555
08023250112, 08023277886, 08033230191
Fax: (046) 210303 * (048) 888171
E-mail: pokobros@infoweb.abs.net
* 30, Creek Road, Fegge, Onitsha, Lagos
Tel: ((046) 210800, 210303, 216022
(048) 886695, 888171, 888555
Contact: Chief (Dr.) P. A. Okonkwo - Chairman/CEO.

POKOBROS FOOD & CHEMICAL INDUSTRIES LIMITED
Business: Flour Milling, Production of Livestock Feeds
Address: Plot P1, Pokobros Avenue, off Atani Road, Harbour Industrial Layout, Onitsha
Tel: (046) 210800, 210303, 216022
(048) 886695, 888171, 888555, 08023277886
Fax: (046) 210303 * (048) 888171
E-mail: pokobros@infoweb.abs.net
Contact: Chief (Dr.) P. A. Okonkwo - Chairman/CEO.

POLAR PHOTOGRAPHIC & COMMUNICATIONS LIMITED
Business: Sales of Photographic Equipment and Materials
Address: 38, Concord Way, Ikeja, Lagos
Tel: (01) 4725237, 4725239, 4616374 **Fax:** (01) 4619155
E-mail: rcn.ng@hyperia.com

POLARIS DISTRIBUTION (NIGERIA) LIMITED
Business: Distribution of Information Technology Products
Address: Consortium House (9th Floor), Plot 1682, Sanusi Fafunwa Street, Victoria Island, Lagos
Tel: (01) 2612702, 616275 **Fax:** (01) 2615024
E-mail: polarisnig@hyperia.com
Contact: Jean Michel Kaikati - Director/CEO

POLFA NIGERIA PLC
Business: Manufacture of Pharmaceutical Drugs; Importation and Marketing of Veterinary Instruments, Medical Equipment, Pharmaceutical Drugs, Industrial & Pharmaceutical Chemicals
Address: Block M, Plot 9, Mushin Road, Isolo, Lagos
Tel: (01) 523730, 521227, 523521, 522368
Fax: (01) 524651
* 18E, Bello Road, Kano
* 135, Aba-Owerri Road, Aba
Contact: Mr. E. Korzeniewicz - MD/CEO

POLLS & RATINGS LIMITED
Business: Opinion & Marketing Research, Monitoring, Human Resources Consultancy
Address: NICON House (5th Floor), 5, Customs St, Lagos
Tel/Fax: (01) 2664787, 2668966, 08023324290
E-mail: prlresearch@consultant.com
Website: www.prlresearch.com
Contact: Mr. Roland Arabome - MD/CEO

POLMAZ LIMITED
Business: Engineering & Marine Services, Pipeline Corrosion Management, Procurement of Tools & Supplies
Address: Okoi Arikpo House (2nd Floor), 5, Idowu Taylor Street, Victoria Island, Lagos

Tel: (01) 2626327-9 (3L), 2703486-7 (2L)
E-mail: info@polmaz.com
Website: www.polmaz.com
Contact: Mr. T. R. K. Omatseye - MD/CEO

POLO LIMITED
Business: Sales & Service of Wrist-Watches, Sales of Gift Items
Address: Polo Towers, 166, Ozumba Mbadiwe Street, Victoria Island, Lagos
Tel: (01) 2621193, 2621189, 2621186, 7741012, 7733543
Fax: (01) 2621191
E-mail: info@pololuxe.com
* NICON Hilton House, Maitama District, Abuja
Tel: (09) 4139294, 4139295 **Fax:** (09) 4139295
Contact: Mr. John O. Obayuwana - Chairman/CEO

POLO SACKS LIMITED
Business: Manufacturing and Marketing of Poly Sacks and Bags, PVC Pipes and Building Materials
Address: RIVOC Rd, Trans-Amadi Ind.Layout, Port Harcourt
Tel: (084) 237607, 232614, 235075 **Fax:** (084) 237608
E-mail: cico@phca.linkserve.com
Contact: Mr. R Chu - MD/CEO

POLY PRODUCTS NIGERIA PLC
Business: Manufacture of Polythene Packaging Materials
Address: Poly House, Plot C, Block 10, Ilupeju Industrial Scheme, State Highway, Ilupeju, Lagos
Tel: (01) 4974583, 4963321, 4975597
Fax: (01) 2613195, 4978551
Contact: Dr. Rupchand I. Bhowani - Vice Chairman/CEO

POLYBAGS INDUSTRIES (NIGERIA) LIMITED
Business: Manufacture of Polyethlene Twines and Ropes, Polypropylene Strapping, Storage Tanks and Pure-Water Rolls, Mattress Edging Tapes, Candle Wicks & Soft Luggage Tapes, Impportters of Plastic Machinery, Flexo Printers, Industrial Raw Materials
Address: Plot 3K, Oshodi Industrial Scheme, Aswani Market Road, off Oshodi-Apapa Expressway, Isolo, Lagos
Tel: (01) 4527167-8 (2L), 2620868, 7762789, 7917511
Fax: (01) 2620868
E-mail: polybaglagos@hotmail.com
Contact: Dr. J. P. Ahuja - MD/CEO

POLYTHENE ENTERPRISES (NIGERIA) LIMITED
Business: Manufacture of Corrugated Paper Cartons, Boxes, Paper Tubes and Bobbins
Address: 4, Obasa Road, off Oba Akran Avenue, Ikeja Industrial Estate, Ikeja, Lagos
Tel: (01) 4961221, 4973420, 7736171 **Fax:** (01) 4967741
Contact: Mr. Robert D' Almeida - GM/CEO

PONTICELLI LIMITED
Business: Oilfield Engineering Services
Address: Plot 100, Rivoc Road, Trans-Amadi Industrial Layout, Port Harcourt
Tel: (084) 236310-23 (14th) (Ext. 3968)
Website: www.ponticellinigeria.com
Contact: Mr. J. Pascal - MD/CEO

POPHAM WALTER ODUSOTE LIMITED
Business: Architecture, Engineering, Project Management
Address: International Plaza (5th Floor), Plot 999C, Danmole Street, Victoria Island, Lagos
Tel: (01) 2623004, 2623012 **Fax:** (01) 2622986
E-mail: pwo@pwoarch.com
Contact: Arc. Okunola Odusote - MD/CEO

POPULARGATES OVERSEAS LIMITED
Business: Contracts, Procurement and Supplies
Address: 32, Bankole Street, Apongbon, Lagos
Tel: 08033033622 **Fax:** (01) 4978139
E-mail: populargatesoverseas@yahoo.com
* 6B, Odanye Close, off Adeniyi Jones Avenue, Ikeja, Lagos
Contact: Bob Okoroji Esq - Director

PORCHESTER INVESTMENTS NIGERIA LIMITED
Business: Distribution and Sales of Fitness Equipment, Office Executive Chairs, Herbal Products, Building of Gyms
Address: 143A, Gbagada Expressway, Anthony, Lagos
Tel: (01) 7745617, 8042975 **Fax:** (01) 2641166, 8047974
E-mail: porchesterafrica@yahoo.com
* Plot 1267, Buchanan Crescent, off Aminu Kano Crescent, Wuse II, Abuja.
Tel: (09) 4134318-9 (2L) **Fax:** (09) 4134319
Contact: Dr. Ola Rahman - Chairman/CEO

PORT HARCOURT FLOUR MILLS LIMITED
Business: Production of Flour and Livestock Feeds
Address: 7/9, Industry Rd/Alfred Diete-Spiff Rd, P/ Harcourt
Tel: (084) 237080-3 (4L), 233853 **Fax:** (084) 239281

PORT HARCOURT INTERNATIONAL AIRPORT HOTEL
Business: Hospitality Services
Address: Airport Road, Omagwa, Rivers State.
Tel: (084) 238036, 238039 **Fax:** (084) 238040

PORT HARCOURT REFINING COMPANY LIMITED
Business: Refining of Crude Petroleum
Address: Alesa-Eleme, Port Harcourt
Tel: (084) 235585, 236420-39(20L) **Fax:** (084) 236431
E-mail: phrc@phca.linkserve.com
* 13, Oju-Olubon Close, off Bishop Oluwole Street, Victoria Island, Lagos
Tel: (01) 614702, 614840, 4702637

PORT HARCOURT SACKS LIMITED
Business: Manufacturing of Polypropylene Woven Sacks
Address: Rumuolumeni, P.M.B. 5006, Port Harcourt
Tel: (084) 231509, 232322, 232923, 236927, 237201, 239190, 239334 **Fax:** (084) 239334
Website: www.eaglecement.com
Contact: Mr. Vincent Nehikhare - MD/CEO

PORTABLE ENGINEERING SERVICES LIMITED
Business: Computer Engineering Services, Networking, System Integration and Maintenance
Address: Plot 1686B, Oladele Olashore St, Victoria Island, Lagos
Tel: (01) 3201155-6 (2L), 7732915 **Fax:** (01) 3201149
E-mail: omatek@infoweb.abs.net
omatek@hyperia.com
* Plot 1087, Kolda Link Street, off Adetokunbo Ademola Crescent, Wuse II, Abuja
Tel: (09) 5235671, 5237300

E-mail: omatekabj@linkserve.com
Contact: Mrs. F. Seriki - MD/CEO

PORT-A-COOL NIGERIA LIMITED
Business: Sales of Ventilation and Cooling Equipment
Address: Cleanjohn HouseAnnex, 90,Ladipo St, Matori, Lagos
Tel: (01) 4523467, 4528407, 4523386, 4525339, 4522186
Fax: (01) 4523098
Contact: Mr. Okwudili Onwudi - Business Manager

PORTCULLIS SECURITY (NIGERIA) LIMITED
Business: Security Guard Services, Sale and Installation of Security Equipment
Address: 159, Igbosere Road, Lagos Island, Lagos
Tel/Fax: (01) 2645610
Contact: Chief (Capt.) A.A. Lisk-Carew (rtd) - Chairman/CEO

PORTLAND ELECTRICAL REPAIRS LIMITED
Business: Repair and Services of Transformers and Mechanical Motors, Airconditioners, Compressors and Electric Alternators
Address: Elephant Cement House, ASSBIFI Road, Central Business District, Alausa, Ikeja, Lagos
Tel: (01) 4986060, 4968061, 7745088-9 **Fax:** (01) 4970704
* 8, Bank Road, Kaduna.
Tel: (062) 213633, 214702
Contact: Engr. Joseph O. Makoju - Chairman
Engr. Emmanuel A. Aduwo - GM/CEO

PORTLAND PAINTS & PRODUCTS NIGERIA LIMITED
Business: Manufacturing of Decorative Paints and Building Finishes, Merchandising of Sanitaryware Equipment/Fittings, Marine Paints and Chemicals, General Building Renovations
Address: Elepahnt Cement House (4th Floor), ASSBIFI Rd, Central Business District, Alausa, Ikeja, Lagos
Tel: (01) 4968181-4 (4 L), 7740413 **Fax:** (01) 4968180
* Shop 23, Wuse Shopping Centre, Maputo Street, Wuse Zone 3, Abuja.
Tel: (09) 5232600
* Opp. Bishop Philips Academy, Iwo Road, Ibadan
Tel: (02) 716542
* 5, Azikiwe Rd, by Leventis Stores, Port Harcourt
Contact: Mr. T. O. Agboola - Chairman
Mr. Yemi Ajayi - Dep. GM.

PORTLAND RENOVATIONS & CONSTRUCTION LIMITED
Business: Building Construction, General Renovations, Maintenance Contracts, Plumbing and Electrical Installations, Interior Decoration
Address: Elephant Cement House (Ground Floor) ASSBIFI Road, Central Business District, Alausa, Ikeja, Lagos
Tel: (01) 4968181-4 (4 L), 7740413, 7745466, 8045551
Fax: (01) 4968180
Contact: Mr. Bayo Osibo - GM/CEO

POS SHOP LIMITED
Business: Provision of Point-of Sales Solutions
Address: 31, Opebi Road (1st Floor), Ikeja, Lagos
Tel: (01) 4727946, 7755663, 08033040576
Fax: (01) 3450577
E-mail: info@pos-shop.com
Contact: Revd. Yinka Akinlade - MD/CEO

POSH INTERNATIONAL COMPANY LIMITED
Business: Importation and Marketing of Bathroom Technologies and Hair-Drying Equipment
Address: Plot 51B, Akanbi Onitiri Close, off Eric Moore Road, Iganmu Industrial Estate, Surulere, Lagos
Tel: (01) 7743533, 5833962, 836307 **Fax:** (01) 5831294
E-mail: posh@micro.com.ng
posh@hyperia.com

POSTAL LIFE & GENERAL INSURANCE COMPANY LTD
Business: Insurance Business (Life & Non-Life)
Address: 142, Awolowo Road, S. W. Ikoyi, Lagos
Tel: (01) 3200176, 4706280, 2692510, 2696070
Contact: Mr. D. O. Balogun - MD/CEO

POTOMAC COMPUTERS LIMITED
Business: Software Development, Sales, Maintenance and Services of Computer Hardware & Accessories, Training, Consultancy
Address: 28, Ogunlana Drive Surulere, Lagos
Tel: (01) 5850870, 5850963, 08023037633, 08033267070
Fax: (01) 5850963
E-mail: potocom2000@yahoo.com
Contact: Isidore N. Alilonu - MD

POULTRY EQUIPMENT FACCO (WEST AFRICA) LIMITED
Business: Sales and Installation of Poultry Cages, Feed-Mill Plants, Storage Silos and Flour-Milling Equipment
Address: Km. 29, Abeokuta Expressway, opp. Lagos State Low-Cost Housing Estate, Ojokoro, Lagos
Tel: (01) 4925720, 4962708, 4967408, 7739619, 7922979, 4718656, 08033589788
Fax: (01) 4936875
E-mail: facco@cybaaspace.net.ng
Contact: Mr. L. B. Adelayo - Chairman/CEO

POWER CONTROL & APPLIANCES LIMITED
Business: Sales of Electricity Distribution & Control Equipment
Address: Plot 1038, Ologun Agbaje Street, off Adeola Odeku Street, Victoria Island, Lagos
Tel: (01) 616298, 619349, 619149, 2627818, 2627897, 08023222789
* 4/6, Happy Home Avenue, Kirikiri Industrial Area, Apapa, Lagos
Tel: (01) 7730529, 7740633, 7752323, 7752424, 7755060
Fax: (01) 5878251

POWER ENERGY (NIGERIA) LIMITED
Business: Oilfield Engineering Services
Address: Fortune Towers (10th Floor), 27/29, Adeyemo Alakija Street, Victoria Island, Lagos
Tel: (01) 2610355, 2612490 Fax: (01) 2613221

POWER GAS ENERGY RESOURCES LIMITED
Business: Energy Engineering Services,Total Energy Solution (Power Plants, Waste Heat Recovery, Supply of Power/Energy), Sales of Generators (Gas/Diesel)
Address: Lennards Compound, Km. 16, Ikorodu Road, Ojota, Lagos
Tel: (01) 7755714, 7131245, 4974609, 4974655, 3205312
E-mail: powergas@beta.linkserve.com
pks@gentec-powergas.com
Contact: Mr. A. Prakash - Project/Worshop Manager

POWERSEAL NIGERIA LIMITED
Business: Manufacturing and Marketing of Paints
Address: 4, Sultan Road, Mallali G.R.A., Kaduna
Tel: (962) 242943, 377003
Contact: Engr. Ibrahim Usman - MD/CEO

POWER SYSTEMS TECHNOLOGY LIMITED
Business: Sales of UPS Power-Control Systems and Computer, Power Engineering and Consultancy Services
Address: 91, Bode Thomas Street, Surulere, Lagos
Tel: (01) 5456212, 7748413, 08033275831
E-mail: powersystems@micro.com.ng
powersystems@hyperia.com

POWERLINE ENGINEERING SERVICES LIMITED
Business: Sales, Repairs & Maintenance of Computers, UPS Stabilizers, Generators, Telecommunication & Industrial Control Equipment, Structured Cabling & Provision of Power Points
Address: Plot 279, Oshodi-Gbagada Expressway (1st Pedro Bus-Stop), Gbagada Phase 1, Gbagada, Lagos
Tel: (01) 5552668, 7742608, 7769570, 08022242594
Fax: (01) 5552668
E-mail: pes@linkserve.com.ng
: sales@powerlineengineering.com
Website: www.powerlineengineering.com
Contact: Mr. Femi Adebayo Davies - Chairman/CEO
Mr. Onyeka Ifeonye - Bus.Dev. Manager

POWERSTEIN LIMITED
Business: Engineering and Construction Services
Address: 32, Ire-Akari Estate Road, Isolo, Lagos
Tel: (01) 4529212, 08033333578, 08037206395
E-mail: pstein@infoweb.abs.net
Contact: Engr. (Chief) Chuba Mbakwe - Chairman/CEO

POWERTRON (NIGERIA) LIMITED
Business: Engineering Contractors (Electrical, Mechanical and Air Conditioning)
Address: 85, Itire Road, Surulere, Lagos
Tel: (01) 5846480, 5831633 **Fax:** (01) 5831633
E-mail: powertronng@yahoo.com
Contact: Engr. E. N. Chukwuneta - Exec. Director

PPC LIMITED (formerly Philips Projects Centre Ltd)
Business: Turnkey, Hospital and Telecommincation Projects, Contract Management, IT Infrastructure Provision/ Supply & Services Management, Private Telecommunications Operation
Address: 8, Kofo Abayomi Street, Victoria Island, Lagos
Tel: (01) 2620811, 2620632, 2619262, 3200516-7(2L)
Fax: (01) 2620631, 2615143
E-mail: enquiry@philips.com.ng
philips@infoweb.abs.net
* 10, Queen Idah Street, Plot 4, Zone A4, Asokoro District, Abuja
Tel: (09) 3144993 **Fax:** (09) 3145081
* 3 (Plot 349), Benjamin Okpara Close, off Olu Obasanjo Road, G.R.A., Phase II, Port Harcourt
Tel: (084) 236918, 237210 (Ext. 21298)
Fax: (084) 236826, 237210 (Ext. 21299)
Contact: Mr Abiodun Disu - MD/CEO
Mr. Adesoji Momson - DGM (Admin/Corp Affairs)

PPI TECHNOLOGY SERVICES NIGERIA LIMITED
Business: Oilfield Engineering Services & Consultancy
Address: Octagon Building (East Wing, 4th Floor), 13A, A. J, Marinho Drive, Victoria Island, Lagos
Tel: (01) 5558327 Fax: (01) 5558328
E-mail: info@ppitech.net
Website: www.ppitech.net
Contact: Mr. Ahmed Ismail - MD/CEO

PR DISTINCTIONS LIMITED
Business: Public Relations, Events Management
Address: 63, Opebi Road, Ikeja, Lagos
Tel/Fax: (01) 4939038-9 (2 L)
Contact: Capt. Toju Ogisi - Chairman
Mrs. Alero Edu - MD/CEO

PRACAM PRODUCTIONS LIMITED
Business: Outdooor Advertising and Print Production
Address: 94, Palm Avenue, Mushin, Lagos
Tel: (01) 4520170, 7929498 **Fax:** (01) 4522839
E-mail: pracam@cyberspace.net.ng
Contact: Mr. Segun Adeneye - CEO

PRAGMATIC TECHNOLOGIES LIMITED
Business: Banking Technologies Services, Sales and Service of Branded Notebook, Banking Equipment, Office Automation and Consumbles
Address: 4, Obanikoro Street, off Ikorodu Road, via Falemi House, Obanikoro, Lagos
Tel: (01) 4979501, 5550801, 08022252939, 08023153055
Fax: (01) 4979501
E-mail: pragmatic.technologies@usa.net
Contact: Mr. Francis Abiodun Marquis - MD/CEO

PRAKLA GEOMECHANIK INTERNATIONAL LIMITED
Business: Water Engineering, Water Resource Management, Environmental Engineering and Consultancy
Address: 3, Gerrard Road, Ikoyi, Lagos
Tel: (01) 4702430, 2691029
E-mail: pgiltd@alpha.linkserve.com
* 2, Edaiken Avenue, G.R.A., Benin City
Tel: (052) 257327 **Fax:** (052) 257348
* 15, Ogbotobo Crescent, off Nnebisi Road, Asaba

PRECIOUS PALM ROYAL HOTELS LIMITED
Business Hospitality Services
Address: Ugbowo, Lagos-Benin Expressway, Benin-City
Tel: (052) 602074, 602075, 602076, 602077
Fax: (052) 602101
E-mail: preciouspalmroyalhotel@yahoo.com
Website: www.preciouspalmroyalhotel.com
Contact: Barr. Jude Nosagie - Chairman

PRECIOUS SAVINGS & LOANS LIMITED
Business: Mortgage Banking, Property Development
Address: 8, Hospital Road, Port Harcourt
Tel: (084) 488087, 08033091474
Contact: Mr. B. O. Whyte - MD/CEO

PRECISION LOSS ADJUSTERS LIMITED
Business: Insurance Loss Adjusting and Claims Investigations, Marine Cargo Surveying, Recovery Agents
Address: 10, Omilani Street, Ijeshatedo, Surulere, Lagos

Tel: (01) 5841163, 5456450
Contact: Chief Joseph Adebiyi Komolafe - Chairman/CEO

PREFAB NIGERIA LIMITED
Business: Manufacturing of Electricity Poles and Tiles
Address: Sharada Industrial Estate Phase I, Kano
Tel: (064) 667435, 08023369594 Fax: (064) 665185
Contact: Alh. Abusaleh S. A. Dantata - MD/CEO

PREMIER AGRO OILS NIGERIA LIMITED
Business: Production of Vegetable Oil
Address: Plot 5, Olubadan Ind. Estate, New Ife Road, Ibadan
Tel: (02) 8102428

PREMIER BROKERS LIMITED
Business: Insurance Broking, Pensions Consultancy
Address: 13, Ogui Road, Enugu
Tel: (042) 257417
E-mail: pmbrokers@infoweb.abs.net
Contact: Chief Ifeanyi Ugwuanyi - MD/CEO

PREMIER HOTEL, IBADAN
Business: Hospitality and Catering Services
Address: Mokola Hill, off Oyo Road, Oremeji, Ibadan
Tel: (02) 2410117, 2410133, 2414304, 2411234, 2414122
Fax: (02) 2414328, 2414582
E-mail: premierhotel@skannet.com
Contact: Mr. 'Bola Jayeola - MD/CEO

PREMIER PAINTS PLC
Business: Manufacturing of Paints and Wood-finishes
Address: Km. 2, Ifo-Ibogun Road, Ifo, Ogun State
Tel: (01) 8112433, 08023218644 **Fax:** (01) 4528834
* 77, Agege Motor Road, Idioro, Mushin, Lagos
Tel: (01) 4528834, 8119444 **Fax:** (01) 4528834
* 45, Hasa Road, opp Sabon-Gari Market, Kano
Tel: (064) 644779
Contact: Chief A. G. O. Bankole - Chairman/CEO

PREMIER PLANT LEASE NIGERIA LIMITED (PPL)
Business: Transportation of Refined Petroleum Products
Address: Km. 20, Badagry Expressway, Okokomaiko, Lagos
Tel: (01) 7740650
Contact: Mr. Martin I. Ikediashi - Chairman/CEO

PREMIER RECORDS LIMITED
Business: Music Repertoire Management, Development, Marketing and Promotion of Artistes' Musical Works , Video Cassette & Compact Disc
Address: 10, Dupe Otegbola Industrial Way, off Lagos-Badagry Expressway, Satellite Town, Lagos
Tel: (01) 5880453, 5891776, 7741698, 08033067241, 08033084140, 08033323452, 08033323467
E-mail: premermusic@multilinks.com
Contact: Mr. T. A. Ejueyitchie - MD/CEO

PREMIER SEED NIGERIA LIMITED
Business: Prodction of Agricultural Seeds
Address: Chikaji Industrial Estate, Zaria
Tel: (069) 331630, 332791, 334804 **Fax:** (069) 334804
E-mail: premier.sed@skannet.com
* 389, Ikorodu Road, Ojota, Lagos
Tel: (01) 4970009, 4972599

PREMIER STANDARD INDUSTRIAL LIMITED
Business: Manufacturers' Representative of Dental Care Products, Offset & Web-Printing Inks
Address: 117, Ikorodu Road, Igbobi-Fadeyi, Lagos
Tel: (01) 5455177
E-mail: psil@hyperia.com
premier@hyperia.com
Contact: Mr. Idowu Adenuga - Chairman/CEO

PREMIER TIMBER INDUSTRIES (NIGERIA) LIMITED
Business: Wood Processing and Production
Address: Km. 33, Benin-Sapele Road, Ologbo, Edo State
Tel: (052) 251746 **Fax:** (052) 256805
* 10/12, Abebe Village Road, Iganmu Industrial Estate, Surulere, Lagos
Tel: (01) 2694386, 5852040 **Fax:** (01) 5852039
Contact: High Chief Adedapo Adekeye - Chairman
Mr Giuseppe Gardino - MD/CEO

PREMIUM AIR SHUTTLE LIMITED
Business: Airline Services
Address: Plto 305, Jide Oki Street, Victoria Island, Lagos
Tel: (01) 2614212, 2614313 **Fax:** (01) 2623241

PREMIUM FOODS LIMITED
Business: Restaurant Services; Conference Centre
Address: Plot 867A, Bishop Aboyade Cole St, Adetokunbo Ademola Street, Victoria Island, Lagos
Tel: (01) 613499, 2623135

PREMIUM INSURANCE BROKERS LIMITED
Business: Insurance Broking
Address: 229, Warri/Sapele Road, Warri.
Tel: (053) 252867, 08023285094
*Leventis Building, 6, Azikiwe Road, Port Harcourt
Tel: (084) 234940
Contact: Chief Emeka Okeke - Chairman/CEO

PREMIUM SECURITIES LIMITED
Business: Stockbroking, Trade & Project Financing, Issuing House, Financial Advisory Services
Address: 27/29, King George V Road, Onikan, Lagos
Tel: (01) 2633301, 2632285 **Fax:** (01) 2637353
E-mail: premsec@cpaaspace.net
Website: www.fbnmb.com/psl
Contact: Mr. Nick Onuoha-Okoro - MD/CEO

PREQUIP TECHNICAL LIMITED
Business: Manufacturing of Hydraulic & Pneumatic Hose and Fitting Assemblies
Address: 48, Siluko Road, Benin City
Tel/Fax: (052) 255911, 08023428387, 08034734781
*1, Waziri Ibrahim Crescent, Kaduna
Tel: (062) 242134
Contact: Eugene C. Anakwenze - Technical Director/CEO

PRESCO INDUSTRIES PLC
Business: Processing, Production and Marketing of Palm Oil and Allied Products, Cultivation of Palm Tree
Address: Obaretin Estate, off Km. 22, Benin-Sapele Road, Benin City
Tel: (052) 342394-5 (2L), 342410
* COWAN Estate, Ajagbodudu, P. O. Box 4063,

Sapele, Delta State.
Tel: (054) 60036, 60040, 60083
*Plot 227, Musa Yar'Adua St Victoria Island, Lagos
Tel: (01) 2619327, 08033323055 **Fax:** (01) 2618473
E-mail: info@presco.plc.com
presco@alpha.linkserve.com
Website: www.presco-plc.com

PRESIDENT PAINTS NIGERIA LIMITED
Business: Manufacturing of Paints
Address: 1, Ladoje Street, Old Abeokuta Road, Gegento Bus Stop, Agege, Lagos
Tel: (01) 4926625, 7943761, 08023039427, 08033003423, 08033003528, 08033003586
*Km 16, Otta-Idiroko Road, Idedo-Otta, Ogun State
Contact: Mr Tunde Senbanjo - Exec. Chairman

PRESIDENTIAL INSURANCE COMPANY LIMITED
Business: Non-Life Insurace
Address: 6, Raymond Njoku Street, Lagos
Tel: (01) 2691290, 2691468, 2691289, 4820563, 7847325-6 8128991 **Fax:** (01) 2691468
E-mail: pic@infoweb.abs.net
picmd@infoweb.abs.net
* 26, Allen Avenue, Ikeja, Lagos.
Tel: (01) 4972082, 8128830
* Angel Plaza, S. L. Akintola Boulevard, Garki II, Abuja
Tel: (09) 2342707
Contact: Mr. O. O. Ajayi - MD/CEO

PRESSED METAL WORKS COMPANY LIMITED
Business: Manufacture of Steel Structures and Tanks (for Road Transport Systems, Refuse Disposal Systems, Agro-Allied, Chemicals Petro-Chemicals and Water Projects)
Address: 212, Moshood, Abiola Way, Ijora, Lagos
Tel: (01) 5451409, 5451410, 5451411
Fax: (01) 5873496, 2621877
Contact: Chief L. Fiorio - MD/CEO

PREST GROUP LIMITED
Business: Cable & Satellite Television Service, Telecommunications, Hospitality Services, Building & Civil Engineering Services
Address: 57, Airport Road, Benin City
Tel: (052) 450002, 450680
E-mail: antonyprest@hotmail.com
Contact: Mr. Anthony Tosan Arthur-Prest - MD/CEO

PRESTIGE ASSURANCE PLC
Business: Insurance
Address: Plot 19, Ligali Ayorinde St, Victoria Is. Annex, Lagos
Tel: (01) 8042804, 8042806, 3204681-3 (3L), 3204688, 3200381 **Fax:** (01) 3204684
Contact: Mr. V. K. Markanda - MD/CEO

PRESTIGE COMMUNICATIONS LIMITED
Business: Advertising, Public Relations and Marketing
Address: 24, John Olugbo Street, Off Unity Rd, Ikeja, Lagos
Tel: (01) 4970943, 08023235892
E-mail: prestigeabe@yahoo.com
Contact: Mr. Tope Abe - MD/CEO

PRESTIGE COSMETICS LIMITED
Business: Manufacturing and Marketing of Cosmetics
Address: 4, Coscharis Street, off Happy Home Avenue, Kirikiri Industrial Estate, Kirikiri, Lagos
Tel: (01) 5454613, 7741704, 775282
Contact: Mr. Ramzi Fawaz - Chairman/CEO

PRESTIGE FIBRES LIMITED
Business: Manufacturing and Marketing of Carpets & Rugs
Address: Plot 2, Block E, Vori Close, off Acme Road, Ogba Industrial Estate, Ikeja, Lagos
Tel: (01) 4921368, 4925684-5 (2L) Fax: (01) 2624138
E-mail: prestige@skannet.net.ng

PRESY & ADENSON LITHOGRAPHIC PACKAGING LTD
Business: Manufacturing of Light Packaging, Printing Services
Address: 9, Modupe Street, off Yaya Abatan Road, Ijaiye-Ogba, Ikeja, Lagos
Tel: (01) 4921174, 4920311, 4922082, 4922078
Fax: (01) 4920020

PREXISE SECURITIES LIMITED
Business: Stockbroking
Address: 88B, Isale-Eko Ave., Dolphin Estate, Ikoyi, Lagos
Tel: (01) 2670763, 7911817
Contact: Mr. Ben O. Enemmo - Chairman

PRICE SECURITIES & TRUST COMPANY LIMITED
Business: Financial Services, Capital Market Activities, Marketing and Commodity Trading
Address: Savannah Bank Building (Ground Floor), 62/66, Broad Street, Lagos Island, Lagos
Tel: (01) 2600134, 2600725, 2600985, 2602184
Fax: (01) 2602184
Contact: Mr. Obinna Okereke - Group Head

PRICEWATERHOUSECOOPERS
Business: Business Risk & Shareholder Value Management; Financial/Accountancy Consultancy Services.
Address: Plot 252E, Muri Okunola Street, off Ajose Adeogun Street, Victoria Island, Lagos
Tel: (01) 3203100, 7744152-4 (2L) **Fax:** (01) 3203101
E-mail: enquiry@ng.pwc.com
Website: www.pwc.com/ng
* 35, Woji Road, G.R.A.,Phase II, Port Harcourt
Contact: Nsa Harrison - Senior Partner
Gabriel A. Ojegbile - Head (Marketing & Research)

PRICEWATERHOUSECOOPERS LIMITED
Business: Management Consultancy Services
Address: Plot 252E, Muri Okunola Street, off Ajose Adeogun Street, Victoria Island, Lagos
Tel: (01) 3203100, 2703100 **Fax:** (01) 3203101
E-mail: enquiry@ng.pwc.com
Website: www.pwc.com/ng
* Katsina House, Ralph Shodeiende Street, off Ahmadu Bello Way, Central Business District, Abuja
Tel: (09) 6709074-5 (2L)
Contact: Mr. Ken Igbokwe - MD/CEO

PRIMA GARNET COMMUNICATIONS LIMITED
Business: Advertising, Public Relations and Marketing; Print Radio and Television Production

Address: Ivory Music House (3rd Floor), IPM Avenue, Central Business District, Alausa, Lagos
Tel: (01) 7730312-4 (3L), 7752917, 08022906634
Fax: (01) 7912485
E-mail: pgarnet@primagarnet.com
Website: www.primagarnetcom
Contact: Mr. 'Lolu Akinwunmi - MD/CEO

PRIMA IMPEX (NIGERIA) LIMITED
Business: Importation of Food Commodities, Frozen Fish, and Plastic Raw Materials
Address: Prima House, 12, Akinwande Street, opp. Strabag Construction off Badagry Expressway, Old Alaba Market, Coker, Lagos
Tel: (01) 7742662, 7740338, 7740477, 7751643, 7752233
Fax: (01) 2670667
Contact: Mr. M. N. Vaswani - Chairman/CEO

PRIME ENERGY & ENGINEERING LIMITED
Business: Sales and Service of Generators
Address: Plot 249A, Muri Okunola Street, Victoria Island Annex, Lagos
Tel: (01) 2621194, 2621195, 4708888
Fax: (01) 2621194, 2621195
E-mail: toc@hyperiacom
*48, Burma Road, Apapa, Lagos
Tel: (01) 5870775, 5874274, 5876925
Contact: Mr. Daniel Ugbosu - Sales Executive

PRIME ENERGY RESOURCES LIMITED
Business: Petroleum Exploration, Consultancy Services, Resources and Environmental Management, Equipment Procurement and Energy Matters
Address: Bankers' House (4th Floor), Plot PC 19, Adeola Hopewell Street, Lagos
Tel: (01) 2623938, 2623435 **Fax:** (01) 2623938
E-mail: primeenergyresources@ryahoo.com
* Mina Hotels Ltd (Suite 2), 23, Igbodo Street, Old G.R.A., Port Harcourt
Tel: (084) 238668, 236356, 236357
* Stonehill House, 27, Deco Road, Warri
Contact: Chief Chambers O. Oyibo - Chairman/CEO

PRIME ENERGY VENTURES LIMITED
Business: Importation of UPS Batteries, Stand-by Power Products, Solar-Power Systems and Computers
Address: Block A (Flat 4), Amuwo Odofin Industrial Estate by Daewoo Autoland, Oshodi Expressway, Lagos
Tel: (01) 8045825, 5843289 **Fax:** (01) 5843289
E-mail: pevl-sps@hyperia.com
Contact: Engr. Hyacinth Udemba - MD/CEO

PRIME LOSS ADJUSTERS LIMITED
Business: Pre-Underwriting Insurance Risks Survey and Loss Adjusting
Address: 7, Akinremi Street, off Obafemi Awolowo Way, Anifowoshe, Ikeja, Lagos
Tel: (01) 4960473, 4968722
Contact: Mr. Ebenezer A. Adebiyi - MD/CEO

PRIME MARKETING ASSOCIATES LIMITED
Business: Shipping, Freight Forwarding, Warehousing
Address: 22, Rhodes Crescent, Apapa, Lagos
Tel: (01) 5457715, 5455824, 5871106, 7757664, 08037231019 **Fax:** (01) 5457715
E-mail: pmalines@starnet.net.ng
Contact: Mr. Ola Sebiomo -MD/CEO

PRIME RESORTS, ABUJA
(Prime Guest Houses & Resorts ltd)
Business: Hospitality & Catering Services, Business-Centre
Address: Plot 679, Ogbomosho Street, off Tafawa Balewa Way, Area 8, Garki, Abuja
Tel: (09) 2343557, 2345697, 2346026-7 (2L)
Fax: (09) 2343665

PRIME SEAFOOD INTERNATIONAL LIMITED
Business: Import & Export o Seafoods, Restaurant
Address: 2, Adetokunbo Ademola Str, Victoria Island, Lagos
Tel: (01) 2618707, 2706655, 4735405

PRIME TECHNOLOGIES LIMITED
Business: Assembly and Repairs of Computer Systems, Manufacture of Computer Cases, Sales of Computer and Accessories, Networking
Address: NIJ Building (1st Floor), 20, Adeyemo Alakija Street, Victoria Island, Lagos
Tel: (01) 2620158
E-mail: primetech@linkserve.com.ng
* Plot 2, National Bank Road, Oregun Industrial Estate, Oregun, Ikeja, Lagos.
Tel: (01) 4937025
* 87, Ogui Road, Enugu
Contact: Mr. Chike Onyekwere - Chairman/CEO

PRIME UNION TRAVELS & TOURS LIMITED
Business: Travel Agency, Tour Operators, Bureau de Change Operations
Address: 37, Ahmed Onibudo Street, Victoria Island, Lagos
Tel: (01) 2616042, 4704196 **Fax:** (01) 2616042
E-mail: primeunin@saleman.net
Contact: Mrs. A. Ayeni - Exec. Director/CEO

PRIMETRUST INSURANCE COMPANY LIMITED
Business: Non-Life Insurance
Address: 2, Raymond Njoku Street, S.W. Ikoyi, Lagos
Tel: (01) 2691048, 2694503 Fax: (01) 2694504
E-mail: primetrustinsurance@yahoo.co.uk
Contact: Mr. 'Yemi Akinyemi - MD/CEO

PRIMLAKS NIGERIA LIMITED
Business: Conglomerate - Trading, Frozen Foods, Fisheries,
Address: 16, Kofo Abayomi Street, Victoria Island, Lagos
Tel: (01) 2622232, 2622259, 2615505
Fax: (01) 2619487
E-mail: primlak@hyperia.com
Contact: Mr H. R. Anil - MD

PRIMUS NIGERIA LIMITED
Business: Building and Civil Engineering, Contracts
Address: Km. 16, Port Harcourt/Aba Expressway, Rumuokwurusi, Port Harcourt
Tel: (084) 612761
E-mail: meridian@phc.i-p.com
Website: ww.portharcourt.i-p.com
Contact: Chief (Hon.) S. O. Worlu, JP - Chairman/CEO

PRINCE HOTEL LIMITED
Business: Hospitality & Catering Services
Address: 1C, Tamandu Road, off Audu Bako Way, Nassarawa, Kano
Tel: (064) 311518, 633393, 639402 **Fax:** (064) 635944
Contact: Mr. Richard Solomon - MD/CEO

PRINCE OF PRINTS LIMITED
Business: Creative Designing, Commercial Printing, Light Packaging and Continuous Computer Stationeries
Address: 58, Karimu Street, Surulere, Lagos
Tel: (01) 5850309, 5851468 **Fax:** (01) 5851468
E-mail: creative@mtrong.ng
Contact: Prince Remi Olowookere - Chairman/CEO

PRINCESS SUITES LIMITED
Business: Hospitality & Catering Services, Car Hire Services
Address: Plot 1760, Lome Street, Wse Zone 7, Abja
Tel: (09) 5238334-6 (2L), 08033118228
Fax: (09) 5237727
E-mail: princesssites@yahoo.com
Website: www.princesssuitesnigeria.com
Contact: Hon. (Princess) V. Ndigwe-Anozodo - Chairman/CEO

PRINCIPAL PROTECTION SECURITY SERVICES INT'L LTD
Business: Sales, Installation and Mintenance of Hitech Electronic Security Gadgets & Equipment
Address: 24A, Isaac John Street, G.R.A., Ikeja, Lagos.
Tel: (01) 4939720, 08023131556-7 (2L)
E-mail: principalprotection@wananet.net

PRINT INKS NIGERIA LIMITED
Business: Manufacture of Inks and Dyes
Address: 385, Ikorodu Road, opp, Ojota New Motor Park, Ojota, Lagos
Tel: (01) 2222024, 4974668, 4977536-7 (2L)
Fax: (01) 2222024
E-mail: printink@vanocomp.com
Website: www.oasisgroup.com
Contact: Chief (Mrs) O. O. Adegbite - MD/CEO

PRINTEX (NIGERIA) LIMITED
Business: Print Production of Flexible Packaging Materials and Labels, Commercial Printing
Address: 7, Segun Irefin St, by Synagogue Church, Egbe Industrial Estate, Ilasamaja, Lagos
Tel: (01) 4827763, 08023049816, 08023156179
Fax: (01) 4827763
E-mail: printexnigltd2001@yahoo.com
Contact: Ms. Paula-Anne Oshilaja - MD/CEO.

PRINTS SPECIALTY LIMITED
Business: Industrial and Commercial Printing Services
Address: Adebola House, 40, Opebi Road, Ikeja, Lagos
Tel: (01) 4976600-9 (10 L) **Fax:** (090) 404759

PRISMA NIGERIA LIMITED
Business: Steeel Converson, Light Industrial Packaging, Import Trade, Financial & Management Cnsulting
Address: 42B, Adelabu Street, Surulere, Lagos
Tel/Fax: (01) 837644, 08033150636
E-mail: kiribaku@yahoo.com
Contact: Abba O. Njoku - Chairman/CEO

PRIVATE NETWORKS NIGERIA LIMITED
Business: Provison of Mobile Telephone Services, Sales and Rentals of Mobile Phones; Consultancy Services
Address: 1, Oremeji St, off Obanle-Aro Avenue, Ilupeju, Lagos
Tel: (01) 7746597, 08027660004-5 (2L) **Fax:** (01) 5551034
E-mail: info@private-networks.net
Website: www.private-networks.net
Contact: AbdulRahman Abiola-Odunowo - Chairman/C.O.O

PROBITY SECURITIES & INVESTMNT LIMITED
Business: Stockbroking, Investment Advisory Services
Address: 31, Oyo Road (2nd Floor), Coca Cola Area, Ibadan
Tel: 08033619993, 08033842786
E-mail: prosil4ever@yahoo.com
Contact: Mr. B. O. Egnlusi - MD/CEO

PROCOMTEL LIMITED
Business: Turnkey Provision of Telecommnication Infrastructre, Importtation & Installation of Galvanised Towers, Masts & Accessories, Galvaanised Equipment Shelters & Base Transmission Stations, RF Supply & Installation
Address: 15, Idejo Street, off Adeola Odeku Street, Victoria Island, Lagos
Tel: (01) 261260, 2627840 **Fax:** (01) 2629205
E-mail: pcomtel@yahoo.com
pcomtel@hotmail.com
Website: www.procomtellimited.com
Contact: Mr. Henry Ojogho - MD/CEO

PROCON GROUP AFRICA
Business: Buiding and Civil Engineering Services
Address: 10, Durban Street, off Adetokunbo Ademola Crescent, Wuse II, Abuja
Tel: (09) 5232337-8 (2 L), 5234498 **Fax:** (09) 5234401
E-mail: procon@proconafrica.com

PROCTER & GAMBLE NIGERIA LIMITED
Business: Manufacture & Marketing of Consumer Health-Care Products, Sanitary Pads & Baby Diapers
Address: Amethyst Block, All Seasons Business Plaza, Lateef Jakande Way, Agindingbi, Ikeja, Lagos
Tel: (01) 7742007, 7742007, 7742616 **Fax:** (01) 3450277
E-mail: oshin.3@pg.com
Contact: Evelyn Oshin - Corporate Affairs Dept.

PRODEC-FUGRO CONSULTANTS LIMITED
Business: Quality, Health, Environmental & Safety Consultancy Services, Laboratory Services.
Address: 11B, Geodetic Road, Rumuobiakani, (By Shell 1A) Trans-Amadi, Port Harcourt
Tel: (084) 238964, 571197 **Fax:** (084) 239328
E-mail: prodec@phca.linkserve.com
Contact: Dr. G. C. Ofunne - MD/CEO.

PRODIGY INTERNATIONAL LIMITED
Business: Internet Services, Thought-Exchange Facilitator
Address: 8, Oduduwa Way, Ikeja G.R.A., Lagoss
Tel: (01) 4970114, 4939653-5 (3 L)
E-mail: info@prodigy2000.com
Website: www.prodigy2000.com
* Plot 144, Kashim Ibrahim Way, Wuse II, Abuja
Tel: (09) 4136940-1 (2 L)

E-mail: abuja@prodigy2000.com
*3/4, Trans-Amadi Industrial Layout, Port Harcourt
Tel: (090) 412792, 412552
E-mail: phc@prodigy2000.com

PROFAB ENGINEERING LIMITED
Bsiness: Engineering & Construction, Welding & Fabrication, Blasting, Coating & Anti-Corrosion Services, Rental of Equipment & Offshore Transport Units
Address: Plot 274, Trans-Amadi Ind. Layout, Port Harcourt
Tel: (084) 231003 **Fax:** (084) 237332
E-mail: profab@hyperia.com

PROFESSIONAL ACCOUNTANCY TUTORS LIMITED
Business: Professional Training Services
Address: 210, Ikorodu Road, Palmgrove, Lagos
Tel: (01) 7730655, 822936, 08023145726, 08023288429, 08033074054, 08033191158, 08056636097
E-mail: pattors2001@yahoo.co.k
* NAOWA Centre, Gado Nasko Barracks, Maitama, Abuja

PROFESSIONAL STOCKBROKERS LIMITED
Business: Stockbroking, Portfolio and Funds Management, Investment Advisory Services
Address: 3-7,Nnamdi Azikiwe Street (3rd Floor), Tinubu Square, Lagos
Tel: (01) 2640322 **Fax:** (01) 865535
Contact: Mr. Adesoye Olanlege - MD/CEO

PRO-FLEX (Gym & Fitness Centre)
Business: Gymnasium and Fitness Centre
Address: 20-24, Ozumba Mbadiwe Ave, opp. Samuel Manuwa Road, by 1004-Flats Estate, Victoria Island, Lagos
Tel: (01) 2618696 **Fax:** (01) 2624946
Website: www.proflexgymn.com

PROFOUND SECURITIES LIMITED
Business: Funds & Investment Management, Stockbroking, Issuing House, Financial Advisory Services
Address: Engineering Centre (7th Floor), Plot PC. 1, Engineering Close, off Idowu Taylor St, Victoria Island, Lagos
Tel: (01) 2646365, 2646366 **Fax:** (01) 2646408
Contact: Mr. Kayode Akin-Ajayi - MD/CEO

PROGENICS CORP. LIMITED
Business: Development, Marketing & Implementation of Applications Software; Sales and Maintenance of Computer Hardware; Network and Communications; IT Consultancy Services
Address: 8, Ibadan Close, off Agbaoku Street, Opebi, Lagos
Tel: (01) 4978304, 4808686, 7947145 **Fax:** (01) 4978304
E-mail: progenix@infoweb.abs.net
sales@progenicscorp.com
Website: www.progenicscorp.com
Contact: Mr. Anthony T. Udoh - MD/CEO

PROGRAFIK LIMITED
Business: Colour Separation, Pre-Press Services, Digital Imaging and Proofing
Address: 14, Ikosi Road, Oregun, Lagos
Tel: (01) 4962205, 4707215 **Fax:** (01) 4974638
Contact: Mr. Jerome Elaiho - Chairman/CEO

PROGRESS ENGINEERS
Business: Civil Engineering Consultancy (Civil, Structures, Foundation, Water Supply, Irrigation, Environment, Geological & Geophysical, Geotechnic, Oilfield).
Address: 4, Babatola Drive, Ikeja, Lagos
Tel: (01) 4976841, 4976888, 08022905609
Fax: (01) 4976888
E-mail: progress@alpha.linkserve.com
* 7, 5th Street, DDPA Estate, Igbdu, Warri
Tel: (053) 255854
Contact: Engr. (Dr.) J. I. Folayan - Principal Partner

PROJECT STRUCTURES LIMITED
Business: Mechanical and Structural Engeineering, Fabrication and Machining of Steel Structures, Farming
Address: 18, Onitsha-Owerri Road, Onitsha
Tel: (046) 214525, 219672
Contact: Mr. Timothy Okeke -MD/CEO

PROMASIDOR NIGERIA LIMITED
(formerly Wonder Foods Nigeria Ltd)
Business: Packaging & Distribution of Milk & Food Drinks
Address: 23, Wharf Road, Apapa, Lagos
Tel: (01) 5457983-7(5L), 5872488, 5871449, 5877864, 2645233-4 (2L) **Fax:** (01) 2645210
E-mail: info@wonderfoods.com
Contact: Mr K. W. Hall - MD/CEO
Mr. Chris Ehimen - National Marketing Manager

PROMINENT SECURITIES LIMITED
Business: Stockbroking, Issuing House, Investment Advisory Services, Portfolio Managemnt
Address: Providence House, 66, Modupe Johnson Crescent, Adeniran Ogunsanya Street, Surulere, Lagos
Tel: (01) 2902767, 5850954 **Fax:** (01) 5840490
E-mail: promsec@infoweb.abs.net
Contact: Mrs. Modupeola Arit Dada - MD/CEO

PROMOMART NIGERIA LIMITED
Business: Monogramming, Screen Printing, Transfer Printing, Production of Signs and Engraving Services
Address: 24, Yesufu Sanusi Street, off Adeniran Ogunsanya Street, Surulere, Lagos
Tel: (01) 4707079, 08023130217, 08033277338
E-mail: promomart@yahoo.com
Contact: Mr. H. O. Feyisitan - MD/CEO

PROMOSERVE LIMITED
Business: Marketing Communications
Address: 49, Bode Thomas Street, Surulere, Lagos
Tel: (01) 5834087, 5847225, 5835320 (DL)
Fax: (01) 5835320
Contact: Prince Kehinde Adeosun - Chairman/CEO

PROMOTEX INDUSTRIAL & CHEMICAL COMPANY LTD
Business: Manufacturing of Soaps and Detergents
Address: Intercontinental Plaza, Plot 999C, Danmole Street, Victoria Island, Lagos
Tel: (01) 617714, 613465, 2622993, 4815985
Fax: (01) 2622983
E-mail: chicason@infoweb.abs.net
* 202 (Km. 11), Old Ojo Road, Ojo, Lagos
Contact: Chief (Sir) Alex Chika Okafor - Chairman/CEO

PROMPT ENTERPRISES LIMITED
Business: Commercial Printing Services, Publishing
Address: 3, St. Finbarr's College Road, Akoka, Yaba, Lagos
Tel: (01) 4707684, 4708494, 5821465, 08033349520
Fax: (01) 820007

PROPERTY DEVELOPMENT COMPANY LTD (PRODECO)
Business: Property Development and Management
Address: Off Seaport Road, Onne, Rivers State

PROSPORTS LIMITED
Business: Distribution and Marketing of Sports Goods, Sports Events Marketing and Managements
Address: Coscharis Plaza, 68A, Adeola Odeku Street, Victoria Island, Lagos
Tel: (01) 2624326

PROTEA HOTEL GROUP
Business: Hospitality, Hotel Management.
Address: Plot 1700, Violet Yough Close, off Adetokunbo Ademola Street, Victoria Island, Lagos
Tel: (01) 3204717, 3204727, 3204737, 3204747
Fax: (01) 3204949
Website: www.proteahotels.com
* 2, Ahmadu Bello Way, opp. Legislative Quarters, Apo, Abuja
Tel: (09) 2311237, 08035973343 **Fax:** (09) 231123
* 3, Isaiah Odolu St GRA, Phase 1, Port Harcourt
Tel: (084) 231557, 08035508230
E-mail: phphapartments@hotmail.com
* Nike Lake Resort, Abakpa-Nike, Enugu
Tel: (042) 557000-19 (20L), 557679, 08036664696
E-mail: nikelake@proteanigeria.com
* The Ranch Resort, Obanliku, Cross River State
Tel: 08035506256, 080934729327
E-mail: gmranch@proteanigria.com

PROVIDENCE CONSULT & SERVICES LIMITED
Business: Marine & Environmental Consultancy Services, Cargo Survey & Superintendence, Fisheries
Address: Development House (7th Floor), 21, Wharf Road, Apapa, Lagos
Tel: (01) 5876192, 5870888, 8119677, 08033084369
Fax: (01) 2621146, 5870888
E-mail: proconslt@yahoo.co.k
Contact: Mr. A. O. A. Olaniyi - Chairman/CEO

PROVIDENCE HOSPITALS LIMITED
Business: Medical and Health Care Services
Address: 77, Itire Road, Surulere, Lagos
Tel: (01) 5835973, 4714367 **Fax:** (01) 5834973
E-mail: pro.hosp@hyperia.com
* 12A, Rafi Shittu St, Alaka Estate, Surulere, Lagos
Contact: Dr. John Esangbedo - Chief Medical Director

PROVIN (NIGERIA) LIMITED
Business: Sales and Support of Power-Protection Equipment
Address: Plot 188, Shittu Animashaun Street, Gbagada Estate Phase II, Gbagada, Lagos
Tel/Fax: (01) 4964071, 5552759, 5552815
E-mail: provinltd@infoweb.abs.net
provinltd@infoweb.com.ng
Contact: Engr. B. A. O. Fisher - Chairman/CEO

PRUDENT BANK PLC
Business: Universal Banking
Address: Plot 708/709, Adeola Hopewell St, V/ Island, Lagos
Tel: (01) 2620161-3 (3 L), 4617783-7 (5 L)
Fax: (01) 2620167, 3200514, 4617140
E-mail: prudentbank@prudentbank.net
Website: www.prudentbank.net
Contact: Mr. Akinsola Akinfemiwa - MD/CEO
Mr Demola Akinbola - Head (Corp. Affairs)

PRUDENT PROPERTY & INVESTMENT COMPANY LTD
Business: Property Development and Management, Investors, General Merchandising
Address: Commercial House (2nd Floor), 80, Allen Avenue, Ikeja, Lagos
Tel: (01) 4965499, 08023100170-1 (2L)
E-mail: prudentpic@onebox.com
Website: www.cpiltd.com
* Millenium Plaza (6th Floor), Plot 24, 4th Avenue, Central Business District, Abuja
Contact: Otunba P. O. Adegbite - Chairman/CEO

PRUDENTIAL SECURITIES LIMITED
Business: Stockbroking, Investment Advisory Services, Treasury and Funds Management, Issuing House, Leasing, Financial/Management Consultants
Address: 19, Tinubu Street, Lagos Island, Lagos
Tel: (01) 2661790, 2664567, 8113701, 08033286011
* Great Nigeria House, Panseke, Ibara, Abeokuta
Tel: (039) 244351, 244356, 08033829016
Contact: Chief B. O. Fagbemi - Exec. Chairman

PRUDENTIAL TRUST COMPANY LIMITED
Business: Consulting, Finance, Information Provision
Address: Princes Court (Suite 7G), Plot PC 37, Ahmed Onibudo Street, Victoria Island, Lagos
Tel: (01) 2703354 Fax: (01) 4617069
E-mail: info@prudentialtrustco.com
Website: www.prudentialtrustco.com
Contact: Mr. Nnamdi Anammah - President/CEO

PSI DENTAL CLINIC LIMITED
Business: Dental Health Care Services
Address: 14B, Agoro Odiyan Street, off Adeola Odeku Street, Victoria Island, Lagos
Tel: (01) 2610797, 5558068
Contact: Dr. Stella Imolorhe - Dental Director/CEO

PUBLIC IMAGE LIMITED
Business: Advertising, Corporate Promotions
Address: 25, Association Avenue, Ilupeju, Lagos
Tel: (01) 4968717, 8044769 **Fax:** (01) 4967399
E-mail: p.image@alpha.linkserve.com
* Plot 500, Tafawa Balewa Way, Area 3, Garki, Abuja
Contact: Mr. Tayo Odunkomaiya - Chairman/CEO

PUBLIC SUPPORT SERVICES LIMITED
Business: Business Findings, Joint Investment & Loans
Address: Atinuke Centre, 129, Okota Road, off Oshodi-Apapa Expressway, Isolo, Lagos
Tel: (01) 4716444, 08023315736
E-mail: pss_ltd@yahoo.com
Contact: Mr. Chris Emeadi - GM

PULSAR LIMITED
Business: Advertising
Address: 6, Market Street, off Abibu-Oki Street, Lagos
Tel: (01) 2641546, 2666737 **Fax:** (01) 2669053
Contact: Mr. Emiko Aruofor - Chairman/CEO

PULSE MARKETING COMMUNICATIONS LIMITED
Business: Advertising & Public Relations; Events Marketing & Management; Public Information Processing; Speciality Printing Services
Address: 4, Jibowu Street, by Jibowu B/Stop, Yaba, Lagos
Tel: (01) 867743, 868272, 4700134 **Fax:** (01) 2693419
Contact: Mrs. Affiong M. Amana - MD/CEO

PUMPCO LIMITED
Business: Sales, Installation and Maintenance of Fuel Pumps
Address: 5, Toyin Street, Ikeja, Lagos
Tel: (01) 4965743, 4971759, 2221552, 7734335, 7749919, 08023003166-7 (2L)
E-mail: pumpcoltd2000@yahoo.com
* Block D2 (Shop 5), Wonderland Shopping Complex opp. Bodija Market, Agbowo, Ibadan

PUNCH NIGERIA LIMITED
Business: Newspaper Publishing and Marketing
Address: 1, Kudeti Street, Onipetesi, off Agege Motor Road, Mangoro B/Stop, Lagos
Tel: (01) 4972815-7 (3L), 4923546, 7745110
Fax: (01) 4920205, 4962350, 4972816
E-mail: dailypunch@the-punch.com
* Halbiz Complex (Suite 6), Plot 567, opp. Minister's Gate, FCDA, Area 11, Garki, Abja
Tel: (09) 3141750-2 (3L)
Contact: Mr. Ademola Osinubu - MD/CEO

PURECHEM INDUSTRIES LIMITED
Business: Manufacture of Chemicals for Textile Specialities, Construction, Metal Treatment, Consumer & Industrial Adhesives, Paint Emulsions & Additives
Address: 19, Town Planning Way (2nd Floor), Ilupeju, Lagos
Tel: (01) 4979341-2 (2 L), 7740172
Fax: (01) 4978286, 2612447, 2618655
E-mail: purechem@linkserve.com.ng
Website: www.purechemindustries.com
* Veepee Industrial Avene, Km. 38, Lagos-Abeokuta Road, Sango-Otta, Ogun State
* Gidan Goldie (Ground Floor), 2B, Niger St, Kano
Tel: (064) 635163, 642408, 649845 **Fax:** (064) 642408
Contact: Mr. S. N. Kirpalani - Chairman
Mr. V. D. Ganglani - MD/CEO

PURIFICATION TECHNIQUES (NIGERIA) LIMITED
Business: Manufacturing, Engineering and Contracting, Consultancy, Road-Construction Technology, Sales of Imported Building Materials and Furniture
Address: Km. 15/16, Lagos-Badagry Expressway, opp. Army Barracks Gate, behind Agip Station, Ojo, Lagos
Tel/Fax: (01) 4818884
E-mail: puritek-ojo@puritek.com
20, Adetokunbo Ademola St Victoria Island, Lagos
Tel: (01) 2622773, 2622774, 615960, 612141
Fax: (01) 2624471
E-mail: puritek@puritek.com

PVC GROUP
Business: Veterinary Services, Sales of Pets & Pet-care Products, Training & Boarding Facilities for Pets
Address: 91, Opebi Road, Opebi, Ikeja, Lagos
Tel: (01) 4961377, 4937132, 2222023, 8119339
E-mail: petcare@infoweb.abs.net
Contact: Dr. Kunle Abiade - MD/CEO

PYRAMID BAG MANUFACTURING COMPANY LIMITED
Business: Manufacturing of Woven Polypropylene Bags
Address: Plots 3 & 8, Block III, Industrial Area 1, OPIC Industrial Estate Agbara, Ogun State
Tel: (01) 7740388 **Fax:** (01) 2880610
E-mail: pyramidbag2000@yahoo.com

PYTHON ENGINEERING COMPANY LIMITED
Business: Building of Houseboats, Construction of Barges and Portakabins, Oil Industry Civil Engineering
Address: 94, Enerhern Road, Warri
Tel: (053) 250824, 252969 **Fax:** (053) 250227
E-mail: python@micro.com.ng
Contact: Rola Zabad - MD/CEO

3Q AVIATION LIMITED
Business: Clearing & Freight Forwarding
Address: SAHCOL Cargo Complex, Port Harcourt International Airport, Omagwa, Rivers State
Tel: (084) 233842, 08033098722, 08035502739
E-mail: threeq@phca.linkserve.com
Website: www.3qaviation.com

Q OIL & GAS SERVICES LIMITED
Business: Oil Services, Enginering, IT, Supply of Manpower, Consultancy
Address: ACB Building, 11, Azikiwe Road, Port Harcourt
Tel: (084) 231953, 235208, 08034070178
Fax: (084) 230373
E-mail: phc@aptech-nigeria.com
Website: www.aptech-globetraining.com
Contact: Mr. V. Ram - MD/CEO

Q SOFTWARE SOLUTIONS LIMITED
Business: IT Education and Training
Address: ACB Building, 11, Azikiwe Road, Port Harcourt
Tel: (084) 230373, 231953, 235208, 08034070170
Fax: (084) 230374
E-mail: phc@aptech-nigeria.com

QED LIMITED
Business: Sales of CCTV Security Systems, Telecommunication Equipment, GSM Phones & Accessories
Address: 5, Obafemi Awolowo Way, opp. Ikeja LG. Council Premises, Ikeja, Lagos
Tel: (01) 7746547, 4934459; 08023009888, 08023029175, 08033066451-2 (2L) **Fax:** (01) 4934460
Contact: Mr. 'Wole Moronfolu -MD/CEO

QINGQI MOTORCYCLES MANUFACTURING CO. LTD
Business: Assembling, Sales and Service of Motorcycles
Address: Plot 1, Block C, Gbagada Industrial Estate, Gbagada-Oshodi Expressway, Gbagada, Lagos
Tel: (01) 5553059, 7742040, 7750555, 7756299
Fax: (01) 5553059

QLINK NIGERIA LIMITED
Business: Importation of Electronic/Electrical Consumer & Office Appliances
Address: 14, Simbiat Abiola Road, Ikeja, Lagos
Tel: (01) 8138458, 08023046274
* 5, Amemosheun Close, Alaba Int'l Market, Lagos
Tel: (01) 7746107, 8110476

QMB TECHNOLOGIES LIMITED
Business: Sales, Installation & Maintenance of Remote-Control Devices for Gates, Garages and Doors
Address: 21, Boyle Street (1st Floor), Onikan, Lagos
Tel: (01) 2645635-6 (2L), 7742660, 08034988888
Fax: (01) 2645753
E-mail: qmbtech@yahoo.com
Contact: Mr. Olumide Anwoju - COO

QUALI FOOD NIGERIA LIMITED
Business: Production of Mineral & Fruit Drinks
Address: Plot 5, Ikosi Road, Oregun, Ikeja, Lagos
Tel: (01) 7734076, 08033858924, 08033969474
E-mail: vkumar_2000@hotmail.com
Contact: Mr. Vijay Kumar - MD/CEO

QUALITEC INDUSTRIES LIMITED
Business: Manufacturing of Colour Coated Coils and Longspan Aluminium Roofing Sheets
Address: 679, Lagos-Abeokuta Expressway, Hamadiya Bus-Stop, Ojokoro, Agege, Lagos
Tel: (01) 7749136, 7749137, 4922399, 4922401
Fax: (01) 4920581, 2882693
Contact: Chief Oluyinka Kufile - Chairman/CEO

QUALITEX TEXTILES LIMITED
Business: Distribution of Textiles (Wax & Fancy Print)
Address: 3, Davies Street, off Marina, Lagos
Tel: (01) 2662795, 2662491, 2662769 **Fax:** (01) 2664021
* Kamjat House, New Ife Road, opp. New Gbagi Market, Ibadan
* 11, Kirikasama St, Maiduguri.
Tel: (076) 235176
Contact: Mr. Jean-Paul Pragout - MD/CEO

QUALITY CONTROL & TESTING LABORATORIES LTD
Business: Importation, Distribtion and Marketing of Testing Systems, Laboratory Equipment and Reagents
Address: Adata Plaza, 10, Balarabe Musa Crescent, Victoria Island, Lagos
Tel: (01) 2619424, 08023046367 **Fax:** (01) 2618997
E-mail: qctlab@yahoo.com
* Plot 173, Trans-Amadi Ind. Layout, Port Harcourt
Tel/Fax: (084) 232535, 08023046367
* Plot 104, Mbale Street, Wuse Zone 4, Abuja
Tel: (09) 3140171
Contact: Mr Tomi Okorodudu - MD/CEO

QUALITY FINANCE LIMITED
Business: Financial Services
Address: 98, Bode Thomas Street, Surulere, Lagos
Tel: (01) 5850753, 4800097, 08033500997
Fax: (01) 5850753
Contact: Dr. Iyayi Efianayi (JP) - Chairman
Mr. G. O. Aigbogun - MD/CEO

QUALITY MOTORS LIMITED
Business: Sales and Service of Motor Vehicles/Accessories
Address: 57, Rasaq Balogun Street, Western Avenue (Alaka Bus-Stop), Surulere, Lagos
Tel: (01) 5851233, 08033026220, 08033186025, 08033263474
Contact: Mr. Goddy Ike Agu - Chairman/CEO

QUALITY RADIATORS LIMITED
Business: Manufacturing and Sales of Radiators for Automobile Vehicles, Plastic Moulded Parts and Jerrycans
Address: Plot 75A, Trans-Amadi Ind. Layout, Port Harcourt
Tel: (084) 232176, 232434, 237467 **Fax:** (084) 237466
Contact: Mr. S. K. Somany - Chairman
Mr. A. C. Garg - MD/CEO

QUANTUM MANAGEMENT & FINANCIAL CONSLTING LTD
Business: Financial & Enterprise Consultancy Services, Investment Banking
Address: 71, Liberty Boulevard, Millionnaires Quarters, Jos
Tel: (073) 463540, 080370022084, 08037003324
Fax: (073) 463540
E-mail: quantumint@onebox.com
Contact: Machar Adams Zaaka - Exec. Chairman

QUANTUM SECURITIES LIMITED
Business: Stokebroking
Address: 24, Sumbo Jibowu Street, off Ribadu Road, S.W., Ikoyi, Lagos
Tel: (01) 2692535, 4742058, 08033315362
Fax: (01) 2692535
E-mail: quantum@infoweb.abs.net
quantum@cyberspace.net.ng
Contact: Chief Jonathan Araui - Chairman
Mr. Sunday Okene - MD/CEO

QUARTERMASTERS LIMITED
Business: Design & Production of Personal Wears, Corporate & School Uniforms, Military/Paramilitary Accessories and Badges, Commercial Monograming and Logo Creation
Address: 120, Bode Thomas Street, Surulere, Lagos
Tel: (01) 5851848, 2905323, 08022905690, 08033521874
Fax: (01) 5851848
E-mail: quartermaster@hyperia.com
Contact: Dr. Chidi Okpaulabu - MD/CEO

QUASAR TECHNOLOGIES LIMITED
Business: Sales and Maintenance of Computer Systems, Information Systems Services
Address: Eleganza Building (8th Floor), 15B, Joseph Street, Lagos Island, Lagos
Tel: (01) 2635182, 2636847 **Fax:** (01) 2635182
E-mail: quasar@infoweb.abs.net
Contact: Jibayo Olumuyiwa Olagundoye - MD/CEO

QUEEN'S PETROLEUM LIMITED
Business: Exploration and Production of Oil and Gas
Address: 6, Louis Solomon Close, off Ahmadu Bello Way, Victoria Island, Lagos
Tel: (01) 2617555, 2616020, 610493, 614312, 615819
Fax: (01) 616622, 614312
Contact: Olorogun M. C. O. Ibru - Chairman/CEO

QUEENSWAY ALUMINIUM COMPANY LIMITED
Business: Manufacturing of Longspan Aluminium and Steel Roofing Sheets and Step Tiles
Address: Plot 9C, Kakuri Ind. Estate, Kaduna South, Kaduna
Tel: (062) 232585, 234253, 234254, 231913
Fax: (062) 231913, 232525
E-mail: queens@skannet.com
* Plot 734, Alexandria Crescent, off Aminu Kano Crescent, Wuse II, Abuja.
Tel: (09) 4138382
* 4, Mai-Malari Road, Bompai Ind. Area, Kano
Tel: (064) 639818

QU-ESS PARTNERSHIP
Business: Chartered Quantity Surveyors, Construction Cost & Development Consultancy, Project Management
Address: 37, Ekololu Street, Surulere, Lagos
Tel: (01) 5851913, 7747950, 08033127341
Fax: (01) 5851913
Contact: J. O. MacGregor - Principal Partner

QUICHI PROPERTIES & INVESTMENTS LIMITED
Bsiness: Property & Estate Development, Furniture & Decor, Hospitality
Address: Plot 1133, Aminu Kano Crescent, Wuse II, Abuja
Tel: (09) 5236832, 08037217000 **Fax:** (09) 5236832
E-mail: quichiinteriors@hotmail.com
* Plot 1192D, Olugbosi Close, Victoria Is., Lagos
* 8, Azikiwe Road, Port Harcourt
Tel: (084) 234722
Contact: Dr. Henry A. Izibili - Chairman/CEO

QUINTESSENCE NIGERIA LIMITED
Business: General Merchandising
Address: Block B, Falomo Shopping Centre, Awolowo Road, Falomo, Ikoyi, Lagos
Tel: (01) 2673048, 2694680
E-mail: qltd@infoweb.abs.net
Website: www.quintessenceltd.com
Contact: Chief (Mrs.) A. T. Oni-Okpaku - MD/CEO

R & D INTERNATIONAL LIMITED
Business: Processing & Exporting of Wood & Components
Address: 395, Old Abeokuta Road, opp. Lagos State Abbatior, Agege, Lagos
Tel: (01) 7762324, 7765666

R. T. BRISCOE (NIGERIA) PLC
Business: Sales & Service of Motor Vehicles, Technical Equipment including Forklifts, Industrial Compressors, Ball and Roller Bearings and Generators, Mining and Drilling Equipment
Address: 16/18, Fatai Atere Way, Matori, Oshodi, Lagos
Tel: (01) 4522175, 4524560, 4524588, 4523201, 4520204, 4522943, 4521365, 4525075, 4524497, 4520174
Fax: (01) 4524519, 4522943
E-mail: briscoemail@rtb.com.ng
Contact: Mr. Jens Erik Mollenbach - MD/CEO
Mr. Rowland O. Eso - DMD

RA-AH INTEGRATED SYSTEMS LIMITED
Business: Information Technology Services (Training, Web & Graphic Design, Hardware Maintenance, Software Development, Typesetting)
Address: 22, Ahmadu Bello Way, Jos
Tel: (073) 456074, 08033229591, 08035076624, 08035888739 **Fax:** (073) 456074
Contact: Engr. Isaac Gimba - MD/CEO

RACE CARGO AIRLINES LIMITED
Business: Carriage of Charter Air Cargo
Address: 17A, Awoniyi Elemo Street, off Osolo Way, Ajao Estate, Apakun-Oshodi, Lagos
Tel: (01) 4520936, 4525147, 4527695, 08033027392
Fax: (01) 4520936
E-mail: losfelix@rclmail.com
losfelix@rclmax.com
* 5, Old Airport Estate Rd, Rumumasi, Port Harcourt
Tel: (084) 230238 **Fax:** (084) 235749
* 18, Apple Avenue, No-Man's-Land, Kano
Tel: (064) 634601 **Fax:** (064) 635944
Contact: Mr. Felix Imonikhe Itonandon - Chairman/CEO

RADAM MARITIME SERVICES LIMITED
Business: Marine Services for the Oil and Gas Industry
Address: Foreshore Towers (10th Floor), 2, Osborne Road, Ikoyi, Lagos
Tel: (01) 2693242, 08033205832 **Fax:** (01) 2694670
E-mail: radam@hyperia.com
Website: www.radam.com
Contact: Rear Admiral Allison Madueke (rtd) - Chairman

RADIAL CIRCLE TELECOMMUNICATIONS LIMITED
Business: Installation & Maintenance of Telecommunication Systems, Security & Surveillance Systems, VSAT, Microwave, Networking & PABX
Address: 56, Balarabe Musa Crescent,by 1004-Flats Estate, off Samuel Manuwa Road, Victoria Island, Lagos
Tel: (01) 611938, 617378, 2613043, 4619507, 4710232
Fax: (01) 611938, 2613043
E-mail: radiacircle@hyperia.com
Website: www.radialcircle.com
Contact: Mr. Richard Oluranti Omole - Chairman/CEO
Mr. Lekan Akande - GM

RADIANT OPTICS LIMITED
Business: Eye Clinic, Optical & Optometric Services
Address: 99, Allen Avenue, Ikeja, Lagos
Tel: (01) 4972355

RADMED DIAGNOSTIC CENTRE LIMITED
Business: Medical Dignostic Services
Address: Ramed House, Plot 1E, Ligali Ayorinde Street, Victoria Island, Lagos
Tel: (01) 2610959, 2619774, 2622889, 5558108-9 (2L)
Fax: (01) 2610959
E-mail: radmed@infoweb.abs.net
Contact: Dr. Adewumi A. Desalu - Chairman
Dr. Adisa A. Senbajo - MD/CEO

RAGOLIS WATERS LIMITED
Business: Bottling and Marketing of Spring Water
Address: 64, Lagos Road, Ikorodu Town, Lagos State
Tel: (01) 7780556, 7780871 **Fax:** (01) 7780626
E-mail: info@ragolis.com
Website: www.ragolis.com

RAHIMBOD INSURANCE BROKERS LIMITED
Business: Insurance Broking
Address: Management House (2nd Floor), 22, Idowu Taylor Street, Victoria Island, Lagos
Tel: (01) 4745353, 08056032406
Contact: Rev. (Dr.) J. A. Akinbobola - CEO

RAHMATIC GROUP
Business: Corporate Consultancy Services in Telecommunication, Investment and Properties
Address: Plot 483, Bangui Street, off Adetokunbo Ademola Crescent, Wuse II, Abuja
Tel: (09) 5230461, 5234090, 5234095 **Fax:** (09) 5240250
E-mail: iamidirs@hotmail.com
Website: www.cashcraft.com
* 6B, Agoro Odiyan Street, Victoria Island, Lagos
Tel: (01) 2629198
Contact: Alh. Idris A. M. Idris - Chairman/CEO

RAHUSA VENTURES NIGERIA LIMITED
Business: Building & Civil Engineering, Electrical Engineering, General Contractor, Sales of Pharmaceutical Products, Motor Vehicles and Furniture
Address: 206, IBB Way, Katsina
Tel: (065) 433637, 433639 **Fax:** (065) 34474
Contact: Alh. M. S. Wada - Chairman/CEO
Alh. H. D . Iliya - GM.

RAILAD LIMITED
Business: Outdoor Advertising Agency
Address: Advertising Centre, Printers Lane, Nigerian Railways Compound, Lagos
Tel: (01) 5456099, 7743429, 831164, 08033258520
Contact: Chukwuma C. E. Moemeke - Exec. Director

RAIN BIRD NIGERIA LIMITED
Business: Sales of Pumps, Water Filters, Chemical-Dosing Pumps, Water-Pumping Machines & Accessories
Address: Plot 908, Lateef Jakande Rd, Agidingbi, Ikeja, Lagos
Tel: (01) 4705880, 3451313, 08033085253
Fax: (01) 3451313
E-mail: rainbird81@yahoo.com
Contact: Mr. Godwin Robinson - MD/CEO

RAINBOW MARITIME (NIGERIA) LIMITED
Business: Clearing and Forwarding Agency, Transport Operators, Consultancy Services
Address: 14, Kareem Akande Street, off Apapa-Oshodi Expressway (Sunrise Bus-Stop), Apapa, Lagos
Tel: (01) 5876809, 8175645, 08033502725
Contact: Chief Dele Akinoso - Chairman/CEO

RAISERS INTERNATIONAL LIMITED
Business: Importation of Printing & Lithographic Equipment
Address: Bankers' House (Ground Floor), Plot PC. 19, Adeola Hopewell Street, Victoria Island, Lagos
Tel: (01) 2623441 **Fax:** (010 2646256
Contact: Mrs. Onikepo Oduekun - MD/CEO

RAJRAB LIMITED
Business: Manufacturing of Pharmaceutical Products
Address: 10, Ogunnipebi St, off Akilo Road, Ogba, Lagos
Tel: (01) 4920875, 4920209 **Fax:** (01) 4920209
E-mail: rajrab@ilorin.skannet.com
* 72-80, Coca-Cola Road, Industrial Estate, Ilorin
Tel: (031) 220926, 223111 **Fax:** (031) 220926
Contact: Elhadj R. Faworaja - Chairman/CEO

RAMADAN PRESS LIMITED
Business: Printing and Publishing
Address: Maiduguri Bye-Pass, Bauchi
Tel: (077) 542623, 541421, 540992, 543579
Fax: (077) 543352
Contact: Alh. Garba Mohammed Noma - Chairman/CEO
Alh. Shehu Mohammed Bukul - Exec. Director

RANA TAHIR FURNITURE LIMITED
Business: Manufacturing and Sales of Furniture
Address: Plot 5, Herbert Macaulay Way, Wuse Zone 5, Abuja
Tel: (09) 5238941
* Sharada Industrial Estate Phase III, Kano
Tel: (064) 663206, 666593 **Fax:** (064) 666593
Contact: Mr. Tahir M. Fadlallah - Chairman

RANAMI ABAH & COMPANY
Business: Estate Surveyors & Valuers
Address: 4, Forces Avenue, G.R.A. Phase I, Port Harcourt
Tel: (084) 230151, 232027, 232785

RANBAXY NIGERIA LIMITED
Business: Production of Pharmaceutical Products
Address: Abimbola House, 24, Abimbola Street, Isolo Industrial Estate, Isolo, Lagos
Tel: (01) 4526359, 4527094 **Fax:** (01) 4526371, 4527545
Contact: Chief Badru Atanda Olaogun - Chairman

RANC LIMITED
Business: Sales, Installation and Supprt of Telecommunication Equipment
Address: 59, Idugbose Estate, off Elf Road, Ogunu, Warri
Tel: (053) 254016, 321027, 321046, 08023084521
E-mail: ranc@alpha.linkserve.com
* 13, Nembe Road, Rumuibekwe Housing Estate, Rumuibekwe, Port Harcourt.
Tel: (084) 572624, 08023132195
* 8, Abel Oreniyi Street, off Salvation Road, Opebi, Ikeja, Lagos.
Tel: (01) 2601600-19 (20 L) (Ext. 65110)
E-mail: ranc@beta.linkserve.com

RANDOM ACCESS COMPUTERS LIMITED
Business: Sales of Computers and Accessories, Networking
Address: 8B, Kasumu Ekemode Street, off Saka Tinubu Street, Victoria Island, Lagos
Tel: (01) 2623796, 2627624, 612422, 4707342, 08023266407, 08033061076
E-mail: random@infoweb.abs.net
randomaccess32@hotmail.com
ral_lagos@yahoo.com
* Fabdal Plaza (Suite 305), Constantine Street, opp. Macdowell, Wuse Zone 4, Abuja
Tel: (09) 5238940

RANGK LIMITED
Business: Maritime Consltancy, Offshor Support Services
Address: 38, Kofo Abayomi Street, Victoria Island, Lagos

Tel: (01) 2610199, 2625480 **Fax:** (01) 2616970, 2623978
E-mail: rangk@rangkltd.com
* 24, Ikwerre Road, Diobu, Port Harcort
Tel/Fax: (084) 239402
Contact: Rear Admiral Godwin N. Kanu (rtd) - Exec. Chairman

RANONA LIMITED
Business: Import and Export
Address: 7A, Creek Road, Apapa, Lagos
Tel: (01) 5452974, 7741599, 08033028928, 08033048420
Fax: (01) 5452975
E-mail: ranoma@hyperia.com
Contact: Mr. Yassir H. Gebara - Chairman/CEO

RANPOLEX NIGERIA LIMITED
Business: Manufacturing of Woven Plastic Mats
Address: 87/88, Sharada Industrial Estate Phase II, Kano
Tel: (064) 660147, 668113, 08033595324
Contact: Anis Sherif Roda - Chairman/CEO

RANSOME-KUTI VETERINARY CONSULTANTS LIMITED
Business: Veterinary Clinic & Consultancy Services, Pet Mart, Grooming & Boarding Facility, Import of Puppies & Kittens, Fumigation & Pest Control
Address: 20B, Elsie Femi-Pearse Str, Victoria Island, Lagos
Tel: (01) 2700596, 4725005, 08023134470
E-mail: rvclimited@21ctl.com
Contact: Dr. Dotun Ransome-Kuti - Managing Partner

RAO INVESTMENT PROPERTY COMPANY LIMITED
Business: Property Investment, Development and Management, Real Estate Agency
Address: 3/5, Ikoyi Crescent, off Osborne Road, Ikoyi, Lagos
Tel: (01) 2672311, 2672987, 7753377, 08033046785

RAPHA SERVICES COMPANY LIMITED
Business: Marine and Maritime Services, Dredging and Reclamation Engineering Services
Address: 31C, Herbert Macaulay St Amadi Flats, Port Harcourt
Tel: (084) 231752, 577823, 08033094870, 08033132281
Fax: (084) 231752
E-mail: rapha@alpha.linkserve.com
Contact: Chief Obinna G. C. Amuchienwa - Chairman/CEO

RAPHSON LABORATORIES LIMITED
Business: Medical Laboratory Diagnostic Services; Sales of Laboratory Equipment, Reagents and Kits,
Address: 9, Adelabu Close, off Ola Ayinde Street, opp. Customs Training College, Ikeja, Lagos
Tel: (01) 4936307, 8150455, 08033043379
Fax: (01) 4936307
E-mail: raphson.nig@usa.net
Contact: Mr. Raphael Okeke - MD/CEO

RAPID VIGIL COMPANY LIMITED
Business: Secruity Guard Services, Security Equipment Sales & Installation, Consultancy & Training
Address: 10, Billy Odumola Street, Juli Estate, off Kudirat Abiola Way, Oregun Ikeja, Lagos
Tel: (01) 2902294, 4735351, 08033158824, 08034709170

RAPIDO VENTURES LIMITED
Business: Sales and Maintenance of Audio-Visual Products & Presentation Equipment, Transporation Services
Address: 122, Wetheral Road, Owerri
Tel: (083) 231716, 233583, 08032034161
Fax: (083) 231275
E-mail: rapido@micro.com.ng
* 134, Obafemi Awolowo Way, Ikeja, Lagos
Tel: (01) 4934545, 4704230, 08032034160, 08033271212
* Plot 7, Cadastral Zone B5, Utako District, off Berger Junction, Abuja.
Tel: (09) 5242125, 6700397, 08033271214
* 172A, Aba Road, Waterlines Junctions, Port Harcourt.
Tel: (084) 572780
Contact: Mr. Frank Nneji - MD/CEO

RAYBROS ENTERPRISES (NIGERIA) LIMITED
Business: Imporation of Generators, Sole Distributor of ROBIN Generators and Power Products
Address: B.363/366, Alaba International Market, Ojo, Lagos
Tel: (01) 5885058, 5880994, 5982455, 2666323, 883903
Fax: (01) 5554320, 5880994
Contact: Chief Raymond Egbuna - Chairman/CEO

RAYCON & COMPANY (NIGERIA) LIMITED
Business: Civil and Mechanical Engineering, Construction of House Boats, Catering Services
Address: 73, Ogunu Road, Ogunu, Warri
Tel: (053) 250935, 252366 **Fax:** (053) 252255
Contact: Mr. Alex Gabriel - MD/CEO

RAYFIELD HOTELS, ABUJA
Business: Hospitality Services
Address: 35, Julius Nyerere Street, Asokoro, Abuja
Tel: (09) 3148531-5 (5L) **Fax:** (09) 3148536
E-mail: rayfieldhotel@hotmail.com

RAYFIELD TRAVELS & TOURS LIMITED
Business: Travel Agency, Tour Packaging, Haulage of Goods
Address: 25, Ahmadu Bello Way, Jos
Tel: (073) 450054-6 (3 L) **Fax:** (073) 452352
E-mail: mathayes@infoweb.abs.net
Contact: Mr. Matthew Hayes Ochepa - Chairman

RAYKON LABORATORIES (NIGERIA) LIMITED
Business: Importation of Pharmaceutical Products
Address: 69, Bode Thomas Street, Surulere, Lagos
Tel: (01) 5833286, 835932, 833689, 08023426161
E-mail: raykonlabs@hotmail.com
* 75, Uselu - Lagos Road, Benin City
Tel: (052) 253050, 08033343128
Contact: Chief Raymond Ajugwo - MD/CEO

RBS MANAGEMENT AND FINANCIAL CONSULTANTS
Business: Management Consultancy Services
Address: 19, Yola Road, opp. College of Education, Yola
Tel: (075) 624896
Contact: A. G. Ribadu - Principal Partner

RCN NETWORK (NIGERIA) LIMITED
Business: Supply, Installation & Maintenance of Telecommnication Equipment, Sales of Photographic Films & Equipment, Copiers & Power Generators
Address: 12C, Oko-Awo Close, Victoria Island, Lagos

Tel: (01) 4616374, 4725237, 4725239 **Fax:** (01) 4619155
* 6, Allen Avene, Ikeja, Lagos
Tel: (01) 4970945
Contact: Mr. S. A. Agboola Abiola - MD/CEO

RCO PROPERTIES & COMPANY
Business: Real Estate Development, Estate Surveyors and Valuers, Rating Surveyors, Estate Agency
Address: RCO Court, 3-5, Sinari Daranijo Street, off Younis Bashorun Street, Victoria Island, Annex, Lagos
Tel: (01) 2624820-2 (3L), 2611134, 616105, 616107, 616109 **Fax:** (01) 2624822
E-mail: rco@infoweb.abs.net
Contact: Chief R. C. Okafor - Principal Partner/CEO

RDI WEST AFRICA LIMITED
Business: International Postgradate Management-Education Consultancy (Executive Programmes), Human Resorces Development Services
Address: 10B, Lalupon Close, off Keffi Str, S.W. Ikoyi, Lagos
Tel: (01) 2672811-2 (2L), 4740937, 08036003373
Fax: (01) 2672812
E-mail: info@rdi-nigeria.com
Website: www.rdiworldwide.net
* Abuja Business School, Millenim Court, Plot 74, Ralph Shodeinde Street, off Ahmadu Bello Way, Central Business District, Abuja
Tel: (09) 2348676, 6714929
Contact: Dr. Fakunle Odifa - Chairman/CEO

RDM LIMITED
Business: Telecommunication and IT Services, Distribution of GSM Phones & Accessories
Address: Plot 283A, Gbagada Estate Phase I, Gbagada Expressway, Gbagada, Lagos
Tel: (01) 5552730-1 (2L), 5552478, 08022241460, 08022241462, 08022900647, 08023139966, 08023192982, 08023222072, 08023222076-7 (2L)
E-mail: rdm@hyperia.com
* Lozumba Plaza, Area 10, Garki, Abuja
Tel: 08023139950
* Blazer Plaza, Rumuola Road, Port harcrout
Tel: (084) 239254, 08022241463, 08023192737

READERSWORLD.COM LIMITED
Business: Bookstore, Library Services, Book Club
Address: Motorways Centre (Wing C), 1, Motorways Avenue, opp. 7Up Factory, Oregun, Lagos
Tel: (01) 7749888, 5557902, 08023068916
E-mail: readerswrld@yahoo.com
books@readers-world.com
Contact: Mr. S. J. George - GM/CEO

READS & MARKS LIMITED
Business: Advertising, Marketing Commnications, Public Relations
Address: 1, Ogboru Street, Indepndence Layout, Enugu
Tel: (042) 152559 **Fax:** (042) 451597

REAL IMAGE SYSTEMS LIMITED
Business: Information Technology Solution Providers, Procurement of Oil & Gas Tools/Equipment
Address: 53, Bekwe4ri Wosu (Igboukwu) Street, D-Line, Port Harcourt
Tel: (084) 231049, 231384, 08033425664
Fax: (084) 231384
E-mail: realimage2000@yahoo.com
Contact: Mr. Okey C. Nwokeikwu - Chairman/CEO

REAL OIL MILLS LIMITED
Business: Processing & Packaging of Vegetable Oils and Fats
Address: 386/394, Ikorodu Road, Ojota, Lagos
Tel: (01) 4978100-1(2L) **Fax:** (01) 4977867
E-mail: realoil@linkserve.com.ng
muyiladoja@realoilmills.com
Contact: Mr. M. A. Ladoja - MD/CEO

REAL SHIPPING COMPANY LIMITED
Business: Shipping Owners & Brokers
Address: 19, Adele Road, off Wreahouse Rd, Apapa, Lagos
Tel: (01) 5455397, 5875657, 5875736
Fax: (01) 5455389, 5872169
Contact: Mr. Tunji Ladoja.- Chairman/CEO

REAL TIME TECHNOLOGY (NIGERIA) LIMITED
Business: Electrical & Mechanical Engineering, Sales and Service of Transformers, Generators, Pumps and Panels, Building Management Consultants
Address: 15, Diya Street, Oremeji, Gbagada, Lagos
Tel: (01) 3205172-3 (2L), 4705385, 5552666
E-mail: rtt_limited@yahoo.com
* Corner Shop 65, Addis Ababa Way, Wuse Zone 4, Abuja.
Tel: (09) 5230495, 5235216
Contact: Engr. I. K. Olagunju - MD/CEO

REALS PHARMACEUTICALS LIMITED
Business: Importation and Marketing of Pharmaceutical Products, Representative of ASTRAZENECA
Address: All-Seasons Plaza (Topaz Block, 2nd Floor), Alh. Lateef Jakande Road, Agidingbi, Ikeja, Lagos
Tel: (01) 3450280, 4935117, 7741205 **Fax:** (01) 3451348
E-mail: reals@skannet.com
Contact: Mr. Ade Popoola - MD/CEO

REAMS NIGERIA LIMITED
Business: General Merchandising, Importation of Chemicals, Bottling of Liquified Petroleum Gas, Drum Re-Conditioning
Address: 118, Old Ojo Road, Amuwo-Kuje, Lagos
Tel: (01) 7741401, 08023040114, 08023342376
Fax: (01) 5891018
Contact: Mr. A. O. Adewale - MD/CEO

RECKITT BENCKISER (NIGERIA) LIMITED
Business: Manufacture & Marketing of Household Goods
Address: Reckitt Benckiser House, 12, Montgomery Road, Yaba, Lagos
Tel: (01) 5851275, 5451848 **Fax:** (01) 5451848
Website: www.reckittbenckiser.com
* Plot C2/3-C3/1, Agbara Industrial Estate, Km 32, Lagos-Badagry Road, Agbara, Ogun State.
Tel: (01) 712092, 712148, 712152, 7749388
* Plot 13, Danco Estate,Enugu Expressway, Onitsha
Tel: (046) 213791
* 9, Industry Road, Aba.

Tel: (082) 228197
Website: www.reckittbenkiser.com
Contact: Mr. Nick Pearson - Ag. MD/CEO.
Chief Ezeoma Onyenro - Human Resources Mgr.

red\line NIGERIA LIMITED
Business: Cargo Consolidation, Clearing and Forwarding, Courier Services, Door-to-Door Delivery Services
Address: Strabag Compound, Coker Rd, off Akinwande St, Badagry Expressway (Coker Bus-Stop), Lagos
Tel: (01) 2880656
* c/o Joe Eboje International Agency Limited, Plot 148, Trans-Amadi Industrial Layout, Port Harcourt
Tel: (084) 333238 **Fax:** (084) 238010
Contact: Mr. Junaid O. Adeniji - Chairman
Mr. Gunter Thoss - MD/CEO

REDINGTON NIGERIA LIMITED
Business: Sales of Information Technology Products
Address: Afprint Compound, 122/132, Oshodi-Apapa Expressway, Isolo, Lagos
Tel: (01) 7763161, 7917787
E-mail: varghese@chanrai.com
Website: www.redingtongulf.com

REEDS & COLLEAGUES LIMITED
Business: Media Consultancy, Public Relations Agency, Advertising Practitioners
Address: 11A, Sanya Olu Street, off Oregun Bus Stop, Oregun, Ikeja, Lagos
Tel: (01) 4931393

REFUGE HOME SAVINGS & LOANS LIMITED
Business: Mortgage Finance
Address: 4, Adeniyi Jones Avenue, Ikeja, Lagos
Tel: (01) 4936732, 4936289, 4723478 **Fax:** (01) 4961478
E-mail: refugedan@yahoo.com
Contact: Mr. Akinola Taiwo - MD/CEO

REFUGE INSURANCE COMPANY LIMITED
Business: All Classes of Insurance including Life & Pensions
Address: Refuge Insurance House, 33, Ikorodu Road, Jibowu, Yaba, Lagos
Tel: (01) 4975845, 4931958, 7917847-8 (2L)
Fax: (01) 4931958
* Halbiz Complex (Suite 4), Plot 567, off Kapital Street, Area 11, Garki, Abuja.
Tel: (09) 3141308
Contact: Mr. Jimmy Orekoya - MD/CEO

REGAL LINK LIMITED
Business: Importation of Computer & Electrical Accessories, UPS, Automatic Voltage Regulation
Address: 61, Princess Street, Lagos Island, Lagos
Tel: (01) 2635914, 08033031848, 08034729356
Fax: (01) 2635914
E-mail: regal@alpha.linkserve.com
Contact: Pastor Nnamdi Ohizu - MD/CEO

REGAL MINERAL INDUSTRIES LIMITED
Business: Processing and Marketing of Solid Minerals
Address: 142/144, Okota Road, Okota, Isolo, Lagos
Tel: (01) 2881143, 2694627-8 (2 L) **Fax:** (01) 2692734
E-mail: regalmineral@yahoo.com
Contact: Dr. Oladiran Fawibe - Chairman/CEO.

REGENCY (OVERSEAS) COMPANY LIMITED
Business: Manufacture of Paints
Address: 13, Abebe Village Road, Iganmu Industrial Estate, Iganmu, Lagos
Tel: (01) 5833684, 5833885
Contact: Major-Gen. F. A. Mujakperuo (rtd) - Chairman
Mr. Farouk Rawas - MD/CEO.

REGENCY FINANCINGS LIMITED
Business: Financial Services
Address: 13, Biaduo Street, off Keffi Street, South-West Ikoyi, Lagos
Tel: (01) 2693591, 2693595, 2693596
Contact: Sir Dave O. Mbanaso - MD/CEO.

REGENCY INSURANCE COMPANY LIMITED
Business: Insurance
Address: 2B, Ebun Street, off Gbagada Expressway, Gbagada Estate Phase I, Gbagada, Lagos
Tel: (01) 4726957-8 (2L), 5821326 **Fax:** (01) 5821402
* 9, Toyin Street, Ikeja, Lagos.
Tel: (01) 4738444
* 94, Malanje Str, Cadastral Zone 4, Wuse, Abuja.
Tel: (09) 5237040
* 26, Ikwerre Road, Port Harcourt.
Tel: (084) 482330
Contact: Mr. Biyi Otegbeye - MD/CEO

REGENT BANK PLC
Business: Commercial Banking
Address: Churchgate Tower, Plot PC. 30, Afribank Street, Victoria Island, Lagos
Tel: (01) 2612554, 2618603, 2629452-3 (2L), 2624449, 2629453, 2629458-9 (2L)
Fax: (01) 2705275, 2705278
E-mail: headoffic@regent-bank.com
Website:: www.regent-bank.com
* 8 (Plot 473), Langtang Close, off Tafawa Balewa Way, Area 3, Garki, Abuja
Contact: Mr. Bhagwan I. Mahtani - Chairman
Mr. Gbolahan O. Folayan - MD/CEO

REIME WEST AFRICA LIMITED
Business: Telecommunication
Address: 2A, Raufu Taylor Close, off Idejo St, V/l, Lagos
Tel: (01) 3204547
E-mail: reime.nigeria@remine.no
Website: www.reime.no

RELIANCE BANK LIMITED
Business: Commercial Banking
Address: 142, Ahmadu Bello Way, Victoria Island, Lagos
Tel: (01) 2610693-8 (6 L) **Fax:** (01) 2611388, 2610258
E-mail: info@reliancebanklimited.com
Website: www.reliancebanklimited.com
* Plot 1145, Aminu Kano Crescent, Wuse II, Abuja
Tel: (09) 4137104-6 (3L), 4137101 **Fax:** (09) 4137107
* 129/131, Olu Obasanjo Road, Port Harcourt
Tel: (084) 232798-9 (2L), 236863 **Fax:** (084) 236863
Contact: Mr. Abayomi O. Majekodunmi - MD/CEO.

RELIANCE EQUIPMENT MANUFACTURING COMPANY LTD
Business: Manufacturing and Marketing of School Equipment, Terrazzo Tiles, Thread & Riser/Angl Steps
Address: 5, Maicibi Close, Kakuri Industrial Estate, Kaduna
Tel: (062) 231690, 230313 Fax: (062) 232599
Contact: Mr. M. O. Titiloye - MD/CEO

RELIANCE HOLDINGS NIGERIA LIMITED
Business: Paper Sales, Printing, Conversion of Paper, Manufacturing of Exercise Books and Envelopes
Address: 25, Maye Street, Yaba, Lagos
Tel: (01) 861802, 860112, 08023114467, 08037174589
Fax: (01) 860027
Contact: Mr. David Oluranti Ademuyiwa - Chairman/CEO.

RELIANCE TELECOMMUNICATIONS NIGERIA LTD (RELTEL)
Business: Fixed Wireless Telephony Service Providers
Address: Reliance House, 219A Moshood Abiola Way, opposite Nigeria Breweries Plc, Iganmu, Lagos
Tel: (01) 4801111-3 (3L), 4800211-2 (3L)
E-mail: sales@reltel.org
Website: www.reltel.org
* 2, Temple Ejekwu Close, off Port Harcourt/Aba Expressway, Rumuogba, Port Harcourt
Tel: (084) 481111-3 (3L)
* 2nd Floor, Joedone Shopping Complex, Limca Road, Onitsha.
Tel: (046) 481111
Contact: Mr Iyke Ejimofor - Admin. Manager

RELIANCE TEXTILE INDUSTRIES LIMITED
Business: Manufacture of Textiles
Address: Plot 6, Block A, Surulere Industrial Road, Ogba Industrial Estate, Ikeja, Lagos
Tel: (01) 4924450, 4924551, 4937809-10 (2L), 7731430, 7740139 **Fax:** (01) 4922476
Contact: Mr. D. N. Budhrani - MD/CEO

REMM OIL SERVICES LIMITED
Business: Machine Shop Fabrication Services, Equipment Rentals
Address: Plot 52, Trans-Amadi Ind. Layout, Port Harcourt
Tel: (084) 232422 **Fax:** (084) 239980
Contact: Mr. A. S. Mildner - Chairman/CEO

REMOTA ENGINEERING (NIGERIA) LIMITED
Business: Sales & Service of Generators & Spare Parts
Address: 8, Louis Solomon Close, off Ahmadu Bello Way, Victoria Island, Lagos
Tel: (01) 2623307-9 (3L) **Fax:** (01) 2623306
E-mail: remota@rcl.nig.com
* 4A, Ndahbrosl Street, Trans-Amadi Industrial Layout, Port Harcourt
Tel: (084) 237476 **Fax:** (084) 237477
Contact: Mr. Tara P. Saha - MD/CEO.

RENART PRINTS LIMITED
Business: Industrial Printing, Monogramming and Engraving, Production of Corporate Gifts & Awards
Address: 184, Herbert Macaulay Street (Adekunle Bus-Stop), Yaba, Lagos
Tel: (01) 4819223, 08023206714
E-mail: renartp@yahoo.com

RENDEZVOUS GROUP HOTELS (NIGERIA) LIMITED
Business: Hospitality & Catering Services
Address: Plot 1/2, Textile Road, Kakuri, Kaduna
Tel: (062) 232017
* Plot 188, Makeri Street, Wuse Zone 6, Abuja
Tel: (09) 5231195

RENENT LIMITED
Business: Cleaning Services and Consultancy, Sales of Cleaning Equipment and Chemicals
Address: 14, Olu Akerele St, off Alhaja Kofoworola Crescent, Obafemi Awolowo Rd (Balogun B/Stop), Ikeja, Lagos
Tel: (01) 4935833, 4977326, 7758554 **Fax:** (01) 4935833
E-mail: renent@infoweb.abs.net
Contact: Mr. Yomi Adewumi - Admin. Manager

REPUBLIC PRESS LIMITED
Business: Publishing of Newspapers, Commercial Printing, Production of Educational Materials & Exercise Books
Address: Financial Trust House (20th Floor), 1-4, Balogun/ Breadfruit Street, Lagos Island, Lagos
* 11/13, Bisi Oladipo St, Mafoluku, Oshodi, Lagos
Tel: (01) 4970719, 967081
Contact: Mr. E. Oladimeji - MD/CEO.

RESANO SECURITIES LIMITED
Business: Stockbroking, Portfolio Management, Investment Advisory Services and Consultancy
Address: New Niger House Annex (3rd Floor), 3/4, Tinubu Street, Lagos Island, Lagos
Tel: (01) 2663810, 2664374 **Fax:** (01) 2641233
Contact: Mr. E. A. Egonmwan - MD/CEO

RESEARCH & DATA SERVICES LIMITED
Business: Publishing, Research, Consultancy & Information Management
Address: Great Nigeria House (18th Floor), 47/57, Martins Street, Lagos
Tel: (01) 2660926, 2664639, 08023053968
Fax: (01) 2660926
E-mail: redasel@infoweb.abs.net
Contact: Mr. Rotimi Osho - GM

RESEARCH & MARKETING SERVICES LIMITED
Business: Marketing Research
Address: 26, Odozie Street, Ojodu, Lagos
Tel: (01) 7741623, 4704403 **Fax:** (01) 2673670
E-mail: rms@rms-africa.com
Contact: Mr. K. A. Tejumola - Group MD.

RESORT SECURITIES & TRUST LIMITED
Business: Capital Market Activities, Issuing House, Portfolio Management, Financial Services
Address: Resort House, 12, Boyle Street, Onikan, Lagos
Tel: (01) 2601925-9 (5L), 4739188, 7747937
E-mail: resortsec@resortgp.com
Contact: Mr. Femi Ekundayo - Chairman/CEO

RESOURCERY LIMITED
Business: IT Consultancy; Systems Networking, Integration, Design and Installation
Address: 18, Adeola Hopewell Street, Victoria Island, Lagos

Tel: (01) 3200300-2 (3L), 4618281-2 (2L), 7740711, 7740712 **Fax:** (01) 4618682
E-mail: info@resourcery.com.ng
Website: www.resourcery.com
* 14, Circular Road, Presidential Hotel Estate, off Aba Road, Port Harcourt.
Tel: (084) 230856, 230858
Contact: Tani Fafunwa - MD/CEO.

RESOURCES IMPROVEMENT & MANUFACTURING CO. LTD
Business: Processing & Production of Oils & Cakes from Palm Kernel, Rubber Seed &Soya Bean; Production of Livestock Feeds, Laundry Soap, Detergent
Address: Akwu-Uru Industrial Estate, Nnewi, Anambra State
Tel: (046) 460173, 460648, 462913-7 (5 L), 462918
Fax: (046) 460972, 462929
E-mail: in<rimco@infoweb.abs.net
* Intercontinental Plaza (2nd Floor), Plot 999C, Danmole St, off Idejo Street, Victoria Island, Lagos
Tel: (01) 2622983, 4815985, 613465, 617714
Fax: (01) 2622983, 7741539
Contact: Chief (Sir) A.C. Okafor - Chairman/CEO.
Engr. L. O. Ilozue - MD.

RESOURCES TRADES & TECHNOLOGIES LIMITED
Business: Sales and Maintenance of Fire-Solutions Equipment & Products
Address: 4, Gapiona Avenue, off Benoni Rd, GRA.,Benin City
Tel/Fax: (052) 258172, 252797 (090) 502092
E-mail: resources@cyberspace.net.ng
* 8, Payne Crescent, Apapa, Lagos
Tel: (01) 5875239, 5453641

RESTRAL LIMITED
Business: Management Consultancy, Franchise Manager of the Franklin Covey Company
Address: St. Nicholas House (12th Floor), 6, Catholic Mission Street, Lagos Island, Lagos
Tel: (01) 2645885, 2632654, 2632239, 2880883, 4705124, 2632850, 2635090 **Fax:** (01) 2632654
E-mail: enquires@restral.com
Website: www.restral.com
Contact: Ifueko Omoigui, Uwa Oboh

REWARD INVESTMENTS & SECURITIES LIMITED
Business: Stockbroking, Portfolio Management, Investment Advisory Services and Consultancy
Address: New Africa House (10th Floor), 31, Marina, Lagos
Tel: (01) 2641273, 2667345, 4718809, 4751550
Fax: (01) 2667345
E-mail: reward@infoweb.abs.net
Contact: Mr. Henry T. Olayemi - MD/CEO.

REWARD TRAVELS & TOURS LIMITED
Business: Travel & Tour Agency
Address: 134/136, Broad Street (1st Floor), Lagos
Tel: (01) 2641959, 2660787, 2667189, 08023521389
Fax: (01) 2667471
E-mail: rewardstravels@linkserve.com
Website: www.rewardsgroup.com

REYNOLDS CONSTRUCTION COMPANY (NIGERIA) LTD
Business: Building & Civil Engineering Contractors
Address: Consortium House, Plot 1682, Sanusi Fafunwa Street, Victoria Island, Lagos
Tel: (01) 4618841-3 (3L) **Fax:** (01) 4618844
E-mail: md@rcc-nigeria.com
Website: www.rcc-nigeria.com
* Plot 564/565, Block A, Central Business District, beh. FEPA Headquarters, Airport Road, Abuja

REYOMS NIGERIA LIMITED
Business: Sales of Mobile Phones & Acccessories, Communications and Security Equipment; Service and Repairs of Communication Terminals; Communication Consultancy
Address: Plot 1398B, Tiamiyu Savage Street, off Ahmadu Bello Way, Victoria Island, Lagos
Tel: (01) 2625947, 2527533-4 (2L), 4616434, 8044728, 08032030872, 08032030874
E-mail: info@reyoms.com
reyomsglobal@yahoo.com
reyoms-baays@theobech.com
reyoms_ltd@virgin.net
Website: www.reyoms.com
* Imperial Hotels Ltd. Plot 226, Sekondi Cr, opp. AP Plaza, off Adetokunbo Ademola Cr, Wuse II, Abuja.
Tel: (09) 5237042, 5232701
Contact: Mr. Abayomi J. Olowo - Chairman/CEO

RHINE INDUSTRIES NIGERIA LIMITED
Business: Import of Jute Bags, Water-Treatment Chemicals, Signage & Printing Material & Motor Batteries
Address: 18, Owukori Crescent, off Ajani Olujare Street, Alaka Estate, Srulere, Lagos
Tel: (01) 5851159, 08023460532
E-mail: rinl@hyperia.com
Contact: Mr. S. D. Olawole - Operation Manager

RHINO LININGS NIGERIA
Business: Corrosion Protection Applications
Address: 337, Herbert Macaulay Street, Sabo-Yaba, Lagos
Tel: (01) 8129218, 08036423300, 08055166640
Website: www.rhinolinings.co.za
Contact: Akinola Oteniya - MD/CEO

RHODIA NIGERIA LIMITED
Business: Import & Sales of Industrial/Laboratory Chemicals
Address: 32B, Ladipo Oluwole Avenue, Ikeja Industrial Estate, Ikeja, Lagos
Tel: (01) 4938312-3 (2L), 7742182 **Fax:** (01) 4967470
E-mail: rhodia.lagos@linkserve.com.ng
Contact: Mr. Phillippe Mattioli - Chairman
Mr. Doherty O. Akinsanmi - MD/CEO.

RICDENIS (NIGERIA) LIMITED
Business: Sales & Repairs of Computers, IT Training
Address: 103, Wetheral Road, Owerri
Tel: (083) 233443, 08037241452 **Fax:** (083) 233443
* 21, Emekuku Street, D/Line, Port Harcourt
Tel: (084) 230424
Contact: Mr. Eric Uzoma Udogwu - Chairman/CEO

RICHLAND COMMUNICATIONS LIMITED
Business: Integrated Marketing Communication, Advertising, Events, Management and Public Relations

Address: 12, Dodo Williams Close, off Rasaq Balogun Street, via Adeniran Ogunsanya Street, Surulere, Lagos
Tel: (01) 5850927, 831922, 7745070 (090) 401307
Fax: (01) 5850927
E-mail: richland@alpha.linkserve.com
Conact: Mrs. Stella Okoli - Chairman
Mr. Ike Modebelu - MD/CEO.

RICHMOND FOODS NIGERIA LIMITED
Business: Production and Processing of Poultry Products
Address: Plot 56, Alade Layout, Ring Road, Ibadan.
* 11B, Thomas Laniyan Street, off Ikorodu Road, Anthony Village, Lagos
Tel/Fax: (01) 4939115, 08033151051
Contact: Mr. Tope Atere - MD/CEO.

RICHSON DRUG COMPANY LIMITED
Business: Importation of Pharmaceuticals, Sales of Medical & Surgical Equipment
Address: 183A, Adeniji Adele Road, Lagos Island, Lagos
Tel: (01) 2667605, 2667607, 2667623, 2667626
Fax: (01) 2667626
Contact: Chief Julius A. E. Nwanya - Chairman/CEO.

RICHTRADE MERCHANDISING (NIGERIA) LIMITED
Business: Sales of Bulk Cement
Address: 12B, Kofo Abayomi Avenue, Apapa, Lagos
Tel: (01) 5870444, 5878579, 5878504
Fax: (01) 5870444, 5871857
E-mail: richtrade@hyperia.com
Contact: Mr. Rashid Alamu Huthman - Chairman

RIC-KEN MERCHANTS LIMITED
Business: Import & Export Trading, Distribution & Marketing of Glue, Markers & Gaskets
Address: LSDPC House (4th Floor, Suite 4), Nnamdi Azikiwe Street, Idumota, Lagos
Tel: (01) 2543198, 2664934, 8114766, 08033088265
E-mail: ric_kenmerchants@yahoo.com
Website: www.ric-ken.com
Contact: Mr. Eric Chika Obele - Chairman/CEO

RIDA NATIONAL PLASTICS LIMITED
Business: Manufacture and Sales of PVC Flooring Materials, Plastic Chairs and Accessories
Address: Plot 8, Industrial Estate, Ilupeju, Lagos
Tel: (01) 8042330, 4963111-5 (5 L) **Fax:** (01) 4963116
E-mail: mp@micro.com.ng
Contact: Mr. M. A. Agha - MD/CEO.

RIETZCOT NIGERIA COMPANY PLC
Business: Manufacturing of Automobile Spare Parts (Radiator Hoses) and Industrial Rubber Components
Address: Km. 38, Abeokuta Motor Road, Otta, Ogun State
Tel: (039) 722412-3 (2 L)
E-mail: rietzcot@infoweb.abs.net

RIGGS SECURITIES LIMITED
Business: Stockbroking, Project Financing
Address: Plot 5, Imam Abibu Adetoro Str (The Penthouse), off Ajose Adeogiun Street, Victoria Island, Lagos
Tel: (01) 4619301-2 (2L), 7749343 **Fax:** (01) 2620604
E-mail: riggs@hyperia.com
Website: www.riggssecurities.com
Contact: Dr. Fredrick Fasheun - Chairman
Mr. Yomi Tokosi - MD/CEO

RIGHTWAY ELECTRONICS COMPANY LIMITED
Business: Importation and Marketing Electronic Appliances
Address: 66, Iweka Road, Onitsha
Tel: (046) 211790, 481175, * (048) 887050, 08033278865, 08034052116
Contact: Chief E. N. Mmuoebonam - Chairman/CEO.

RIGIDPAK CONTAINERS LIMITED
Business: Manufacturing of Corrugated Paper Packaging
Address: 1, 2 & 3, Old Jos Road, Kaduna Street
Tel: (069) 332034, 334473, 330308 **Fax:** (069) 332689
E-mail: rigcosales@skannet.com
* APCO Building, beh Zenith Bank 20, Oba Akran Avenue, Ikeja, Lagos
Tel: (01) 496811-4 (4 L) (Ext. 129)
Contact: Mr. Kirit Shah - Chairman
Mr. Gautam Datta - GM/CEO

RIKIJI & SONS GROUP
Business: Processing & Cotton Lint
Address: 2/3, Industrial Layout, Magami Road, Gusau
Tel: (063) 201732, 202188 **Fax:** (063) 201732
Contact: Alh. Garba Rikiji - Chairman
Alh. Shehu Imam - Ag. GM

RIMI HOLDINGS LIMITED
Business: Trading; Transportation; Marketing of Petroleum Products
Address: 40, Maiduguri Road, opposite NNPC Depot, Hotoro Quarters, Kano
Tel: (064) 645554, 637070, 637195, 330374, 08023279935 08023279936
Contact: Alh. Auwalu Yusuf Rimi - Chairman
Aih. Abdullahi Hussaini Ahmad - MD/CEO.

RIPPCON NIGERIA LIMITED
Business: Networking, Sales of Computers, Radio & Telecommunication Systems, Software Development
Address: 156, Ogunlana Drive, Surulere, Lagos
Tel: (01) 5832560, 5851353, 5851491, 7743014, 8042285, 4705816 **Fax:** (01) 5832560
E-mail: info@rippcon.com
rippcon@rippcon.com
Contact: Engr. Alfred O. Boye - Group MD/CEO.

RISK CONSULTANTS LIMITED
Business: Insurance Broking
Address: 83, Ladipo Street, Matori, Mushin, Lagos
Tel: (01) 524123, 524946, 08033011202
E-mail: riskconsultantsltd@hotmail.com
Contact: Gbenro Oluwole - Chairman/CEO.

RISK WATCH INSURANCE BROKERS LIMITED
Business: Insurance Broking and Risk Management
Address: UBA House (3rd Floor), 57, Marina, Lagos
Tel: (01) 2640066, 2640644 **Fax:** (01) 2640191
E-mail: riskwatch@watchrisk.com
Cotnact: Mrs. Morin Babalola - MD/CEO
Mr. Yambo Bammeke - GM

RISKTECH INSURANCE BROKERS LIMITED
Business: Insurance Broking and Consultancy
Address: 6, Animashaun Street, off Bode Thomas Street, Surulere, Lagos
Tel: (01) 5851740, 831606, 5851414 **Fax:** (01) 5851740
E-mail: risktech@infoweb.abs.net
Contact: Mr. Dele Adelodun - MD/CEO

RISONPALM LIMITED
Business: Palm Plantation, Processing and Marketing of Palm Oil and Allied Products
Address: Nucleus Estate, Ubima, Rivers State
* 35, Aba Road, Port Harcourt
Tel: (084) 486958, 231315 **Fax:** (084) 231315
Contact: Mr. Victor N. Uchendu - Co Sec./Legal Adviser

RITA LORI HOTELS LIMITED
Business: Hospitality Services
Address: Taoridi Street, off Babs Animashaun Road, Census Area, Surulere, Lagos
Tel: (01) 2885136, 831783, 831775, 830559
* Ahmadu Bello Way, Garki II, Abuja

RITZOIL LIMITED
Business: Facilities Engineering & Condition Monitoring, Certification of Lifting Equipments and Pressure Vessels
Address: 9, Ukwerre Street, DDPA Estate, Warri
Tel/Fax: (053) 255504
E-mail: ritzoil@yahoo.co.uk
enoch@infoweb.abs.net
Contact: Engr. Enoch A.Nwobi - Chairman/CEO

RIVBANK INSURANCE COMPANY LIMITED
Business: Insurance
Address: 14, Aba Road, Port Harcourt
Tel: (084) 335100, 335102, 335462, 481711
* Federal Mortgage Bank Building (3rd Floor), Adekunle Fajuyi Road, Ibadan
Tel: (02) 2312308, 08033264450
Contact: Deacon J. A. Ademulegun - MD/CEO

RIVEROAKS DRAKE & SWEENEY LIMITED
Business: Consultancy Services
Address: 68, Mississippi St, Ministers Hill, Maitama, Abuja
Tel: (09) 4139455-6 (2 L) **Fax:** (09) 4139456

RIVERS TRANSPORT COMPANY LIMITED
Business: Transportation of Passengers
Address: Waterlines Complex, Olu Obasanjo Rd, Port Harcourt
Tel: (084) 233702, 239432
Contact: Mr. H. I. R. Wilcox - Asst. GM.

RIVERS VEGETABLE OIL COMPANY LIMITED
Business: Manufacturing of Vegetable Oil, Laundry Soap, Glycerine, Baker's Fat and other Vegetable Oil Products
Address: Plot 80, Trans-Amadi Ind. Layout, Port Harcourt
Tel: (084) 238880, 238881, 571468 **Fax:** (084) 239153
E-mail: rivoc@phca.linkserve.com
rivoc@rivoc.com
Website: www.rivoc.com
Contact: Mr. Ashok Agarwal - MD/CEO

RIVTRUST SECURITIES LIMITED
Business: Stockbroking, Investment Advisory Services, Portfolio Management and Capital Market Research
Address: 39, Campbell Street, Lagos Island, Lagos
Tel: (01) 2637296, 2645683 **Fax:** (01) 2637297
E-mail: rivtrust@infoweb.abs.net
Contact: Rear Admiral Peter I. Eluma (rtd.) - Chairman
Mr. Alex Adeusi - MD/Chief Operating Officer

RIZROSE COMMUNICATIONS LIMITED
Business: Advertising, Marketing Communications
Address: 5, Chilak Close, off Maduagwu Moronu Street, off Adelabu Street, Surulere, Lagos
Tel: (01) 831609, 840114, 4937311
Fax: (01) 2693810, 2618387

RIZZ FOAM & CHEMICAL INDUSTRIES LIMITED
Business: Manufacturing of Foam Products
Address: Behind Kapital Insurance Co. Ltd. Head Office, 116, Hadejia Road,
Tel: (064) 636883, 317479, 08023080578, 08023835160, 08033237607
E-mail: rizzfoam@yahoo.com
* 103, Ibrahim Taiwo Road, Sani Ngogo, Kano
Tel: (064) 641538
Contact: Mr. Arinze C. Atuchukwu - Chairman/CEO

RO PONIG LIMITED
Business: Aviation Services; Logistics Support; Supply and Maintenance of Aircraft; Sales of Spares
Address: 150, Obafemi Awolowo Way, Ikeja, Lagos
Tel: (01) 4965638, 4960558 **Fax:** (01) 4965638
Contact: Col. Willie M. Haywood (rtd.) - MD/CEO

RO/RO OCEANIC SHIPPING SERVICES NIGERIA LIMITED
Business: Shipping Agency, Ship Brokers & Charterers
Address: 17, Burma Road, Apapa, Lagos
Tel: (01) 5878438, 5453433, 5872311
Fax: (01) 5873805, 5453435
E-mail: agency.lagos@rorolagos.com
Website: www.rorolagos.com

ROAD TRUCKERS (NIGERIA) LIMITED
Business: Auto Body Building, Motor Vehicle Sales/Repairs
Address: Plot 1302A, Akin Adesola St Victoria Island, Lagos
Tel: (01) 2624068-9 (2L), 08023137210, 08023137217
Fax: (01) 2620867
E-mail: road1302@mwebafrica.com
roadtruckers@hotmail.com
* 282, Murtala Mohammed Way, Alagomeji-Yaba, Lagos
Tel: (01) 2880196, 7730724, 08023238000, 08036672223
Contact: Chief Oladele Benson - Chairman/CEO

ROADMARKS NIGERIA LIMITED
Business: Integrated Logistics, Haulage, Garage/Workshop Services, Petroleum Downstream Operations
Address: 22, Simbiat Abiola Road, Ikeja, Lagos
Tel: (01) 4961762, 4961764, 08033059115, 08033132905
E-mail: roadmarks98@yahoo.com
* 180, Aba Road, Port Harcourt
Tel: (084) 231801, 08033419177 **Fax:** (084) 231801
Contact: Ola Olunubi - MD/CEO.

ROADS NIGERIA PLC
Business: Civil Engineering Contractors, Construction of Roads, Bridges, Dams and Airfields
Address: Bye-Pass Road, Sokoto
Tel: (060) 235736, 235751, 233011 **Fax:** (060) 234233
* 41B, Marine Road, Apapa, G.R.A., Apapa, Lagos
Tel: (01) 5873567, 5870404
Contact: Mr. J. M. Dansu - MD/CEO

ROBATEK NIGERIA LIMITED
Business: Manufacture of Various Industrial and Domestic Plastic Goods and Items
Address: Plot 1303A, Akin Adesola St Victoria Island, Lagos
Tel: (01) 2622232, 2622259, 2615505 **Fax:** (01) 2619487
E-mail: primlak@hyperia.com
* Plot E, Kirikiri Industrial Estate, Alahun Osumba Street, via Maza-Maza, Lagos
Tel: (01) 7760370
Contact: Mr. Abhijit Sanyal - MD/CEO

ROBBIALAC NIGERIA LIMITED (Sub of Berger Paints Nig Plc)
Business: Manufacturing of Paint
Address: Oba Akran Avenue, Ikeja Industrial Estate, Lagos
Tel: (01) 4978350 **Fax:** (01) 4976987
E-mail: berger@hyperia.com
Website: www.bergerprocol.com

ROBERT-JOHNSON NIGERIA LIMITED
Business: Marketing and Maintenance of Currency-Counting Machines and Office Automation
Address: 286, Ikorodu Road, Anthony, Lagos
Tel: (01) 4931682, 4932527, 4977104, 5550962, 7744747
Fax: (01) 4931681
* 33, Sanagana Street (formerly Ikot Ekpene Street), Diobu Port Harcourt
Tel: (084) 484470
* Plot 1, Road B, NITEL/Sumal Road, Oluyole Estate, Ibadan.
Tel: (02) 2319079
Contact: Soji Arowolo - MD/CEO

ROBEY BOILER & SITE SERVICE LIMITED
Business: Sales, Installation and Maintenance of Boilers
Address: 12/14, Agege Motor Road, Idi-Oro, Mushin, Lagos
Tel: (01) 4705740, 4527661, 4529029, 7748358
Fax: (01) 2693259
E-mail: rolg@infoweb.abs.net

ROBICON ALUMINIUM EXTRUSION COMPANY LIMITED
Business: Aluminium Extrusion and Anodising; Sales of Aluminium Profiles; Casting of Aluminium Billets
Address: Plot 8, Block C, Acme Road, Ogba Industrial Estate, Ikeja, Lagos
Tel: (01) 4922258, 4922761, 7741909 **Fax:** (01) 4922258
Contact: Pastor. Felix Daniels - MD/CEO

ROBINS BEGG CONSULTING LIMITED
Business: Management Consulting (Training, Recruitment, Business Advisory Services, Strategy, Evaluation & Development, Organisational & Industrial Psychotherapy)
Address: 19, Campbell Str (1st Floor), Lagos Island, Lagos
Tel: (01) 8045676, 08033087178
E-mail: info@robinsbeggconsulting.com
Website: www.robinsbeggconsulting.com
Contact: Mr. Abraham Laleye - MD/CEO

ROCANA NIGERIA LIMITED
Business: Outdoor Advertising, Screen & Offset Printing, Reprographic Press, Production of Advertising Materials
Address: 69, Ogui Road, Enugu
Tel: (042) 250615, 250619 **Fax:** (042) 251282
E-mail: rocana@infoweb.abs.net
Website: www.rocana-ng.com
* 17,Olaide Street, off Ladele Dada Street, Ikate, Surulere, Lagos.
Tel: (01) 5456709, 08023103939, 08035051184
Contact: Rotarian Rob O. Oji - Chairman/CEO

ROCH TOOLS AND PRODUCTS LIMITED
Business: Foundry Services, Production of Wrought Iron, Fittings, Furniture, Gates, Fence Rails etc., General Fabrication, Machine Shop
Address: 33, Abimbola Street, Isolo Industrial Estate, Ilasamaja, Lagos
Tel: (01) 4520462, 4524917, 4529470 **Fax:** (01) 4524917
E-mail: printex@hyperia.com
Contact: Ms. Paula-Anne Oshilaja - Chairman
Mr. Itua Ighodalo - MD/CEO

ROCK & POWER ENGINEERING LIMITED
Business: Sales of Electricity Transformers, Feeder Pillars and Low Voltage Panels
Address: J12, Nnamdi Azikiwe Exp, Kurmi-Mashi, Kaduna
Tel: (062) 410932, 411355, 419932, 08023222864
Fax: (062) 410932
Contact: Engr. A. O. Nwaekwe - President

ROCKPETERS NIGERIA LIMITED
Business: Sales of Machine/Technical/Engineering Tools & Industrial Machines
Address: Rockpeters House, Plot 4, Oshodi-Apapa Expressway (Westminster Bus-Stop), Apapa, Lagos
Tel: (01) 5875747, 5876707, 4810245 **Fax:** (01) 5876707
E-mail: rokpetersnigltd@yahoo.com
Contact: Mr. Peter E. Ndulue - Chairman/CEO

ROCKSON ENGINEERING COMPANY LIMITED
Business: Electrical, Mechanical & Civil Engineering, Engineering Construction, Installation, Commissioning, Operations & Maintenance of Gas Turbines
Address: Plot 267, Trans-Amadi Ind. Layout, Port Harcourt
Tel (084) 234162, 08034071113 **Fax:** (084) 234602
E-mail: sales@rocksonengineering.com
Website: www.rocksonengineering.com
Contact: Sir J. I. A. Arumemi-Johnson - Chairman/CEO

ROCKVIEW HOTEL, ABUJA
Business: Hospitality Services
Address: Plot 789, Cadastral Zone A8, off Adetokunbo Ademola Crescent, Wuse II, Garki, Abuja
Tel: (09) 4136722-38 (17L) **Fax:** (09) 4136768, 4136720
E-mail: info@rockviewhotelsltd.com
rockview_reservations@yahoo.com
Website: www.rockviewhotelabuja.com

ROCKY ELECTRONIC CASH & CARRY LIMITED
Business: Sales of Electronic Products
Address: 1087, Adeola Odeku Street, Victoria Island, Lagos
Tel: (01) 2621931, 2622926, 7754399, 08033338846
Fax: (01) 2621931
Contact: Mr. E. N. S. Morah - MD/CEO

RODCO NIGERIA LIMITED
Business: Manufacturer of Ruber Latex Compounds, Latex Gloves, Balloons and Industrial Fillers, Distributors of Fragrances & Chemical Ingredients for Toiletries & Cosmetics, Specialty Chemicals, Flavours and Food Ingredients
Address: 42, Ogudu Road, Ojota, Lagos
Tel: (01) 4965398, 4938209 **Fax:** (01) 4960194
E-mail: rodconig@linkserve.com.ng
* Km. 45, Benin-Sapele Road, by Oghara Junction, Sapele, Delta State
Tel: (054) 60044, 60045 **Fax:** (054) 60048
Contact: Rodney A. Okpu-Hecksher - Chairman/CEO

RODNEY EMMANUL TECHNOLOGIES LIMITED
Business: Supply of Scientific & Technological Equipment
Address: Foreshore Towers (11th Floor), 2A, Osborne Road, Ikoyi, Lagos
Tel: (01) 2672067 **Fax:** (01) 2672068
E-mail: rodemmatech@vgccl.net
Contact: Air Vice Marshal E.I. Ombu (rtd). - Chairman/CEO

ROE LIMITED
Business: Sales of IT Products, Support Services
Address: Amazing Grace Plaza (3rd Floor), 2E-4E, Ligali Ayorinde Street, Victoria Island, Lagos
Tel: (01) 2696049, 2694411, 4617390-3 (4L), 4619530-1 (2L), 4734985 **Fax:** (01) 2690210, 2695924
E-mail: roe@roeltd.com
* 14, Fanaha Suites, Plot 1147, Adetokunbo Ademola Crescent, beh AP Plaza, Wuse II, Abuja.
Tel: (09) 5235308
Contact: Mr Ositah Egbuche - Chairman

ROGA GROUP OF COMPANIES
Business: Corporate Business Promotions, Engraving and Screen Printing Services, Public Relations & Consultancy Services, Award & Incentive Services, Sales of Water Treatment
Address: Olabode House, 217/219, Ikorodu Road, Obanikoro, Lagos
Tel: (01) 4978019, 4962059 **Fax:** (01) 4962059
Contact: Mr. Richard Ogunde - Chairman

ROGERS ALL STARS NIGERIA LIMITED
Business: Production and Promotion of Audio Records
Address: 12A, Okolo Street, Onitsha
Tel: (046) 412096
Contact: Chief R. E. Okonkwo - Chairman/CEO

ROGETS CONSULTING
Business: Tax Consulting, Financial Management Consulting
Address: BAICO Plaza (8th Floor), 12, Abibu-Oki Street, off Marina, Lagos Island, Lagos
Tel: (01) 2643748, 08033054474
E-mail: vemeana@yahoo.com

ROJENNY GAMES & TOURIST VILLAGE
Business: Leisure & Entertainment Sevices, Hospitality Services, Sports Facilities
Address: Km. 11, Onitsha-Owerri Road, Onitsha
Contact: Chief Rommy Ezeonwuka - Chairman/CEO

ROKANA INDUSTRIES PLC
Business: Manufacturing and Marketing of Household Products, Toiletries and Hygiene Products
Address: Plot 4, Ajayi Street, by Lagos Hilton Hotel, off Ogundana St, off Allen Avenue, Ikeja, Lagos
Tel: (01) 4967481, 08033427557, 08036686576
Fax: (01) 4970100
E-mail: rokana@infowb.abs.net
* Plot 5, Mission Rd, Umualum-Nekede, via Owerri
Tel: (083) 234631, 234894 **Fax:** (083) 234909
Contact: Engr. Charles C. Ugwuh - Chairman/CEO

ROKINGS INSURANCE BROKERS LIMITED
Business: Insuranc Broking
Address: 53B, Akpakpava Street, Benin City
Tel: (052) 252028, 08023242117
E-mail: rokings@yahoo.com
Contact: Sir. R. K. Igunbor - Chairman/CEO

ROLAY ENGINEERING COMPANY LIMITED
Business: Manfacturing of Solar Energy, Electronic & Electrical Equipment and Electronic Printed Circuit Boards; Stockist of Electronic Tools & Components; Payphone Operations; Building Projects
Address: 32, Iwo Road, Ibadan
Tel: (02) 8108329 **Fax:** (02) 8109051
Contact: Engr. (Dr.) Abraham O. Ajayi-Obe - Chairman/CEO.

ROMA U. A. AGENCIES NIGERIA LIMITED
Business: Importation of Rugs, Carpets and Underlay
Address: Shops H46/H47, Alaba Int'l Market, Ojo, Lagos
Tel: (01) 3456032
E-mail: romacarpets@yahoo.com
Contact: Mr. R. Ukah - Chairman/CEO.

ROMAPLAST NIGERIA LIMITED
Business: Manufacturers of Bottle-Grade PVC Compounds
Address: 10, Duala Road, Apapa, Lagos
Tel: (01) 875175, 873709, 874135, 5454729-20 (2 L)
* 19/23, Okoduwa Street, Kirikiri Ind Estate, Lagos.
Tel: (01) 7742811
Contact: Mr. M. S. Fawaz - Chairman/CEO

RO-MARONG NIGERIA LIMITED
Business: Large-Format Digital Printing, Sole Agent for RISO Printing Machine, Manufacturing of Metallic Sponge
Address: Brossette Compound, 311, Apapa Road, Apapa, Lagos
Tel: (01) 7912371-9(3 L), 7768577, 7768572
Fax: (01) 7912371
Website: www.romarong.net
Contact: Mr. Maged Bahson - Chairman/CEO

ROMAY ENTERPRISES LIMITED
Business: Importation, Manufacturing and Marketing of Cosmetics, Hair Care Products and Hair Weave-on
Address: 12A, Bankole Street, off Issa Williams Street, off

Broad Street, Balogun, Lagos
Tel: (01) 2666601, 2660673, 2666823 **Fax:** (01) 2646439
Contact: Chief (Dr.) R. O. Chinwuba - Chairman/CEO.

ROMEK & COMPANY LIMITED
Business: Engineering Services
Address: 12, Arochukwu Street, Rumumasi, Port Harcourt
Tel: (084) 333981, 08033097307, 08033385304
* Km. 3, East-West Road, off Rumuokoro Junction, Port Harcourt
Contact: R.A. Okwuka - Chairman/CEO

ROMSON OILFIELD SERVICES LIMITED
Business: Oilfield Engineering Services
Address: Plot 20, Chief Benson Anorue Street, off Ajao Estate, Apakun-Oshodi, Lagos
Tel: (01) 4520592, 4520965, 4520877, 4520987, 7740383, 4520626-32 (7L) **Fax:** (01) 452980
E-mail: tgimajic@cyberspace.net.ng
Contact: Mr. C. G. Vink - Chairman

ROOFCO NIGERIA LIMITED
Business: Manufacturing of Galvanized Iron Roofing Sheets
Address: L-14, Kachia Road, Kakuri Industrial Area, Kaduna
Tel: (062) 231155, 2322341 **Fax:** (062) 231155
E-mail: roofcong@inet-global.com
Contact: Alh. Abdulahi Kaloma Ali - MD/CEO

ROOMANS ENELI FLYNN INSURANCE BROKERS LIMITED
Business: Insurance Broking and Pension Consultancy
Address: 49, Awolowo Road, S.W. Ikoyi, Lagos
Tel: (01) 2693559, 2692737, 2692618 **Fax:** (01) 2691654
Contact: Chief (Dr.) Sunday Dankaro - Chairman
Mr. P. V. S. Sagar - MD/CEO

ROPE & RIGGING NIGERIA LIMITED
Business: Manufacturing of Ropes and Strings
Address: Maritime House, Kirikiri Lighter Terminal Phase I, Oshodi Expressway, Kirikiri Wharf, Apapa, Lagos
Tel: (01) 5872491, 5872582, 5873561, 5871684, 5877376
Fax: (01) 5876355, 5877376, 5873450
E-mail: aerogroup@infoweb.abs.net
* Investment House, 3, Grace Avenue, Elelenwoo, Port Harcourt
Tel: (084) 332934, 239428, 238005, 338095, 612480-2 (3 L)
Fax: (084) 238006, 238024
Contact: Chief Victor I. Odili - Chairman/CEO.

ROSA FAIR LIMITED
Business: Advertising & Market Research, Events Marketing, Designs & Print Production, Promotions
Address: 1/3, Ade Adesanya Street, off Nuru Oniwo Street, Aguda, Surulere, Lagos
Tel: (01) 831530, 847248
Contact: Austin O. Asomaku - MD/CEO.

ROSAAB INDUSTRIAL DESIGN LIMITED
Business: Signs Manufacturing, Sign-Related Services
Address: Plot B, Ikosi Rd, Oregun Ind, Estate, Oregun, Lagos
Tel: (01) 4961872-3 (2L), 4706573, 8118611
E-mail: signs@rosaab.com
Contact: Mr. Abiodun Odojukan - Exec. Chairman
Mr. Ibidapo Odojukan - MD/CEO

ROSABEL ADVERTISING LIMITED
Business: Advetising and Marketing Communications
Address: Rosabel Court, 31, Aromire Avenue, Ikeja, Lagos
Tel: (01) 4976210-3 (4 L) **Fax:** (01) 4976214
E-mail: info@rosabelleoburnett.com
Contact: Chief Babalola Akinola Odunsi - Chairman
Mr. Kofoworola Babatunde Adelaja - MD/CEO.

ROSABOL NIGERIA LIMITED
Business: Supply & Installation of Marble & Granite Building Materials, Suply & Installation of Ceiling Tiles, Manufacture of Marble/Granite Furniture
Address: 9/11, Morison Crescent, off Oregun Road, Oregun Industrial Estate, Alausa, Ikeja, Lagos
Tel/Fax: (01) 4972417
* Plot 367, Cadastral Zone A6, off Nnamdi Azikiwe Road, Maitama, Abuja. **Tel:** (09) 5213328
Contact: Mr. Adekoyejo Branco Rhodes - MD/CEO.

ROSAK ASSOCIATES LIMITED
Business: Photography
Address: 11, Ribadu Road, Ikoyi, Lagos
Tel: (01) 2690821 **Fax:** (01) 2690820
* 1, Rumuodalu/Market Road, Port Harcourt

ROSAN VENTURES LIMITED
Business: Assembly, Sales & Service of Computers; Lithographic Printing Services
Address: 28, Akinremi Street, off Obafemi Awolowo Street, Anifowoshe, Ikeja, Lagos
Tel: (01) 4965715, 4936609, 3453497 **Fax:** (01) 4936609
E-mail: rosan@intracom5.com
Contact: Mr. Anietie B. Essien - Chairamn/CEO.

ROSEAT INSURANCE BROKERS LIMITED
Business: Insurance Broking and Consultancy
Address: 2, Alh. Tokunbo Alli Street (3rd Floor), off Toyin Street, Ikeja, Lagos
Tel: (01) 4977929
E-mail: roseat2000@hotmail.com
* Suite 24, Lumumba Shopping Complex, Area 10, Garki, Abuja
Contact: Rose A. Okon - MD/CEO.

ROSECOM.NET NIGERIA LIMITED
Business: Internet Service Provider,
Address: Plot 138B, Adetokunbo Ademola Crescent, Wuse II, Abuja
Tel: (09) 4131844-5 (2L), 080331544421
Fax: (09) 4132657
E-mail: info@rosecom.net
Website: www.rosecom.net
Contact: Sulieman Yahyah - Chairman

ROSS CLAYTON LIMITED
Business: Data Communication & Data Management Consultants, Internet Service Provider
Address: Plot PC. 10, Engineering Close, Victoria Island, Lagos
Tel: (01) 2623235, 2620074 **Fax:** (01) 2623235
E-mail: rcl@rcl.nig.com
Website: www.rossclayton.com
* 1, Ohaeto Lane, D-Line, Port Harcourt
Tel: (084) 330446

* Ersico Bonpet Plaza (2nd Floor), Herbert Macaulay Way, Wuse Zone 5, Abuja
Contact: Mr. Babatunde Sowobi - Chairman/CEO

ROTIMI OBEISUN INVESTMENT LIMITED
Business: Shipping, Clearing & Forwarding, Supply of Raw Materials and Industrial Chemicals, Agro-Allied Manufacturing & Consultancy, Project Financing and Investments, Civil Contractors
Address: Timsed House, Plot 2, Blocks A & B, Salimonu St, off Oladunni Ayandipo Rd, New Bodija Estate, Ibadan
Tel: (02) 8102133, 8104177, 8103266 **Fax:** (02) 8102974
* Km. 5, Old Lagos Road, Podo Village, Ibadan
Tel: (02) 2316734, 2316742 **Fax:** (02) 2318008
* 41, Hospital Road, opposite Oti Carpets, Tin Can Island Expressway, Olodi-Apapa, Lagos
Contact: Bashorun Rotimi Obeisun - Chairman/CEO

ROTIX (NIGERIA) LIMITED
Business: Production of Ring Binders, Conference Folders, Desk Pads & Lever Arch Files, Sales & Service of Paper-Shredding Machine
Address: 7, McNeil Road, Sabo-Yaba, Lagos
Tel: (01) 861506, 4731040, 08033152481
Fax: (01) 865586
Contact: Mr. A. A. Onaolapo - Chairman/CEO

ROYAL CERAMICS LIMITED
Business: Manufacturing and Marketing of Ceramic Wall Tiles and Sanitary Ware
Address: Baban Tunga Village, 7 Km from Zuma Rock (towards Kaduna), Abuja-Kaduna Expressway, P. O. Box 003, Suleja, Niger State
Tel: (09) 8500803, 8500832, 6702772, 6707735
E-mail: rclsv@yahoo.com
rclsv@hyperia.com
* 14, Ademola Street, off Awolowo Road, S.W. Ikoyi, Lagos
Tel: (01) 2694152-6 (5L), 08034021000, 08034692932
Fax: (01) 2691314
E-mail: fc@linkserve.com.ng
fcltd@hyperia.com
Contact: Alh. M. O. Idrisu - Chairman/CEO

ROYAL COMMUNICATIONS LIMITED
Business: Outdoor Advertising and Production Agency, Sales of Corporate Gifts
Address: 104, Western Avenue (3rd Floor), Ojuelegba, Surulere, Lagos
Tel: (01) 5847142, 08033288505, 08033306302
Contact: Mr. Olayinka Adepoju - MD/CEO

ROYAL COURIER SERVICES LIMITED
Business: Express Courier Services, Consolidations, Freight Forwarding, Procurement, Logistics
Address: 57, Allen Avene, Ikeja, Lagos
Tel: (01) 4974793, 4938588, 08032030887
Fax: (01) 4938383
E-mail: info@royalcourier.net
Website: www.royalcourier.net
* 13, Ogui Road, Enugu
Tel: (042) 258150, 08033128799
Contact: Mr. Okey Dimoji - MD/CEO

ROYAL CREST FINANCE LIMITED
Business: Stockbroking, Funds and Portfolio Management, Money Market Operations
Address: LSDPC House (3rd Floor), 17, Nnamdi Azikiwe/Alli Balogun Street, Lagos Island, Lagos
Tel: (01) 2661340, 2669760, 2640664 **Fax:** (01) 2644586
Contact: Chief S. O. Ikeneku - MD/CEO

ROYAL CROSS MEDICAL CENTRE
Business: Healthcare & Medical Services
Address: 10, Nojeem Maiyegun Road, Obalende, Lagos
Tel: (01) 2693761, 2691927
Contact: Dr. Doyin Okupe - Chairman
Dr. Seyi Roberts

ROYAL EXCHANGE ASSURANCE (NIGERIA) PLC
Business: Life & General Insurance Business
Address: New Africa House, 31, Marina, Lagos
Tel: (01) 2663120, 2663191, 2663197, 2663218
Fax: (01) 2664431
* 34/36, Oshodi-Apapa Expressway, Oshodi, Lagos
Tel: (01) 4968010-6 (7L) **Fax:** (01) 4968017
* Plot 2404, HMacaulay Way, Wuse Zone 6, Abuja
Contact: Mr. James O. Ayo - MD/CEO.

ROYAL FOAM PRODUCTS NIGERIA LIMITED
Business: Manufacturing and Marketing of Foam Products
Address: Plot 46/47, Sharada Industrial Estate Phase II, Kano
Tel: (064) 666706, 661831; **Fax:** (064) 664694
Contact: Mr. Fouad Zoueihed - MD/CEO.

ROYAL PRESS LIMITED
Business: Printing Services, Digital Colour Separation
Address: 52, St. Finbarr's College Road, Akoka, Yaba, Lagos
Tel: (01) 4972466, 4975379 **Fax:** (01) 4972465
* Plot 477, Airport Road, Central Business District, Garki, Abuja.
Tel: (09) 5230045 (090) 802548
Contact: Mr. Ayo Osho - GM/CEO

ROYAL PROPERTIES INTERNATIONAL LIMITED
Business: Estate Agency, Property Development
Address: NCWS House, Plot PC. 14, Ahmed Onibudo Street, Victoria Island, Lagos
Tel: (01) 2617215, 4618489, 4708733 **Fax:** (01) 618146

ROYAL SALT LIMITED
Business: Refining and Sales of Edible Salt
Address: 14, Ademola Street, S.W. Ikoyi, Lagos
Tel: (01) 2694152-5 (4 L) **Fax:** (01) 2691314
* Northern Warehouse, Kirikiri Lighter Terminal Phase I, near Tin-Can Island, Apapa, Lagos
Tel: (01) 5878449, 7756725
Contact: Alh. Nasidi Ibrahim - Chairman/CEO

ROYAL SAVINGS & LOANS LIMITED
Business: Mortgage Banking
Address: Isoken Plaza, 3, Effurun/Sapele Rd, Effurun, Warri
Tel: (053) 254319-21 (3L) **Fax:** (053) 252646
Contact: Engr. T. I. Imasuen - Chairman/CEO.

ROYAL STRIDE NIGERIA LIMITED
Business: Provision of Mobile Telephone Services and

Satellite Telephone Services via INMARSAT; Sales and Service of GSM Phones and Accessories
Address: 57, Allen Avenue, Ikeja, Lagos
Tel: (01) 4931999, 4938588, 4974793; 08034007465
Fax: (01) 4938383
E-mail: rstride@infoweb.abs.net
Website: www.royalstride.com
* Plot 874B, Adetokunbo Ademola Cr, Wuse II, Abuja.
Tel: (09) 5238539 (090) 802898
Contact: Air Cmdre Emeka S. Omeruah - Chairman
Mr. Okey Dimoji - MD/CEO.

ROYAL SUITES LIMITED
Business: Sales of Fitted Kitchens, Furniture, Sanitary Wares, Ceramic Tiles, Lighting Fittings, Bathroom Furniture & Accessories
Address: Plot 1378D, Joseph Nahman Close, off Karimu Kotun Street, Victoria Island, Lagos
Tel: (01) 2624833, 7914203 **Fax:** (01) 2624833
E-mail: 7914203@multilinks.com
Website: ww.royalsuitesnigeria.com
Contact: Arc T. K. Sulaiman - Chairman/CEO

ROYAL TROPICANA HOTEL, KANO
Business: Hospitality & Catering Services, Conference Facilities
Address: 17/19, Niger Street, Kano
Tel: (064) 639350, 639352, 647494, 639359
Fax: (064) 639358
E-mail: royaltrop@yahoo.com
Contact: Alh. Abdullahi Aliyu - Chairman/CEO

ROYAL TRUST ASSURANCE LIMITED
Business: Insurance Business
Address: Bookshop House (8th Floor), 5052, Broad Street, Lagos Island, Lagos
Tel: (01) 2645583-5 (3 L) **Fax:** (01) 2645586
E-mail: royaltrust@nigol.net.ng
* 9, Mbonu Street, D-Line, Port Harcourt
* Russl Centre, Plot 2425, Herbert Macaulay Way, Zon 4, Wuse, Abuja
Contact: Chief (Dr.) B. A. Adigun - Chairman
Mr. Tunde Oyolola - MD/CEO

ROYAL UNITED NIGERIA LIMITED
Business: Distribution and Sales of Portland Cement, Iron Rods, Automobile Tyres and Batteries, Ceramic Wall & Floor Tiles
Address: Plot 88, Ajose Adeogun St, Victoria Island, Lagos
Tel: (01) 2623430-1 (2L), 2629112-3 (2L)
Fax: (01) 2624173
E-mail: royalunited@aol.com
Website: www.royalnigeria.com
Contact: Alh. Aliko Dangote - Chairman
Alh. M. Noureddine - MD/CEO

ROYALSEC SERVICES COMPANY LIMITED
Business: Security Guard Services, Sales and Maintenance of Security Systems and Equipment
Address: 55, Itire Road, Ekololu Bus-Stop, opposite Mobil Filling Station, Surulere, Lagos
Tel: (01) 5841630, 5455698, 5456341, 4706137, 08022231255, 08028284416 **Fax:** (01) 5456341

* Wuse Shopping Mall (Suite C9), Plot 2233, Maputo Street, Zone 3, Wuse, Abuja
Tel: 08033139080
* 8C, Okarki Street, New Layout, Borokini, off Harold Wilson Drive, Port Harcourt
Contact: Mr. Rotimi S. Isola - MD/CEO

ROYALTON HOTELS LIMITED
Business: Hospitality & Catering Services
Address: Plot 1907, Gongola St, Area 2, Section 1, Garki, Abuja
Tel: (09) 2344914-7 (4L), 2346850-2 (3L)
Fax: (09) 2344913
E-mail: royalton9@hotmail.com
Contact: Engr. E. O. Obiajunwa - Chairman/CEO

ROYAS EXCLUSIVE FURNISHINGS LIMITED
Business: Furniture & Furnishing, Interior Decorators
Address: Plot 598, Kashim Ibrahim Way, Wuse II, Garki, Abuja
Tel: (09) 5236920, 08033139224
* 19, Zaria Road, Gyadi-Gyadi, Kano
Tel: (064) 667348, 08037877329
Contact: Muhammad Imam - Chairman/CEO

ROYE IBRU ASSOCIATES
Business: Architectural Consultants, Project Managers
Address: 5C, Marine Road, Apapa, Lagos
* 201, Central Ugbowo-Lagos Road,, Benin-City
Tel: (052) 600261
* 9, Amigbo Street, Port Harcourt
Contact: Arc. Felix Ovuoderoye Ibru - Principal Partner

RTB MARINE LIMITED
Business: Sales & Service of Outboard Motor Boat Engines
Address: Plot K9, Oshodi-Apapa Expressway, beside Union Bank, Isolo, Lagos
Tel: (01) 7741753, 4526576 **Fax:** (01) 4525453
Contact: Mr. Olayinka Olumide Akinkugbe - MD.
Miss Dupe Olaniyan - Operations Manager

RTB TELECOM LIMITED
Business: Consultancy, Supply, Installation, Repairs and Maintenance of Radio & Telecommunication Equipment
Address: 18, Fatati Atere Way, Matori Industrial Scheme, Oshodi, Lagos
Tel: (01) 4823540, 7757875, 08032030913, 08035551555
Fax: (01) 3203365, 4524519, 4524519
E-mail: telecom@rtb.com.ng
Contact: Mr. Jens Erik Mollenbach - Chairman
Mr. J. O. Nielsen - MD.

RUFF 'N' TUMBLE
Business: Fashion Sales Outlet for Children
Address: 23A, Isaac John Street, Ikeja G.R.A., Lagos
Tel/Fax: (01) 4932387
E-mail: rufntumble@gatimo.com
Website: gatimo.com
Contact: Mrs. N. Ogunlesi - MD/CEO

RUMBU SACKS LIMITED
Business: Production of Woven Polypropylene Sacks & Mats
Address: Opp. Sir Sanusi Gen. Hospital, Tokarawa, Km. 4, Hadejia Road, Kano

Tel: (064) 314114, 08023341174
E-mail: rumb@ecnx.net
Contact: Alh. Sani Ahmed Mukthar - MD/CEO

RURU ENGINEERING SERVICES LIMITED
Business: Sales & Service of Dredgers, Gas Turbines, Gas Compressors & Fire Pumps, Consultancy/Training
Address: 37, Eboh Road, Okumagba Layout, Warri
Tel/Fax: (053) 250762, 251775
E-mail: ruru.b@warri.rcl.nig.com
Contact: Prof E. Paive - Chairman/CEO.

RUTAM TRAVELS LIMITED
Business: Travel Agency and Car Hire Services
Address: Federal Palace Hotel (Suite 366), Ahmadu Bello Way, Victoria Island, Lagos
Tel: (01) 2623116-25 (10 L)(Ext 366) **Fax:** (01) 2617934
Contact: Dr. Alex A. Thomopulos - Dir./Group Co-ordinator

RYDER FENDT (NIGERIA) LIMITED
Business: Sales & Service of Tractors, Automobiles and Hospital Equipment
Address: Plot 691, Tundunfulani, Minna
Tel: (066) 220515 **Fax:** (066) 220454
Contact: Alh. Shafi Ndayako - Chairman/CEO

S & D GROUP
Business: Venture Capital, Information Technology Consultancy, Financing, Trading
Address: Kajola House, 62/64, Campbell Street, Lagos
Tel: (01) 2635371, 2635338, 2631406, 2631299, 8047915, 08022234692
E-mail: info@sdc-consult.com
Contact: Mr. O. Olusanya - Group MD.CEO

S & S WIRELESS LIMITED
Business: Sales of Telecommunication Equipment, GSM Phone & Accessories
Address: 7, Adelabu Street, Surulere, Lagos
Tel: (01) 8048899, 8129119, 8047668, 8111118, 0808129119
* 60, Ogunlana Drive, Surulere, Lagos
Tel: (01) 7923000, 814866, 8111118, 08037178880
Fax: (01) 8129119
E-mail: partypacks@yahoo.com
Contact: Mr. Seinde Olusola - MD/CEO

S. OJOLOWO TECHNICAL COMPANY LIMITED
Business: Fire and Security Protection Services, Building Construction
Address: 6, Charles Amu Avenue, Alasia, Oshodi, Lagos
Tel: (01) 4976842, 08023014770, 08033012751
Fax: (01) 4976842
E-mail: sot_co@yahoo.com
Contact: Chief Solomon A. Ojolowo - Chairman/CEO.

S. RODA & SONS LIMITED
Business: Manufacturing of Plastic Mats
Address: Plot 17/18, Sharada Industrial Estate Phase I, Kano
Tel: (064) 661694, 664713 **Fax:** (064) 661694

S. C. JOHNSON NIGERIA LIMITED
Business: Manufacturing & Marketing of Industrial & Domestic Products
Address: 13/14, Abimbola Street, Isolo Ind. Estate, Lagos
Tel: (01) 4520575, 4524210, 4524213, 4524216
Fax: (01) 4522154
E-mail: kesurua@infoweb.abs.net
Contact: Mr. Godwin O. Oteri - MD/CEO.

S. C. C. (NIGERIA) LIMITED
Business: Drilling of Boreholes, Water Engineering Services, Water & Sewage Treatment Works, Building & Road Construction
Address: 7, Olosa Street, Victoria Island, Lagos
Tel: (01) 2622153-4 (2L), 2622197, 2622230
Fax: (01) 2611290
* Plot 471, Lobito Crescent, off Adetokunbo Ademola Crescent, Cadastral Zone A8, Abuja
Tel: (09) 4132701, 4137108, 5237108 **Fax:** (09) 4137109
Contact: Mr. Aviram - Deputy MD

S. G. INTERNATIONAL AGENCIES LIMITED
Business: Shipping and Airfreighting Services, Clearing and Forwarding
Address: NACFA Compound, Cargo Section, Aminu Kano International Airport, Kano
Tel: (064) 638353, 647640 **Fax:** (064) 638353
E-mail: sginterkano@yahoo.com
* Eleganza Plaza (Libra Block, 1st Floor), 1, Commercial Road, Apapa, Lagos
Tel: (01) 5876643, 08033006886
Contact: Alh. Sanusi Wakili - MD/CEO

S. O. M. ANENE & PARTNERS
Business: Estate Surveyors & Valuers
Address: Russel Centre, Plot 2425, Herbert Macaulay Way, Zone 4, Wuse, Abuja
Tel: (09) 5235033, 5234672, 08033118303, 08033141875, 08044106101

SA & C LIMITED
Business: Marketing Communications
Address: Yinka Folawiyo Plaza (6th Floor), 38, Yinka Folawiyo (Warehouse) Road, Apapa, Lagos
Tel: (01) 5870136, 5870443 **Fax:** (01) 5870509
Contact: Mr V. O. Afowowe - Chairman/CEO

SA'A PHARMACEUTICAL PRODUCT LIMITED
Business: Manufacturing of Pharmaceutical Products
Address: Plot 100, Sharada Industrial Estate, Phase II, Kano
Tel: (064) 668799, 668807, 08023810660
Fax: (064) 668807.

SA' ADATU PLASTICS MANUFACTURING COMPANY LTD
Business: Manufacturing of Industrial & Domestic Plasticwares
Address: Plot 06, Sharada Industrial Estate Phase I, Kano
Tel: (064) 665282, 665549 **Fax:** (064) 665549
Contact: Alh. Gambo Mohammed - Chairman/CEO

SAAP-TECH NIGERIA LIMITED
Business: Structured Cabling, Systems Integration, Communication, High-Power Solutions
Address: 32, Musa Yar'Adua Street, off Idowu Martins Street, Victoria Island, Lagos
Tel: (01) 2620336, 262483-5 (3 L), 6194040, 619404

Fax: (01) 2620346
E-mail: infosales@saap-tech.com
Website: www.saap-tech.com
Contact: Mr. Fola Adeola - Chairman
Mr. Chima Onyekwere - MD/CEO

SABEANAT NIGERIA LIMITED
Business: Marketing of Dairy Products and Raw Materials
Address: 11, Akinsanya Street, off Isheri Road, by FRSC Compound, Ojodu, Lagos
Tel: (01) 5557476-8 (3L), 7919797 **Fax:** (01) 5557490
E-mail: customercare@sabeanatgroup.com
Website: www.sabeanatgroup.com
Contact: Mr. Sam. O. Oburoh - Chairman/CEO

SABIPLAST NIGERIA LIMITED
Business: Manufacture of Polythene Bags
Address: 4C, Independence Road, Bompai Ind. Estate, Kano
Tel: (064) 644636, 635111, 637111, 644637, 316931, 08033173583 **Fax:** (064) 644637
* 2, Sassandra Street, Wuse Zon 6, Abuja
Tel: 08023003812
Contact: Alh. Sabiu Bako - Chairman/CEO

SABIU BAKO TRADING COMPANY LIMITED
Business: Building & Civil Engineering, General Contractors & Procurers, General Merhcandising, Import & Export, Plasticware Products Manufacturers
Address: 4C, Independence Road, Bompai Ind. Estate, Kano
Tel: (064) 644636, 635111, 637111, 644637, 316931, 08033173583 **Fax:** (064) 644637
* 2, Sassandra Stret, Wuse Zone 6, Abuja
Tel: 08023003812
Contact: Alh. Sabiu Bako - Chairman/CEO

SABOW BAKING & FOOD INDUSTRIES LIMITED
Business: Baking and Confectionery
Address: 20/22, Kadiri Street, off Ajayi Street, Aguda-Titun, Ogba-Ikeja, Lagos
Tel: (01) 7737784, 4923659, 4923711, 08023162102, 08023162100 **Fax:** (01) 4923711
E-mail: sabowbakess@yahoo.com
Contact: S. B. Owoeye - Chairman/CEO

SABRU NIGERIA LIMITED
Business: Ship Charterers, Brokers & Agents, Customs Agents
Address: Sabru House, 3, Mubi Road, Yola
Tel: (075) 625658 **Fax:** (075) 625567
* 14, Warehouse Road, Apapa, Lagos
Tel: (01) 5876069, 5876070 **Fax:** (01) 5870521
Contact: Alh. Sadiq Ahmed (Ciroma Ganye) - Chairman
Alh. U. A. Sadiq - MD/CEO

SABSUN NIGERIA LIMITED
Business: Security Printing, Hologram Solutions (Product & Document Authentication), Pre-Paid Card Marketing
Address: 61, Tejuosho Street, Surulere, Lagos
Tel: (01) 4738352, 7748811, 08033082323
E-mail: sabsun_ng@yahoo.co.uk
Contact: Mr. Ayodele Simon Awoluja - Chairman/CEO

SACKS & MOTORS NIGERIA LIMITED
Business: Manufacturing of Woven Sacks, Sales of Motor Vehicles
Address: 105, Murtala Mohammed Way, Fagge 'C', Kano
Tel: (064) 634653, 649282
Contact: Alh. Hamisu Sankaka - MD/CEO.

SADEL INTERNATIONAL LIMITED
Business: Outdoor Advertising Agency, Production of Packaged Water, Car-Care Services
Address: 223, Egbeda Road, Idimu, Lagos
Tel: (01) 4736061, 7747087, 08023180971, 08033193935
E-mail: sadelbus@yahoo.com
Contact: Mr. S. A. Bakare - Chairman/CEO.

SADIQ PETROLEUM NIGERIA LIMITED
Business: Exploration, Refining and Marketing of Petroleum
Address: Plot 278, Ajose Adeogun St, Victoria Island, Lagos
Tel: (01) 2622058, 2621627, 2621589, 2642071, 4617753.
Fax: (01) 2621627, 4617752
E-mail: sadiqpetro@hyperia.com
Contact: Mr. Peter Eloka Okocha OON - Chairman/CEO

SAFA FOAM PRODUCTS (NIGERIA) LIMITED
Business: Manufacturing and Marketing of Foam Products
Address: 2, Maicibi Close, Kakarui Industrial Estate, Kaduna
Tel: (062) 231240, 231241, 08033111328
Fax: (062) 231186
Contact: Alh. Sule Katagum, OFR - Chairman
Alh. Adib M. Safa - MD/CEO

SAFA STEEL & CHEMICAL MANUFACTURING LIMITED
Business: Manufacturing and Distribution of Steel and Chemicals; Oil Industry Engineering Services.
Address: Plot 89, Industrial Area, Sharada Phase II, Kano
Tel: (064) 629865
* 184/195, Happy Home Avenue, Kirikiri Industrial Estate, Lagos
Tel: (01) 5454775-8 (5 L) **Fax:** (01) 5454774
* Plot 65, Trans-Amadi Ind Layout, Port Harcourt.
Tel: (084) 230471, 08034023030
Contact: Mr. Adib M. Safa - Vice Chairman/CEO.
Engr. I. Kobeissi - MD

SAFAAR INTERNATIONAL (NIGERIA) LIMITED
Business: Construction, Supply and Furnishing
Address: 39, Joel Ogunnaike Street, Ikeja, G.R.A, Lagos
Tel/Fax: (01) 4975976

SAFE ASSOCIATES LIMITED
Business: Accounting & Management Tutorial Services
Address: 31, Ore-Ofe Street, Onitolo, opp. Lagos State Polytechnic, Gbaja, Surulere, Lagos
Tel: (01) 7742190, 4811988, 08022252931, 08023177050, 08033024864, 08033304599
E-mail: safetuition@onebox.com
safeican@yahoo.com
Wesbite: www.safe-associates.com

SAFE NIGERIA LIMITED
Business: Building and Civil Engineering, Road Construction, Water Distribution Enginering, Rural Electrication Services
Address: 15A, Oko-Awo Close, off Karimu Kotun Street, Victoria Island, Lagos

Tel: (01) 2626375, 612319 **Fax:** (01) 2882543
E-mail: chateno@hyperia.com
* 43, Eric Manuel Street, off Bode Thomas Street, Surulere, Lagos.
Tel: (01) 836119, 836490
Contact: Chief Frank Ogieva Omosigho - Chairman/CEO

SAFEPOINT INVESTMENTS COMPANY LIMITED
Business: Financial Services and Bureau de Change, Property Development and Management, Travel Agency
Address: Oxford House (Basement), Bank Rd, Dugbe, Ibadan
Tel: (02) 2410649, 2410752, 08023066679, 08037220536
Fax: (02) 2410823, 2410856
E-mail: bakosile@infoweb.abs.net
Website: www.safepointexpress.com
* NIM Building (2nd Floor), Plot 22, Idowu Taylor Street, Victoria Island, Lagos.
Tel: (01) 7749396
Contact: Mr. Banjo Akosile - Chairman/CEO

SAFEQUIP (NIGERIA) LIMITED
Business: Sales, Installation and Maintenance of Electronic Security Equipment, Fire Detection and Extinguishing Systems and Rapiscan Screening Machines
Address: Block A (Unit 14), Falomo Shopping Centre, Awolowo Road, S. W. Ikoyi, Lagos
Tel: (01) 2670651, 2673675, 08023048551
Fax: (01) 2673675
E-mail: topsymide@nova.net.ng
Contact: Mr Abayomi Jolaoso - MD/CEO

SAFETRUST SAVINGS & LOANS LIMITED
Business: Mortgage Finance Services
Address: Safetrust Centre, 18, Keffi Street, S. W. Ikoyi, Lagos
Tel: (01) 2691442, 2691443, 2690792, 2671520, 267521, 2691483 **Fax:** (01) 2694258
E-mail: safe@infoweb.abs.net
Contact: Mr. Danjuma Saleh - Chairman/CEO

SAFETY ENGINEERING & FIRE CONSULTANTS (NIG.) LTD
Business: Safety and Environmental Consultancy Services
Address: 118, Bode Thomas Street, Surulere, Lagos
Tel: (01) 5847909, 5843400, 5841699, 08023113753, 08033066649 **Fax:** (01) 5843400
E-mail: sefc@infoweb.abs.net
Contact: Mr. Evaristus Ovbiye Uzamere - Chairman/CEO

SAFEWAY TRAVEL LIMITED
Business: 213, Herbert Macaulay Streeet, Yaba, Lagos
Tel: (01) 7745464, 5872163, 08023521130, 08023594768
Fax: (01) 5872163
E-mail: safetravels@hyperia.com
: www.safewaytravls.com

SAFIRE FURNISHINGS NIGERIA LIMITED
Business: Importation, Manufacturing and Sales of Furniture, Interior Decorating and Furnishing
Address: Plot 1066, Adetokunbo Ademola Cr, Wuse II, Abuja
Tel: (09) 5232229, 5232783 **Fax:** (09) 5232418, 5232783
Contact: Arc. Okwy Adogu - MD/CEO

SAFMARINE NIGERIA LIMITED
Business: Shipping (Containerised & Bulk Cargo), Ocean Liners and Ship Owners
Address: Maersk House (3rd Floor), 121, Louis Solomon Close, Ahmadu Bello Way, Victoria Island, Lagos
Tel: (01) 2626410-9 (10 L) **Fax:** (01) 2626424
E-mail: lossclmk@africa.safmarine.com
Website: www.safmarine.com
* 1, Worlu Rd, off Olu Obasanjo Rd, Port Harcourt
Tel: (084) 461100-5 (6L), 461117 **Fax:** (084) 461106
E-mail: phcscl@africa.safmarine.com
Contact: Mr. E. F. Ajayi - Head (Commercial)

SAFOLE NIGERIA LIMITED
Business: Sales and Service of Computers, Software Development and Marketing, Systems Engineering and Support, IT Education and Training Services
Address: 133, Old Ojo Road (Church Bus-Stop), Amuwo-Kuje, Festac Town, Lagos
Tel: (01) 4806183, 5883501, 7736524, 08023182254
Fax: (01) 5883501
E-mail: safoleng@yahoo.com
Contact: Mr. S. A. Fawole - Chairman/CEO
Mrs. Ajibola J. Onanuga - GM.

SAFRAS VENTURES LIMITED
Business: Clearing and Forwarding
Address: 4/5, Apapa-Oshodi Expressway (Coconut Bus-Stop), Olodi, Apapa, Lagos
Tel: (01) 7746306, 5450598
Contact: Alh. Kola Oladepo - Chairman/CEO

SAGAOLA MINING & ENGINEERING NIGERIA LIMITED
Business: Mining Consultancy, Water Resources Development, Rural Electrification
Address: 4, Jos-Bukuru Way, Bukuru, Jos
Tel: (073) 281219
E-mail: sagaola@yahoo.com
Contact: Chief Ndam Gambo - MD/CEO

SAGE BUSINESS GROUP (Robert Ade-Odiachi & Company)
Business: Sales and Management of Accounting Software, Audit and Accountancy, Taxation Services.
Address: 4, Park Lane, Apapa, G.R.A., Apapa, Lagos
Tel: (01) 5450986, 5451795, 5452310, 5451833
Fax: (01) 5452911
E-mail: lagos@inpactint.com
Contact: Mr. Robert Ade Odiachi - Managing Partner

SAGETO LIMITED
Business: Building & Civil Engineering Construction, (Mechanical & Electrical Engineering contracting, Estate (Properties) & Turnkey Projects
Address: Plot 411, Nouakchott Street, Zone 1, Wuse, Abuja
Tel: (09) 5233777, 5234128-9 (2 L), 08033144171
Fax: (09) 5234777
E-mail: sageto@hotmail.com
Website: www.sageto.com
Contact: Salim Abou Jaoud - Chairman/CEO

SAHANA INDUSTRIAL PRODUCTS LIMITED
Business: Aluminium Fabrication
Address: Km. 6, Hadejia Road, Kano
Tel: (080) 28324217
Contact: Naman Jebara - MD/CEO

SAHARA BELLS COMMUNICATIONS LIMITED
Business: Provision of Satellite Communication Services, Sales of Satellite-Based Telecommunication Equipment, Satellite Internet Access Provider
Address: 11, Awolowo Road, S. W. Ikoyi, Lagos
Tel: (01) 8042444, 2694953 **Fax:** (01) 2694953
E-mail: info@saharabell.com
Website: www.saharabell.com
* Wadata House (2nd Floor), Plot 1247, Aminu Kano Crescent, Wuse II, Abuja
Tel: (01) 5238138, 5238158
Contact: Mr. Sam Igwe - MD/CEO

SAHEL ENGINEERING SERVICES LIMITED
Business: Cutting of Granite Blocks, Production of Granite Floor Tiles and Slabs
Address: Industrial Area, beh. Railways Station, Bauchi
Tel: (077) 541328, 545572, 08023531016
Fax: (077) 541328
E-mail: saheligeng@yahoo.com
Contact: Dr. Soleh M. Toro - Chairman/CEO

SAIDI HOTELS LIMITED
Business: Catering Services and Hotel Management
Address: 271, Murtala Muhammed Way, Benin City
Tel: (052) 252125, 250460, 08023155913
Fax: (052) 250588
E-mail: saidi@saidihotelsltd.com
Website: www.saidihotelsltd.com
Contact: Mr. Ghassan Saidi - Chairman/CEO

SAIL INTERNATIONAL LIMITED
Business: Importation of Electronics, House-Hold Appliances, Audio-Visual Cassettes and Cleaners, Automototive Batteries, Tubes and Tyres
Address: 135/137, Nnamdi Azikiwe Street, Idumota, Lagos
Tel: (01) 2660227, 2662013, 2661187 **Fax:** (01) 2660227
E-mail: sail@alpha.linkserve.com
Contact: Engr. Nnamdi Anozie - Chairman/CEO

SAIL SEA SHIPPING COMPANY LIMITED
Business: Shipping Agents, Clearing and Forwarding, Customs Bonded Terminal, Warehousing
Address: 4, Burna Road (3rd Floor), Apapa, Lagos
Tel/Fax: (01) 5458769
E-mail: anosailsea@yahoo.com
Contact: Chief (Engr.) Anthony A. Anochie - Chairman

SAIMA NIGERIA LIMITED
Business: Shipping Agency, Haulage Service
Address: 11B, Burma Road, Apapa, Lagos
Tel: (01) 5871393, 7747206 **Fax:** (01) 5455551
E-mail: saimaoperations@hyperia.com
* Km. 16, PHarcourt/Aba Expreesway, Port Harourt
Tel: (084) 610603, 610426
E-mail: ssaima_ph@phca.linkserve.com

SAINGENES NIGERIA LIMITED
Business: Importation & General Trading
Address: Lennards Comp'd, Km. 16, Ikorodu Rd, Ojota, Lagos
Tel: (01) 7756254, 7755154, 08033070441
E-mail: saingenes@hotmail.com
Contact: Mr. A. Roop Kumar - Director

SAINT FLAIRS AWARDS LIMITED
Business: Marketing, Promotional Product Business, Awards, Leather Goods, Household/Office Utensils and Electronics
Address: 7, Majekodunmi Street, off Allen Avenue, (by Oshopey Plaza), Ikeja, Lagos
Tel: (01) 4937015, 4937029, 4721656 **Fax:** (01) 4937029
E-mail: st.flairs@alpha.linkserve.com
saintflairs@stflairsgrp.com
Contact: Cheif Ralphs Okey Nwosu - Chairman/CEO

SAINT NICHOLAS HOSPITAL
Business: Medical Practice and Healthcare Delivery Services
Address: 57, Campbell Street, Lagos Island, Lagos
Tel: (01) 2600070-9 (10L), 2635576, 08022908484, 08033075560, 08035251295 **Fax:** (01) 2633915
E-mail: info@saintnicholashospital.com
Website: www.saintnicholashospital.com
Contact: Chief (Dr.) Moses A. Majekodunmi - Chairman

SAIPEM CONTRACTING NIGERIA LIMITED
Business: Oilfield Engineering/Construction Services
Address: Plot 99, Ajose Adeogun St, Victoria Island, Lagos
Tel: (01) 2619368, 2621076-9(4L), 2624336-7(2L) 7746094-5(2L)
Fax: (01) 2610319, 2610957, 2615731, 2618272
* Mile 4, Ikwerre Road, Rumolumeni, Port Harcourt
Contact: Mr. P. Varone - MD/CEO

SAKEY ENGINEERING SERVICES LIMITED
Business: Water Engineering Services, Hardware Sales and Services, Borehole Drilling, Water Treatment Plant, Water-Bottling and Packaging Equipment, Water Treatment Chemicals
Address: 5, Alabi Street, off Toyin Street, Ikeja, Lagos
Tel: (01) 4972382, 8044220, 08023305450, 08033041773
Fax: (01) 4972382
E-mail: sakeyoke@beta.linkserve.com
Contact: Engr. S. A. Oke - Chairman/CEO

SAKKWATO SAVINGS & LOANS LIMITED
Business: Mortgage Finance
Address: Sossco Building, 8, Sani Abacha Way, Sokoto
Tel: (060) 236987
Contact: Dr. Sambo Junaidu - Chairman
Alh. Abdullahi Bakale - GM/CEO

SALCO NIGERIA LIMITED
Business: Import and Export, Trading
Address: 42/15, Massalachin Juma's Street, Jos.
Tel: (073) 454330, 458250, 08037022061, 08037149860, 08037149870 **Fax:** (073) 460501
E-mail: salco@infoweb.abs.net
Contact: Dr. Dimeji D. Lawuyi - MD/CEO

SALENAB NIGERIA LIMITED
Business: Supply of Medical Laboratory Equipment, Consumables and Reagents, Maintenance of Laboratory Equipment
Address: 49, Morison Crescent, Oregun Industrial Estate, off Kudirat Abiola Way, Alausa, Ikeja, Lagos
Tel: (01) 4966241, 4938057 **Fax:** (01) 4938057
E-mail: info@salenab.com

sales@salenab.com
Website: www.salenab.com
Contact: Mr. Farid Abou-Hassan - MD/CEO

SALIENT RUBBER PRODUCTS LIMITED
Business: Manufacturing of Industrial and Automotive Rubber Products
Address: 4, Dabara St, Olowogbowo, Lagos Island, Lagos
Tel: (01) 2664877, 2640343, 2663219 **Fax:** (01) 2610768
E-mail: salient@simbaonline.net
Contact: Mr. S. A. Hathiramani - MD/CEO

SALIMPEX LIMITED
Business: Importation, Distribution and Marketing of Nutritional Pharmaceutical Products
Address: 28, Adele Road, Apapa, Lagos
Tel: (01) 5873964, 5873581 **Fax:** (01) 5451978

SALINI NIGERIA LIMITED
Business: Construction and Civil Engineering, Power Generation Engineering Services
Address: Plot 655 (11), Blantyre Street, off Adetoknbo Ademola Crescent, Wuse II, Abuja
Tel: (09) 5230571, 5236057, 5238428 **Fax:** (09) 5230579
*18, Dakar St, off Odduwa Rd, GRA, Apapa, Lagos
Tel: (01) 5450731, 5875981 **Fax:** (01) 5453067

SALLYMAN (NIGERIA) LIMITED
Business: Shipping and Airfreighting, Clearing & Forwarding, Transportation
Address: 1A, Marine Road, Apapa, Lagos
Tel: (01) 5876598, 5452477 **Fax:** (01) 5457153
E-mail: sallyman@infoweb.abs.net

SALOROG GROUP OF COMPANIES LIMITED
Business: Manufacturers of Industrial Chemicals
Address: Km. 164, Auchi-Okene Rd, Okpella, Auchi, Edo State
Tel: (057) 200144, 200305, 200371, 200561
* Oworonshoki Expressway, off Ogudu Bye-Pass, Ogudu, Lagos.
Tel: (01) 4938045, 4976782
Contact: Alh. Abdulazeez Orogho - MD/CEO

SAM PHARMACEUTICALS LIMITED
Business: Manufacturing and Importation of Pharmaceuticals
Address: Great Nigeria House (11th Floor), 47/57, Martins Street, Marina, Lagos
Tel: (01) 2665755, 2664516 **Fax:** (01) 2621237
Contact: Mr. S. Bhojwani - Chairman
Mr. Mishra Manoj - Marketing Manager

SAM UDO-AKAGHA & PARTNERS
Business: Estate Surveyors, Valuers & Agents, Chartered Surveyors, Property Developers and Managers
Address: 3, Military Street (Suite C5), Onikan, Lagos
Tel: (01) 2634288, 2632225 **Fax:** (01) 2634288
E-mail: samakagha2000@yahoo.com
Contact: Mr. S. Udo-Akagha - MD.

SAMACO RECORDS AND VIDEO LIMITED
Business: Sales of Video Films and Compact Disc, Outdoor Video Coverage, Disc Jockeying, Business Centre
Address: 22, Ojuelegba Road, Surulere, Lagos
Tel: (01) 832583 **Fax:** (01) 4978134
Contact: Mr. Sam Azumara - Chairman/CEO

SAMAKOL PRINTERS NIGERIA LIMITED
Business: Industrial and Commercial Printing Services, Production of Light Packaging
Address: 2, Adeknle Kuye Street, Aguda, Surulere, Lagos
Tel: (01) 830432, 831460, 843598, 08035521966
Contact: Mr. Samuel Akinola Kolade - Chairman/CEO

SAMANJA ELECTRONICS SERVICES LIMITED
Business: Sales and Maintenance of Computers, Printers and Accessories, Internet Service Provider
Address: 8A, Race Course Road, Kano
Tel: (064) 640693-4 (2 L) **Fax:** (064) 642056
Website: www.ecnx.net
Contact: Jihad N. Jaafar - MD/CEO

SAMBROS INDUSTRIES LIMITED
Business: Sales of Automobile Paints, Auto Refurbishing, Fabrication and Electroplating
Address: 9, Emeka Orazulume Street, Umumejiaka Uruagu, Nnewi, Anambra State.
Tel: (046) 460930, 460698, 462439 **Fax:** (046) 462439
E-mail: sambros@infoweb.abs.net
Website: www.sambrosgroup.com
* 10, Amazon Street, off Alvan Ikoku Way, Ministers Hill, Maitama District, Abuja.
Tel: (09) 4139509
Contact: Mr. S. E. Orazu - Chairman/CEO

SAMCHAM HOLDINGS LIMITED
Business: Ship Owners/Agents, Ship Charterers, Clearing and Forwarding, Airfreighting, Warehousing.
Address: 11, Adele Road, Apapa, Lagos
Tel: (01) 5874002, 5453017, 5453018
Fax: (01) 5875016
E-mail: samcham@hyperia.com
Contact: Mr. Samuel Okunselor - Chairman/CEO

SAMEK GROUP
Business: Conglomerate - Construction, Investment & Finance, Brokers, Drilling & Allied Services
Address: 15, Samek Road, off Okigwe Road, Owrri
Tel: (083) 230891
Contact: Dr. Sam Igwe Eke - Exec. Chairman

SAMHAYS LIMITED
Business: Distribution and Sales of Automobile Paints
Address: 9, St Finbar's College Road, Akoka, Lagos
Tel: (01) 4975535, 4971352, 5821292-3 (2L)
Fax: (01) 4975534-5 (2 L)
E-mail: samhays@hyperia.com
Contact: Mr. Samuel Nsoedo - Chairman/CEO

SAMOL LIMITED
Business: Marketing of Dairy Products (ROYAL DELITE Full Cream Instant Milk)
Address: 3A Prince's Court, 37, Ahmed Onibudo Street, Victoria Island, Lagos
Tel: (01) 2622170, 612378, 619616
* 23, NRC Compound, Apapa, Lagos.
Tel: (01) 5874640

SAMORE NIGERIA LIMITED
Business: Property Development and Management
Address: Oshopey Plaza (2nd Floor, Front Wing), 17/19, Allen Avenue, Ikeja, Lagos
Tel: (01) 4939043
E-mail: samore@nigerianet.com
Contact: Mr. Oluwasanmi Lawal - Chairman/MD/CEO

SAMPAL ENGINEERING SERVICES INTERNATIONAL
Business: Civil/Structural Engineering Consultancy Services and Project Management
Address: 52, Oladipo Labinjo Crescent, off Bode Thomas Street, Surulere, Lagos
Tel: (01) 5833666, 4707471, 832384. **Fax:** (01) 5833666
E-mail: sesi@metrong.com
* Plot 540, Adetokunbo Ademola Cr, Wuse II, Abuja.
Tel: (09) 5328486
Contact: Engr. S. B. Adegbayibi - Snr. Partner

SAMROSE AGRO-INDUSTRIAL COMPANY LIMITED
Business: Hatchery, Piggery and Fishing, Livestock Feed Milling, Agro-Allied Business
Address: 10, Alimosho Road, Dopemu, Agege, Lagos
Tel: (01) 4962950, 08034044710
E-mail: samagrose@yahoo.com
Contact: Chief Samuel M. Amoye - Chairman/CEO

SAMSTAR LIMITED
Business: Manufacturing of PVC Storage Tanks, Household Plastic Products & Coolers
Address: 56B, Fagge Takudu, Kantin Kwari Market, Kano
Tel: (064) 635163, 649845
* Plot 25, Challawa Industrial Estate, Kano

SAMSUNG NIGERIA LIMITED
Business: Engineering Procurement, Construction, Installation
Address: Amazing Grace Plaza (2nd Floor), 2E-4E, Ligali Ayorinde Street, Victoria Island, Lagos
Tel: (01) 3200659 **Fax:** (01) 2615529
Contact: Mr. S. A. Bamidele - Business Dev. Manager

SAMUEL ETOMI & ASSOCIATES
Business: Chartered Quantity Surveyors, Constrution Cost Consultants, Project Manager
Address: 23, Ologun Agbaje Street, Victoria Island, Lagos
Tel: (01) 4619690-1 (2L), 2621207, 2624123
Fax: (01) 2621218
E-mail: samtoni@hotmail.com

SAMUEL UKPONG & COMPANY
Business: Estate Surveying & Valuation, Property and Facility Management, Project Development & Management, Property Taxation
Address: 20, King George V Road (1st Rooad), opp. Ghana High Commission, Onikan, Lagos
Tel: (01) 2631867, (08033480212 **Fax:** (01) 2636308
Contact: Mr. Samuel Ukpong - Principal Partner
Mr. Imo Ekanem - Managing Director

SAMUELSON MANAGEMENT LIMITED
Business: Management Consultancy Services, Sale of Time-Management Products
Address: 8B, Ademola Street, off Awolowo Road, S. W. Ikoyi, Lagos
Tel: (01) 2691124 **Fax:** (01) 2692087, 2691124
E-mail: samuelson@nova.net.ng
Contact: Mr. Tony Epelle - Management Consultant/CEO

SAMVIC'S EXQUISITE FURNITURE LIMITED
Business: Sales of Furniture & Furnishings, Interior Design & Decoration
Address: 19, Sanusi Fafunwa Street, Victoria Island, Lagos
Tel: (01) 2613509, 2703602, 08033005759
Fax: (01) 2617014
E-mail: samvics@onebox.com
Contact: Mr. Samuel Igboku - MD/CEO

SANACO MOTORS NIGERIA LIMITED
Business: Sales of Fire-Fighting Tankers, Trucks & Equipment
Address: 58, Ali Akilu Road, Kaduna
Tel: (062) 248177, 248178 **Fax:** (062) 247056
Contact: Alh. Ibrahim Saminaka - Chairman/CEO

SANBROS TRUST & SECURITIES LIMITED
Business: Stockbroking
Address: 28, Berkely Street, Onikan, Lagos
Tel: (01) 2636450, 2634205, 08023460639
Fax: (01) 2631038, 2636527
Website: www.sanbrostrust.com
Contact: Mr. Olumide Victor Oke - Manager

SANDAJI CHALETS NIGERIA LIMITED
Business: Hospitality and Catering Services
Address: Millionaire Quarters, along Jos Road, Lafia
Tel: (047) 21802
Contact: Alh. Usman Abubakar - Chairman

SANDERTON VENTURES LIMITED
Business: Building Construction and Engineering
Address: Plot 2, Lateef Jakande Rd, Agidingbi, Ikeja, Lagos
Tel: (01) 2632532, 2636485, 3450183, 7742503-4 (2L), 08023127990 **Fax:** (01) 3450180-1 (2L)
E-mail: info@royalsanderton.com
* Plot 1207, Yakubu Gowon Way, Asokoro, Abuja
Tel: (09) 3148120, 3148119 **Fax:** (09) 3148119
E-mail: sandertonabj@micro.com.ng
Contact: Mr. Olu Fagbemi - Chairman/CEO

SANDRICH LIMITED
Business: Sales of Corporate Gifts & Promotional Items, Production & Sales of Uniforms, Safety Wears, T-Shirts & Face Caps
Address: 26, Industrial Avenue, Ilupeju Ind. Estate, Lagos
Tel: (01) 4962225, 08023080178, 08042139505
E-mail: sandrichgifts@yahoo.com
Contact: R. B. Olumegbon - Chairman/CEO

SANI BROTHERS TRANSPORT LIMITED
Business: Haulage Contractors
Address: C9, Zaria Road, Naibawa Quarters
Tel: (064) 662944, 666589, 669756, 08023202105, 08023202490, 08023106996, 08023110124
Contact: Alh. Aliyu Y. Sulaiman - Gen. Manager

SANKARA NIGERIA LIMITED
Business: Sales/Service of Tractors & Agricultural Implements

Address: 7/8, B.U.K. Road, Gyadi-Gyadi, Kano
Tel: (064) 665710, 666422 **Fax:** (064) 662614, 664908
E-mail: sankara@ecnx.net
dsankara@yahoo.co.uk
Contact: Alh. Danladi Abdullahi Sankara - Chairman/CEO

SANKEY LIMITED
Business: Sales & Maintenance of Medical & Laboratory Equipment, Ecology, Health Services
Address: 10, Stephen Osibote Close, off Oludegun Street, Ire-Akari Estate Road, Okota Layout, Isolo, Lagos
Tel: (01) 4523026, 4524276, 5559136
Fax: (01) 4521277, 4526422
E-mail: sankey@linkserve.com
sankey@infoweb.abs.net
Contact: Mr. Vincent O. Sankey - Chairman/CEO
Mr. David Smith - MD

SANS FRONTIERS INVESTMENT LIMITED
Business: Building Engineering and Civil Construction, Sales of Furniture and Office Furnishings, Stockist of Building Materials, Procurement
Address: 52B, Itolo St, off Eric Moore Road, Surulere, Lagos
Tel: (01) 7745912

SANTA SEDE NIGERIA LIMITED
Business: Trucking; Plant & Equipment Leasing, Car Hire
Address: Plot 207/208, Trans-Amadi Ind.Layout, Port Harcourt
Tel: (084) 238809, 239934, 238807, 08033131190
Website: www.santa-ng.org
Contact: Mr. U. Santiago - CEO

SANTANA FOODS LIMITED
Business: Food Processing, Production of Mineral Water, Dairy Products and Fruit Juice
Address: Plot 4, Sharada Industrial Estate Phase I, Kano
Tel: (064) 663857, 668515 **Fax:** (064) 668515
Contact: Engr. T. T. C. Maduba - Chairman/CEO

SAP (SYSTEM APPLICATION PRODUCTS) NIGERIA LTD
Business: Marketing and Support of Strategic Enterprise Management
Address: The Octagn (3rd Floor), 13A, A.J. Marinho Drive, Victoria Island Annex, Lagos
Tel: (01) 2626827-8 (2 L), 3200889, 3200890, 7746646
Fax: (01) 2626828
E-mail: info@sap.com
Website: www.sap.com/africa

SAPID AGENCIES LIMITED
Business: Clearing & Forwarding, Container Terminal Operation, Warehousing, Transportation, Cargo Consolidation
Address: LSDPC Alaka Shopping Complex (Suite 9), by Bode Thomas Street, Surulere, Lagos
Tel: (01) 5850159, 5850306, 7740680 **Fax:** (01) 5834297
* 441/443, Old Ojo Road, off Badagry Expressway, Abule-Osun, Ojo, Lagos
Contact: Mr. William Nkemdirim - Chairman
Mrs. Ureh Nkemdirim - CEO.

SARA PRODUCTS LIMITED
Business: Manufacturing and Marketing of Foam Products
Address: Plot 4, Amodu Tijani Street, Victoria Island, Lagos
Tel: (01) 2612853, 2613090, 2614700 **Fax:** (01) 2614699
* 184/185, Happy Home Avenue, Kirikiri Industrial Estate, Lagos
Tel: (01) 5454775-6(2L), 5454778, 7742130-1(2L)
Fax: (01) 5454774
E-mail: safahassan@hotmail.com
Contact: Mr. Hassan Safa - ED
Mr. J. F. Oginni - Marketing Manager

SARGOM FIRE & SECURITY EQUIPMENT LIMITED
Business: Sales of Fire-Fighting & Secuirty Equipment
Address: Plot D40, S. L. Akintola Boulevard, Garki II, Abuja

SARM NIGERIA LIMITED
Business: Sales, Installation and Maintenance of Fire Detection and Protection Equipment, Electrical & Mechanical Engineering Services
Address: Plot 4, Balogun Street, opp. Neimeth Factory, Oregun Industrial Estate, Ikeja, Lagos
* 11, Military Street, Onikan, Lagos
Tel: (01) 2637470, 7754424 **Fax:** (01) 2634290

SARO AGROCHEMICALS LIMITED
Business: Marketing of Crop Protection Chemicals, Exportation of Raw Cocoa Beans
Address: Saro's Place, Plot 2068, Block 18C, Amuwo/Festac New Access Rd, Amuwo-Odofin New Town, Lagos
Tel: (01) 4702458, 5893137 **Fax:** (01) 5888055, 2690915
E-mail: saro@micro.com.ng
* 14, Bethel Clinic Way, by NACB, Ibi Road, Wukari, Taraba State.
Tel/Fax: (041) 20088
Contact: Mr. L. A. Bakare - Chairman
Mr. O. R. Sarumi - MD/CEO

SAS SPACE DESIGN
Business: Architecture and Interior Design, Consultancy, Development
Address: 2A, Raufu Taylor Close, off Idejo Street, off Adeola Odeku Street, Victoria Island, Lagos
Tel: (01) 2626627, 3200461, 08023687211
Fax: (01) 2626628
E-mail: jimi.soyebo@sas-spacedesign.com
Website: www.sas-spacedesign.com
Contact: Mr. Jimi Soyebo - Principal Partner

SASISA NIGERIA LIMITED
Business: Sales & Supply of Fertilizer and Cotton, General Merchandising, Importers and Exporters
Address: Plot 89, Sharada Industrial Estate Phase 1, Kano
Tel: (064) 664503, 640040, 08044123314
Fax: (064) 664503
Contact: Alh. Sirajo Mohammed - Chairman/CEO

SATEC ENGINEERING LIMITED
Business: Water Resources Engineering, Sewage Treatment and Disposal, Water/Sewage Treatment Plants
Address: 40, Burma Road, Apapa, Lagos
Tel: (01) 5870221 **Fax:** (01) 5870231
E-mail: satecng@infoweb.abs.net
Contact: Alh. Isa Tahir - Chairman
Engr. Martins O. Okwor - MD/CEO

SATELLITE COMMUNICATIONS LIMITED
Business: Media Relations Consultancy, Publishing
Address: 20, Obanikoro Street, off Ikorodu Road, Obanikoro, Lagos
Tel: 080234146073, 0033735117 **Fax:** (01) 820522
E-mail: grandtransport2001@yahoo.com
Contact: Mr. Peter C. Nwazie - Chairman/CEO

SATELLITE PRESS LIMITED
Business: Publishing-Newspaper, Magazine, and Book Publishing, Commercial Printing and Light Packaging, Typesetting and Design
Address: Plot 8C, Metal Box Road, off Acme Road, Ogba Industrial Scheme, Ogba, Ikeja, Lagos
Tel: (01) 4924399, 4973549 **Fax:** (01) 610977
Contact: Mr. Emmanuel C. Nwachukwu - Ag. CEO.

SATELLITE TELECOMMUNICATIONS LIMITED
Business: Sales and Service of Telecommunication (PABX) Equipment, Security and Surveillance Gadgets, Radio Communications Equipment, Satellite Dishes and Accessories, GSM Handsets and Accessories
Address: 217, Ikorodu Road, Obanikoro, Lagos
Tel: (01) 4932045, 8046983 **Fax:** (01) 4932045
Contact: Eze Okey Chukwuji - Chairman/CEO

SAVANNAH SHIPPING COMPANY (NIGERIA) LIMITED
Business: Exportation of Seafoods
Address: 16, Kofo Abayomi Street (Ground Floor, Flat 2), Victoria Island, Lgaos
Tel: (01) 2622232, 2622259, 2615505 **Fax:** (01) 2619487
E-mail: primlaks@hyperia.com
Contact: Mr. H. K. Ram - Director

SAVANNAH BEVERAGES LIMITED
Business: Production of Mineral Water & Carbonated Drinks
Address: 19/21, Dantata Rd, Bompai Industrial Estate, Kano
Tel: (064) 641058, 641769 **Fax:** (064) 643318, 641058
E-mail: savair@gulonline.com
Contact: Alh. Abdul Ringim - MD/CEO

SAVANNAH CHEMICAL INDUSTRIES LIMITED
Business: Sales of Industrial Chemicals, Processing and Sales of Vegetable Oil
Address: Km 4, Onitsha-Owerri Road, Onitsha
Tel: (046) 213503, 219393
* 16/18, Oyefeso Avenue, off Ikorodu Road, Obanikoro, Lagos
Tel: (01) 4936032, 4936049, 4970408

SAVANNAH HOSPITALS MEDICAL APPLICATIONS LTD
Business: Sales, Installation and Maintenance of Medical Systems and Equipment
Address: Plot 1438, Sanusi Fafunwa St, Victoria Island, Lagos
Tel: (01) 2620958, 2623988 **Fax:** (01) 2613274
* 17A, Yandutse Road, Kano.
Tel/Fax: (064) 632603
Contact: Mr. Oluwole Durojaiye - Dep. GM

SAVANNAH SUGAR COMPANY LIMITED
Business: Sugar Processing and Cubing
Address: Numan, P.O.Box 2230, Numan, Adamawa State
Tel: (075) 625707, 625517, 625970, 625971, 624646
Fax: (075) 625517
Contact: Alh. Suleiman Abdullahi - MD/CEO
Mal Ahmed Waziri - Public Relations Officer

SAVANNAH SUITES & RESTUARANTS LIMITED
Business: Hospitality and Catering Services
Address: Faskari St, off J.S. Tarka Way, Area 3, Garki, Abuja
Tel: (09) 2342840-3 (4 L), 2342025
Fax: (09) 2341520, 2342025
Contact: Chief Edward Ogunkoya - Chairman
Sir Chika Chiejina - MD/CEO

SAWYERR GROUP
Business: Manufacturer of Plastic Products, PVC Sheetings, Fabrication of Spare Parts, Engineering Services
Address: Plot 1, Block K, Isolo, Ind. Estate, Apapa-Oshodi Expressway (Sadiku Bus-Stop), Ilasamaja, Lagos
Tel: (01) 4522305, 522305, 522476 **Fax:** (01) 4522574
Contact: Mr. G. O. Sawyer - Chairman/CEO

SCANA LIMITED
Business: Borehole Drilling, Fabrication, Installation and Maintenance of Water Storage Tanks and Treatment Plants, Water Supply and Network and Distribution, Geological and Geophysical Surveys
Address: 66, Oyo Road, Samonda, Ibadan
Tel: (02) 8100106, 8104777 **Fax:** (02) 8100106
E-mail: scana@skannet.com
Contact: Mr. B. S. Adebowale - MD/CEO

SCANINK NIGERIA LIMITED
Business: Manufacture and Marketing of Printing Ink
Address: Plot 8, Block O, New Oluyole Industrial Estate, Scheme II, Ibadan
Tel: (02) 2317219, 2317721, 2310631 **Fax:** (02) 2314392
* 23, Burma Road, Apapa, Lagos
Tel: (01) 5804080-4 (5L) **Fax:** (01) 5877722, 2647747
Contact: Dr. G. E. O. Shofolu - MD/CEO

SCANWATER (NIGERIA) LIMITED
Business: Design and Construction of Water Treatment Plants, Investigation and Drilling of Boreholes, Operation and Maintenance of Water Treatment Plants, Pipeline Design and Construction
Address: 13, Town Planning Way, Ilupeju, Lagos
Tel/Fax: (01) 4936070
E-mail: md@scanwater.com
fathy-mobarak@yahoo.com
Website: www.scanwater.com
Contact: Ambassador J. T. F. Iyalla - Chairman
Mr. F. M. A. Mobarak - MD/CEO

SCARLET COMMUNICATIONS LIMITED
Business: Printing and Publishing, Public Relations and Consultancy Services
Address: Plot 6, F Layout, off Bosso Road, Minna
Tel: (066) 224157, 224894-5 (2L)
Contact: Alh. D. Illiyasu - MD/CEO

SCG CONSULTING
Business: Corporate Management Consultancy, Human Resource Management and Development, Systems Consulting, Executive Search and Selection

Address: 6, Chief Onitana Street. off Adebola Street, off Adeniran Ogunsanya Street, Surulere, Lagos
Tel: (01) 5847414, 5851539 **Fax:** (01) 5847414
E-mail: scg@alpha.linkserve.com
Contact: Ndubisi Anekwe - Director/CEO

SCHNEIDER ELECTRIC NIGERIA LIMITED
Business: Manufacturing & Marketing of Electrical Engineering Equipment (Medium & Low Voltage Distributors, Industrial Control & Automation, Programmable Logic Controllers, Motion Control), Consultancy Services for Services for Electrical Projects
Address: Eleganza Biro Plaza (8th Floor), Plot 634, Adeyemo Alakija Street, Victoria Island, Lagos
Tel: (01) 2702973-5 (3L) **Fax:** (01) 2702976
E-mail: steve_Iyonng@yahoo.com
Contact: Steve Lyon - National Sales Manager

SCHLUMBERGER OILFIELDS SERVICES NIGERIA LIMITED
Business: Comprehensive Oilfield Services
Address: 17/19, Idowu Taylor Street, Victoria Island, Lagos
Tel: (01) 2615275, 2619200, 2614442, 2626241-53(13L)
Fax: (01) 2612141, 2621172, 2619102, 2623669, 2617869
Contact: B. Decoste - Marketing Manager

SCHLUMBERGER NETWORK SOLUTIONS
Business: Telecommunication Engineering and Networking, Domestic Satellite Communications, Information Security and Secure Connectivity
Address: ICON House (3rd Floor), Plot 999F Idejo/Danmole Street, Victoria Island, Lagos
Tel: (01) 2610446, 2623668 **Fax:** (01) 2621034
E-mail: info@lagos.omnes.slb.com
Website: www.omnes.slb.com
* 161, Trans-Amadi Ind. Layout, Port Harcourt
Tel: (084) 332217, 331353
Contact: Africanus Mensah - MD/CEO
Trevor Lobo - Finance Director

SCHUKAS RAPIDKILL LIMITED
Business: Pest & Weed Control Services, Industrial Cleaning, Sewage Engineering Services
Address: 34, Deco Road, Warri
Tel: (053) 250163, 08023117586
* 6, Ogele Street, off Okporo Road, by Trinity School, Gojin Estate, Port Harcourt.
Tel: 08037237086
Contact: Sir Peter C. Chukwu - Chairman/CEO

SCHWARTZ GROUP OF COMPANIES
Business: Oil & Gas Exploration and Engineering Services; Waste Management & Environmental Protection Services; IT Engineering & Consultancy Services; Internet Service Provider; Broadcasting and Cable Television
Address: Plot208, Aba-P H Expressway, Port Harcourt
Tel: (084) 236754-5 (2L), 237808-9 (2L)
Fax: (084) 237809
E-mail: comtrends@supernet300.com
Website: www.schwartzgroup.com
* Etiebet's Place (8th Floor), 21, Mobolaji Bank Anthony Way, Ikeja, Lagos
Tel: (01) 4976493, 4976500 **Fax:** (01) 4976491
* CTL House, Plot 1221, Aminu Kano Crescent, Wuse II, Abuja.
Tel: (09) 4139921-3 (3L) **Fax:** (09) 4139923
Contact: Engr. Uzo Udemba - Chairnan/CEO
Mr. Neil Glynn - GM

SCHWARTZ KRISTOFFEL ENGINEERING SERVICES LTD
Business: Oilfield Engineering Services, Erosion Control
Address: 400 (Km. 16), Port Harcourt/Aba Expressway, Elem Junction, Port Harcourt
Tel: (084) 237809, 610395

SCIB NIGERIA & COMPANY LIMITED
Business: Insurance Broking
Address: 66, Adeniran Ogunsanya Street, Surulere, Lagos
Tel: (01) 5456430-3 (4L), 4704357-8 (2L)
Fax: (01) 5456439
E-mail: scibng@linkserve.com.ng
* Orosi House (6th Floor), 28, Forces Avenue, Old G.R.A., Port Harcourt
Tel: (084) 232124, 575499
Contact: Mr. F. O. Ogunlana - Chairman/CEO

SCIENTIFIC INFORMATION LIMITED
Business: Sales, Installation and Training in Telecommunication and Information Technology
Address: 22, Ajao Rd, off Adeniyi Jones Avenue, Ikeja, Lagos
Tel/Fax: (01) 4932488
E-mail: scientific@micro.com.ng
Contact: Dr. Oboyerulu E. Agboje - Chairman/CEO

SCIRROCCO INTERNATIONAL LIMITED
Business: Manufacturing and Marketing of Tea Bags
Address: Plot 85, Tokarawa Ind Estate, off Hadejia Rd, Kano
Tel: (064) 310636 **Fax:** (064) 640790
Contact: Alh. Muktar Halilu - MD/CEO

SCOA NIGERIA PLC
Business: Conglomerate - Assembly, Maintenance, Marketing and Leasing of Automobiles; Sales & Service of Generators, Engineering & Construction Equipment; Power Projects; Production & Marketing of Furniture; Supply of Medical & Security Systems; General Merchandising.
Address: 67, Marina, Lagos
Tel: (01) 2665015, 2663133, 2669704, 2668906, 2644484
Fax: (01) 2668835, 2669180, 2646790
* Plot 258, Central Business District, beh. Central Mosque, Wuse, Abuja
Tel: (09) 4139924
* 13, Azikiwe Road/Forces Avenue, Port Harcourt.
Tel: (084) 230058, 234652, 235465, 239068, 239074
* 51/53, Tafawa Balewa Road, Kano
Tel: (064) 630907, 633252, 633462, 636558, 647437
* 70, Warri/Sapele Road, Warri.
Tel: (053) 250944, 252221
* 1, Ali Akilu Road, Kaduna.
Tel: (062) 240765
Contact: Dr Massad F. Boulos - Group MD/CEO
Mr G. Tali - Group Sales Co-ordinator

SCOA AGRIC/TRAC (Div of SCOA Nig. Plc)
Business: Sales, Repair and Maintenance of Agricultural

Equipment, Tools and Machinery, Chemicals, Construction Equipment
Address: Apapa Expressway, Isolo Industrial Estate, Lagos
Tel: (01) 4521539, 4521803, 4521774 **Fax:** (01) 4521683
E-mail: trac@rcl.nig.com
scoatrac@scoaplc.com
Website: www.scoaplc.com
* Plot 258, Centra Area, beh. Central Mosque, Wuse, Abuja.
Tel: (09) 5239371
Contact: Dr. Massad F. Boulos - MD/CEO

SCOA EQUIP (Div of SCOA Nig. Plc)
Business: Sales, Repair, Leasing and Maintenance of Medical Equipment, Air Conditioners, Manufacture and Sales of Office, Home and Medical Furniture, Technical Tools, Building Materials, Industrial Safety and Security Equipment
Address: 10, Creek Road, Apapa, Lagos
Tel: (01) 5872795, 5450646 **Fax:** (01) 5450646
E-mail: scoaequip@scoaplc.com
Website: www.scoaplc.com
Contact: Dr. Massad F. Boulous - MD/CEO

SCOA INDUSTRIES (Div of SCOA Nig. Plc)
Business: Assembling of Vehicles & Tractors, Manufacturing of Auto Spare Parts, Building of Buses & Trailers
Address: 10, Dillion Street, Kirikiri Ind Estate, Apapa, Lagos
Tel: (01) 5870651, 5804180-4 (5 L) **Fax:** (01) 5870681
Website: www.scoaplc.com
* 13, Azikiwe Road, Port Harcourt
Tel: (084) 234652, 330138
Contact: Dr. Massad F. Boulos - Group MD/CEO

SCOA MOTORS (Div of SCOA Nig. Plc)
Business: Sales, Leasing and Maintenance of Motor Vehicles
Address: Lapal House, 235, Igbosere Road, Marina, Lagos
Tel: (01) 2635961, 2661687, 2647761, 2601193, 2620194
Fax: (01) 2646790, 2668906
E-mail: scoamotors@scoaplc.com
Website: www.scoaplc.com
Contact: Dr. Massad F. Boulos - Group MD/CEO

SCOA PETROLEUM SERVICES
Business: Provision for Wellhead Equipment and other Ancillary Services to the Petroleum Sector
Address: 67, Marina, Lagos
Tel: (01) 2663133, 2665015, 2665019
Fax: (01) 2668835, 2669180
Website: www.scoaplc.com
* Plot 258, Central Area, beh Central Mosque, Abuja.
Tel: (09) 5239371
Contact: Dr. Massad F. Boulos - Group MD/CEO

SCOA POWER (Div. of SCOA Nigeria Plc)
Business: Sales & Service of Generators & Generator Parts
Address: 37, Creek Road, Apapa, Lagos
Tel: (01) 5871769, 5876454, 5873623, 5877322, 5877333, 0803663333, 08034008722 **Fax:** (01) 5450646
E-mail: scoapower@scoaplc.com
cummins@scoaplc.com
powerports@scoaplc.com
Website: www.scoaplc.com

SCOA TRADING/SCOA EXIM (Div of SCOA Nig. Plc)
Business: General Merchandising & Distributive Trade; Import & Export of Agrochemicals, Supermarket
Address: 1, Dillion Street, Kirikiri, Apapa, Lagos.
Tel: (01) 5878000, 7741030
E-mail: scoatrac@scoaplc.com
Website: www.scoaplc.com
* LAPOINTE, 743, Adetokunbo Ademola Street, Victoria Island, Lagos
* Plot 258, Central Business District, beh. Central Mosque, Wuse, Abuja.
Tel: (09) 4139924
* 13, Azikiwe Road/Forces Avenue, Port Harcourt.
Tel: (084) 230058, 234652, 235465, 239068, 239074
* 51/53, Tafawa Balewa Road, Kano
Tel: (064) 630907, 633252, 633462, 636558, 647437
* 70, Warri/Sapele Road, Warri.
Tel: (053) 250944, 252221
* 1, Ali Akilu Road, Kaduna
Tel: (062) 240765
Contact: Dr Massad F. Boulos - Group MD/CEO
Mr Joseph Achkar - Co-ordinator

SCOTTS INDUSTRIES LIMITED
Business: Manufacturing of Stationery Products, PET Preforms, PET Bottles and Domestic Plastic Items
Address: Plot 27C, Fatai Atere Way, Matori Industrial Estate, Mushin, Lagos
Tel: (01) 44710124, 520261, 2663267 **Fax:** (01) 2615637
E-mail: scotts@beta.linkserve.com
Contact: Mr. Rajath Mendonca - Manager

SDEM ERECTORS NIGERIA LIMITED
Business: Steel Fabrication, Site Equipment Leasing, Project Erection, Design and Engineering
Address: 11, Awolowo Road, S.W., Ikoyi, Lagos
Tel: (01) 2672928, 2692640, 2693890 **Fax:** (01) 2692640
E-mail: sdeml@sdem.com
* Km.16, Aba Rd, near Eleme Junction, Port Harcourt
Tel/Fax: (084) 613206
Contact: Mrs. Adebo-Kiencke - Chairman
Mr. Vincent Gueneau - MD/CEO

SDI & ASSOCIATES LIMITED
Business: Public Relations Consultancy, Events Marketing
Address: 55, Raymond Njoku Street, S. W. Ikoyi, Lagos
Tel: (01) 2695867, 2696710 **Fax:** (01) 2695867
Contact: Mr. Sani Irabor - MD/CEO

SDI BROADBAND LIMITED
Business: Provision of Infrastructure of Mobile Cellular Networks Fixed and Private Wireless Networks
Address: NCWS House (2nd Floor), Plot PC. 14B, Ahmed Onibudo Street, Victoria Island, Lagos
Tel: (01) 4701674, 4617705 **Fax:** (01) 4619418
E-mail: sdibroadband@signalalliance.com
Contact: Collins Onegbu - MD/CEO
Yemi Soyibo - Business Dev. Manager

SDV (NIGERIA) LIMITED
Business: Clearing and Forwarding, Express Services, Heavy Lift, Oil Projects
Address: 26, Creek Road, Apapa, Lagos

Tel: (01) 5803470-4 (5L) **Fax:** (01) 5874542
E-mail: (Transport): itd@sdv.com.ng
Contact: Mr. F. Lavanant - MD

SEA PETROLEUM & GAS COMPANY LIMITED
Business: Independent Marketing and Supply of Petroleum Products, Marine Services, Vessel Hiring/Leasing, Equipment Supply and Logistics Support
Address: Km. 14, Lekki-Epe Expressway, Ikota, Lagos
Tel: (01) 2614638, 7742990, 7740965, 3204220-1 (2L), 619763, 612276 **Fax:** (01) 2614638
E-mail: spglekki@compuserve.com
* Plot 330, Mike Akhigbe Drive, off Trans-Amadi Industrial Layout, Phase II, Port Harcourt
Tel/Fax: (084) 239274
* Plot 494, Funmilayo Ransome-Kuti Road, Area 3, Garki, Abuja
Tel/Fax: (09) 5239191
Contact: Princess Stella Ada Oduah - Chairperson/CEO

SEA SANDY INVESTMENTS LIMITED
Business: Importation and Sales of Printing Papers, Stationeries and Gift Items
Address: 27, Osolo Way, off International Airport Road, Ajao Estate, Apakun-Oshodi, Lagos
Tel: (01) 4522022, 4522228 **Fax:** (01) 4522022
E-mail: sandy@hyperia.com
Contact: Mr. Emeka Nnama - MD/CEO

SEA TRUCKS (NIGERIA) LIMITED
Business: Marine Oilfield Services, Shipyard, Marine Vessels Repair & Maintenance
Address: 4A, Onitana Street (formerly Less Rd), Ikoyi, Lagos
Tel: (01) 2691347, 2694337, 7739654-6 (3L)
Fax: (01) 2692476, 2694505
* Onne Free Zone, Onne, Port Harcourt
* Enerhen/Effurun Road, Warri
Tel: (053) 250273, 252410, 252742, 254098
Contact: Mr. B. Bos - MD/CEO

SEACRAFTS NIGERIA LIMITED
Business: Marine Transportation Services
Address: 57A, Emekuku Street, D-Line, Port Harcourt
Tel: (090) 500117
Contact: Otunba Olusola Adekanola - Chairamn/CEO

SEAGULL TECHNICAL SERVICES LIMITED
Business: Sales of Petroleum-Handling Equipment & Accessoreis, Pipeline Constructon, Calibration Services, Petroleum Consultancy Services, Sales of Garage/Station Equipment
Address: Km. 16, Kachi Road, (Refinery Junction), Mahutu Village, Kaduna
Tel: (062) 514149, 412361 **Fax:** (062) 412361
* 102/104, New Ipaja Road, Alimosho Bus-Stop, Agege, Lagos

SEAFOOD PRODUCTS LIMITED
Business: Importers and Marketers of Frozen Foods and Fish
Address: Apapa-Oshodi Expressway, Ijesha-Tedo
Tel: (01) 5454727, 5454728, 5456229-30 (2 L), 5456228
Fax: (01)5454726
E-mail: seafood@linkserve.com.ng

SEALAND OILFIELD SERVICES LIMITED
Business: Oilfield Engineering Services
Address: Plot 1020, Ologun Agbaje St, Victoria Island, Lagos
Tel: (01) 2621450, 612065

SEAPORT MARITIME SERVICES LIMITED
Business: Shipping, Chartering, Agency & Ship Management, Oil Trading
Address: 69, Payne Crescent, Apapa, Lagos
Tel: (01) 5873253, 5873185 **Fax:** (01) 5876857, 2619690
Contact: Mr. Toufic Abdallah - Chairman/MD

SEAVIEW PROPERTIES LIMITED
Business: Real Estate Agency, Property Development and Management, Project Management and Environmetal Services, Management of Waste
Address: Seaview Plaza, 216, Broad Street, Lagos
Tel: (01) 2641438, 2662290, 2663239, 2664741, 7730353
Fax: (01) 2665556, 2662470

SEAWAVE GROUP OF COMPANIES
Business: Shipping, Marine and Oil Services
Address: 39, Ladipo Labinjo Crescent, off Bode Thomas Street, Surulere, Lagos
Tel/Fax: (01) 5836497
E-mail: seawavegroups@hotmail.com
Contact: Otunba Adenike Wole-Ajibode - Chairman/CEO

SEBAYA GROUP LIMITED
Business: Interior Designing, Decoration/Furnishing, Sales of Imported Security Doors and Industrial Machinery
Address: 19/21, Adeola Adeoye St, off Olowu St, Ikeja, Lagos
Tel: (01) 4973326, 4936780 **Fax:** (01) 4937507, 4938520
E-mail: sebaya@micro.com.ng
Contact: Mr. Yinka Odunnubi - Chairman/CEO
Mr. Babatunde Okunuga - Marketing Director

SEC EQUIPMENT NIGERIA LIMITED
Business: Sales and Maintenance of Satellite Communication Networks and Soltions
Address: 14C, Agoro Odiyan Street, Victoria Island, Lagos
Tel: (01) 2695903, 2623262

SECOND HAND EQUIPMENT & ASSET BROKERAGE LTD
Business: Databank Services of Used Equipment & Properties
Address: 21, Boyle Street (1st Floor), Onikan, Lagos
Tel: (01) 2645635-6 (2 L) **Fax:** (01) 2645753
E-mail: sheabltd@yahoo.com
sheabltd@nova.net.ng
Website: www.sheab.gq.2onu
Contact: Mr. Biobaku - MD/CEO

SECURE LOSS AJUSTERS LIMITED
Business: Insurance Loss Adjusting, & Consultancy, Marine Cargo Superintendence, Marine/Aviation loss
Address: Block A (Flat 29), Eko Court Complex, Kofo Abauyomi Stret, Victoria Islan,d Lagos
Tel: (01) 2622217, 4819306, 08033326222
Fax: (01) 2622217
* 49, Aba Road, Port Harcourt

SEC-TECH NIGERIA LIMITED
Business: Sales and Services of Security Equipment, Consultancy

Address: 207, Ikorodu Road, Obanikoro, Lagos
Tel: (01) 8013144 **Fax:** (01) 8048009
E-mail: iykeneth4@yahoo.com

SECURITIES SOLUTIONS LIMITED
Business: Stockbroking, Issuing House, Fund Management
Address: Foreshore Towers (5th Floor), 2A, Osborne Road, Ikoyi, Lagos
Tel: (01) 2696211, 4703449 **Fax:** (01) 2696211
Contact: Chief Bayo Kuku - Chairman
Mohammed W. Ibrahim - GM/CEO

SECURITY TRADING & INVESTMENT LIMITED
Business: Stockbroking, Portfolio Management, Investment Advisory Service
Address: Reinsurance House (7th Floor), 46, Marina, Lagos
Tel: (01) 4714778, 08023023489, 08033050639
Contact: Matthew Etareri - Chairman
David Odiwo - ED (Operations)

SECURITIES TRANSACTIONS & TRUST COMPANY LTD
Business: Stockbroking, Investment Advisory Services, Fund and Assets Management
Address: Foreshore Towers (12th Floor), 2A, Osborne Road, Ikoyi, Lagos
Tel: (01) 2695479-81 (3 L), 2694005, 2690861
Fax: (01) 2694392
E-mail: sectrust@hyperia.com
info@sectrust-nigeria.com
Website: www.sectrust-nigeria.com
www.sectrust-online.com
Contact: Mr. Moses Kragha - Chairman
Mr. Godwin N. Obaseki - MD/CEO

SECURITY HAZARDS EXPERTS LIMITED
Business: Sales & Installation of Security Devices
Address: 228A, Gbagada Expressway, Gbagada, Lagos.
Tel: (01) 4935184, 7747815, 7753333, 7759041, 08023146736, 08024040111, 08034040111.
E-mail: she228a@yahoo.com
* Block 3, Suit 13, Abari Shopping Complex, opp. Ibro Hotels, Wuse Zone 5, Abuja.
Tel: 08023146736
* 4C, Ogoja Road, Abakaliki.
Tel: (043) 210833, 210333, 210666, 210777

SECURITY ASSURANCE PLC
Business: Insurance
Address: 15, Jibowu St, off Ikorodu Rd, Jibowu-Yaba, Lagos
Tel: (01) 4704212, 8114133, 8114135, 8158448
E-mail: security@infoweb.abs.net
* 47, Ikwerre Road, Mile 1, Diabu, Port Harcourt
Tel: (080) 33097387
Contact: Mr. E. I. Ijewere - Chairman
Mr. Y. A. Alao - MD/CEO

SECURITY SWAPS LIMITED
Business: Stockbroking, Issuing House
Address: Okoi Arikpo House (1st Floor), 5, Idowu Taylor Street, Victoria Island, Lagos
Tel: (01) 2620353-4 (2L), 2624440, 2703595-8 (4L)
Contact: Mr. Abiodun M. Dabiri - Chairman
Mr. Folabi Owolabi - MD/CEO

SEDCO FOREX OF NIGERIA LIMITED
Business: Drilling Rig Services, Offshore Drilling & Well Construction, Provision of Deepwater Driill Vessels & Semi-Submersible Rigs
Address: Plot 2/3, Rumuwoke, opp. Shell Residential Area, Aba-Port Harcourt Expressway, Rumuibekwe, Port Harcourt
Tel: (084) 610633, 612857 **Fax:** (084) 612861
* Km. 2, Refinery Road, Warri.
Tel: (053) 232711
* Lake Chad Club Road, Old GRA Maiduguri
Tel: (076) 233538
Contact: Mr P. Tremeter - MD

SEE SWEET & BAKERY LIMITED
Business: Production of Confectionery
Address: 8, Bompai Road, Kano
Tel: (064) 632733 **Fax:** (064) 632739
E-mail: sweetbakery2k@yahoo.com
Contact: Mr. A. Ahmed Berjoui - MD/CEO

SEEDED VENTURES LIMITED
Business: Manufacturing and Marketing of Plastic Mats
Address: Plot 114, Sharada Industrial Estate Phase III, Kano
Tel: (064) 663579 **Fax:** (064) 665783
Contact: Alh. Adamu Mohammed Gumel - Chairman/CEO

SEEPC NIGERIA LIMITED
Business: Ptoduction of SANDERS Livestock Feeds & Concentrates, Poultry Farming
Address: Plot 4A, Block D, Wempco Road, Ogba Industrial Estate, Ikeja, Lagos
Tel: (01) 4924438-9(2L), 7739403, 7754191, 08022921038, 08034441950, 08035350545
Fax: (01) 4922164, 7747020
E-mail: seepcgm@multilinks.com
* Km. 66, Enugu-Port Harcourt Expressway, Aba
Tel: (082) 226168, 440258
* 23A, Kachia Road, opp. Queen Amina College, Kaduna.
Tel: (062) 232917, 235540
Contact: Mr. Don Spencer - Group MD/CEO

SEFAM COMPANY LIMITED
Business: Telecommunication &Electrical Engineering Services
Address: Oshopey Plaza (3rd Floor), 17/19, Allen Avenue, Ikeja, Lagos
Tel/Fax: (01) 4932143
E-mail: sefam@nigerianet.com

SEG-MAHSEN AND COMPANY NIGERIA LIMITED
Business: Construction, Water/Process Engineering and Technical Procurement, Sales and Installation of Pumps, Water Treatment Services, Sales of Power Plants, Generators and Transformers, Oil and Gas Services, Sales of Ductile-Iron Pipe and Spiral-Welded Steel Pipes, Valves & Fittings
Address: 1, Dawodu Lane, off Moshood Abiola Way, by Ilogbo Bus-Stop, Ebute Metta (West), Lagos
Tel: (01) 5851879, 5841757, 7739129
Fax: (01) 5851879, 2694437
E-mail: segmahsn@infoweb.abs.net
Contact: Chief (Dr.) M. O. Abraham - MD/CEO

SELINA VENTURES LIMITED
Business: Computer Sales, Maintenance, Training and Consultancy, Contract Management, Employment Bureau, Pest Control & Business Bureau Services.
Address: Plot 300, Adeola Odeku St, Victoria Island, Lagos
Tel: (01) 2618367-8 (2L), 2610086 **Fax:** (01) 2615511
E-mail: manger@selinaventures.com
Contact: Dr. Gabi A. Williams - Chairman/CEO

SEM-EDO WIRE INDUSTRIES LIMITED
Business: Manufacture of Steel Wires
Address: Along Jemila Road, Oregbeni Estate, Ikpoba Hill, Benin City
Tel: (052) 243890, 223262, 229171

SEMYNA OIL & GAS LIMITED
Business: Oil & Gas Support Services (Pipelines)
Address: Prince's Court (Suite 4E), 37, Ahmed Onibudo Street, Victoria Island, Lagos
Tel: (01) 7749303, 2616042, 08023065608
E-mail: semynaoilgas@hotmail.com
Contact: Mr. S. Yinka Jinadu - Chairman/CEO
Olubunmi O. Martins - Business Dev. Director

SENFORCE INSURANCE BROKERS LIMITED
Business: Insurance Broking
Address: Plot 1501, Bishop Aboyade Cole St, V/Island, Lagos
Tel: (01) 4616675, 4818620 **Fax:** (01) 2627866
* Plot 1046, Ahmadu Bello Way, Garki, Abuja
Tel: (09) 3141940, 3142120
* 22, Force Road, Port Harcourt
Tel: (084) 232669, 234528
Contact: Mr. Felix Epebinu - GM/CEO

SENIL POWER PROTECTION SYSTEMS LIMITED
Business: Sales and Maintenance of UPS and Voltage Stabilizers, Electrical Systems Design, Site Preparation, Installation Commissioning and Training
Address: 10A, Ajanaku Street, Awuse Estate, off Salvation Road, off Opebi Road, Ikeja, Lagos
Tel: (01) 4933094, 4967127, 4967488, 2694197
Fax: (01) 4970184, 2694197
Contact: Chief S. O. Fajinmii - President/CEO

SERIC IMPIANTI INTENRATIONAL NIGERIA LIMITED
Business: Oifield Engineering Services
Address: 169A, Aba Road, Port Harcourt
Tel: (084) 235126, 238255
E-mail: seric@phca.linkserve.com

SERVICES & TRADE LIMITED
Business: Importation of Specialised Coatings and Paints
Address: 1, Tafawa Balewa Crescent, off Adeniran Ogunsanya Street, Surulere, Lagos
Tel/Fax: (01) 5830652, 7915859
E-mail: cep@cyberspace.net.ng
sentra@linkserve.com

SESANTECH INDUSTRIES NIGERIA LIMITED
Business: Marketing of Industrial and Refrigerant Gases, Processing of Liquefied Petroleum Gas and Natural Gas, Sales, Commissioning and Services of Electrical Systems
Address: Km. 40, Lagos-Abeokuta Express Road, near Gateway Hotel, Sango-Otta, Ogun State
Tel: (039) 722472-3 (2L), 08033445459 * (01) 2885714
Fax: (039) 722467 * (01) 2885714
Contact: Mayor Ezekiel O. Moyegun - Chairman/CEO

SESSY-ADE (NIGERIA) LIMITED
Business: Importation of Automotive Batteries & Spare Parts
Address: 3, Ashogbon Street, Idumota, Lagos
Tel: (01) 2667197, 2667604
Contact: Mr. Sesan Adekunle - MD/CEO

SETRACO NIGERIA LIMITED
Business: Construction and Civil Engineering Services
Address: Plot 192, Block 11, Makeni Street, Wuse Zone 6, Garki, Abuja
Tel: (09) 5233454-5 (2L), 5234946-7 (2L)
Fax: (09) 5234945
E-mail: setraco@micro.com.ng
* 37, John Olugbo Street, Ikeja, Lagos
Tel: (01) 4961844, 8116924 **Fax:** (01) 4961844
* 24, Boundary Road, G.R.A., Benin City
Tel: (052) 250517, 255321 **Fax:** (052) 255321
Contact: Mr. Said Khalaf - Vice Chairman/CEO

SETRAD NIGERIA LIMITED
Business: Manufacturing of Furniture, Service Trade and Development
Address: Plot 86, Sharada Industrial Estate Phase II, Kano
Tel/Fax: (064) 666082, 08023110526
Contact: Alh. Farouk A. Aliyu - MD/CEO

SETRAMECH LIMITED
Business: Civil Engineering, Electro-Mechanical Contractors
Address: 24, Cameron Road, Ikoyi, L agos
Tel: (01) 2690764, 2690766, 2693877, 08023557466
Fax: (01) 2690764, 2690766
E-mail: setramech@micro.com.ng
Contact: Mr. Nabil Dawalibi - MD/CEO

SEVELLE NIGERIA LIMITED
Business: Importation and Distribution of Writing Materials and other Corporate Gift Items
Address: Alfaco House, Plot E, Ikosi Rd,Oregun Industrial Estate, Ikeja, Lagos
Tel: (01) 4971350-1 (2 L) **Fax:** (01) 4971350, 5557979
E-mail: sevelle@groupalfa.com
Website: www.gropalfa.com
Contact: Mr. F. Jarmakani - MD/CEO

SEVEN-UP BOTTLING COMPANY PLC
Business: Bottlimg & Marketing of Carbonated Soft Drinks.
Address: Seven-Up Building, 247, Moshood Abiola Way, Ijora, Lagos.
Tel: (01) 5803420-9 (10L) **Fax:** (01) 5873712, 5877146
Website: www.sevenup.org/up
* Ikeja Bottling Plant, Mobolaji Johnson Avenue, Alausa, Oregun, Lagos.
Contact: Mr Anwar El-Khalil - Chairman
Mr Faysal El-Khalil - MD/CEO

SEYDEL NIGERIA LIMITED
Business: Manufacturing and Sales and Sizing and Process-

ing Chemicals for Textile Industries, Plastic Products, Glue and Adhesives (Solid Bond) and Construction Chemicals.
Address: 3, Blind Centre Road, Cappa-Oshodi, Lagos
Tel: (01) 4527128, 4527470, 7743151, 4523387
Fax: (01) 4522951
E-mail: seydel@melsonsgroup.com
Contact: Mr. M. U. Melwani - MD/CEO

SFICO LIMITED
Business: Sales and Service of Office Equipment
Address: 100, Obafemi Awolowo Way, Ikeja, Lagos
Tel: (01) 4976137, 4931235, 4714267 **Fax:** (01) 4971808
* 6, Oremeji St, off Simbiat Abiola Way, Ikeja, Lagos
Tel: (01) 4930135
Contact: Mr. S. O.Obembe - MD/CEO

SGS INSPECTION SERVICES NIGERIA LIMITED
Business: Inspection; Testing, & Verification Services; Marine, Industrial, & Engineering Services; ISO Certification Consultancy, Staff Recruitment.
Address: Intercontinental Plaza (4th Floor), Plot 999C, Danmole Street, Victoria Island, Lagos.
Tel: (01) 2620735-7(3L), 2620739, 2625347-50(4L), 611188, 610792 **Fax:** (01) 2620732
Website: www.sgs.com
* 13/15, Wharf Road, Apapa, Lagos
Tel: (01) 5803860-9(10L) **Fax:** (01) 5452655
* 1, Wogu Street, D-Line, Port Harcourt.
Tel: (084) 232961, 233558, 234481, 234783, 238349
* 87, Effurun - Sapele Road, Warri.
Tel: (053) 250378, 256067, 256088, 257091
Contact: Mr Rod E. Grinsell - MD/CEO

SHAFOL INVESTMENT LIMITED
Business: Fast-Food Outlet Management
Address: 2A, Opebi Rd, Toyin/Allen Rondabout, Ikeja, Lagos
Tel: (01) 4931726, 8169361
* 18/20, Itire Road, Surulere, Lagos
Tel: (01) 5846323, 833623
Contact: Mrs. Folake Kassim Kuku - Director (Corp Affairs)

SHAGALINKU HOTEL & CONFERENCE CENTRE, BIRNIN KEBBI.
Business: Hospitality and Catering Services
Address: P. O. Box 603, Birnin Kebbi
Tel: (068) 321092, 321030, 321607, 321051
Fax: (068) 321005
E-mail: kebbicybercafe@mailnigeria.com
Contact: Alh. Umaru Hairi Shagalinku - Chairman/CEO

SHAGOYA NIGERIA LIMITED
Business: Manufacture of Plasic Products, Cosmetics and Industria/Hygiene Products
Address: 18, Oshunketian Street, off Aiolal Bus-Stop, Alapere, Ketu, Lagos
Tel: (01) 4703451, 8046538, 08033039608
E-mail: shagoyanigltd@yahoo,com
Contact: Engr. Adegoke Okunola - Chairman/MD

SHALOM INVESTMENT & SECURITIES LIMITED
Business: Stockbroking , Portfolio Management, Investment Advisory Services
Address: Investment House Annex (Suite 6), 21/25, Broad Street, Lagos Island, Lagos
Tel: (01) 2669941, 2640570, 08023116692
Fax: (01) 2669941
E-mail: shalomsec@linkserve.com
Contact: Air Vice Marshal Larry Koinyan (rtd.) - Chairman
Solomon Adegboju - GM/CEO

SHARON REGENCY HOTELS, ABUJA
Business: Hospitality & Catering Servcies, Car-Hire Services
Address: Plot 1312, Nairobi Street, off Parakou Crescent, off Aminu Kano Crescent, Wuse II, Abuja
Tel: (09) 5232642-3 (2L) **Fax:** (09) 5234713

SHANNA NIGERIA LIMITED
Business: Automobile Distribution, Sales and Servicing, Supply of Spare Parts
Address: Plot 71, Atbara Street, Wuse II, Abuja
Tel: (09) 4139074-5 (2 L)
Contact: Capt. Paul Adamu Nwachukwu - Chairman/CEO

SHARADA OIL MILLS LIMITED
Business: Extraction of Groundnut Oil & other Vegetable Oils
Address: 41, Sharada Industrial Estate Phase III, Kano
Tel: (064) 666143, 663650
Contact: Munir H. Muhammad - GM

SHEBAG HOLDINGS LIMITED
Business: Sales of Drilling Rigs and Allied Equipment
Address: 3A, Ali Akilu Road, Kaduna
Tel: (062) 247383, 217216 **Fax:** (062) 217216
E-mail: shebag@micro.com.ng
Contact: Alh. Sheriff Balogun - MD/CEO

SHELL PETROLEUM DEVELOPMENT COMPANY OF NIGERIA LIMITED
Business: Exploration, Development & Production of Crude Oil & Gas. Operators of National Crude Oil & Gas Joint Ventures
Address: Freeman House, 21/22, Marina, Lagos
Tel: (01) 2601800 (19 L), 2601600-24 (25 L), (01) 27xxxxx, * (084) 42xxxx, * (053) 44xxxx
Fax: (01) 2645303
E-mail: spdc@shell.com
* Plot 510, Gana Street, Maitama District, Abuja
Tel: (09) 5230585, 5230609
Contact: Mr. Basil Omiyi - MD/CEO
Mr. Don Boham - Corp. Ext. Relations Mgr

SHELL NIGERIA EXPLORATION & PRODUCTION CO. LTD
Business: Exploration and Production of Oil and Gas
Address: NAL Towers, 20, Marina, Lagos
Tel: (01) 2601600, 2601820 **Fax:** (01) 2637165
Website: www.snepco.shell.com
Contact: Mr. Basil Omiyi - Chairman
Dr. Kisito O. Okpere - Exec. Director/CEO

SHELL NIGERIA GAS LIMITED
Business: Tranmission, Distribution and Marketing of Natural Gas
Address: Freeman House, 21/22, Marina, Lagos
Tel: (01) 2601800-18 (19 L), 2601600-24 (25 L)
Fax: (01) 2645303

E-mail: shellnigeriagas@spdc.shell.com
Contact: Mr. Egbert U. Imomoh - Chairman
Mr. F. I. Okonkwo - Manager (External Relations)

SHELTARCH ASSOCIATES
Business: Architectural Consultancy, Project Management
Address: 11, Mustafa Umaru Road, Maiduguri
Tel: (076) 231925
* 25, Oju-Olubun Close, Victoria Island, Lagos
Tel: (01) 2612185, 2615964
* 24A, Waff Road, Kaduna
Tel: (062) 211826
Contact: Arc. B. I. Bunu - Principal Partner

SHELTER CLAY PRODUCTS LIMITED
Business: Manufacturing of Burnt Bricks and Clay Pots
Address: Opp. NNPC Depot, Km. 15, Suleja Road, Minna
Tel: (066) 220703, 222392

SHELTER WORKS LIMITED
Business: Consultants and Project Managers, Building and Civil Engineering Contractors
Address: 26, Michael Adekoya Street, Ilupeju, Lagos
Tel: (01) 4930056, 4961721 **Fax:** (01) 4961721
Contact: Olusegun Amusat - MD/CEO

SHEMPATE LIMITED
Business: Manufacturing of Motor-Vehicle Parts
Address: Plot 9/13, Maicibi Close,
Kakuri Industrial Estate, Kaduna
Tel: (062) 237287

SHEPHERDS INSURANCE BROKERS LIMITED
Business: Insurance Broking, Life and Pension Consultancy
Address: 71, Apapa Road, Ebute-Metta (West), Lagos
Tel: (01) 836087
Contact: Alh. M. A. Mustapha - MD/CEO

SHERATON LAGOS HOTEL & TOWERS
Business: Hospitality & Catering Services, Conference & Banqueting Facilities
Address: 30, Mobolaji Bank-Anthony Way, Ikeja, Lagos
Tel: (01) 4978660-9 (10 L), 4970311, 4970313, 4970314, 4970319, 4970325 **Fax:** (01) 4970321-2 (2L)
E-mail: reserveationslagosnigeria@sheraton.com
sheraton@nigol.net.ng
Website: www.sheraton.com/lagos
www.starwoodhotels.com
Contact: Mr. Goodie Ibru - Chairman
Mr. Laurent Certelet - GM/Area Manager

SHIFA PLASTIC INDUSTRIAL COMPANY (NIGERIA) LTD
Business: Manfuacture of Plastic Products
Address: Kessingsheen Plaza, Ikotun-Egbe Road, NNPC Junction, Ejigbo, Lagos
Tel: (01) 4746168, 08037171292
E-mail: shifanig@yahoo.com

SHINCO NIGERIA LIMITED
Business: Construction
Address: Rayfield Industrial Estate, Jos
Tel: (073) 280903, 280908
Contact: Alh. Ibrahim Sani - Director

SHERLATON RESTAURANT
Business: Resturant Services
Address: 108, Awolowo Road, S. W. Ikoyi, Lagos
Tel: (01) 2691275, 2691282 **Fax:** (01) 2690598

SHIELD INSURANCE BROKERS LIMITED
Business: Insurance Broking
Address: 2A, Keffi Street, S. W. Ikoyi, Lagos
Tel/Fax: (01) 2670982, 2693171

SHIP & SHORE SERVICES LIMITED
Business: Oilfield Services
Address: LSDPC Luxury Flats (Block A, Flat 1), 24, Adeola Odeku Street, Victoria Island, Lagos
Tel: (01) 2613366, 2610558, 614050
Fax: (01) 2611484, 2613035
E-mail: ship&shore@linkserve.com.ng

SHIPPING MAGNATE LIMITED
Business: Airfreight and Oceanfreight, Global Logistics, Customs Brokerage, Haulage, Packaging and Removals, Groupage, Door-to-Door Services
Address: 9, Chief Onitana Street, off Adebola Services, off Adeniran Ogunsanya Street, Surulere, Lagos
Tel: (01) 5842182, 4819451, 832637, 08023063839
Fax: (01) 5849512
E-mail: smagnate@elkapyra.com
smagnate@yahoo.com
smagnate@mail.com
Contact: Arc. T. C. Awagu - Chairman
Mr. E. O. Ochi - MD/CEO

SHIPS OF TARSHISH LIMITED
Business: General Merchandising
Address: Lafayette Mall, Plot 1436, Sanusi Fafunwa Street, Victoria Island, Lagos
Tel: (01) 4712509
E-mail: traders@tarshish-ltd.com
Contact: Mr. Bolaji Akinyemi - Chairman/CEO

SHIRORO HOTEL LIMITED, MINNA
Business: Hospitality and Catering Services
Address: Nnamdi Azikiwe Way, Western Bye-Pass, Minna
Tel: (066) 221498, 222021 **Fax:** (066) 221622

SHONGAI PACKAGING INDUSTRY LIMITED
Business: Manufacturing of Crates, Jar, Labels, Domestic and Flexible Packaging Materials
Address: Km. 38, Lagos-Abeokuta Road, Sango-Ota
Tel: (039) 722204, 722206, 722208 * (01) 7739803-4 (2L), 7738838, 08022910400, 08022910402, 08022910404
Fax: (039) 722435 * (01) 2617511
E-mail: shongai@sonagrpnig.com
Contact: Alh. M. L. Kassim - Chairman
Mr. R. Oldfield - MD.

SHONNY INVESTMENT PROPERTIES COMPANY LIMITED
Business: Property Development, Estate Agency, Conference Facilities
Address: Elephant House (18th Floor), 214, Broad St, Lagos
Tel: (01) 2667353, 2667320 **Fax:** (01) 2663442
E-mail: trolope@cyberspace.net.ng
Contact: Chief (Mrs.) A. O. Shonibare - Chairman

SHONUBI MEK-IND ASSOCIATES
Business: Engineering Consultants, Project Managerrs
Address: 8, Ilupeju Bye-Pass, Ilupeju, Lagos
Tel: (01) 4962715, 4963850
Contact: Engr. (Dr.) F. A. Shonubi - Managing Partner/CEO

SHORELINE CHEMICALS & OIL SERVICES LIMITED
Business: Dredging Services; Marine Transportation and Construction Equipment Leasing; Supply of Sand, Chemicals, Mechanical and Electrical Equipment, Spares and Tools to Oil Companies
Address: 24, Oromineke Layout, D-Line, Port Harcourt
Tel: (084) 239429 **Fax:** (084) 230733
E-mail: shoreline@hyperia.com
Contact: Dr. Olumide O. Amos-Oluwole - MD/CEO

SHOREMAN AGRO PRODUCTS NIGERIA LIMITED
Business: Livestock Farming, Agro-Allied Manufacturing
Address: 5/7, Mohammed Taofeeq Street, Shogunle, Lagos
Tel: (01) 4964340, 4963744, 4934903, 7742033
* 110/120, Ikotun-Idimu Rd, (Alake B/Stop), Lagos
Tel: (01) 7742033
Contact: Alh. Mohammed Taofeeq Elebute - Chairman/CEO

SHOTE & COMPANY
Business: Estate Surveyors and Valuers
Address: 77B, Bode Thomas St, by Mr. Bigg's, Surulere, Lagos
Tel: (01) 4705579, 5834099, 7736972, 833141, 833742, 833746 **Fax:** (01) 5834099
E-mail: shoteandco@linkserve.com
Contact: Mr. Adetola Olanipekun Shote - CEO

SHOUR INDUSTRIAL ENTERPRISES LIMITED
Business: Manufacturing and Marketing of Furniture
Address: 5, Bompai Road, Kano
Tel: (064) 637706, 638509
Contact: Mohammed D. Fawaz - MD/CEO

SIDEX NIGERIA LIMITED
Business: Importation and Sales of Automobile Spare Parts
Address: 19, Akinyemi Crescent/Badejo Kalesanwo Road, Matori Industrial Estate, Mushin
Tel: (01) 4528551, 4527657, 7748511, 522563
Fax: (01) 4527657
E-mail: sidex@hyperia.com

SIDMACH TECHNOLOGIES NIGERIA LIMITED
Business: Computer Maintenance and Support; System Integration and Networking, Software Development, IT Consultancy Services and Training
Address: 28, Otuntona Crescent, Gbagada Estate Phase I, Gbagada, Lagos
Tel: (01) 7740392, 2880251, 4700594 **Fax:** (01) 2880251
E-mail: corporate@sidmach.com
Contact: Mr. A. P. S Arogndade - Chairman/ED (Operations)

SIEMENS LIMITED
Business: Electrical &Electronic Engineering; Solar Energy, Information, Telecommunication and Medical Equipment; Automation, Industrial Projects and Technical Services for Oil, Gas and Petrochemical Industry, Lighting Engineering.
Address: Siemens House, Plot 3F, Block A, Oshdoi Scheme, Oshodi-Apapa Expressway, Lagos
Tel: (01) 4500207, 4523010 **Fax:** (01) 4500163, 4525129
E-mail: e.seidel@hyperia.com
* N'djamena Cr, off Aminu Kano Cr, Wuse II, Abuja.
Tel/Fax: (09) 6083100
* 31, King Perekule St, GRA Phase II, Port Harcourt.
Tel: (084) 233261 **Fax:** (084) 440227
* 30, Giwa Amu Road, G.R.A., Benin City
Tel: (052) 251597, 257504 **Fax:** (052) 251504
Contact: Mr. E. Seidel - MD/CEO
Chief R. O. Odusanya - Head (Corp. Comm.)

SIFAX NIGERIA LIMITED
Business: Shipping, Ship Charterers, Container Terminal Operators, Clearing & Forwarding, Sea & Air Freight, Warehousing, Groupage & Haulage Services, Plant Hire
Address: 41, Calcutta Crescent, Apapa, Lagos
Tel: (01) 5452774, 5870186, 5878080, 5878289, 4713358, 7911459, 7912218 **Fax:** (01) 5878289
E-mail: sifaxshippingng@yahoo.co.uk
Website: www.sifax.biz
Sifax/NPA Container Terminal, Trinity Bus- Stop, Apapa-Oshodi Expressway, Olodi-Apapa, Lagos
Contact: Mr. T. Y. Afolabi - MD/CEO

SIFUL NIGERIA LIMITED
Business: Importation of Pharmaceutical Raw Materials and Finished Products, Medical Equipment, Industrial Chemicals, Building Materials, Equipment and Machinery, Special Chinese Traditional Remedies and General Goods
Address: 30, Adeola Hopewell Street, Victoria Island, Lagos
Tel: (01) 2624524-6 (3 L) **Fax:** (01) 2612296
Contact: Dr. Wu Hui Ya - MD/CEO

SIGMA SECURITIES LIMITED
Business: Stockbroking, Investment Advisory Services, Portfolio Management
Address: 1-9, Berkley St (11th Floor, Suite 17), Onikan, Lagos
Tel: (01) 2631510, 2632757, 2630144 **Fax:** (01) 2630144
E-mail: sigmasec@cyberspace.net.ng
* NSITF/Labour House (3rd Floor), Central Business District, Garki, Abuja
Tel: (09) 2349496, 2349497 **Fax:** (09) 2349497
Contact: Said M. Ahmed - Chairman
Umaru H. Modibbo - MD/CEO

SIGNAL & CONTROL SYSTEMS LIMITED
Business: Supply, Installation and Maintenance of Communication and Electronic Systems, Training
Address: Turaki Ali House, 3, Kanta Road, Kaduna
Tel/Fax: (062) 247891, 08034080134
E-mail: mals@signal-control.com
Website: www.signal-control.com
* Block B (Shop 9), Festac '77 Hotel, off Lagos-Badagry Expressway, Amuwo-Odofin, Lagos
Tel: (01) 5884049, 5884111
Contact: Aliyu Usman - MD/CEO

SIGNAL ALLIANCE LIMITED
Business: Structured Cabling, Networking, Provision of Software Solutions

Address: NCWS House (2nd Floor), Plot PC, 14B, Ahmed Onibudo Street, Victoria Island, Lagos
Tel: (01) 4701674, 4619418, 4617704 **Fax:** (01) 4619418
E-mail: info@signalalliance.com
Website: www.signalalliance.com
Contact: Collins Onuegbu - MD/CEO

SIGNAL INSURANCE COMPANY LIMITED
Business: General Insurance Business
Address: 19, Military Street, Onikan, Lagos
Tel: (01) 2602117-8 (2L), 8117095-6 (2L), 2645784
Fax: (01) 2645786
E-mail: toyeodunsi@signalinsurance.com
Contact: Mr. Oluseyi Osho - Chairman
Mr. Olatoye Odunsi - MD/CEO

SIGNAL HEALTH NIGERIA LIMITED
Business: Marketing of Pharmaceutical Products
Address: 4, Ola-Ayeni Street, Ikeja, Lagos
Tel: (01) 4960549, 4970893 **Fax:** (01) 4975964
E-mail: info@tanuscomms.com
Contact: Dr. Yemi Ogunbiyi - MD/CEO

SIGNAL INVESTMENT & TRUST COMPANY LIMITED
Business: Stockbroking
Address: L.8, Ahmadu Bello Way/Katsina Road Roundabout, Kaduna
* Suite 28-35B (Entrance 4, Race Course Bus-Stop Wing, Tafawa Balewa Square Complex, Lagos
Tel: (01) 2634230, 2632081 **Fax:** (01) 2632981
Contact: Alh. A. Onigbanjo - MD/CEO

SIGNALHOUSE CONSULTING LIMITED
Business: IT Consultancy & Computer Forensic Services, IT Security, Audit & Control, Corporate Training, Financial Consultancy, CAAT Audit & Fruad Examination
Address: 13, Mojidi Street, off Toyin Street, Ikeja, Lagos
Tel: (01) 4978012, 8119808, 08033008104
Contact: Mr. Greg Ezeilo - Managing Consultaant

SIGNATURE FOLIO COMMUNICATIONS LIMITED
Business: Design and Printing of Corporate Gifts and Promotional Items, Sports Merchandising, Consultancy
Address: 12, Sumbo Jibowu Street, off Ribadu Road, S. W. Ikoyi, Lagos
Tel: (01) 2670029, 4703555; **Fax:** (01) 2695149
* 5, Katsina-Ala Road, Maitama District, Abuja
Tel: (09) 4139090-1 (2 L)

SIGNET INVESTMENT & SECURITIES LIMITED
Business: Stockbroking, Financial Services
Address: Church House (Signet Suite), 29, Marina, Lagos
Tel: (01) 2630965, 2632642 **Fax:** (01) 2647467
E-mail: signet@rcl.nig.com
Contact: Mr. Oladipo Abiose Aina - MD/CEO

SIGNONAFRICA COMMUNICATIONS LIMITED
Business: Deployment of VSAT, Wireless Internet Service Provider, Website Design, Training, Registration & Hosting, Sales of Internet Phone Equipment, Internet Wireless Connection
Address: 156, Obafemi Awolowo Way (3rd Floor), Ikeja, Lagos
Tel: (01) 4723065, 8112883, 08033071186, 08033486535
E-mail: info@signonafrica.com
Website: www.signonafrica.com
Contact: Mr. Godwin Okafor - President/CEO

SIKON SECURITIES & INVESTMENT TRUST LIMITED
Business: Stockbroking, Financial Advisory Services
Address: 38/40, Strachan Street, off Igbosere Road, Lagos
Tel: (01) 2645716-8 (3 L) **Fax:** (01) 2645718
E-mail: sikon@nova.net.ng
Contact: S. A. Onomakpome - Chairman

SILAS INDUSTRIAL & TRADING COMPANY LIMITED
Business: Sales of Food Products, Bakery Materials, Food Condiments and Spicies
Address: 36, Oguta Road, Onitsha
Tel: (046) 214724, 215239 **Fax:** (046) 216245
E-mail: sindgroup@infoweb.abs.net
silas@infoweb.abs.net
Contact: Chief (Sen.) Ezeugo S. Iyinagoro - Chairman/CEO

SILCAL INDUSTRIES LIMITED
Bisiness: Importation and Marketing of Cosmetic Products, Motorcycles and General Goods
Address: Eko Court Complex, Block A (Shop 1), Kofo Abayomi Street, Victoria Island, Lagos
Tel: (01) 2626280-1 (2L) **Fax:** (01) 2613230
E-mail: sanjit@linkseve.com
Contact: Mr. R. S. Arora - MD/CEO

SILHOUETTE INTERNATIONAL LIMITED
Business: Wood Processing, Manufacturing and Marketing of Furniture, Interior Decorations
Address: Plot 102/105, Trans-Amadi Ind.Layout, Port Harcourt
Tel: (084) 461237, 08033144253, 08037402288
E-mail: robert@courdeau.com
*Plot 1059, Adetokunbo Ademola Cr, Wuse II, Abuja
Tel/Fax: (09) 5232537
Contact: Mr. Robert Matossian - GM

SILICON ENGINEERING LIMITED
Business: Manufacture and Marketing of Engineering Equipment, Low and High-Voltage Switchgear Panels; Power Systems Engineering; Industrial Control and Automation
Address: 2B, Dillion St, Kirikiri Industrial Estate, Apapa, Lagos
Tel: (01) 5454685, 7746438, 7946436, 08023038839, 08033029386 **Fax:** (01) 5454685
E-mail: siliconpower@yahoo.com
* Plot 1503, Abidjan Street, near Customs Headquarters, Wuse Zone 3, Abuja
Tel: (09) 5235678
Contact: Engr. (Dr.) I. A. Ndubuisi - Chairman/CEO

SILKY TOUCH EMPORIUM
Business: Professional Clotheirs, Fashion House
Address: 14B, Karimu Kotun Street, Victoria Island, Lagos
Tel: (01) 2624374, 5558391, 08033007733
Fax: (01) 2625998
E-mail: silkytouch@hyperia.com
* Plot 1, House 4, Chief Aguma Street, off Aba Road, Port Harcourt.
Tel: (084) 239743

* 10, Usuma Street, Maitama, Abuja
Tel: (09) 4138776, 08033007733
* 15, Allen Avenue, Ikeja, Lagos
Tel: (01) 4970277, 4966458
Contact: Ogbuefi Victor C. Okolie - Chairman/CEO

SILMA TRAVELS LIMITED LIMITED
Business: Travel Agency
Address: 37, Campbell Street, Lagos Island, Lagos
Tel: (01) 7922855, 08023378461
Contact: Mr. E. A. Imoukhede - Chairman/CEO

SILVER FINANCIAL SERVICES LIMITED
Business: Stockbroking Financial Services
Address: Bookshop House (6th Floor), 50/52, Broad St, Lagos
Tel: (01) 2669131, 2666487, 2664412 **Fax:** (01) 2664412
E-mail: silverfs@infoweb.abs.net
* Akure Shopping Centre (Suite 11), Akure-Owo Road, Akure.
Tel: (034) 240344, 241043
Contact: Mr. Akintade Akinkugbe - MD/CEO

SILVER INDUSTRIES NIGERIA LIMITED
Business: Manufacturing and Marketing of Plastic Mats
Address: 151, Old Cemetery Road, Bompai Ind. Estate, Kano
Tel: (064) 649666, 631184 **Fax:** (064) 641140
Contact: Wassif M. Khartoun - Chairman/CEO

SILVER PLASTICS LIMITED
Business: Manufacturing of Plastic Mats
Address: 100, Maganda Road, Bompai Ind. Estate, Kano
Tel: (064) 630370, 646613 **Fax:** (064) 646613
Contact: Ali M. Khatoun - Exec. Director
Issam Zein - GM

SILVERBIRD COMMUNICATIONS LIMITED
Business: Radio Broadcasting Services
Address: 17A, Commercial Avenue, Sabo-Yaba, Lagos
Tel: (01) 7740511, 7740513 Fax: (01) 3425239
Contact: Mr. Ben Murray-Bruce - Group Chairman

SILVERBIRD PRODUCTIONS LIMITED
Business: Television Broadcasting & Syndication, Organisation of Beauty Pageants and Model Shows, Events Promotion
Address: 1, Rythm Avenue, Lekki Beach, off Lekki-Epe Expressway, Lagos
Tel: (01) 5555475, 7740512 Fax: (01) 5555386
E-mail: info@silverbirdTV.com
Contact: Mr. Ben Murray-Bruce - Group Chairman

SILVERTRUST INSURANCE BROKERS LIMITED
Business: Insurance Broking
Address: Suite B5, Falomo Shopping Complex, Ikoyi, Lagos
Tel: (01) 2671271, 2693856 **Fax:** (01) 2693856
Contact: Mr. A. I. Oyetola - MD/CEO

SIMBA TECHNOLOGY (NIGERIA) LIMITED
Business: Systems Integration, Communication Solution Provider, Turnkey IT Solutions, Distribution of IT Products and Communication Equipment
Address: 77/79, Eric Moore Road, Iganmu Industrial Estate, Surulere, Lagos
Tel: (01) 5835202, 5841958, 5456441, 7740120
Fax: (01) 5851016
E-mail: sales@simbaoline.net
Website: www.simbatechnology.com

SIMBABE BALLOONS & ACCESSORIES
Business: Sales of Balloons & Decorative Accessories, Sales of Christmas Trees & Accessories
Address: 164, Ogunlana Drive, Surulere, Lagos
Tel: (01) 5456773, 5851788, 7749686, 08023341938, 08023356835 **Fax:** (01) 5841992
E-mail: simbabe@nova.net.ng
simbabe2@hotmail.com
Contact: Mrs. Ronke Osunsan - MD/CEO

SIMIDIA S & I INTERNATIONAL COMPANY LIMITED
Business: Mechanical & Civil Engineering
Address: Plot 127, off Trans-Amadi Road, by Coca Cola Plant, Port Harcourt
Tel: (084) 230787, 235324 Fax: (084) 236626

SIMOCH INTERNATIONAL LIMITED
Business: Sales of Computer Hardware and Software, and Accessories, Engineering and Consultancy Servcies, Networking
Address: 24, Ogunlana Drive, Surulere, Lagos
Tel: (01) 5840918, 5851282, 833334, 08033067614, 08033299433, 08042119102
E-mail: simoch@infoweb.abs.net
Contact: Chief S. U. Ochuba - Chairman/CEO

SIMON OKEKE & ASSOCIATES
Business: Estate Surveyor and Valuers, Chartered Surveyors, Real Estate Consultants and Agents
Address: 7A, Hall Lane, Oduduwa Rd, Apapa G.R.A., Lagos
Tel: (01) 5454331, 7745066 **Fax:** (01) 5454331
E-mail: sivik@micro.com.ng
Contact: Simon Nsobundu Okeke - Chairman/CEO

SIMON SITTE NIGERIA LIMITED
Business: Sales of Drilling, Industrial & Water Treatment Chemicals, Corrosion Control Materials & Consultants, Electrical & Mechanical Engineers
Address: 128, PTI Road, Effurun, Warri
Tel: (053) 257522, 0035508511 Fax: (053) 254642
E-mail: simonsitte@yahoo.com
Contact: Mr. Simon A. Asite - Chairman/CEO

SIMPOLY INDUSTRIES NIGERIA LIMITED
Business: Manfacturing of Water Poly Tanks, Ice Coolers, Portable Toilets, Plastic Pallets & Courier Boxes
Address: Km. 16, Ikorodu Road, beh. Philips Factory, Ojota, Lagos
Tel: (01) 4971457, 4975584, 7760674
Fax: (01) 4971550, 4971555
E-mail: anil@somotexnig.com
Contact: Mr. Anil Mohinani - MD/CEO

SIMS NIGERIA LIMITED
Business: Importation and Marketing of Electronic and Electrical Appliances; Sales of Electrical Materials and Agricultural Equipment
Address: 2, Ogui Road, Enugu

Tel: (042) 250145, 251614 **Fax:** (042) 256659
E-mail: sims@micro.com.ng
* 43, Ibrahim Taiwo Road, Kano.
Tel: (064) 641069
* 72/74, Iweka Road, Onitsha.
Tel: (046) 410005
Contact: Mr. Simeon Eyisi - Chairman/CEO
Mr. Aloy Umeodinka - Marketing Manager

SINGAFRIQUE ENGINEERING LIMITED
Business: Building & Civil Engineering, Roof Construction & Maintenance, Building Renovation
Address: 7, D'Alberto Road, Palm Grove Estate, off Ikorodu Road, Ilupeju, Lagos
Tel/Fax: (01) 4931463, 08023156634
E-mail: rnisel@hotmail.com
* 50, Psychiatric Hospital Road, Rumuigbo, Port Harcourt
* News Engineering Plaza (1st Floor), Herbert Macaulay Way, Wuse Zone 4, Abuja

SIO INDUSTRIES LIMITED
Business: Manufacture of Polypropylene Woven Sacks, Ball Twins, Laminated Sacks, School and Sports Bags,and Sport Wears
Address: Group House, 4/6, Ikoyi Road, Obalende, Lagos
Tel: (01) 2692667, 2692664-9 (6L), 2691825
Fax: (01) 2692683
* Km 129, Benin-Asaba Expressway, Asaba
Tel: (056) 280850-4(5L), 280164, 280184, 281131
3, Lagos Street, Asata, Enugu
Contact: Chief (Dr.) Sonny I. Odogwu - Chairman
Mr P. Zemanek - Factory Tech, Manager

SIO LIMITED
Business: Property Development, Road Maintenance
Address: 25, Boyle Street, Onikan, Lagos
Tel: (01) 2631484, 2692665 **Fax:** (01) 2692666
* Plot 1301, Akin Adesola Street, Victoria Is, Lagos
Tel: (01) 3201273-5 (3L), 7747030 **Fax:** (01) 2623924
Contact: Chief (Dr.) Sonny I. Odogwu - Chairman
Mr. Kenny Odogwu - MD/CEO

SIOTEL NIGERIA LIMITED
Business: VSAT and Internet Service Provider
Address: 5A, Karimu Kotun Street, Victoria Island, Lagos
Tel: (01) 3201260-3 (4 L), 2622511 **Fax:** (01) 2622511
E-mail: info@siotel.net
sales@siotel.net
Website: www.siotel.net
www.siotel.com
* Asokoro Shopping Complex, Plot 155, T. Y. Danjuma Street, Asokoro, Abuja
Tel: (09) 3140631-4 (4 L)
E-mail: sales@abuja.siotel.com
* 9, Agudama Avenue, D/Line, Port Harcourt.
Tel: (084) 572918-9 (2L)
Contact: Chief S. D. Odogwu - Chairman
Mr Kenny E. Odogwu - MD/CEO

SIPERCO NIGERIA LIMITED
Business: Production and Manufacturing of Cosmetics, Baby Care and Beauty Products, Importation and Marketing of Cosmetics Raw Materials
Address: 359/361, Old Ojo Road, off Badagry Expressway, Satellite Town, Ojo, Lagos
Tel/Fax: (02) 4706060, 7738615, 08023044511
Contact: Mr. Ali Safieddine - MD/CEO

SIRAJ (NIGERIA) LIMITED
Business: Engineering Consultancy Services
Address: Plot 3162B, IBB Way, by Rhine Str, Maitama, Abuja
Tel: (09) 41333329, 08033154424 **Fax:** (09) 4135012
Contact: Engr. Mojidi Abou Najm - MD/CEO

SIRPI-ALUSTEEL CONSTRUCTION LIMITED
Business: Steel Fabrication and Construction (Onshore, Offshore and Swamp Operations)
Address: 2, East-West Road, Rumuodara, Port Harcourt
Tel: (084) 611430-1 (2L), * (082) 440107, 440126, 440470, 440878 **Fax:** (082) 440069, 440467
E-mail: sirpi-ph@phca.linkserve.com
* 67, Liverpool Road, Eket, Akwa Ibom State
Tel: (082) 443623
* 54, Effurun Road, Warri.
Tel: (053) 254757
Contact: Mr. Henry MacPepple - Chairman/CEO

SKEIN NIGERIA LIMITED
Business: Sales and Services of Generators and Electrical Equipment, Engineering Project Management
Address: 76B, Adeniran Ogunsanya Street, Surulere, Lagos
Tel: (01) 5850409, 7747797 **Fax:** (01) 5850410
E-mail: skein@infoweb.abs.net
* Plot 519, Koforidua Street, by Michael Okpara Way, Wuse Zone 2, Abuja.
Tel: (09) 5237522
Contact: Engr. Obidi Ezenwa - MD/CEO

SKENCOURT LIMITED
Business: Import and Export, Stockist of Iron Building Materials, General Merchandising
Address: Oluwalogbon Motors Premises, Plot A, Obafemi Awolowo Way, Alausa, Ikeja, Lagos
Tel: (01) 4939841-3(3L) **Fax:** (01) 4970027
Contact: Chief S. O. Bakare - Chairman

SKETCH BOX LIMITED
Business: Distribution and Sales of Suspended Ceilings, Partition Systems and General Building Products
Address: 72, Queen's Street, Alagomeji-Yaba, Lagos
Tel: (01) 866999, 2881750, 4936666
* Plot 6\539, Nelson Mandela Street, Asokoro District, Abuja.
Tel/Fax: (09) 3148857

SKETCH PRESS LIMITED
Business: Newspaper Publishing, Printing Services
Address: Oba Adebimpe Road, Ibadan
Tel: (02) 2414983, 2414851
Fax: (02) 2413820, 2411289, 2411604
E-mail: sketch@skannet.com
* 88/92, Broad Street, Lagos.
Tel: (01) 2661521
Contact: Chief Adewole Atandeyi - Chairman/CEO
Mrs. Dupe Ajayi Gbadebo - MD/Editor-in-Chief

SKF NIGERIA LIMITED
Business: Sale and Marketing of SKF Bearing, Seals and Allied Products
Address: Elephant Cement House (3rd Floor), ASSBIFI Rd, Central Business District, Alausa, Ikeja, Lagos
Tel: (01)7742546 **Fax:** (01) 5557558, 7742546
E-mail: skfngr@infoweb.abs.net
Contact: Alh. Layi Adegbite - GM/CEO

SKG-PHARMA LIMITED
Business: Production & Marketing of Pharmaceutical Products
Address: Welcome House, Plot 2, Oba Akran Avenue, Ikeja Industrial Estate Ikeja, Lagos
Tel: (01) 4960841, 4961745, 4961628, 4961665, 4962718
Fax: (01) 4962671
E-mail: office@rumon.nigeria.com
Contact: Mr. B. A. Voakes - MD/CEO
Mr. S. O. N. Akpa - GM(Sales/Marketing)

SKYBLIND (NIGERIA) LIMITED
Business: Sales of Furniutre, Carpets, Curtains & Accessoris Interior Decotion Services, Import Trading
Address: L5, Ahmadu Bello Way, Kaduna
Tel: (062) 210241, 248656, 08023239544, 08034086033
Website: www.skyblind.com
Contact: Mr. Augustine Achilike -President/CEO

SKYBRIGHT INDUSTRIES LIMITED
Business: Manufacturers of Automobile Silencers, Metal Office-Filling Cabinets and Office Furniture
Address: 5, Kayode Adebanji Street, Ashamu Estate, Oke-Afa, Isolo, Lagos
Tel: (01) 4705226, 4809446, 08023012605, 08033265343
Fax: (01) 2880494
Contact: Chief Innocent T. Ogene - Chairman

SKYLINE GROUP OF COMPANIES
Business: Airline Services, Aviation Consultancy
Address: 28, Creek Road, Apapa, Lagos
Tel: (01) 5874658 **Fax:** (01) 7746136
* Domestic Terminal, M.Mohammed Airport, Lagos
* Presidential Hotel, Aba Road, Port Harcourt
Tel: (084) 231908 (Ext. 256)
* Nnamdi Azikiwe International Airport, Abuja
Tel: (09) 8100267

SKYLINK TELECOMMUNICATIONS LIMITED
Business: Telecommunication Engineering Services, Equipment Sales & Service, Internet Service Provider
Address: 11, Military Street, Onikan, Lagos
Tel: (01) 2636665, 2636635 **Fax:** (01) 2636684
E-mail: skylink@hyperia.com
Contact: Engr. Ambrose Nwankwo - Chairman/CEO

SKYMILES TRAVELS & TOURS LIMITED
Business: Travel Agency
Address: 35, Opebi Road, Opebi, Ikeja, Lagos
Tel: (01) 4961912, 4703921 **Fax:** (01) 4937138
E-mail: skymilestravels@hotmail.com
Contact: Mr. Abiodun Kassim - GM

SKYMIT MOTORS LIMITED
Business: Sales of Automobiles, Real Estate Development and Management, Travels & Tours
Address: 20, Mobolaji Bank-Anthony Way, Ikeja, Lagos
Tel: (01) 4966462, 4966468, 4961912, 08033075072, 08033219079 **Fax:** (01) 4937128
E-mail: sales@skymitmotorsltd.com
Website: www.skymitmotorsltd.com
Contact: Mr. Tayo Ayeni - Chairman/CEO

SKYPOWER AVIATION HANDLING COMPANY LIMITED
Business: Aviation/Air Cargo Handling and Warehousing.
Address: SAHCOL Warehouse Complex, Cargo Terminal, Murtala Mohammed Airport, Ikeja, Lagos
Tel: (01) 4934857, 4973767, 08023040600
Fax: (01) 4935298
E-mail: info@sahcol.com
Website: www.sahcol.com
* Nnamdi Azikiwe International Airport, Abuja
Tel: (09) 8100202
* Aminu Kano International Airport, Kano
Tel: (064) 649278
* Port Harcourt Int'l Airport, Omagwa, Rivers State
Tel: (084) 771554

SKYPOWER EXPRESS AIRWAYS NIGERIA LIMITED
Business: Airline Services
Address: 84, Awolowo Road, S. W. Ikoyi, Lagos
Tel: (01) 2693275-6 (2L), 4614035, 08033740572
Fax: (01) 2693253
E-mail: skypower@vgccl.com
* Kaduna International Airport, Kaduna
Tel: (062) 243521
Contact: Mr T. N. Ike - GM
Capt. S. Ohiomah - Director of Operations

SKYROUTE AGENCY LIMITED
Business: Clearing and Forwarding Agency
Address: 450, Airport Road, No-Man's Land, Kano
Tel: (064) 638704, 08033173673, 08044122552
Fax: (064) 638704, 643164
E-mail: skyrouteagltd@hotmail.com
Contact: Prince D. A. Tokula - Chairman/CEO

SKYVIEW ESTATES LIMITED
Business: Property Development and Advisory Services
Address: 13, Agoro Odiyan Street, Victoria Island, Lagos
Tel: (01) 2620683-4 (2L), 2626963-4 (2L)
Fax: (01) 2616489
E-mail: skyview@intracom.net.ng
* Plot 252, Sapara Williams Close, off Idowu Martins Street, Victoria Island, Lagos
Tel: (01) 2626963-4 (2L), 8129455, 08022245431
Fax: (01) 2626963-4 (2L)
Contact: Mr. Oba Otudeko - Chairman
Mr. Kunle Fashogbon - Property Manager

SKYVIEW-O NIGERIA LIMITED
Business: Telecommunication Service Delivery & Consultancy
Address: Bookshop House, 50/52, Broad Street, Lagos
Tel: (01) 2601310, 2601313 **Fax:** (01) 2601312, 7590329
E-mail: sales@skyview-o.com
Website: www.skyview-o.com
* Bamcar Shopping Complex (1st Floor, Shop 01) Wuse Zone 5, Abuja.

Tel: (09) 5239747, 2727575
* 16, Railway Close, D-Line, Port Harcourt
Tel: (084) 236014-6 (3 L)
Contact: Ozumba A. Otiji - MD/CEO

SLEEP COMFORT COMPANY LIMITED
Business: Furniture Manufacturing
Address: 231A/233, Moshood Abiola Way, Ijora, Lagos
Tel: (01) 836513, 836979, 844799
Contact: Carlos F. Chidiac - MD/CEO

SLOK GROUP
Business: Oil & Gas Industry Services, Banking, Insurance, Aviation, Shipping Services, Manufacturing, Printing, Publishing, Import and Export, General Merchandise
Address: Slok House, 10, Randle Road, Apapa, Lagos
Tel: (01) 5875311, 5870240, 5452136
Fax: (01) 5874571, 5452137
E-mail: slokgroup@nova.net.ng
slokgroup@teleplex.net
Contact: Dr. Orji Uzor Kalu, MON - Founder
Mr. Emeka Abone - GM

SMAB INTER TRADE LIMITED
Business: Importing & Assembly of Motorcycles
Address: Plor 47, Sharada Industrial Estate, Kano
Tel: (064) 660905, 660907, 08023273251
Fax: (064) 660907
E-mail: smabintertrade@yahoo.com
Contact: Alh. A. Shehu Mohammed - MD/CEO

SMAGH & COMPANY NIGERIA LIMITED
Business: Corporate Printers, General Contracts & Supplies
Address: 59, Ilesanmi Street, Surulere, Lagos
Tel: (01) 5456469, 8135748, 08042114719
E-mail: smagh@infoweb.abs.net

SMART MARK LIMITED
Business: Importation, Distribution and Marketing of Watches and Personal-Care Products
Address: 58, Akanbi Onitiri Close (4th Floor), off Eric Moore Road, Iganmu, Lagos
Tel: (01) 7748326, 7739367, 7731016 **Fax:** (01) 5802607
E-mail: smartmk@infoweb.abs.net

SMARTCARD NIGERIA PLC
Business: Design and Implementation of Electrionic Card (Valucard) Payment System
Address: 3, Idowu Taylor Street, Victoria Island, Lagos
Tel: (01) 7742441, 4701627, 4701268 **Fax:** (01) 2625590
Contact: Dr. J. P. Merino - MD/CEO

SMARTPAY NIGERIA LIMITED
Business: Processing of Electrionic Payments for Banks ('Smartpay'), Provision of Cstomised Electronic Solutions & Platforms
Address: CSS Bookshop House (13th & 14th Floors), 50/52, Broad Street, Lagos
Tel: (01) 2631734, 2634970 Fax: (01) 2647016
E-mail: info@smartpay.org
Website: www.smartpay.org
Contact: Mr. Alex Nwuba - MD/CEO

SME MANAGER LIMITED
Business: Private Placement of Eqity, Investment Advisors
Address: C & C Towers (8th Floor), Plot 1684, Sanusi Fafunwa Street, Victoria Island, Lagos
Tel: (01) 2620696, 2620699, 3200897-8 (2L)
E-mail: info@sm-aca.com.ng
Website: www.sme-aca.com.ng

SMIEC CHEMICAL ENGINEERING & CONSTRUCTION COMPANY LIMITED
Business: Engineering and Construction, Dredging and Marine Services, Oil and Gas, Telecommunications, Aviation Services, Agro-Allied Activities
Address: 30, Adeola Hopewell Street, Victoria Island, Lagos
Tel: (01) 2624521-7 (7 L) **Fax:** (01) 2624219
E-mail: smiecengineering@aol.com
* 165, Woji Road, G. R. A. Phase II, Port Harcourt
Tel/Fax: (084) 238702
Contact: Chief Hope O. Uzodinma - Chairman

SMILE DENTAL PRACTICE
Business: Dental Clinic
Address: Plot 1210, Yakubu Gowon Crescent, Asokoro, Abuja
Tel/Fax: (09) 3142670

SMIT NIGERIA LIMITED
Business: Oil Industry Services
Address: 5A, Aerodrome Road, off Wharf Rd, Apapa, Lagos
Tel: (01) 5870667, 5804168 **Fax:** (01) 5804168
E-mail: smit@hyperia.com

SMOOTHWAY INSURANCE BROKERS LIMITED
Business: Insurance Broking, Risk Advisory Services
Address: Aiyede House (Upper Rear Suite), 10, Abeokuta Street, Ebute-Metta (East), Lagos
Tel: (01) 8043387, 860595, 08023198711
Fax: (01) 861809
Contact: Mr. Akinola Odusami - MD/CEO

SMURFIT PRINT NIGERIA PLC
Business: Manufacturing of Corrugated Packaging Cartons
Address: 76/84, Lagos-Abeokta Expressway, Dopemu, Lagos
Tel: (01) 4924493, 4924749, 4926411 **Fax:** (01) 4926515
Contact: Chief F. O. Isikwei - MD/CEO

SNC LAVALIN NIGERIA LIMITED
Business: Engineering, Procurement, Management Consultancy Services, Drilling Services
Address: 19A, Mekuwen Road (Unit 3), off Oyinkan Abayomi Drive, Ikoyi, Lagos
Tel: (01) 2693277, 2692243 **Fax:** (01) 2693032
E-mail: snc_lavalin_nigeria@hotmail.com
snc_lavalin_nigeria@yahoo.com
Contact: Alh. (Brigadier) Abba Kyari (rtd) - Chairman
Chief Lucky A. Egwakhide - MD/CEO

SNIG NIGERIA LIMITED
Business: Fabrication and Technical Engineering Services, Pipeline Construction
Address: 56, Onumini Ahia, Ogidingba, Trans-Amadi Industrial Layout, Port Harcourt
Tel: (084) 237400, 231308 **Fax:** (084) 231308
E-mail: snig@phca.linkserve.com.

SO & U SAATCHI & SAATCHI
Business: Marketing Communications
Address: 2, Oyetola Street, off Ajanaku Street, via Thomas Ajufo Street, off Opebi Road, Ikeja, Lagos
Tel: (01) 4979361, 4930450-1 (2L), 7731547, 7741754
Fax: (01) 4973798
E-mail: info@sousaatchi.com
Contact: Mr. V. G. Osibodu - Chairman
Mr. Udeme Ufot - MD/CEO

SOBARSON NIGERIA LIMITED
Business: Importation and Distribution of Food Commodities
Address: Eleganza Plaza (Virgo Block, 1st Floor), 1, Commercial Road, Apapa, Lagos
Tel: (01) 5450962, 5454449 **Fax:** (01) 5454449
* Plot 318, Adeyemo Akapo Street, Omole Estate Phase I, Ikeja, Lagos
Contact: Chief S. O. N. Emeasoba - Chairman/CEO

SOCATEC ELECTRICAL INDUSTRIES NIGERIA LIMITED
Business: Manufacturing and Marketing of Electrical Appliances and Fittings
Address: 146, Olojo Drive, Ojo-Alaba, Lagos
Tel: (01) 5871949, 880988, 885081
Contact: Mr. Sunday Onyia - Chairman/CEO

SOCIETE BANCAIRE NIGERIA LIMITED
Business: Merchant Banking
Address: Plot 1683, Sanusi Fafunwa St Victoria Island, Lagos
Tel: (01) 2621120-4 (5L), 2621126
Fax: (01) 2621132, 2621135
E-mail: sbnl@alpha.linkserve.com
Contact: Mal. I. Shuaibu - Ag MD/CEO

SOCIETE GENERALE BANK (NIGERIA) LIMITED
Business: Commercial Banking
Address: Sarah House, 13, Martins Street, Lagos
Tel: (01) 2660315, 2661881, 26654900, 2661934, 2661978
E-mail: infoosgbn@sgbn.com.ng
Website: www.sgbn.com.ng
Contact: Mr. Robert Mbonu - MD/CEO
Mrs S. Odumosu - Head (Corp. Affairs)

SOCKETWORKS LIMITED
Business: Software Development, IT Outsourcing
Address: Marbl House (2nd Floor), 1, Alfred Rewane (Kingsway) Road, Falomo, Ikoyi, Lagos
Tel: (01) 4812439, 08033141234
E-mail: info@socketworksglobal.com
Website: www.socketworksglobal.com
Contact: Dr. Aloy Chife - MD/CEO

SOCOMEX NIGERIA LIMITED
Business: Importation and Sales of Pharmaceuticals
Address: John Holt Compound, Plot 3/4, Adewunmi Industrial Estate, Oregun, Ikeja, Lagos
Tel: (01) 4703716, 8183973
Contact: Mr. Vincent A. D'Silva - MD

SOCOPAO VENTURES LIMITED
Bsiness: Clearing & Forwarding
Address: Socopao House, 10, Bashir Oweh Street, off Simbiat Abiola Road, Ikeja, Lagos
Tel: (01) 4931655, 4936391 Fax: (01) 4936391
Contact: Otunba Akeem A. Adigun - Chairman/CEO

SODIK BAG MANUFACTURERS LIMITED
Business: Manufacture of Synthetic-Fibre Travelling Bags
Address: Group House, 4/6, Ikoyi Road, Obalende, Lagos
Tel: (01) 683735, 683736 **Fax:** (01) 683738
* Km. 129, Benin-Asaba Expressway, Asaba
Tel: (046) 280850, 280852, 280854 **Fax:** (046) 280853

SODIK ELECTRICAL & ENGINEERING LIMITED
Business: Manufacture and Assembly of Motor Control Centres, Bus Bar Chambers, Fire-Resistant Steel Cabinets, Metal Enclosures, Electric Motors, Contractors and Relays, High-Voltage Switchgear, Starters and Control Apparatus
Address: 1, Happy Home Avenue, Kirikiri Industrial Estate, Apapa, Lagos
Tel: (01) 5455419, 4814214, 08042113608
Fax: (01) 5455418, 2692666
E-mail: informsodik@yahoo.com
Contact: Chief (Dr.) Sonny Iwedike Odogwu - Chairman
Mr. Kenny Odogwu - CEO.

SOFISTICAT LIMITED
Business: Design and Sales of Fashion Wears Corporate Gifts Accessories and Cosmetics
Address: 4, Mobolaji Bank-Anthony Way, Maryland, Ikeja, Lagos
Tel: (01) 961819, 967323, 4970395 **Fax:** (01) 967317
* 6-10, Samuel Anibaba St, Aiyedere-Ketu, Lagos
* 3, Ribadu Road, S. W. Ikoyi, Lagos.
Tel: (01) 686160
* Allen/Opebi Roundabout, Ikeja, Lagos
Contact: Mr. Lanre Ogunlesi - CEO.

SOFITAM NIGERIA LIMITED
Business: Supply and Maintenance of Petroleum Equipment, Industrial and Fire-Fighting/Safety Equipment
Address: Plot 2/4, Amuwo-Odofin Industrial Scheme, Apapa-Oshodi Expressway, Amuwo-Odofin, Lagos
Tel: (01) 5847673, 7740600, 4711242 **Fax:** (01) 5847673
E-mail: info@sofitamnigeria.com
* 55A, Tafawa Balewa Road, Kano
Tel/Fax: (064) 644608
* 10, Forces Avenue, Port Harcourt
Tel/Fax: (084) 235430
* Michael Okpara Street, Wuse Zone 2, Abuja
Tel: (09) 5232502 **Fax:** (09) 5232503
E-mail: info@sofitamnigeria.com
Contact: Mr. D. de Smeytere - MD/CEO

SOFT SOLUTIONS LIMITED
Business: Software Development & Implementation, Anti-Virus Helpdesk, Network Security, Network Management
Address: 5, Alh. Tokan Street, off Western Avenue, Alaka Estate, Surulere, Lagos
Tel: (01) 5841409, 5850465, 5851011, 5851081
Fax: (01) 2693362, 5851348
E-mail: postmaster@ss-limited.com
Website: www.ss-limited.com
Contact: Mr. Steven Edge - MD/CEO.

SOFTWARE TECHNOLOGY PARK LIMITED
Business: IT Education & Training , Software Solution
Address: 40, Saka Tinubu Street, Victoria Island, Lagos
Tel: (01) 4708056, 7782930
Website: www.stpl-ng.com
* 7, Agoro Odiyan Street, off Adeola Odeku Street, Victoria Island, Lagos
Tel: (01) 7731751-2 (2 L)
E-mail: visland@aptech-nigeria.com
Website: www.aptech-globaltraining.com
* Oyo House (2nd Floor), opp Fed.Min.of Finance, Central Business District, Garki, Abuja
Tel: (09) 2344151
E-mail: abuja@aptech-nigeria.com
Contact: Mr. Vincent Fernandez - MD/CEO

SOFTWORKS LIMITED
Business: Enterprise Business Solutions, Enterprise Infrastructure Solution, Enterprise Application Solution
Address: Plot 242, Kofo Abayomi Street, Victoria Is. Lagos
Tel: (01) 2611729, 2619954, 3200580-4 (5L)
Fax: (01) 2619945
E-mail: info@softworksng.com
Website: www.softworksng.com
Contact: Mr. Ini Akpan - MD/CEO

SOIMI (NIGERIA) LIMITED
Business: Engieering Service for the Oil, Petrochemcial & Gas Industry, (Construction, Project Management, Prefabrication Maintenance & Service, Engineering & Procurement, Electrical Installation & Hook-up)
Address: Consortium House, Plot 1682, Sanusi Fafunwa Street, Victoria Island, Lagos
Tel: (01) 2616855, 2631216 **Fax:** (01) 2613216
* Plot 60, Trans-Amadi Ind. Layout, Port Harcourt
Tel: (084) 330644, 238871, 237709 **Fax:** (084) 238871
Contact: Mr. Stefano Piotti - GM/CEO

SOKO-TECH (NIGERIA) LIMITED
Business: Electrical, Mechanical and Telecommunication Engineering Services
Address: 35, Abosede Kuboye Crescent, off Imam Dauda Street, Iganmu, Lagos
Tel: (01) 832642, 832892; Fax: (01) 832632
* OAU Quarters, Zone A7, Wuse II, Abuja
Tel: (09) 5236046
Contact: Engr. C. E. Ogoro - MD/CEO.

SOKOTO FURNITURE FACTORY LIMITED
Business: Manufacturing and Marketing of Furniture
Address: 1, Furniture Factory Road, Sokoto
Tel: (060) 232204, 232539 **Fax:** (060) 233078
E-mail: sokfur@yahoo.com
Contact: Alh. Muhammad Lemo Abubakar - GM/CEO

SOKOTO HOTEL LIMITED
Business: Hospitality and Catering Services
Address: Kano Road, Sokoto
Tel: (060) 238148, 232126
Contact: Amina O. Joshua - GM/CEO

SOKOTO INVESTMENT COMPANY LIMITED
Business: Development Finance Institution, Portfolio Investment, Project Financing, Promotion of Local Investments
Address: 8, Kano Road, Sokoto
Tel: (060) 232836, 235821 **Fax:** (060) 235629
Contact: Alh. Shehu Dange - Sole Administrator

SOKOTO LEATHER AND TANNING INDUSTRIES LIMITED
Business: Production of Leather
Address: State Highway, Ilupeju Ind. Estate, Ilupeju, Lagos
Tel: (01) 493877 (090) 408567
Contact: Mr. S. Haider - MD/CEO

SOLA BADMUS & COMPANY
Business: Estate Surveyors and Valuers, Plant and Machinery Valuation, Auctioneering, Estate Agency
Address: Waterfront Plaza (1st Floor), Plot O, 1st Avenue, opposite Mr. Biggs, Festac Town, Lagos
Tel: (01) 5883729, 7731656, 08023071614, 08042132353
* Goodness Place (Suite 383), Plot 627, Sokode Crescent, opposite F.I.R.S., Wuse Zone 5, Abuja
Tel: (09) 5236591
Contact: Mr. A. M. Badmus - Principal Partner

SOLA ENITAN & COMPANY
Business: Estate Surveyors & Valuers, Property & Facility Management, Estate Agency
Address: 26, Ilepeju Bye-Pass, Ilupeju, Lagos
Tel: (01) 4937619, 08023050130 Fax: (01) 4937619
E-mail: solaenitan@yahoo.com
Website: www.solaenitan.com
Contact: Mr. Sola Enitan - Managing Partner

SOLAR ELECTRIC SYSTEMS LIMITED
Business: Marketing, Installation and Maintenance of Alternative (Solar, Wind, Hydro) Power Systems
Address: J.D. Gomwalk House (6th Floor), Jos
Tel/Fax: (073) 450102
E-mail: solect@infoweb.abs.net
Contact: M. O. Lawal - MD/CEO.

SOLAR ENERGY ADVANCED POWER SYSTEMS LIMITED
Business: Importation and Assembly of Solar Energy Equipment, Electricity Generation Services, Solar-Powered Boreholes
Address: Shamrock House, Plot 10, Apapa-Oshodi Expressway, Coconut Bus-Stop, Apapa, Lagos
Tel: (01) 5450046, 5871599, 5875200, 4816149, 7912558, 08033150399, 08033378898 **Fax:** (01) 5871599
E-mail: solar_energy2002@yahoo.com
solar_energy2002@linkserve.com
Contact: Chief Vincent E. Ajede - Chairman/CEO

SOLAR PRODUCTIONS LIMITED
Business: Film & Television Programme Production, Broadcast Consultancy, Equipment Supply & Hire, Industrial Photography
Address: 8A, Town Planning Way, Ilupeju, Lagos
Tel: (01) 4961336, 823734
E-mail: solarpro@infoweb.abs.net
Contact: Adegboyega Adelaja - MD/CEO

SOLAR TURBINES SERVICES NIGERIA LIMITED
Business: Sales & Maintenance of Power-Generating Turbines

Address: Plot 36, Trans-Amadi Ind. Layout, Port Harcourt
Tel: (084) 230186-7 (2 L) **Fax:** (084) 230185

SOLARMATE ENGINEERING LIMITED
Business: Design, Supply and Installation of Solar-Power Systems
Address: 435/437, Herbert Macaulay Street, Yaba, Lagos
Tel: (01) 7740887, 2880165, 867836 08033016045
Fax: (01) 3425159, 4974607
E-mail: solarmate@metrong.cm
Contact: Engr. Dotun Tokun - MD/CEO.

SOLEL BONEH (NIGERIA) LIMITED
Business: Building & Civil Engineering Services
Address: 82, Younis Bashorun Street, off Ajose Adeogun Street, Victoria Island, Lagos
Tel: (01) 4618841-3 (3L) **Fax:** (01) 4618844
E-mail: md@rcc.nigeria.com
Website: www.rccnigeria.com
* Plot 564/565, Block A, beh. FEPA Headquarters, Airport Road, Central Business District, Abuja
* Oyo Road, opp. University of Ibadan, Ibadan

SOLGAS PETROLEUM LIMITED
Business: Prospecting, Exploration, Production and Exploitation of Crude Oil & Natural Gas
Address: Fortune Towers (1st Floor), 27/29, Adeyemo Alakija Street, Victoria Island, Lagos
Tel: (01) 617334, 2620651-2 (2 L), 2620624
Fax: (01) 2620662
E-mail: solgas@hyperia.com
Contact: Owelle Oscar Udoji - MD/CEO

SOLID BASE NIGERIA LIMITED
Business: Sales of Power Control & Protection Equipment, Contracting, Solid Mineral Mining, Engineering Consultancy Services
Address: 25A, Fatai Atere Way, Matori Ind Estate, Lagos
Tel: (01) 4526782, 523018 **Fax:** (01) 4526782
E-mail: solidbase@theobech.com
solidbasenig@yahoo.com
* 3, Oghene Drive, G.R.A. Phase 2, Port Harcourt
Tel: (084) 237697
Contact: Mr. Kadiri P. Otaru - Chairman/CEO.

SOLID HOMES LIMITED
Business: Real Estate Development & Managemant
Address: 1A, Kayode Abraham Street, off Ligali Ayorinde Street, Victoria Island, Lagos
Tel: (01) 7739620, 3200633, 2901035 **Fax:** (01) 3200633
E-mail: info@solidhomesltd.com
Website: www.solidhomesltd.com
Contact: Engr. Oladipo Ashafa - MD/CEO

SOLID TRUST INSURANCE BROKERS LIMITED
Business: Insurance Broking and Consultancy Services
Address: Elephant House (2nd Floor), 239/241, Ikorodu Road, Ilupeju, Lagos
Tel: (01) 4978448, 4978450 **Fax:** (01) 4978448
Contact: Mrs. Funmi Juwah - MD/CEO.

SOLIDARITY INTERNATIONAL VENTURES LIMITED
Business: Importation of Fertilizer Blending Plants, Incinerators, Agricultural Machinery and Fertilizers
Address: Solidarity House, Plot 717, Minna Street, Area 8, Garki, Abuja
Tel: (09) 2340267-8 (2L) **Fax:** (09) 2340269
E-mail: info@solidarityinternational.com
Website: www.solidarityinternational.com
* Stereo House, Industrial Layout, Western Bye-Pass, Minna.
Tel: (062) 223090, 222324

SOLID-ROCK SECURITIES & INVESTMENT LIMITED
Business: Stockbroking, Investment Advisory Services, Portfolio Management
Address: Stock Exchange House (Level 18), 2/4, Customs Street, Lagos Island, Lagos
Tel: (01) 2660408, 2661464 Fax: (01) 2666813
E-mail: solid_rockng@yahoo.com
Contact: Rear Admiral A. A. Madueke (rtd) - Chairman
Mr. A. C. Nwaobi - MD/CEO

SOLLATEK (NIGERIA) LIMITED
Business: Marketing of Power Protection Equipment, and Solar Energy Equipment
Address: Jagal House, Jagal Road, off Ikosi Road, Oregun Industrial Estate, Oregun, Ikeja, Lagos
Tel: (01) 4961510, 4865745, 4973390-4 (5 L)
Fax: (01) 4970090
E-mail: sollatek@jagal.com
snl@linkserve.com.ng
* Jagal House, Plot 550, Usuma St, Maitama, Abuja
Tel: (09) 4133489 **Fax:** (09) 4133490
Contact: Mr. Anwar Jarmakani - Group Exec. Chairman
Mr. Kevin Meachim - GM

SOLTAN TRAVELS & TOURS LIMITED
Business: Travel Agency, Tour Packaging, General Handling Services for Airlines
Address: Glitter House, 214C, Eti-Osa Way, Dolphin Estate, Ikoyi, Lagos
Tel: (01) 2693358, 4718295, 08023254002
Fax: (01) 2693590
E-mail: soltan@hyperia.com
Website: www.soltan.asfa.net
* Shop A10, AEPB Concession Shops, Kwame Nkrumah Crescent, opp. Swiss Embassy, beh. ECOWAS Secretariat, Asokoro, Abuja
Tel: (09) 3142196
Contact: Mrs. Victori Soluade - MD/CEO.

SOLUS SCHALL NIGERIA LIMITED
Business: Oil Industry Engineering Services, Diving
Address: Plot 68, Trans-Amadi Ind. Layout, Port Harcourt
Tel: (084) 331983, 237911
* Edewor Shopping Centre, Warri-Sapele Road, Effurun, Warri.
Tel/Fax: (053) 252372

SOLUTION TECH LIMITED
Business: Information & Communication Technology
Address: 85, Simpson Street, Ebute-Metta, Lagos
Tel: (01) 7743401, 7750856 **Fax:** (01) 5550467
E-mail: info@solutiontechltd.com
Contact: Inibehe Otoho - MD/CEO.

SOMATRADE NIGERIA LIMITED
Business: Consultancy Services in Trade, Maritime, Finance and Management
Address: 1A, Oyekan Road, off Akerele Rd, Surulere, Lagos
Tel: (01) 831213, 849785, 5891345 **Fax:** (01) 849785
E-mail: somatrade@theobech.com.ng
* 135, Royce Road, Owerri
Contact: Hon. (Chief) Chris C. Asoluka - Chairman/CEO

SOMENI NIGERIA LIMITED
Business: Construction/Upgrading of Piplines & Flowstation, Oilfield Servics, Civil, Mechanical & Electrical Services, Manpower Supply
Address: Plot 1, Effurun/DSC Effurun G.R.A. Extention, Effurun, Delta State
Tel: (053) 254238, 257325, 257327
E-mail: contact@someni.com
Contact: Mr. Robinson Edevwie - GM

SOMOTEX (NIGERIA) LIMITED
Business: Distribution and Sales of LG, WHIRLPOOL and PHILIPS Electronic Products & Home Appliances
Address: Km 16, Ikorodu Road, behind Philips, Ojota, Lagos
Tel: (01) 4971548-9 (2L), 7760691, 7761263, 7731936
Fax: (01) 4971550, 4971555
Website: www.lgeafrica.com
Contact: Mr. Anil Moninani - MD/CEO

SON INTERNATIONAL AGENCIES (NIGERIA) LIMITED
Business: Shipping and Airfreighting, Clearing & Forwarding, Warehousing, Transport
Address: Nasco House, 29, Burma Road, Apapa, Lagos
Tel: (01) 5872743, 08033322816
E-mail: son@cyberspace.net.ng
* 8, Elelenwo Road, off Aba Road, Port Harcourt
Contact: Elder S. O. Saseyi - Chairman/CEO.

SONA BREWERIES PLC
Business: Brewing of Alcoholic and Non-Alcoholic Drinks
Address: N.C.W.S. House, Plot PC 14, Ahmed Onibudo Street, Victoria Island, Lagos
* Km 40, Lagos-Abeokuta Road, Sango-Ota
Tel: (039) 720324, 720436, 720541, 722195, 721313-4(2L)
Fax: (039) 721313
E-mail: sona@beta.linkserve.com
* Km. 40, Lagos-Abeokuta Road, Sango-Otta
Tel: (039) 722195
Contact: Mr A. K. Mirchandani - MD/CEO

SONJET INTERNATIONAL LIMITED
Business: Import of Electronics, Curtain Materials & Rails
Address: A54, & A63, Alaba Int'l Market, Ojo-Alaba, Lagos
Tel: (01) 7731215
Contact: Bro. S. E. Eze - Chairman/CEO

SONY MUSIC ENTERAINMENT (NIGERIA) LIMITED
Business: Manufacture and Distribution of Pre-Recorded Music and Video Cassettes, Cassette Custom Pressing, Sales of Compact Discs, Musical Equipment Rental and Hire
Address: 107A, Adeniyi Jones Avenue, Ikeja, Lagos
Tel: (01) 4975925, 4975926, 963514, 997567
Contact: Chief (Mrs.) Keji Okunowo - MD/CEO

SONGHAI ENRGY SERVICES LIMITED
Business: Hiring of Tug Boats and Barges
Address: 28, Warri/Sapele Road, Warri
Tel: (053) 256644
E-mail: seswarri@onebox.com
* Plot 144, Trans-Amadi Ind. Layout, Port Harcourt
Tel: (084) 239661
Contact: Capt. F. Oyewo - GM

SONNEX PACKAGING LIMITED
Business: Prodction of PET Preforms & Bottles, Coextruded Films, BOPP Films/Laminates
Address: Km. 16, Ikorodu Road, beh. Philips Factory, Ojota, Lagos
Tel: (01) 4971457, 4975584, 7740528, 7765133
Fax: (01) 4971550, 4971555
E-mail: rohit@somotexnig.com
Contact: Mr. Anil Mohinani - MD/CEO

SO-SAFE WATER TECHNOLOGIES LIMITED
Business: Sales of Water Packaging Machineries, Treatment Plants, Borehole Drilling Equipment, UV-Sterilizers, Water Filtration & Purification Systems and Water Bottling Plants
Address: 28, Ysufu Sanusi Street, off Adeniran Ogunsanya Street, Surulere, Lagos
Tel: (01) 4750049, 4807220, 7920411, 8169730, 08033020158, 08033085989
Fax: (01) 5874865, 5878268
E-mail: kingsmat@yahoo.co.uk
service@kingsmat.com
Contact: Chief M. C. I nyama - MD/CEO

SOSAPLAST (NIGERIA) LIMITED
Business: Manufacture of PVC Shoes and Slippers
Address: Plot 1, Block C, Fatai Atere Way, Matori Industrial Estate, Mushin, Lagos
Tel: (01) 4524913, 4524595, 4529003, 526216
Fax: (01) 4529003
Contact: Mr. Tarik El-Abdallah - MD/CEO

SOSOLISO AIRLINES LIMITED
Business: Aviation Business, General Passenger, Cargo and Charter Services
Address: Valley View Plaza (4th Floor), 99, Opebi Road, Ikeja, Lagos
Tel: (01) 4971491-2 (2 L), 4704386 **Fax:** (01) 4971491
E-mail: fly@sosolisoairline.com
* Murtala Muh'd Airport (Terminal II), Ikeja, Lagos.
Tel: (01) 4704386
* Nnamdi Azikiwe International Airport, Abuja
Tel: (09) 8100122
* Port Harcourt International Airport, Prt Harcourt.
Tel: (084) 571946 08023127433
* Dial Travels Bureau Limited, 15, Azikiwe Road, (UTC Bus-Stop), Port Harcourt.
Tel: (084) 234529
Contact: Mr. Oscar Ikwuemesi - MD/CEO.

SOTAEN NIGERIA LIMITED
Business: Importation and Sales of Cars, Trucks and Heavy-Construction Equipment, Clearing and Forwarding, Warehousing and Transportation, Farming

Address: 10, Aerodrome Road, Apapa, Lagos
Tel: (01) 5455471, 5457068-9 (2L) **Fax:** (01) 5455471
E-mail: soatan.ap@rcl.nig.com
Contact: Chief Solomon Osayande Agbontaen - Chairman

SOTONIA FISHERIES LIMITED
Business: Fish Merchants, Cold Storage Facilities, Trawling
Address: 60, Airport Road, Warri
Tel: (053) 251858, 251489 **Fax:** (053) 254950

SOUCHE INSURANCE BROKERS LIMITED
Business: Insurance Broking & Risk Management Consultants
Address: 223, Ikorodu Road, Obanikoro, Lagos
Tel: (01) 4930589, 08023589064 **Fax:** (01) 4961618
E-mail: souinb@yahoo.net
Contact: Sim Ozo Okeke - Chairman/CEO

SOUL PUBLICATIONS LIMITED
Business: Publishing of Magazines
Address: 42, Olowu Street, Ikeja, Lagos
Tel: (01) 4972964, 4977164, 08033037011
Contact: Chief Godwin Anabor - President/Publisher

SOUND INSURANCE BROKERS LIMITED
Business: Insurance Broking
Address: 29B, James Watt Road, Benin City
Tel: (052) 251455, 254897 **Fax:** (052) 255274
Contact: Mr. J. I. Idehen - MD/CEO

SOUTH AFRICAN AIRWAYS (NIGERIA)
Business: International Airline Services
Address: 28, Adetokunbo Ademola St, Victoria Island, Lagos
Tel: (01) 7743197, 7743573, 2620609, 2625928, 2625783-4
Fax: (01) 2625929
* Murtala Mohammed Int'l Airport, Ikeja, Lagos
Tel: (01) 7746200
E-mail: saagsa@beta.linkserve.com

SOUTHERN AIRLINE
Business: Aircraft Services
Address: 18A, Oko-Awo Close, off Karimu Kotun Street, Victoria Island, Lagos
Tel: (01) 2619966
* General Aviation Terminal, Murtala Mohammed Airport, Ikeja, Lagos

SOUTHERN ALUMINIUM PRODUCTS LIMITED
Business: Fabrication of Alminim Building Materials
Address: 5, First Avenue, Independence Layout, Enugu
Tel: (042) 458272-4 (3L)
E-mail: southalu@infoweb,abs.net
Contact: Engr. Frank Anozie - Chairman/CEO

SOUTHERN ROSE HEALTHCARE SERVICES LIMITED
Business: Health Maintenance Organisation
Address: Plot 71B, Molade Okoya-Thomas Street, off Ajose Adeogun Street, Victoria Island, Lagos
Tel: (01) 2611012, 2614828, 3204066, 08023230550, 08033075733
Fax: (01) 3204066
Website: www.sothernrosehealth.com
Contact: Dr. Obi Anyanyo - Chairman
Mr. Preye B. Zuobai - MD/CEO

SOUTHERN STAR SHIPPING COMPANY (NIGERIA) LTD
Business: Shipping Services and Shipping Agent
Address: Flour Mills Building, 2, Old Dock Road, Apapa, Lagos
Tel: (01) 5450972, 5452667, 5803370-9 (10L) (Ext. 110)
Fax: (01) 5870395, 5871602, 5872749
Contact: Capt. D. M. Osah - MD/CEO

SOUTHGATE TECHNOLOGIES LIMITED
Business: Sales of Computers and Communication Equipment, Networking, Systems Integration, Structured Cabling and Software Development
Address: 92A, Younis Bashorun Street, off Ajose Adeogun Street, Victoria Island, Lagos
Tel: (01) 2626728-9 (2L), 4618544-5 (2L)
Fax: (01) 2626728
E-mail: southgate@beta.linkserve.com
enquiry@sothgtech.com
Website: www.southgtech.com
Contact: F. Folajomi Sarumi - Chairman/CEO

SOVERAN NIGERIA LIMITED
Business: Services to the Oil Industry, Industrial Procurement
Address: Foreshore Towers (Suites 7 & 8), Pees Galleria (2nd Floor), 2A, Osborne Road, Ikoyi, Lagos
Tel: (01) 2695520, 2670276, 2695709, 2671847
E-mail: soveran@hyperia.com

SOVEREIGN TRUST INSURANCE COMPANY LIMITED
Business: Insurance
Address: 35, Adetokunbo Ademola St,Victoria Island, Lagos
Tel: (01) 2623940, 2620594, 2623949, 2620716, 2612720
Fax: (01) 4617200
E-mail: sti@cyberspace.net.ng
Website: www.sovereigntrustinsurance.com
* Block B (Flat 3), Stallion Estate, Lobito Crescent, off Adetokunbo Ademola Cresc., Wuse II, Abuja
Tel/Fax: (09) 4135117
* 92, Aba Road, Port Harcourt
Tel/Fax: (084) 571315
* 2, Creek Road, Apapa, Lagos
Tel/Fax: (01) 5874895, 7748222
Contact: Chief Ephraim F. Faloughi - Chairman
Mr. Oluseun A. Ajayi - MD/CEO

SOWSCO WELL SERVICES NIGERIA LIMITED
Business: Oilfield Services (Pumping, Cementing, Stimulation, Sand Control, Well-Head Maintenance, Testing, Pipeline Pigging), Engineering Consultancy
Address: Plot 212, Trans-Amadi Ind. Layout, Port Harcourt
Tel: (084) 236774, 08034022380 **Fax:** (084) 238581
Contact: Mr. Samuel Adegboyega - MD/CEO

SPA WATERS LIMITED
Business: Production and Bottling of Table Water
Address: SPA Complex, Plot B, Olympic Street, off Alakoso Avenue, off Festac Access Road, Amuwo-Odofin Industrial Area, Lagos
Tel: (01) 2882196, 4802333, 5892123, 5890552-3 (2L)
Fax: (01) 2885885, 5882969
E-mail: spawaters@hotmail.com
Contact: Dr. Ausbet Nnamdi Ajagu - Exec. Chairman
Mr. J. Olorunda - Operation Manager

SPACE DYNAMICS LIMITED
Business: Procurement & Activation of ETACs/GSM Lines, Sales & Repairs of Mobile Phones & Accessories
Address: 2A, Raymond Njoku Street, S. W. Ikoyi, Lagos
Tel: (01) 2694935. 2671789 **Fax:** (01) 2694935
E-mail: spacedy@cyberspace.net.ng
Contact: C. J. Okekearu - MD/CEO

SPACE WORLD AIRLINE
Business: Domestic & International Airline Services
Address: 634, Olu Obasanjo Road, Port Harcourt
Tel: (084) 239781, 08023575022, 08023334193, 08033008017, 08033044379,
E-mail: spaceworldinternational@yahoo.com
* Port Harcourt International Airport
Tel: 08033404538, 08033414880, 08036695766, 08037027102
* 26, Obafemi Awolowo Way, Ikeja, Lagos
Tel: 08033007150

SPAR AEROSPACE (NIGERIA) LIMITED
Business: Sales of Satellite and Communication Equipment
Address: 46, Saka Tinubu Street, Victoria Island, Lagos
Tel: (01) 2624700 **Fax:** (01) 2622172
E-mail: info@gstelecom.com
* Plot 844E, Komoe Street, off Limpopo Street, Cadastral Zone A6, Maitama, Abuja
* Plot 213, Trans-Amadi Ind. Layout, Port Harcourt
Contact: Mr. John Neville - Chairman
Mr. Steve Chapman - MD/CEO

SPARK POWER GENERATORS LIMITED
Business: Sales, Installation and Service of Industrial and Domestic Power Generators, Sales of Spare Parts
Address: 107, Bode Thomas Street, Surulere, Lagos
Tel: (01) 5850245, 5850594, 5851026 **Fax:** (01) 5850244
Contact: Engr. Isaac O. Ayelabola - Chairman/CEO

SPARKLIGHT ENGINEERING COMPANY LIMITED
Business: Civil Engineering & Construction Works and Consultancy.
Address: Olatunji House (1st Floor), 299, Ikorodu Road, Idiroko Bus-Stop, Maryland, Lagos
Tel: (01) 4930036, 4972251 **Fax:** (01) 4972251
E-mail: sparklight@hyperia.com
Contact: Engr. Toyin Adeyinka - Group Chairman/CEO

SPARNOON NIGERIA LIMITED
Business: Distribution and Marketing of Structured Cabling Systems, Server Racks and Printers
Address: First Bank Building, 2B, Adewunmi Industrial Estate, Oregun Road, Ikeja, Lagos
Tel: (01) 4938098, 4938099, 4937340 **Fax:** (01) 4937340
E-mail: sparnoon@cscng.com
Website: www.sparnoon.co.uk
Contact: Chief Rasheed A. Gbadamosi - Chairman
Mr. Lucky P. C. Ajieh - CEO

SPEAKEEZEE LTD (Cellular & Paging Systems)
Business: Sales and Installation of Cellular Phones & Paging Systems, Airtime Retailing and Customer Care
Address: 92, Awolowo Road, S. W. Ikoyi, Lagos
Tel: (01) 2693925, 2695857, 3204142-3 (2L)
08034007562, 08033078211-3 (3L)
Fax: (01) 2692700
E-mail: speak@rcl.nig.com
* Millenium Verdict Plaza, Adetokunbo Ademola Crescent, Wuse II, Abuja. **Tel:** 08033078214
* NMA Shopping Hall, 8, Old Aba Road, Rumuogba, Port Harcourt. **Tel:** 08033078216
Website: www.speakeezee.com
Contact: Otunba Dotun Olakunri - MD/CEO

SPECIALITY DRILLING FLUIDS LIMITED
Business: Oilfield Tools and Equipment Rentals, Drilling Services and Products Supply, Environmental Pollution Control
Address: Plot 184C, Trans-Amadi Ind. Layout, Port Harcourt
Tel: (084) 231322 **Fax:** (084) 235915
Contact: Mr. Tony Eze - MD/CEO

SPECOMIL TEXTILES LIMITED
Business: Production of Textile Piece Goods (Wax Print and African Print)
Address: Awosika Avenue, Ikeja Industrial Estate, Ikeja, Lagos
Tel: (01) 4979170-3 (4L), 4963135 **Fax:** (01) 4964631
E-mail: specong@linkserve.com.ng
Contact: Mr. Johnson W. H. Chiang - MD/CEO

SPECTRA NIGERIA LIMITED
Business: Processing & Production of Vegetable Oil and Food Beverages
Address: Plot 1, Abisola Alimi Crescent, beside New Abbatoir, Oko-Oba, Agege, Lagos
Tel: (01) 4921035, 4924930, 4701592, 4924890, 4741767
Fax: (01) 4924288
E-mail: spectra@alpha.linkserve.com
Website: www.spectra-ng.com

SPECTRUM BOOKS LIMITED
Business: Publishing of Books
Address: Spectrum House, Oluyole Industrial Estate, Ring Road, Ibadan
Tel: (02) 2310145, 2311215, 2310058
Fax: (02) 2318502, 2312705
E-mail: joopberkhout@spectrumsafari.com.ng
publishing@spectrumbooksonline.com
admin 1@spectrumbooksonline.com
Website: www.spectrumsafari.com
Contact: Chief Joop Berkhot - MD/CEO
Mr. Edeman Igbinosun - Marketing Director

SPECTRUM COMMUNICATIONS SERVICES LIMITED
Business: Planning, Supply and Installation of Telecommunication Equipment
Address: 9, Bombay Crescent, Apapa, Lagos
Tel: (01) 5453275, 5452734 **Fax:** (01) 5453275
E-mail: spectrum@hyperia.com
Contact: Wenike Oruwariye - Operations Director

SPEEDY WORLD LIMITED
Business: Clearing Agency, Importation of General Goods
Address: 12B, Obanta Avenue, Wemabod Estate, off Ajao Road, off Adeniyi Jones Avenue, Ikeja, Lagos
Tel/Fax: (01) 4937991
Contact: Travis Ojo - MD/CEO

SPEEDMARK SERVICES LIMITED
Business: Express Courier & Cargo Services
Address: 1 & 2, Jibowu Street, off Ikorodu Road, Jibowu-Yaba, Lagos
Tel: (01) 862648, 08033320114 **Fax:** (01) 5878867
Contact: Mr. S. O. Ilodibe - MD/CEO

SPEEDY PRINTS LIMITED
Business: Comemercial & Security Printing Services, Print-Production & Delivery of Itemized Bills for Telecommunication Service Providers
Address: 5A, Oko Awo Close, off Adetokunbo Ademola Street, Victoria Island, Lagos
Tel: (01) 3200414-5 (2L), 2705304-5 (2L), 2705153, 0802315153 **Fax:** (01) 2705153
E-mail: sales@speedyprints-ng.com
Website: www.speedyprints-ng.com
Contact: Tokunbo Talabi - Chairman/CEO

SPIDER INTERNATIONAL LIMITED
Business: Assembling and Marketing of Water Pumps, Transportation Services
Address: 34A, Boundary Road, G.R.A., Benin City
Tel: (052) 256753 **Fax:** (052) 250739
* 1A, Babatunde Oki Street, off Town Planning Way, Ilupeju, Lagos.
Tel: (01) 7747501, 2692164

SPIE BATIGNOLLES NIGERIA LIMITED (SPIBAT)
Business: Civil and Industrial Engineering Contractors
Address: Port Harcourt Bonny Island, Abuja
E-mail: spibatho@infoweb.abs.net
Contact: Mr. Jean Francois Picard - MD/CEO

SPINET FURNISHING LIMITED
Business: Manufacture and Sales of Home and Office Furniture, Wrought Iron; Interior Decoration
Address: 26, Adeniran Ogunsanya Street, Surulere, Lagos
Tel: (01) 5845650, 836522
E-mail: spinetinternational@hyperia.com
Contact: Hon. Gbolahan Funsho - MD/CEO

SPINTEX MILLS NIGERIA LIMITED
Business: Manufacture of Yarn and Synthetic Fibres
Address: Plot 37/39, Iganmu Ind. Estate, Iganmu, S/L, Lagos
Tel: (01) 5850303, 5850294, 7740943, 7747064
Fax: (01) 5834549, 5850303, 7781164
E-mail: spintex@infoweb.abs.net
* Plot 333, LSDPC Ind Estate, Odogunyan, Ikorodu
Tel: (01) 7740943 **Fax:** (01) 7781164
Contact: Mr. M. G. Menon - MD/CEO

SPIROPOULOS, ADIELE, OKPARA & COMPANY
Business: Chartered Accountants
Address: 127, Douglas Road (2nd Floor), Owerri
Tel: (083) 230759, 230754

SPRADIT COMPUTERS LIMITED
Business: Sales and Service of Computers, Printers and Consumables, Networking and Consultancy
Address: 124, Bode Thomas Street, Surulere, Lagos
Tel: (01) 4705288, 5850039, 5850878 **Fax:** (01) 5850039
* Garki II Corner-Shops (Suite 30A), Ladoke Akintola Boulevard, Garki II, Abuja
Tel: 08033232624
E-mail: spardit@micro.com.ng
Contact: Barr. Omolola Adekunle - MD/CEO

SPRING WATERS (NIGERIA) LIMITED
Business: Bottlers of SWAN Natural Spring Water
Address: 4/6, Beach Road, Jos
Tel: (073) 458583-5 (3L) **Fax:** (073) 458589
* UAC Building, 6, Akinyemi Crescent, Matori Industrial Estate, Mushin, Lagos
Tel: (01) 5451276, 5451278, 7736312
* Kerang Village, Mangu LGA Plateau State
Contact: Engr. J. B. Effiong - MD/CEO

SPRINGBOARD TRUST & INVESTMENT LIMITED
Business: Capital Market Operations
Address: NIJ House (1st Floor), 20, Adeyemo Alakija Street, Victoria Island, Lagos
Tel: (01) 26622799, 2627783, 2629617-8 (2L), 4616761-2, 4712058 **Fax:** (01) 2627953
E-mail: springboard@infoweb.abs.net
Contact: Engr. S. O. Oke - Chairman
Mr. Shehu Yakubu-Concern - MD/CEO

SPRINGFOUNTAIN LIMITED
Business: Management Consultants, Financial Advisors, Chartered Accountants, Issuing House, Information Technology
Address: 2A, Idowu Olaitan Street,Gbagada Estate Phase II, Gbagada, Lagos
Tel: (01) 4702062, 4702263, 5552888 **Fax:** (01) 5552888
Contact: Mr. B. A. Fagbemi - MD/CEO

SPROKETS NIGERIA LIMITED
Business: Sales and Installation ACE Security & Safety Glass Laminates
Address: Unity House (6th Floor), 37, Marina, Lagos
Tel: (01) 2667307, 08033082531, 08023070330
E-mail: sprokets@beta.linkserve.com
Contact: Mr. Daniel Usiade - MD/CEO.

ST. MARY'S INDUSTRIAL COMPLEX LIMITED
Business: Manufacturing of Poly Bags and Rolls, and Plastic Packaging Products
Address: 57, Nnobi Road, Nwewi, Anambra State
Tel: (046) 460018, 463959, 463971 **Fax:** (046) 463959
E-mail: stmarys@infoweb.abs.net
Contact: Mr. C. A. Nwafor - Chairman/CEO

ST. MICHAEL'S PHARMACEUTICALS LIMITED
Business: Importation and Marketing of Pharmaceuticals, Medical Equipment and Consumables
Address: 17A, Adeola Hopewell Street, Victoria Island, Lagos
Tel: (01) 2882858, 4737017, 5558499 **Fax:** (01) 2643326
* 39, Iduganran Street, Idumota, Lagos

ST. MIRA NIGERIA LIMITED
Business: Manufacture and Sales of Pharmaceuticals
Address: 9, Alh. Bashorun Street, S. W. Ikoyi, Lagos
Tel: (01) 2694358, 2693894 **Fax:** (01) 2694149
* 111, Herbert Macaulay Str, Ebute-Metta, Lagos
Contact: Mr. Raj Bhojwani - Chairman/CEO

STABILINI VISINONI LIMITED
Business: Building and Civil Engineering Construction
Address: Plot 8, Adeyanju-Daniel Street, off Km. 5, Oshodi-Apapa Expresway, Awodi-Ora, Kirikiri, Lagos
Tel: (01) 2645219, 2645220, 4817861, 5875502
Fax: (01) 2645219, 2645220
E-mail: svl@infoweb.abs.net
* 4, Gana Street, Maitama District, Abuja
Tel: (09) 4138797, 4133635 **Fax:** (09) 4133634
Contact: Dr. B. O. Babalakin - Chairman
Mr. Mariano Visinoni - Director/Contract Manager

STAFFORD CHEMICALS & INDUSTRIES LIMITED
Business: Manufacture of Marketing of Industrial Chemicals
Address: 4, Commercial Road, Apapa, Lagos
Tel: (01) 5452050-2 (3 L), 5452058-9 (2 L), 5451719, 5451717 **Fax:** (01) 5452054, 2664781
E-mail: info@doyin.net
doyin@hyperia.com
Website: www.doyin.net
Contact: Prince (Dr.) Samuel Adedoyin - Chairman/CEO

STAG ENGINEERING (NIGERIA) LIMITED
Business: Electrical and Mechanical Engineering Services; Sales and Service of Industrial Machinery and Precision Optical , Geophysical and Electro-Medical Hospital Equipment; Industrial Diesel Generating Plants and Machinery Spare Parts; Water and Sewage Treatment Plants
Address: Plot 5, Benson Anorue Street, Ajao Estate off International Airport Road, Apakun-Oshodi, Lagos
Tel: (01) 4522917, 4521720, 4522807, 77442300
Fax: (01) 4521598, 4523391
Contact: Engr. A. A. Jagun - MD/CEO

STALLION ASSURANCE LIMITED
Business: Non-Life Assurance
Address: 334, Herbert Macaulay Street, Yaba, Lagos
Tel: (01) 7730524, 4822406 **Fax:** (01) 81298433
Contact: Major Gen. A. B. Mamman (rtd) - Chairman
Dr. A. U. Okafor - Vice Chairman/CEO

STALLION HOME SAVINGS & LOAN LIMITED
Business: Mortage Finance Services
Address: 2A, Akerele Street (Boskono Bus - Stop), by Ogunala Drive, Surulere, Lagos
Tel:: (010 7740551, 08023036800-1 (2L)
* Abuja Shopping Mall, Zone 3, Wuse, Abuja
Tel: (09) 5237993

STALLION MOTORS LIMITED
Business: Sales and Service of Motor Vehicles, Sales of Auto Spare Parts
Address: Block A, Gbagada Industrial Estate, Oworonsoki - Oshodi Expressway, Gbagada, Lagos
Tel: (01) 4960586, 7742040
E-mail: contact@stallion.com.ng
Akin Adesola/179A-D, Kofo Abayomi Street, Victoria Island, Lagos.
Tel: (01) 2612539, 4700099, 7751774

STALLION PLASTICS LIMITED
Business: Manufacturing of Plastic Products - HDPP-CP Moulded Household Furniture & Containers
Address: Plot 439/445, Apapa-Oshodi Expressway (Cele Bus-Stop), Odo-Eran, Itire, Lagos.
Tel: (01) 7732636, 7732646, 7760587

STALLION PROPERTY & DEVELOPMENT COMPANY LTD
Business: Property Development, Acquisition and Facility Management
Address: Stallion House, 2, Ajose Adeogun Street, Victoria Island, Lagos
Tel: (01) 2621908, 2613388, 2621909 **Fax:** (01) 2616508
E-mail: info@stallionproperty.com
Website: www.stallionproperty.com
Contact: Chief O. C. Harry - Chairman
Mr. Nasir Usman - Ag. MD/CEO

STALLION SEAFOODS LIMITED
Business: Importation and Sales of Frozen Seafoods, Fishing and Trawling
Address: 419/425, Apapa-Oshodi Expressway (Berliet Bus-Stop), Ilasamaja, Lagos

STANBIC BANK NIGERIA LIMITED
Business: Universal Banking
Address: Plot 688, Amodu Tijani Close, off Sanusi Fafunwa Streeet, Victoria Island, Lagos
Tel: (01) 2709660-9 (10 L) (Ext. 180 & 182)
Fax: (01) 2692469
E-mail: nigeriainfo@stanbic.cocm
Website: www.stanbic.com.ng
Contact: Mr Milton A. Weeks - MD/CEO

STANBIC EQUITIES LIMITED
Business: Stockbroking, Issuing House
Address: Plot 688, Amodu Tijani Close, off Sanusi Fafunwa Streeet, Victoria Island, Lagos
Tel: (01) 2709660-9 (10 L) (Ext. 180 & 182)
Fax: (01) 2692469
E-mail: kutif@stanbic.cocm
Contact: Mr. Folajimi Kuti - Chief Operating Officer

STANDARD ADJUSTERS & COMPANY LIMITED
Business: Insurance Loss Adjusting
Address: Unity House (10th Floor), 37, Marina, Lagos
Tel: (01) 8169025, 2666439
Contact: Mr. Babalola Ogunleye - MD/CEO

STANDARD ALLIANCE INSURANCE COMPANY LIMITED
Business: Insurance
Address: Plot 281, Ajose Adeogun St, Victoria Island, Lagos
Tel: (01) 2623927, 4616201-2 (2L), 7741644-5 (2L)
Fax: (01) 2623928, 4616203, 4619199
E-mail: standardallicance@standardalliancegrp.com
Website: www.standardalliancegrp.com
* Plot 1182, Olusegun Obasanjo Crescent, off Ibrahim Babangida Way, Wuse Zone 2, Abuja.
Tel: (09) 4130221-2 (2L), 5232140, 5232142
* 10, Woji Road, G.R.A. Phase II, Port Harcourt
Tel: (084) 483667, 331174, 232791
* 73. Ibrahim Taiwo Road, Kano.
Tel: (064) 316874, 642058
Contact: Mr. G. Oghenetega Emerhor - Vice Chairman
Mr Yinka Bolarinwa - MD/CEO

STANDARD ASSOCIATED EXAMINING BOARD
Business: Conduct of Educational Examinations
Address: 561, Agege Motor Road (Ladipo Bus-Stop), Lagos
Tel: (01) 4975738, 7754841
E-mail: info@saebusa.com
saebusa@hotmail.com
Website: www.saebusa.com
Contact: Dr. A. Adetunji - Registrar

STANDARD BISCUIT (NIGERIA) LIMITED
Business: Manufacturing and Marketing of Biscuits
Address: 37/43, Enu-Owa Street, Idumota, Lagos
Tel: (01) 2666070, 2666075, 7740137 **Fax:** (01) 2666075
E-mail: standbis@beta.linkserve.com
Contact: Chief H. B. Chanrai - Chairman
Mr. P. B. Rege - GM/CEO

STANDARD CHARTERED BANK NIGERIA LIMITED
Business: Commercial Banking
Address: 105B, Ajose Adeogun St, Victoria Island, Lagos
Tel: (01) 3202000-29 (30L), 3201631-35 (5L), 2626801-5 (5L), 2626815-20 (6L) **Fax:** (01) 2626814
* Ogun State House, 4th Avenue, Cadastral Zone AO, Central Business District, Abuja
Tel: (09) 2344534, 2343731-2(2L)
* Plot 7, Ttrans-Amadi Ind. Layout, Port Harcourt
Tel: (084) 483345
Contact: Mr. David D. Cutting - MD/CEO

STANDARD CONSOLIDATED DREDGING & CONSTRUCTION COMPANY LIMITED
Business: Building and Civil Engineering Works, Production and Supply of Concrete Blocks, Culvert/Drainage Rings and Electrical Poles, General Merchandising
Address: SCDC House, 2B, Adewunmi Industrial Estate, Oregun Road, Oregun, Lagos
Tel: (01) 4971189, 08033600816 **Fax:** (01) 4971189
E-mail: scdcltd@yahoo.com
Contact: Chief J. A. Awoyinka - Chairman/CEO
Mr. Ayodele James - GM

STANDARD CONSTRUCTION LIMITED
Business: Total Engineering Solutions, Consultancy Services
Address: Gidan Buhari, 12/13, Zoo Road, Kano
Tel: (064) 664068, 664539, 668160 **Fax:** (064) 666284
E-mail: standardconltd@yahoo.com
*Plot 766, Mabushi, beh VIO Office, Mabushi, Abuja
Tel: (09) 3144230, 5239533 **Fax:** (09) 3144231
* 19B, Olosa Street, Victoria Island, Lagos
Tel: (01) 3204550 **Fax:** (01) 3204264
Contact: Alh. Sani Buhari - Exec. Chairman
Alh. Aminu Buharii - MD/CEO

STANDARD FLOUR MILLS LIMITED
Business: Flour Milling
Address: 15, Creek Road, Apapa, Lagos
Tel: (01) 5877486, 5877487

STANDARD GROUP OF HOTELS
Business: Hospitality & Catering Services, Confrence & Banqueting Facilities
Address: 3/5, Ifelodun Street, off Sadiku Street, Ilasamaja, Mushin, Lagos
Tel: (01) 4521503, 4521649, 08034026708
E-mail: standardgroupofhotels@yahoo.co.uk
Contact: Mr. Olusegun Fatusi - Chairman
Mr. Patrick Adebayo Ayoola - MD/CEO

STANDARD INDUSTRIAL DEVELOPMENT COMPANY LTD
Business: Manufacturing of Galvanized Pipes, Z Purlins, Black Pipes and Hollow Sections
Address: Plot D17, Acme Road, Ogba Industrial Scheme, Ogba, Ikeja, Lagos
Tel: (01) 4920151, 4920152, 4921076
Contact: Mr. Mon. O Chinke - Manager (Gen. Affairs)

STANDARD INSURANCE CONSULTANTS LIMITED
Business: Insurance and Reinsurance Broking
Address: House 130A, Association Road, Dolphin Scheme, Ikoyi, Lagos
Tel: (01) 2693457, 2691703 **Fax:** (01) 2691703
* Plot 855, Tafawa Balewa Way (Exec. Suite 106), Area 11, Garki, Abuja.
Tel: (09) 2347717, 4135070
Contact: Alh. Ahmed Olaniyi Salawudeen - President/CEO

STANDARD LIFE ASSURANCE COMPANY LIMITED
Business: Life Assurance and Pension Fund Management
Address: Plot 285B, Ajose Adeogun St, Victoria Island, Lagos
Tel: (01) 7748195, 4617678-9 (2L), 3200254
Fax: (01) 3200253
E-mail: standardlife@standardalliancegrp.com
* Plot 1182, Olusegun Obasanjo Crescent, off IBB Way, Wuse II, Abuja.
Tel: (09) 4130221-2 (2L), 4132783
* 199, Evo Road, G.R.A Phase II, Port Harcourt
Tel: (084) 484159
Contact: Mr. Austin Enajemo-Isire - MD/CEO

STANDARD PACKAGING NIGERIA LIMITED
Business: Manufacturers of Plasticwares and Woven Sacks
Address: 15, Creek Road, Apapa, Lagos
Tel: (01) 5450810-1 (2L) **Fax:** (01) 5450789
* Old Lagos Road, Alomaja Village, Ibadan
Tel: (02) 3211812

STANDARD PETROCHEMICAL INDUSTRIES LIMITED
Business: Design and Construction of Integrated Methanol/ MTBE Plants, Petrochemical Engineering Consultancy Services
Address: 27/29, Adeyemo Alakija Street (2nd Floor), Victoria Island, Lagos.
Tel: (01) 2620037, 2620092 **Fax:** (01) 2620128
* Eteo/Ogu, Tai-Eleme L.G.A. Port Harcourt
Contact: Mr. Danjuma C. Nwachukwu - Chairman/CEO

STANDARD PLASTICS & FOOTWEAR LIMITED
Business: Manufacturing of Plastics.
Address: Plot 29, Dantata Road, Bompai Ind. Estate, Kano
Tel: (064) 631431, 646362, 645901 **Fax:** (064) 638185
Contact: Madam Bonnie Lau - Chairman/CEO

STANDARD SYSTEMS INTEGRATED ARCHITECTURAL PRODUCTS
Business: Architectural Products (Longspan Roofing Sheet, Curtain Wall, Windows & Doors Partitions and

Suspended Ceiling)
Address: PLot 4, Block A, Apapa-Oshodi Expressway, Amuwo-Odofin Ind. Estate, Amuwo-Odofin, Lagos
Tel: (01) 8044514
Contact: Mr. Femi Frank Afolabi - MD/CEO

STANDARD TRUST ASSURANCE PLC
Business: Insurance
Address: 209, Herbert Macaulay St, Ebute-Metta, Yaba, Lagos
Tel: (01) 7731880-1 (2L), 7740571, 7741181, 861384, 864703, 864971, 868995 **Fax:** (01) 867947
* 66, Ogbia (Mbonu) Street, D-Line, Port Harcourt
Tel: (084) 238637
E-mail: staco@nova.net.ng
Contact: Alh. M. A. Shittu - Chairman
Mr. S. O. Oyefeso - MD/CEO

STANDARD TRUST BANK PLC
Business: Commercial Banking
Address: Standard Place; PLot 1662, Oyin Jolayemi Street, Victoria Island, Lagos
Tel: (01) 2625080-9 (10L), 3201414-28 (15L), 4618900-9
Fax: (01) 2620371
Website: www.standardtrustbank.com
* Admiralty House, 202, Olu Obasanjo Way, Port Harcourt
* Plot 832, Adetokunbo Ademola Crescent, off Ahmadu Bello Way, North Wuse 11, Abuja
Contact: Mr. Tony O. Elumelu - CEO
Mr. Ikemefuna Mordi - Head (Corp. Affairs)

STANDARD UNION SECURITIES LIMITED
Business: Stockbroking, Portfolio Management, Financial Advisory Services
Address: African Alliance Building (1st Floor), F1, Sani Abacha Way, Kano
Tel: (064) 644592, 649184, 646423, 08033138447, 08033210027 **Fax:** (064) 648178
Contact: Ibrahim Ali Amin - Chairman
Rabiu Ibrahim - MD/CEO

STANLEY BRIDAL SHOP
Business: Sales of Wedding Rings, Wears and Accessories
Address: 101, Nnamdi Azikiwe Street, Lagos Island, Lagos
Tel: (01) 2667176
Contact: Mr. J. Nwosu - Chairman/CEO

STANLEY MORGAN INSURANCE BROKERS LIMITED
Business: General Insurance & Special Risks Broking, Life & Pensions Consultancy
Address: 130, Broad Street (2nd Floor), Lagos
Tel: (01) 2643950, 4709066 **Fax:** (01) 2643950
E-mail: stanleymorgan@hotmail.com
Contact: Mr. Ademola Denloye - Chairman

STANMARK COCOA PROCESSING COMPANY LIMITED
Business: Cocoa Processing and Exportation
Address: Km. 5, Ondo/Akure Road, Ile-Oluji, Ondo
Tel: (034) 610109, 610106, 610852, 610854, 243388
Fax: (034) 243424
E-mail: stanmark@cadburynig.com
Contact: Mr. Bunmi Oni - Chairman
Mr. M. Segun Oyewole - MD/CEO

STANN NIGERIA LIMITED
Business: Sales of Auto Spare Parts
Address: Isaacstann Close, off WEMPCO Road, Ogba Industrial Estate, Ogba, Ikeja, Lagos
Tel: (01) 4808056, 4971315, 5557557, 08023103781

STANQUEEN INVESTMENTS LIMITED
Business: Sales & Repairs of Mobile Phones & Accessories
Address: 1A, Mojidi Street, off Toyin Street, by Fumman Drinks, Ikeja, Lagos
Tel: (01) 4933446, 8119131, 08023120366, 08033158119
E-mail: stanqeenltd@onebox.com
* G17, Alaba International Market, Ojo, Lagos
Tel: 08022914122, 08033158119

STANWAL SECURITIES LIMITED
Business: Stockbroking
Address: Stock Exchange House (12th Floor), 2/4, Customs Street, off Tinubu Square, Lagos
Tel: (01) 2640906, 2664223 **Fax:** (01) 2664223
Contact: Chief (Dr.) Walter I. Ofonagoro - Chairman
Mr. Augustine O. Ofonagoro - MD/CEO

STAR INSURANCE BROKERS LIMITED
Business: Insurance Broking, Life & Pensions Consultancy
Address: Tom Jones Memorial Hall & Library (3rd Floor), 80, Nnamdi Azikiwe Street/Idumagbo Avenue, Idumota, Lagos
Tel: (01) 2662113, 08033046701
Contact: Chief J. E. Muoghalu - Chairman
Chief E. C. M. Akamobi - MD/CEO

STAR MAJESTY FURNITURE INDUSTRIES LIMITED
Business: Furniture
Address: Novena Majesty Plaza, (1st & 2nd Floor,) 141, Ahmadu Bello way, Victoria Island, Lagos
Tel: (01) 2611442, 4708046, 2617978, 2616101

STAR MODERN PAPER MILL LIMITED
Business: Manufacturing of Exercise Books and Envelopes, Colour Separation Services
Address: 50, Weatherhead Road, Sabon-Gari, Kano
Tel: (064) 634585, 644922, 645083, 08037016124, 08044115412 **Fax:** (064) 644922
Contact: Chief (Sir) Vincent Okena (KSM) - Chairman/CEO

STAR MOTELS (NIGERIA) LIMITED
Business: Catering Services, Restaurant Business
Address: 7C, Creek Road, Apapa, Lagos
Tel: (01) 5878413 **Fax:** (01) 5452802
E-mail: starmotels@yahoo.com
starmotels@nova.net.ng
Contact: Maen Mansour - MD/CEO

STAR-AP JOINT VENTURE
Business: Oilfield Engineering Services
Address: Plot 1438, Sanusi Fafunwa Street, Victoria Is, Lagos
Tel: (01) 2620958, 2623988 **Fax:** (01) 2615274
* Plot 27, Trans-Amadi Ind. Layout, Port Harcourt
Tel: (084) 571256, 231219, 231189
* 49, nerhen Road, Effurun, Warri
Tel: (053) 250368
Contact: Mr. Peter Okocha, OON - Chairman/CEO

STAR PAINTS INDUSTRIES LIMITED
Business: Manufacture of Paints and Coatings
Address: 8/10, Aerodrome Road, Apapa, Lagos
Tel/Fax: (01) 5451850, 5451860
E-mail: info@starpaints.com
Website: www.starpaints.com
Contact: Mr. Jean Claude Hakim - Chairman
Mr. Ghassan A. Cheaib - MD/CEO

STAR PAPER MILL LIMITED
Business: Paper Recycling and Conversion
Address: 114/116, Aba-Owerri Road, Umungasi, Aba
Tel: (082) 225658, 225208, 225421 **Fax:** (082) 221472
E-mail: star@alpha.linkserve.com
Website: www.starpaperml.com
Contact: Chief Echeme Nnana Kalu - Chairman

STAR POWER NIGERIA LIMITED
Business: Sales and Service of Generations
Address: Okoi Arikpo House (2nd Floor), 5, Idowu Taylor Street, Victoria Island, Lagos
Tel: (01) 2623307, 4701073 **Fax:** (01) 2623308
E-mail: remota@hyperia.com

STARCOM MEDIA LIMITED
Business: Integrated Markting Communications
Address: 57, Adeknle Fajuyi Way, G.R.A, Ikeja, Lagos
Tel: (01) 4977553-4 (2L)

STARCOMMS LIMITED
Business: Wireless Telephone Service Provider
Address: Starcomms House, Plot 1261C, Bishop Kale Close, off Saka Tinubu Street, Victoria Island, Lagos
Tel: (01) 8041028-9 (2 L), 8041080, 8041234
Fax: (01) 8041235
* AIB Plaza, AIB Terrace, Akin Adesola Street, Victoria Island, Lagos
* Buffalo House, 2, Allen Avenue, Ikeja, Lagos

STARGATE TELECOMMUNICATIONS LIMITED
Business: Sales, Installation and Repairs of Cellular (GSM) Phones and Accessories
Address: Princes Plaza, 2, Araromi Street, off Moloney Street, Onikan, Lagos
Tel: (01) 2613953, 08033062255, 08039802255
E-mail: stargetelecoms@yahoo.co.uk
Contact: Mr. Ademola Oyenuga - Chairman

STARLINE NIGERIA LIMITED
Business: Conglomerate (Manufacturing, Trading, Real Estate, Finance Investments)
Address: 152, Azikiwe Road, Aba
Tel: (082) 221686, 230488, 230645, 220214
Fax: (082) 221686
E-mail: starlineo@yahoo.com
* 8, Forcados Road, Apapa G.R.A, Lagos
Tel: (01) 5870662, 5870705, 2880833 **Fax:** (01) 5870705
Contact: Mazi Clement Ikechukwu Ownna - Chairman/CEO
Chief Damian Nwosu - GM (Admin./Personnel)

STARLING NIGERIA LIMITED
Business: Supply of Pharmaceutical and Health Products, and Medicinal Herbs (Swedish Bitters)
Address: 17, Alh. Tokan Street, Alaka Estate, off Western Avenue, Surulere, Lagos
Tel: (01) 7743976, 833794 **Fax:** (01) 5833675
Contact: Mrs. V. I. Cole - Chairman
Mr. Louis Oputa-Otutu - MD/CEO

STARPOINT COMMODITIES LIMITED
Business: Importation of Printing Papers and Boards
Address: 25, Fatai Atere Way, Matori Industrial Estate, Mshin, Lagos
Tel: (01) 4527146, 521965, 7914645 **Fax:** (01) 4527146
* Bookshop House (12th Floor), 50/52, Broad St, Lagos
Tel: (01) 2633268, 2636097 **Fax:** (01) 2633268
Contact: Olugbenga Obisesan - Chairman/CEO

STARTECH CONNECTIONS LIMITED
Business: Private Telecom Operator, Broadband Fixed Wireless Access Provider, VSAT Supplier and Internet Service Provider
Address: Plot 83, Ralph Shodeinde Street, opp. Fed Min. of Finance, off Ahmadu Bello Way, Central Business District, Abuja
Tel: (09) 2221083 **Fax:** (09) 2221099
E-mail: info@startechconnections.com
Website: www.startechcconnections.com
Contact: Ms. Anne J. Bresnahan - MD/CEO

STATOIL NIGERIA LIMITED
Business: Exploration & Production of Petroleum & Gas
Address: 1A, Bourdillion Road, Ikoyi, Lagos
Tel: (01) 2690491-8 (8L) **Fax:** (01) 2691245

STATUS FURNITURE COMPANY LIMITED
Business: Sales of Furniture for Homes and Offices
Address: 387, Badagry Expressway (Oluti B/Stop), Ojo, Lagos
Tel: (01) 7755927
* 23, Olojo Drive, by Volkswagen, Ojo-Alaba, Lagos
Tel: (01) 7766205
E-mail: statusnigeria@yahoo.co.uk
statusnigeria@cyberspace.net.ng

STB CAPITAL MARKETS LIMITED
Business: Financial Advisory Services, Capital Market Operations, Stockbrokage
Address: Standard Place; PLot 1662, Oyin Jolayemi Street, Victoria Island, Lagos
Tel: (01) 2625080-9 (10L), 3201414-28 (15L), 4618900-9
Fax: (01) 2620371
E-mail: enquiries@standardtrust.com
Website: www.standardtrustbank.com

STB-McCANN LAGOS
Business: Advertising, Marketing and Communications
Address: STB House, 356, Murtala Mohammed Way, Yaba, Lagos
Tel: (01) 5834103, 4703376, 3425025, 2901537, 7742363, 7744311 **Fax:** (01) 5830009, 3425049
E-mail: stb-mccann@cyberspac.net.ng
Website: www.stbmccan.com
Contact: Mr. Steve E. Omojafor - MD/CEO

STEAM BROADCASTING & COMMUNICATIONS LIMITED
Business: Radio Broadcasting Services (COOL FM)

Address: AIM Plaza, Plot 267B, Etim Inyang Crescent, off Muri Okunola Road, Victoria Island, Lagos
Tel: (01) 26223051-4 (4L) **Fax:** (01) 2610393, 2614779
E-mail: coollagos@coolfm.us
* Plot 592, Independence Ave, Central Area, Abuja
Tel: (09) 2340073-4 (2L) **Fax:** (09) 2340067
E-mail: coolabuja@coolfm.us

STEBU LIMITED
Business: Sales & Service of Computers and Accessories, IT Consultancy, Networking, Internet Service
Address: 14, Ositelu Street (2nd Floor), off Simbiat Abiola Road, Ikeja, Lagos
Tel: (01) 4971184, 4810372
E-mail: mailinto@stebu.com
* 7, Otigba Street, Ikeja, Lagos
Tel: (01) 4971184, 4810372
Contact: Mr. Gift Omamuli - Gen. Manager

STEEL & ENGINEERING SERVICES (WEST AFRICA) LTD
Business: Steel Processing, Fabrication and Distribution
Address: SESWA House, Limca Way, Plot 2, Block J, Isolo Industrial Estate, Isolo, Lagos
Tel: (01) 4522868, 4526320, 4522881, 4709081, 4709118
Fax: (01) 4522881
E-mail: seswa@beta.linkserve.com

STEEL & WIRE MANUFACTURING COMPANY LIMITED
Business: Sales and Service of Workshop Machine Tools and Technical Products
Address: 380, Ikorodu Road, Maryland, Lagos
Tel: (01) 4971907, 4962172, 4716355 **Fax:** (01) 2617663
E-mail: sales@psltd.com

STEEL CITY ESTATE LIMITED
Business: Real Estate Development & Management
Address: Plot 11, Block R, Oladimeji Adeyemo St, Oroki Housing Estate, off Osogbo-Iwo Exp/way, Osogbo
Tel: (035) 240150, 243697, 08023281988, 08033329030

STEEL WORKS LIMITED
Business: Fabrication, Distribution and Sales of Roller Shutters, Steel Products and Portakabins
Address: Oluyole Industrial Estate, Ibadan
Tel: (02) 2315083-93 (11L), 2315073 **Fax:** (02) 2317269
E-mail: zardgroup@hyperia.com
* 4, Adetokunbo Ademola Cr, Wuse II, Abuja.
Tel: (09) 5235196
* 1, Old Aba Road, Port Harcourt.
Tel: (084) 234582

STEELWAYS NIGERIA LIMITED
Business: Manufacture & Fabrication of House-Boats, Ferries, Tug Boats, Fuel & Water Tanks, Caravans, Fences, Gates & Steel Doors, Oilfield Services
Address: Plot E, Ikosi Road, Oregun Industrial Estate, Oregun, Ikeja, Lagos
Tel: (01) 4960127, 4967637, 4821512, 7755065, 08033051797, 08033089203 **Fax:** (01) 4961590
E-mail: steelways@nova.net.ng
* Merogun Waterside, Warri
Tel: (053) 255404, 08023018574, 080332443217
Contact: Mr. Wesam Jarmakani - GM/CEO

STEPHENSON BROTHERS LIMITED
Business: Sales of Measuring Equipment, Petroleum Vending Machines, Watches, Calculators, Digital Diaries and Cameras
Address: 8, Sumbo Jibowu Street, off Ribadu Road, S.W. Ikoyi, Lagos
Tel: (01) 267348-9 (2L) **Fax:** (01) 2673097
* Office 60, Federal Palace Hotel, Ahmadu Bello Way, Victoria Island, Lagos
Tel: (01)2611048 **Fax:** (01) 2619080
E-mail: sbl@beta.linkserve.com
Contact: Prince Ademola Dada - Chairman/CEO

STERLING ASSURANCE NIGERIA LIMITED
Business: Insurance (General Business)
Address: Capital Building, 332, Ikorodu Road , (Idiroko Bus-Stop), Maryland, Lagos
Tel: (01) 4930227, 4976544, 7730406, 8045079
Fax: (01) 4933656
E-mail: sterling@intracom.net.ng
* 2, Ikwerre Road, Port Harcourt.
Tel: (084) 235929
* Wuraola Building, New State Hospital Roundabout, Ring Road, Ibadan.
Tel: (02) 2315434, 2311373
Contact: Mr. M. O. A. Dada - Chairman
Mr. M. O. Bammeke - MD/CEO

STERLING COMMUNICATIONS LIMITED
Business: Telecommunications; Internet Service Provider
Address: 18, Sunday Adigun Street, Central Business District, Alausa, Ikeja, Lagos.
Tel: (01) 4939612
E-mail: info@stercom.com
Contact: Marc Adebesin - System Engineer.

STEYR NIGERIA LIMITED
Business: Assembly & Manufacture of Motor Vehicles, Tractors, Trucks, Buses &Motorcycles
Address: Fritz Felsinger Road, Industrial Estate, Bauchi
Tel: (077) 542204, 542491, 542524, 542639
Fax: (077) 543048
* Plot 5, Akinyemi Crescent, off Fatai Atere Way, Matori Industrial Estate, Oshodi, Lagos
Tel: (01) 4528644-5 (2L), 2885867 **Fax:** (01) 45288643
Contact: Mr. T. A. Ojeleye - Ag. MD

STI STEPHENSON LIMITED
Business: Sales of colour Photo Laboratory Machines and Spare Parts . Fabrication of Machine Parts
Address: 10, New Market Road, Onitsha.
Tel: (046) 412552, 481018, 08033279438
E-mail: sti.abakwamsteve@yahoo.com
* 3, Offorjindu St, Odume Layout, Obosi, Anambra

STILLWATER GROUP OF COMPANIES
Business: Conglomerate
Address: 40, Isaac John Street, Ikeja G.R.A., Lagos.
Tel: (01) 4977094, 4826554, 08033087337
Fax: (01) 4977094
E-mail: stillwater@beta.linkserve.com
stillwaterb@yahoo.com
Contact: Dr. Femi Bamigboye - Chairman/CEO

STIRLING BEVERAGES LIMITED
Business: Distilling of Alcholoci Spirits and Wines
Address: Km. 14, Idiroko Road, Iju-Ota, Ogun State
Tel: (01) 7944428, 7922367, 08033166542
Contact: Chief A. O. Abudu - Chairman

STIRLING CIVIL ENGINEERING (NIGERIA) LIMITED
Business: Building and civil Engineering Contractors
Address: Km. 6, Mando Road, Kaduna
Tel: (062) 318370, 318059, 318374, 318497
Fax: (062) 318370
* Plot 214, off Parakou Crescent, Wuse II, Abuja
Tel: (09) 5230650, 5234053 **Fax:** (09) 5234958
Contact: Alh. Muhammad Gambo Jimeta (IGP rtd.)-Chairman
Mr. O. Coss - MD/CEO

STIRLING TRUST COMPANY LIMITED
Business: Import & Export Trade Financing, Funds & Portfolio Management, Trade & LPO Financing, Contracting, Joint Venture Projects, Equipments & Vehicle Leasing, General Services
Address: NITP Franklin Akinyemi House, Plot PC. 10, Engineering Close, off Idowu Taylor Street, Victoria Island, Lagos
Tel: (01) 4617591, 2705446-7 (2L)
E-mail: stc@tbplc.org
Contact: Chief (Dr.) Senator Jacob Tilley-Gyado - Chairman
Mr. Patrick A. Iniovosa - GM

STOIRIN MARITIME SERVICES LIMITED
Business: Shipping Agents & Brokers; Cargo Handling and Freight Forwarding . Warehousing, Packaging & Removals. Transportation.
Address: 2/8, Calcutta Crescent (Maisonette 3), Apapa, Lagos
Tel: (01) 5454040, 7917274, 8044683 **Fax:** (01) 5454040
E-mail: stoirinmaritime@hyperia.com
Contact: Mr. Ademola Lawal Mumuney - MD/CEO.

STONEHILL NIGERIA LIMITED
Business: Importation and Assembly of Fire-Fighting & Safety Equipment; Contractual Procurement of Industrial SpareParts; Importation of Cement.
Address: 27, Deco Road, P.M.B. 1022, Warri
Tel: (053) 251608, 253368, 254233-5 **Fax:** (053) 251035
E-mail: stonehill@warri.rcl.nig.com
Contact: Mr. Gregory J. Akpeokhai - Chairman/CEO.

STOP CENTRE (A Div. of Eta Noel Ltd.)
Business: Retail Trading.Greeting Cards and Gift Items
Address: 1, Allen Avenue, Ikeja, Lagos.
Tel: (01) 4972757, 08033077302 **Fax:** (01)4967932
E-mail: stopcentre@micro.com.ng
* 5, Amodu Ojikutu Street, Victoria Island, Lagos
Tel: (01) 613591
Contact: Mrs. Simi Onabanjo - MD/CEO.

STOP OVER MOTELS LIMITED
Business: Hotel Services and Conference facilities
Address: Ajao Estate, Apakun-Oshodi, Lagos
Tel: (01) 4523839, 4523642, 4523563, 4707557-8(2L)
Fax: (01) 4523839
E-mail: stopovermote@micro.com.ng
Contact: Mrs K. O. Fischer - CEO.

STRABAG CONSTRUCTION (NIGERIA) LIMITED
Business: Building & Civil Engineering Contractors
Address: Off Kubwa Express Road, Abuja
Tel: (09) 5210746, 5211039, 5239593 **Fax:** (09) 5239489
* Oshodi - Apapa Expressway (Sunrise Bus-Stop), Olodi - Apapa, Lagos
Tel: (01) 4701545, 5876423-4(2L), 5876414
* 2B, Akorolo Close, opp Police Post, Elekahia Road, Port Harcourt.
Tel: (084) 237890
Contact: Mr. W. Schmaus - Exec. Director

STRETCH FIBRES LIMITED
Business: Manufacture of Fishing nets, Sports & Safety Nets
Address: Great Nigeria House (20th Floor), 47/57, Martins Street, Lagos
Tel: (01) 2661259, 2661269, 2665671, 2665668
Fax: (01) 2666380
* Plot 118, Trans-Amadi Ind. Layout, Port Harcourt

STRIDES ARCOLAB (NIGERIA) LIMITED
Business: Import of Pharmaceuticals & Healthcare Products
Address: 28, Ajasa Street (Ground Floor), Onikan, Lagos
Tel: (01) 2636449, 2633485, 2636411, 7735757
Fax: (01) 2636678
Contact: Alh. Kasimu Haruna - Chairman
Mr. Sanjiv Raj Kapoor - MD/CEO

STRIKA ENTERTAINMENT (NIGERIA) LIMITED
Business: Entertainment, Enlightenment Productions (
Address: 13B, Bishop Oluwole Street, Victoria Island, Lagos
Tel/Fax: (01) 2618657
E-mail: naija.info@spastrikas.com
Contact: Mr. Richard Akerele - Chairman
Mr. H'Tomi Davies - MD/CEO

STRUCTEC (Div of CFAO Nig Plc)
Business: Design & Construction of Water Projects/ Schemes, Waterproofing Projects, Supply & Installation of Pumps, Solar Equipment & Pumps, Construction Equipment, Waterproofing Felt, Waterproofing Additives & Admixtures, Ingersoll-Rand Drilling Rigs
Address: Plot 2 & 4, Block D, Amuwo-Odofin Ind. Scheme, Apapa-Oshodi Expressway, Amuwo-Odofin, Lagos
Tel: (01) 5801739, 5847709, 5453781-2 (2L), 4701505, 4705702 **Fax:** (01) 5801739
* 8, Azikiwe Road, Port Harcourt
Tel: (084) 2315885, 236140-2 (3 L)
* Plot 568 Michael Okpara Street, opp. Ibro International Hotel, Wuse Zone 2, Abuja
Tel/Fax: (09) 5232503
Contact: Chief Molade Okoya-Thomas, MFR - Chairman
Mr. C. M. Villa - MD/CEO

STUDENTS PYE NIGERIA LIMITED
Business: Accounting Tutorial Services
Address: PYE House, 14, Oweh Street, off Ikorodu Road, Fadeyi, Lagos
Tel: (01) 7745383, 7734536, 08033067325, 08033491371,
* c/o Pilot Finance Ltd, Cultural Centre (Suite SBB), Area 7, Garki, Abuja
Tel: (09) 2347853

STUDIO PRESS (NIGERIA) PLC
Business: Production of Light Packaging Materials & Labels
Address: Plot B, Israel Adebajo Close, off Ladipo Oluwole Avenue, Ikeja Industrial Estate, Lagos
Tel: (01) 4968137-9 (3L) **Fax:** (01) 4974399
E-mail: mail.spn@micro.com.ng

SUB-SAHARAN PRESS LIMITED
Business: Publishers of Newsmagazine
Address: 23, Adeniyi Jones Avenue, Ikeja, Lagos
Tel: (01) 7756204, 7756205, 4804268, 2882143
E-mail: theweekmagazine@yahoo.com
Contact: Mr Peter Eloka Okocha - Chairman
Mr. Clement Okitikpi - MD/CEO

SUBURBAN TRUST SAVINGS & LOANS LIMITED
Business: Mortgage Banking
Address: 4B, Mobolaji Bank-Anthony Way, Maryland, Ikeja, Lagos
Tel: (01) 4938278, 4931688, 8124399 **Fax:** (01) 4931688
Contact: Chief A. O. Olafisoye - Chairman
Mr. F. A. Adeduro - MD/CEO

SUDELETTRA NIGERIA LIMITED
Business: Electrical & Mechanical Engineering Services
Address: Km. 16, P.Harcourt/Aba Expressway, Port Harcourt
Tel: (084) 611681
E-mail: sen@infoweb.abs.net
* 122A, Tombia St, G. R. A. Phase I, Port Harcourt
Tel: (084) 237788
* Plot 2A, Agodogba Avenue, Park View Estate, Ikoyi, Lagos.
Tel/Fax: (01) 2692974

SUFFOLK PETROLEIUM SERVICES LIMITED
Business: Oilfield Drilling & Engineering Services
Address: Plot 20, East-West Rd, Rumuodara, Port Harcourt

SULTEC INTERNATIONAL COMPANY LIMITED
Business: Manufacture and Installation of Pumps, Compressors, Paper & Pulp Machines, Steam Boilers, Water & Waste Water Treatment Plants, Katadyn Filters
Address: 6B, Ademola Street, South-West Ikoyi, Lagos
Tel: (01) 2692011, 688889, 08033160381-2 (2L)
Fax: (01) 2691904
Contact: Mr. Barrie Bould - MD/CEO

SUMAL FOODS LIMITED
Business: Manufacturing of Chewing Gum & Confectionery
Address: Plot 2A, Block J, Oluyole Industrial Estate, Town Planning Way, off Ring Road, Ibadan
Tel: (02) 2310186, 2310195, 2312904, 314541, 314559
Fax: (02) 2311935, 2312046
Contact: Mr. S. J. Nassar - MD/CEO

SUMMA GUARANTY & TRUST COMPANY PLC
Business: Issuing House, Stockbroking, Financial Advisory Services, Economic Consultancy, Portfolio Management
Address: LSDPC Luxury Flats (Suite F2), 24, Adeola Odeku Street, Victoria Island, Lagos
Tel: (01) 2625067 **Fax:** (01) 2625068
E-mail: summa@summaguaranty.com
Website: www.summaguaranty.com
Contact: Dr. Herbert O. Orji - Chairman
Mr. Alex A. Duruike - MD/Chief Operation Officer

SUMMIT FINANCE COMPANY LIMITED
Business: Stockbroking, Financial Services
Address: Summit House, 6, Ajele St, off Broad Street, Lagos
Tel: (01) 2601220-2 (3L), 2647872, 2634309, 2885161
Fax: (01) 2634309, 2647872
Contact: Mr. Raymond C. Obieri - Chairman
Mr. Albert Owolabi - MD/CEO

SUMMIT INSURANCE COMPANY LIMITED
Business: Non-Life Insurance and Special Risks
Address: Summit Centre, 9, Bishop Aboyade Cole Street, Victoria Island, Lagos
Tel: (01) 2618477, 2617512, 612090 **Fax:** (01) 2618333
Contact: Mrs. A. A. Awogboro - Chairperson
Mr. B. A. Atiku - Ag. MD/CEO

SUMMIT OIL INTERNATIONAL LIMITED
Business: Oil Exploration & Production
Address: 362, Herbert Macaulay Street, Yaba, Lagos
Tel: (01) 867850, 8004450-4 (5L), 7741270
Contact: Alh. L. K. O. Abiola - MD/CEO

SUMMIT PUBLICATIONS LIMITED
Business: Publishing of Newsmagazine
Address: 30, Emina Crescent, off Toyin Street, Ikeja, Lagos
Tel: (01) 4960289
E-mail: source@nigol.net.ng
Contact: Comfort Obi - CEO

SUN IMPEX LIMITED
Business: Importation of Plastic Raw Materials, Tanks, Bicycles, Cosmetics and General Merchandise
Address: 154, Inuwa Wada Lane (off Civic Centre Road), behind Ibrahim Taiwo Road, Kano
Tel: (064) 646584, 649824, 648481, 643147, 08037221900, 08044121343, 08044121662
Fax: (064) 637633, 631162
E-mail: sunimpex@hotmail.com
sunimpexltd@yahoo.com
Contact: Mr. Sunil V. Bellani - Chairman/CEO
Mr. Girish H. Sharma - GM

SUN INSURANCE NIGERIA PLC
Business: All Classes of Insurance
Address: 14/16, Abibu-Oki Street, (3rd & 5th Floor) off Marina, Lagos
Tel: (01) 2663068, 2661992, 2660804 **Fax:** (01) 2664365
E-mail: sun-insuranceplc@hyperia.com
Contact: Otunba (Dr.) Adekunle Ojora, CON - Chairman
Mr. S. B. Ifatujosin - MD/CEO

SUNBEAM ADVERTISING AND PUBLICITY LIMITED
Business: Advertising Agency, Publishing
Address: 7, Upper Campos St, off Bamgbose Street, Lagos
Tel: (01) 2631300, 2631961
Contact: Mrs. Toluwalope Adewusi - MD/CEO

SUNBO ONITIRI & COMPANY
Business: Estate Surveyor and Valuers, Property Manage-

ment, Agency, Valuation and Maintenance
Address: 26, King George V Road (3rd Floor), Onikan, Lagos
Tel: (01) 2645042, 2646749, 2646783, 612773, 08023054899, 08023234135
E-mail: soc@theobech.com
Contact: Chief Sunbo Onitiri - Principal Partner

SUNCOAST (NIGERIA) LIMITED
Business: Sales & Service of Computer, Development & Marketing of Software, Systems Support Services
Address: Eleganza Plaza (Pisces Block, Ground & 1st Floor), 1, Commercial Road, Apapa, Lagos
Tel: (01) 5450647, 5450679, 5450478
Fax: (01) 2693122, 5450647

SUNCOAST INVESTMENTS LIMITED
Business: Capital Market Operators, Financial Consultants, Investment Advisors, Portfolio Managers
Address: Unity House (13th Floor), 37, Marina, Lagos
Tel: (01) 2661404 **Fax:** (01) 2643420
* 40,Usuma Street, Maitama District, Abuja
Contact: Tobias Ikwuegbu - GM/CEO

SUNFLAG GROUP OF COMPANIES
Business: Conglomerate, Manufacturers of Textile Goods
Address: Plots 37-39, Iganmu Ind. Estate, Iganmu, Lagos
Tel: (01) 7748843, 5455237, 5830208, 5832312, 5850294, 5874011 **Fax:** (01) 5831314, 5850303
Contact: Mr. V. K. Kapur

SUNFLEX NIGERIA LIMITED
Business: Manufacturer of Venetian, Vertical, Roller Window Blinds, Furnishing and Carpeting Services
Address: 18, Mojidi Street, off Toyin Street, Ikeja, Lagos
Tel: (01) 4936230, 7742733, 8129191, 08023117304
Fax: (01) 4936230
E-mail: sunflex@gacom.net
sunflexkb@yahoo.com
Contact: Mr. Kingsley Bolaji Obiekwe - Chairman/CEO.

SUNGAS COMPANY NIGERIA LIMITED
Business: Importation, Transportation, Distribution and Marketing of Bulk & Bottled LP-Gas, Design & Construction of LPG Plants, Sales & Service of Appliances and Equipment
Address: 1, Obasa Road, off Oba Akran Avenue, Ikeja, Industrial Estate, Ikeja, Lagos
Tel: (01) 4937842 **Fax:** (01) 4937841
E-mail: sungas@intracom.net.ng
* 7, Reclamation Road, Mobil Depot, Port Harcourt
Contact: Dr. J. A. Ibidapo - Chairman
Mrs. O. O. Akinbobola - MD/CEO

SUNGLAD NIGERIA LIMITED
Business: Shipping, General Merchandising
Address: 11, Randle Road, Apapa, Lagos
Tel: (01) 5451748, 5457043 **Fax:** (01) 5451748
E-mail: sunglad@cyberspace.net.ng
Contact: Chief Eziuche Nwoke - Chairman/CEO

SUNGLASS LIMITED
Business: Processing and Production of Glass Containers
Address: Plot H8, Kudenda Industrial Area, off Nnamdi Azikiwe Expressway, Kaduna
Tel: (062) 236809, 236840, 236841, 234555
Fax: (062) 236801
E-mail: sunglass@hyperia.com
sunglass@wwlkad.com
* 1, Mobolaji Johnson Avenue, beh. 7-Up Factory, Oregun, Ikeja, Lagos
Tel: (01) 4930025

SUNNIL NIGERIA LIMITED
Business: Import & Export, Sales of Welding Electrodes, Grinding Wheels, Vehicle Tubes, Textiles & Goods
Address: 9, Creek Road, Apapa, Lagos
Tel: (01) 5878148, 7760648, 08033021669
Fax: (01) 5878148
E-mail: tckim2000@yahoo.co.kr
Contact: Mr. Kim - Managing Director

SUNNEX INTERNATIONAL (NIGERIA) LIMITED
Business: Importation and Sales of Decorative Lightings
Address: 20 & 24, Alaba Int'l Market Rd, Ojo-Alaba, Lagos
Tel: (01) 2630860, 08033038409 **Fax:** (01) 2630126
E-mail: sunnex@hyperia.com

SUNNY MOTORS LIMITED
Business: Sales and Services of Motor Vehicles
Address: Plot 45, Alh. Tokan St, Alaka Estate, near National Stadium, Western Avenue, Surulere, Lagos
Tel: (01) 4701550, 5837296, 5830435, 5830433, 08033016289, 08034030150 **Fax:** (01) 5830433
E-mail: sunnymotors@nova.net.ng
Contact: Mr. Sunny Asemota - Chairman/CEO

SUNPLAST INDUSTRIES LIMITED
Business: Manfacturing of Plasticware
Address: Plot 4C, Block H, Apapa-Osodi Expressway, Sadiku-Ilasamaja, Lagos
Tel: (01) 7743975, 4523580

SUNRISE DMB & B LIMITED
Business: Advertising & Marketing Communication Consultancy Services
Address: 21, Balogun Street, off Kudirat Abiola Way, near Radio Bus-Stop, Alausa, Ikeja, Lagos
Tel: (01) 4966197, 4967717, 4970689 **Fax:** (01) 4934701
E-mail: sunrisedmbb@nova.net.ng
Contact: Mr. May Nzeribe - Chairman/CEO

SUNROSE CONSULTING LIMITED
Business: Human Resources Consultants (Executive Recruitment, /Training, Outsourcing, Personnel Policy & Procedure Development, Strategic Planning)
Address: NICON House (3rd Floor), 5, Customs Street, off Marina, Lagos Island, Lagos
Tel/Fax: (01) 2643281
E-mail: sunroseco@yahoo.com
Contact: Mr. Olumuyiwa Sofowora - Prin. Consultant/CEO

SUNSEED NIGERIA PLC
Business: Processing and Production of Vegetable Oil
Address: Kewalram Compound, 8A, Karimu Kotun Street, Victoria Island, Lagos
Tel: (01) 2620328-9 (2L)

Website: www.chanrai.com
* New Jos Road, Dakace, P.O. Box 240, Zaria
Tel: (069) 332040, 332621, 334956, 335114
Fax: (069) 332472, 332621

SUPADET HOLDINGS LIMITED
Business: Sales and Installation of Radio Communication Equipment
Address: 12, Oteomi St, off Isolo Rd, Papa-Ajao, Mushin, Lagos
Tel: (01) 4524721, 4528655, 4528910, 4528905-6 (2 L), 4527664 , 4527748 **Fax:** (01) 4528656, 4528936
E-mail: supadet@hyperia.com
supadet@infoweb.abs.net
Contact: Prince Adesupo Adetunji - Chairman/CEO

SUPERB ELECTRICAL & ELECTRONIC COMPANY LTD
Business: Distribution & Sales of Automatic Voltage Regulators, UPS and Antennae
Address: 49, Iga-Idungaran Street, Idumagbo, Lagos
Tel: (01) 2643424, 7733549, 08033086023, 08033162513

SUPERCOR INDUSTRIES LIMITED
Business: Manufacturing of Fibre Cement Products
Address: Industrial Estate, Bauchi
Tel: (077) 543285, 542171 **Fax:** (077) 543398
* Eleganza Plaza (Libra Block, 1st Floor), Aerodrome Road, Apaapa, Lagos
* Port Harcourt Expressway, Ariria Junction, Aba
Tel: (082) 222412
Contact: Dr. Umaru A. Alkaleri - Chairman
Dr. Ramesh C. Shishu - MD/CEO

SUPERFINE FURNITURE & TRADING COMPANY LIMITED
Business: Production and Marketing of Furniture
Address: Old Airport Road, Jos
Tel: (073) 461687, 08037010788
Contact: Mr. Pius G. Korinjoh - Chairman/CEO

SUPERFINE INDUSTRIES (NIGERIA) LIMITED
Business: Manufacture of Domestic & Industrial Plastic Wares
Address: 22, Abimbola Street, Isolo Ind. Estate, Isolo, Lagos
Tel: (01) 4527034, 4524478, 4520831, 7753660
Fax: (01) 4527034
E-mail: nane5h@hotmail.com
Contact: Mr. D. S. Mirami - Chairman

SUPERFLUX INTERNATIONAL LIMITED
Business: Printing of Security Documents, Sales and Installation of Payment Systems and Pre-Paid Telephony Infrastructure, Transaction Processing
Address: 5A, Oko-Awo Close, off Karimu Kotun Street, Victoria Island, Lagos
Tel: (01) 3200414-5 (2L), 2705304-5 (2L), 2705153, 08023126833 **Fax:** (01) 2705153
E-mail: superflux2@yahoo.com
sales@superflux-ng.com
Website: www.superflux-ng.com
Contact: Mr. Tokunbo Talabi - President/CEO

SUPERIOR EQUIPMENT LIMITED
Business: Sales and Service of Computer & Accessories, Networking & System Intergration, IT Consultancy
Address: 285B, Corporation Drive, Dolphin Estate, Ikoyi, Lagos
Tel: (01) 2693753, 2693754, 2693755 **Fax:** (01) 2693754
E-mail: info@superior-equipment.com
Contact: Mrs. Nkoli Oyeka - MD/CEO

SUPERIOR MOTORS (NIGERIA) LIMITED
Business: Sales of Motor Vehicles
Address: 39, Alh. Tokan Street, Alaka Estate, Western Avenue, Surulere, Lagos
Tel: (01) 5454521, 5454588
Contact: Chief Oscar P. Udoji - MD/CEO

SUPERMARITIME (NIGERIA) LIMITED
Business: Shipping Services & Ship Chartering, Clearing and Forwaring, Warehousing, Halage, Stevedoring
Address: 10, Obanta Street, (Beula Suites), Entrance by Oduduwa Road, Apapa GRA, Apapa, Lagos
Tel: (01) 2645191-2 (2L), 2644858-9 (2L)
Fax: (01) 5876845
E-mail: vessel@supmanig.net
* 11B, Adetokunbo Ademola Cr.Wuse II, Abuja.
Tel/Fax: (09) 5239383
* 1, Worlu Road/Olu Obasanjo Road, Port Harcourt
Tel: (084) 334406, 334658
* 57, Effurun/Sapele Road, opp. PZ, Effurun, Warri.
Tel: (053) 251495, 250552
Contact: Chief (Mrs.) Edna Aleyideino - Chairman
Mr. Fred T. Roller - GM/CEO

SUPERTEX LIMITED
Business: Manufacturing and Marketing of Textile Wax Prints
Address: 1, Mohammed Ladan Road, Kakuri Industrial Estate, Kaduna South, Kaduna
Tel: (062) 231450, 232346, 230069 **Fax:** (062) 232127

SUPRA COMMERCIAL TRUST LIMITED
Business: Stockbroking, Financing
Address: NIM Building (2nd Floor, Suites 13 & 14), Plot 22, Idowu Taylor Street, Victoria Island, Lagos
Tel/Fax: (01) 4617747

SUPRA INVESTMENT LIMITED
Business: Financial and Management Advisory Services
Address: 11B, Karimu Kotun Street, Victoria Island, Lagos
Tel: (01) 2622865, 2623684 **Fax:** (01) 2623098
E-mail: suprainv@cyberspace.com
Contact: Mr. Andy Esemegie - MD/CEO

SUPREME FINANCE & INVESTMENT COMPANY LIMITED
Business: Financial Services, Investment Management, Insurance Broking
Address: Great Nigeria House (14th Floor), 47/57, Martins Street, Lagos
Tel: (01) 2660661 **Fax:** (01) 2668576
Contact: Mr. Tunde Ajayi - Chairman/CEO

SUPREME SAVINGS & LOANS LIMITED
Business: Mortgage Banking & Finance Services
Address: Falomo Shopping Centre (Suite A10), Awolowo Road, Ikoyi, Lagos
47/57, Martins Street, Lagos
Tel: (01) 8118127, 683795, 08023186262 **Fax:** (01) 683795
E-mail: ssll@webaccessng.com
Contact: Engr. L. Onalaja - MD/CEO

SUPREME INSURANCE BROKERS LIMITED
Business: Insurance Brokerage
Address: Tisco House (1st Floor), 23, Association Avenue, Ilupeju, Lagos
Tel: (01) 4932585
Contact: Mr. Somope Oladejo - MD/CEO

SUPREME TRADING COMPANY LIMITED
Business: Importation of Pharmaceutical Products, Surgical Dressings and Office Automation
Address: 18, Ilupeju Bye-Pass, Ilupeju, Lagos
Tel: (01) 4978556 **Fax:** (01) 4525639
E-mail: supreme@beta.linkserve.com
Website: www.suprempharmaceuticals.com
*5, Eastern Bye-Pass,Ogbunabali, Diobu, P/Harcourt
Tel: (084) 232662
Contact: Emile E. Batruny - MD/CEO

SUPREMETECK NIGERIA LIMITED
Business: Information Communication Technology, VSAT Access Solution Provider
Address: 100, Awolowo Road, S.W. Ikoyi, Lagos
Tel: (01) 8118528, 08034105255
E-mail: tolutunde@hotmail.com
Contact: Tunde Olutunde - MD/CEO

SURFACE DOCTOR
Business: Surface Restoration & Refinishing
Address: 5B, Oko-Awo Street, Victoria Island, Lagos
Tel: (01) 2624541, 4934555 **Fax:** (01) 2624542, 4934556
Contact: Mr. Morrison Odion Okunbo - MD/CEO

SURPORT SERVICES LIMITED
Business: Stockbroking
Address: Lapal House (2nd Floor), 241, Igbosere Rd, Lagos
Tel: (01) 2646797-8 (2 L), 4705429 **Fax:** (01) 2646798
E-mail: dipwil@yahoo.com
Contact: Mr. Oladipo Williams - CEO

SURVEILANCE & COMMUNICATION TECHNOLOGIES LTD (SurComTec)
Business: Design, Procurement and Installation of Electronic Security Systems & Equipment, Central Alarm Monitoring
Address: 12, Waziri Ibrahim Crescent, off Elsie Femi-Pearse Street, Victoria Island, Lagos
Tel: (01) 7744200, 7753606, 2613037, 2615852
Fax: (01) 7595396
E-mail: cctvnig@beta.linkserve.com
* Survellance Place, 56, Mbonu Street, D-Line, Port Harcourt.
Tel: (084) 231863
Contact: Engr. Hilary C. Obi - Chairman/CEO

SVACO IMPORT & EXPORT COMPANY LIMITED
Business: Manufacturing, Distribution and Sales of Plastic Footwear and Polythene Products
Address: Plot 5, Ayodele Diyan Road, Ikeja Industrial Estate, Ikeja, Lagos
Tel: (01) 4963803 **Fax:** (01) 4963489

SVENGALI DESIGNS LIMITED
Business: Manufacture and Sales of Furniture and Lightings, Wrought-Iron Works, Interior Decor Consultancy
Address: 9, Agoro Odiyan Street, Victoria Island, Lagos
Tel: (01) 2629275, 2629584, 611747 **Fax:** (01) 2622308
E-mail: sven@infoweb.abs.net
Website: www.svengali-ng.com
Contact: Mr Anselm Tabani - MD/CEO

SWANEESE
Business: Sales of Home Wares and Appliances
Address: 59, Awolowo Road, S. W. Ikoyi, Lagos
Tel: (01) 2691570, 0803307854, 0055120776
Fax: (01) 2691570
* Plot 351, Aminu Kano Crescent, Wuse II, Abuja
Tel: (09) 5231048

SWAP TECHNOLOGY & TELECOMMUNICATIONS LTD
Business: Distribution & Sales of Mobile Phones and GSM Airtime, Telecommunicatio Services
Address: 7, Oyin Jolayemi Street, Victoria Island, Lagos
Tel: (01) 3200612, 08023053052 **Fax:** (01) 3201713
E-mail: swap-ng@excite.com
Website: www.swap-ng.com
Contact: Mr. Tunde Titilayo - MD/CEO

SWEDE CONTROL INTERTEK LIMITED
Business: Pre-Shipment Inspection of Goods, Quality Control
Address: Plot 1709, Olugbosi Close, off Bishop Oluwole Street, Victoria Island, Lagos
Tel: (01) 2619897, 2619963 **Fax:** (01) 2620198
E-mail: swedecontrol@yahoo.com
Contact: R. A. Onikede - Executive Manager
R. O. Olanegan - Asst. Manager (Admin.)

SWEET APPLE SERVICES LIMITED
Business: Shipping and Clearing & Forwarding Agents
Address: 14, Industry Road, Port Harcourt
Tel: (084) 233411, 234303, 08033108650
E-mail: sweetapples@infoweb.abs.net
Contact: Mr. Dennis Okwu - MD/CEO

SWEET SENSATION CONFECTIONERY LIMITED
Business: Fast-Food Outlets
Address: 3, Opebi Road, Ikeja, Lagos
Tel: (01) 7748777
E-mail: ssc@micro.com.ng
* 26, Adetokunbo Ademola St, Victoria Island, Lagos
Tel: (01) 7740276 **Fax:** (01) 2622270
* 14, Town Planning Way, Ilupeju, Lagos
Tel: (01) 4961336, 7730571
Contact: Mrs. Kehinde Kamson - CEO

SWIFT FREIGHT INTERNATIONAL NIGERIA LIMITED
Business: Air & Sea Freight Services, Logistics
Address: NAHCO Cargo Complex (Ground Floor, Wing B), Murtala Muh'd International Aairport, Ikeja, Lagos
Tel: (01) 7737616, 7745865, 7749684 **Fax:** (01) 2702949
E-mail: swiftlagos@infoweb.abs.net
Website: www.swiftfreight.com
Contact: Mr. Behram Baluch - MD/CEO

SWIFT TRAVELS LIMITED
Business: Travel Agency, Packaging of Tours
Address: 17, East Pavillion, Tafawa Balewa Square, Race

Course, Lagos Island, Lagos
Tel: (01) 2634442, 2634449, 2634445, 2646647, 2634442, 08034103873 **Fax:** (01) 2646647
E-mail: swiftrvl@yahoo.com

SWISS NOVA CHEM LIMITED (formerly Clariant Nig. Ltd)
Business: Manufacturing and Distribution of Auxiliaries for the Textile, Leather, Paper and other Industries
Address: Plot 9, Block A, Gbagada Industrial Estate, Gbagada, Lagos
Tel: (01) 4978860-62 (3 L), 7730305-6 (2 L), 7749104
Fax: (01) 5874351, 2222500
E-mail: vicoda@infoweb.abs.net
Contact: Dr. Liman Ciroma - Chairman
Mr. H. M. Fritschi - MD/CEO

SWISS PHARMA NIGERIA LIMITED
Business: Manufacture, Importation & Marketing of Pharmaceuticals, Chemicals & Flavours
Address: 5, Dopemu Road, Agege, Lagos
Tel: (01) 4920543, 4920544, 4921100, 4923444, 4925767
Fax: (01) 4921974, 4964136
E-mail: swisspharma@hyperia.com
Contact: Mr. A. F. Spinnler - MD/CEO
Mr. C. Cummings - Commercial Director

SWISS SPECIALITY CHEMICAL LIMITED
Business: Importation and Sales of Dyestuff & Chemicals for the Textile Industry, Pigments for Makers of Inks, Paints & Plastics, Home & Personal Care Products, Manufacturers' Representative
Address: Syngenta House, 387, Agege Motor Rd, Challenge, Mushin, Lagos
Tel: (01) 4523511, 4523523, 4523534, 4523541, 7743119, 7746435-6 (2L) **Fax:** (01) 4523562, 4523569
Contact: Mr. Rolf Streib - Chairman
Mr. Jean J. Kaspar - MD/CEO

SWISSAIR/SABENA (NIGERIA)
Business: International Airline Services
Address: Churchgate Towers, Plot PC. 30, Afribank Street, Victoria Island, Lagos
Tel: (01) 2617738, 2617752, 2611665, 2619367, 2619700
Fax: (01) 2613760, 2611659
Website: www.swissair.com
www.sabena.com
Contact: Mr G. Philips - GM
Mr. I. Adedeji - Sales Manager

SWISSCO NIGERIA LIMITED
Business: Marketing and Distribution of Ethical Pharmaceutical Products, Sales and Marketing of Soap
Address: Jagal Road, off Ikosi Road, Oregun Industrial Estate, Oregun, Lagos
Tel: (01) 4973390-4 (5L), 4973396, 4930519
Fax: (01) 4970090
Contact: Mr. Anwar Jamarkani - Group Exec. Chairman
Mr. Donald Spencer - Group MD/CEO

SWISSTRADE SECURITIES (NIGERIA) LIMITED
Business: Manufacturing & Installation of Security Doors
Address: Topaz Plaza (Suite B5), Km. 18, Lagos-Epe Expressway, opp. Alpha Beach Junction, Idado, Lekki, Lagos
Tel: (01) 7730468, 7752471, 4618470, 08033051809, 08033079797 **Fax:** (01) 2630143
E-mail: swistrade@yahoo.com

SWORD SWEET CONFECTIONERIES NIGERIA LIMITED
Business: Manufacturing of Sweets and Confectionery
Address: Plot 6, Olubadan Ind. Estate, New Ife Road, Ibadan
Tel: (02) 8103240, 8102019, 08033243373, 08033246660, 08033777687, 08042117709
Fax: (02) 2411330, 8103229
E-mail: swordsweet@intracom5.com
sscnl@yahoo.com
Contact: Mr. Yousef Fawa - Director (Operations)

SYBASE NIGERIA LIMITED
Business: Information Technology Solution Provider (e-Tranzact: Functional Electronic Payment)
Address: Fortune Towers (5th Floor), 27/29, Adeyemo Alakija Street, Victoria Island, Lagos
Tel: (01) 2625120, 2610226 **Fax:** (01) 2625120
Website: www.sybase.com.ng
Contact: Mr. Valentine Obi - MD/CEO

SYKOBIN INVESTMENT LIMITED
Business: Shipping, Airfreight, Clearing, Forwarding, Haulage, Warehousing; Engineering and Construction
Address: 74B, Marine Road, Apapa G. R. A., Lagos
Tel: (01) 5870428, 5870586 , 4706814 **Fax:** (01) 5870586
E-mail: sykobingroup@linkserve.com
Website: www.sykobingroup.com
Contact: Okenze S. I. Obinna - Chairman/CEO

SYNCO INTERNATIONA LIMITED
Business: Import and Export, General Commerce, Contractors
Address: 76, Ogui Road, Enugu
Tel/Fax: (042) 253479
Contact: Chief S. N. C. Ogbuanu - Chairman/CEO

SYNDICATED METAL INDUSTRIES LIMITED
Business: Fabrication of Aluminium Doors, Windows, Curtain Walls, Office Partitioning, Suspended Ceilings & Cashier's Cubicles
Address: Secretariat Road, opp. Onward Paper Mill, Alausa, Lagos
Tel: (01) 7740657-8 (2L), 08034403732
Fax: (01) 2694093, 5846154
E-mail: dcpl@beta.linkserve.com
* 6, Old Aba Road, Rumuogba, Port Harcourt
Tel: 08034070165
* Plot 541, Aminu Kano Crescent, opp. Amal Court, Wuse II, Abuja.
Tel: (09) 5239006, 5239762
Contact: Chief R. A. Gbadamosi - Chairman
Mr. Paul N. B. Erinne - MD/CEO

SYNERCOM LIMITED
Business: Information Management and Consultancy Services, Systems Integration & Network Planning, Electronic Document Management and Workflow Solutions, Network Security and Enterprise Anti-Virus Solutions
Address: Great Nigeria House (16th Floor), 47/67, Martins Street, Lagos

Tel: (01) 2661269, 2643160 **Fax:** (01) 2661269, 2902006
E-mail: info@subeny.com
synercom@subeny.com
synercom@intracom.net
Website: www.subeny.com
Contact: Mr. V. B. Adeyemi - Chairperson
Mr. Adewale Adebiyi - MD/CEO

SYNERGY SYSTEMS LIMITED
Business: Marketing, Implementation & Support of *SAGE Enterpriese Solutions* & *Version One's Dp* Archive, Fax, Mail Form, Information Technology Consulting & Traning, Broadband Internet Service Provider, Provision of Network Infrastructure & Virtual Private Networks (VPN), Hardware Sales
Address: Ibu-Owa House (1st & 2nd Floors), 41, Osolo Way, off International Airport, Isolo, Lagos
Tel: (01) 3205404-5 (2L), 8168855-6 (2L)
Fax: (01) 4527518
E-mail: info@synergysystemsng.com
Contact: Mr. E. E. Obijiofor - Chairman/CEO

SYNETICS TECHNOLOGIES LIMITED
Business: Sales & Services of Computers, Software Development and Implementation
Address: 33, Akin Adesola Street, Victoria Island, Lagos
Tel: (01) 3200312, 3204768-9 (2L) **Fax:** (01) 3204352
Website: www.syneticstechnologies.com
Contact: Mr. O'tega Emerhor - Chairman
Mr. Kingsley Odoh - MD/CEO

SYSDATA LIMITED
Business: Sales of Information Technology Products
Address: 13, Adebola Street, off Adeniran Ogunsanya Street, Surulere, Lagos
Tel: (01) 5834178, 5847564, 4700051 **Fax:** (01) 5841266
E-mail: info@beta-computers.com
Website: www.beta-computers.com
* Plot 17, Yusuf Maitama Sule Street, off Yakubu Gowon Crescent, Asokoro, Abuja
Tel: (09) 6702552, 6702551, 3143516 **Fax:** (09) 3143516
E-mail: bclabj@beta-computers.com
Contact: Mr. Will E. Anyaegbunam - MD/CEO

SYNGENTA NIGERIA LIMITED
Business: Distribution and Sales of Agro-chemicals, Animal & Public Health Products
Address: 387, Agege Motor Road, Mushin, Lagos
Tel: (01) 4523511, 4523523, 4523534, 4523541, 7746435-6
Fax: (01) 4523562, 4523569
* 3, Akilu Road, P.O.Box 1050, Kaduna
Tel: (062) 248482
* Ballon House, E9/205B, Iwo Road, Ibadan
Tel: (02) 711433
* 3, Ahmadu Bello Way, P.O.Box 430, Jimeta Yola
Tel: (075) 624341
Contact: Alh. Ahmed Joda - Chairman
Sir P. N. Ikemefuna - MD/CEO

SYSTEM METAL INDUSTRIES LIMITED
Business: Aluminium Roofing Sheets & Cooking Utensils
Address: Ikot-Ishie, off Murtala Muhammed Highway, Calabar
Tel: (01) 232065, 235905

SYSTEMCARE & SOFTWARE LIMITED
Business: Software Development, System Support Services, Computer Training
Address: 4, Norman Williams Street, S. W. Ikoyi, Lagos
Tel: (01) 2671137-8 (2L), 685697 **Fax:** (01) 2671137
E-mail: systemcare@hyperia.com
Contact: Mr. Anthony Awosiyan - MD/CEO

SYSTEMPLUS LIMITED
Business: Sales of Internet Telephony Equipment
Address: 4, Dipeolu Street, off Obafemi Awolowo Way, behind Tantalizers - Allen Avenue, Ikeja, Lagos
Tel: (01) 4936340, 4939425 **Fax:** (01) 4972678
E-mail: systemplusng@yahoo.com
Website: www.systemplusng.com

SYSTEMS FOR TELECOMMUNICATIONS INTERNATIONAL LIMITED (STI)
Business: Telecommunication Engineering, Sales and Maintenance of Telecommunication Equipment
Address: Adem House, Lagos-Badagry Expressway (Odun-Ade Bus-Stop) Lagos
Tel: (01) 2880566, 4808057 **Fax:** (01) 2880566
E-mail: sti@infoweb.abs.net
* 8, Ogoloma/Amadi Street, Oroworukwu, off St. John's Port Harcourt.
Tel: (084) 333010
Contact: Chief P. C. Asiodu - Exec. Chairman
Engr. (Dr.) E. C. Nwankwo - MD/CEO

SYSTEMS TECH TONER CARTRIDGE REMANUFACTURERS LIMITED
Business: Remanufacturing of Printer-Toner Cartridges, Computer Services
Address: 21, Bola Ajibola Street, off Ogundana Street, off Allen Avenue, Ikeja, Lagos
Tel: (01) 4935953-3 (4L) **Fax:** (01) 4935993
E-mail: systech@nigol.net.ng
info@systemstonercartridge.com
Website: www.systemstonercartridge.com
* Sky Memorial Complex, 158, Michael Okpara St, opp. The Young Motors, Wuse Zone 5, Abuja
Tel: (09) 2346490-4 (5L)
Contact: Chief Michael Ade-Ojo - Chairman
Mr. Benson Kola Majekodunmi - MD/CEO

SYSTEMSPECS LIMITED
Business: Marketing & Support of *SunSystems* Software Packages & *HumanManager* Suite
Address: 136, Lewis Street (5th - 8th Floor), Lafiaji, Lagos
Tel: (01) 2633785, 2633786, 2633900 **Fax:** (01) 2632622
E-mail: sales@systemspecs.com.ng
secretary@systemspecs.com.ng
Website: www.systemspec.com.ng
Contact: John Tani Obaro - MD/CEO
Mojisola Sode - GM (Technical Services)

SYSTEMTECH SERVICES LIMITED
Business: Sales and Maintenance of Computers and Peripherals, Software Development, Networking, Integration, UPS, Consultancy Services and Training
Address: 126, Ogunlana Drive, Surulere, Lagos
Tel: (01) 4713740, 4713893, 5454157, 5454207,

08034708511, 08034713740 **Fax:** (01) 5454157
E-mail: systemtech@infoweb.abs.net
info@systemtech-ng.com
Website: www.systemtech-ng.com
Contact: Emeka Madubuike - MD/CEO
Oladimeji Suberu - ED/Head - System Dev

T. A. BRAITHWAITE (INSURANCE BROKERS) & CO. LTD
Business: Insurance Broking
Address: 47, Marina (6th Floor), Lagos Island, Lagos
Tel: (01) 2661337, 2661348, 2660598, 2661852, 2664813
Fax: (01) 2666313, 2693381
E-mail: tabins@micro.com.ng
Contact: Mr. Talabi Adebayo Braithwaite - Chairman
Mr. James Akinola Bello - MD/CEO

T. A. C (TIGER) PLASTICS INDUSTRIES NIGERIA LIMITED
Business: Manufacturers of Plastic Products
Address: 62, Town Planning Way, Ilupeju Ind. Estate, Lagos
Tel: (01) 4965228 **Fax:** (01) 4971600
Contact: Mr. Barnabas Nwokeji - Manager (Admin./Accts)

T. F. MAKINDE (LOSS ADJUSTING) LIMITED
Business: Loss Adjusting
Address: SW9/1525A, Aba Alamu Road, Apata, Ibadan
Tel: (02) 2313225, 08023074644, 08033602190
Fax: (02) 2313225
E-mail: levanchrismak@yahoo.com
Contact: Pastor T. F. Makinde - Chairman/CEO

TAAK LIMITED
Business: Sales of Hospital Allied Equipment, Office Equipment, Computers, Peripherals & Accessories
Address: 21B, Idowu Martins Street, Victoria Island, Lagos
Tel: (01) 2614818, 2629421, 2629423, 7741913
Fax: (01) 2614818
E-mail: taak_haal@micro.com.ng
taakhaal@linkserve.com
Contact: Mrs. Tokunbo A. Akinosho - MD/CEO

TABANSI AGENCIES LIMITED
Business: Recording and Publishing of Music & Songs, Production of Video Films, Import and Export
Address: 22, Limca Road, Onitsha
Tel: (046) 487269, 08033125197 **Fax:** (046) 487269
E-mail: tabansiagencies@lycos.com
Contact: Chief (Dr.) G.A.D. Tabansi - Chairman/CEO

TABSON GASES & WELDING PRODUCTS LIMITED
Business: Production of Industrial & Domestic Gases, Sales of Welding Equipment, Electrodes & Consumables
Address: M5, Cadastral Zone 07, Gba Zango, Kubwa, Abuja
Tel: (080) 34081179
E-mail: tabson607@hotmail.com
* Jadesola Shopping Complex, Old Ife Road, (Olaogun Bus-Stop), Ibadan
Tel: (080) 23348835

TAFAK INDUSTRIES NIGERIA LIMITED
Business: Manufacture of Stormline Window Louvre Frames
Address: Plot 33, Chief T. O. Doherty Industrial Layout, Oregun Industrial Estate, Ikeja, Lagos
Tel/Fax: (01) 4936886
E-mail: tafakindustries@yahoo.com
Contact: T. A. F. Akinyemi - Chairman/CEO

TAFAWA BALEWA SQUARE INVESTMENTS LIMITED
Business: Property Development and Management
Address: Tafawa Balewa Square Complex, Race Course, Lagos
Tel: (01) 2630175, 2631907 **Fax:** (01) 2633933
Contact: Mrs. Aisha Inok Bakari - MD/CEO

TAG (NIGERIA) LIMITED
Business: Design, Installation and Maintenance of Central Airconditioners, Plumbing and Electrical Works, Mechanical Engineering
Address: 60A, Apapa Road, Ebute-Metta, Lagos
Tel/Fax: (01) 5851260, 5835813, 5850150
E-mail: tag@europe.com
tagnig@mail.com
Contact: Alh. Shehu Musa - Chairman
Alh. Ahmed Haidar - MD/CEO

TAHAL CONSULTANTS (WEST AFRICA) LIMITED
Business: Management Consultancy Services
Address: Plot 1145, Aminu Kano Crescent, Wuse II, Abuja
Tel: (09) 4137316, 4137317 **Fax:** (09) 4137317
E-mail: tahal_ng@hotmail.com

TAHIR GUEST PALACE
Business: Hospitality & Catering Services
Address: 4, Ibrahim Natsungune Road, off Ahmadu Bello Way, Nassarawa, Kano
Tel: (064) 632057, 649710, 641630, 646988, 638912-3 (2L), 646284, 317245-6 (2L) **Fax:** (064) 646284
E-mail: tahir@ecnx.net
Contact: Mr. Rana Tahir - Chairman

TAHIR OIL MILLS LIMITED
Business: Processing & Sales of Vegetable Oils, Cakes and Seeds; Sales of Oil Milling Equipment
Address: 92/93, Tafawa Balewa Rd, Bompai Ind Estate, Kano
Tel: (064) 314175, 646521-3 (3L) **Fax:** (064) 645717
Contact: Alh. Haruna Tahir - Chairman/CEO
Alh. Sani Aliyu Sumaila - GM

TAIJO WONUKABE LIMITED
Business: Advertising, Public Relations and Event Management, Print Production, Graphics & Design
Address: 2, Anifowoshe Street, off Adebola Street, off Adeniran Ogunsanya Street, Surulere, Lagos
Tel: (01) 5844982, 2229942
E-mail: info@taijowonukabe.com
Website: www.taijowonukabe.com
Contact: Taiwo Obe - MD/CEO
Chido Nwakanma - ED/COO

TAJU INDUSTRIES NIGERIA LIMITED
Business: Manufacture of PVC Footballs, Baby Dolls and Toys, and Polythene Bags
Address: 17, Docemo Street, Idumota, Lagos
Tel: (01) 2665229, 2666664 **Fax:** (01) 2645255, 2666664
* Plot 7, Kolawole Shonibare Street, off International Airport Road, Ajao Estate, Isolo, Lagos
Tel: (01) 4524958, 521353
Contact: Dr. Tajudeen Okoya - Chairman/CEO

TALAFON TELECOMMUNICATIONS LIMITED
Business: Provision of Card-Phone Services, Telecommunication Equipment Outsourcing, Consultancy
Address: Adetokunbo Ademol Crescent, Wuse II, Abuja
E-mail: talafon@talatel.com
Website: www.talatel.com
Contact: Brig-Gen. Ahmed A. Abdullahi (rtd.) - Chairman
Engr. Abdullahi Adamu

TALAMIZ OIL MILL LIMITED
Business: Seed Oil Milling, Production of Refined Vegetable Oil, Cake and Meal
Address: Sharada Road, Dan Agundi, Kano
Tel: (064) 667090, 666990 Fax: (064) 667290
E-mail: talamiz@yahoo.co.uk
* Km. 12, Hadejia Rd, Gunduwawa Ind. Estate, Kano
Tel: (064) 310114
Contact: Alh. Mohammed Badaru Abubakar - Chairman

TALINET LIMITED
Business: Sales and Installation of Telecommunications Terminal Equipment, Internet Facilities Provider, Cyber Cafe/Telecentre
Address: Big Leaf House (2nd Floor, Left Wing), 7, Oyin Jolayemi Street, Victoria Island, Lagos
Tel: (01) 2610371, 3200386, 616510 **Fax:** (01) 2610371
E-mail: talinet@nova.net.ng
talinet@hotmail.com
Contact: Mr. Clem Agba - Chairman
Mr. Tom Obaseki - MD/CEO

TALKWORLD LIMITED
Business: Operation of International Pre-Paid Calling Cards and *Talkworld* Commnication Centres
Address: 48, Adeniran Ogunsanya Street, Surulere, Lagos
Tel: (01) 8902934
Contact: Mr. Olubola Sanu - MD/CEO

TALKLAND TRADE ALLIANCE LIMITED
Business: Importation of Electronics, Broadcasting Equipment & Home Appliances, Sales of Electronics Telecommunication and Sec urity Equipment
Address: 78, Allen Avenue, Ikeja, Lagos
Tel: (01) 4968504, 7730538
Contact: Mr. Young Oguntibeju - GM

TALON NIGERIA LIMITED
Business: Agricultural Research, Development and Consultancy, Fisheries, Agro-Allied Business
Address: 16, Aerodrome Road, Apapa, Lagos
Tel: (01) 5875952, 7747160, 08022234100, 08022234105, 08023254967 **Fax:** (01) 5876580, 7912125
E-mail: talon@cybaaspace.net
lanretalabi@netscape.net
Contact: Dr. S. O. Talabi - Chairman/CEO

TAMARIN HOTELS LIMITED
Business: Hospitality Services
Address: 158, Adekunle Fajuyi Way, G.R.A., Ikeja, Lagos
Tel: (01) 4979160-9 (10L)

TAMUNO GEORGE & COMPANY
Business: Chartered Accountants, Auditing and Accounting Services, Finance & Management Consultancy
Address: 11A, Alfred Rewane (Kingsway) Rd, Ikoyi, Lagos
Tel: (01) 2694241, 2694242, 2615173 **Fax:** (01) 2694141
Website: www.tgeorge-co.com
Contact: Mr. T. N. George - MD/CEO

TAN'MO PHARMACEUTICALS LIMITED
Business: Marketing of Pharmaceutical Products
Address: 9B, Abimbola Awoliyi Close, off Kasumu Ekemode Street, off Saka Tinubu Str, Victoria Island, Lagos
Tel: (01) 2700191, 7764391 **Fax:** (01) 2614994
E-mail: info@tanmopharm.com
Website: www.tanmopharm.com

TANDATA SYSTEMS LIMITED
Business: Sales of UPS, Industrial Batteries, Stabilizers, Lightning & Voltage Surge Protectors
Address: 106, Norman Williams Street, S.W. Ikoyi, Lagos
Tel: (01) 2693300, 2964693 **Fax:** (01) 2694693, 7599729
E-mail: tandata@nova.net.ng
Contact: Mrs. B. O. Ikupa - Chairman/CEO
M.O. Abiola - GM (Engineering & Operations)

TANO AGENCY AND SHIPPING COMPANY LIMITED
Business: Clearing and Forwarding Agency, Shipping/Consultancy Services, Supply of Industrial Materials, Projects Handling
Address: 3, Itapeju Street, Apapa, Lagos
Tel: (01) 5870759, 5874848, 7749949, 7756536, 08023200354 **Fax:** (01) 5870759, 5874848
E-mail: jintano@linkserve.com
Contact: Mr. J. B. Tanaruno - Chairman/CEO

TANORTH TANNERY LIMITED
Business: Tannery
Address: Plot 70, Sharada Industrial Estate Phase III, Kano
Tel: (064) 667350-2 (3 L) **Fax:** (064) 666812, 669580
Contact: Mohammed Osman El-Tayeb - Chairman
Hussuin Fahez Mahaloude - MD/CEO

TANTALIZERS NIGERIA LIMITED
Business: Catering Services, Fast-Food Outlets
Address: Makay Plaza, 21,Road, I Close, Festac Town, Lagos
Tel: (01) 4707102, 4707383 **Fax:** (01) 5893282
E-mail: tantalizers@tantalizersnig.com
Contact: Mr. Folu Ayeni - Chairman
Mrs. Bose Ayeni - MD/CEO

TANU GROUP (NIGERIA) LIMITED
Business: Manufacturing of Adhesives and Glues, Importation of Automobile Batteries and Bakery
Address: Km. 1, Opobo Road, Ehere Village, Ogbor Hill, Aba
Tel: (082) 220798, 226766, 226300 **Fax:** (082) 226751
Contact: Sir T. C. Umeweni KSC - Chairman/CEO

TANUS COMMUNICATIONS LIMITED
Business: Advertising, Event Management, Media/Public Consultancy, Printing and Publishing
Address: 4, Ola-Ayeni Street, Ikeja, Lagos
Tel: (01) 4960549, 4970893 **Fax:** (01) 4975964
E-mail: info@tanuscomms.com
Website: www.tanuscomms.com
Contact: Dr. Yemi Ogunbiyi - Exec. Chairman

TAPROM ENGINEERING LIMITED
Business: Marketing of Hydraulic Equipment (Pumps, Motors, Valves, Cranes, Forklifts, Crushers)
Address: 12, Abraham Adesanya Street, (formerly Douala Road), Apapa, Lagos
Tel: (01) 5870324, 5871005, 5804102, 7762672, 08023138191 **Fax:** (01) 5458990
E-mail: t_opute@tapromeng.com
Website: www.tapromeng.com
Contact: Mr. Yausa Emejonm - Chairman
Mr. Tahiru Opute - MD/CEO

TARA SYSTEMS LIMITED
Business: Software Development, Communications Systems Integration, Oracle Relational Database Management and Training, Internet Service Provider
Address: 6, Broad Street (9th Floor), Lagos
Tel: (01) 2600340 **Fax:** (01) 2600349
Website: www.metrong.com
Contact: Mr. Seni Williams - MD/CEO

TARABA INVESTMENT & PROPERTIES LIMITED
Business: Investment Banking, Development Finance Institution, Investment Promotion
Address: Investment House, 134, Hammaruwa Way, Jalingo
Tel: (079) 22602, 22635 **Fax:** (079) 22635

TARABAROZ FISHERIES LIMITED
Business: Fishing and Shrimping
Address: Tin-Can Island Port (2nd Gate), Apapa, Lagos
Tel: (01) 5452568, 5804574, 5878011 **Fax:** (01) 5878223
Contact: Barr. Musa Danjuma - Chairman
Mr. G. Singh - MD/CEO

TARAKU MILLS LIMITD
Business: Processing of Vegetable Oils, Feeds & Meals
Address: Km. 74, Makurdi-Enugu Road, Taraku, Benue State, P.O.Box 1917, Makurdi
Contact: Dr. Allan Ajonye - Chairman
Mr. Jonathan I. Ichaver - MD/CEO

TARGET INTERNATIONAL LIMITED
Business: Finance, Trade and Procurement, Importation and Marketing of Airconditioners, Medical Equipment, X-Ray Films and Consumables
Address: 22, Kofo Abayomi Avenue, Apapa, Lagos
Tel: (01) 5878373, 5455715, 08023093163, 08023146065, 08032085660, 08033342076 **Fax:** (01) 5878373
E-mail: taargtint2002@yahoo.com
targtint@nova.net.ng
* 93, Cameron Road, Aba
Contact: Mazi E. K. O. Ivi - Chairman/CEO

TARGET TRAVEL LIMITED
Business: Travel Agency
Address: Big Leaf House (1st Floor), 7, Oyin Jolayemi Street, Victoria Island, Lagos
Tel: (01) 2612496, 2616549, 4618910, 4618911, 7745482, 08033024237, 08033074171, 08033182644, 08033223072, 08033475672 **Fax:** (01) 2627819
E-mail: taarget_travl@hotmail.com
target@intracom.net.ng
Contact: Mrs. M. O. Adekunle - MD/CEO

TARPAULIN INDUSTRIES (W. A.) LIMITED
Business: Manufacture of Tarpaulin and Industrial Uniforms
Address: 8, Burma Road, Apapa, Lagos
Tel: (01) 5876470, 5876024, 5874623 **Fax:** (01) 5874197
Contact: Mr. A. Agudah - MD/CEO

TAS SYSTEMS LIMITED
Business: Sales & Service of Radio Communication Equipment
Address: Communication House, Km. 17, Lagos-Badagry Expressway (Agric Bus-Stop), opp Volkswagen Football Ground, Ojo, Festac Town, Lagos
Tel: (01), 08033192791, 08033221647, 08033243642, 08034044159, 08044180592 **Fax:** (01) 5891240
E-mail: taslinky2k@hotmail.com
Contact: Chief (Dr.) R. O. Attah - Chairman/CEO

TASADOS (NIGERIA) LIMITED
Business: Project Managers, Building & Estate Development
Address: Plot 245, Malanje Street, Wuse Zone 4, Abuja
Tel: (09) 2340168, 5232332, 08034445566, 08034446655

TASK GRAPHICS LIMITED
Business: Digital Colour Separation (Scanning, Photo-Image Manipulation, Design and Proof)
Address: 93A, Opebi Road, Ikeja, Lagos
Tel: (01) 7733445, 08033023175, 08033257549,
Contact: Mr. Amos Edeaghe - Chairman/CEO

TASK SYSTEMS LIMITED
Business: Distribution, Sales and Maintenance of Computer Systems, Peripherals, Software and Accessories. Computer Engineering, Training
Address: 25A, Karimu Kotun Street, Victoria Island, Lagos
Tel: (01) 2621997, 2621232-3 (2L), 2622872, 7754001
Fax: (01) 2622871
E-mail: sales@task.com.ng
Website: www.task.com.ng
* Technology House, 22B, Old Aba Road, Artillery Junction, Port Harcourt
Tel: (084) 610805, 610807, 610811
* Plot 653, Djibouti Close, Zone A8, off Adetokunbo Ademola Crescent, Wuse II, Abuja
Tel: (09) 5238613, 5238614 **Fax:** (09) 5238614
E-mail: task.ab@task.com.ng
Contact: Mr. Leo Stan Ekeh - Chairman
Mr. Dave Ibelegbu - MD/CEO

TASTEE POT LIMITED
Business: Fast-Food Outlets, Catering Services
Address: 49C, Marina, by Martins Street, Lagos
Tel: (01) 2641616, 2642626, 2664826
* 21, Opebi Road, Ikeja, Lagos
Tel: (01) 4702258, 4930565, 4930935

TASTY TIME NIGERIA LIMITED
Business: Production of Foods, Drinks and Plastic Products
Address: 15/17, Ogaolosinrin St (Olude B-Stop), Ipaja, Lagos
Tel: (01) 7745518

TATEC INTERBIZ LIMITED
Business: Civil Power, Marine and Mechanical Engineering Consultancy Services, Export/Import of Agro-Allied Products and Solid Minerals

Address: 30/32, Creek Road (2nd Floor), Apapa, Lagos
Tel: (01) 4817663, 5451233, 5457508, 7741779, 7748099, 7749622, 7753045 |**Fax:** (01) 5451037, 5451233
E-mail: tatecprojects@tatec.net
Website: www.tatec.net
Contact: Mr. Tunde Abrahams - Chairman/CEO

TAURUS NIGERIA LIMITED
Business: Shipping, Clearing & Forwarding
Address: 18A, Pelewura Crescent, off Kofo Abayomi Avenue, Apapa, Lagos
Tel: (01) 5803790-4 (L), 5871264 **Fax:** (01) 5871064
* 22, Circular Road, Presidential Estate, G.R.A. Phase II, Port Harcourt
Tel: (084) 232251, 08033017231

TAVIA TECHNOLOGIES LIMITED
Business: E-Commerce Consultancy Services, Web & Wireless Solutions, Website Design Services
Address: Motorways Centre (Penthouse B), 1, Motorways Avenue, opp. 7up Factory Alausa, Lagos
Tel: (01) 4934145-6 (2L), 7736783, 08032090302
Fax: (01) 4934148
E-mail: info@taviatech.com
Website: www.taviatech.com

TAYLEK DRUGS COMPANY LIMITED
Business: Manufacture & Distribution of Pharmaceutical Products and Cosmetics
Address: Plot 8, Block M, Abimbola Street, Isolo Industrial Estate, Isolo, Lagos
Tel: (01) 4525961, 4526037 **Fax:** (01) 4528797
E-mail: taylek@infoweb.abs.net
taylek@multilinks.com
Contact: Ambassador T. A. Olu Otunla - Chairman
Mr. Stonjan Satej - MD/CEO

TAYLOR COMMUNICATIONS SOLUTIONS LIMITED
Business: Wireless Internet Access and Telecommunications
Address: Western House (18th Floor), 8/10, Broad St, Lagos
Tel: (01) 2630553, 2631097
E-mail: tcsnetwork@execs.com
adegoketaylor@hotmail.com
Contact: Mr. Adegoke Taylor - Chairman/MD

TBWA\CONCEPT LIMITED
Business: Advertising, Marketing and Communications
Address: 77, Samuel Adedoyin Avenue, off Ajose Adeogun Street, Victoria Island, Lagos
Tel/Fax: (01) 2610745, 2619071
E-mail: info@tbwaconcept.com
Website: www.tbwaconcept.com
Contact: Mr. Kelechi Nwosu - Client Services Direcror

T-COMMS NIGERIA LIMITED
Business: Mobile Trunking Radio Network Services, Sales of Digital-Wireless Telecommunication Equipment, Internet Services
Address: 16/17, Water Corporation Road, Victoria Is., Lagos
Tel: (01) 3204164, 7901265
E-mail: t-comms@usa.net
Website: www.t-comms.org
Contact: Mr. Imoukhede Ohikhuare - Chairman

TDI COMMUNICATIONS LIMITED
Business: Sales & Installation of Telecommunication Equipment, Provision of Community Networks/Rural Telephony Services, Pre & Post-Paid Telephony and Internet Services
Address: WAPIC House, 119, Awolowo Road, Ikoyi, Lagos
Tel: (01) 2694529, 2670355, 08033963990
Fax: (01) 2670355
E-mail: telekomdirect@hotmail.com
* McLewis Plaza (Suite A33), IBB Way, Wuse II, Abuja
Tel: (09) 5237744
Contact: Mr. E. Bassey Udosen - MD/CEO

TDT LIMITED
Business: Colour-Processing Laboratory, Photography, Digital Colour Separation
Address: TDT Photo Plaza, 51, Kofo Abayomi Avenue, Apapa, Lagos
Tel: (01) 5455819, 5455820 **Fax:** (01) 5455820
E-mail: tdtgraphics@metrong.com

TECHNAE (NIGERIA) LIMITED
Business: Manufacturers of Neon Signs, Illuminated & Non-Illuminated Plastic/Metal/Flex-Face Signs, Bill-boards & Directory Signs
Address: 6/8, Warehouse Road, Apapa, Lagos
Tel: (01) 5452935, 5877230 **Fax:** (01) 5450026-78 (2 L)
Contact: Mr. A. R. B. Adewale - Chairman/CEO

TECHNO OIL LIMITED
Business: Marketing of Petroleum Products, Lubricants & Chemicals
Address: 26, Pelewura Way, Apapa, Victoria Island, Lagos
Tel: (01) 5878387, 5453707, 8042877, 08033007940
Fax: (01) 5453916, 5450026
E-mail: info@technooil.com
sales@technooil.com
Website: www.technooil.com
Contact: Dr. J. C. Nnadi - Chairman
Mrs. Nkechi. O. Obi - GM/CEO

TECHNOCRIME NIGERIA LIMITED
Business: Security Services, Consultancy
Address: 77, Awolowo Road (3rd Floor), by Mobil Filling Station, S. W. Ikoyi, Lagos
Tel: (01) 7741898, 730532, 4705008, 2881203
E-mail: techsecu@nigol.net.ng
* 45, Isiokpo Street, D-Line, Port Harcourt
* Bataiya Plaza (Suite 28), opp. Corporate Affairs Commission, Plot 1271, Area 11, Garki, Abuja
Contact: A. U. Azuya - Chairman
Patricia Aghayere - Chief of Biz. Dev & Strategy

TECHNO-LOGIC NIGERIA LIMITED
Business: Technical Education Centre, System Implementation, Internet Services, Network Design, Networking and Data Communication, Structured Cabling, Application Software Development and Consultancy, Prometric & VUC Testing Centre
Address: 8B, Oko-Awo Close, off Karimu Kotun Street, Victoria Island, Lagos
Tel: (01) 2610467 **Fax:** (01) 2610462

E-mail: info@techno-logic.com
Website: www.techno-logic.com
Contact: Mrs. Josephine Mikkelborg - MD/CEO

TECHNOLOGY DISTRIBUTIONS LIMITED
Business: Infomation Technology Products Distribution
Address: 13A, Idowu Martins Street, Victoria Island, Lagos
Tel: (01) 2626051-3 (3L), 2624828-30 (3L), 3201490
Fax: (01) 2626054
E-mail: td@tdafrica.com
td@nigol.net.ng
* Plot 633, Djibouti Street, Wuse II, Abuja.
Tel: (09) 5236139 **Fax:** (09) 5236140
E-mail: tdad@tdafrica.com
* 10, Simbiat Abiola Road, Ikeja, Lagos.
* 3, Babatunde St, off Ogunlana Drive, S/L, Lagos.
Tel: (01) 2881156
* Technology House, 22, Old Aba Rd, P/ Harcourt.
Tel/Fax: (084) 611932.
Contact: Chief Leo Stan Ekeh - Group MD/CEO
Mrs. Chioma Ekeh - MD

TECHNOLOGY EXCHANGE LIMITED
Business: Information & Technology Management Services
Address: 54, Corporation Drive, Dolphin Estate, Ikoyi, Lagos
Tel: (01) 2697440, 2694352 **Fax:** (01) 2694352
E-mail: technex@cyberspace.net.ng
technex@technex.com
Website: www.techexng.com
Contact: Engr. (Dr.) Temilola Kehinde - Chairman/CEO

TECHO-QUIP LIMITED
Business: Design, Fabrication, Installation and Service of Agro-Allied Processing & Industrial Machines
Address: 14/16, Olushola Ikare Street, off Ogidan Street (Alake Bus-Stop), Idimu, Lagos
Tel: (01) 2904714, 7745648, 08022904222, 08033056708
E-mail: techoquip@yahoo.com
Website: www.techoquipltd.com
Contact: Engr. (Dr.) S. I. Makinwa - Chairman/CEO

TECIL COMPUTERS LIMITED
Business: Sales of Computers and Peripherals, IT Training
Address: Gotheg Plaza, 14, Port Harcourt/Aba Express Road, 1st Artillery Junction, Rumuogba, Port Harcourt
Tel: (084) 610820, 08033154116, 08043126888, 08046101062 **Fax:** (084) 239613

TECNO MECHANICAL (NIGERIA) LIMITED
Business: Manufacturig of Silencer Cabins for Generation
Address: Km. 50, Lagos-Abeokuta Road, Pakoto Area, Ifo, Ogun State
Tel: (01) 4704799, 08034016620 **Fax:** (01) 4972755
E-mail: thermocoustic@hotmail.com
Contact: Prince Doyin Adesida - Sales Manager

TECNOBAT FITTINGS & FIXTURES LIMITED
Business: Manufacturing & Marketing of Furniture, Importation of Furniture Fittings & Fixtures
Address: 46, New Market Road, Onitsha
Tel: (046) 410555, 08033133633 **Fax:** (046) 414635
E-mail: tecnobatltd@aol.com
Contact: H.R.H Igwe Peter C. Ezenwa - Chairman

TECO GROUP
Business: Projects Development Engineers; Palm Oil Mills and Palm Kernel Plants; Oil & Gas Services, Foundry & Metallurgical Works; Sales of Poultry-Processing Equipment, Pumps, Electric Motors & Automation Products, Manpower Services, Turnkey Projects Management & Training
Address: Obafemi Awolowo House (1st Floor), 29/31, Obafemi Awolowo Way, Ikeja, Lagos
Tel: (01) 4936619, 2885009 **Fax:** (01) 4936619
E-mail: tecogroup@cyberspace.net.ng
tecogroup@beta.linkserve.com
Website: www.tecolimited.com
* Teco Industrial Estate, Akure-Benin Expressway, Owo, Ondo State.
Tel: (051) 241455, 241108, 241621 **Fax:** (051) 241621
Contact: Engr. Charles A. Aladewolu - Chairman/CEO

TECON OIL SERVICES LIMITED
Business: Oil Industruy Services
Address: 47, Yeshayahu Lasode Crescent (behind Mobil Station), Victoria Island Annex, Lagos.
Tel: (01) 2618371, 4803413, 7918094 **Fax:** (01) 2618371
E-mail: teconoilng@micro.com.ng
ccm.teconoilng@micro.com.ng
* Plot 41, Trans-Amadi Ind. Layout, Port Harcourt
Tel: (084) 483006-7 (2L), 480863 **Fax:** (084) 485273
E-mail: teconph@infoweb.abs.net
* 69/71, Airport Road, Warri
Tel/Fax: (053) 255831, 255832, Shell Ext. 50448
E-mail: teconwr@infoweb.abs.net
Contact: Casmir Maduafokwa - President/CEO

TEEOMY SYSTEMS LIMITED
Business: Sales, Maintenance and Repairs of Computers, Software Engineering, Computer Engineering and Networking, Training
Address: 18, Otigba St, Obafemi Awolowo Way, Ikeja, Lagos
Tel: (01) 4935906, 08023229297, 0033597089
Contact: Mr. Tunde Omitogun - Chairman

TEFLON INTERNATIONAL NIGERIA LIMITED
Business: Manufacture of Plastic Shopping Bags & Disposable, Single-Use Sterile Syringes
Address: 13-15, Wharf Road, Apapa, Lagos
Tel: (01) 5877526, 5875413, 5874279 **Fax:** (01) 5877526
Contact: A. O. Martins - Group Executive Director

TEHILA COMMUNICATIONS LIMITED
Business: Sales of GSM Phones & Accessories
Address: 2/4, Abebe Village Road, Iganmu, Lagos
Tel: (01) 5456258, 08022008888 Fax: (01) 5837187

TEJU GROUP OF COMPANIES
Business: Manufacturing, Healthcare and Medical Services, Petroleum Products Distribution and Marketing, Farming, Hotel/Property Development and Management.
Address: 18/22, Ilupeju Bye-Pass, Ilupeju, Lagos
Tel: (01) 4960262, 4964420, 4960855
E-mail: tejufoam@nova.net.ng
Contact: Oba (Dr.) Adewale A. Tejuoso - Chairman
Prince (Dr.) Lanre Tejuoso - Exec. Director

TEJUDE PHOTO COMPANY LIMITED
Business: Importation and Sales of Photographic Materials, Equipment and Accessories, Sales of NORITSU Minilabs and Accessories
Address: 108B, Ojuelegba Road, Surulere, Lagos
Tel: (01) 480049, 08033019197, 08046130646, 08055158748
E-mail: tejude@linkserve.com.ng
Contact: Mr. Ted O. Offor - Chairman

TEKNO NIGERIA LIMITED
Business: Sales of Furniture
Address: 30, Allen Avenue, Ikeja, Lagos
Tel: (01) 8178198
E-mail: teknonig@infoweb.abs.net

TEKNOKLEEN LIMITED
Business: Sales and Distribution of Industrial Cleaning Machines, Products and Accessories, Home, Office and Industrial Cleaning Services, Training Courses for Cleaning Staff, Pest Control Services
Address: 37A, Bode Thomas Street, Surulere, Lagos
Tel: (01) 5456237, 5830154, 7744948, 08023116411
Fax: (01) 5850837
E-mail: tekno@infoweb.abs.net
* Plot 283, Addis Ababa Cr, Wuse Zone 4, Abuja.
Tel: (09) 5230912
Contact: Iheanyi Nzekwe - MD/CEO

TELECOM TECHNOLOGIES INTERNATIONAL LIMITED
Business: IT and Telecommunication Engineering Services
Address: Yashua Plaza, beside AP Plaza, Adetokunbo Ademola Crescent, Wuse II, Abuja
Tel: (09) 6707976
E-mail: info@ttilimited.com
* Stallion House (13th Floor), 2, Ajose Adeogun Street, Victoria Island, Lagos
Tel: (01) 2626942, 614923 **Fax:** (01) 614923
Contact: Chief Johnson Ndubuisi Asinugo - Chairman/CEO

TELEDOM INTERNATIONAL LIMITED
Business: Provision of IP Broadband Wireless Access Solutions, Wireless LAN and Internet Facilities, VSAT/DVB Systems Integration, Turnkey IT Projects, Human Resource Development
Address: 24, Bamishile Street, off Allen Avenue, Ikeja, Lagos
Tel: (01) 4976220, 4976229, 4977892, 7730528, 8129467, 08023010709 **Fax:** (01) 4976229
E-mail: teledom@rcl.nig.com
Website: www.teledominternational.com
Contact: Dr. Emmanuel E. Ekuwem - Vice Chairman/CEO

TELEMOBILE (NIGERIA) LIMITED
Business: VSAT Private Network Links, Phone-Links, Phone-Link Systems, Radio Communication Engineering, Value-Added Internet Networks, Sales & Installation of PABX Systems
Address: 30, Plateau Road/Creek Road, Apapa, Lagos
Tel: (01) 5874418, 5874402, 7738654, 08034040407
Fax: (01) 5871401
E-mail: sbabalola@telemobile-nigeria.com
Contact: Alh. S. O. Babalola - Chairman/CEO
Mr. D. O. Ibrahim - Finance/Admin. Manager

TELGATE COMMUNICATIONS LIMITED
Business: Sales of Mobile Phones and Radio Network Systems, Telecentre Services, Sales & Installation of Covert Security Systems and IPSky V-SAT, Internet Services
Address: Glitter House, 214C, Eti-Osa Way, Dolphin Estate, Ikoyi, Lagos
Tel: (01) 4614334, 4711331, 2645252, 2693597
Fax: (01) 2693590, 4614335
E-mail: info@telgateonline.net
telgate@telgteonline.net
Website: www.telegatecom.net
* Flat 4, Grema Estate, Obinuchi Street, GRA Phase II, Port Harcourt
Contact: Col. Babatunde O. Soluade (rtd.) - Chairman/CEO

TELIPOINT NIGERIA LIMITED
Business: Provision of Telecommication Services (Payphone, Voice, Mail, Paging and Smartcard Applications)
Address: 48, Raymond Njoku Street, S.W. Ikoyi, Lagos
Tel: (01) 2690855, 08034007630
Fax: (01) 2693646, 2693149
E-mail: telecard@infoweb.abs.net
Contact: Dr. Folarin Gbadebo-Smith - Chairman
Mr. Francis Chikelu - Chief Operating Officer

TELL COMMUNICATIONS LIMITED
Business: NewsMedica Publishing
Address: Textile Labour House, 10, Acme Road, Ogba Industrial Estate, Ogba, Ikeja, Lagos
Tel: (01) 7747910, 4932497, 7745582, 4932498, 4923499
Fax: (01) 4932494
E-mail: tell@cyberspace.com.ng
tell@infoweb.abs.net
editor@tell.org
tel-lib@beta.linkserve.com
Website: www.tell.org
Contact: Nosa Igiebor - Editor-In-Chief
Onome Osifo - Whiskey - Managing Editor

TELNET NETWORK SERVICES
Business: Telecommunications Network Services
Address: Plot 242, Kofo Abayomi St, Victoria Island, Lagos
Tel: (01) 2611729, 2619954, 3200580-4 (5L)
Fax: (01) 2619945
E-mail: info@iteco.com
Website: www.telnetng.com
Contact: Mr. Uche Ejiogu - MD/CEO

TEMPAS CONSULTANTS
Business: Civil and Structural Engineering Consultants
Address: 4A, Iya Oloye Crescent, off Ikorodou Road, Onigbongbo, Maryland, Lagos
Tel: (01) 4964993, 4964255 **Fax:** (01) 4964255
Contact: Engr. Y. K. Adeyemo - Partner
Engr. H. F. Adigun - Partner

TEMREX NIGERIA LIMITED
Business: Financial Intermediation, Export of Agricultural Commodities
Address: ED House (7th Floor), 47, Marina, Lagos
Tel: (01) 2663656, 2664231, 08033232689
Fax: (01) 2664231

E-mail: temrex@hyperia.com
Contact: Mr. Remi Olufe - Exec. Chairman

TENDERLOIN ENTERPRISES LIMITED
(Whispering Palms Holiday Resort)
Business: Holiday Resort, Hospitality Services
Address: Iworo, off Lagos-Badagry Expressway, Badagry L.G.A., Lagos State
Tel: (01) 7741279, 08033256216, 08037228283
E-mail: whisperingpalms2002@yahoo.com
whisperingpalms2003@yahoo.com
* 1, James Robertson Street, Surulere, Lagos
Tel: (01) 7741279, 5851597
Contact: Prof. Deji Femi-Pearse - Chairman/CEO

TENEX GROUP NIGERIA LIMITED
Business: Import & Export, Whole Plant Consultancy
Address: 11A, Olosa Street, off Karimu Kotun St, V/I, Lagos
Tel: (01) 2621199 **Fax:** (01) 2624579
E-mail: tenexgroup@nigol.net.ng
Website: www.tenexgroupng.com
Contact: Chief Tochukwu E. Anako - Chairman/CEO

TEPSI (INVESTMENT) LIMITED
Business: Security Surveillance and Communication Equipment Sales and Installation, Consultancy
Address: 28, 7up Road, Oluyole Estate, Ibadan
Tel: (02) 2319081, 090-418764, 08023218536, 08034535090, 0042690822 **Fax:** (02) 2314977
E-mail: Tepsi@skannet.com
Contact: Mr Rotimi Ibironke - MD/CEO

TEQUILA\1:1 NIGERIA
Business: Direct Marketing Communications, Relationship Marketing, Data Bureau Services
Address: 22A, Olatunbosun Street, Sam Shonibare Estate, Mobolaji Bank-Anthony Way, Lagos
Tel: (01) 4978408, 4978409, 4700093, 5550519, 08033214092 **Fax:** (01) 4978409
E-mail: teqim@infoweb.abs.net
onetoone@intracom.net.ng
Website: www.tequila121.com
Contact: Mr. George E. Thorpe - Chairman
Mr. Rotimi Olaniyan - MD/CEO

TERMEX LIMITED
Business: Sales & Service of Computer Hardware, Peripherals, Consumables and Networking Equipments
Address: 47, Awolowo Road, S. W. Ikoyi, Lagos
Tel: (01) 2673816-7 (2 L), 2904028, 4701473, 4732643, 08023034403 **Fax:** (01) 2673817
E-mail: sales@termex.com
termex@linkserve.com
Website: www.termex.com
* 21, Kodesoh Street, Ikeja, Lagos
Tel: (01) 4701473, 4932473
Contact: Mr. W. K. O. Badiru - Chairman/CEO

TERRA ENERGY SERVICES LIMITED
Business: Oilfield Engineering Services
Address: Plot 147A, Younis Bashorun Street, Victoria Island, Lagos
Tel: (01) 4619245, 7732076 **Fax:** (01) 4616305

TERYTEX NIGERIA LIMITED
Business: Manufacturing of Towels, Bedsheets, Napkins and Hank Yam
Address: 134, Barde/Independence Road, Bompai Industrial Estate, Kano
Tel: (064) 646293, 634461, 08023147288
E-mail: terytex@hotmail.com
Contact: Mr. P. H. Kabra - MD/CEO

TESNIC NIGERIA LIMITED
Business: Sales, Supply, Repairs, Servicing & Maintenance of Audio-Visual Aids, Training Equipment, Presentation Aids, Medical & Surgical Equipment, Office-Services Equipment and Accessories
Address: Obafemi Awolowo House, 29, Obafemi Awolowo Way, Ikeja, Lagos
Tel: (01) 4975215, 7927902, 08037212638
Fax: (01) 4972047
E-mail: tes_nic@yahoo.com
* Plot 814, Uyo Crescent, off Obafemi Awolowo Street, Area 11, Garki, Abuja.
Tel: (09) 2346073
Contact: Dr. Jude I. Duru-Onweni - Exec. Chairman

TESS TRAVELS LIMITED
Business: Travel Agents and Tour Operations
Address: Broking House, 1, Alh. Jimoh Odutola Road, Dugbe, Ibadan
Tel: (02) 2410942 **Fax:** (02) 2410230
* Shop 19A, Tafawa Balewa Square Complex, Lagos
Tel: (01) 2634849, 2634083 **Fax:** (01) 2633540
Contact: Mrs. Teresa Ezobi - MD/CEO

TETHYS PLANTGERIA COMPANY LIMITED
Business: Offshore Oilfield Engineering Services
Address: Plot 278, Trans-Amadi Ind. Layout, Port Harcourt
Tel: (084) 233285, 236956 **Fax:** (084) 236778
E-mail: comet@micro.com.ng
* NAL-COMET House, 4, Hinderer Road, Apapa G.R.A., Apapa, Lagos
Tel: (01) 5874926, 2645201, 2634284
Contact: Mr. Musa Danjuma - Chairman/CEO
Mr. P. L. Carrodano - MD/CEO

TETRA PAK (WEST AFRICA) LIMITED
Business: Manufacture of Paper Packaging Products for Liquid Foods and Drinks
Addresss: Elephant Cement House (3rd Floor), ASSBIFI Rd, Central Business District, Alausa, Ikeja, Lagos
Tel: (01) 4922857-8 (2L) **Fax:** (01) 4922858
Website: www.tetrapak.com

TETRAZZINI CHICKEN RESTAURANT
Business: Operation of Fast-Food Outlets
Address: 4, Osolo Way, Off Murtala Mohammed International Airpot Road, Ajao Estate, Lagos
Tel: (01) 4701227, 4824376
E-mail: info@tetrazzinifood.com
Website: www.tetrazzinifood.com
Contact: Princess Rachael Okonkwo - MD/CEO

TEXACO NIGERIA OUTER SHELF LIMITED
Business: Exploration and Production of Oil & Gas

Address: 36, Gerrard Road, Ikoyi, Lagos
Tel: (01) 2671816, 2690227-36 (10 L) **Fax:** (01) 2693990

TEXACO NIGERIA PLC
Business: Blending of Lubricants; Manufacture of Greases and Petroleum Jelly; Marketing & Distribution of Refined Petroleum Products
Address: 8, Macarthy Street, Lagos
Tel: (01) 2600540-9 (10L), 4614500 **Fax:** (01) 2632231
* 5, Alapata St, (off Dockyard Road), Apapa, Lagos
Tel: (01) 5455492
Contact: Mr. James J. Harkness - MD/CEO
Mrs. U. C. Ifejika - Company Secretary

TEXEN LIMITED
Business: Design and Marketing of Men's Garments & Accessories
Address: 130, Obafemi Awolowo Way, Lagos
Tel: (01) 4973119
Contact: Mr. N. Tex Egbedi - Chairman/CEO

TFP GLOBAL NETWORK LIMITED
Business: Production of Film, Documentaries and Commercials, Studio Facilities and Movie Editing, Equipment Leasing, Distribution of Films
Address: 2, Alh. Shittu Street, off Nuru Oniwo Street, by NEPA Bus-Stop, Aguda Surulere, Lagos
Tel: (01) 470374, 08023062814, 08033329711
E-mail: tecobenson2@yahoo.com
Contact: Mr. Teco Benson - MDCEO

THE ANCHOR NEWSPAPER LIMITED
Business: Newspaper Publishing
Address: 100, Kudirat Abiola (Oregun) Road, Pacific Holdings Building, Oregun, Ikeja, Lagos
Tel: (01) 4971381 **Fax:** (01) 4971380
E-mail: info.anchor@prodigy2000.com
Contact: Nata Nwose - Business Dev. Manager

THE ASSOCIATION OF NIGERIAN CO-OPERATIVE EXPORTERS LIMITED (ANCE)
Business: Exporters of Agricultural Commodites, Clearing Agents
Address: ANCE Building, Magazine Road, Jericho, Ibadan
Tel: (02) 2412600, 08037182714 **Fax:** (02) 2411050
* 17, Wharf Road, Apapa, Lagos
Contact: Chief J. O. Olorunyolemi - Chairman
Prince O. Abiba - GM/CEO

THE BEDDING GROUP
Business: Metal Fabricators, Road Construction
Address: 55, Adeniyi Jones Avenue, Ikeja, Lagos
Tel: (01) 4973118, (090) 401401, 402865
Fax: (01) 4960508
Contact: Mr. Sylvester Osadolor Odigie - MD/CEO

THE BRIDGE CLINIC LIMITED
Business: Medical & Healthcare Services (Reproductive Health Consultants & Specialists)
Address: Plot 1397A, Tiamiyu Savage Street, off Olosa Street, Victoria Island, Lagos
Tel: (01) 2623268, 2610686, 7745626, 4710990
Fax: (01) 2616505
E-mail: bridge@om.metrong.com
Website: www.thebridgeclinic.com
Contact: Dr. Richardson Ajayi - Medical Director/CEO

THE CANDEL COMPANY LIMITED
Business: Formulation, Marketing and Distribution of Agricultural Chemicals
Address: 8B, 2nd Close, off Ligali Ayorinde Avenue, Victoria Island, Lagos
Tel: (01) 4619170-2 (3L) **Fax:** (01) 4617173
E-mail: candel@cyberspace.net.ng
Contact: Charles Anudu - MD/CEO

THE CARDIAC CENTRE
Business: Medical Consultancy and Health Science
Address: 12, Idowu Martins Street, Victoria Island, Lagos
Tel: (01) 2621234, 262144, 2610445 **Fax:** (01) 2610442
E-mail: cardiaccentre@linkserve.com.ng
Contact: Dr. Adeyemi Onabowale - MD/CEO

THE CAXTON PRESS (WEST AFRICA) LIMITED
Business: Printing of Textbooks, Sales of Stationery Items
Address: Cocoa House, Oba Adebimpe Rd, Dugbe, Ibadan
Tel: (02) 2414183, 2414229, 2410869, 2414491
Fax: (02) 2413000
* Eleyele Road, Ibadan
Contact: Engr. Oni Abiola - Chairman
Mr. O. A. Adesina - MD/CEO

THE CHAIR CENTRE LIMITED
Business: Importation and Marketing of Office Equipment
Address: House of His Glory, Lekki-Epe Expressway (Jazz Bus-Stop), Lekki, Lagos
Tel: (01)5555201-4 (4L), 4707251
E-mail: cclagos@yahoo.com
Website: www.chaircentre.com
Contact: Mrs. Ibukunoluwa Awosika - MD/CEO
Bose Ikemefuna - GM

THE COOPERS GROUP LIMITED
Business: Manufacturing, Import & Export Managers, Commodity Brokers, Management & Marketing Services Consultants, Estate Developers, Clearing & Forwarding Agents
Address: Coppers House, 3, Bishop Anyogu Street, Uwani, Enugu
Tel: (042) 253051, 259592, 08033419851
Fax: (042) 253048
E-mail: coopers@infoweb.abs.net
*104, Western Avenue, Ojuelegba, Surulere, Lagos
Tel: (01) 5847753, 08037055874
Contact: Chief Ben Ezeibe - Chairman/CEO

THE CORNERSTONE ORGANISATION GROUP
Business: Financial Service; Real Estate Developers, Business Development; Import of Foods; Cement Distribution
Address: 38/40, Burma Road, Apapa, Lagos
Tel: (01) 8733911, 873888

THE CORPORATE FINANCE GROUP LIMITED
Business: Investment Banking and Venture Capital Services, Issuing House, Broker-Dealer, Investment Managers & Advisors

Address: Cowrie Creek View, 84, Ozumba Mbadiwe Street, beh. Mr. Bigg's Building, Victoria Island, Lagos
Tel: (01) 7737157, 3200881, 08034002028
E-mail: info@i-cfg.com
Website: www.i-cfg.com
Contact: Mr. Oba Otudeko, MFR - Chairman

THE DAILY TIMES OF NIGERIA PLC
Business: Newspaper, Magazine & Book Publishing, Property Development, Printing and Packaging
Address: Lateef Jakande Road, Agidingbi, Ikeja, Lagos
Tel: (01) 4975598, 4977283, 34050597, 3453169
* 3/5/7, Kakawa Street, off Marina, Lagos
Contact: Dr. Yemi Farounbi - Chairman

THE DENTAL SURGERY, KADUNA
Business: Provision of Dental Health Care
Address: 7, Wurno Road, G.R.A., opp. Kaduna Media Corporation, Kaduna
Tel: (062) 249738, 370742

THE DESIGN CENTR LIMITED
Business: Sales of Office Furniture
Address: The Beach Plaza, Plot 1412, Ahmad Bello Way, Victoria Island, Lagos
Tel: (01) 4702270, 2705895, 4709776, 7765785, 08033251418

THE DIET COMMUNICATIONS LIMITED
Business: Pulishing
Address: 61, Queen's Street, Sabo-Yaba, Lagos
Tel: (01) 5450538, 5450736, 866142 **Fax:** (01) 5450558
Website: www.dietnews
Contact: Mr. Tom Borha - GM

THE EXECUTIVE CYBERSCHUUL, LAGOS
Business: Infotech Training, Telecommunication and Computer Consulting, Internet Applications, Website and Network Designs
Address: 152, Ikorodu Road, (2nd Floor), Onipanu, Lagos
Tel: (01) 4971004, 08023224572 **Fax:** (01) 4972358
E-mail: tec@cyberschuul.com
Website: www.cyberschuul.com
Contact: Engr. Titi Omo-Ettu - Managing Partner/CEO

THE GRAND MIRAGE HOTEL, ABUJA
Business: Hospitality & Catering Services, Conference Facilities
Address: Plot 691, Port Harcourt Crescent, off Gimbiya Street, off Ahmadu Bello Way, Garki II, Abuja
Tel: (09) 3141311-2 (2L) **Fax:** (09) 3141310
E-mail: thegrandmirage@linkserve.com
* The Grand Mirage Hotel, Lokoja
Contact: Mr. C. D. Adeola - Chairman/CEO

THE GREAT WALL CHINENE RESTAURANT
Business: Catering & Restaurant Services
Address: Landmark Plaza, Plot 3124, IBB Way, Maitama, Abuja
Tel: (09) 4132372, 4132895, 670279, 08033493514
Fax: (09) 4132895
E-mail: gwcr@hotmail.com
* 72, Awolowo Road, S.W. Ikoyi, Lagos
Tel: (01) 2694822

THE GSM CENTRE LIMITED
Business: Distribution of GSM Mobile Phones &Accessories
Address: 7, Saka Tinubu Street, Victoria Island, Lagos
Tel: (01) 2622809, 2617261, 7753802, 7756707-9 (3 L), 775710, 08022240021 **Fax:** (01) 2617261
* Lansar House, Plot 218, Aba Road, Artillery Junction, Port Harcourt
* Plot 590H, Adetokunbo Ademola Crescent, Wuse II, Abuja
* City Plaza (Front Shop 2), Plot 596, Ahmadu Bello Way/M.Buhari Way Junction, Garki II, Abuja

THE HAJAIG GROUP
Business: Building & Civil Engineering Contractors, Manufacturing of Terrazzo Floor Tiles & Concrete Products, Confectioners, Engineering Services
Address: 16, Maigarin Road, Industrial Area, Bauchi
Tel: (077) 542039
58A, Tafawa Balewa Rd, Bompai Ind Estate, Kano
Tel: (064) 641442, 641443
E-mail: ajhajaig@inet-global.com

THE HERITAGE HOSPITAL & CARDIAC CENTRE
Business: Medical Consultancy and Health Services
Address: 12, Idowu Martins Stret, Victoria Island, Lagos
Tel: (01) 2610442
E-mail: cardiaccentre@linkserve.com
Contact: Dr. Adeyemi Onabowale - MD/CEO

THE HOUR GLASS GALLERY
Business: Art Gallery, Design & Printing Services
Address: 5, Biadou Street, off Keffi Street, S.W. Ikoyi, Lagos
Tel: (01) 2696250, 2707253, 080332016103
E-mail: hourglass@yahoo.com
Contact: Mr. Dozie Igweze

THE HONDA PLACE LIMITED
Business: Exclusive Distributors of Honda Motor Cars & Spare Parts
Address: Plot 270A, Ajose Adeogun St, Victoria Island, Lagos
Tel: (01) 2611974, 2618605, 2618090, 2623378, 7740202, 7740222, 7740737, 7744444, 7740774-6 (3L), 7751774, 7758080, 7759161, 7759166, 08022905224, 08022908474 **Fax:** (01) 2617737
E-mail: contact@honda.com.ng
hondathp@aol.com
hondanigeria@aol.com
* 7, Olu Obasanjo Road, Port Harcourt
Tel: (084) 328317
Contact: Mr. H. S. Vaswani - DMD

THE HUMANA HOSPITAL
Business: Medical and Health Care Services
Address: 9, Ashabi Cole Street, off Lateef Jakande Road, Central Business District, Alausa, Ikeja, Lagos
Tel: (01) 7745655
Contact: Chief (Dr.) Victor Obiakor - Chairman/Medical Dir.

THE JAZZHOLE LIMITED
Business: Sales of Music Recordings, Books and Magazines, Book & Poetry Readings, Recording Label
Address: Block C (Suite 4), Falomo Shopping Centre, Falomo, Ikoyi, Lagos

Tel: (01) 2692762, 4750168, 08033161857
Fax: (01) 2692762
E-mail: 105271@compuserve.com
Website: www.glendora-eculture.com
Contact: Mr. Olakunle Tejuosho - Director

THE K. O. K. VENTURES LIMITED
Business: Mechanical, Electrical & Civil Engineers
Address: 9, Trinity Close, Olodi-Apapa, Lagos
Tel: (01) 4802866, 0803300484, 08033041807, 08055222276 **Fax:** (01) 7747462
E-mail: kokengineers@yahoo.com
Contact: Chief Kalu Okereke Kalu - Chairman/CEO

THE INVESTORS' ADVISERS LIMITED
Business: Stockbroking, Financial Services
Address: Lapal House (4th Floor, Suite 5), 235, Igbosere Road, Lagos Island, Lagos
Tel/Fax: (01) 2636544
Contact: Mr. Bokime Bassey - MD/CEO

THE KING'S LIMITED
Business: Distribution of Enviro-Save Autocare Products, Sales & Installation of Cabl TV, Sales of FlatFix Autocare Products
Address: Block 13 (Suite 15), Sura Shopping Complex, Simpson Street, Lagos Island, Lagos
Tel: (01) 3202094, 3202164, 08023034646
Fax: (01) 3202164
E-mail: thekings@hyperia.com
Contact: Mr. Mike Itegboje - MD/CEO

THE LAGOON RESTAURANT
Business: Restuarant, Casino, Banquet Hall and Conference Facilities
Address: IC, Ozumba Nbadiwe Street, Victoria Island, Lagos
Tel: (01) 2611616, 2611888, 2616036, 08034002266
Contact: Mr. Marcel Chagoury - MD/CEO

THE LION OF AFRICA INSURANCE COMPANY LIMITED
Business: All Classes of Insurance Business
Address: St. Peter's House, 3, Ajele Street, Lagos
Tel: (01) 2600950-9 (10L), 2630902, 8043279-80 (2L)
Fax: (01) 2636111
E-mail: lionfinancial@asonnet.com
Contact: Mr. Godwin A. Alegieuno, FCA, FCCA - MD/CEO
Mrs. E. N. Adigwe - DGM/Chief Dev. Officer

THE MARKET RESEARCH CONSULTANCY LIMITED
Business: Marketing Research
Address: 10, Adeboye Sholanke St, off Allen Ave, Ikeja, Lagos
Tel: (01) 7741758, 4930601 **Fax:** (01) 4930601
E-mail: mrcreserach@hotmail.com
mrc@nigerianet.com
Contact: Mr. Sola Akinnagbe - Chairman/CEO

THE MONITOR NEWSPAPERS LIMITED
Business: Newspaper Publishing
Address: Lister House, M.K.O. Abiola Way (Ring Rd), Ibadan
Tel: (02) 2318869, 2318870, 2318871, 310145
Fax: (02) 2318545, 2318546
Contact: Alh. Abdul-Azeez Arisekola Alao - Chairman
Mr. Liadi Tella - MD/CEO

THE MOORHOUSE, LAGOS (Sofitel Hotels & Resorts)
Business: Hospitality, Hotel Services
Address: 1, Bankole Oki Road, Ikoyi, Lagos
Tel: (01) 2670231-9 (9L), 2690796, 2690937, 2693571, 4615409, 08035534685 **Fax:** (01) 2695263, 2690937
E-mail: mhsofitel@hyperia.com
Website: www.sofitel.com
www.hotelweb.fr

THE NEON GROUP
Business: Production & Supply of Illuminated & Non-Illuminated Signs & Paints
Address: Neon House, Km. 16, Lagos-Badagry, opp. Ojo Army Barrack, Ojo, Lagos
Tel: (01) 8127502, 4815031, 08033447944, 0034712246
E-mail: neonchidi@yahoo.com
Contact: Engr. Mensah F. C. Emegwalu - Chairman/CEO

THE NEW CARGO HANDLING COMPANY LIMITED
Business: Stevedoring and Shore Handling
Address: 17, Apapa-Oshodi Expressway (Coconut Bus-Stop), Olodi-Apapa, Lagos
Tel: (01) 4820868
Contact: Chief Fabian Umunnakwe - MD/CEO

THE NIGERIAN BANK FOR COMMERCE AND INDUSTRY
Business: Development Banking
Address: 2, Yola Street, Garki Area 7, Abuja
Tel: (09) 2346600
* 26, Idejo Street, Victoria Island, Lagos
Tel: (01) 612134, 610459, 6135511, 616769
Fax: (01) 614902
E-mail: nbci@intracomm5.com
Contact: Mr. A. I. Obi - Head (Corporate Affairs)

THE NIGERIAN GENERAL INSURANCE COMPANY PLC
Business: All Classses of Insurance
Address: 1, Nnamdi Azikiwe Street, Tinubu Square, Lagos
Tel: (01) 2663552, 2663757, 2663873, 2664698
E-mail: odua@odu-a.com
* 17, Kodesoh Street, Ikeja, Lgaos
Tel: (01) 961441-2 (3L)
* Cocoa House (1st Floor), Ibadan
Tel: (02) 2410759, 2414256
* 3, Kanta Road, Kaduna
Tel: (062) 212090
* 71, Warri/Sapele Road, Warri
Tel: (053) 231664
* 83, Ibrahim Taiwo Street, Kano
Tel: (064) 634039
Contact: Mr. J. A.Olanihun - MD/CEO

THE NIGERIAN SECURITY PRINTING & MINTING CO. LTD
Business: Production of Currency Notes & Coins, Printing of Security Documents, Commercial Printing
Address: 54, Samuel Ladoke Akintola Boulevard, Garki 11, Abuja
Tel: (09) 3149139-46 (8L) **Fax:** (09) 3149148
E-mail: nspmc@nspmc.com.ng
Website: www.nspmc.com.ng
* 26, Ahmadu Bello Way, Victoria Island, Lagos
Tel: (01) 2620646-7 (2L), 2620672-4 (3L), 2620670
Fax: (01) 2618570, 2620644, 261019, 2614139

THE NUCLEUS MARKETING COMPANY LIMITED
Business: Advertising, Marketing Communication
Address: 16, Awori Crescent, off Coker Road/Obokun Street, Ilupeju, Lagos
Tel: (01) 49668493, 4979363, 4710922 **Fax:** (01) 4968493
E-mail: thenucleus@linkserve.com
Contact: Mr. Ladi Owodunni - Chairman/CEO

THE OIL RESOURCES DEVELOPMENT CO. (NIGERIA) LTD
Business: Engineering, Oilfield Services, Petroleum Consultancy, Management Consultancy, General Contact Services and Supplies
Address: Izzi Shopping Plaza (1st Floor, Right Wing), Aba/P Harcourt Expressway, Eleme Junction, Port Harcourt
Tel: (084) 487155, 488765, 611367, 08037113535, 08056636181
E-mail: tordcoilresources@yahoo.com
Contact: Mr. Gregory J. Omoregie - Chairman/CEO

THE OKOMU OIL PALM COMPANY PLC
Business: Development of Oil Palm Plantations, Production of Palm Produce, Rubber Plantation
Address Okomu Oil Palm Estate, Okomu-Udo, Ovia South-West L.G.A; Edo State
Tel: (052) 250118
* 11B, Chief Alonge Avenue, off Central Roa, G.R.A., Benin City
Tel: (052) 255101, 254597 **Fax:** (052) 251880
E-mail: okomu@infoweb.abs.net
okomu@yahoo.co.uk
Contact: Mr. T. J R. Havard - MD/CEO
Mr. P. I. K Uwadia - Company Sec./Registrar

THE PEACH COMPANY LIMITED
Business: Sales of Seat and Chairs
Address: Plot 240A, Kofo Abayomi St, Victoria Island, Lagos
Tel: (01) 2610649, 4701708, 611008, 08023223843
E-mail: peach@infoweb.abs.net

THE PEN SHOP LIMITED
Business: Corporae Gifts, Public Relations and Promotions
Address: 57, Western Avenue, Surulere, Lagos
Tel: (01) 2613224, 08037122866 **Fax:** (01) 2666919
E-mail: penshop@infoweb.abs.net
Contact: Olakunle A. Sodipo - Chairman/CEO

THE PENINSULA WATERFRONT/PENINSULA RESORT
Business: Hospitality
Address: Plot 8, Ozumba Mbadiwe Ave, Victoria Island, Lagos
Tel: (01) 2617168, 2621895 **Fax:** (01) 2617168
Contact: Mr. Niyi Onibudo - MD

THE POST PUBLISHING COMPANY LIMITED
Business: Newspaper Publishing
Address: 7, Warehouse Road, Apapa, Lagos
Tel: (01) 5453351-2 (2 L) **Fax:** (01) 5453436
* 24, Ikwerre Road, Port Harcourt.
Tel: (084) 230495
* Plot 646, Block 10, Abeokuta Street, off Ogbomosho Street, Area 8, Garki, Abuja
Tel: (09) 2347083
Contact: Chief Sonny I.Odogwu - Chairman/Publisher
Mr. Ogbuagu Anikwe - MD/Editor-In-Chief/CEO

THE QUADRANT COMPANY
Business: Public Relations Consultancy
Address: 52, Isaac John Street, Ikeja G.R.A, Ikeja, Lagos
Tel: (01) 4970550-2 (3 L), 4970218 **Fax:** (01) 4965820
E-mail: tqc@infoweb.abs.net
Contact: Biodun Shobanjo - Chairman
Jimi Awosika - Supervising Director

THE ROSE OF SHARON
Business: Supply of Tee-Shirts & Promotional Items, Monogramming, Heat-Transfer & Screen Printing
Address: 13, Adeniran Ogunsanya Street, Surulere, Lagos
Tel: (01) 5834151, 7744139 **Fax:** (01) 5834432
E-mail: rsharonfashion@yahoo.com
Contact: Mrs. Folorunsho Alakija - Chairman/CEO

THE SHOPS LIMITED
Business: Advertising and Marketing Communications
Address: 4, Modupe Str, off Folu Agoro St, Somolu, Lagos
Tel: (01) 4701254, 5455054
Contact: Gbemi Sagay - MD/CEO

THE SOUND CENTRE
Business: Acoustics, Audio-Visuals, Consultancy
Address: The Green House, Plot 1607, Omegabank Avenue, off Adeola Hopewell Street, Victoria Island, Lagos
Tel: (01) 2704456, 4619671, 4703095, 0033069044
E-mail: thesondcentre@vgccl.net
Contact: Mr. Lanre Kupoluyi - MD/CEO

THE SUN PUBLISHING LIMITED
Business: Tabloid Newspaper Publishing, Printing Services
Address: 2, Coscharis Street, Kirikiri Industriaal Layout, Apapa, Lagos
Tel: (01) 3203229, 3203230, 3205754, 5875561, 7900632
Fax: (01) 3205754, 5875561
E-mail: thesun@sunnewsonline.com
Website: www.sunnewsonline.com
* Plot 695, Lafia Close, Area 8, Garki, Abuja
Tel: (09) 2346381
Contact: Mr. Mike Awoyinfa - MD/Editor-in-Chief

THE TALL & WIDE COMPANY LIMITED
Business: Advertising, Marketing Communicaations & Public Relations Agency, Research & Surveys, Design & Print Production, Supply of Promotional Gift Items
Address: 21, Adeboye Sholanke Street, off Allen Avenue, Ikeja, Lagos
Tel: (01) 4815227, 4930145, 08033074699
E-mail: tall_wide@hotmail.com
Contact: Mr. Toye Arulogun - MD/CEO

THE TENT EVENT LIMITED
Business: Rental & Managment of Eqipment for Events
Address: 47, James Robertson Street, Surulere, Lagos
Tel: (01) 5851378, 833574 **Fax:** (01) 5851378

THE TICKET CENTRE LIMITED
Business: Travel Agency
Address: Crusader House, 16A, Commercial Avenue, Sabo-Yaba, Lagos
Tel: (01) 3425300-1 (2L), 8129000-1 (2L)
Contact: Mr. Victor Uchendu - MD/CEO

THE TOURIST COMPANY OF NIGERIA PLC
Business: Hotel Management and Catering Services
Address: 6-8, Ahmadu Bello Way, Victoria Island, Lagos
Tel: (01) 2623116-25 (10L), 2626180-6 (7L), 2626190-9 (10L), 26239115-7 (3 L)
Fax: (01) 2623912
E-mail: fedpalhotel@micro.com.ng
Contact: Mr. Goodie M. Ibru - Chairman
Mr. Mr. J. M. Provis - GM

THE UNITED AFRICAN INSURANCE BROKERS LIMITED
Business: Insurance & Reinsurance Broking
Address: Ashakun House (5th Floor), 13/15, Lake Street, off Broad Streeet; Lagos
Tel: (01) 2647218, 2647219 **Fax:** (01) 2647220
E-mail: uaib@aol.com
Contact: Chief (Dr.). Sonny I. Odogwu - Chairman

THE WEST AFRICAN ENGINEERING CO. (NIGERIA) LTD
Business: Importation, Distribution, Sales and Installation of Electrical & Mechanical Materials and Equipment, Non-Radioactive Lightning Preventors and Fire-Alarm Materials
Address: 30, Wharf Road, Apapa, Lagos
Tel: (01) 5877463, 5877468, 5875530, 7748331
Fax: (01) 2645069, 5875530
E-mail: weaco@infoweb.abs.net
Website: www.lagosstate.gov.ng
Contact: Mr. Nicholas O. Onukwufor - Exec. Director

THE YINKA LAYINKA COMPANY LIMITED
Business: Media Management Consultancy, Multi-Media Procurement & Installation Services, Film Producers
Address: 8, Oyediran St, off Bode Thomas St, Surulere, Lagos
Tel: (01) 3209655, 8042433, 08023210092, 08033217355, 08056147524 **Fax:** (01) 8101354
E-mail: yourme@yahoo.co.uk
Contact: Mr. Yomi Layinka - MD/CEO

THEMES & SCHEMES LIMITED
Business: Industrial Printing, Production of Light Packaging, Digital Colour Separation, Consultancy Services
Address: 11, Bariga Rd, by Adesina Bus-Stop, Bariga, Lagos
Tel: (01) 4716987, 4971788, 4973037, 7741480
E-mail: sales@themesnschemes.com
* 32, Abiodun Street, Shomolu, Lagos
Contact: Mr. Segun Folarin - Chairman/CEO

THEOBECH SYSTEMS LIMITED
Business: Provision of Internet Services, Computer Software Development, Computer and Telecommunication Consultancy, Networking
Address: Plot 1398, Tiamiyu Savage St, Victoria Island, Lagos
Tel: (01) 3204169-70 (2L), 614140, 08033343028
Fax: (01) 614140
E-mail: info@theobech.com
Website: www.theobech.com
Contact: Dr. Theodora Onyekuru - MD/CEO

THERAPEUTIC LABORATORIES (NIGERIA) LIMITED
Business: Manufacturing of Pharmaceutical Products, Importation and Distribution of Pharmaceutical Raw Materials and Pharmaceuticals Manufacturing Machinery
Address: 372, Ikorodu Road, Maryland, Ikeja, Lagos
Tel: (01) 4973068, 4934445, 7737234 **Fax:** (01) 4934445
E-mail: theralab@hyperia.com
Contact: Chief Alex Akinyele - Chairman
Mr. J. T. Lalvani - MD/CEO

THERMO ACOUSTIC PRODUCTS LIMITED
Business: Manufacturing and Marketing of Thermo-Acoustic Insulation Fibres
Address: Km. 50, Lagos-Abeokuta Road, Pakoto Area, Ifo L.G.A., Ogun State
Tel: (039) 340595, 340599 * (01) 4704799, 08034016620
Fax: (01) 4972755
E-mail: thermocoustic@hotmail.com
Contact: Prince Doyin Adesida - Sales Manager

THERMOSTEEL NIGERIA LIMITED
Business: Industrial Laboratory & Environmental Consultancy
Address: 65, Enerhen/Effurun Road, Warri
Tel: (053) 253836, 250445
E-mail: tsteel@linkserve.com.ng
Contact: Mauro Zamblera - Chairman/CEO

THERMOTEC ENGINEERING COMPANY LIMITED
Business: Importation & Marketing of Power-Control Equipment, Industrial Stabilizers (AVR), Electrical Distribution Products, Generators, Airconditioners
Address: Great Nigeria House (7th Floor), 47/57, Martins Street, Lagos
Tel: (01) 2661694, 2664426 **Fax:** (01) 2664426
Contact: Chief E. N. Nwobi - Chairman

THOMAS FRENCH (NIGERIA) LIMITED
Business: Marketing of Curtain Tapes, Tracks &Accessories
Address: 13, Olutunda Street, off Coker Road, Ilupeju, Lgaos
Tel: (01) 4934699, 4960408, 4962525 **Fax:** (01) 4962525
E-mail: thomas.french@skannet.com
* c/o Apex Paints Ltd, Adanla House, 1, Commercial Layout (Benjamin Bus-Stop), Eleyele, Ibadan
* c/o Tower Galvanised Products (Nig.) Ltd. 4, Mai-Malari Road, Bompai Industrial Area, Kano
Tel: (064) 630869

THOMAS FURNITURE COMPANY LIMITED
Business: manufacturing & Sales of Furniture
Address: Jubilee House, 98, Ring Road, Ibadan
Tel: (02) 3211384 Fax: (02) 2311480
* Eko Hotel Shopping Complex (Units 9/10), 1, Ajose Adeogun Street, Victoria Island, Lagos
Tel: (01) 2626959, 4730627 Fax: (01) 2626959

THOMAS INSURANCE BROKERS COMPANY LIMITED
Business: Insurance Broking
Address: 3, Ibezim Obiajulu Street (Ground Floor), off Adelabu Street, Surulere, Lagos
Tel: (01) 5454698, 4717422, 8118555, 835581, 08033096507 **Fax:** (01) 5454698
E-mail: tibcool@yahoo.com
Contact: Mr. Femi.Thomas - MD/CEO

THOMAS KINSLEY SECURITIES LIMITED
Business: Stocbroking, Issuing House, Portfolio & Asset

Management, Research and Consultancy
Address: Bookshop House (6th Floor), 50/52, Broad St, Lagos
Tel: (01) 2635918, 2632028, 2633947 **Fax:** (01) 2637134
E-mail: tk_sec2002@tahoo.com
Contact: Chief (Sir) Kingsley I. Ikpe - Chairman/CEO

THOMAS WYATT NIGERIA PLC
Business: Production of Exercise Books, Office & Domestic Stationery, Toilet Rolls and Facial Tissues
Address: 10, Abebe Village Road, Iganm Industrial Estate, Iganmu, Lagos
* 6, Eze Iweka Road, off Owerri Road, Awoda Industrial Layout, Onitsha
Tel: (046) 210908

THORBURN INVESTMENTS NIGERIA LIMITED
Business: Investments, Joint Ventures
Address: New Africa House (12th Floor), 31, Marina, Lagos
Tel: (01) 2632341, 2661019 **Fax:** (01) 2645069

THREE POINTS INDUSTRIES LIMITED
Business: Production of Insecticides, Fabric Starch and Cleaning Powder
Address: Lagos State Small-Scale Industries Estate, off Fatai Atere Way, Matori, Mushin, Lagos
Tel: (01) 2901779

THREE STARS INVESTMENT LIMITED
Business: Stockbroking, Portfolio Management, Investment Advisory Services
Address: 130, Ahmadu Bellow Way, Victoria Island, Lagos
Tel: (01) 2621174-5 (2L), 2623780-7 (8L)(Ext. 2570, 2558), 4705461, 08023072025, 08033030108, 08033267901
Fax: (01) 2621175
E-mail: cisl@hyperia.com
Contact: Alh. Hassan Momodu - Chairman
Mr. Abdul R. Lawani - MD/CEO

TIANSHI HEALTH PRODUCTS COMPANY LIMITED
Business: Importation & Sales of Food Supplements, Health Care Products and Appliances
Address: Plot 1692B, Buraimah Kenku Street, off Sanusi Fafunwa Street, Victoria Island, Lagos
Tel: (01) 3200024 Fax: (01) 3200023
E-mail: tiensnig@linkserve.com
Website: www.tiens.com
www.tianshi.com
Contact: Mr. Paul Wang - MD/CEO

TICON INVESTMENTS LIMITED
Business: Importation and Marketing of Office Automation, Printers and Computers, Networking,Financing
Address: 67E, Bello Road, opp. Wema Bank, Kano
Tel: (064) 631685, 633922, 643486, 08023085781, 08023085786, 08033022362, 08034050510
Fax: (064) 631685
E-mail: ticontech@yahoo.com
Contact: Engr. Theo W .Nwokoye-Obiajulu - Chairman/CEO
Mrs. Joy I. Nwokoye-Obiajulu - MD

TIDDO SECURITIES LIMITED
Business: Stockbroking, Portfolio Management
Address: Labour/NSITF House (1st Floor, Left Wing), Muhammadu Buhari Way, Central Area, Garki, Abuja
Tel: (09) 2348168-9 (2L) **Fax:** (09) 2348168
E-mail: tiddosecltd@yahoo.com
Contact: Alh. Bashiru M. Tukur - Chairman
Alh. Yusufu Aliyu Modibbo - MD/CEO

TIDEMARK NIGERIA LIMITED
Business: Shipping, Ship Brokerage & Liner Agency, Stevedoring, Clearing & Forwarding
Address: 304, Aba Road, Rumuokwurusi, Port Harcourt
Tel: (084) 610081 **Fax:** (084) 610996
* 25, Musa Yar'Adua Street, Victoria Island, Lagos
Tel: (01) 616970 **Fax:** (01) 616268
Contact: Mr. Emenike Nwokeoji - MD/CEO

TIDEX NIGERIA LIMITED
Business: Marine Transportation
Address: 8, Louis Solomon Close, off Ahmadu Bello Way, Victoria Island, Lagos
Tel: (01) 2622084 **Fax:** (01) 2613045
E-mail: kemeghe@tidewater.co.uk
Contact: Capt. R. E. Manchester - MD/CEO
Capt. M. Karimo - Dep. MD

TIDY INSURANCE BROKERS LIMITED
Business: Insurance Broking
Address: Merchant House (3rd Floor), 37, Adekunle Fajuyi Road, opp. Queen's Cinema, Ekotedo, Ibadan
Tel: (02) 2411448, 2413082 **Fax:** (02) 2411357
E-mail: niyarotidy@yahoo.com
Contact: Dr. K. S. Oyegbite - Chairman
Elder Niyi Arogundade - MD/CEO

TIE COMMUNICATIONS LIMITED
Business: Advertising & Marketing Communications, Printing Services
Address: 26, Ajani Olujare Street, Alaka Estate, off Western Avenue, Surulere, Lagos
Tel: (01) 7744967, 5850629, 830521 **Fax:** (01) 5850629
E-mail: tiecommunications@siotel.com
Contact: Pastor Esko Mfon - Chairman/CEO
Mr. Vincent Udi - Media Manager

TIGER SHIPPING COMPANY LIMITED
Business: Shipping, Freight Forwarding, Hualage, Warehousing, Procurement
Address: Kariko Towers (1st Floor), 9, Wharf Road, Apapa, Lagos
Tel: (01) 5870105, 5870110, 08033076389
Fax: (01) 5872327
E-mail: info@tigershipping.com
Website: www.tigershipping.com
Contact: Mr. Ademola Oyewumi - MD/CEO

TIGON INDUSTRIES LIMITED
Business: Manufacturing of Industrial Chemicals, Starch and Adhesives
Address: 9, Kareem Giwa Street, Abule-Osun, off Badagry Expressway, opp. Trade Fair Complex, Ojo, Lagos.
Tel: (01) 885731, 884999, 885690 **Fax:** (01) 884031

TILLEY-GYADO GROUP OF COMPANIES
Business: Conglomerate - Building & Civil Engineering

Contractors, Farming, Trading
Address: Tilley Gyado House, 12, Alli Akilu Street, Makurdi
Tel: (044) 532463
* 10, Thomas Sankara Street, Asokoro, Abujaa
* LSDPC Luxry Flats, Block B (Flat 13), 24, Adeola Odeku Street, Victoria Island, Lagos
Tel: (01) 2617316 **Fax:** (01) 2611114
Contact: Chief (Dr.) Sen. Jack Tilley - Gyado - Group MD

TILLYARD & PARTNERS
Business: Chartered Quantity Surveyors, Project Management, Cost Consultants
Address: 241, Igbosere Road, Lagos Island, Lagos
Tel: (01) 2636358, 2636726, 2636940 **Fax:** (01) 2636290
E-mail: info@tillyardnigeria.com
Contact: Mr. John Tuffrey - Chairman/CEO

TIM INDUSTRIES LIMITED
Business: Production of Office Pins, Staple Pins & Paper Clips, Toilet Rolls & Tissue Paper and Candles, Electroplatins Services
Address: 10, Sez Crescent, off Ladi Kwali Way, beh. Sheraton Hotels & Towers, Wuse Zone 4, Abuja
Tel: (09) 5234160, 08034511667 **Fax:** (09) 5234160
* 26, Bukuru Bye-Pass, Rayfield Ind Layout, Jos
Tel: (073) 465225
Contact: Lt. Gen. J. T. Useni (rtd) - Chairman
Mr. A. T. Bigun - MD/CEO

TIMBERWOOD LIMITED
Business: Wood Processing and Drying
Address: Billingsway (Opp. Tractor & Equipment), Junction of Olanrewaju Street, Oregun, Lagos
Tel: (01) 7746336, 4717059, 2613068 **Fax:** (01) 2694078
Contact: Major Gen. Adeyinka Adebayo (rtd.) - Chairman
Mrs. Nike Makinde - MD/CEO

TIME INSURANCE BROKERS LIMITED
Business: Insurance Broking
Address: 44, Association Avenue, by Obanikoro Bus-Stop, Ilupeju, Lagos
Tel: (01) 4933717
Contact: Dr. Paul A. Aifuwa - President
Mrs. Austin U. Ogboli - MD/CEO

TIMES PRESS LIMITED
Business: Industrial and Commercial Printing Services
Address: Lateef Jakande Road, Agidingbi, Ikeja, Lagos
Tel: (01) 4975598, 4977283
Contact: Dr. Yemi Farounbi - Chairman

TIMICOM TELECOMMUNICATIONS LIMITED
Business: Telecommunications, Internet Service Provider, Operation of Pre-Paid Phone Cards
Address: 37, Joel Ogunnaike St, Ikeja G.R.A., Ikeja, Lagos
Tel: (01) 4967208, 4975307-9 (3L), 7742098
Fax: (01) 4975308, 7743555
Contact: Mr. Adedeji Doherty - Chairman
Mrs. Abidemi Kalenikanse - CEO

TINEX NIGERIA LIMITED
Business: IT Consultancy Services and Training, Sales & Service of Computer Hardware & Software, OMR & OCR Machines, Printing of Computer Stationery, OMR & OCR Forms
Address: 35, Adeniyi Jones, Ikeja, Lagos
Tel: (01) 4960990, 4732444 **Fax:** (01) 4975250
E-mail: tinex@beta.linkserve.com
Contact: Mr. Olugbenga Okunsanya - Chairman/CEO

TINO ELECTRONICS NIGERIA LIMITED
Business: Sales of Consumer Electronic & Electrical Appliances
Address: 59, Raymond Njoku Street, off Awolowo Road, S. W. Ikoyi, Lagos
Tel: (01) 2690806, 2690809, 08022902969, 08023407184, 08033028409, 08033346657 Fax: (01) 2690809
Contact: Mr. Timothy Ofoezue - Chairman/CEO

TINUBU ASSOCIATES UNLIMITED
Business: Company Secretariat Services
Address: Barbinder Chambers, Elepehant Cement House, (5th Floor), ASSBIFI Road, Central Business District, Alausa, Ikeja, Lagos
Tel: (01) 4922943-7 (5L) **Fax:** (01) 4922941, 2617193

TISCO NIGERIA LIMITED
Business: Manufacturing, Importation and Marketing of Pharmaceutical & Hygiene Products
Address: TISCO Plaza, 1, NERDC Road, Plot 6, Block B, Central Business District, Alausa, Ikeja, Lagos
Tel: (01) 4932845 **Fax:** (01) 4932844
E-mail: tisconigeria@yahoo.com
* Plot 1818, State Ind. Estate, Ilesha Road, Akure
Tel: (034) 242966
Contact: Mr. I. S. Tapere - Chairman/CEO

TITAN ENGINEERS & CONSTRUCTORS LIMITED
Business: Engineering, Procurement, Construction & Project Management (Oil & Gas Processing Facilities, Pipeline & Utility Construction, Civil & Infrastructural Engineering, Water & Waste Treatment Management)
Address: 3, Evo Road, G.R.A. Phase II, Port Harcourt
Tel: (084) 230513-4 (2 L), 238782, 461531-2 (2L)
Fax: (084) 238781
E-mail: tec@phca.linkserve.com
Website: www.titanprojects.com
Contact: Mr. Rudi Meyenburg - MD/CEO

TLG ENGINEERING NIGERIA LIMITED
Business: Network Management & Solutions, Structred Cabling, Computer Systems, Communications/VoIP, UPS & Power Systems
Address: 32, Mba Street, off Tafawa Balewa Crescent, off Adeniran Ogunsanya Street, Surulere, Lagos
Tel: (01) 5850280, 4703661, 08023116982
Fax: (01) 5850280
E-mail: tlgengineeering@yahoo.com
Contact: Engr. Emmanuel Chidi Elele - MD/CEO

TMC SAVINGS & LOANS LIMITED
Business: Mortgage Finance Services
Address: ASEI World Centre, 57, Aba Road, Port Harcourt
Tel: (084) 237630-1 (2L) **Fax:** (-084) 237630
* Linkage Plaza, 25, Akin Adesola Street, Victoria

Island, Lagos
Tel: (01) 2621262, 2621263 **Fax:** (01) 2615480
Contact: Mr. Ben Okutu - MD/CEO

TNT NEWSPAPERS LIMITED
Business: Publishing of Newspapers and Magazines
Address: 13, Ize Iyamu Street, off Billingsway, Oregun Industrial Estate, Oregun, Lagos
Tel: (01) 2644833
Contact: Dr. Christopher Kolade - Chairman
Mr. Muyiwa Adetiba - Publisher/CEO

TNT/IAS CARGO AIRLINES (NIGERIA) LIMITED
Business: Courier & Cargo Services/Deliveries
Address: 2nd Roundabout, Epe Expressway, Lekki, Lagos
Tel: (01) 5555-TNT, 5555517-20 (4L), 7748906
Fax: (01) 5555513
E-mail: enquires@ias-ng.com
Website: www.tnt.com
www.iasexpress.com
* NAHCO Shed, Murtala Mohammed International Airport, Ikeja, Lagos.
Tel: (01) 4701783
* 21/22, Marina, Lagos
Tel: (01) 2632800, 2621210 **Fax:** (01) 2621211
* Shopping Complex (Shop 4) Wuse Zone 3, Abuja
Contact: Mr. Larry Chinekezi - MD/CEO
Chibisi Ohakah - Corp. Affairs/Marketing Manager

TOCARO EMERGENCY MEDICAL SERVICES LIMITED
Business: Emergency Medical Services, Medical Air Evacuation Services, Local and International Medical Escort Services
Address: Plot 1618, Danmole Street, Victoria Island, Lagos
Tel: (01) 2624330-1 (2L), 4619937, 612694, 613364, 08033069933 Fax: (01) 2624331
E-mail: tocarco@infoweb.abs.net
Contact: Mr. Robert Reinich - Exec. Director/CEO
Mr. J. D. I. Nwosu - GM

TODAY'S CARS LIMITED
Business: Importation and Marketing of Cars
Address: 35, Mobolaji Bank-Anthony Way, Ikeja, Lagos
Tel: (01) 4974059, 4974060, 08033044414
Fax: (01) 4939914, 4978560
Contact: Chief Albert Barry Ezenwa - Chairman/CEO
Mr. Patrick A. Unoagu - AGM. (Group Accounts)

TODAY'S COMPUTERS LIMITED
Business: Website Design & Internet Connectivity Services, Sales & Service of Computers, Networking, Training
Address: 33, Rumuola Road, Port Harcourt
Tel: (084) 570677, 08033165949, 08037080369
E-mail: webmaster@hotgist.com
Website: www.hotgist.com

TODSEN ENTERPRISES LIMITED
Business: Importation of Motor Vehicles and Motorcycle Tyres & Tubes and Filters
Address: 4, Edoezemewi Road, Anambra State
Tel: (046) 460311, 461397 **Fax:** (046) 460842
E-mail: todsen@infoweb.abs.net
Contact: Mr. Anthony O. Obiora - MD/CEO

TOE INDUSTRIES LIMITED
Business: Environmental & Civil Engineering, Fire Protection, Procurement Contracting, Computers
Address: Block 3 (Top Floor), Edewor Shopping Centre, Effuru/Sapele Road, Warri
Tel/Fax: (053) 256811, 08023094679
* 7, Port Harcourt/Aba Expressway, Port Harcourt
Tel: (084) 579919
Contact: Mr. Anthony Uwaya - Chairman/CEO

TOEM TECHNOLOGIES LIMITED
Business: Sales of Electronic Cards, Computers, Indoor & Outdoor Electronic Displays and Banking Equipment, Document Imaging Technology, Production of Identity Cards, Distribution of Card Printers
Address: Bankers House (3rd Floor), Plot PC. 19, Adeola Hopewell Street, Victoria Island, Lagos
Tel: (01) 8042985 **Fax:** (01) 2623441, 3200776
E-mail: toemzebra@yahoo.com
Website: www.toemtechnologies.com
Contact: Mr. Chris Oshai - MD/CEO

TOFA GENERAL ENTERPRISES LIMITED
Business: Paper Converters
Address: 496, Hotoro Commercial Layout, Kano
Tel: (064) 649822, 649930, 08044117192, 08044117568
Fax: (064) 648489
E-mail: tofa@ecnx.com
* Tofa Paper Mill Ltd, 1, Dutse Road, Kawaji/Jiginya, off Hadejia Road, Kano
Tel: (064) 642040, 649822
Contact: Alh. Isiyaku Umar - Chairman/CEO
Mr. B. A. Brebson - Printing Manager

TOKI HOTELS LIMITED
Business: Hospitality & Catering Services
Address: 68/70, Nkpogu Road, off Trans-Amadi Industrial Layout, Port Harcourt
Tel: (084) 231635 **Fax:** (084) 230451
E-mail: tokihotels@yahoo.co.uk
Contact: Dr. (Mrs.) L. I. MacDonald, JP- Chairman/CEO

TOKI-LINKWORLD GROUP
Business: Manufacturing & Marketing of Pharmaceutical Products and Cosmetics
Address: Plot 1, Olajuwon Street, off Ojuelegba Road, opp. Tejuosho Market, Surulere, Lagos
Tel: (01) 7744317, 7914378, 08023082381
Fax: (01) 525499
Website: www.tokilinkworld.com
Contact: Chief Oluyombo A. Akoni - Chairman

TOKKE MARITIME SERVICES LIMITED
Business: Shipping, Clearing and Forwarding, Transportation and Brokerage
Address: NPA Commercial Building (Room 33-36), Tin Can Island, Apapa, Lagos
Tel: (01) 5871918, 4713616, 08023223620
E-mail: bamagaco.agile@comp.com
* 6, Industry Road, Port Harcourt
Tel: (084) 485016
Contact: Alh. Abdullahi A. Bamanga - Exec. Chairman
Alh. Bello Hamidu

TOKY CHEMICAL MANUFACTURERS LIMITED
Business: Manufacture of Healthcare Products, Printing Inks and Paints
Address: Toky Avenue, Igboho Crescent, Km. 40, Lagos-Abeokuta Expressway, Sango-Otta, Lagos
Tel: (01) 920600, 08023274189, 08033044576
* Abuja Shopping Mall (Suite B15), Maputo Street, Wuse Zone 3, Abuja.
Tel: (09) 5236712
Contact: Engr. O. A. Oni - Chairman/CEO

TOLARAM GROUP OF COMPANIES
Business: Conglomerate, Manufacture of Clay & Burnt Bricks Blocks & Tiles
Address: Great Nigeria House (20th Floor), 47/57, Martins Street, Lagos
Tel: (01) 2660372, 2661269, 2665668
Fax: (01) 2668637, 2666380
* Baiyeku Road, Igbogbo, Ikorodu, Lagos
Tel: (01) 2660372

TOMBIZ GROUP OF COMPANIES
Business: Importation Consultancy, Shipping & Financial Services, Construction Management, Sewage Services, Marketing of Agricultural Products
Address: Nasco House, 29, Burma Road, Apapa, Lagos
Tel: (01) 5876985, 5873996 **Fax:** (01) 5876985
E-mail: tombizgroup@yahoo.com
Contact: Hon. Chief (Dr.) Tom U. B. Egbuwoku - Chairman
Arc. Mazino Y. Egbuwoku - MD

TOMBRA LIFE SUPPORT COMPANY LIMITED
Business: Medical Technology Speciality Services
Address: Administration Building (Suite 214), Trade Fair Complex, Lagos-Badagry Expressway, Ojo, Lagos
Tel: (01) 4707845, 5880803 **Fax:** (01) 5880803
E-mail: tombralife@yahoo.com
tombra@alpha.linkserve.com

TOMBULCO (NIGERIA) LIMITED
Business: Mining, Processing and Marketing of Solid Minerals, Consultancy Services, Development of Mineral Resources, Water Engineering Services, Environmental Management
Address: 1, Olusolape Ige Avenue, NNPC Bus-Stop, Oke-Afa, Isolo, Lagos
Tel: (01) 775282
Contact: Elder (Dr.) W. I. Aderonpe - Chairman/CEO

TOM-TAN NIGERIA LIMITED
Business: Marketing of Petroleum Products and Liquefied Petroleum Gas
Address: Plot 11, Block C, Amuwo-Odofin Ind. Scheme, off Festac Link Road, Amuwo-Odofin, Lagos
Tel: (01) 4701891

TONIMAS NIGERIA LIMITED
Business: Transportation and Marketing of Petroleum Products, Blending of Lubricants
Address: 11, Port Harcourt Road, Aba
Tel: (082) 234665, 234912, 232968 **Fax:** (082) 234912
E-mail: tonimasnigltd@yahoo.com
Contact: Chief (Sir) Anthony Enukaeme - MD/CEO

TOOLS & ALLIED PRODUCTS NIGERIA LIMITED
Business: Sales and Service of Machinery, Engineering Tools & Equipment, Foundry & Material Equipment
Address: 126, Obafemi Awolowo Way, Ikeja, Lagos
Tel: (01) 4978377, 4965926, 08033018399, 08033019346
Fax: (01) 5453549
E-mail: toolsal@infoweb.abs.net
Contact: Mr. Femi Taiwo - Chairman/CEO

TOP FEEDS LIMITED
Business: Manufacturing and Marketing of Livestock Feeds
Address: Ogorode Road, Sapele, Delta State
Tel: (054) 341036, 341363, 342102, 342628, 08035350545, 0035844767 **Fax:** (054) 342422
E-mail: lifesapele@infoweb.com.ng
* 10A, Adetokunbo Ademola St, Victoria Is, Lagos
Tel: (01) 2611862, 2880473, 7754191, 613671, 611383, 08022921038, 08035350545
E-mail: lifelagos@infoweb.com.ng
africadon@infoweb.abs.net
africadon@aol.com
Contact: Mr. Donald Spencer - MD/CEO
Mr. Shekhar Oke - GM

TOP NORTH ENGINEERING LIMITED
Business: Sales of Generators and Power Systems
Address: 32, Balarabe Musa Crescent, off Samuel Manuwa Road, near 1004-Flats Estate, Victoria Island, Lagos
Tel: (01) 7753197, 2626351-4 (4 L), 2610754
Fax: (01) 2626351
E-mail: tnotch@infoweb.abs.net

TOP RANK HOTELS LIMITED
Business: Hospitality & Catering Services
Address: Plot 892, Gimbiya Street, off Ahmadu Bello Way, Garki II, Abuja
Tel: (09) 3148301-4 (4L), 08033495495, 08044129947
Fax: (09) 3148304
E-mail: toprkng@yahoo.com
Contact: Mr. Obasi O. Obasi - GM

TOP SECURITIES & INVESTMENT LIMITED
Business: Stockbroking, Financial Services
Address: Elephant Cement House (3rd Floor), ASSBIFI Road, Central Business District, Alausa, Lagos
Tel: (01) 7745088, 4968060-5 (6 L) (Ext. 8302)

TOPAZA NIGERIA LIMITED
Business: Production of Ceramics, Bricks & Clay Products
Address: 1, Abimbola Shodipe Street, by Western Avenue, Surulere, Lgaos
Tel: (01) 5837744, 5836695, 5840791

TOPCLASS COMPUTERS NIGERIA LIMITED
Business: Strategic Power-Protection Management, Distribution, Marketing/Sales, Installation, Maintenance and Repairs, Software Development, Training and Consultancy
Address: Topclass House, 10/11, Sabbath Close, Ijeshatedo, off Apapa-Oshodi Expressway, Ijesha Bus-Stop, Ijesha-Tedo, Lagos
Tel: (01) 5850723, 5850253, 836460, 4710385-6 (2L), 4710331 **Fax:** (01) 5850723

E-mail: topclassnet2000@yahoo.com
titssl@yahoo.com
Contact: Dr. P. N. Azonobi - Chairman/CEO

TOPCOM (NIGERIA) LIMITED
Business: Telephony Operation, Internet Service Providers
Address: 39A, Bishop Aboyade Cole Str, Victoria Is, Lagos
Tel: (01) 2610624-5 (2L), 7736249 **Fax:** (01) 2611095
* 16, Choba Street, D-Line, Port Harcourt

TOPE OLOYEDE & COMPANY
Business: Estate Agency, Surveying & Valuation, Property Development & Management, Consultancy
Address: Olatunji House (2nd Floor), 299, Ikorod Road (Idiroko Bus-Stop), Maryland, Lagos
Tel: (01) 4961472, 4965275, 4967219, 08033165305
Fax: (01) 4967219
Contact: Chief B. A. Oloyede - Principal Partners

TOPKLASS TRADING COMPANY LIMITED
Business: Fashion & Furniture Sales
Address: 64, Toyin Street, Ikeja, Lagos
Tel: (01) 4932379, 08023207155, 0033025650, 08042116063
E-mail: topklasssboutique@yahoo.com
Contact: Mr. L. V. Obiajulu - MD/CEO

TOPMOST FINANCE & INVESTMENTS LIMITED
Business: Capital Market Operations, Investment & Fund Management;Financial Consultancy
Address: Bookshop House (12th Floor), 50/52, Broad Street, Lagos
Tel: (01) 2633268, 2630697 **Fax:** (01) 2633268
E-mail: topmost@hyperia.com
Contact: Felix Olusegun Fagbohungbe, SAN - Chairman
Emmanuel Olugbenga Obisesan - MD/CEO

TOPTECH ENGINEERING LIMITED
Business: Sales & Maintenance of UPS & Staabilizers, Structured Cabling, Preparation of IT Suites
Address: 9, Olufunmilola Okikiola Street, off Toyin Street, Ikeja, Lagos
Tel: (01) 3453313, 4930876, 7739586, 08033056190, 0033056197 **Fax:** (01) 3453314
E-mail: info@toptech-ng.com
Website: www.toptech-ng.com
Contact: Mr. Johnson Oboni - Chairman
Mr. A. A. Odeyinka - MD/CEO

TOPTREE OIL MILLS NIGERIA LIMITED
Business: Refining of Vegetable Oil, Production of Soap
Address: Km. 5, Aba/Enugu Expressway, Aba
Tel/Fax: (082) 440018
Contact: Owelle Andy Okaje - MD/CEO

TOPWAY PHARMACEUTICAL INDUSTRIES LIMITED
Business: Manufacturing of Pharmaceutical Products
Address: 2, Ebun Street, Abule-Ijesha, Yaba, Lagos
Tel: (01) 2694699
E-mail: topway@linkserve.com.ng
* Ilishan-Iperu Road, Ilishan, Ogun State
Tel: (037) 630089, 630574
Contact: Chief (Mrs.) Olamide T. Adegbenro - MD/CEO

TORNADO INTERNATIONAL ASSOCIATES LIMITED
Business: Consultancy, Engineering, Procurement and Inspection Services to the Chemical, Petrochemical, Power Engineering and Oil Sectors, Sales, Installation & Services of Telecommunication Equipment
Address: Tornado House, 3, Sefia House, off Third Marine Gate, Warri
Tel: (053) 255523, 254922 **Fax:** (053) 255523
Contact: Prince J. O. Enosegbe - Chairman/CEO

TOSYKAY NIGERIA LIMITED
Business: Importation, Distribution and Sales of Pharmaceutical & Nutritional Products
Address: Plot 13, Jide Rowland Street, Ajao Estate, Apakun-Oshodi, Lagos
Tel: (01) 4523810 **Fax::** (01) 4523810, 4922263
E-mail: doopsies@yahoo.com
tosykay@alibaba.com
Contact: J. A. Ogundipe - MD/CEO

TOTAL ALUMINIUM SYSTEMS LIMITED
Business: Manufacturing of Longspan Aluminium Roofing Sheets
Address: 2, Akilo Road , Ogba, Ikeja, Lagos
Tel: (01) 4701631, 4924421, 4924888 **Fax:** (01) 618005
E-mail: totalum@nova.net.ng
* 4, Lumumbashi Street, Wuse Zone 3, Abuja
Tel: (09) 5233512

TOTAL HEALTH TRUST LIMITED
Business: Health Maintenance Organisation, Healthcare Provision and Consultancy Services
Address: 2, Marconi Rod, Palmgrove Estate, off Ikorodu Road, Palmgrove, Lagos
Tel: (01) 7747150, 4701813, 4709877
E-mail: info@totalhealthtrust.com
Website: www.totalhealthtrust.com
Contact: Dr. E. B. Mama - Chairman
Dr. O. A. Awosika - MD/CEO

TOTAL MARKETING COMMUNICATIONS LIMITED
Business: Advertising, Marketing Communication Agency
Address: 17, Buraimoh St, off Ikorodu Rd, Obanikoro, Lagos
Tel: (01) 4936040, 7743844 **Fax:** (01) 4936040
Contact: Mr. Demola Fowler - Chairman/CEO

TOTAL NIGERIA
Business: Exploration & Production of Oil & Gas
Address: 35, Kofo Abayomi Street, Victoria Island, Lagos
Tel: (01) 2623720-39 (40L) **Fax:** (01) 2623744
* 25, Trans-Amadi Industrial Layout, Port Harcourt
Tel: (084) 236310-23 (14L)

TOTAL OFFICE CONCEPT LIMITED
Business: Marketers of *Steelcase Inc.* Office Products and Furniture, Design and Planning of Office Space, Installations and Project Maintenance
Address: Plot 249A, Muri Okunola Street, Victoria Island, Annex, Lagos
Tel: (01) 2621194, 4709696, 4708888, 4718231
Fax: (01) 2621194
E-mail: toc@21ctl.com
Contact: Mr. Wale Ajisebutu - MD/CEO

TOTAL TELECOM SOLUTIONS LIMITED
Business: Sales, Installation & Service of Radio Communication Equipment
Address: 62, Akanro Street, off Apapa-Oshodi Expressway, Ilasamaja, Lagos
Tel: (01) 4712743, 4813170, 7947078, 08033046261, 08033918017
E-mail: sognigeria@yahoo.co.uk
Contact: Mr. Sunday O. Gbenjo - Chairman/CEO

TOTALFINAELF NIGERIA PLC
Business: Marketing of Petroleum Products
Address: Total House, 4, Afribank St, Victoria Island, Lagos
Tel: (01) 2600280-9 (10L), 2621780-9 (10L), 4617041-4
Fax: (01) 2621810, 2621811
Contact: Mr. Jean-Denis Royere - MD/CEO
Mr. O. A. Apampa - Head (Marketing Div.

TOWER ALUMINIUM NIGERIA PLC
Business: Manufacture & Marketing of Aluminium Products
Address: 9, Oba Akran Avenue,Ikeja Ind.Estate, Ikeja, Lagos
Tel: (01) 4937232, 4971325, 4969611-5 (5L)
Fax: (01) 4971320, 4971325
E-mail: tower2@linkserve.com.ng
tower3@betalinkserve.com
Contact: Mr. D. N. Sabarwal - MD/CEO

TOWER BUILDING PRODUCTS (Div of Tower Aluminium Plc)
Business: Manufacturing of Alumininium/Steel Corrugated and Fabricated Sheets
Address: 9, Oba Akran Avenue,Ikeja Ind Estate, Ikeja, Lagos
Tel: (01) 4972436-7 (2 L), 4968611-5 (5 L), 4967241, 4976661, 7740238 **Fax:** (01) 4976661, 4971320
E-mail: tbpikeja@@infoweb.abs.net
* Cocoa House (2nd Floor), Oba Adebimpe Road, Dugbe, Ibadan.
Tel: (02) 2410886
* Iluobe Filling Station, Kashim Ibrahim Way, Wuse II, Abuja.
Tel: (09) 5233488
Contact: Chief (Dr.) E. A. O. Shonekan - Chairman
Mr. D. N. Sabarwal - Group MD

TOWER EXTRUSIONS (Div of Tower Aluminium Plc)
Business: Manufacture of Extruded Aluminium Profiles for Windows and Doors
Address: 9, Oba Akran Avenue,Ikeja Ind Estate, Ikeja, Lagos
Tel: (01) 4968611-5 (5 L) **Fax:** (01) 962801
* Abeokuta Expressway, Dopemu, Agege, Lagos
Tel: (01) 4920937, 4920738 **Fax:** (01) 4920946
E-mail: towerex@micro.com.ng
Contact: Chief (Dr.) E.A.O. Shonekan - Chairman
Mr. D. N. Sabarwal - MD/CEO

TOWER GALVANISED PRODUCTS (NIGERIA) LIMITED
Business: Manufacturing of Black Pipes, Furniture Pipes, Hollow Sections, Headpans and Steel Products
Address: Plot 9C, Industrial Area, Kaduna South, Kaduna
Tel: (062) 232175, 232053, 231436, 08035232328-9 (2L)
Fax: (062) 231435
E-mail: towergal@skannet.com
* 4, Maimalari Rd, Bompai Industrial Area, Kano
Contact: Mr. V. M. Patel - MD/CEO

TOWER HOLLOWARE (Div of Tower Aluminium Plc)
Business: Manufacturing and Marketing of Aluminium Utensils and Containers
Address: 9, Oba Akran Avenue,Ikeja Ind.Estate, Ikeja, Lagos
Tel: (01) 4968614, 4974295
Fax: (01) 4971320, 4971325

TOWRY-COKER ASSOCIATES
Business: Chartered Architects, Engineers, Urban Planners, Project Managers & Development Consultants
Address: Towry Towers, Plot 1, Towry Close, off Idejo Street, Victoria Island, Lagos
Tel/Fax: (01) 2611389
E-mail: info@towrycoker.com
Website: www.towrycoker.com
Contact: Arc. Lanre Towry-Coker - Principal Partner

TOYIBAT GROUP OF COMPANIES
Business: Conglomerate, Mining, Consultants
Address: 1/3, Alhaja Toyibat Yusuf Adeniji Street, Medina Estate, via General Hospital, Ifako, Gbagaada, Lagos
Tel: (01) 4800301, 5552244, 08033005767
Fax: (01) 5552551
E-mail: gatewaymining@yahoo.com
Contact: Alhaja Toyibat Yusuf Adeniji - Chairperson/CEO

TOYOTA NIGERIA LIMITED
Business: Marketing of Toyota Brand of Automobiles, Spare Parts & Accessories
Address: Plot 2, Block G, Isolo Expressway, Isolo, Lagos
Tel: (01) 4528320, 4527912, 524532, 4529326
Fax: (01) 4524637
E-mail: toyota@toyotanigeria.com
Website: www.toyotanigeria.com
Contact: Mr. F. O. Owolawi - MD/CEO
Mr. I. O. Chigbu - Marketing Manager

TQM CONSULTS LIMITED
Business: Human Resources & Management Consultancy Services, Training
Address: Elephant House (Wing E, Entrance B, 3rd Floor), ASSBIFI Road, Central Business District, Alausa, Ikeja, Lagos
Tel: (01) 4968060, 5557453, 7745088
Contact: Chief Adeyemi Soladoye - Chairman/CEO

TRAB INVESTMENTS NIGERIA LIMITED
Business: Engineering, Construction, Procurement
Address: 17, Adeola Odeku Street, Victoria Island, Lagos
Tel: (01) 611672, 2611764 **Fax:** (01) 2881307
E-mail: trab@infoweb.abs.net
Contact: Mr. Barth M. Onuoha, Jnr. - Chairman/CEO

TRACMASTER LIMITED
Business: Distribution & Sales of Hand-Pallet Trucks, Ceiling Materials, Security Doors, Airconditioners & Refridgerating Appliances, Industrial Equipment and Machinery
Address: D1, Alh. Masha Road, near Adeniran Ogunsanya Street, Junction, Surulere, Lagos
Tel: (01) 5456090-1 (2L), 5850050, 5852397, 4710446, 7751676, 2882104
Fax: (01) 5456091

TRACTOR & EQUIPMENT NIGERIA LIMITED
Business: Sales & Support of Caterpillar Mining, Construction Equipments, Lift Trucks & Generators
Address: Billingsway (off Secretariat Road), Oregun Industrial Estate, Oregun, Lagos
Tel: (01) 4930430-6 (7L), 2642332
Fax: (01) 4971911, 4964499
Contact: Mr. Steve A. Scott - MD
Mr. Austin Oyowe - GM (Sales)

TRADE BANK PLC
Business: Commercial Banking
Address: 2, Ilofa Road, Ilorin, Kwara State
Tel: (031) 220062, 223524, 223529 **Fax:** (031) 223532
* Great Nigeria House (3rd Floor), 47/57, Martins Street, Lagos
Tel: (01) 2667100, 2661895 **Fax:** (01) 2669768
E-mail: trade.bnk@infoweb.abs.net
* Gateway Plaza, Plot 208, 4th Avenue, Central Business Area, Abuja
Tel: (09) 5233562-4 (3L) **Fax:** (09) 5234752
Contact: Mr. S. E. Kolawole - MD/CEO
Tunde Olofintila - PRO

TRADE FAIR SERVICES LIMITED
Business: Country Agent to International Trade Fair Companies
Address: 5, Oregun Road, by Radio Bus-Stop, Alausa,Lagos
Tel: (01) 4970860, 4965778 **Fax:** (01) 4936473
E-mail: itua@infoweb.abs.net
info@nigeria.messefrankfurt.com
Contact: Mr. Augustus Itua - Chairman/CEO
Miss Omonigho Itoya - Trade Fair Office

TRADE WINGS LIMITED
Business: Importation & Distribution of General Merchandise
Address: 36, Offin Road, Oke-Arin, Lagos Island, Lagos
Tel: (01) 2640750, 2640970, 4749191 **Fax:** (01) 2640740
E-mail: tradewings@hyperia.com
* 102, Asa Road, Aba
Tel: 08023520723
* Singer Market, opp. Union Bank, Kano
Tel: 08023747920

TRADEWAYS EXPRESS INTERNATIONAL LIMITED
Business: Express Courier, Import Express, Cargo Handling, Warehousing Services
Address: 2, Oludegun Avenue, opp. Domino Stores, off International Airport Road, Mafoluku, Lagos
Tel: (01) 4973867, 4705774, 4802916, 08033943449
Fax: (01) 4973400
E-mail: trace@tradewaysexpress..com
Website: www.tradewaysexpress..com
Contact: Mr. Larry Chinekezi - MD/CEO

TRAINING & CONFERENCE CENTRE, OGERE
Business: Provision of Facilities for Residental Courses, Seminars, Conference and Workshops
Address: The Centre, Lagos-Ibadan Expressway, Ogere Remo, Ogun State
Tel: (037) 620107-9 (3L), 620741-3 (3L), 08034620107-9
Fax: (037) 620605
* St. Peter's House (8th Floor), 3, Ajele Street ,off Broad Street, Marina, Lagos
Tel: (01) 2601640-3 (4 L)
E-mail: nodistractions@tccogere.com.ng

TRANE AGENCIES
Business: Shipping, Clearing & Forwaring, Warehousing, Logistic Services
Address: 282, Gbagada Expressway, Gbagada Estate Phase I, Lagos
Tel: (01) 4930554, 4935178, 8042411, 08033086309
Fax: (01) 4930554
E-mail: tranex@tranex.com.ng
Contact: Chief A. O. Olatunji - Chairman
Mrs. C. E. Iheme - GM/CEO

TRANS AFRICA EXPRESS LIMITED
Business: Courier & Air Cargo Services
Address: 3, Babatola Drive, off Obafemi Awolowo Way, behind Obafemi Awolowo House, Ikeja, Lagos
Tel: (01) 4960800, 4960595 **Fax:** (01) 4960800
E-mail: transafrica@infoweb.abs.net
transafricaairexpress@yahoo.com
Website: www.transafrica.com
Contact: Mr. William T. Ejuetami - MD/CEO

TRANS ATLANTIC SHIPPING AGENCY LIMITED
Business: Shipping Agency, Clearing & Forwarding, Warehousing and Collateral Management
Address: 36, Kofo Abayomi Avenue Apapa, Lagos
Tel: (01) 5872290, 5877718, 5874317, 5873065, 0033053711 **Fax:** (01) 5872643, 5450709
E-mail: info@tasal.com
Contact: Alh. Umaru A. Shinkafi, CON - Chairman
Chief Uche U. Ohafia - MD/CEO

TRANS CITY TRANSPORT COMPANY
Business: Transportation (Passenger-Buses), Hiring Services
Address: Eleyele, Ibadan
Tel: (02) 2414331
Contact: Deacon P. A. Adeniran -GM/CEO

TRANS INTERNATIONAL BANK PLC
Business: Commercial Banking
Address: TIB House, Oba Adepimpe Road, Ibadan
Tel: (02) 2413135, 2413165, 2414647 **Fax:** (02) 2412327
E-mail: transbk@tib.nig.com
27, Karimu Kotun Street, Victoria Island, Lagos
Tel: (01) 3204095, 4738263, 4738275 **Fax:** (01) 3204094
Contact: Mr. B. A. Osunkunle, JP - MD/CEO

TRANS METRO VENTURES LIMITED
Business: Sales, Engineering & Maintenance of Computers
Address: 117, Lewis Street, by P & T, Obalende, Lagos
Tel: (01) 2635657, 2647446, 8902552, 8903670, 08033291731
Fax: (01) 2634009
Contact: Mr. T. T. Balogun - MD/CEO

TRANS WONDERLAND (NIGERIA) PLC
Business: Recreational & Hospitality Activities; Transportation, Leisure & Recreational Consultancy Services
Address: Old Airport Bodija U.I.P.O. Box 208498, Ibadan
Tel: (02) 8104253
Contact: Engr. Bode Owoeye - GM/CEO

TRANS-CLASS WORLD SERVICES NIGERIA LIMITED
Business: Maritime Services, Telecommunications
Address: Nnewi Building, 1-3, Creek Road, Apapa, Lagos
Tel: (01) 4700456, 5871513, 5871514 **Fax:** (01) 5871514
* 6, Burma Road, Apapa, Lagos
Contact: Chief Chukwunwike Emenuga - CEO

TRANS-MEDIA GROUP
Business: Maritime Services, Import & Export, Industrials, General Contractors & Merhcants, Advertising
Address: Trans-Media Group House, 125A, Market Rd, Aba
Tel: (082) 231274
Contact: Chief (Dr.) Jerry Kalu - MD/CEO

TRANS-NATIONWIDE EXPRESS PLC
Business: Air Express and Courier Service, Shipping, Freight Forwarding, Travel Agency
Address: Plot 282, Gbagada Estate Phase I, Gbagada Expressway, Lagos
Tel: (01) 4930554, 4714983, 8042411 **Fax:** (01) 4935178
E-mail: tranex@tranex.com.ng
Website: www.tranex.com.ng
Contact: Chief A. O. Olatunji - Chairman
Mrs. C. E. Iheme - GM/CEO

TRANS-NIGERIA ASSURANCE COMPANY LIMITED
Business: All Classes of Insurance
Address: Premium House, Premium Place, Jericho, Ibadan
Tel: (02) 2412350, 2413624, 2413789
Contact: Mr. Olu Ogunniran - MD/CEO

TRANS-ROYAL COMPANY LIMITED
Business: Shipping & Airfreighting, Import & Export, Petroleum & Allied Services
Address: Union Bank Building (1st Floor), 6, Ijora Causeway, Ijora, Lagos
Tel: (01) 5870189, 885891, 08033152429
E-mail: trans-royal@yahoo.com
Contact: Mr. Simeon O. Ebbah - Exec. GM

TRANS-SAHARAN AIR LIMITED
Business: Domestic & International Airline Services
Address: Audu Lukat House, 8, Lagos Street, Kano
Tel: (064) 318187 **Fax:** (064) 647015
E-mail: transsaharan@hotmail.com
Contact: Salihu Belel Yunusa - Chairman/CEO

TRANS-WORLD SECURITY SYSYEMS LIMITED
Business: Sales and Service of Security Equipment, Manufacture of Intruder Alarm Panel, Guard Services, Central Monitoring Service, Training
Address: 31, Allen Avenue, Ikeja, Lagos
Tel: (01) 49383004826509, 8124241, 08023046969
Fax: (01) 2631150
E-mail: tss@alpha.linkserve.com
oekhomu@aol.com
Contact: Chief (Dr.) Ona Ekhomu - Chairman/CEO

TRANSAFRICA FINANCIAL SERVICES LIMITED
Business: Capital Market Operation, Project Finance & Infrastructure, Portfolio Management, Finance Advisory Services
Address: AIICO Plaza (2nd Floor), Plot PC. 12, Afibank Street, Victoria Island, Lagos
Tel: (01) 4618932, 4711251, 08023324154, 0803315123
Fax: (01) 4618932
E-mail: info@transafricafinancial.com
Website: www.transafricafinancial.com
Contact: Mr. John Agboiboh - Head (Admin)

TRANSALTIC NIGERIA LIMITED
Business: Customs Clearing and Forwarinding Agency
Address: Development House (6th Floor), 21, Wharf Road, Apapa, Lagos
Tel/Fax: (01) 5452595
E-mail: transaltic@linkserve.com
transaltic2004@yahoo.com
Contact: High Chief Nathaniel Adesiyakan - Chairman/CEO
Chief Adeduro Adesiyakan - MD

TRANSCAN GRAPHICS LIMITED
Business: Colour Separation Servicesss, Printing and Desktop Publishing
Address: 91, Akerele Street, Surulere Lagos
Tel/Fax: (01) 5850538
E-mail: transcangl@hotmail.com
Contact: Mr. Stephen G. Taylor - CEO

TRANSCAP NIGERIA LIMITED
Business: Shipping
Address: 28, Burma Road, Apapa, Lagos
Tel: (01) 5453981, 5453164 **Fax:** (01) 5876419
E-mail: info@transcap-ng.com
Contact: Mr. Mr. Francois Lavanant - CEO

TRANSCAP TRAVEL BUREAUX (Div of CFAO Nig. Plc)
Business: Travel Agency and Airport Services
Address: 1, Davies Street, off Marina, Lagos
Tel: (01) 2660330, 2665071, 2665071, 262887, 26655063, 2665067 **Fax:** (01) 2662887
E-mail: transcap@nova.net.ng
transcaplos@yahoo.com
Contact: Chief Molade Okoya-Thomas, MFR - Chairman
Mr. R. Grant - Group MD/CEO

TRANSCHEM NIGERIA LIMITED
Business: Supply and Installation and Security Equipment, Importation and Sales of Water Treatment Chemicals, Production of Airfresher, Nylon and Starch
Address: 208/212, Broad Street, Lagos
Tel: (01) 2661590, 2667042 **Fax:** (01) 2643003
E-mail: ipec_industries@hotmail.com
Contact: Alh. Nuhu Aliu - Chairman
Mr. Emmanuel Ayodele - MD/CEO

TRANSCOASTAL NIGERIA LIMITED
Business: Onshore & Offshore Oil Industry Services (Steel Fabrication, Installation and Refurbishment of Platforms and Pipelines; Project Management, Hook-up & Commissioning, Sand-Blasting & Painting
Address: 25, Ologun Agbaje Street, off Adeola Odeku Street, Victoria Island, Lagos
Tel: (01) 2624904, 2624906, 4712329 **Fax:** (01) 2624906
E-mail: transcoastalng 1@yahoo.com
pailag@hyperia.com
pailag@vgccl.net

Contact: Mr. Iyke Ejizu - Chairman
Mr. Mike Robertson - MD/CEO

TRANSCON GROUP
Business: Health Care, Oil & Gas, Communication, Properties & Investments
Address: 18, Kofo Abayomi Avenue, Apapa, Lagos
Tel: (01) 5872927, 5874063, 5874065, 2906216, 08033037099 **Fax:** (01) 5872927, 5453312, 2906216
E-mail: transcongroup@yahoo.com
Contact: Dr. E. E. Sowho - Group MD/CEO

TRANSCONTINENTAL EXPRESS SERVICES LIMITED
Business: Courier Services
Address: Ikeja Shopping Plaza (Suite A204), 81, Mobolaji Bank-Anthony Way, Ikeja, Lagos
Tel: (01) 4932199, 4935581, 4977045 **Fax:** (01) 4932199
E-mail: tesogar@yahoo.com
Contact: Mr. Francis Ugbong Ogar - MD/CEO

TRANSGLOBAL INSURANCE BROKERS LIMITED
Business: Insurance Broking
Address: Big Leaf House (4th Floor), 7 (Plot 1663), Oyin Jolayemi Street, Victoria Island, Lagos
Tel: (01) 2612263, 2614133, 2625727 **Fax:** (01) 2617908
E-mail: info@transglobal.com.ng
Website: www.transglobal.com.ng
* 19, Blantyre Street, off Adetokunbo Ademola Crescent, Wuse II, Abuja
Tel: (09) 5236237-8 (2L) **Fax:** (09) 5238660
Contact: Chief I. C. Ogbue - Chairman
Mr. Adeniyi S. Olatimilehin - GM/CEO

TRANSGLOBE INVESTMENT & FINANCE COMPANY LTD
Business: Stockbroking, Trustees, Investment Management, Issuing House, Nominees, Consultancy
Address: 21, Boyle Street, Onikan, Lagos
Tel: (01) 2668407, 683460, 683565 **Fax:** (01) 2668407
E-mail: trasnglobe@infoweb.abs.net
Contact: Nze (Dr.) C. O. Maduako - Chairman
Mr. Francis O. Chimezie - Group MD/CEO

TRANSMARINE NIGERIA LIMITED
Business: Shipping, Ship Chartering, Clearing and Forwarding
Address: 17, Bornu Crescent, Apapa, Lagos
Tel: (01) 5452680 **Fax:** (01) 5875011
Contact: Chief G. A. Hassan - Chairman
Mr. S. A. Ogunsanya - MD/CEO

TRANSPHARM NIGERIA LIMITED
Business: Sales, Installation & Service of Medical and Laboratory Equipment
Address: Plot 311A, Adeniyi Street, off Isheri Road, Ogba Industrial Estate, Ikeja, Lagos
Tel: (01) 4922879, 4924052, 4925449, 7767194
Fax: (01) 4925449
E-mail: transgroup 1@yahoo.com
Contact: Prince Felix Awofisayo - Chairman/MD

TRANSPROJECT NIGERIA LIMITED
Business: Construction and Civil Engineering Contractors
Address: 90, Raymond Njoku Road, S. W. Ikoyi, Lagos
Tel: (01) 2694874, 688166, 2671255 **Fax:** (01) 2694874
Contact: Arc. Y. Mohammed - Chairman
Engr. Tanko Abdullahi - Exec. Director

TRANSRAPID NIGERIA LIMITED
Business: Turn-Key Project Development and Procurement Services, Civil Engineering & Building Construction, Marketing of Pharmaceuticals, Medical & Laboratory Reagents
Address: Plot 311-A, Abisogun Leigh St/Adeniyi Street off Isheri Road, Ogba Industrial Estate, Ikeja, Lagos
Tel: (01) 4922879, 4924052, 4925449, 7767194
Fax: (01) 4922879
E-mail: transgroup@yahoo.com
transgroup@linkserve.com
* Oyebode Plaza (1st Floor), B.C.G.A. Road, beh. Olorunda L.G. Secretariat, Igbonna, Osogbo
Tel: (035) 240540
Contact: Prince Felix A. Awofisayo - Chairman/MD

TRANSTEC GROUP OF COMPANIES
Business: Sales of Occupational & Safety Wears, Sales, Installation & Service of Computers & Accessories
Address: 24, Constitution Road, Kaduna
Tel: (062) 248719, 08037054651 **Fax:** (062) 248719
E-mail: transteccomputers@yahoo.com

TRANSWORLD INVESTMENT LIMITED
Business: Stockbroking
Address: BAICO Plaza (6th Floor), 12, Abibu-Oki Street, off Marina, Lagos
Tel: (01) 2662275, 2642550, 08023232001, 0033032481
Fax: (01) 2662275
E-mail: transworld00@hotmail.com
Contact: Mr. Niran Davies - Chief Operation Officer

TRANTER INTERNATIONAL LIMITED
Business: IT Solutions, Computer Training and Certification, Datacomms/Telecoms/Computer Engineering Services, Electrical/Mechanical and Structural Engineering, Civil & Building Engineering, Procurement & Supply Services, Logistics Support
Address: 3-6, Alh. Adejumo Avenue, off State Highway, opp. Bhojsons, Ilupeju Ind Estate, Oshodi, Lagos
Tel: (01) 4973363, 4961582, 4975905-6 (2L)
Fax: (01) 4973363
E-mail: info@tranterserve.com
Website: www.tranterserve.com
www.executrain.com
* Plot A42, Birabi Street, opp Hotel Presidential, G.R.A. Phase II, Port Harcourt
Tel: (084) 232223, 232228, 232234-5 (2L)
Contact: Mr. E. O. Ayoola - Chairman/CEO

TRAVELEX RETAIL NIGERIA LIMITED
Business: Distribution & Sales of Travellers' Cheques, 'Travelex' Money Transfer
Address: Mamman Kontagora House (13th Floor), 23, Marina, Lagos
Tel: (01) 2662193, 2666764 **Fax:** (01) 2669199

TRAVELLERS PALACE HOTEL LIMITED
Business: Hospitality Services
Address: 8, Agbo Ogbuefi Street, Woliwo, Onitsha

Tel: (046) 211013
Contact: P. C. Ezeanuna - Chairman/CEO

TRAVELTRON LIMITED
Business: Travel Agency
Address: Plot 1038A, Ologun Agbaje Street, off Adeola Odeku Street, Victoria Island, Lagos
Tel: (01) 2625680, 4616799 **Fax:** (01) 2625681
E-mail: traveltron@yahoo.com
traveltronlimited@yahoo.com
Contact: Kehinde Durosinmi-Etti - Chairman
Adeshina Bashir - MD/CEO

TRAWL ATLANTIC LIMITED
Business: Fish Trawling and Shrimping
Address: 10/12, Acme Crescent, off Acme Road, by Industrial Cartons Ltd., Ogba Ind. Estate, Ikeja, Lagos
Tel: (01) 7742648 **Fax:** (01) 4922640
E-mail: trawlatlantic@hyperia.com
Contact: Mrs. E. Jituboh - MD/CEO

TRAWLER MANUFACTURING LIMITED
Business: Manufactureing of Fibre-Glass Fishing Trawlers
Address: Enerhen/Effurun Road, opp. Leventis Stores, Warri
Tel: (053) 250273, 252410, 252742, 254098

TRENDS VENERATE LIMITED
Business: Tannery, Exportation of Hides and Skin, Importation of Commodities
Address: 15S, Niger Street, Kano
Tel: (064) 645164
Contact: Alh. Lawal Sule Garo - MD/CEO

TRENKO INTERNATIONAL NIGERIA LIMITED
Business: Importation, Distribution and Marketing of Rice
Address: 1, Oju Olobun Close, off Bishop Oluwole Street, Victoria Island, Lagos
Tel: (01) 2626332, 2614229, 2614743 **Fax:** (01) 2626332
E-mail: trenko@hyperia.com
Contact: Adetunji Adebayo - Chairman/CEO

TREVI FOUNDATIONS NIGERIA LIMITED
Business: Foundation Engineering, Oil Servicing
Address: Plot 4, Block B, Gbagada Ind Area, Gbagada, Lagos
Tel: (01) 5550981-2 (2L), 7918881-3 (3L)
Fax: (01) 5550983
E-mail: tfnl@hyperia.com
trevinig@micro.com.ng
Website: www.trevispa.com
Contact: Engr. (Dr.) Leonardo Biserna - MD/CEO
Engr. Enrico Rovati - GM

TRIACTA CONSTRUCTION LIMITED
Business: Engineering Construction
Address: 139, Murtala Mohammed Way, Kano
Tel: (064) 631832 **Fax:** (064) 647672
E-mail: triacta@ecnx.net
Contact: Mr. Elie A. Fahat - MD/CEO

TRIANA LIMITED
Business: Shipping & Agency Services, Chartering, Freight Forwarding, Customs Agents, Container Handling, Warehousing, Cargo Consolidation & Handling, Air Freight & Charters and Special Projects
Address: 18/20, Commercial Road, Apapa, Lagos
Tel: (01) 5803040-2 (3L), 5871826, 5873468, 5873475, 5876693, 5877019, 5877671
Fax: (01) 5876161, 5876348
E-mail: triana@alpha.linkserve.com
Contact: Mr. M. P., Aguba - MD/CEO
Mr. D. K. Ebinum - Head (Com. & Special Projects)

TRICONTINENTAL OIL SERVICES LIMITED
Business: Contracts and Supplies to Upstream Oil & Gas Industry
Address: Elephant Cement House, ASSBIFI Road, Central Business District, Alausa, Ikeja, Lagos
Tel: (01) 4965379, 4972666 **Fax:** (01) 4930444
E-mail: tricontinental @nova.net.ng
* 41/43, Oroigwe Road, Elimgbu, Rumoukurushi, Port Harcourt. **Tel:** (084) 239661, * (082) 440027
Contact: Chief Olabintan Famutimi - Chairman/CEO
Mr. Dayo Bankole - Sales Engineer/Admin. Mgr

TRIDENT STEEL WORKS (NIGERIA) LIMITED
Business: Manfacturing of Steel & Wire Products, Oilfield Steel Works
Address: Plot 55, Trans-Amadi Ind. Layout, Port Harcourt
Tel: (084) 237171, 232561, 571097
Fax: (084) 233819, 235453
E-mail: trident@tridentnigeria.com
Website: www.tridentnigeria.com
* Plot IN/66A, Niger Bridge Head Industrial Layout, Atani Road, Onitsha
Tel: 08033122432

TRIDOK NIGERIA LIMITED
Business: Metal Pretreatment & Corrosion Control, Sales of Chemical Treatment and Coatings
Address: 320, Agege Motor Rd, Challenge, Mushin, Lagos
Tel: (01) 4527181, 520888 **Fax:** (01) 4527184, 4528999

TRIMCO LIMITED
Business: Crushing and Processing of Palm Kernel, Exportation of Palm Kernel Cake
Address: Plot 55, Happy Home Avenue, Kirikiri Industrial Estate, Mazamaza, Lagos
Tel: (01) 5871624, 5870816, 8044884 **Fax:** (01) 5877512
* Km. 5, Aponmu Road, off Ondo Road, opp. Limca Factory, Akure
Tel: (034) 231677, 231827
Contact: Mr. H. A. Safieddine - Chairman
Mr. F. Reda - MD/CEO

TRINICLE NIGERIA LIMITED
Business: Sales & Lease of Photocopiers, Paper Shredders and Office Automation Equipment
Address: Plot 474/110, Trans-Amadi Industrial Layout, Port Harcourt
Tel: (084) 231449, 231467 **Fax:** (084) 231316
E-mail: trinicle@phca.linkserve.com
* Plot 1673, Oyin Jolayemi Street, Victoria Is, Lagos
Tel: (01) 2701273, 4726785, 08033078813
* Peoples Shopping Complex, Plot 1263, Jere Street, Garki II, Abuja
Tel: (09) 6710727
Contact: Engr. (Mrs) Stella Okene - Chairman/CEO

TRINITAS INTERNATIONAL LIMITED
Business: Manufacturing and Marketing of Paints
Address: Km. 10, LASU-Isheri Road (Obadore Bus-Stop), TopCharm Avenue, off Rafiu Egemu Street, Obadore, Lagos
Tel: (01) 7744659, 08034703200 **Fax:** (01) 4924615
E-mail: topcharm@yahoo.co.uk

TRIPOD HOLDINGS LIMITED
Business: Holding Company, Venture Capital, Trade & Investment, Consultancy Services
Address: NICON House (6th Floor), 5, Customs Street, off Marina, Lagos
Tel: (01) 2663148, 2669749, 2665598, 2665858, 2663655
Fax: (01) 2669947
E-mail: rimsec@linkserve.com.ng
Contact: Mr. Emmanuel Ocholi - Chairman/CEO
Mr. Wale Oyejola - GM

TRIPLE A OUTDOOR LIMITED
Bsiness: Outdoor Advertising Agency
Address: 51A, Faramobi Ajike Str, Anthony Village, Lagos
Tel: (01) 4932208, 7744517, 08034749322, 08037260789
E-mail: woleolaleye@yahoo.com
* 3, Dutse Close, Nassarawa G.R.A., Kano
Tel: (064) 645882
Contact: Mr. Oluwole Olaleye - Exec. Chairman

TRIPLE 'E' SYSTEMS ASSOCIATES LIMITED
Business: Consultancy Services in Energy, Engineering, Environment and Computer Applications
Address: Goodwill House, 278, Ikorodu Road, beside Mobil Station, Anthony, Lagos
Tel: (01) 4974751, 7917078 **Fax:** (01) 4937140
E-mail: triple-e@cyberspace.net.ng
triple-e@triplesys.com
Website: www.triplesys.com
Contact: Lt. Gen. M.I. Wushishi (rtd.) - Chairman
Dr. Felix Babatunde O. Dayo - MD/CEO

TRIPLE P (NIGERIA) LIMITED
Business: Processing of Expanded Polystyrene, Production of Ceiling Tiles, Cool Boxes and Insulation Panels
Address: Plot 71, Sharada Industrial Estate Phase III, Kano
Tel: (064) 660901-2 (2L), 664244, 08046120567

TRIPOD HOLDINGS LIMITED
Business: Capital Venture, Trade & Investment, Consultancy
Address: 1A, Monrovia Street, off Aminu Kano Crescent, Wuse II, Abuja
Tel: (09) 4130453, 4137125 **Fax:** (09) 4137126
* NICON House (6th Floor), 5, Customs Street, off Marina, Lagos
Tel: (01) 2663148, 2663665, 2665598, 2665858, 2669749
Fax: (01) 2669847
E-mail: rimsec@linkserve.com.ng
Contact: Mr. Emmanuel Ocholi - Chairman/CEO

TRIPPLE GEE & COMPANY PLC
Business: Manufacturing of Computer Stationery, Self-Adhesive Labels and Flexible Packaging Materials, Security Printing, Sales of Computer Systems
Address: Plot 9, Kareem Giwa Street, (opp Trade Fair Complex). Km. 11, Lagos-Badagry Expressway, Abule-Oshun, Lagos
Tel: (01) 8042442, 8043222 **Fax:** (01) 3204088, 3205564
E-mail: info@3geegroup.com
* Plot 11, Area 7A, Cornershop, beh. National Arts & Culture Council, off Festival Road, Garki, Abuja
Tel: (09) 2345366, 2346846
Contact: Chief Gani G. Giwa - MD/CEO

TRIPPLESEA LIMITED
Business: Sales of Information Technology Products, Distribution & Sales of Automatic Voltage Regulators, GSM Phones & Accessories
Address: 17, Oremeji St, off Simbiat Abiola Rd, Ikeja, Lagos
Tel: (01) 4826184, 7731615, 08023708596
Fax: (01) 3209257
E-mail: trippleseamarketing@yahoo.com
Contact: Mr. Chike Charles Chidozie - Chairman/CEO

TRISTAR COMMODITIES (NIGERIA) LIMITED
Business: Importation and Sales of Frozen Foods
Address: Plot 239, Kofo Abayomi St, Victoria Island, Lagos
Tel: (01) 2613416, 2614896 **Fax:** (01) 2610887
Contact: Mr. B. Jimoh

TRISTAR INTERNATIONAL PRODUCTS & EQUIPMENT COMPANY LIMITED
Business: Importation & Marketing of General Merchandise
Address: Plot 39, Trans-Amadi Ind. Layout, Port Harcourt
Tel: (084) 230727, 230043, 571627 **Fax:** (084) 230727
E-mail: gerl@ph.rcl.nig.com
Contact: Alh. Bashir Adaba - Chairman/CEO

TRI-T ENGINEERING SERVICES LIMITED
Business: Sales & Maintenance of Information Technology Products, Office Equipment, Networking, Software, Consultancy
Address: Tinuose House, 45, Murtala Mohammed International Airport Road, Ajao Estate, Isolo, Lagos
Tel: (01) 4522607, 4803930, 08023000017, 08022233366
E-mail: tri-teng@eudoramail.com
Contact: Mr. Oluwatosin Adebajo - MD/CEO

TRITECH COMPUTERS LIMITED
Business: Sales of Servers, IT Workstations & Laptops, Storage Solutions, Networking & Systems Integration (NetSys), IT Infrastructure Support, Software Services, Website Design, Hosting & Domain-Name Registration
Address: 101A, Adeniyi Jones Avenue, Ikeja, Lagos
Tel: (01) 4922564, 4922650, 3453695 **Fax:** (01) 4922651
E-mail: info@tritech-computers-ltd.com
Website: www.tritech-computers-ltd.com
* Plot 1125, Kmusa Traore Street, Asokoro, Abuja
Tel: (09) 3140850, 6714176 **Fax:** (09) 3140851
Contact: Dr. Fola O. Awokoya - MD/CEO

TRITEL NETWORKS LIMITED
Business: Information & Commnication Technology
Address: Plot 93, Younis Bashorun Str, Victoria Island, Lagos
Tel: (01) 2619890 **Fax:** (01) 2611450
Website: www.tritel.co.uk
Contact: Mr. Ezekiel Y. Ajanya - MD/CEO

TRITHEL INTERNATIONAL COMPANY LIMITED
Business: Management and Environmental Consultancy Services (Quality Management, Strategic Management, Human Capital Services, Environmental & Engineering Services, Diagnostic Studies, E-Business, Business Excellence & Consulting)
Address: 104, Opebi Road, Ikeja, Lagos
Tel: (01) 2220064-5 (2L), 08022239566, 0023049966, 08023049968 **Fax:** (01) 2220065
E-mail: trithel@trithelconslting.com
Website: www.trithelconsulting.com
Contact: Chief J. J. Akpieyi, FSChE - Chairman/CEO

TRIUMPH NIGERIA LIMITED
Business: Manufacturing of Corrugated Cartons and Iner Packaging
Address: 26, Dantata Road, Bompai Industrial Estate, Kano
Tel: (064) 635986, 647020 **Fax:** (064) 632536
* 2, Oyeleke Street, Alausa, Ikeja, Lagos
Tel: (01) 7740259, 4966490
Contact: Mr. Milind M. Vyavaharkar - MD/CEO

TRIUMPH PUBLISHING COMPANY LIMITED
Business: Printing, Publishing, Manufacturing of Stationery
Address: 1, Kofar Mazugal Road, Faggae Quarters, Kano
Tel: (064) 633875, 630273, 630060, 649733, 649592, 08037876695 **Fax:** (064) 630273
E-mail: triumph@gamji.com.kano
Website: www.gamji.com/triumph.htm
* Opp. NYSC Secretariat, Area 3, Garki, Abuja
Tel: (09) 2342501
Contact: Alh. Bello Bashir Gwarzo - MD/CEO
Alh. Muktari Magaji - Editor-in-Chief

TRIUMPH BANK PLC
Business: Merchant Banking
Address: 186, Awolowo Road, Ikoyi, Lagos
Tel: (01) 2673894-8 (5L), 2691560-4 (5L)
Fax: (01) 2694242, 2694184, 2690604
E-mail: mis@triumphbank.com.ng
Website: www.triuphbank.com.ng
* 345B, Olu Obasanjo Road, GRA Phase 11, Port Harcourt
Tel: (084) 238939, 239251, 239252, 238941
Fax: (084) 238941
* Plot 2105, H. Macaulay Way, Wuse Zone 6, Abuja.
Tel: (09) 5235174 **Fax:** (09) 5235175
Contact: Mr. Francis O. Atoju - MD/CEO
Mr. Ray Mgbeokwere - Head (Legal & Ext. Affairs)

TROPICAL COMMERCIAL BANK PLC
Business: Commercial Bank
Address: 72B, Murtala Muhammed Way, Kano
Tel: (064) 640050-4 (5L), 631991 **Fax:** (064) 644506
E-mail: tcbplc@samdav.com
* Eleganza Plaza, 1, Commercial Rd, Apapa, Lagos
Tel: (01) 5874365, 5450340 **Fax:** (01) 5450308
Contact: Alh. Lawan Zakarian Gana - MD/CEO
Abubakar Shehu Minjibir -Prin.Mgr. (Corp. Affairs)

TROPICAL EXPRESS NIGERIA LIMITED
Business: Courier & Cargo Services, Freight Forwarding
Address: 12, Mobolaji Bank-Anthony Way, Onigbongbo, Maryland, Ikeja, Lagos
Tel: (01) 4939380-2 (3 L), 4966987, 4966891
Fax: (01) 4966903
E-mail: info@tropicalexpress.ng.com
E-mail: tropex@cyberspace.net.ng
* Neighbourhood Centre (Kiosk 5), opp. Open University, Area 3, Garki, Abuja
Tel: (09) 2343336
Contact: Chief F. R. A. Willaims - Chairman
Mr. Enoma Agbontaen - MD/CEO

TROPICAL FIRE PREVENTION SERVICES LIMITED
Business: Marketing of Fire-Extinguishers and Safety Equipment, Fire Prevention Services
Address: Alexander House, 9/10, Badagry Expressway, Orile-Iganmu, Lagos
Tel: (01) 7744387, 2671284; **Fax:** (01) 2671286
* Erisco Bonpet Plaza, Plot 2357, Herbert Macaulay Way, opp. Old Wuse Market, Wuse Zone 5, Abuja
Tel: (09) 5234670, 5234671; **Fax:** (09) 5234671
Contact: Alh. Abubakar Bashir - Chairman
Chief Eric Umeofia - Vice Chairman/CEO

TROPICAL SERVICES NIGERIA LIMITED
Business: Oilfield Support Services - Global Procrement, Rig Safety Maintenance, Safety/Fire & Gas Detention Systems
Address: 6, Omoku Street, D-Line, Port Harcourt
Tel: (084) 239620, 08035091061 **Fax:** (084) 239621
E-mail: tsnl@phca.linkserve.com
* 31, Ladipo Oluwole Avenue, off Adeniyi Jones Avenue, Ikeja, Lagos
Tel: (01) 4971096, 7742639 **Fax:** (01) 4971454
E-mail: tsnl72@yahoo.com
Contact: Mr. Bola Adejobi - Chairman/CEO

TROPICS FINANCE & INVESTMENT COMPANY LIMITED
Business: Funds Management, Trade Finance, Money Market Operations, Nominee Holdings
Address: Amazing Grace Plaza, Plots 2E-4E, Ligali Ayorinde Street, Victoria Island, Lagos
Tel: (01) 2624553 **Fax:** (01) 2624554
E-mail: tropics@linkserve.com
Contact: Mr. Erastus B. O. Akingbola - Chairman
Mrs. Anthonia T. O. Akingbola - MD/CEO

TROPICS SECURITIES LIMITED
Business: Stockbroking, Portfolio Management
Address: The Penthouse, Amazing Grace Plaza, Plots 2E-4E, Ligali Ayorinde Street, Victoria Island, Lagos
Tel: (01) 2624553 **Fax:** (01) 2624554
E-mail: tropics@alpha.linkserve.com
Contact: Mr. E. B. O. Akingbola - Chairman
Mrs. A. T. O. Akingbola - Exec. Director/CEO

TRUE TALES PUBLICATIONS LIMITED
Business: Publishing of Magazines, Trading, Home Video Film Production, Contracting
Address: True Tales Plaza, 2/4, Aromolaran Close, off Aina Street, Ojodu Bus-Stop, Ojodu Estate, Ikeja, Lagos
Tel: (01) 4925188
Contact: Dr. Emmanuel Ibe Kachikwu - Founder
Mr. Kayode Ajala - MD/CEO

TRUPAK TECHNOLOGIES
Business: Computer Software Development/Consultancy
Address: 8, Ladipo Adeyemi Street, Anthony Village, Lagos
Tel: (01) 4931494, DL 4979419 **Fax:** (01) 4931493
E-mail: austin@trupak.net
Website: www.trupak.net
Contact: Dr. Austin E. Osuide - MD/CEO

TRUST BANK OF AFRICA LIMITED
Business: Merchant Banking
Address: Waterfront Plaza, (1st Floor), Plot 270A, Ozumba Mbadiwe Avenue, Victoria Island, Lagos
Tel: (01) 2709550-69 (20L) **Fax:** (01) 2625196
Website: www.trustbankng.com
* Plot 444 Constitution Avenue (Next to NDIC), Central Area, Phase II, Abuja
* Admiralty Building, Plot 202, Olu Obasanjo Road, Port Harcourt
Contact: Mr. Adam Gramston - MD/CEO
Mrs. M. S. Ladipo - GM (Corporate Banking)

TRUST WORLD ELECTRONICS LIMITED
Business: Sales of Consumer Electronic Appliances & Phone
Address: 12, Calcutta Crescent, Apapa, Lagos
Tel: (01) 5878876-7 (2L), 08023070607, 08033437766
Contact: Mr. Joe Ugwushie - Exec. Director/CEO

TRUST YIELDS SECURITIES LIMITED
Business: Stockbroking
Address: Stock Exchange House (20th Floor), 2/4, Customs Street, off Marina, Lagos
Tel: (01) 2661541, 2694198 **Fax:** (01) 2694198
E-mail: trustyields@metrong.com
Contact: Alh. R. Ola Yussuff - Chairman/CEO
Mr. Tunde Alade-Dauda - Chief Ops. Officer

TRUSTHOUSE INVESTMENTS LIMITED
Business: Investments, Stockbroking, Financial Services
Address: 3, Sumbo Jibowu Street, off Ribadu Road, S. W. Ikoyi, Lagos
Tel: (01) 2691281, 2691284 Fax: (01) 2691265
E-mail: trushouse@hyperia.com
Contact: Mr. Luke O. Okonkwo - Chairman/CEO

TRUSTVILLE PROPERTIES DEVELOPMENT CO. LTD
Business: Development, Sales & Management of Properties, General Business
Address: 40B, Raymond Njoku Street, S. W. Ikoyi, Lagos
Tel: (01) 2695824, 4614846 **Fax:** (01) 2695824
E-mail: ppty@hyperia.com
* 32A, Emekuku Street, D-Line, Port Harcourt
Tel: (084) 231882
Contact: Mr. Onyekwere Ogba - Chairman
Mr. Joseph Ezeru Obi - MD/CEO

TRUST-WORLD INSURANCE COMPANY LIMITED
Business: All Classes of Insurance
Address: 213, Herbert Macaulay Street, Yaba, Lagos
Tel: (01) 4804622, 865276, 866010 **Fax:** (01) 865267
E-mail: trustworldins@cyberspace.net.ng
* Industrial Aluminium Plaza, opp. NITEL Corporate Headquarters, Plot 887, Emeka Anyaoku Street, Area 11, Garki, Abuja
Tel: (09) 2340563, 08037018579
Contact: Dr. A. T. Adeleke - Chairman
Mr. E. Olu Omirin - MD/CEO

TRUSTY-STEP NIGERIA LIMITED
Business: Floors and Surfaces Anti-Slip Treatment Services
Address: 5B, Oko Awo Street, off Adetokunbo Ademola Street, Victoria Island, Lagos
Tel: (01) 2620679, 3204215, 08023102622, 08038118111
Fax: (01) 2624542, 3204215
E-mail: safety_tsn@yahoo.co.uk
* Plot 37, Trans-Amadi Ind. Layout, Port Harcourt
Tel/Fax: (084) 238708
Contact: Mr. Morrison Odion Okunbor - MD/CEO

TRUVISION LIMITED
Business: Eye Care Services, Fitting of Contact Lens
Address: 37, Igbosere Road, Lagos Island, Lagos
Tel: (01) 2633754 **Fax:** (01) 2633113
E-mail: truvision@beta.linkserve.com
* Plot 590F, Adetokunbo Ademola Crescent, Wuse II, Abuja.
Tel: (09) 5238761
Contact: Dr. Nkem Okoroafor - Chairman/CEO

TRW STOCKBROKERS LIMITED
Business: Stockbroking, Issuing House, Equity Research and Portfolio Management
Address: Kajola House, 62/64, Campbell Street, Lagos
Tel: (01) 2646976, 2637743, 2649999 **Fax:** (01) 2645363
E-mail: trw@linkserve.com
* Plot 3 (Suite 3), Area 7 Cornershops, Garki, Abuja
Contact: Barr. Solomon Eghobamien - Chairman
Mr. Azubuike Okpalaoka - MD/CEO

TRY 'N' CARRY LIMITED
Business: Sales of Electronics and Kitchen Equipment
Address: 7, Ado Avenue, off Commercial Rd, Apapa, Lagos
Tel: (01) 5871927, 5871722
Contact: Mr. Hassan H. Zein - Chairman
Mr. Ramzy Yatim - MD/CEO

TRYFAM NIGERIA LIMITED
Business: Publishing, Graphics Design, Colour Separation, Corporate & Commercial Printing Services
Address: 23, Park Lane, Apapa, G.R.A., Lagos
Tel: (01) 5872120, 08023186277, 08023242942, 0802352402, 08033211859, 08033304456, 08055268428 **Fax:** (01) 5450879
E-mail: tryfam@micro.com.ng
Contact: Mr. Herbet Umaru Anderson - Chairman
Mrs. Binta Mohammed - MD/CEO

TSL (NIGERIA) LIMITED
Business: Import & Export, Indenting Agents
Address: 4, Osolo Way, off International Airport Road, Ajao Estaate, Isolo, Lagos
Tel: (01) 4522795, 7741133 **Fax:** (01) 2610069
Contact: Chief H. O. Onyekuru - Chairman/CEO

TUDAKA PETROLEUM & GAS COMPANY LIMITED
Business: Marketing of Petroleum Products, Bottling of LP Gas
Address: Western House (8th Floor, Suite 802), 8/10, Broad

Street, Lagos Island, Lagos
Tel: (01) 2635258, 2634517
* Plot 4, T.A. Doherty Industrial Layout, behind National Station, off Oregun Road, Ikeja, Lagos
Tel: (01) 4933786-7 (2 L)
Contact: Chief Tunde Afolabi - Exec. Chairman

TULIP PRESS LIMITED
Business: Printing, Manufacturing of Light Packaging
Address: Plot 1127, Aminu Kano Crescent, Wuse II, Abuja
Tel: (09) 5238705-6 (2L), 08033139362, 0803750336
Fax: (09) 5237624
Contact: Dr. Remi Oyewumi - Exec Director/CEO

TUNG TRAVEL AND TOURS LIMITED
Business: Travel Agency and Consultancy
Address: 23, Sinari Daranijo Street, off Younis Bashorun Street, Victoria Island Annex, Lagos
Tel: (01) 2620364, 7742377
Contact: Mr. Francis Barde - Co-ordinator

TUNJI ADENIYI & COMPANY
Business: Estate Agency, Estate Surveying & Valuation, Property Management
Address: Nigeria Airways Building (1st Floor), 24, Ahmadu Bello Way, Kaduna
Tel: (062) 241112, 247760, 08023225648
Fax: (062) 241112
E-mail: tunji.adeniyi@skannet.com
Contact: Mr. Tunji Adeniyi - Principal Partner

TUNJI IJAOLA & CO
Business: Chartered Accountants, Due Dilligence Services
Address: Ebani House, (Right Wing, 2nd Floor), 149/153, Broad Street, Lagos Island, Lagos
Tel: (01) 8150232, 0802314927
Contact: Mr Tunji Ijaola - MD/CEO

TUNNEX LABORATORY ENGINEERING LIMITED
Business: Sales of Laboratory Equipment & Chemicals, Sales & Installation of Laboratory Furniture & Fittings
Address: 111, Demurin Street (Oba-Nle Aro Bus-Stop), Ketu, Lagos
Tel: (01) 8147607, 08033060580
E-mail: tunnexlab@hotmail.com
Contact: Mr. Olatunji Ayo Olaleye - Chairman/CEO

TUNS HOLDINGS LIMITED
Business: Production of Vegetable Oil, Livestock & Agricultural Products, PVC Pipes and Ballpoint Pens.
Address: Km 9, Ikirun Road, Osogbo.
Tel: (035) 240400, 240408, 243300 **Fax:** (035) 241188
* Chicken House, Plot 16, Omole Layout, Isheri Road, Ikeja, Lagos.
Tel: (01) 4712321, 4922008-9 (2L), 8045205
Fax: (01) 4922011
* Chicken House, Plot 472, Ibrahim Babangida Way, Wuse II, Abuja
Tel: (09) 5234072 **Fax:** (09) 5234985
Contact: Chief Tunde Badmus - Chairman/CEO

TURNERS BUILDING PRODUCTS (AREWA) LIMITED
Business: Manufacturing of Roofing & Cieling Sheets
Address: 19/20, Textile Road, Kakuri Indstrial Estate, Kaduna
Tel: (062) 232739, 08033111244, 08035901585
E-mail: tbp4175@mail.com
Contact: Hajia Maryam Mohammed - MD/CEO

TURNING-POINT NEWSPAPERS LIMITED
Business: Newspaper Publishing (The Comet)
Address: 23/25, Ijora Causeway, Ijora, Lagos
Tel: (01) 2882726, 2882728, 2882926, 5455627-9 (3 L)
E-mail: mail@cometnew.com.ng
* Plot 1707, Jos Street, Area 3, Garki, Abuja
Tel/Fax: (09) 2343202
Contact: Mr. Lade Bonuola - Vice Chairman/CEO

TUTTO CHICCO LIMITED
Business: Importation/Sales of Items & Toys for Children
Address: 42, Randle Road, Apapa, Lagos
Tel: (01) 5451432, 5454312
* Elpina Plaza (Shop 16), Plot 642C, Akin Adesola Street, Victoria Island, Lagos

TWENTY-FIRST CENTURY COMMUNICATIONS LIMITED
Business: Advertising and Marketing Communications
Address: 1, Akinwale St off CMD Avenue, Ikosi-Ketu, Lagos
Tel: (01) 4930833, 08023039978, 08023257062
E-mail: stcent@yahoo.com
Contact: Chief Allan Ola Olabode - Vice Chairman/CEO

TWIN PRUDENTIAL VENTURES LIMITED
Business: Procurement, Supply, Installation & Maintenance of Airconditioners, Procurement & Supply of Oil Tools & Equipment, Mechanical & Electrical Parts
Address: 2, Toyin Street, Ikeja, Lagos
Tel: (01) 4721388, 08033044412
E-mail: twinprudential@yahoo.com
Contact: Mr. Kehinde O. Oluseye - Chairman/CEO

TWT COMMUNICATIONS LIMITED
Business: Advertising, Marketing Communication & Public Relations Consultancy
Address: 75B, Akinola Cole Crescent, off Adeniyi Jones Avenue, Ikeja, Lagos
Tel: (01) 2881679, 4707806 **Fax:** (01) 2881679
E-mail: twt@infoweb.abs.net
twtcommunications@yahoo.com
Contact: Taiwo Ola, Jnr. - MD/CEO
Femi Oyeniyi - ED (Client Services)

TYME RESOURCES AND COMPANY LIMITED
Business: Construction Services, Metal Fabrication, Civil, Electrical and Mechanical Engineering, Equipment Supplies, Maintenance and Allied Services, Fertilizer Distributorship
Address: 52, Norman Williams Street, S. W. Ikoyi, Lagos
Tel: (01) 2693150, 2692751 **Fax:** (01) 2693150
E-mail: temec@beta.linkserve.com
* House 7, Close B, off 2nd Avenue, F.H.A. Estate, Rumueme, Port Harcourt.
Tel: (084) 440516
Contact: Chief (Dr.) E. M. E. Ugenyi - Chairman/CEO

TYPHA CENIA NIGERIA LIMITED
Business: Oilfield Engineering Services

Address: 5, Uloho Close, off Enerhen-Effurun Road, Warri
Tel: (053) 250980

U. B. A. CAPITAL & TRUST LIMITED
Business: Asset Management, Pension Administration & Management, Executorship of Wills, Trust of Consortium Lending, Advisory Services
Address: 22B, Idowu Taylor Street, Victoria Island, Lagos
Tel: (01) 2700750-6 (7L) **Fax:** (01) 2700762
E-mail: info@ubatrustees.com
info@ubacaptrust.com
Website: www.ubatrustees.com
www.ubacaptrust,com
Contact: Mr Tomi Soyode - MD/CEO

U. I. VENTURES LIMITED
Business: Hospitality Services, Consultancy and Training, Printing
Address: Conference Centre Building, Chapel Road, University of Ibadan, Ibadan
Tel: (02) 8100041, 8102297 **Fax:** (02) 8104663
Contact: Sir. Remi Omotosho - Chairman
Mr. Samuel F. Olatunde - MD/CEO

U. O. O. GROUP OF COMPANIES
Business: Manufacturing, Merchandising, Poultry Farming &Agro-Allied Business
Address: 4, Balogun Square, Lagos Island,
Tel: (01) 2660941, 2663857, 2661256 **Fax:** (01) 2661256
E-mail: uoolagos@infoweb.abs.net
uoo_nigerialtd@hotmail.com
Contact: Chief Nzedioranma Uche Okafor - Chairman/CEO

UAC OF NIGERIA PLC
Business: Conglomerate - Manufacturing & Processing, Distribution/Warehousing, Logistics & Marketing, Agro-Industries, Property Development/Management, Computer Services
Address: Niger House (3th Floor), 1/5, Odunlami St, Lagos
Tel: (01) 2663010, 2663081, 2663325, 2663349
Fax: (01) 2661747, 2664255
Contact: Lt. Gen. M. I. Wushishi (rtd.), CFR - Chairman
Mr. J. A. Ajayi - MD/CEO
Miss Duro Onabolu - Group Public Rel. Adviser

UAC AGRO INDUSTRIES (Div. of UAC of Nig. Plc)
Business: Producers of Chicken, Day-Old Chicks, Eggs & Livestock Feeds
Address: 32, Commercial Road, Apapa, Lagos
Tel: (01) 5451277-8 (2L) **Fax:** (01) 5451278
*Maya Village, Near Lanlate
Contact: Miss Duro Onabolu - Group Public Rel. Adviser

UAC FOODS (Div. of UAC of Nig. Plc)
Business: Manufacturing and Marketing of Convenience Foods, Food & Meat Processing, Integrated Poultry Farming
Address: Km. 16, Ikorodu Road, Ojota, Lagos
Tel: (01) 4933017, 2222012, 7745955 **Fax:** (01) 4973922
E-mail: uacfoods@uacnplc.com
uacfcare@uacnplc.com
Contact: Lt. Gen. M. I. Wushishi (rtd), CFR. - Chairman
Mr. J. A. Ajayi - MD/CEO

UACN PHARMACEUTICAL & PERSONAL PRODUCTS LTD (Div. of UAC of Nig. Plc)
Business: Manufacturing and Marketing of Pharmaceutical and Personal-Care Products
Address: 1/3, Industrial Avenue, Ilupeju Ind Estate, Lagos
Tel: (01) 4932986-9 (4 L)
Contact: Mrs. O. A. Adetayo - MD/CEO
Miss Duro Onabolu - Group Public Rel. Adviser

UACN PROPERTY DEVELOPMENT COMPANY PLC (Div. of UAC of Nig. Plc)
Business: Properties Acquisition, Development, Sales and Leasing
Address: Niger House (3th Floor), 1/5, Odunlami St, Lagos
Tel: (01) 2660889, 2662257, 2663010, 2663349, 7919009
Fax: (01) 2662681
E-mail: updc@uacnplc.com
Contact: Lt. Gen. M. I. Wushishi (rtd.), CFR - Chairman
Mr. Stephen Shuaibu Mayaki - MD/CEO

UAS INVESTMENT LIMITED
Business: Shipping, Export and Courier Services
Address: 3, Adegbola Street, off 1, Obafemi Awolowo Way, Ikeja, Lagos
Tel: (01) 4813947, 8136598, 08023318861
Contact: Mr. Alhassan Charles Idoko - GM

UBA SECURITES SERVICS LIMITED
Business: Issuing House, Share Registration Services, Advisory Services
Address: 97/105, Broad Street, Lagos
Tel: (01) 2667415, 2667419, 4741053

UBINI INDUSTRIAL (NIGERIA) LIMITED
Business: Sales of General Steel & Oilfield Materials, Equipment Leasing, Labour Contractors
Address: Km. 1, Refinery Road, Warri
Tel: (035) 250580, 254935, 255478 **Fax:** (035) 254935
E-mail: ubini@skannet.com
ubini@infoweb.abs.net
Contact: Chief J. D. Ubini - Chairman/CEO
Mr. Steve Osungbuwa - GM

UBOSI ELEH + COMPANY
Business: Estate Surveyors and Valuers, Property Management, Real Estate Investment Advisers, Estate Agency, Feasibility Studies.
Address: 27, Obafemi Awolowo Way (2nd Floor), Ikeja, Lagos
Tel: (01) 4966790, 4968445-6 (2L), 4702186, 4801807
Fax: (01) 4968446
E-mail: ubosieleh@alpha.linkserve.com
* Plot 572, Adetoknbo Ademola Crescent, Cadastral Zone A8, Wuse II, Abuja
Tel: (09) 5230132, 5231435
Contact: Mr. Chudi S. Ubosi - Partner
Mr. Emeka D. Eleh - Partner

UDESCO MANUFACTURING COMPANY LIMITED
Business: Production and Marketing of Cosmetics
Address: 15, Udegboka Street, Nkpor, Onitsha
Tel: (046) 217524
Contact: Chief Ambrose Udegboka - Chairman/CEO

UDEZE INVESTMENTS & INDUSTRIAL COMPLEX LIMITED
Business: Manufacturing of Plastic Goods and Wire Products
Address: Plot D, Bridge Head Industrial Layout, Onitsha
Tel: (046) 212602, 484213
Contact: Elder. F. I. Udeze - MD/CEO

UDOETUK & ASSOCIATES
Business: Estate Surveying & Valuation
Address: Sunshine Suites (2nd Floor), 42, Bishop Oluwole Street, Victoria Islaand, Lagos
Tel: (01) 2612841, 2624651, 4708783, 08023107703, 08023118380, 08033139352
Fax: (01) 2612841
E-mail: udoetuk@infoweb.abs.net

UGEN & ASSOCIATES COMPANY LIMITED
Business: Building of Vehicle Bodies, Fabrication of Aluminium Doors and Windows and. Allied Materials
Address: 199, Muyibi Street, via Peoples Bus-Stop, Olodi, Apapa, Lagos
Tel: (01) 5871469, 08023045239, 08033262356
Contact: Mr. E. T. Okolo - Director/CEO

UGO GARMENTS INDUSTRIES LIMITED
Business: Design & Production of Garments
Address: 17, Niger Street, Onitsha
Tel: (046) 210799, 212464
* Banex Plaza, Plot 750, Aminu Kano Crescent, Wuse II, Abuja

UGOCHUKWU GROUP OF COMPANIES
Business: Conglomerate - Manufacturers, Real Estate Owners & Managers, Insurance Brokerage and Commerce
Address: 17, Calcutta Crescent, Apapa, Lagos
Tel: (01) 5870310, 5876935 **Fax:** (01) 876793
* Nassarawa Road, Ind. Layout, Kakuri, Kaduna
Contact: Mr. Obiora C. Ugochukwu - Group Chairman/CEO

UGOCHUKWU CHEMICAL INDUSTRIES LIMITED
Business: Manufacture of Foam Products & Ind. Chemicals
Address: 17, Calcutta Crescent, Apapa, Lagos
Tel: (01) 5876935, 5870310
Contact: Mr. Obiora C. Ugochukwu - Group Chairman/CEO

UIDC SECURITIES LIMITED
Business: Stockbroking, Investment Advisory Services, Portfolio Managememnt, Capital Market Operation
Address: Great Nigeria House (6th Floor), 47/57, Martins Street, Lagos Island, Lagos
Tel: (01) 2667733, 2662677
Contact: Mr. M. Atsepoyi-Akpieyi - Chairman
Mr. Okon Edet Etu - GM/CEO

ULTICARE-LYKA PHARMACEUTICALS LIMITED
Business: Manufacturing of Pharmaceutical Products
Address: 8A, Akanbi Onitiri Close, off Eric Moore Road, Surulere, Lagos
Tel: (01) 5454140-2 (3L), 5456074, 2646071, 7942322
Fax: (01) 5456074, 5454143-4 (2L), 2646066
E-mail: ulticarepharm@yahoo.com
chrismatel@hyperia.com
* Km. 10, Ibusa-Asaba Road, Ibusa, Delta State
Tel: 08033276431
* 13, Creek Road, Apapa, Lagos
* Plot 304, New Hospital Road, Gyadi-Gyadi, Kano
Contact: Mr. Peter Eloka Okocha, OON - Chairman
Mr. E. D. C. Ilozor - MD/CEO

ULTIMATE AIR SERVICES LIMITED
Business: Travel Agency
Address: Anon Furniture House, Plot 672, Ogbomosho Street,Area 8, Garki, Abuja
Tel: (09) 2902972, 5236659, 08037880995, 08042104095
E-mail: ultimate_air@yahoo.com
* 56, Opebi Road, Ikeja, Lagos
Tel: 08033505780
Contact: Mrs Aloba Opeseyitan - MD/CEO

ULTIMATE NEONS LIMITED
Business: Design, Manufacturing and Installation of Flexy, Neon, Metal & Plastic Signages
Address: 25, Oju-Olobun Close, Victoria Island, Lagos
Tel: (01) 2620610, 2622165 **Fax:** (01) 2621947, 5878013
E-mail: peregrine@alpha.linkserve.com
Contact: Ariyo Salami - Chairman
Bashir Mustapha - MD/CEO

ULTIMATE PERCEPTION LIMITED
Business: Outdoor Advertising (Customised Billboards at Filling Station Pump Tops)
Address: 5, Olufunmilola Okikiolu St,off Toyin St,Ikeja,Lagos
Tel: (01) 4739343, 08023983820
E-mail: up-_kj@yahoo.com
Contact: Mr H. B. Affinnih - MD/CEO

ULYSSES NIGERIA LIMITED
Business: Manufacture and Distribution of Hygiene Products
Address: 227, Apapa Road, Iganmu Industrial Estate, Iganmu, Lagos
Tel: (01) 5837815, 5873416, 7749553, 08033127822
Fax: (01) 5836071
E-mail: ulysses@infoweb.abs.net
Contact: Mr. G. M. E. Osadebe - Chairman
Mr. M. Thadani - MD/CEO

UMM VENTURES LIMITED
Business: Manufacturing of Conference Folders, Customised Bags, Briefcases, Wallets, Travel & School Bags, Book/Bible Carrier and Corporate Gift Items
Address: 5, Oregun Road, Alausa, off Obafemi Awolowo Way (Radio Bus-Stop), Ikeja, Lagos
Tel: (01) 4977516, 7737205, 080231221157, 08023789803
E-mail: ummleatherworks@yahoo.com
Contact: Mr. Dayo Gbohunmi - MD/CEO

UNCLE EAGLE & ASSOCIATES NIGERIA LIMITED
Business: Processing of Colour Films, Commercial & General Photography, Business Bureau Services
Address: 26, Obafemi Awolowo Way, Ikeja, Lagos
Tel: (01) 4974204, 4966249, 8173015
* 109, Allen Avenue, Ikeja, Lagos
Contact: Chief Michael Ajayi Ayeni - Chairman/CEO
Mr. Festus O. Sada - Accountant

UNDERWATER ENGINEERING (COMPANY) NIGERIA LTD
Business: Salvage, Repairs and Dry-Docking of Ships and

Marine Vessels, Underwater Repairs and Hull Cleaning, Underwater Inspection/T.V., Camera Services, Wreck Removal, Heavy Lift Discharging, Ultrasonic Guaging, Testing of Cargo Derricks, Pipeline Laying and Integrity Surveys, BOV Services, Construction, Rehabilityation and Refurbishment of Platforms
Address: 44, Kofo Abayomi Avenue, Apapa, Lagos
Tel: (01) 5877514, 5873806 **Fax:** (01) 5877514
Website: www.underwater-engineering.com
* 2, Ikwerre Road, Port Harcourt
Tel: (084) 236853
Contact: Rear Admiral Ndubuisi G. Kanu (rtd) - Chairman
Mr. Christ Duru - MD/CEO

UNECON ASSOCIATES LIMITED
Business: Engineering Consultancy Services, Mechanical, Electrical Water and Sanitary Engineering Services
Address: 18, Johnson Street, Ilupeju Estate, Lagos
Tel: (01) 4973980, 4974069 **Fax:** (01) 4973981
E-mail: unecom@infoweb.abs.net
Website: www.unecon.com
* 2, Adelabu Road, G.R.A. Ibadan
Tel: (02) 2310089
* Suite 60, Nouakchott Street, Wuse Zone 1, Abuja
Tel: (09) 3145998
Contact: Engr. I. C. Okechkwu - Principal Partner/CEO

UNEX SECURITIES & INVESTMENT LIMITED
Business: Stockbroking, Portfolio Management, Investment Advisory Services
Address: 3, Biaduo Street, off Keffi Street, S. W. Ikoyi, Lagos
Tel: (01) 2690288, 2690289 **Fax:** (01) 2690289
E-mail: unex@asonnet.com
unex@nipost.nigpost.com
Contact: Chief Lloyd Iyeimo - Chairman
Dr. Francis N. Chukujama - MD/CEO

UNIC INSURANCE PLC
Business: All Classes of Insurance Business
Address: NGC Building, Plot 144, Oba Akran Avenue, Ikeja, Lagos
Tel: (01) 4968230-9 (10L), 4964474, 7731518-23(6L), 7742383-5(3L)
E-mail: unic@unicinsurance.com
Website: www.unicinsurance.com
* 2, Tinubu Square, Lagos
Tel: (01) 2632103, 2636432 **Fax:** (01) 2664282
* Plot 1046, Ahmadu Bello Way, Garki, Abuja
Contact: Mr. David M. Martin - MD/CEO
Mr T. O. B. Ogboi - ED (Marketing)

UNICHEALTH
Business: Health Maintenance Urganisation
Address: Plot 144, Oba Akran Avenue, Ikeja, Lagos
Tel: (01) 2709728
E-mail: enquire@unichealth.com
Contact: Dr. Abiodun Osiyemi - Business Dev. Manager

UNICENT ENTERPRISES LIMITED
Business: Import & Export, General Merchandising, Clearing & Forwarding, Warehousing, Haulage
Address: Glass House (2nd Floor), 7A, Asa Afariogun Street, off Osolo Way, Ajao Estate, Isolo, Lagos
Tel: (01) 4521359, 4528483, 4706013 **Fax:** (01) 4521359
E-mail: unicent@yahoo.com
* 3, Greek Souls Boulevard, by 277, Aba Road, Rumuogba, Port Harcourt.
Tel: (084) 613175
Contact: Chief I. N. Okoye - Chairman/CEO
Mr. Anthony Okoye - GM

UNI-CHARTERED INSURANCE BROKERS LIMITED
Business: Insurance Broking and Consultancy
Address: 122, Murtala Mohammed Way, opp. General Post Office, Ebute - Metta, Lagos
Tel: (01) 860176, 866620, 4707338
* S7/705, Idowu Street, Felele Layout, Ibadan
Tel: (02) 2310025
Contact: Chief B. A. A. Coker - Chairman/CEO

UNICHEM NIGERIA LIMITED
Business: Importation of Chemicals, Dyestuffs & Diagnostics
Address: SCDC House, Plot 2B, Adewunmi Industrial Estate, Oregun Road, Ikeja, Lagos
Tel: (01) 4971192, 4971201
Fax: (01) 2691736, 2693849
Contact: Alh. Femi Okunnu - Chairman
Mr. S. J. Ashton - MD/CEO

UNI-CONTROL LIMITED
Business: Sales of Electrical Materials
Address: 61, Oroyinyin Street, beh. Jankara Market, Lagos
Tel: (01) 2667670, 08033058558
E-mail: nicontrol@yahoo.com
Contact: Mr. Uche Ezikeoha - MD/CEO

UNIGLOBAL COMMODITIES PLC
Business: Manufacturing and International Trading
Address: Plot 170B, Gbagada Estate Phase I, Gbagada Expressway, Lagos
Tel: (01) 5552338, 7747066 **Fax:** (01) 5552212
E-mail: commerz@beta.linkserve.com
Contact: Dr. F. A. O. Alade - Chairman/CEO
Mr. Bayo Adegoke - Business Dev. Manager

UNIK INDSTRIES LIMITED
Business: Manufacturing of Footwear, Shoe Soles & Bags
Address: 357, Agege Motor Road, Mushin, Lagos
Tel: (01) 4523572, 520926, 521629, 4711150

UNILEVER NIGERIA PLC
Business: Manufacturing and Marketing of Consumer Products (Home Care & Personal Care Products, and Foods)
Address: 1, Billingsway, Oregun, Ikeja, Lagos
Tel: (01) 4972315-6 (2 L), 4972318-9 (2 L), 4977300
Fax: (01) 4972313
* Plot 534, Zone AO, Airport Road, beh. Protea/ Bolingo Hotel, Central Business District, Abuja.
Tel: (09) 2344141, 2344156, 5239757
* 2, Industrial Road, Aba.
Tel: (082) 220611, 220895, 224370
* 4, Oba Akenzua Crescent, Onireke, Ibadan
Tel: (02) 2411712, 2411925, 2412008
* 4/6, Beach Road, Jos.

Tel: (073) 452974, 453060, 455002
Contact: Mr Gunender Kapur - Vice Chairman/CEO
Mr Yemi Adeboye - Corp. Relations Manager

UNILINKS NIGERIA LIMITED
Business: Planning and Construction of Water Resources, Borehole Drilling, Construction of Storage Tanks and Treatment Plants, and Pipe Laying, Maintenance of Water Works
Address: 8, Aina Eleko Str, Onigbongbo, Maryland, Lagos
Tel: (01) 4963954, 4520659, 08033151363
Website: www.niwasa.nig.org
* 136, Town-Hall Rd, Ojowo, Ijebu-Igbo, Ogun State
* S7/356, Oshodi Street, Challenge, Ibadan
Contact: Mr. A. A. Akinyemi - Chairman/CEO
Mr. J. M. Alaba - Project Director

UNIMARK LIMITED
Business: Advertising Production
Address: Usmobill House, 81/2A, Bauchi Road, Jos
Tel/Fax:: (073) 452025
E-mail: unimarkltd@yahoo.com
Contact: Haroun Audu - MD/CEO

UNION ADHESIVE & CHEMICAL COMPANY LIMITED
Business: Plastic Packaging and Foam Products
Address: 31/33, Hospital Road, off Apapa-Oshodi Expressway, Tin Can Island, Apapa, Lagos
Tel: (01) 5450184, 5804112 **Fax:** (01) 5873939
E-mail: unionadhesive@yahoo.com
* 43, Ahmadu Bello Way, Jos
Contact: Mr. Iheanacho C. Ugochukwu - Chairman
Mr. C. M. Okereke - AGM. (Marketing)

UNION ASSURANCE COMPANY LIMITED
(Sub. of Union Bank of Nig. Plc)
Business: All Classes of Insurance (Life & Pension, Medical, General & Special Risk)
Address: Stallion Plaza, (13th Floor), 36, Marina, Lagos
Tel: (01) 2643859-61 (3L), 2640277 **Fax:** (01) 2643862
E-mail: hotline@unionassuranceng.com
Website: www.unionassuranceng.com
* UBN Plc Abuja Area Office Building, Area 3, Garki, Abuja.
Tel/Fax: (09) 2341141, 2343262
* UBN Plc Port Harcourt Area Office Building, Plot 468, Trans-Amadi Industrial Layout, Port Harcourt.
Tel/Fax: (084) 233652
* UBN Plc, M/Mohammed Way, Yankura Area, Kano
Tel: (064) 632772, 645499
Contact: Mr. G. A. T. Oboh - Chairman
Mr. T. E. Eke - MD/CEO

UNION AUTOMOBILES LIMITED
Business: Sales of Motor Vehicles
Address: 60, Adeola Odeku Street, Victoria Island, Lagos
Tel: (01) 2617891

UNION AUTOPARTS MANUFACTURING COMPANY LTD
Business: Manufacturing of Auto Batteries & Spare Parts
Address: 60/61, Igwe Orizu Rd, Otolo, Nnewi, Anambra State
Tel: (046) 460894, 460296, 460665, 461683
Fax: (046) 462894
E-mail: sales@ibeto.com
ibeto@infoweb.abs.net
Website: www.ibeto.com
* 4A, Adeola Hopewell St, Victoria Island, Lagos
Tel: (01) 2616637, 2619194, 2625915-6(2L)
Fax: (01) 2619667, 2703590
Contact: Chief C. M. Ibeto - Chairman/CEO
Mr Emma Agu - GM

UNION BANK OF NIGERIA PLC
Business: Commercial Banking, Financial Services Conglomerate
Address: Stallion Plaza, 36, Marina, Lagos
Tel: (01) 2644149, 2664815, 2644373, 2664268
Fax: (01) 2669873, 2644306
E-mail: info@unionbankng.com
Website: www.unionbankng.com
Contact: Mr. Godwin A. T. Oboh - Group MD/CEO
Kabir Dangogo - AGM (Corporate Affairs)

UNION COLOURS & CHEMICALS LIMITED
Business: Manufacturing and Marketing of Paints
Address: Km. 32, Lagos-Abeokuta Expressway, Caaso Bus-Stop, Alagbado, Agege, Lagos
Tel: (01) 4921517
E-mail: unioncolours@aol.com
Contact: Mr. Babawande Majekodunmi - Chairman
Mrs. Abiola Ajayi-Majebi - Director

UNION COMMERCIAL INSURANCE BROKERS LIMITED
Business: Insurance Broking
Address: Poatson Building, 142, Oba Akran Avenue, Ikeja Industrial Estate, Ikeja, Lagos
Tel (01) 4930921, 7737214, 08033254191
Fax: (01) 4930921
E-mail: ucib@beta.linkserve.com
Contact: Chief (Dr.) J. C. Dugad - Chairman
Dr. Dotun R. Ogunwoolu - MD/CEO

UNION DICON SALT PLC
Business: Processing of Crude Salt; Wholesale of Domestic and Industrial Salt
Address: Union Dicon House, Plot 8, Block A, Ilasamaja Industrial Estate, Itire, Surulere, Lagos
Tel: (01) 4526454, 4526502, 4526452
Fax: (01) 4526445
E-mail: diconslt@alpha.linkserve.com
* 1, Reclamation Road, Port Harcourt
Tel: (084) 238113, 238456
* 60, Ibrahim Taiwo Road, Kano
Tel: (064) 639451
* Plot 1A, S. L. Akintola Boulevard, Garki II, Abuja
* 44, New Market Road, Onitsha
Contact: Mr Johan Claerhout - MD/CEO
Mr Dansule Muazu - Head (Marketing)

UNION FREIGHT FORWARDERS LIMITED
Business: Clearing & Forwarding, Cargo Handling
Address: 2, Odual road, off Aggrey Road, Port Harcourt
Tel: (084) 333048
* 17, Toyin Street, Ikeja, Lagos. **Tel:** (01) 4978053
* 7, Deco Road, Warri. **Tel/Fax:** (053) 253973
Contact: Mr. Roland U. Okpoko - Chairman/CEO

UNION HOMES SAVINGS & LOANS LIMITED
(Sub. of Union Bank of Nig. Plc)
Business: Mortgage Banking
Address: Royal House, 153, Ikorodu Road, Onipanu, Lagos
Tel: (01) 5870562; **Fax:** (01) 4972186
E-mail: info@unionhomes-ng.com
Website: www.unionhomes-ng.com
* 150/162, Broad Street, Lagos
Tel: (01) 2640275 (DL), 2660153, 2660282, 2662814
* Union Bank Building,37, Murtala Mohammed Way, Kano.
Tel: (064) 649194, 648228
* Falomo Shopping Complex, Awolowo Road, Ikoyi, Lagos.
Tel: (01) 683596
* Plot 2370, Herbert Macaulay Way, Old Wuse Market B/Stop, Wuse Zone 6, Abuja
Tel: (09) 5235375-6 (2L)
Contact: Mr. Onyemauwa N. Chionuma - MD/CEO
Mrs. O. A. Ogunkoya - AGM(Treasury)

UNION MERCHANTS BANK LIMITED
(Sub. of Union Bank of Nig. Plc)
Business: Banking, Stock and Portfolio Management
Address: 4, Davies Street, off Marina, Lagos
Tel: (01) 2667313, 2668484, 2663787
Fax: (01) 2662803, 2660874
E-mail: unionmbl@micro.com.ng
Contact: Mr. Steve Osuji - Head (Corpporate Affairs)

UNION PETROLEUM SERVICES NIGERIA LIMITED
Business: Marketing of Petroleum Products
Address: Octagon House (8th Floor), 13, A. J. Marinho Drive, Victoria Island, Lagos
Tel: (01) 3200927, 4617657 **Fax:** (01) 4617656
E-mail: ups@infoweb.abs.net
Website: www.unionpetroleum.com

UNION PRODUCTS LIMITED
Business: Manufacturing and Marketing of Stailness Steel Utensils and Kitchenware
Address: Plot 1A, Block 1, Oluyole Industrial Estate, off Ring Road, Ibadan
Tel: (02) 2317821
Contact: Mr. H. R. M. Shamdasani - Chairman

UNIPUMPS NIGERIA LIMITED
Business: Manufacturing and Assembling of Hand-Operated Pumps and Water Purification Equipment
Address: Agbeloba House, Quarry Road, Abeokuta
Tel: (039) 244053, 242547, 243658, 242005
Fax: (039) 242005
E-mail: unipump@hyperia.com
* 389, Ikorodu Road, Ojota, Lagos
Tel: (01) 4970009, 4972598-9 (2L) **Fax:** (01) 4970009
* 7, Urum Street, Trans-Ekulu, Abakpa, Enugu
Tel: 08033418526

UNIQUE ALUMINIUM PRODUCTS LIMITED
Business: Fabricators of Aluminium Building Materials
Address: Block J, Plot 1, Oluyole Ind.Estate, Dugbe, Ibadan
Tel: (02) 2314350, 2313182
* 62B, Opebi Road, Ikeja, Lagos.
Tel: (01) 820457
Contact: Mr. Tunde Ibrahim - ED

UNIQUE EYE CENTRE LIMITED
Business: Optometrists, Opticians, Medical & Optitcal Services
Address: 21, Obalende Road, Ikoyi, Lagos
Tel: (01) 2672540, 2695139, 08033466876
Fax: (01) 2672540
E-mail: unique_eye@hyperia.com
Contact: Dr. Joe Owie - MD/CEO

UNIQUE GENERATORS LIMITED
Business: Sales & Service of Generators
Address: Plot 116, Trans-Amadi Ind. Layout, Port Harcourt
Tel: (084) 230862, 484414, 09034070160

UNIQUE INSTRUMENTS & SCIENCE COMPANY LIMITED
Business: IVF Instrumentation, Distribution, Installation and Maintenance of Laboratory Equipment, Laboratory Consultancy Service
Address: Adebayo House (Ground Floor), 100, Murtala Mohammed Way, Lagos
Tel: (01) 8183395, 08033010234
E-mail: bayo-adeyeloja@uniqueinstrumentltd.com
Website: www.uniqueinstrumentltd.com
Contact: Mr. Bayo Adeyelofa

UNIQUE LEATHER FINISHING COMPANY LIMITED
Business: Tanning
Address: Plot 55-62, Sharada Industrial Estate Phase II, Kano
Tel: (064) 669557 **Fax:** (064) 669911
Contact: Mr. G. Helmut - GM

UNIQUE PHARMACEUTICALS LIMITED
Business: Manufacture of Intravenous Fluids and Intravenous Antibiotic Preparations & Formulations
Address: 11, Fatai Atere Way, Matori, Mushin, Lagos
Tel: (01) 4520290, 4520658, 4523977, 4525678, 7740161
Fax: (01) 2615782, 4524028
E-mail: unique@cybaaspace.net
* Veepee Industrial Avenue, Km. 38, Abeokuta Express Road, Sango Otta, Ogun State
Tel: (039) 722161, 722197, 722302 * (01) 7740162
Contact: Mr. L. C. Wadhwani - MD/CEO

UNIQUE SECURITY & INVESTIGATION SERVICES LIMITED
Business: Security Guard Services & Consultancy, Training of Security Personnel, Corporate Investigation Services, Installation of Security Gadget
Address: 27, Kakawa Street (2nd Floor), Lagos Island, Lagos
Tel/Fax: (01) 2636846
E-mail: uniquesecurity@hyperia.net
Contact: Brigadier-Gen. Fred Chijuka (rtd) - Chairman

UNISTEEL WORKS LIMITED
Business: Steel Fabrication, Construction of Oil Tankers, Tippers & Trailers, Water Tanks & other Steel Structures
Address: Textile Road, Kakuri Industrial Estate, Kaduna South, Kaduna
Tel/Fax: (062) 232213
Contact: Alh. Hassan Hadejia - Chairman
Mr. G. PIizzinat - MD/CEO

UNITAB NIGERIA LIMITED
Business: Retail Sales of Automotive Batteries and Tyres, Manufacturing of Plastic Containers
Address: Stallion House, 2, Ajose Adeogun Street, Victoria Island, Lagos
Tel: (01) 2601290-9 (10L) **Fax:** (01) 860158
E-mail: info@unipetrol.org
Website: www.unipetrol.org
Contact: Mr. E. A. O. Shomade - GM/CEO
Mr. A. O. Nzekwu - Asst. GM

UNITED AIR EXPRESS LIMITED
Business: Aircraft Charter
Address: Olatunji House (4th Floor), 259, Ikorodu Road, (Idiroko Bus-Stop), Maryland, Lagos
Tel: (01) 4966641, 4964240 **Fax:** (01) 4966641
E-mail: tr1bello@hotmail.com
Contact: Engr. T. R. Bello - Chairman/CEO
Engr. Goddy Ehiwe - ED.

UNITED BANK FOR AFRICA PLC
Business: Comprehensive/Universal Banking
Address: UBA House, 57, Marina, Lagos
Tel: (01) 2644651-700 (50L), 2644754-9 (5L), 08025606000, 08035606000 **Fax:** (01) 2644722
E-mail: info@ubagroup.com
Website: www.ubagroup.com
Contact: Alh. Aliyu Dikko - MD/CEO
Mrs. Funmi Olayinka - Head (Corp. Affairs)

UNITED BEVERAGES COMPANY LIMITED
Business: Bottling of Carbonated Drinks
Address: Jekayinfa Village, Old Ijebu-Ode/Lagos Road, Alomaja, Ibadan
Tel: (02) 2312501, 2312297
E-mail: ubc@modandolagroup.com.ng
Contact: Sir (Chief) Bode Akindele - Chairman/CEO

UNITED BIOCHEMICAL INDUSTRIES LIMITED
Business: Manufacturing of Pharmaceuticals
Address: Niger Bridge Head Industrial Layout, Onitsha
Tel: (046) 212703
Contact: Chief I. B. Igwe - MD/CEO

UNITED COURIER LIMITED
Business: Courier Services
Address: 14A, Oshodi-Apapa Expressway, Oshodi, Lagos
Tel: (01) 4931622, 4931134 **Fax:** (01) 4931622
Contact: Mr. O. Willoughby - MD/CEO

UNITED DISTILLERS & VINTNERS NIGERIA LIMITED
Business: Distillers Of Acholic Spirits and Wines
Address: Km. 14, Idiroko Road, Iju-Ota, Ogun State
Tel: (01) 2882302 **Fax:** (01) 4976668
E-mail: udvl200@yahoo.com

UNITED FISHERIES LIMITED
Business: Fishing and Trawling, Sales of Frozen Seafoods
Address: 36, Warehouse Road, Apapa, Lagos
Tel: (01) 5451247

UNITED FREIGHT SERVICES LIMITED
Business: Clearing & Forwarding, Freights & Cargo Handling
Address: W. Biney Building, 34/36, Burma Rd, Apapa, Lagos
Tel: (01) 5870414, 5450148, 08033028342
Fax: (01) 5452398
Contact: Mr. Okpor - MD/CEO

UNITED GASES LIMITED
Business: Production of Industrial and Domestic Gases
Address: Plot 13, Challawa Industrial Estate, Kano
Tel: (064) 649228 **Fax:** (064) 642752
E-mail: ugl@rcl.nig.com
Contact: Mr. D. P. Ashar - MD/CEO

UNITED GEOPHYSICAL (NIGERIA) LIMITED
Business: Oil Exploration; Seismic Data Acquisition
Address: 7, Remi Fani-Kayode Avenue, G. R. A. Ikeja, Lagos
Tel: (01) 4960701, 4970121, 4974218, 4937695, 7918464
Fax: (01) 4934892
* Merogun Waterside, off McDermott Road, Warri
Tel: (053) 254583

UNITED INFORMATION TECHNOLOGIES LIMITED
Business: Assembling of IT Products (Desktop Computers, Notebooks, Servers and UPS)
Address: 16A, Sasegbon Street, off Oduduwa Crescent, Ikeja G.R.A, Lagos
Tel: (01) 4939098, 4939099, 08037253734
E-mail: info@unitecpc.com
Website: www.unitecpc.com

UNITED MODERN INSURANCE BROKERS LIMITED
Business: Insurance Broking
Address: 2, Jibowu Street, off Ikorodu Road, Jibowu, Yaba
Tel: (01) 4707172, 5878867, 8044781 **Fax:** (01) 5878867
E-mail: umib@infoweb.abs.net
Contact: Chief (Dr.) Augustine E. Ilodibe, MFR - Chairman
Mr. Stephen O. Ilodibe - MD/CEO

UNITED NIGERIA TEXTILES PLC
Business: Manufacturing of Textile Products
Address: Plot O, Industrial Estate, Kaduna South, Kaduna
Tel: (062) 234100-7 (8L)
Fax: (062) 231412, 232279
E-mail: untplckad@micro.com.ng
*BOI House (2nd Floor), 63/71, Broad Street, Lagos
Tel: (01) 2640971-5 (5L), 2661174, 2661245, 2662455
Fax: (01) 2640979, 2660427, 2667370, 268198
* 31, Unity Road, Kano.
Tel: (064) 632368, 634823 **Fax:** (064) 648773
36, New Market Road, Onitsha.
Tel: (046) 211406
Contact: Mr. Yue Shing Wong - MD/CEO
Mr. F. T. Lo - AGM (Marketing)

UNITED PARCEL SERVICE (UPS)
Business: Courier & Cargo Services
Addrress: Plot 16, Oworonsoki Expressway, Gbagada Industrial Estate, Gbagada, Lagos
Tel: (01) 5553000-5 (6L), 7740453, 7740454, 4701917, 4701907 **Fax:** (01) 5553006, 7740452
Website: www.ups.com

UNITED PREFAB COMPANY (NIGERIA) LIMITED
Business: Manufacturing of Fibreglass Baths and Related

Products
Address: Plot 141/149, Trans-Amadi Ind.Layout,Port Harcourt
Tel: (084) 330158, 482240
Contact: Mr Godswill A. Ofoije - Chairman/CEO

UNITED PROPERTY DEVELOPERS COMPANY LIMITED
Business: Real Estate Construction, Development and Management
Address: Yinka Folawiyo Plaza (8th Floor), 38, Yinka Folawiyo Avenue, Apapa, Lagos
Tel: (01) 5450436-40 (5L)
Fax: (01) 5450204, 5450274
Contact: Alh. (Chief, Dr.) W. I. Folawiyo, CON - Chairman
Mr R. A. Adegbite - Co-ordinator (Projects)

UNITED SECURITIES LIMITED
Business: Data Management & Securities, Register Administration Services
Address: Niger House (5th Floor), 1/5, Odunlami St, Lagos
Tel: (01) 2640710-4 (5L) **Fax:** (01) 2640709
E-mail: hh@hamiltonhammer.com
Contact: Femi Akinsanya - Chairman/CEO

UNITED STEEL CONVERTERS LIMITED
Business: Manufacture of Galvanised Roofing Sheets
Address: 4, Balogun Square, Lagos
Tel: (01) 2660941, 2663857, 2661256 **Fax:** (01) 2661256
* 214, Port Harcourt Road, Aba
Tel: (082) 440409, 225250 **Fax:** (082) 233508
E-mail: uoolagos@infoweb.abs.net
Contact: Chief Nzedioranma Uche Okafor - Chairman/CEO

UNITED SURGICALS LIMITED
Business: Sales of Medical & Laboratory Equipment and Consumables
Address: Surgical House, opp. WAEC Office, Ali Akilu Road, Kawo, Kaduna
Tel: (062) 241039, 311566, 317197 **Fax:** (062) 311566
* Sky Memorial Complex, Herbert Macaulay Way/ Michael Okpara Street, Wuse Zone 5, Abuja
Tel/Fax: (09) 5236666

UNITED SWITCHGEARS & CONTROLS LIMITED
Business: Electrical Engineering, Supply of Electricity Control Equipment, Generator Rentals
Address: Plot 98, Fatai Irawo Street, off International Airport Road, Ajao Estate, Apakun-Oshodi, Lagos
Tel/Fax: (01) 4522426
E-mail: uscl@infoweb.abs.net
Contact: Engr. L. A. Emodi - Chairman/CEO

UNITED TECH SUPPLY COMPANY LIMITED
Business: Sales of Machinery, Safety Equipment and Hoses
Address: Plot 79, Trans-Amadi Ind. Layout, Port Harcourt
Tel: (084) 330065 **Fax:** (084) 237427
Contact: Chief A. N. Iheoma - MD/CEO

UNITED TECHNOLOGIES LIMITED
Business: Assembly and Distribution of Airconditioners
Address: 3, Molade Okoya-Thomas Street, beh. Zenitrh Bank Head Office, Victoria Island, Lagos
Tel: (01) 4707752, 08023130365, 08034030600
Fax: (01) 4619259
E-mail: unitecltd@yahoo.com
* 20, Bola Tiyamiyu Street, Molipa Layout, Ijebu-Ode, Ogun State
Tel: (037) 430701, 431854, 432401-2(2L)
Contact: Mr. Aderemi Abdul - Chairman/CEO

UNITED TELESYS LIMITED
Business: Sales, Installation and Maintenance of Satellite Communication Equipment, Communication Solution Provider
Address: Chevron Drive, off Lekki-Epe Expressway, Lekki, Lagos
Tel: (01) 2620640

UNITED TRUST ASSURANCE COMPANY LIMITED
Business: All Classes of Insurance
Address: 31, Akin Adesola Street, Victoria Island, Lagos
Tel: (01) 2612947, 2612968, 2629068, 2629075, 2629157, 2629260 **Fax:** (01) 2612943
E-mail: info@unitedtrustassure.com
Website: www.unitedtrustassure.com
Contact: Don O. Agbo -MD/CEO

UNITED WIRE PRODUCTS LIMITED
Business: Manufacturing of Nails, Welded Mesh, Black Binding Wire, Welding Electrodes, Straightened and Cut Wires, Straining-Up Wires, Chain-Link Fencing and Barbed Wire
Address: Plot 7, Maicibi Close, Industrial Area, Kaduna South, Kaduna
Tel: (062) 232964, 231595 **Fax:** (062) 232373
E-mail: uwpl@wwlkad.com
Contact: Mal. D. H. Abdu - Chairman
Mr. K. R. Rao - MD/CEO

UNITEX LIMITED
Business: Production of Wax Print Textiles
Address: 1, Mohammed Ladan Road, Kakuri Industrial Estate, Kaduna South, Kaduna
Tel: (062) 230069, 231450, 232346 **Fax:** (062) 232127

UNITEX TELECOMMUNICATIONS LIMITED
Business: Telecommunication Services, Installation of Satellite Communication Equipment
Address: 3A, Ibrahim Taiwo Road, Kano
Tel: (064) 635617, 648081, 08032032471
Fax: (064) 648081
E-mail: asg@yahoo.com
Contact: Alh. Idris Sule Gobir - Exec. Chairman

UNITOP INTERNATIONAL LIMITED
Business: Leasing & Maintenance of Marine Equipment, Marine Engineering & Construction, Engineering, Fabrication & International/Local Prcurement
Address: 23A, Ogun Road, Warri
Tel: (053) 253370, 256580, 08033104141, 08033355591
Fax: (053) 253370
E-mail: unitop50@hotmail.com
Contact: Mr. Sylvester Emeka - MD/CEO

UNITRUST INSURANCE COMPANY LIMITED
Business: Insurance Business
Address: Unitrust House, 105B, Ajose Adeogun Street,

Victoria Island, Lagos
Tel: (01) 2625523-7 (5L), 2629143-6 (4L), 08036000060
Fax: (01) 2625528
E-mail: unitrust@hyperia.com
Website: www.unitrustinsurance.com
Contact: Mr. Jihad El-Matni - MD/CEO

UNITY LIFE & FIRE INSURANCE PLC
Business: All Clases of Insurance
Address: 9, Nnamdi Azikiwe Street (7th & 8th Floor), Tinubu Square, Lagos
Tel/Fax: (01) 2662783, 2662948, 2667044, 7734226
Contact: Chief (Dr) Hope Uzodinma - Chairman
Mr. Okey Nwadioha - MD/CEO

UNIVERSAL ASSOCIATES COMPANY LIMITED
Business: Processing & Exportation of Sea Foods
Address: Plot 1303A, Akin Adesola Street, Victoria Island, Lagos
Tel: (01) 2622232, 2622259 **Fax:** (01) 2619487
* Plot 1, Block M, 27, Abimbola Street, Isolo Industrial Estate, Ilasamaja, Lagos
Tel: (01) 5872711, 5874221, 5872690 **Fax:** (01) 5871249
Contact: Mr. K. N. Hegde - MD

UNIVERSAL BROADCASTING SERVICES LIMITED
Business: Television Broadcasting, Events Promotion & Production, Post-Production
Address: 9/11, Catholic Mission Street, Lagos
Tel: (01) 2635631, 2635880, 2645380 **Fax:** (01) 2632833
E-mail: superscreent@yahoo.com
Contact: Otukayode Otufale - Exec. Chairman

UNIVERSAL CHEMICAL & EXPLOSIVE COMPANY LTD
Business: Sales of Explosive and Accessories (for Quarries, Mining, Oil Prospecting and Engineering Firms)
Address: 25, Boyle Street (3rd Floor), Onikan, Lagos
Tel: (01) 2632714, 2632793, 2636053 **Fax:** (01) 2636980
* 98, Ibrahim Taiwo Road, Ilorin.
Tel: (031) 222394
* 113, New Lagos Rd, Benin City.
Tel: (052) 259133
Contact: Alh. (Chief) Raimi Oladimeji - Chairman
Mr. Jacques J. Engels - Exec. Vice Chairman

UNIVERSAL DRILLING FLUIDS LIMITED
Business: Sales of Oilfield Drilling Chemicals
Address: Liberty House (7th Floor), 1, St; Gregory's Road, Obalende, Lagos
Tel: (01) 2690054, 7752566, 08034000441

UNIVERSAL FISHING COMPANY LIMITED
Business: Importation of Frozen Fish
Address: Plot 1303, Akin Adesola Stt, Victoria Island, Lagos
Tel: (01) 2615505, 2622259, 2622232 **Fax:** (01) 2619487
E-mail: primlaks@hyperia.com
Contact: Alhaja H. O. Agoro - Chairman
Mr. B. C. P. Gowda - MD/CEO

UNIVERSAL FURNITURE LIMITED
Business: Manufacturers of Exclusive Chrome, Metal and Wooden Furniture
Address: Km. 16, Ikorodu Road, Ojota, Lagos
Tel: (01) 4931285, 4963457, 4974567.
Fax: (01) 4930103, 4932670, 2619477
* Plot 1247, Aminu Kano Crescent, Wuse II, Abuja
Tel: (09) 5230197, 5230198 **Fax:** (09) 5230198

UNIVERSAL GASES LIMITED
Business: Production of Industrial, Household (LPG) & Medical Gases
Address: AIICO Plaza (2nd Floor), Plot PC. 12, Afribank Street, Victoria Island, Lagos
Tel: (01) 2620339, 2620340, 7742397, 7742398
Fax: (01) 2613064, 2622093
* Km. 1, Ijoko Road, Sango-Otta
Tel: (039) 721103 * (01) 7742396 **Fax:** (039) 721103
Contact: Dr. Matthew O. Eshalomi - Chairman
Mr. Murli Mirchandani - MD/CEO

UNIVERSAL INVESTMENT & DEVELOPMENT CO. PLC
Business: Development Finance and Equity Investment, Financial Consultancy Services
Address: 21, Ogunu Road, Warri
Tel: (053) 250629, 255215, 254244, 321286-7 (2L)
Fax: (053) 255215
Contact: Dr. F. F. O. Abudu - MD/CEO

UNIVERSAL MOTORS & ENGINEERING COMPANY LTD
Business: Reconditioning of Engines, Mechanical Engineering Services
Address: 115, Oguta Road, Onitsha
Tel: (046) 213862, 219017
Contact: Chief P. O. Onuegbu - Chairman/CEO

UNIVERSAL NATURAL BEVERAGES LIMITED
Business: Bottling of Natural Mineral Water
Address: Plot P1, 10800, Zawan, Jos
Tel: (073) 280393, 281205

UNIVERSAL POWER SYSTEMS NIGERIA LIMITED
Business: Sales and Service of Generators and Transformers
Address: 1C, Block E, Fatai Atere Way, Matori Industrial Estate, Mushin, Lagos
Tel: (01) 4527108, 520750, 4524193 **Fax:** (01) 4527108
E-mail: unipower@infoweb.abs.net
* Plot 808, Ona Crescent, off Lake Chad Street, Maitama District, Abuja.
Tel/Fax: (09) 4130154
Contact: Mr. Leye Kupoluyi - MD/CEO
Mr. Segun Afolayan - Manager (Sales & Mkting)

UNIVERSAL RUBBER COMPANY LIMITED
Business: Manufacturing of Automotive/Industrial Rubber Products, Sales and Service of Conveyor Belts, Vehicle Tyres and Earth-Moving Machinery Tyres, Relugging/Repairs of Tyres
Address: Lagos Expressway Roundabout, Challenge, Ibadan
Tel: (02) 2311191, 2314875, 2314090, 2318000, 2318003, 08023080873, 08033442867 **Fax:** (02) 2314090
* 114, Lagos-Badagry Expressway (Agbolu Bus-Stop), opp. Festac Town Second Gate, Lagos
Tel: (01) 883120
* KW. 20, Ibrahim Taiwo Rd, Tundun Wada, Kaduna
Tel: (062) 411542
Contact: Otunba Amos O. Adegoke - Chairman/CEO

UNIVERSAL SPINNERS LIMITED

Business: Spinning of Yarn
Address: 1, Independence Road, Bompai Ind. Estate, Kano
Tel: (064) 648034, 648031, 648065, 632904, 632922
E-mail: util@compuserve.com
Contact: Alh. (Dr.). Aminu Dantata - Chairman
Mr. C. Ja'afar - MD/CEO

UNIVERSAL STEELS LIMITED

Business: Manufacture of Steel Products & Enamelware
Address: Universal Steels Crescent, off Surulere Industrial Road, Ogba Industrial Estate, Ikeja, Lagos
Tel: (01) 4925364, 4961074
Fax: (01) 4964631, 4970175
E-mail: usteelng@linkserve,com.ng
Contact: Mr. Stephen S. T. Young - MD/CEO

UNIVERSAL TEXTILES INDUSTRIES LIMITED

Business: Manufacturing and Marketing of Textile Products
Address: 1, Independence Road, Bompai Ind. Estate, Kano
Tel: (064) 645394, 647201, 630218, 630586-7 (2L)
Fax: (064) 630585
E-mail: util@compuserve.com
universal@ecnx.com
Contact: Alh. (Dr.) Aminu Dantata - Chairman
Mr. C. Ja'far - MD/CEO

UNIVERSAL TRUST BANK PLC

Business: Commercial Banking
Address: 4/6, Ajose Adeogun Street, Victoria Island, Lagos
Tel: (01) 2637849, 2631123, 2622281, 3200905-14(10L), 3200905, 4617179
Fax: (01) 2612950, 2616003, 615812
E-mail: info@utb.com.ng
Website: www.utb.com.ng
Contact: Mr. Kris C. Nwosu - MD/CEO
Mr. Akaninyene Esiere - Corporate Affairs

UNIVERSITY PRESS PLC

Business: Publishing, Distribution & Sales of Books & Educational Materials
Address: Three Crowns Building, Jericho, Ibadan
Tel: (02) 2411356, 2412313, 2412386
Fax: (02) 2411356, 2412056
E-mail: unipress@skannet.com.ng
Website: www.universitypressplc.com
Contact: Alh. Waheed A. Olajide - MD/CEO

UNIWORLD LIMITED

Business: Advertising & Marketing Communication Agency
Address: 143, Ojuelegba Road, Surulere, Lagos
Tel: (01) 842528, 837048, 08023507939, 08037165159
E-mail: uniworld@yahoo.com
Contact: Sir G. C. Maduwuba - MD/CEO

U-NUEL AND COMPANY LIMITED

Business: Commoditiy Exporters and General Merchants, Civil Engineering Contractor, Sales of Aluminium Building Products, Property Consultants
Address: 91, Zik Avenue, Uwani, Enugu
Tel: (042) 252397, 08033134248
E-mail: u_nuel@onebox.com
Contact: Mr Emmanuel A. Umahi - Chairman/CEO

UPS NIGERIA LIMITED

Business: Sales & Repairs of UPS & Voltage Stabilizers, Sales of UPS Batteries, Computer Site Electrification/ Preparation
Address: 6, Seinde Callisto Crescent, behind Gas Oil Ltd., off Oshodi-Apapa Expressway, Oshodi, Lagos
Tel: (01) 2229962, 4930083, 8044797, 08023230282
Fax: (01) 2229962, 4930260
E-mail: unlpower@infoweb.abs.net
Contact: Mr Moses Adebayo - MD/CEO

URBAN FIRE LIMITED

Business: Sales of Industrial Safety & Fire-Fighting Equipment
Address: 93, Clegg St, off Western Avenue, Surulere, Lagos
Tel: (01) 5851887
E-mail: urbanfire2001@yahoo.com
Contact: Chief J. A. Odey - Chairman/CEO

URBAN SHELTER LIMITED

Business: Property Development and Management
Address: Shiper's Plaza, Plot 438, Michael Okpara Street, Wuse Zone 5, Abuja
Tel: (09) 5234147, 5239862 **Fax:** (09) 5236922
E-mail: estate@urbanshelternigeria.com
Website: www.urbanshelternigeria.com
* UBA House (5th Floor), 57, Marina, Lagos
Tel: (01) 2644922, 2666468 **Fax:** (01) 2665973
Contact: Mal. Ibrahim Aliyu - Chairman
Mal. Musa Dangogo Aliyu - MD/CEO

URBANE STOCKBROKERS LIMITED

Business: Stockbroking
Address: 207, Ikorodu Road, Obanikoro, Lagos
Tel: (01) 8043144

UREN ENGINEERING CONSTRUCTION COMPANY LIMITED

Business: Civil (Building), Mechanical, Electrical Engineering
Address: 32, Okota Road, Isolo, Lagos
Tel: (01) 7744648, 520233, 523882 **Fax:** (01) 523882
E-mail: urennig@yahoo.com
Contact: Rev. (Engr.) Emmanuel O. Adebajo - Chairman/CEO
Engr. Bolaji A. Adebajo - GM

UREN UNITED FOOD PROCESSING COMPANY LIMITED

Business: Food Processing and Production
Address: 58/60, Omoboriowo Street, Ikotun, Lagos
Tel: (01) 7743979
Contact: Mr. A. S. Bankole - Chairman/CEO

URU INDUSTRIES LIMITED

Business: Manufacturing of Automobile Cables
Address: 122, Owerri Road, Umudim, Nnewi, Anambra State
Tel: (046) 460594, 462154, 463154, 460825
Fax: (046) 463573
E-mail: otccable@infoweb.abs.net
* 19, Church Street, Idumota, Lagos
Contact: Sir. D. C. Ofordeme - Chairman/CEO

USAMA INDUSTRIES LIMITED

Business: Transportation , Tranning of Hides & Skins
Address: Plot 83, Sharada Industrial Estate Phase II, Kano
Tel/Fax: (064) 661440
Contact: Nasidi Usama - Chairman

USCCO NIGERIA LIMITED
Business: Structural Steel Construction, Production of Agricultural Machinery, Animal Husbandry
Address: Ebony Paints Road, Awkunanaw, Enugu
Tel/Fax: (042) 453624
Contact: Engr. Pius U. Okeke - Chairman/CEO

USG TECHNOLOGY LIMITED
Business: Information Technology Training & Consultancy
Address: Olajuwon House, 15/17, Opebi Road, Ikeja, Lagos
Tel: (01) 4932401-6 (6L), 4932193
E-mail: info@usgtechnology.com
training@usgtechnology.com
Website: www.usgtechnology.com
* 1, Benin - Lagos Road, by NITEL Exchange, opp Uniben Main Gate, Ugbowo, Benin City
Tel: (052) 602855
Contact: Mr. Lambert Ugorji - MD/CEO

USMAD NIGERIA LIMITED
Business: Sales of Building Materials, Importers and Exporters, General Contractors
Address: Km. 1, Badagry Expressway, by Makanjuola Market, opp. Alexander House, Sari-Iganmu, Orile, Lagos
Tel: (01) 7745456, 7753794
Contact: Alh. Usman Adisa - Chairman/CEO

USP LIMITED
Business: Brand Management Consultancy
Address: 4, Thomas Ajufo St, off Opebi Road, Ikeja, Lagos
Tel: (01) 4705254, 4933305 **Fax:** (01) 4932175
E-mail: uspltd@hyperia.com
Website: www.uspltd.com
Contact: Mr Akin Kekere-Ekun - Chairman
Mr Kayode Muyiwa - MD/CEO

UTB TRUSTEES LIMITED
Business: Pension & Funds Management; Finance Advisory Services, Equipment Leasing, Trusteeship
Address: 214, Etim Inyang Crescent, Victoria Island, Lagos
Tel: (01) 2612150, 261825
Contact: Mr. J. O. Afolabi - MD/CEO

UTC NIGERIA PLC
Business: Conglomerate - Foods Processing, Fast Foods, Bakery, Retailing & Farming; Water, Power, Automotive & Mechanical Engineering; Lift Installation & Maintenance, Vehicle Leasing, Manufacture & Installation of Aluminium Products
Address: 27, Wharf Road, Apapa, Lagos
Tel: (01) 5451531-5 (5L) **Fax:** (01) 5870152
E-mail: utcho@beta.linkserve.com
Contact: Chief. C. H. Okolo - Group MD/CEO
Mr. Emman Obinyan - GM (Corporate Dev.)

UTC ALUMINIUM (Div. of UTC Nigeria Plc)
Business: Fabrication of Aluminium Building Materials
Address: 27/29, Creek Road, Apapa, Lagos
Tel: (01) 5452710, 5452712, 5452714, 5877346, 8118760
Fax: (01) 5452713, 5877346
E-mail: utcalu@linkserve.com
Contact: Mr. E. O Poluyi - GM

UTOBRAS (NIGERIA) LIMITED
Business: Importation & Marketing of Luxury Buses, Refuge Compactors, Agricultural Tractors & Household Equipment
Address: Plot 634, Adeyemo Alakija Street, Eleganza Biro Plaza, 6th Floor C5, Victoria Island, Lagos
Tel: (01) 2702936, 7749041, 08033144257
Fax: (01) 2702936
E-mail: utabras@linkserve.com
*78, Murtala Mohammed Way, Ebute-Metta, Lagos
Tel/Fax: (01) 862662,4729028, 7730501
Contact: Mr. Frank Utomi - MD/CEO

UZOH VITSON AND ASSOCIATES LIMITED
Business: Stockist of Industrial Fittings (Galvanized Steel, UPVC Pipes & Fittings, Sanitary Wares, Tiles, Water Pumps and Tanks)
Address: Kofoworola House (Shop No. 10) 33, Badagry Expressway, Odun-Ade Bus-Stop, Coker, Lagos
Tel: (01) 2881306, 7919091, 08033011096, 08033255969
Fax: (01) 2881306, 5556077
E-mail: uzohvitson@yahoo.com
uzohvitson@infoweb.abs.net
Contact: Chief Vitus Chukwudubem Uzoh - Chairman/CEO

V. I. P. INDUSTRIES LIMITED
Business: Manufacturing of Cosmetics
Address: 34, Idowu Oshifodunrin Street, Ire-Akari Estate, Isolo, Lagos
Tel: (01) 4525705, 525491, 7732054 **Fax:** (01) 525491
Contact: Mr. Dominic Umeh - Chairman/CEO

VAL INSURANCE LIMITED
Business: General Business Insurance
Address: 7, Bompai Road, Kano
Tel: (064) 632178, 634009, 08037038058
Fax: (064) 632446
Contact: Alh. Nafi'u Rabiu - Chairman
Nnamdi R. Ononwu - GM/CEO

V-MOBILE NIGERIA LIMITED
Business: Global System of Mobile (GSM) Telecommunication Service Provider
Address: Plot 1678, Olakunle Bakare Street, off Sanusi Fafunwa Street, Victoria Island, Lagos
Tel: (01) 2610126-8 (3L), 2610130-1 (2L), 3200474-8 (5L)
Fax: (01) 2610127, 2610148, 3200477
Contact: Mr. Willem Swart - MD/CEO
Mr. Lawrie Golding - Chief Marketing Manager

VALAGH & COMPANY LIMITED
Business: Importation and Sales of Water Chemical Pumps, Electric Variable & Geared Motors; Flow Meters, Vavles & Accessories and Chlorinator
Address: 1147/149, Akowonjo Road, Akowonjo, Lagos
Tel: (01) 4922386, 883055 **Fax:** (01) 4930419
E-mail: valagh@usa.net
Contact: Mr. A. G. Agha - Chairman/CEO

VALCOM TECHNOLOGIES LIMITED
Business: Importation of Oilfield Equipment and Accessories
Address: Prince's Court (2nd Floor, Room 2A), 37, Ahmed Onibudo Street, Victoria Island, Lagos

Tel: (01) 2622571 **Fax:** (01) 2622854
E-mail: valcomng@lagosmail.sprint.com

VALE COMMUNICATIONS LIMITED
Business: Information & Public Relations Management Production & Sales of Diaries, Marketing of Leather Essentials & General Gift Items
Address: 10, Biaduo St, off Keffi Street, S. W. Ikoyi, Lagos
Tel: (01) 2692547, 2692543 **Fax:** (01) 2692547
Contact: Chinedu Ibeji - MD/CEO

VALENCIA HOTELS
Business: Hospitality Services
Address: Plot 799, Blantyre Street, off Adetokunbo Ademola Crescent, Wuse II, Abuja
Tel: (09) 5240669, 5240670, 5241582-3 (2L)
Fax: (09) 5239986
E-mail: info@valenciahotelsabuja.com
Website: www.valenciahotelsabuja.com

VALLAN VENTURES LIMITED
Business: Processing of Palm Kernel
Address: 134, Happy Home Avenue, Kirikiri Industrial Estate, Apapa, Lagos
Tel: (01) 7740223

VALMON SECURITIES LIMITED
Business: Stockbroking, Fund & Portfolio Management, Investment & Financial Advisory Services
Address: Ebani House Complex (2nd Floor), 149/153, Broad, Street, Lagos
Tel: (01) 2662496, 2662571 **Fax:** (01) 2662571
E-mail: valsl@infoweb.abs.net
Contact: Chief Luke E. Okafor - Exec. Chairman

VALUE MART LIMITED
Business: Supermarket
Address: 24, Akin Adesola Street, Victoria Island, Lagos
Tel/Fax: (01) 2623297

VALUELINE SECURIES & INVESTMENT LIMITED
Business: Financing, Stockbroking, Management Consultancy
Address: 1A, Kaduna Street, Port Harcourt
Tel: (084) 233067, 233483, 08023035564, 08033411598, 08046104625 **Fax:** (084) 233483
* 67, Douglas Road, Owerri
Tel: (083) 232155, 233944
Contact: Chief O. E. Amaonwu - Chairman
Mr. S. O. Enyinnaya - MD/CEO

VALUEPLUS NIGERIA LIMITED
Business: Business Promotions, Investment Lottery
Address: 4, Turton St, off Thorburn Ave, Sabo-Yaba, Lagos
Tel: (01) 7747066, 2882616 **Fax:** (01) 2882616, 3422212
E-mail: gugroup@beta.linkserve.com
Contact: Dr. F. A. O. Alade - Chairman
Mr. A. D. Olaniyan - Exec. Director/CEO

VAMED ENGINEERING NIGERIA LIMITED
Business: Medical Design & Engineering, Procurement, Supply & Installation, Construction, Training and Consultancy
Address: 92B, Buchanan Close, off Aminu Kano Crescent, Wuse II, Abuja
Tel: (09) 4132112-3 (2L) **Fax:** (09) 4132117

VAN FRANK LIMITED
Business: IT Support, Sales of Storage Management Systems
Address: 2, Tokunbo Alli Street, off Toyin St, Ikeja, Lagos
Tel: (01) 4930980, 4709255 **Fax:** (01) 4930980
Contact: Mr. Awele Osadebe - MD/CEO

VAN INVESTMENTS LIMITED
Business: Clearing & Forwarding, Warehousing, Import & Export
Address: Nnewi Building (4th Floor, left Wing), 1/3, Creek Road, Apapa, Lagos
Tel: (01) 5453757, 5457740 **Fax:** (01) 5457793
E-mail: vaninvestment@yahoo.com
* 13, Okilton Drive, Rumuokwuta, Port Harcourt
Contact: Chief Anayo Nwadike - Chairman/CEO

VAN LEER CONTAINERS (NIGERIA) PLC
Business: Manufacturing & Marketing of Metal Drums & Plastic Containers
Address: 1, Alapata Road, (off Dockyard Rd), Apapa, Lagos
Tel: (01) 5873007, 5877024, 5877085 **Fax:** (01) 5873084
E-mail: vanleer@linkserve.com.ng
Contact: Mr. G. A. Sangosanya - MD/CEO
Mr. G A. Ikem - Commercial Manager

VAN VLIET TRUCKS (NIGERIA) LIMITED
Business: Truck Sales and Marketing, Design and Construction of Trailers & Tankers, Sided Body, Flat Beds, Surface and Underground Tanks, Repairs and Maintenance of Trucks, Panel Beating & Spray Painting, Steel Fabrication Works
Address: Plot 29, Abimbola St, Isolo Ind Estate, Isolo, Lagos
Tel: (01) 4528009, 4523766, 4528888, 7745858
Fax: (01) 4529013
E-mail: vanvliet@infoweb.abs.net
* Plot 1115, Adetokunbo Ademola Crescent, Wuse II, Abuja.
Tel: (090) 803290
Contact: Engr. Dayo Adetunmbi - Chairman/MD
Mr. Seye Adetunmbi - GM

VANGUARD INSURANCE BROKERS LIMITED
Business: Insurance Broking
Address: 7, Kolawole Odunsi St, off Unity Rd, Ikeja, Lagos
Tel: (01) 4978262, 4712251 **Fax:** (01) 4978262
E-mail: vanguardbrokers@yahoo.com
* 94, Malanje St, Cadastral Zone A4, Wuse, Abuja
Contact: Mr. Adebayo O. Itiola - Chairman
Mr. Modupe F. Sipe - MD

VANGUARD MEDIA LIMITED
Business: Publishing
Address: Vanguard Avnue, off Mile 2/Apapa Expressway, Kirikiri Canal, Apapa, Lagos
Tel: (01) 5871200, 5875847, 5871781, 5871787, 7742861
Fax: (01) 5877970
E-mail: vanguard@linkserve.net.ng; vanguard@nova.net.ng
Website: www.vanguardngr.com
Contact: Mr. Sam Amuka - Publisher/CEO

VANNI INTERNATIONAL SECURITY SYSTEMS LIMITED
Business: Security & Cash-in-Transit Services
Address: 1, Vanni Close, off Surulere Industrial Road, Ogba Industrial Scheme, Lagos
Tel: (01) 962264, 961918
Contact: Chief Victor Imianvan - Chairman/CEO

VASONS CONCEPT GROUP
Business: Consulting Engineers (Civil, Structural, Environmental), Project Management
Address: 3, Adegbola Street, off Anjorin Street, Lawanson, Surulere, Lagos
Tel: (01) 5830449, 835309, 4711033, 08033231985
E-mail: vasonsconcept@yahoo.com
Contact: Engr. (Chief) R. O. Shoderu - Principal Partner
Engr. V. O. Oyenuga - Partner

VASO-VIN COMMERCIAL COMPANY NIGERIA LIMITED
Business: Importation of Marble & Palladiana; Terrazo-Polishing Machine and Spare Parts; Terrazo & Marble Works
Address: 38, Ozomagala St/Modebe Avenue Junction, off St. Andrew's Anglican Church, Odoakpu, Onitsha
Tel: (046) 217672, 212276, 08033360720
Contact: Mr. Vincent Okeke - Chairman/CEO

VAST INTERNATIONAL COMPANY LIMITED
Business: Planning, Designing Building & Installation of Stadia Scoreboards, Floodlights, Running Tracks & Swimming Pools
Address: 28, Bassie Ogamba Street, off Adeniran Ogunsanya Street, Surulere, Lagos
Tel: (01) 5851245, 5850430, 08023041066, 08023069850, 08033254230, 08037027253, 08042107084, 08045049166, 08055235889, 08055245695
Fax: (01) 5833237
E-mail: vastinternational@yahoo.co.uk
Website: www.vastinternational.com
Contact: Mr. Obiora Okoye - MD/CE3O

VDT COMMUNICATIONS LIMITED
Business: Data Communication Services
Address: Marble House (7th Floor), 1, Alfred Rewane Road, (formerly Kingsway, Road) Famolo, Ikoyi,
Tel: (01) 2696786, 2696775, 4705501 **Fax:** (01) 2690900
E-mail: bitcomsys@aol.com
Contact: Biodun Omoniyi - MD/CEO

VEBUS LIMITED
Business: Sales of UPS Equipment & Back-Up Systems
Address: Plot 284B, Ajose Adeogun St, Victoria Island Lagos
Tel: (01) 2622539, 2623845 **Fax:** (01) 2623138, 2623846
* 170, Aba Road, Port Harcourt
* 140C, Airport Road, Warri
Contact: Mr. George U. Nkwo - Chairman/CEO

VEEPEE INDUSTRIES LIMITED
Business: Manufacture of Flexible Packing Materials
Address: Km. 38, Abeokuta Motor Road, Sango Otta
Tel: (039) 722209, 722212, 722104, 722301, 722051
Fax: (039) 2692051, 4973110
E-mail: veepee@alpha.linkserve.com
Contact: Mr. R. V. Vaswani - MD/CEO

VEGO PRODUCTS LIMITED
Business: Manufacture of Cosmetics & Body-Care Products
Address: Plot 13, Block XII, Industrial Estate, off Ota-Idiroko Road, Ota, Ogun State
Tel: (01) 7740477, 7740653 * (039) 722131, 722456
Fax: (039) 722142
Website: www.vegoplast.net
* 43, Commercial Avenue, Sabo-Yaba, Lagos
* 270, Aba-Owerri Road, Abayi, Aba
Contact: Mr. Babatunde Bajulaiye - Group Sales Director

VEITGUNS COMMUNICATIONS LIMITED
Business: Sales, Installation & Maintenance of Telecommunication Terminal Equipment, CDMA'S GSM Phones & Accesories
Address: Valley View Plaza, Ikeja, Lagos
Tel: (01) 8124475, 08023225721
E-mail: veitguns@yahoo.com
* 18, O la Ayeni Str, Computer Village, Ikeja, Lagos
Contact: Mr. Wale Thomas - MD/CEO

VELTROP LIMITED
Business: Swimming Pool Equipment Supply & Engineering, Water/Sewage Treatment Plants & Engineering
Address: 2B, Chief Aguma Street, Ogbunabali, Port Harcourt
Tel/Fax: (084) 611178, 08033040240
E-mail: veltrop@hyperia.com
* 6, Chikwe Close, Rumukurushi, Port Harcourt
Contact: Mr. Kaodi Nduaka - Chairman/CEO

VENIVIC MCMXCVIII
Business: Health Club and Spa
Address: 52, Kofo Abayomi Street, Victoria Island, Lagos
Tel: (01) 2625785, 08033282582
E-mail: urbanspa2000@yahoo.com
Contact: Ms. Arinola Adeniyi - MD/CEO

VENI VICI
Business: Health Club and Spa
Address: 52, Kofo Abayomi Street, Victoria Island, Lagos
Tel: (01) 2625785
E-mail: venivici@beta.linkserve.com

VENTROM NIGERIA LIMITED
Business: Importation of Computer Systems & Accessories
Address: Coutinho Building, 30/32, Creek Rd, Apapa, Lagos
Tel: (01) 4809954, 4809958, 8042098
E-mail: ventrom@yahoo.com
Website: www.ventronltd.com
Contact: Chief (Dr.) Amobi Uwaleke - Exec. Chairman

VENTURE CAPITAL PARTNERS LIMITED
Business: Asset Management, Provision of Corporate (Business) Training Solutions
Address: 24, Sumbo Jibowu Street, off Ribadu Road, S.W. Ikoyi, Lagos
Tel: (01) 2694127, 2694302 **Fax:** (01) 2694302
E-mail: vcpng@infoweba.abs.net
Contact: Mr. Ayodeji Akindolie - Chairman
Mr. Bolade Oyebolu - MD/CEO

VENTURE TRUST COMPANY LIMITED
Business: Financing of Import & Export Trade, LPO and

Lease; Portfolio Management, Contracting
Address: Ivie House, 4/6, Ajose Adeogun Street, Victoria Island, Lagos
Tel: (01) 2613246, 2622278, 2622281 **Fax:** (01) 2613246
Contact: Chief (Dr.) Senator Jacob Tilley-Gyado - Chairman
Mr. Ademola Shefiu Ali - GM/CEO

VENTURES & TRUSTS LIMITED
Business: Venture Capital & Investment Management
Address: 5A, Adeyemo Alakija Street, Victoria Island, Lagos
Tel: (01) 2620300-2 (3L), 2620602-3(2L) **Fax:** (01)2620303
E-mail: vt@infoweb.abs.net
Contact: Mr. Femi T. Akingbe - MD/CEO

VENUS PROCESSING & PACKAGING COMPANY LIMITED
Business: Manufacture of Individually Quick-Frozen Pineapple Cubes & Pulps, Other Fruits and Vegetables
Address: 16, Kofo Abayomi St,Victoria Island, Lagos
Tel: (01) 2622232, 2622259, 2615505 **Fax:** (01) 2619487
E-mail: primlaks@hyperia.com
Contact: Mr. Anil R. Hemnani - Director
Mr. S. Murali - Group Controller

VERONA INDUSTRIES LIMITED
Business: Importation of General Merchandise
Address: 42/44, Ijora Oloye Street, Ijora, Lagos
Tel: (01) 5872305, 5878138, 7755854
Fax: (01) 2620523, 2617631
Contact: Mr. N. Paryani - Manager

VESA FOOD AGENCIES LIMITED
Business: Importation of Frozen Foods and Fish
Address: 24, Oregun Road, Oregun, Ikeja, Lagos
Tel: (01) 4979251, 7747896

VETCO GRAY NIGERIA LIMITED
Business: Sales and Maintenance of Oilfield Equipment
Address: Ahmadu Bello Way, Victoria Island, Lagos
Tel: (01) 2615881, 2615935 **Fax:** (01) 2615029
* Plot 114, Trans-Amadi Ind. Layout, Port Harcourt
Tel: (084) 236674-5 (2L), 238020
Contact: Otunba A. O. Ojora, OFR - Chairman

VIBON NIGERIA LIMITED
Business: Importation of General Merchandise
Address: 50, Opebi Road, Ikeja, Lagos
Tel: (01) 4960175, 4964189, 4967892
E-mail: viboninvestment@yahoo.com

VIBRANT INSURANCE BROKERS LIMITED
Business: Insurance Broking
Address: 23, off Calabar Street, High-Level, Makurdi
Tel: (044) 531127, 532380, 532520
Contact: Elder Olusola Morakinyo - Chairman/CEO

VIC LAWRENCE & ASSOCIATES LIMITED
Business: Training, Business Development, Consultancy
Address: VLA House, Plot 1646, Oko Awo Street, Victoria Island, Lagos
Tel: (01) 4616360-2 (3L), 7742422 **Fax:** (01) 4616363
E-mail: vic@hyperia.com
Website: www.viclawrence.com
Contact: Mr. Dominique Abudu - MD/CEO

VICKERS WORLD TRADE LIMITED
Business: Trading Importation of Raw Steel Billets
Address: Plot 1232, Bishop Oluwole St Victoria Island, Lagos
Tel: (01) 2620191 **Fax:** (01) 2647246
Contact: Mr. Yomi Edu - Chairman/CEO

VICKY OPTICAL SERVICES & MANUFACTURING LIMITED
Business: Eye Care Services (Testing & Examination), Optometric Services, Manufacturing & Dispensing Optical Services
Address: 21/21A, Tafawa Balewa Square Complex, Race Course, Lagos Island, Lagos
Tel: (01) 2635103, 4802261, 08023465593
Contact: Mrs. V. A. Balogun - MD/CEO

VICODA LIMITED
Business: Importation of Textile Machinery and Accessories, Manufacturing of Textile Chemicals & Dyes, Colour Separation and Printing Services
Address: Plot 9, Block a, Gbagada Industrial Estate, off Gbagada Expressway, Gbagada, Lagos
Tel: (01) 7730305-6 (2L), 7733169, 7749104, 08037160390
Fax: (01) 5875440
E-mail: vicoda@infoweb.abs.net
* Gidan Bamaiyi, M1, Ahmadu Bello Way, Kaduna
Tel: (062) 248753
* Supreme Plaza (Shop 18), Ladoke Akintola Boulevard, Garki II, Abuja.
Tel: (09) 2341743

VICTA TECHNOLOGIES LIMITED
Business: Sales of Colour Plastic-ID Card Printers, Production of Plastic ID Cards, Sales, Maintenance & Repairs of Computers and Peripherals, Supply of Office Equipment
Address: 6, Oba Akran Avenue, Ikeja, Lagos
Tel: (01) 4962572, 4803773, 08033032288, 08033006133
Fax: (01) 4960171
E-mail: victatech@yahoo.com
victa@supernet300.com

VICTORIA BEACH HOTEL LIMITED
Business: Hotel Services (Mainland Hotel, Lagos)
Address: 2/4, Murtala Mohammed Way, Oyingbo, Lagos
Tel: (01) 7741388, 7745941, 800300-19 (20L), 861600
Fax: (01) 860556
E-mail: mainlandhotel@beta-leventis.net
Contact: Dr. J. U. Aire - Chairman
Dr. S. Constantinidis - MD/CEO

VICTORIAL CONTINENTAL HOTELS & TOURS
Business: Hospital & Catering Services
Address: Plot 18/19, Dideolu Estate, Water Corporation Rd, off Ligali Ayorinde Street, Victoria Island, Lagos
Tel: (01) 3204178-80 (3L), 4705767 **Fax:** (01) 3204630
E-mail: info@victoriacontinentalhotels.com
Website: www.victoriacontinentalhotels.com

VICTORIA GARDEN CITY COMMUNICATION CO. LIMITED
Business: Wireless Telephone Service Provider
Address: VGC Shopping Complex (Shop 10B), Victoria Garden City, Lekki Expressway, Lagos
Tel: (01) 4618005 **Fax:** (01) 4618007

VICTORIA ISLAND CONSULTANCY & HOSPITAL SERVICES LIMITED

Business: Hospital and Medical Consultancy Services
Address: Fabac Centre, 3B, Ligali Ayorinde St, V/Is, Lagos
Tel: (01) 4612069-70 (2L), 4619284-6 (3L), 7748276
Fax: (01) 2612712
Contact: Dr. F. B. A. Coker - Chairman/Medical Director
Dr. O. A. Balogun - MD

VICTORIA LIGHTS & FURNITURE (NIGERIA) LIMITED

Business: Sales of Furniture, Lights and Carpets
Address: 20, Oroyinyin Street (3rd Floor), Lagos
Tel: (01) 2610814, 2621376, 7751810, 7902888
Fax: (01) 2610815
E-mail: kmsharma@vicfur.com
Contact: Alh. Abdul Wahab Olaitan - Chairman
Mr. Kishore Shalmar - MD/CEO

VIDAC EQUIPMENT NIGERIA LIMITED

Business: Import and Export, Sales of Agricultural, Industrial, Construction and Mechanical Equipment
Address: 129, Okota Road, off Cele Bus-Stop, off Oshodi - Apapa Expressway, Isolo, Lagos
Tel: (01) 5556209, 7916812, 08023133366, 08033790054
Fax: (01) 5556209
E-mail: info@vidacequip.com
vidacequip@hotmail.com
Website: www.vidacequipng,com
* 32, Benue Crescent, Wadata, Makurdi
Tel: (044) 533080 **Fax:** (044) 531821
Contact: Chief Vidan Uchechukwu Agbani - MD/CEO

VIDEONET LIMITED

Business: Importation, Sales and Rentals of Video Films
Address: 12, Festival Road, off Adetokunbo Ademola Street, Victoria Island, Lagos
Tel/Fax: (01) 2880925
Contact: Dr. Femi Aribisala - Chairman/CEO
Mr. Ernest W. Oboh - GM

VIDEPAT ENTERPRISES NIGERIA LIMITED

Business: General Merchandising, Sales of Wire Netting and Building Materials
Address: 17, Idumagbo Avenue, Idumota, Lagos
Tel: (01) 2666930, 2636122, 2640969, 2669855
E-mail: videpat@alpha.linkserve.com
* 5, Idumagbo Avenue, Lagos Island, Lagos
Contact: Mr. Patrick N. Ezeadum - MD/CEO

VIGEO LIMITED

Business: Marketing Support Services (Sales of Diaries and Corporate Gifts, Design of Sales Incentive Programme, Merchandising, Signages, Events & Lifestyle Marketing Service, Sports Marketing, Conferences, Seminars & Exhibitions Management, Training, Awards Services), Technical Support Services (Materials Procurement Services, Safety Equipment Services, Safety & Environment Management Services), Project Managers
Address: Vigeo House, 31A, Adeniyi Jones Avenue, Ikeja, Lagos
Tel: (01) 4961118, 4965605, 4930531-3 (3L), 7733376, 7741059 **Fax:** (01) 4972060, 2693920
E-mail: vigeo@vigeo.com.ng
Website: www.vigeoholdings.com
* Plot 278, Aba-Port Harcourt Expressway, opp. Shell Residential Area, Port Harcourt
* Plot 212, Shehu Shagari Way, Asokoro, Abuja
Contact: Mr. Victor G. Osibodu, MER - Chairman/CEO

VIGILANT INSURANCE COMPANY LIMITED

Business: General Insurance Business
Address: 284, Ikorod Road, Anthony, Lagos
Tel: (01) 4939839, 4961771, 4967398, 4978241, 4978692
Fax: (01) 4977898
E-mail: info@vigilantinsurance.com
Website: www.vigilantinsurance.com
* Plot 516, Sultan Abubakar Way (2nd Floor), Wuse Zone 2, Abuja.
Tel: (09) 2901455, 5233083
Contact: Chief Adewale Teluwo - Chairman
Mr. Tope Smart - MD/CEO

VIGILANT INTERNATIONAL AGENCIES (NIGERIA) LTD

Business: Security Guard Services
Address: 16, Ezinifite Street, Bridge Head Approach, Onitsha
Tel: (046) 212337
Contact: Chief F. A. Okadigbo - Chairman/CEO

VIK INDUSTRIES LIMITED

Business: Manufacturing of Domestic Plastic Storage Products
Address: 25, Asa Afariogun Street, off Osolo Way, Ajao Estate, Lagos
Tel: (01) 4522696, 4523171, 7741552 **Fax:** (01) 2695549

VIKING CONTAINER & MARINE SERVICES LIMITED

Business: Repair and Conversion of Sea-Freight Containers, Plant Hire
Address: 2/4, Steve Ajose Street, off Dillion Street, Kirikiri, Apapa, Lagos
Tel: (01) 5450213, 5875622, 5450073
Fax: (01) 5450223, 5872953
E-mail: vicomar@micro.com.ng
Contact: Mr. P. D. Taylor - MD/CEO

VIKREN CORPORATION NIGERIA LIMITED

Business: Exportation of Gum-Arabic
Address: Chartered Bank Building (5th Floor), 19, Martins Street, Lagos
* 19, Club Road, Kano.
Tel: (064) 638170
Contact: Mr. Vinod Kirplani - Chairman/CEO

VIMBA INTERNATIONAL NIGERIA LIMITED

Business: Importation of Safes and Office Equipment
Address: 5, Jaiyeola Ajatta Street, off M. M. International Airport Road, Ajao Estate, Apakun-Oshodi, Lagos
Tel: (01) 4524340, 4703184, 08033074800
Fax: (01) 2632195
* Plot 2302, H.Macaulay Way, Wuse Zone 6, Abuja
Tel: (09) 5235484, 6700282
Contact: Mr. Victor Mbatu - MD/CEO

VINA INTERNATIONAL LIMITED

Business: Manufacturing and Marketing of Home, School & Office Furniture, Portakabins and Kitchen Closets

Address: Plots 4, 5 & 6, First Rd, Oluyole Ind. Estate, Ibadan
Tel: (02) 2315073, 2315083, 2315093 **Fax:** (02) 2317269
E-mail: admin@vinaltd.com
zardgroup@hyperia.com
* 4, Adetokunbo Ademola Cresc, Wuse II, Abuja.
Tel: (09) 5235196 **Fax:** (09) 52343143
* 14A, Akin Adesola St, Victoria Island, Lagos
Tel: (01) 7731155
* Fmr Airport Hotel, 1, Old Aba Rd, Port Harcourt.
Tel: (084) 234582
Contact: Mr. Eli Zard - MD/CEO

VINAS INDUSTRIES LIMITED
Business: Manufacturing and Marketing of Zip, Audio & Video Tapes, Recording of Tapes
Address: 25, Nottidge Street, Onitsha
Tel: (046) 485128
Contact: Mr. Vincent Chuwuzubelu - Chairman/CEO

VINNA INVESTMENTS LIMITED
Business: Import and Export, General Merchandising
Address: Maggi House, 30, Clifford House, Aba
Tel: (082) 231898 **Fax:** (082) 233485
* 143, opp. Old Minna Garage, Suleja, Niger State
Tel: (09) 8500011
* 10/8, Bauchi Road, opp. First Bank, Jos
Tel: (073) 610464
Contact: Chief Vincent Ezenwu - MD/CEO

VINOTEL HOTELS, ABUJA
Business: Hospitality & Catering Services
Address: 57, Nelson Mandela Str, Area F, Asokoro, Abuja
Tel: (09) 3142801-3 (3 Lines)
Contact: Mr. U. D. Okafor - Chairman/CEO

VINZ INTERNATIONAL NIGERIA LIMITED
Business: Computer Sales and Services
Address: 15, Toyin Street, Ikeja, Lagos
Tel: (01) 4968436, 4971072, 7749844, 7911760
Fax: (01) 4971072
E-mail: vinz@cyberspace.net.ng
Contact: Mr. Osy Gbemudu - Chairman/CEO

VIRGIN ATLANTIC AIRLINE (NIGERIA)
Business: International Airline Services
Address: The Ark Tower, Plot 17A, Ligali Ayorinde Street, Victoria Island, Lagos.
Tel: (01) 3202750, 3202747, 4612750, 4612747
Fax: (01) 3202745
Website: www.virgin.com/atlantic
* Plot 175, Aba Rd, G.R.A Junction, Port Harcourt
Tel: (084) 467000-6 (7L) **Fax:** (084) 467009

VIRGIN GROUP OF COMPANIES LIMITED
Business: Petroleum & Petrochemicals, Marine Transport & Services, Printing & Publishing, Import & Export of Fashion Materials, Lube Blenders, Oil & Gas Merchants, Telecommunications
Address: 1, Kofo Abayomi Avenue, Apapa, Lagos
Tel: (01) 5450468, 5450469, 5874582 **Fax:** (01) 5874582
E-mail: virgingroup@nova.net.ng
virgingroup@hotmail.com
Contact: Engr. Best Ezeani - MD/CEO

VISA INVESTMENTS & SECURITIES LIMITED
Business: Securities Trading, Investment Management, Trade Finance, Financial Advisory Services
Address: 2 (Plot 1302), Akin Adesola Street, Victoria Island, Lagos
Tel: (01) 2615318, 2613549, 2613833 **Fax:** (01) 2617136
E-mail: visa@hyperia.com
Contact: Alh. Ibrahim Katune - Chairman
Alh. Ibrahim Babayo - GM/CEO

VISANA NIGERIA LIMITED
Business: Manufacturing of Electrical Fittings & Lamps
Address: 21, Alao Street, Ajao Estate, Isolo, Lagos
Tel: (01) 7741206, 08023095263, 08033107045, 08034534461, 08042103130 **Fax:** (01) 2623434
E-mail: visana@msn.com
Contact: Mr. N. L. Chulani - MD/CEO

VISION RESERVOIR MANAGEMENT TECHNICAL (VRMT) INTERNATIONAL
Business: Petroleum, Geoscience & Engineering Consultancy
Address: Plot 1, East-West Road, Eleme, Port Harcourt
Tel: (084) 611469, 613400, 486136
Contact: Dr. Felix Njoku - MD/CEO
Mr Ernest Ihejirika - GM

VISION TRUST & INVESTMENT LIMITED
Business: Stockbroking, Investment Advisory Services, Portfolio Management
Address: Ashakun House (Ground Floor), 13/15, Lake Street, off Broad Street, Apongbon, Lagos
Tel: (01) 2642980, 2666448, 2640255, 08023519348, 08033077421, 08033078360, 08033485280
E-mail: visiontrust@hyperia.com
Contact: Mr. George O. Ibhade - MD/CEO

VISIONQUEST COMMUNICATIONS LIMITED
Business: Information & Communication Technology
Address: 58, Mbonu Street, D-Line, Port Harcourt
Tel: (084) 574045, 08033099713, 08033333343
E-mail: visionquest82000@yahoo.com
Website: www.visionquest.com
Contact: Mr. Emeka Nworji (JP) - MD/CEO

VISTA INTERNATIONAL LIMITED
Business: Importation of Paperline Papers, Boards and Stationery, Marketing of Office & Copier Papers, Exercise Books and Computer Stationery
Address: Block 1, Plot 44, Jimoh Odutola Road, off Eric Moore Road, Surulere,
Tel: (01) 5456378-80 (3L), 4707561-2 (2L)
Fax: (01) 5456381
E-mail: vistaint@multilinks.com
Contact: Mr. Anup Varyani - MD/CEO

VISTAR SERVICES LIMITED
Business: Telecommunication Engineering Services, Distribution of GSM Phones
Address: Foreshore Towers (9th Floor), 2A, Osborne Road, Ikoyi, Lagos
Tel: (01) 2693791, 08034007627 **Fax:** (01) 2695367
E-mail: vistarvsl@yahoo.com
Contact: Mr. David Pelemo - GM

VISUAL ADVERTISING COMPANY LIMITED
Business: Outdoor Advertising
Address: 12, Moshood Bakare Street, Gbagada/Pedro Phase I, Lagos
Tel: (01) 823231
Contact: Mr. Akintunde Yeku - MD/CEO

VITA CONSTRUCTION LIMITED
Business: Construction and Civil Engineering Contractors
Address: Vita Tower, 13, Elsie Pearse St, Victoria Is, Lagos
Tel: (01) 2623242, 08034021923 **Fax:** (01) 2623242
* Plot 629, Abeokuta Street, Area 8, Garki, Abuja
Tel: (09) 2340637, 2342595
Contact: Mr. V. A. Varnavas - Chairman/CEO
Mr. Y. N. Christodoulou - Dep. MD

VITABIOTICS NIGERIA LIMITED
Business: Manufacturing of Pharmaceutical Products
Address: 35, Mobolaji Johnson Avenue, Oregun Industrial Estate, Oregun, Ikeja, Lagos
Tel: (01) 4973717-8 (2L) **Fax:** (01) 4960852
Contact: Dr. K. T. Lalvani - Chairman

VITAFOAM NIGERIA PLC
Business: Manufacture & Distribution of Foam Products
Address: Oba Akran Avenue, Ikeja Ind. Estate, Ikeja, Lagos
Tel: (01) 4972570-8 (9L) **Fax:** (01) 4972563
E-mail: vitafoam@vitafoamng.com
* Industry Road, Aba.
Tel: (082) 220570, 228656
* Plot 13, Maimalari Road, Bompai Industrial Estate, Kano.
Tel: (064) 637773, 645023
Contact: Mr. A. Akinbowale - MD/CEO
Mr. B. A. Lasisi - ED (Personnel)

VITAL FOODS LIMITED
Business: Manufacturing and Marketing of Confectionery
Address: Plot 2B, Block 1, Oluyole Industrial Estate, Ring Road, Ibadan
Tel: (02) 2315579
Contact: Mr. N. J. Nassar - MD/CEO

VITAL MEDIX NIGERIA LIMITED
Business: Marketing of Pharmaceutical Products
Address: Elephant Cement House (2nd & 6th Floors), ASSBIFI Road, Central Business District, Alausa, Ikeja, Lagos
Tel: (01) 5557809, 5557257, 08033023203
Fax: (01) 5557256
E-mail: vitamofen@aol.com
Contact: Mr. Abimbola Owolabi - Chairman
Mrs. Biola Akinsanya - MD/CEO

VITAL PHARMACEUTICALS & HEALTHCARE LIMITED
Business: Importation and Distribution of Pharmaceuticals and Healthcare Products
Address: 28, Ajasa Street, Onikan, Lagos
Tel: (01) 2636449, 2633485, 2633877, 2636411
Fax: (01) 2636298, 2636678
E-mail: vitalnig@metrong.com
Contact: Alh. Kasumu Haruna - Chairman
Mr. Sanjiv Raj Kapoor - MD/CEO

VITALITY COMPUTERS LIMITED
Business: Sales of Computer Accessories, Installation of Internet, Training, Maintenance Systems
Address: 168, Awolowo Road, (1st Floor), S.W. Ikoyi, Lagos
Tel: (01) 2693715 **Fax:** (01) 2695544
Contact: Dr. Obioha N. Ugoji - Chairman/CEO

VITAMALT PLC
Business: Brewing & Bottling of Non-Alcoholic Malt Drink
Address: Km. 32, Lagos-Badagry Expressway, Agbara Industrial Estate, Agbara, Ogun State
Tel: (01) 4724358, 4748441 **Fax:** (01) 5559857
Contact: Mr. O'tega Emerhor - Chairman
Mr. Yomi Oladipupo - MD/CEO

VIVA INSURANCE BROKERS LIMITED
Business: Insurance Broking
Address: Waterfront Plaza, Plot 270, Ozumba Mbadiwe Avenue, Victoria Island, Lagos
Tel: (01) 2619836, 2613472 **Fax:** (01) 2621059

VIVA METAL & PLASTICS INDUSTRIES LIMITED
Business: Manufacturing, Marketing and Exportation of various types of PE Poly Bags
Address: Off Km. 11, Hadejia Road, Gunduwawa, Kano
Tel: (064) 310541, 08034080823 **Fax:** (064) 638185
E-mail: office@decent-polybag.com
Website: www.decent-polybag.com
Contact: Miss Bonnie Lou - MD/CEO

VIVA SECURITIES LIMITED
Business: Stockbroking
Address: LSDPC House (9th Floor), Nnamdi Azikiwe/Alli Balogun Street, Marina, Lagos
Tel: (01) 2663437, 2667879 **Fax:** (01) 2663437
E-mail: viva@hyperia.com
Contact: Mr. Gbogai M. Umoru - MD/CEO

VIVALDI INTERNATIONAL LIMITED
Business: Marketing and Maintenance of Airconditioning Equipment and Home Appliances
Address: 13, Creek Road, Apapa, Lagos
Tel: (01) 5875179, 5871944, 5874082, 5877689
Fax: (01) 5875437
E-mail: dizpharm@hyperia.com
Contact: Mr. Peter E. Okocha OON - Chairman
Chief P. M. Porbeni - GM/CEO

VIVID IMAGINATION LIMITED
Business: Fashion Designers, Tailoring Services, Import & Export
Address: Fameli House, 250, Ikorodu Rd, Obanikoro, Lagos
Tel: (01) 4935912, 4965153 **Fax:** (01) 4965153

VK PLASTIKS LIMITED
Business: Extrusion of Polythene Sheeting & Recycling of Films
Address: 46/50, Alimosho Road, Alimosho, Lagos
Tel: (01) 7915714, 08037164158
E-mail: vkexalon@yahoo.com
Contact: Chief Bayo Akinyemi - Chairman/CEO

VOEN ASSOCIATES
Business: Architects, Planners & Development Consultants

Address: Foreshore Towers (14th Floor), 2A, Osborne Road, Ikoyi, Lagos
Tel: (01) 2671831, 2691150
* 18, College Road, Benin City.
Tel: (052) 255347

VOEST-ALPINE (NIGERIA) LIMITED
Business: Power Generation and Distribution, Industrial Consultants, Water/Sewage Treatment Plants, Hospital Construction
Address: 5, Park Lane, Apapa G. R. A. Lagos
Tel: (01) 5874862, 5875580, 7742330
Fax: (01) 5870928, 5875580

VOLKSWAGEN OF NIGERIA LIMITED
Business: Sales and Services of Volkswagen Vehicles
Address: Volkswagen Estate, Km. 17, Lagos-Badagry Expressway, Ojo, Lagos
Tel: (01) 5880772, 5882482, 2885915 **Fax:** (01) 2885915
Contact: Chief Y. C. Onwuchekwa - MD/CEO

VOLKSWAGEN CENTRE (Sub. of Stallion Group)
Business: Comprehesive Maintenance of VOLKWAGEN Vehicles; Sales of Spare Parts
Address: Plot 1, Block B, Gbagada Industrial Estate, Lagos
Tel: (01) 4960586, 7732661-2(2L), 7742040, 08034799999.
E-mail: vwcentre@stallion.com.ng

VONO PRODUCTS PLC
Business: Manufacturing of Foam Products, Beds, Beddings and Specialised Furniture for Schools & Hospitals
Address: 326/328, Agege Motor Road, Mushin, Lagos
Tel: (01) 4520329, 4520330, 4528143, 4528455, 520407
Fax: (01) 4528142
E-mail: vonoproducts@siotel.com
* Plot 1529, Nouakchott St, off Olusegun Obasanjo Way, Wuse Zone 1, Abuja.
Tel: (09) 5238437
Contact: Rev. R. O. Oloidi - MD/CEO
Mr F. A. Shittu - Marketing Manager

VOSAN & BAACON LIMITED
Business: Supply of Medical & Laboratory Equipment, Healthcare Consultancy Services
Address: Vosan House, Vosan Villa, 5-7, Vosan Drive, Independent Layout, Enugu
Tel: (042) 454540 **Fax:** (042) 455558
Contact: Mr. Vincent O. S. Ngodo - MD/CEO

VOYAGER TRAVELS LIMITED
Business: Travel Agency
Address: Plot 1661, Oyin Jolayemi Street (2nd Floor), Victoria Island, Lagos
Tel: (01) 3204317, 4613723, 5558437-8(2L)
Fax: (01) 4613723
E-mail: voyagen@hyperia.com
Contact: Miss Ibikemi Adefolu - MD/CEO

VT LEASING LIMITED
Business: Equipment Leasing
Address: NCWS House (The Penthouse), Plot PC.14, Ahmed Onibudo Street, Victoria Island, Lagos
Tel: (01) 2629027, 4707901, 612192, 618662, 08023121872
Fax: (01) 2613259
E-mail: vtlease@infoweb.abs.net
Contact: Mr. Akin O. Opeodu - MD/CEO

VTL INSURANCE BROKERS LIMITED
Business: Insurance Brokage
Address: 29, Kakawa Street, Lagos Island, Lagos
Tel: (01) 4816049, 8147533 **Fax:** (01) 2613259
Contact: Mr. Akin Opeodu - Chairman
Mr. Emmanuel Eneanya - MD/CEO

VULCAN GASES LIMITED
Business: Manufacturing of Oxygen/Acetylene Gases
Address: 19, Inuwa Abdulkadir Road, Kakuri Industrial Area, Kaduna South, Kaduna
Tel: (062) 232184 **Fax:** (062) 233490
Contact: Chief E. O. Adesoye - Chairman
B. K. Olayemi - GM/CEO

W. J. BUSH AND COMPANY (NIGERIA) LIMITED
Business: Manufacturing of Perfumes, Cosmetics, Airfreshner & Soap
Address: 108/180, Mission Road, Bompai Ind., Estate, Kano
Tel: (064) 634024, 648574 **Fax:** (064) 647434
E-mail: wjbushnig@ecnx.net
* 37, Tapa Street, Epetedo, Lagos Is, Lagos
Tel: (01) 2637217 **Fax:** (01) 2646185
Contact: Alh. Ado Bayero (Emir of Kano) - Chairman
Mr. S. O. C. Malaussene - MD/CEO

W.S.T.C. FINANCIAL SERVICES LIMITED
Business: Funds Management, Stockbroking & other Capital Market Activities, Corporates & Trade Finance, Financial Advisory Services, Equipment Leasing
Address: 28B, Adesola Hopewell Str, Victoria Island, Lagos
Tel/Fax: (01) 4618490, 4619989
E-mail: wstc@hyperia.com
Contact: Mr. Oluwatofarati Agusto - MD/CEO

W. W. WHYTE & COMPANY LIMITED
Business: Engineering Contractors, Swamp Mechanical Works, Oil Servicing, Equipment and Vehicle Hire
Address: Plot 183, Trans-Amadi Ind. Layout, Port Harcourt
Tel: (084) 238015, 231878, 231879 **Fax:** (084) 238015
Contact: Tonye William-Whyte - Chairman

WADOF SOFTWARE CONSULTING LIMITED
Business: IT Consultancy & Training, Software Development
Address: 19, Fola Jinadu Crescent, Gbagada Estate Phase I, Gbagada, Lagos
Tel: (01) 4938747, 4701927, 08033054052, 08033289680
E-mail: info@wadof.com
Website: www.wadof.com
Contact: Wahab Aminu-Sarumi - MD/CEO

WADOYE NIGERIA LIMITED
Business: Courier Services, Freight Forwarders, Haulage
Address: 2, Olaide Tomori Street, off Simbiat Abiola Road, Ikeja, Lagos
Tel: (01) 4932698, 49355719 **Fax:** (01) 4976073
E-mail: wadoye@beezlink.com
Website: www.wadoye.com
Contact: Alh. Haruna Waidi - Chairman/CEO

WAFO NIGERIA LIMITED
Business: Security Guard Services and Consultancy
Address: Plot 16, Okeho Street, Ire-Akari Estate, Isolo, Lagos
Tel: (01) 4524337, 8040065, 08023309819, 08035537783
Fax: (01) 4524337
E-mail: wafo@hyperia.com
Contact: Dr. Feyi W. Olatoyinbo - Chairman/CEO

WAHUM GROUP OF COMPANIES
Business: Manufacturing Conglomerate
Address: 2, Adeniyi Jones Avenue, Ikeja Ind Estate, Lagos
Tel: (01) 4978770-4 (5L) **Fax:** (01) 4961802, 4528689
E-mail: wahum@wtcn.org

WAHUM PACKAGING LIMITED
Business: Manufacture of Corrugated Cartons, Trays, Layers and Partitions
Address: 3, Adeniyi Jones Avenue, Ikeja Industrial Estate
Tel: (01) 4978770-4 (5L) **Fax:** (01) 4528689
E-mail: wahum@wtcn.org
* Plot 2, Block B, off Acme Road, Ogba Industrial Estate, Ikeja, Lagos.
Tel: (01) 4926329, 4963207, 4978770-4 (5 L)(Ext 242)
Fax: (01) 4961802, 4963654

WAKIT ENTERPRISES LIMITED
Business: Sales and Services of Technical, Industrial, Petroleum, Gas & Service Station Equipment
Address: 8, Olanrewaju Street, opp. Archbishop Aggey Memorial School, Ilasamaja, Mushin, Lagos
Tel: (01) 4521274, 4523537, 4960770, 4960873, 4961249
Fax: (01) 4963131
Contact: Engr. Akin Laguda - Chairman/CEO
Mr. Moruf Rabiu - Company Superintendent

WAKMEED MERCHANT & COMPANY LIMITED
Business: Importation of Electronic Mosquito Repellent, Anti-Mosquito Mats and Perfumed Vapourisers
Address: 15, Iga Idungaran Street, Idumota, Lagos
Tel: (01) 2664753
Contact: Kamowu E. Oyenuga - Chairman/CEO

WALE ADENUGA PRODUCTION LIMITED
Business: Independent Production of Television Programmes
Address: 16, Murtala Muhammed International Airport Road, Mafoluku - Oshodi
Tel: (01) 7746744
E-mail: papaajasco@yahoo.com

WALL STREET TRUST COMPANY LIMITED
Business: Funds Management, Capital Market Operations, Corporate & Trade Finance, Financial Advisory Services, Equipment Leasing
Address: 28B, Adeola Hopewell St, Victoria Island, Lagos
Tel: (01) 2620770, 2620771, 611309, 4618490
E-mail: wstc@linkserve.com.ng
Contact: Alh. Falalu Bello - Chairman
Mr. Oluwatofarati Agusto - MD/CEO

WALVIS NIGERIA LIMITED
Business: Marine Transportation Services
Address: 4A, Less Roa, Ikoyi, Lagos
Tel: (01) 2691347, 2691706, 2694691, 2693236, 2692796
Fax: (01) 2692476, 2694505
E-mail: seatruck@hyperia.com

WANDEL INTERNATIONAL (NIGERIA) LIMITED
Business: Marketing of AIWA Electronics, Agricultural Machinery, Bicycles and Diesel Engines
Address: 77/79, Eric Moore Road, Iganmu Industrial Estate, Surulere, Lagos
Tel: (01) 5456440-4 (5L), 7740120 **Fax:** (01) 5851016
E-mail: wandelnig@simbaonline.com
Contact: Mr. V. Grover - MD/CEO

WAPCIPCO LIMITED
Business: Real Estate Development, Importation of Electrical Appliances, Institutional Investors
Address: WAPCIPCO House, Plot 22/23, Balogun Street, Oregun Industrial Estate, Oregun, Lagos
Tel: (01) 4967129
Contact: Mr. Daniel Emile Bassil - Chairman/CEO

WAPIC INSURANCE PLC
Business: All Classes of Insurance Business
Address: WAPIC House, 119, Awolowo Road, Ikoyi, Lagos
Tel: (01) 8119857-8 (2L), 4615153 **Fax:** (01) 2693838
E-mail: wapic@alpha.linkserve.com
Website: www.wapicinsurance.com
* Intercontinental Plaza, Plot 207, Cadastral Zone A0, Central Business District, Abuja
Tel: (09) 2346568, 6713597 **Fax:** (09) 2346561
Contact: Engr. H.U.F. Enuha - Chairman
Mr. Segun Balogun - MD/CEO

WARRI BOTTLING COMPANY LIMITED
Business: Bottling of Carbonated Drinks
Address: 81, Effurun/Sapele Road, Warri
Tel: (053) 253945, 250257 **Fax:** (053) 250263
Contact: M. N. Kapadia - MD/CEO

WARRI REFINING & PETROCHEMICALS COMPANY LTD
Business: Refining of Crude Oil, Production of Petrochemicals
Address: Ekpan-Warri, P.M.B. 44, Effurun, near Warri
Tel: (053) 254160-4 (5L), 252535, 250812, 253701, 252006, 252571 **Fax:** (053) 254222
* 13, Oju-Olobun Close, Victoria Island, Lagos
Tel: (01) 2614702, 2612239, 2614840, 2619861
Contact: Engr. B. E. Idahosa - MD/CEO

WARRY-GEE MAYO & COMPANY (NIGERIA) LIMITED
Business: Customs Clearing & Freight Forwarding, Haulage, Export & Import Consultancy, General Supplies
Address: Eleganza Plaza (Leo Block, 1st Floor), 1, Commercial Road, Apapa, Lagos
Tel/Fax: (01) 5451738
E-mail: warrygee@yahoo.com
Contact: A. D. Warigon - Chairman/CEO

WARSUN NETWORK SOLUTIONS LIMITED
Business: Satellite Communications (VSAT) Engineering, Internet Gateway Services
Address: Plot 242B, Muri Okunola St, Victoria Island, Lagos
Tel: (01) 3200430-3 (4L) **Fax:** (01) 3200434
Website: www.warsun.com
Contact: Mr. S. A. Imudia MD/CEO

WASA-DELMAS NIGERIA LIMITED
Business: Shipping Services
Address: 26, Creek Road, Apapa, Lagos
Tel: (01) 5803480-2 (3L), 7752680 **Fax:** (01) 5875552
E-mail: info@wasadelmas.com.ng
Contact: Mr. Bernard Martineau - MD/CEO
Mr. Peter. Bleasdale - GM

WASCO NIGERIA LIMITED
Business: Waste Management Consultancy, Sales of Waste-Mnagemnt Systems & Mobile Coolers
Address: 1, Brewtech Street, off Adenekan Street, Okota-Isolo, Lagos
Tel: (01) 4523511, 4528875, 7742359, 7743119, 7746435
Fax: (01) 4528875
E-mail: wasconig@beta.linkserve.com
Website: www.mobicool.co.za
Contact: Mr. Norbert K. Weidlich - MD/CEO

WASCO OILS SERVICES COMPANY NIGERIA LIMITED
Business: Oilfield Engineering Services, Supply of Oilfield Tools and Equipment
Address: Plot 56/57, Ordinance Road, Trans-Amadi Industrial Layout, Port Harcourt
Tel/Fax: (084) 239660, 331050

WASHAMAN DRYCLEANERS NIGERIA LIMITED
Business: Drycleaning and Laundry Services
Address: Shifau House, 48/50, Oluwaleyimu Street, off Toyin Street, Ikeja, Lagos
Tel: (01) 4936496, 7915148, 08023830236, 08035081083
Contact: Mr. Tolu Akinbami - MD/CEO

WASTE MATTERS NIGERIA LIMITED
Business: Municipal & Industrial Waste Management Services, Remediation & Audit
Address: Olatunji House, 299, Ikorodu Road, (Idiroko Bus-Stop), Maryland, Lagos
Tel/Fax: (01) 5833911
E-mail: wastermatters@eudoramail.com
Contact: Mr. Ken A. Edike - Chairman/CEO
Mr. Sunny Obi - Operations Director

WATA TIMBER COMPANY LIMITED
Business: Processing of Timber, Sales of Industrial Tools
Address: 40, Burma Road, Apapa, Lagos
Tel: (01) 5870891, 5453157 **Fax:** (01) 5453624
Contact: Alh. (Chief) A. K. Akhigbe - MD/CEO

WATER SEARCH NIGERIA LIMITED
Business: Water Exploration, Exploitation & Treatment Engineering Services; Water Storage; Construction of Water Treatment Plants & Towers; Flood Mitigation and Drainage Design Network
Address: Block D (Suite 7), Falomo Shopping Centre, Ikoyi, Lagos
Tel/Fax: (01) 2694657
E-mail: water2000@infoweb.abs.net
Contact: Mr. Gerhard Seedorff - MD/CEO

WATDRILL ENGINEERING & GEOTECH SERVICES LTD
Business: Water-Borehole Drilling, Water & Geotechnical Engineering Services
Address: Shehu Laminu Way,by JAMB Office, Maiduguri
Tel: (076) 235339 **Fax:** (076) 235394

WATER SERVICES ENGINEERING LIMITED
Business: Drilling & Servicing of Water Borehole; Design, Construction & Servicing of Water Treatment Plant; Supply, Installation and Servicing of Pumps; Project Evaluation; Construction of Tanks
Address: 119, Idimu Rd, Abule-Odu Bus/Stop, Idimu, Lagos
Tel: (01) 7915140, 08023036717
E-mail: waterservicesengineeringltd2002@yahoo.com

WATERFORD LIMITED
Business: Manufacturing of Corn & Cassava Starch and Modified Starches
Address: 21, Olosa St, off Karimu Kotun St, Victoria Is.Lagos
Tel: (01) 2624834-7 (4L) **Fax:** (01) 2614859
E-mail: waterfold@hyperia.com
Contact: Mr. Ashok Mahtani - MD/CEO

WATERPARKS LIMITED
Business: Tourism, Recreational and Entertainment Services
Address: 31/37, Toyin Street, Ikeja, Lagos
Tel: (01) 4972279, 4937813, 08023094311
Fax: (01) 4972279
E-mail: waterparks@eudoramail.com
*Water Parks Island, Jabi Lake, Kado Estate, Abuja
Tel: (09) 5239835
Contact: Otunba Feyisayo Winfunke - President/CEO
Mr. Olaleye Oshingbule- GM

WATERPIT NIGERIA LIMITED
Business: Ground Water Engineering, Management and Development
Address: 11, Abuloma Road, Trans-Amadi Industrial Layout, Port Harcourt
Tel: (084) 234319, 483986 **Fax:** (084) 234319
E-mail: waterpit2003@yahoo.com
Contact: Mrs. E. T. Abibo - CEO

WATERTECH (NIGERIA) LIMITED
Business: Water Treatment and Purification Technologies
Address: 17, Murtala Mohammed International Airport Road, Ajao Estate, Isolo, Lagos
Tel: (01) 4520435, 4520436, 7741542 **Fax:** (01) 4520436
E-mail: sales@watertechng.com
Website: www.watertechng.com
Contact: Mr. Augustine A. Egbo - Chairman/CEO

WATERWELL SERVICES LIMITED
Business: Sales of Production & Drilling Chemicals, Blending Plant, Laboratory Testing Services
Address: Alexander House (3rd Floor), 9/10, Badagry Expressway, Orile-Iganmu, Lagos
Tel: (01) 5834527, 7740788, 7912174, 08022905752
Fax: (01) 5834527, 7912175
E-mail: waterwellservices@yahoo.com
Contact: Mr. Peter Oba - Chairman/CEO

WATSON & SONS (ELECTRO-MEDICAL) NIGERIA LTD
Business: Sales, Installation and Service of Medical Diagnostic, Dental and Physiotheraphy Equipment
Address: 35, Park Lane, off Liverpool Rd, Apapa, G.R.A.,

Apapa, Lagos
Tel: (01) 5870192, 5453366, 5452575 **Fax:** (01) 5870196
E-mail: imaging@watsonmedical.com
Contact: Major Gen. Henry E. O. Adefope - Chairma
Mr. U. N. Okezie - MD/CEO

WATYEM-DKS ENTERPRISES LIMITED
Business: Cocoa Merchants
Address: 1, Kayode St, off Ikorodu Road, Onipanu, Lagos
Tel: (01) 7746091, 7731061 **Fax:** (01) 2885434
* 105, Idanre Road, Akure
Tel/Fax: (034) 244774, 242607

WAVETECH PHONEHOUSE LIMITED
Business: Sales of Mobile Phones and Accessories; Fixed Wireless Technology Operators' Agents
Address: 48, Awolowo Road, S.W. Ikoyi, Lagos
Tel: (01) 4615972-3 (2L), 08034007631, 08032031172
E-mail: wavetechphonehouse@yahoo.com
* Iluobe Complex (1st Floor), Plot 596, Kashim Ibrahim Way, Wuse II, Abuja
Tel: (09) 5230896, 08032031182
Contact: Mr. Ben Ekejiuba - CEO

WAXTALL LIMITED
Business: Manufacturing of Plain & Customised Floor Mats
Address: 66, Campbell Street (1st Floor), Lagos
Tel: (01) 2646941, 2634057 **Fax:** (01) 2646941
E-mail: waxtall@rcl.nig.com
logomats@skannet.com
oba@ghotekmail.com
Contact: Miss Obafunmilola Adesola - MD/CEO

WAYNE (WEST AFRICA) LIMITED
Business: Importation, Sales, Installation and Maintenance of Gasoline Dispensing Pumps, Service Station Equipment, Grease Pumps, Submersible Pumps, Metering Equipments and Air Compressors
Address: 20, Creek Road, Apapa, Lagos
Tel: (01) 5876644, 5876760 **Fax:** (01) 5876748
E-mail: nigerparts@hyperia.com
Contact: Mr. O. A. Alakija - Chairman
Prince V. K. Adesulure - GM

WEARNES NIGERIA LIMITED
Business: Marketing, Installation & Maintenance of Computer Systems, Information Technology Consultancy
Address: Wey House (1st Floor), 117, Tokunbo Street, Lagos
Tel: (01) 2630562, 2636020 **Fax:** (01) 2647742
E-mail: wearness@alpha.linkser.com
Contact: Mr. Ogugua Chioke - Chairman/CEO

WEATHERFORD NIGERIA LIMITED
Business: Completion and Oilfield Services
Address: 21, NEW Road, Plot 37, Trans-Amadi Industrial Layout, Port Harcourt
Tel: (084) 236711, 238977 **Fax:** (084) 238977, 236541

WEATHERHEAD INDUSTRIES LIMITED
Business: Manufacturing of Paints and Allied Products
Address: 2, Alahun Osumba Street, off Badagry Expressway, Maza-Maza, Lagos
Tel: (01) 4922557

* Dumez Junction, Suleja, via Abuja
Contact: Rev. (Dr.) L. M. A. Ezeanochie - Chairman

WECO ENGINEERING & CONSTRUCTION COMPANY LTD
Business: Mechanical, Electrical and Instrumentation Projects; Land and Swamp Pipelines; Fabrication of Onshore/Offshore Oil & Gas Structures
Address: Plot 110, Trans-Amadi Ind. Layout, Port Harcourt
Tel: (084) 237610, 237611, 231493 **Fax:** (084) 235675
E-mail: wecoeng@phca.linkser.com
Contact: Mr. Saadeh Amin Habib - MD/CEO

WECO SYSTEMS INTERNATIONAL LIMITED
Business: IT Integratioin Services
Address: Plot 200B, Etim Inyang Cr., Victoria Island, Lagos
Tel: (01) 4619064, 3200747, 3200891, 3200892
Fax: (01) 4619130
E-mail: wecosys@wecosystems.com
Website: www.wecosystems.com
Contact: Mr. Uchenna Obidike - MD/CEO

WEDOTABARY NIGERIA LIMITED
Business: Manufacturing of Chalk; Cotton Ginning
Address: 5, Sabon-Gida Kanar Road, Jos
Tel: (073) 280505, 280777 **Fax:** (073) 280777
E-mail: wedotebary@yahoo.com
Contact: Mr Dong Dalyop - MD/CEO

WEGAS ELECTRONICS WORKS LIMITED
Business: Manufacturing and Sales of Music Instrucments
Address: 2, Market Street, off Cardoso Road, (Oja Bus-Stop), Otto Wolff, Ajegunle, Apapa, Lagos
Tel: (01) 5872793, 5872759, 08033018736, 08033017836
Contact: Pastor Young Onwudinanti - MD/CEO

WELLHEAD DREDGING (NIGERIA) LIMITED
Business: Dredging and Land Reclamation Engineering
Address: 36, Deco Road, Warri
Tel: (053) 253305
Contact: Chief Peter O. Ukuwrere - Chairman/CEO

WELLSTOCKED NIGERIA LIMITED
Business: Sales & Service of Business Machine (Photocopiers, Printers, Fax Machines), Computers, Domestic Appliances, Papers and Consumable
Address: Reinsurance House (6th Floor), 46, Marina, Lagos
Tel: (01) 2633455, 2633438, 2633340, 08023011537, 08035100065 **Fax:** (0) 2632664
Contact: Mr. Olapoju O. Oladinni - Chairman/CEO

WELTEK LIMITED
Business: Oilfield Engineering (Instrumentation & Control)
Address: Plot 35, Trans-Amadi Ind. Layout, Port Harcourt
Tel: (084) 237902-3 (2 L) **Fax:** (084) 237904
E-mail: weltek@phca.linkserve.com
Website: www.weltekng.com
Contact: Mr P. J. Egbe - MD/CEO

WEMA BANK PLC
Business: Commercial Banking
Address: Wema Towers, 54, Marina, Lagos
Tel: 01) 2668105, 2668303, 2668043, 2667216
E-mail: info@wemabank.com

Website: www.wemabank.com
Contact: Alh. Musiliu Alade Adeleke - MD/CEO
Mr Eddy A. Ademosu - Snr Manager (Public Rel.)

WEMA SECURITIES & FINANCIAL PLC
Business: Financial Services (LPO/Import Financing, Leasing and Treasury Services, Capital Market Operations)
Address: Leventis Building, 42/43, Marina, Lagos
Tel/Fax: (01) 2640407, 2640409
* Plot 24, Trans-Amadi Ind. Layout, Port Harcourt
Tel: (084) 232767, 238130
* c/o Wema Bank Plc Plot 464, Constitution Road, Central Business District, Abuja
Tel: (09) 5233364, 2221120

WEMA TRUSTEES LIMITED
Business: Management of Pension Schemes & Provident Schemes/Funds, Trusteeship, Nominee Services, Company Secretarial Services, Asset Management and Investment Advisory Services
Address: Leventis Building (1st Floor), 42/43, Marina, Lagos
Tel: (01) 7733355, 2640411

WEMABOD ESTATES LIMITED
Business: Real Estate Development and Management
Address: Western House (5th Floor), 8/10, Broad Street, Lagos
Tel: (01) 2635577, 2635509, 2634761, 2636160, 2636022
Contact: Otunba Alaba O. Shonibare - Chairman
Mr. S. O. Aseweje - MD/CEO

WEMTRACO (NIGERIA) LIMITED
Business: Electrical, Civil & Mechanical Engineering Services; Sales & Service of Refrigeration and Airconditioning Equipment and Spare Parts
Address: 70, Cemetery Road, Warri
Tel: (073) 253607, 08035514056, 08037461145
E-mail: wemtraco@skannet.com
wemtraco@yahoo.com
Contact: Mr. Wilson Mayaki - Chairman/CEO

WEMY INDUSTRIES LIMITED
Business: Manufacturing of Disposable Baby Nappies, Body Wipes & Sanitary Pads
Address: 110/113, Demurin Street, Oba-Nle-Aro Bus-Stop, Alapere, Ketu, Lagos
Tel: (01) 4964418, 4808137 **Fax:** (01) 4960973
E-mail: wemi@infoweb.abs.net
wemydrbrowns@yahoo.com
Contact: Pastor Ademola W. Odunaiya - Chairman/CEO

WERAG (NIGERIA) LIMITED
Business: Manufacture of Lockeset and Iron -Mongery
Address: 7 (PLot 1A), Fatai Atere Way, Matori Indstural Estate, Oshodi, Lagos
Tel: (01) 522925, 4520450 **Fax:** (01) 2690038
Contact: Mr. A. Azuh - MD/CEO

WESCO ENGINEERING LIMITED
Business: Civil & Mechanical Engineering Services
Address: 87, Effurun/Sapele Road, Effurun, Warri
Tel: (053) 256657, 253317 **Fax:** (053) 254525
Contact: Mr. A. H. Yassin - Operations Manager

WESPRO NIGERIA COMPANY LIMITED
Business: Haulage Services
Address: Zard Building, 9, Obafemi Awolowo Road, Dugbe Ibadan
Tel: (02) 2411806
Contact: Chief (Dr.) Raymond Zard - MD/CEO

WEST AFRICA AIRLINES (NIGERIA) LIMITED
Business: International Airlines Service
Address: 3 (Plot 1661), Oyin Jolayemi Str, Victoria Is, Lagos
Tel: (01) 47517552-3 (2 Lines), 7920559, 4616797
Fax: (01) 4616798
Website: www.westafrican-airlines.org
Contact: Olorogun O. C. J. Ibru - Chairman
Mr. Minna Oforukuma - Exec. Director

WEST AFRICA INTERNATIONAL LIMITED
Business: Import & Export, General Merchanding
Address: 66, Calcutta Crescent, Apapa, Lagos
Tel: (01) 5453106

WEST AFRICA MILK COMPANY (NIGERIA) PLC
Business: Manufacturing & Marketng of Evaporated/ Powered Milk and Fresh Dairy Products
Address: Plot 7B, ACME Road, Ogba Industrial Estate, Ogba, Ikeja, Lagos
Tel: (01) 4920500-3 (4L), 4976880-1 (2L), 4930491, 4930497-8 (2L) **Fax:** (01) 4930500
E-mail: milk@wamco.com.ng
Contact: Mr. C.H.M.Ruygrok - MD/CEO
Dr. E. I. Uraih - Marketing Manager

WEST AFRICA OFFSHORE LIMITED
Business: Offshore Oil Drilling Services, Marine and Special Transportation
Address: 28, Omerelu Street, G.R.A.Phase I, Port Harcourt
Tel: (084) 237494, 235956, 231652 **Fax:** (084) 237784
E-mail: voc<114506,33546>@compuserve.com
* 60, Enerhen Road, Warri
Tel: (053) 254394, 252901, 252464 **Fax:** (053) 254412

WEST AFRICA RESEARCH LIMITED
Business: Investment & Capital Market Research, Undertaking of Due Diligence, General Financial Consultancy
Address: New Africa House (8th Floor), 31, Marina, Lagos
Tel: (01) 2641933
E-mail: bisi@warltd.com
Contact: Mr. Adebisi Ajiboye - MD/CEO

WEST AFRICAN BITUMEN EMULSION CO LTD (WABECO)
Business: Bitumen Blending Into Emulson and Cutbacks; Bitumen Supplies; Refined Petroleum Products Terminal Operation; Sales of Petroleum Products and Lubricant
Address WABECO Depot, Ibafon Jetty, Tincan Island Port Complex, Apapa, Lagos.
Tel: (01) 5454248, 5457228, 5457230, 5454247, 7739240
Fax: (01) 5454247, 5457230
E-mail: wabeco@mail.micro.com.ng
* 11, Maicibi Close, Kaduna South, Kaduna
Tel: (062) 232087, 234054 **Fax:** (062) 234053
Contact: Engr. S. I. C. Okoli - Exec. Chairman
Mr. L. Adoh - MD/CEO

WEST AFRICAN BOOK PUBLISHERS LIMITED
Business: Book Publishing, Marketing of Diaries, Corporate Gift Items and Street Maps
Address: 28/32, Industrial Avenue, Ilupeju Ind. Estate, Lagos
Tel: (01) 4977700-4 (5L), 4702757, 7754518, 08033124113
Fax: (01) 2616702
E-mail: westbook02md@yahoo.com
w_bookafricapubl@hotmail.com
* Wadata House, Plot 1247, Aminu Kano Crescent, Wuse II, Abuja.
Tel: (09) 6708969
Contact: Mr. Bashir A. Idris-Animashaun - Chairman/CEO
Mrs. Folashade B. Omo-Eboh - MD

WEST AFRICAN BUILDING MATERIALS LIMITED
Business: Manufacture of Galvanised Iron Sheets
Address: 2, Adeniyi Jones Avenue, Ikeja Ind. Estate, Lagos
Tel: (01) 4977770-4 (5L) **Fax:** (01) 4961802

WEST AFRICAN DRYDOCKS LIMITED
Business: Shipyard; Maintenance & Repairs of Marine Vessels
Address: 4A, Less Road, Ikoyi, Lagos
Tel: (01) 2691347, 2691706, 7739654, 7739656
E-mail: waventures@hyperia.com

WEST AFRICAN FERTILIZER COMPANY LIMITED
Business: Mining and Industrial Mineral Processing
Address: 14, Ademola Street, S.W. Ikoyi, Lagos
Tel: (01) 2694152-5 (4L), 7756742 **Fax:** (01) 2691314
* Km. 169, Auchi-Okene Road, Okpella, Edo State
Contact: Alh. M. Idirisu - Chairman
Mr Santanam - MD/CEO

WEST AFRICA FREIGHT & COASTAL LINES LIMITED
Business: Shipping, Ship Managers, Agents & Consultancy
Address: 39, Adele Road, Apapa, Lagos
Tel: (01) 5450601, 5450613, 5872053
Fax: (01) 5450613, 2611766
Contact: E. O. Sowade - MD/CEO

WEST AFRICAN GLASS INDUSTRIES PLC
Business: Production and Marketing of Sheet Glass
Address: Trans-Amadi Industrial Layout, Port Harcourt
Tel: (084) 300250, 334103, 330092

WEST AFRICAN MARINE PRODUCTS LIMITED
Business: Importatation of Frozen Fish and Fish Meal
Address: 29, Adetokunbo Ademola St, Victoria Island, Lagos
Tel: (01) 2617542 **Fax:** (01) 2616018
* Apapa-Oshodi Expressway (Agunlejika B/Stop), Ijeshatedo, Lagos
* 5, Warri/Sapele Road, Warri
* Trans Amadi Industrial Layout, Port Harcourt
Contact: Mr. Slava Rodnov - MD/CEO

WEST AFRICAN NEON INDUSTRIES LIMITED
Business: Manufacture of Illuminated and Non-Illuminated Signs
Address: Km. 16, Lagos-Badagry Expressway (Neon Bus-Stop), opp. Ojo Barracks, Ojo, Lagos
Tel: (01) 881395 **Fax:** (01) 882451
Contact: Nze M. C. Okoye - Chairman
Mensah F. C. Emegwalu - MD/CEO

WEST AFRICAN NGO NETWORK
Business: Outreach & Advocacy, Content & Website Development, IT Connectivity & Networking (LAN/WAN), ICT Training & Consultancy
Address: ICON House (2nd Floor), Plot 999F, Idejo Street, Victoria Island, Lagos
Tel: (01) 2624505, 2610990, 3204587, 3204771
Fax: (01) 3204588
E-mail: info@wangonet.org
Website: www.wangoent.org
* Russel Centre, Plot 2425, Herbert Macaulay Way, Zone 4, Wuse, Abuja
Contact: Mr. Tunji Lardner - MD/CEO

WEST AFRICAN OILFIELD SERVICES LIMITED
Business: Oilfield Engineering Services
Address: Plot 72/73, Trans-Amadi Ind. Layout, Port Harcourt
Tel: (084) 232066, 232075 **Fax:** (084) 232066
* 31C, Raymond Njoku Street, S. W. Ikoyi, Lagos
Tel: (01) 2690988 **Fax:** (01) 680551
Contact: Mr. M. A. Ibrahim - MD/CEO

WEST AFRICAN PORTLAND CEMENT PLC
Business: Manufacture of Cement, Manufacture & Distribution of Sandtex Decorative Paints, Electrical Repair Services, Transport Services, Kraft Bag Production
Address: Elephant Cement House, ASSBIFFI Road, Ikeja, Central Business District, Alausa, Lagos
Tel: (01) 7745088-9 (2L), 4968060-9(10L)
Fax: (01) 4970704
Contact: Mr. Ray Harding - Ag. MD/CEO
Mr. Ademola Idowu - GM (Sales/Marketing)
Mr. J. A. Salako - Public Affairs Manager

WEST AFRICAN PROVINCIAL INSURANCE CO. PLC
Business: Insurance (Non-Life)
Address: 27/29, King George V. Road, Onikan Lagos
Tel: (01) 2636433, 2636435, 2634958 **Fax:** (01) 2633688
* 29, Ikwerre Road, Port Harcourt.
Tel: (084) 332864
* 65, Ibrahim Taiwo Road, Kano.
Tel: (064) 626570
Contact: Mr. C. O. Idowu Silva - MD/CEO

WEST AFRICAN RUBBER PRODUCTS LIMITED
Business: Producers of Rubber Footwear and other Products
Address: Plot 68, Ikorodu Industrial Estate, Odogunyan, Ikorodu, Lagos

WEST AFRICAN SEASONING COMPANY LIMITED
Business: Manufacturing of Food-Seasoning Products
Address: 37, Creek Road, Apapa, Lagos
Tel: (01) 5804920-8 (9L) **Fax:** (01) 5804927, 5804928
Contact: Kunio Egashira - President
Keij Kaneko - MD/CEO

WEST ATLANTIC AGENCIES LIMITED
Business: Fishing, Ship Owners, Importer, Exporter, Oil Services
Address: Ibru Jetty Complex, Oshodi-Apapa Expressway, Ibafon Apapa, Lagos
Tel: (01) 5455442, 5455458, 5451303
Fax: (01) 2611071, 5451303

WEST ATLANTIC SYSTEMS NIGERIA LIMITED
Business: IT Services (Computers, Telecommunication Infrastructure, GSM Services), Oil & Gas Production Services, Property & Estate Developers
Address: 36, Moshood Abiola Crescent, off Toyin Street, Ikeja, Lagos
Tel: (01) 4978004, 4971811 **Fax:** (01) 4978004
E-mail: westarng@yahoo.com
info@west-atlantic.zzn.com
Website: www.west-atlantic.zzn.com
* 112A, Aba Road, opp.NITEL, Port Harcourt
Tel: (084) 234729
Contact: Engr. Abis Igoni - Chairman/CEO

WEST END LIMITED
Business: Catering Consultants, Management Services and Supplies
Address: 31/32, Trans-Amadi Industrial Layout, Rumuobiakani, Port Harcourt
Tel: (084) 231213, 239138, 08023150101, 08035084725
Fax: (084) 231213
* Plot 12/78, Km. 2, Refinery Road, Effurun, Warri
* Ogunpa Oyo, P.O.Box 513, Ibadan.
Tel: (02) 2414846
Contact: Mr. Faris Haddad - MD/CEO

WESTAC ENGINEERING (NIGERIA) LIMITED
Business: Manufacturing & Assembling of Diesel Generating Sets and Power Systems
Address: 385, Ikorodu Road, Opp. New Garage, Ojota, Lagos
Tel: (01) 4970242, 08023179608, 08033589447
Fax: (01) 4970242
E-mail: nigeria@westac.co.uk
Contact: Christopher Taylor - Chairman
Tony Shirliff - MD/CEO

WESTCOTT NIGERIA LIMITED
Business: Sales, Installation and Maintenance of Training & Office Equipment
Address: 98/100, Bamgbose Street (near Campos Square), Lagos Island, Lagos
Tel: (01) 2633462, 08033007302, 08033280630
E-mail: westcott@hyperia.com
Contact: Mr. Emmanuel Onovo - Chairman
Mr. Sylva Mbaogu - MD/CEO

WESTERN AFRICA WELL SERVICES NIGERIA LIMITED
Business: Servicing of Oil Wells
Address: 4, Onne-Eleme Road, off Aba Expressway, near Eleme Junction, Port Harcourt
Tel: (084) 612967-9 (3L), 611481-2 (2L), 612050

WESTERN ATLAS INTERNATIONAL NIGERIA LIMITED
Business: Oilfield Services (Data Processing, Seismic Survey, Logging Services)
Address: 17, Mekuwen Road, Ikoyi, Lagos
Tel: (01) 2693254, 2691772 **Fax:** (01) 2692042
* Plot 468, Trans-Amadi Ind. Layout, Port Harcourt
Tel: (084) 232480, 234510, 236135 **Fax:** (084) 236135
Contact: Mr. Gray Jones - President/CEO

WESTERN METAL PRODUCTS COMPANY LIMITED
Business: Manufacture of Corrugated Galvanized Roofing Sheets & Galvanized Buckets
Address: 18, Wempco Road, Ogba Ind.Scheme, Ogba, Lagos
Tel: (01) 4920261
Contact: Mr. Lewis Tung - MD

WESTERN PACIFIC COMMUNICATIONS LIMITED
Business: Telecommunication Services
Address: 37B, Raymond Njoku Street, S. W. Ikoyi, Lagos
Tel: (01) 2690794, 4615642-3 (2L), 08034008971-2 (2L), 08037008975 **Fax:** (01) 4617220
E-mail: info@wpcgroup.com
Website: www.wpcgroup.com
Contact: Chief Akanni Aluko - Chairman
Mr Abdulgafar Williams - MD/CEO

WESTEX MOTORS NIGERIA LIMITED
Business: Sales & Services of Motor Vehicles
Address: 142, Ahmadu Bello Way, Victoria Island, Lagos
Tel: (01) 2621407, 2611123 **Fax:** (01) 2611388
E-mail: westex@nova.net.ng
* Plot 1, Block A, Gbagada Industrial Estate, Oworonsoki Expressway, Gbagada, Lagos
Tel: (01) 4960586, 2621407, 2611123 **Fax:** (01) 2611388

WESTMART NIGERIA LIMITED
Business: Manufacture of Polythene Bags & Sheetings, Film Printing Services; Import & Export, Contractors
Address: 75A, Iju Road, Agege, Lagos
Tel: (01) 4926057, 08023160693, 08033071201
Fax: (01) 4926057
E-mail: boladeladipo@yahoo.com
Contact: Mr. Bolade Ladipo - Chairman/CEO

WESTON PORKKA NIGERIA LIMITED
Business: Building, Sales & Maintenance of Industrial, Commercial & Domesic Airconditioning & Refrigeration Equipment, Sales & Service of Hospital, Laboratory & Kitchen Equipment
Address: 5, Western Avenue, Ojuelegba, Surulere, Lagos
Tel: (01) 833955, 08033066417 **Fax:** (01) 833955
E-mail: westonporkka@yahoo.com
Contact: Prince Olukayode A. Aiyeola - Chairman/CEO
Mrs. F. Ajewole - Project Manager

WESTOWN NIGERIA LIMITED
Business: Hospitality, Cleaning Services, Sales of Cleaning Equipment & Chemicals, Janitorial Supplies
Address: 14/16, Mojidi Street, off Toyin Street, Lagos
Tel: (01) 4973314 **Fax:** (01) 4979492
E-mail: westown@micro.com.ng
Website: www.westown.net
* Plot 627, Herbert Macaulay Way, Berger Junction, Wuse Zone 5, Abuja.
Tel: (09) 5234557
* 33B, Ohaeto Street, behind Allstates Trust Bank, D-Line, Port Harcourt.
Tel: (090) 405839
Contact: Mr. Anthony Ayeni - Chairman/CEO

WESTRON GROUP OF COMPANIES
Business: Electrical/Mechanicl Engineering & Contracting, Finance, Property Development & Management
Address: Great Nigeria House (20th Floor), 47/57, Martins

Street, Lgaos
Tel: (01) 2660045, 2660464 **Fax:** (01) 2669019
E-mail: westron@beta.linkserve.com
Contact: Chief George Igboegwu - Chairman/CEO
Mr Henry Okoh - Manager

WHASSAN-EUREST NIGERIA LIMITED
Business: Catering Services
Address: 52, Adetokunbo Ademola St, Victoria Island, Lagos
Tel: (01) 2610352, 2615464 **Fax:** (01) 2614194
E-mail: whassan@beta.linkserve.com
E-mail: whassan@hyperia.com
* Plot 16, Chief Nwuke Street, Trans-Amadi, Port Harcourt.
Tel: (084) 232774, 232775
* Blcok B, 123, Edewor Estate, Warri
Tel: (053) 253234, 253297
Contact: Chief C. S. Sankey - Chairman
Mr. Bimal Saxena - GM/CEO

WHITE GOLD GINNERY NIGERIA LIMITED
Business: Cotton Ginnery
Address: Plots 7 & 10, Challawa Industrial Estate, Kano
Tel: (064) 637931, 646369, 310174, 310929, 08037870254
E-mail: whitegoldnigeria@hotmail.com
Contact: Mr. Mustapher Tahir - Chairman/CEO

WHITEHALL MULTINATIONAL LIMITED
Business: Sales of Electrical Materials and Equipment
Address: 71A, Marine Road, Apapa, G.R.A. Lagos
Tel: (01) 5872546, 5872543, 5455955, 08033077508
Fax: (01) 5872543, 5455954
E-mail: white@nova.net.ng
Contact: Mr. Gabriel Onyema - GM/CEO

WHITESANDS INSURANCE BROKERS LIMITED
Business: Insurance Broking and Consultancy
Address: Turaki Ali House (5th Floor), 3, Kanta Rd, Kaduna
Tel: (062) 248366, 246200-4 (5 L) **Fax:** (062) 248345

WHITEWOOD ASSOCIATE INTERNATIONAL LIMITED
Business: Sports Marketing, Television Production & Programming; Public Relations Services, Events Marketing & Management
Address: 1, Joel Ogunnaike Street (Bungalow 4), Ikeja GRA, Lagos
Tel: (01) 4977848, 4960526 **Fax:** (01) 4977848
E-mail: wwood@infoweb.abs.net
Contact: Mr. Ose Elakhe Imoukhuede - Chairman/CEO

WHIZ PRODUCTS (WEST AFRICA) LIMITED
Business: Blending & Marketing of Lubricants and Hydraulic Fluids, Production of Adhesives, Gasket Cement and Car-Care Products
Address: 4, Pokobros Industrial Avenue, off Atani Road, Harbour Industrial Layout, Onitsha
Tel: (046) 216002, 217425, 210800
Fax: (046) 217425, 212973
* 10, Omilani Street, Onireke, Ojo, Lagos
Tel: (01) 7748342, 4800191 **Fax:** (01) 7748342
* Whiz Filling Station, Ahmadu Bello Way, Wuse II, Abuja
Contact: Chief (Dr.) P. A. Okonkwo - Chairman/CEO

WHIZ-TECH LIMITED
Business: Sales of Computers and Accessories
Address: 1, Oremeji St, off Simbiat Abiola Road, Ikeja, Lagos
Tel: (01) 4964753, 4935502, 08033252002
Fax: (01) 4964753
Contact: Mr. Wale Ogundeji - MD/CEO

WIGGINS TEAPE PLC
Business: Manufacture, Conversion & Sales of Paper & Allied Products, Printing & Publishing
Address: 19, Fatai Atere Way, Matori Industrial Estate, Mushin, Lagos
Tel: (01) 4528209, 4527241, 4523739 **Fax:** (01) 4522092
* Suite 21, Zone 1, Cornershop, Nonakehott Street, off Olusegun Obasanjo Way, Wuse Zone 1, Abuja
Tel: (09) 5232111
Contact: Mr. P. M. Mbu - Vice Chairman/CEO
Mr. G. O. V. Ekpere - Head (Sales/Marketing)

WILLBROS (NIGERIA) LIMITED
Business: Oil Industry Services; Marine Transportation.
Address: Plot 256, Kofo Abayomi St, Victoria Island, Lagos
Tel: (01) 2614877, 2614990 **Fax:** (01) 2615676
* East-West Road, Choba, Port Harcourt

WILLIAMS & PARTNERS
Business: Estate Surveyors/Valuers, Property Management
Address: 2nd Avenue, 22 Rd, House 1, Festac Town, Lagos
Tel: (01) 5883562, 8116372, 08023070968, 08033339350
* Cornershop 1, Garki Modern Market, Abuja
Tel: (090) 803223
Contact: Okpala C. K. William - Principal Partner

WILLMERC LA CUISSON LIMITED
Business: Production of Soya Meal and other Food Cereals
Address: 21/23, Paul Avenue, Yakoyo-Ojodu, Ikeja, Lagos
Tel: (01) 7747276, 08033333220
Contact: Mr. Arnold Adadevoh - MD/CEO

WINCO FOAM INDUSTRIES LIMITED
Business: Manufacturing and Marketing of Foam Products
Address: 17/19, Orishigun St, off Ikorodu Rd, Ketu, Lagos
Tel: (01) 4701342, 4712170, 4750317, 4970032, 2880730, 08022900836 **Fax:** (01) 4970032
E-mail: winco-foam@intacom5.com
winco-foam@intracom.net.ng
* Plot 231, Pokobros Ave, Awka Ind Layout, Akwa.
Tel: (048) 552271, 552369
Contact: Chief G. I. Okafor - Chairman/CEO

WINCOTECH LIFTS LIMITED
Business: Sales, Installation, Maintenance and Service of Elevators, Escaltors and Moving Walkways
Address: Novacoke Compound, Plot 54, Akanbi Onitiri Close, off Eric Moore Road, Iganmu, Lagos
Tel: (01) 5830934 **Fax:** (01) 5836323

WINDSBROW CONSULT LIMITED
Business: Sale of Security & Communication Equipment, Consultancy
Address: Doyin Motors Premises, Plot 27, Iganmu Ind Estate, Lagos-Badagry Expressway, Orile, Lagos
Tel: (01) 7741436, 830690, 5851690, 4707192

Fax: (01) 5851690
E-mail: windsbrow@hyperia.com
Contact: Mr. Ayorinde Adedoyin - MD/CEO

WINELIGHT ANALYTICAL SYSTEMS (NIGERIA) LIMITED
Business: Sales & Maintenance of Laboratory Analytical Equipment and Instruments
Address: 2, Bola Crescent, Anthony Village, Lagos
Tel: (01) 4932700, 4974810, 4937251, 08022901866
Fax: (01) 4931738, 4937005
E-mail: info@winelightnig.com
winelightnigeria@yahoo.com
Website: www.winelightnig.com
Contact: Hon. Tobi Oduyale - MD/CEO

WINPAL LIMITED
Business: Supply of Aviation Equipment, Production of Chemicals (Degreasers, Detergent & Coolant)
Address: 311, Apapa (Wharf) Road, Apapa, Lagos
Tel: (01) 5803310-13 (4L) **Fax:** (01) 5875374
* 42, Effurun Road, opp. Urhobo College, Warri
Tel: (053) 253019
Contact: Mr. Paul Akpofure - Chairman/CEO

WINTECK (NIGERIA) LIMITED
Business: Sales and Service of Scientific, Medical, Engineering and Technical Equipment, Laboratory Design and Furnishing
Address: N5B/1906, Iwo Road, by Ilorin/Lagos Expressway Junction, Ibadan
Tel: (02) 8104782, 8108564, 08023047647, 08023049041-2, 08034303447 **Fax:** (02) 8104782
E-mail: winteck@winteck-ng.com
winteck@skannet.com
* Plot 82, Utako District, Cadastral Zone B5, Abuja
* 7, Block 13, Makera Road, Kakuri, Kaduna
Tel: (062) 232808
Contact: Engr. M. D. Akinjo - MD/CEO

WIRELINE & TESTING /GEOQUEST/NETWORK SOLUTIONS (Div. of Schlumberger Oilfield Services Ltd.)
Business: Computer & IT Services; Oilfield Services
Address: 161, Trans-Amadi Industrial Layout, Port Harcourt
Tel: (084) 237951-2(2L), 237951, 232969, 232979
* 17/19, Idowu Taylor Street, Victoria Island, Lagos
Tel: (01) 2612141, 2626241-53(13L), 2619200
* Plot 999F, Idejo Street, Victoria Island, Lagos
Tel: (01) 2610446-7(2L) **Fax:** (01) 2621034

WIRELESS TRADE NIGERIA LIMITED
Business: Distribution of Telecommunication Terminal Equipment
Address: Eleganza Biro Plaza, Plot 634, Adeyemo Alakija Street, Victoria Island, Lagos
Tel: (01) 2702959, 2706767, 4748070
E-mail: infonigeria@wirelesstradegroup.com
Website: www.wirelesstradegroup.com
Contact: Lukman Akanbi -MD/CEO

WIRE-TEK INTERNATIONAL COMPANY LIMITED
Business: Salees of Electrical & Technical Equipment, Engineering, Leasing of Vehicles & Heavy-Duty Equipment
Tel: (084) 231548, 08033100780 **Fax:** (080) 234196
E-mail: wireteks@yahoo.com
Contact: Chief Eldelis Osita Nweke - Chairman/CEO

WISEWAY INSURANCE BROKERS LIMITED
Business: Insurance Broking
Address: Old Leventis Building (3rd Floor), 5, Lebanon Street, Ibadan
Tel: (02) 2414442 **Fax:** (02) 2411286
* 1, Fawole St, off Ikorodu Road, Obanikoro, Lagos
Tel: (01) 4935466
Contact: Mr. Jide Sanya - MD/CEO

WISLER STEEL NIGERIA LIMITED
Business: Iron Materia Stockist
Address: 148, Effurun-Sapele Road, Warri
E-mail: jk@hyperia.com
* Steelways Compound, Plot E, Ikosi Road, Oregun Industrial Estate, Ikeja, Lagos
Tel: (01) 4960178
Contact: Ilia Todorov - Chairman
Mr. Jasper Kakashe - MD/CEO

WITT & BUSCH LIMITED
Business: Sales & Maintenace of Generators & Technical Equipment
Address: Union Dicon Salt Compound, Ilasamaja Industrial Scheme, off Apapa Expressway, Iyana Itire, Lagos
Tel: (01) 2645232, 2645242-3 ()2L, 7754819
Fax: (01) 2645222

WIZCOUNT COMPANY LIMITED
Business: Sales & Services of Computer Systems & Peripherals
Address: 7B, Ahmed Onibudo Street, Victoria Island, Lagos
Tel: (01) 2623463-4 (2L), 2620994, 3200280
Fax: (01) 2622073
E-mail: magic@alpha.linkserve.com
* Chigola Street, Wuse Zone 6, Abuja
Contact: Mr. Avi Zabuski - Vice Chairman
Mrs. Maimuna Musa Shuaibu - CEO

WOO INTERACTIVE LIMITED
Business: Interactive Multimedia Development, Website Design & Development, Digital Video Creation, 3-Dimensional Animation for Television & Multimedia, Corportate Identiy Development, Training
Address: 12, Adegoke St, off Alh. Masha Rd, Surulere, Lagos
Tel: (01) 4702169, 775827
E-mail: info@woo-interactive.com
Website: www.woo-interactive.com
Contact: Mr. Emeka J. Onuoha - Chairman/CEO
Mr. Chubike Agu - Manager (Multimedia Services)

WOODLINE INDUSTRIES LIMITED
Business: Manufacture of Toothpicks, Drinking Straws, Cotton Buds, Lolly Sticks, Bamboo & Wooden Products
Address: Obasanjo Farms Road, Otta,Ogun State
Tel: 08033071231
Contact: Mr. Biodun Dabiri - Chairman

WOODPECKERS NIGERIA LIMITED
Business: Manufacturing of Office and Home Furniture, Interior Decoration, Supply of Home Appliance,

Processing & Export of Furniture Component Parts
Address: 2, Vori Close, off Acme Road, Ogba Industrial Estate, Ikeja, Lagos
Tel: (01) 4923431 **Fax:** (01) 4528022
E-mail: info@woodpeckers-ng.com
woodpeckers-92@yahoo.com
Website: www.woodpeckers-ng.com
Contact: Chief Stephen U. Ibegbu - Chairman/CEO

WOOLLEN & SYNTHETIC TEXTILE MANUFACTURING LTD
Business: Manufacturer of Textile Piece Goods
Address: 88, Oba Akran Avenue, Ikeja Ind Estate, Ikeja, Lagos
Tel: (01) 4962903, 4964804, 4962243 **Fax:** (01) 4964398
E-mail: wstm@infoweb.abs.net
Contact: Chief H. B. Chanrai - Chairman
Mr. A. Ghosh - GM

WORLD BOOK FAMILY LEARNING CENTRE
Business: Distribution and Sales of Books for All ages
Address: 13, Soji Adepegba Close, Allen Avenue,Ikeja, Lagos
Tel: (01) 4936404
* 4, Abayomi Akinmosa Crescent, Idi-Ishin, Jericho, Ibadan.
Tel: (02) 2414285, 2414087

WORDSMITHES PRINTING & PACKAGING LIMITED
Business: Printing, Publishing, Digital Colour Separation, LIght Packaging
Address: Wordsmithes House, Plot 246, Amuwo-Festac Access Road, off Oshodi-Apapa Expressway, Amuwo-Odofin, Lagos
Tel: (01) 5890502, 5885761, 7742724, 3454510-4 (5L)
Fax: (01) 5885761
E-mail: wsmithes@alpha.linkserve.com
Website: www.linkserve.net/wsmithes

WORLD ENVIRONMENTAL SYSTEMS (NIGERIA) LIMITED
Business: Environmental & Engineering Consultancy Services (Landfill Design, Baseline Studies, Site Remediation, GIS Mapping) Waster Management, Hazard Communication Safety Supplies
Address: Plot 9, Ladipo Oluwole Avenue, off Adeniyi Jones Avenue, Ikeja, Lagos
Tel: (01) 4930243, 08023057419, 08033052059
Fax: (01) 4930243
E-mail: weslagos@aol.com
Contact: Mr. Dare Obasanya - Chairman/CEO
Mr. Kehinde Awosika-Olumo - MD

WORLD INFORMATION AGENTS LIMITED
Business: Newspaper Publishing
Address: 13, Ize Iyanmu Street, off Balogun Street, Oregun, Ikeja, Lagos
Tel: (01) 7742003
E-mail: alaroye@alaroye.com

WORLD MARITIME LIMITED
Business: Maritime Services, Air & Sea Freight Handling, Import and Export, Shipping Agents
Address: 52, Eagle Cement Road, off Ada George Road, Mile 4, Rumuepirikom, Port Harcourt
Tel: (084) 231954, 08033420558
Contact: Mr. Clement Utua - Chairman/CEO

WORLD TRADE CENTER OF NIGERIA (Ltd/Gte)
Business: Trade and Investment Promotion, Opportunities Disseminationa, Hosting and Sponsoring of Trade Missions, Workshops and Seminars on Trade
Address: Western House (8th Floor), 8/10, Broad St, Lagos
Tel: (01) 2635276, 2647279, 4744404, 08034717416
Fax: (01) 2647279
E-mail: worldtradelagos@yahoo.co.uk
Website: www.wtca.org
Contact: Lt. Gen. T.Y. Danjuma (rtd.) GCON - Chairman
Mr. John Adeyemi Adeleke - Exec. Director/CEO

WORLD TRADE CORPORATION LIMITED
Business: Freight Forwarders, Warehousing
Address: 38/40, Burma Road, Apapa, Lagos
Tel: (01) 5453845, 5455840
Contact: Alhaja (Mrs.) Toyin Adeyemi - MD/CEO

WORLD WEB LIMITED
Business: Internet Service Provider
Address: 11, Ali Akilul Road, Kaduna
Tel: (062) 243210, 243564, 243565, 08023278068
Fax: (062) 243564
E-mail: csupport@wwlkad.com
Website: www.wwlkad.com
Contact: Mr. Daniel Omale Chairman/CEO

WORLDMARK (NIGERIA) LIMITED
Business: Sales of Security and Office Equipment
Address: 1/3 (163), Badagry Expressway, opp Festac Town 1st Gate, Amuwo-Odofin, Lagos
Tel: (01) 5880445, 2885851, 08023137397, 08023311331, 08033344309 **Fax:** (01) 5880445, 2882851
Contact: Mr. P. E. Omokwale - MD/CEO

WORLDMARK INSURANCE BROKERS LIMITED
Business: Insurance Broking, Life & Pension Consultancy
Address: Shippers' Plaza, Michael Okpara Street, Wuse Zone 5, Abuja
Tel/Fax: (09) 5230407, 5238034
E-mail: worldmarkinsurancebrokers@yahoo.co.uk

WORLDWIDE INDUSTRIAL SUPPORT SERVICES LTD
Business: Sales & Installation of Crop & Food Processing Equipment, Farm Machinery & Agro-Industrial Implements, Turnkey Solutions
Address: Plot 6, Badejo Kalesanwo Street, Matori Industrial Estate, Mushin, Lagos
Tel: (01) 4721081, 7740274, 08023398756, 08023576314, 08023820081, 08033777286, 08037881641
E-mail: agricworldwide@yahoo.com
Contact: Mr. Abiodun George Bell - GM (Projects/ Services)

WORLDWIDE INSURANCE COMPANY LIMITED
Business: Insurance
Address: ANCE Buidling, Magazine Road, Jericho, Ibadan
Tel: (02) 2413718, 2413728 **Fax:** (02) 2414588
E-Mail: worldins@skannet.com
Website: www.worldwideinsurance.netfirms.com
* Co-operative Bank Building, 30, Marina, Lagos
Tel: (01) 2661098, 2669334
* Co-operative Bank Building, Aguiyi-Ironsi Street, Maitama District, Abuja.

Tel: (09) 4134120
* 47, Ikwerre Road, Port Harcourt.
Tel: (084) 231168
Contact: Mr. A. A. Ajaja - Chairman
Dr. F. M. Epetimehin - MD/CEO

WORLDWIDE PETROLEUM SERVICES (WEST AFRICA) LTD
Business: Oilfield Services
Address: 26, Moloney Street, Onikan, Lagos
Tel: (01) 2630715, 2634606 **Fax:** (01) 2630715
* 175, Trans-Amadi Ind. Layout, Port Harcourt
Tel: (084) 331157, 229851, 238013
* c/o Baker Yard, Edewor Shopping Complex, Warri
Tel: (053) 251344

WORLDWIDE SPORTS LIMITED
Business: Television Production, Sports Marketing and Events Management, Management of Sport People, Sports Consultancy, Public Relations and Advertising Agency
Address: 2, Oweh Street, by WAEC Roundabout, Jibowu, Yaba, Lagos
Tel: (01) 4728398
E-mail: wwsport@usa.net
Contact: Chief Segun Odegbami, MON - Chairman/CEO

WYSE ASSOCIATES LIMITED
Business: LED Compound, Maryland
Address: LED Compound, Maryland, Lagos
Tel: (01) 4702349, 4934797, 08037171965
E-mail: info@wyseassociates
Website: www.wyseassociates.com

WYTAK PRESS LIMITED
Business: Flexible Packaging Converters, Printing & Packaging (Rotogravure, Flexo, Offset)
Address: Plot 1, Block F, Oluyole Industrial Estate, Ibadan
Tel: (02) 2314542-3 (3L) **Fax:** (02) 2317917
E-mail: wytak@hyperia.com
Contact: Elie Joseph Taktouk - MD/CEO

X LEVEL LIMITED
Business: Laser Engraving and Production of Awards & Plagues, Sales of Shelving Systems, Signage Products, Robotic Signage & Banners
Address: 256, Herbert Macaulay Street, Yaba, Lagos
Tel: (01) 8151688, 8172072, 8179617, 08033058395
E-mail: yemi-o@nigol.net.ng
Website: www.light-level.com
Contact: Mrs. L. Osilaja - MD/CEO

X-CEL COMPUTER COMPANY LIMITED
Business: Sales and Maintenance of Computers, Software Development, Training
Address: 26, Beirut Road, Kano
Tel: (064) 643935, 641642, 08033251289
Fax: (064) 641642
E-mail: x-cel@yahoo.com
Contact: Engr. Isa El-Hassan - MD/CEO

XCEL INTERNATIONAL LIMITED
Business: Sales & Maintenance of Computer Hardware, Networking, Training, Leasing, Mail Order Services
Address: 280, Effurun-Warri Road, Warri
Tel: (053) 250982, 255304, 08023259937
E-mail: xcel@compuserve.com
* POWA Plaza (Suite 56), Otigba Str, Ikeja, Lagos
Tel: (01) 4810025, 08023406898
Contact: Mr. P. Olaniyan - Chairman/CEO

XHS (NIGERIA) LIMITED
Business: Sales & Services of High-Tech Office Eqiupment
Address: Block C, Plot 3, 12/14, Fatai Atere Way, Matori Scheme, Oshodi, Lagos
Tel: (01) 4521500, 4521514, 4521532, 4521543, 4525265, 7731868 **Fax:** (01) 4521569
E-mail: xhs@xeroxnigeria.com
mktxerox@xeroxnigeria.com
Website: www.xeroxnigeria.com
*Plot 1950, Mich Opara Ave, Wuse Zone 5, Abuja
Tel: (09) 5234968-70 (3L) **Fax:** (09) 5234983
Contact: Mr. Jeff Hitchman - MD/CEO

XLR8 LIMITED
Business: Accelerated Communications Solutions
Adddress: Plot 661, Oluwatoyin Eleoramo Street, Omole Phase 2, Ikeja, Lagos
Tel: (01) 7214255, 08033909590
E-mail: calixthus.okoruwa@xlr8.com.ng
Website: www.xlr8.com.ng
Contact: Mr. Calixthus Okoruwa - MD/CEO

XPRESS PARTNERS LIMITED
Business: Courier Servces, Bulk Haulage of Goods siness: Courier Services, Bulk Haulage of Goods
Address: Xpress House, Gas Plant Road, off Otunba Jobifele Way, Central Business District, Alausa
Tel: (01) 7741072, 4703786, 345111, 08033061150
Fax: (01) 3450133
E-mail: xpress@xpresspartners.ltd
Contact: Mr. Babatope Akinyele - Chief Executive

XTRASERV NIGERIA LIMITED
Business: Airgreight, Clearing & Forwarding, Shipping and Cargo Superintedence, Road Haulage
Address: 78/80, Wimer Crescent, Olodi-Apapa, Lagos
Tel: (01) 2905872, 7921850, 08023125113-4 (2L), 08033902517
Contact: Mr. S. Obisanya - MD/CEO

YABAK TELECOMMUNICATIONS LIMITED
Business: Importation, Sales, Installation and Maintenance of Telecommunication and Radio Equipment
Address: 62B, Opebi Road, Ikeja, Lagos
Tel: (01) 4974276, 4970400, 7946877 **Fax:** (01) 4974276
* 8, First East Circular Road, Benin City
Tel: (052) 450579, 08023532470
Contact: Mr. Frank Ize-Iyamu - President/CEO

YAMACO (Div of John Holt Plc)
Business: Sales and Service of Motorcycles, Power Products, Outboard Engines, Almarine Boats.
Address: John Holt Complex, Plot 3/4, Adewunmi Estate, Oregun Road, Ikeja, Lagos
Tel: (01) 4968000-4 (5L), 4967312
Fax: (01) 4976571, 2660830

Website: www.jhplc.com
* c/o John Holt Distribution, 16, Niger Street, Kano
Tel: (064) 633295
* Plot 23, Kolokuma Street, Borokiri, Port Harcourt
Tel: (084) 233541, 335857, 232517 **Fax:** (084) 231226
Contact: Mr. James McLardy - Group MD/CEO

YAMAGUCHI INTERNATIONAL NETWORK NIGERIA LTD
Business: E-Commerce, V-SAT/Satellite Solutions, Web Design, Hosting and Management, Networking, Internet Service Provision
Address: Western House (4th Floor, Suite 409), 8/10, Broad Street, Lagos
Tel: (01) 2632220, 4735807, 8160482, 08023338648, 08023559467 **Fax:** (01) 7597396
E-mail: info-nigeria@yamaguchigroup.net
Website: www.yamaguchigroup.net
* 7, Joyce B Road, opp. Town Planning, off Ring Road, Ibadan
Contact: Mr. Stephen Adeoshun - MD/CEO
Mr. Ajibade Adeoye - Operations Manager

YAMAHA MANUFACTURING (NIGERIA) LIMITED
Business: Assembling of Motorcycles, Maintenance of Yamaha Generators
Address: Yamaco Division, John Holt Compound, Plot 3/4, Adewunmi Ind. Estate, Oregun Road, Ikeja, Lagos
* 4122/420, Lagos-Abeokuta Expressway, Abule-Egba, Agege, Lagos
Tel: (01) 4967312, 498000-4 (5L)
Fax: (01) 4976571, 2660830
Website: www.jhplc.com
Contact: Mr. G. O. Aghuno - GM

YANKARI INSURANCE COMPANY LIMITED
Business: All Classes of Insurance (except Life & Pension)
Address: Rock Top House, 1, Ahmdu Bello Way, Bauchi
Tel: (077) 542926, 543067, 543065 **Fax:** (077) 542926
* UPS Building,Plot 781, Obafemi Awolowo Street, Area 11, Garki, Abuja
* 7B, Ibrahim Taiwo Road, Kano.
Tel: (064) 634702
* Kano Road, P.O. Box 356, Azare, Bauchi State
Contact: Alh. Aminu Ahmed - Chairman
Yahaya Mahmood Sheik - MD/CEO

YANKARI NATURAL SPRING WATER COMPANY LIMITED
Business: Bottlers of Spring Water
Address: 10, Gombe Road, Bauchi
Tel: (077) 543709, 542977
* 22/24, Calcutta Crescent, Apapa, Lagos
Tel: (01) 5870851

YANKARI SAVINGS & LOANS LIMITED
Business: Mortgage Banking
Address: 10, Yan Doka Road, Bauchi
Tel: (077) 543754, 544869, 08023250920
Fax: (077) 541520
E-mail: ysl@37.com
* Opp. NTTC, along Gombe-Biu /Road, Gombe
Tel: (072) 222147
Contact: Alh. Sabiu Mohammed - Ag. Chairman
Alh. Muhammadu Gambo Mu'azu - MD/CEO

YAOLAT TECHNOLOGIES NIGERIA LIMITED
Business: Sales, Installation and Maintenance of Computers and Office Equipment
Address: 19, Oyabiyi Street, off Ojuelegba Road, opp. Tejuosho Market, Surulere, Lagos
Tel: (01) 5836062, 5844452 **Fax:** (01) 5836062
E-mail: yaolat-tech@usa.net
yaolat@nova.net.ng
Contact: Mr. Y. O. Aladetan - MD/CEO

YARESH INTERNATIONAL LIMITED
Business: Industrial Cleaning & Pest Control Services
Address: 8B, Ondo Street, off Apapa Road, by Railway Recreation Club, Ebute-Metta (West), Lagos
Tel: (01) 8043427, 08033048177
* Suite G20, Area 1Recreation Park, Garki, Abuja
Contact: Evangelist Ola Kazim - MD/CEO

YAROSON PARTNERSHIP LIMITED
Business: Consulting Engineers
Address: 18, Aliyu Turaki Road, Kaduna
Tel: (062) 248624, 216931, 248217 **Fax:** (062) 248624
* 87, Apapa Road, (Suite II), Ebute Metta, Lagos
* Bataiya Plaza (2nd Floor, Suite 22), Area 11, Garki, Abuja

YASAVA LIMITED
Business: Aerospace Consultancy; Sales, Lease & Management of Aircraft
Address: 27, Boyle Street, Onikan, Lagos
Tel: (01) 2600846, 7756621 **Fax:** (01) 2631660
E-mail: jets@yasava.com
Website: www.yasava.com
Contact: Prof. John Godwin Obe - Chairman
Mr. Christopher Mbanefo - MD/CEO

YCN MINERAL PROCESSING COMPANY LIMITED
Business: Mining & Processing of Solid Minerals, Manufacturing of Woven Polypropylene Sacks
Address: 5/7, Morison Crescent, Oregun Ind. Estate, Lagos
E-mail: ycnsolidminerals@mail.com
Contact: Prof G. O. Olusanya, OON - Chairman
Mr. S. O .Olabode - MD/CEO

YEMOSA INTERNATIONAL (NIGERIA) LIMITED
Business: General Merchandising , Property Developers, Importers & Exporters
Address: Yemosa Shopping Mall, Akowonjo Road, Egbeda Bus-Stop, Egbeda, Lagos
Tel: (01) 4733682, 08022903107, 08023163709
* 5, Adelabu Close, off Ola Ayinde St, Ikeja, Lagos
Tel: (01) 4971377, 7221830
Contact: Mr. Paul O. Omoruyi - Chairman/CEO

YESIN INTERNATIONAL LIMITED
Business: Engineering, Dredging Stock Piling, Marine Services & Shipping, Pipelines & Flowlines, Swamp/Land Construction, Shore Protection, Road Construction, Procurement
Address: 44, Epirikom Road, Mile 4, Wimpey Junction, Port Harcourt
Tel: (084) 231746, 235561, 235563, 234464, 234499, 08033385514, 08037110210

Fax: (084) 231746, 235563
E-mail: yesin@hyperia.com
yesininternationalltd@yahoo.com
* 2, Maple Swamp Road, opp. St. Andrew's Cathedral Church, off Okere Road, Warri
Tel: (053) 256003
Contact: Mr. Alfred Yesin - Chairman/CEO

YF POWER NIGERIA LIMITED
Business: Generation of Electricity
Address: Yinka Folawiyo Plaza (10th Floor), 38, Yinka Folawiyo Avenue, Apapa, Lagos
Tel: (01) 5450436-40 (5L) **Fax:** (01) 5450204, 5450274
E-mail: info@yinkafolawiyo.org
Website: www.yinkafolawiyo.org
Contact: Alh. (Chief) Dr. W. I. Folawiyo, CON - Chairman
Alh. T. B. Folawiyo - MD/CEO

YIFA NIGERIA LIMITED
Business: Importation, Distribution and Sales of Generators
Address: 33A, Kofo Abayomi Street, Victoria Island, Lagos
Tel: (01) 7749428 **Fax:** (01) 2622896
E-mail: yifa@cyberspace.net.ng
Website: www.yifa.com

YINKA CRAIG & ASSOCIATES LIMITED
Business: Corporate Relations Consultancy, Events Management
Address: LSDPC Flats (Blocks A, Flat 18), 24, Adeola Odeku Street, Victoria Island, Lagos
Tel: (01) 2610684, 2880190 **Fax:** (01) 2610684
E-mail: info@yinkacraig.com
Website: www.yinkacraig.com
Contact: Mr. Yinka Craig - Chairman/CEO

YINKA FOLAWIYO GROUP OF COMPANIES
Business: Conglomerate - Import, Export; Petroleum Exploration, Production and Product Marketing; Real Estate Development & Management, etc
Address: Yinka Folawiyo Plaza, 38, Yinka Folawiyo Avenue (fmr. Warehouse Road), Apapa, Lagos
Tel: (01) 5450436-40 (5L) **Fax:** (01) 5450204, 5450274
Contact: Alh. (Chief) Wahab I. Folawiyo CON - Chairman
Mr. Bolarin St. Samuel - Manager (Public Relations)

YINKA FOLAWIYO ELECTRICAL & MECHANICAL CO. LTD
Business: Electrical & Mechanical Engineering Services
Address: Yinka Folawiyo Plaza, 38, Yinka Folawiyo Avenue, Apapa, Lagos
Tel: (01) 5450436-40 (5L) (Ext. 164), 5450193, 5450221
Fax: (01) 5450204, 5450274
E-mail: yfem@yinfol.com
Contact: Alh. (Chief) Wahab I. Folawiyo CON - Chairman
Mr Patrick. Spence - GM

YINKA FOLAWIYO PETROLEUM COMPANY LIMITED
Business: Recovery, Sales and Marketing of Gasoline; Crude Oil Exploration and Marketing
Address: Yinka Folawiyo Plaza, 38, Yinka Folawiyo Avenue, Apapa, Lagos
Tel: (01) 5450436-40 (5L) **Fax:** (01) 5450204, 5450274
E-mail: info@yinkafolawiyo.org
Website: www.yinkafolawiyo.org
Contact: Alh. (Chief) Dr. W. I. Folawiyo, CON - Chairman
Alh. T. B. Folawiyo - MD/CEO

YINKA OMILANI & ASSOCIATES
Business: Loss Adjusting, Superintending and Marine Surveying, General Recovery Services
Address: 13, Abraham Adesanya Road, Apapa, Lagos
Tel: (01) 5873342, 5873297 **Fax:** (01) 5876696
* 2, Ikwerre Road, Port Harcourt.
Tel: (084) 230069
Contact: Chief Olayinka O. Omilani - Chairman
Mr. Shade Ajayi - GM/CEO

YINKA SONAIKE & COMPANY
Business: Chartered Estate Surveyors, Valuation Consultancy
Address: 102, Adeniyi Jones Avenue, Ikeja, Lagos
Tel: (01) 4937898, 4937899 **Fax:** (01) 4937899
E-mail: ysco@nova.net.ng
Contact: Mr. Yinka Sonaike - Principal Partner

YOBE FLOUR & FEED MILLS COMPANY
Business: Milling of Flour and Feeds
Address: Maiduguri Road, Potiskum, Yobe State
Tel: (074) 420802, 420722
Contact: H. E. Alh. Aliyu Sale Bagare - Chairman
Mr. Attila Borszeki - MD/CEO

YOBE INVESTMENT COMPANY LIMITED
Business: Development Finance Institution
Address: 3, Amusement Part Street, Games Village, off Maiduguri Road, Damaturu
Tel: (074) 522720 **Fax:** (074) 522397
Website: www.yobeinvestment.com
Contact: Alh. Muhammad Mairami Goniri - Chairman
Mal. Hassan Mamman - MD/CEO

YOBE SAVINGS AND LOANS LIMITED
Business: Mortgage Banking
Address: 4, Ahmadu Bello Way, Damaturu
Tel: (074) 521241, 521242 **Fax:** (074) 521241
Contact: Alh. Bukar Adam - Chairman
Mal. Usman K. Hardo - GM/CEO

YODESONS GROUP OF COMPANIES
Business: Cable Distributorship; Power Engineering; Hoteliers; Insurance Brokerage; Packaging Industry; Mortgage Finance; Petroleum Marketing; Clearing and Forwarding
Address: 28 (Plot 19), Badejo Kalesanwo Street, Matori Industrial Estate, Mushin, Lagos
Tel: (01) 4522821, 4522821, 4527896, 452898, 523923
Fax: (01) 4522849
E-mail: yodesons@nova.net.ng
yodeons@yahoo.com
* Plot 192, Jebba Close, Area 2, Garki, Abuja
Tel: (09) 2349983
* 169, Aba Road, Port Harcourt.
Tel: (084) 330228
Contact: Otunba S. K. Onafowokan - Group Exec. Chairman

YOMATECH NIGERIA LIMITED
Business: Mechanical, Piping, Welding & Fabrication, E/I Construction, Revamping & Maintenance, Man-

power Supply, Maintenance of Housing Facilities, Gas Plaants, Flow Stations & Power Generation Sets, Procurement
Address: 160A, NTA/Choba Road, Mgbuoba, Port Harcourt
Tel: (084) 231818, 575801 **Fax:** (084) 231818
E-mail: enquiry@yomatech.com

YOSCO (NIGERIA) LIMITED
Business: Sales and Repairs of Cellular Phones and Accessories
Address: 4/6, Obagi Street, G.R.A. Phase II, Port Harcourt.
Tel: (084) 234160, 08032034399
Contact: Mrs. Ladi Anne Yougha - Chairperson/CEO

YOUNESCO LIMITED
Business: Clearing & Forwarding, Import & Export, General Contractors and Merchants, Manufacturing of Plastic Products, Warehousing
Address: 9B, Niger Street, Kano
Tel: (064) 648668, 645434 **Fax:** (064) 647939
Contact: Khaled Barakat Chami - CEO

YOUNG SHALL GROW MOTORS LIMITED
Business: Road Transportation Services
Address: Plot A, Close A, Satellite Town, Lagos
Tel: (01) 2901007, 5891294, 5893352-3 (2L), 7740912
Fax: (01) 5890741
E-mail: youngshallgrowmotors@yahoo.com
* 169A, Lagos-Badagry Expressway, Maza-Maza, Amuwo, Lagos
Tel: (01) 882580
Contact: Chief Vincent A. Obianodo - Chairman/CEO

YUKIMS NIGERIA LIMITED
Business: Importation of Plastic-Production Machinery
Address: 2A, Oyeleke Street, Alausa, Ikeja, Lagos
Tel: (01) 7743950 **Fax:** (01) 5557569
E-mail: yukim@alpha.linkserve.com
* Plot 43, Oregun Road, Ikeja, Lagos
Tel: (01) 7743950, 7755680, 7758801 **Fax:** (01) 5557569
Contact: Mr. I. K. Kim - MD/CEO

YUSFAITH LITHOGRAPHIC INDUSTRIES LIMITED
Business: Lithographic and Screen Printing; Lithographic Materials Distribution
Address: 36, Awofeso Street, Palmgrove, Somolu, Lagos
Tel: (01) 8042990, 08033063330 **Fax:** (01) 8047951
E-mail: yusfaith@yahoo.com
Contact: Alh. F. Ola Oreniwa - Chairman/MD
Mrs. N. B. Onabajo - CEO

ZABADNE & COMPANY LIMITED
Business: Sales and Services of Electrical and Electronic Domestic Appliances and Household Goods
Address: Plot E, Block IV, Industrial Street, Ilupeju Industrial Estate, Ilupeju, Lagos
Tel: (01) 4960582, 4960572
E-mail: zabadne2000@nova.net.ng
Contact: Walid Zabadne - MD/CEO
Nazir Obaji - GM

ZABTEX COMAPNY NIGERIA LIMITED
Business: Manufacturing and Marketing of Socks
Address: Rayfield Industrial Estate, Jos
Tel: (073) 280903, 280908 **Fax:** (073) 280457
Contact: Alh. Ibrahim Sidi - Director

ZACCHI & KROME LIMITED
Business: Corporate Promotions; Graphic Art, Printing and Publishing
Address: 4, Ilupeju Bye-Pass, Ilupeju, Lagos
Tel: (01) 5550294-7 (4L), 4970103
Fax: (01) 5550294, 4970103
E-mail: zackrome@infoweb.abs.net
Contact: Mr. Teni Zaccheaus - Chairman/CEO

ZAKHEM CONSTRUCTION NIGERIA LIMITED
Business: Civil and Mechanical Engineers and Contractors, Pipeline Works and Water Projects
Address: Stallion House (5th Floor), 5, Ajose Adeogun Street, Victoria Island, Lagos
Tel: (01) 2610396, 2616676 **Fax:** (01) 2617543
Contact: Abdallah S. Zakhem - Chairman
Wadih F. Ghabriel - GM

ZAMFARA STATE INVESTMENTS & PROPERTY DEVELOPMENT COMPANY LIMITED
Business: Development Finance Institution, Investment Promotion, Portfolio Investment
Address: Gidan Bala Waiman, Zaria Road, Gusau
Tel: (063) 201619, 204819 **Fax:** (063) 204032
Contact: Alh. Sani Salihu Anka - Chairman
Alh. Umaru Ibrahim Kanoma - MD/CEO

ZAMFARA TEXTILE INDUSTRIES LIMITED
Business: Manufacturing and Marketing of Textile Products
Address: Zaria Road, P. O. Box 164, Gusau
Tel: (063) 200036, 201136

ZARANDA HOTEL, BAUCHI
Business: Hotel & Tourism Services
Address: Km. 4, Bauchi - Jos Road, Bauchi
Tel: (077) 543590-9 (10L), 542480

ZARD HOLDINGS LIMITED
Business: Conglomerate - General Merchandising, Manufacturing, Agriculture & Food Processing.
Address: 9, Obafemi Awolowo Road, Gbagi, Ibadan
Tel: (02) 2412695, 2413160, 2414722 **Fax:** (02) 2413839
E-mail: zardgroup@skannet.com
rayzard@skannet.com
Contact: Chief (Dr.) Raymond Zard - MD/CEO

ZARIA PHARMACEUTICAL COMPANY LIMITED
Business: Manufacturing and Marketing of Pharmaceuticals and Medical Consumables (Disposable Syringes)
Address: Dakace Ind. Layout, Old Jos Road, Dakace, Zaria
Tel: (069) 332959 **Fax:** (069) 332355

ZARTECH LIMITED
Business: Livestock Production, Food Processing
Address: 7Up Road, off Ring Road, Oluyole Industrial Estate, Ibadan
Tel: (02) 2314680, 2314685, 2316849, 2317802, 2317805
Fax: (02) 2317528, 2316129
E-mail: info@zartechltd.com

E-mail: farms@hyperia.com
* Plot 792, off Adetokunbo Ademola Crescent, NITEL Junction, near Rockview Hotel, Cadastral Zone A8, Wuse II, Abuja
Tel: (09) 4130022 **Fax:** (09) 4130023
* 10, Olusegun Obasanjo Road, Port Harcourt
Tel: (084) 234612, 235121
Contact: Chief (Dr.) Raymond Zard - Chairman/CEO

ZEALETT CARGOES LIMITED
Business: Clearing & Forwarding Agency, Warehousing
Address: Motorways Centre (Block B, 1st Floor), 1, Motorways Avenue, opp. 7Up Factory, Oregun, Lagos
Tel: (01) 4740481, 4973533, 08033319722, 08056018136
Fax: (01) 4973038
E-mail: zealett@yahoo.com
*28, Shiaba Street, Agege, Lagos.
Tel: (01) 4926466
Contact: Tosin O. Fadare - MD/CEO

ZEB EJIRO PRODUCTION LIMITED
Business: Professional Film, TV & Radio Script Writing, Production of Movies, Drama & TV Commercials, Artiste Management & Promotions, Adveritising & Public Relations Consultancy
Address: 29, Olufemi St,off Ogunlana Drive, Surulere, Lagos
Tel: (01) 5850976, 2909555, 08023085942, 30803286755
E-mail: zeb4nigeria@yahoo.com
zebejiro@yahoo.com
Website: www.nigeria.arts.net
Contact: Mr. Zeb Ejiro - President/CEO

ZEBENCO INDUSTRIES NIGERIA LIMITED
Business: Import and Export
Address: 18, Old Market Road, Onitsha
Tel: (046) 410466, 485381, 211404, 08033330352
E-mail: m.zeb1@aol.com
Contact: Mr. Chizoba Zebe Okpala - CEO

ZECO (NIGERIA) LIMITED
Business: Supply of Industrial Bearing & Accessories, Belts & Chains
Address: A8, Junction Road, Kaduna
Tel: (062) 240502 **Fax:** (062) 246220
E-mail: zeconigltd@yahoo.com
* Plot 280, Trans-Amadi Industrial Layout, beside Trans-Amadi Post Office, Port Harcourt
Tel: (084) 235623
* 55, Port Harcourt Road, Aba
Tel: (082) 228369

ZEE HOLDINGS LIMITED
Business: Veterinary Clinics, Livestock Breeding & Marketing, Sales of Livestock Drugs, Agrovet Consulting, Pest & Rodent Control Services; Security Services.
Address: 3, Walter Carrington Crescent, near American Embassy, Victoria Island, Lagos
Tel: (01) 610091, 2621577 **Fax:** (01) 2621577
E-mail: jiyore2000@yahoo.com
Contact: Dr. J. E. Iyore - MD/CEO

ZEEK SHIPPING (NIGERIA) LIMITED
Business: Shipping, Ship Chartering, Marine Transportation
Address: 25, Rhodes Crescent, Apapa, Lagos
Tel: (01) 5804135, 08033449988

ZENBOOK INTERIOR CONSTRUCTIONS LIMITED
Business: Interior Design and Construction, Installation of Fire Resistant Partitioning and Suspended Ceilings, Interior Furnishing, Aluminium Works
Address: 29, Norman Williams Streert, S. W. Ikoyi, Lagos
Tel: (01) 4745383, 7762994, 08033046886, 08033360181
Fax: (01) 4745383
E-mail: info@zenbrook.com
zenbrook@udeya.net
Website: www.zenbrook.com
* The Grand Mirage Complex (Office Suite 3), Port Harcourt Crescent, Area 11, Garki, Abuja
Tel: (09) 3141311, 3141312, 3140885
Contact: Chief (Engr.) Olufemi Odeyale - Chairman/CEO

ZENINA LIMITED
Business: Manufacturing of Printing Inks and Paints
Address: Plot C26, Amuwo-Odofin Industrial Estate, off Festac Access Road, Festac Town, Lagos
Tel: (01) 4705007, 3203342 **Fax:** (01) 882024
E-mail: zenina@infoweb.abs.net
Contact: Engr. E. I. Nwizu - Chairman/CEO

ZENITH CONTAINERS COMPANY LIMITED
Business: Manufacturing and Marketing of Polythene Bags
Address: Plot 136, Trans-Amadi Ind.Layout, Port Harcourt
Tel: (084) 232301, 237992, 232960 **Fax:** (084) 237992
E-mail: zcon@hyperia.cm

ZENITH HOTELS LIMITED
Business: Hotel and Catering Services
Address: 28, Adeniran Ogunsanya Street, Surulere, Lagos
Tel: (01) 5831781, 8165704, 08023024408
* Jade Gardens, 98, Effurun/Sapele Road, opp Our Lady's High School, Effurun, Warri
Tel: (053) 250773, 08035974079
Contact: Apostle S. E. K. Obrutse - Chairman

ZENITH INTERNATIONAL BANK PLC
Business: Commercial Banking Services
Address: Plot 84, Ajose Adeogun St, Victoria Island, Lagos
Tel: (01) 2620727, 2703132-4 (3L), 2703136-42 (7L) 4618301, 4618311, 4618321 **Fax:** (01) 2618212
E-mail: enquiry@zenithbank.com
Website: www.zenithbank.com
Contact: Mr Jim Ovia - MD/CEO
Mr Tony Chiejina - Head (Corporate Comms)

ZENITH NIGERGROUP COMPANY LIMITED
Business: Surveying, Mapping and Exploration Servces, Consultancy Service, Environmental Management
Address: Olatunji House, 299, Ikorodu Road (Idiroko Bus-Stop), Maryland, Ikeja, Lagos
Tel: (01) 4962629, 4817439 **Fax:** (01) 4962629
E-mail: zenithlos@yahoo.com
* Plot 25, Trans-Amadi Ind. Layout, Port Harcourt
Contact: Mr. S. O. Joda - Chairman/CEO

ZENITH PLASTIC LIMITED
Business: Manufacturing and Marketing of Plastic Footwear

Address: Km. 16, P.Harcourt/Aba Expressway, Port Harcourt
Tel: (084) 613139

ZENITH SHIPPING COMPANY LIMITED
Business: Shipping, Export, Clearing and Forwarding, Petroleum Services
Address: 98, Adetola Street, Aguda, Lagos
Tel: (01) 5850737, 5457586, 7741882, 08037759015
Fax: (01) 5851084
E-mail: zenithshipping@hyperia.com
Contact: Mr Innocent Obelle - Chairman/CEO

ZENITH TRAVELS & TOURS LIMITED
Business: Travel Agency, Tour Operators
Address: 67, Bamgbose Street, Lagos Island, Lagos
Tel: (01) 4812373, 7942316, 08022235119, 08023129906, 08033254992, 98955469754 **Fax:** (01) 2641166
E-mail: zenith_travels@yahoo.co.uk
Contact: Mr. Ayodele Olonilua - Chairman/CEO

ZENON LABORATORIES & CHEMICAL INDUSTRIAL NIGERIA LIMITED
Business: Manufacturing of Cosmetics & Haircare Products
Address: 7/8, Oyadiran Estate, Sabo-Yaba, Lagos
Tel: (01) 7738013, 08033138001
Contact: Mr. John E. Edeoghon - Director (Operations)

ZENON PETROLEUM & GAS LIMITED
Business: Petroleum Products Marketers & Terminal/Depot Onwers/Operators
Address: 7 (Plot 10), Tiamiyu Savage Street, off Olosa Street, Victoria Island, Lagos
Tel: (01) 2626391, 2626392, 2620792 **Fax:** (01) 2620971
* Ibru Jetty Complex, Oshodi-Apapa Expressway, Ibafon, Apapa, Lagos
* Plot 859, Usman Dan Fodio St, Maitama, Abuja
Tel: (09) 3142084-5(2L)
Contact: Mr. Femi Otedola - Chairman/CEO
Mr. K. K. Otaru - GM (Abuja)

ZENTEC NIGERIA LIMITED
Business: Importation & Sales of Plumbing Materials & Tools, Building Materials and Water Pumps
Address: Block 8, Extension (Shop 6), Agric Market, Badagry Expressway, Coker, Orile, Lagos
Tel: (01) 5452165, 5450826, 7747158 **Fax:** (01) 5452165
Contact: Mr. Charles Ezenduka - Chairman/CEO

ZEPOL ADVERTISING LIMITED
Business: Adveritising Agency
Address: 1, Oremeji Street, off Palm Avenue, Mushin, Lagos
Tel: (01) 4527240, 4524788, 08022245089
Fax: (01) 4524788
E-mail: zepol@zepoladvertising.com
zepol@linkserve.com.ng
Contact: Mr Jide Jopez - MD/CEO
Mr Tunde Ogungbile - GM

ZEROCK CONSTRUCTION NIGERIA LIMITED
Business: Building & Civil Engineering Services
Address: Fleet House (2nd Floor), Plot 105, Olu Obasanjo Road, Port Harcourt
Tel: (084) 572744, 461222-4 (3L)

ZEVIS GROUP LIMITED
Business: Importation and Sales of Pharmaceutical Products
Address: 79, Adeniran Ogunsanya Street, Surulere, Lagos
Tel: (01) 5851363
* Zevis House, Onitsha-Asaba Expressway Housing Estate, Onitsha
Tel: (046) 219416, 219613
Contact: Mr. Elvis Eze Emecheta - Chairman/CEO

ZIATECH NIGERIA LIMITED
Business: Sales & Maintenance of Generators, Water Pumps, & Low/High Voltage Switchgears; Rural Electrification & Water Projects, Sales of Body-Care Products
Address: 11, Adekunle Fajuyi Way, Ikeja G.R.A., Lagos
Tel: (01) 4933366, 4967521, 7753811 **Fax:** (01) 4967521
E-mail: ziatech@hyperia.com
Contact: Mr. Ziad Jarmakani - Chairman
Mr. Adham Henaoui - CEO

ZIHABIT LIMITED
Business: Building Construction, Renovation of Buildings, Civil Works Rural Electrification Engineering
Address: Plot 443, Jos Street, Area 3, Garki, Abuja
Tel: (09) 2344261, 2344278 **Fax:** (09) 2344262
E-mail: zihabit@yahoo.com
zihabit@hotmail.com
Contact: Arc. P. Z. Iyortyer - Chief Executive

ZIKLAG LIMITED
Business: Design, Supply & Installation of Marble, Granite and P.O.P. Ceilings, Designers and Fixers, Publishers and Printers
Address: Ziklag House, Plot 34, Oregun Road, Oregun Lagos
Tel: (01) 4702130, 4960585
Fax: (01) 4975140, 4979668, 4979669
E-mail: ziklag@nova.net.ng
kiti@ziklag.com
Contact: Mr. Akitoye Branco-Rhodes - Chairman
Mr Tunji Oyegbami - Group GM

ZINOX TECHNOLOGIES LIMITED
Business: Information Technology, Products Manufacturing, Installation & Sales (PCs, Laptops, Servers, UPS)
Address: 13A, Idowu Martins Street, Victoria Island, Lagos
Tel: (01) 2611139, 2611350, 3200641-2(2L)
Fax: (01) 3200642, 5558095
E-mail: enquries@zinoxtechnologies.com
* 1A, Pa Oshunkeye Cr., Gbagada Estate, Lagos.
Tel: (01) 4713774-5(2L)
* Plot 452, Kontagora Closd, Area 3, Garki, Abuja
Tel: (09) 2340234, 0803321773
E-mail: abuja@zinoxtehnologies.com
* 228, Old Aba Road, 2nd Artillery Junction, Port Harcourt.
Tel: (084) 311790, 612084
Contact: Mr. Leo Stan Ekeh - Chairman/CEO
Mr. Anosike Emelonye - Director (Business Dev.)

ZITADEL LIMITED
Business: Environmetal, Waste Management and Security Consultancy, Engineering/Technical Support.
Address: 4, Nkpogu Road, Trans-Amadi Industrial Layout, Port Harcourt

Tel: (084) 237700, 239494 **Fax:** (084) 239494
E-mail: zitadel@infoweb.abs.net
Contact: Mr. Nik C. Odinuwe - Chairman/CEO

ZODIAC TRAVELS AND COMMUNICATIONS.LIMITED
Business: Travel & Tourism, Air Cargo Services, Real Estate
Address: 38, Toyin Street, Ikeja, Lagos
Tel: (01) 4967088, 4966106, 4978071 **Fax:** (01) 4978071
Contact: Chief Godson Ewulum - Chairman/Group CEO

ZUBEE INTERNATIONAL COMPANY LIMITED
Business: Manufacturing of Biscuits, Importation and Marketing of Building Materials
Address: 44, Ozomagala Street, Odoakpu, Onitsha
Tel: (046) 210183, 218576 **Fax:** (046) 218576
Contact: Mr. Nnamdi Okafor - MD/CEO

ZUKUS INDUSTRIES LIMITED
Business: Marine Technical & Wireline Engineering Services, Well Testing/Pumping Services, Hot Oil Services
Address: EVOC Yard, off Enerhen Road, Warri
Tel: (053) 250880, 320237 **Fax:** (053) 250880
E-mail: zukub@linkserve.com.ng
Contact: Mr. Chinye I. Uzor - MD/CEO

ZUS BUREAU LIMITED
Business: Publishing, Media Research & Consultancy
Address: 6, Maduagwu Moronu Street, off Ibezim Obiajlu Street, off Adelabu Street, Surulere, Lagos
Tel: (01) 831190, 844790, 08023513708
E-mail: zusbureau@yahoo.com
Contact: Mr. Chris A. Doghuje - MD/CEO

ZWISCHENSTUCK ENGINEERING (NIGERIA) LIMITED
Business: Sales of Swimming Pool Equipment, Waste-Water and Sewage Treatment: Sales of Water Pumps & Filtration Equipment
Address: 19, Afariogun/Seriki Aro Avenue, Ikeja, Lagos
Tel/Fax: (01) 4976333
* Plot C6, Ewet/Itian Housing Estate, Uyo
Contact: Mr. Joseph B. Edet - MD/CEO

Printed by Libri Plureos GmbH in Hamburg,
Germany